MW01071539

JAMESTOWN PEOPLE
TO 1800

Landowners, Public Officials,
Minorities, and Native Leaders

JAMESTOWN PEOPLE TO 1800

Landowners, Public Officials, Minorities, and Native Leaders

Martha W. McCartney

Genealogical Publishing Company

Copyright © 2012
Martha W. McCartney
All Rights Reserved.
No part of this publication may be reproduced
in any form or by any means, including electronic
reproduction or reproduction via the Internet,
except by permission of the publisher.

Published by Genealogical Publishing Company
3600 Clipper Mill Rd., Suite 260
Baltimore, MD 21211
Library of Congress Catalogue Card Number 2010938190
ISBN 978-0-8063-1872-1
Made in the United States of America

Index compiled by Carolyn L. Barkley

Artwork on cover and title page: Louis Hué Girardin, a professor at the College of William and Mary, produced a watercolor painting that depicted urban Jamestown as it appeared in 1803. That rendering shows the Amblers' two-story house with a mansard roof; the Travises' hip-roofed dwelling on the waterfront; and the tower of Jamestown's ancient church (courtesy of the Special Collections, John D. Rockefeller, Jr. Library, The Colonial Williamsburg Foundation).

DEDICATED TO

MADELEINE, LAUREL, AND NICHOLAS

CONTENTS

Preface. ix
Introduction. xi
Sources and Abbreviations xxv
Glossary xxvii
Jamestown's History. 3
Biographical Dictionary 29
Index 467

PREFACE

Jamestown Island's history has intrigued successive generations of scholars and antiquarians. The approach of the 400th anniversary of the establishment of America's first permanent English settlement prompted the National Park Service to sponsor a collaborative study known as the Jamestown Archaeological Assessment. This multidisciplinary project involved personnel from the Colonial Williamsburg Foundation, the College of William and Mary, and the National Park Service, as well as consultants who were committed to studying Jamestown Island's historical continuum. The research team included prehistoric and historical archaeologists, historians, paleo-botanists, geophysicists, geologists, architectural historians, reference librarians, computer specialists, and curators of artifact collections. The resulting research, which included environmental reconstruction, sheds new light on how the island's acreage was developed over time. Thanks to archaeological fieldwork and the use of remote sensing techniques such as ground-penetrating radar, subsurface cultural resources were identified so that they could be tested and then preserved for future generations.

Prior to the Jamestown Archaeological Assessment, there had been no comprehensive reconstruction of property ownership and land use patterns from the first decade of settlement through the modern period. My work as project historian involved use of a diverse body of primary and secondary documentary, cartographic, pictorial, and iconographic sources that ranged from the early seventeenth century through the twentieth century. The Jamestown Archaeological Assessment culminated in the production of annotated technical reports that summarize the findings of each of the project's teams of specialists.

The historical biographies included in this volume fall into two basic categories. One group consists of Jamestown Island landowners and residents through 1800, whether enslaved or free. The other is composed of public officials such as governors, members of the Council of State, and burgesses, and Native American leaders who visited Jamestown, Virginia's capital city through 1699. Many of the biographies produced as part of the Jamestown Archaeological Assessment have been expanded. Also included are biographies of public officials, many of whom never owned land on Jamestown Island but spent extended periods of time there. There are listings for more than a thousand individuals whose activities brought them to the capital city and more than a hundred Native American leaders who visited Jamestown to transact business on their people's behalf. Also included are a hundred or more Africans and African Americans, many of whom were enslaved. Much of this information was drawn from the records generated by the overarching branches of government and by the court justices of eastern Virginia's counties. Overseas sources also have been used extensively. As individual biographies clearly demonstrate, there are enormous differences in the extent to which county records have been preserved. Because relatively complete biographies of people associated with Jamestown's earliest years were published in *Virginia Immigrants and Adven-*

turers 1607–1635: A Biographical Dictionary (Baltimore: Genealogical Publishing Co., 2007), information about those individuals is summarized herein. It should be noted, however, that extensive use of county records and other sources has resulted in the augmentation of some of those biographies.

INTRODUCTION

Broad waterways, which serve as natural boundaries and conduits of transportation, divide Tidewater Virginia into five distinct regions. When viewed from north to south, the regions consist of the Northern Neck, the Middle Peninsula, the James-York Peninsula, and the Southside. The Eastern Shore, a peninsula bound on the east by the Atlantic Ocean and on the west by the Chesapeake Bay, also lies within the Tidewater. Surviving court records suggest that the colonial Virginians who had the means to acquire land usually focused their attention on a specific region. Their political and economic activities and social contacts also tended to be concentrated within a specific area, and they tended to patent or purchase acreage in counties that were contiguous. Thus, regional patterns played an important role in the way seventeenth-century Virginians conducted their daily lives.

TIDEWATER VIRGINIA'S REGIONS

The Northern Neck: The region traditionally known as the Northern Neck is bound on the north by the Potomac River, on the south by the Rappahannock River, and on the east by the Chesapeake Bay. In September 1649 Charles II, though exiled and king in name only, granted the Northern Neck to seven men as a proprietary territory. Much of the region had not been mapped, and as settlement spread in a westerly direction, questions arose about where the proprietors' territory ended. By 1681 control of the Northern Neck Proprietary had descended to one man, Thomas Lord Culpeper, who received a new charter in 1688. At his death, his five-sixths interest in the proprietary descended to his daughter, Catherine, and her husband, Thomas Lord Fairfax. When Lord Fairfax died in January 1710, his son, Thomas, who was a minor, inherited his father's title along with his legal interest in the Northern Neck. In May of that year, Thomas inherited the remaining one-sixth interest from his grandmother. As Virginia's frontier moved in a southerly and westerly direction, definition of the territory's boundaries became increasingly important. A survey was undertaken in 1736, a year after Lord Fairfax had visited his territory and reserved for himself a tract of 12,588 acres near Great Falls, in what was to become Fairfax County. A second survey was conducted with great difficulty in 1746, establishing a line between the sources of the Potomac and Rappahannock rivers. When Lord Fairfax died in 1781, the Northern Neck Proprietary ceased to exist. All the land that he had granted to settlers remained in their hands, and acreage that had not been assigned to anyone came under the control of the new Commonwealth of Virginia. In 1699 the Northern Neck included King George, Lancaster, Northumberland, Richmond, Stafford, and Westmoreland counties. As settlement spread west beyond the head of the Potomac River, the Northern Neck eventually included more than a dozen additional counties.

The Middle Peninsula: The Middle Peninsula, which is bound on the north by the Rappahannock River and on the south by the York River, extends from the Chesapeake Bay on the east to Essex County on the west. The Middle Peninsula's counties are descendants of Charles River (or York) County, one of Virginia's eight original shires. In 1699 the Middle Peninsula included Essex, Gloucester, King and Queen, and Middlesex counties. King William County was later formed from the southern part of King and Queen County, and Mathews County was formed from the northern part of Gloucester County.

The James-York Peninsula: The James-York Peninsula, the area first settled by European colonists, borders north upon the York River and south upon the James, and extends from the Chesapeake Bay on the east to Henrico County on the west. The northerly portions of four of Virginia's eight original shires or counties (Charles City, Elizabeth City, Henrico, and James City), established in 1634, lay within the James-York Peninsula, whereas Charles River (York) and Warwick counties lay wholly within the peninsula. In 1634 Charles City, Henrico, and James City's territory was vast and spanned both sides of the James River, encompassing territory now considered part of the Southside. Until the mid-twentieth century, when two of the James-York Peninsula's counties became incorporated cities, the region included Charles City, Elizabeth City, Henrico, James City, New Kent, Warwick, and York counties. The city of Williamsburg, chartered in 1699, was formed from land that lay in James City and York counties.

The Southside: The region generally known as the Southside includes counties that are located on the lower side of the James River. It extends in a westerly direction from the James River's mouth to the east side of the Appomattox River. On April 18, 1637, King Charles I granted one of his favorites, Henry Lord Maltravers, the Duke of Norfolk's son, a large proprietary territory on the south side of the James River. Maltravers' acreage encompassed what was then Upper and Lower Norfolk counties (later, Nansemond, Norfolk, and Princess Anne counties) and parts of Isle of Wight County and Carolina. Governor John Harvey's eagerness to assist Maltravers thoroughly alienated the Council of State, whose members strenuously objected to the loss of Virginia territory and potential tax revenues. Meanwhile, those who had patented land in the region were concerned about the validity of their land titles. In 1700 Dr. John Cox, as Maltravers' heir, tried in vain to assert a claim to Norfolk County. Until the mid-twentieth century the Southside encompassed Isle of Wight, Nansemond, Norfolk, Prince George, Princess Anne, and Surry counties. Nansemond, Norfolk, and Princess Anne counties eventually became incorporated cities.

The Eastern Shore: Virginia's Eastern Shore is delimited on the east by the Atlantic Ocean and on the west by the Chesapeake Bay. It extends in a northerly direction to Virginia's boundary line with Maryland. The Eastern Shore includes two counties: Accomack and Northampton.

VIRGINIA'S ORIGINAL COUNTIES AND THEIR IMMEDIATE DESCENDANTS

In 1634 the Virginia colony was divided into eight shires or counties that were vast in size and extended to the limits of the colony. As the population grew and settlement spread, each of the original counties was subdivided. Thus, over time,

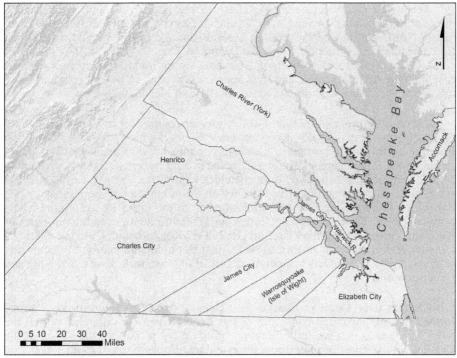

In 1634 Virginia was subdivided into eight shires or counties.
Map by Gregory J. Brown.

the number of counties slowly but surely rose. Convenient access to a county seat, where local justices convened, taxes were collected, and elections were held, was a driving force. When establishing new counties, the burgesses preferred to use natural boundaries (like rivers and lesser streams) to delimit them (HEN I:8, 224; II:18). In 1699, when the capital city moved from Jamestown to Williamsburg, the colony had 23 counties. Just as the formation of new counties was a matter of practicality, the creation of new parishes was prompted by the obligation to attend and support the Established Church. Researchers should bear in mind that because county and parish boundary lines changed over time, information on their ancestors might be found in one or more neighboring locations.

Shortly after war broke out between the North and South, Richmond, at the head of the James-York Peninsula, became the Confederacy's capital city. In spring 1862, when Union Army troops left their stronghold at Fort Monroe and began moving up the peninsula, county justices throughout the James-York and Middle peninsulas decided to send their records to Richmond for safekeeping. A notable exception was York County, whose clerk reportedly loaded the record books into a boat and took them across the York River. When Richmond's tobacco warehouses were set ablaze in April 1865 by Confederate troops who realized that their capital city was about to fall into Union hands, flames quickly spread to the General Court building where many of eastern Virginia's antebellum court records were stored. Some regions suffered more record losses than others. With rare exception, the early records taken to Richmond for safekeeping were destroyed. The antebellum records of all but two counties in the Southside escaped damage, as did those of the Eastern Shore and most of Northern Neck's counties.

Accomack County: Accomac (Accawmacke), one of the eight original shires or counties, originally encompassed Virginia's Eastern Shore peninsula. It was renamed Northampton County in 1643. Around 1663 Accomack County was formed from the northernmost portion of Northampton County (HEN I:224, 249). Accomack County borders north upon Maryland, south upon Northampton County, east upon the Atlantic Ocean, and west upon the Chesapeake Bay. Accomack County's court records are well preserved, as are those of Northampton.

Caroline County: Much of the territory encompassed by Caroline County originally was part of "Old" Rappahannock County, which was formed in 1656 from the northwestern portion of Lancaster County. "Old" Rappahannock County straddled the Rappahannock River and included land in the Northern Neck and the Middle Peninsula. When "Old" Rappahannock County became extinct in 1692, Essex County was created out of its territory on the south side of the Rappahannock River. In 1727 Caroline County was formed from the upper or westernmost portions of Essex, King and Queen, and King William counties; additional parts of King and Queen were added later on (HEN IV:240). Although Caroline County's records are fragmentary, much can be learned through examination of documents associated with its antecedents, notably "Old" Rappahannock, Essex, and King and Queen counties.

Charles City County: Charles City County, one of the eight original shires formed in 1634, spanned both sides of the James River. On the north side of the river, it extended in a westerly direction from a point just above the mouth of the Chickahominy River and ran upstream just above Eppes Island. On the lower side of the James, it extended from Upper Chippokes Creek on the east to the east side of the Appomattox River. By 1656 colonists living on the lower side of the James River began clamoring for the creation of a new county, but the assembly was disinclined to act. In 1702 Prince George County was created out Charles City County's territory on the lower side of the James River. Charles City County was enlarged in 1721 when the boundary between Charles City and James City counties was adjusted, and the Chickahominy River became the dividing line (HEN I:224, 426, 497; III:223; IV:94). Charles City County's antebellum court records are fragmentary, as are those of its immediate descendant, Prince George County.

Charles River County: Charles River County, one of Virginia's eight original shires or counties, was formed in 1634 (HEN I:224). In 1643 its name was changed to York County (see **York County**).

Elizabeth City County: In 1634 Elizabeth City County, one of the eight original shires, straddled the James River. It included territory on the upper side of the James River and ran from Newport News Point on the west to Old Point Comfort on the east. It also extended northward to the York River, taking in Fox Hill and the plantations along the Back and Poquoson rivers, and abutted south on the James River. Elizabeth City County's size was reduced significantly in 1636 when its territory on the south side of the James River was split off to form New Norfolk County and its descendants (HEN I:224, 247; III:95–96). In 1952 Elizabeth City County merged with the city of Hampton. Elizabeth City County's antebellum court records are fragmentary but some of its early records survive.

Essex County: In 1692 Essex County was formed from the part of "Old" Rappahannock County that lay on the lower side of the Rappahannock River. In 1728

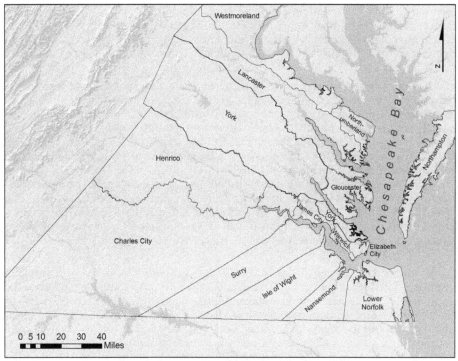

**The boundary lines of Virginia counties in 1653–1654.
Map by Gregory J. Brown.**

Essex County was reduced in size when Caroline County was formed from portions of Essex, King and Queen, and King William counties; additional parts of King and Queen were added later (HEN III:104). Essex County's antebellum court records are extensive, as are those of its antecedent, "Old" Rappahannock.

Gloucester County: In 1651 Gloucester County, which extended from the York River to the south side of the Piankatank River, was formed from the northerly part of York (formerly Charles River) County, one of Virginia's original shires. Gloucester County abuts east upon the Chesapeake Bay and west upon Poropotank Creek, which separates Gloucester from King and Queen County, formed in 1691 (HEN I:224, 374). Mathews County was created out of the northernmost part of Gloucester County in 1791 (HEN XIII:162). Portions of Gloucester County's antebellum court records were lost during a courthouse fire, and many of the county's remaining records were destroyed when Richmond burned. Significantly, Gloucester County's early plat books have survived.

Henrico County: In 1634, when the Virginia colony was divided into eight shires or counties, Henrico County's territory spanned the James River and extended from the falls to Shirley Hundred (Eppes) Island and the Appomattox River, interfacing with Charles City County (HEN I:224). Goochland County was formed from the westernmost part of Henrico County in 1728, and in 1749 Chesterfield County was created out of Henrico's territory on the lower side of the James River. As settlement spread west, Goochland County gave rise to several other counties.

Henrico County's antebellum court records sustained significant losses when the British burned Richmond, the county seat, during the Revolutionary War. Though Henrico's colonial court records are incomplete, they are extensive. Moreover, many of Henrico County's eighteenth- and nineteenth-century plats have survived.

Isle of Wight County: In 1634 the county or shire of Warisqueak (Warrosquoyacke, Warresqueak), which was located on the south side of the James River, extended from Lawnes Creek on the west, downstream to the Pagan River on the east. It abutted north upon the James River and extended south to what became known as Carolina. In 1637 Warisqueak County's original name was changed to Isle of Wight, and in 1643 the county's boundary lines were reaffirmed. Part of Nansemond County's territory was added to Isle of Wight in 1655–1656, and in 1674 the two counties' limits were described. During the eighteenth century a portion of Isle of Wight's land was added to Brunswick County (HEN I:224, 247, 249, 404, 423; II:318; IV:355). During the mid-eighteenth century Isle of Wight's southerly territory was split off to form much of Southampton County. Isle of Wight County's antebellum court records are extensive.

James City County: In 1634 James City County's territory was vast and spanned both sides of the James River. James City County's limits extended on the north side of the James from just above the Chickahominy River (on the west) to Skiffs Creek (on the east), and on the south side of the James from Upper Chippokes Creek (on the west) to Lawnes Creek (on the east), taking in what in 1652 became Surry County. James City County's boundary lines were adjusted in 1721, when the Chickahominy River became its westernmost boundary. In 1767 another boundary adjustment was made. This time, the territory between Skimino and Ware creeks was taken from New Kent County and added to James City. Simultaneously, Diascund Creek became the boundary line between James City and New Kent counties, with the result that some land on the west side of Diascund Creek became part of New Kent (HEN I:224 IV:94; VIII:208). Jamestown (often identified as "James City") served as the Virginia colony's capital city from 1607 to 1699, at which time the newly established city of Williamsburg became the seat of government. The corporate limits of urban Jamestown were defined by natural boundaries. The capital city was delimited on the south by the James River, on the north by Back Creek, on the east by Orchard Run and Kingsmill Creek, and on the west by the Thoroughfare. Jamestown Island is located in James City County. Almost all of James City County's antebellum court records have been lost or destroyed, although some seventeenth- and eighteenth-century deeds and wills can be found in collections of private papers, most notably, the Ambler Papers, which are preserved at the Library of Congress.

Kecoughtan: During the early seventeenth century, the territory that became known as Elizabeth City was called Kecoughtan, the name of the natives who had been living there when the first European colonists arrived. Around 1619 the area was renamed Elizabeth City at the request of the area's European inhabitants (see **Elizabeth City County**).

King and Queen County: In 1691 King and Queen County, a descendant of York (formerly Charles River) County, was formed from New Kent County. King and Queen's territory is bound on the north by the Piankatank River and portions of Essex and Middlesex counties, and on the south by the York River and its tributary, the Mattaponi River, and King William County. It is bound on the east by Poropo-

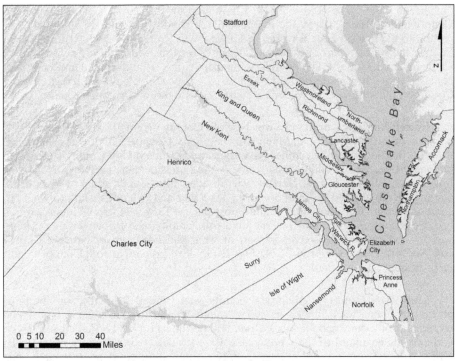

The boundary lines of Virginia counties in 1699.
Map by Gregory J. Brown.

tank Creek and Gloucester County, formed in 1651; it is bound on the west by Caroline County, a descendant of "Old" Rappahannock County and its antecedent, Lancaster County (HEN I:224; III:94). Most of King and Queen County's antebellum court records have been destroyed, although those of one of its antecedents, York County, are well preserved.

King George County: King George County was formed from Richmond County in 1720, and part of Westmoreland County was added later on. In 1730 Prince William County was formed from the westernmost part of Stafford County (HEN IV:95, 303). King George County's antebellum court records are fragmentary although those of two of its antecedents, Westmoreland and Richmond counties, are intact.

King William County: King William County, a descendant of York (formerly Charles River) and New Kent counties, was formed in 1701. It was created from that portion of King and Queen County which originally included Pamunkey Neck, the territory defined by the Pamunkey and Mattaponi rivers (HEN I:224; III:211). King William's antebellum court records are incomplete. Many were lost in a courthouse fire, followed by the burning of Richmond in 1865.

Lancaster County: In 1651 Lancaster County was formed from the northernmost part of York (formerly Charles River) County and the southern part of Northumberland County, formed in 1648. It is bound on the north by Northumberland County and on the south by the Rappahannock River. It extends in an easterly direction to the Chesapeake Bay and interfaces with Richmond County on the west. In 1658 the western part of Lancaster County's territory was split off to form "Old" Rappahannock County. The boundary line between Northumberland and Lancaster counties was confirmed and ratified in 1670 (HEN I:374, 427; II:285). Lancaster County's antebellum court records are intact, as are those of its antecedents.

Lower Norfolk County: Lower Norfolk County originally lay within the corporation of Elizabeth City and then Elizabeth City County, which was established in 1634. In 1636, when the James River became Elizabeth City County's southerly boundary line, the land on the south side of the James became known as New Norfolk County. In 1637 New Norfolk was divided into Upper and Lower Norfolk counties. Both abutted north upon the James River and extended south to what became known as Carolina. The westernmost part of Lower Norfolk County, which became extinct in 1691, was renamed Norfolk County, and Princess Anne County was formed from the easternmost part of what had been Lower Norfolk County (see **Norfolk County**) (HEN I:224, 247; III:95–96). Lower Norfolk County's court records are well preserved.

Middlesex County: Middlesex County was formed from the southernmost portion of Lancaster County's territory around 1669. Middlesex County is bound on the north by the Rappahannock River and on the south by the Piankatank River, and extends eastward to the Chesapeake Bay. It abuts Essex County on the west (HEN II:329). Some of Middlesex County's antebellum court records have been preserved, and those of its antecedent, Lancaster County, are intact (see **Lancaster County**).

Nansemond County: The territory that in 1646 became known as Nansemond County originally lay within the corporation of Elizabeth City and then Elizabeth City County, which was established in 1634. In 1636, when the James River became Elizabeth City County's southerly boundary line, the land on the south side of the James became known as New Norfolk County. By 1637 New Norfolk was divided into Upper and Lower Norfolk counties. In 1646 the name of Upper Norfolk County (the westernmost jurisdiction) was changed to Nansemond County. It abutted north on the James River and extended southward to what became known as Carolina. The dividing line between Nansemond and Isle of Wight counties was settled and described more explicitly in 1674 (HEN I:224, 323; II:318). In 1769 a small part of Nansemond County's land was added to neighboring Isle of Wight County, and later, part of Nansemond was made part of Southampton County. In July 1972 Nansemond County became the independent city of Nansemond, which in January 1974 merged with the city of Suffolk. Almost all of Nansemond County's antebellum court records have been lost or destroyed, probably while Suffolk, the county seat, was occupied by the Union Army. However, Nansemond residents' interaction with their neighbors in nearby Isle of Wight and Norfolk counties sometimes made its way into the records of those counties, which have been preserved.

New Kent County: New Kent County was formed around 1654 from York (formerly Charles River) County, one of Virginia's original shires, established in 1634. New Kent's boundaries extended from the west side of Skimino Creek (where it interfaced with York County's boundary line) to the heads of the Pamunkey and Mattaponi rivers. It also extended northward to the west side of Poropotank Creek.

New Kent's vast territory took in what became Hanover County in 1720 and Louisa County in 1742. New Kent County's northerly territory enveloped Pamunkey Neck, which eventually became King William County, and the region that in 1691 became known as King and Queen County (HEN I:224, 388; IV:95). Most of New Kent County's antebellum court records have been lost or destroyed, although those of its antecedent, York or Charles River County, are well preserved.

New Norfolk County: New Norfolk County originally lay within the corporation of Elizabeth City and then Elizabeth City County, established in 1634. In 1636, when the James River became Elizabeth City County's southerly boundary line, the land on the lower side of the James became known as New Norfolk County. In 1637 New Norfolk was divided into Upper and Lower Norfolk counties, and New Norfolk County became extinct (see **Nansemond County** and **Norfolk County**) (HEN I:224, 247; III:95–96). Portions of New Norfolk County's court records are preserved as part of Lower Norfolk and Norfolk counties' records.

Norfolk County: The territory on the Southside that in 1691 became known as Norfolk County originally lay within the corporation of Elizabeth City and then Elizabeth City County, established in 1634. In 1636, when the James River became Elizabeth City County's southerly boundary line, the land on the lower side of the James became known as New Norfolk County. A year later New Norfolk County was divided into Upper and Lower Norfolk counties. Then, in 1691 Lower Norfolk County, the easternmost of the two jurisdictions, was divided again. The western part of Lower Norfolk County was renamed Norfolk County, whereas the eastern part of Lower Norfolk's territory became Princess Anne County (HEN I:224, 247; III:95–96). Norfolk County became extinct in 1963 when it was consolidated with the city of South Norfolk to form the city of Chesapeake. The court records of Lower Norfolk and Norfolk counties are largely intact.

Northampton County: Northampton County, which is located on the Eastern Shore, was known as Accawmacke (Accomac) until 1643 and included the Eastern Shore peninsula in its entirety. In 1663 Northampton County was subdivided and the northernmost part became known as Accomack County (HEN I:249). Northampton County's court records are intact, as are those of its antecedent, Accomack County.

Northumberland County: Northumberland County, which is located in the Northern Neck, was formed around 1648 from Chickacoan, the region between the Potomac and Rappahannock rivers. In 1651 Lancaster County was formed from the southern part of Northumberland County and the northern part of York (formerly Charles River) County. Two years later Westmoreland County was created out of the northwestern portion of Northumberland County. In 1664 part of Westmoreland County was split off to form Stafford County. Middlesex County was formed from the southernmost portion of Lancaster County's territory around 1669. The boundary between Northumberland and Lancaster counties was confirmed in 1670 (HEN I:352; II:285). Later, Fairfax, Prince William, Loudoun, and Fauquier counties were formed from the Northern Neck Proprietary's westerly territory. Northumberland County's court records are intact.

"Old" Rappahannock County: In 1658 the original or "Old" Rappahannock County was formed from the westernmost portion of Lancaster County. It straddled the Rappahannock River and included land in the Northern Neck and the Middle

Peninsula. "Old" Rappahannock County became extinct in 1692 and its territory was subdivided. Richmond County was formed from "Old" Rappahannock's land on the upper side of the Rappahannock River and Essex was created out its acreage on the south side of the river. In 1720 King George County was created out of Richmond County's territory, and part of Westmoreland County was added later on. In 1728 Caroline County, a descendant of "Old" Rappahannock County, was formed from portions of Essex, King and Queen, and King William counties. Parts of King and Queen County eventually were added (HEN I:427; III:104). Seventeenth-century or "Old" Rappahannock County should not be confused with today's Rappahannock County, which was established in 1833 and formed from Culpeper County. "Old" Rappahannock's records, though covering a relatively brief period, are relatively complete.

Prince George County: Prince George County, which is located on the south side of the James River, was formed in 1702. It is descended from Charles City County, one of Virginia's original shires, which spanned both sides of the James. As early as 1656, Charles City County colonists living on the lower side of the river began asking the assembly to form a new county from their territory. The assembly refused to do so but held court sessions on both sides of the river. Prince George County is bound on the east by Upper Chippokes Creek and on the west by the Appomattox River. It borders the James River on the north and originally extended in a southerly direction toward Carolina (HEN I:426, 497; III:223). Prince George County's antebellum court records are fragmentary.

Princess Anne County: Princess Anne County's territory is descended from the corporation of Elizabeth City and Elizabeth City County, established in 1634. It also was part of New Norfolk County, which was formed in 1636 and subdivided into Upper and Lower Norfolk counties in 1637. Both jurisdictions abutted north upon the James River and extended south to what became known as Carolina. In 1691 Lower Norfolk County became extinct. Its easternmost territory became known as Princess Anne County and its westernmost acreage became known as Norfolk County (HEN I:224; II:247; III:95–96). Princess Anne County was consolidated with the city of Virginia Beach in 1963 and Princess Anne became extinct. Princess Anne County's antebellum records are incomplete, although those of its antecedents, Lower Norfolk and Norfolk counties, are well preserved.

Richmond County: In 1692 Richmond County was formed from the portion of "Old" Rappahannock County that lay on the upper side of the Rappahannock River. Then, in 1720 King George County was formed from the westernmost portion of Richmond County (HEN IV:95). Richmond County borders Westmoreland and Northumberland counties on the north and the Rappahannock River on the south. It abuts Lancaster County on the east and King George County on the west. Richmond County's antebellum court records are well preserved.

Stafford County: Stafford County, formed by 1664, is descended from the northwestern part of the territory encompassed by "Old" Rappahannock County, a descendant of Lancaster County (HEN II:239). Many of Stafford County's antebellum court records have been destroyed. Some of the county's court records have been preserved at the Huntington Library in San Marino, California.

Surry County: In 1652 Surry County, which is located on the lower side of the James River, was formed from the southerly part of James City County, one of the colony's original shires. Surry sent its first representatives to the assembly in 1652. Although Surry County originally extended southward as far as Carolina, its eastern and western boundaries have remained fixed at Lawnes Creek on the east and Upper Chippokes Creek on the west. Sussex County eventually was created out of Surry County's southernmost territory, and during the early eighteenth century part of Surry's acreage was added to Brunswick County (HEN I:373; IV:355). The court records of Surry County are remarkably well preserved and provide many useful insights into the lives of its early residents. However, because Surry's territory was part of James City County from 1634 to 1652, and most of James City's antebellum court records have been lost or destroyed, there are major gaps in what is known about that period (see **James City County**).

Upper Norfolk County: see Nansemond County.

Warwick County: In 1634 the westerly part of the Corporation of Elizabeth City was split off to become the shire of Warwick River or Warwick River County. Its territory extended from Skiffs Creek and Mulberry Island on the west, to Maries Mount and Newport News Point on the east. It was bound on the south by the James River and on the north by York (formerly Charles River) County. In 1643 the name Warwick River County was shortened to Warwick County. At that time, the county's original boundaries were reaffirmed and described more explicitly (HEN I:224, 249–250). In 1958 the city of Warwick was consolidated with the city of Newport News, engulfing all of Warwick County, which became extinct. Warwick County's antebellum court records are fragmentary, although some of its early records survive.

Westmoreland County: Westmoreland County was formed in 1653 from the western part of Northumberland County, a descendant of the region called Chicacoan. Westmoreland County abuts north on the Potomac River and south on Richmond County, a descendant of "Old" Rappahannock County. Its original boundaries extended from the Machodoc River (on the east) to the falls of the Potomac River (on the west). Part of King George County, formed in 1720 from Richmond County, eventually was added to Westmoreland County (HEN I:381; IV:95). Westmoreland County's antebellum court records are intact.

York County: In 1634 Charles River County was formed from the land bordering the York River, from the New Poquoson River (by 1670 known as the Poquoson) westward to the limits of the colony. In 1636 the name of Charles River County was changed to York County. As time went on, York County's vast territory was subdivided. In 1651 Gloucester County, which extended from the York to the Piankatank rivers, was formed from the northerly part of York County. In 1654 New Kent County was formed from the westernmost part of York County. New Kent's size was reduced in 1688 when King and Queen County was formed. In 1790 Mathews County was formed from the northeastern part of Gloucester County (HEN I:224, 374, 388; III:94; XIII:162). York County's antebellum court records are essentially intact.

OBSERVATIONS

Extensive research in Virginia's seventeenth-century records has led to a broader understanding of the colony's formative years and hints at larger issues that may have played a role in the colony's development. For example, during the years

Virginia was under the sway of the Commonwealth government (1652–1660), a significant number of colonists who resided in Nansemond and Isle of Wight counties, home to a significant number of Virginians with Puritan leanings, began patenting land in the Northern Neck. Did they anticipate that the monarchy was likely to regain control and that there would be renewed pressure to support and attend the Established Church? Were they concerned about retributive justice? Or were they simply eager to be closer to Maryland, which had a substantial Puritan population? These questions remain to be answered. Another issue has come to light. A close examination of seventeenth-century land records reveals that most of the people investing in acreage on the Middle Peninsula were residents of the James-York Peninsula. In many instances the original patentees' descendants were the ones who became established on acreage that once had been on the colony's frontier.

County records and those of the overarching branches of government demonstrate that during the early seventeenth century there was a considerable amount of interaction between settlers living in Elizabeth City and those residing across the Chesapeake Bay on the Eastern Shore. Later in the century, colonists living in the Northern Neck frequently interacted with those living on Virginia's Eastern Shore.

During the seventeenth century conflict of interest does not seem to have been considered a serious issue, as many high-ranking officials simultaneously held multiple public offices. Public service yielded fees of office, which sometimes were lucrative, but holding office also presented the more successful with an opportunity to protect their business interests. Male freeholders could serve as court justices in any of the counties in which they owned land. In fact, some individuals served as a justice in two counties' courts simultaneously. Rarely did county justices recuse themselves from deliberations. There were no residency requirements associated with holding office as a burgess. Thus, a man could serve as a burgess for any of the counties in which he owned land, although he could not represent two counties at the same time.

Although the 1646 treaty was supposed to give Virginia's tributary Indians protection from their enemies and land was assigned to certain tribes, the natives' right to seek justice was very limited. As time went on and settlement became widespread, Indian leaders sometimes made treaties with county courts or came before a county court to have their grievances addressed. The Treaty of Middle Plantation, signed in 1677 and expanded in 1680, was supposed to give Virginia's tributary Indians legal rights comparable to those of English citizens. Records generated by Virginia's county courts and those of higher ranking officials reveal that Virginia's natives sometimes availed themselves of that privilege. County records also contain a wealth of information about the manner in which the colonists interacted with their Indian neighbors. Likewise, African Americans, if free, sometimes came into court seeking justice. Thus, governmental records provide a wealth of information on the Virginia colony's people.

*　*　*

Note: Within each chapter of this volume, asterisks have been used as a means of clustering family groups.

*　*　*

ACKNOWLEDGMENTS

The support provided by personnel involved in the Jamestown Archaeological Assessment—notably colleagues in the employ of the National Park Service, the Colonial Williamsburg Foundation, and the College of William and Mary—underpinned my research on Jamestown Island's people and the land they occupied. The able assistance, encouragement, and logistical support provided by Colonial Williamsburg reference librarians Susan Shames, Dell Moore, Marianne Martin, and George Yetter were invaluable. Thanks also to Marian Hoffman of the Genealogical Publishing Company for her careful and supportive editing, Carolyn L. Barkley for preparing the index to this book, and Gregory J. Brown for providing maps that illustrate how the boundary lines of Virginia counties evolved over time. The digital data included in each base map was taken from the *Atlas of Historical County Boundaries* (The Newberry Library, Dr. William M. Scholl Center for American History and Culture, http://publications.newberry.org/ahcbp) and ESRI common files, ArcGIS Online Map and Task Services, World Shaded Relief.

SOURCES AND ABBREVIATIONS

AMB: Ambler Papers 1636–1809. Library of Congress, Washington, D.C. Transcripts and microfilm, Rockefeller Library, Colonial Williamsburg Foundation, Williamsburg, Virginia.

AMB-AF: John Ambler Papers, 1770–1860, James City, Louisa, Amherst, Henrico and Hanover Counties. Records of Antebellum Southern Plantations for the Revolution Through the Civil War, Series E, Part 1. Microfilm, University of Virginia, Charlottesville, Virginia.

AMB-E: Ambler, Edward. Appraisal of Edward Ambler's estate, 1769. Transcript, Rockefeller Library, Colonial Williamsburg Foundation, Williamsburg, Virginia.

AMB-EJ: Ambler, Eliza Jaquelin. Letter dated October 10, 1798. Rockefeller Library, Colonial Williamsburg Foundation, Williamsburg, Virginia.

AMB-JJ: Ambler, John Jaquelin. History of Ambler Family in Virginia, 1826. Microfilm on file at the Library of Virginia, Richmond, Virginia. History of the Ambler Family in Virginia, 1828. Alderman Library, University of Virginia, Charlottesville, Virginia.

AMES 1: Ames, Susie M., ed. *County Court Records of Accomack-Northampton, Virginia, 1632–1640*. Washington: American Historical Association, 1954.

AMES 2: Ames, Susie M., ed. *County Court Records of Accomack-Northampton, Virginia, 1640–1645*. Charlottesville: University Press of Virginia, 1973.

AND: Andrews, Charles, ed. *Narratives of the Insurrections, 1665–1690*. New York: Charles Scribner's Sons, 1967.

BEV: Beverly, Robert II. *History of the Present State of Virginia (1705)*, L.B. Wright, ed. Chapel Hill: University of North Carolina Press, 1947.

BILL: Billings, Warren M., ed. *The Papers of Sir William Berkeley 1605–1677*. Richmond: Library of Virginia, 2007.

BOD: Boddie, John B. *Seventeenth Century Isle of Wight County, Virginia*. 2 vols. Chicago: Chicago Law Printing Company, 1938; repr., Baltimore: Genealogical Publishing Company, 1980.

BRO: Brown, Alexander G. *The Genesis of the United States*. 2 vols. Boston and New York: Houghton, Mifflin and Company, 1890; repr., Bowie, MD: Heritage Books Inc., 1994.

BRU: Bruce, Philip A. ed. "Viewers of the Tobacco Crop." *Virginia Magazine of History and Biography* 5:119–123.

BRYDON: Brydon, George M. *Virginia's Mother Church*. Richmond: Whittet and Shepperson, 1947.

BURGESS: Burgess, Lewis W. *Virginia Soldiers of 1776*. Richmond: Richmond Press Inc., 1929.

BYRD: Byrd, William II. *The Secret Diary of William Byrd of Westover, 1709–1712*. Louis B. Wright and Marion Tinling, eds. Richmond: The Dietz Press Inc., 1941.

BYRD 2: Byrd, William II. *Another Secret Diary of William Byrd of Westover, 1739–1741*. Maude H. Woodfin, ed., and Marion Tinling, trans. Richmond: The Dietz Press Inc., 1942.

CBE: Coldham, Peter W. *The Complete Book of Emigrants, 1607–1660*. Baltimore: Genealogical Publishing Company, 1987.

CHAPMAN: Chapman, Blanche A. *Wills and Administrations of Elizabeth City County, Virginia, 1688–1800*. Baltimore: Genealogical Publishing Company, 1980.

CHURCH: Church, Randolph W. *Virginia Legislative Petitions*. Richmond: Virginia State Library, 1984.

CJS: Barbour, Philip, ed. *Travels and Works of Captain John Smith, President of Virginia and Admiral of New England, 1580–1631*. 3 vols. Chapel Hill: University of North Carolina, 1986.

CLAGHORN: Claghorn, Charles E. *Naval Officers of the American Revolution: A Concise Biographical Dictionary*. Metuchen, N.J.: Scarecrow Press Inc., 1988.

CLARE: Clarendon Manuscripts, Bodelian Library, Oxford University, Oxford, England.

CLARK: Clark, William Bell, ed. *Naval Documents of the American Revolution*. 9 vols. Washington, D.C.: U.S. Government Printing Office, 1966.

CO: Colonial Office Papers. The National Archives, Kew, England. Survey Reports and microfilms, Rockefeller Library, Colonial Williamsburg Foundation, Williamsburg, Virginia.

CUSTIS: Custis, John Parke. Letter to George Washington, May 12, 1778. Virginia Historical Society, Richmond, Virginia.

DAVIES: Davies, K. G. *The Royal African Company*. London, New York, Toronto: Longmans, Green and Co., 1957.

DES: Descognet, Louis B., ed. *English Duplicates of Lost Virginia Records*. Princeton: privately published, 1958.

DOR: Dorman, John F., ed. *Adventurers of Purse and Person, Virginia 1607–1624/5*. 4th ed. 3 vols. Baltimore: Genealogical Publishing Company, 2004–2007.

DUNN: Dunn, Richard, ed. *Warwick County, Virginia, Colonial Court Records in Transcription*. Baltimore: Clearfield Company, 2000.

DURAND: Dauphine, Durand de. *A Brief Description of America with a Longer One of Virginia and Maryland,* Gilbert Chinard, trans. New York: Press of the Pioneers, 1934.

EAE: Coldham, Peter W. *English Adventurers and Emigrants, 1609–1660: Abstracts of Examinations in the High Court of Admiralty with Reference to Colonial America.* Baltimore: Genealogical Publishing Company, 1984.

EEAC: Coldham, Peter W. *English Estates of American Colonists.* Baltimore: Genealogical Publishing Company, 1980.

EJC: McIlwaine, H. R. *Executive Journals of the Council of Colonial Virginia.* 5 vols. Richmond: Virginia State Library, 1925–1945.

FLEE: Fleet, Beverley, comp. *Virginia Colonial Abstracts.* 3 vols. Baltimore: Genealogical Publishing Company, 1988.

FONT: Fontaine, John. *The Journal of John Fontaine, An Irish Huguenot Son in Spain and Virginia, 1710–1719.* Williamsburg: Colonial Williamsburg Foundation, 1972.

FOR: Force, Peter, comp. *Tracts and Other Papers, Relating to the Origin, Settlement and Progress of the Colonies in North America.* 4 vols. 1836; repr., Gloucester, MA: Peter Smith, 1963.

HAI: Haile, Edward W., ed. *Jamestown Narratives: Eyewitness Accounts of the Virginia Colony: The First Decade, 1607–1617.* Champlain, VA: Roundhouse, 1998.

HALL: Hall, Clayton C., ed. *Narratives of Early Maryland, 1633–1684.* New York: Charles Scribner's Sons, 1946; repr., Barnes and Noble, 1959.

HART: Hartwell, Henry et al. *The Present State of Virginia and the College [1697] by Henry Hartwell, James Blair and Edward Chilton.* Princeton: Princeton University, 1940.

HEITMAN: Heitman, F. B. *Historical Register of Officers During the War of the Revolution.* New York: Garland Publishing, 1967.

HEN: Hening, William W., ed. *The Statutes at Large: Being a Collection of All the Laws of Virginia.* 13 vols. Richmond: Samuel Pleasants, 1809–1823; repr., Charlottesville: University Press of Virginia, 1969.

HIN: Hinshaw, William W., ed. *Encyclopedia of American Quaker Genealogy.* Vol. 6. Ann Arbor: Edwards Brothers Inc., 1950.

HODGES: Hodges, Graham R. *The Black Loyalist Directory: African Americans in Exile After the American Revolution.* New York and London: Garland Publishing, 1996.

HOWARD: Billings, Warren M. ed. *The Papers of Francis Howard, Baron Howard of Effingham, 1643–1695.* Richmond: Library of Virginia, 1989.

HUD: Hudgins, Dennis. *Cavaliers and Pioneers: Abstracts of Virginia Land Patents and Grants.* Vol. 4. Richmond: Virginia Genealogical Society, 1994.

JAM: Jameson, J. Franklin, ed. *Narratives of New Netherland, 1609–1664.* New York: Charles Scribner's Sons, 1909; repr., Barnes and Noble, 1959.

JHB: McIlwaine, H. R. et al., eds. *Journals of the House of Burgesses, 1619–1776.* 13 vols. Richmond: Virginia State Library, 1905–1915.

LC: Lord Chamberlain's Accounts. The National Archives, Kew, England. Survey reports and microfilms, Rockefeller Library, Colonial Williamsburg Foundation, Williamsburg, Virginia.

LEDERER: John Lederer, *The Discoveries of John Lederer with Unpublished Letters by and about Lederer to Governor John Winthrop, Jr. and an Essay on the Indians of Lederer's Discoveries,* William P. Cumming, ed. Charlottesville: University Press of Virginia, 1958.

LEE: Lee Manuscripts 1638–1837. Virginia Historical Society, Richmond, Virginia.

LEF: Lefroy, J. H., comp. *Memorials of the Discovery and Early Settlement of the Bermudas or Somer Islands, 1511–1687.* Toronto: Bermuda Historical Society, University of Toronto Press, 1981.

LEO: Leonard, Cynthia M., comp. *The General Assembly of Virginia, July 30, 1619–January 11, 1978, A Bicentennial Register of Members.* Richmond: Virginia State Library Board, 1978.

LJC: McIlwaine, H. R., ed. *Legislative Journals of the Council of Colonial Virginia.* 3 vols. Richmond: Virginia State Library, 1918; repr., 1979.

LNC: Walter, Alice Granbery, comp. *Lower Norfolk County Court Records: Book A 1637–1646 and Book B 1646–1651/2.* Virginia Beach: privately published, 1978; repr., Baltimore: Clearfield Company, 1994.

MARSHALL: Marshall, James H., comp. *Abstracts of the Wills and Administrations of Northampton County, Virginia, 1632–1802.* Rockport, ME: Picton Press, 2001.

MCGC: McIlwaine, H. R., ed. *Minutes of the Council and General Court of Colonial Virginia.* Richmond: The Library Board, 1924; repr., Richmond: Virginia State Library, 1979.

MCGH: McGhan, Judith, indexer. *Virginia Will Records from the Virginia Magazine of History and Biography, the William and Mary College Quarterly, and Tyler's Quarterly.* Baltimore: Genealogical Publishing Company, 1982.

MEADE: Meade, Bishop William. *Old Churches, Ministers and Families of Virginia.* 2 vols. Baltimore: Genealogical Publishing Company, 1992.

MHS: Aspinall, Thomas et al. *Collections of the Massachusetts Historical Society* (Fourth Series) 9:1–164.

MIN: Minchinton, Walter et al., eds. *Virginia Slave-Trade Statistics, 1698–1775.* Richmond: Virginia State Library, 1984.

MOR: Morrison, J. H., comp. *Prerogative Court of Canterbury: Letters of Administration 1620–1630 (Inclusive), Abstracts Translated from the Original Latin.* London: privately published, 1935.

MORTON: Morton, Richard L. *Colonial Virginia.* University of North Carolina Press, Chapel Hill, North Carolina, 1956.

NEAL: Neal, Rosemary C., comp. *Elizabeth City County, Virginia (Now the City of Hampton), Deeds, Wills, Court Orders, Etc. 1634, 1659, 1688–1701.* Bowie, MD: Heritage Books, 1987.

NEI: Neill, Edward D. *Virginia Carolorum: The Colony Under the Rule of Charles the 1st and 2nd.* New York: J. Munsell's Sons, Albany, 1886; repr., Bowie, MD: Heritage Books, 1996.

NEVILLE: Neville, John D. *Bacon's Rebellion, Abstracts of Materials in the Colonial Records Project.* Williamsburg: The Jamestown Foundation, 1976.

NN: Northern Neck Grants. Virginia Land Office 1692–1862. Microfilm on file at Library of Virginia, Richmond, and Rockefeller Library, Colonial Williamsburg Foundation, Williamsburg, Virginia. Database and digital images. Library of Virginia. http://ajax.lva.lib.va.us/.

NUG: Nugent, Nell M. et al. *Cavaliers and Pioneers: Abstracts of Virginia Land Patents and Grants [1623–1732].* 3 vols. Vol. 1: 1623–1666. Richmond: Dietz Printing Company, 1934 (repr., Genealogical Publishing Company, 1963); Vol. 2: 1666–1695. Richmond: Virginia State Library, 1977; Vol. 3: 1695–1732. Richmond: Virginia State Library, 1979.

OCAL: O'Callaghan, E. B., ed. *Documents Relative to the Colonial History of the State of New York, Procured in Holland, England and France.* Vol. 1. Albany: Weed, Parsons and Co., 1856.

PALM: Palmer, William P. *Calendar of Virginia State Papers.* 11 vols. New York: Kraus Reprint, 1968.

PARKS: Parks, Gary, ed. *Virginia Land Records.* Baltimore: Genealogical Publishing Company, 1982.

PB: Virginia Land Office Patent Books 1619–1660. Microfilm on file at Library of Virginia, Richmond, and Rockefeller Library, Colonial Williamsburg Foundation, Williamsburg, Virginia. Database and digital images. Library of Virginia. http://ajax.lva.lib.va.us/.

PERRY: Perry, William S., comp. *Historical Collections Relating to the American Colonial Church.* Vol. I, Virginia. New York: AMS Press, 1969.

PRICE: Price, Jacob M. *Perry of London.* Cambridge, MD, and London, England: Harvard University Press, 1992.

RAIMO Raimo, John W. *Biographical Directory of American Colonial and Revolutionary Governors, 1607–1789.* Westport, CT: Meckler Books, 1980.

RUT: Rutman, Darrett B. et al. *A Place in Time: Middlesex County, 1650–1750.* New York: Norton Publishers, 1984.

SAIN: Sainsbury, William Noel et al. *Calendar of State Papers, Colonial Series, America and the West Indies.* 22 vols. Vaduz, Liechtenstein: Kraus Reprint, 1964.

SAL: Salley, Alexander S., comp. *Narratives of Early Carolina.* New York: Charles Scribner's Sons, 1911; repr., Barnes and Noble, 1967.

SCHRE: Van Schreeven, William J. et al. *Revolutionary Virginia: The Road to Independence.* 8 vols. Charlottesville: University Press of Virginia, 1973–1979.

SHELLEY: Shelley, Fred, ed. "The Journal of Ebenezer Hazard in Virginia, 1777." *Virginia Magazine of History and Biography* 62:400–423.

SHEP: Sheppherd, Samuel. *The Statutes at Large of Virginia*. 3 vols. New York: AMS Press, 1970.

SHEPPERSON: Shepperson, Archibald Bolling. *John Paradise and Lucy Ludwell of London and Williamsburg*. Richmond: The Dietz Press Inc., 1942.

SMITH: Smith, Annie L., comp. *The Quitrents of Virginia*. Gloucester County, VA: privately published, 1957; repr., Baltimore: Genealogical Publishing Company, 1980.

SPVB: Chamberlayne, Charles, ed. *Vestry Book of St. Peter's Parish, 1684–1786*. Richmond: Library of Virginia, 1937.

SR: Virginia Colonial Records Project Survey Reports. Rockefeller Library, Colonial Williamsburg, Virginia. Database and digital images. Library of Virginia. http://ajax.lva.va.us/.

STAN: Stanard, William G. and Mary Stanard, comps. *Colonial Virginia Register*. Albany: privately published, 1902; repr., Baltimore: Genealogical Publishing Company, 1965.

TRAVIS: Travis, Robert J. *The Travis (Travers) Family and Its Allies*. Savannah, GA: privately published, 1954.

TYLER: Tyler, Lyon G. *Cradle of the Republic*. Richmond: The Hermitage Press Inc., 1906.

VAL: Torrence, Clayton P., ed. *The Edward Pleasants Valentine Papers*. Vol. 4. Richmond: The Valentine Museum, 1927.

VI&A: Martha W. McCartney. *Virginia Immigrants and Adventurers 1607–1635: A Biographical Dictionary*. Baltimore: Genealogical Publishing Company, 2007.

WASH: Washburn, Wilcomb E. "Sir William Berkeley's 'A History of our Miseries.'" *William and Mary Quarterly* (Third Series) 14:403–413.

WASHINGTON: Washington, George. *The Writings of George Washington from Original Manuscript Sources*. John C. Fitzpatrick, ed. Washington, D.C.: U. S. Government Printing Office, 1936.

WAT: Waters, Henry F. *Genealogical Gleanings in England, New Series*. 2 vols. Boston: New England Historic Genealogical Society, 1901, 1907; repr., Baltimore: Genealogical Publishing Company, 1969.

WINFREE: Winfree, Waverley K. *The Laws of Virginia Being a Supplement to Hening's The Statutes At Large, 1700–1750*. Richmond: Virginia State Library, 1971.

WISEMAN: Wiseman, Samuel. *Samuel Wiseman's Book of Record, 1676–1677*. Microfilm, Rockefeller Library, Colonial Williamsburg Foundation, Williamsburg, Virginia.

WITH: Withington, Lothrop. *Virginia Gleanings in England*. Baltimore: Genealogical Publishing Company, 1980.

MANUSCRIPTS AND MAPS

Ancteville, Chevalier de. Journal of the Chesapeake Campaign, 1781. Archives of the Navy No. B4-184, ff 145,157. Transcript, Rockefeller Library, Colonial Williamsburg Foundation Research Archives.

Anonymous, 1677 Treaty. Library of Congress, Miscellaneous Virginia Records 1606–1692, Bland Manuscripts, XIV, ff 226–233.

Carson, Jane. "Green Spring Plantation in the Seventeenth Century." Manuscript, Rockefeller Library, Colonial Williamsburg Foundation, Williamsburg, Virginia, 1954.

Desandrouin, Jean Nicholas. Plan du terein a la Rive Gauche de la Riviere de James, 1781–1782. Rockefeller Library, Colonial Williamsburg Foundation, Williamsburg, Virginia.

Girardin, Louis. Amoenitates Graphicae, 1805. Rockefeller Library, Colonial Williamsburg Foundation, Williamsburg, Virginia.

Griffin, Corbin. February 2, 1701, will. Huntington Library, San Marino, California.

Lawrence, Richard. A Mapp of Paradise belonging to Mr. Richard Lee, July 22, 1672. Alderman Library, University of Virginia, Charlottesville, Virginia.

Pindavako, Indian treaty between Pindavaco, the protector of the young king of Chiskyacke and representatives of Edward Wyatt, October 29, 1655. Brock Box 256 f 1. Huntington Library, San Marino, California.

Scarborough, Edmund. Report of Colonel Edmund Scarburgh [Scarborough] to the Governor and Council of Virginia on his Expedition into Maryland in October, 1663. In Ralph T. Whitelaw, *Virginia's Eastern Shore*. Gloucester, Massachusetts: P. Smith, 1968.

Senior, John. Survey of Richard Kemp's Land, 1642. Rockefeller Library, Colonial Williamsburg Foundation, Williamsburg, Virginia.

Smith, John et al. April 4, 1745, deed of John Smith and wife, Mary, and Martha Jaquelin, to Richard Ambler. New York Historical Society, New York.

Soane, John. This parcel containing 285 acres surveyed for Lady Berkeley the last of October 1679. Virginia Historical Society, Richmond, Virginia.

Soane, John. Land for William Sherwood, 1681. Library of Congress, Washington, D.C., and Rockefeller Library, Colonial Williamsburg Foundation, Williamsburg, Virginia.

Soane, John. Survey for Thomas Lord Culpeper, 1683. Library of Congress, Washington, D.C., and Rockefeller Library, Colonial Williamsburg Foundation, Williamsburg, Virginia.

Soane, John. Plot of 660 acres for Christopher Wormeley, 1684. Robinson Papers, Rockefeller Library, Colonial Williamsburg Foundation, Williamsburg, Virginia.

Soane, John. The Plott of 76 acres of lands survey'd on 12th of December 1690 for Henry Jenkins. Library of Congress, Washington, D.C., and Virginia Historical Society, Richmond, Virginia.

Thompson, James. Property of Champion Travis Esquire Surveyed & Delineated the 20th of M[ ] [1780]. Rockefeller Library, Colonial Williamsburg Foundation, Williamsburg, Virginia.

Tucker, St. George Jr. Journal of the Siege of Yorktown and the Surrender of Cornwallis, 1781. Rockefeller Library, Colonial Williamsburg Foundation, Williamsburg, Virginia.

Wormeley, Christopher. Last will and testament, June 20, 1690. Brock Box 222, Brock Collection, Huntington Library, San Marino, California.

Yates, William. Last will and testament, September 5, 1764, proved October 8, 1764. Brock Box 221, Brock Collection, Huntington Library, San Marino, California.

MISCELLANEOUS PUBLISHED SOURCES

Billings, Warren G., ed. "Some Acts Not in Hening's, April 1652, November 1652, and July 1653." *Virginia Magazine of History and Biography* 83:65–72.

Brown, William H., ed. "Conference Between Penn and Talbot at Newcastle in 1684." Maryland Historical Society 3:21–32.

Bruce, Philip A., ed. "Bacon's Men in Surry." *Virginia Magazine of History and Biography* 5:368–373.

Bruce, Philip A., ed. "Bacon's Rebellion." *Virginia Magazine of History and Biography* 1:167–186.

Bruce, Philip A., ed. "Colonial Letters &c." *Virginia Magazine of History and Biography* 5:42–53.

Bruce, Philip A., ed. "Defense of Colonel Edward Hill," *Virginia Magazine of History and Biography* 3:239–347; 342–349.

Bruce, Philip A., ed. "Diary of Captain John Davis of the Pennsylvania Line." *Virginia Magazine of History and Biography* 1:1–16.

Bruce, Philip A., ed. "Historical Notes and Queries." *Virginia Magazine of History and Biography* 1:453–476.

Bruce, Philip A., ed. "The Indians of Southern Virginia." *Virginia Magazine of History and Biography* 7:337–357.

Bruce, Philip A., ed. "Indians of Southern Virginia, 1650–1711: Depositions in the Virginia and North Carolina Boundary Case," *Virginia Magazine of History and Biography* 8:1–11.

Bruce, Philip A., ed. "Letters of Lafayette." *Virginia Magazine of History and Biography* 6:55–59.

Bruce, Philip A., ed. "Papers Relating to the Administration of Governor Nicholson and to the Founding of William and Mary College." *Virginia Magazine of History and Biography* 7:275–286.

Bruce, Philip A., ed. "Persons Who Suffered by Bacon's Rebellion." *Virginia Magazine of History and Biography* 5:64–70.

Bruce, Philip A., ed. "Robert Beverley," *Virginia Magazine of History and Biography* 5:405–407

Bruce, Philip A., ed. "Robert Beverley and his Descendants." *Virginia Magazine of History and Biography* 2:405–412.

Bruce, Philip A., ed. "Title to Green Spring." *Virginia Magazine of History and Biography* 5:383–387.

Chandler, J. A. C. et al., eds. "George Wilson." *William and Mary Quarterly* (Second Series) 5:266–267.

Chandler, J. A. C. et al., eds. "Letters of William Byrd II and Sir Hans Sloane Relative to Plants and Minerals of Virginia." *William and Mary Quarterly* (Second Series) 1:186–200.

Chilton, W. B., ed. "The Brent Family." *Virginia Magazine of History and Biography* 16:96–102.

Clayton, John. Map of Jamestown and May 12, 1688, letter to Robert Boyle. Boyle Papers 39, Item 3, ff 160–162. Archives of the Royal Society of London, London.

James, Edward W. "Henry Woodhouse." *William and Mary Quarterly* (First Series) 1:227–232.

Johnson, Christopher. Letter to his wife, July 16, 1781. Virginia Historical Society, Richmond, Virginia.

Maxwell, William, ed. "Jamestown." *Virginia Historical Register* 2:138–139.

Maxwell, William, ed. "A Tour in the United States of America &c by J. F. D. Smyth." *Virginia Historical Register* 6:10–17.

Maxwell, William, ed. "Lord Cornwallis's Movements and Operations in Virginia in 1781." *Virginia Historical Register* 6:181–202.

Maxwell, William, ed. "Original Letters: Samuel Athawes to Edward Ambler." *Virginia Historical Register* 3:25–29.

Mumford, William. *Reports of Cases Argued and Determined in the Supreme Court of Appeals of Virginia*. 6 vols. Richmond: N. Pollard Printer, 1921.

Rowland, Kay Mason, ed. "Mercer Land Book." *William and Mary Quarterly* 13 (First Series):165–168.

Stanard, William G., ed. "Appraisal of Estate of Philip Ludwell, Esquire, Deceased." *Virginia Magazine of History and Biography* 21:395–416.

Stanard, William G., Ed. "Diary of Colonel William Bolling of Bolling Hall." *Virginia Magazine of History and Biography* 43:237–250.

Stanard, William G., ed. "January 29, 1737." *Virginia Magazine of History and Biography* 12:352.

Stanard, William G., ed. "Letters of William Byrd, First." *Virginia Magazine of History and Biography* 26:17–31.

Stanard, William G., ed. "Lord Culpeper." *Virginia Magazine of History and Biography* 41:196

Stanard, William G., ed. "Minutes of the Council and General Court." *Virginia Magazine of History and Biography* 24:238–249.

Stanard, William G., ed. "Notes to Council Journals." *Virginia Magazine of History and Biography* 33:183–193.

Stanard, William G., ed., "Old Rappahannock County Records, Volume 1656–1664," *Virginia Magazine of History and Biography* 38:391.

Stanard, William G. ed. "Papers from the Virginia State Auditors Office Now in the State Library." *Virginia Magazine of History and Biography* 25:376–388.

Stanard, William G., ed. "Philip Ludwell to Edward Jenings, 1709, in regard to a Negro Plot." *Virginia Magazine of History and Biography* 19:23–24.

Stanard, William G., ed. "Proprietors of the Northern Neck." *Virginia Magazine of History and Biography* 33:333–358.

Stanard, William G., ed. "The Randolph Manuscript". *Virginia Magazine of History and Biography* 18:1–24, 241–255.

Stanard, William G., ed. "Travis Family." *William and Mary Quarterly* (First Series) 17:141–144.

Stanard, William G., ed. "Virginia Gleanings in England." *Virginia Magazine of History and Biography* 13:402–409.

Stanard, William G., ed. "Virginia Gleanings in England." *Virginia Magazine of History and Biography* 14:419–426.

Stanard, William G., ed. "Virginia Gleanings in England." *Virginia Magazine of History and Biography* 19:282–291.

Stanard, William G. "Virginia in 1637." *Virginia Magazine of History and Biography* 9:175–176.

Stanard, William G. "Virginia in 1638." *Virginia Magazine of History and Biography* 10:427–428.

Stanard, William G., ed. "Virginia in 1638–1639." *Virginia Magazine of History and Biography* 11:48–49.

Stanard, William G., ed. "Virginia in 1639." *Virginia Magazine of History and Biography* 12:392.

Stanard, William G., ed. "Virginia in 1650." *Virginia Magazine of History and Biography* 17:136–140.

Sully, Robert. Letter to Lyman Draper, October 1854. Wisconsin Historical Society, Madison, Wisconsin. Facsimiles of paintings and sketches on file at National Park Service Visitor Center, Jamestown.

Theatre Data Base: http://www.theatredatabase.com/17th_century/sir_william_davenant.html

Tyler, Lyon G., ed. "The Armistead Family." *William and Mary Quarterly* (First Series) 6:31–32.

Tyler, Lyon G., ed. "The Armistead Family." *William and Mary Quarterly* (First Series) 7:226–234.

Tyler, Lyon G., ed. "Cole Family." *William and Mary Quarterly* (First Series) 5:177–181.

Tyler, Lyon G., ed. "Diary of John Blair." *William and Mary Quarterly* (First Series) 7:133–153.

Tyler, Lyon G., ed. "Gooch Family." *William and Mary Quarterly* (First Series) 5:110–112.

Tyler, Lyon G., ed. "Historical and Genealogical Notes." *William and Mary Quarterly* (First Series) 4:65–69.

Tyler, Lyon G., ed. "Historical and Genealogical Notes," *William and Mary Quarterly* (First Series) 20:218–222.

Tyler, Lyon G., ed. "James City County Petitions." *Tyler's Historical Quarterly* 2:177–193.

Tyler, Lyon G., ed. "Lt. Colonel Walter Chiles." *William and Mary Quarterly* (First Series) 1:75–78.

Tyler, Lyon G., ed. "Ludwell Family," *William and Mary Quarterly* (First Series) 19:199–214.

Tyler, Lyon G., ed. "Micajah Perry." *William and Mary Quarterly* (First Series) 17:264–268.

Williams, Neville. "The Tribulations of John Bland, Merchant." *Virginia Magazine of History and Biography* 72:19–41.

Wise, Jennings Cropper. "The Northampton Protest." Transcription in *Ye Kingdome of Accawmake or the Eastern Shore of Virginia in the Seventeenth Century*, Baltimore: Regional Publishing Company, 1961.

HISTORICAL NEWSPAPERS

Boston Gazette, January 29–February 5, 1729. Microfilm, Swem Library, College of William and Mary, Williamsburg, Virginia.

Dixon, John. *Virginia Gazette*. Williamsburg: *Virginia Gazette*, 1777–1780. Microfilms, Rockefeller Library, Colonial Williamsburg Foundation, Williamsburg, Virginia.

Pinkney, John. *Virginia Gazette*. Williamsburg: *Virginia Gazette*, 1775. Microfilms, Rockefeller Library, Colonial Williamsburg Foundation, Williamsburg, Virginia.

Purdie, Alexander. *Virginia Gazette*. Williamsburg: *Virginia Gazette*, 1775. Microfilms, Rockefeller Library, Colonial Williamsburg Foundation, Williamsburg, Virginia.

Purdie, Alexander and John Dixon. *Virginia Gazette*. Williamsburg: *Virginia Gazette*, 1772–1773. Microfilms, Rockefeller Library, Colonial Williamsburg Foundation, Williamsburg, Virginia.

Richmond Times-Dispatch. May 25, 1822, article on Jamestown Day. National Park Service Archives, Yorktown, Virginia.

Richmond Whig. October 24, 1862, edition. Richmond: *Richmond Whig*, 1862. Microfilm, Swem Library, College of William and Mary, Williamsburg, Virginia.

Rind, William. *Virginia Gazette.* Williamsburg: *Virginia Gazette*, 1772. Microfilms, Rockefeller Library, Colonial Williamsburg Foundation, Williamsburg, Virginia.

Virginia Gazette and Weekly Advertiser. Richmond: *Virginia Gazette and Weekly Advertiser*, 1784. Microfilms, Rockefeller Library, Colonial Williamsburg Foundation, Williamsburg, Virginia.

COUNTY RECORDS

Throughout this volume, reliable transcriptions of early court records or microfilmed copies of the original records have been utilized. References to specific record books have been provided. That said, the loss of some counties' antebellum court records, like the loss of so many early patents, sometimes has presented insurmountable challenges.

GLOSSARY

Ancient Planter: someone who came to Virginia prior to Sir Thomas Dale's May 1616 departure and had lived in the colony at least three years when applying for a patent. Ancient planters were eligible for 100 acres of land and had a few other privileges.

Administrator: the person appointed by court officials to settle an estate. A female administrator sometimes was termed an **administratrix**.

Burgess: an elected official who represented his community in the legislature.

Cape Merchant: the Virginia Company's official merchant in the Virginia colony.

Caveat: an instrument filed by a party intent upon halting the patenting process until his opposition could be entered.

Churchwarden: the "chairman" or headman of a parish vestry.

Court Commissioner or Justice: local officials who performed judiciary functions.

Decedent: a legal term used in reference to a deceased person.

Escheat: the reversion of land to the Crown or other granting party (in the case of Proprietary territories) when a patentee failed to leave heirs or was found guilty of a major crime.

Established Church: the Anglican Church, which was the Virginia colony's state church until the time of the American Revolution.

Executor: an individual designated by the maker of a will to settle his/her estate. A female executor sometimes was termed an **executrix**.

Factor: a merchant's agent or representative.

Fee Simple Ownership: outright ownership of a piece of property, including the right to sell.

First (1st) Supply: the first group of new colonists to arrive in Jamestown after the initial establishment of settlement. They landed in January 1608.

Freedom Dues: the allotment of corn and clothes usually provided to a newly freed servant who had completed his/her agreed-upon term of service.

Guardian: a person appointed to oversee the general welfare and material assets of an underage orphan.

Headright: an entitlement to 50 acres of land, awarded to someone who paid for his own (or another person's) transportation to Virginia.

Hogshead: the large cask or barrel-like containers into which dried tobacco leaves were packed and then shipped out of the colony.

Hundreds: a seventeenth-century term used in reference to a large plantation. Prior to the formation of county government, the leaders of Hundreds were authorized to settle petty disputes and perform other functions associated with leadership.

Indenture: a service contract or agreement made between a master and servant.

Indentured Servant: a person of either sex who agreed to work for a specified amount of time in exchange for transportation, food, shelter, and clothing. A guardian could sign a contract on a minor child's behalf.

Intestate: someone who died before making a will.

Legatee: an heir.

Life-rights: the right to possession for one's lifetime.

Nuncupative Will: a will made verbally in the presence of witnesses.

Old Style and New Style Calendar Dates: The Old Style, or Julian, Calendar was in general use in England until 1752. With the Old Style Calendar, March 25th was the first day of the new year: New Year's Day.

Parish: the geographic area served by a church.

Particular Plantation: a settlement whose cost was underwritten by private investors who usually outfitted and sent a group of prospective colonists to Virginia.

Patentee: a person to whom a tract of un-owned land was assigned by means of a patent.

Plant: to clear, develop, or settle upon unclaimed or vacant land, a requirement for validating one's title; synonymous with "seat."

Probate: the process whereby the real and/or personal assets of a deceased person are documented, his/her just debts are paid, and distribution is made to legitimate decedent's heirs.

Reversionary Heir: the individual or individuals to whom a decedent's estate would revert if the primary heirs were deceased.

Seat: to clear, develop, or settle upon un-owned or vacant land, thereby validating one's claim; synonymous with "plant."

Second (2nd) Supply: the second group of new colonists to arrive in Jamestown after the initial establishment of settlement. They landed during the latter part of 1608.

Son-in-Law, Daughter-in-Law: this term often was applied to stepchildren but also could refer to members associated with a family through marriage.

Testator: the maker of a will.

Third (3rd) Supply: the third group of new colonists to arrive in Jamestown after the initial establishment of settlement. Some of these people reached Virginia in 1609 and the remainder, who were shipwrecked in Bermuda, landed in May 1610.

Tobacco Inspector: an appointed official authorized to examine casks or hogsheads of tobacco that had been prepared for export. His job was to assure that the tobacco being sent out of the colony was of saleable quality and did not include trash.

Tobacco Note: a certificate obtained from a tobacco inspector certifying that an individual had available a certain number of hogsheads of saleable tobacco. Tobacco notes were used as a medium of exchange, much like currency.

Vestry: a small committee of elected church officials who were responsible for overseeing the business of their parish. Colonial vestries, always male, were responsible for maintaining church property and, during the early seventeenth century, for seeing that moral laws were enforced. Vestrymen also were responsible for public welfare.

JAMESTOWN PEOPLE TO 1800

Landowners, Public Officials, Minorities, and Native Leaders

JAMESTOWN'S HISTORY

Jamestown, the Virginia colony's capital for nearly a century, was a community where socioeconomic status, gender, and ethnicity were important determinants. The men, women, and children whose biographies are included in this volume were part of a complex multicultural society that evolved not only in response to the colony's growth and development but also to leadership philosophies and directives from overseas. The capital city's population soared whenever the assembly and courts were in session. Visitors and inhabitants included public officials of divergent rank and status, Indian leaders, merchants and mariners, planters, titled men and women, clergy, tavern-keepers, slave traders, and a myriad of skilled workers. Also present were pirates, foreign and naturalized citizens, jailbirds, indentured servants, slaves, religious dissenters, and newly arrived immigrants. Contrary to popular belief, after the capital moved to Williamsburg, Jamestown continued to be a small but viable community that enjoyed representation in the assembly until 1776.

The Virginia Adventure

Captain Christopher Newport, commander of the small fleet that brought the Virginia Company of London's first colonists across the Atlantic, set sail from England on Saturday, December 20, 1606. The 104 men aboard the *Susan Constant, Discovery*, and *Godspeed* were embarking on an adventure that changed the course of history. Captain Newport had unrivaled experience in navigating the American coastline, and it was with confidence that officials of the Virginia Company chose him to convey their colonists to Virginia. Bartholomew Gosnold and Gabriel Archer had been to New England and were familiar with its natives and their language. Captain John Smith and others in the group were acquainted with the narratives of the men involved in the attempts to plant a colony on Roanoke Island. Thus, some of the first colonists had an idea of what to expect once they reached land. That Smith and Newport were able to communicate with the natives suggests that they had at least a minimal working knowledge of the Algonquian language.

The three ships arrived safely in the Chesapeake Bay on April 26, 1607, after a difficult 18-week crossing. Cramped quarters, seasickness, boredom, and food inferior to their usual fare probably made the would-be colonists fractious and somewhat apprehensive about what lay ahead. Nearly half of Virginia's first settlers were gentlemen, scholars, artisans, and tradesmen, not laborers or sturdy yeoman farmers whose basic skills and physical conditioning would have been invaluable in a wilderness environment. Captain John Smith, an experienced explorer and soldier-of-fortune, was an exception, and in time his survival skills proved invaluable. As soon as Captain Newport reached Virginia, he opened a sealed box containing the names of the seven men the Virginia Company had handpicked to serve as the colony's first council. Exercising their right to elect their own president, the members of the council chose Edward Maria Wingfield, Virginia's first chief executive. Later, Virginia Company officials selected the colony's governor, who had the right to choose members of his council and other subordinates. Importantly, the Virginia Company's instructions to its first colonists brought to the New World the rudiments of English common law.

Planting the Colony

During the colonists' first few days in Virginia, they sailed inland to explore the countryside. When they went ashore, they found magnificent timber, fields covered with brilliantly colored flowers, lush vegetation, fertile soil, and an abundance of wildfowl, game, and seafood. The Virginia wilderness also had large meadows that would make excellent pasturage for cattle. As the colonists moved up the broad river called the Powhatan, later the James, they encountered natives whose bodies were ornamented with brightly colored furs and jewelry of bone, shell, and copper, and whose hair was adorned with feathers and animal horns. According to John Smith, some of the Indians welcomed the newcomers hospitably, offering food and entertainment. Others discharged arrows and then fled from the colonists' retaliatory gunfire.

On May 12th, after nearly three weeks of exploring, Newport's fleet arrived at a promontory the men called Archer's Hope, naming it after Gabriel Archer, who favored building their settlement there. But because the water was too shallow for their ships to anchor near the shore, they continued on upstream. The May 13, 1607, landing of the colonists on a small, marsh-rimmed peninsula almost enveloped by the James River heralded the establishment of the first permanent English settlement in America. There, within the territory of the Pasbehay (Paspahegh) Indians, the small vessels came to rest at a site where, according to George Percy, "our shippes doe lie so neere the shoare that they are moored to the Trees in six fathom water." John Smith said that President Wingfield "would admit no exercise at armes, or fortification but the boughs of trees cast together in the forme of a halfe moone," a lunette. Within days, the Indians became increasingly bold in their interactions with the colonists and on May 26, 1607, when they attacked the slightly crafted retreat, the settlers found it difficult to defend themselves. Afterward, Wingfield decided that a new, more substantial fort should be built, one that had palisades and mounted ordnance. According to Gabriel Archer, construction of a palisaded fort got underway on Thursday, May 28, 1607; it was finished by June 15th. The colonists' first real fort was triangular and had mounted artillery and "three bulwarks at every corner like a half-moon." After the fort was built, the settlers worked diligently, cutting down trees so that they would have room "to pitch their Tents." They also prepared the ground for corn and fabricated some clapboard that could be taken back to England. Then came the summer sicknesses. According to George Percy, by August the settlers had begun dying in droves. Some succumbed to the bloody flux, burning fevers, and swellings, and others died of wounds they received from the Indians. However, most of the men succumbed to famine. After successive changes in leadership, John Smith became president. His pragmatic, though unpopular, approach included the imposition of military discipline and forcing the colonists to plant crops, build houses, and work toward their own support.

Native Life at the Time of Colonization

In 1607, when the English established their first permanent settlement, Tidewater Virginia's natives were under the sway of Wahunsunacock or Powhatan. He was a paramount chief, who reigned over 32 districts that encompassed more than 150 villages whose inhabitants paid him tribute and supported him in times of war. John Smith described Powhatan as a monarch to whom many lesser kings (or werowances) were subservient. Thus, the people of the Powhatan Chiefdom were members of a society in which rank and status were important. Scholars believe that the Powhatan Chiefdom took form during the 1570s, when Powhatan inherited the right to lead six or more small chiefdoms within a vast territory that extended from the falls of the James River northward to the York. Around the time the first colonists arrived, Powhatan was trying to seize control of the Chickahominy, a strong native group governed by a council of eight elders rather than by a solitary, all-powerful leader. He also attempted to assert his supremacy over some of the lesser chiefdoms between the Rappahannock and Potomac rivers. By the close of 1608 Powhatan controlled almost all of the sub-chiefdoms or districts located in Virginia's coastal plain. He lived at Werowocomoco, on the north side of the York River at Purton Bay, but in 1609 he withdrew to Orapax, a Powhatan Indian "hunting town" that lay between the Chickahominy River's headwaters and the Pamunkey River. Powhatan died in 1618, a year after the demise of his daughter, Pocahontas. Archaeologists believe that at the time of initial European contact, the Powhatan Indians were conducting seasonal hunting expeditions inland to, and perhaps beyond, the fall line. That probably increased tensions with native peoples who lived further inland.

Captain John Smith and other early writers recorded their observations about native life, but they surely overlooked many subtle, more important differences between the Indians and the Europeans. The Powhatans considered land merely a part of the earth, like the sky, water, and the air, and therefore available to all for subsistence. Thus, the European concept of *owning* land was foreign to them. The two cultures also had vastly different views of religion. The Powhatans, while open to the idea of a Christian deity, were reluctant to renounce their own gods. Although both cultures viewed accumulated wealth as an emblem of social status, they had a much different concept of inheritance. With the Powhatans, it passed through the female line rather than the male. For example, Powhatan's chiefdom could descend to his next oldest brother or the son of his eldest sister but not to his own children. In light of the vast differences between the two peoples and their mutual lack of understanding, they were destined to collide.

Bad Timing: Climatic Conditions at the Time of European Contact

The University of Arkansas's study of tree-ring data from a bald cypress near Jamestown Island reveals that the first European colonists arrived during a period of severe drought that lasted from 1606 to 1612, the driest period in 770 years, and that conditions were particularly severe in eastern Virginia. Drought conditions would have created a crisis for natives and colonists alike, because plant materials would not have been readily available for subsistence, which, in turn, would have affected the availability of game animals and fish. Thus, when the first Virginia colonists arrived, the natives they encountered would have experienced a bad crop year and probably were dealing with food shortages. Also, water quality would have been at its poorest. Regional drought would have increased the salinity of Virginia's tidal waterways, especially near Jamestown Island, which lies squarely within the James River's oligohaline zone, where the exchange between fresh and salt water is minimal.

Newly Arrived Colonists Strain Resources

In early January 1608, 120 weak and famished immigrants (the 1st Supply) landed in Jamestown. Approximately nine months later, 70 more colonists arrived in the 2nd Supply, which included two women—the first female colonists. Finally, in May 1609 a 3rd Supply set out for Virginia. The fleet of nine ships got caught in a hurricane, and in August seven of the ships limped into Jamestown with 200–300 passengers. One small vessel was lost at sea and the flagship *Seaventure* ran aground in Bermuda, stranding Sir Thomas Gates and the other men chosen to serve as the colony's principal leaders. In Jamestown the struggle to survive proved so arduous that the winter of 1609–1610 became known as the Starving Time and nearly led to the colony's extinction. Gates and the others stranded in Bermuda managed to make their way to Virginia in two vessels that they fabricated from the island's native cedar wood. When they reached the colony in late May 1610, the conditions they found were horrific.

Military Governance

Within a day of his arrival in Jamestown, Sir Thomas Gates began forcing the colonists to work toward their own support. He also devised a strict code of military justice, *The Lawes Divine, Morall, and Martiall, &c.*, which he completed on May 24, 1610. However, Gates lacked the provisions he needed to revive the colony and decided to evacuate the surviving settlers to Newfoundland, where they could secure sustenance and safe passage back to England. Only the timely arrival of Governor and Captain General Thomas West, Lord Delaware, on June 9, 1610, averted the abandonment of the colony. The next day, the colonists heavy-heartedly returned to Jamestown.

On June 12, 1610, Delaware endorsed the code of conduct that Sir Thomas Gates had formulated, and in mid-June he sent Sir George Somers to Bermuda to retrieve additional provisions. Then, in late July he dispatched Gates to England to bring back more settlers and supplies, and to report that the colony needed farmers and laborers who could produce a dependable food supply and women so that families could be established.

During the time Delaware was in the colony, he accomplished a great deal. He had the settlers build new, more weatherproof houses in Jamestown, and he strengthened the colony's defenses. He also made some important organizational changes. Ultimately, ill health forced Lord Delaware to leave Virginia, and he departed on March 28, 1611, only ten months after his arrival. Approximately two weeks later, Sir Thomas Dale arrived. Like Delaware, he endorsed martial law, and on June 22, 1611, he enlarged and enhanced the strict code of conduct that Gates had devised. Many of these regulations were harsh and were enforced with the death penalty, but they enabled the colony to survive.

When Gates returned in August 1611 with more colonists, provisions, and livestock, Dale began implementing some of the Virginia Company's instructions. They included planting several settlements toward the head of the James River, away from Jamestown Island's salt marshes. In 1614 he also sent some colonists to the Eastern Shore to extract salt from seawater, so that fish could be preserved.

Gates left Virginia in August 1614, and when Dale departed in May 1616, he left Captain George Yeardley in charge. Yeardley was replaced by Samuel Argall, who was appointed deputy governor in early 1617 and reached Virginia on May 15, 1617. Argall, like the other "hard-liners," believed that martial law was essential to the colony's success.

Ralph Hamor's Observations

In 1614 Ralph Hamor reported that Jamestown Island was thickly wooded when the colonists first arrived. He said that with much labor, forested land had been cleared and converted into good ground for corn and gardens. He credited Sir Thomas Gates with making Jamestown a success. He said that the community "hath in it two faire rowes of howses, all of framed Timber, two stories, and an upper Garrett or Corn loft high, besides three large and substantiall store houses, joyned together in length some hundred and twenty foot and in breadth forty." He added that the town had been "newly and strongly impaled" and that a new gun platform had been built in the fort's west bulwark. Beyond the fort, there were some "very pleasant, and beautifull howses," two blockhouses, and some farmhouses. Hamor claimed that Sir Thomas Dale had given every new immigrant a "handsome howse," 12 acres of land, and some livestock. The presence of numerous 12-acre farmsteads in the eastern end of Jamestown Island, tracts that were seated at a very early date, may reflect Dale's strategy for assisting newcomers.

Genesis of the Tobacco Economy

Between 1611 and 1614, John Rolfe, through experimentation, developed a strain of sweet-scented tobacco that quickly became a lucrative money crop, so much so that it attained acceptance as currency. Many colonists, lured by the prospect of wealth, planted tobacco instead of food crops and then complained bitterly about hunger while awaiting supplies from England. They also bartered with the Indians for corn and other food but sometimes took it by force, making enemies in the process. In 1619 Secretary of the Colony John Pory declared that Virginia was ideal for agriculture but admitted that the colony's riches lay in tobacco. The boom in tobacco prices continued until around 1630, when overproduction glutted the market. Even so, tobacco remained the staple crop of the Chesapeake colonies, and by 1639 the quantity exported annually rose to a million-and-a-half pounds.

The rapidly expanding tobacco market created substantial opportunities for those who immigrated to Virginia and became planters. Also, the relatively high price of tobacco during the 1620s led to a search for ways to increase productivity. At first the labor shortage was so critical that employers often worked alongside their servants. Between 1620 and 1670 the annual rate of productivity per worker more than doubled and shipping costs were halved. During that same period, prices dwindled but tobacco production remained profitable because planters were able to produce more of the crop with fewer hands.

Establishment of the Headright System

In 1618, when a change in the Virginia Company's leadership led to a major transformation of its management philosophy, Virginia entered a new phase of its history. Among the changes wrought by the Company's Great Charter was the establishment of representative government. Another was the institution of the headright system, which fueled the colony's expansion and strengthened its economy. During the early to mid-seventeenth century, many people owned two or more tracts of land and circulated among them. New immigrants, lured to Virginia's vast wilderness by the opportunity to own land on which they could profitably cultivate tobacco, had little interest in settling in towns. Before long, their disinclination became a deeply ingrained tradition.

The Burgeoning Need for Workers

Between 1630 and 1680, tobacco consumption rose in response to lower prices, and planters rushed to meet that demand and added to their workforce. An estimated 75,000 whites emigrated from the British Isles to the Chesapeake colonies during that period. Approximately half to three-quarters of these people were indentured servants, many of whom were poor, unskilled youths. Planters were especially eager to procure males to toil in the tobacco fields, and during the 1630s six times as many men as women became indentured servants. Between 1640 and 1680, only one out of every four servants was female. This ratio, which left many men without an opportunity to marry and rear a family, perpetuated the need for immigrant labor. So did the fact that many servants died before they became "seasoned," that is, adjusted to the climate and the hardships of living in a wilderness environment.

In the beginning many of Virginia's indentured servants were from the English middle class and were respectable citizens who simply lacked the means to pay for their own transportation or outfit themselves for life in the colony. Many were young men in their late teens or early twenties and represented a cross-section of society, ranging from the younger sons of prominent families, yeoman farmers, husbandmen, artisans, and laborers, to former prison inmates. Men and women willing to become indentured servants, and sometimes minors' legal guardians, usually signed a contract or "indenture," agreeing to exchange a certain number of years of work for transportation to Virginia. These contracts could then be sold to planters who needed workers. Those who acquired indentured servants were supposed to provide them with food, clothing, and shelter and could discipline them within the limits of the law. Servants (especially men and boys) usually worked as field hands from dawn to dusk, six days a week, throughout the growing season. Skilled or literate servants often could negotiate shorter terms because they were capable of performing tasks considered more valuable.

The First Africans

In August 1619 an event occurred that irrevocably changed the course of Virginia history. It was then that a Dutch frigate, the *White Lion*, fresh from a plundering expedition in the West Indies, sailed into Hampton Roads with 20-some Africans. Governor George Yeardley and cape merchant Abraham Peirsey met the ship at Old Point Comfort in Kecoughtan and bartered with its captain, exchanging victuals for the Africans. It is open to conjecture whether this very first group of African natives stepped ashore at Old Point Comfort or was transferred directly to the ship that Yeardley and Peirsey were aboard. Shortly thereafter, most (if not all) of the newly arrived African men and women were brought up to Jamestown and sold into servitude.

Three or four days after the *White Lion* departed, its consort, the *Treasurer,* came in. According to John Rolfe, Governor Yeardley sent his father-in-law, Lieutenant William Peirce, and a Mr. Ewens (probably William Ewens) to Old Point Comfort to meet the incoming ship, but it set sail before they arrived. Rolfe said that the *Treasurer* left hastily because Kecoughtan's inhabitants refused to sell its captain and crew the food stuffs they desperately needed.

Nearly 30 Africans were aboard the *Treasurer,* and official testimony from a member of the ship's crew indicates that 10 or more of them were left in Virginia. The March 1620 census reveals that 32 Africans (15 men and 17 women) were then living in the colony, presumably the 20-some from the *White Lion* and the 10 or so from the *Treasurer.* The 1625 muster reveals that a woman named Angelo, who had come to the colony on the *Treasurer,* was living in Jamestown at that time. After the *Treasurer* left Virginia, it landed in Bermuda, whose governor acquired 14 Africans. Governor Nathaniel Butler referred to them as "slaves," a term suggesting that he did not perceive them as servants who had a prospect of freedom.

In recent years scholars have surmised that Virginia's first Africans probably were captured in Angola, on the West Coast of Africa, and were removed from the *San Juan Batista,* a Portuguese slave ship that was overtaken by English corsairs. There is some evidence that the Africans had been baptized and made Christians in accord with Portuguese law, even though the Dutch and Portuguese seem to have considered them slaves. It is estimated that between 1617 and 1621 approximately 50,000 slaves were exported from Angola, including approximately 4,000 baptized Christians.

Many of the Africans who came to Virginia during the seventeenth century brought along a specialized knowledge of agriculture and other practical skills that made a significant contribution to the developing colony. Of immediate use was their familiarity with the cultivation of tobacco. Men and women from agrarian tribes, who had been servants or agriculturists in their homeland, probably found it somewhat easier to adjust to the New World because they would have had some preparation for working in agricultural fields. But those accustomed to a higher position in the social order would have found life especially difficult. The Africans' distinctive appearance, unfamiliar language, and exotic cultural background surely set them apart from the other colonists and would have placed them at a decided disadvantage in bargaining for their freedom.

The Institution of Representative Government

On April 19, 1619, Virginia's new governor, Sir George Yeardley, arrived in the colony. As soon as he assumed the reins of government, he suspended *The Lawes Divine, Morall, and Martiall.* He also placed renewed emphasis on Jamestown, the capital city. Yeardley subdivided the colony into four vast corporations or boroughs that spanned the James River. Then, he invited each settlement to send two delegates or burgesses to Jamestown to convene in an assembly. The capital city's provost marshal (then its chief law enforcement officer) was supposed to serve as the assembly's sergeant-at-arms, a tradition that endured. On July 30, 1619, delegates or burgesses from 11 of the colony's 12 communities gathered in the church as members of the New World's first legislative assembly. Also present were Governor Yeardley and his six councilors. Captain William Powell and Ensign William Spence attended on behalf of Jamestown Island's inhabitants. After the Reverend Richard Buck offered a prayer for guidance, the speaker, John Pory, who had served in the Parliament and therefore had experience in a representative assembly, read aloud excerpts from the Virginia Company's Great Charter, enacted in November 1618. He also reviewed two of the four books of laws that had been sent to the colony. Then, the burgesses formed two committees to study the remaining books of laws. The committees had no right to challenge the rules set down for governing the colony, but they could petition for any changes they felt were necessary. Afterward, the burgesses drafted some laws, all of which were subject to the monarch's approval.

At the assembly's 1619 session, legislation was enacted against idleness, gambling, intoxication, and "excesse in apparel," as well as against theft, murder, and other criminal offenses. Trade with the Indians was to be regulated by the colony's governing officials, and a restriction was imposed on the number of natives allowed to live and work within the settlements. The colonists were supposed to provide their households with a year's supply of corn (or maize), storing some for use in times of need, and to plant vineyards, mulberry trees, and silk flax. Tobacco growers were obliged to follow certain procedures when preparing their crops for market. No one was allowed to venture further than 20 miles from home, visit Indian towns, or undertake a voyage longer than seven days without the governing officials' permission. A few disputes were aired before the assembly. One concerned a disagreement between two Indian interpreters. Another involved Captain William Powell of Jamestown and his servant, Thomas Garnett, who allegedly had misbehaved with a woman servant. Powell also sought to recover funds he was owed for clearing some acreage. The burgesses made plans to meet again in 1620.

According to Captain John Smith, by 1622 courts had been set up "in convenient places," perhaps a reference to the right of private plantations' leaders to arbitrate disputes among their people. By February 1623 the governor and his council began convening regularly as a judicial body. Although they met in Jamestown, surviving records fail to disclose precisely where they gathered to conduct business. By 1625 there were local courts in two of the colony's corporations, and there was one on the Eastern Shore. The Virginia Company's charter was revoked in May 1624, at which point Virginia became a Crown colony. Thereafter, the monarch chose the colony's governor and his councilors. The governor, in turn, appointed lesser officials.

The Link Between Church and State

When the first legislative assembly convened, 12 of the 34 laws the burgesses enacted dealt with religion, morality, or other forms of personal discipline. Each of the colony's four corporations was to have "a godly and learned minister," who was provided with a hundred-acre glebe (home farm) and six servants to work his land. Two churchwardens chosen by the corporation's clergyman were responsible for maintaining the church, reporting wrongdoers, and collecting church taxes or dues. Those who persisted in "skandulous offences" could be excommunicated, which brought certain arrest and confiscation of all personal property. Plans were made to establish a college and university in Henrico where young Indians could be converted to Christianity. During the early seventeenth century, writers often used Biblical metaphors (particularly those of the Old Testament) to describe their sufferings. Days in the church calendar were used to identify secular dates upon which rent and taxes were due and public events occurred. Thus, the State Church and religious law permeated daily life.

Official records for the years 1622–1632 reveal that churchwardens routinely reported those who got drunk, swore, or committed other acts deemed unseemly. Wrongdoers received what was considered appropriate punishment, often a whipping or a lesser form of public humiliation. Sometimes slanderers were obliged to kneel and offer a public apology, but gossipy or combative women might be dunked in the nearest river. When county courts were established, some of the church's responsibilities for maintaining public morality were transferred to the local judiciary, to whom the churchwardens reported directly. Later, vestries, elected by freeholders, chose their own churchwardens.

The Capital Becomes an Urban Community

Governor Francis Wyatt made purposeful efforts to strengthen Jamestown's development and give structure to the capital city. William Claiborne, who became the colony's official surveyor when Wyatt took office in 1621, probably was responsible for laying out the streets and lots of what was known as the New Town during the second quarter of the seventeenth century. Although relatively little is known about how Jamestown was organized functionally, archival records suggest that during the 1620s public activities (both sacred and secular) were concentrated in the immediate vicinity of the fort, however that term was defined physically. Meanwhile, in the New Town, residential and commercial development was intensified between Orchard Run and the church, where lots and streets were laid out in a more-or-less orderly fashion. Almost all of the patents that were issued in 1624 for New Town lots cited legislation that had been passed earlier "to encourage building." This suggests that the urbanized area's development was undertaken purposefully. During this period small farmsteads were situated in outlying "suburbs" that were located in the eastern half of the island and to the west, near the isthmus then leading to the mainland.

By 1624 several New Town lots of half-acre or less had been laid out along the waterfront, abutting south upon a roadway that traced the river bank. Forming the rear boundary of these lots was Back Street, which also contained rows of lots, most of which were elongated. Almost all of the New Town's lot owners were well-to-do merchants, prominent public officials, or both. Most (if not all) of these people had constructed buildings on their property prior to obtaining their patents. One such New Town resident was fort-captain William Peirce, whose "new dwelling" in 1624 served as the collection point for the tobacco levied as taxes. In 1629 Peirce's wife, Joan, "an honest and industrious woman" who had lived in the colony for nearly 20 years, reportedly had "a garden at Jamestown containing 3 or 4 acres," from which she gathered nearly 100 bushels of excellent figs in a year. Her claim that she could "keep a better house in Virginia for 3 or 4 hundred pounds than in London," despite having gone to the colony with "little or nothing," attests to the economic opportunities that awaited new immigrants.

At the periphery of the urbanized area's smaller lots were a few larger parcels. Captain John Harvey and Dr. John Pott had lots of six acres or more in the vicinity of Orchard Run, whereas Sir George Yeardley and Captain Roger Smith owned property that lay somewhat inland and to the northwest, beyond the New Town's waterfront lots. Yeardley's seven-plus acres touched upon another Harvey patent and extended toward the Back River, while Smith's four acres abutted north upon Yeardley and south upon the Government (or Governor's) Garden. In the "outback" but also near at hand was an 80-acre farm that belonged to Richard Kingsmill and bordered the west side of the creek that eventually assumed his name.

By the early 1620s, masters of incoming ships were required to open their cargoes in Jamestown and conduct business with its storekeepers before proceeding elsewhere. This policy, which was in effect through the 1660s, would have made Jamestown the colony's premier commercial center. It also would have brought a steady stream of visitors to the island. In 1626 New Town resident George Menefie, owner of a waterfront lot and a forge, was appointed the corporation of James City's official merchant, a post he retained for nearly two decades. Although many of the artisans who served the greater Jamestown community owned property on the east side of Orchard Run, beyond the New Town's limits, an exception was gunsmith John Jackson, whose waterfront lot was next door to two merchants. Wassill Rayner, a brewer or distiller, lived nearby. Archaeological evidence suggests that other skilled workers (likely indentured servants) literally set up shop in Jamestown on property that was owned by others.

European Intrusion into Native Land

During the first quarter of the seventeenth century, when the Virginia colonists discovered that enormous profits could be reaped from cultivating tobacco, they established plantations along the banks of the James River inland to the fall line and across the Chesapeake Bay, on the Eastern Shore. This rapid encroachment upon native territory precipitated a major Indian attack on March 22, 1622, with the result that more than one-third of the colonists lost their lives. By then, Powhatan and his brother, Opitchapam, were dead and Opechancanough had become paramount chief. Opechancanough was a forceful and charismatic native leader, who lived on an island in the Pamunkey River. The colonists retaliated forcefully.

Settlement along the James River was so well established by 1629–1630 that the colonists decided to venture into the countryside along the lower side of the York River, homeland of the Chiskiack Indians. In February 1633 Virginia's burgesses resolved to commence construction of a palisade across the James-York Peninsula, cordoning off an area that was reserved exclusively for the colonists' habitation. They established homesteads at Middle Plantation and Chiskiack and then moved eastward toward the mouth of the York River. But they also began pushing in a westerly direction, up the York River's lower bank and across to the opposite shore. By the 1640s settlement had spread into the Powhatan Chiefdom's heartland, north into the Middle Peninsula, and south of the James River. Most of the men who claimed literally thousands of acres of land were members of the planter elite who were heavily involved in the colony's political affairs.

The Establishment of County Government

In 1634 the colony was subdivided into eight shires or counties. It was then that James City, Charles City, Elizabeth City (Kecoughtan), Henrico, Warwick, York (Charles River), Isle of Wight (Warresqueak), and Accomack (Accomac) counties were formed, replacing the four corporations that were established in 1619. There were 4,914 settlers in the Virginia colony in 1634, and new immigrants were arriving constantly.

According to law, each of Virginia's eight counties had a court with justices (or commissioners) of the peace, a sheriff, a clerk, and lesser functionaries, such as constables and tithe-takers. All of these appointees served at the pleasure of the governor. County justices were authorized to take depositions, settle petty disputes and minor criminal cases, and try civil cases involving less than £10. They usually convened monthly to hear the civil and criminal matters that fell within their purview. Individual justices could resolve minor disputes, take depositions, or issue warrants, whereas sheriffs served warrants, arrested defendants, conducted assembly elections, and collected taxes. The clerk of court kept the minutes of court proceedings and recorded deeds, wills, and other legal transactions. The establishment of county courts, whose authority increased over time, relieved the Quarter Court—which consisted of the governor and his council—of many routine matters. It also freed the Quarter Court to handle important cases and to function as an appellate body. When the Quarter Court needed a jury, James City County's sheriff (who also served as sergeant-at-arms) impaneled those he considered "the most able and discrete men" in Jamestown, a practice that originated in tradition. Decisions made by the Quarter Court could be appealed to the monarch. Each county had a lieutenant, who was responsible for organizing the local militia and seeing that his men were properly armed and drilled regularly. Burgesses were elected at the county seat, which was at the hub of local life.

Jamestown was at the heart of the colony's most populous region in 1634 when county government was established. It also was the location at which the governor and his council convened to conduct business and sit as justices in the Quarter Court. As the colony's capital city, Jamestown had representation in the assembly and was James City County's seat. Whenever the assembly or Quarter Court convened, or the county court was in session, there was an influx of visitors who would patronize the community's popular taverns and numerous merchants and artisans. Ferries transported passengers to and from the lower side of the James River. Also located in Jamestown was one of Virginia's five tobacco storage warehouses, where outbound shipments of the crop were inspected and repacked before being sent abroad.

The Capital as an Urban Community

In February 1636 legislation was passed to promote urban development in Jamestown, and those willing to erect buildings were offered "a convenient portion of ground for housing and a garden plot." As a means of quelling land speculation, lots that were patented but stood vacant for six or more months could be reassigned. In 1639 Sir John Harvey, the incumbent governor, informed the Privy Council that "twelve houses and stores" had been built in Jamestown and that there was not "one foote of ground for half a mile altogether by the rivers side . . . but was taken up and undertaken to be built on." He added that the colony's secretary, Richard Kemp, had erected a brick house that was "the fairest ever known in this country" and that "others have undertaken to build frame houses to beautify the place." The colony's assembly responded by formally declaring that Jamestown should remain "the chief town and residence of the Governor."

Around 1641–1642 the king ordered incoming governor, Sir William Berkeley, to encourage the growth of towns. He also authorized the colony's officials to relocate the capital city, if they so desired. But the assembly affirmed its preference for Jamestown and again enacted legislation designed to promote its development. A flurry of patentees, who were warned to use or lose their land, laid claim to small lots in the western end of the island. During the mid-1640s plans were made to establish public flax-houses, one of which was to be in Jamestown. One writer, who lauded Virginia's economic opportunities, said that most skilled workers could expect to earn a good living in Virginia, with the exception of brewers, whose customers often failed to pay their bills. He cited as an example the experience of Jamestown's two or three brew-house proprietors. One was John Moon, whose brew-house was located on Back Street.

Jamestown at mid-century flourished with both foreign and domestic trade and in 1648 one man reported that "at last Christmas we had trading here ten ships from London, two from Bristol, twelve Hollanders, and seven from New England." A 1649 law designated as Jamestown's official marketplace the territory between Sandy Bay (on the west, by the isthmus) and Orchard Run (on the east), from the James River (on the south) to the Back River (on the north), enveloping what eventually became the town's corporate limits. All transactions that occurred within that market zone between 8 AM and 6 PM, Wednesdays and Saturdays, were legally binding. During the 1650s a number of waterfront lots in the New Town changed hands through litigation, inheritance, or outright purchase. Patents for relatively large parcels in the extreme ends of the island were issued during this period. Most of Jamestown's more affluent property owners, especially public officials and merchants, had outlying plantations in one or more nearby counties.

Native Resistance

On April 18, 1644, when the Indians of the Powhatan Chiefdom made a second major attempt to drive the colonists from their homeland, an estimated four to five hundred settlers lost their lives or were taken prisoner. Especially hard hit were those living in the upper reaches of the York River, in what became New Kent County, and on the south side of the James, near the Nansemond and Elizabeth rivers. Opechancanough, who had led the 1622 Indian attack, was credited with leading the second assault. By March 1645 the construction of four military outposts had gotten underway. They were located at the falls of the James and Appomattox rivers, on the Pamunkey River near Manquin Creek, and on the Chickahominy River near Diascund Creek. There, armed men were supposed to keep watch over the frontier and control access to the colonized area. In 1645 Governor William Berkeley led an expedition against the Pamunkeys and, while storming Opechanca-nough's stronghold, captured the aged Indian leader, who was brought to James-town and imprisoned. Later, Opechancanough was mortally wounded when he was shot in the back by a guard. It was an inglorious end for a mighty chief who had led his people for more than two decades. Official records reveal that Pamunkey warriors were captured and taken to the "Western Island" or Tangier, where they were abandoned.

The 1646 Indian Treaty: Racial Separation

In October 1646 Necotowance, the late Opechancanough's immediate successor, concluded a formal peace agreement with the Virginia government, which promised to protect his people from their enemies. In return the Indians agreed to pay an annual tribute to the Crown's representatives, an acknowledgment of their subservient position. They also began allowing the governor to appoint or confirm their leaders. This was an especially important concession, one that hastened the disintegration of the Powhatan Chiefdom, for it disjoined the native groups formerly unified under a powerful paramount chief. Secretary of the Colony Thomas Ludwell later recalled that Governor Berkeley and his council believed that freeing all of the native groups formerly subservient to the Pamunkey was the most effective way to render them powerless. As he put it, the Indians "like to warr with each other and destroy themselves more in a year than we can do it." This "divide and conquer" approach quickly evolved into the establishment of tribal lands or preserves that dispersed the natives into small clustered groups. It also restricted them to certain areas and allowed European settlement to spread more freely.

Under the terms of the 1646 treaty, the natives agreed to withdraw from the James-York Peninsula inland to the fall line, and to abandon their territory on the lower side of the James River, south to the Blackwater River. The treaty specified that settlers had to vacate the territory on the north side of the York River, east of Poropotank Creek. Those who had seated land there prior to October 5, 1646, the day the treaty was signed, were given until March 1, 1647, to remove or slaughter their cattle and hogs. Colonists venturing into the restricted area without securing official permission were presumed guilty of a felony, unless they went there to fell trees or cut sedge, a type of rush-like plant found in wet ground. All trade with the Indians was to be conducted through Fort Royall on the Pamunkey River, and at Fort Henry at the head of the Appomattox River. Natives who needed to enter the ceded territory on official business were obliged to procure from either of those two forts (or checkpoints) the special striped coats that were to serve as badges of safe conduct. Otherwise, the natives could be lawfully slain. In November 1647 two additional points of entry were established.

Despite the terms of the 1646 treaty, on September 1, 1649, the territory on the north side of the York River that had been reserved for the natives' use was thrown open to settlement. This policy change coincided with official abandonment of the military outposts established in 1645 and 1646. Would-be patentees moved into the wilderness to the north and west, establishing homesteads, and they also penetrated deeply into the countryside below the James. "Seating" (or development) requirements were extremely lax and, with the exception of those patenting lots in urban Jamestown, only one acre had to be placed under cultivation and one house built to substantiate a land claim. Those patenting new acreage had three years in which to seat it. If they failed to do so, their land reverted to the Crown, whose representatives could assign it to another.

The Evolving Role of Government and the Implications for Virginia Society

Scholars agree that the rise of representative government occurred gradually, in part because the Crown failed to interfere in its evolution. In 1643 Virginia's Grand Assembly became bicameral, for the burgesses began meeting apart from the governor and his council. The Council of State, assembly, and Quarter Court (later known as the General Court) had clerks who kept their official records. The office of the Secretary of the Colony maintained copies of patents and grants. Virginia's legal system was based upon English law, and the assembly enacted legislation to meet the colony's changing needs.

The development and maturation of the colony and its governmental systems coincided with an increase in the stratification of Virginia society as a whole. The result was that those in its upper ranks, socially and economically, possessed many important advantages. County officials were appointed by the governor and his council, who also filled lesser positions. All of these men derived fees and privileges from performing their duties. Members of the assembly, though elected, were drawn from the upper ranks of society. Often, they were able to use their official positions to further their own economic interests and political aspirations. For instance, when land was sought as the prospective site of a planned town or tobacco inspection warehouse, acreage that belonged to a high-ranking official was the most likely to be selected. Familial, political, and social connections among the colony's leaders enabled them to enhance and perpetuate their role in the governmental establishment. These connections also extended into the affairs of the church, to which official interest was linked, and often the same men who held office as burgesses, naval officers, or county officials (such as justices, sheriffs, or tobacco inspectors) served as parish vestrymen. Thus, Virginians at the lower end of the socioeconomic scale had a very limited opportunity to enhance their personal fortunes.

Scholars generally agree that between 1640 and 1660 the status of Africans and African Americans in Virginia society began to erode, with the result that black and white servants were treated dissimilarly. In time, blacks in servitude gradually came to be regarded as "servants for life," a custom that eventually attained lawful status. This coincided with a shortage of white indentured servants and an increase in the number of workers of African descent. Ultimately, this fueled development of the plantation system.

The Commonwealth Period

Even before England became embroiled in a bloody civil war, tensions between royalists and the supporters of Parliament (dubbed the Roundheads) reached the colonies. Virginians by and large were sympathetic to the monarchy, and in 1649, after they learned that King Charles I had been beheaded, the burgesses met in Jamestown to proclaim Charles II's right to the throne. They also declared that anyone openly questioning Charles II's right of succession would be considered treasonous. Governor William Berkeley, who was fiercely loyal to the Crown, welcomed royalists to Virginia, and the colony became a haven for those in exile. After Cromwell's forces emerged triumphant, a Parliamentary fleet set sail for Virginia to proclaim the supremacy of the Commonwealth government. Governor William Berkeley was obliged to surrender the colony and relinquish his position as chief executive. The articles of surrender he signed in Jamestown on March 12, 1652, acknowledged that Virginia was under the purview of the Commonwealth's laws, which had not been imposed upon the colonists through the use of military might. In 1659 the Commonwealth government strengthened the Navigation Acts, intended to restrict Virginia's trade with foreign nations. This prompted Sir William Berkeley to remind his superiors that the articles of surrender he had signed guaranteed Virginians free trade with "all nations in amity with the people of England." When word reached Jamestown in 1660 that the monarchy had been restored and that King Charles II was installed upon the throne, celebrants marked the occasion with drinking, trumpeting, and the firing of guns.

Virginia's Government During the Commonwealth Period

After Governor William Berkeley surrendered the colony to Oliver Cromwell's agents, Virginia's burgesses were allowed to conduct business as usual, but they could not enact legislation that was contrary to the laws of the Commonwealth. Virginia's charter was to be confirmed by Parliament, and the legality of the colonists' land patents was to be upheld. Like all English citizens, Virginia colonists were entitled to free trade and no taxes could be imposed upon them without their assembly's consent. All publicly owned arms and ammunition had to be surrendered. The clergy could continue using the Book of Common Prayer as long as they omitted all references to the monarchy. Anyone refusing to subscribe to the Articles of Surrender had to leave Virginia within a year. While the colony was under the sway of the Commonwealth government, the governor and his council were appointed by the burgesses, from whom they derived their authority. But after Charles II ascended to the throne and Virginia again became a royal colony, the monarch again began appointing the governor and his council. Scholars believe, however, that the independence the assembly had enjoyed during the 1650s was never totally undone. By the mid-seventeenth century, the colony's population had grown significantly and settlement had spread into the hinterlands. As a result, new counties were formed as were new parishes. During the late 1650s consideration was given to limiting the number of burgesses that each county could send to the assembly, but the proposed act (formulated as a cost-cutting measure) failed to pass.

The 1650s and 1660s

While Virginia was under the sway of the Commonwealth government, the colony's leaders more actively pursued the preservation of native lands. In 1656 the burgesses acknowledged that disputes over land were at the root of many clashes between the colonists and the Indians, and so they enacted legislation stipulating that Indians could not sell their acreage without the assembly's consent. High-ranking officials also decided not to issue new patents until the Indians had been allocated tribal land. Each native group's preserve or reservation, issued on the basis of 50 acres per warrior, was to be surveyed and laid out as an aggregate. The Indians were authorized to hunt and gather outside of the territory ceded to the government in 1646, with the exception of land that the colonists had enclosed with fences. In October 1649 the government decided to allocate five thousand acres to the leaders of three Indian tribes (the Pamunkey, the Weyanoke, and the "Northern Indians," probably the Chiskiack), whose territory was surrounded by patented land.

In November 1652 the assembly resolved to assign the natives tracts of land that were reserved exclusively for their occupancy. Henceforth, no one was supposed to intrude upon tribal land without the consent of the Council of State or a locality's justices. Just as specific tracts had been assigned to the Pamunkey, Weyanoke, and likely the Chiskiack in 1649, acreage was allocated to the Accomack, Chickahominy, Moratticund, Mattaponi, Nansemond, Nanzattico, Portobago, Rappahannock, Totusky, and Upper Nansemond (Mangomixon). Most of these native preserves lay within the Middle Peninsula or the Northern Neck, although the Chickahominy were given land in Pamunkey Neck, and the Nansemond and Accomack received acreage within their original territory. Deeds and patents that mention the reservations' boundary lines suggest strongly that some (if not all) of the tribal preserves were surveyed and physically demarcated. From time to time, county justices reaffirmed the bargains settlers sometimes made with their Indian neighbors. For instance, in 1655 Pindavako, protector of the young King of the Chiskiack Indians, made a treaty in Gloucester County, confirming a colonist's right to use part of the land that had been assigned to the Chiskiack. Surviving records from Northern Neck and Middle Peninsula counties contain similar agreements and reveal that Indian leaders occasionally came into court to complain about trespassers. Often, the disputes involved unscrupulous planters who made dishonest bargains. Sometimes Indians were called to account for giving refuge to a runaway servant or killing livestock. Fortunately, relations between the colonists and their Indian neighbors were somewhat more peaceful on the Eastern Shore.

Updating the Colony's Laws

In 1662 Virginia's legal code was revised extensively and then summarized. For the first time each county could send only two burgesses to the assembly. Jamestown, as the capital city, retained its ancient right to representation, and any hundred-acre tract on which a hundred tithable (that is, taxable) citizens took up residence was entitled to the same privilege. County courts were to have eight justices, and the first man appointed to office was to serve as sheriff. Vestries could have no more than twelve members. Tax rates were established by law, and county courts were authorized to issue marriage licenses. When the assembly formally adopted English common law in 1662, legislation was enacted to regulate local elections and set public officials' fees. Procedures were established for probating estates, determining land ownership, setting the prices tavern-keepers and millers could charge, and formalizing land transfers. Not unexpectedly, these duties added to the county court's workload.

To discourage the "idleness and debaucheryes" attributable to drunkenness, local court justices were ordered to see that their county seat had no more than one or two taverns. A limited number of taverns were permissible at ports, ferry landings, and major roads, where they were necessary "for the accommodation of travelers." Other issues the burgesses addressed in 1662 included relations with the Indians, the treatment of indentured servants, controlling the quality of tobacco, and proper observance of the Sabbath. Every four years vestrymen had to "procession" (walk) the boundaries of land within their parish, renew boundary markers whenever necessary, and have disputed property lines surveyed. A procedure was established for appointing the surveyors of public highways, whose duties were defined by law. Every county seat was supposed to have a pillory, stocks, whipping post, and ducking-stool near the courthouse, and local courts' meeting dates were established. Half of each county's eight justices were "of the quorum," that is, one or more of them had to be present at every court session. Plaintiffs and defendants were supposed to summarize their cases in writing and were guaranteed the right to trial by jury. The Quarter Court, renamed the General Court in 1662, continued to serve as an appellate body but could send cases back to the county courts.

Jamestown After the Restoration

In 1662 Governor William Berkeley was ordered to see that towns were established on each of the colony's rivers, commencing with the James. He also was told to set a good example by building some houses in the capital city and urging his council members to follow suit. In December the assembly responded by enacting legislation that was intended to promote Jamestown's development. It called for the construction of 32 brick houses of prescribed specifications, utilizing workmen whose wages were set by law. Each of the colony's 17 counties was supposed to build a prototypical brick house. Private citizens who did so would receive a public subsidy and were allowed to erect a storehouse. The construction of frame houses was prohibited, and townspeople were ordered to pull up all of the old stakes of the wharves "before the town" because they endangered the ships landing there. Patents were issued for several half-acre lots along the waterfront and on Back Street. Again, governing officials were allowed to reassign undeveloped lots to others.

In September 1663 the burgesses decided to compensate counties that already had erected brick houses in Jamestown, and it was agreed that four should be built each year, until every county had fulfilled its obligation. Until then, all 17 of these "country houses" were to be held as common land. Archival records reveal that two units of a four-bay brick row house on Back Street were constructed with public funds and two with private money. Although private participants in the building program were not supposed to be compensated until their work was complete, at least four men were censured for accepting funds without fulfilling their commitments. Archaeologists have found evidence of these "false starts," buildings of the prescribed size that proceeded no further than construction of their brick foundations. Legislation was passed authorizing the construction of a statehouse, which by 1665 reportedly was underway. A hall for merchants and their representatives (or factors) also was being built. By that date Jamestown was said to have approximately 20 houses. Within the capital city's corporate limits, but inland and somewhat behind the urbanized area, were two large tracts owned by prominent merchants who had developed their property into working plantations. Neither had frontage on the James River, but they bordered the Back River, which was navigable.

Despite a promising start to urbanizing Jamestown, work was disrupted in the mid-1660s thanks to the onset of the second Anglo-Dutch war and the king's orders to put the colony into a defensive posture. This led to the construction of a tetragonal earthen-walled fort on a waterfront lot in the New Town, a military feature that was intended to protect commercial shipping but also would have been costly to build. In 1667 a string of costly disasters put an end to the government's efforts to improve the capital city. In April a storm yielding hail "as big as Turkey Eggs" ruined spring crops, killed young livestock, and "brake [*sic*] all the glass windowes and beat holes through the tiles of our houses." Then, in June, the Dutch attacked the tobacco fleet near Newport News Point, causing the loss of more than 20 ships. That was followed by a midsummer rainy spell that severely damaged crops. Finally, on August 27th a violent hurricane struck, which reportedly lasted for 24 hours, destroying 10,000 houses and causing severe flooding. Together, these catastrophic events weakened the colony's economy and the colonists' morale.

Although the threat of foreign invasion abated temporarily, by September 1672 the third Anglo-Dutch war had gotten underway and a decision was made to construct brick forts at several sites, one of which was Jamestown. In July 1673, when the Dutch assaulted the tobacco fleet near Old Point Comfort, a number of ships "got above the fort" at the western end of Jamestown Island and were safe. Hardly had hostilities ceased when Virginians became caught up in the popular uprising known as Bacon's Rebellion.

Bacon's Rebellion's Impact on the Capital City

By the mid-1670s Governor William Berkeley had been in office for nearly 30 years, during which time members of the planter elite had solidified their political power. As a result, many colonists perceived senior officials as opportunists who profited handsomely from performing duties that were a public trust. The settlers also chafed under the restraints of the Navigation Acts. As taxes soared, rumors spread about Indian troubles in the New England colonies. There were sporadic outbreaks of violence on the fringes of Virginia's frontiers, where Indians who lived above the fall line sometimes attacked outlying homesteads. Hostile natives also fell upon the colony's tributary Indians, who were east of the continuously advancing frontier.

In March 1676 Virginia's governing officials, who were obliged to protect the colonists and the tributary Indian tribes, decided to construct defensive garrisons at nine locations that were considered strategically important. These small, fortified buildings, erected at public expense, were costly and therefore were extremely unpopular. Moreover, it soon became painfully clear that they were useless against highly mobile bands of natives whose strategy was to orchestrate ambushes. Many colonists became increasingly frustrated by what they perceived as their aging governor's failure to take effective action. As the rumors spread of Indian troubles in the New England colonies and native attacks became more and more frequent on the fringes of Virginia's frontiers, colonists became increasingly fearful. A significant number of settlers, especially those in the upper reaches of the Rappahannock River, abandoned their homesteads.

Young Nathaniel Bacon, a burgess and council member whose Henrico County plantation had come under attack, eagerly offered to lead a march against the Indians. Governor Berkeley ordered him to cease and desist and summoned him to

Jamestown. When Bacon continued on his way, Berkeley responded by declaring him a rebel. Thus began the popular uprising known as Bacon's Rebellion, which during 1676 spread throughout Tidewater Virginia and left a bloody imprint on the region.

In early June 1676 Bacon and 50 armed men slipped into Jamestown under the cover of darkness and met with two of his confederates, innkeeper Richard Lawrence and William Drummond I, whose homes were in the western end of the island near the church. When Bacon was captured he begged for the governor's forgiveness, whereupon Berkeley pardoned him and restored him to his council seat. However, after Bacon left Jamestown he rallied an army of 500 to 600 supporters, and on June 23rd he returned to confront the colony's governing officials. When Bacon entered Jamestown he sent some of his men to the fort, to the riverfront, and to the ferry landing—locations he considered strategic. Then, he ordered the rest of his supporters to the statehouse, where he demanded a commission authorizing him to undertake action against the Indians. Governor William Berkeley at first demurred, but when Bacon's followers reiterated his demands at gunpoint and threatened to kill members of the council and assembly if they refused to cooperate, they acquiesced. Bacon prevailed upon the burgesses to include some of his ideas in the legislation they were considering. One new law gave colonists the right to claim land that the Indians had vacated. This, in essence, gave them the right to drive the natives from their reservations and then claim the land themselves. Another new law expanded Jamestown's corporate limits to include the entire island. This would have allowed any free white male who owned land on the island to serve as Jamestown's burgess, not merely those whose property lay within the city limits. A third new law authorized all freemen who lived on Jamestown Island and paid taxes there to participate in the election of Jamestown's burgess.

On June 26th Governor Berkeley withdrew to his plantation, Green Spring. Meanwhile, Bacon and his men began roving about the countryside, trying to rally support. When Berkeley and his supporters suddenly became aware of their own vulnerability, they withdrew to the Eastern Shore and took refuge at Arlington, John Custis II's Northampton County plantation. Berkeley returned to Jamestown on September 7, 1676, and found the capital city in control of Bacon's men. Although he offered to pardon those willing to surrender their arms, many of the men fled, fearing repercussions. Toward the middle of the month, Bacon and his men took up a position on the isthmus that linked Jamestown Island to the mainland. They constructed a defensive trench, using the wives of Berkeley's supporters as a human shield, and then began firing two great guns at Jamestown, wreaking destruction. After Berkeley abandoned the capital a second time, Bacon and his men swarmed in and put numerous buildings to the torch. Among the buildings they destroyed were the statehouse, the church, and some of the brick houses that had been erected with public funds. Then they withdrew to Green Spring. Heady with success and invigorated by their own lawlessness, Bacon's followers turned into an unruly mob that made little distinction between friend and foe.

On October 26, 1676, Nathaniel Bacon died from natural causes and the rebellion quickly lost support. Governor Berkeley's men seized the opportunity to quell the uprising and during November and December captured many of the rebel leaders, who were hastily tried in court-martial hearings and quickly executed. Special commissioners appointed by the king and given the task of determining the underlying causes of the popular uprising arrived in Virginia in January 1677. They asked the freeholders of each county to submit a petition explaining why they were dissatisfied with the Berkeley government. When the Virginia assembly convened in late February 1677, the burgesses agreed to extend a pardon to all but 23 men already convicted of treason. More lenient penalties, such as fines, were deemed suitable punishment for other participants in the rebellion. Plundered goods were to be restored to their rightful owners and those who had sustained losses in the rebellion were given the legal right to sue for damages. In time, Jamestown's church was restored, the statehouse was replaced, and some of the capital city's buildings were rebuilt or renovated, but the community never recovered its former vitality.

Bacon's Rebellion's Impact on the Native Population

In early 1676 Cockacoeske, queen of the Pamunkey Indians, was summoned to Jamestown, where high-ranking officials asked her to provide warriors to oppose hostile tribes on the frontier. After reminding council members that 20 years earlier her husband, Totopotomoy, and a hundred of his warriors had perished while assisting the English, she reluctantly agreed to provide a dozen warriors, a fraction of the number officials presumed were under her command. In August 1676 the rebel Nathaniel Bacon, eager to demonstrate his prowess as an Indian fighter, turned his wrath on a convenient target, the Pamunkeys, who in March had signed a peace agreement with the Berkeley government. Bacon and his followers pursued the Pamunkey Indians into the Middle Peninsula's Dragon Swamp and indiscriminately killed men, women, and children, took captives, and plundered the natives' goods. Bacon then set out for Jamestown, displaying his Pamunkey prisoners. After Bacon's death and a change in the colony's leadership, Cockacoeske appeared before the assembly and asked for the release of her people and restoration of their belongings. Although the burgesses were unresponsive, the king's special commissioners felt that she should be rewarded for her loyalty to the Crown, for she had honored her treaty with the Berkeley government and forbidden her warriors to fire on Bacon and his men when they attacked.

The Treaty of 1677

On May 29, 1677, Virginia's governing officials executed a formal peace agreement with some of the colony's Indian tribes. At what later became the site of Williamsburg, several native leaders affixed their signature marks to the Treaty of Middle Plantation, acknowledging their allegiance to the Crown. They also conceded that their land rights were derived from the monarch. Certain tribes were placed under the queen of the Pamunkey Indian's aegis, "as anceintly they had beene." The Virginia government's obligation to protect the tributary Indians surely would have been perceived as advantageous, given the natives' diminished strength. One of the 1677 treaty's most important provisions (from the natives' perspective) was that colonists were not supposed to seat land within three miles of an Indian town. In reality, however, the natives received very little protection from land-hungry settlers. Another provision of the 1677 treaty was that the signatory tribes, like other English subjects, were entitled to receive protection from their enemies and had the right to make use of the colony's judicial system. In 1680 the treaty was expanded to include several more native groups. At the suggestion of the king's special commissioners, some of the native leaders who had signed the original 1677 treaty were singled out for recognition, but special attention was given to the Pamunkey queen, who had demonstrated her loyalty to the English.

Even before an expanded version of the 1677 treaty had been signed, Virginia officials realized that some of the Indians placed under the queen of the Pamunkey Indian's rule, notably the Chickahominys and Rappahannocks, resented the attempt to force their subservience. They stubbornly refused to cooperate with her, claiming they had not agreed to such subjection when subscribing to the peace treaty. In a list of grievances Cockacoeske and her son, a youth called Captain John West, presented to the governor and his council on June 5, 1678, Cockacoeske alleged that the Chickahominys were unwilling to pay tribute, obey her orders, or live in her village. Great mutual enmity was apparent in the list of nine grievances, for the Chickahominy were accused of poisoning one of Cockacoeske's Great Men and plotting revenge on eight more, whereas the Chickahominy claimed that Cockacoeske had "cutt off soe many Chickahominy heads."

The Pamunkeys' interpreter, Cornelius Dabney, also dispatched a personal letter to Colonel Francis Morrison, which corroborated Cockacoeske's allegations against the Chickahominy. He alluded to some misunderstandings with the current governor, blaming the problems on the malice of the Chickahominy Indians' interpreter, Richard Yarborough, who, Dabney claimed, was attempting to undermine peaceful relations with the tributary Indians. Dabney said that he intended to resign as interpreter when the assembly met. He acknowledged the plight of the tributary Indians who were caught between the colonists' spreading settlement and hostile outlying tribes, and said that the "Senecas having put our Indians into a feare, dare not go so high to hunt."

Some government officials claimed that the 1677 treaty created more problems than it had solved, for when tributary Indian leaders took their disagreements to court, the justices made enemies of whomever they sided against. Also, the Virginia government was obligated to protect the tributary tribes from the warlike natives above the fall line, who not only attacked frontier settlers but sometimes preyed upon the tributary tribes. To meet this need for defense, in December 1679 the assembly decided to establish garrisons at the heads of certain rivers. In 1682, however, the assembly decided to abolish this latest series of forts, opting instead to have groups of horse soldiers patrol the frontier. As late as 1699 hostile Indians from the interior of the continent posed a threat to settlers living along the fringes of the colony's frontier.

Minutes of the Council of State reveal that from time to time natives exercised their legal right to file formal complaints against settlers who trespassed, allowed their livestock to damage the Indians' crops, or committed other infractions of the law. Occasionally they also sought protection from aggressive non-tributary tribes, such as the Susquehannocks, who lived beyond the fringes of the colony's frontiers. During the early 1680s Seneca attacks on the tributary tribes increased to the point that the Virginia government had to intervene. In mid-November 1683 the Seneca reportedly descended upon the Mattaponi Indian town on the Mattaponi River and then laid siege to a Chickahominy or Rappahannock fort that was nearby. Afterward, the Mattaponi took refuge with the Pamunkey Indians, whereas the Rappahannock, whom government officials urged to unite with the Nanzattico, were taken to Portobago.

However, the legal system could also work against the natives. When a group of Indian warriors descended on a frontier family's home in 1704 and several people were slain, the Nanzattico (a tributary tribe) became prime suspects. Several warriors, who were rounded up and questioned, confessed to the killings. When local justices convened as a court of oyer and terminer on October 5, 1704, all but one of the accused were convicted of murder and sentenced to death. Forty others were brought to Williamsburg, where they were tried in accord with a 1663 law that held natives accountable for wrongful actions committed by other members of their group. In May 1705 the House of Burgesses concluded that all of the male Nanzattico were guilty by association and, therefore, all males age 12 or older should be deported and sold as servants. Those under the age of 12 were to be bound out until age 24. Ultimately, almost all of the Nanzattico were transported to Antigua, where they were sold into servitude. Meanwhile, 13 Nanzattico children were distributed among the members of the Council of State. Thus, during 1705 the Nanzattico as a group essentially ceased to exist.

Prelude to Change

When the first of three town acts was passed in 1680 in response to pressure from abroad, Jamestown was one of twenty 50-acre sites selected for urbanization. Shortly thereafter, Virginia's governor was ordered to see that the capital city was rebuilt as soon as possible. This prompted a group of townspeople to ask the assembly to define Jamestown's legal limits, which traditionally extended from Sandy Bay to Orchard Run and from the Back River to the James, encompassing several hundred acres. During this period attorney William Sherwood, who married a wealthy widow, began consolidating small lots and larger parcels within urban Jamestown. When the Rev. John Clayton made a primitive sketch of Jamestown Island in 1688, he indicated that a row of houses stood along the waterfront, west of Orchard Run. He also showed a brick house that was located on the west side of Kingsmill Creek's mouth. Clayton disdainfully described the crescent-shaped brick fort that had been built in 1673 as a defense against the Dutch as "a silly sort of fort," better suited for shooting at ducks than firing upon an enemy! Clayton said that Jamestown had between 16 and 18 houses, most of which were brick and located on the waterfront. He said that they were occupied by a dozen families who got "their liveings by keeping ordinaries at extraordinary rates." One such tavern-keeper was jailer Henry Gawler, who sometimes played host to tributary Indian leaders visiting Jamestown on official business. Another was Colonel Thomas Swann I, whose tavern was burned during Bacon's Rebellion but later was rebuilt. In 1695 Jamestown's householders persuaded the assembly to pass a law prohibiting swine from running at large within the city limits. However, the governor and council disallowed the law, perhaps reflecting their disdain for the community. It was around this time that a new gun platform was built in Jamestown, and King Charles II considered designating the town an Anglican see or bishop's seat.

Government at the End of the Seventeenth Century

At the close of the seventeenth century, Jamestown residents Henry Hartwell and Edward Chilton, and James City Parish's rector, the Rev. James Blair, prepared an official report at the request of officials in England. Their narrative, which described conditions in Virginia, provided an overview of the way the government conducted business. It also demonstrated that the colony's highest-ranking officials had to spend lengthy periods of time in Jamestown when performing their duties. The governor, as chief executive, had the right to grant land, fill public offices, and issue warrants for government funds. He also presided over the Council of State and the General Court, and could summon or dismiss the burgesses, veto the laws they passed, and call for elections. As commander-in-chief of the armed forces, the governor made sure that the colony's defenses were maintained, and he commissioned all military officers. His power was restrained by the monarch.

The Council of State was supposed to advise the governor on matters that ranged from military and trade policies to the State Church. Council members also sat as justices in the General Court, the colony's highest-ranking judicial body, which sometimes acted in an appellate capacity, and councilors served as the colony's secretary, escheator, and auditor. The secretary maintained copies of important public documents, whereas the escheator kept a record of all land that had reverted to the Crown and therefore was available to would-be patentees. The auditor accepted the tax revenues that local sheriffs collected from their jurisdiction's inhabitants. He also received the customs duties collected by naval officers, who were council members and inspected all seagoing vessels entering and leaving Virginia. Councilors served as superior military officers, colonels who were in command of county militia units. If a county was too distant from a colonel's home, the governor usually appointed a local military leader who was designated a major. The governor, with input from his colonels and majors, commissioned captains and lieutenants, who headed local military companies and units directly under their charge. Members of the Council of State were handsomely compensated for performing their numerous duties. They also were privy to "insider information" that they could use to their own advantage. For instance, because they had convenient access to the escheator's records, they usually knew when desirable land reverted to the Crown and could patent it before others learned that it was available. As military officers, council members sometimes agreed to outfit the militia or undertake fort construction, which entitled them to compensation from public funds. If land was needed for a planned town or construction of a tobacco inspection warehouse, a council member's property usually was selected.

At the close of the seventeenth century, the assembly consisted of two burgesses from each county and one from Jamestown. As soon as the governor called the assembly into session, elections were held at county seats. Free white adult males had the right to vote and hold office in every county in which they (or their spouses) owned a certain minimum amount of real estate. Thus, a man could vote in several localities' elections and hold office in a jurisdiction in which he did not reside. Highly successful planters and merchants often owned land in two or more counties and therefore had a greater opportunity to wield their influence over local and regional affairs. For instance, Miles Cary II, who resided in Warwick County but owned a lot in urban Jamestown, served briefly as the capital city's burgess in the 1693 term. Daniel Parke II, who in 1693 was elected a burgess for both Jamestown and York County, was allowed to choose which jurisdiction he preferred to represent. Conflict of interest does not seem to have mattered, for prominent individuals often held two or more public offices for which they were compensated. The assembly chose its own speaker and formed standing committees. Because Jamestown was the capital of Virginia from 1607 to 1699 and James City County's seat from 1634 to ca. 1715–1721, many local men played an official role in both governments. The James City County sheriff served as sergeant-at-arms to the General Court and the assembly, and as jailer, he had custody of both judicial bodies' prisoners. Clergy were paid for offering prayers at assembly meetings, and citizens were compensated for serving as official messengers, furnishing candles and writing materials, and occasionally providing room-and-board to tributary Indians and others who came to town on official business. A drummer was paid for summoning the burgesses to their meetings, and sometimes the assembly and General Court rented space in which to convene.

The Capital Moves to Williamsburg

Construction of the College of William and Mary at Middle Plantation and an arsonist's destruction of the colony's statehouse in September 1698 ultimately sealed Jamestown's fate. Although one writer at the close of the seventeenth century said that the town had 20 to 30 houses and another called it "one of the largest and most beautiful places in the country," Lieutenant Governor Francis Nicholson claimed that it was "reduced to so mean a condition that it cannot give entertainment to the people attending both a General Assembly and a General Court." The assembly convened in Jamestown from April 27 to April 29, 1699, and while they were in session, Governor Nicholson sent word that he wanted them to meet at the College of William and Mary on May 1st. An act was then presented before the burgesses, calling for the colony's capital city to be moved from Jamestown to Middle Plantation. The proposed legislation stressed the new location's desirable characteristics and described how the new planned community would be laid out. A group of college students appeared before the assembly in a carefully orchestrated May Day celebration. They urged the burgesses to make Middle Plantation the new capital and pointed out that the makings of a city were already there: a church, two mills, several stores, an ordinary, and of course, the college. After two weeks of deliberation and the drafting of some amendments, the burgesses agreed, and on June 8, 1699, the governor approved the law that made Williamsburg the new capital.

By the close of 1700, the assembly and the Council of State had begun meeting at the College of William and Mary. Although plans were made for the General Court to convene there too, its sessions continued to be held in Jamestown, which was still the seat of the James City County court. In December 1700 plans were made to transfer the records of the Secretary's Office and the assembly's records to the College of William and Mary, and during 1701 powder, shot, cannon, and other materiel were fetched from Jamestown. In 1703, four years after the decision was made to move the capital to Williamsburg and construction of a new statehouse already was underway, Queen Anne informed Virginia's governing officials that she wanted Jamestown rebuilt as the colony's capital. Council minutes hint at the leaders' uneasiness when they informed the queen that they had already moved the capital, pointing out that she had failed to disallow the legislation effecting the transfer.

Representation in the Assembly

Another politically charged issue that arose during 1703 was whether Jamestown would continue sending a delegate to the colony's assembly, a privilege the old capital city had enjoyed since 1619. Lieutenant Governor Francis Nicholson adamantly opposed letting the former capital have its own delegate and refused to permit it. However, Jamestown's freeholders dispatched petitions to England, seeking official intervention. When Governor Edward Nott took office in 1705, the assembly asked him to allow Jamestown to elect a burgess. He agreed and representation was restored after a hiatus of more than two years. Jamestown continued sending a delegate to the assembly until 1776.

The Old Capital Begins to Fade

In 1705, when a new town act was passed, Jamestown again was designated an official port and market days were established. However, by that time Edward Jaquelin had begun accumulating much of the acreage that lay within urban Jamestown's legal limits, and the Travis and Broadnax families had come into possession of almost all of the island's remaining land. Although a handful of people retained their Jamestown lots for several more decades, the old capital city began receding into the rural landscape. According to the Rev. John Fontaine in 1716, Jamestown "now is all gone to ruin." In 1724 the Rev. Hugh Jones described the former capital even more disparagingly, for he said that at present it consisted "of nothing but Abundance of Brick Rubbish, and three or four good inhabited Houses."

In 1706 James City County's court justices asked the assembly to allow them to use bricks from the old, burned-out statehouse to construct a new county courthouse in Jamestown. Nine years later some of the county court's justices asked Lieutenant Governor Alexander Spotswood to make Williamsburg the new county seat. However, a number of Jamestown property owners vigorously opposed the change. Despite the opposition, sometime after 1715, but before 1721, a James City County courthouse was erected in Williamsburg. City and county officials shared this building for more than 20 years "on courtesie."

Legalized Racial Discrimination

In 1705 the assembly updated the legal code to address the colony's changing needs, and several laws were enacted that affected the lives of all non-whites. Enslaved blacks were relegated to the status of personal property that could be bought and sold, and Indians were deprived of the legal rights they had formerly enjoyed. This change occurred at a time when the tributary Indians were making increased use of the colony's judicial system instead of settling their own disputes. Under the 1705 legal code, Indians and other non-whites were prohibited from testifying in court, a restriction that prevented them from collecting debts. It also kept Indian bond servants from suing for their freedom if their masters detained them after their contract expired. Interracial marriage became illegal, and non-whites were declared ineligible to hold any public office whatsoever. A 1711 law required both tributary and non-tributary Indians to wear badges when they ventured into colonized areas, and three years later a law was passed prohibiting the use of the titles "king" and "queen" in reference to native leaders. Thus, as Virginia's Indians became increasingly acculturated and assumed a more visible (but less forceful) role in society, and as they declined in population and strength, they became legally susceptible to the same types of discrimination to which blacks and other minorities were subjected.

Jamestown During the Eighteenth Century

In 1729 Richard Ambler of Yorktown married Elizabeth, the eldest daughter of Edward Jaquelin, who had consolidated several tracts within urban Jamestown and created a successful working plantation. When Jaquelin died in 1739, his property descended to his daughter, Elizabeth, and her second oldest son, John Ambler I. Between 1745 and 1753 Richard Ambler managed to combine several urban parcels in the western end of Jamestown Island with acreage he had purchased in the island's southeastern end. This not only created a large plantation, it also gave Ambler and his heirs control of almost all of Jamestown Island's frontage on the James River and more than half of the land bordering the Back River. Ambler erected a large Georgian mansion on his property in urban Jamestown, intending it as a family seat for his son, John I.

Meanwhile, members of the Travis family, who by 1682 had begun consolidating their holdings into a plantation that enveloped the northeastern part of Jamestown Island, had possession of two waterfront lots in urban Jamestown. During the 1750s Edward Champion Travis was actively involved in the slave trade and served as the former capital city's burgess. Although he eventually moved to a riverfront plantation in York County, he retained his property on Jamestown Island. Others who owned lots within urban Jamestown during the second half of the eighteenth century included members of the Ludwell, Custis, Burwell, and Harris families. The island, which had access to deepwater shipping, continued to function as a port, and until around 1748–1750 James City Parish's parishioners attended services at the church that stood at the western end of Jamestown Island. The ferries that had run from the western end of Jamestown Island to Swann's Point and Crouch's Creek, in Surry County, continued to operate until 1779.

The American Revolution Impacts Jamestown Island

At the beginning of the Revolutionary War, a battery was built at the western end of Jamestown Island, overlooking the river. By that time the island, with the exception of a few urban lots, was owned by the Amblers and Travises, whose houses stood amidst the vestiges of old Jamestown. Captain Edward Travis IV, an American naval officer whose ancestral plantation was located at the eastern end of Jamestown Island, coordinated extensive ship repair activities on the island during the 1770s and rented the Amblers' Georgian mansion. A major battle took place on the mainland in early July 1781, and British troops camped on Jamestown Island while waiting to cross the James River. A prisoner-exchange cartel (negotiated by American General Nathanael Greene and British General Charles Lord Cornwallis) made provisions for the Southern Department's detainees to be swapped at Jamestown. "Cartel vessels" reportedly landed in Jamestown periodically between mid-July 1781 and November 1782, with prisoners who were being repatriated. Some of the prisoners were wounded or in poor physical condition. On August 7, 1781, Surgeon General Goodwin Wilson sent word to Colonel William Davies that one of General Lafayette's aides wanted a flag of truce so that he could transport the wounded from Jamestown to Richmond, where they would be able to receive medical treatment. When Louis Hue Girardin painted a picture in 1803 of Jamestown's ruinous church, he showed the Travis family's urban dwelling and the Amblers' towering Georgian mansion.

The War of 1812's Impact

During the War of 1812, the British invaded the James River basin. By June 1813 a large number of British barges, an armed brig, and six or seven tenders were moving freely up and down the James River, plundering waterfront homes and sometimes venturing inland. John Ambler II was away on July 1, 1813, when the British invaded his ancestral home in urban Jamestown. According to official correspondence, a raiding party landed and "after plundering the plantation, destroyed Lieut. Ambler's Household furniture of every description." The British reportedly carried off whatever they could and laid waste to the rest. John Henry Strobia, who visited Jamestown Island in 1817, commented that there were only "two or three old houses, the ruins of an old steeple, a churchyard and faint marks of rude fortifications."

Consolidation

By 1822 Edward Ambler II had sold his 900-acre Jamestown Island plantation to Thomas Wilson, who quickly disposed of it. It was purchased by David Bullock of Richmond, a prominent attorney and the city's former mayor, who probably placed the Ambler property in the hands of a tenant or farm manager. In 1831 Bullock bought the Travis family's acreage in the northeastern end of Jamestown Island. It was the first time since Virginia was colonized that almost all of Jamestown Island was owned by one individual. At the close of 1892, Jamestown Island—with the exception of the state-owned church property—came into the hands of Edward E. Barney and his wife, Louise. They deeded a 22½-acre tract to the Association for the Preservation of Virginia Antiquities (now known as Preservation Virginia) in 1893, and in 1934 the United States government acquired the rest of the Barneys' land.

A

Thomas Abbay: Thomas Abbay, a gentleman, arrived in Jamestown in 1608 in the 2nd Supply of new settlers. Captain John Smith included some of Abbay's writings in his *Proceedings* (VI&A 77).

Jeffrey Abbott (Abbot): Jeffrey Abbott (Abbot), a gentleman and soldier who had served in Ireland and in the Netherlands, arrived in Jamestown in January 1608 in the 1st Supply of new colonists. Captain John Smith described him as an intelligent, loyal, and hardworking man. Sometime prior to 1611 Abbott was executed for plotting against the government (VI&A 77).

Samuel Abbott: Samuel Abbott secured a patent for approximately one-tenth of an acre of land, probably in urban Jamestown. On September 22, 1694, the clerk in the Secretary of the Colony's office described the Abbott patent as illegible (PB 2:367–368; NUG I:226).

Abell: An inventory of the late Richard Ambler's slaves on Jamestown Island and in the Governor's Land, compiled on February 15, 1768, included Abell, an enslaved boy, who was identified as Sarah's child (York County Wills and Inventories 21:386–391).

Aberdeen: On February 15, 1768, when an inventory was made of the late Richard Ambler's slaves on Jamestown Island and in the Governor's Land, an adult male slave named Aberdeen was listed (York County Wills and Inventories 21:386–391).

Abochancano (see Opechancanough)

Richard Abrell (Abrahall, Abraell): Richard Abrell served in the assembly in 1661–1662, representing New Kent County (LEO 39; York County Record Book 1 [1648–1657]: 131). His name's absence in surviving patents and in the records of New Kent County's antecedent, York County, raises the possibility that the burgess identified as Richard Abrell actually was Robert Abrell.

Robert Abrell (Abrahall, Abraell): Robert Abrell was named York County's undersheriff in May 1648. From time to time he appeared before the county court, alternately as plaintiff and defendant. His reputation was questioned in 1648 when Abraham Moon accused him of taking bribes while carrying out his official duties; proof was lacking and he was absolved of any wrongdoing. When New Kent County was formed, Abrell served as one of its burgesses and attended the assembly sessions held in 1654–1655 and 1660. During the 1650s, while the Commonwealth government was in power, Robert Abrell began speculating in real estate, laying claim to large tracts of land on both sides of the York River and its tributaries, the Mattaponi and Pamunkey rivers. He continued to acquire land during the 1660s, 1670s, and early 1680s, securing large patents in York, Gloucester, and New Kent counties. Abrell held the rank of colonel when he posted a bond in 1670 on another man's behalf. The following year he brought suit against George Lee, a merchant and Jamestown property owner, and in 1672, while he was sheriff of New Kent County, he sued John Payne of Old Rappahannock County. In 1673 Abrell was ordered to investigate two people's deaths and the role Anthony Arnold might have played in those deaths. In September 1674 Abrell was ordered to survey the several parcels of land he owned on the upper side of the Mattaponi River, seemingly because of a land dispute. On one occasion he was assaulted by George Morris (Morrice), who was forced to apologize (LEO 32, 36; MCGC 209, 249, 294, 316, 328, 361–362, 375, 378, 380, 398, 415, 417, 443; PB 2:309–310; 3:30, 225, 337; 4:146, 259, 467, 476; 5:238, 264, 334; 6:554, 654, 686; 7:111, 311; York County Court Orders 2 [1646–1648]:297, 352, 360; Record Book 2 [1648–1657]:401, 411). The year of Abrell's death is uncertain.

Accapataugh (Native American): In May 1657 Accapataugh made a peace agreement with the justices of Old Rappahannock County. On May 27, 1658, Naeheoopa, then king of the Rappahannock Indians, was among the natives confirming a land transaction made by the tribe's late king, Accapataugh, and Colonel Moore Fauntleroy (Old

Rappahannock County Deed Book 1656–1664: 10–11, 26–27).

George Acrig: In 1608 George Acrig, a gentleman and a soldier, was among those given the task of building a house for Powhatan (VI&A 78).

Adam: According to Captain John Smith, during the latter part of 1608 Adam and Francis, "two stout Dutchmen" or Poles (probably Germans) who had been living with Powhatan, came to the fort in Jamestown asking for firearms and clothing. Smith considered their request a ruse because some of the Indians accompanying Adam and Francis stole some weapons. On another occasion Adam went to the glasshouse with Francis, who was disguised as an Indian. In 1610, when Lord Delaware arrived, Adam and Francis fled to Powhatan. Lord Delaware realized that Adam and Francis were as likely to betray him as they had Captain John Smith and therefore had them executed (HAI 304, 325, 337).

[No First Name] Adams: On February 16, 1624, Mr. Adams, whose first name is unknown, was living in the Jamestown household of Goodman Stoiks, probably John Stoaks (Stoiks, Stokes) (VI&A 78).

Ann Adams (Addams): Ann Adams was living in urban Jamestown on February 16, 1624. She was still there in January 1625 and was identified as a servant in Ralph Hamor's household (VI&A 78).

Peter Adams: On February 10, 1677, Governor William Berkeley issued a proclamation in which he named those who were exempt from the king's pardon due to their role in Bacon's Rebellion. Peter Adams, who was among those listed, was supposed to be brought before a court to stand trial (NEVILLE 61).

Robert Adams: Robert Adams, a servant, was living at Martin's Hundred at the time of the March 22, 1622, Indian attack and was evacuated to Jamestown Island. By 1623 he had married and returned to Martin's Hundred. When Indians again attacked the settlement, he received a gunshot wound. In 1624 Adams served as a burgess for Martin's Hundred. He died sometime prior to January 21, 1629, at which time his widow was authorized to settle his estate (VI&A 79; LEO 5).

Thomas Adams: On October 26, 1670, the late Thomas Adams' executors were ordered to pay a debt to Thomas Hunt of urban Jamestown (MCGC 236).

Henry Adling: Henry Adling came to Virginia in 1607 in the 1st Supply of Jamestown colonists (VI&A 80).

Richard Alder (Aldon): In 1624 Richard Alder, who came to Virginia in 1620, was a servant in William Peirce's household in urban Jamestown. A year later he was a member of Peirce's household on Mulberry Island (VI&A 80).

Richard Alford: In 1625 Richard Alford, a 26-year-old indentured servant, was living on Captain Roger Smith's plantation on the lower side of the James River. He also spent time in urban Jamestown, probably in Smith's home, and often provided court testimony about residents of the capital city. In 1627 Alford was identified as a Virginia Company tenant who had been assigned to Captain Samuel Mathews (VI&A 81).

Alice: When an inventory was made on February 15, 1768, of the late Richard Ambler's slaves on Jamestown Island and his leasehold in the Governor's Land, one of the people listed was a female slave named Alice. In 1769 she was living in the Governor's Land and was attributed to the late Edward Ambler I's estate. Alice was described as a girl (York County Wills and Inventories 21:386–391; AMB-E).

Alice: When an inventory was made on February 15, 1768, of the late Richard Ambler's slaves on Jamestown Island and his leasehold in the Governor's Land, an enslaved girl named Alice was listed. In 1769 she was living on Jamestown Island and was attributed to the late Edward Ambler I's estate (York County Wills and Inventories 21:386–391; AMB-E).

Jeremy (Herome) Alicock (Allicock): Jeremy Alicock, a gentleman, came to Virginia in 1607 in the first group of Jamestown colonists. He was wounded and died on August 14, 1607. Edward Maria Wingfield spoke appreciatively of Alicock (VI&A 81).

Arthur Allen (Allin) II: Arthur Allen II was the son and principal heir of Arthur Allen I, who by 1649 had settled in Surry County and become a highly successful merchant-planter. Around 1670, when Arthur Allen II was age 19, he inherited the land his late father had patented between Lawnes and Lower Chippokes creeks, some acreage on the Blackwater River, and a large parcel on Upper Chippokes Creek. He also inherited the fine brick mansion that his father had built in 1665, the family seat that eventually became known as Bacon's Castle. Arthur Allen II became a county justice as soon as he attained his majority. Thanks to his steadfast loyalty to Governor William Berkeley, some of rebel Nathaniel Bacon's followers seized and occupied his home during the latter part of 1676. Later, Allen sued some of the men who had inflicted significant damage on his residence. In January 1677 Governor William Berkeley ordered Allen and two other men to confiscate the estate of Robert Kay, an accused rebel. Arthur Allen II, like his late father, speculated in real estate, sometimes acquiring large tracts of land on the Blackwater River. He also patented some land on the Nansemond River, acreage that straddled the boundary between Isle of White and Nansemond counties. Allen, who married Catherine (Katherine), the daughter and heir of neighbor and burgess Lawrence Baker, served as a Surry County burgess and attended the assembly sessions held in 1680–1682, 1684, 1685–1686, 1688, and 1691–1692. He and three other men were identified as surveyors in 1680 and 1693. He was suspended from holding the office of surveyor in 1685 because he disputed the governor's prerogative, but he was elected speaker of the assembly during its 1686 session. When the burgesses convened for the 1691–1692 session, Allen refused to take the required oaths and was replaced by Benjamin Harrison II. Allen, who served as an attorney from time to time, was a militia captain and became the Upper James River District's customs officer. One of his friends was John Thompson, a Surry County merchant who conducted trade in London.

When the assembly enacted town-founding legislation and each of Virginia's counties was supposed to set aside 50 acres for urban development, Captain Arthur Allen II was ordered to lay off part of John Pitt's land, what was known as Pates Field, into a town site. Pitt's acreage, sometimes called Newtown, eventually became the community known as Smithfield. Allen identified himself as a resident of Lawnes Creek Parish in Surry in 1692 when he disposed of some of his land in Isle of Wight County. On November 5, 1693, Catherine and Arthur Allen II sold some of the acreage they had inherited from her father, Captain Lawrence Baker. Later, the Allen couple got rid of the acreage in which they and William Edwards II had invested, land that was on the Black-

water River. From time to time Major Arthur Allen II was named to the College of William and Mary's board of governors. In 1704 he was designated surveyor of Isle of Wight and Surry counties. His will was presented to Surry County's justices in July 1710 (LEO xiii, 46–49, 51; Isle of Wight County Deed Book 2 [1688–1704]:44, 298, 381–382, 450; 3 [1704–1715]:9; Orders 1693–1695:6; Surry County Deeds, Wills, &c. Book 1:91, 172; 4:140, 335; Order Book III:167–169; SR 384, 660, 4362, 4786, 6579; PB 2:197; 5:236; 6:650, 652, 654; 7:16, 109; 8:127, 174–175, 219, 365; 9:330, 332; EJC I:198, 204, 366, 372, 507; II:233, 271, 348, 350, 354; III:33, 49, 59, 62, 64, 77, 131, 157, 249; CO 1/39 f 24).

William Allen: In early 1624 William Allen was living in Elizabeth City. Within a year's time he had moved to Flowerdew Hundred, where he was one of Abraham Peirsey's servants. When the assembly convened on October 16, 1629, Allen, then a free man, represented Henry Throgmorton's plantation at Shirley Hundred (VI&A 82; LEO 8).

* * *

Isaac Allerton: Isaac Allerton, who was born in Massachusetts, spent time in Connecticut before moving to Virginia. In 1656 the Machodoc Indians filed a petition in Northumberland County's court, claiming that he was then residing on their land. In 1659 he disposed of some of his land on the Machodoc River, and in 1662, around the time he began serving as a Northumberland County justice, he secured a patent for acreage on the Lower Machodoc River in Westmoreland County. During the early 1660s he married Elizabeth, the daughter of Captain Thomas Willoughby of Lower Norfolk County, who had outlived her first two husbands, Dutch merchant Simon Overzee and Major George Colclough of Northumberland County. In 1664 Allerton served as administrator for the estate of Simon Overzee, who traded extensively in Virginia, especially Lower Norfolk County, and he assisted his wife, Elizabeth, while she was serving as George Colclough's administratrix. In fact, while Allerton was a Westmoreland County burgess in 1667, he was still involved in the settlement of the decedents' estates. Allerton appeared in court numerous times, attempting to recover debts or to defend himself or others against suits. In 1670 he and John Lee purchased two acres on the eastern branch of the Nominy River and built a mill. After Lee's death Allerton retained his legal interest in the property. In 1667 Major Isaac Allerton was part of a group known as the Association of Northumberland, Westmoreland, and Stafford Counties, which was given the responsibility of building a fort to protect against a Dutch invasion. In August 1677, while he was a Westmoreland County court justice, he testified before a local jury about some of rebel Nathaniel Bacon's men who had seized control of the homes that belonged to colonels John Washington and Nicholas Spencer. Allerton's house also was overrun by Bacon's followers, who stole some of his goods.

During the early 1680s Allerton patented 2,172 acres of land on the south side of the Rappahannock River in Old Rappahannock County. Then, a decade later he laid claim to three tracts in Westmoreland County on the Lower Machodoc and Nominy cliffs and more than 2,000 acres in Stafford County on Aquia Creek. Allerton served as a burgess on behalf of Northumberland County and attended the sessions held in 1668–1674, 1676, and 1677, but he represented Westmoreland County in 1680–1682, 1684, and 1696–1697. In August 1675 he and Colonel John Washington were ordered to summon militia officers from the regiments on the north side of the Rappahannock and south side of the Potomac to determine which Indian group was responsible for attacking some settlers in Stafford County. In 1679 Lieutenant Colonel Allerton and two other men were authorized to see that a fort was built on the Potomac River at Niabsco and equipped to accommodate a garrison of men. A year later he and Colonel Richard Lee were authorized to negotiate with Northumberland County officials about collaboratively building a town at Yeocomoco (Yeocomico). Allerton was named to the Council of State in 1683 and thereafter was a colonel. He also was naval officer and receiver for Northumberland County and was escheator for Old Rappahannock County. During the mid-1680s he became high sheriff and served several terms. One of his tasks was to hire a large boat and oarsmen to take Colonel Richard Lee to Maryland on official business. Isaac Allerton died in 1702 (LEO 39–43, 46–47, 57; STAN 42; HEN II:433; Northumberland County Wills, Inventories &c. 1652–1658:101; Record Book 1658–1662:21, 36; 1662–1666:168; 1666–1670:34–36; Order Book 1652–1665:107, 351, 398, 412, 415; 1666–1678:76, 79, 86, 106, 163, 302, 325; 1678–1698:73; Stafford County Record Book 1686–1693:108a, 210a; Old Rappahannock County Deeds and Wills 1677–1682:319; Order Book 1686–1692:163; Westmoreland County Deeds, Wills, Patents &c. 1653–1659:103; Deeds, Wills &c. 1661–1662:16–16a; Deeds, Patents &c.

1665–1677:94a–95, 170–170a, 199a–200, 231a–232, 325a–326; Deeds and Wills 1701–1707:115; Order Book 1662–1664:41a; 1676–1689:50, 83, 146, 152, 187, 247, 263, 360, 367, 407, 488, 523, 617; PB 4:434; 7:198, 292; NN 1:28–32; 2:74–75, 94–95; DOR 1:476; 3:651–652).

Willoughby Allerton: Willoughby, the son of Isaac and Elizabeth Allerton, was born around 1664. He was a resident of Westmoreland County, where he became a militia captain in 1698, county justice in 1699, and sheriff in 1700. Allerton married Colonel William Fitzhugh's daughter, Rosamond. After her death in 1700 he wed the widowed Sarah Taverner Travers, and upon being widowed a second time, he married Hannah Keene Bushrod, who also was a widow. In June 1699, when Allerton disposed of some acreage on the Lower Machodoc River, he identified himself as a resident of Cople Parish. He represented Westmoreland in the assembly in 1699 and attended the 1710–1714 sessions. His will, which was proved on April 8, 1724, named his wife, Hannah, her children by John Bushrod, and his own children, Isaac II and Elizabeth Allerton (LEO 59, 66–67; Westmoreland County Deeds and Wills 1691–1699:186a–187; 1723–1738:9–10; Richmond County Wills and Inventories 1699–1709:42v; MEADE II:193; DOR 3:653–654, 656).

* * *

Thomas Allnutt (Alnutt): In February 1624 Thomas Allnutt and his wife, Joan (Joane), were living within the Neck O'Land behind Jamestown Island, but by January 1625 they had moved to urban Jamestown. Thomas died prior to August 21, 1626, and by February 5, 1627, Joan had married Thomas Bagwell, an ancient planter (VI&A 82–83).

Thomas Allomby (Allainby, Allamby): In December 1682 Thomas Allomby patented a tract of land on the James River in Elizabeth City County, acreage that formerly had been owned by William Brooks alias Morgan. In 1684 Allomby served as a burgess for Elizabeth City County, and in 1688 he became a justice in the local court. The following year official records identified him as Sebastin Perrin's guardian. Allomby was returned to the assembly and served in 1688 and 1691–1692. He also was designated a trustee of the new town that was to be established in Elizabeth City County, which became the city of Hampton. Captain Thomas Allomby died intestate, and on January 27, 1693, his widow, Elizabeth, was designated administratrix. Elizabeth City County's justices ordered some local men to appraise the decedent's estate on behalf of his widow and orphan; the appraisal was completed by February 10th. Mrs. Elizabeth Allomby quickly remarried and by June 10, 1693, had wed Walter Innis, a surgeon. In November 1697 Charles Goring, who had married the late Thomas Allomby's daughter, Eleanor (Ellynor), brought suit against Mrs. Elizabeth Innis in an attempt to recover two-thirds of her late father's estate. A year later Mrs. Innis was sued by the orphans of a man who had named her late husband as guardian of his children (LEO 47, 49–50; NEAL 3, 9, 18, 22, 29, 96, 225, 242; PB 7:217; CHAPMAN 1, 154).

James Alsop (Allsop, Alsope): On December 7, 1664, James Alsop purchased part of a waterfront lot in urban Jamestown from John Barber I and his wife, Letitia. He developed his property, and on November 24, 1671, the vestry of James City Parish was authorized to compensate him for providing room and board to the Rev. Samuel Jones, James City Parish's new rector. On August 16, 1670, Alsop bought a tract of Surry County land that he and his wife, Judith, then sold to Edward Howell on March 16, 1674. In 1675 Alsop went to court in Surry, where he won a judgment against bricklayer John Bird, who was involved in the construction of buildings in Jamestown and elsewhere. He also helped settle the late Bennett Marjoram's estate in Surry. According to court testimony that was taken in early March 1674, a Surry County man took a boat to James Alsop in Jamestown so that it could be "trimmed," that is, be outfitted with sails. That statement raises the possibility that Alsop had a sail loft on his waterfront lot in the capital city. Court testimony taken in the wake of Bacon's Rebellion suggests strongly that Alsop sympathized with the rebel Nathaniel Bacon and was among those who seized Governor Berkeley's goods and stashed them at innkeeper Richard Lawrence's house in Jamestown. On May 21, 1679, Alsop's executor, Thomas Holiday (Holliday), sold the decedent's quarter-acre lot to William Briscoe, a blacksmith. Thus, the decedent was in possession of his Jamestown lot at the time of his death and likely had been residing there (AMB 27, 57, 133; MCGC 288, 403; Surry County Deeds and Wills 1671–1684:46, 73, 130, 178, 193, 203, 205; Order Book 1671–1691:193).

* * *

Richard Ambler: Richard, the son of John and Elizabeth Birkard Ambler of York, England, was born on December 23, 1690. He immigrated to Virginia in 1716 and became established at Yorktown. His descendants described him as about 5 feet 11 inches tall and "inclined to be fat." They also said that he was a highly successful merchant who was "saving and thrifty." Ambler's well-documented ability to accumulate wealth attests to his business acumen. In 1729 he married Elizabeth, the eldest daughter of Edward and Martha Cary Thruston Jaquelin of Jamestown Island. Richard and Elizabeth produced three sons and a daughter: Edward I, John I, Jaquelin, and Elizabeth II, who was born in 1731 and died in 1740. Richard Ambler's father-in-law, Edward Jaquelin, who owned a plantation in urban Jamestown, died in November 1739. His heirs included Richard's wife, Elizabeth, and her sisters: Martha, a spinster known for her fastidiousness, and Mary, who in November 1739 wed John Smith. Thus, Edward Jaquelin's only grandchildren at the time of his death were the offspring of his daughter Elizabeth and her husband, Richard Ambler. According to a family history written in 1826, Edward Jaquelin left his Jamestown plantation to his grandson John Ambler I; however, a contemporary narrative, also done by a family member, states that he left the property to his eldest daughter, Elizabeth, who passed it on to son John Ambler I. Edward Jaquelin gave son-in-law Richard Ambler life-rights to a small parcel in the western end of Jamestown Island, next to the ferry landing. Twenty years later, Richard transferred it to his son John Ambler I.

In 1745 Richard Ambler began purchasing pieces of land that adjoined his late father-in-law's plantation. On January 1, 1745, he bought from Norfolk merchant Christopher Perkins approximately 298 acres in the eastern end of Jamestown Island, acreage that previously had belonged to William Broadnax I and his son William II. Then, on April 24, 1745, he procured fee simple ownership of the Jamestown lot in which Edward Jaquelin had given him life-rights. By consolidating the Jaquelin and Perkins landholdings, Richard Ambler amassed just over 698 acres of land in the southeast, central, and western portions of Jamestown Island. This gave him control of almost all of the island's frontage on the James River and more than half of the land bordering the Back River. On October 6, 1753, Richard Ambler purchased from Edward Champion Travis a half-acre lot in ur-

ban Jamestown, a parcel that was situated
directly in front of the site on which he built
a Georgian mansion and dependencies. Ambler's purposeful land acquisitions and the
construction of a substantial dwelling attest
to his desire to provide a suitable family seat
for his second oldest son, John I, who came
of age in 1756. Richard Ambler's almost
continuous presence in Yorktown until his
death in 1765 demonstrates that he, personally, never intended to move to Jamestown.

In 1748 several local citizens asked the
House of Burgesses to move the Jamestown
ferry's landing from Richard Ambler's
property on Jamestown Island to another location, insisting that the causeway to the island was too costly to maintain. He filed a
counter-petition and the ferry stayed where
it was. On December 13, 1755, Richard Ambler gave his eldest son, Edward I, and
brother-in-law John Smith a life-interest in
lots adjoining the ferry-landing in the western end of Jamestown Island. As the Jamestown ferry accommodated a steady stream
of travelers, the lots Ambler gave to his eldest son and son-in-law would have had
considerable commercial potential and protected his own interests.

When Richard Ambler of Yorktown
made his will on January 23, 1765, he distributed the acreage he owned in several Virginia counties among his sons. Although
Edward was the eldest and principal heir and
inherited residential and commercial property in Yorktown, Richard left his son John I
almost all of his land on Jamestown Island,
his plantation on Powhatan Swamp, and a
310-acre leasehold in the Governor's Land.
John Ambler I also stood to receive his late
father's household furnishings in Jamestown and the slaves that were on all of his
James City County property. The testator
bequeathed to his son John I two acres of
land that adjoined Jamestown's ferry landing, noting that he had inherited it from his
late father-in-law, Edward Jaquelin; he also
acknowledged that he had given life-inter-
ests in the parcel to his eldest son, Edward,
and brother-in-law John Smith. Richard
Ambler died in February 1766, predeceas-
ing his wife, Elizabeth, who died on September 25, 1769. An inventory of his personal effects in Yorktown reflects his
material wealth and affluent lifestyle. The
men who appraised Ambler's estate credited
him with 63 slaves who were associated
with his Jamestown Island property and his
leasehold in the mainland, and another 14
slaves at his quarter on Powhatan Swamp.
Significantly, the value of Richard Ambler's
James City County slaves was comparable

to the combined worth of the slaves on the
plantations he owned in Hanover, Louisa,
and Warwick counties (AMB-EJ; AMB-JJ 25;
Smith et al. 1745; AMB 53, 106, 107, 115, 116,
123; York County Wills and Inventories 21:278–
282, 386–391; JHB 1742–1749:300, 305, 310;
Stanard, "Notes to Council Journals," 187;
MEADE I:95).

Edward Ambler I: Edward Ambler I, Richard and Elizabeth Jaquelin Ambler's eldest
son, was born in 1733 and at age 18 married
Mary, the daughter of Wilson Cary of Ceeley's in Elizabeth City County. Their son
and principal heir, John II, was born in 1762.
According to grandson John Jaquelin Ambler, Edward Ambler I, who was approximately 6 feet tall, was partial to red cut-vel-
vet suits trimmed with gold lace. Edward I
inherited his late father's Yorktown mansion
in 1766 and was living there when his
younger brother, John Ambler I, died in
1766. Edward I and his family quickly
moved into John I's Georgian mansion in urban Jamestown, and Edward I completed
John I's unexpired term in the assembly,
representing the former capital city in the
sessions of 1767 and 1768. Edward Ambler
I's life, like that of his brother, John I, was
abbreviated and he died on October 30,
1768, after "a tedious illness." He was survived by his widow, Mary, and their minor
children. Two months after Edward's death,
one of the outbuildings on the Ambler plantation in Jamestown burned to the ground.
According to the *Virginia Gazette*, a valuable male slave perished while attempting to
save some of his belongings. In 1768 and
1769 Edward Ambler I's estate was credited
with 1,050 acres of land, which would have
included his plantation on Jamestown Island, his leasehold in the Governor's Land,
and his quarter on Powhatan Swamp; he also
had a large number of slaves.

After her husband's death, Mrs. Mary
Cary Ambler and her children continued to
reside on Jamestown Island. They were living there when the Revolutionary War began
but withdrew to Hanover County, a position
of greater safety, when Jamestown Island's
proximity to the James River's channel
made it strategically important to the military. Ebenezer Hazard, who visited Jamestown Island on June 10, 1777, commented
that the old capital city was in ruinous condition. He said, "In the midst of this Desola-
tion appears a large Brick House (delight-
fully situated, with large Rooms, well
papered, lofty Ceilings, Marble Hearths, and
other Indications of Elegance & Taste)" but
"decaying fast." He noted that it was the
dwelling of "a Mrs. Ambler (who has fled

from James Town)" and added that the mansion was then serving as the ferry house. In late 1779 Mrs. Ambler agreed to lease her late husband's Jamestown Island plantation to Captain Edward Travis IV for four years but retained a percentage of the orchard's profits and the right to pasture cattle on the property. Travis was obliged to pay all of the taxes on the plantation and was prohibited from subletting it without Mrs. Ambler's written permission. When Mrs. Mary Cary Ambler left Jamestown, she took along a collection of manuscripts that her late husband's family had accumulated—the Ambler Papers, now housed at the Library of Congress. In 1781 Mrs. Ambler died in Hanover County at her late husband's plantation, The Cottage. After the war her remains were brought to Jamestown for final interment (Stanard, "Notes to Council Journals," 187; AMB 129; AMB-JJ 50–51; Ambler, October 10, 1796; Purdie and Dixon, *Virginia Gazette,* December 29, 1768; November 17, 1775; Williamsburg-James City County Tax Lists 1768–1769; Shelley, "The Journal of Ebenezer Hazard," 411, 414–415).

John Ambler I: John Ambler I, the second oldest son of Richard and Elizabeth Jaquelin Ambler, was born on December 31, 1735, and was educated in England at Cambridge's Trinity College and earned a law degree at the Inner and Middle Temples. He also traveled throughout Europe and reportedly had mastered seven languages by the time he returned to Virginia. Ambler took up residence in the Georgian mansion his father had built for him in urban Jamestown and served as the former capital's burgess from 1759 to 1761 and in 1765 and 1766. While he held office, the legislature considered building a tobacco inspection warehouse on his property in Jamestown. In November 1762 Ambler commenced leasing acreage in the Governor's Land, the same property his maternal grandfather, Edward Jaquelin, had rented from the government. John Ambler I was collector of customs for the York District. While he was living in Jamestown, his mansion caught fire and, according to his great-nephew, half of it burned. After John Ambler I, who was unmarried, contracted consumption (tuberculosis), he withdrew to Barbados, hoping to recover his health. He died there on May 27, 1766, having outlived his father by only three months; he named his older brother, Edward I, as his executor and heir to his real and personal property. John Ambler I was interred in the churchyard in Jamestown. His epitaph described him as a man who was peerless in attending to family and social duties (STAN 152, 154, 173; Stanard,

"Notes to Council Journals," 187; JHB 1758–1761:223, 231; 1761–1765:72; 1766–1769:13; MEADE I:11, 104; AMB-JJ 36, 50; Purdie and Dixon, *Virginia Gazette,* October 17, 1766).

Jaquelin Ambler: Jaquelin Ambler, the youngest son of Richard and Elizabeth Jaquelin Ambler, was born on August 9, 1742, and attended the College of William and Mary. He married Rebecca Burwell of Gloucester County on May 24, 1764, and in 1766, when his father died, became collector of customs in Yorktown. He inherited nine acres of land in Yorktown, along with part of the family's mercantile business. Jaquelin Ambler took an active role in the American Revolution, served on the Council of State, and became treasurer of Virginia. He died on February 10, 1798. He and his wife, Rebecca, produced several children (AMB 123; MCGH 661; AMB-JJ4).

John Ambler II: John Ambler II, the son of Mary Cary and Edward Ambler I, was born on September 25, 1762. As the couple's only surviving son, he inherited the late Edward Ambler I's immense ancestral estate, which included land in several Virginia counties, literally hundreds of slaves, a large quantity of livestock, and investments in the Dismal Swamp Canal, the Richmond Dock, and three banks. The decedent's properties included his plantation and Georgian mansion on Jamestown Island, the Maine farm, and Powhatan in James City County; Westham in Richmond; The Cottage in Hanover County; the Mill Farm, Loheland, and Nero's in Louisa County; Glenambler and St. Moore in Amherst County; an estate in Frederick County; 1,015 acres in Piedmont Manor; 10,000 acres in the Manor of Leeds; the Mill Tract in Henrico County; and lots in Yorktown, Manchester, and Richmond. James City County real estate tax rolls compiled in 1782, a few months before John Ambler II came of age, indicate that he owned 1,275 acres of local land. Included were 900 acres on Jamestown Island and 375 acres on the mainland (his forebears' 310-acre leasehold in the Governor's Land, which he was renting from the government, the 24-acre Glasshouse parcel, and some additional acreage on the mainland). In 1782 the tax assessor credited John Ambler II (then a minor) with 22 slaves and 20 cattle. By 1788 Ambler had acquired fee simple ownership of the acreage he had been renting on the mainland, which had reverted to the Commonwealth of Virginia and been sold as government surplus property.

John Ambler II married Frances Armistead in 1782, took up residence in Jamestown shortly thereafter, and repaired whatever wartime damage the family dwelling had sustained. Frances and John Ambler II produced a daughter, Mary Cary II, and a son, Edward II. After Frances's death John married Lucy Marshall, with whom he had a son, Thomas Marshall Ambler. Lucy, like Frances Ambler, seemingly died of malaria, and in 1799 John Ambler II married a third time. He took as his bride the widowed Catherine Bush Norton, with whom he had seven children (John Jaquelin, Catherine Cary, Elizabeth, Philip St. George, Sarah Jaquelin, Richard Cary, and William Marshall). It was their son John Jaquelin Ambler who chronicled the family's history in 1826 and 1828.

John Ambler II's plantation accounts reveal that while he and his household resided in Jamestown, he procured much of the family's clothing, shoes, and household furnishings from London but relied heavily upon merchants in Richmond, Williamsburg, and Cobham for household necessities, alcoholic beverages, and other everyday items. A tailor in Richmond fashioned some of the Amblers' wearing apparel, but James Galt of Williamsburg repaired and cleaned John II's gold watches and mended his incense case. He had his blacksmithing done at nearby Green Spring plantation, and he paid local men, such as William Wilkinson Jr., for repairing his saddle, mending farming equipment, and making a wheat machine. His household's medical needs, such as dentistry and smallpox vaccinations, were met by local practitioners. Wheat and pork produced on Jamestown Island and at the Ambler farm on the mainland were sold in bulk to local customers. John Ambler II's business records reveal that he operated a thriving and productive working plantation. In 1784 he was assisted by farm manager William Chick and 38 slaves. Later, he employed overseer Henry Taylor. During the 1780s the number of slaves under John Ambler II's control slowly but surely increased, as did the size of his livestock herd, making him one of James City County's wealthiest farmers. In 1797 Captain John Ambler II of Jamestown was in command of the local cavalry, an office he still held in 1801. He also served as a county justice of the peace. Before the close of the eighteenth century he undertook the construction of a log-and-stone causeway that connected Jamestown Island to the mainland, a span that was subject to tidal flooding.

John Ambler II's decision to spend less time in Jamestown coincided with his 1799 marriage to Catherine Bush Norton, for he was convinced that the island was unhealthy. In 1806 he reportedly purchased an elegant house in the Shockoe section of Richmond and moved his family there. However, the Amblers continued to spend their winters in Jamestown and Williamsburg. In 1805 artist Louis Girardin published a work entitled *Amoenitates Graphicae* and adorned it with a sophisticated watercolor painting. In a position analogous to the Ambler house was a large, two-story dwelling with a mansard roof. In May 1807, while John Ambler II owned his 900-acre plantation on Jamestown Island, a centenary celebration or jubilee was held there to commemorate the first colonists' arrival.

John Ambler II, who held the rank of colonel during the War of 1812, was stationed at Camp Bottoms Bridge in New Kent County and at Frazier's Tavern in Henrico. On July 1, 1813, a British raiding party came ashore in Jamestown and reportedly carried off whatever they could and laid waste to everything else. In 1815 Colonel John Ambler II, who still resided in Richmond, transferred his 900-acre Jamestown Island tract to his son Edward Ambler II but retained his property on the mainland and his quarter at Powhatan, eventually giving both to his daughter Mary, the wife of John Hill Smith of King and Queen County, a Williamsburg attorney. John Ambler II revered his forebears and had the churchyard in Jamestown enclosed with a brick wall to preserve the ancestral graves it contained (James City County Land Tax Lists 1782–1820; Personal Property Tax Lists 1782–1798; Petitions, November 22, 1813; Executive Papers, July 27, 1785; October 8, 1797; August 27, 1801; April 10, 1797; EJC III:124; HEN X:189; XI:406; SHEP I:237; PALM 10:240; AMB-JJ 57, 59–60, 62, 66, 69–70; AMB-AF; Ewing, *Virginia Gazette*, May 17, 1855).

Edward Ambler II: Edward Ambler II, the son of John Ambler II and his wife Frances Armistead, was born in Jamestown and lived there until his father moved to Richmond. He attended the College of William and Mary and in 1809 returned to Jamestown. Like his forebears, he took an active role in public life and became a James City County court justice. Although he had very little military experience, when the War of 1812 commenced, he persuaded his father to seek a commission for him as a major of infantry or a cavalry captain. Edward Ambler II did not gain outright ownership of his father's Jamestown Island plantation and property on the mainland until 1815, by which time he was a resident of Lynchburg. He retained the ancestral plantation in

Jamestown until 1821, then sold it to Thomas Wilson. Edward Ambler II, after being widowed, married Sarah Taylor Holcombe of Amelia County (AMB-JJ 65–66, James City County Personal Property Tax Lists 1809–1815; Land Tax Lists 1809–1821; Executive Papers, February 20, 1813).

John Jaquelin Ambler: John Jaquelin Ambler, the son of John Ambler II and his third wife, Catherine Bush Norton, was born in Williamsburg on March 9, 1801. When he compiled two detailed histories of the Ambler family, he indicated that his father, John Ambler II, left Jamestown because he attributed his first two wives' untimely deaths to its unwholesome summers. Ambler attended the College of William and Mary and spent much time with Bishop James Madison and his family. John Jaquelin Ambler had three brothers (Philip St. George, Richard Cary, and William Marshall), three sisters (Catherine Cary, Elizabeth, and Sarah Jaquelin), two older half-brothers (Edward II and Thomas Marshall Ambler), and a half-sister (Mary Cary, who married John Hill Smith) (AMB-JJ; AMB-JJ4).

* * *

Charles Amry: On September 5, 1677, Charles Amry paid George Marable I of Jamestown for appearing as a witness in a suit he filed in Surry County (Surry County Order Book 1671–1691:160).

Amy (Amey): On February 15, 1768, when an inventory was made of the late Richard Ambler's slaves on Jamestown Island and his leasehold in the Governor's Land, an adult female slave named Amy was listed. In 1769 she was living at Powhatan and was attributed to the late Edward Ambler I's estate (York County Wills and Inventories 21:386–391; AMB-E).

Amy (Amey): On February 15, 1768, when an inventory was made of the late Richard Ambler's slaves at his quarter called Powhatan, a young female slave named Amy was living there. In 1769 Amy was identified as Hannah's daughter and was living on Jamestown Island. She was attributed to the late Edward Ambler I's estate (York County Wills and Inventories 21:386–391; AMB-E).

Louis Floxel d'Ancteville: The Chevalier Louis Floxel d'Ancteville, who was in Rochambeau's Army and arrived on Jamestown Island in July 1781, shortly before the British Army departed, recorded his observations in a journal. He said that they had left "indelible traces" of their presence and that "All means of devastation had been employed" to "this small city, one of the oldest in America" (Ancteville, "Journal").

William Anderson: William Anderson, a planter, began patenting land on the Eastern Shore in 1660 and added to his holdings in 1676 and 1686. He served as a burgess for Accomack County and attended the assembly sessions held in 1685–1686 and 1688. A document on file in the British Archives suggests strongly that he was a religious dissenter. In 1689 the Rev. Francis Makemie (a Presbyterian minister) and six other non-Anglican clergy from Virginia and Maryland sent a petition to authorities in England protesting Governor Francis Howard's confinement of Anderson, then an assembly member. They added that Anderson previously had been allowed to exercise liberty of conscience in religion. Anderson was returned to the assembly and represented Accomack County in the sessions held in 1691–1692 and 1695–1696. On July 23, 1698, William Anderson made his will, which was proved on October 4, 1698. He left his 1,000-acre plantation at Matchatanck and a sloop to the Rev. Francis Makemie and his wife, Naomi, Anderson's daughter. The Makemies also stood to inherit Anderson's 950-acre plantation at Pocomoke. Anderson made bequests to his granddaughters, Elizabeth, Naomi, and Comfort Taylor, the children of Elias and Comfort Taylor. He left life-rights in his plantation at Accomson to his wife, Mary, and gave some land at Sikes Island to his daughter Comfort. He made more modest bequests to his nephews Anderson, Thomas, William, and Mathew Parker; to his sister, Comfort Scott; and nephew William Hope, the son of George and Temperance Hope (LEO 48–50, 54; Accomack County Wills &c. 1692–1715:209; SR 3571, 6885; PB 4:460; 6:609; 7:538).

Joachim (Jocomb, Joakim, Jockey, Jenkin) Andrewes (Andrews, Andrus): Sometime prior to February 20, 1619, Joachim Andrewes, an ancient planter, patented 12 acres in the eastern end of Jamestown Island. He also had a 100-acre patent in Archer's Hope, the plantation that became known as Jockey's Neck. In 1624 Andrewes and his wife were living in urban Jamestown as members of Captain William Peirce's household. By early 1625 Joachim was listed among those who had died in Pasbehay, just west of Jamestown Island (VI&A 84).

Robin Andrews (Native American): On January 7, 1690, Robin Andrews, an Indian servant employed by Richard Willis, made a formal complaint to the justices of Old Rappahannock County's court. He claimed that although he was free "by the Laws of this Colony," he was being detained by his master. The justices ordered Andrews' overseer to summon Willis to the next session of court to respond to the complaint. Otherwise, Robin Andrews was to be set free (Old Rappahannock County Order Book 1687–1692:193).

William Andrews (Andrewes, Andros) II: William Andrews II, one of ancient planter William Andrews I's four sons, was born around 1632 and made his home on Old Plantation Creek in Northampton County. He followed in his father's footsteps by becoming a commissioner of the county court, and in April 1655, around the time of his father's death, he became sheriff. Over the years he acquired substantial quantities of land in Northampton County. William Andrews II became a captain and then a major in the Northampton County militia. In January 1652 he married Elizabeth, the daughter of George and Alisha Travellor, and after being widowed he wed Dorothea Robins Evelyn. Andrews served in the assembly in 1663–1664, representing Northampton County. On July 24, 1673, he made his will, which was proved on August 28, 1674 (LEO 39; VI&A 86; Northampton County Deeds, Wills &c. 5 [1654–1655]:47, 52, 137; Deeds and Wills 6:18; Order Book 1657–1666:133; 10 [1664–1674]:210–212; 11 [1678–1683]:293; Wills and Orders 13 [1678–1683]:245, 285; MCGC 213; PB 3:311; 5:226, 514, 538; DOR 1:76–77).

William Andrews (Andrewes): On December 3, 1659, Edward Prescott, a mariner and the owner of a lot in urban Jamestown, successfully sued William Andrews (HEN I:549). The defendant may have been William Andrews II of Northampton County.

Governor Edmund Andros: Sir Edmund Andros, Virginia's governor from September 1692 to 1698, took an active role in running the colony's government. In 1693 he had a gun platform built in Jamestown to accommodate a dozen cannon that were mounted on ship's carriages; he also had a vault built for the storage of ammunition. In 1693 he secured a 99-year leasehold in the Governor's Land, and a year later he gave a silver paten to the parish church at Jamestown. Andros was held in high esteem by William Sherwood, a resident of Jamestown, who in 1697 bequeathed him money

to buy a mourning ring. According to the outspoken Rev. James Blair, Governor Andros squandered a lot of money in his attempts to fortify Jamestown. In March 1697 Andros compiled an account of the military stores at Jamestown and Gloucester Point, and he responded to a list of queries about the state of the colony. Andros was in office in 1698 when the colony's statehouse burned and afterward had all of the public records that were salvaged taken to Mrs. Sherwood's house in Jamestown. Andros died in England on February 27, 1714 (EJC I:269, 271, 406; SAIN 14:132; 16:132; CO 5/1359 f 117; STAN 17; MCGH 873; AMB 65; PERRY 1:14).

Angelo: Angelo, a black woman, came to Virginia on the *Treasurer* in 1619 and was one of the colony's first Africans. In February 1624 she was living in urban Jamestown in the household of Captain William Peirce, and she was still residing there in January 1625. In late August or early September 1619, Peirce and his son-in-law, John Rolfe, met the *Treasurer* when it arrived at Old Point Comfort and bartered for some of the Africans who were aboard (VI&A 86).

Anthony: Anthony came to Virginia in 1621 at the expense of William Spencer of Jamestown Island and probably was one of his servants (VI&A 87).

Mary Anthrobus: William Sherwood, a resident of urban Jamestown who died in 1697, made a monetary bequest to Mary Anthrobus, one of his indentured servants. She was to receive payment as soon as she was free (AMB 65; MCGH 873).

Appenmaw (Native American): In June 1668 Owasewas, Appenmaw, and Chicatomen were identified as Wicocomoco (Wecocomaka, Wicocomocoe) leaders or Great Men. They were summoned to court by Northumberland County's justices, who wanted to have an Indian named Noroas brought to them. The justices indicated that Adam Pettegrew believed that Noroas was detaining a runaway maidservant. Because neither Noroas nor the maidservant appeared, the court justices decided that all three Great Men should be held (Northumberland County Order Book 1666–1678:40).

William Appleby (Apleby): William Appleby died in Jamestown sometime after April 1623 but before February 16, 1624 (VI&A 88).

John Appleton: John Appleton's name appeared in Westmoreland County's records in

1668 because a gentleman named Richard Cole, who was at his house, became inebriated and made slanderous remarks about Governor William Berkeley and other high-ranking officials. Eyewitnesses claimed that on another occasion Cole accused Appleton's wife of whoredom and slandered Colonel Peter Aston and Westmoreland County's court commissioners. In 1670 John Appleton was designated a justice of Westmoreland County's court and in 1671 became sheriff. He was paid for conducting coroner's inquests during 1673. Appleton served in the assembly in 1674, representing Westmoreland County. He married Frances, the widow of burgess Valentine Peyton, who died around 1664–1665. On February 18, 1676, Captain John Appleton, when testifying in court, indicated that he was age 36. He died sometime prior to April 24, 1676, at which time an inventory of his estate was presented to county officials. On May 10th the widowed Mrs. Frances Appleton verified the accuracy of the appraisal. Colonel John Washington, who was planning to marry her, deeded a tract of land to two trustees as part of their marriage contract. By August 1677 the couple had wed and Washington had begun serving as the late John Appleton's administrator. Two years earlier Appleton had served as a witness when Washington made his will. Captain John Appleton's widow, Frances, outlived John Washington and by March 1680 had married William Hardidge, her fourth husband (LEO 40; Westmoreland County Deeds, Patents &c. 1665–1677:17–18a, 25–26, 92a, 98, 168, 185a, 260a, 266a–267, 274–275a, 326a, 365a–367; Order Book 1676–1689:161, 180, 218).

Henry Applewaite (Applewhaite, Applewayte): Henry Applewaite, a merchant, purchased a tract of land in Isle of Wight County in March 1665. He was living in the county in June 1670 when he filed suit against Richard Lawrence, proprietor of a popular inn in urban Jamestown. The case was postponed and in October 1670 was dismissed. By 1674 Applewaite had acquired some additional land in Isle of Wight. He served as one of the county's burgesses and attended the assembly sessions held in 1684, 1685–1686, 1688, and 1691–1692. Over the years he steadily added to his landholdings in Isle of Wight County. He patented three large tracts near Kinsale Swamp and some additional acreage on the branches of the Blackwater River. In 1693 Applewaite was identified as an official surveyor, a position that would have facilitated his ability to speculate in undeveloped land. During 1695 he added to his landholdings, and in 1700 he gave halves of

a tract he owned on the Blackwater River to his sons Thomas and William. By 1699 Henry Applewaite had become a trustee for the town of Newport (later known as Smithfield); he was still serving in that capacity in February 1703. When Applewaite made his will on August 26, 1703, he left tracts of land to his sons, Thomas, William, and John, and made bequests to his daughter, Anne, and grandson, Henry Applewaite. The decedent designated his wife as his executrix but failed to mention her name. His will was recorded on May 9, 1704 (LEO 47–50; Isle of Wight County Will and Deed Book 1 [1662–1688]:331–332; 2 [1688–1704]:190, 315; 3 [1704–1715]:462; Orders 1693–1695:6; PB 6:520, 643; 7:119, 320, 334; 9:181; BODIE 649; MCGC 222, 228; SMITH 3).

Gabriel Archer: Gabriel Archer, a gentleman, came to Virginia in 1607 in the first group of Jamestown colonists. He was made Secretary of the Colony in September 1607 but in early 1608 returned to England with Captain Christopher Newport. Archer was back in the colony by 1609 and died in Virginia during the winter of 1609–1610 (VI&A 88).

Samuel Argall (Argal, Argoll, Argyle): Samuel Argall, a mariner, brought Lord Delaware to Jamestown in March 1610. Afterward, he made an exploratory voyage to the New England coast and visited the Chesapeake Bay and its tributaries. Argall returned to England but was sent back to the colony. He favored martial law and the policies that had been implemented by Sir Thomas Gates and Sir Thomas Dale. Argall was appointed deputy governor in 1617, held office for approximately two years, and later claimed that he had greatly improved conditions in the colony. One of his accomplishments was building a frame church in Jamestown. Argall left for England in early April 1619 but had sent out the *Treasurer*, which captured some Africans under questionable circumstances and brought them to Virginia in late summer. Despite his detractors, some of whom were politically powerful, Samuel Argall was knighted at Rochester in 1622, but he eventually was made to account for his actions in Virginia. When he died in England in 1625–1626, he was still under a cloud of suspicion (VI&A 88).

Symon Armested: On May 23, 1625, Symon Armested testified before the General Court about some business dealings that involved Mr. Welch and a Mr. Beaumont, master of a ship bringing some servants to Virginia (VI&A 90).

William Armiger (Armager): William Armiger, a mariner, came to Virginia sometime prior to 1651 but was in England in August 1675 when he witnessed a legal document for a Westmoreland County woman. He returned to Virginia prior to the close of Bacon's Rebellion and in July 1677 testified before Westmoreland County's justices about an event that had occurred at Colonel John Washington's house. Armiger said that as the popular uprising drew to a close, he and another man had disarmed some of Bacon's supporters, who had seized Washington's home. Between June 1680 and May 25, 1681, William Armiger married Susanne, the widow of English merchant William Fisher, who moved to Virginia around 1676. Official records reveal that in 1680 Mrs. Susanne Fisher hosted one or more assembly meetings in her home, which was located on a half-acre waterfront lot in urban Jamestown. During 1682 Captain William Armiger, then sheriff of James City County, was compensated for furnishing candles to the assembly and the governor's council. He also allowed government officials to meet in his Jamestown home, probably the residence acquired through his marriage to the widowed Susanne Fisher. Armiger was compensated for having the furniture that was used in the courthouse repaired and for obtaining a picture of the king's arms that was to be displayed there. He was residing in Jamestown in 1682 when he attested to the capital city's legal limits. During the 1680s Armiger's name appeared numerous times in official records. He sued several prominent Jamestown landowners, initiating the litigation in York County's monthly court, and he pursued one of his wife's debtors, a Westmoreland County man. Secretary of the Colony Nicholas Spencer acted as the Armiger couple's attorney in a suit against another Westmoreland County resident, who owed money to Mrs. Armiger's late husband. Like many of Jamestown's residents, Armiger possessed both urban and rural property. Besides his land in urban Jamestown, he had a 102-acre leasehold in the Governor's Land, and he patented a 225-acre tract in Charles City County. Documentary records associated with the Virginia slave trade reveal that Captain William Armiger's ship, the *Two Brothers*, was used to import large numbers of Africans directly from their homeland. According to maritime records, in 1701 Yorktown was the *Two Brothers'* port of call. Armiger's business interests extended to the Northern Neck and other locations that were a considerable distance from Jamestown. Susanna Fisher Armiger seems to have predeceased her husband, for he eventually was credited with her half-acre lot on the waterfront. Because William Armiger died without heirs, by 1729 his land had escheated to the Crown. Later, his Jamestown acreage came into the hands of the Travis family, who developed it into an urban townstead (York County Deeds, Orders, Wills 6:302, 353, 367, 393, 412, 417; Westmoreland County Order Book 1676–1689:206, 221, 232, 310; Deeds, Wills, Patents &c. 1665–1677:259a, 324a–325; Old Rappahannock County Order Book 1683–1685:56, 92; Lancaster County Order Book 1680–1687:70; Northumberland County Order Book 1678–1698:263, 271; SR 668, 4194, 10722; EJC I:174, 191, 256; MIN 5; PB 31:635; NUG III:361–362; PB 31:635; AMB 23; JHB 1660–1693:119).

* * *

Anthony Armistead (Armstead, Armsted, Armestead): Anthony Armistead was the son of William Armistead I, who settled in Elizabeth City County around 1635. He seems to have inherited some of his late father's property on the Middle Peninsula, two large tracts on the East River and Mobjack Bay in what is now Mathews County. However, the only land Anthony seems to have patented personally was some Elizabeth City County acreage that had escheated to the Crown. In January 1677 Captain Anthony Armistead participated in a court-martial hearing held aboard Captain Martin's ship while at anchor in the York River. During those deliberations several participants in Bacon's Rebellion were tried and condemned to death. Captain Armistead went on to serve as an Elizabeth City County justice and sheriff. He was elected to the assembly and represented Elizabeth City in the sessions held in 1680–1682, 1693, 1695–1696, 1696–1697, 1698, and 1699. He began attending the assembly meetings held in 1703–1705 but died during the fourth session. Anthony Armistead and his wife, the former Hannah Ellyson, produced several children, some of whom went on to achieve prominence. He was involved in a suit concerning a shipment of tobacco, which was aired before the High Court of the Admiralty. In July 1698 Anthony and Hannah Armistead sold a piece of New Kent County land that she had inherited from her late father, Robert Ellyson. On October 26, 1726, Hannah made her will, which was proved on December 19th. She made bequests to her sons Anthony II and Robert and to her granddaughter, Judith Armistead (LEO 45, 53–54, 56, 58–59, 62; PB 2:331; 7:129; Elizabeth City County Book 1704–1730:160;

1715–1721:19; MCGC 454, 527; SR 8523, 10086; NEAL 4, 10, 30, 71, 101, 257).

William Armistead (Armstead, Armsted, Armestead) II: William Armistead II, the son of Anthony and Hannah Ellyson Armistead and grandson of immigrant William Armistead I, served as a burgess for Elizabeth City County and attended the assembly meetings held in 1691–1692 and 1693. In 1696 he patented some Elizabeth City acreage adjacent to his father's property, and in 1700 and 1713 he acquired some additional land in the county. By 1693 he had begun serving as a local justice and militia captain. In 1695 Commissary James Blair informed his superiors that Captain Armistead and his son had attacked and beaten the Rev. James Wallace at Kecoughtan; however, he failed to disclose what sparked the violence. Major William Armistead II made his will on January 5, 1714, and died shortly thereafter. He made bequests to his mother, Hannah, to his wife, Rebecca, and to his sons, Anthony II, Hind, John, Moss, Robert, and William III, and stipulated that his unborn child was to share in the estate (LEO 50, 52; Elizabeth City County Book 1715–1721:19; PB 9:52, 257; 10:95; SR 587; NEAL 16, 32, 88, 280).

John Armistead (Armstead, Armsted, Armestead): John Armistead, the brother of William Armistead II, son of Anthony Armistead I, and grandson of immigrant William Armistead I of Elizabeth City County, moved to what was then Gloucester (later Mathews) County. He settled on land bordering the Piankatank River, acreage he patented in 1679. He also owned and repatented the acreage on the East River and Mobjack Bay that his grandfather had patented in 1651. John Armistead became Gloucester's high sheriff and in 1672 served as surety for Thomas Pate, the late John Pate's administrator. Correspondence generated during Bacon's Rebellion suggests that Captain Armistead's Gloucester County plantation was damaged by Nathaniel Bacon's followers. Armistead served as a burgess for Gloucester County and attended the assembly sessions held in 1680–1682 and 1685–1686. In 1688 he was named to the Council of State. The justices of Middlesex County's monthly court, when discussing the estate of the late Major Robert Beverley I, noted that some of the decedent's cattle were at Colonel John Armistead's North River quarter. In 1694 he was identified as one of the late Christopher Robinson's executors. Armistead died in Virginia sometime after 1697 (LEO 45, 48; STAN 42; Middlesex County Order Book 1680–1694:477, 704; Stafford County Record Book

1686–1693:108a; PB 2:331; 6:536, 657, 666, 674; 7:2, 532–533; 8:140; Elizabeth City County Book 1715–1721:19; SR 749, 6618; MCGC 319, 323).

* * *

Anthony Arnold: Although Anthony Arnold patented 500 acres in Westmoreland County in May 1665, by the early 1670s his name was associated with New Kent County, his place of residence. During 1673 and 1674 Arnold began having disagreements with some of his neighbors. He was sued by Major William Wyatt, one of his creditors, and Captain Joseph Pickis's widow tried in vain to recover a large debt attributable to her late husband's estate. Arnold also was ordered to return to the Monguy (leader) of the Chickahominy Indians some goods (shell money, animal hides, and other items) that he had received in compensation for a man who was killed. On one occasion Arnold was summoned to appear before the General Court. His failure to appear antagonized the court's justices and the plaintiffs, as well as members of the Council of State. Arnold was censured, which seems to have fueled his resentment of authority and may have resulted in his supporting the rebel Nathaniel Bacon's cause. After the popular uprising was quelled, Anthony Arnold was taken into custody and imprisoned at Governor William Berkeley's home, Green Spring plantation. Although he was put on trial there on March 9, 1676, found guilty, and sentenced to death, he was not executed. When Governor Berkeley issued a proclamation on February 10, 1677, in which he listed those exempt from the king's pardon due to their role in Bacon's Rebellion, one named was Anthony Arnold, who was still incarcerated. Arnold was released by one of Berkeley's successors and in 1703 patented 150 acres near his dwelling in Pamunkey Neck, then part of New Kent County. Interestingly, Arnold's home near the Herring Creeks was close to the Chickahominy Indians' village, which was located on land they had been assigned by the government (NEVILLE 61; PB 5:36; 9:546; MCGC 344, 361–363, 386, 389, 400, 457, 530).

Elizabeth Arrundell (Arundel, Arundelle, Arundell, Arondell, Arndell): Elizabeth Arrundell, who came to Virginia in 1620, was living in Elizabeth City at Buckroe in 1624. By January 1625 she had moved to urban Jamestown, where she was a servant in Sir George Yeardley's household. She may have been related to Richard Arrundell, also a Yeardley servant. In 1626 a man testifying against Joan Wright, who was accused of witchcraft, claimed that Wright had predicted Elizabeth's death (VI&A 91).

John Arrundell (Arundel, Arundelle, Arundell, Arondell, Arndell): In 1621 John Arrundell came to Virginia with his father, Peter, a Virginia Company investor. Both were trained silk workers who in February 1624 were residing on the Virginia Company's land at Buckroe, in Elizabeth City. During the late 1620s and early 1630s, John Arrundell, who was a gentleman, possessed two leaseholds and a patent, all of which were in Elizabeth City. In September 1632 he was identified as a commissioner of Elizabeth City's local court, and in February 1633 he served as a burgess for the lower parish of Elizabeth City (VI&A 91; LEO 12).

Richard Arrundell (Arundel, Arundelle, Arundell, Arondell, Arndell): Richard Arrundell, who came to Virginia on the *Abigail*, was living in urban Jamestown in February 1624 and was a servant in Sir George Yeardley's household. He was still residing there on January 24, 1625. He may have been related to Elizabeth Arrundell, also a servant in the Yeardley household (VI&A 92).

Richard Arthur: On January 31, 1625, Richard Arthur appeared before the General Court, which convened in Jamestown, and testified in litigation involving Captain Wilcox (Wilcocks) and John Crowdick (VI&A 92).

John Asbie: According to George Percy, John Asbie, who was in the first group of Jamestown colonists, died of the bloody flux on August 9, 1607. His name was not included in the list of settlers compiled by Captain John Smith (VI&A 92).

Peter Ascam (Ascomb, Ascombe) I: Peter Ascam I came to Virginia sometime prior to December 1621 and resided on Jamestown Island. He died after August 5, 1623, but before February 16, 1624, and was survived by his widow, Mary, and their two young children, Peter II and Abigail (Abigall). By January 1625 Mary Ascam had married Peter Langman (VI&A 92–93).

Ascomowett (Native American): In 1649 the colony's governing officials gave Ascomowett, the king of the "South Indians" or Weyanoke, a 5,000-acre tract for his people. The land they were assigned was on the south side of the James River, beyond the boundaries established by the 1646 treaty. Ascomowett's acreage was to be laid out and surveyed and assigned to his people permanently. The Indians were to be reimbursed for any land that settlers already had seated, if it lay within the boundaries of the tract the natives had been assigned (Billings, "Some Acts Not in Hening's, April 1652, November 1652, and July 1653," 171).

Ann Ashley: In 1624 and 1625 Ann Ashley, a maidservant, was living in John Burrows' household in urban Jamestown (VI&A 93).

Peter Ashton: By 1654 Peter Ashton already had begun patenting land in the Northern Neck, where he secured 400 acres on the Wicocomoco River in Northumberland County. The following year he secured 500 acres in Westmoreland County. As time went on, he continued to add to his landholdings in the Northern Neck, on one occasion patenting 2,000 acres in Westmoreland County near the Potomac Indians' town. Although Ashton served as a burgess for Elizabeth City County in 1656, by 1657 he seems to have moved to Northumberland, where his name began appearing regularly in local court records when he served on juries or as an attorney, witnessed public documents, and participated in lawsuits. He became a county justice, was appointed sheriff in March 1658, and by 1663 was designated high sheriff. He also was a captain in the militia. In 1660 Ashton joined Henry Corbin and William Thomas in patenting 900 acres in Northumberland County. He and three co-investors acquired another 485 acres in 1662 and in 1665 patented 500 acres on the Potomac River in Westmoreland County. Finally, in 1668 he patented 2,000 acres at the head of the Upper Machodoc River in Stafford County. These land acquisitions attest to Ashton's ability to generate disposable income, thanks to his success as a planter, service as a public official, and speculation in real estate. He also earned headright certificates by paying for the transportation of new immigrants.

Peter Ashton of Great Wicocomoco became a Northumberland County burgess in 1660 and continued to serve as a county justice, sometimes hosting court meetings in his home. In 1663 he accepted funds that were to be used toward building a county courthouse, prison, stocks, pillory, and ducking stool. He launched an inquiry into the death of a seaman who died of a gunshot wound, and he was among those mediating a dispute between the king of the Potomac Indians and Major General Manwarring Hammond. In 1664 Ashton was paid for providing waterborne transportation to some people summoned to Jamestown for a court case. When merchant John Le Briton of Jersey set sail for England, he designated Captain Peter Ashton as his attorney. In 1667, when the threat of a Dutch invasion forced the colony into a defensive posture, the Association for Northumberland, Westmoreland and Stafford Counties—which included Colonel Peter Ashton and several other high-ranking militia officers—was given the task of seeing that a fort was built on the Potomac River and furnished with men and munitions. Later in the year Ashton supplied a set of weights and measures to the county and served as Northumberland's collector of revenue. In 1668 Aston sold much of the land on which he lived but reserved three acres and a room in an existing house. By 1669 he had become deputy escheator, a public office that perhaps led to his being slandered by a drunken merchant, Richard Cole of Westmoreland County. In early 1669 Ashton assisted William May and Nicholas Meriwether of Jamestown in settling the estate of Thomas Woodhouse, also of the capital city, by collecting debts in Northumberland and Westmoreland counties. Peter Aston died intestate sometime prior to November 28, 1669. He may have had living heirs, for Major Isaac Allerton and Captain Thomas Brereton served as executors-in-trust to the decedent's estate. By July 1671 Brereton and John Ashton were serving as co-executors of the late Peter Ashton's estate (LEO 33, 36; PB 3:320; 4:206, 312, 418, 476; 5:494; 6:157, 179; Northumberland County Record Book 1652–1658:139, 144, 146; 1658–1662:85; 1662–1666:116, 130, 138, 146, 168; 1666–1670:34–36, 57, 83, 99; Deeds and Wills 1670–1672:186, 191–192; Order Book 1652–1665:138, 142, 350, 363, 368–370, 375, 415; 1666–1678:22, 26, 78, 88, 103, 107, 115, 126, 129; Westmoreland County Deeds, Wills, Patents &c. 1653–1659:94, 102; Deeds, Wills &c. 1661–1662:16–16a, 23a, 49a; Deeds and Wills No. 1 [1653–1671]:281–282; Deeds, Patents &c. 1665–1677:23a, 25).

Walter Aston I: Walter Aston I came to Virginia in 1627–1628 and in March 1630 served as the burgess for Shirley Hundred (Eppes) Island. In the February 1632 and 1633 sessions of the assembly, he represented the settlers living at Shirley Hundred and the Island, Chaplin's Choice, and Jordan's Journey. In 1639 Aston became one of Charles City County's tobacco inspectors and a justice of the county court, and in 1641 he and three other men obtained the assembly's permission to explore the countryside at the head of the Appomattox River. Aston was returned to the assembly in 1642 and 1643. He used his first wife, Warbowe, as a

headright when patenting some land and by 1638 had married a woman named Hannah. Walter Aston I died on April 6, 1656, at age 49 and was buried at Westover Church in Charles City County. His son, Walter II, was his primary heir. Walter Aston I's domestic complex was excavated by state archaeologists during the 1980s (VI&A 94; LEO 9–12, 20–21; SR 3482).

Peter Atherton (see William Nelson alias Peter Atherton)

John Atkins: John Atkins, who made his will on September 3, 1623, probably resided in or near the capital city, for he asked to be buried "in the usual place" in Jamestown. His will was witnessed by Christopher Davison, Edward Sharples, and Peter Stafferton, all of whom resided in urban Jamestown. Atkins, a planter, asked Luke Boyse of Bermuda Hundred to see that his tobacco crop was harvested and that his just debts paid. When English officials appointed an administrator for Atkins' estate on October 2, 1624, Atkins was described as a bachelor who had died in Virginia (VI&A 95).

Richard Atkins: Richard Atkins and his child died in Jamestown sometime after April 1623 but before February 16, 1624 (VI&A 95).

William Atkins: On April 25, 1625, William Atkins, who lived near Jamestown, testified before the General Court. The nuncupative will he made in March 1626 mentioned his wife and children, who were in England (VI&A 96).

Attahune (Native American): In 1662 Attahune, leader of the Nanzattico Indians, relinquished part of the tribal preserve or reservation that had been allocated to his people during the 1650s. Patents and deeds reveal that the Nanzatticos' land, which was located in the upper reaches of the Rappahannock River, not only encompassed acreage on the river's upper side, traditionally known as Nanzattico, but also extended to the lower side of the river, abutting Portobago Bay and Portobago and Goldenvale creeks. In 1669 the Nanzattico and Portobago tribes collectively had 110 warriors, probably fewer than they had a decade earlier. Based upon the 1669 population, they would have been eligible for 5,500 acres of land under the colonial government's system of allocating 50 acres per bowman. To the west of the Nanzattico were the Nansemond, whose town in 1667 encompassed an estimated 5,275 acres, an amount that suggests they had 55–56 warriors. Thus, in the Portobago Bay–Nanzattico area, in what are now Caroline and Richmond counties, nearly 11,000 acres of land had been assigned to the Indians as preserves (MCGC 493; HEN II:274–275).

Nicholas Atwell: On January 21, 1629, Nicholas Atwell testified that he had heard John Lightfoot bequeath his entire estate to William Spencer. Atwell, like the testator and his heir, probably resided in the eastern end of Jamestown Island (VI&A 97).

Richard Auborne (Awborne): Richard Auborne, who became clerk of the General Court in April 1667 and held office for many years, owned land on the west side of Lawnes Creek in Surry County and further south on the Blackwater River. In 1670 he and Richard James I, a Jamestown merchant, patented 1,000 acres of land in Northumberland County. A year later Auborne and John Winsloe acquired 2,000 acres in the upper part of New Kent County, and in 1673 he patented 300 acres of wasteland near the French Ordinary in York County. Much of the property Auborne patented was escheat land, acreage that had reverted to the Crown. He probably was privy to insider information, gathered through his association with high-ranking officials.

When Richard Lawrence, a Jamestown innkeeper, appeared before the justices of the James City County court during 1671–1672, he accused Richard Auborne of causing John Senior's death. Auborne was arrested but released after he posted a bond. In October 1672 the attorney general presented the case against Auborne, but it was dismissed for lack of grounds for an indictment. In May 1673 the General Court again sided with Richard Auborne, overturning a James City County court decision in favor of Richard Lawrence, who went on to become one of the rebel Nathaniel Bacon's most ardent supporters. Auborne was closely associated with James City County sheriff Francis Kirkman, with whom he patented some acreage in Archer's Hope, and with Colonel William White, owner of a lot in urban Jamestown, who joined him in investing in some Surry County land. Auborne also acquired and quickly resold some property in Westmoreland County.

On September 19, 1676, when Nathaniel Bacon's rebels torched urban Jamestown, Richard Auborne was renting a unit in a brick row house on Back Street. Auborne's clashes with Richard Lawrence, his unflagging loyalty to Governor William Berkeley,

and his position as clerk of the General Court would have made his dwelling a likely target. After Bacon's Rebellion was quelled, several people sought to lease the ruins of the house Auborne had occupied, a structure that was privately owned. Richard Auborne turned vigilante in the wake of Bacon's Rebellion and was among those accused of plundering the homes of paroled Bacon supporters. He went on to become clerk of the York County court in 1679 and clerk of the assembly in June 1680. He also was appointed clerk for the Committee for Propositions and Grievances. By January 24, 1681, Richard Auborne's health was failing. He died in York County three months later and his widow and administratrix, Mary, surrendered the official records that were in his possession. She also made arrangements for his estate to be appraised and set sail for England shortly thereafter. Among those who presented claims against the late Richard Auborne's estate were mariner and merchant William Armiger and attorney William Sherwood, both of Jamestown (JHB 1660–1693:73, 78, 122, 142–143, 152; 1924:513; AMB 10, 16; York County Deeds, Orders, Wills 5:121; 6:23, 82, 282, 302–303, 345, 365, 367, 393; Westmoreland County Deeds and Wills No. 1 [1653–1659]:66–66a; CO 1/40 f 5; MCGC 225, 264, 276, 313, 318, 341, 344, 360, 513; NUG II:71).

Robert Austin (Austine, Aston, Austen): In 1624 Robert Austin, an indentured servant, resided in urban Jamestown in William Peirce's household. By early 1625 he had moved to Mulberry Island, where he and another Peirce servant shared a home. Austin made his will on September 18, 1626, and by October 2, 1626, was dead (VI&A 97).

Henry Awbrey (Aubrey, Awbry, Awrrey): Sometime prior to 1665 Henry Awbrey took up residence in Old Rappahannock County. He purchased a 200-acre plantation on the south side of Occupacy Creek in November 1679, land that had escheated to the Crown because its former owner, John Bagwell, had been found guilty of counterfeiting. Awbrey bought an additional 200 acres a few months later. Surviving patents reveal that by 1680 he owned land on the south side of the Rappahannock River, near Gilsons and Piscataway creeks. He served as a county justice throughout the 1680s. As a burgess for Old Rappahannock County, he attended the assembly sessions held in 1680–1682, 1684, 1688, and 1691–1692. Old Rappahannock County court records reveal that Awbrey was active in the community. From time to time he went to court to recover debts but he also authenticated appraisals of estates and performed other public duties. He was instrumental in helping the Rappahannock Indians move from their old fort on the Mattaponi River to a safer location on Portobago Bay, a site then known as the Portobago Fort. In 1684 Awbrey was paid for finding an interpreter to assist the Rappahannock Indians and for allowing his boat to be used for their transportation to Portobago. In 1691 he began serving as a trustee for the planned town at Hobbes Hole, what became known as Tappahannock. By May 1692 the section of Old Rappahannock County in which Henry Awbrey lived had been made part of the newly formed Essex County. He immediately began serving as a justice in the new county court and became high sheriff. When Awbrey prepared his will on August 1, 1694, he noted that he was sick and weak. He bequeathed to his wife, Mary, life-rights in the plantation on which they lived and named his son, Richard, as reversionary heir. He specified that his personal belongings, household furnishings, livestock, and servants were to be divided between his wife and son. The testator's granddaughter, Mary (Richard's child), was to receive some pewter dishes after her grandmother's death. On September 10, 1694, Essex County's justices validated the late Henry Awbrey's will and appointed his widow, Mary, and son, Richard, as joint executors (LEO 46–47, 49–50; Old Rappahannock County Deeds and Wills 1665–1677:19; 1677–1682:243, 266–267; Will Book 1682–1687:6–7, 12–13, 97–100; Order Book 1683–1685:1, 14; 1687–1692:42, 146, 153, 236–237; Essex County Order Book 1692–1695:1–2, 90, 154, 157–158, 209, 227, 235; 1695–1699:13; Deeds and Wills 1692–1695:24, 181–186; PB 7:53; 8:40).

Rev. Justinian Aylemer (Aylmer): In 1666 the Rev. Justinian Aylemer, rector of Hampton Parish, married Frances Armistead. He became rector of James City Parish but by September 29, 1671, had died. His widow, Frances, married Captain Christopher Wormeley II, who sued for Aylemer's back pay as parish priest (MCGC 277; Tyler, "The Armistead Family," 31).

B

***

Nathaniel Bacon: Nathaniel Bacon, the son of an English clergyman, was born in 1620 and was a cousin of the rebel Nathaniel Bacon. After immigrating to Virginia, he rose in wealth and prominence, in part propelled by successive marriages to two wealthy widows. By 1654 he had married Mrs. Ann Smith, whose daughter, Ann, married Isle of Wight County burgess George Fawdon. After the death of his first wife, Nathaniel Bacon wed Richard Kingsmill's daughter, Elizabeth, the widow and heir of William Tayloe. Thanks to their marriage, Bacon came into possession of Tayloe's Kings Creek plantation in York County. Bacon's prowess as a planter and the lucrative fees he received as a high-ranking government official helped enhance his fortune significantly. In 1663 he renewed his patent for 1,075 acres in Isle of Wight County, and in 1666 he claimed 1,000 acres in New Kent and 700 acres in Nansemond. In 1656 and 1659 Bacon served as a burgess for York County. From 1657 through the 1680s Bacon was a member of the Council of State, and from 1675 to 1687 he served as the colony's auditor general. In 1661 he and Elizabeth, sold her share of the late Richard Kingsmill's "Island House" tract (a large plantation on Jamestown Island) to Nicholas Meriwether.

On April 6, 1671, Colonel Nathaniel Bacon and Miles Cary I's executor purchased from Henry Randolph one unit in a long row house in the western end of Jamestown Island, property that by 1683 had come into the hands of Philip Ludwell I. Bacon, a close associate of Governor William Berkeley, was part-owner of the ship *Lady Frances*. During the early 1670s Bacon made numerous appearances before the General Court, recovering debts and reporting on the estate accounts he had audited. It was there that he aired a dispute with Colonel Thomas Swann, owner of a popular tavern in urban Jamestown, and he audited the claims that William Drummond I of Jamestown made against another man. Some of these issues and Bacon's steadfast loyalty to Governor Berkeley undoubtedly put him at odds with the rebel Nathaniel Bacon's supporters. In 1676, when Virginia was in the throes of the popular uprising known as Bacon's Rebellion, Bacon's Kings Creek plantation was plundered, and in September Bacon was detained there by the rebel Thomas Whaley. Meanwhile, Bacon's wife, Elizabeth, was one of the women the rebel Nathaniel Bacon seized and used as a human shield when his men were erecting a fortification at the entrance to Jamestown Island.

In July 1680 Colonel Bacon and George Lee asked the Council of State and the assembly for a 50-year lease for "the ruins of two brick houses burnt in the late Rebellion" and the land on which they were situated. Both men expressed a preference for the same houses, which were neighboring units at the east end of a long row house on Jamestown's Back Street. One dwelling formerly had been occupied by clerk of the council Richard Auborne and the other by Arnold or Arnall Cassinett (Cossina). Bacon, when asked to choose one of the two structures, selected the Auborne house. When giving Bacon and Lee leases for their respective properties, the burgesses reminded them of the need to rebuild the houses within the specified time and to keep them in good repair. They also were told that their leases were valid only if the structures were "country houses," that is, government-owned property. As it turned out, both were privately owned and Bacon seems to have let the matter drop.

On May 29, 1683, Colonel Nathaniel Bacon patented nearly 3½ acres of land in the western end of Jamestown Island, property that formerly belonged to Richard Lawrence, an innkeeper and one of the rebel Nathaniel Bacon's staunchest supporters. On September 20, 1683, Governor Thomas Lord Culpeper informed his superiors that—in response to the king's desire to see Jamestown rebuilt—Auditor General Bacon recently had constructed two good houses, as had others. Throughout the latter part of his life, Colonel Bacon continued to play an active role in governmental affairs. In 1680 he was paid for supplying food and military stores to one of the frontier forts built as a defense against the Indians. The Council of State convened at Bacon's home in July 1686 and March 1689; in 1687 Bacon served as council president. Colonel Nathaniel Bacon, who had outlived his second wife, Elizabeth, made his will on March 15, 1692. Among those to whom he made bequests were Lady Frances Berkeley and her husband, Philip Ludwell I; Lieutenant Governor Francis Nicholson; Elizabeth Pettus; and several members of the Burwell family. Bacon died on March 16, 1692, and shortly thereafter his will was presented to the justices of York County. He left all of his otherwise undesignated real and personal property to his niece Abigail Smith Burwell of Gloucester County (his sister's child and the wife of his great-nephew, Lewis Burwell II), with the understanding that the inheritance was to descend to her sons, Nathaniel and James. Besides the property left to his niece and her children, Bacon made a bequest to Lewis Burwell II, who, as executor, settled claims against Bacon's estate in 1694. In August 1692 Lieutenant Governor Francis Nicholson used Colonel Nathaniel Bacon's Kings Creek residence on the York River as a readily identifiable landmark when ordering mariners to take their vessels upstream to positions of greater safety (MCGH 159, 452; STAN 17, 22, 37, 73; Isle of Wight Book A:93; NUG I:478, 486; II:2, 265; HEN II:560, 568; MCGC 52, 251, 253, 259, 270, 274, 276, 289, 302, 344, 412, 484, 486, 491, 514, 516, 518; PB 4:397; 7:300; AMB 11; York County Deeds, Orders, Wills 6:258; 9:116–118; Essex County Deeds and Wills 1692–1695:50–51; Isle of Wight County Deeds, Wills & Guardian Accounts Book A:92–93; Orders 1693–1695:37; LJC 10, 86; EJC I:10, 78; CO 5/1356 f 68; JHB 1660–1693:142–143, 152; FOR I:9:8; I:11:41; DOR 1:433–434; 2:419–420; LEO 33, 35–36).

Elizabeth Kingsmill Tayloe Bacon (Mrs. William Tayloe [Taylor, Tayler], Mrs. Nathaniel Bacon) (see Elizabeth Kingsmill): Richard Kingsmill's daughter, Elizabeth, who was born in 1624, outlived her brother, Nathaniel, and sometime prior to September 1638 inherited the bulk of her late father's Jamestown Island acreage. By that date she had married William Tayloe, who had purchased the Kings Creek plantation in York County from John Uty's son and heir. In 1647 Tayloe became a York County burgess, and in 1651 he was named to the Council of State. Although the Tayloes resided on the Kings Creek plantation, they may have occupied Elizabeth's Jamestown Island plantation from time to time or simply placed it in the hands of a tenant. After William Tayloe's death in 1655, Elizabeth inherited his Kings Creek plantation. She remarried, becoming the second wife of Colonel Nathaniel Bacon, who moved to the Kings Creek property. In 1676, when the rebel Nathaniel Bacon and his men built a trench across the isthmus leading into Jamestown Island, they placed Elizabeth and the wives of other council members on the ramparts to shield themselves from Governor Berkeley's loyalists' attack. On November 6, 1661, Nathaniel and Elizabeth Kingsmill Tayloe Bacon sold her share of her late father's Jamestown Island plantation to Nicholas Meriwether. The deed cited an agreement made on April 30, 1661, whereby the Bacons promised to sell the property for an unspecified sum. When Meriwether patented the Bacons' land, it was noted that the acreage was "formerly planted and seated by Richard Kingsmill Deceased" and that Elizabeth was his "only Daughter and Heir." Elizabeth died in 1691 at the age of 67. Her tombstone, which has been moved to St. Paul's Church in Norfolk, bears the Kingsmill and Tayloe arms (MCGH 159; FOR I:9:8; NUG I:125, 394; STAN 36, 66; AMB 11, 12; PB 4:397; DOR 2:419–420; VI&A 447).

***

***

Nathaniel Bacon (the rebel): In 1670 Nathaniel Bacon, Thomas Bacon's son, married Elizabeth, the daughter of Sir Edward Duke and his wife, Ellen. The young couple went to Virginia in 1674, by which time Nathaniel had run through his patrimony and had ruined his reputation in England. In fact, Elizabeth's father so strongly disapproved of the marriage that he disinherited her. However, after Sir Edward's death his son and primary heir, Sir John Duke, took pity on his sister, Elizabeth, and decided to give Nathaniel Bacon £800 if he would endow his wife (and any children they had) with certain land in Suffolk, England. Bacon agreed and posted a £1,000 promissory note guaranteeing to do so. Court testimony reveals, however, that Bacon quietly conveyed the Suffolk land to Sir Robert Jason, who never fully paid for the property. Jason, on the other hand, claimed that he had been duped by Bacon, who had transferred the property to one of his own friends. Thomas Bacon, Nathaniel's father, testified that he was aware that the transaction with Jason was incomplete but didn't know the particulars. On November 8, 1674, Nathaniel Bacon, who was then living in Virginia, agreed to sell the Suffolk land to Thomas Jarvis I, an Elizabeth City County merchant and mariner, in exchange for a substantial sum. Afterward, Bacon, who was the cousin of Colonel Nathaniel Bacon and Governor William Berkeley, acquired a plantation called Curles (or Longfield) in Henrico, and by 1675 he had secured an appointment to the Council of State. A year later he became a burgess for Henrico County. After Bacon's plantation at the head of the James River was attacked by Indians, he grew extremely impatient while waiting for Governor Berkeley to respond. Ultimately, Bacon led the popular uprising known as Bacon's Rebellion and, contrary to Governor Berkeley's orders, undertook marches against Indian tribes that were tributaries to the Crown. Although the Council of State pardoned Bacon for his disobedience and Berkeley restored him to his council seat, the rebel rallied an army of supporters and in June 1676 returned to confront the colony's governing officials. Bacon had his men build a trench across the isthmus that connected Jamestown Island to the mainland and from that position shelled the town. He also seized the wives of certain council members and placed them on the ramparts to serve as a human shield. On September 19, 1676, after Berkeley abandoned Jamestown, Bacon and his men put the capital city to the torch, destroying the church, statehouse, and numerous other buildings. Nathaniel Bacon died from natural causes and the rebellion subsided, owing to a lack of strong leadership. His estate was seized because he was considered guilty of treason. His widow, Elizabeth, married Thomas Jarvis I and in 1684 initiated a lawsuit in an attempt to reclaim the land her brother had given her (NUG III:27; CO 5/1307 ff 61–62; 5/1371 f 218; STAN 40; MCGC 516; FOR I:8:15–16, 21, 23, 26; 9:8–9; 11:24–26; WASH 17–18; LEO 41; SR 690, 3720, 4559, 10072, 10518, 10605; NEVILLE 61).

Elizabeth Duke Bacon (Mrs. Nathaniel Bacon Jr., Mrs. Thomas Jarvis I, Mrs. Edward Mole [Hole]): Elizabeth, the daughter of Sir Edward Duke and Ellen Panton of Benhall, in Suffolk, England, married Nathaniel Bacon in 1670 and moved to Virginia in 1674. Elizabeth's father's disapproval of Bacon was so great that he disinherited her. However, her brother, Sir John Duke, took pity on her and decided to give Nathaniel Bacon £800 if he would endow his wife (and any children they had) with some land in Suffolk, England. Bacon agreed and posted a promissory note but sold the property to Sir Robert Jason, perhaps without Elizabeth's knowledge. Later he told his father, Thomas Bacon, that Jason had never fully paid for the property, which was in the hands of tenants. In 1673 Thomas Jarvis I, an Elizabeth City County merchant and mariner, went to England intending to purchase some land and chose the Suffolk property that Nathaniel Bacon held on behalf of his wife, Elizabeth. When Jarvis returned to Virginia, he and Bacon made a sales agreement on November 8, 1674, and a significant amount of money changed hands. When Jarvis was back in England in 1676, he informed Thomas Bacon that he was in the process of purchasing his son's Suffolk property. The two men drafted an agreement taking into account Sir Robert Jason's legal interest in the land. Meanwhile, Nathaniel Bacon, who had gotten caught up in what became known as Bacon's Rebellion, died in late 1676 before a deed was signed. Sometime prior to November 25, 1679, the widowed Elizabeth Duke Bacon married Thomas Jarvis I and accompanied him to England, where he died in April 1684. A few months later Elizabeth initiated a lawsuit against Sir Robert Jason, intending to claim a legal interest in the land that her brother had bestowed upon her and her heirs. Although the matter dragged on in court, Jason eventually vacated his claim and Elizabeth Duke Bacon Jarvis returned to Virginia. Court testimony taken in 1684 and 1685 reveals that Nathaniel and Elizabeth Duke Bacon produced two daughters. One of them, Mary, was living in England in January 1685 when Charles Blois, who identified himself as her guardian, testified in a lawsuit that had been initiated by her mother, Elizabeth, by then the wife of Thomas Jarvis I. By 1688 the twice-widowed Elizabeth had married her third husband, Edward Mole (Hole). In 1692 William Sherwood of Jamestown served as her attorney (WITH 443; MCGC 520; EJC I:261; SR 10072, 10518, 10605, 10730).

* * *

Thomas Baglen: On January 24, 1625, Thomas Baglen was a resident of Jamestown Island (VI&A 99).

James Bagnall (Bagnell): In 1646 James Bagnall served as a burgess for Isle of Wight County. He acquired some land on the lower side of the Rappahannock River in 1652, in the newly formed Lancaster County, and moved there, establishing a plantation. He became a county justice and in August 1652 hosted a meeting of the monthly court at his home. Bagnall attended the 1654–1655 assembly session, representing Lancaster County. He and Anne (Ann), the daughter of the Rev. Robert Braswell (Bracewell) of Isle of Wight County, posted their marriage bonds in 1667. In March 1674 James and Anne Braswell Bagnall sold a plantation she had inherited from her late father to a man then occupying the property. By 1675 Bagnall was widowed, and he married Richard Izard's daughter, Rebecca. In March 1676 he patented 300 acres in Isle of Wight County, land that had descended to him from Captain John Upton. A year later he was among those who signed a petition asking for clemency on behalf of William West, an accused supporter of the rebel Nathaniel Bacon. In 1680 James Bagwell sold a two-

acre mill seat to William West, noting that it was part of a larger tract that had belonged to the Rev. Robert Braswell, part of whose acreage had escheated to the Crown (LEO 25, 32; Lancaster County Deeds &c. 2 [1652–1657]:1; Order Book 1656–1666:126; Isle of Wight County Wills and Deeds 2:52, 135; I:311; PB 1:894; 3:153; 6:606; BODIE 163, 569, 588, 627).

Anthony Bagness (Bagley): During the summer of 1608, some Nansemond and Chesapeake Indians reportedly shot at Anthony Bagness, one of the first Jamestown colonists, and struck his hat. Later in the year Bagness accompanied Captain John Smith on his second exploratory voyage in the Chesapeake Bay and spent Christmas 1608 (January 1609) at Kecoughtan. Bagness was coauthor of an account that Smith included in some of his published narratives (VI&A 99).

Henry Bagwell: Henry Bagwell, an ancient planter shipwrecked in Bermuda, reached Virginia in 1610 and during the mid-1620s lived at West and Shirley Hundred. When a list of patented land was sent back to England in May 1625, Bagwell was credited with 50 acres within the corporation of Charles City. He moved to the Eastern Shore and in 1630 and 1632 served as a burgess for Accomack. Over the years he was entrusted with the settlement of estates. By 1637 he had married Alice, Benjamin Stratton's widow. Bagwell continued to play an active role in public life and became clerk of the local court. He was still alive in April 1645 but died intestate sometime prior to April 28, 1663 (VI&A 99; NUG I:43, 112, 295; MCGC 180; AMES 1:14, 16, 67, 94, 96, 148; LEO 9, 11; MARSHALL 1, 3, 18, 21, 71, 243; DOR 1:90–91).

John Bagwell: On September 28, 1677, Governor Herbert Jeffreys and the General Court's justices learned that John Bagwell, who had been found guilty of rebellion and treason due to his involvement in Bacon's Rebellion, had failed to comply with the sentence he had received. Bagwell, who was ordered to appear before the justices of Old Rappahannock County with a rope around his neck and apologize on bended knee, came to court wearing small tape instead of a rope halter. Major Robert Beverley was ordered to investigate the matter and determine whether Bagwell and the county justices had demonstrated contempt of the law (MCGC 534).

Thomas Bagwell: In February 1624 ancient planter Thomas Bagwell was living at West and Shirley Hundred, but by early 1625 he had moved to the Neck O'Land behind Jamestown Island. Sometime prior to February 5, 1627, he married Thomas Allnutt's widow. In March 1629 Bagwell served on a jury and as a burgess for Pasbehay. In May 1638 he received a patent for 450 acres on the Appomattox River (VI&A 100; LEO 8).

* * *

Arthur Bailey (Bayly, Baily, Bayley): In 1637 Arthur Bailey, a prosperous English merchant with headquarters in London, patented two large tracts near the falls of the James River but sold part of his land within a year. Then, on September 22, 1638, he patented a half-acre waterfront lot in urban Jamestown in response to the assembly's efforts to encourage development in the capital city. Bailey, who also acquired the land called Arrahattocks, moved to Curles Neck in Henrico County and in 1643 represented that area in the assembly. In July 1654 Arthur Bailey and several other merchants trading in Virginia asked the Commonwealth government's permission to ship shoes and gunpowder to the colony, where both were needed. When Mrs. Ann Talbott patented a waterfront lot in urban Jamestown in March 1655, her property was said to abut east upon the lot of Thomas Bailey, Arthur Bailey's kinsman. In 1658 a Captain Arthur Bailey, who was then in England, described himself as a trader to Virginia. In 1675 a merchant named Arthur Bailey, perhaps a direct descendant of the Henrico County burgess, was conducting business in Lancaster County but was based in England. By 1699 he was trading as Arthur Bailey and Company of London and had become the son-in-law of merchant Robert Bristow, who had lived in the Northern Neck but returned to England in 1677 (Stanard, "Council and General Court Records,"191; "Virginia in 1656–1658," 158; PB 1:598; 3:331; NUG I:78–79, 86, 97, 121, 305, 447, 471; HEN I:239; WITH 114, 266; WAT 1446, 1448; SR 633; LEO 21; Lancaster County Wills 1674–1689:7; Essex County Order Book 1699–1702:66, 109).

Thomas Bailey (Bayly, Baily, Bayley): Thomas Bailey, who by March 1, 1655, was in possession of a half-acre lot abutting the James River in urban Jamestown, was from Henrico County. He was a kinsman of London merchant Arthur Bailey, from whom he may have inherited his lot. Sometime after October 1660 but before April 7, 1671, Thomas Bailey occupied a unit in a brick row house in the western end of Jamestown Island. He may have been a tenant of Henry

Randolph—who, like Bailey, was from Henrico—or of Thomas Woodhouse, who formerly owned a unit in the building. In 1704 a Thomas Bailey was credited with 251 acres of land in Henrico County (PB 3:331; NUG I:305; MCGC 514; SMITH 4; JHB 1619–1660:96, 101; 1660–1693:8).

* * *

John Bailey (Baily, Bayly, Bayley, Bailie, Baile): John Bailey, an ancient planter and resident of Hog Island, acquired some land in the eastern end of Jamestown Island sometime prior to 1618. He may have been one of the men to whom Sir Thomas Dale or Deputy Governor Samuel Argall gave land before the headright system was established. At John's death, which occurred before February 20, 1620, his Virginia land descended to his daughter and sole heir, Mary, who also was an ancient planter. In 1624 Mary's guardians, Robert Evers and Richard Bailey (and Richard's surrogate, Edward Grindon), preserved her legal interest in her late father's real estate by placing it in the hands of tenants. Evers personally occupied one of Mary's patents on Jamestown Island, and in 1626 Grindon leased her Hog Island acreage to Sir George Yeardley. In May 1625 Mary Bailey was credited with 500 acres at Hog Island, property that had been planted or seated. Mary married Randall Holt (Howlett) I sometime prior to 1629 and produced a son and heir, Randall Holt II. She died sometime prior to August 1643 (VI&A 100).

Richard Bailey (Bayly, Bayley, Baylie, Bailey) I: Richard Bailey I, who appears to have been a merchant trading to Bristol, England, represented Accomack County in the assembly sessions held in 1693 and 1696–1697. One of the vessels in which he had a financial interest was the *Expectation*. Bailey made his will on November 15, 1707, which was proved on June 1, 1708. He designated his wife, Ursilla, and son, Richard II, as his executors. He made bequests to his wife and to his sons, Richard II, Edmund, Henry, and Whittington, and his daughters, Lacy, Ursilla, and Joyce. The testator asked his father and brother to oversee his will (LEO 52, 56; Accomack County Wills &c. 1692–1715:441; SR 730, 3851, 5393, 5674, 6491).

William Bailey (Baylie, Baly, Baley): In 1608 William Bailey, a gentleman, arrived in Jamestown as part of the 1st Supply of new settlers (VI&A 102).

William Bailey (Baylie, Baly, Baley): William Bailey, an ancient planter, came to Virginia in 1610 and lived in Jamestown. By January 1625 he was residing at West and Shirley Hundred with his wife, Mary, and son, Thomas. During 1625 William, who was then age 41, informed the justices of the General Court that he had seen Indians attack and kill a man at Shirley Hundred. When a list of patented land was sent to England in May 1625, Bailey was credited with 50 acres in Great Weyanoke and 100 acres in Charles City, near Bailey's Creek. He died prior to July 9, 1635, when his son, Thomas, patented 150 acres, a third of which he had inherited from his late father (VI&A 102).

John Baird: John Baird, a carpenter, purchased two lots in urban Jamestown from John Howard on May 6, 1710. He and his wife, Margaret, sold both parcels, which were in the western end of Jamestown Island, to Edward Travis III on January 13, 1717 (AMB 82, 92).

Henry Baker I: In 1693 Henry Baker, a merchant, served as a burgess for Isle of Wight County and simultaneously as a justice of the county court. By 1694 he had become the county's high sheriff. Baker patented 350 acres in Surry County in 1684, and on at least one occasion served as the attorney of Samuel Swann of Surry. In 1694 Henry Baker and his wife, Mary, who were still residents of Isle of Wight, disposed of a tract of land in adjoining Nansemond County. In June 1699, while Baker was a colonel in the Isle of Wight County militia, he patented 522 acres in Nansemond County, near Buckland. As time went on, he continued to enhance the size of his landholdings. By 1712 Baker was dead. Survivors included his widow and executrix, Mary, and their son, Henry II, then a resident of Nansemond County. In 1704 Colonel Henry Baker was credited with 850 acres in Surry, whereas his son, Henry II, paid quitrent on acreage in Isle of Wight and Nansemond (LEO 52–53; Isle of Wight County Deed Book 1 [1688–1704]:97, 99–100, 208, 221; 2 [1704–1715]:9, 55, 234; Orders 1693–1695:1, 33–34, 58; BODIE 643; PB 7:371; 9:195, 537; SMITH 4).

John Baker: John Baker, a young joiner from London, arrived in Jamestown on September 5, 1623, and took the oath of supremacy. In 1625 he was living on the Eastern Shore, where he was a servant in Captain William Eppes's household (VI&A 103; CBE 68; MCGC 6).

Lawrence Baker: Lawrence Baker came to Virginia sometime prior to May 1643 when he and James Taylor patented 500 acres near the head of Lawnes Creek, in what was then James City (later, Surry) County. The two men repatented their acreage in June 1650, an indication that they had not developed their property. When Surry County was formed in 1652, Baker, a planter, was made a justice of the monthly court, a position he still held in 1668. On January 16, 1654, James Baker testified that his brother, Lawrence, had signed a certain legal document. In 1667 Captain Lawrence Baker patented 2,050 acres of Surry County land. He served as a burgess for Surry County from 1666 to 1676, succeeding William Cockerham, who retired after the 1665 session. In 1671 he was one of the men the justices of the General Court ordered to audit some accounts. On November 29, 1672, Captain Baker obtained a judgment against bricklayer John Bird in Surry County's monthly court. He died in 1681 and was survived by his wife, Elizabeth, and daughter, Catherine (Katherine), who was married to Arthur Allen II of Bacon's Castle. In 1693 the Allens sold some of the property Catherine had inherited from her parents (LEO 40; Surry County Order Book 1671–1691:17, 348; Deeds, Wills, &c. Book 1:25, 48; 4:335; SR 13853; PB 2:18, 221; 6:167; BILLINGS 348–349; MCGC 214, 273, 278).

Thomas Baker: Thomas Baker, a 22-year-old skinner from Staffordshire, arrived in Jamestown in 1619 on the *Bona Nova* (VI&A 103). He probably was a Virginia Company tenant or servant.

Thomas Baker (Backer): On March 22, 1677, Thomas Baker was hauled before Governor William Berkeley and the Council of State, where he was accused of supporting the rebel Nathaniel Bacon's cause. During a military tribunal it was decided that Baker would be released if he took an oath of obedience and paid a substantial fine: 2,000 pounds of pork that could be used by the king's soldiers (MCGC 461, 533).

Thomas Baldridge: In 1650 Captain Thomas Baldridge simultaneously served as a Northumberland County burgess and county justice. He continued to hold office and represented Northumberland County in the 1651–1652 assembly session. By 1653, when Westmoreland County was formed out of the northwestern portion of Northumberland, Baldridge had attained the rank of major in the local militia. He died sometime prior to July 20, 1654, when Northumberland's justices stipulated that his will could not be proved nor an administrator appointed until John Tew, his greatest creditor, was able to appear in court. The justices noted that Tew had married Grace Bowman, who formerly had been betrothed to Baldridge. On August 20, 1657, James Baldridge, the late Major Thomas Baldridge's brother, received permission from Westmoreland County's justices to serve as his administrator. He also was authorized to serve as administrator for their cousin, Thomas Baldridge, who had moved from Barbados to Virginia. James Baldridge, when settling Major Baldridge's estate, made reference to the decedent's son, James, who stood to receive half of a patent assigned to his late father (LEO 28; Northumberland County Deeds and Orders 1650–1652:41; Wills, Inventories &c. 1652–1658:41, 77; Order Book 1652–1665:9, 55; Westmoreland County Deeds, Wills, Patents &c. 1653–1659:29, 83; Order Book 1676–1689:147).

Robert Baldry (Baldrey, Baldrye): In 1645 Robert Baldry, a resident of York County, brought suit against an indentured servant, a seamstress who had failed to fulfill her contract. In January 1648 Baldry was replaced as constable for the upper part of York Parish. Later in the year he and another man were ordered to appraise the late Gabriel Smith's estate. In 1652 he leased his 1,050-acre patent on the south side of the Potomac River to Richard Cole, a York County merchant. In 1657, when Edward Barnes was censured for fathering an illegitimate child, he was ordered to do penance "before the Congregation att the next meeting att Robert Baldry's house," an indication that church services were then being held in the Baldry home. Baldry appears to have been a builder, for in early 1657 he was paid for constructing the county courthouse and jail. When he witnessed a document later in the year, he endorsed it with an "x," perhaps because he was illiterate or unable to see well enough to write. Robert Baldry served as a burgess for York County in 1660 and from 1669–1674. He died in January 1676 (LEO 36, 40; York County Deeds, Orders, Wills 1 [1633–1657]:141; 2 [1645–1649]:321, 355; 2 [1648–1657]:429; 3 [1657–1662]:1–3).

John Baldwin (Baldwine, Baldwyn, Bauldwin): John Baldwin, who came to Virginia in 1622 as a free man, had friends or family members in Bermuda. During the mid-1620s he resided on the lower side of the James River on the Treasurer's Plantation, which belonged to the colony's treasurer, George Sandys. A letter Baldwin sent to a friend in Bermuda around 1623 described the many hardships he endured

while living there. On May 20, 1637, when John Baldwin disposed of a plot of ground in the eastern end of Jamestown Island, he was described as a gentleman. In 1653 he served as a burgess for Lancaster County, a duty for which he was compensated out of the county levies. His name disappeared from the Lancaster County records in 1654, perhaps because in 1656 he had moved back to Jamestown Island, where he had patented a 15-acre parcel near the isthmus that led to the mainland. Baldwin also became involved in a lawsuit in Surry County. When he made his will sometime prior to 1677, he named John Fulcher as his heir (VI&A 105; LEO 31; Lancaster Deeds &c. Book 2 [1652–1657]:90–93, 244).

Henry Ball (Baul, Baule): Henry Ball served as a burgess for Warwick County in 1646 (LEO 25; STAN 66). Despite a diligent search, no further information has been found.

* * *

William Ball I: By 1662 William Ball I, a merchant and planter, had begun serving as a Lancaster County justice. He went on to become high sheriff. In 1663 he patented 300 acres and established a family seat at what became known as Balls Point, adding another 240 acres in 1667. Because a Dutch invasion was expected in 1667 and high-ranking officials decided to have fortifications built on the Corotoman River and at other strategically important locations, local military officers convened at Ball's house. As time went on, Ball invested in land in New Kent and Old Rappahannock counties, and he enhanced the size of his home tract. He went on to become a Lancaster County burgess and attended the assembly sessions held in 1670–1676 and 1677. In November 1671 Colonel Ball received permission to keep a ferry on the Corotoman River, from William Wroughton's property to John Carter's landing. A year later Ball and his son, William II, served together as justices of the monthly court. In 1677 William Ball I, who was again high sheriff, was ordered to collect taxes that could be used to cover the cost of quelling Bacon's Rebellion. When Colonel Ball made his will on October 5, 1680, he bequeathed life-rights in his 540-acre plantation to his wife, Hannah I, during her widowhood but named his son, Captain William Ball II, as reversionary heir to the property. He divided his 1,600 acres at the head of the Rappahannock River between his sons, Joseph and William II, to whom he also gave unequal shares of his merchandise and debts. He left each of his sons, who were to serve as co-executors, some servants and slaves. However, he left only £5 to his daughter, Hannah II, the wife of Captain David Fox, stating that it was more than she deserved. William Ball I's will was proved on November 10, 1680. The widowed Hannah Ball I continued to manage the property she had inherited and in 1688 and 1689 was paid by the county for keeping a ferry. In 1691 part of her land was laid out as a town site. When the widowed Hannah Ball I made her will in December 1694, she treated her daughter, Hannah Fox, as generously as she treated her surviving son, Joseph, and the heirs of her deceased son, William II. In October 1695 she enhanced her bequests by means of a codicil, leaving personal property to son Joseph as well as to her grandsons William III, James, and Richard, the children of her deceased son, William II. In October 1695 Mrs. Ball's will and codicil were proved by son Joseph, daughter Hannah Fox, and grandson William Ball III. A portion of her will (probably the codicil) was nuncupative and was proved by a black servant named Bess, who lived with the testator. Hannah Ball I's son Joseph seized the household furnishings that had been left to his sister, Hannah II, which prompted her husband, Captain David Fox, to take legal action (NUG I:491; II:20, 163, 283; PB 5:300; LEO 38, 42, 45; Lancaster County Wills 1675–1689:70–71; 1690–1709:52–54; Order Book 1656–1666:175, 370; 1666–1680:147, 209, 226, 288, 375, 480; 1686–1696:93, 114, 170, 324, 338, 350; Northumberland County Order Book 1652–1665:303, 321; 1666–1678:174; Westmoreland County Deeds, Patents &c. 1665–1677:347a–350; HEN II:256–257).

Joseph Ball: In 1680 William Ball I named his son Joseph as a co-executor and left him part of his merchandise, slaves, and other personal property, and half of a large tract on the Rappahannock River in Richmond County. In 1684 Joseph Ball became a Lancaster County justice, and in May 1685 he commenced serving as high sheriff. In 1687 he compiled a list of the tithables living in White Chapel Parish and in 1698 was still serving as county justice. When Hannah I, Joseph Ball's mother, made her will in 1694, she named him as one of her principal heirs. He and his sister, Hannah Fox, and nephew William Ball III saw that the decedent's will and codicil were proved. Major Joseph Ball served as a burgess for Lancaster County in 1698 and by 1700 held the rank of colonel in the militia. He served another term in the assembly, attending the sessions held in 1700–1702 (Lancaster County Wills 1675–1689:70–

71; Wills 1690–1709:52–54; Inventories & Wills 1650–1705:90; Order Book 1680–1687:160, 202; 1687–1696:21, 35, 179, 324; 1696–1702:37, 75, 128; LEO 58, 60).

William Ball II: In 1680 Captain William Ball II, the son of Colonel William Ball I, inherited his late father's 540-acre plantation in Lancaster County, half of his 1,600 acres on the Rappahannock River, and a substantial portion of his late father's merchandise and debts. Captain Ball, who served as a county justice during the 1670s, 1680s, and early 1690s and became high sheriff in 1683, represented Lancaster County in the assembly sessions that were held in 1680–1682, 1685–1686, 1688, 1691–1692, and 1693. He also appeared in court from time to time, serving as an attorney. In June 1694 he began serving another term as Lancaster County's high sheriff. However, he made his will in September 1694, indicating that he was very ill, and by November was dead. Ball left his wife, Margaret, life-rights in his mill and the 277-acre plantation on which they were living at the time of his death. She also had the right to use the rest of his substantial landholdings for her own benefit. Ball named as reversionary heirs his sons, William III, Richard, Joseph, George, James, David, Stretchley, and Samuel, and his daughter, Margaret. He designated as executors his sons Richard and William III and three friends, one of whom was brother-in-law Captain David Fox (LEO 38, 42, 45, 48–50, 53; Lancaster County Wills 1675–1689:70–71; Wills 1690–1709:46–47; Inventories & Wills 1650–1705:90; Order Book 1666–1680:437, 480; 1680–1687:84, 116; 1686–1696:179, 294, 298; Northumberland County Order Book 1666–1678:142, 221).

* * *

* * *

Thomas Ballard I: Thomas Ballard I, who was born in England, served as a James City County justice in 1664 and as sheriff in 1670. In 1666 he became a burgess, representing James City County, and in 1670 he was named to the Council of State. He also represented James City County in the assembly during the 1680s. In July 1667 Thomas Ballard I purchased 130 acres at Middle Plantation, acreage that had belonged to Nicholas Watkins and had descended to his daughter, Elizabeth, and her husband, George Richman (Richmand) of Nominy in Westmoreland County. Ballard, however, took up residence in York County, having purchased William Pryor's riverfront plantation. Ballard, a respected citizen, frequently was ordered to audit accounts and arbitrate disputes. In April 1670 he made a claim against the estate of Jonathan Newell, a Jamestown merchant. Because of Ballard's loyalty to Governor William Berkeley, the rebel Nathaniel Bacon declared him a traitor. When Bacon's men captured the wives of several prominent men in September 1676 and placed them on the ramparts of a fortification they were building across the entrance to Jamestown Island, Thomas Ballard I's wife, Anna, was one of the women behind whom the rebels hid. Early in 1677, when the king's troops were sent to the colony to restore order, Ballard was ordered to find land on which they could grow corn for subsistence. Although he continued to serve on the Council of State after Bacon's Rebellion had been quelled, ultimately he clashed with Lieutenant Governor Herbert Jeffreys, one of the special commissioners sent to investigate the underlying causes of the popular uprising. In 1674 Thomas Ballard I made arrangements to purchase 330 acres of land at Middle Plantation, part of the Ludwells' Rich Neck tract. Plats made by Robert Beverley I in 1674 and 1678 reveal that the parcel included only 284 acres of usable land. During the 1680s Ballard served as a James City County burgess and from 1680 to 1682 was speaker of the assembly. In 1685 he was on the committee responsible for renting one of William Sherwood's Jamestown houses for official meetings. Ballard died in Virginia in 1689. His York River plantation descended to his son, Thomas II, as did his land at Middle Plantation (HEN II:249–250; Charles City County Order Book 1:103; MCGC 211, 218, 235, 329, 340, 342, 373, 516; FOR I:9:8; SAIN 10:341; CO 1/2 f 304; JHB1660–1693:72; LJC 93; STAN 39, 84; LEO 38, 45, 47–48; NEVILLE 46, 53–54, 70, 75, 86, 90, 99, 174, 255–256, 286, 299, 320, 368; Westmoreland County Deeds, Patents &c. 1665–1677:61a–62; York County Deeds, Orders, Wills 6:430).

Thomas Ballard II: Thomas Ballard II, the son and primary heir of Anna and Thomas Ballard I, inherited his late father's 330 acres at Middle Plantation and his plantation on the York River. He served as a York County burgess and attended the assembly sessions held in 1691–1692, 1693, 1696–1697, 1698, and 1699. In 1693 the College of William and Mary was erected on the Ballard land at Middle Plantation. Thomas Ballard II was relatively short-lived. He prepared his will on September 26, 1706, and died sometime prior to June 18, 1711. The testator left to his eldest son, Mathew, a York

River plantation that extended in a westerly direction from what became known as Ballard's Creek (on the east) to the easternmost limits of Bellfield, the Digges plantation. Thus, by the early eighteenth century, the Ballards' York River plantation encompassed all of William Pryor's patent, which had been purchased by Thomas Ballard I, and the eastern part of Captain Francis Morgan's plantation (LEO 51–52, 57–59; JHB1660–1693:72; LJC 93; York County Deeds, Orders, Wills 14:89–90, 92).

* * *

John Bamford (Bramford, Brampford): John Bamford, who set out for Virginia with cape merchant Abraham Peirsey, arrived in Jamestown on July 31, 1622. During the mid-1620s he was living at Flowerdew Hundred and was one of Peirsey's servants (VI&A 106).

John Banckton (Bankton?): John Banckton came to Virginia with William Felgate and arrived in Jamestown on July 31, 1622 (VI&A 106).

Phillip Bandage: Phillip Bandage, a young cook from Somersetshire, arrived in Jamestown in 1619 and probably was one of the Virginia Company servants or tenants who reached Virginia in November of that year (VI&A 106).

William Banks (Bancks, Binks, Byncks, Bincks): In February 1624 Goodman William Banks and his wife, Ann, were living on the lower side of the James River, across from Jamestown. In December 1624 Banks agreed to rent a house and land on Jamestown Island from John Lightfoot. However, in January 1625 William and Ann were residing on the Governor's Land and were described as Thomas Swinhowe's servants (VI&A 107).

Francis Banks: Francis Banks came to Virginia in 1623 and during the mid-1620s was a servant in Edward Bennett's house in Warresqueak. When Banks testified before the General Court in 1625, he claimed that Jamestown merchant John Chew had taken a sentinel from the capital city's fort with him to the store in Warresqueak. Two years later Banks verified John Uty's allegation that a man had refused to perform military duties (VI&A 106).

Christopher Bankus: Christopher Bankus came to Virginia in 1622 and in January 1625 was a servant in the urban Jamestown household of Captain Roger Smith. He may have been Christopher Banks, a planter who in 1631 sought relief from paying customs duties (VI&A 107).

John Baptista: On January 20, 1677, John Baptista, a Frenchman and one of the rebel Nathaniel Bacon's most devoted followers, was tried at a martial court held at James Bray's house in Middle Plantation. He admitted his guilt and was sentenced to be hanged. On February 10, 1677, Governor Berkeley issued a proclamation noting that Baptista already had been executed and that his estate was not exempt from seizure (MCGC 454, 527; SR 660; NEVILLE 61, 274).

* * *

John Barber I: In 1664 and 1665 John Barber I acquired two waterfront lots in urban Jamestown. He disposed of one parcel but retained the other, using it to build a personal residence. In October 1667 Barber was fined for building a wharf "before the town," contrary to law, which raises the possibility that he was engaged in mercantile activities. Sometime prior to July 21, 1657, he acquired some land in the eastern end of Jamestown Island, rural acreage formerly owned by Major Robert Holt. Barber was still in possession of the property in 1667 and probably used it for grazing livestock or other agricultural purposes. He died sometime prior to October 3, 1671, when his widow and administratrix, Letitia, appeared in court to conduct business on his behalf. By October 1672 Letitia Barber had married David Newell, the brother of Jamestown merchant Jonathan Newell, who owned a large parcel on the upper side of Back Street that formerly had belonged to John Knowles. The late John Barber I's principal heir was his son, John Barber II. The decedent apparently did business with Henry Corbyn and Cuthbert Potter of Lancaster County, who made claims against his estate (AMB 18, 27, 83; PB 4:150; 5:228; 6:42; NUG I:347, 468; II:12; JHB 1660–1693:48; MCGC 240, 262, 281, 314).

John Barber II: John Barber II inherited his late father's Jamestown Island landholdings, which included three-quarters of an acre on the west side of Orchard Run in urban Jamestown. When the widowed Letitia Barber remarried around 1672, she probably vacated the dwelling she had shared with her late husband, John Barber I, making it available to John Barber II. By April 6, 1671, John Barber II (also known as Captain John Barber) had wed Elizabeth, the widow of Captain Edward Streater (Streeter), and brought suit against Thomas Bowler, a

debtor to the Streater estate. Even though Elizabeth was deceased, Barber initiated litigation and eventually won the case. On February 7, 1678, John Barber II sold his late father's Jamestown lot to Thomas Rabley (MCGC 206–207, 240, 251; AMB 83).

* * *

Thomas Barber (Barbar): In October 1672 Thomas Barber was sued by the mother of a young male servant whose contract he had bought from a person unauthorized to sell it. In March 1676 Barber and another man, who were then in England, sued Robert Spring; however, the matter was referred to York County's justices for arbitration. At issue was an unfavorable agreement made by Barber's attorney that involved the purchase of some New Kent County land. By 1687 Barber had begun serving as a justice in York County's court. Among his duties was compiling a list of Hampton Parish's tithables. In 1691 he became high sheriff and also held the rank of captain in the militia. Court records suggest that in 1695 he married Prudence, one of the late Francis Read's former servants. In 1696 Captain Barber served as a churchwarden of Hampton Parish, and in 1700 he was on a commission that tried some men accused of piracy. Barber became a York County burgess and served in the assembly sessions of 1680–1682, 1685–1686, 1688, 1691–1692, 1693, 1695–1696, 1700–1702, 1703–1705, and 1705–1706. In November 1707 he was on a commission given the responsibility of trying some Tuscorora Indians accused of murdering a New Kent County man. Thomas Barber died sometime prior to June 24, 1709, at which time an inventory of his estate was presented to the justices of York County's monthly court (LEO 46, 48–49, 51, 53, 55, 61, 63–64; MCGC 312, 441, 447–448, 450; EJC I:66; II:165; York County Deeds, Orders, Wills 8 [1687–1691]:6, 118, 179; 9 [1691–1694]:28, 53, 120; 10 [1694–1697]:137, 148, 159, 246, 329, 348, 371, 505).

William Barber (Barbar) I: On August 20, 1654, William Barber purchased some Surry County land from William Corker, who had acquired it from Thomas Rabley of Jamestown. Three months later Barber sold it to two other men, who were Surry residents. From 1662 to 1667 Barber represented York County in the assembly. In March 1663, while he was a lieutenant colonel in the militia, he served on the committee responsible for seeing that a statehouse was built in Jamestown. He also patented 596 acres of land in York County and in 1664 disposed of his plantation on Totuskey Creek in Old Rappahannock (later, Richmond) County. Barber purchased Thomas Rolfe's plantation in Surry County in 1674. Barber's daughter, Mary, was married to John Baskerville, whereas his son, William Barber II, and his grandson, William Barber III, were residents of Richmond County (Surry County Deeds, Wills &c. 1652–1672:55; 1671–1684:51; NUG I:480; HEN II:205, 249–250; WITH 82; LEO 40; Old Rappahannock County Deeds and Wills 1656–1664:303; Richmond County Deed Book 2 [1693–1695]:50–55).

John Bargrave: In June 1623, after William Nuce's death, Captain John Bargrave was appointed marshal of Virginia. He received a letter from Sir Nathaniel Rich containing recommendations about how the colony should be managed (VI&A 109).

Richard Barefoot: Richard Barefoot arrived in Jamestown on April 17, 1619 (VI&A 109).

Anthony Barham (Baram, Barram): Anthony Barham came to Virginia sometime prior to 1624 and in January 1625 was living on Mulberry Island with his wife, Elizabeth. He owned 100 acres of land in Warresqueak but continued to live on Mulberry Island and served as its burgess in 1630. When Barham prepared his will on September 6, 1641, he made bequests to his wife and daughter, who were both named Elizabeth; to his brother-in-law Richard Bennett; and to Captain William Peirce's wife, Joan, of urban Jamestown (VI&A 110; LEO 9).

Christopher Barker: At the time of the March 1622 Indian attack, Christopher Barker was one of Captain John Ward's servants. He left Ward's employ later in the year and in January 1625 was living in urban Jamestown, where he was one of Thomas Allnutt's servants. In 1626 Barker, who was accused of leaving Allnutt without cause, told the General Court that he was obliged to serve Captain Ward for four years and that he had fulfilled his contractual obligation. The General Court's justices decided that Barker, like Ward's other servants, would be freed if he posted a bond (VI&A 110).

William Barker: William Barker, a mariner, came to Virginia sometime prior to January 1626 and had some business dealings with Lady Temperance Yeardley. Over the years he appeared in court, often testifying about maritime matters. By 1634 Barker had come into possession of Powle-Brooke, a plantation in Charles City (later, Prince George)

County, and a year later he joined two merchants in patenting the acreage that became known as Merchants Hope. Shortly thereafter he patented some adjacent acreage, which he added to the Merchants Hope grant. Barker frequently took shipments of tobacco to England and returned with manufactured goods. His mercantile activities most likely prompted him to purchase a waterfront lot in urban Jamestown in 1638, presumably because it was advantageous to have a base of operations in what was then the colony's sole port of entry. In 1645–1646 Barker served as a burgess for Charles City County, and in 1654 he purchased 150 acres of land on the lower side of the James River at "Smith's Fort," the Surry County plantation that originally belonged to Pocahontas's son, Thomas Rolfe. In 1656 Barker identified himself as commander of the *William* of London when testifying before Northumberland County's justices. Two years later, when he authorized someone to serve as his attorney in Virginia, he indicated that he was from Ratcliffe, in Middlesex County, England. Barker eventually seems to have begun using Northumberland County as his home base, for in 1656 he was authorized to accept its "castle duties" or the gunpowder that incoming ships were obliged to pay to their port of entry. A suit against Barker, undertaken in 1657, suggests that he was importing and selling indentured servants in Northumberland County. A case that was tried by Northumberland's justices in January 1682 implies that Alexander Pattison was then his business partner (VI&A 112; LEO 24; Northumberland County Wills, Inventories &c. 1652–1658:94, 106; Order Book 1652–1665:95, 123; 1678–1698:118; PB 1:320–321, 475, 609, 622, 645, 654).

Henry Barker: In February 1624 Henry Barker was living in urban Jamestown in Captain William Holmes' household (VI&A 111).

Stephen Barker: Stephen Barker arrived in Jamestown in 1622 and in 1625 was living at Martin's Hundred with his partner, Humphrey Walden. By 1629 Barker had moved to the Neck O'Land behind Jamestown Island. While residing there he witnessed Abraham Porter's nuncupative will and agreed to allow Edward Wigg to marry his maidservant, if the prospective bridegroom reimbursed him for the woman's transportation costs. Barker was still living in Virginia in May 1634 (VI&A 111).

John Barnard: In January 1627 the General Court acknowledged that Captain John Harvey of urban Jamestown owed money to

John Barnard for his services (VI&A 113). Throughout the years Harvey was in the colony, he demonstrated a prolonged interest in industrial activities. Therefore, Barnard probably was an artisan or skilled worker.

William Barnard (Bernard): William Barnard came to Virginia in 1622 as a free man, and during the mid-1620s he was residing at Basses Choice. Barnard, who became a successful planter and continued to reside in Warresqueak or Isle of Wight County, was named to the Council of State in 1641, and on August 10, 1642, he patented 1,200 acres of land at the head of Lawne's Creek. He eventually moved to Nansemond County and died in Virginia on March 31, 1665 (STAN 35; VI&A 113; PB 1:798).

Lancelot (Launcelott) Barnes: Lancelot Barnes, who came to Virginia sometime prior to 1628, was associated with the corporation of Elizabeth City. In March 1630 he served as a burgess for the lower part of Elizabeth City. In February 1632 he patented a 100-acre tract acquired from Captain William Tucker, and a year later he obtained a 100-acre leasehold in the Indian Thicket, acreage that formerly was part of the Virginia Company's land in Elizabeth City. Barnes died sometime prior to May 30, 1634 (VI&A 113; LEO 9).

Richard Barnes: Richard Barnes, who criticized the colony's governor, was brutally punished and then banished from Jamestown Island, unarmed. Sometime prior to May 5, 1624, he sent a petition to Governor Francis Wyatt, pleading for mercy (VI&A 114).

Robert Barnes: In 1608 Robert Barnes, a gentleman, arrived in Jamestown in the 1st Supply of new colonists (VI&A 114).

John Barnett: In 1624 John Barnett was living on the Eastern Shore in Captain William Eppes's household, but by January 1625 he had moved to Jamestown, where he was a household head. Prior to October 13, 1627, he married Samuel Kennell's widow, who ran afoul of the law by disposing of her late husband's estate before satisfying his debt to Abraham Peirsey. The General Court decided that Barnett was not at fault (VI&A 114).

Thomas Barnett (Barnet, Barnitt): During the mid-1620s Thomas Barnett was a servant at Sir George Yeardley's plantation, Flowerdew Hundred, and resided in his household in urban Jamestown. In October 1626 Barnett testified before the General Court about a document that he had seen in England. In 1632 he served as a burgess for Stanley Hundred, where Yeardley had formerly owned property. In November 1636 the Rev. Thomas Butler of Elizabeth City named Barnett as overseer of his will and made a bequest to his wife, Mary. Barnett served as Captain Samuel Mathews' attorney in 1640 and represented Warwick County in the assembly in 1642 (LEO 11, 20; VI&A 115; MCGC 119, 470).

Dr. Philip Barraud: On October 28, 1798, Dr. Philip Barraud of Williamsburg, a physician, wrote a letter in which he described a visit to John Ambler II's home on Jamestown Island and his experience when traversing Ambler's slippery log-and-stone causeway (Barraud, October 28, 1798).

Thomas Barrett (Barret): In 1619 Thomas Barrett, a weaver, arrived in Jamestown on the *Bona Nova* and probably was a Company servant or tenant (VI&A 115).

William Barrett: In June 1648 William Barrett patented 700 acres on the east side of the Chickahominy River that included the old Warraney Indian town. His acreage probably was located on the west side of Diascund Creek's mouth, in what was then James City County but later became New Kent. Barrett represented James City County in the assembly sessions of 1645, 1646, and 1649. In 1638 and 1658 he testified about some hogsheads of tobacco that he had shipped to England (LEO 23, 25, 27; PB 2:141; SR 3499, 5725). William Barrett may have been the same individual who on February 16, 1624, was living at Flowerdew Hundred, in what is now Prince George County (VI&A 115).

Robert Barrington: In July 1628 Robert Barrington, who was appointed clerk of the assembly, patented 250 acres of land abutting Powhatan Swamp and the Back River. During 1629 and 1630 Barrington served as a burgess, representing Jamestown Island. In April 1641 Barrington was obliged to relinquish his 250-acre patent because it was determined that Governor John Harvey had wrongfully given him part of the Governor's Land, a publicly owned property. In exchange for clearing and developing the 250 acres, Barrington received a 500-acre parcel (VI&A 115; LEO 7, 9).

Richard Bartlett: In April 1625 Richard Bartlett of Warresqueak agreed to build a house for John Chew, a merchant. Chew owned a waterfront lot in urban Jamestown, some acreage at Hog Island, and a store in Warresqueak. It is unclear which property he was having developed (VI&A 116).

Edward Bartley (Bartlett?): In 1625 Edward Bartley served as a burgess for Hog Island. On July 5, 1627, Mrs. Jane Martiau delivered an inventory of Lieutenant Edward Bartley's estate. He may have been the man identified as Lieutenant Bartlett of Bermuda Hundred, who in 1619 agreed to accept the 11 Virginia Company men who came to Virginia with Captain Christopher Lawne (VI&A 116; LEO 6).

Thomas Barwick: In June 1622 the Company of Shipwrights outfitted Captain Thomas Barwick and 25 men and sent them to Virginia to build watercraft and settle in a community. Barwick and his crew decided to live on Jamestown Island, where they commenced building homes and reportedly built a few shallops. However, by December 1623 he and several others became ill and died. In July 1629 Barwick's widow, Elizabeth, asked Virginia's governor to see that his estate was inventoried and said that he had died six years earlier, around Christmas, that is, in January 1623 (VI&A 116).

Nathaniel Basse (Bass, Base): Nathaniel Basse came to Virginia sometime prior to November 1619 and established a plantation called Basses Choice in Warresqueak. He and his wife, the former Mary Jordan, produced at least seven children. During the March 1622 Indian attack, Basse's house was burned and several people were killed. In 1624 and 1625 Basse represented Basses Choice in the assembly, and in 1626 he and three other men were authorized to serve as justices in the community and were empowered to try all but capital offences. In 1627 Basse ransomed some English prisoners from the Nansemond Indians, against whom he led an offensive. In 1628 and 1629 he served as a burgess for Warresqueak (Isle of Wight) and in 1632 became a court commissioner. Finally, in February 1632 he was named to the Council of State. Two of Basse's sons, Edward and John, married Indian women, one of whom was the daughter of the Nansemond king (VI&A 117–118; LEO 5–8, 31).

* * *

William Bassett I: In 1665 Captain William Bassett, a militia officer and merchant, was among those hired to build a fort at Old Point Comfort. His wife, Bridget (Bridgett),

was the daughter of Miles and Anne (Ann) Taylor Cary. Bassett owned land on the Chickahominy River in James City County, acreage that he patented in 1638. By 1664 he had some property on the lower side of the Pamunkey River in New Kent, and he enlarged his holdings in 1669. He also invested in a 3,000-acre tract, sharing ownership with Philip Ludwell I. In March 1672 Mrs. Bridget Bassett, Captain Bassett's widow, asked the General Court to see that his estate remained intact until it could be determined whether she was to receive her dower third or a legacy under her late husband's will. She returned to court in November 1672, renounced her husband's will, and was given a dower share of his estate plus a living allowance for herself and their son, William II (Bruce, "Historical Notes and Queries," 456; PB 1:641; 5:161; 7:643; SR 10919; DOR 1:434; 3:295; MCGC 214, 234, 280, 286, 293, 317, 335, 488, 514).

William Bassett II: William Bassett II, the son of Captain William Bassett I and the former Bridget Cary, was born around 1670 and lived in Blisland Parish in eastern New Kent County, probably on some of the acreage he inherited from his late father. By 1688 William II had laid claim to 2,048 acres on the lower side of the Pamunkey River, establishing the plantation known as Eltham, which became the Bassett family seat. William Bassett II, first a lieutenant and then a colonel of the county militia, served as a burgess for New Kent County and attended the assembly sessions of 1693, 1695–1696, 1696–1697, 1698, 1699, and 1700–1702. In 1704 he paid quitrent on 1,500 acres of land in King William County and 4,100 acres of land in New Kent County, whereas his son, William III, paid taxes on 550 acres in New Kent. William Bassett II was married to Joanna, the daughter of Lewis Burwell II and his wife, Abigail. He became a member of the Council of State and served from 1702 to 1723. Bassett died on October 11, 1723, at Eltham (LEO xix, 52–54, 56, 58–60; DOR 1:433–434; 3:295, 300; SMITH 6; PB 1:641; 5:161; 6:248; 7:643; 8:419; 9:601; SR 384, 715, 729, 748, 1437, 1667, 3919, 10919).

* * *

Hastings Bateman: On July 31, 1622, Hastings Bateman set out for Virginia on the *James* and arrived in Jamestown on July 31, 1622. He probably was related to John Bateman, who came at the same time (VI&A 119).

John Bateman: John Bateman went to Virginia with merchant Richard Stephens on the *James* and arrived in Jamestown on July 31, 1622. He probably was a kinsman of Hastings Bateman, who came on the same vessel (VI&A 119).

Thomas Bates: On June 21, 1640, it was decided that Thomas Bates, an indentured servant belonging to William Beard, was to be whipped in Jamestown for committing adultery with Beard's wife, Margaret (MCGC 475).

John Bath (Buth, Booth?): John Bath, a leather-fellow, arrived in Jamestown on September 12, 1623. He became ill while staying in Richard Stephens' house in urban Jamestown and by February 16, 1624, was dead. In January 1625 one of Stephens' servants testified that Bath had made a written will bequeathing his estate to a woman in England, but upon further reflection he had asked another Stephens servant to destroy it (VI&A 119). Bath may have been a leather merchant or he may have had specialized knowledge of leather processing.

Henry Batt (Batte, Battes, Batts, Bats): When Henry Lound of Henrico County's Varina Parish made his will in 1678, he named the children of his daughter, Mary, and her husband, Henry Batt, as his reversionary heirs. Captain Henry Batt, who took an active role in governmental affairs in Charles City County, often was called upon to witness documents or inventory estates. In 1678 he became a county justice and also served as a tax collector for Appomattox Parish. In December 1679, while Batt was still a county justice, he rented a house at the falls of the Appomattox River for four months' occupancy by the rangers the assembly had placed there to keep watch over the frontier. In 1692 Henry Batt and James Thweatt of Bristol Parish in Charles City County disposed of a piece of land in Westover Parish. Batt witnessed legal documents in Henrico County in 1678, 1686, 1691, and 1695 and represented Charles City County in the assembly sessions held in 1685–1686, 1691–1692, and 1695–1696. He served on a jury appointed by the General Court in 1691 and in 1694 was censured for failing to initiate litigation against two men who allegedly had undertaken incestuous marriages. In April 1695 Henry Batt patented two tracts of land in Charles City County, within what became Prince George County. One, a 270-acre parcel, was on the lower side of the Appomattox River and the other was on Bailey's Creek and contained 700 acres. Batt left Virginia before the opening of the

second session of the 1695–1696 assembly. When he testified before an English court in 1695, he identified himself as a Virginia merchant and said that he had gone to the colony 45 years ago and had resided there for 40 years (LEO 48, 50, 54; Henrico County Wills, Deeds, Etc. 1677–1692:385; Will and Deed Book 1688–1697:203, 656; Court Orders 1678–1693:55; Charles City County Will and Deed Book 1692–1694:159–160; Order Book 1676–1679:254, 337–338, 340, 343, 350, 417; DOR 3:166–168; EJC I:204, 316; PB 8:411; SR 10094).

Michael Batt: During the mid-1620s Michael Batt, and his wife, Ellen (Ellin), were living on the Governor's Land, just west of Jamestown Island, and were Thomas Swinhowe's servants. On January 10, 1627, Michael received permission to move to the lower side of the James River. His wife, Ellen, was still alive in February 1629 and was named as one of Jamestown merchant Thomas Warnett's heirs. On September 20, 1643, Michael Batt patented an acre of land on Jamestown Island near the Back River. His acreage lay within the capital city's corporate limits (VI&A 120).

William Batt (Batte): In 1636 William and Henry Batt, who may have been kinsmen, served as witnesses when Edward Abbes, a Virginia colonist, made his will. By 1643 William Batt had begun investing in land in the Middle Peninsula, acquiring a 250-acre tract that bordered the North River and Mobjack Bay in what later became Gloucester County. Six years later he laid claim to 120 acres on Lower Chippokes Creek in Surry County and was living there in 1652–1653. In January 1653 he purchased a 275-acre plantation from Henry Banister. Batt, a successful planter, served as a burgess for Surry County in 1654–1655. In January 1656 he bought Captain William Powell's plantation on Lower Chippokes Creek and sold the Banister property to another man. Batt may have relocated, because he was an Elizabeth City County justice and sheriff in 1657, and in 1659 he began representing Elizabeth City in the assembly (LEO 32, 35; SR 3978; PB 1:901; 2:161; Surry County Deed Book 1 [1652–1663]:21, 28, 31, 91–92, 125, 128; CHAPMAN 151, 156).

John Battail (Battaile): John Battail was sworn in as one of Old Rappahannock County's two undersheriffs (deputies) in May 1684 and was responsible for the territory that lay on the south side of the Rappahannock River. By June 1687 he had married Catherine (Katherine), one of the late Robert Taliaferro I's daughters. It was then that Battail went to court to seek possession of her inheritance, which was in the hands of her guardian, Robert Taliaferro II. The justices decided to partition the assets that Catherine and her brother, Charles, stood to inherit. When John Battail appeared before the justices of Stafford County's monthly court in 1687, he sought to confirm the sale of a slave that his wife had inherited. During the 1680s his name appeared numerous times in Old Rappahannock County's court records, almost always in connection with debts he was trying to collect. In 1690 he was Old Rappahannock County's subsheriff, and in 1691 he purchased a town lot at Hobbes Hole, the community that became known as Tappahannock. When Essex County was formed in 1692 out of part of what had been Old Rappahannock County, Captain Battail commenced serving as one of the new jurisdiction's justices and held office for more than a decade. Within two years he became high sheriff. Battaile represented Essex County in the assembly sessions held in 1693 and 1696–1697. On October 26, 1694, he and Nicholas Meriwether's son and heir, Francis Meriwether of urban Jamestown, patented 1,091 acres in Gloucester County. In 1698 Battaile and his wife, Catherine, witnessed a deed whereby bride-to-be Susanna Goss transferred some of her personal property to her children. In September 1699 he purchased 500 acres in Richmond County but continued to live in Essex, where he was reappointed a justice in 1699. Simultaneously he sold some of his Essex acreage to a fellow justice, Thomas Gregson (LEO 52, 56; Stafford County Record Book 1686–1693:47–47a; Old Rappahannock County Order Book 1683–1686:27, 130; 1687–1692:27–28, 101, 152, 237; Essex County Order Book 1692–1695:13, 114, 154, 159, 174, 221, 240; 1695–1699:40–41, 87; Deeds and Wills 1692–1695:272, 351; 1695–1699:236, 344; 1699–1702:1, 44; Richmond County Deed Book 3 [1697–1704]:85; NUG II:395; PB 8:393).

[No First Name] Batters: Lieutenant Batters received land in the eastern end of Jamestown Island during Deputy Governor Samuel Argall's government, 1617–1618. Sometime prior to January 24, 1625, he sold his acreage to David Ellis (VI&A 120).

Thomas Batts: Sometime prior to November 24, 1674, Thomas Batts of Henrico County and Francis Kirkman, the James City County sheriff and a friend of Governor William Berkeley, patented 1,000 acres of escheat land on the south side of the Chickahominy River swamp. Because Batts and Kirkman failed to improve their property, it

escheated to the Crown (MCGC 394).

John Baugh: In 1635–1636 John Baugh, the late Mathew Smallwood's administrator, filed a suit against one of the decedent's creditors. In May 1638 he patented 250 acres in Henrico County, on the upper side of the Appomattox River, near Abraham Peirsey's property. In 1645 Baugh patented 100 acres in Bermuda Hundred and in 1650 claimed another 100-acre tract on the Appomattox. He served as a burgess for Henrico County in 1642 and 1645 (LEO 20, 23; PB 1:559; 2:27, 219; 6:427; SR 4890).

James Baughan (Boughan) II: James Baughan II inherited half of a 1,000-acre tract that his father, James I, and Thomas Harper had patented on the Piscataway Creek. Because the late James Baughan I died before the land had been partitioned, in January 1679 John II agreed to take that portion which abutted the creek's main swamp. In June 1684 Baughan became Old Rappahannock County's constable but was replaced a year later. He ran afoul of local officials in 1688 because his taxes were in arrears. He may have salvaged his reputation in 1691 when he reported a couple of people who had served alcoholic beverages in their homes, contrary to a September 1668 act of the assembly. In 1695 he was living on the plantation at Piscataway that he had inherited from his father. By that time the property was in the newly formed Essex County. Baughan served as an attorney numerous times, and in 1697 his brother, John, designated him the executor of his estate. James Baughan II became a county justice in 1697 and represented Essex County in the assembly sessions held in 1698 and 1699. In 1699 he sold some of his land to burgess and justice Thomas Gregson. By 1700 Baughan had become Essex County's sheriff. When testifying in court in October 1700, he said that he was age 45 or thereabouts (LEO 58–59; Old Rappahannock County Deeds and Wills 1677–1682:196–197; Order Book 1683–1686:30, 96; 1687–1692:102, 194; Essex County Order Book 1692–1695:15, 188; 1695–1699:138, 152, 163; 1699–1702:1, 12, 27, 41, 73; Deeds and Wills 1692–1695:390; 1695–1699:86–87, 154, 172; 1699–1702:1, 9–10, 36, 63).

Mary Bawdreye: Mary Bawdreye died in Jamestown sometime after April 1623 but before February 16, 1624 (VI&A 121).

John Baylor: According to nineteenth-century historian Bishop William Meade, John Baylor was born in England in 1650 and came to Gloucester County with his elderly father. The younger Baylor became actively engaged in transatlantic trade, owned several ships, and kept stores in Gloucester, King and Queen, and New Kent counties. He represented Gloucester County in the assembly in 1692–1693, an indication that he owned land in the county or perhaps was married to someone who did. Baylor married Lucy Todd O'Brien of New Kent County in 1698. He was identified as a resident of Gloucester County when he and two other men were authorized to act as the agents of Robert Bristow, a London merchant. In October 1703 Baylor patented 2,717 acres that were located in King and Queen and Essex counties on the Mattaponi River and Piscattaway (Piscataway) Creek. A year later all of the property was said to be in Essex County. Baylor's name appeared in Essex County records in 1702 when one of his servants, a runaway, was captured, but Baylor himself was attributed to Gloucester County. In 1704 he paid quitrent on 3,000 acres in King and Queen County, where he and Colonel James Taylor acquired 2,763 acres in May 1706. In 1715 Baylor was credited with 1,330 acres in King and Queen County, land that was adjacent to that of James Taylor and Colonel John Walker. Finally, in July 1719 he patented 400 acres in King William County. An inventory of Baylor's estate, taken shortly after his death, included personal property worth an estimated £6,500 (LEO 52; STAN 88; PB 9:641, 721; 10:250, 427; SMITH 7; Essex County Deeds, Wills C [1699–1702]:122; Lancaster County Deeds II [1694–1702]:441; MEADE I:464).

Richard Baynes: On February 24, 1622, Richard Baynes, who was in his mid-30s and was a servant in Dr. John Pott's household in urban Jamestown, was summoned to court and accused of being involved in killing a calf that belonged to someone else (VI&A 121).

Gabriel Beadle: In 1608 Gabriel Beadle, a gentleman and Virginia Company investor, reached Jamestown in the 2nd Supply of new settlers. According to Captain John Smith, he assisted in felling trees and making clapboard (VI&A 121).

John Beadle: John Beadle, a gentleman and Virginia Company investor, arrived in Jamestown in 1608 in the 2nd Supply of new colonists (VI&A 121).

George Beale: George Beale, a blacksmith from Staffordshire, England, arrived in Jamestown in 1619 on the *Bona Nova*, a vessel that brought a large group of Virginia

Company servants and tenants to the colony (VI&A 121).

Thomas Beale: Thomas Beale, who was born in England, was named to the Council of State in 1662. By 1668 he and another man had invested in 1,500 acres in the Northern Neck. In May 1671 he was identified as a lieutenant colonel when he and his wife, Alice, initiated a suit against Thomas and Jane Wardley, a married couple. At issue were some disparaging remarks that Mrs. Wardley reportedly made about the Beales. The General Court's justices ordered her to appear at the next meeting of York County's court to ask for the Beales' forgiveness; she refused to comply and twice was summoned to appear before the General Court. In October 1671 Thomas Beale asked the General Court to order a survey of Colonel Moore Fauntleroy's orphans' land because he hoped to secure a patent for some adjacent acreage. A few months later Robert Beverley I sued Beale, who was then serving as security for Elizabeth Newell, her late husband's administratrix. By June 1675 Colonel Beale and fellow councilor James Bray I were involved in a dispute that was subject to arbitration by two of their peers; the matter was supposed to be resolved to Bray's satisfaction. On February 10, 1677, Governor William Berkeley issued a proclamation in which he named those who were exempt from the king's pardon on account of their role in Bacon's Rebellion, and one of those listed was council member Thomas Beale (NEVILLE 61; STAN 38; LEO xix; MCGC 207, 261–262, 267, 280, 291, 326–327, 338, 415, 452; PB 6:176; SR 660, 4201, 11483). Beale seems to have escaped punishment.

William Beard: In June 1635, when William Beard patented some land in Pasbehay, adjacent to his leasehold in the Governor's Land, he used the headright of his late wife, Joan (Joane). Later, Beard was obliged to surrender his newly acquired acreage because it was found to lie within the boundaries of the Governor's Land, which was publicly owned property. Although Beard made his will in December 1636, he survived for another decade. He made bequests to several people, including his "wicked wife Margaret," whom he termed a whore and ordered to vacate their house within three months of his death. The widowed Margaret Beard ran afoul of the law in July 1640, for she became pregnant. She also failed to report some runaway servants and on October 13, 1640, received a whipping in Jamestown (VI&A 122).

Jacob (Job) Beazley (Beasly, Beasley, Beaslie, Bearly): When George Fawdon and Mrs. Ann Smith signed a marriage contract in 1654, he gave his bride-to-be 1,500 acres on the James River in Isle of Wight's Upper Parish, adjacent to "Job Beazlies plantation." Jacob Beazley, who served as a burgess for Isle of Wight County in 1656, patented 600 acres on the second swamp of the Blackwater River, and his headright was used by another patentee in 1655 (LEO 33; Isle of Wight County Deeds, Wills & Guardian Accounts Book A:92; PB 3:348, 385).

Theophilus Beaston (Beastone, Beriston, Berristone, Boriston): Theophilus Beaston, an ancient planter, was an indentured servant in Sir George Yeardley's household at Flowerdew Hundred in February 1624. He moved briefly to Shirley Hundred, but by January 1625 was residing with Yeardley in urban Jamestown. In May 1625 Theophilus Beaston was credited with 100 acres of land in Charles City. He died prior to February 9, 1633, having bequeathed some tobacco to Theophilus Stone, an orphan (VI&A 122).

Thomas Beckett (Leckett?): In November 1693 Thomas Beckett sought compensation from the assembly for some work he had done on the colony's statehouse. He reportedly had bricked up a chimney, done some whitewashing, and excavated a vault beneath the powder house. The burgesses were reluctant to pay him for all of his work because some of it was done without their authorization. Beckett may have been the man identified as Thomas Leckett, who during 1695 was renting a Jamestown lot from Francis Meriwether. In 1670 a man named Thomas Beckett, who was then in England, testified in a court case involving the *Black Eagle*, a unsafe ship that had made a number of voyages to Virginia. He indicated that he was age 44 and from Stepney (LJC 206–207; AMB 56; SR 4024, 11040).

Robert Beckinham (Beckingham): On November 17, 1674, Richard James I, a Jamestown merchant, sued Robert Beckinham in the General Court for reasons that are unclear. By that date Beckinham had married Raleigh Travers I's widow, Elizabeth (MCGC 393; Stanard, "Travis Family," 246).

Robert Beheathland (Behethlem): Robert Beheathland, a gentleman, came to Virginia in 1607 in the first group of Jamestown colonists. In 1620 Captain Beheathland identified himself as one of Lord Delaware's associates when signing a petition in England asking for Sir George Yeardley's removal as governor. Beheathland, who by 1627 was dead, was survived by his widow, Mary, an ancient planter, and his two daughters, Mary and Dorothy, who were from a previous marriage. Mrs. Mary Beheathland, upon being widowed, married Thomas Flint (Flynt) of Elizabeth City and in 1628 complained to the governor about Flint's inappropriate behavior with her stepdaughter Dorothy. By 1638 Dorothy Beheathland had wed Randall Crew. Her sister, Mary Beheathland, married Captain Thomas Bernard (VI&A 124; WAT 100; DOR 1:218–219; SR 4106).

Ann Behoute: Ann Behoute, one of Gabriel Holland's servants, came to Virginia in 1625 and resided in his house on Jamestown Island. She died, and in January 1627 Holland, as a court-appointed administrator, presented an inventory of her goods (VI&A 124).

Richard Belfield: Richard Belfield, a goldsmith, arrived in Jamestown in 1608 in the 1st Supply of new colonists (VI&A 124).

Henry Bell: Henry Bell, a tradesman, came to Virginia in 1608 in the 2nd Supply of new colonists and would have lived in Jamestown (VI&A 124).

John Bell (Bel): John Bell, a husbandman, arrived in Jamestown in 1619. On March 22, 1622, when the Indians attacked William Farrar I's house on the Appomattox River, Bell, an indentured servant in the employ of John England, was killed (VI&A 124).

Richard Bell: Sometime prior to June 27, 1635, Richard Bell purchased 200 acres of James City County land from Alexander Stonar of Jamestown Island (VI&A 125).

Ann Belson: In October 1640 Ann Belson, an indentured servant who had served Theodore Moses since 1633, asked to be freed from her remaining year of service. She claimed that Moses had failed to teach her to read and give her instruction in religion and had put her to work at hard labor. The General Court, after hearing two witnesses' testimony, decided to free Belson and let her have custody of her inheritance, which Moses had been keeping (VI&A 125).

Ben: When Richard Ambler made his will on January 23, 1765, he mentioned a carpenter known as "Old Ben." On February 15, 1768, when an inventory was made of Ambler's slaves on Jamestown Island and his leasehold in the Governor's Land, an adult male slave named Ben was listed and identified as a carpenter. In 1769 Old Ben, the carpenter, was attributed to the estate of Richard Ambler's son, Edward Ambler I, and was living on Jamestown Island (York County Wills and Inventories 21:378–382, 386–391; AMB-E).

Ben: On February 15, 1768, when an inventory was made of the late Richard Ambler's slaves on Jamestown Island and his leasehold in the Governor's Land, an adult male slave named Ben was listed. He may have been the man identified as "Young Ben," a carpenter who was living on Jamestown Island in 1769 and attributed to Edward Ambler I's estate (York County Wills and Inventories 21:386–391; AMB-E).

Ben: On February 15, 1768, when an inventory was made of the late Richard Ambler's slaves on Jamestown Island and his leasehold in the Governor's Land, an adult male slave named Ben was listed. In 1769 he may have been the individual identified as Ben who was then living on Jamestown Island and was part of Edward Ambler I's estate. (York County Wills and Inventories 21:386–391; AMB-E). This man named Ben should not be confused with the carpenters known as "Old Ben" and "Young Ben."

Ben: In 1769 a child named Ben was living on the Governor's Land with his mother, an enslaved woman named Lucy. Both were attributed to the late Edward Ambler I's estate (AMB-E).

James Benn (Ben) I: James Benn I, who served as an Isle of Wight County burgess during the 1690s, was the son of cooper Christopher Benn and his wife, Anne. In 1640 Christopher received 50 acres at the head of Pagan Creek from his landlord, Captain John Upton, and in 1657 he bought some additional acreage from Thomas Harris of Chippokes in Surry County. Christopher Benn died sometime prior to September 1670 when John Vicars patented 200 acres of land in Isle of Wight County on behalf of his orphan, James Benn I. The decedent's acreage would have escheated to the Crown had not Vicars intervened. When James Benn I attained his majority, he occasionally performed duties for the local court, and by 1684 he had become a county justice. He went on to become a burgess and represented Isle of Wight County in the assembly sessions held in 1691–1692 and 1696–1697. On one occasion in 1690 he served as the agent of Jamestown jailer and tavern-keeper Henry Gawler. When Captain James Benn I made his will on February 6, 1696, he divided his land among his sons James II, Ar-

thur, and George, and made bequests to his wife and executrix, Anne, and to his daughters, Mary, Sarah, Jeane, and Anne. He also left a remembrance to Mary Knight. Benn died prior to April 9, 1697, when his will was proved. By May 5th his estate had been appraised. The decedent was survived by his son and heir, George Benn (LEO 50, 56; Isle of Wight County Will and Deed Book 1 [1688–1704]:35, 63, 110, 126, 213, 361; 2:381–382; PB 6:307; BODIE 516, 597, 608).

* * *

Edward Bennett: Edward Bennett, a London merchant with extensive trading interests in the Netherlands and Virginia, was among those who in 1621 founded the plantation called Bennett's Welcome or Warresqueak. Bennett seems to have placed his land in the hands of tenants, who paid their rent with money and labor. He had a land dispute with Jamestown merchant Ralph Hamor and ultimately made a claim against Hamor's estate. He also had some business dealings with Sir George Yeardley. Edward Bennett, a burgess in 1628, went to England to seek a more favorable tobacco contract from the king. When he testified in court in August 1635, he said that he was age 35. He died in England sometime prior to June 3, 1651, when his daughter Mary was given administration of his estate. In 1658 Mary Bennett, who married Thomas Bland, and her sister, Silvestra, who married Nicholas Hill, inherited equal shares of their late father's 1,500 acres in Isle of Wight County, Virginia (VI&A 125; LEO 7; DOR 1:228–229).

Richard Bennett I: Sometime prior to March 1628 Richard Bennett I, a nephew of British merchant Edward Bennett, came to Virginia with his first cousin, Robert. After settling in Warresqueak, Richard Bennett I commenced serving as a burgess in 1629 and as a justice of the Warresqueak (later, Isle of Wight County) court. In time, Bennett became a very successful merchant and planter and began patenting vast tracts of land along the Nansemond and Elizabeth rivers. He continued to deal with the family-owned mercantile group with which he was associated, and he had business dealings with Jamestown merchant George Menefie, whose will he oversaw in 1645. Bennett was named to the Council of State in 1639 and served until 1651. A land transaction that occurred in 1692 reveals that in 1642 Bennett patented a 2,000-acre tract in what eventually became Essex County. Bennett, whose Puritan beliefs set him apart from those of the colony's officially sanctioned religious denomination, the Church of England, moved to Maryland in 1648 and settled on the Severn River in Anne Arundel County. In September 1651 he was one of three commissioners the government of the Commonwealth of England sent to Virginia and Maryland to compel both colonies to submit to the Commonwealth's laws. After Sir William Berkeley surrendered to the Parliamentary fleet, Bennett was elected Virginia's governor and served from April 1652 to March 1655. It was then that Berkeley sold Bennett the westernmost of the three brick row houses he had built in urban Jamestown in the western end of Jamestown Island. Around 1662 Richard Bennett I gave his daughter, Anna (Anne), and her husband, Theodorick Bland of Westover, his row house in Jamestown. Earlier on, Bennett had disposed of the 24-acre Glasshouse tract at the entrance to Jamestown Island. After the monarchy was restored, Richard Bennett I was appointed to Virginia's Council of State, serving from 1665 through 1667. He also held the rank of major-general from 1662 to 1672. Like many of his contemporaries, he speculated in real estate. Although he lived on a plantation on the Nansemond River, he bought and sold land in the Northern Neck and the Middle Peninsula. In 1658 he conveyed a large tract at Nimcock to John Carter I. Bennett was sympathetic to the Quaker denomination (the Society of Friends), whose religious convictions were compatible with his own Puritan persuasions, but when he made his will, he bequeathed 300 acres to his parish in Nansemond County, stipulating that the acreage be used toward the relief of the poor. William Edmundson, Quaker missionary George Fox's traveling companion, described Bennett as "a solid, wise man [who] received the truth and died in the same." When Richard Bennett prepared his will on March 15, 1674, he bequeathed money to several people, including his daughter, Anna, and cousin, Sylvester Hill, but he bequeathed the bulk of his landholdings to Richard Bennett III, his grandson. Richard Bennett I died within a year, and his will was proved in Nansemond County's monthly court on April 12, 1675 (VI&A 126; LEO 8; Old Rappahannock County Deeds and Wills 1656–1664:33; Essex County Deeds and Wills 1692–1695:115–118; MCGC 503).

Robert Bennett: The Virginia Company authorized Robert Bennett to trade in Virginia, and by June 1623 he was living at Bennett's Welcome in Warresqueak. He ran afoul of Virginia law when he sold Sir George Yeardley some wine, contrary to the

trading restrictions on imported goods. Robert Bennett died sometime prior to November 20, 1623, probably on Jamestown Island. Jamestown merchant John Chew was named his administrator, probably because he was part of the Bennett family's trading network (VI&A 127).

* * *

Philip Bennett: In December 1643 Philip Bennett patented 515 acres of land on Bennett's Creek in Lower Norfolk County. He served as a burgess for Lower Norfolk and attended the assembly sessions of 1645 and 1645–1646. He added to his landholdings on Bennett's Creek in 1648, acquiring an aggregate of 1,430 acres. When John Watkins made his will in February 1648, he nominated his friends Philip Bennett and Edward Lloyd as the overseers of his estate (LEO 23–24; Lower Norfolk County Book B:128; PB 1:932; 2:60, 148).

Robert Bennett: On February 16, 1624, Robert Bennett reportedly was residing on Jamestown Island in Ensign William Spence's household (VI&A 127).

Thomas Bennett: In September 1632 Thomas Bennett served as a burgess for Mulberry Island, in what was then the corporation of Elizabeth City but later became Warwick County. He may have been the individual whose headright was used by Richard Bennett in 1636 (VI&A 129; LEO 11; NUG I:45).

William Bennett: William Bennett, a boatbuilder, came to Virginia sometime prior to March 23, 1624, and obtained household items from Jamestown merchant John Chew. In December 1627, Bennett was residing in the home of Dr. John Pott in urban Jamestown. In exchange for the medical treatment, room, and board he received, he agreed to make Pott a boat like the one he had fabricated for Edward Sharples (VI&A 129).

William Bennett: William Bennett, who came to Virginia on the *Gift of God*, died in Jamestown sometime after April 1623 but before February 16, 1624 (VI&A 129).

William Bentley (Bently, Bentlie): William Bentley, a tailor, came to Virginia in 1624 as a free man. He patented 50 acres of land in Elizabeth City at Blunt Point shortly after his arrival, but he lived in the household headed by Pharaoh Flinton. When a list of patented land was sent back to England in May 1625, Bentley was credited with his 50 acres at Blunt Point. In 1629 he ran afoul of the law when he fought with a neighbor, who then died. Although Bentley was indicted and a jury found him guilty of manslaughter, he received benefit of clergy and was freed. In October 1629 Bentley was elected a burgess for Nutmeg Quarter. On January 27, 1652, he was sued by John Bland, who was trying to recover a debt from the late John King's estate. Bentley, as King's executor, denied any knowledge of an agreement the decedent had made to purchase tobacco from France and Spain (VI&A 129; LEO 8; SR 12548).

John Berkeley: John Berkeley, his son, Maurice, and 20 others went to Virginia in 1621 to build an ironworks for the Virginia Company's investors. Company officials agreed to provide the Berkeleys and some of their servants with free transportation and provisions. They also instructed Governor Francis Wyatt to give land to John Berkeley and to appoint him to the Council of State. However, on March 22, 1622, when the Indians attacked the Falling Creek ironworks, 22 people (including John Berkeley) were killed (VI&A 130; STAN 30; LEO xix).

* * *

Sir William Berkeley: William, the son of Sir Maurice Berkeley of Bruton, in Somerset, England, was the brother of Sir John Berkeley and belonged to a family that for several centuries enjoyed great influence at the English court. He was a graduate of Oxford University and Merton College and while he was young held a seat on the Privy Council. A skilled playwright and a polished courtier, he was knighted by King Charles I on July 27, 1639, and was appointed a commissioner of Canadian affairs. By March 8, 1642, Sir William Berkeley had arrived in Virginia as governor. In June the assembly presented him with some property in urban Jamestown: two houses and an orchard that probably had belonged to Sir John Harvey, his debt-ridden predecessor in office, who had lost "all that capital, messuage or tenement now used for a court house." Sometime prior to July 1644, Governor Berkeley purchased a Jamestown lot containing a well-known brick house that Richard Kemp had built. By 1645 Berkeley had begun building a brick row house in urban Jamestown, in the western end of the island. The March 1655 deeds whereby he later disposed of his row house reveal that at least two of its three units had been used as an interim statehouse.

Governor Berkeley earned the admiration of the people by capturing Opechancanough, the paramount chief credited with leading the 1644 Indian attack. At the onset of the English civil war, when the salary of Virginia's royal governor was suspended, the burgesses passed legislation giving Berkeley income from locally generated taxes on tobacco, wheat, and other agricultural commodities. On June 4, 1643, he received a patent for 984 acres called Green Spring, and by February 27, 1645, he had begun building a brick manor house on the property. Construction at Green Spring coincided with his building a brick house in Jamestown, a structure that perhaps replaced the dwelling erected by former governor John Harvey. On June 6, 1646, the Council of State reassigned Berkeley the Green Spring acreage he had received in 1643, noting that when his property was surveyed it was found to contain 1,090 acres, not 984. By 1649 Berkeley had moved into his residence at Green Spring, which became his country estate, but it is likely that he maintained some accommodations in Jamestown. Governor William Berkeley's first wife, whose identity is uncertain, was residing in Virginia in May 1650, when she received a letter from Virginia Ferrar. A letter written by the governor's brother, Sir John Berkeley, suggests that the Berkeley couple wed sometime between October 25, 1649, and May 9, 1650. Governor Berkeley, like some of his predecessors, strongly promoted the development of staple commodities. He set about enlarging his landholdings in the Green Spring neighborhood, in 1651 acquiring 5,062 acres that lay between the head of Powhatan Swamp and Jones Creek. In October 1652 he added another 1,000 acres.

After the civil war in England came to an end, a parliamentary fleet set sail for Virginia to assert its authority over a colony known as a royalist stronghold. In April 1652 Berkeley, who had governed Virginia for a decade, was obliged to surrender the colony, relinquish his office, and sign a document acknowledging Virginians' retention of their rights as citizens of the Commonwealth of England. Although the articles of surrender stated that its terms had not been imposed by force, the colonists had to relinquish all publicly owned arms and ammunition. Virginia's charter and the legality of its land patents were to be upheld. Berkeley and his councilors were told to subscribe to the articles of surrender or leave the colony within a year. Although Berkeley decided to stay on in the colony, in 1655 he elected to dispose of his three-bay brick row house in Jamestown. He then retired to Green Spring, where he channeled his energies into agricultural and industrial experimentation.

When Commonwealth Governor Samuel Mathews died, Sir William Berkeley was elected governor and was authorized to see that a statehouse was built. Funds were to be raised by means of private subscriptions rather than through a public levy. Official records suggest that Berkeley took no immediate action, perhaps because he was awaiting instructions from the recently restored king. In 1662 the Privy Council instructed Berkeley to see that towns were built on each of the colony's rivers, commencing with the James. He was told to set a good example by building some houses there himself and to ask his councilors to follow suit. Since the burgesses preferred to enhance Jamestown's development rather than to begin a new town, in December 1662 they enacted legislation specifying that 32 brick houses were to be built in the capital city. Each of Virginia's 17 counties was responsible for building a brick house, and private individuals were encouraged to do so as well. Fragmentary assembly minutes for September 16, 1663, suggest that by that date little or no progress had been made toward building a statehouse. A committee of burgesses was delegated to negotiate with the governor about construction of a statehouse. Whether Berkeley sold part of his urban property to the government or chose to convert an existing building into a statehouse is open to conjecture.

In 1662 Governor William Berkeley, who was then in England, presented an address to the Privy Council, and in 1663 he published his text in a promotional pamphlet, "A Discourse and View of Virginia." He promoted the exploitation of the colony's natural resources and asked that skilled workers and tools be sent to Virginia. During the late 1660s he was ordered to place the colony in a defensive posture, as a Dutch attack was expected. He purchased three contiguous row house units, which he disposed of in 1670, around the time he wed Frances Culpeper Stephens, a wealthy and genteel widow nearly half his age. In 1672 Berkeley bought another row house unit, one that Thomas Ludwell and Thomas Stegg II had built around 1667. In 1674 the assembly acknowledged the validity of Berkeley's title to Green Spring, noting that he had spent a great sum of money developing his land. They may have been referring to a building campaign that probably followed on the heels of Berkeley's marriage to Lady Frances.

During the mid-1670s, when Virginians became embroiled in the popular uprising that became known as Bacon's Rebellion,

Governor Berkeley found himself facing a large band of men led by his young cousin, Nathaniel Bacon. During the conflict Berkeley had to withdraw for the safety of Arlington, Colonel John Custis II's house on the Eastern Shore. While Berkeley was gone, Bacon and his followers put Jamestown to the torch. After the rebel leader became mortally ill, Berkeley's supporters set about quelling the uprising and brought the accused perpetrators before a military tribunal. Berkeley informed the king's commissioners that Bacon had burned five of his houses, the church, and twenty houses that belonged to other gentlemen. In early 1677 Governor William Berkeley was relieved of his duties and recalled to England. He prepared his will on March 20, 1677, naming his widow as his principal beneficiary, and by November 1678 was dead. He was buried in England (HEN I:267, 363–368, 407, 427–428; II:13, 38, 172–176, 204–205, 552, 560; MCGC 480, 484, 494, 497–498, 503, 514–515, 521; AMB 4, 10, 24; Clarendon MS 24 f 51; 82 ff 275–276; JHB 1619–1660:96–97, 104; 1660–1693:8, 13, 23, 25–26; FOR I:9:10;10:4; II:8:14; III:10:50; NUG I:160, 173, 340, 390, 415; PB 4:101–102; SAIN 10:167–168; CO 1/19 ff 200–203; 1/41 ff 28, 32ro; 5/1354 ff 265, 273–274; 5/1355 f 230; WASH 84–91; Stanard, "Historical and Genealogical Notes and Queries," 200; Bruce, "Bacon's Rebellion," 170–174; FER 1168; BILLINGS 617–622).

Frances Culpeper (Culpepper) Stephens Berkeley (Mrs. Samuel Stephens, Mrs. William Berkeley, Mrs. Philip Ludwell I): Frances Culpeper, who was baptized on May 27, 1634, at Hollingbourne, Kent, England, was the cousin of Sir Thomas Culpeper and Samuel Filmer. She was said to be intelligent, high-spirited, and shrewd. She married Samuel Stephens, the governor of Albemarle, who on January 1, 1653, signed a marriage contract agreeing to give her his Warwick County plantation, Boldrup, if he died before they produced heirs. Stephens died sometime prior to March 1670, and in June 1670 the widowed Frances, who was 36 years old at the time, married Governor William Berkeley, who was then 64 and residing at Green Spring plantation. They had signed a premarital agreement whereby Sir William would provide her with a life estate of £600 in annual income. On April 20, 1671, Lady Frances and Sir William Berkeley conveyed her plantation, Boldrup, to Colonel William Cole, noting that she had inherited the property from her late husband, Samuel Stephens. This infusion of wealth, when combined with the proceeds of Sir William's sale of three brick row houses in

Jamestown, provided the Berkeleys with the funds they needed to significantly enhance the development of Green Spring.

Throughout Bacon's Rebellion, Lady Frances Berkeley was fiercely loyal to Sir William, and when he died in England in 1677 he left her almost all of his estate. Therefore, she would have inherited Green Spring plantation along with a row house unit he still owned in urban Jamestown, property that he purchased from Thomas Ludwell on March 17, 1672. After the popular uprising was quelled, Lady Frances was sued by Sarah Drummond, whose late husband had been executed by Governor Berkeley for his role in Bacon's Rebellion. Mrs. Drummond claimed that Lady Frances had unlawfully detained some of the late William Drummond I's goods. Lady Frances Berkeley refurbished the Green Spring mansion soon after the rebellion subsided and planned to rent the property to Virginia's future governors. She informed a friend that she hoped the rental income would provide her with enough money to live comfortably in England. In October 1680, three years after Sir William Berkeley's death, Lady Frances married Philip Ludwell I, one of her late husband's staunchest supporters, and moved into his home at Rich Neck, near Middle Plantation (later, Williamsburg). Despite her remarriage she continued to identify herself as Lady Frances Berkeley. Although she became pregnant, she produced no living children. Therefore, when she died in 1691 her real and personal estate descended to her husband, Philip Ludwell I, and his heir, a son by his marriage to Lucy Higginson Burwell (CO 1/42 ff 288, 291; MCGC 514–515, 534; NUG II:48; HEN II:319–325, 558–560; DOR 3:105, 248; Stanard, "Proprietors of the Northern Neck," 352; SHEP 453–454; MORTON 238; Bruce, "Title to Green Spring," 356; CARSON 6; EEAC 22).

* * *

Thomas Bernard (Barnard): Thomas Bernard patented 500 acres in August 1637, land that was on Back Creek in what was then Warwick River (later, Warwick) County. In 1638 officials in England ordered Virginia's governor to return Colonel Samuel Mathews' estate to Thomas Bernard and Humphrey Lloyd. Bernard, who had married Robert Beheathland's daughter Mary, laid claim to 1,050 acres at the mouth of Back Creek in December 1641. Then, in September 1645 he received a patent for 500 acres of land on the south side of the Warwick River; it was adjacent to the late Thomas Flint's land on which Bernard's

house was located. Thomas Bernard served as a burgess for Warwick County in the assembly sessions of 1640, 1644, 1645, and 1645–1646 and during the late 1640s was county sheriff. He died prior to May 14, 1651, when his estate was inventoried, and the appraisal was endorsed by his widow, Mary. When London merchant Robert Nicholson prepared his will on November 10, 1651, he made bequests to Thomas Bernard's widow, Mary, and her daughters. One daughter, Beheathland Bernard, was given some expensive jewelry (LEO 18, 22–24; PB 1:464, 761; 2:44; SR 4106, 4544; WAT 100; DOR 1:218–219; DUNN 24, 164, 175–176).

Mr. Bernardo: Mr. Bernardo, an Italian artisan, was outfitted by the Virginia Company and sent to Virginia to produce glass that could be sold profitably. On February 16, 1624, he and his wife were living at Glasshouse Point, where a glass furnace had been built. By February 4, 1625, the Bernardo couple and their child had moved to the Treasurer's Plantation on the lower side of the James River. Later in the year Mr. Bernardo received a pass to go to England but was obliged to post a bond with the glassworks' investors. His wife, Peirce, stayed on in Virginia. In October 1627 she testified that she had formerly lived with Captain William Norton, late overseer of the glassworks, and that he had not paid Thomas Wilson for his work (VI&A 131).

Sir John Berry: Sir John Berry, commander of the *Bristol* and the fleet of ships that brought 1,000 men to Virginia to suppress Bacon's Rebellion, arrived in Virginia in January 1677. He was one of three special commissioners whom King Charles II sent to the colony to investigate the underlying causes of the popular uprising. One of the commissioners' principal goals was to forge a peace agreement with the neighboring Indians, that is, native groups who lived in or near the Tidewater region. On February 27, 1677, the king's commissioners urged assembly members to act quickly in securing a treaty with the natives. They proffered that the Indians, if loyal allies of the Virginia government, would provide outlying settlers with the best protection against the stronger, more hostile tribes that lived in the interior of the continent. They also pointed out that on-going conflict with the natives deprived the colony of their trade and labor, and they reminded the burgesses that it was Governor Berkeley who first conquered the Indians and made peace with them. On May 29, 1677, the Treaty of Middle Plantation was signed in a ceremony that was witnessed by

Sir John Berry, Colonel Francis Morrison (Moryson), and members of the Council of State. Afterward, the commissioners recounted how they had complied with the king's instructions after Sir William Berkeley left the colony. Sir John Berry eventually was accused of seizing the executed rebel William Drummond I's wine and brandy, along with some of his other goods. In November 1677 Berry was ordered to return everything to Mrs. Sarah Drummond except the beverages (CO 5/1355 ff 83, 88, 196; NEVILLE 9, 12, 74, 112, 200).

Christopher Best: On April 1, 1623, Christopher Best, a surgeon and indentured servant then in Virginia, sent a letter to his master, John Woodall. Best, who in February 1624 was living in urban Jamestown in John Pountis's household, practiced his profession in the capital city and rendered assistance to several Jamestown residents. During 1625 the General Court mentioned some of the people indebted to Best, who apparently died prior to September 19, 1625, when the court's justices discussed the disposition of some recently arrived medical supplies that Woodall had sent to him (VI&A 133).

Betsey: On February 15, 1768, when an inventory was made of the late Richard Ambler's slaves on Jamestown Island and his leasehold in the Governor's Land, an enslaved girl named Betsey was listed and identified as Sarah's child. In 1769 Betsey was living on Jamestown Island and was attributed to the late Edward Ambler I's household (York County Wills and Inventories 21:386–391; AMB-E).

Betty: On February 15, 1768, when an inventory was made of the late Richard Ambler's slaves on Jamestown Island and his leasehold in the Governor's Land, an adult female slave named Betty was listed. In 1769 an enslaved woman named Betty was living on Jamestown Island and was attributed to the late Edward Ambler I's household (York County Wills and Inventories 21:386–391; AMB-E).

Betty: When an inventory was made of the late Richard Ambler's slaves on Jamestown Island and his leasehold in the Governor's Land on February 15, 1768, Betty, a female slave, was listed. In 1769 Betty, who was described as a girl living on the Governor's Land, was included in the late Edward Ambler I's estate (York County Wills and Inventories 21:386–391; AMB-E).

Betty: On February 15, 1768, when an inventory was made of the late Richard Ambler's slaves at his quarter called Powhatan, an adult female slave named Betty and her young child were living there. She was still there in 1769 and was attributed to the late Edward Ambler I's estate (York County Wills and Inventories 21:386–391; AMB-E).

* * *

Robert Beverley I: Robert Beverley I, who immigrated to Virginia prior to 1655, was responsible for maintaining the records in the Secretary's Office. During the 1650s he indicated that he had transcribed numerous patents that previously had been maintained as loose leaves suspended on a string. Beverley constantly added to his landholdings during the 1670s and 1680s, often patenting escheat land, undoubtedly availing himself of information he acquired while working in the Secretary's Office. He also was a highly successful planter and claimed large quantities of land under the headright system. Much of the acreage he patented was in the Middle Peninsula. For example, Beverley patented large tracts on the Mattaponi River and in Old Rappahannock County, where he amassed 8,000 acres in 1670; he also owned land in Lancaster and Gloucester counties. During the early 1670s Robert Beverley I made several appearances before the General Court, sometimes as a litigant, and on other occasions to arbitrate disputes. In November 1671 he audited the contested accounts of two Jamestown residents, Thomas Rabley and Rabley's former guardian, Theophilus Hone. Beverley was a surveyor and from time to time laid out large tracts of land. He commenced compiling a "title book," that is, a compendium of his landholdings. By 1673 he had become a justice in Middlesex County's monthly court, and a year later he was county coroner and captain of the militia. By 1675 he was designated a surveyor of the county's highways. He was named the clerk of Middlesex County's court but served very briefly, having been replaced by James Blackmore. In December 1675 Beverley and his wife, Margaret, were named as two of Blackmore's heirs.

The rebel Nathaniel Bacon declared Robert Beverley I a traitor, for he remained loyal to Governor William Berkeley throughout Bacon's Rebellion. However, after the popular uprising was quelled, Beverley broke the law by plundering the belongings of those he considered Bacon's partisans. In 1676 Beverley was a member of the Council of State, and in 1677 he became clerk of the assembly. Because of his vigilante-style actions after Bacon's Rebellion, he lost his council seat when Berkeley left office. Beverley also clashed with Lieutenant Governor Herbert Jeffreys. He returned to Middlesex County, and although Berkeley had designated him high sheriff, Jeffreys appointed another man to office. In August 1680 Colonel John Burnham and Major Robert Beverley I were authorized to purchase 50 acres from Ralph Wormeley II, land that was to be surveyed and laid out into the site of a planned town, what became known as Urbanna. During the early 1680s, while Beverley was clerk of the assembly, he ran afoul of the law for plant-cutting, that is, purposefully destroying part of the year's tobacco crop in order to inflate the price. Although he was jailed in Middlesex until he could be brought to Jamestown, he escaped, and ultimately the penalties against him were withdrawn. In 1681 Beverley was the churchwarden of Christ Church Parish in Middlesex County. He continued to serve as clerk of the assembly and during 1685–1686 was elected Middlesex County's burgess; however, he was disqualified from continuing his clerkship. Part of his income was derived from having one of his clerks make copies of assembly records for the county courts. A document dated August 1, 1686, in the records of Stafford County reveals that the king sent word to Lord Effingham, Virginia's lieutenant governor, informing him that Beverley was unfit to serve as clerk of the assembly or hold any other public office. The king's agent alleged that Beverley had disrupted the assembly by promoting disputes and said that he should be prosecuted if he was found to have altered the records with which he was entrusted.

Toward the end of his life, Robert Beverley I married Theophilus Hone's daughter, Catherine I, and produced a daughter, Catherine II. He made his will on August 26, 1686, and died on March 15, 1687, leaving life-rights to his plantation and personal possessions to his wife, Catherine I. After Catherine I's death, the testator's daughter Mary was to receive one-third of his personal estate and his daughter Catherine II was to receive two-thirds. Robert Beverley I was survived by his widow and daughters as well as sons Robert II, Peter, and Henry (Harry), his administrators and the reversionary heirs to his real estate. The widowed Catherine Hone Beverley married Christopher Robinson of Middlesex County sometime after 1693 but retained possession of her late husband's real and personal property. Because the decedent was in the habit of keeping the assembly records at his plan-

tation, they had to be retrieved and brought to Jamestown. According to contemporary sources, the documents were packed in hampers and brought in by Christopher and Ralph Wormeley. After Beverley's death his estate was paid for making copies of the assembly's laws and propositions. In the wake of Catherine Hone Beverley Robinson's death and that of her second husband, Christopher Robinson, daughters Mary and Catherine Beverley II initiated legal action in order to gain custody of their inheritance (NUG I:320; II:61, 73, 77, 138, 140, 142, 152, 163, 185, 190, 192, 201, 226; MCGC 236, 265, 316, 285, 289, 326, 335, 362, 386, 394, 404, 415, 520, 531; HEN II: 454, 456, 546, 552; III:552; STAN 40, 81, 84; LEO 42–45, 48; CO1/2 f 304; 5/1355 f 326; 5/1356 f 3; 5/1407 f 81; 391/3 f 318; SAIN 10:341; 11:256; 12:357; LJC 86; EJC I:81; Wormeley 1686; ASPIN 172; Bruce, "Robert Beverley," 405–407, 412; "Persons Who Suffered by Bacon's Rebellion," 66; Middlesex County Order Book 1673–1680:1, 22, 31–32, 36, 47, 62, 224; 1680–1694:35, 243, 274, 288, 304; Stafford County Record Book 1686–1693:15–15a; Lancaster County Order Book 1680–1687:264).

Henry (Harry) Beverley: The name of Henry or Harry Beverley, Robert Beverley I's son, appeared numerous times in Essex County's records during the late seventeenth and early eighteenth centuries. During the mid-1690s he sold several Essex County properties that had belonged to his late father. In 1700, when he disposed of three more pieces of land that he had inherited from his late father, his wife, Elizabeth, relinquished her dower share. The Beverley couple was then living in Middlesex County. The following year Beverley took the oath of office as surveyor of the lower (or eastern) part of Essex County (Essex County Deeds and Wills 1695–1699:16–17; 1699–1702:46–48; Order Book 1699–1702:54, 99).

Peter Beverley: Peter Beverley, the brother of Robert Beverley II, was clerk of the assembly in 1693 and 1695–1696 and also served as clerk of the General Court in 1698. Both positions would have required him to spend a significant amount of time in urban Jamestown. In 1690 the London firm Micajah Perry and Company brought suit against Peter, Robert II, and Henry Beverley in Middlesex County's monthly court, in an attempt to recover the cost of providing them with lodging, probably while they were in Jamestown on official business and staying in a company-owned house that was on the waterfront. In 1692 and 1693 the courts of Middlesex and Stafford counties paid Captain Peter Beverley for making copies of laws enacted by the assembly. A year later he was identified as the guardian of his sister Catherine Beverley II. On September 3, 1694, Captain Beverley and his brother, Robert II, who were administrators of their late father's estate, took legal action against Christopher Robinson's executors. They contended that their late stepmother, the former Catherine Hone, and her new husband, Christopher Robinson, took custody of the late Robert Beverley I's estate and never rendered an accurate accounting (EJC I:392–393; LEO 52–54, 56; Middlesex County Order Book 1680–1694:477, 669, 685, 706–707; 1694–1705:56; Stafford County Record Book 1686–1693:271a).

Robert Beverley II: Robert Beverley II, son of the assembly clerk Robert Beverley I, was born in 1673. He was educated in England and when he returned to Virginia became a volunteer scrivener in the office of the Secretary, where land records were kept. In 1690 the London firm Micajah Perry and Company brought suit against Robert, Peter, and Henry Beverley in Middlesex County's monthly court, in an attempt to recover the cost of providing them with lodging, probably while they were in Jamestown on official business. By April 4, 1694, Robert Beverley II had been appointed clerk of the James City County court and had patented a lot in urban Jamestown. Because his father died in 1687, he already had inherited 300 acres in Gloucester County and 6,500 acres in King and Queen and Essex counties. Beverley began acquiring land on his own and in 1692 bought some acreage in Essex County. In 1696 he patented 2,359 acres between the Rappahannock and Mattaponi rivers and 5,000 acres in New Kent. Two years later he laid claim to 570 acres in Elizabeth City County. Between 1700 and 1729 he patented a massive quantity of land, including 813 acres in Elizabeth City County; 4,254 acres in King and Queen; 1,650 acres in King William and Spotsylvania; and 24,000 acres in Spotsylvania. In 1697, three years after he acquired a lot in Jamestown, Robert Beverley II married Ursula, the 16-year-old daughter of William Byrd I and sister of William Byrd II of Westover. The Beverley couple was living in Jamestown in 1698 when their son, William, was born. Ursula died in childbirth and was interred in the churchyard in Jamestown. Robert Beverley II never remarried. He retained his Jamestown lot until May 1718, but it is uncertain how long he resided in the capital city after his wife's demise. His increasingly active role in public life would have required his

presence in Williamsburg, Virginia's new capital city, for extended periods of time and would have made a local residence useful.

After the statehouse burned on October 20, 1698, Robert Beverley II, as clerk of the General Court, and his brother Peter, then clerk of the assembly, were ordered to ask Mrs. Rachel Sherwood of Jamestown if she would rent a couple rooms in her house for the storage of official records. Between 1699 and 1706 Robert Beverley II served several terms as Jamestown's burgess. When first elected in 1699, he and Bartholomew Fowler were locked in a tie vote and the House of Burgesses chose Beverley. A year later, when a new election was held, Beverley and Benjamin Harrison received an equal number of votes. Again, when the House of Burgesses was called upon to decide who should represent Jamestown, Beverley was chosen. In 1702 his compensation as a burgess became the center of a debate over whether James City County citizens who lived in Williamsburg were obliged to contribute toward the support of Jamestown's delegate to the assembly. From time to time Beverley, a staunch supporter of former governor William Berkeley, clashed openly with Governor Francis Nicholson. As a result, in 1703 Nicholson dismissed him as clerk of the King and Queen County court. At the heart of the two men's disagreement was Beverley's opposition to Nicholson's decision to move the seat of government from Jamestown to Williamsburg. In May 1706 Robert Beverley II, as one of the James City County justices, asked the House of Burgesses for permission to salvage bricks from the ruinous statehouse so that they could be used in building a new county courthouse in Jamestown. The request was approved. However, sometime after 1715 but before 1721, a James City County courthouse was erected in Williamsburg, where the city's justices shared the building with those of the county. On May 6 and 7, 1718, Robert Beverley II, by then a resident of King and Queen County, disposed of his Jamestown lot and its improvements (JHB 1695–1702:141; 1702–1712:204; LJC 459; LEO 59–60, 64; STAN 94–95, 97; SAIN 20:333, 737; BEV xiv–xv, xxix; AMB 48, 53, 97–98, 106–107; NUG II:377, 395; III:6, 9, 22, 34, 205, 233, 285, 360, 395; EJC I:392–393; Stanard, "Notes and Queries," 244; Middlesex County Order Book 1680–1694:477; Essex County Order Book 1692–1695:20; Deeds and Wills 1692–1695:35–37; Westmoreland County Order Book 1676–1689:632).

* * *

William Beverley: William Beverley witnessed Sir William Berkeley's will on March 20, 1677 (HEN II:560).

Pierre Biard: Father Pierre Biard, a Jesuit priest from New France, and two other Jesuits were among the 15 men Samuel Argall captured in July 1613 at Mount Desert, a fledgling Catholic colony in what is now Maine. Argall took them to Jamestown, where they were detained aboard ship during 1613 and 1614. Biard later said they were in constant fear of being hanged by Sir Thomas Dale, who frequently threatened their lives. Argall finally persuaded Dale to let him take the men to England, so that they could return to their native country. He transported Father Biard to Wales, where he was released after 9½ months of living in captivity (VI&A 133).

Thomas Bibbie: On July 31, 1622, Thomas Bibbie set sail from England with William Rowley, who resided in Jamestown (VI&A 134).

Richard Biggs I: Richard Biggs I came to Virginia in 1610, and during the mid-1620s he, his wife, and sons were living at West and Shirley Hundred. He served as a burgess for Shirley Hundred in 1624 and 1625 and was among those who signed a document rebutting a Virginia Company official's claims that prior to 1619 conditions in the colony were good. When a list of patented land was sent back to England in May 1625, Richard Biggs was credited with 150 acres in Charles City, land that had been planted. When he made his will in September 1625, he bequeathed most of his real and personal possessions to his wife, Sarah, and son, Richard II, and left six acres to his sister, Rebecca Rose. Biggs died within a few months of making his will (VI&A 134; LEO 5–6).

Billy: On February 15, 1768, when an inventory was made of late Richard Ambler's slaves on Jamestown Island and his leasehold in the Governor's Land, a male slave named Billy was listed. In 1769 Billy, who was described as a boy attributed to the estate of the late Edward Ambler I, was living at Powhatan, where the Amblers had a subsidiary farm or quarter (York County Wills and Inventories 21:386–391; AMB-E).

John Bird (Burd, Byrd): John Bird, a bricklayer and resident of Southwark Parish in Surry County, constructed two or more buildings in Jamestown during the 1660s and early 1670s. One individual for whom he built a brick house was merchant Richard

James I. Another was for Colonel Thomas Swann, the owner of a popular tavern in the capital city. However, Bird failed to complete some of the construction projects he undertook and, as a result, was sued by several people. He also incurred a substantial amount of debt. Two of his creditors were James Alsop and Colonel Thomas Swann, both of whom were Jamestown property owners. On the other hand, John Bird sued John Page of Jamestown and several Surry County residents in order to collect debts. Bird's wife, Ann, who had his power-of-attorney, occasionally appeared in court on his behalf (MCGC 334, 357–358; Surry County Order Book 1671–1691:2–3, 34, 74, 100, 112, 114, 171, 203, 314, 343, 352, 412, 420, 685; Deeds, Wills &c. 1652–1672:302).

John Bishop (Bishopp, Bushopp) I: In 1631 John Bishop I testified in an English court in a case that involved transatlantic commerce. He patented some land in Surry County in 1638, acreage that was at the head of Crouches Creek and close to College Run, and he enlarged his holdings five years later. Over the years Bishop continued to add to his holdings in that vicinity. He may have been related to Colonel Henry Bishop, who acquired Chippokes plantation in 1646. On March 28, 1655, William and Temperance Bretton (Britton) of Maryland sold a tract of Surry County land to John Bishop, then described as a resident of the county. The acreage that he and co-investor Thomas Bins purchased was known as Grindall's or Grindon's Olde Fort or the "middle plantacon," a parcel that originally was part of the Treasurer's Plantation and by 1649 had come into the hands of George Evelin. Despite the fact that Bishop owned a substantial amount of land in Surry County, he served as a burgess for Charles City County in 1644 and in 1652 and 1653, while the Commonwealth government was in power. He would have been eligible to do so if he or his wife owned property in Charles City. In 1652 Bishop, who continued to live in Surry, served on a jury that was investigating the cause of a man's death, and he also purchased some livestock. He was a highly successful planter and would have generated the disposable income he needed to accumulate land. When he testified in court in 1654, he identified himself as a resident of the Crouches Creek area. John Bishop I died sometime prior to March 1658 and was survived by a son, John Bishop II, whose name was associated with Charles City County (LEO 22, 29, 31; STAN 64, 68, 70; Westmoreland County Deeds, Wills, Patents &c. 1653–1659:45; NUG I:98, 148, 165, 216, 281, 367; PB 1:441,

604, 915, 929; 2:8, 323; 3:222; 4:263; Surry County Deed Book 1 [1652–1672]:17, 21, 29, 57, 70, 71, 82; SR 4016, 10719).

James Biss (Bisse): Captain James Biss began living in Charles City County sometime prior to 1663 when his name began appearing in court records. In June 1677 he and three other men were interrogated about some testimony they gave to the special commissioners King Charles II sent to the colony to investigate the underlying causes of Bacon's Rebellion. During the late 1670s Biss frequently transacted business that involved Charles City County's court justices, for he settled and audited estates, compiled inventories, and served as an attorney. One of the people he represented was Colonel Arthur Allen of Bacon's Castle. Biss went on to become a justice of the Charles City County court and was the county's high sheriff in 1676. He patented some land on the north side of the James River, abutting Kittewan Creek, and served as a burgess for Charles City County in 1680–1682. He patented some escheat land in Charles City in 1687, acreage that was east of Weyanoke and bordered Kittewan Creek. Captain Biss added to his holdings in 1692. In July 1694 he and two other Charles City County justices appeared before the Council of State, where they were queried about why they had delayed the attorney general's suits against two men who allegedly had made incestuous marriages (LEO 45; NUG I:230, 307, 374; PB 7:130, 564; 8:218; SR 661; Charles City County Order Book 1661–1664:414; 1664–1665:513, 544; 1677–1679:199, 229, 276, 295, 312, 333, 352, 411; 1650–1696:5; EJC I:316).

William Black (Blacke, Blackey, Blackley, Blacky): In 1640 William Black or Blackley, who seems to have been a planter, purchased 100 acres on Queens Creek in York County. His wife, Margaret, was the sister of Thomas Gybson (Gibson) of York County. Although Black's patents have been lost or destroyed, an April 1648 patent to Lewis Burwell I and another man reveal that his land was on the south side of the Pamunkey River in what by 1654 had become New Kent County. Black's acreage may have adjoined the stream that by 1651 had become known as Black's Creek, a tributary of the Pamunkey River. Black served as a burgess for New Kent County and attended the assembly sessions held in 1658, 1659, and 1666–1676 (LEO 34–35, 39; PB 2:119, 310; York County Deeds, Orders, Wills 1 [1633–1657]:75; 2 [1645–1649]:60, 114; 2 [1657–1662]:146).

Susan Blackwood: Susan Blackwood came to Virginia in 1622. In February 1624 she was living on the Maine, where she was a servant in Dr. John Pott's household. By January 1625 she was living in the Pott residence in urban Jamestown (VI&A 138).

Mary Blades: In March 1672 Mary Blades, one of John Knowles' servants, fatally stabbed Philip Lettice. She was found guilty of murder and sentenced to hang. The incident occurred in urban Jamestown, where Knowles resided (MCGC 329; PALM I:8).

* * *

Archibald Blair: Dr. Archibald Blair, the Rev. James Blair's brother, was born in Scotland around 1690 and was considered one of Virginia's most competent physicians. He married William Wilson's twice-widowed daughter, Mary, who had outlived William Roscoe and her second husband, Miles Cary II, who died in February 1709. As late as 1723 Blair was conducting business on behalf of Mary's first husband's estate, and she seems to have retained a dower interest in her second husband's lot in urban Jamestown. In 1710 some of Dr. Archibald Blair's slaves were implicated in a plot that involved an attempt to escape to freedom. Blair was on intimate terms with members of the colony's elite families, such as the Ludwells, Burwells, Harrisons, and Byrds. Those connections probably played a role in his being recommended for appointment to the Council of State; however, his nomination was unsuccessful, perhaps because his brother was a councilor. In 1718 Dr. Blair represented Jamestown in the assembly, an indication that he or his wife, Mary, had a legal interest in land in the former capital city. Blair was returned to the assembly but began serving as a James City County burgess, attending the sessions held in 1720–1722 and 1723–1726. He was elected to represent Jamestown in the sessions held between 1728 and 1734 but died before the commencement of the 1734 session. Dr. Archibald Blair's son, John, completed his 1734 term in the assembly. Mary Wilson Roscoe Cary Blair died in 1741 (DOR 3:297; BYRD 51, 67, 91–92, 157, 162, 265, 404; STAN 102–103, 105–107; LEO 69–70, 72, 74; SR 383, 732, 5095).

John Blair: In 1734 John Blair, the son of Dr. Archibald Blair and nephew of the Rev. James Blair, completed his late father's term in the assembly as Jamestown's representative, but in 1736 and 1737 he served as the City of Williamsburg's delegate. John

Blair's 1751 diary reveals that he made trips to Jamestown from time to time. In 1752 he was a James City County justice of the peace (BYRD 51; LEO 74; STAN 108, 110; EJC V:391; Tyler, "Diary of John Blair," 141).

James Blair: The Rev. James Blair was born in Scotland in 1655 and in 1673 received the Master of Arts degree from the University of Edinburgh. He was an ordained Anglican minister, and when he moved to England around 1682, he became acquainted with the Bishop of London. In 1685 Blair immigrated to Virginia. On October 21, 1687, he patented 453 acres of land in Henrico County at Varina, near the site of the parish glebe. In April 1690 he and two other real estate speculators patented a 130-acre strip of land between the Henrico Glebe and Two Mile Creek, anticipating that part of their acreage would be selected as the site of a planned town. In 1689 the Bishop of London designated the Rev. James Blair as his commissary or official representative in Virginia. In that capacity Blair began holding convocations—meetings of the colony's clergy. These gatherings gave rise to the idea of having a college in Virginia where clergy could be trained. Blair served as commissary for 54 years. In 1689 he was appointed to the Council of State, which convened at Jamestown. He also was the rector of James City Parish from 1694 until 1710, when he became rector of Bruton Parish. He served there until his death in 1743. In 1687 the Rev. James Blair married Sarah, the daughter of Colonel Benjamin Harrison of Wakefield in Surry County and the sister of Philip Ludwell II's wife, Hannah. Blair's marriage into the Harrison family allied him with Virginia's planter elite. Sarah's adamant refusal to use the word "obey" when taking her wedding vows created a stir. While the Rev. James Blair was a councilor, he and Sarah resided at Rich Neck, near Middle Plantation (later, Williamsburg). From time to time he apparently experienced some medical problems that kept him from his ministerial duties. His brother, Dr. Archibald Blair, a physician, was held in high esteem.

The Rev. James Blair, Henry Hartwell, and Edward Chilton were asked to report on conditions in Virginia. Their account, published in 1697, contains important information about the colony. When Blair made a trip to England, his salary was divided among the clergy who served as his substitutes at the church in Jamestown, in the assembly, and in the Council of State. He was one of William Byrd II's friends and sometimes visited Westover. In June 1701 Blair was reappointed to the council as Edward

Hill's replacement. He quarreled openly with three Virginia governors and, by using his influence with the Bishop of London, was instrumental in having them removed from office. Governor William Gooch, who intensely disliked Blair, described him as "a very vile old ffellow." In 1697 the outspoken Blair declared that Lieutenant Governor Edmond Andros had wasted a great deal of money by replacing the old brick fort in Jamestown with a poorly designed gun platform. He also believed that the powder house Andros had constructed was useless. In 1704 Blair complained about Governor Francis Nicholson, whom he said behaved badly, and in 1718 he had problems with Lieutenant Governor Alexander Spotswood, who wanted Blair removed from the council. Sarah died in 1712 and was interred in the churchyard in Jamestown. From September 1740 to July 1741, the Rev. James Blair, as council president, served as acting governor. He died on November 14, 1743, and was interred in Jamestown, next to his wife, Sarah, who predeceased him by 31 years (PERRY I:14; CO 5/1307 f 22–23; 5/1318 f 268; 5/1339 ff 36–37; STAN 19, 42; EJC I:325, 360, 440; NUG II:313, 341; SAIN 15:584, 655; 22:158; BYRD 25; Stanard, "Lord Culpeper,"19, 61; HART xxii–xxviii; GOOD 251; Bruce, "Papers Relating to the Administration of Governor Nicholson," 278).

* * *

[No First Name] Blake: A man whose surname was Blake served as a burgess for Nansemond County in 1656 (LEO 33). He may have been John Blake, who held office from 1666 to 1676.

Bartholomew Blake: Bartholomew Blake, a smith sent to Virginia in 1621 by the Company of Shipwrights, was promised 25 acres of land on completion of his five-year contract. When he testified in court in 1623, he was described as a carpenter. It is probable that Blake (like others who came to Virginia on behalf of the Company of Shipwrights) resided on Jamestown Island. He died there sometime after February 16, 1624, but before January 24, 1625 (VI&A 138).

John Blake: In 1658 Captain John Blake patented 400 acres on Mathews Creek, a tributary of the southern branch of the Nansemond River. He also acquired 150 acres on Parkers Creek. As time went on, Blake continued to add to his holdings. In 1662 he patented another 300 acres on Mathews Creek, and he and a partner, Edward Ison, laid claim to 2,500 acres elsewhere in Nansemond County. John Blake represented Nansemond County in the assembly and held office from 1666 to 1676. He may have been the same individual who was a burgess for Nansemond in 1656. During 1672 Blake acquired an additional 200 acres, and two years later he patented tracts of 1,050 acres and 800 acres on Mathews Creek, as well as 450 acres on the western branch of the Nansemond River. He and a partner also patented 3,000 acres elsewhere in Nansemond County. On February 9, 1698, an inventory was made of John Blake's possessions in Isle of Wight County (PB 4:208–209; 5:22, 28; 6:435, 500–501; LEO 33, 38; Isle of Wight County Wills and Deeds 2:397).

Charles Blanckevile: On March 17, 1677, Governor William Berkeley and the Council of State members, who had convened as a tribunal, were informed that Charles Blanckevile had supported the rebel Nathaniel Bacon's cause by stirring up discontent in Elizabeth City County. They decided to leave Blanckevile's fate in the hands of the justices of his home jurisdiction, Elizabeth City County. He was to be compelled to appear in court with a rope around his neck and, while kneeling, to ask to be pardoned for rebellion and treason (MCGC 460, 530).

* * *

Adam Bland: During the second and third quarters of the seventeenth century John Bland I's son, John Bland II of Kimoges in Charles City County, owned a lot in urban Jamestown, perhaps the waterfront lot on which archaeologists have found the remains of a large warehouse with a brick foundation. In 1644 John Bland II's brother, Adam, who was in Jamestown at that time, received a large shipment of goods. Adam Bland died around 1647 while on his way to Virginia; he was unmarried (DOR 1:325; Surry County Deeds and Wills 1671–1684:229; HEN II:199; Williams, "The Tribulations of John Bland, Merchant," 30–40).

Edward Bland: Edward Bland, a London merchant and one of John Bland I's sons, purchased from Thomas Hill of Jamestown 3,000 acres known as Upper Chippokes. In August 1650 Bland and three other adventurers set out from Fort Henry and explored the territory beyond the head of the Appomattox River. When he was named John Bland I's administrator in July 1652, he was described as a bachelor, but soon after he married a cousin, Jane Bland. Edward Bland died sometime prior to May 9, 1652, when his widow repatented his land. Later, she

married John Holmwood (PB 3:200; EEAC 7; NUG I:175; DOR 1:327; SR 13838).

John Bland II: During the second and third quarters of the seventeenth century, John Bland I's son, John Bland II, owned a lot in urban Jamestown, perhaps the waterfront lot on which archaeologists have found the remains of a large warehouse with a brick foundation. In 1644 John II's brother Adam received a large shipment of goods in Jamestown, which were described in detail in a bill of lading. In 1663 another Bland brother, Theodorick, received high praise from the Virginia assembly for working closely with John II in obtaining substantial quantities of commodities that were considered essential to the colony's well-being. In August 1678 John Bland II, who described himself as a London merchant, executed a document giving his wife, Sarah, his power of attorney. In 1679 Bland was still in possession of his Jamestown lot, a mill on Herring Creek, and several plantations (Berkeley, Kimoges, Jordan's Point, Westover, Upper Chippokes, Sunken Marsh, Basses Choice, and Lawnes Creek) when his wife, Sarah, came to Virginia to conduct business on his behalf and claim the land that he was supposed to inherit. Sarah and John Bland II's son, Giles, quarreled openly with Secretary Thomas Ludwell and eventually was executed for his role in Bacon's Rebellion (VI&A 139; Surry County Deeds, Wills &c. 1671–1684:229; Isle of Wight County Will and Deed Book 1 [1662–1688]:410–411; DOR 1:325–327, 329; CO 5/1355 f 57; HEN II, 199; Williams, "The Tribulations of John Bland, Merchant," 30–40; CBE 7).

Giles Bland: Giles, the son of Sarah and John Bland II, immigrated to Virginia in 1674. Acting as his father's attorney, he brought suit against his aunt Anna Bland, the widow and executrix of his uncle Theodorick Bland. Giles Bland was appointed the collector of customs, thanks to his family's political connections, but within a short time he was queried by Governor William Berkeley about the way he was carrying out his duties. Ultimately, Bland was suspended from office. Later, he was arrested because of debts he owed to merchant Richard James I of urban Jamestown and was required to post a bond guaranteeing that he would pay them. However, he failed to do so and had to forfeit his bond. Giles Bland became enraged and sent a letter to the king complaining about Governor Berkeley and council members Philip Ludwell I and Joseph Bridger. He also declared that he would not be accountable to the governor. Shortly thereafter, Bland got into a drunken quarrel with Secretary Thomas Ludwell at Ludwell's house. After hurling insults at Ludwell and challenging him to a duel, he nailed his glove to the statehouse door. As a result, in October 1674 Secretary Ludwell had him arrested for slander, jailed, and then brought before the General Court, where he was fined £500 and ordered to make a public apology. When he did so, it was with biting sarcasm. In May 1676 Sarah Bland asked the king to release her son from the fine the Berkeley government had imposed. Giles Bland's problems quickly multiplied, for he sided with the rebel Nathaniel Bacon and took an active role in Bacon's popular uprising. When Bland and some of Bacon's compatriots seized one of the king's ships and took it to Accomack, hoping to capture Governor Berkeley, they were taken into custody by Thomas Gardner. Afterward they were imprisoned, probably at Green Spring plantation, the Berkeley home. Bland was tried there on March 8, 1677, found guilty by a jury, and executed on March 27th. His estate was subject to seizure, for he was declared exempt from the king's pardon (SAIN 10:42; MCGC 390, 399, 418, 423, 448, 452–453, 515, 518; CO 5/1355 ff 57, 60, 65; 5/1306 f 61; Surry Deeds, Wills &c. 1671–1684:229; SR 6618; NEVILLE 61; DOR 1:329; MCGC 457, 529).

Theodorick Bland I: In March 1660 Theodorick Bland I, the son of John Bland I, commenced serving as a burgess for Charles City and was chosen speaker of the assembly. He represented Henrico County in the assembly sessions of 1661–1662, and in 1665 he became a member of the Council of State. Bland lived in Charles City County at Berkeley during the 1660s, and in 1666 he acquired Westover. He married Anna, the daughter of Commonwealth governor Richard Bennett, who conveyed to them a unit in a brick row house in the western part of urban Jamestown. Bland sometimes served as an attorney, and in 1660 he filed suit against William Drummond I, a Jamestown resident and nearby property owner. In 1670 he also brought suit against innkeeper Richard Lawrence of Jamestown. Theodorick Bland I was held in high esteem by high-ranking government officials because he and his brother John II procured essential goods for the colony during the early 1660s, when shortages were severe. As a reward, he was authorized to receive the impost on imported tobacco. In 1662, when plans were made to strengthen Jamestown as an urban community, a law was passed that required each of Virginia's counties to build a brick house in the capital city. In February 1663, while he was a Charles City County justice, Bland

was authorized to undertake construction of the county's obligatory brick house. When Theodorick Bland I died on April 23, 1671, Berkeley and Westover descended to his sons, Theodorick II and Richard. While Anna Bennett Bland was serving as her late husband's administratrix in 1675, she sued William Brown I of Surry County in an attempt to recover some debts (STAN 39, 73; MCGC 222, 409, 484, 488, 503, 507; HEN I:549; II:9; Charles City County Order Book 1:34; LEO 36, 38).

William Bland: The Rev. William Bland, successively the rector of James City Parish and Bruton Parish, married William Yates's daughter, Elizabeth. Yates left his son-in-law a substantial bequest in 1764. At the time of the Revolutionary War, Bland was the owner of Jockey's Neck plantation, which was near Jamestown and the James City Parish glebe. Elizabeth Yates Bland died in December 1772. In 1779 the Rev. Bland was assaulted by Edward Champion Travis of Jamestown Island, who reportedly gave him a severe beating. Later, Bland sued for damages (James City County Land Tax Lists 1782; Desandrouins 1781–1782; Yates, October 8, 1764; Bland n.d.; Purdie and Dixon, *Virginia Gazette,* December 17, 1772; Rind, *Virginia Gazette,* December 17, 1772).

* * *

Peregrine (Perregrin, Perigreene, Perrygreene) Bland: Peregrine Bland served as a burgess for Charles River (York) County in 1640. He patented 1,000 acres on the north side of the Piankatank River in August 1642. By 1651 his acreage was included in Lancaster County. Bland died sometime prior to November 1656. In 1646 he witnessed a document that was signed in York County (LEO 18; PB 1:805; 2:344; 4:66; 8:319; York County Deeds, Orders, Wills 1 [1633–1657]:162).

Edward Blaney (Blany, Blanye, Blanie, Blainy, Blayny): Edward Blaney, a merchant and the Virginia Company's factor, came to Virginia in 1621. He was responsible for the Company's store of goods and was supposed to send home any marketable commodities produced by Company servants and artisans. He also was authorized to trade with the Indians. By April 1623 Blaney, who was an aspiring planter, had married the late Captain William Powell's widow, Margaret, a resident of Jamestown. She made a trip to England to assert a claim to part of her late husband's land on Hog Island, acreage that Captain Samuel Mathews tried to claim. She also had possession of the late Captain Powell's plantation, which his orphans stood to inherit. Blaney served as a burgess, representing the merchants in 1623 and Jamestown in 1624; in January 1626 he was named to the Council of State. In February 1624 when he was age 28, he headed a large household in urban Jamestown, occupying the Powell property. By 1625 he had shifted most of his servants to the Powell plantation on the lower side of the James River, maintaining it for his stepchildren. Edward Blaney became a successful planter, but he continued to generate income as a merchant. He died before February 6, 1626. His widow, Margaret, quickly remarried, this time taking as her husband Captain Francis West, the late Lord Delaware's brother. She died prior to March 1628, by which time West (then interim-governor) had married Sir George Yeardley's widow, Lady Temperance (VI&A 139–140; LEO 5–6).

Thomas Blayton: On February 10, 1677, Governor William Berkeley issued a proclamation naming those exempt from the king's pardon due to their participation in Bacon's Rebellion. Berkeley listed Thomas Blayton but noted that he needed to be brought before a court (NEVILLE 61).

John Blesse (Bliss): John Blesse, a young Virginia Company servant who came to Virginia in 1619, was from Sussex, England. In April 1623 he was described as a smith who had been assigned to Sir Francis Wyatt. Therefore, he almost certainly lived in Jamestown or on the nearby Governor's Land (VI&A 140).

[No First Name] Blewitt (Bluett, Blewett, Bluett, Bluet): According to Virginia Company records, Captain Blewitt came to Virginia in 1619 and was accompanied by the men who were to be employed in Southampton Hundred's ironworks. Blewitt was appointed to the Council of State but died a short time after his arrival. He may have been Benjamin Blewitt, the father of Elizabeth, a young marriageable woman who came to the colony in 1621 (VI&A 140; STAN 29; LEO xix).

Humphrey (Henry) Blunt: On July 6, 1610, Humphrey Blunt, one of Sir Thomas Gates's men and a resident of Jamestown, went to the lower side of the James River to recover a longboat. He was captured there and killed by the Indians (VI&A 142; HAI 434–435).

Bob: On February 15, 1768, when an inventory was made of the late Richard Ambler's slaves on Jamestown Island and his leasehold in the Governor's Land, an adult male slave named Bob was listed. In 1769 Bob was living at the quarter called Powhatan and was attributed to Edward Ambler I's estate (York County Wills and Inventories 21:386–391; AMB-E).

Bob: In 1769, when an inventory was made of the late Edward Ambler I's estate, a slave named Bob was living on Jamestown Island and was identified as the son of a woman known as Chubby (AMB-E).

Humphrey Bock: Humphrey Bock came to Virginia in 1622 and accompanied a Mr. Spencer, probably William Spencer of Jamestown Island (VI&A 142).

Lawrence Bohun (Bohune, Bohunne): Dr. Lawrence Bohun, a London physician, came to Virginia in 1610 and resided in Jamestown. He returned to England, and in 1619 he and some co-investors made plans to transport 300 people to the colony. A year later he was appointed to the Council of State. He also was named the colony's physician-general, which entitled him to medical assistants, servants, and 500 acres of office land. Dr. Bohun made his will on March 10, 1620, and set sail for Virginia in mid-December 1620. However, he was killed in the West Indies on March 19, 1621, when the vessel he was aboard was attacked by the Spanish. On October 31, 1621, Dr. Bohun's widow, Alice, asked to be compensated for his substantial investment in the Virginia Company. She also wanted Company officials to free her son, Edward Barnes, a Virginia Company servant, from his seven years of service (VI&A 142–143; STAN 30; LEO xix).

Robert Bolling: Robert Bolling, who was born in London on December 26, 1646, immigrated to Virginia at age 14. In 1675 he married Jane, the daughter of Thomas Rolfe and granddaughter of John Rolfe and Pocahontas. A year later Jane Rolfe Bolling gave birth to a son named John. After her death around 1677, Bolling married Anne (Ann), the daughter of Major John Stith Sr. of Westover Parish in Charles City. Together they produced five sons and two daughters. In 1697 Bolling patented 300 acres on the east side of City (Cabin) Creek. He gradually enhanced his plantation's size, securing the acreage upon which he established his family seat, Kippax, later known as Farmingdale. Bolling also owned 500 acres in Henrico County. Colonel Robert Bolling represented Charles City County in the assembly sessions held in 1688, 1691–1692, and 1699 and was county sheriff in 1692 and 1699. In 1692 he and two other men endorsed the Rev. John Banister's list of "Physiological Collections," a document that was being sent back to England. In 1702, when Prince George County was formed from Charles City's territory south of the James River, he became a justice and surveyor. He patented 365 acres on a branch of Rohoick Creek in Prince George County in October 1703 and was credited with 831 acres in 1704. He went on to serve as a burgess for Prince George County in 1704–1705, and in 1705 was appointed county lieutenant. In May 1705 he patented 50 acres in Henrico County, and in May 1706 he laid claim to 1,973 acres in Prince George County, acreage that extended southward as far as the Nottoway River. According to William Byrd II of Westover, Colonel Robert Bolling was actively involved in Indian trade. Archaeologists have found large quantities of glass beads on his plantation, which was relatively close to a well-established trading path that extended in a southwesterly direction from the falls of the Appomattox River. Bolling died on July 17, 1709, after a lengthy illness. According to William Byrd II, he suffered from dropsy (LEO 49–50, 59; DOR 3:27–28; NUG I:61, 75, 298, 469; III:13; PB 9:85, 571, 646, 714; SR 66; Charles City County Wills and Deeds 1692–1694:185; Order Book 1676–1679, passim; SR 66; BYRD 8, 305).

Stith Bolling: Stith Bolling moved to Surry County sometime prior to 1711, and by 1716 he had been chosen a county justice of the peace. On February 20, 1717, he was authorized to keep the ferry from Swann's Point to Jamestown. In 1725 he witnessed a deed whereby William and Mary Hartwell Macon sold some Surry County property to Robert Carter of Lancaster County (Surry County Court Records 1700–1711:152, 156; 1712–1718:86; Order Book 1713–1718:108; Deeds, Wills, &c. 7 [1715–1730]:605).

Amias (Annis) Bolt (Boult): Amias Bolt arrived in Virginia in 1619 and in 1624 was living at Flowerdew Hundred. By January 22, 1625, he had moved to West and Shirley Hundred, where he was a household head (VI&A 143).

* * *

Francis Bolton (Boulton): In 1628 the Rev. Francis Bolton, rector of James City Parish from 1628 to 1633, was authorized to lease the parish glebe to tenants (VI&A 143).

Joseph Bolton (Boulton): Joseph, brother of the Rev. Francis Bolton, rector of James City Parish from 1628 to 1633, came to Virginia as the clergyman's servant. He was sponsored by the Company of Mercers (VI&A 143).

* * *

John Bond I: In July 1650 John Bond I patented 760 acres in Lancaster County, acreage that was located on the north side of the Rappahannock River, on the Corotoman River's eastern branch. Like many of his contemporaries, he seems to have been investing in land on Virginia's frontier. Bond was living in Isle of Wight County in 1651 when he loaned £250 (a substantial sum) to William Garnett, master of the *Comfort*, which had managed to reach Virginia but was in need of extensive repairs. It is unclear whether Bond had invested in the cargo aboard Garnett's ship or enabled him to make it seaworthy. John Bond served as a burgess for Isle of Wight County and attended the assembly sessions of 1654–1655, 1656, 1658, 1659, 1660, and 1661–1662. In 1665 he was identified as a major when he sold a grist mill on Pagan Creek to Thomas Harris, who later disposed of it. When Major John Bond I made his will, which appears to have been lost or destroyed, he named his wife, Dorothy, as his executrix. On September 23, 1669, Francis England and Arthur Smith agreed to serve as her security. In 1683 Dorothy Bond, who identified herself as Major John Bond's widow, joined her son, John II, in selling a piece of property to Joseph Bridger (LEO 32–36, 38; Isle of Wight County Will & Deed Book 1 [1662–1688]:38–39, 116–117, 505–506; Administrations and Probates 18; PB 2:217; SR 4015).

[No First Name] Booth (Boothe): According to Captain John Smith, Sergeant Booth, one of the Jamestown colonists, was involved in a march against natives known as the Ozinies (VI&A 145). He may have been John Booth, a laborer who came to Virginia in 1608 in the 1st Supply.

Henry (Henery) Booth (Bowth): In 1619 officials at Bridewell decided that Henry Booth, a thief, would be sent to Virginia. When census records were compiled in 1624, he reportedly was living just west of Jamestown Island, on the Maine, where Captain Roger Smith had some servants. Simultaneously, he was attributed to Smith's household in urban Jamestown, where he was living a year later. In 1626, when Booth received an eye injury and was unable to pay his medical bill, he was described as a poor Virginia Company man. He eventually gained his freedom and by 1630 had at least one indentured servant (VI&A 145).

John Booth (Bouth): John Booth, a laborer, arrived in Jamestown in 1608 in the 1st Supply of new settlers (VI&A 145).

John Booth (Buth): John Booth, a member of Ensign Spence's household, died on Jamestown Island sometime after April 1623 but before February 16, 1624. Simultaneously, he was listed among the living (VI&A 145).

Reynold Booth: Reynold Booth, who arrived in Virginia in 1609, lived in Jamestown. He returned to England, and in 1620, when testifying in court, he described the circumstances under which some of the first Africans had been captured and brought to Virginia in 1619. In February 1624 Booth and his wife, Elizabeth, and their daughter, Mary, were living in Elizabeth City. In September 1626 Sergeant Booth testified against Joan Wright, an accused witch, and claimed that she had put a curse on him (VI&A 145–146).

Robert Booth (Bouth) I: Robert Booth moved to York County sometime prior to 1645. In January 1646 he received a certificate that entitled him to 150 acres of land, and by 1647 he had become the county's clerk of court. As a burgess for York County, he attended the assembly sessions of 1653 and 1654–1655 and also served as a justice in the county court. By 1651 Booth had patented 800 acres on the west side of Skimino Creek, land that fronted on the York River. In July 1652, while the Commonwealth government was in power, he received two patents, each of which was for 400 acres on the lower side of Queens Creek in York County. A year later he successfully laid claim to an 880-acre tract to the southeast of the Old Warrany Indian Town, in what was then York County. In 1654 Booth brought suit against a Northumberland County man but died prior to October 26, 1657, when his widow, Francis, relinquished her legal interest in some land that the decedent had sold to Gyles Mode. In November 1672 Robert Booth II, the son and heir of Robert Booth I, was awarded his late father's patent for 1,000 acres of land in New Kent County. The General Court's justices noted that the decedent had seated the land, which rightfully descended to his son (LEO 31–32; Northumberland County Order Book 1652–1665:58;

York County Deeds, Orders, Wills 1 [1633–1657]:189; 2 [1645–1649]:53, 75, 90, 273; 3 [1657–1662]:5; MCGC 322; PB 2:317; 3:194, 201–202).

Daniel Boucher: On November 13, 1633, William Parke, a Virginia resident, identified Daniel Boucher as purser of the ship *Blessing*. By 1653 Boucher had settled in Isle of Wight County, which he represented in the assembly. He patented a large tract of land on the Blackwater River in 1654 and renewed his patent a decade later, an indication that he had failed to seat it. Boucher made his will on December 4, 1667, and died sometime prior to May 1, 1668, when it was proved. The testator noted that his wife, Elizabeth, had predeceased him and made bequests to his daughter, Elizabeth, and the grandchildren of his late wife. He specified that if his daughter, Elizabeth, died without heirs, his kinsman Robert Boucher would inherit her portion of the estate. He also named several other people as heirs, notably, Hodges Councill Jr., William and Mary Hunt (William Hunt Sr.'s children), Elizabeth Munger (John Munger's daughter), and Elizabeth Davis (John Davis's daughter). At Daniel Boucher's request, an inventory was taken of his estate on March 11, 1668, the day he died. On August 20, 1668, the county court appointed John Hardy and Thomas Taborer to represent Elizabeth Boucher's interest in her late father's estate. In July 1669 she renewed his patent for land on the Blackwater River (VI&A 146; LEO 31; Isle of Wight County Will and Deed Book 2:53, 57; Administrations and Probates:16; SR 3969; PB 5:199; 6:233).

George Bourcher: On August 8, 1626, George Bourcher testified about a conversation he overheard at George Menefie's forge in urban Jamestown (VI&A 147).

James Bourne: In June 1608 James Bourne, a gentleman and one of the first Jamestown settlers, accompanied Captain John Smith on two exploratory voyages within Chesapeake Bay. Later, Smith described him as a soldier (VI&A 147).

Robert Bourne (Borne): In 1650 Robert Bourne, a London merchant, testified about some tobacco that had been put aboard the *Eagle* while he was in Virginia. By 1653 he had moved to the colony and taken up residence in York County. In 1655 he and Daniel Parke I patented 580 acres on an old mill swamp near Middle Plantation, renewing their claim in 1658, probably because they had not seated their land. Bourne and Henry

Tyler disposed of some jointly owned land in 1657. Robert Bourne began serving as a York County justice in 1656 and held office for several years, becoming sheriff in 1659. In 1658 he represented the county as a burgess. Over the years he witnessed documents and testified in court. Robert Bourne was alive in May 1659 but died prior to April 1661, when a coroner's jury determined that his death was accidental. Court testimony reveals that his body was found on the shore of the York River, below the high water mark. This raises the possibility that he had drowned or perhaps fallen ill while near the water. Although Robert Bourne died intestate and may not have been married at the time of his death, a June 1681 deed reveals that his property descended to John Bourne (LEO 34; SR 4014, 8641; PB 4:14, 338; York County Deeds, Orders, Wills 1 [1633–1657]:132, 200, 230, 321, 335, 490; 3 [1657–1662]:17, 48, 55–56, 118; 6:315–317).

Jeoffrey Bowe: On October 3, 1672, Jeoffrey Bowe was penalized by the General Court because his wife, Sarah, had slandered Mrs. Deacon by calling her a whore. Bowe's fine was to go toward construction of a brick fort that was to be built in Jamestown. If he failed to pay what he owed, Sarah was to be ducked in the river after she had given birth to the child she was carrying (MCGC 313).

Robert Bowland: Around 1779 one of Edward Champion Travis's Jamestown Island slaves, 35-year-old Robert Bowland, fled to the British. In 1783 the British evacuated from New York an estimated 3,000 African Americans from Virginia who had accepted Lord Dunmore's promise of freedom and acted as loyalists during the Revolution. One of those evacuees was Robert Bowland, who reportedly had fled "about 3½ years ago." He and his fellow passengers aboard the *L'Abondance* headed for Port Matoon in Nova Scotia (HODGES 208).

John Bowler: In 1662 John Bowler became an apprentice to George Lee, an English merchant, who sent him to Virginia in 1663 and entrusted him with his merchandise and plantation. Bowler was supposed to assist Lee's agent and factor, Robert Whitehaire, and eventually assume his duties, which included selling goods and servants. However, Bowler sometimes failed to present a satisfactory account of his dealings as Lee's factor, perhaps because he sometimes purchased and resold goods on his own behalf. When George Lee and William Nevett sued the owners of the *Elizabeth* in October 1670,

they identified John Bowler and two other men as their factors in Virginia. In September 1671, Bowler, who was then in England, testified on behalf of Lee and Nevett. He was still abroad on November 23, 1671, when he was sued by John Lightfoot. Later, Bowler's attorney, Daniel Wild, reported that he had died at sea while returning to Virginia. Sarah Bowler, as her late son's administratrix, laid claim to some goods and personal property that George Lee insisted were his; Lee, in turn, filed a counter suit (MCGC 285, 327; SR 10440,10035, 10038, 10049, 10051, 10429, 11482, 12555). John Bowler of Virginia may have been the son of the late John Bowler, who in 1634 was identified as a merchant from Oldham in Lancashire, then trading in Virginia (SR 10914).

Thomas Bowler: In 1662 Thomas Bowler, a Lancaster County merchant and the proprietor of Thomas Bowler and Company, leased an Old Rappahannock County plantation and an adjoining parcel from Thomas Paine for a term of a thousand years. Simultaneously, he purchased servants (both white and black) to work the land. As time went on, Bowler acquired additional acreage in the county. By January 1665 he had moved to Old Rappahannock County and become a court justice. A document filed in Northumberland County in 1664 suggests that he may have been involved in the slave trade. Many of Bowler's business dealings involved planters in Lancaster County. He had a disagreement with Jamestown lot owner John Barber II in April 1670, a dispute that ended up in court. A year later he had a legal dispute with John Leare, a Nansemond County gentleman, and summoned a Northumberland County man to court as a witness. Bowler brought suit against Hubert Farrell, who allegedly made slanderous statements about Bowler's wife, Tabitha, while she was at the home of William White in urban Jamestown. In 1674 Thomas Bowler patented 1,134 acres of land that Robert Beverley I agreed to survey but failed to do so. Two years later surveyor James Minge placed a lien against Bowler's property, hoping to recover the sum he was owed. In March 1676 Bowler asked to be named the guardian of John Edloe, an orphan, but his request was denied because his wife was the orphan's half-sister. In February 1677, while Thomas Bowler was on the Council of State, he was denied the king's pardon because he stood accused of supporting the rebel Nathaniel Bacon. Moreover, his estate was subject to seizure. When Bowler made his will in March 1679, he left his home plantation and manor house in Old

Rappahannock County to his son, James, then a minor, along with half of a 1,000-acre tract called Mary Gold. He bequeathed to his daughter Anne the remaining half of the Mary Gold property and left to his unmarried daughter Elizabeth, the child of a previous marriage, a 500-acre plantation, some livestock, and some of her late mother's personal effects. He bestowed the rest of his estate to his "Dear and most Excellent Wife," Tabitha, and asked his friends Colonel Nicholas Spencer and Captain Thomas Gouldman to serve as his executors. Thomas Bowler died prior to July 1679. However, his estate was not settled for many years (MCGC 207, 240, 251, 368, 386–387, 436, 450; STAN 40; CO 1/39 f 65; Old Rappahannock County Deeds and Wills 1656–1664:217–220, 246–247, 330; Deeds and Wills 1665–1677:79–81, 98–100; Deeds and Wills 1677–1682:133–137, 344; Order Book 1686–1692:149; Northumberland County Record Book 1662–1666:130; Order Book 1666–1678:192; Lancaster County Order Book 1656–1666:187, 228, 283; NEVILLE 61).

Sarah Bowman: On February 6, 1626, Sara Bowman was identified as a servant of John Burrows, who owned property on Jamestown Island and on the lower side of the James River (VI&A 148).

Cheney (Chyna, Chene, Cheyney) Boyse (Boise, Boys, Boice, Boyce): Cheney Boyse, an ancient planter, went to England but returned to the colony in May 1617 and settled at West and Shirley Hundred. In 1629, 1630, and 1632 he served as a burgess for West and Shirley Hundred (now Eppes) Island. In May 1636 he patented a large tract of land on the lower side of the James River, on the east side of Merchant's Hundred (Powell's) Creek, in the immediate vicinity of what had been Samuel Macock's 2,000-acre plantation. In 1641 Boyse was among those who testified against ex-governor John Harvey, who had allowed part of the Governor's Land, a publicly owned tract, to be patented by private individuals (VI&A 148; LEO 8–9, 11).

Humphrey (Humpry) Boyse (Boise, Boys, Boice, Boyce): Humphrey Boyse died on Jamestown Island sometime after April 1623 but before February 16, 1624 (VI&A 149).

John (Johnny) Boyse (Boise, Boys, Boice, Boyce): John Boyse served as a burgess for Martin's Hundred in the July 1619 session of the assembly. Like others whom the Society of Martin's Hundred sent to establish their plantation, he would have lived on the Governor's Land before seating the acreage the Society had been assigned. In May 1621 Boyse, as warden (or custodian) of Martin's Hundred, informed Company officials that plots of ground had not yet been assigned to specific people. When the Indians attacked Martin's Hundred in March 1622, John Boyse and his wife were listed among those slain. However, he survived and his wife was captured and detained by the Pamunkey Indians. Boyse apparently was a relatively successful planter, for he was able to export substantial quantities of tobacco. He went to England and made his will on August 7, 1649, on the eve of his return to Virginia (VI&A 149; LEO 3).

Luke Boyse (Boise, Boys, Boice, Boyce): Luke Boyse came to Virginia in one of the ships that brought the Society of Martin's Hundred's settlers. In April 1620 Virginia Company officials noted that Boyse was supposed to be the bailiff of Martin's Hundred but had broken his contract and settled elsewhere. He was living at Bermuda Hundred in September 1623 and represented that community in the assembly, serving in 1624 and 1625. Boyse became ill and died at his Bermuda Hundred home on June 21, 1626. When making a nuncupative will, he left his real and personal property to his wife, Alice, and their child. In February 1627 Alice Boyse, as her late husband's administratrix, presented the General Court with an inventory of his estate. She remarried before the estate had been settled, taking as her new husband Mathew Edloe (Edlowe) I. When the Boyse couple's daughter, Hannah, patented some land in 1635, she identified herself as their child (VI&A 150; LEO 5–6).

Henry Bradford (Brodsul): In 1625 Henry Bradford was a servant in William Peirce's household in urban Jamestown, and in January 1627 he was fined for being drunk. Court testimony Bradford gave during 1627 suggests that he was a cow-keeper. By December 9, 1628, he was dead (VI&A 151).

John Bradford (Braford?): John Bradford came to Virginia in 1621 at the expense of Sir George Yeardley. By September 20, 1628, his headright had been assigned to Thomas Flint (VI&A 151). John Bradford may have been the John Braford who was killed in the March 1622 Indian attack on Yeardley's plantation, Flowerdew Hundred.

Thomas Bradley: In 1608 Thomas Bradley, a tradesman, arrived in Jamestown in the 2nd Supply of new settlers (VI&A 152).

John Bradwell: On May 20, 1637, John Bradwell and John Radish patented 16 acres in the eastern end of Jamestown Island, adjacent to Mary Holland's property (PB1:423; VI&A 153).

John Bradye: On October 13, 1640, John Bradye and William Wootton, who were indentured servants, were identified as the instigators in a plot that involved running away and enticing others to join them. Both men were sentenced to be whipped from the gallows to the courthouse door. Bradye also was to be branded on the shoulder, placed in irons, and made to serve the colony for seven years. By 1658 he had moved across the James River to Surry County. On May 3, 1658, he testified in court about a trip he made from Surry to the storehouse at Goose Hill, in the eastern end of Jamestown Island (MCGC 467; Surry County Deeds, Wills, &c. 1652–1672:119).

Christopher Branch: During the mid-1620s Christopher Branch was living at the College or Arrohattock with his wife, Mary, and their son, Thomas. He was still residing there in October 1634 when he secured a 21-year lease for a nearby tract of land. In 1635 he patented some acreage called Kingsland that was located on the lower side of the James River. In 1640 Branch, who was then a tobacco viewer and burgess for Henrico County, testified about the estate of Thomas Sheffield, a casualty of the March 1622 Indian attack. When Branch made his will in 1678, he was still living at Kingsland (VI&A 153; LEO 18).

John Branch: John Branch served as a burgess for Elizabeth City County in 1642 and 1643. His plantation was mentioned in the patents that William Armestead (Armistead) and Thomas Watts secured in 1636 and 1638 for land on the Broad Creek and the Back River in Elizabeth City County (LEO 20–21; PB 1:342, 370, 564).

John Brashear (Brasseur, Brassier, Brassieur): In April 1667 John Brashear patented 400 acres in Nansemond County, part of the acreage that he had inherited from Robert Brashear, who had claimed it in 1638. He was identified as a resident of Nansemond in October 1668 when he leased some land to John Rawlings, acreage that was on Burchen Swamp of Upper Chippokes Creek. Sometime prior to June 6, 1672, Brashear married Mary, the daughter of Colonel Robert Pitt, an Isle of Wight County burgess and merchant; she inherited some of her late father's property around

1674. In April 1682 Brashear purchased and then repatented 235 acres in Surry County, at the head of Upper Chippokes Creek, land that formerly had belonged to Edward Travis and a member of the Johnson family. He also came into possession of some acreage that had descended to Mary Pitt Brashear from George Stevens, who seems to have been her maternal grandfather. Finally, in 1700 Brashear patented an additional 37 acres in Nansemond County. He represented Nansemond in the assembly sessions held in 1680–1682, 1684, 1685–1686, 1691–1692, 1695–1696, and 1696–1697. He or perhaps a descendant may have owned some land in Essex County in 1704, when a list of quitrents was compiled (LEO 45, 47–48, 50, 54, 56; PB 1:736; 3:33; 6:72; 7:134; 9:259; SMITH 11; Isle of Wight Administrations and Probates:34; BODIE 510, 706; Surry County Deed Book 1 [1652–1672]:317).

Brass (Brase): On September 19, 1625, the General Court ordered Captain Nathaniel Basse to provide some clothing to a black man servant from Portugal, who had been brought to the colony by a Captain Jones and sold to Basse. The justices told Basse to take the items from Jones' sea chest and have the servant pay for them with his labor. They also decided that Brass should be assigned to Lady Temperance Yeardley temporarily and that she should to pay him 40 pounds of tobacco a month for his work. On October 3rd, the General Court's justices revisited the matter and decided that the man servant known as Brass should be assigned to the incumbent governor, Sir Francis Wyatt, and that the sale Captain Jones made to Captain Basse was null and void. Virginia Company documents reveal that Jones was authorized to sail under a commission Captain Powell had received from the Low Countries (VI&A 155; MCGC 71–73; VCR 4:567–570).

Robert Braswell (Bracewell): In 1652 Robert Braswell was identified as an Isle of Wight County merchant who lived on the Pagan River. He was elected to the assembly in 1653, while the Commonwealth government was in power, but was declared ineligible to serve because he was a clergyman and rector of Isle of Wight's Lower Parish. Although none of Braswell's patents seem to have survived, in 1662 his acreage was used in reference to another Isle of Wight patentee's property. When the Rev. Robert Braswell made his will on February 15, 1667, he made bequests to his married daughters, Jane Stoikes, Rebecca West, and Ann Bagnall (the wife of burgess James Bagnall), and to their children. He also made bequests to his sons Richard and Robert, and appointed two guardians for his own minor children. The decedent's will was proved on May 1, 1668, and an account of his estate was presented to the county court on January 10, 1669. By that time Braswell's sons had been appointed executors, although they had not attained their majority; however, George Gwilliam and Richard Izard were to serve as overseers of the decedent's will (LEO 31; Isle of Wight Will and Deed Book 1 [1662–1688]:52, 80, 457; Administrations and Probates:16; SR 6578; PB 4:576; HEN I:378).

* * *

James Bray I: James Bray I, who immigrated to Virginia sometime prior to 1657, patented 1,250 acres in New Kent County. The following year he acquired an additional 100 acres, using his wife, Angelica, as a headright. Bray was named to the Council of State in 1670 and was steadfast in his loyalty to Governor William Berkeley. In 1671 Bray purchased 290 acres of land in Middle Plantation near the head of Archer's Hope (College) Creek, in James City County. Later in the year he and John Page of Jamestown inventoried the late Richard Stock's estate. Court testimony dating to November 1674 reveals that Bray performed many tasks for Jamestown merchant George Lee, owner of a townhouse in the capital city, and that at one point Bray and Lee became embroiled in a dispute that required arbitration. He also had a disagreement with Thomas Beale. By the mid-1670s James Bray I and wife, Angelica, were residing at Middle Plantation. She was one of the women seized by the rebel Nathaniel Bacon's men in September 1676 and used as a human shield while they built a defensive work at the entrance to Jamestown Island. On January 20, 1677, when a court-martial hearing was held at the Bray home in Middle Plantation, Bacon supporter William Drummond I was tried and sentenced to hang. The following day Governor Berkeley paused at the Bray residence but continued on to the home of Colonel John Page, where he spent the night. In February 1677 Bray was asked to obtain land at Middle Plantation for the king's troops' use in growing food crops. In 1688 he became one of James City County's burgesses but resigned at the commencement of the 1691–1692 session, refusing to take the required oaths. When he died around 1691, he was in possession of acreage in Middle Plantation and in Charles City and New Kent counties. The decedent was survived by his wife, Angelica, three sons (James II, Thomas I, and David I), and a daughter

(Ann). Although his will appears to have been lost or destroyed, excerpts of that document were included in a transcript of litigation undertaken by some of his heirs in 1732 (NUG I:161; III:18; PB 2:54, 59; WINFREE 383; FOR I:9:8; MCGC 257, 393–394, 454; JHB 1660–1693:72; EJC I:284; II:435; SAIN 10:341; 17:309; 22:158; HEN II:546, 549, 569; IV:377–378; VI:412; STAN 39, 86; LEO xix, 49–50; AND 98).

James Bray II: Around 1697 James Bray II of James City County married Thomas Pettus II's widow, the former Mourning Glenn, and acquired her legal interest in her late husband's realty. He also seized Pettus's personal property and household possessions before they had been inventoried by court-appointed commissioners. In 1700 Bray purchased the other Pettus heirs' legal interest in the 1,280 acres known as Littletown and Utopia, on the east side of College Creek, and developed them into a family seat. He also had a brick house and lots in Williamsburg. James Bray II served as a James City County justice of the peace and represented the county in the assembly sessions held in 1700–1702. He was involved in the slave trade and on July 23, 1700, licensed his slave ship at Jamestown. Governor Francis Nicholson, who was in office from 1698 to 1705, intensely disliked Bray, who seems to have been fractious and quarrelsome. In 1705 Bray berated Thomas Cowles, a fellow county justice, so vigorously that he resigned. On November 17, 1725, James Bray II made his will, which was presented for probate on March 14, 1726 (York County Deeds, Wills, Orders 11:30; MIN 4–5; STAN 94–95; LEO 60; FOR I:9:8; WINFREE 382).

* * *

Robert Bray: Robert Bray, who was a native of Bedfordshire, England, and the son of Edward Bray, came into possession of land in Lower Norfolk County sometime prior to 1676, when he served as a burgess. Over the years he witnessed the wills made by Elizabeth Keeling, Richard Poole, Thomas Lambert, and Francis Aldridge. Almost all of those who had personal dealings with Bray were residents of the Lynnhaven area. Elizabeth and Thorowgood Keeling referred to him as their father-in-law, probably their stepfather. On April 24, 1681, when Robert Bray made his will, he designated his wife, Ann, as his executrix and made bequests to his cousins Edward and John Bray, several friends, and some of his servants. He left the plantation he had recently purchased from Richard Carver to his brother, Plomer (Plumer, Plummcr) Bray, who owned acreage on Lynnhaven Bay. He also made bequests to his brother-in-law Thomas Tomkings and his kinsman John Boodington, who were in Bedfordshire, and identified Anthony Lawson as his close friend. Robert Bray's will was proved on June 15, 1681 (LEO 39; Lower Norfolk County Book E:91, 167; Wills and Deeds Book 4:16, 38, 54, 101; PB 5:475; 6:37).

Samuel Bray: In 1699 Samuel Bray, who lived Charles City County or James City, was executed in Jamestown for murdering his wife, Sarah (EJC I:440; II:20).

Thomas Breman (Breeman, Bremor, Bremo, Bremore): In 1650 Thomas Breman patented 500 acres on the Ware River and Craney Creek Swamp in what later became Gloucester County, purchasing the acreage from Secretary Richard Kemp's estate. Then, in March 1653 he patented 300 acres in Gloucester County, adjacent to the property he already owned. Finally, in 1654 he patented 600 acres on the north side of the Severn River and in 1656 acquired another 300 acres adjacent to his own land. Captain Breman served as a burgess for Gloucester County and attended the 1654–1655 assembly sessions. When he made his will, which appears to have been lost or destroyed, he bequeathed his land to his wife, Margaret. After her death, his acreage escheated to the Crown, an indication that they had failed to leave surviving heirs (LEO 32; PB 2:308; 3:11, 326; 4:106; 6:381).

* * *

Giles (Gyles) Brent I: Giles Brent I and his sister Margaret settled in St. Mary's City, Maryland, where they became close associates of Lord Baltimore's brother, Governor Leonard Calvert. When Calvert went to England in spring 1643, Brent served as deputy governor. Sometime prior to January 1645, he married young Mary Kittamaquund, the daughter of Kittamaquund, the tapac (tayac) or emperor of Maryland's Piscataway Indians. After the couple moved to Virginia, Brent asked Calvert to give him Mary's cattle or their equivalent value in tobacco. Giles Brent I patented a tract in Stafford County, across from the Piscataway Indians' town on the Maryland shore. As time went on, he acquired numerous pieces of property along the Potomac. Brent and his household—which included his Indian wife, Mary, their children, and his sister Mary—

were living on his Westmoreland County plantation called Peace. When Giles Brent I made plans to go to England in mid-April 1654, he made a legal agreement with his sister Mary, asking her to see that his children were educated and that his wife, Mary, had living space in the family home. Brent assigned some of his land to his sister Mary and gave her his personal estate in Virginia and Maryland, but he specified that it was to be used for the support of his wife and children. Brent and his wife, Mary, gave two calves to their daughter, Mary. After Mary Kittamaquund Brent's death, which had occurred by 1655, Giles Brent I remarried, taking as his wife the widowed Frances Harrison, with whom he failed to produce living heirs. Brent's sister Mary was living at Peace, the family home, in July 1657 when she named her sister, Margaret, and brother, Giles I, as her heirs. In August 1658 Giles Brent I executed two deeds of gift in which he bestowed upon his son Giles II a black servant named Joan, and upon his daughter, Mary, a piece of land on the south and southwest side of the Aquia River. In 1663 when Brent's sister Margaret made her will, she named him as an heir and designated his children, Giles II, Mary, and Richard, as reversionary heirs. When Giles Brent I made his will on August 31, 1671, he was living in Stafford County at a plantation known as The Retirement. He bequeathed livestock to his married daughter, Mary Fitzherbert, son Giles Brent II, and two male friends, but left virtually all of his landholdings in Virginia, Maryland, and England to his son Giles II. The testator, whose will was proved on February 15, 1672, assigned reversionary rights to his late father's heirs if Giles Brent II failed to produce direct descendants. In 1684 George Talbot, who was defending the Calverts' claim from William Penn, commented that "Capt. Brent who in the right of his wife the Piscataway Emperor's daughter and only Child pretended a right to the most part of Maryland but could doe noe good . . . after a great bustle about it" (HALL 131–132, 135–136; *Maryland Historical Magazine* 3, "Conference Between Penn and Talbot, at New Castle in 1684," 30; Chilton, "The Brent Family," 96–102; Rowland, "Mercer Land Book," 165–168; PB 2:359; 3:134, 192, 303, 308; 4:421; 5:652; Westmoreland County Deeds, Wills, Patents &c. 1653–1659:16–17, 105–105a, 112).

Mary Brent (Mrs. Giles Brent I) (see Mary Kittamaquund)

Giles (Gyles) Brent II: Giles Brent II, the son of Giles Brent I and his Piscataway Indian wife, Mary Kittamaquund, was born around 1652. In 1658 Giles Brent I executed a deed of gift, bestowing upon son Giles II the labor of a black servant named Joan. Giles Brent II was his father's principal heir and ultimately inherited his land in Virginia, Maryland, and England. His acreage on Aquia Creek in Stafford County was known as the Rock Patent. In 1675 Colonel George Mason, Captain George Brent II, and a party of armed men from the Northern Neck, enraged over an attack on an outlying homestead, crossed into Maryland. They assaulted some Susquehannock Indians who were staying in a cabin, and then laid siege to the Piscattoway (Piscatoway) Indians' fort, in which some Susquehannocks had taken refuge. According to a contemporary account by Thomas Mathew, many of the Indians escaped despite a prolonged attack and withdrew to Virginia, where they began preying on settlers living beyond the falls of the James and York rivers. Mathew concluded that this sequence of events gave rise to Bacon's Rebellion. By 1676 Giles Brent II had become a staunch supporter of the rebel Nathaniel Bacon. However, when he learned that Governor William Berkeley had declared Bacon an outlaw, he set out for Tindall's Point in Gloucester County with an estimated 1,000 men. Although Brent's men intended to confront Bacon's followers, they fled when they were confronted with the prospect of vigorous opposition. Lancaster County records reveal that in 1677 the county justices tried to recover the weapons that had been given to the local militia. They also were obliged to deal with the claims filed by local citizens who were trying to recover the cost of confiscated food stuffs and horses. In 1688 Giles Brent II served as a burgess for Stafford County. He died in Middlesex County on September 2, 1689 (LEO 49; Stafford County Record Book 1686–1693:131–131a; Lancaster County Order Book 1666–1680:382–385, 447; Chilton, "The Brent Family," 96–102; AND 16–20; Westmoreland County Deeds, Wills, Patents &c. 1653–1659:112).

* * *

* * *

Thomas Brereton (Brerreton, Brewerton) I: Thomas Brereton I was clerk of the General Court from 1654 to 1661 and often spent time in Jamestown. Between 1657 and 1668 he patented massive quantities of land in New Kent County and in Northumberland, where he was appointed a county justice in 1663 and served successive terms. Sometimes Brereton also served as a juryman in Northumberland and Lancaster counties. A deed he and his wife, Jane, witnessed in 1668 indicates that they were living in Little Wicocomico. Brereton's business dealings involved people in several counties, including Lower Norfolk County, which was a considerable distance from his home. One of the merchants with whom he dealt was Peter Knight of Jamestown, who often did business in Northumberland County. When Brereton disposed of a piece of property in 1671, he identified his late wife, Jane, as the daughter of Colonel William Claiborne and indicated that the 1,450 acres he was selling had been granted to her in 1657. In November 1671 Thomas Brereton I of Little Wicocomico was prompted to make his will, perhaps on account of his wife's death or his own ill health; however, he survived for another 12 years. Throughout the 1670s and early 1680s, Major Thomas Brereton continued to serve as a justice in Northumberland County, and he was co-executor of Peter Ashton's estate. In November 1672 he was authorized to receive payment for furnishing a drum, probably to the local militia. In December 1677 he was placed in command of some men who participated in an offensive against the Susquehannock Indians. By August 1680 he held the rank of colonel in the local militia. During 1680, when the assembly decided to establish an urban community in every county, Colonel Thomas Brereton, who had surveyed the proposed town site, was ordered to send a plat to Colonel Richard Lee and Lieutenant Colonel Isaac Allerton. Brereton was sworn in as high sheriff in April 1683 and was still alive the following November. However, by June 4, 1684, he was dead, at which time his will was proved and his son, Thomas II, became his executor and heir to his real estate. The decedent left his personal estate to his son, Thomas II, and his daughter, Elizabeth (Northumberland County Wills, Inventories &c. 1652–1658:78, 87, 144; Record Book 1662–1666:168; 1666–1670:67–68; Deeds and Wills 1670–1672:179, 205; Order Book 1652–1665:276, 282, 306, 364, 415; 1666–1678:2, 60, 112, 163, 173, 176, 199, 208, 275, 282, 324–325, 329; 1678–1698:64, 73, 78, 175, 205, 229, 253, 263, 310; Lancaster County Order Book 1656–1666:346; 1666–1680:69; PB 4:202, 225, 474, 477; 5:325; 6:77, 191, 203; Westmoreland County Deeds, Wills, Patents &c. 1653–1659:100; Deeds, Wills &c. 1661–1662:37a, 49a).

Thomas Brereton (Brerreton, Brewerton) II: When Thomas Brereton I made his will in 1671, he left a share of his household furnishings, goods, and livestock to his son, Thomas Brereton II, who was then a minor. However, the testator lived until late 1683 or early 1684, by which time his son had attained his majority and was able to serve as executor. In 1680–1682 Captain Thomas Brereton II served as a burgess for Northumberland County, and he went on to serve as a court justice. During the mid-1680s his name began appearing in Lancaster County's records, but he continued to be closely associated with Northumberland County. Brereton died prior to August 1699, at which time his widow, Mary, presented his will and was named executrix (LEO xxii, 46; Northumberland County Deeds and Wills 1670–1672:179, 205; Order Book 1678–1698:229, 253, 263, 310; 1699–1700:1, 45, 53; Lancaster County Order Book 1680–1687:211).

* * *

* * *

John Brewer (Bower, Brower) I: John Brewer came to Virginia sometime prior to 1622, when he identified himself as an ancient planter and adventurer in New England. In January 1629 he was described as a merchant when he purchased 1,000 acres called Stanley Hundred, property formerly owned by Sir George Yeardley. In 1630 Brewer was elected a burgess, representing the settlers along the Warwick River. He may have been seriously ill in September 1631, for he was prompted to make his will, designating his wife, children, and brother as heirs. However, in 1632 Brewer served as a justice of the Warwick River court, and in February 1633 he became a member of the Council of State. He died in Virginia sometime prior to July 11, 1635, by which time his widow, Marie (Mary), had married the Rev. Thomas Butler of Denbigh. John Brewer's son John II went on to become an Isle of Wight County burgess (VI&A 155; LEO 9; STAN 32).

John Brewer (Bower, Brower) II: John Brewer II was the son of merchant, burgess, and councilor John Brewer I and his wife, Marie (Mary) of Stanley Hundred. John II and his siblings, Roger and Margaret, were minors in 1635 when their father died. John Brewer II inherited his late father's acreage at Stanley Hundred and went on to enhance its size in 1653 through the acquisition of 300 acres he purchased from George Lobb. Brewer served as a burgess for Isle of Wight County in 1658. On June 9, 1669, his nuncupative will was entered into the records of Isle of Wight County's court. At that time, Margaret Skyner, who identified herself as the decedent's 46-year-old sister, indicated that Brewer wanted his estate to be divided between his wife and sons John III and

Thomas. James Valentine, who was age 24, corroborated Skyner's statements. On July 14, 1671, John Brewer II's estate was appraised by three local men. That document was presented to the county court on October 19, 1671, by Mrs. Ann Holliday, who identified herself as the widow and administratrix of the late John Brewer II (LEO 34; VI&A 155–156; Isle of Wight Will and Deed Book 1 [1688–1704]:16; 2 [1704–1715]:68, 100; Deeds, Wills, & Guardian Accounts Book A:51; PB 5:364).

* * *

* * *

Edward Brewster: Edward Brewster came to Virginia with Thomas West, Lord Delaware, in 1610. After they landed in Jamestown, Delaware made Brewster captain of his company and sent him to the falls of the James River. In May 1611 Sir Thomas Dale had Brewster and his workers repair the church in Jamestown. Captain Edward Brewster left Virginia but returned in August 1618 as one of Lord Delaware's officers. Delaware died on the way to the colony and Brewster tried to take custody of his goods once they arrived in Jamestown. However, Deputy-Governor Samuel Argall seized Delaware's belongings and put his men to work on his personal projects. When Brewster protested, Argall had him tried at a court-martial hearing. Although Brewster was condemned to death, Argall offered him a reprieve if he agreed to leave the colony and never speak of him unfavorably. Brewster reached England and in May 1619 appealed his sentence to officials of the Virginia Company (VI&A 156).

Mr. and Mrs. Richard Brewster: In 1622 Richard Brewster, an ancient planter, stated that he had resided in Jamestown for seven years but was not present in August 1618 when Lord Delaware's ship arrived. He mentioned Argall's trial of Captain Edward Brewster, his kinsman, and said that Edward had been mistreated. In April 1624 he asked to be relieved from paying taxes because of the losses he had sustained during the 1622 Indian attack. When a list of patented land was sent back to England in May 1625, Richard Brewster was credited with 100 acres in Archer's Hope; however, in December 1626 he was living at Pasbehay and paying rent to the governor. In 1629 and 1630 Brewster was a burgess for the settlers living in the Neck O'Land, and in 1633 he represented the territory between Harrop and Martin's Hundred. Finally, in 1644 he served as a burgess for James City County. In February 1638 Brewster acquired a patent for 500 acres known as the Great or Barren Neck, using the headrights of his wife, his two children, and his brother, Henry. In 1642 Brewster was obliged to purchase Captain Francis Pott's interest in the Barren Neck, which had descended to him from his brother, Dr. John Pott. In 1646 Brewster enlarged his 500-acre tract through the addition of another 250 acres. References to his possession of the property persisted into the 1670s (VI&A 157; LEO 8–9, 12, 22; NUG I:80–81, 174; II:207; PB 1:520).

* * *

William Brewster: William Brewster, a gentleman, came to Virginia in 1607 and was one of the first Jamestown settlers. On August 7, 1607, he was wounded by the Indians. He died in or near Jamestown, where he was buried (VI&A 158).

Edward Bricke (Britt): Edward Bricke was living in urban Jamestown in 1624 and was one of Captain William Peirce's servants. Court testimony taken two years later states that in 1620 he made an accounting of some tobacco that John Rolfe received (VI&A 158).

Joseph Bridger I: Joseph Bridger I commenced serving in the assembly in 1658, representing Isle of Wight County. In March 1664 he and two other men patented a large quantity of land in Isle of Wight, on the Blackwater River. Two years later he enhanced the size of his holdings, this time gaining land on a "white marsh." His residence, which bore that name, may have been in that vicinity. Bridger served in the assembly from December 1660 to 1670 and was a member of the Council of State from 1673 to 1686. He was on the commission that in 1664 adjusted the boundary line between Virginia and Maryland, and in 1666 he was adjutant general of the Virginia militia. In 1672 he married Hester, the daughter of Robert Pitt and the granddaughter of William and Mary Pitt of Bristol, England, and in 1675 he was made commander of the Isle of Wight militia. When Bridger and his father-in-law, Colonel Robert Pitt, had a disagreement in 1673 over a large tract of land formerly owned by Captain John Upton, Pitt asked that the matter be settled by a jury. In 1680 Bridger sold John Pitt his interest in two large tracts that he had patented in 1664 with two other men. Colonel Joseph Bridger was a council member at the time of Bacon's Rebellion, and in March 1676 he was among those placed in overall command of the local

militia. A fort was to be built at Currawaugh or New Dursley (Dursly), property that Bridger owned on the west side of the Dismal Swamp. Bridger staunchly supported Governor William Berkeley, and as a result his cattle were seized by Bacon's men and some of his property was destroyed. He also was among those who fled to the Eastern Shore after Bacon's followers gained control of the capital city, and in early 1677 he witnessed the will Governor Berkeley made before leaving for England to explain his actions. In 1680 Colonel Bridger was placed in command of the militia from Lower Norfolk, Nansemond, and Isle of Wight counties.

On September 20, 1683, Colonel Joseph Bridger reportedly was in the process of building "houses" in Jamestown, probably in response to the king's order that council members do so. When Bridger prepared his will on August 3, 1683, he named his wife, Hester, as his executrix and left her life-rights in his real estate, some household furniture, a horse, two servants, and her apparel and jewelry. He made bequests to his mother, Mrs. Mary Bridger; to his daughters, Martha Godwin, Mary, Elizabeth, and Hester; and to his sons, Samuel, William, and Joseph II. However, on October 18, 1683, Bridger added a codicil to his will, disinheriting his son and primary heir, Joseph II, on account of his disobedience and "divers dissolute courses of life." The testator designated his wife, Hester, as his executrix and asked that she be assisted by Thomas and John Pitt and Arthur Smith, all of whom were prominent public officials. Colonel Joseph Bridger was survived by his wife and their seven children. He died on April 15, 1686, and was buried at his home, White Marsh. An inventory of his estate reveals that he had a large, well-furnished dwelling with numerous rooms. On November 25, 1692, after Bridger's death, the Council of State convened in his accommodations in Jamestown, an indication that he had erected one or more buildings there. In 1739 the *Virginia Gazette* reported that a large quantity of old English coins had been found in the ruins of Colonel Bridger's house in Isle of Wight. Some dated to the reigns of Queen Elizabeth and Kings James I and Charles I. The *Gazette's* editor speculated that the money may have been hidden for security's sake (NUG I:433; HEN 2:225, 328; NEIL 303; CO 5/1356 f 68; EJC I:9; LJC 35; MCGH 162, 167–168; Isle of Wight Will and Deed Book 1 [1662–1688]:128, 242, 250–251, 255–263, 296–297, 504–505; Deed Book 1 [1662–1688]:453–454; 2 [1688–1704]:407; 2 [1704–1715]:87; LEO xix, 34, 38; Parks, *Virginia Gazette*, April 6, 1739; STAN 39).

Bridget (Bridgett): On February 15, 1768, when an inventory was made of the late Richard Ambler's slaves on Jamestown Island and his leasehold in the Governor's Land, a female slave named Bridget was listed. In 1769 she was included in the late Edward Ambler I's estate and was described as a girl living on the Governor's Land (York County Wills and Inventories 21:386–391; AMB-E).

Edward Brinton (Brynton): Edward Brinton, a mason, arrived in Virginia in 1607 and was one of the first Jamestown settlers. According to Captain John Smith, when Brinton learned that some Dutchmen sent to build a house for Powhatan were furnishing the Indians with weapons, he tried to return to Jamestown to inform the authorities. However, he was caught and killed by the Indians on his way home (VI&A 159).

* * *

William Briscoe (Brisco): William Briscoe, a blacksmith, purchased a quarter-acre lot in urban Jamestown in May 1679. In November 1681 Briscoe, then a resident of the capital city, appointed an attorney to represent him in Surry County's monthly court. Earlier in the year, when John Soane made a plat of William Sherwood's landholdings in urban Jamestown, "Briscoe's Orchard" was shown prominently at a location astride Orchard Run, a small tributary of the James River. In April 1682, when urban Jamestown's landowners sought to have the community's boundaries legally defined, the easternmost limit of the town was "ye run or slash by Wm. Briscoe ye smith." In November 10, 1682, the assembly authorized payment to Briscoe for work the blacksmith had done at the prison in Jamestown. Two years later he was paid for irons he had provided for securing prisoners. On September 20, 1686, Briscoe was summoned before escheator John Page to testify about whether Colonel William White had disposed of his Jamestown lots before he died.

In September 1683 William Briscoe patented 12 acres of escheat land on the east side of Orchard Run, acreage that formerly belonged to the late William Penn (Pinn). Briscoe's business interests extended into the Northern Neck and Middle Peninsula, and in October 1691 he patented 153 acres in Middlesex County, acreage that had been abandoned. In 1684 he sued a Norfolk County burgess, William Robinson, who had married the widow of Richard Hill of Westmoreland County. In 1685 and again in

1688 Briscoe hired a Westmoreland County attorney, Original Brown, to handle a case against a local woman. Sometime prior to July 10, 1695, William Briscoe of Jamestown made his will, in which he bequeathed all of his land in the capital city "adjoyning to Mr. Henry Hartwell" to his widowed daughter-in-law, the former Ann Holder. The acreage she stood to inherit included the quarter-acre lot Briscoe had bought in 1679 and some adjoining acreage that he had purchased from Thomas Holiday, property that included a brick house that had been rented to Joseph and Elizabeth Rabley Topping. Original Browne served as the late William Briscoe's attorney in Westmoreland County's monthly court and tried to collect debts that were due to his estate (Ambler MS 23, 27, 35, 37, 53, 57, 133, 134; PB 7:328; NUG II:269, 372; JHB 1660–1693:174, 256; Surry County Deeds and Wills 1671–1684:295; Westmoreland County Order Book 1676–1689:355, 473, 511, 680; 1691–1699:73a).

[First Name Unknown] Briscoe (Brisco): The son of Jamestown lot owner and blacksmith William Briscoe married Ann Holder, who outlived him. The first name of the younger Briscoe and the date of his death are uncertain. However, by 1695 his widow, Ann, had married James Chudley (AMB 53, 57).

Ann Holder (Holden, Holdinge) Briscoe (Brisco) (see Ann Holder)

* * *

Peter (Peeter) Brishitt (Briskitt): Peter Brishitt died in Jamestown sometime after April 1623 but before February 16, 1624 (VI&A 160).

Richard Brislow: Richard Brislow, a laborer, arrived in Jamestown in January 1608 in the 1st Supply of new settlers (VI&A 160).

Robert Bristow: Robert Bristow patented a 12-acre lot on Back Street in urban Jamestown. He acquired his lot from Captain Francis Pott, the brother and principal heir of Dr. John Pott, who came into possession of the property between 1635 and 1640. Sometime after 1640 but before 1656, Robert Bristow's widow, Joane, disposed of his lot in the capital city (NUG I:340; PB 4:69).

Robert Bristow I: Robert Bristow I, who was born in 1634, came to Virginia around 1660. He acquired and developed large tracts of land in the Northern Neck and Middle Peninsula, in Lancaster, Northumberland, and Gloucester counties. By 1665 he had married Avarilla (Averilla), the daughter of Thomas Curtis, who owned land on the James-York Peninsula and in Gloucester County. Because Bristow sided with Governor William Berkeley during Bacon's Rebellion, he was captured and imprisoned by Bacon. Bristow returned to England in 1677, after the popular uprising was quelled, and became an important merchant and a London alderman. His daughter was married to merchant Arthur Bayly. While Bristow was away, his attorney brought suit in Middlesex County's monthly court. Officials in England debated whether Major Robert Bristow had been a sufferer in Bacon's Rebellion or one of the rebel's leading supporters. From time to time Bristow's name appeared in local court records, usually because he was pursuing debtors. Robert Bristow and his wife, Avarilla, had two children, Robert II and Avarilla. Robert Bristow I died in England in 1706–1707 and was survived by his then wife, Susanna (DOR 1:786–789; SR 664, 1453; PB 4:464; 5:523; CO 5/1371 f 181; Middlesex County Order Book 1673–1680:118, 135, 139, 141, 194; Lancaster County Order Book 1674–1680:337; 1696–1702:60; Northumberland County Order Book 1652–1665:287; SR 5726; NEVILLE 92–93).

Peter Bristow: Peter Bristow arrived in Jamestown on July 31, 1622, with Mr. Spencer, probably William Spencer, who lived in the eastern end of Jamestown Island (VI&A 160).

Walter Broadhurst (Brodhurst) I: In 1652 and 1653 Walter Broadhurst I represented Northumberland County in the assembly. He also became a justice of the county court, and shortly thereafter he was chosen high sheriff. He appeared in court from time to time, serving as an attorney or testifying in cases that were being deliberated. At times he also served as a mediator. In 1655 he was appointed a justice of Westmoreland County, which in 1653 was formed out of part of northwestern Northumberland County, and held office for several years. Broadhurst was respected by his contemporaries and often was placed in positions of trust. When testifying in court in 1654, he indicated that he was around 36. However, when he returned to court two years later, he again gave his age as 36. Walter Broadhurst I made his will on January 26, 1659, and by February 12th was dead. He nominated his wife, Anne, as executrix and gave her life-rights in their land until she remarried or his sons came of age. The testator named his son Gerrard as heir to his land in Nominy and stipulated

that if he died without heirs, the acreage would descend to son Walter II. If both sons were to die, the testator's land was to descend to his daughter, Elizabeth. Walter Broadhurst I instructed his wife to dispose of whatever he had in England, using the proceeds for the benefit of his children. In April 1661 executrix Anne Broadhurst presented an inventory of her late husband's estate. In August she followed it with a list of the disbursements she had made on his behalf. Later, the twice-widowed Anne, who had outlived Henry Brett and Walter Broadhurst I, married Lieutenant Colonel John Washington I, a widower. In January 1670, when Washington rented the Broadhurst plantation to Lewis Markham for three years, he indicated that its dwelling was furnished and that livestock were pastured on the property. Markham was allowed to have half of the profits produced by the ordinary, but Washington was allowed to keep the courthouse and prison, a shop, and a loft (LEO 31; Northumberland County Deeds and Orders 1650–1652:76; Wills, Inventories &c. 1652–1658:4; Order Book 1652–1665:9, 108, 148, 167, 217, 262; Westmoreland County Deeds, Wills, Patents &c. 1653–1659:13, 15, 36, 54, 100, 102, 116a, 121; Deeds, Wills &c. 1661–1662:47a–48a; Deeds, Patents &c. 1665–1677:49a–51).

* * *

William Broadnax (Brodnax) I: William Broadnax I was born on February 28, 1676. He married and fathered three children: Edward, Elizabeth, and William II. Around 1720, after being widowed, he married Rebecca, the widow of Edward Travis II and the mother of Edward Travis III. She may have been the sister of John Champion, who is buried in the Travis graveyard on Jamestown Island. In 1706 William Broadnax I commenced serving as a James City County justice of the peace, and he was elected Jamestown's burgess in 1718, serving intermittently through 1726. William Broadnax I purchased two waterfront parcels in the capital city from James and Ann Holder Briscoe Chudley. He also began enhancing the size of his holdings in the south-central part of Jamestown Island, finally accumulating a total of 127.7 acres. Part of the land he owned included Fox Island. Broadnax also may have acquired the 12-acre tract of escheat land that William Briscoe left to daughter-in-law Ann. Rebecca Travis Broadnax died on December 19, 1723, at the age of 46. When William Broadnax I died on February 16, 1727, he left his son and namesake, William Broadnax II, as his principal heir (STAN 102–103, 105–106; PALM I:99;

LEO 70, 72; DOR 2:359; AMB 106–107; Tyler "The Broadnax Family," 56; DOR 2:359).

William Broadnax (Brodnax) II: William Broadnax II inherited his late father's rural landholdings on Jamestown Island and his acreage within the limits of urban Jamestown. He also was heir to at least one town lot in the western end of the island, property that had belonged to Jamestown ferryman Edward Ross. Broadnax purchased 100 acres in the eastern end of Jamestown Island from Philip Ludwell II, along with some additional land. Then, on April 22, 1736, he bought William Sarson's 107-acre tract from Francis Bullifant. Broadnax was a wealthy and prominent citizen, with substantial landholdings on the south side of the James in Brunswick County. He represented Jamestown in the February 1, 1728, session of the legislature and in 1731 was one of James City County's justices of the peace. On January 1, 1744, when William Broadnax II sold all of his property on Jamestown Island (both rural and urban) to Christopher Perkins, a Norfolk County merchant, his wife, Ann, relinquished her dower interest in the property. Broadnax also conveyed to Perkins a slave named William Liverpool (STAN 107; EJC 4:236; HUD V:136; AMB 77, 97–98, 106–107, 250).

John Broadnax: In 1690 John, the brother of William Broadnax I, patented a substantial quantity of land on the south side of the James River, within what was then Henrico County but later Chesterfield. He also owned or rented property in urban Jamestown and hosted meetings of the Committee for Public Claims during 1693 and 1696. In 1710 at least one of Broadnax's slaves was involved in a planned escape. An African slave named Jamy, who reportedly played an active role, was arrested and detained. In 1719 Edward Travis III, whose plantation was in the eastern end of Jamestown Island, purchased some of John Broadnax's personal property (NUG II:345, 396; JHB 1695–1702:8, 49, 62; Stanard, "The Randolph Manuscript," 23; Tyler, "Historical and Genealogical Notes," 142).

* * *

William Broadribb: William Broadribb inherited some land from Thomas Hunt of urban Jamestown during the fourth quarter of the seventeenth century. His guardian was Henry Hartwell, also a Jamestown resident. In 1699 Broadribb obtained a 21-year lease for a mill seat on Powhatan Creek, which he sublet to John Tullitt of Jamestown. By May 1699 Broadribb was serving as a churchwarden for James City Parish, an indication that he was a respected member of the community. He made his will in early May 1703 and died within a month. He was survived by his wife, Lydia, two daughters, and a son. Broadribb designated Benjamin Eggleston of Powhatan Plantation, Mrs. William Drummond II of the Mainland, and George Marable II of Jamestown as his trustees. In 1708 Broadribb's trustees sold to Joseph Chermaison the Glasshouse tract, which Emanuel Dees had commenced leasing in 1703. Lydia, the widow of William Broadribb, married the Rev. Christopher Smith sometime after 1703 but before 1709 (Surry County Order Book 1671–1690:509; AMB 77, 78; MCGH 676; LJC 263).

William Brocas (Brocus): William Brocas, who was named to the Council of State in 1637 and served until 1652, was born in England. A year later he patented a large tract of land at the head of "Otterdams" in Warwick County and a smaller parcel on a tributary of the Warwick River. By July 1638 he had become a member of the Charles River (York) County court; like other justices, he occasionally hosted court sessions in his home. At times he speculated in real estate, and he seems to have sold indentured servants. On January 30, 1647, Captain William Brocas and his wife, Mary, sold two black male servants to Thomas Harrison, master of the *Honour*, and shipped some of their tobacco to England aboard the ship. By June 7, 1648, Brocas had remarried, this time taking as his bride a woman named Elinor (Elnor), who was the aunt of Edwin and Martha Connaway's daughter, Eltonhead. Like many of his contemporaries, during the early 1650s Captain Brocas began patenting land on Virginia's frontier. In July 1650 he acquired some acreage that was 35 miles above the mouth of the Rappahannock River. Then, in 1652 he and his wife, Elinor, secured patents for hundreds of acres near the Rappahannock's mouth. Finally, in 1653 he laid claim to an additional parcel on the lower side of the Rappahannock. All of the remote acreage in which Brocas invested was on the south side of the Rappahannock River. In October 1652 he was awarded a land certificate in Lancaster County's monthly court and within a few months added to his holdings in that area. Brocas's land, like the other Lancaster County property in which he invested, abutted the Rappahannock River. A document signed by Sir Henry Chicheley and his wife, Lady Agatha, Colonel Ralph Wormeley's widow, reveals that in 1652 Captain

William Brocas was one of Lady Agatha's trustees. Brocas died in Virginia sometime prior to May 1655 and left his entire estate to his wife, Elinor. John Jackson, the decedent's nephew, was identified as his sister's son. An inventory of William Brocas's estate reveals that he was a wealthy and erudite man, who owned white and African servants and a large herd of livestock. In his possession were books written in Spanish, Italian, and Latin, raising the possibility that he was fluent in several languages. His household furnishings included several silver vessels. Brocas had property on the upper side of the York River in York County, in territory that later became Middlesex and then Lancaster County. By 1657 his widow, Elinor, who had married burgess John Carter, was deceased (STAN 33; LEO xix; Lancaster County Deeds &c. 1652–1657:16, 129–131, 133, 189–192, 202–204; 1654–1661:161; Order Book 1666–1680:58; PB 1:533, 554; 2:222; 3:34, 130, 224; SR 10473, 12537; York County 1633–1657:49, 54, 61, 115, 121; 1646–1648:203; 1648–1657:406, 432).

William Brockenbrough: On January 14, 1798, William Brockenbrough informed a friend that a schoolmate, Weylie, "now lives at Jamestown" with the Amblers. Brockenbrough and Weylie attended the College of William and Mary with Edward Ambler II, the son of John Ambler II (Stanard, "Letters from William and Mary, 1795–1799," 238).

Thomas Brodsil: On August 22, 1625, Thomas Brodsil testified that he had witnessed a bargain between John Hall and Thomas Passmore, both of whom were residents of eastern Jamestown Island (VI&A 161). Brodsil may have lived there too.

John Bromfield: John Bromfield married Bridget, one of the guardians of the late Rev. Richard Buck's children, who already had outlived husbands John Burrows and William Davis. In 1655 Bromfield sued Elizabeth Buck Crump in an attempt to recover what he presumed was his late wife's interest in the Buck property in Archer's Hope, where he also owned land. It was then determined that Bridget had only held a life-interest in the Buck estate. During the late 1670s John Bromfield was clerk of the Isle of Wight County court (HEN I:405; PB 4:81; VI&A 177).

Richard Brooks: In 1635 Richard Brooks, who was 30 years old, immigrated to Virginia on the *David*. On January 22, 1641, he secured a 21-acre leasehold in the Governor's land, a parcel that was near the Glass-

house tract. On August 28, 1643, Brooks patented a one-acre lot in urban Jamestown that was located on a point of land between the Doctors and Gallows swamps. Brooks's parcel probably was absorbed into the 120 acres John Phipps patented in 1656, which included Dr. John Pott's acreage. In 1652 Richard Brooks acquired some land near the palisade at Middle Plantation (CBE 166; NUG I: 127, 139, 154, 266; PB 2:11).

William Brooks (Brookes, Broockes) alias Jones alias Morgan (see William Morgan)

Thomas Broomer: On June 21, 1682, Thomas Broomer was ordered to deliver military stores to John Page of urban Jamestown (EJC I:25).

[No First Name] Brown: On June 12, 1610, Thomas West, Lord Delaware, designated a Mr. Brown as clerk of the council. Therefore, he would have lived in Jamestown (VI&A 163).

Devereau (Deverax, Devereaux, Deveroux, Deborae, Devercux) Brown (Browne): Devereau Brown came to Virginia prior to the early 1660s and became a merchant and planter. A Northampton County court document reveals that in 1662, while he was conducting business, he mistakenly sent Mr. Anscomb's goods to Thomas Martin and Ambrose Johnson. Brown served as a burgess for Accomack County in 1663–1666 but retired after the 1666 session. His mercantile enterprises seem to have flourished during the 1660s and 1670s, and records on file in the British Archives document his numerous shipments of tobacco. Sometimes he served as the factor of British merchant Thomas Webb, who did business along the Rappahannock River. From time to time Brown undertook lawsuits, and on at least one occasion, he used the General Court as an appellate body. In 1670 Brown patented 3,700 acres at Pocomoke in Accomack County and married the widowed Tabitha Scarborough Smart, Colonel Edmund Scarborough II's daughter. After the colonel's death his son Charles and sons-in-law Devereau Brown and John West were named administrators and commenced settling his estate. On September 21, 1671, the three men informed the General Court that the decedent had patented, but deserted, several large tracts of land in Northampton County. Therefore, they sought—and received— permission to patent the acreage themselves. In 1671 and 1672 Brown joined his wife's brothers, Charles and Edmund Scarborough III, in patenting tracts of 3,000 acres and

4,500 acres in Northampton County. Independently, he patented 3,600 acres on Deep Creek in 1672. After Devereau Brown's death, his widow, Tabitha, sought the General Court's help in settling his estate. She eventually married John Custis II of Arlington (LEO 37; PB 6:392, 398, 401, 405; SR 4199, 4200, 10041, 10044, 10056, 10060, 10431, 10470, 10478, 10499, 13574, 13799; NUG I:328, 393, 455; II:107, 109, 237, 243; MCGC 237–238, 256, 268–269, 271, 291, 298, 374, 376, 384–385, 394, 397, 413–414; MARSHALL 54, 151–152).

John Brown (Browne): John Brown (Browne) came to Virginia in 1621 and by the mid-1620s was living at Chaplin's Choice, where he was a household head. On December 4, 1626, he was identified as a servant of Rowland Truelove and Company who already had served for five years. John Brown was freed of two additional years he was supposed to serve, and on October 16, 1629, he represented West and Shirley Hundred (Eppes) Island in the assembly. He died prior to June 5, 1632, by which time his widow had married Richard Cocke, who took custody of Brown's orphans' estate (VI&A 164; LEO 8; PB 3:133; MCGC 201; DOR 1:120–121).

Henry Brown: Captain Henry Brown was named to the Council of State in 1634 and served until 1641, having been removed and then reinstated. He lived on the plantation known as Pipsico, acquiring 2,250 acres there in July 1637. Then he added the property that became known as Four Mile Tree. The Brown property was located on the lower side of the James River in what was then James City County but later Surry. Colonel Brown and his wife, Ann, disposed of a piece of property in 1657. He died in Virginia before November 1662, when his widow, Ann, signed a marriage contract with Colonel Thomas Swann; Brown's son, Berkeley, was party to the agreement. The late Henry Brown's plantation descended to Lieutenant William Brown I, a kinsman (STAN 33; LEO xix; PB 1:441, 929; 2:8; MCGC 492, 498–499; Surry County Deed Book 1 [1652–1672]:114–116, 195).

* * *

William Brown (Browne) I: William Brown I of Four Mile Tree in Surry County, a burgess who represented Surry County in 1661–1662, 1671–1673, 1677, and 1679, was a highly successful planter. He acquired land in the Northern Neck and on Diascund Creek in James City County. He also patented land on the Blackwater River and in Isle of Wight County. In 1677 Brown was among those who signed the James City County grievances, a list of complaints about how the colony was being governed. He was returned to the assembly and represented Surry County, serving in 1681–1682. In November 1682 Brown, who then owned part of a row house in urban Jamestown, requested 2¼ years' compensation for renting his dwelling to the General Court as an office; he also asked to be paid for providing accommodations to the Secretary's Office. On April 7, 1685, Brown and his wife, Elizabeth, sold George Lee their ¾-acre lot in urban Jamestown. The tract, which contained the easternmost bays of a long row house on Back Street, was described as formerly belonging to Thomas Woodhurst (Woodhouse?). This raises the possibility that Elizabeth Brown was Woodhurst's widow or daughter. The deed the Browns executed in 1685 made reference to two row house bays, one that was ruinous and one that was habitable. Both structures had been put to the torch in 1676 when Nathaniel Bacon's men set the capital city ablaze. In 1691, 1692, and 1694 William Brown I was paid for providing a storehouse for the ammunition belonging to the fort at Jamestown. As he had already sold his ¾-acre row house lot to George Lee, it is uncertain where his storehouse was located. When Brown made his will on December 4, 1704, he left his acreage in James City (then occupied by John Child) to his grandson, Henry. It is uncertain whether the testator was referring to property in urban Jamestown or in James City County. William Brown I's will was presented for probate on July 3, 1705 (LEE 51 f 668; STAN 73, 80, 82–83; NUG II:61, 222; III:45, 62; SAIN 10:44; JHB 1660–1693:174, 254; EJC I:187, 255, 315; Surry County Will Book 5:305; LEO 36, 40, 42–44, 46).

Henry Brown II: In 1705 Henry II, the grandson of William Brown I, inherited the James City property that had belonged to his late grandfather. It is uncertain whether the decedent's acreage was in Jamestown or James City County. Henry Brown II made his will on September 23, 1734, and died early in 1735 (Surry County Will Book 5:305; 8:458).

* * *

Thomas Brown (Browne): Thomas Brown died on Jamestown Island sometime after April 1623 but before February 16, 1624 (VI&A 165).

John Browning (Browninge): John Browning came to Virginia in 1621 and in 1625 was living at Basses Choice, where he and partner Henry Woodward headed a household. In 1628 he purchased a 400-acre tract called Hampton Key in the corporation of James City, property that had belonged in succession to Treasurer George Sandys and Edward Grindon. In 1629 Browning was identified as a married man. He bought 250 acres that lay contiguous and upstream from his Hampton Key property, acreage that had belonged to John Uty, and he also acquired Uty's property at Hog Island. In October 1629 Browning served as a burgess for the corporation of Elizabeth City, an indication that he or his wife owned property in that jurisdiction. However, in March 1630 he began representing the territory between Archer's Hope and Martin's Hundred in the corporation of James City. John Browning died sometime prior to 1646 when his son and heir, William Browning, repatented his James City County acreage (VI&A 166; LEO 8–9, 11; NUG I:4, 105, 168).

Robert Browning: On November 22, 1671, Robert Browning lost a lawsuit to William Drummond I of urban Jamestown (MCGC 284).

* * *

Richard Buck: The Rev. Richard Buck and his wife, the former Maria Thorowgood, left England in June 1609 and were aboard the *Seaventure* when it wrecked in Bermuda. In May 1610 Buck, who arrived in Jamestown and replaced the late Rev. Robert Hunt, served as chaplain to the colony's first assembly and as rector of the church in Jamestown. He had use of the James City glebe, and he patented 750 acres in Archer's Hope. The Bucks preferred to live on Jamestown Island, and in December 1620 purchased William Fairfax's 12-acre homestead. Mrs. Buck died in Jamestown, perhaps around 1620 when her son Peleg was born. She was the mother of three other Virginia-born children (Mara, Gercian, and Benomi), and the stepmother of Elizabeth Buck, who remained behind in England for a while. The Rev. Buck died sometime after December 1622 but before April 1623, and his minor children went to live with Mrs. Mary Ascam (Ascomb, Ascombe), a widow. Later, Gercian went to live with John Jackson, Peleg moved into the home of Thomas Alnutt, Benomi found shelter with Richard Kingsmill, and Mara commenced living with John and Bridget Burrows. Elizabeth, the Rev. Richard Buck's eldest daughter, came to Virginia around 1625 and married Sergeant Thomas Crump, with whom she

produced a son, John. She went on to marry Mathew Page. On September 1, 1636, when Gercian Buck acquired 500 acres in the Neck O'Land from his brother-in-law Thomas Crump, he was described as a resident of Jamestown Island. He died sometime prior to May 29, 1638, after naming his brother Peleg as his heir. Therefore, Peleg inherited their late father's property and the 500 acres that had belonged to his brother Gercian. Although Elizabeth inherited life-rights to her late father's acreage in Archer's Hope, which she occupied, litigation that occurred after her death reveals that the Rev. Buck specified that his reversionary heirs must be male. In late 1654, when Peleg, the last of the Buck brothers, died, grandson John Crump inherited the deceased clergyman's property on Jamestown Island and on the mainland (VI&A 167–169).

Benomi (Benomy) Buck: Benomi, the orphaned son of the Rev. Richard and Maria Buck, lived with the widowed Mrs. Mary Ascam (Ascomb, Ascombe) in urban Jamestown but later went to live with Richard Kingsmill, whose plantation was in the western end of Jamestown Island. After Kingsmill's death and the marriage of his widow, Jane, to Ambrose Harmar, the issue arose of providing custodial care to Benomi, who came of age in 1637 but was considered mentally impaired. Although English officials designated Ambrose Harmar as the youth's legal guardian, Virginia governor John Harvey devised a plan whereby Benomi would divide his time between the households of Richard Kemp and George Donne, each of whom would receive a custodial fee. Official records reveal that Kemp took care of Benomi for a year but then turned him over to the county sheriff until Donne returned from overseas. Harmar reached Virginia, having reaffirmed his right to guardianship, but Benomi, who had been left in Mrs. Jane Kingsmill Harmar's custody, died shortly thereafter (VI&A 168). Undoubtedly, people's eagerness to serve as Benomi's guardian was linked to his status as a Buck heir and the opportunity to receive a custodial fee.

* * *

Elizabeth Buck: Elizabeth Buck, a maidservant of Colonel Thomas Swann of urban Jamestown and Swann's Point in Surry, was killed accidentally sometime prior to March 1655 (HEN I:406).

[No First Name] Buckingham: When the Indians attacked Weyanoke on March 22,

1622, one of Sir George Yeardley's people, a servant named Buckingham, was killed. He may have been Edward Buckingham, a former inmate of Bridewell prison, who was sentenced to transportation to Virginia (VI&A 169).

Andrew Buckler: In 1608 Andrew Buckler, who resided in Jamestown, accompanied Captain John Smith and some others on a visit to Werowocomoco (VI&A 169).

John Buckmaster (Buckmuster): During the mid-1620s John Buckmaster was living on Jamestown Island and was one of Thomas Passmore's servants. Later, Passmore used Buckmaster's headright when patenting some land. In March 1625 Buckmaster testified against a fellow servant, alleging that he rarely worked a full day (VI&A 169).

* * *

John Buckner I: John Buckner I moved to Gloucester County sometime prior to 1667 and settled on some land he had patented. In October 1669 he and another man staked a claim to 1,000 acres on the Cheesecake Branches of the Piankatank River, in what was then Gloucester County. As time went on, Buckner patented land near Purton Bay and along the North River, and he also owned some acreage in what became Essex County. By 1678 he was serving as Gloucester County's clerk of court and was among those authorized to appraise the estate of the late Colonel Peter Jennings. He also became a burgess and served in the assembly in 1680–1682 and 1693, representing Gloucester County. On February 21, 1683, the Council of State censured John Buckner and his servant, printer William Nuthead, for printing the November 1682 acts of the assembly and several other groups of official papers with neither authorization nor a license. Both men were ordered to post a bond guaranteeing that they would never do so again, and Nuthead eventually moved to St. Mary's City, Maryland. Buckner, who was still serving as Gloucester County clerk, was a respected member of his community. When William Buckner of Stafford County executed a land transaction in 1692, he said that the property had been given to him by his father, John. In 1694 John Buckner I, then a resident of Essex County, was among the prominent citizens authorized to make a supplementary accounting of the late Robert Beverley I's estate. He died sometime prior to September 1695, at which time his sons and executors, William, John II, and Thomas

Buckner, were ordered to meet at the decedent's plantation and inventory his estate. The late John Buckner I's inventory was presented to Essex County's justices on February 10, 1696. He was survived by his widow, Ann (CO 1/51 ff 98–99; 5/1405 f 63; York County Deeds, Orders, Wills 6:483; LEO 45, 53; Middlesex County Order Book 1673–1680:128; Order Book 1680–1694:708, 718; Stafford County Record Book 1686–1693:273; Essex County Deeds and Wills 1692–1695:19–21, 138–139; 1695–1699:6; Order Book 1692–1695:259; 1695–1699:1; PB 6:144–145, 240; 7:115, 212, 513, 518; MCGC 295, 431; EJC I:39, 493).

Thomas Buckner: Thomas Buckner was the son of Gloucester County's clerk of court, John Buckner I. When Edward Porteus of Gloucester's Petsworth Parish made his will in 1694, he named Thomas Buckner and his wife, Sarah—who served as a witness—among his heirs. In September 1695 Thomas and his brothers, William and John II, were to meet at their late father's plantation in Essex County to inventory his estate. In 1698 Thomas Buckner represented Gloucester County in the assembly. When quitrents were compiled in 1704, he was credited with 850 acres in Gloucester County's Petsworth Parish and 2,000 acres in Essex County. He served as a Gloucester County justice from 1702 to 1705. In 1727 he witnessed a deed when his mother, Ann, bestowed a gift of land upon his brother John II (LEO 58; Essex County Order Book 1692–1695:259; Deed Book 1724–1728:270; SMITH 14; SR 4793; PB 9:145).

William Buckner: William Buckner, the son of Gloucester County's clerk of court, John Buckner I, represented York County when the assembly convened in 1698. He became a captain and then a major in the county militia. He was among those authorized to try pirates in the Admiralty Court and over the years performed other official duties. By 1701 Buckner had become the lower York River's official Collector of Customs, and in 1705 he was a York County justice. He purchased an acre of land on the east side of Yorktown Creek's mouth in July 1711 and made an agreement with the seller, John Lewis, to build a windmill and keep it in good repair for seven years. Sometime prior to July 1727, when Ann Buckner of Gloucester County transferred some land to her son Thomas, she acknowledged that her son William had received 500 acres of land from his late father, John Buckner I (LEO 58; SR 384, 3627; Essex County Deed Book 1724–

1728:270; EJC I:370, 392, 444, 449, 458; II:50, 63, 66, 132, 180–181, 260, 309; York County Deed Book 2:374–375).

* * *

Ralph Buckridge: Ralph Buckridge, a gentleman from Sutton in Berkshire, arrived in Jamestown on September 5, 1623, and took the oath of supremacy (VI&A 169).

James Budworth: Nathaniel Jeffreys, a resident of Jamestown Island, agreed to let James Budworth, an indentured servant, serve John Southern for four years commencing on December 21, 1626. Because Jeffreys failed to deliver Budworth on time, the General Court decided that Jeffreys had to provide Southern with two years' use of another servant and that Budworth had to serve Southern for two years before he would be freed (VI&A 169).

Silvester (Sylvester) Bullen: On November 30, 1624, Silvester Bullen, a servant in the household of Jamestown Island carpenter Richard Tree, testified that John Danes transported timber to Captain John Barwick, overseer of the men whom the Company of Shipwrights sent to Virginia. In January 1625 Bullen was living in the eastern end of Jamestown Island (VI&A 170).

Francis Bullifant: Between April 1667 and April 1736, Francis Bullifant of Jamestown acquired William Sarson's 107-acre patent in the eastern end of Jamestown Island. He may have come into possession of the property through his marriage to Joyce Hopkins, whose kinsman, John, owned 100 acres of contiguous land by January 1702. On April 22, 1736, Bullifant sold the Sarson acreage to William Broadnax II. In 1693, when Bullifant was paid for delivering messages for the colony's assembly, he was a resident of urban Jamestown. On December 30, 1693, he commenced renting from William Sherwood two acres in the western end of the island, part of a 28½-acre parcel that Sherwood had leased to John Hopkins for three lifetimes. Bullifant was obliged to plant apple trees on Sherwood's property, maintain its buildings, and put rings in his hogs' snouts. Sherwood retained the right to use a half acre as a landing. Francis and Joyce Hopkins Bullifant were in residence on the Sherwood parcel when they began renting it. Although it is uncertain how they used the Sarson property in the eastern end of Jamestown Island, it was known to be valuable grazing land (AMB 48, 49, 77, 106–107; PB 6:42; NUG II:12; LJC 143).

Hugh Bullock (Bullocke): Hugh Bullock came to Virginia prior to 1626 and reportedly planted 5,500 acres of land. In 1628 he secured a 14-year patent or monopoly for an engine that he had invented, a machine that purportedly would square timber. Bullock's exclusive rights, awarded by the king, gave him a monopoly in England, Ireland, Wales, Virginia, and the Caribbean Islands. Captain Bullock was named to the Council of State in 1631, and in March 1634 he patented 2,250 acres of land in Elizabeth City. He returned to England, and when testifying in court on January 23, 1635, he identified himself as a Virginia planter and 59-year-old resident of London. In 1649 Bullock, who was still living in London, made his will, dividing his estate between his son, William, and grandson, Robert. The testator died in 1650 while in his early 70s, leaving an annual pension to his widow, Mary. In 1666 Robert Bullock, who had come of age and intended to go to Virginia, claimed that his late grandfather's neighbors had intruded upon his 5,500-acre plantation and seated part of the land to which he was entitled (VI&A 171; STAN 32; PB 1:159; SR 654, 4004, 4154).

Robert Burde (Byrd, Bird): On February 5, 1628, Robert Burde was described as one of Edward Sharples' servants in Jamestown (VI&A 173).

William Burdett (Burchitt, Burditt): William Burdett came to Virginia at age 16 and in early 1625 was living on the Eastern Shore, where he was a servant on Captain William Eppes's plantation. In December 1633 Burdett was appointed a commissioner of the Accomack County court and a year later became a vestryman. Sometime after February 19, 1634, Burdett married Frances (Francis) Blore Sanders, a wealthy widow who had outlived ancient planter John Blore (Blower) and mariner Roger Sanders (Saunders). Some of the Burdett couple's contemporaries were hauled into court for wagering that they would never wed. When Frances and William Burdett did marry, they executed a prenuptial agreement. By 1634 William Burdette had obtained a leasehold on Old Plantation Creek, the first of his many land acquisitions. He also continued to serve as a county justice, and in 1639 he was elected a burgess. He outlived his wife, Frances, who died in 1641. He married another widow, Alice or Alicia Travellor, whose brutal treatment of a young servant is well documented. When William Burdett made his will on July 22, 1643, he identified himself as a resident of Northampton County and made bequests to his wife, Alice, and Thomas Burdett, his only son; by early October 1643 he was dead. An inventory of the decedent's estate reflects his wealth. The widowed Alice Travellor Burdett later married Captain Peter Walker I and, upon his death, wed Colonel John Custis II (VI&A 174, 699–700; DOR 1:78; LEO 17; PB 1 Pt. 1:157; Pt. 2:657, 713; AMES 1:xxxii, 7–8, 11, 39, 108, 153; 2:271–272, 293–295, 307–308).

William Burfoot: On February 6, 1626, William Burfoot was identified as an indentured servant of John Burrows of Jamestown Island, who used him as a headright (VI&A 174).

Thomas Burgess (Burgis, Burges): Thomas Burgess came to Virginia sometime prior to 1628 and had a personal or business relationship with Thomas Warnett, a Jamestown merchant. In 1628 and 1630 Burgess represented Warresqueak (Isle of Wight) in the colony's assembly (VI&A 174; LEO 7, 9).

John Burland: John Burland, a vintner from Yorkshire, England, came to Virginia in 1619 as a Virginia Company servant. His contract was let to Captain William Norton, a sometime resident of Jamestown Island who oversaw the glassworks and some of the Company's other industrial activities. In February 1624 Burland was living on the lower side of the James River at the Treasurer's Plantation. He went to court in October 1625 in an attempt to recover the funds he was owed by Captain Norton's estate. In 1628 he served as a burgess for that portion of the corporation of James City which lay on the lower side of the James River. On May 20, 1634, John Burland leased from Michael Ratcliff 25 acres of land in Chiskiack near Uty's (Kings) Creek (VI&A 174; LEO 7).

John Burnham: John Burnham became a Middlesex County justice sometime prior to February 2, 1673. He went on to serve in the assembly and represented Middlesex County in 1676 and 1680–1682. In 1676 he succeeded Ralph Wormeley II, who was named to the Council of State, and by October 1677 he had been designated a colonel in the militia. In 1678 John Jeffreys, a London merchant with strong ties to Virginia, designated Burnham as his attorney. As Jeffreys' agent, Burnham executed an agreement with Middlesex County justice and physician Walter Whitaker, accepting his real and personal estate as collateral to cover debts. In August 1680 Colonel John Burnham and Major Robert Beverley I were authorized to

purchase 50 acres from Ralph Wormeley II, land that was to be surveyed and laid out into a town site. Burnham died prior to February 7, 1681, when his will was presented to the Middlesex County court. Major Lewis Burwell II, who indicated that he was a kinsman, asked to be appointed one of the decedent's administrators. However, Ralph Wormeley II contested the will's legitimacy and insisted that the matter be forwarded to the General Court. He contended that Burnham's land should escheat to the Crown and said that he already had filed a claim to it. As late as 1690 Burnham's property was still part of his estate (LEO 38, 45; Middlesex County Order Book 1673–1680:1, 80, 103, 128, 149, 224; 1680–1694:11–12, 48, 55, 479).

Rowland Burnham: In August 1643 Rowland Burnham patented 450 acres in York County on what already was known as Burnham's Creek. He served as a burgess for York County and attended the assembly sessions of 1644, 1645–1646, and 1649. Simultaneously, he served as a justice in the county court and became a tax collector. Over the years he made numerous appearances in court, providing testimony or serving as a witness. Burnham, like many of his peers, invested in land on Virginia's frontier. In 1651 he patented 1,400 acres on the south side of the Rappahannock River, 20 miles above its mouth, and in 1659 he laid claim to another 850 acres in the same vicinity. A lawsuit undertaken in England in 1653 reveals that Rowland Burnham and Colonel Richard Lee had made an agreement with British merchant and slave trader John Jeffries whereby they would take delivery of 100 white male servants they could sell on the Rappahannock and York rivers. The men, who were being transported from Ireland to Virginia, were described as Irish Tories (LEO 22, 24, 27; PB 1:884; 2:319, 339; SR 10594; York County Deeds, Orders, Wills 2 [1645–1649]:47, 430). It is likely that they were Irish loyalists to the monarchy who went overseas after Oliver Cromwell instituted the Commonwealth government.

Anthony Burrin (Burrows?): On February 16, 1624, Anthony Burrin was living on the lower side of the James River on one of the plantations west of Gray's Creek. Since John Burrows' plantation, Burrows Hill, was in that vicinity, Anthony may have been the same Anthony Burrows who was simultaneously attributed to John Burrows' household in Jamestown (VI&A 175).

* * *

Christopher Burroughs (Burrows, Burrough): Christopher Burroughs, who in 1636 patented some land on the lower side of the James River in what was then Elizabeth City County, laid claim to some acreage on Bennett's Creek in 1638. He was named to the Lynnhaven Parish vestry in August 1640, but in April 1641 his parish's churchwardens accused him of committing fornication with Mary (Marie) Somes, one of Captain John Sibley's servants. The justices of Lower Norfolk County's monthly court, who chose public shaming as punishment, ordered the couple to stand in the aisle of their parish church during Sunday services, wrapped in a white sheet and holding a white wand. In 1642 Burroughs served as the attorney of his brother, William Burroughs, in the sale of his plantation, and when testifying in court he indicated that he was in his 30s. His indiscretion with a maidservant did not hurt his political career, for he attended the assembly sessions of 1645, 1645–1646, and 1652, representing Lower Norfolk County. Burroughs sold part of his land to Thomas Bullock and in 1651 patented two tracts of land in Lower Norfolk County, one of 354 acres and another of 150 acres. He was a justice in the county's monthly court in 1652 and also was in command of the militia on the eastern shore of the Lynnhaven River. He died during the year, and in January 1653 the justices of Lower Norfolk County appointed his widow, Mary, as his executrix and ordered four local men to see that his estate was appraised (LEO 23–24, 29–30; Lower Norfolk County Record Book A:44, 76, 87, 110, 163; B:65–65a; Deeds and Wills C:10, 14, 21–22, 31, 33, 55; PB 1:341, 628; 2:347).

Benomi (Benomy) Burroughs: Benomi Burroughs was the eldest son of Lower Norfolk County burgess Christopher Burroughs, who died in late 1652 or early 1653. Benomi's name first appeared in the records of the newly formed Princess Anne County in October 1691, when he witnessed a legal document. In April 1693 he patented 150 acres in Princess Anne County, near the northern branch of the Currituck, and represented the county in the assembly sessions held in 1695–1696, 1696–1697, 1698, and 1699. When Benomi Burroughs and his wife, Mary, disposed of some land on the eastern side of the Lynnhaven River in September 1701, they indicated that it had formerly belonged to Benomi's uncle, William Burroughs. They also stated that Benomi's late father, Christopher Burroughs, had disposed of the property without the right to do so. On March 6, 1706, when he made his will, Benomi Burroughs indicated that he was the eldest son of Christopher Burroughs of Dam Neck. He made bequests to his sons, Robert and Benjamin, and to his daughters, Mary, Barbary (Barbara), and Elizabeth. He named his wife, Mary, as one of his heirs and designated her as his executrix. The testator's will was proved on December 4, 1706 (LEO 54, 56, 58–59; PB 8:275; Princess Anne County Deed Book 1:11, 292, 452).

* * *

John Burrows (Burrough, Burras, Burrowes, Bourrows): Ancient planter John Burrows, a tradesman, arrived in Jamestown in 1608 in the 2nd Supply of new settlers and was still living on the island in 1618. During the mid-1620s Burrows and his wife, Bridget, lived on Jamestown Island, occupying the former residence of the late Rev. Richard Buck while taking care of the deceased clergyman's daughter Mara. Burrows patented and seated a 150-acre tract on the lower side of the James River, a plantation he called Burrows Hill, but in August 1626 he moved to the Neck O'Land behind Jamestown Island so that he could tend to the Buck orphans' cattle. Late in 1628 he succumbed to a stab wound he received during an altercation with a servant boy. John Burrows' widow, Bridget, married William Davis, who died sometime prior to March 27, 1643. Afterward, she wed John Bromfield, who outlived her and attempted to recover what he presumed was her legal interest in the Buck property in the Neck O'Land. It was then determined that as one of the Buck children's guardians, she had had only a life interest in the Buck estate (VI&A 176–177).

Robert Burt (Burte): Robert Burt, an indentured servant, came to Virginia in 1617 at the expense of Richard Kingsmill of Jamestown Island (VI&A 177).

George Burton: George Burton, a gentleman and soldier, arrived in Jamestown in 1608 as part of the 2nd Supply of new settlers. In 1620 he was identified as a Virginia Company investor (VI&A 177).

Jane Burtt: In February 1624 Jane Burtt was one of Governor Francis Wyatt's servants and lived in urban Jamestown (VI&A 178).

Henry Burton: The James City County court's decision in favor of Henry Burton against George Marable I of urban Jamestown was upheld by the General Court on March 20, 1676 (MCGC 447).

* * *

Lewis Burwell I: Lewis Burwell I, the son of Edward and Dorothy Bedell Burwell, married Robert Higginson's daughter, Lucy. In September 1652 he was living in Gloucester County when he designated Walter Broadhurst I, Northumberland County's high sheriff, as his attorney. Like many of his contemporaries, Burwell speculated in real estate and invested in land in the Northern Neck, then part of the colony's frontier. One of the large tracts he acquired was on the Lower Machodoc or Trent River in Westmoreland County. After Burwell's death in November 1653, his widow, Lucy, married William Bernard and then Philip Ludwell I. She died in November 1675 (WITH 286; DOR 1:261, 432, 434; NUG I:266; Northumberland County Wills, Inventories &c.1652–1658:4; Order Book 1652–1665:249; Westmoreland County Deeds, Patents &c. 1665–1677:22a–23, 133–135).

Lewis Burwell II: Prior to March 1692 Lewis Burwell II married Abigail Smith of Gloucester, Colonel Nathaniel Bacon's niece and heir to most of his real and personal property. Bacon, when making his will, stipulated that his estate was to pass from Abigail to her sons, Nathaniel and James, and he had made a bequest to Abigail's grandson and his great-nephew, Lewis Burwell III. As it turned out, Abigail Smith Burwell outlived Colonel Bacon by only a few months, for she died on November 12, 1692. At that point, life-rights in the property she had inherited would have descended to her husband, Lewis Burwell II, and afterward to her sons, Nathaniel and James. In July 1694 Lewis Burwell II, acting as Colonel Nathaniel Bacon's executor, brought suit against a Middlesex County man and another individual in Isle of Wight County. A year earlier he sued people in Lancaster County who owed funds to Bacon's estate. Thanks to Colonel Bacon's bequests, Lewis Burwell II had possession of the decedent's lot in urban Jamestown and therefore would have been eligible to hold office as the capital city's representative. In 1698 Burwell served as Jamestown's burgess. However, he resided at Colonel Bacon's Kings Creek Plantation in York County, and he owned vast quantities of land in several other Tidewater counties. It is uncertain how he used the Bacon property in Jamestown, which in the late seventeenth century contained a house. Burwell was named to the Council of State in 1702 but by autumn 1710 was beginning to have medical problems, which became increasingly acute. On October 11,

1710, he made his will and two days later he asked to be relieved of his duties as member of the council. According to William Byrd II of Westover, Burwell received medical treatment from Dr. Archibald Blair, a highly respected physician. Even so, he died on December 19, 1710. Burwell's will, which was proved on February 19, 1711, in the court of York County, mentioned his sons, Nathaniel and James; four daughters; grandson Lewis III (Nathaniel's son); and Philip Ludwell II. The testator bequeathed his landholdings to his sons and grandson and indicated that Colonel Nathaniel Bacon's estate was to be divided among his children (LEO 58; BYRD 28, 265; STAN 17, 44; York County Deeds, Orders, Wills 9:116–118; 14:64; CO 5/1312 f 105; Middlesex County Order Book 1680–1694:698; Lancaster County Order Book 1686–1696:271, 280; Isle of Wight County Orders 1693–1695:37; MCGH 452; DOR 1:433).

Nathaniel Burwell: Nathaniel, the eldest son of Lewis II and Abigail Smith Burwell, resided on Carter's Creek in Gloucester County. By 1692 he had married Elizabeth, the daughter of Robert "King" Carter of Corotoman. As one of his parents' principal heirs, he inherited part of Colonel Nathaniel Bacon's estate. From 1710 to 1712 Nathaniel Burwell served as Jamestown's burgess, an indication that he owned property within the urban community, presumably a legal interest in the lot that was part of the late Colonel Bacon's estate. Nathaniel Burwell died in 1734 (BYRD 7, 29; York County Deeds, Orders, Wills 14:64; LEO 65; DOR 1:282, 296, 434–435, 437, 443, 445–446, 450, 843).

James Burwell: In 1710 James Burwell, the second oldest son of Lewis Burwell II, inherited a legal interest in the lot in urban Jamestown that his mother was given by her uncle, Colonel Nathaniel Bacon. Burwell resided on the Kings Creek Plantation in York County, where he died in 1719 (York County Deeds, Orders, Wills 14:64; 15:334, 424, 426).

Lewis Burwell III: Lewis III, the son of Nathaniel and Elizabeth Carter Burwell and great-nephew of Colonel Nathaniel Bacon, inherited a share of the Bacon property. In 1736, within two years of his father's death, Lewis III became Jamestown's burgess and served in that capacity through 1740. His eligibility to represent Jamestown in the assembly most likely indicates that he owned land there, most likely the urban lot that he inherited from Colonel Bacon. Lewis Burwell III also was a James City County court justice. In 1744 he was elected a burgess for James City County but died before taking office (York County Deeds, Orders, Wills 9:116–118; 14:64; LEO 76; STAN 108, 110, 112, 116; EJC IV:413).

* * *

Thomas Bushrod (Bushrode): When George Ludlow of York County made his will in September 1655, he bequeathed £75 to Thomas Bushrod and gave him his sixteenth-part interest in the ship *Mayflower.* When Bushrod was deposed by the justices of York County's monthly court on January 25, 1658, he indicated that he was age 53. In September 1657 Bushrod married Mary Peirsey Hill, Abraham Peirsey's daughter and Captain Thomas Hill's widow, and represented York County in the assembly sessions held in 1659 and 1660. In 1665 he and his brother, Richard, patented 300 acres on the Nominy and Potomac rivers, in what was then Northumberland but later became Westmoreland County. On October 24, 1673, Bushrod obtained a judgment against the estate of Jonathan Newell, a Jamestown merchant and the owner of a large parcel in the New Town. On April 4, 1674, while he was serving as the attorney of Thomas Lawrie of Edinburgh, he won a suit against Samuel Austin and William Drummond I of Jamestown, who was one of the rebel Nathaniel Bacon's supporters. When Bushrod designated Malachi Peale of Westmoreland County as his attorney in 1674, he identified himself as a merchant and resident of Essex Lodge in York County. After being widowed, he married Elizabeth Farlow and continued to live at Essex Lodge, which belonged to his late wife's son, Thomas Hill II. Thomas Bushrod made his will on December 18, 1676, and died prior to April 24, 1677. He asked to be buried beside his first wife, Mary, if he was living at Essex Lodge at the time of his death (LEO 35–36; Westmoreland County Deeds, Patents &c. 1665–1677: 216a; Order Book 1676–1689:685, 701; York County Deeds, Orders, Wills &c. 3 [1657–1662]:14; 6 [1677–1684]:5; SR 3131; PB 5:15; 6:235; DOR 3:506, 805–806; MCGC 352, 365; SR 3131).

John Bustone: In 1673 John Bustone, Richard Lawrence's runaway servant, stole a shallop and lost it. After he was apprehended and brought to justice, he was ordered to serve five extra years (MCGC 348, 382).

Nathaniel Butler: Captain Nathaniel Butler, Bermuda's governor from 1619 to 1622, visited Virginia in the winter of 1622 and stayed for approximately three months. He later wrote a scathing account of life in the colony, which he called the "Unmasking of Virginia." A number of burgesses and ancient planters rebutted Butler's allegations (VI&A 180).

William Butler (Buttler): By 1636 William Butler, a merchant, had become involved in the tobacco trade and may have been living in Virginia. He was licensed to sell tobacco in Gloucestershire, England. Butler represented James City as a burgess in the January 12, 1641, session of the assembly. He went to England later in the year, when he and Edward Major proved the will made by Anthony Barham of Mulberry Island. Barham bequeathed a generous sum to both men, who were to serve as his executors in Virginia. He also left a wine cup to Butler's daughter, Sara. In August 1643 William Butler patented 700 acres on Lawnes Creek, in what was then James City County but later became Surry, and in 1653 and 1658 he represented Surry County in the assembly. He appeared in court from time to time to witness wills, serve as an attorney, and arbitrate disputes. He also became a county justice. By January 24, 1659, Major William Butler was dead and his widow had married William Marriot. In March 1673 a William Butler (probably the burgess's son) patented part of the late Major William Butler's land on Lawnes Creek (STAN 61; LEO 20, 31, 34; PB 1:900; 6:440; SR 3502, 3989, 10933; Surry County Deed Book 1 [1652–1663]:79, 89, 99, 101, 136, 141, 151).

* * *

William Byrd I: By 1671 William Byrd I had inherited Westover and some land near the falls of the James River from Thomas Stegg II. He became a highly successful merchant and planter and in 1677 commenced serving successive terms as a Henrico County burgess. His wife, Mary, was the daughter of Warham Horsemenden (Horsmanden). Byrd was highly critical of Governor William Berkeley and seems to have sympathized with the rebel Nathaniel Bacon. In 1679 officials in England withdrew permission for Byrd to seat land at the head of the James, for the Indians had begun attacking frontier settlers. In 1681 Byrd was named to the Council of State, and in 1687 he became auditor general and receiver general, positions that gave him considerable political power. When Byrd came to Jamestown on official business, he may have stayed at Henry Gawler's tavern, which was located in a row house on the waterfront, for in 1689 he had a case of French claret sent there for use of the council. Byrd's correspondence reveals that he often did business with Perry and Lane, the firm that during the fourth quarter of the seventeenth century owned a row house unit next door to Henry Gawler's tavern. During the 1680s William Byrd I acquired a considerable amount of land in Henrico County, which then spanned both sides of the James, and he patented land in Nansemond and Charles City counties. He also laid claim to a massive tract in King William and in what became Goochland County. He was heavily involved in seeing that Jamestown was fortified against a foreign invasion. In 1695 he inspected the 20-year-old brick fort in Jamestown, which had become ruinous, and the following year he was authorized to purchase small guns for the newly built platform that replaced the fort. During 1699 he made an official visit to Jamestown so that he could inspect its fortifications. Afterward, he submitted a report on their condition and on the quantity of military stores on hand. In 1698 Byrd was reimbursed for partially financing construction of Jamestown's new gun platform. Between 1699 and 1704 the Council of State occasionally convened at Westover, William Byrd I's home. He died on December 4, 1704, leaving his son and namesake, William II, as principal heir. The decedent's daughter, Ursula, married Robert Beverley II in 1697 and lived in urban Jamestown in a house in the western end of the island. She died in childbirth and was buried in the churchyard in Jamestown (SAIN 10:404–405, 498; STAN 22–23, 41, 82–83; NUG II:258, 275, 297, 305; III:11, 65, 86; EJC I: 25, 114, 322, 344, 423–424; II: 127, 151, 383, 406; PALM I:59; Stanard, "Minutes of Council and General Court," 228; "Letters of William Byrd I," 27; LEO 43–45, 56; WITH 509).

William Byrd II: William Byrd II of Westover Plantation in Charles City County was born on March 28, 1674, and was educated in England. In 1692 he served his first term as a burgess. The 1704 quitrent rolls reveal that he then owned 19,500 acres of land in Henrico County, 100 acres in Prince George, and 300 acres in Nansemond. Byrd was a council member and served as receiver general from 1705 to 1716. In 1706 he married Lucy, the daughter of Jane Ludwell and her husband, the notorious Daniel Parke II. She also was the niece of Philip Ludwell II of Jamestown and Green Spring Plantation. Byrd agreed to accept his late father-in-law's debts along with his assets. It was a decision he lived to regret, for the amount of debt against the Parke estate was much larger than Byrd had anticipated. In 1708 Byrd described the medicinal properties of "Jamestown" (gimson) weed, which he said was poisonous but would cure burns. In August 1711, when a French invasion was anticipated, William Byrd II sent 25 men to Jamestown to work on a gun battery that was being constructed, and he furnished 2,000 palisades that were to be erected there and outside of Williamsburg. Although Byrd does not appear to have owned property in urban Jamestown, he frequently visited the former capital and probably secured room and board in one of its taverns. On the other hand, he would have had custody of any real estate his late father-in-law had owned and was on cordial terms with the Ludwells. In 1709 Byrd wrote of attending church in Jamestown, where the Rev. James Blair conducted services. In 1724, eight years after his wife Lucy's death in London, Byrd married Maria Taylor. He continued to acquire land and in 1738 patented nearly 5,000 acres of new land in Brunswick County. Four years later he laid claim to 105,000 acres there. He died on August 26, 1744 (SMITH 15; BYRD ix–xi, 25, 102, 393, 401; STAN 23, 45; NUG III:99; LJC 529; HUD IV:150–151, 158, 197; V:16; Chandler, "Letters of William Bird II and Sir Hans Sloane," 190; BEV xiv; Stanard, "Diary of Colonel William Bolling," 244).

* * *

C

William Cadwell: On January 11, 1627, William Cadwell appeared before the General Court in Jamestown and substantiated Robert Dennys' claim that Edward Pritchard's will was authentic (VI&A 181).

Edward Cage (Cadge): On March 12, 1624, Edward Cage, a Virginia Company investor, testified before the General Court. In April 1625 he and his partner, Nathaniel Jefferys (Jeffries, Jeffreys), were residing in urban Jamestown when the General Court ordered Cage to inventory the late John Pountis's estate. In 1638 Cage was described as one of Virginia's chief merchants and planters (VI&A 181).

Mr. Calcker (Calcar): On February 16, 1624, Mr. Calcker, his wife, and their child were living in the urban Jamestown household of Captain William Holmes. On March 23, 1624, it was reported that Mr. Calcker had sold his bed, bedclothes, and pewter to John Chew (VI&A 182).

Christopher Calthrop (Colethorpe): Christopher Calthrop came to Virginia in 1622, settled in Kecoughtan (Elizabeth City), and lived with Captain Isaac Whittaker for a couple years. In early 1625, when a muster was made, Calthrop was residing on the west side of the Hampton River in Lieutenant Thomas Purfoy's home. On September 20, 1628, Calthrop obtained a leasehold for acreage near the fields called Fort Henry, property that was still in his possession in the 1630s. In July 1635 he received a patent for 500 acres in the area known as the New Poquoson. He attained the rank of captain and served as a burgess for York County in 1644, 1646, 1652–1653, and 1660, although in 1645 he represented Elizabeth City. By 1661 Calthrop had gone to Carolina, where he died in 1662. He was survived by his widow, Ann (VI&A 182; LEO 22–24, 30–31, 36).

* * *

George Calvert I (Lord Baltimore I): Sir George Calvert, the first Lord Baltimore, was a member of the Virginia Company and in 1622 was admitted to the New England Company. His first wife, Anne Mynne, died on August 8, 1621, having produced at least a dozen children. Calvert received a grant to Newfoundland in 1623. He became a Roman Catholic, was elevated to the Irish peerage, and remarried. During the summer of 1628 he and his second wife, Joane, and some of his children set sail for Newfoundland. However, the harsh winter weather prompted them to leave in August 1629. In October the Calverts and 40 members of their household arrived in Jamestown, but Sir George continued on to England. He asked the Privy Council to order Virginia governor John Harvey to assist his wife, Joane, in collecting debts and securing safe passage to England, and to help her dispose of her servants, if she saw fit. Lady Baltimore probably was a guest in Governor Harvey's home in urban Jamestown, for he often entertained high-ranking visitors. Calvert asked the king for some Virginia land, with the same proprietary privileges he had enjoyed in Newfoundland. However, his refusal to take the oaths of allegiance and supremacy, which he considered at odds with his faith, sparked controversy. King Charles I loaned the *St. Claude* to Calvert so that he could bring his wife and the rest of their entourage back to England. The ship went down off the English coast and all aboard were lost. Sir George Calvert died in April 1632, having received a charter for the proprietary colony that became known as Maryland (VI&A 183–184).

Cecil (Cecilius, Cecill) Calvert (Lord Baltimore II): Cecil, the second Lord Baltimore, set about utilizing the charter that his late father, George Calvert I, had negotiated for the Maryland colony. When he paused at Old Point Comfort on February 24, 1634, on the way to Maryland, he thanked Governor John Harvey for helping him oust William Claiborne from Kent Island and for supporting the new colony's interests. Calvert proved loyal to Harvey and in December 1635 asked English authorities to reinstate him as Virginia's governor (VI&A 183).

Leonard Calvert: Leonard Calvert and his brother, George Calvert II, set out from England in October 1633 and reached Maryland, the Baltimore family's new proprietary territory, on March 27, 1634. As soon as they arrived, they commenced establishing the settlement known as St. Mary's City, and Leonard Calvert became Maryland's first governor. During the late 1630s Maryland's assembly forced him to govern in accord with the laws of England, not in an arbitrary, feudalistic fashion. Leonard Calvert arrived in Virginia in 1644, in the wake of violent clashes between Maryland's Catholics and Protestants, conflict fueled by William Claiborne. According to Secretary of the Colony Richard Kemp, Calvert, who reached Virginia a few months after the 1644 Indian attack, assisted the colonists by attacking the Chickahominy Indians in their homeland. Calvert died in 1647. Margaret Brent served as his administratrix in Maryland, but her brother, Giles Brent I, acted as her attorney in Virginia and pursued debts that were owed to Calvert's estate (VI&A 184; Northumberland County Order Book 1652–1665:25).

* * *

Delpheus Cann: Mr. Delpheus Cann, a merchant, lived in urban Jamestown during the mid-1620s. He served on the jury investigating John Verone's death and was involved in litigation that concerned Robert Bennett and Thomas Edwards (VI&A 185).

Ralph Cannion: On February 5, 1628, Ralph Cannion, who was living in Jamestown, was identified as one of Edward Sharples's servants (VI&A 185).

* * *

David Cant I: David Cant I, who was named as an overseer of mariner Thomas Wilson's will in 1654, served as a burgess for Gloucester County in 1660 and 1661–1662 and by 1663 had attained the rank of major. He owned acreage at the head of Nimcock Creek in what was then Lancaster County but later became Middlesex, and in 1663 he patented two tracts in what was then Gloucester County: 600 acres on the south side of the Piankatank River and another 542 acres near its head. Major Cant died sometime prior to March 1672, having produced at least two sons, David II and John (LEO 36, 38; PB 5:300, 357; 6:154, 448; SR 3127).

John Cant: John Cant was the son of Major David Cant I, who owned land on the south side of the Piankatank River in what was then Gloucester County, and acreage at the head of Nimcock Creek, in a part of Lancaster County that later became Middlesex. When Major Cant died, his son John inherited his Lancaster County property, whereas son David Cant II inherited his land in Gloucester. In January 1675 John Cant's name appeared in Middlesex County court records when he undertook some litigation. As time went on, he became more involved in public life. By 1688 he had become a surveyor of Middlesex County's highways, and in 1690 he became a court justice. In 1693 he represented Middlesex County in the assembly. Cant was alive in early March 1694 but died prior to May 14th, when his will was proved and three men were ordered to inventory his estate. In February 1695 John Grymes was functioning as Cant's executor (LEO 52–53; Middlesex County Order Book 1673–1680:25; 1680–1694:345, 504, 678, 690, 693; 1694–1705:19; PB 5:310, 357; 6:154, 448; SR 3127).

* * *

William Cantrell (Cantrill): William Cantrell, a gentleman and Virginia Company investor, arrived in Jamestown in 1608 in the 1st Supply of new colonists (VI&A 185).

John Capper: On September 17, 1607, John Capper, one of the first Jamestown colonists, testified that Edward Maria Wingfield had given Mr. Croft a copper kettle and that Croft had not stolen it (VI&A 186).

William Capps (Caps, Cappe, Capp): Ancient planter William Capps, who came to Virginia in the 3rd Supply of new colonists, also invested in the colonization of New England. He was fiercely critical of Governor George Yeardley and seems to have been one of the Virginia government's harshest critics. He resided in Elizabeth City on the east side of the Hampton River, and when the assembly first met in July 1619, he represented the settlers at Kecoughtan. During the early 1620s he sent several letters to Virginia Company officials complaining about public policies. In 1624 he received a patent for some land on the west side of the Hampton River in Elizabeth City, and in 1627 he was a member of the Council of State. He was still alive on March 21, 1634, and patented some land on the Back River in Elizabeth City (VI&A 186; STAN 31; LEO 3). Capps may have produced descendants, for the name "William Capps" is found in the records of Lower Norfolk County and Princess Anne County, formed in 1691.

George Caquescough (Native American): In early August 1659, George Caquescough, a Machodoc Indian, was accused of murdering colonist John Cammel. Caquescough and three of his tribesmen (Pantatouse, Chakingatough, and Yeotassa) were brought before the justices of Northumberland County, which had convened as a court of oyer and terminer. Caquescough was indicted but he pled "not guilty" when asked whether he had murdered Cammel by striking him forcefully on the head. Even so, a jury held him responsible and sentenced him to be hanged. The three other warriors were implicated in the murder and found guilty, but not punished. All four men had been taken to Northumberland's justices by their own people, although a fifth warrior was not brought in. Nearly two years later Northumberland's court justices surmised that the Machodoc were conspiring with other Indians "to make a Warr upon us." Therefore, they decided that some local men, with the assistance of the militia, would drive the tribe from the land they called home (Northumberland County Order Book 1652–1665:216, 239).

Stephen Carleton: On February 10, 1677, Governor William Berkeley issued a proclamation in which he named those who were exempt from the king's pardon on account of their role in Bacon's Rebellion. One of those named was Stephen Carleton, whom Berkeley said needed to be brought before a court (NEVILLE 61).

Henry Carman: Henry Carman, a youth detained in Bridewell prison, was transported to Virginia as an indentured servant. He lived at West and Shirley Hundred during 1624 but later was sent to Peirsey's (formerly Flowerdew) Hundred, where he resided in Samuel Sharpe's household. Carman soon ran afoul of the law, for he got one of Abraham Peirsey's maidservants pregnant. Carman was assigned to William Farrar of Jordan's Journey and put to work on behalf of his master, Samuel Sharpe, who was then absent from Virginia (VI&A 188).

Edward Carter: Edward Carter, who was born in England, represented Upper Norfolk (later, Nansemond) County in the assembly in 1658 and 1659. He was named to the Council of State in 1659 and served until 1677. When Colonel Carter patented some Nansemond County land in September 1665, reference was made to some adjoining property that he already owned. In December 1660, while he was a resident of Nansemond County, he purchased a plantation on the north side of the Rappahannock River in Lancaster County. Then, in April 1665 he secured a patent for 1,650 acres on the north side of the Rappahannock, property that included part of a sprawling Indian village known as Morraticund. Throughout the mid-to-late 1670s Carter supplemented his earnings by importing and selling goods, especially cloth, upholstery fabric, and articles of clothing. In 1676 he testified in a chancery case that involved a man he thought incapable of serving as a factor, and he witnessed a will in Lower Norfolk County in 1677. In 1678 Carter was one of several men who asked the king for relief from customs duties. One of his friends was Daniel Parke I, who bequeathed him £5 to buy a mourning ring. Colonel Edward Carter died in England in 1682, naming his widow, Elizabeth, as executrix. She authorized Colonel Cuthbert Potter to act as her attorney when selling some of her late husband's land in Nansemond County (LEO 34–35; STAN 38; Lancaster County Deeds and Wills [1661–1702]:359–361; Lower Norfolk County Wills and Deeds 4:84; PB 5:29, 209; SR 663, 3720, 3774, 3793a, 5586, 5589, 5590, 5594, 5726, 10059; NEAL 68).

* * *

John Carter I: John Carter, who was born in England, served as a burgess for Lower Norfolk County in 1642 and 1643. He represented Nansemond County in 1649 but moved to Lancaster County, where in January 1653 his name and landholdings were mentioned in local court records. Carter, who was a major in the militia, purchased several thousand acres on the Corotoman River in August 1653 and established a major plantation. By April 1654 he held the rank of colonel. When the justices of Lancaster County decided a case in February 1656 involving Captain William Brocas's estate, they noted that John Carter had married Brocas's widow, Elinor. In April 1656 Carter, who was a merchant, borrowed some of the tobacco he had given his children, John II and Elizabeth, using 10 African servants as collateral. Edward Eltonhead, to whom Richard Kemp, Ralph Wormeley, and William Brocas were in debt, initiated a lawsuit in England in 1648 in an attempt to recover what he was owed. A decade later Eltonhead sued his debtors' widows, one of whom was Elinor Brocas Carter. John Carter I was named to the Council of State and served in 1657–1658 while the Commonwealth government was in power. In 1658 he purchased a tract of Lancaster County land at Nimcock from former governor Richard Bennett and his wife, Mary Ann, residents of the Nansemond River area. Carter served as a Lancaster County burgess in 1654–1655, 1658, 1659, and 1660 and by 1662 was a justice of the county court. In 1664 the justices of Lancaster County acknowledged a debt to Colonel Carter, who had supplied the matchcoats given to some local Indians. Carter died in late 1669, leaving three sons: John II, Robert, and Charles. Because John Carter II died without surviving male heirs, the Corotoman estate eventually descended to his brother Robert (LEO 20–21, 27, 32, 34–36; STAN 37; Lancaster County Deeds &c. Book 2 [1652–1657]:23, 33, 65–66, 131a, 255; [1654–1661]:25–26; Deeds and Wills [1661–1702]:359–362, 412–416; Order Book 1656–1666:175, 300; 1666–1680;1, 114, 119, 133; Old Rappahannock County Deeds and Wills 1656–1662:33, 51; SR 10473, 12537).

John Carter II: John Carter II, who was his father's primary heir, served as a Lancaster County militia officer. He represented the county in the assembly sessions held in 1676 and 1680–1682. He also served as a court justice for many years and in 1673 became Lancaster County's high sheriff. A document submitted to Lancaster County's justices in July 1677 reveals that a large quantity of cornmeal was taken from Carter's mill, a well-known local landmark, for consumption by the soldiers suppressing Bacon's Rebellion. By 1678 Carter, who was a merchant, had become a resident of Gloucester County. He married Elizabeth Hull, with whom he produced his only child,

Elizabeth Carter. He wed again in 1684, taking Elizabeth Travers as his second wife. In 1688 he became a justice of Westmoreland County's monthly court and served for a year or two. On June 4, 1690, Colonel John Carter II made his will, stating that he was ill. He died within a week, having freed some of his servants and slaves. The testator named his wife, Elizabeth, as an heir but referred to the terms of their marriage contract. He was especially generous to his daughter, Elizabeth, who was then a minor, but he left his real estate to his brothers, Robert and Charles. When daughter Elizabeth came of age, she was to serve as her late father's executrix. In January 1691 Robert Carter compiled an inventory of his late brother's personal estate, which reflected his immense wealth. John Carter II's widow, Elizabeth, married Christopher Wormeley II but died in 1693 (LEO 41, 45; Middlesex County Order Book 1673–1680:127; Lancaster County Wills 1690–1709:3–5, 22–29, 32–34; Order Book 1666–1680:238, 262, 292, 375; 1686–1696:129, 149–150; Westmoreland County Order Book 1676–1689:643, 701).

Robert Carter: Robert "King" Carter, the son of John Carter I of Corotoman, inherited the bulk of his late father's estate. In 1684 he began serving as a justice in Lancaster County's monthly court and was still holding office in May 1700. One of his duties as a justice was seeing that a new county courthouse was built at Queen's Town. Carter served in the assembly and attended the sessions held in 1691–1692, 1695–1696, 1696–1697, 1698, and 1699, representing Lancaster County. He was elected speaker of the 1695–1696 and 1699 sessions. He was named to the Council of State in 1699 and served until 1732. In 1726, while Carter was president of the Council of State, he became acting governor when Governor Hugh Drysdale died. In 1701, when Robert Carter was preparing to marry the former Elizabeth (Betty) Landon, the widow of Richard Willis of Middlesex County, he executed a marriage contract, giving her part of his land. He identified the late John Carter II, deceased in 1690, as his eldest brother, from whom he had inherited part of the acreage he was giving his bride-to-be. While Carter served two terms as Lord Fairfax's agent for the Northern Neck Proprietary, he acquired massive quantities of land, including the James City County estate that became known as Carter's Grove. Robert Carter died on August 4, 1732, in Lancaster County (LEO xix, 50, 54, 56, 58–59; STAN 43–44; Lancaster County Deeds and Wills [1661–1702]:412–416; Wills 1690–1709:3–5, 22–29, 32–34; Order Book

1680–1687:148; 1686–1696:166; 1696–1702:51, 68, 100, 110).

* * *

William Carter: In February 1623 William Carter, who was living in Dr. John Pott's house in urban Jamestown, was questioned about his role in killing one of Sir George Yeardley's calves. Later, he testified about events that occurred in June 1623 while he stood watch at Jamestown's fort. By early 1625 he had moved to the eastern end of Jamestown Island. He may have married later in the year, for a reference was made to Goodwife Carter's house, which was located in that area. During 1625 Carter assisted Jamestown gunsmith John Jefferson in repairing a weapon and gave medicine to a sick cow that belonged to the Rev. Richard Buck's orphans. On August 14, 1626, William Carter was identified as one of the servants George Menefie employed in his forge in Jamestown. A coworker, Martin Turner, bequeathed his bed to Carter, who later claimed that Captain Hamor tried to confiscate it. In 1629 Carter's wife was accused of making a slanderous statement about her cousin, Goodwife Gray, while visiting Mr. Cheesman's house in Elizabeth City. In 1636 William Carter patented 700 acres of land on the lower side of the James River, using the headrights of his first, second, and third wives: Avis Turtley, Ann Mathis, and Alice Croxon (VI&A 190–191).

John Cartwright: On March 10, 1622, John Cartwright witnessed John Rolfe's will. In February 1624, he was a servant in the urban Jamestown household of Captain William Peirce, Rolfe's father-in-law (VI&A 191).

William Carver: Captain William Carver served as a burgess between 1665 and 1669, representing Lower Norfolk County. His contemporaries described him as a valiant and strong mariner. Carver became one of the rebel Nathaniel Bacon's staunch supporters and in 1676 Bacon sent him to the Eastern Shore to capture Governor William Berkeley, who had retreated to Colonel John Custis II's plantation, Arlington. During the failed attempt, Carver was among the men "taken miraculously" and quickly executed for their role in Bacon's Rebellion. When Governor Berkeley issued a proclamation on February 10, 1677, listing the names of those who were exempt from the king's pardon, he indicated that Carver was dead and that his estate was subject to seizure. In October 1677 Carver's son and heir, Richard, sought to recover the decedent's estate, which had been inventoried by the authorities. He indicated that his late father, who had resided in Lower Norfolk County, had a large plantation there (LEO 39; SR 600, 660, 661, 662, 749, 1453, 6618; NEVILLE 61, 274).

Richard Carwithey: On March 12, 1627, Richard Carwithey, a sailor, was in urban Jamestown where he testified before the General Court about an incident that involved the ship *Saker* and occurred in the West Indies (VI&A 191).

Henry Cary (Carey): Henry, the son of Thomas Cary of Warwick County, was born around 1650. He served as a county justice and became a militia captain. He was a skillful and respected builder who oversaw the construction of a courthouse at Yorktown in 1694, a fort on the York River in 1697, and the first capitol building in Williamsburg between 1701 and 1703. He also saw that the Wren Building was rebuilt after it burned in 1705 and was responsible for construction of the Governor's Palace. In May 1706 the Council of State authorized Henry Cary to move military materiel from Jamestown to Williamsburg, and afterward he was paid for the hiring carts that were used. In 1711 Cary was censured for his extravagance in building the Governor's Palace and for using public funds to support his own household (EJC II:382; III:88, 99, 118, 180, 192, 202–203, 272, 293; HEN III:226, 485; DOR 3:294–295).

* * *

Miles Cary (Carey) I: Miles Cary I, the grandson of Bristol innholder Henry Hobson, married Anne, the daughter of Thomas Taylor of Windmill Point in Warwick County. In 1644 Cary patented 3,000 acres of land in Westmoreland County, then a frontier area, and during the 1650s he began acquiring acreage in Warwick County, which he made his permanent home. He took an active role in public life and served as a court justice and major, lieutenant colonel, and colonel in the county militia. In 1660 and 1661–1662 Cary served as one of Warwick's burgesses, and in 1663 he was named to the Council of State, on which he remained for the rest of his life. He became collector of customs and escheator general, both positions that generated lucrative fees. When a turf fort was being built on urban Jamestown's waterfront in 1665, Colonel Miles Cary I was ordered to hire sloops to retrieve the ordnance at Old Point Comfort. The following year a decision was made to fortify Old Point Comfort, and Cary was or-

dered to assist his son Thomas in its construction. When Miles Cary I made his will, he left two houses in England to his daughter, Bridget (Bridgett), and designated his son Thomas as legal guardian of his younger sons, Miles II and William, who were living in Virginia. Cary died on June 10, 1667, of wounds he received at Old Point Comfort when the Dutch attacked Virginia's tobacco fleet, which was anchored there. At the time of Cary's death, he had four plantations in Warwick County. On April 6, 1671, Colonel Nathaniel Bacon and the executors of Colonel Miles Cary I of Warwick County purchased from Henry Randolph one unit of a row house in urban Jamestown. It is unclear why the Cary executors made the purchase, unless Randolph was indebted to Cary's estate or Bacon and Cary had jointly invested in the row house (WITH 2831; MCGC 233–234, 292, 484, 486–488, 503, 507–508, 513–514, 517; NUG I:244, 326, 353–354, 374, 533; II:263; STAN 39, 73; PB 7:294; LEO 36, 40; DOR 3:293–294).

Miles Cary (Carey) II: Miles Cary II of Warwick County, one of Miles Cary I's sons, served as county justice and a lieutenant colonel and commander-in-chief of the militia. He became a Warwick County burgess in 1680 and served in the assembly sessions held in 1680–1682, 1684, 1688, 1691–1692, 1698, 1699, 1700–1702, and 1703–1705. He also served briefly as Jamestown's burgess in 1693. Cary, who was well educated, was the colony's surveyor general from 1692 to 1708. He became Register of the Admiralty Court in 1698 and in 1705–1706 served as trustee and then rector of the College of William and Mary. Cary patented substantial quantities of land in Warwick and York counties, much of which he inherited from his late father, and he stood to receive his father's lot in urban Jamestown. Miles Cary II's first wife, Mary, the daughter of Lieutenant Colonel Thomas Milner of Nansemond County, died in October 1700. He then married Mary, the daughter of William Wilson of Ceeley's and the widow of William Roscoe. Mary and Miles II's marriage license is dated April 13, 1702. After Miles Cary II's death on February 16, 1709, his widow, Mary, married Dr. Archibald Blair, a noted physician and the brother of James City Parish's rector, the Rev. James Blair. Dr. Blair represented Jamestown in the assembly just as Miles Cary II had, and served in 1718 and from 1728 to 1734. He probably was eligible because Mary had a dower interest in the lot her late husband, Miles Cary II, owned within the capital city, for land ownership was prerequisite to service as a burgess (LEN 46–47, 49, 51–52, 58–59; STAN 26, 88, 94–97; LEO 69–70, 72, 74; NUG II:247, 368; III:40, 393; DOR 3:294, 296–297; Smith 17; CO 5/1309 f 100; CHAPMAN 161).

William Cary (Carey): William Cary, the son of Miles Cary I and his wife, the former Anne Taylor, inherited his father's plantation on Skiff's Creek in Warwick County. Over the years he held the rank of major and lieutenant colonel in the county militia and also served as a justice, sheriff, and coroner. He was elected to the assembly and represented Warwick County in the sessions held in 1691–1692, 1693, 1699, 1703–1705, 1705–1706, 1710–1712. In 1700 he was named to a commission whose purpose was to put pirates on trial. When Cary made his will on August 26, 1711, while living on Mulberry Island, he made bequests to his wife, Martha I, sons Harwood, Miles, William, and John, and a daughter, Martha II. On May 7, 1713, the executrix Martha Cary I presented the decedent's will to the county court. Although the will had not been endorsed by witnesses, it was accepted as valid. In 1706 Martha II, the daughter of William and Martha Cary of Elizabeth City County, married Edward Jaquelin of Jamestown Island. She had already outlived her former husband, John Thruston of Martin's Hundred (LEO 51–53, 59, 63–64, 66–67; DOR 3:297, 302; EJC I:444, 446; II:66; DUNN 2, 106, 186–187, 200, 216).

* * *

Caskameno (Caskamino, Esquire John) (Native American): On May 27, 1658, Caskameno, one of the Rappahannock Indians' Great Men or leaders, was among the natives confirming a land transaction that the Rappahannock's late king, Accapataugh, and Colonel Moore Fauntleroy had made in 1657. In 1660 Caskameno presented a sow to Fauntleroy as a gift for his daughter, Mary (Old Rappahannock County Deed Book 1656–1664:10–11, 26–27, 106).

George Cassen: George Cassen, a laborer and one of the first Jamestown colonists, was involved in Indian trade. According to William White, Cassen was ambushed by the natives while he was on a trading mission. Afterward, they tortured and then executed him (VI&A 191).

Thomas Cassen: Thomas Cassen, one of the first Jamestown colonists, was a laborer (VI&A 192).

William Cassen: According to Captain John Smith, William Cassen, a laborer, was one of the first Jamestown colonists (VI&A 192).

Arnold (Arnall) Cassinett (Cassina, Cossina): On March 6, 1675, Arnold Cassinett was ordered to free Edward Rawlins, an indentured servant he had obtained from innkeeper Richard Lawrence of Jamestown. Minutes of the General Court reveal that Rawlins signed a contract agreeing to become an apprentice to a ship carpenter, but the ship carpenter assigned him to Lawrence. Lawrence, in turn, sold Rawlins' contract to Arnold Cassinett, who employed him as "a common servant." The justices of the General Court ordered Cassinett to release Rawlins immediately and give him his freedom dues. At the time of Bacon's Rebellion (1675–1676), Cassinett was residing in urban Jamestown in the easternmost bay of a row house on an easterly extension of Back Street. His dwelling was destroyed by fire on September 19, 1676, when Nathaniel Bacon and his followers put the capital city to the torch. Afterward, several people sought to lease the ruins of the house Cassinett had been renting (JHB 1659–1693:73, 78, 152; EJC I:187, 255; MCGC 407).

Vincencio (Vicentio) Castine (Castillian): In 1621 Vincencio Castine, an Italian glassmaker, was outfitted with provisions and the tools of his trade and sent to Virginia. He and his fellow glassworkers were supposed to make tumblers and glass beads that could be used in trading with the Indians. The glassmakers and their families were entrusted to the care of Captain John Norton of Jamestown. The first furnace the glassworkers built at Glasshouse Point, just west of Jamestown Island, exploded within two weeks and Vincencio was suspected of cracking it with an iron crowbar. The glassmaking venture proved unsuccessful and the workers began clamoring to go home. After Captain Norton died, Treasurer George Sandys took over management of the glassworks project and the furnace was rebuilt. In February 1624 Vincencio, whom the census-taker identified as Italian, was residing at Glasshouse Point, but a year later he was living on the lower side of the James River on Sandys' property, the Treasurer's Plantation. On May 23, 1625, Mrs. Vencentia Castine, who may have accompanied her husband to Virginia in 1621, testified in court about the demise of John Clever at the Treasurer's Plantation. On February 20, 1626, she tried to recover some tobacco she was owed by Thomas Swift (Swyft), also a resident of the Treasurer's Plantation (VI&A 192).

Robert Castle: In March 1656 Robert Castle patented an island in the Chickahominy River, low-lying ground that was marsh-covered. In September 1664 he was identified as the guardian of William Gray, a Surry County orphan. On February 25, 1662, Castle bought a waterfront lot in urban Jamestown, purchasing it from Thomas Woodhouse. When he repatented the parcel a year later, after enactment of the 1662 building initiative, the lot's boundaries were redefined. By 1665 plans were made to build a fort on the acreage that adjoined the east side of Robert Castle's lot. The fort's use as a licensing center for trading vessels probably influenced how Robert Castle developed his property. Archaeologists have determined that a unit of a brick row house was constructed on Robert Castle's lot, perhaps during his period of ownership (PB 5:272; NUG I:154, 327; Surry County Deeds and Wills 1652–1672:240).

William Caswell: On April 23, 1670, Captain William Caswell acknowledged a debt to the orphans of William Edwards I, who owned some lots in urban Jamestown (MCGC 216).

George Catchmaid (Catchmaie, Catchmade): In 1660 George Catchmaid served as a burgess for Lower Norfolk County, but he represented Nansemond County in 1661–1662. He patented 3,333 acres on the north side of Roanoke Sound in Carolina in April 1663, receiving his grant from Sir William Berkeley. In March 1664 Catchmaid sold his acreage to George Durant, who already owned land in that vicinity. Catchmaid became speaker of the Carolina assembly in 1666. He died sometime prior to 1688 when his nephew, Edward Catchmaid, sued Timothy Biggs, who had married George Catchmaid's widow (LEO 36, 38; PB 5:330; BODIE 134–135).

Dorcas Catesbie: Dorcas Catesbie left England on July 31, 1622, with William Rowley and his family and probably was a servant in their household on Jamestown Island (VI&A 193).

Catherine (Native American): On May 29, 1677, the queen of the Weyanoke Indians, whose native name is unknown, went to Middle Plantation (later, Williamsburg) and signed the Treaty of Middle Plantation, using a curvilinear symbol as her mark. She

also endorsed the expanded version of the treaty, which was consummated between March 18 and June 19, 1680. In recognition of her loyalty to the Crown, King Charles II authorized the fabrication of a purple robe lined with scarlet shalloon (a twill-woven woolen), a crimson ermine-trimmed cap, and a coronet. The Weyanoke queen was described as a "woman of a most exact proportion of parts, pretty tall of stature and slender of body, also of a pleasing aspect and demeanor." When the king's commissioners asked her name, she said that she would like to be called "Catherine," which they indicated was the name of King Charles II's consort (CO 5/1371; LC 5/108 f 8; 9/275 ff 264ro–267ro; SR 5736, 5743).

John Catlett (Catlet) II: John Catlett II was the son and principal heir of John Catlett I, a surveyor who began patenting land in Old Rappahannock County in 1650 and eventually acquired literally thousands of acres on both sides of the Rappahannock River. The elder John Catlett settled near Occupacia Creek and was a colonel in the Old Rappahannock County militia at the time of his death around 1671. He was survived by his wife, Elizabeth, son John Catlett II, daughters Elizabeth and Sarah, and one or more other children. By 1684 John Catlett II had begun serving as a surveyor of Old Rappahannock County's highways. During the 1680s he performed many public services as an agent of Old Rappahannock County's justices, for he often served on juries and inventoried estates. In 1691 he purchased a lot in the planned town at Hobbes Hole, a community that became known as Tappahannock, and in 1692 he was appointed a trustee. In May 1692 Captain Catlett became a justice in the court of Essex County, which was descended from a portion of Old Rappahannock County. He held that position for many years and also served several terms as a burgess, representing Essex County in the assembly sessions held in 1693, 1695–1696, 1696–1697, and 1700–1702. By 1692 he held the rank of colonel in the local militia, and in 1700 he became Essex County's coroner. His land was mentioned as a reference point in a land transaction that occurred in January 1699. Shortly thereafter he was named as one of his brother's heirs. John Catlett II continued to serve as an Essex County court justice and in 1699 was the presiding justice (LEO 53–54, 56, 60; Old Rappahannock County Deeds and Wills 1656–1664:132–133; 1665–1677:136–143; 1677–1682: 294, 316; 1683–1686:27, 45, 82; Order Book 1683–1686:151; 1687–1692:20, 71, 80, 91, 236; Essex County Order Book 1692–1695:1, 51, 99,

154, 220; 1695–1699:1, 31, 40; Deeds and Wills 1692–1695:325–326; 1695–1699:298, 336; 1699–1702:1, 25–26, 36, 46, 73, 128; Richmond County Deed Book 1 [1692–1693]:24–26; PB 2:224; 3:114, 360; 4:546, 548; 5:477, 623, 625; 6:12, 66; 9:616).

Bryan Caught (Cawt): Bryan Caught, a boat builder, was living in Richard Stephens' household in urban Jamestown on February 16, 1624. In early January 1625 he agreed to build a shallop for John Uty, for whom he already had fabricated a boat. On January 3, 1625, Caught testified that John Gill and James Calver were supposed to give him a tobacco note on behalf of Captain Hamor (VI&A 193).

Robert Cauntrie (Chantry, Channtree): In 1624 Robert Cauntrie, a servant in his teens, was attributed to two locations: Edward Blaney's household in urban Jamestown and Captain William Powell's plantation on the lower side of the James River, then in Blaney's hands. Because Blaney married Powell's widow and purposefully moved some of the decedent's workers to his plantation, Cauntrie may have been a Powell servant (VI&A 193).

Nathaniel Causey (Cawsey): Nathaniel Causey arrived in Jamestown in 1608 in the 1st Supply of new settlers. Although very little is known about his early years in the colony, by December 1620 he had received a patent for some land on the north side of the James River, just east of West and Shirley Hundred. He and his wife, Thomasine, were living at their plantation, Causey's Cleare (or Care), when the Indians attacked in March 1622. Causey, though wounded, fought off the Indians, who fled. Afterward, he and his wife moved to nearby Jordan's Journey, where they stayed on. In 1624 and 1625 Causey served as a burgess for Jordan's Journey and nearby Chaplain's Choice. In August 1626 he was named a commissioner for the monthly court then serving the communities along the upper James River. He also served as overseer of the Truelove Company's property in Virginia. He died sometime prior to February 7, 1634, when his heir, John Causey, disposed of the Causey's Care plantation (VI&A 193; LEO 5–6).

Thomas Causey (Cawsey): Thomas Causey came to Virginia in 1620 and in February 1624 was living on Hog Island; shortly thereafter he moved to Jordan's Journey. In 1635 he patented 150 acres called the Indian Field, acreage that abutted Jordan's Journey and Chaplain's Choice in Charles City County, and a year later he doubled the size of his landholdings. In July 1637 he further enhanced the amount of property he owned. These acquisitions, which occurred in rapid succession, suggest that Causey was a highly successful planter or was a man of means when he came to the colony. By October 1639 Causey had moved to Martin's Hundred, where he was living when he disposed of his 500 acres in Charles City County. In 1640 he served as a burgess for James City County, representing the settlers living in Martin's Hundred (VI&A 194; LEO 18; NUG I:21, 37, 161). No known connection between Nathaniel and Thomas Causey has come to light.

William Cawfield (Caufield): In January 1652 Lieutenant William Cawfield purchased 1,100 acres of land from Robert Shepard, acreage that was located on the west side of Lawnes Creek's mouth in Surry County. In September 1654 Cawfield, a planter and resident of Chippokes Parish in Surry, executed a deed of trust in which he deeded his property to two other men, thereby preserving the legal interests of his wife, Dorcas, and their children, Robert and Elizabeth. Cawfield served as a burgess for Surry County and attended the assembly sessions held in 1658, 1659, 1660, and 1661–1662. He also functioned as an attorney from time to time but in 1667 named his son, Robert, as his attorney. Major William Cawfield was still alive in 1668 (LEO 34–36, 40; Surry County Record Book 1 [1652–1663]:19, 52, 126, 173; 2 [1664–1671]:236, 282, 313).

Thomas Ceely (Seely, Seelie): On October 16, 1629, Thomas Ceely began serving as a burgess for the Warwick River communities, then the westernmost part of the corporation of Elizabeth City. He was among those ordered to find men to plant at Chiskiack, on the York River, in exchange for some land. In March 1630 Ceely served as a burgess for the Denbigh area, and in 1632 he represented the settlers along the Warwick River. Simultaneously, he was named a commissioner of the Warwick River court (VI&A 195; LEO 8–10).

Henry Ceny: In March 1630, September 1632, and February 1633, Henry Ceny served as a burgess for the settlers living in Archer's Hope, which included the James City Parish glebe (VI&A 195; LEO 9, 11–12). In 1634 the area Ceny represented became part of James City County.

Chakingatough (Native American): In early August 1659 Chakingatough, Pantatouse, Yeotassa, and George Caquescough, who were Machodoc Indians, were brought before the justices of Northumberland County, where they were accused of murdering John Cammel, a colonist. A jury found all four Indians guilty and sentenced Caquescough to be hanged but released Chakingatough and the other two men. All four warriors had been brought to Northumberland's justices by their own people. According to Northumberland's court justices, when John Cammel was slain, one Machodoc Indian, who was implicated in the crime, was not brought in. Because the justices decided that the Machodoc were conspiring with other natives "to make a Warr upon us," they concluded that some local men, with the assistance of the militia, should drive the Indians from their tribal land (Northumberland County Order Book 1652–1665:216, 239).

Edward Challis (Challice): Edward Challis came to Virginia sometime prior to 1639, at which time Edward Sanderson listed him as a headright when patenting some land on the Chickahominy River in James City County. On August 28, 1643, Challis patented a one-acre waterfront lot close to the isthmus that connected Jamestown Island to the mainland. Most of those who patented lots in that area were artisans or tradesmen. In 1683, when James City County's official surveyor prepared a plat of the Governor's Land, Edward Challis was credited with a 65-acre leasehold that abutted the James River. Within Challis's leasehold, which was located in the western part of the Governor's Land, archaeologists have identified numerous fragments of a distinctive type of locally made, coarse earthenware pottery, along with wasters. A kiln was not found, perhaps because it had eroded into the James River. It is unclear whether Edward Challis or one of his servants was a potter. On May 12, 1693, Challis was authorized to receive compensation for delivering official messages on behalf of the government (PB 2:12; NUG I:112, 154; Soane 1683; LJC 143; VDHR 1974). The Challis site is on the National Register of Historic Places.

Thomas Chamberlain (Chamberlin, Chamberlaine, Chamberlayne): Thomas Chamberlain, the son of Edmund Chamberlayne of Maugersbury, Gloucestershire, was born around 1653. In 1675, when he was sued by Richard Hill in the General Court, he was ordered to procure some goods from England on Hill's behalf. Some-

time prior to July 28, 1675, Chamberlin wed Mary, Abraham Wood's daughter and the widow of John Bly. She later inherited some of her late father's land in Charles City and Henrico counties. When testifying in court in 1684, Thomas Chamberlain described himself as a London mariner. Later in the year he also was identified as a major in the militia. In 1686 Thomas and Mary Chamberlain sold some of the land she had inherited from her father. Four years later Chamberlin secured a patent for 856 acres on the lower side of the Appomattox River, a tract called Rehoweck, in what was then Charles City County but later became Prince George. He served as a justice and sheriff of Henrico County, but he represented Charles City County in the assembly sessions held in 1695–1696. He also settled and inventoried estates and witnessed wills in Henrico County. In 1702 he patented a Henrico County tract that consisted of 509 acres on the west side of Proctor's Creek, and two years later he paid quitrent on 1,000 acres in Henrico County. Mary Wood Bly Chamberlain predeceased her husband, Thomas, and on September 22, 1709, he married Elizabeth Stratton, the daughter of Martha Sheppey and Edward Stratton Jr. In December 1719 the widowed Elizabeth Stratton Chamberlain presented her late husband's will to the Henrico County court (LEO 54; DOR 3:165, 167, 676–677; Henrico County Order Book 1678–1693:47–48; Deeds and Wills 1677–1692:224, 278, 379, 397; 1697–1704:175, 220, 264; 1706–1709:119, 163, 188; 1710–1714:137; Minute Book 1719–1724:3; SMITH 17; PB 8:38; 9:442; SR 2006; MCGC 411).

Alice Chambers: Alice Chambers came to Virginia in 1623 and in 1625 was living in urban Jamestown, where she was a servant in cape merchant Abraham Peirsey's household. She became pregnant and, on October 10, 1626, was arrested on a charge of whoredom. She was found guilty of committing fornication with Henry Carman, a young servant and resident of West and Shirley Hundred. Alice and Henry were ordered to serve their respective masters an additional seven years (VI&A 196).

Robert Chambly (Chambley): Robert Chambly, a gentleman, served on the jury that in 1624 investigated the drowning death of George Pope, a Jamestown Island youngster. In January 1625 Chambly was fined for neglecting jury duty (VI&A 197).

John Champion: John Champion, who was born on November 10, 1660, may have been a brother of Elizabeth, the wife of Edward Travis II of Jamestown Island. On May 5, 1678, Champion served as a witness when Travis gave his wife, Elizabeth, his power of attorney. He may have been a kinsman of the John Champion who patented some acreage in Northumberland County in 1688 and 1691, but was in Lancaster County during the early 1680s. John Champion died on December 16, 1700, and was interred in the Travis family graveyard in the eastern end of Jamestown Island (NUG III:4; DOR 2:359; Surry County Deeds, Wills &c. 1671–1684:170; Lancaster County Order Book 1680–1687:44; Tyler, "Historical and Genealogical Notes," 142).

William Champion: On November 15, 1677, William Champion deeded to Edward Travis II a 12-acre tract of land on Jamestown Island. At that point the Champion parcel became part of the Travis family's plantation in the eastern end of Jamestown Island (NUG II:252; PB 7:228–229). William Champion may have been Edward Travis II's brother-in-law and John Champion's brother.

Robert Chancellor: In 1787 Robert Chancellor, a free white male of tithable age, was one of the overseers employed by John Ambler II for his Jamestown Island plantation (James City County Personal Property Tax Lists 1787). He does not appear to have owned land in James City County.

Chanco (Chauco) (Native American): Chanco, an Indian youth who had been converted to Christianity and was living at Pace's Paines near Jamestown, traditionally has been credited with warning the colonists of the March 22, 1622, attack. In April 1623 the paramount chief Opechancanough sent Chanco and Comahum as his emissaries to Martin's Hundred to make an overture for peace. Both natives were taken into custody and brought up to Jamestown (VI&A 197).

John Chandler (Chaundler, Chandeler): John Chandler, an ancient planter, came to Virginia in 1609. In 1625, when he was an indentured servant in Thomas Willoughby's household in the corporation of Elizabeth City, he was age 24. By August 1632 Chandler had gained his freedom and was leasing some land that bordered the Back River in Elizabeth City, acreage that belonged to Captain Richard Stephens. Chandler patented 1,000 acres on the west side of Harris Creek in Elizabeth City County in July 1636, and he represented Elizabeth City in the assembly sessions of 1645–1646 and 1647–1648. By August 1646 he had acquired acreage on the lower side of the

James River. He moved there and began serving as a justice of Lower Norfolk County's monthly court, a position he held for many years. In June 1647 he was ordered to collect information on the tithable individuals living on the eastern branch of the Lynnhaven River, an indication that he resided in that vicinity. The following year he was ordered to make a list of those who owed quitrent. Chandler served as a burgess for Lower Norfolk County in 1649. In 1651 he was a justice in Lower Norfolk County's monthly court but held office very briefly. His interests seem to have shifted to Northumberland County, where he patented 1,500 acres on the Wicocomoco and Chicacoan rivers and another 350 acres on the southeast side of the Chicacoan (LEO 24, 26–27; VI&A 198; Lower Norfolk County Record Book B:33a, 40, 52, 162, 167a, 176, 188a; C:23, 25, 51; PB 1:109, 116, 386; 4:110–111).

Samuel Chandler: On March 24, 1642, Samuel Chandler was an executor of the late Lady Elizabeth Dale, who owned land at Goose Hill in the eastern end of Jamestown Island and fronting on the James River (VI&A 239–241; MCGC 499).

Isaac (Isaak) Chaplin (Chapline, Chaplain, Chaplaine, Chaplyn): Isaac Chaplin came to Virginia in 1610–1611 and may have been associated with Bermuda Hundred. He established a plantation of his own, Chaplin's Choice, and as a burgess represented it and nearby Jordan's Journey in 1624 and 1625. In May 1625, when a list of patented land was sent back to England, Ensign Isaac Chaplin was credited with 200 acres in the territory of Great Weyanoke and 50 additional acres in the corporation of Charles City. Despite some legal problems, in August 1626 he was made a justice of the monthly court that served the communities near the head of the James River. In December 1628 the General Court learned that Chaplin had been lost at sea (VI&A 198; LEO 5–6).

Benjamin Chapman: On June 16, 1714, Benjamin Chapman was authorized to keep the ferry from Swann's Point to Jamestown (Surry County Order Book 1713–1718:33).

Francis Chapman: In December 1620 ancient planter Francis Chapman received a patent for a 100-acre parcel adjacent to Richard Pace's property. He was living in urban Jamestown in early 1624 but within a year had moved to his own property. On January 21, 1628, Richard Richards and Richard Dolphenby, who had come into possession of Chapman's land, jointly conveyed it to Isabell Smythe Pace Perry, who owned an adjacent piece of property. The men's land became part of the settlement known as Paces Paines (VI&A 199).

William Chapman: On June 5, 1646, Richard Clarke patented 1½ acres near "the Friggott," in the western end of Jamestown Island. His acreage included a half-acre lot that formerly belonged to William Chapman and contained a cow pen (PB 2:47; NUG I:160).

Charles: On February 15, 1768, when an inventory was made of the late Richard Ambler's slaves on Jamestown Island and his leasehold in the Governor's Land, a boy named Charles was listed and described as Hannah's child. In 1769 Charles was living on Jamestown Island and was identified as Hannah's son and part of Edward Ambler I's estate (York County Wills and Inventories 21:386–391; AMB-E).

Stephen Charlton (Charleston): On May 4, 1635, when he testified before the justices of Accomack County's monthly court and described an event he had witnessed at Thomas Evans' house, Stephen Charlton indicated that he was age 33. Later in the year he was named to the parish vestry. On January 2, 1638, Charlton and another man were ordered to inventory the estate of Henry (Henrie) Charlton, probably a kinsman. Stephen Charlton patented 1,050 acres on Nuswattocks Creek and during the early 1640s made arrangements for John Knight, a New England carpenter, to build a house and mill on his property; the two men may have made an agreement during one of Charlton's trading voyages to New England. One of Charlton's trading partners was Captain John Stone, whose mercantile activities involved transatlantic trade, commerce in the West Indies, and trade with the Eastern Shore's Indians. Charlton owned the pinnace *Elizabeth* and had a store on his property. While trade with the Dutch was legal, he shipped Virginia tobacco on the *Water Duck* of Rotterdam, exchanging it for pipes of wine, Holland sheets, and other items. Among the merchandise he sold was trading cloth, used as a medium of exchange with the natives. Court testimony that occurred in April 1639 and February 1640 reveals that Charlton was involved in the sale of a silver crucifix to a Mr. Stringer of Accomack, almost certainly John Stringer. Charlton continued to acquire land on the Eastern Shore. By February 1640 he had become a member of Accomack County's monthly court, and at the

end of April 1644, he was designated a regional military commander. He married John Severne I's widow, Bridgett, who in July 1645 patented 500 acres on Hungars Creek on behalf of her son, John Severne II. In 1645, 1647–1648, and 1652 Stephen Charlton served as a burgess for Northampton County. Henry Norwood, who had been shipwrecked on the Eastern Shore in 1649 and befriended by that area's Indians, was led to Charlton's house in Northampton County, where he was treated hospitably and provided with food and clothing. Norwood described Charleton's kind treatment in a narrative that later was published. Sometime after May 25, 1652, Stephen Charleton married the twice-widowed Ann Huffe West, who had outlived Stephen Huffe and surgeon Anthony West. Stephen Charlton of Nuswattocks made his will on October 28, 1654, which was proved on January 29, 1655. He made bequests to his wife, Ann; to his daughters, Bridgett and Elizabeth; to his nephew, John Walton; and to several friends and godchildren (LEO 23, 26, 30; VI&A 730; FOR III:10:48–49; AMES 1:28, 34, 39, 96, 144–145, 159; 2:228–233, 359; Northampton County Orders, Deeds, Wills 2:193, 196, 365; Deeds, Wills, Orders 4 [1651–1654]:23, 67–68; Deeds, Wills &c. 5 [165–1655]:56, 58; Order Book 1657–1664:35; DOR 3:509–510; DEVRIES 64; NUG I:79, 82, 129, 200, 412; PB 1:783; 2:30; MARSHALL 38–39, 54).

* * *

Edmund (Edmond, Edward) Cheesman (Chisman, Cheasman, Cheaseman) I: Edmund Cheesman I, a resident of Elizabeth City during the mid-1620s, began patenting land in York County in 1638. Much of his property was in the New Poquoson Parish, in eastern York County, and on Cheesman Creek, but he also had acreage on Milford Haven in what became Gloucester County and then Mathews. He married John Lilly's widow, Mary, who became a member of the Quaker faith. By 1652 Cheesman had become a justice in York County's court. As time went on, Mary Cheesman's religious beliefs proved problematic, for when it became illegal for groups of Quakers to assemble, the Cheesman couple received a warning from York's justices. On April 1, 1662, Edmund Cheesman I signed a 21-year lease with his brother, John, renting all of his York County property. If John Cheesman and his wife, Margaret, were to die while the lease was in effect, the property was to descend to Edmund Cheesman I and then to his sons, Edmund II and Thomas. Edward Cheesman I patented 300 acres on the upper side of Cheesman's Creek in 1668, land that had been claimed by his brother, John, but deserted. He made his will on March 26, 1673, and died prior to February 23, 1674 (VI&A 201; York County Deeds, Orders, Wills 1:130; 2:180; 3:125, 127, 162–164; DOR 1:570; PB 1:718; 2:262; 5:121; 6:273).

Edmund (Edmond, Edward) Cheesman (Chisman, Cheasman, Cheaseman) II: Edmund Cheesman II, a resident of York County and the son of Edmund I, began serving as a court justice in 1670. He became an ardent supporter of the rebel Nathaniel Bacon and was among those captured by Governor William Berkeley's men. Cheesman died in prison before he could stand trial. When Governor Berkeley issued a proclamation on February 10, 1677, naming those who were exempt from the king's pardon, one of those listed was Edmund Cheesman II, who already was deceased. His personal effects were inventoried and then confiscated. His wife, Lydia, who was in her late 20s, went on to marry Thomas Harwood (DOR 1:571; NEVILLE 61; SR 235, 660, 749; PB 6:288; HEN II:375).

Thomas Cheesman (Chisman, Cheasman, Cheaseman): Thomas Cheesman was the son of Edmund Cheesman I and brother of Edmund Cheesman II. As his father's heir and a reversionary heir of his uncle, John Cheesman, he inherited a substantial amount of land in York County. Thomas Cheesman became a county justice in 1680 and went on to become a militia captain and vestryman of Charles Parish. In September 1680 he patented some acreage in Gloucester County on Milford Haven, part of which had been claimed by his father earlier on. During Bacon's Rebellion, which got underway in 1676 and ended in 1677, Captain Thomas Wilford was captured by Governor Berkeley's men who ambushed some of the rebels holed up in Captain Thomas Cheesman's house on the York River. Thomas Cheesman served as a burgess for York County and attended the assembly sessions held in 1685–1686. In January 1690 he indicated that he was around age 38. When quitrents were compiled in 1704, Cheesman was credited with 1,800 acres in York County and 650 acres in Gloucester County's Ware Parish. Cheesman was married to the former Elizabeth Read, Nicholas Martiau's granddaughter. His will, dated January 25, 1701, was proved on July 18, 1715 (LEO 48; York County Deeds, Orders, Wills 3:162–164; 8:385; 14 [1709–1716]:434–436; DOR 1:571–572; PB 7:47, 62; 8:300; AND 80–81).

John Cheesman (Chisman, Cheasman, Cheaseman): John Cheesman came to Virginia in 1621 and settled in Elizabeth City, where he patented 200 acres of land in 1624. In early 1625 Cheesman was sharing a dwelling with his brother, Edward Cheesman I. On April 25, 1625, the General Court identified him as Lieutenant John Cheesman. In May 1625 he was credited with 200 acres on the south side of the James River in Elizabeth City, land that had been claimed but not seated. He was a successful merchant and planter, who continued to acquire land; in 1635 he patented acreage on the New Poquoson River in Charles River (York) County, along what became known as Cheesman's Creek. During the early 1650s he invested in land on Mobjack Bay in what became Gloucester and then Mathews County. Cheesman rose in wealth and prominence and in 1643 served as a burgess for York County. In time, he became a captain and lieutenant colonel of the militia. He also became a county justice, tobacco viewer, and finally a member of the Council of State in 1652. Cheesman went to England in 1661 and leased his York County property to his brother, Edmund I, for 21 years. He stipulated that if he were not to survive the length of the lease, Edmund I and his sons, Edmund II and Thomas, would inherit it. John Cheesman died in England sometime prior to September 20, 1678, when his wife, Margaret, was identified as a widow (VI&A 201; LEO 21; STAN 36; York County Deeds, Orders, Wills 3:162–164; DOR 1:568–569; PB 1:47, 471–472, 492, 770; 3:116–117; 4:554).

* * *

Joseph Chermaison (Chermeson): In October 1703 Joseph Chermaison, a Frenchman, was residing in York County at Stephen Fouace's plantation. He had in his possession some money that was supposed to go to the minister at Manakin Town, a French settlement above the falls of the James River. By June 1708 Chermaison had purchased the Glasshouse tract from William Broadribb's executor. After Joseph Chermaison's death, which occurred sometime prior to January 1713, his widow, Elizabeth, served as his executrix and, in that capacity, sold the Glasshouse tract to Edward Jaquelin. The widowed Elizabeth Chermaison eventually married Claude Rouniere, another Frenchman. In June 1714 a child named Elizabeth Chermaison (probably Joseph and Elizabeth I's daughter) was credited with 100 acres of land in York County (EJC II:339; AMB 78; NUG II:140).

Thomas Chermant: Thomas Chermant came to Virginia with Edward Grendon I of Jamestown Island and set sail from England on July 31, 1622 (VI&A 202).

Anthony Chester: Anthony Chester, captain of the *Margaret and John*, left England in mid-December 1620 with Dr. Lawrence Bohun. Their ship was attacked by the Spanish in the West Indies, and on March 19, 1621, Dr. Bohun was killed. Later, one of Captain Chester's passengers produced a narrative of his adventures, which was published in 1707 in the Dutch language. It included a description of the March 22, 1622, Indian attack. Although the writer's accuracy has been questioned, Chester's presence in the colony around the time of the native assault is documented (VI&A 202).

John Chew: John Chew came to Virginia in 1622 and became the factor or business agent of the Bennetts, a prominent English mercantile family that established the settlement in Warresqueak known as Bennett's Welcome. In 1624, while he was living at Hog Island, Chew served as a burgess for Warresqueak. By January 24, 1625, he had married a woman named Sarah. Later in the year he patented a small waterfront lot in urban Jamestown, where he built a store. Although John Chew took an active role in the capital city's civic affairs, in 1625 and 1628 he again served as a burgess for Hog Island, where he and his wife, Sarah, resided. Together they produced a son, Samuel, who was born around 1626. Governor John Harvey described John Chew as one of the "ablest merchants in Virginia." In 1630 Chew established a plantation on the York River at Chiskiack and eventually moved there. In 1643 and 1644 he served as a York County burgess and donated part of his land as a parish glebe. John Chew's wife, Sarah, died sometime prior to April 3, 1651, when he signed a marriage contract with the widowed Mrs. Rachel (Rachael) Constable. However, he died around 1652, shortly after his remarriage. By 1659 John Chew's son, Samuel, who was his principal heir, had moved to Maryland, which he made his permanent home (VI&A 202–203; LEO 5–8, 21–22).

Henry Cheyney: Henry Cheyney, a merchant from York, England, arrived in Jamestown on September 12, 1623, and took the oath of supremacy (VI&A 203).

King of the Chicacoan and the Wicocomoco (Wecocomaka, Wicocomocoe) Indians (Native American): In March 1655 Governor William Berkeley and his council issued an order granting the king of the Chicacoan and the Wicocomoco (Wecocomaka, Wicocomocoe) Indians the land on which they were living. The order made reference to a specific act of assembly and stated that the land would be surveyed for them. On January 20, 1664, the acreage the Indians had been awarded, a 4,400-acre tract that had been delimited, was confirmed to them (Northumberland County Record Book 1622–1666:142). It is likely that in March 1655 the leader or werowance of the Chicacoan and Wicocomoco (Wecocomaka, Wicocomocoe) Indians was Machywap, who in November 1655 was identified as their king. *See Machywap.*

Chicatomen (Native American): Northumberland County court records dating to June 1668 reveal that three Wicocomoco (Wecocomaka, Wicocomocoe) Indian Great Men, Owasewas, Appenmaw, and Chicatomen, had been ordered to bring in a warrior named Noroas. The justices wanted Noroas taken into custody because a colonist named Adam Pettegrew believed that he was harboring a runaway maidservant. Because neither Noroas nor the maidservant could be found, the court justices decided that all three Great Men should be detained (Northumberland County Order Book 1666–1678:40).

Sir Henry Chicheley: Sir Henry Chicheley, the son of Thomas Chicheley of Wimple in Cambridge, England, immigrated to Virginia in 1649, shortly after King Charles I was beheaded. He was Edward Digges I's cousin and a close associate of Governor William Berkeley. Around 1651 Chicheley married the former Agatha Eltonhead, Ralph Wormeley I's widow, whose son, Ralph Wormeley II, was an infant. Before the couple wed they signed a prenuptial agreement whereby Chicheley agreed to convey Agatha's former husband's real and personal property to Ralph Wormeley II when he came of age. Chicheley moved into Rosegill, the Wormeley estate, and enjoyed its profits for more than 20 years. He represented Lancaster County in the assembly in 1656, while the Commonwealth government was in power, and during the 1660s his name appeared many times in records generated by the county court. In 1666 he paid poll taxes on 52 people who were associated with the Lancaster County property he managed. When Chicheley went abroad in 1662, he authorized merchant Cuthbert Potter to serve as his attorney and noted that Potter was then at Rosegill. Chicheley became a member of the Council of State in 1670 and served until 1683; he also held the rank of lieutenant general. In 1674 he became a justice for Middlesex County, where he owned two plantations, Timber Neck and Nimcock. Chicheley was intensely disliked by the rebel Nathaniel Bacon, who declared that he was a traitor and allowed his men to loot his home. Chicheley himself was captured and imprisoned for 20 weeks at the Mehixon Fort, in the upper reaches of the Pamunkey River, but survived the ordeal despite his advanced age. In March 1677 he signed a document in which he agreed to account for the income he had received over the years from the late Ralph Wormeley I's estate and the disbursements he had made on his stepson's behalf. Attached to the agreement was a lengthy list of valuable personal property that Ralph Wormeley II, as his father's heir, expected to receive. In December 1678 Sir Henry Chicheley commenced serving as deputy governor. While he was in office, the low price of tobacco prompted large groups of planters to destroy the year's crop, thereby reducing the supply and forcing a price increase. In 1679 Chicheley commissioned Edward Hill II of Shirley Plantation as attorney general, and he advocated abolition of the quitrent. Chicheley died on February 5, 1683 (WITH 421; STAN 16, 39; MCGC 515, 521; Bruce, "Persons Who Suffered by Bacon's Rebellion," 64; SAIN 10:360; ASPIN 169, 172, 174; WASH 409; LEO xix, 33; Old Rappahannock County Deeds and Wills 1656–1664:171–172; Middlesex County Order Book 1673–1680:11, 38, 68, 104–107; Lancaster County Order Book 1666–1680:18).

William Chick: In March 1784 William Chick, an overseer or farm manager on John Ambler II's Jamestown Island plantation, paid someone for building a flat, a watercraft suitable for shallow waters. In 1784, 1785, and 1786 Chick was listed in the James City County Personal Property Tax rolls as a free white male tithe (James City County Personal Property Tax Lists 1784–1786; Ambler, March 29, 1784).

* * *

Walter Chiles I: On March 1, 1638, Walter Chiles I of Bristol, England, patented 400 acres of land in Charles City County, acreage that abutted the Appomattox River. He used the headrights of his wife, Elizabeth, and sons, Walter II and William, plus those of four other people. Chiles, a merchant and planter, served as a Charles City County burgess in 1642–1643. However, in November 1645 he commenced representing James City County, an indication that he or his wife

was a property owner, and held office in 1646 when a major Indian treaty was signed. Later he became a James City Parish churchwarden, an indication that he was then living in the parish. By 1649 Chiles, who was still a James City burgess, had patented 813 acres on the south side of the Appomattox River, in what was then Charles City County but is now Prince George. On March 23, 1649, Governor William Berkeley sold Chiles, who was identified as a merchant, a 3½-acre lot in urban Jamestown, which contained a fine brick house that had belonged successively to Secretary Richard Kemp and Sir Francis Wyatt. Walter Chiles I and his wife, Elizabeth, resided on his property in urban Jamestown. In 1651 he was appointed to the Council of State and became a lieutenant colonel in the militia. In 1653 he served as a burgess for James City but resigned on July 6th, after he was elected speaker of the assembly. Because his ship, the *Leopaldus*, was involved in trading with the Dutch, contrary to law, he was censured for violating the navigation acts and temporarily deprived of the right to hold office. Sometime prior to March 10, 1653, Chiles acquired 70 acres at Black Point in the eastern end of Jamestown Island. In April 1653 he purchased two servants from William Edwards I, father and grandfather of William Edwards II and III, who owned two lots in urban Jamestown. He also obtained some livestock and furniture from William, son of John Corker, who patented two Jamestown lots. When Walter Chiles I died in 1653, all of his landholdings descended to his eldest son, Walter II. A land transaction reveals that Walter Chiles I's widow, Elizabeth, and her new husband, Edward Hill I, retained a legal interest in the Kemp dwelling she and her late husband had bought from Governor William Berkeley (HCA ff 268, 273; HEN I:239, 358, 377–378, 382; Tyler 1892–1893:75; Surry County Deeds, Wills &c. 1652–1672:8, 28, 263; JHB 1619–1660:86, 91; NUG I:103–104, 186, 231; II:112; PB 3:8; 6:413; AMB 4, 6, 24; STAN 36, 61, 63–64, 70; Stanard, "Minutes of Council," 122; LEO xix, 20–21, 24–25, 27, 31).

Walter Chiles II: Walter Chiles II, the son of Elizabeth and Walter Chiles I, was born prior to 1638, at which time he was living in Virginia. By 1656 Walter Chiles II had inherited his late father's property on Jamestown Island and moved there. He and his wife, Mary, the daughter of Colonel John Page of Middle Plantation, probably occupied the brick house that Secretary Richard Kemp built in urban Jamestown. Chiles was living in the capital city in October 1656 when a Surry man sent him a sail for his boat, and his land was used as a reference point in 1660 when John Fitchett patented a neighboring lot. From 1659 through 1666 Chiles served as Jamestown's burgess but retired after the June 1666 session. During at least part of the time he held office, he was a justice in James City County's court. On May 20, 1670, Walter Chiles II patented a 70-acre tract at Black Point, in the extreme eastern end of Jamestown Island, acreage that he had inherited from his father. He probably placed some of his indentured servants on his 70 acres and on his leasehold in the Governor's Land. Walter Chiles II was a respected member of the Jamestown Island community and by 1671 had become a member of the James City Parish vestry. He was called upon to inventory the estate of the late Thomas Hunt of urban Jamestown and was designated his executor and his orphan's guardian. In April 1671 Chiles patented 1,500 acres in Westmoreland County for his sons, John and Henry. His name appeared for the last time in official records on May 25, 1671, when the justices of the General Court asked him to arbitrate a dispute. Chiles prepared his will on November 15, 1671, and designated his second wife, Susanna, as executrix. He died later in the year and she began implementing the terms of his will, which required her to sell all of his property on Jamestown Island. A deed executed on November 20, 1673, by Susanna and her new husband, the Rev. James Wadding, reveals that Walter Chiles II, after inheriting the Kemp house, built a brick house on an adjacent parcel. In 1673 the Kemp house was in Thomas Sully's possession, whereas the dwelling that Chiles had built was occupied by Major Theophilus Hone. Among the late Walter Chiles II's properties was a 200-acre leasehold in the Governor's Land, in which Susanna retained a legal interest (MCGC 217, 247, 259, 285;DOR 2:494; Surry County Deeds, Wills &c. 1652–1672:84; NUG I:103–104, 339; II:112; AMB 6, 24; LEE L51 ff 672–673; HEN I:506–507; II:196–197; STAN 74, 77; Charles City County Order Book:33; Lee 51 f 673; PB 6:413; 7:228–229; LEO 35–36, 38).

John Chiles (Childs, Giles): John Chiles was the son of Walter Chiles II. In September 1693 when he and his wife, Mary, sold Governor Edmund Andros the residue of his late father's 99-year lease for acreage in the Governor's Land, Walter II's widow, Susanna, agreed to the transaction. However, in November 1697 John Chiles asked for a new piece of rental property in the mainland, that is, the Governor's Land. In 1699 Chiles served as a messenger for the assem-

bly, and in December 1704 he reportedly was occupying William Brown I's land in James City, perhaps his acreage on Diascund Creek in James City County, for Brown already had disposed of his lots in urban Jamestown (SAIN 16:8; JHB1695–1702:141; Surry County Will Book 5:305; LEE L51 ff 672–673).

* * *

Edward Chilton: By 1682 Edward Chilton had begun serving as clerk in the Secretary of the Colony's office, where he entered important public documents into the record books and saw that the volumes were maintained properly. In 1682 Chilton was lauded for alphabetizing the records in his custody. He went on to become clerk of the assembly and during the 1690s, while he was a resident of Charles City County, served as Virginia's attorney general. In April 1683 Chilton patented a lot in urban Jamestown. He was married to Hannah, the daughter of Edward Hill III of Shirley Plantation, and sometimes conducted business on his father-in-law's behalf. During the 1680s and 1690s Edward Chilton began patenting escheat land in New Kent County, probably making use of information he obtained while working in the Secretary's office. In 1697 Edward Chilton, Henry Hartwell (also of Jamestown), and the Rev. James Blair prepared a report on the status of the colony, a published work that describes the colony's economic and political attributes. Chilton was a strong advocate of the admiralty court, a judicial body on which his father-in-law served as judge (HEN III:562; PB 7:292; JHB1660–1693:174; EJC I:200, 495, 529; 1918:92; STAN 25; Charles City County Wills and Deeds 1692–1694:183; York County Deeds, Orders, Wills 9:115,124; NUG II:284, 293; SAIN 15:655; CO 5/1309 f 100).

Chiste Cuttewans (Native American): On November 17, 1662, Chiste Cuttewans and two other Great Men of the Wicocomoco (Wecocomaka, Wicocomocoe) Indian Town acknowledged that Robert Jones was authorized to use their land in exchange for 12 matchcoats, cloth garments often used as trade goods (Northumberland County Record Book 1658–1662:86).

Chubby: On February 15, 1768, when an inventory was made of the late Richard Ambler's slaves on Jamestown Island and his leasehold in the Governor's Land, an adult female slave named Chubby and her child were listed. In 1769, when an inventory was made of the late Edward Ambler I's estate,

Chubby was living on Jamestown Island with her child, John (York County Wills and Inventories 21:386–391; AMB-E).

* * *

James Chudley (Chudleigh): Sometime after 1687 but before 1695, James Chudley married Ann Holder Briscoe, a widow who had inherited some acreage in urban Jamestown from three family members: her late father, Richard Holder; her brother, John Holder; and her late father-in-law, William Briscoe. Ann's acreage, which fronted on the James River, bordered Orchard Run and consisted of several contiguous parcels. On February 5, 1697, James and Ann Holder Briscoe Chudley sold part of her property to William Edwards III. The Chudleys were then residing upon the residue of the eight-plus acre tract that Ann had inherited from her father and brother. When Jamestown merchant William Sherwood made his will in 1697, he referred to the Chudleys' orchard near Orchard Run (AMB 21, 22, 38, 53, 57, 63, 65, 133).

Ann Holder (Holden, Holdinge) Briscoe (Brisco) Chudley (Chudleigh) (see Ann Holder)

* * *

Richard Church: Richard Church probably was living in Lower Norfolk County in 1662 when he witnessed William Odeon's will. In April 1668 he patented 550 acres of land in the county on the south side of the Elizabeth River's eastern branch, later adding 1,000 acres to his holdings. In 1676 he served as a burgess for Lower Norfolk County and in 1685–1686 authenticated Richard Hill's will. Church was a burgess for Norfolk County in 1699, and a year later he witnessed documents generated in the newly formed Princess Anne County. He inventoried the estate of the late Thomas Walke of Princess Anne in 1703. Church, who resided in Norfolk County, made his will on January 5, 1705, and perhaps on account of failing health, gave his power of attorney to his son-in-law, Richard Corbin (Corbitt), on September 3, 1705. The testator made bequests to his wife, Elizabeth, and to his daughters Abigail and Patience Church, Sarah Nichols, Ann Trevathan, and Mary Murrow. He also named his son, Joseph Church, his daughter Mrs. Corbin, and his grandchildren as legatees, and designated his wife and son as co-executors of his estate. By February 15, 1706, Richard Church was dead (LEO 41, 59; Lower Norfolk County Book D:368; Norfolk County Wills and Deeds 4:236; 7:106; Princess

Anne County Deed Book 1:274, 384, 438; PB 6:148; 7:398).

William Churchill: In November 1675 William Churchill, newly designated under-sheriff of Middlesex County, took the oath of office. He served in that position for several years and was returned to office in 1687, around the time when he and several others appraised the late Robert Beverley I's estate. Churchill served as a factor for London merchants John and Jeffrey Jeffreys, who were investors in the Royal African Company and maintained a store at his plantation. With the assistance of William Killbee, he seems to have sold indentured servants and enslaved Africans as well as goods. Churchill served as a county justice for many years and represented Middlesex in the assembly sessions held in 1691–1692. He compiled a list of the tithables in Middlesex County's lower precinct in 1690. A year later, when he was churchwarden of Christ Church Parish, he reported an unmarried woman who had given birth to a child. When the ship *Wolfe* ran aground, William Churchill agreed to pay the men who put it afloat if they would become his servants for a limited time. In 1694 he was acting as Jeffrey Jeffreys' factor when he sued the Rev. Samuel Gray and his wife, who were residents of Middlesex County. Three years later Churchill represented John and Jeffrey Jeffreys in litigation he pursued in Lancaster County's monthly court. He also participated in suits in Essex County and served as one of Christopher Robinson's executors. In 1705 William Churchill succeeded burgess Edwin Thacker, who died before the final session of the assembly, and he served on the Council of State from 1705 to 1710. In 1706 he was one of several men given the responsibility of determining which of the Rappahannock River's branches should be considered the main one. At issue was ascertaining the course of the Northern Neck Proprietary's boundary line (LEO xix, 50, 62; Middlesex County Order Book 1673–1680:44, 160, 176; 1680–1694:296, 303, 343, 409, 466, 470, 510, 553, 701, 714; 1694–1705:69, 276–277; Lancaster County Order Book 1686–1696:263; 1696–1702:17, 20, 23; Essex County Order Book 1692–1695:235, 239, 244; SR 5754; EJC III:86).

William Claiborne (Claiborn, Clayborne, Cleyborn): William Claiborne, the Virginia Company's official surveyor, arrived in Virginia in October 1621. He had some previous experience in colonization ventures and was an ancient planter and adventurer in New England. Claiborne was supposed to live in Jamestown and perform surveys for three years. By 1623 he had been named to the Council of State. He delimited several lots in urban Jamestown and plotted the boundaries of some 12-acre homesteads in the eastern end of the island. By June 1624 he had patented two parcels of land in the corporation of Elizabeth City. In 1625 Claiborne became secretary of state, a position he held for a decade. His interest in Indian trade and exploration soon became evident, and in 1629 he received permission to trade with the Dutch and with other English colonies. Because he was in control of Kent Island, which formed the base of his Indian trading operations, he vehemently opposed the Calverts' colonization of Maryland. Although he was ousted from Kent Island, he rallied a group of Protestants who in 1644 attacked Maryland, then a Roman Catholic colony. In 1642 Claiborne became treasurer of Virginia, a position he held until 1660. When Governor Berkeley surrendered the colony, known as a royalist stronghold, to a Parliamentary fleet in 1652, Claiborne was one of the Commonwealth government's representatives. Afterward, he again served as secretary of state, holding office from 1652–1660. During the 1650s he patented vast tracts of land on the colony's frontier— in the Northern Neck, Middle Peninsula, and Pamunkey Neck—in time amassing more than 16,000 acres. After he was replaced as secretary, he was elected a burgess for New Kent County and served in 1660 and from 1666 to 1676. William Claiborne died in Virginia in 1677, by which time he had established a family seat in Pamunkey Neck, at the head of the York River (VI&A 205; LEO 36, 39).

Clara (Clary): On February 15, 1768, when an inventory was made of the late Richard Ambler's slaves at his quarter called Powhatan, Clara, a female slave, was living there. She was still there in 1769 and was described as a girl who was part of Edward Ambler I's estate (York County Wills and Inventories 21:386–391; AMB-E).

Ambrose Clare: In May 1671 Jamestown merchant Jonathan Newell successfully brought suit against Ambrose Clare and recovered some funds he was owed. In 1667 the two men, as partners, had patented 2,500 acres in New Kent County's St. Peter's Parish. Later, Clare was sued by William Sawyer (MCGC 260, 275; PB 6:95; 7:18; 8:121).

Bridgett Clark (Clarke): On February 16, 1624, Bridgett Clark was identified as a servant in Mary and Peter Ascam's home in urban Jamestown (VI&A 207).

George Clark (Clarke): The dwelling of George Clark, a Jamestown Island gunsmith, was located near Sandy Hill, not far from the urban Jamestown workshop of fellow gunsmith John Jackson. In July 1623 Clark and another man slaughtered one of Sir George Yeardley's calves and hid the meat in Clark's loft. Both men were convicted of the crime, but Clark was reprieved, probably because of his specialized skills. In February 1624 Clark was living at Warresqueak, but by late November he had returned to Jamestown. George Clark died in Jamestown sometime prior to January 24, 1625 (VI&A 207).

John Clark (Clarke): John Clark, a tradesman, came to Virginia in 1608 in the 2nd Supply of new settlers and lived in Jamestown (VI&A 208).

John Clark (Clarke): John Clark, a 35-year-old English pilot, left London on March 17, 1611, and arrived in Virginia in early May. In June, when he boarded a Spanish ship at Old Point Comfort, he was seized and taken to Havana, Cuba, where he was interrogated. He then described Jamestown and the forts at Old Point Comfort. In 1612 Clark was taken to Madrid, Spain, where he was interrogated for a second time. Thanks to a prisoner exchange agreement between the Spanish and English governments, Clark was released and allowed to return to England. In 1620 he came to the New World as pilot of the *Mayflower*. By 1623 he had immigrated to Virginia and died shortly thereafter, leaving a widow and children (VI&A 208).

John Clark (Clarke): John Clark, a 33-year-old butcher from Oxfordshire, went to Virginia in 1619 on the *Bona Nova*, which arrived in Jamestown in mid-November 1619. He probably was a Virginia Company servant or tenant (VI&A 208).

John Clark (Clarke): On May 18, 1622, John Clark was identified as a sawyer employed by the Company of Shipwrights. He worked under the supervision of Thomas Nunn, who resided on Jamestown Island. On May 2, 1625, Clark was arrested and placed in the custody of the provost marshal (VI&A 208).

Richard Clark (Clarke): On June 5, 1646, Richard Clark patented a 1½-acre lot in urban Jamestown, having purchased part of it from William Chapman. Relatively little is known about Clark except that in 1635 George Menefie listed him as a headright when patenting a lot in the capital city. During the early 1670s Clark made several appearances before the General Court, where he served as the attorney of George Lee, a London merchant who by 1681 was living in Jamestown. He also functioned as the attorney of Sarah Bland, who came to Virginia to tend to the business interests of her husband, John Bland I, a powerful British merchant. By the early to mid-1670s Richard Clark had moved to New Kent County, where he became established in the vicinity of Ware Creek. In 1673 he made a complaint about a fence erected by Colonel Daniel Parke I, who owned Mount Folly, and in 1677 he filed a petition with the king's special commissioners, alleging that a group of armed men (Berkeley loyalists) came to his house and "took away 4 English servants, 7 negroes and all household goods, beds and linen to a value of about £400." Among those absconding with Clark's goods were Richard Auborne of urban Jamestown and Robert Beverley I. Richard Clark prepared his will on August 25, 1686, and died a short time later. His daughter, Margaret, the wife of Jamestown tailor John Howard, served as his administratrix (PB 2:47; NUG I:24, 160; MCGC 249, 273, 349, 382, 386; Surry County Deeds, Wills &c. 1671–1684:287; BOD II:583; NEVILLE 67; WITH 60).

Thomas Clark (Clarke): Thomas Clark was listed among those who died in Jamestown sometime after April 1623 but before February 16, 1624 (VI&A 209).

Thomas Clark (Clarke): In February 1624 Thomas Clark, one of Vice Admiral John Pountis's servants, was living in urban Jamestown. He died at sea in May 1625 while returning to Virginia. His inventory and appraisal, compiled by Farrar (Pharaoh) Flinton and Joseph Cobb, were presented to the General Court on November 28, 1625. Among Clark's creditors were William Webster (purser of the *Elizabeth*), Richard Wake (a shipboard surgeon), and Thomas Weekes (VI&A 209).

Thomas Clarke: In 1672 Thomas Clarke, a Surry County bricklayer, reportedly owed money to innkeeper Richard Lawrence of urban Jamestown. In 1679 Clarke lost a lawsuit to Nicholas Wyatt, who took action against him in Surry County. When Clarke testified in court in July 1683, he identified himself as a bricklayer (Surry County Deeds, Wills &c. 1652–1672:256; Order Book 1671–1691:5, 8, 235, 446).

John Claus: On February 5, 1628, John Claus was identified as an indentured servant of Edward Sharples of urban Jamestown (VI&A 209).

* * *

Rev. John Clayton: The Rev. John Clayton, a dedicated naturalist and Anglican clergyman, was the rector of James City Parish. When he prepared a written description of Virginia in 1684, he commented on life in the colony and made note of flora and fauna. He said that the Back River's channel (behind Jamestown Island) would accommodate a ship of 20 to 30 tons and that there was a large oak tree midway between the Back River and a brick house located near the mouth of Kingsmill Creek. In 1688 Clayton described and made sketches of the various types of fences that could be seen on Jamestown Island and said that he told property owner William Sherwood that he should drain his marsh (Pitch and Tar Swamp), which cut a broad swath across the island. When Clayton made a map of Jamestown Island in 1688, he identified the sites upon which the turf fort (built around 1665) and the brick fort (built in the early 1670s) were located. He also indicated that a row of houses then lined the bank of the James River, just west of the turf fort, and he showed a substantial brick house at the mouth of Kingsmill Creek (Clayton 1688; FOR III:12:3).

John Clayton II: John Clayton II of Williamsburg, son of the Rev. John Clayton, was born in 1665. He served as the attorney of London merchant Micajah Perry, who owned part of a brick row house and a waterfront lot in urban Jamestown. During the 1720s Clayton served as a James City County burgess. On May 6, 1710, he witnessed John Howard's deed to John Baird, which involved two Jamestown lots changing hands. The following year, while he was serving as attorney, he carried a message from William Byrd II of Westover to the governor about furnishing palisades that were to be used in defending the colony's old and new capitals (AMB 82, 101; STAN 103, 105–107; Byrd 1941:401).

* * *

Francis Clements (Clemons): Surry County records reveal that sometime prior to December 1690 Henry Hartwell, a resident of urban Jamestown, gave his power of attorney to Captain Francis Clements, who then owned land in Southwark Parish. The names of Clements and his wife, Elizabeth, appeared in Surry records two years later when they witnessed a deed whereby Thomas Flood's land was transferred to a kinsman. In 1693 Nicholas Meriwether of James City County, whose sister Ann was then married to Francis Clements, referred to Clements as his brother when authorizing him to act as his attorney. He also sold Clements 651 acres in Surry, acreage known as the Indian Spring. Clements represented Surry County in the assembly in 1693. When he sold some of his acreage to a local man two years later, he indicated that he had purchased it from Godfrey Lee of Donol Commons in London. In 1698 Clements, who was then serving as the Council of State's clerk, received a modest bequest from his friend John Thompson, a merchant. Clements continued to acquire acreage, some of which was on the Nottoway River in what was then Surry County. He moved to Isle of Wight County sometime after 1711 and was living there in 1715 when his third wife, Lydia, authorized a local resident to act as her attorney. Francis Clements I died there in 1717. When his son, Francis II, made his will in April 1721, he bequeathed his late father's Indian Spring tract in Surry to the vestry and churchwardens of Southwark Parish for use as a glebe (Surry County Deeds, Wills &c. 1687–1694:181, 188, 272, 320; 1694–1709:100; 1709–1715:81, 258; TOR 86; WITH 122; LEO xxii, 52; PB 7:703; 9:725; 10:184; SR 4786; BODIE 214; Isle of Wight County Will and Deed Book 2 [1666–1719]:632; 3 [1726–1734]:520).

Thomas Clayton: In 1682 Thomas Clayton was among those who testified about Jamestown's corporate limits. As a burgess from 1680 to 1682, he represented the capital city, an indication that he or his wife owned property there. In November 1682 he was paid for hosting assembly committees (AMB 23; JHB 1660–1693:174; LJC 19; LEO 45).

* * *

Jeremiah (Jeffrey, Jeremy, Jeremie, Joreme, Jereme) Clements I: Sometime prior to November 1607 Jeremiah Clements I married his wife, Elizabeth I. When she came to Virginia in 1617, she was accompanied by her children, Elizabeth II, Jeremiah II, Ezeckiell, and Nicholas Clements, and two servants. Jeremiah Clements I died sometime prior to March 1, 1620. By February 1624 his widow, Elizabeth I, had married Captain Ralph Hamor (Hamer) and was living in urban Jamestown with her children Elizabeth II and Jeremiah Clements II. Hamor died, and by February 1628 Elizabeth I had married Captain Tobias Felgate. She made plans to go to England but died before March 30, 1630 (VI&A 210).

Jeremiah (Jeffrey, Jeremy, Jeremie, Joreme, Jereme) Clements II: Jeremiah II, the son of Jeremiah Clements I and his wife, the former Elizabeth Fuller, was born in England and was baptized on November 8, 1607. He came to Virginia with his mother and siblings in 1617 and in February 1624 was living in urban Jamestown with his mother, stepfather Captain Ralph Hamor, and sister, Elizabeth II. On August 26, 1633, Jeremiah Clements II patented 350 acres on Upper Chippokes Creek within what was then James City County but later Surry. When patenting some additional land on Upper Chippokes Creek in June 11, 1635, he used the headright of his wife, Edye, with whom he produced a daughter, Elizabeth. In 1641–1642 Jeremiah Clements II served as a James City County burgess, but by March 17, 1658, he was deceased (VI&A 211; LEO 20).

* * *

Phettiplace (Petiplace, Pettiplace, Phetiplace) Close: Phettiplace Close came to Virginia in 1608 and during the mid-1620s lived on the lower side of the James River at Paces Paines. When a list of patented land was compiled in May 1625, Close was credited with 100 acres in Henrico, on the south side of the James River near the falls. In January 1627 he was authorized to move from Paces Paines to Blunt Point, and in early December 1628 he was given a patent for 100 acres near the mouth of the Warresqueak (Pagan) River in exchange for his acreage in Henrico. The swap was made because of the "danger of planting" the original tract. In January 1629 Close began serving as a burgess for Mulberry Island, and in September 1632 he represented the area from Denbigh Plantation to Water's Creek. He was still alive in 1635 and was in possession of some land in Elizabeth City County (VI&A 212; LEO 8, 11).

Rev. John Clough: The Rev. John Clough, rector of James City Parish, was described by the rebel Nathaniel Bacon as a supporter of Governor William Berkeley. When Bacon seized control of Jamestown, Clough was captured and condemned to death. Although he was detained, he was eventually released (SR 6618, 7366).

Cockacoeske (Native American): Cockacoeske, queen of the Pamunkey Indians, was a descendant of Opechancanough, brother of the paramount chief, Powhatan. She succeeded her husband, Totopotomoy, who led the Pamunkey from ca. 1649 to 1656, when he was killed in the Battle of Bloody Run. The Pamunkeys, like other native subscribers to the Treaty of 1646, were tributaries to the English crown. By the time Cockacoeske began her rule, the ancient Powhatan chiefdom had disintegrated and the Indians of Virginia's coastal plain were no longer subordinate to a paramount native leader.

Early in 1676 Cockacoeske was summoned to Jamestown to appear before a committee of the Council of State. She reportedly entered the room with regal bearing, flanked by her interpreter and her son, Captain John West, a youth who was the offspring of an English colonel. Her head was crowned with a broad braid adorned with black-and-white shells, and she wore a full-length deerskin mantle with cut edges resembling deep, twisted fringe. Cockacoeske, with "a majestick air," took a seat at the council table. She spoke only through her interpreter, though her listeners believed that she understood the English language. Cockacoeske, when asked for warriors to oppose hostile frontier tribes, fell silent. She became agitated when pressed further, then cried out, "Tatapotamoi Chepiack" ("Totopotomoy is dead"), reminding the council that her husband and a hundred of his warriors had perished while helping the English. Resignedly, she agreed to provide a dozen warriors, a fraction of the number then under her command.

Although the Pamunkey Indians signed a peace treaty with the Virginia government in March 1676, Nathaniel Bacon and his followers attacked them, took captives and plunder, and seized their land. In February 1677 Cockacoeske asked the Virginia assembly for her people's release and the restoration of the Pamunkey's property. Although the burgesses were unresponsive, the commissioners King Charles II sent to investigate Bacon's Rebellion concluded that Cockacoeske should be rewarded for her loyalty to the English. At their suggestion, a jeweled cornet, regal attire, and jewelry were ordered for the Pamunkey queen, who was described as "of meane or indifferent stature and somewhat plump of body." She was to receive a cap of crimson velvet trimmed with ermine fur; a gold and silver brocade "Indian gown," lined with cherry-colored sarcenet, a soft silk; a robe fabricated of scarlet cloth, lined with purple

manto; and a necklace and a bracelet of false stones, probably paste jewels. Gifts also were commissioned for her son, Captain John West; her interpreter, Cornelius Dabney; and her chief counselor, Seosteyn.

Cockacoeske was an astute leader and skillful politician. When the Treaty of Middle Plantation was signed on May 29, 1677, she saw that certain Indian tribes were "reunited" under her subjugation. But certain native groups, free of Pamunkey domination since 1646, stubbornly refused to become subservient or pay tribute. This prompted Cockacoeske to have her interpreter compile a list of grievances she sent to governing officials in early June 1678. She then had him dispatch to England a letter in which she professed her loyalty to the Crown and complained about the tribes who disobeyed her orders. The letter, signed "Cockacoeske Queen of Pamunkey," included her signature mark, the same W-like symbol that she had affixed to the Treaty of Middle Plantation. Cockacoeske was unsuccessful in recapturing the chiefly dominance enjoyed by her people's leaders during the first half of the seventeenth century. However, the Pamunkey were under her sway until her death in 1686 (FOR 1:8:14–15; Lederer 16; HEN I:323–329; JHB 1660–1693, 89; AND 125–127; EJC I:79; CO 1/42 ff 177, 270; 5/1371 f 365; LC 5/108 f 8; 9/275 ff 264ro–267ro; SR 5736, 5743). *See Totopotomoy (Cockacoeske's husband) and John West ("Captain John West") (Cockacoeske's son)*

Nicholas Cocke (Cock): On September 20, 1668, Nicholas Cocke, an alien who had lived in Virginia for a long time, went to Jamestown where the General Court's justices declared him naturalized and granted him denization. By 1677 Cocke had become a resident of Middlesex County, where in September 1683 he patented 346 acres of land near that of Robert Beverley I (Northumberland County Record Book 1666–1670:51; Middlesex County Order Book 1673–1680:73; PB 7:318).

* * *

Richard Cocke (Cock, Coxe?) I: On December 24, 1627, Richard Cocke I, purser of the *Thomas and John*, testified before the General Court in Jamestown. Sometime prior to June 5, 1632, he married John Brown's widow, the former Temperance Bailey. He settled the estate of his wife's late husband and became conservator of his orphans' inheritance. Cocke may have been the Richard Coxe who in 1632 represented

Weyanoke in the assembly. In March 1637 Cocke patented 3,000 acres in Henrico County; when he repatented 2,000 acres of that tract in March 1640, reference was made to the plantations called Bremo, Malvern Hill, and Curles. Cocke became a tobacco viewer in 1640 and represented Henrico County in the assembly sessions held in 1644, 1646, and 1654–1655. He also became a militia commander. Around 1652 he married Mary, the daughter of Lieutenant Colonel Walter Aston I of Charles City. Cocke died sometime after October 4, 1665, when he made his will. He was survived by his widow, Mary, and children: Thomas, two sons named Richard, and a daughter, Elizabeth (VI&A 214; DOR 1:120–122; LEO 11, 22, 32; PB 1:413, 707; 3:133; MCGC 158, 186, 201; Henrico County Miscellaneous Court Records I [1650–1807]:27–28).

Thomas Cocke (Cock) I: Thomas Cocke I, the son of Temperance Bailey and her husband, Richard Cocke I, was born around 1639. By 1672 he was making his home at Henrico County's Pickthorn Farm but later moved to Malvern Hill, one of his father's plantations. He commenced patenting land in western Charles City County and in Henrico. Thomas Cocke I began serving as a Henrico County justice in 1678, became sheriff and coroner in 1680, and in 1688 again held office as sheriff. He was a respected citizen who assisted the General Court in arbitrating disputes. As a burgess for Henrico County, he attended the assembly session held in 1677–1678 and in 1677 was given some additional time to seat some frontier land that he had patented. Over the years he continued to acquire acreage and during the 1680s and 1690s patented three large tracts of land on the north side of the James River in Henrico County. While residing at Malvern Hill, Cocke operated its flour mill, tanneries, and looms for weaving. In 1695 he received an award from the assembly because of the fine quality linen that had been produced at Malvern Hill. Thomas Cocke I made his will on December 10, 1691, and by April 1, 1697, was dead. He married twice and left several children, notably Thomas II, Stephen, James, William, Agnes, and Temperance (LEO 43; DOR 1:122–123; Henrico County Wills and Deeds 1677–1692:327; 1688–1697:245, 684–685; MCGC 386–387, 456; PB 6:563; 7:557, 668; 8:1, 138).

James Cocke (Cock): James Cocke, the son of Thomas Cocke I, was born around 1667. In January 1692 he married Elizabeth, the daughter of Quaker John Pleasants.

Through that union he came into possession of the plantation known as Curles, which had belonged to his grandfather, Richard Cocke I. During the 1690s James Cocke patented some land in Charles City and Henrico counties. He served as a burgess for Henrico County and attended the assembly sessions held in 1696–1697 and 1699, in 1699 serving with his brother Thomas Cocke II, who replaced William Randolph. James Cocke went on to become the county's clerk of court, serving from 1692 to 1707. In 1702 he patented a large tract in Henrico County near White Oak Swamp, and in 1704 he paid quitrent on 1,506 acres of land in Henrico County. His will was proved on November 6, 1721 (LEO 56, 59; DOR 1:124–125; Henrico County Wills and Deeds 1688–1697:357, 712; Minute Book 1719–1724:141; PB 8:60; 9:86, 491).

Thomas Cocke (Cock) II: Thomas Cocke II, the son of Thomas Cocke I, was born around 1662. He served as a Henrico County militia captain in 1698 and as county sheriff in 1699. He was elected to the assembly in 1698, and when Henrico burgess William Randolph vacated his seat in 1699, Cocke was elected in his place. He went on to represent Henrico County in the assembly sessions held in 1699 and 1700–1701. He was a wealthy and successful planter who over the years continued to acquire land, often in Henrico and Charles City counties. He also repatented some of the land to which his late father had laid claim. Thomas Cocke II married the former Mary Brasseur of Nansemond County and after her death wed Frances, the widow of John Herbert. Cocke's marriages to women who lived in the Southside, near the mouth of the James River, most likely prompted him to patent tracts of land in Norfolk County during the 1690s. He appears to have lived in the Southside during the early 1690s, for he made several appearances in court, where he reported on a ship that had run aground. He made his will on January 16, 1707, added a codicil a month later, and died sometime prior to April 1, 1707 (LEO 58–60; DOR 1:123–24; Henrico County Wills and Deeds 1706–1709:24; PB 7:556, 584; 8:247, 428; 9:198, 373, 403; EJC I:234, 300, 359, 446).

* * *

William Cockerham (Cockeram) I: William Cockerham I's name began appearing in Surry County's court records in 1652, when the county was first formed, often because he was witnessing documents. In November 1654, when Robert Sheppard's widow, Elizabeth, signed a marriage contract with Thomas Warren of Smith's Fort plantation, Cockerham agreed to serve as a trustee of Sheppard's estate, representing his orphans' legal interest. In 1656 he secured a patent for 1,230 acres on the south side of the James River in Surry County, acreage adjoining that of merchant John Bland. Then, in 1666 he patented 850 acres on the Blackwater River in Surry. By 1660 Cockerham had become a Surry County justice, and he went on to serve as a lieutenant and then as a captain in the militia. He represented the county in the assembly sessions held between 1662 and 1665 but retired after the 1665 session. When William Cockerham I died between 1668 and 1669, he appears to have been a widower. He was survived by sons William II and Thomas (LEO 40; Surry County Deed Book 1 [1652–1672]:10, 50, 54, 102, 165, 192, 313, 332; PB 4:105; 5:640; 6:650).

St. Leger Codd: St. Leger Codd, the eldest son of William Codd of Watringbury Parish, Kent, England, lost his father in late 1652 or early 1653. Afterward, he came to Virginia and commenced acquiring land. Although Codd's patent or patents have been lost or destroyed, in 1678 his landholdings were mentioned in descriptions of neighboring properties. His plantation was in Lancaster County on a branch of the Corotoman River, close to the boundary line separating Northumberland and Lancaster counties. During the late 1660s Codd's name appeared occasionally in Lancaster County's records, usually when legal disputes were being settled. In May 1670 he was sued by his stepchildren, William and Elizabeth Fox, the offspring of his wife, Anne, and her former husband, the late David Fox I. By 1671 St. Leger Codd was serving as a justice of Northumberland County's monthly court. A year later he successfully sued a Northumberland County man who had spread a rumor that Codd had abused his indentured servants and killed one or more of them. In February 1675 when Codd bought a tract of Northumberland County land from Elizabeth Pettigrew, he was ordered to have it surveyed. He was a military officer, and when forts were to be built at the heads of the colony's rivers in July 1676, 11 men were taken from his militia company. By December 1677 he had begun serving as a Northumberland County court justice, an office he held for many years. In 1678 Codd paid taxes on eight tithables that lived at his quarter in Lancaster County and was still in possession of the property in December 1686. In 1679 Colonel Codd and two others were given the responsibility of building

and equipping a garrison that was to be situated on the Potomac River at Niabsco. In 1680 he was elected to assembly seats in both Lancaster and Northumberland counties but he chose to represent the latter. He attended only the June 1680 and April 1682 sessions as Northumberland's representative and then in 1684 began serving on behalf of Lancaster County. By October 1679 St. Leger Codd had married Anna, the widow of Theodorick Bland. In 1682 the couple became involved in a contentious lawsuit with her sister-in-law, Sarah Bland, and Thomas Povey, John Bland's executor. The litigation dragged on for at least four years and resulted in an appeal to the king. In 1685 Codd, who was represented by Christopher Robinson, was sued by John Jeffreys, a British merchant, who called for his arrest because he had failed to obey a court summons. In 1686 Codd asked the Northumberland County court justices to see that his land was surveyed, seemingly because of a dispute with a neighboring property owner. By summer 1687 his financial problems had become so serious that he "in a private clandestine manner conveyed himself, his Wife & family" out of the county, allegedly eluding his creditors and taking as much of his personal estate as he could. Among those to whom Codd owed money were John Jeffreys, William Sherwood (a Jamestown merchant), Nicholas Spencer, and John Strechley, all of whom attached his personal estate (LEO 46–47; PB 6:635; SR 678, 1456, 4564; HEN II:433; Lancaster County Order Book 1666–1680:120, 131, 147, 218, 451, 517; 1680–1687:62, 108, 140, 196, 198, 227, 267; 1686–1696:34–36, 47, 52, 65, 86; Northumberland County Order Book 1666–1678:121, 146, 196, 199, 218, 274, 302, 323; 1678–1698:66, 78, 177, 232, 234; HEN II: 433; Charles City County Order Book 1676–1679:407).

Daniel (Daniell) Cogan (Coogan, Coogin, Coogen, Gookin, Gookins, Cookins, Goegin) (see Daniel Gookin II)

Coght (Native American): In September 1660 the Mattaponi (Mattapony) Indians' king and Great Men or leaders denied that they had tried to claim some Old Rappahannock County land on which Francis Brown had established a plantation. Coght's name was affixed to an affidavit the Indians signed (Old Rappahannock County Deed Book 1656–1664:111).

George Colclough (Collclough): In 1650 George Colclough obtained a land certificate from the Northumberland County court, entitling him to patent 300 acres. In 1652 he was identified as a resident of Wicocomoco (Wicocomocoe) when he purchased a tract known as Hulls Thicket, and a year later he bought some land that abutted the Potomac River. As time went on, Colclough continued to add to his holdings. In 1656 he was identified as a colonel and a county justice when he and Colonel Thomas Speke served as overseers of Colonel John Mottrom's will. Colclough was then married to Mottrom's widow, Ursula, who was entitled to a dower third of the decedent's estate. She also had children from her former marriage to Richard Thompson. In 1657 Colclough was taken to court and was accused of slandering Hugh Lee and other prominent citizens. Perhaps in an attempt at retribution, in 1658 he sent a petition to Governor Samuel Mathews II stating that a document damaging to his reputation was being circulated. Colclough's fellow justices refused to take depositions from those whom he accused of slander, claiming that there was no legal basis requiring them to do so. After Colclough's wife, Ursula, died, he married Elizabeth, the daughter of Captain Thomas Willoughby of Lower Norfolk County and the widow of Simon Overzee, a prominent Dutch merchant. George Colclough served as a burgess for Northumberland County and attended the assembly sessions held in 1659. When he sold some land in January 1661, he identified himself as a resident of Little Wicomico. He died intestate sometime prior to July 21, 1662, when his widow, Elizabeth, received a commission of administration. An inventory of his estate reveals that he owned two working plantations and a well-furnished home; his estate was still being settled in 1663. By February 1664 Colclough's widow, Elizabeth, had married Isaac Allerton, her third husband (LEO 35; Northumberland County Deeds and Orders 1650–1652:42; Wills, Inventories &c. 1652–1658:26, 37–38, 76, 87, 122–124; Record Book 1658–1662:8, 68, 82; 1662–1666:101; Order Book 1652–1665:105, 115, 116, 176, 181, 185–186, 281, 316, 354, 449; 1666–1678:12; Westmoreland County Deeds, Wills &c. 1661–1662:18a; DOR 3:651–652).

Josiah Cole: Josiah Cole and Thomas Thurston, who were Quaker ministers, were incarcerated in Jamestown because they were religious dissenters. On November 27, 1657, they described the capital city's jail as "a dirty dungeon." It probably was a windowless basement in one of Jamestown's brick buildings. The General Court's justices later decided that the two men would

be sent to Maryland (MCGC 506; Tyler, *Cradle*, 61).

* * *

William Cole (Coale) I: William Cole I arrived in Virginia in 1618 and during the mid-1620s lived in Elizabeth City. In early 1625 he headed a household that included 27-year-old Francis Cole. In May 1625, when a list of patented land was sent back to England, William Cole I was credited with 50 acres in Elizabeth City, land that had been planted (seated). On October 16, 1629, he served as a burgess for the settlers in Nutmeg Quarter, a community that by 1634 was in Warwick River (later, Warwick) County. He died sometime prior to September 15, 1664, at which time some land he had patented in Accomack County escheated to the Crown and was assigned to another man (VI&A 215; LEO 8; PB 5:215; DOR 1:713).

William Cole II: In April 1671 William Cole II, the son of William Cole I, purchased the Warwick County plantation known as Boldrop from Governor William Berkeley and his wife, Lady Frances, who had inherited it from her late husband, Samuel Stephens. Cole also acquired a 1,433-acre tract called Newportes News. He married in succession Anne, the daughter of Edward Digges I of York County, and Martha, the daughter of Colonel John Lear of Nansemond County. Cole was named to the Council of State and served from 1675 to 1692. He was appointed Secretary of State on October 22, 1689, but on April 15, 1692, asked to be relieved of his duties due to ill health. Besides serving as secretary, Cole was Collector of the Lower District of the James River and commander of the Warwick County militia. In 1693 he was named a trustee of the College of William and Mary. Colonel William Cole II died on March 4, 1694, at age 56 and was buried at his plantation, Boldrop. At the time of his death he owned Boldrop, the Cary plantation known as Windmill Point, and part of the Gookin tract, Newportes News. Cole married three times and was survived by his wife, Martha (STAN 21, 40; LEO xix; HEN II:119–120; DOR 1:714–715). Boldrop, the Cole plantation, which is located in the city of Newport News, is on the National Register of Historic Places.

* * *

Anthony Coleman: Sir John Harvey, Virginia's governor from 1632 to 1639 and an avid proponent of industrial development, sold the Glasshouse tract to Anthony Coleman, who bequeathed it to William Coleman and Edward Knight. On September 21, 1643, Coleman obtained a lease for a large parcel in the Governor's Land, next to Sir Francis Wyatt's leasehold. In July 1651 Thomas Ludwell came into possession of the Coleman acreage (PB 1:891; 3:26, 367–368; NUG I:145; AMB 78).

William Coleman: William Coleman and Edward Knight inherited Anthony Coleman's Glasshouse tract sometime prior to 1655. When they sold the property to John Senior, Joseph Knight served as William Coleman's attorney (PB 3:367; NUG I:313).

[No First Name] Colfer: Mr. Colfer, one of the overseers of Lady Elizabeth Dale's Virginia property, loaned corn to a man who was killed during the March 1622 Indian attack. On March 7, 1625, the General Court decided that Charles Harmer, Lady Dale's current overseer, would be compensated from the decedent's estate. Lady Dale owned land on Jamestown Island, on the Eastern Shore, at Coxendale, and in Charles City near Shirley Hundred (VI&A 215).

Samuel Collier: In December 1608 Samuel Collier, a youth and one of the first Jamestown colonists, accompanied Captain John Smith on an overland journey to Werowocomoco on the York River. He stayed behind with Powhatan so that he could learn the Indian language. In 1623 Smith said that Collier had been accidentally slain by an English sentinel (VI&A 216).

[No First Name] Collins: According to George Percy, during the winter of 1609–1610, the infamous "Starving Time," a man named Collins, who lived in Jamestown, murdered his wife and salted her flesh, preserving it as food. Percy said that Collins confessed to the crime under torture. He was executed, having been suspended by the thumbs with weights on his feet (VI&A 216).

[No First Name] Collins: Mr. and Mrs. Collins died in Jamestown after April 1623 but before February 16, 1624 (VI&A 216).

William Colston (Coulson, Costnol): In 1683 William Colston served as the attorney of Edward Chilton of Jamestown in a matter that was aired in Old Rappahannock County's monthly court. He also interacted regularly with Henry Gawler, another Jamestown resident. Sometime prior to September 1686 Colston married Ann Hull. In 1688 he received a certificate that entitled him to patent 1,800 acres of land; almost all the head-

rights he used were for Africans. He did business in Lancaster County and in 1687 brought suit against a local resident. In 1684 William Colston began serving as Old Rappahannock County's clerk of court. He retained that position until around 1691–1692, at which time the county became extinct and Essex and Richmond counties were formed. He also served as a burgess for Old Rappahannock County and attended the assembly sessions held in 1691–1692. In 1691 he purchased a lot in the town at Hobbes Hole that became known as Tappahannock. In 1693, while he was clerk of Richmond County's monthly court, Colston attended the assembly on the newly formed county's behalf. He was still clerk in December 1699 when he witnessed John Parker's will and agreed to serve as his executor. He also agreed to serve as custodian of the tobacco John Parker was bequeathing to Thomas Parker I's orphan, Thomas II. Colston's name appeared frequently in local court records, for he witnessed documents and performed other duties for his fellow citizens. In 1694 he patented some land on Totosky Creek in Richmond County. He represented Richmond County in the assembly in 1698 and 1699 and in March 1700 witnessed the will made by Francis Stone, a county resident. One of William Colston's forebears or kinsmen may have been a merchant, for in 1639 a man of that name was co-owner of *Le Prudence*, a ship involved in trade between Virginia and London (LEO 50, 52–53, 58–59; STAN 88, 92; Old Rappahannock County Wills 1682–1687:14, 59–60, 118; Deeds and Wills 1677–1682:365; 1682–1688:161; Deeds 1688–1691:158; Order Book 1683–1686:1, 88, 106, 158; 1687–1692:18, 42, 60–61, 68, 236–237; NN 2:57–58; SR 4117, 6590; Middlesex County Order Book 1680–1694:276, 393, 612; Lancaster County Order Book 1686–1696:58, 77; Essex County Order Book 1692–1695:48; Deeds and Wills 1692–1695:145, 274, 339; 1699–1701:33; Richmond County Deed Book 1 [1692–1693]:1; 2 [169–1695]:56–58, 107; 3 [1697–1704]:124).

Comahum (Native American): In April 1623 Comanum, a native leader or Great Man, and the youth named Chanco (Chauco) went to Martin's Hundred so that they could deliver a message to the settlers living there. Comahum, who was implicated in the killings that occurred at the plantation during the March 1622 attack, was taken into custody and sent to Jamestown in chains. Later, he and Chanco were allowed to return to the Pamunkey Indians' stronghold (VI&A 218).

Austen Combes: On February 16, 1624, Austen Combes was a servant in Sir George

Yeardley's household in urban Jamestown (VI&A 218).

Edward Constable: In 1624 Edward Constable, a 47-year-old scissors-maker of St. Clement Danes, Westminster, testified in litigation involving the ships *Treasurer* and *Neptune*, which were bound for Virginia in 1618–1619. Constable and his wife, Sibell, who was age 36, were passengers on the *Treasurer*, a vessel that the Earl of Warwick had declared he was assigning to his cousin Captain Samuel Argall (VI&A 219).

Robert Constable (Cunstable): On September 12, 1623, Robert Constable, a gentleman and the brother of Philip Constable and a Mrs. Place of Dinsdale, arrived in Jamestown. In early 1624 Robert Constable was living in the Jamestown Island household of John Osbourne. Later in the year he inherited a sow from John Phillimore, also a Jamestown Island resident (VI&A 219).

William Constable (Cunstable): On August 31, 1625, William Constable informed the Ferrars, who were major Virginia Company investors, that he and Arthur Swaine were dispatching a ship, the *Flying Hart* of Flushing, to Virginia. The vessel, which was poorly provisioned, arrived in Virginia in December 1625. On March 13, 1626, the General Court acknowledged that Constable stood to inherit some tobacco, a bequest from Robert Wright of Jamestown Island, a sawyer. He also was supposed to collect a debt from Captain Crowshaw's estate (VI&A 220).

Arthur Cooke: Arthur Cooke came to Virginia on the *Furtherance* and died in Jamestown sometime after April 1623 but before February 16, 1624 (VI&A 220).

Christopher Cooke: Christopher Cooke, one of Sir Francis Wyatt's servants, accompanied him to Virginia in 1621. In January 1625 he was residing in urban Jamestown in the Wyatt household (VI&A 220).

Edward Cooke: In February 1624 Edward Cooke was a servant in Sir Francis Wyatt's household in urban Jamestown (VI&A 220).

John Cooke: On June 20, 1620, John Cooke received a certificate from Governor George Yeardley acknowledging that he had fulfilled his obligation to the Virginia Company. On January 3, 1625, Cooke sued Peter Langman of urban Jamestown, a debtor. On the other hand, he was sued and jailed by Lewis Baily in 1628. By June 22, 1635, Cooke was dead and his widow, Jane, had

married Alexander Stoner, a brick-maker who owned land on Jamestown Island and in the Neck O'Land. Later on, when the Stoners patented some land, they used Jane's headright and that of her late husband, John Cooke (VI&A 221).

John Cooke: During the mid-1620s John Cooke lived on Jamestown Island and was a servant in John Burrows' household (VI&A 221).

Mordecai (Mordecay) Cooke: Mordecai Cooke began patenting land on Mobjack Bay in 1650. He gradually added to his holdings on the Middle Peninsula's Ware and North rivers, in what became Gloucester and Mathews counties. In August 1674 he witnessed the will made by Henry Gray of Gloucester and in December 1677, when Joseph Hayes made his will, Cooke agreed to serve as trustee and assist in the settlement of the testator's estate. Mordecai Cooke served as a burgess for Gloucester County and attended the assembly sessions held in 1695–1696, 1696–1697, 1699, 1700–1702, and 1710–1712. He also served as a Gloucester County justice from 1702–1714 (LEO 54, 56, 59–60, 67; PB 2:255; 3:375; 7:63; 9:542; SR 3555, 3717; MASON 121).

Richard Cooke: In February 1633 the justices of the General Court decided that Richard Cooke was entitled to compensation from Captain John Preene's estate for rental of warehouse space, cooperage, and court appearances he had made on Preene's behalf, and for bringing a boat up to Jamestown. It is unclear where Cooke's warehouse was located (VI&A 221).

Roger Cooke: According to Captain John Smith, Roger Cooke, a gentleman, was one of the first Jamestown colonists and arrived in 1607 (VI&A 221).

Thomas Cooke: In 1635 and 1637 Thomas Cooke of "James Cittie" served as clerk of the assembly. By the early 1640s he had moved to the Eastern Shore, where he occasionally testified in court. After the death of George Dawe, Northampton County's clerk of court, sometime prior to January 1641, Cooke commenced filling the decedent's position and served until spring 1642. He seems to have been associated with Secretary Richard Kemp, who in 1638 listed him as a headright when purchasing some patented land from George Menefie. Thomas Cooke died intestate sometime prior to January 3, 1645, and was living on the Eastern Shore at the time of his death (LEO 15; HEN

I:223; Northampton County Orders, Wills, Deeds &c. II:76; NUG I:104; AMES 2:24, 61, 77–78, 81, 110, 116, 130, 147, 151, 235, 455).

William Cooke: In February 1624 William Cooke was living in Elizabeth City. Later in the year he and Mr. Thomas Hethersoll borrowed a boat from Jamestown Island carpenter Richard Tree so that they could transport their goods to Blunt Point. However, the two men reportedly lost Tree's boat when they carelessly abandoned it and went ashore at Martin's Hundred (VI&A 222).

Richard Cookeson: On July 22, 1640, Richard Cookeson was identified as a runaway servant who belonged to William Peirce, the owner of land in urban Jamestown (MCGC 467).

William Cookeson (Cookson): On January 24, 1677, William Cookeson, one of the rebel Nathaniel Bacon's most ardent supporters, was tried at a martial court held at Green Spring plantation. He admitted his guilt and was sentenced to be hanged. Governor William Berkeley later indicated that he had been captured twice. When Governor Berkeley issued a proclamation on February 10, 1677, he noted that Cookeson had been executed and that his estate was subject to seizure (MCGC 455, 528; NEVILLE 61, 275).

William Cooksey: In early 1624 William Cooksey, his wife, and his infant were living in the Jamestown Island household of John Haul (Hall). On January 24, 1625, when a muster was made, William was still there but his wife and child were not, perhaps because they were deceased (VI&A 222).

[No First Name] Cooper: A man identified only as Cooper, who had been with Captain John Smith in Virginia, signed his narrative, *True Travels*, in 1629 (VI&A 222). He may have been Thomas Cooper (Couper, Cowper), one of the first Jamestown colonists (VI&A 223).

George Cooper: In May 1675 George Cooper was appointed sub-sheriff of Northumberland County. Three years later, when John Jeffreys and Company, a British mercantile firm, sued Cooper for unpaid debt, Cooper contended that he had already paid what he owed. By 1680 Captain Cooper had acquired some land in Stafford County, but he relinquished his property in 1688, the same year he acquired 176 acres in Northumberland County and was identified as a surveyor. He was still conducting surveys in the Northern Neck in 1691. In 1680 Colonel St. Leger Codd was ordered to give George Cooper some muskets to be used by the men in the Potomac River garrison. In March 1690 he initiated a suit in Old Rappahannock County's monthly court. He also did business in Lancaster County during the mid- to late 1670s, and his name appeared occasionally in claims against decedents' estates. In 1688 he filed a petition in which he insisted that when he had been paid for performing a public service, the tobacco he received in payment was rotten and worthless. Captain Cooper served as a burgess for Northumberland County and attended the assembly sessions held in 1691–1692 and 1699. He also served as a county justice. Like most of his contemporaries, he appeared in court from time to time, defending himself from creditors or trying to recover debts. In 1684 he took some of the county militia's arms into his custody and had them repaired. By October 1699 he had achieved the rank of lieutenant colonel, and he owned some land in Richmond County near Totosky Creek. When he made his will on November 18, 1708, he identified himself as a resident of Great Wicocomoco and left the plantation on which he lived to St. Stephen's Parish for a glebe (LEO 50, 59; Old Rappahannock County Order Book 1687–1692:154; Lancaster County Wills 1674–1689:16, 131; Order Book 1680–1687:21; 1687–1696:72; Essex County Order Book 1692–1695:43; Richmond County Deed Book 3 [1697–1704]:75; Northumberland County Order Book 1666–1678:230; 1678–1698:73, 153, 206, 213, 246, 271; 1699–1700:1, 39, 76–77; NN A:69, 105; 1:124; Westmoreland County Order Book 1676–1689:688; FLEET I:515).

Joseph Copeland: When National Park Service archaeologists conducted excavations during the 1930s on a waterfront lot that had belonged to Mrs. Ann Talbott in 1655 and to George Marable I in the 1660s and 1670s, they found part of a pewter spoon bearing the maker's mark of Isle of Wight County craftsman Joseph Copeland and the date 1675. It is unclear whether the Copeland spoon was manufactured by Joseph Copeland I, the son-in-law of Isle of Wight County burgess Thomas Taborer of Basses Choice, or by Joseph Copeland II, who prepared his will in February 1726 and died sometime prior to July, leaving his wife, Mary, and at least two children. On November 21, 1690, when William Edwards II patented a waterfront lot in urban Jamestown, reference was made to the "great gum" tree on Joseph Copeland's lot (PB 8:42; NUG II:342; MCGH 194, 197; Isle of Wight Deeds and Wills II:350; BOD 214–215).

Copsco (Native American): When John Spencer of Westmoreland County sold 200 acres to Joseph Taylor in May 1708, he indicated that it was in Cople Parish, near the home of King Copsco, a native leader (Westmoreland County Deeds, Patents &c. 1665–1677:128).

Henry Corbin (Corben, Corbyn): Henry Corbin, who was born in England, was elected a burgess for Lancaster County and served in the assembly's 1659–1660 session. In December 1660 he and his wife, Alice, sold their 300 acres on Morratico Creek to Raleigh Travers. Corbin was one of the men who in 1661 mediated a dispute between the king of the Potomac Indians and Major General Hammond. In September 1662, while Corbin was a justice of Lancaster County's monthly court, he submitted Sir William Berkeley's claim for compensation from local taxes. In 1663 Corbin was appointed to the Council of State. He continued to participate in Lancaster County's court proceedings and his name appeared regularly during the 1660s. He also made occasional appearances before the justices of Westmoreland County. In 1664 he represented London merchant John Jeffreys in a suit being aired before the justices of Northumberland County. In 1671 Corbin sued Letitia, the widow of John Barber II of urban Jamestown, in an attempt to recover funds from the decedent's estate. Corbin, who had custody of the late Captain John Whitty's funds, was obliged to pay one of the decedent's creditors, William Drummond I of Jamestown. By that time Whitty's widow, Susan, had wed William Corker of Jamestown. Henry Corbin Esq. died in Virginia on January 8, 1676, and by June 1677 his widow had married Henry Creete. Corbin's name appeared in Lancaster County records in 1674, when Colonel William Travers served as his attorney, and in 1677, when Corbin's executors made a claim against Robert Beckingham's estate. Some of Corbin's land was located in what later became Richmond County (MCGC 218, 262, 270, 274, 281; STAN 38; LEO 35–36; Old Rappahannock County Deeds and Wills 1656–1664:123; Lancaster County Wills 1674–1689:39; Order Book 1656–1666:175, 190; 1666–1680:2, 97, 100, 103, 106, 187, 277, 288; Northumberland County Order Book 1652–665:402; Westmoreland County Deeds, Wills &c. 1661–1662:49a; Deeds, Patents &c. 1665–1677:24a; Order Book 1676–1689:76).

* * *

John Corker: John Corker represented Pasbehay in the assembly in 1632, and the following year he attended on behalf of Jamestown Island, Pasbehay, and the settlements along the Chickahominy River. In 1633 he was ordered to maintain an account of the tobacco collected to pay for the construction of a fort at Old Point Comfort. In 1645 Corker served as burgess for James City, the same year he became clerk of the assembly, a post he held until the close of 1653. In February 1637 or 1638 he patented six acres near Goose Hill, in the eastern end of Jamestown Island. Then, on August 3, 1640, he claimed a tiny lot in urban Jamestown, property he was obliged to develop within six months or forfeit; it is not known whether he made the improvements needed to secure his title. In April 1652, when Corker became the General Court's clerk, he began identifying himself as a resident of Surry County. The following year he represented Surry in the assembly and became clerk of the county's monthly court. His name appeared in Surry's legal records in September 1654 when James Jolley, who was visiting Corker's house, made slanderous remarks about how William Edwards I defrauded Lieutenant Colonel Walter Chiles I. In 1656 John Corker was designated a Surry County justice of the peace. He increased his landholdings in Surry County and in 1657 patented 1,150 acres near Gray's Creek. His business dealings in Surry reveal that he interacted regularly with Jamestown lot owners Richard Webster and Thomas Woodhouse. In 1670 Corker and William Thompson I (Thomson), who rented Colonel Thomas Swann's ordinary in Jamestown, proved Thomas Warren's will. Corker's wife was named Dorothy (PB 1:521, 730–731; NUG I:81,124, 374; LEO 23–31; STAN 57–58; Chandler 1924:161; HEN I:202, 222, 289, 370, 377; MCGC 213; Surry County Deeds, Wills 1652–1672:6, 13, 31, 53, 76, 98; LEO 11–12, 23–31). John Corker's political career and business dealings suggest that he was associated with the Jamestown area during the 1630s and 1640s but by the early 1650s had moved to Surry.

William Corker: William Corker, the son of Jamestown lot owner John Corker, had business dealings with several people who had property in the capital city. In April 1653, when he was indebted to Walter Chiles I, his attorney was William Edwards I, the father of William Edwards II, a Jamestown lot owner. In 1654 Corker sold to William Barber (or Barker) his interest in some Surry County land that he owned jointly with Thomas Rabley, a Jamestown lot owner. He then purchased 150 acres from Thomas Rolfe, which he retained for 20 years and then sold to William Barber. By the mid-1650s Corker had patented 1,850 acres of land in Surry. He also owned property in James City County and served as one of its delegates in the 1658 session of the assembly. In 1664 Corker was a James City justice, but by 1668 he had become a resident of Southwark Parish in Surry. Sometime prior to April 1670 he married Captain John Whitty's widow, Susan, the daughter of Arthur Blackmore of St. Gregory in London. In 1675 John White, the son of Captain John White of Surry County, sued William Corker, as did Captain Robert Spencer. When Corker died in 1676 he was indebted to Richard Holder and Nicholas Meriwether, both of urban Jamestown, who may have had a claim on his James City County property. He bequeathed his real and personal estate on the lower side of the James River to his wife and his daughters, Lucy and Susanna. In 1676 John White, who described himself as Lucy Corker's brother but actually was her half-brother, left her a gold ring and half of his estate. The decedent was the son and heir of Captain John White of Surry and the stepson of William Corker (Surry County Deeds, Wills &c. 1 [1652–1672]:28, 54–55, 263, 315; 2 [1671–1684]:51, 140, 152, 203; NUG II:95; MCGC 215–218, 257, 407, 413; Charles City County Order Book 1:33; CBE 7; HEN I:439;LEO 34; JHB1660–1693:69).

* * *

Richard Cornish alias Williams: In November 1624 Richard Cornish alias Williams, captain of the *Ambrose*, was summoned before the General Court, where he was accused of sexually assaulting William Cowse, a cabin boy. Cowse's allegations were verified by one of his shipmates. Sometime prior to February 8, 1625, Cornish was hanged in Jamestown (VI&A 226).

Charles Lord Cornwallis: In late May 1781 Charles Lord Cornwallis and his army of seasoned veterans arrived in Petersburg, where they joined forces with Phillips' men, temporarily under the command of General Benedict Arnold. This union of forces created a British Army of 7,000 men. Cornwallis and his men then crossed the James River in pursuit of the Marquis de Lafayette. While the British occupied Williamsburg, they visited Jamestown Island and destroyed some of the Allies' horse-boats. On June 30, 1781, Cornwallis notified his superiors that he was moving to Jamestown so that his men

could cross to the lower side of the James River. By July 4, 1781, the main body of the British Army was encamped on the Ambler farm on the mainland, and they had taken possession of Jamestown Island. Cornwallis's men on the mainland were positioned to provide coverage to "a ford into the island of James-town," a probable reference to the low-lying isthmus. Meanwhile, Lafayette, who had heard that the bulk of the British Army already had crossed the James, resolved to draw closer to Jamestown so that his men could attack any remaining enemy troops. He dispatched General Anthony Wayne and a detachment of men to Jamestown but held the greater part of his force in abeyance. When Lafayette arrived at Green Spring plantation and moved to a vantage point on the river bank, he realized that he had been privy to false intelligence, for the British had not departed from Jamestown Island. He ordered two battalions of Virginia troops to cover General Wayne's troops' retreat. Wayne's men, however, continued on toward Jamestown and, too late, realized that they had entered a trap. Although the Americans withdrew, their losses were heavy. On the night of July 7th, the British departed from Jamestown Island. Cornwallis's army was conclusively defeated at Yorktown in October 1781 (MAX 186, 202).

* * *

Arent (Around) Corstenstam (Corsten Stam, Corstin Stam, Corssin Stamm, Curson Stame, Van Corensten, Costence?): On October 11, 1638, Derek and Arent Corstenstam patented a half-acre waterfront lot in urban Jamestown. The brothers' patent stated that they had to develop their parcel within 12 months or face forfeiture. On October 23, 1639, they received a patent for 860 acres of land in Elizabeth City County, which abutted south upon the James River and lay between Newport News Point and Salters Creek. In January 1640 Arent Corstenstam appeared before Accomac County's justices, where he sought headright certificates for several people: himself, his wife, his brother Derrick, and two others. On May 26, 1641, Arent Corstenstam, who was then living in Accomack County, used his real and personal estate in Virginia as collateral when securing a debt to Captain William Douglas and Company. In December he identified himself as an Accomack County merchant when he leased to Samuel Lucas a plantation he had obtained from Nathaniel Littleton. In March 1642 Corstenstam was obliged to defend himself against a suit undertaken by Stephen Charlton. According to Adriaen Van der Donck's July 2, 1649, narrative, Arent Corstenstam (Van Corensten) was a Dutch merchant who in 1646 transported mineral samples from New Netherland to Holland aboard Captain George Lamberton's ship (PB I:603, 629; NUG I: 104–105, 340, 455; AMES 2:58, 98–99, 142–145, 145, 148–151; JAM 229).

Derrick (Derricke, Dirck) Corstenstam (Corsten Stam, Corstin Stam, Corssin Stamm, Curson Stame, Van Corensten, Costence?): On October 11, 1638, Derek and Arent Corstenstam patented a half-acre waterfront lot in urban Jamestown, acreage they were obliged to improve within 12 months. On October 23, 1639, the Corstenstam brothers received a patent for 860 acres of land in Elizabeth City County, below Newport News Point. Then, in January 1640 Arent Corstenstam, when obtaining headright certificates, listed the name of his brother, Derrick, and indicated that he had covered the cost of his transportation. Derrick Corstenstam appeared before Accomack County's justices on May 10, 1642, and admitted that he had not satisfied his debt to Nathaniel Littleton. He returned to court in May 1643 and acknowledged a debt to Northampton County mariner Thomas Hunt. This time, Corstenstam identified himself as a merchant of Amsterdam, Holland. In September 1664 a Derrick Costence (perhaps Derrick Corstenstam) was listed among the headrights of John Dolby, who patented land in Accomack County (PB I:603, 629; NUG I: 104–105, 340, 455; AMES 2:58, 265, 295–296; JAM 229).

* * *

John Countwayne (Countrivane, Countway): John Countwayne died in Jamestown between April 1623 and February 16, 1624 (VI&A 227).

William Courtney: In October 1790 William Courtney of Stafford County filed a pension claim for a war wound he received in Jamestown (HEN XIII:210).

Thomas Cowles: In 1698 Thomas Cowles represented James City County in the assembly. On December 9, 1700, when he was a James City County justice and sheriff, he held elections for Jamestown's seat in the assembly and reported that there was a tie vote between two candidates. In 1702 Cowles again was chosen sheriff. Three years later he resigned his position because

of the abuse he allegedly received from fellow justice James Bray II, who was known for his violent temper (SAIN 18:728, 737; 20:268; LEO 58; EJC II:261–262, 435).

Christopher Cowling: Christopher Cowling, who was born in England, was named to the Council of State and was in Virginia in 1630, while Sir John Harvey was governor (STAN 32; NEILL 78 ftnt). Whatever records that may have been associated with Cowling seem to have been lost or destroyed.

William Cowse (Couse): In November 1624 William Cowse, a cabin boy, appeared before the General Court in Jamestown, where he alleged that he had been sexually assaulted by Captain Richard Cornish alias Williams, master of the *Ambrose*. Cornish was found guilty and executed. On February 8, 1625, when Cowse was ordered to decide whether he preferred to serve Captain Ralph Hamor or Captain John West, he chose Hamor, with whom he had been staying on Hog Island (VI&A 228).

Richard Coxe (Cocke?): On September 4, 1632, when the assembly convened, Richard Coxe served as a burgess for the settlers living in Weyanoke (VI&A 228; LEO 11).

David Crafford (Crawford): David Crafford became a resident of York County sometime prior to November 1, 1665, when he was appointed constable. On August 7, 1667, he purchased 86 acres of land in James City County, part of Thomas Loving's acreage in Martin's Hundred Parish. Then, in 1669 he acquired 135 acres from Richard Whitaker. Crafford seems to have moved to James City County shortly thereafter, for on February 26, 1672, when he bought 75 acres of York County land on the east side of Felgates Creek, he was identified as a planter "of Merchants [Martin's] Hundred." Crafford, a successful planter, continued to buy and sell land. In October 1672 he patented 1,000 acres in New Kent County, bordering Matadequin Creek, and four years later he acquired another large tract in that vicinity. Finally, in 1685 he obtained 1,300 acres on Whiting Swamp and some additional acreage in the upper part of New Kent. One of the tracts he owned eventually became the site of Newcastle Town, a small urban community. During the 1670s and 1680s David Crafford made repeated appearances in York County's monthly court, where he initiated lawsuits or served as an executor or court-appointed administrator. In 1679 he disposed of his James City County property.

Court testimony suggests strongly that by the 1680s David Crafford had personal residences in York and New Kent counties and commuted between the two. In 1691–1692 he served as a burgess for New Kent County and was a member of St. Peter's Parish in New Kent. In 1681 he executed a deed of gift, bestowing upon his daughter Sarah and her heirs approximately 500 acres of land on the lower side of the Pamunkey River, adjoining the mouth of Herring Gut. By that time Crafford had become a very wealthy planter. One of his daughters, Elizabeth, married into the Meriwether family and another wed a clergyman, the Rev. James Bricken (Britain, Brechen). Some acreage that Crafford owned on Mechumps Creek, in what became Hanover County, became the seat of the county court. Crafford made his final court appearance in York County on January 24, 1698 (York County Deeds, Orders, Wills 6:495; 8:183, 192; LEO 50; PB 10:341; NUG II:25, 112, 171, 231, 253, 293–294; III:195; York County Deeds, Orders, Wills 4:37, 52; 5:6, 101; 6:112, 131, 139–146, 274, 283, 302, 347, 467–468, 477, 491, 500; 8:155–156, 183; MCGC 213; WINFREE 265–267).

William Crafford (Crawford) I: In 1688 William Crafford I served as a burgess for Lower Norfolk County. He was returned to the assembly in 1695–1696, this time representing the newly named Norfolk County. When Crafford testified before the General Court in May 1691, he said that he was age 54 and was a Lower Norfolk County justice. On September 26, 1699, William Crafford of Norfolk County made his will, which was proved on March 16, 1700. Although the document is fragmentary, it contains some information about his family. The testator made a bequest to his wife, Margaret, and to his grandchildren, Abigail and William Crafford III. He designated his wife as executrix in Virginia, but asked James Cocke of Plymouth to serve as executor of his overseas interests. He wanted his trusted friends Thomas Hodges, Samuel Bouch, and a Mr. Scott to serve as overseers of his Virginia estate. A suit against William Crafford I that was pending in April 1700—a bond that had been posted to guarantee the lading of the ship *Adventure*—was dismissed because he was dead. William Crafford I's son, Captain William Crafford II, represented Norfolk County beginning in 1712 and in 1704 paid quitrent on 2,650 acres of land in Princess Anne County, which descended from Norfolk County (LEO 49, 54; Norfolk County Will Book 6:181; EJC I:179; II:52, 55; SMITH 23).

William Crafford (Crawford): In 1696–

1697 William Crafford served as a burgess for New Kent County (LEO 56). He may have been related to David Crafford, a wealthy landowner who established a home in New Kent during the 1670s and became a burgess, or perhaps to William Crafford I of Lower Norfolk County.

William Crapplace (Crakeplace): William Crapplace came to Virginia in 1622 with five servants. When he presented a petition to Governor Francis Wyatt in 1623, he was identified as groom of the king's chamber and keeper of his house at Roiston. Crapplace asked for his goods, which were being detained by the master of the ship that had brought him to the colony. In December 1623 Sir George Yeardley asked to be released from a bond he had posted to cover a debt to William Crapplace. Crapplace died in Jamestown sometime prior to February 16, 1624 (VI&A 230).

Randall Crew: Randall Crew, who came to Virginia in 1621, was living at Shirley Hundred during the mid-1620s and was a servant in the widowed Katherine Bennett's household. By January 1627 Crew had obtained his freedom and married Elizabeth, Captain Robert Smalley's widow. He testified on behalf when she accused Deputy Governor Samuel Argall of seizing her late husband's oxen. Elizabeth died prior to July 1638, by which time Crew had married Dorothy Beheathland. He served as a burgess for Upper Norfolk County in 1640, 1643, and 1644. He seems to have left in the wake of the April 18, 1644, Indian attack and moved to Warwick River County, which he represented in the assembly from 1645 to 1648. Crew died in 1649 (VI&A 232; LEO 18, 21–22, 24–26).

James Crewes (Crews): James Crewes, who became one of the rebel Nathaniel Bacon's most loyal supporters, was elected a burgess for Henrico County in 1676. On January 24, 1677, he was tried at a martial court held at Green Spring plantation. Crewes admitted his guilt and was sentenced to be hanged two days later. Governor William Berkeley described him as a colonel and Bacon's "trumpet," who went about the countryside promoting the insurrection. On February 10, 1677, Governor Berkeley issued a proclamation, noting that Crewes already had been executed and that his estate was not exempt from seizure (LEO 41; MCGC 455, 528; NEVILLE 61, 275). Crewes may have been the same individual who in 1652 provided testimony about Francis Giles' death at Jordan's Point (SR 10005).

Zachary (Zacharia) Crispe (Cripps): Zachary Crispe came to Virginia in 1621 and during the mid-1620s resided on the lower side of the James River, on the Treasurer's Plantation, where he appears to have been a tenant. He appeared twice before the General Court in 1629, by which time he had received a patent for 100 acres at the mouth of the Warwick River. On October 16, 1629, Crispe served as a burgess for the settlements along the Warwick River, and in February 1633 he represented Stanley Hundred. In September 1632 he was named a commissioner of the Warwick River area's monthly court, and in 1640 he served as a burgess for Warwick County. He was still serving as a justice of the Warwick River County court in 1647 and may have been alive in 1650 (VI&A 233; LEO 8, 12, 18; DUNN 182).

[No First Name] Crosby (Crosbie): When Edward Travis I patented 196 acres in the eastern end of Jamestown Island on March 10, 1652—land he gradually developed into a manor plantation—he noted that his acreage abutted "west upon David Ellis his land and Mr. Crosbys Land." Although Crosby's identity is uncertain, only two men bearing that surname have been found in mid-seventeenth-century Virginia records. One is Thomas Crosby of Curles Neck in Henrico County, who on January 16, 1637, joined Jamestown merchant Arthur Bayly in patenting 800 acres in Henrico County. The other is Daniel Crosby, who in September 1654 patented 150 acres of land in Northumberland County (PB 1:512; 3:158; 4:288; 5:342; NUG I:78, 121, 270–271, 503).

* * *

Raleigh (Raugley, Rawleigh) Croshaw (Crawshawe, Croshair, Crowshawe): Raleigh Croshaw, a gentleman and Virginia Company investor, came to Virginia in 1608 in the 2nd Supply of new colonists. He was a supporter of Captain John Smith and was involved in Indian trade. Sometime prior to 1624 he received a patent for 500 acres of land in Elizabeth City at Fox Hill, near Old Point Comfort. In 1624 he was elected a burgess for Elizabeth City but died sometime prior to December 1624. In May 1625, when a list of patented land was sent back to England, Croshaw was credited with his 500 acres at Fox Hill. His son, Joseph, who was born around 1612, produced several children, including Unity, who married John West II (VI&A 230; LEO 5; DOR1:773).

Joseph Croshaw (Crawshawe, Croshair, Crowshawe): Joseph, the son of ancient planter Raleigh Croshaw, was born around 1612 and became an avowed Royalist. In 1656, while he was a York County justice and sheriff, he was elected to the assembly, representing York County. Samuel Mathews II, who was governor at the time, suspended him from his office as a county justice because of his vocal opposition to the succession of Lord Protector Richard Cromwell, Oliver Cromwell's son. Croshaw was returned to the assembly in 1659 and 1660 and again became a county justice. On December 20, 1662, he was authorized by his fellow York County justices to hire workmen to build a brick house in urban Jamestown, one of the structures that each of Virginia's counties were required to erect as part of the 1662 building initiative. Major Joseph Croshaw produced several children, one of whom was Unity, who married John West II and eventually inherited the Croshaw home tract, Poplar Neck, in York County. Unity's marriage to West was marred by his liaison with Cockacoeske, the queen of the Pamunkey Indians (York County Deeds, Orders, Wills &c. [1657–1662] 3:38a, 183; PB 2:201, 352; LEO 33, 35–36; DOR 1:769–770).

* * *

Thomas Cross (Crosse): In 1620 Thomas Cross came to Virginia on the *Abigail* and in 1624 was living on the Governor's Land, where he was an indentured servant in Thomas Swinhow's household. In October 1624 Cross informed the justices of the General Court about John and Alice Proctor's cruel treatment of their servants. In 1625 Cross was living on Dr. John Pott's leasehold on the Governor's Land (VI&A 235).

Richard Crouch: Richard Crouch, a carpenter, arrived in Jamestown on September 12, 1623. In February 1624 he was living on the mainland just west of Jamestown Island (VI&A 235).

Thomas Crouch (Crouth): In 1624 Thomas Crouch, an indentured servant, was living in urban Jamestown in Edward Blaney's household. Simultaneously, he was attributed to the Blaney plantation on the lower side of the James River. This suggests that Blaney was shifting him from one location to the other, as the need arose. In 1625 Crouch was residing on the Blaney property on the lower side of the James (VI&A 235).

Hugh Crowder (Cruder): Hugh Crowder came to Virginia in 1619 and during the mid-1620s lived on the lower side of the James River, within the corporation of James City and east of Gray's Creek. In 1625 he served as a burgess for that area. Crowder was eager to relocate, for the land he was leasing from Captain John Huddleston reportedly was barren. He declined the acreage he was offered at Martin's Hundred and at the College, and in November 1626 he was given permission to relocate to Captain Francis West's land on the west side of Lower Chippokes Creek. Crowder died intestate sometime prior to April 21, 1628 (VI&A 235, 405; LEO 6).

* * *

Thomas Crump (Crompe, Crumpe, Crampe, Crumfort): Thomas Crump was living on the Eastern Shore in early 1624, but by January 1625 he had moved to Jamestown Island and begun taking an active role in public life. He also married the late Rev. Richard Buck's daughter Elizabeth, who seems to have come to Virginia a year or two after her father's death. The Crumps resided on Jamestown Island and until around 1632 probably occupied the Buck property in the eastern end of Jamestown Island, acreage in which Elizabeth had a legal interest. Together Thomas and Elizabeth produced a son, John. Thomas Crump represented Jamestown in the assembly's February 1632 session, but in September he commenced serving as the Neck O'Land's delegate. By 1633 he had patented some acreage there, abutting the Buck estate. Thomas Crump died sometime prior to 1652 and was survived by his widow, Elizabeth, and their son, John, who was the Rev. Richard Buck's surviving male heir. In 1655 John Bromfield, whose late wife, Bridget, had been one of the Buck orphans' guardians, sued Elizabeth Buck Crump in an attempt to recover what he believed was Bridget's legal interest in the Buck landholdings in Archer's Hope. Upon being widowed, Elizabeth Buck Crump married Mathew Page I sometime prior to December 2, 1657, having conveyed to him the Neck O'Land acreage that she owned outright (VI&A 236–237; LEO 10–12).

John Crump (Crompe, Crumpe, Crampe, Crumfort): On December 4, 1654, John Crump, Thomas and Elizabeth Buck Crump's son, sold his late maternal grandfather's 12-acre parcel in the eastern end of Jamestown Island to Edward Travis I. By that date all of the Rev. Richard Buck's sons (Benomi, Gercian, and Peleg) were dead

and John Crump, as his grandson and the only surviving male heir, would have been legally able to dispose of the property. When John Crump died in 1655, he bequeathed his property to his wife and daughter, both of whom were named Elizabeth (NUG I:299; II:76, 252; PB 3:306; 6:298; 7:228–229; DOR 1:427–428, 785).

* * *

Thomas Crust: Thomas Crust came to Virginia in 1620 and on January 24, 1625, was an indentured servant living in household of John Southern in urban Jamestown (VI&A 237).

* * *

Alexander Culpeper (Culpepper): In 1671, while Governor William Berkeley held office, King Charles II appointed Alexander Culpeper as Virginia's surveyor general. He served successive terms, holding office until 1692. Culpeper, who was Lady Frances Berkeley's cousin, was a staunch supporter of Sir William Berkeley and in 1677 began serving as the administrator of the deceased governor's estate in Virginia. Culpeper's brother, Thomas Lord Culpeper, became governor. The Culpeper brothers and Lord Fairfax retained the Northern Neck Proprietary, even though Virginia officials asked the king to nullify their patent (MCGC 515; STAN 26; SR 235, 375, 377, 662, 663, 664, 1458, 3442, 3456, 5578, 7473, 7478, 12501, 13607, 13620).

Frances Culpeper (Culpepper): Frances Culpeper, the cousin of Alexander and Thomas Culpeper, married Samuel Stephens. Through a premarital agreement, she was entitled to Boldrup, the plantation they occupied in Warwick County. At Stephens' death, she married Governor William Berkeley. Upon being widowed, she wed Philip Ludwell I (HEN II:321–323). *See Frances Culpeper Stephens Berkeley.*

Thomas Lord Culpeper (Culpepper): King Charles II selected Thomas Lord Culpeper as Governor William Berkeley's successor. Although he was named governor in 1678, he did not come to Virginia until 1680. He sued acting governor Herbert Jeffreys' estate in an attempt to recover part of the compensation to which he felt he was entitled. Culpeper favored urban development in Virginia and had been ordered to see that Jamestown, the capital city, was rebuilt as soon as possible. Governor Culpeper ignored the seriousness of the colony's economic problems and went to England, leaving Sir Henry Chicheley in charge as deputy governor. Although Chicheley had orders not to convene the assembly, during the winter of 1681–1682 economic conditions deteriorated and planters began circulating petitions urging the passage of legislation that limited tobacco production. By April 1682 Chicheley had been persuaded to summon the legislature. But just as the burgesses began converging on Jamestown, he received word from Culpeper that he was not to convene the assembly until November. The burgesses, upon learning that their session had been postponed, became angry. Within a week gangs of planters, frustrated with the government's inaction, began going from plantation to plantation in Gloucester, New Kent, and other places, destroying tobacco plants. Chicheley ordered local militia commanders to prevent further trouble, but plant cutting began anew in August and plants were often uprooted at night. By the time the destruction ceased, much of the year's crop lay in ruins.

While Governor Culpeper was in office, he generated two documents that provide a wealth of information on Jamestown. In March 1683 he described the damage that resulted from a fire ignited by an electrical storm. He said that the corps de gard (or guard house) was destroyed within two hours and two other buildings that contained powder and firearms were also burned. Culpeper said that soldiers quickly extinguished the blaze. Sometime prior to September 20, 1683, Thomas Lord Culpeper, who was living at Green Spring, reviewed his instructions, making note of how he had implemented them. He indicated that the Privy Council had ordered the members of his council to build houses in Jamestown and that colonels Nathaniel Bacon and Joseph Bridger had done so, as had William Sherwood. He added, however, that only the prospect of reaping a profit would encourage more people to rebuild. On September 20, 1683, when Culpeper drafted a formal report for submission to his superiors, he stated that he had lifted the suspension of the town act. Culpeper returned to England twice during his governorship and died there in 1719 (Surry County Deeds, Wills, &c. 1671–1684:23; MCGC 493, 520, 522; SAIN 10:341; 11:153, 497; CO 5/1355 ff 258, 326; 5/1356 #68; Beverley 1947:95; Culpeper March 18, 1683; STAN 17).

* * *

Cupid: On February 15, 1768, when an inventory was made of the late Richard Ambler's slaves on Jamestown Island and his leasehold in the Governor's Land, an adult male slave named Cupid was listed. He probably was the youth called Cupid that Ambler mentioned in his 1765 will and left to his son, John (York County Wills and Inventories 21:378–382, 386–391).

John Currer: On March 28, 1672, William Drummond I, who had a dwelling in the western end of Jamestown Island near the church, and a plantation in the Governor's Land, made a claim against the estate of John Currer (MCGC 303).

John Curtis (Curtys): In August 1656 John Curtis, a surveyor and resident of Lancaster County, took the required oath. Throughout the 1660s he performed surveys for county residents and began speculating in real estate, sometimes generating income by leasing his land to tenants. By 1656 Curtis had commenced serving as a justice in Lancaster County's monthly court, an office he held for many years. He made numerous court appearances as the late Abraham Moone's administrator, and in 1657 he became a Lancaster Parish vestryman. In May 1659 Curtis was elected to the assembly and represented Lancaster County in both sessions that were held in 1660. In September 1660 he and his wife, Anne, disposed of a piece of land, and the following year he sold a large parcel in Westmoreland County. In 1669 John Curtis obtained from the Lancaster County court a license that allowed him to keep a tavern. When applying, he noted that he lived on a major road. Curtis died intestate sometime prior to September 13, 1671, at which time Richard Robinson began serving as administrator of his estate (LEO 36; Lancaster County Deeds &c. 1652–1657:253, 284; 1654–1661:141, 147; 1661–1702:382–383, 390; 1656–1661:81, 129; Order Book 1656–1666:1; 1666–1680:1, 104, 200, 206; Northumberland County Order Book 1652–1665:315; Westmoreland County Deeds and Wills No. 1 [1653–1671]:199–200).

* * *

John Custis (Custise) II: John Custis II, who was born in the Netherlands around 1628 and came to Virginia with his uncle, John Custis I, in 1648, was the son of Henry and Joan Custis, who had a victualing house in Rotterdam. John II's sister, Anne, married Argoll (Argall) Yeardley in 1649 and moved to Northampton County, on Virginia's Eastern Shore. By July 1651 John Custis II had wed burgess Robert Eyre's widow, Elizabeth, a resident of Lower Norfolk County. In

February 1652 he appeared before the justices of Northampton County and secured a land certificate that entitled him to patent 600 acres. When John Custis II and his brother, William, were naturalized on March 13, 1652, they indicated that they had been residing in Virginia for four years. John Custis II secured his first patent in July 1653, securing 100 acres of land in Northampton County. In October of that year, when suing Cuthbert Potter in Lancaster County's court, he identified himself as a Northampton County merchant. In 1657 John Custis II, his uncle, John Custis I, and his cousin, Joseph Custis, signed a legal document in Lancaster County, absolving Luke Billington from all debts.

In November 1663 John Custis II assisted the General Court's justices by translating a Dutch document, and in 1677 he was named to the Council of State. In February 1669 Colonel John Custis II patented some additional land in Northampton County. He was identified as a surveyor in 1674 and was called upon to audit two people's accounts. As time went on, Custis continued to acquire land, sometimes in massive quantities. He also built an elaborate brick manor house on his Eastern Shore plantation, Arlington. During 1676, while the colony was in the throes of Bacon's Rebellion, Governor William Berkeley and some of his loyalists withdrew to Arlington, where they stayed for five months. While Berkeley was in seclusion there, Major Robert Beverley I seized Bacon supporter Sands Knowles and his servants and delivered them to the Custis plantation. Giles Bland and Captain William Carver set out in two ships, intending to confront Berkeley and his supporters, but shortly after they arrived at Arlington, their plans went awry and they were captured and executed.

On September 29, 1683, Colonel John Custis II sold to Henry Hartwell a half-acre waterfront lot in urban Jamestown. When Hartwell secured a patent for a larger parcel on the waterfront on April 20, 1689, it included the acreage that he had bought from Custis in 1683. On April 17, 1684, two days after Governor Francis Howard took office, Custis was ordered not to leave Jamestown, but surviving assembly records fail to explain why he was detained. Later, he was mistakenly reported dead and replaced as a councilor. Custis responded to the situation in an April 30, 1685, letter he dispatched to the king, professing his loyalty to the Crown. He identified himself as a former council member, major general, surveyor, and collector of the king's customs, all of which positions had been assigned to others. He also pointed out that during Bacon's Rebellion he had entertained Governor Berkeley and 50 men at his home for a period of five months and that he had placed a ship and two sloops in the king's service. He added that he had been very ill but had recovered. John Custis II patented more land on the Eastern Shore. He also continued to be involved in mercantile activities and sued those who were in his debt. Among those who owed him money was Robert Beverley I. John Custis II died on January 29, 1696, and was interred at his Northampton County plantation, Arlington. His will, made on March 18, 1691, was proved on February 10, 1696. He made generous bequests to his wife, the former Tabitha Scarborough, John Smart's widow, and he left the bulk of his real estate to his son, John III, but gave land to other family members. The testator named his grandson, John Custis IV, as reversionary heir to Arlington and other pieces of property. The widowed Tabitha Scarborough Smart Custis married Edward Hill of Charles City County in 1699 (STAN 41; FOR III:10:49; NUG I: 251; II: 69, 207, 230, 242–243, 268, 364; PB 3:57; HEN I:499; II:552; MCGC 385, 518, 531, 584; PB 7:701; AMB 40; JHB 1660–1693:191; CO 1/57 f 265–266; SR 678, 1456; Northampton County Orders, Deeds, Wills &c. 4 [1651–1654]:65, 106, 188; 6 [1655–1656]:17; Lancaster County Deeds and Wills 1652–1657:88; Old Rappahannock County Deeds and Wills 1656–1664:19; Middlesex County Order Book 1680–1694:353, 357, 362; Lower Norfolk County Book B:184; C:4, 9, 23, 29; MARSHALL 151–152).

John Custis III: John Custis III, the son of John Custis II of Arlington, served as a Northampton County burgess in 1677. He was returned to office in 1684 but was disqualified on account of his position as county sheriff, the official who conducted local elections. When a new writ was issued, he was reelected and returned to the assembly. Custis served as a burgess in the assembly sessions that were held in 1685–1686, 1693, 1695–1696, 1696–1697, 1698, and 1699. He was named to the Council of State and served from 1699 to 1713. He was captain of the Accomack County militia and deputy commander of the Eastern Shore until 1692, when he was temporarily suspended from office. He was commander-in-chief of the Eastern Shore in 1699. John Custis III made his will on December 3, 1708, and died in Virginia on January 26, 1714. He bequeathed to his wife, Sarah, the use of his dwelling and plantation at Hungars and numerous slaves, and an abundance of material goods. He also made generous bequests to his sons, John IV, Henry, and Hancock, and to his daughters, Elizabeth (the wife of Thomas Custis) and Sorrowful Margaret (the wife of William Kendall). The testator seems to have had some afterthoughts, for he added three codicils to his will, making the last one on March 20, 1712 (STAN 41, 43; LEO 42, 47–48, 52–54, 56, 58–59; DOR 3:337–338; MARSHALL 204–205).

John Custis IV: John Custis IV, the son of John Custis III and grandson of John Custis II, married Daniel Parke II's daughter, Frances I. According to William Byrd II of Westover, who was married to Frances I's sister, Lucy, the Custis couple's marriage was extremely unhappy. However, they produced a daughter, Frances II, and a son, Daniel Parke Custis. When Daniel Parke II died, he left his daughter, Frances I, his property in Virginia and England, along with his outstanding debts. It was probably through Parke's dower agreement with Custis or his bequest to daughter Frances I that Parke's York County land near Williamsburg came into Custis's hands. Major John Custis IV represented the College of William and Mary in the 1718 session of the assembly, and in 1720 he acquired some escheat land in Middle Plantation near the Page holdings. By 1727 he had become a resident of Williamsburg. An avid horticulturist, he was proud of the quality of the tobacco he was able to produce on his York River plantation. In 1738, when he became interested in purchasing some land that belonged to Mrs. Mary Whaley, Custis developed a contentious relationship with Whaley's attorney, Edward Jaquelin of Jamestown. John Custis IV prepared his will on November 14, 1749, and by April 9, 1750, was dead. His principal heir was his son, 40-year-old Daniel Parke Custis, who inherited John Custis II's remaining lots in Jamestown. John Custis IV's will contained some controversial provisions. He freed Jack (John), a son he had with his slave woman, Alice, and instructed his executor (Daniel Parke Custis, John's half-brother) to build Jack a handsome house designed by John Blair, on a site near the head of Queens Creek. Jack also was to receive an annuity, some livestock, furniture, and clothing, along with the right to use some marshland adjoining Queen Mary's Port (Capitol Landing). After Jack's death, the land was to pass to Daniel Parke Custis (BYRD xi, 82, 249; NUG III:225; STAN 101; SR 4655; York County Wills and Inventories 20 [1745–1759]:431; Judgments and Orders 2 [1752–1754]:76; SR 4655).

Daniel Parke Custis: Daniel Parke Custis was born on October 15, 1710, and was christened on October 28th. He was the son of John Custis IV and his wife, Frances I, Daniel Parke II's daughter. When Daniel matured, he married Martha Dandridge and produced a son, John Parke Custis. Upon being widowed, Martha wed George Washington (BYRD xi, 82, 249).

John Parke Custis: John Parke Custis, the orphaned son of Daniel Parke Custis and his wife, Martha Dandridge, became the stepson of George Washington. On May 11, 1778, he sought Washington's advice on whether he should dispose of the lots he had inherited in urban Jamestown. Washington agreed, but urged him to trade them for other pieces of real estate, for he felt that the value of currency was unstable. When John Parke Custis died at Eltham in 1781, he was age 26. He left behind a widow and four children, whom he entrusted to Washington's care (BYRD 249; WASHINGTON 13:56–58; CUSTIS, May 12, 1778).

William Custis II: William Custis II and his brother, John Custis II, who were born in Holland of English Protestant parents, were naturalized in March 1652, when they indicated that they had been residing in Virginia for four years. William Custis II patented 200 acres in Accomack County around the time he was naturalized. Then, in 1669 he patented 300 acres on Mesangoe Creek. During the 1680s he acquired 1,350 acres in Accomack County, near Nussawaddox; 800 acres on Freaks Island; and 36 acres known as Sandy Hills and Cooney Island. Some of the land he acquired formerly had belonged to Colonel Edmund Scarborough II, whose estate he inventoried in 1671. In October 1674 Custis, who had served as guarantor, was ordered to see that Captain Daniel Jenifer appeared in court. Six months later Custis was ordered to pay a large bond because Jenifer had failed to appear. He also was obliged to inventory John Culpeper's estate. William Custis II served as a burgess for Accomack County in 1677. When Colonel William Custis II made his will on November 27, 1725, he designated his wife and daughter, both of whom were named Bridget, as joint executrixes and left them the bulk of his estate. He named his granddaughter, Joanna Custis Hope, the child of the testator's deceased daughter, Joanna Mary Hope, as a reversionary heir and left her some slaves. Custis died sometime prior to November 1, 1726, when his will was proved (LEO 42; MCGC 256, 388, 405–406; Northampton County

Orders, Deeds, Wills &c. 4 [1651–1654]:188; Accomack County Wills and Deeds 1676–1690:423; Wills, Deeds &c. 1715–1729:107; PB 4:224; 6:265; 7:173, 500, 592).

*** *

Robert Cutler: Robert Cutler, a gentleman, arrived in Jamestown in 1608 in the 1st Supply of new settlers (VI&A 239).

D

Cornelius Dabney (Dabony, Dabamy, Debony): In early 1676 Cockacoeske, queen of the Pamunkey Indians, was summoned to appear before a committee of the Council of State. When she arrived in Jamestown, she was accompanied by her interpreter, Cornelius Dabney, and her son, a youth called Captain John West. During the meeting Cockacoeske insisted on speaking only through Dabney, but Virginia officials believed that she could understand English. Although the Pamunkey Indians had signed a peace treaty with the Virginia government in March 1676, they were attacked by Nathaniel Bacon and his followers. Therefore, the special commissioners King Charles II sent to investigate Bacon's Rebellion concluded that Cockacoeske and her entourage should be rewarded for their loyalty in the face of adversity. At their recommendation a gray suit and scarlet stockings were ordered for interpreter Cornelius Dabney, and he was present on May 29, 1677, when the Treaty of Middle Plantation was signed. Thanks to that peace agreement, certain Indian tribes were involuntarily "reunited" under the queen of the Pamunkey Indian's subjugation. Because some of them refused to comply or to pay tribute to Cockacoeske, she had Dabney, as her interpreter, compile and send a list of grievances to governing officials in early June 1678. She also had him prepare a letter to Colonel Francis Morrison (Moryson), one of the king's special commissioners, in which she professed her loyalty to the Crown. Dabney accompanied it with a letter of his own, which supported Cockacoeske's allegations against the uncooperative tribes. He also told Morrison that he was unable to send him the elk he had requested. In 1668 Cornelius Dabney patented 300 acres of land on the upper side of Totopotomoy Creek, in what is now Hanover County (FOR 1:8:14–15; AND 125–127; EJC I:79; CO 1/42 ff 177, 270; 5/1371 f 365; LC 5/108 f 8; 9/275 ff 264ro–267ro; SR 5736, 5743; NUG II:31, 77, 237, 282).

Francis Dade I: Around 1652 Francis Dade I married Beheathland Bernard, the daugh-

ter of burgess Thomas Bernard and his wife, Mary, Robert Beheathland's daughter. In 1658 Major Francis Dade served as a burgess for Warwick County and was named speaker of the assembly. For reasons that are open to conjecture, he assumed the name "John Smith" and moved to Westmoreland County, giving his power of attorney to Major Edward Griffith of Mulberry Island in Warwick County. He went to England but died in 1663 while returning to Virginia. He made a nuncupative will in which he identified himself by his real name. Francis Dade I was survived by his widow, Beheathland, who was his reversionary heir, and a son, Francis Dade II, who inherited his late father's land in Westmoreland and Stafford counties. The widowed Beheathland Bernard Dade went on to marry Major Andrew Gilson, a Lancaster and Stafford County justice and sheriff of Old Rappahannock County (LEO 34; NN 1:188–189; 2:30; Westmoreland County Deeds. Wills &c. 1661–1662:27–27a; Deeds and Wills 1:201–202m 215–217; DOR 1:218–220).

Edward Dale: In December 1655 Edward Dale, a merchant, was made the sheriff of Lancaster County. Shortly thereafter, he became the clerk of court and served until at least March 1671. In May 1670 he took an oath as high sheriff and served as a county justice until at least 1682. One Sunday, when he was attending a service in the St. Mary White Chapel parish church, Richard Price, a boisterous local citizen, entered the pew reserved for the county's justices and shoved Dale aside. Later, a warrant was issued for Price's arrest, so that he could be brought before the General Court in Jamestown. In November 1671, when forts were to be built as a defense against the Dutch, Major Edward Dale was designated as Lancaster County's commissioner. He served as a burgess for Lancaster in 1676 and 1677, and from 1680 to 1682. In January 1677 he and Colonel William Ball were instructed to appear before the assembly. While John Strechley, Lancaster's new clerk of court, was in England in 1683, Dale was asked to teach the interim (or deputy) clerk how to maintain the county's records properly. In 1691 Major Dale sued his brother-in-law, John Pinkard II, in an attempt to recover his wife's share of her late father's estate. When Edward Dale made his will on August 24, 1694, he indicated that he was a resident of Lancaster County and lived on the Rappahannock River. He bequeathed his real and personal estate to his wife, describing her as an honest and gentle woman to whom he had been married for many years. After her death the plantation on which they lived was to go to two of their grandchildren, Peter and Joseph Carter. He also made bequests to his grandson John Carter and granddaughters, Elizabeth and Katherine Carter. The testator also mentioned his daughter Elizabeth (the wife of William Rogers), daughter Katherine (the wife of Thomas Carter), and grandson Edward Carter. Edward Dale died sometime prior to March 10, 1695, when his will was presented to the county court (LEO 38, 42–43, 45; Lancaster County Deeds &c. 1652–1657:231, 240; 1654–1661:228; 1661–1702:390; Order Book 1656–1666:172, 386; 1666–1680:4, 106, 142, 151, 180, 206, 209, 265, 421, 476; 1680–1686:32, 84, 104; 1686–1696:159, 188, 213, 262; Wills 1690–1709:42, 56, 95; SR 660, 3793a).

Sir Thomas Dale: Sir Thomas Dale, who served in the Netherlands with Sir Thomas Gates and had extensive military experience, married Elizabeth Throgmorten in February 1611 and came to Virginia a month later. He enhanced the code of military justice that Gates had instituted and implemented the Virginia Company's plan to establish settlements toward the head of the James River. Dale resided at Bermuda Hundred much of the time he was in Virginia, although he had a farmstead in the eastern end of Jamestown Island at Goose Hill. Under Dale's leadership, a stable, munitions house, sturgeon house, forge, barn, and wharf were erected in Jamestown. He also saw that the church and storehouses were repaired. When Gates left Virginia in 1614, Dale became marshal or deputy governor, a title he held until May 1616 when he returned to England. By instituting martial law, enforceable by harsh penalties, Dale compelled the Virginia colonists to work toward their own support and produce their own food supply. Dale died on August 9, 1619, in the East Indies, leaving his widow, Lady Elizabeth, as sole heir to his Virginia property. She had a legal interest in several tracts of land in Henrico, Charles City, and on the Eastern Shore and also had a 12-acre

parcel in the eastern end of Jamestown Island at Goose Hill. Over the years she employed overseers to manage her acreage. When Lady Elizabeth Dale made her will in 1640, she bequeathed almost all of her Virginia land to her Throgmorten and Hanby kin. The exception was her land at Goose Hill, which she instructed her executors to sell. Although Sir Thomas Dale's administrative policies were harsh and strongly criticized, he usually is credited with saving the Virginia colony from extinction (VI&A 239–241; STAN 28).

John Danes: According to court testimony taken on November 30, 1624, John Danes sometimes transported timber for Thomas Barwick of Jamestown Island, who oversaw the Company of Shipwrights' men in Virginia (VI&A 243).

Richard Daniel (Danyell): In 1622 Richard Daniel was identified as owner of the *Furtherance*. He was in Jamestown on August 4, 1623, and served on a jury (VI&A 243).

Daphne: On May 31, 1793, two of Champion Travis's slaves, Daphne and Nelly, allegedly attacked and killed their overseer, Joel Gathright. The women had been plowing the fields of Travis's Jamestown Island plantation when Gathright began berating them for allowing sheep to get into a cornfield. When Nelly hotly denied the accusation, the overseer began flailing her with a small cane. She was able to flee from his blows, despite her pregnancy, but when she stumbled and fell, he struck her repeatedly. When Nelly regained her footing, she began to fight back, at which point Daphne entered the fray. The two women then knocked Gathright to the ground and began beating him with sticks and branches. Two young slaves heard Gathright's cries and ran for help, but by the time someone came to his aid, he was almost dead. According to the James City County coroner, the left side of Gathright's skull had been crushed with a large stone.

When an inquisition was held in Jamestown, the slave women, who were tried by James City County's court justices without legal representation, were allowed to question those testifying against them. Ultimately, they were found guilty of murder and sentenced to hang. Daphne was led to the gallows on July 19, 1793, but Nelly's execution was delayed. Although the circumstances surrounding the case are open to conjecture, the slaves' plight seems to have aroused some public sympathy. In September 1793 a group of neighborhood men asked Governor Henry Lee to commute Nelly's sentence. But another group of citizens filed a counter-petition, recommending that clemency be denied. William Lee of Green Spring, who favored execution, contended that "the alarming commotions in this neighborhood and the dangerous example of such a murder" might inspire other slaves to rise up against their owners. Governor Lee apparently agreed with his cousin, William, for he postponed Nelly's hanging only long enough for her baby to be born. Her death sentence was carried out on October 4th. As was customary in a capital crime, the slaves' owner was compensated for their value as personal property (PALM VI:461–465, 521, 532–533, 543).

William Davenant: Sir William Davenant, England's poet laureate, had close ties to the monarchy and fled to France after King Charles I's beheading in January 1649. In 1650 he received a commission from the exiled King Charles II, designating him governor of Maryland, and he was named to Virginia's Council of State. However, while he was en route to the colonies, his ship was captured by a Parliamentary fleet and he was imprisoned. Davenant seemingly never came to Virginia and died in England on December 7, 1668 (LEO xix; STAN 36; http://www.theatredatabase.com; Stanard, "Virginia in 1650," 136–140).

Joseph Davenport: On April 7, 1694, Joseph Davenport was deputy clerk of the James City County court (AMB 48).

David: In 1769 David, an adult male slave, was living on Jamestown Island and was included in the late Edward Ambler I's estate (AMB-E).

Edward Davis: Sometime prior to March 28, 1689, Edward Davis, Lionel Delawafer, and Andrew Hinson, who were accused of piracy, were incarcerated in Jamestown and their goods were seized. Although the three men were released, thanks to pressure from British merchant Micajah Perry and others, their money and some of their goods were kept. They were also forced to pay room and board for the time they were jailed. The accused pirates may have been detained in Sheriff Henry Gawler's home, part of a brick row house that was located on urban Jamestown's waterfront and was next door to a unit owned by Micajah Perry's firm (CO 5/1305 ff 13–14; 1357 f 228; PRO T 11/12 f 395).

Hugh Davis: On September 7, 1630, the General Court's justices decided to have Hugh Davis whipped for having sexual relations with a black woman (VI&A 245).

Hugh Davis: On August 18, 1697, William Sherwood bequeathed money to Hugh Davis so that he could purchase a mourning ring (AMB 65; MCGH 873).

* * *

James Davis: Captain James Davis, who in 1607 was captain of St. George's Fort in Sagadahoc, Maine, returned to England. In 1609 he set sail for Virginia in Sir Thomas Gates' fleet, which brought the 3rd Supply of Jamestown colonists. Shortly after Davis arrived in Virginia, George Percy, then president of the colony, sent him to the mouth of the James River to take command of Algernon Fort. Sir Thomas Dale later placed Davis in charge of Coxendale, near Henrico. Davis died between April 1623 and February 16, 1624, at one of the communities on the lower side of the James River, east of Gray's Creek. Rachell Davis, like her husband, James, was an ancient planter. She died sometime prior to March 6, 1633. James and Rachell Davis's land allotment as ancient planters descended to their son, Thomas (VI&A 245; DOR 1:804–805).

Thomas Davis (Davies): Thomas, the son of ancient planters Captain James Davis and his wife, Rachell, was born in 1613. In 1633–1634 he patented 300 acres in Warresqueak, using his parents' land rights and the headrights he received for transporting people to the colony. As time went on, Davis disposed of his acreage in Warresqueak and moved to Nansemond County, formerly known as Upper Norfolk County. However, he continued to invest in land in Isle of Wight County and may have patented some acreage in the Northern Neck. In 1639, when Davis made a sworn statement before the Admiralty Court, he identified himself as a 26-year-old merchant from Chuckatuck in Virginia. He went on to become a justice of the Nansemond County court, but at his own request he was relieved of his position in October 1660 (VI&A 246; PB 1:128, 424, 502, 613; 2:21, 70–71, 198, 354; 3:67, 256; DOR 1:805–806; EAE 85; JHB 1660–1693:9).

Robert Davis: In 1607 Captain Robert Davis was sergeant major of St. George's Fort, an English outpost established in what is now Maine. He returned to England in 1608 when the fort was abandoned but in 1609 set out for Virginia in Sir Thomas Gates' fleet, which brought the 3rd Supply. Robert was the brother of Captain James Davis, who also was at St. George's Fort and came to Virginia in 1609 (VI&A 248).

***

James Davis: On April 24, 1745, James Davis witnessed the deed that was made when Edward Jaquelin's heirs conveyed to Richard Ambler a two-acre parcel in urban Jamestown. It was part of the land on which Ambler built a manor house for his second oldest son, John Ambler I (Smith et al. 1745).

Jane Davis: Jane Davis came to Virginia in 1622 and in January 1625 was a servant in Sir Francis Wyatt's household in urban Jamestown (VI&A 246).

Joan (Jone) Davis (Davies): In February 1624 Joan Davis was a maidservant in the urban Jamestown household headed by the late Christopher Davison's widow. By February 1625 Joan was residing on Hog Island and appears to have been free (VI&A 246).

John Davis (Davies, Davys): John Davis, one of Ralph Hamor's servants, came to Virginia sometime prior to February 1624 and resided on Hog Island. When John, a minor, received a bequest from the estate of his brother, Walter, in January 1625, Ralph Hamor served as his legal guardian. On January 10, 1627, John Davis, who had come of age, tried to recover the value of some barrels of corn that had belonged to his late brother and had been taken to Jamestown after the March 1622 Indian attack. He also tried to collect a debt that was accruable to the decedent's estate. John Davis was arrested for indebtedness in January 1628, but the General Court decided that he was to be compensated for clearing some land at Martin's Hundred that had belonged to his brother and another man. In July 1635, when Benjamin Harrison purchased 100 acres of land in Warresqueak from John Davis of Chiskiack, it was noted that John, as his brother's heir, had received the acreage by means of a 1633 court order (VI&A 247).

John Davis: On July 25, 1776, John Davis of Surry County was given a military trial in Jamestown, where he was accused of passing counterfeit money. He was found innocent and released (Dixon, *Virginia Gazette*, August 3, 1776).

John Davis: Captain John Davis, an American military officer, kept a diary in which he described what he called the Battle of Jamestown, the conflict that occurred on July 6, 1781, and became more commonly known as the Battle of Green Spring. Davis

indicated that the British had been on Jamestown Island the day the battle occurred but left. On September 2nd he noted that they had returned. A week later Davis helped transport the Allied Army's baggage across the James River (Bruce, "Diary of Captain John Davis of the Pennsylvania Line," 2–10).

Richard Davis: On March 22, 1670, the justices of the General Court acknowledged that Richard Davis's servant was named Richard Mopeson (SAIN 9:382).

Robert Davis (Davies, Davys): Robert Davis, one of John Rolfe's servants, witnessed his March 10, 1622 will, which was made in urban Jamestown. On July 17, 1622, Mr. Harwood, a member of the Virginia Company, asked for Davis's release and said that he had outfitted himself to come to Virginia, had served Rolfe for three years, and was eager to have his own land. In February 1624 Robert Davis was living in the Governor's Land, where he was a member of Richard Atkins' household. Around January 1637 Robert Davis, who was then age 36 and a resident of Warresqueak, said that he had lived in Virginia more than 20 years (VI&A 248).

Thomas Davis (Davies): When the assembly convened in its first session in July–August 1619, Thomas Davis, who represented Martin's Brandon, admitted that Captain John Martin's men took some of the Indians' corn by force. The plantation's delegates were challenged and ultimately unseated because Martin refused to relinquish a clause in his patent that exempted the Martin's Brandon colonists from having to obey the colony's laws (VI&A 248; LEO 3).

Thomas Davis (Davies, Davys): In September 1645 Thomas Davis secured a patent for 475 acres on Waters Creek in Warwick County, and he was living there in August 1650 when he served as an attorney. Davis enhanced the size of his holdings on Waters Creek by patenting another 300 acres in January 1655. In 1656 and 1658 he served as a burgess for Warwick County and was the county's sheriff in 1663–1664. He died sometime prior to November 2, 1671. Davis may have been a son of the Thomas Davis who came to Virginia in 1623, lived in Elizabeth City during the mid-1620s, and was identified as a captain and 40-year-old household head in 1625 (VI&A 248; LEO 33–34; DUNN 165; PB 1:37; 2:34; 4:24; MCGC 283, 508).

Thomas Davis (Davies): In March 1659 Thomas Davis was sued by Elizabeth Perry of Surry. He identified himself as the son of the late John Davis in May 1673 when he appealed a York County court decision in favor of Robert Weeks (HEN I:516; MCGC 341).

Thomas Davis (Davies): On May 11, 1699, Thomas Davis, a ferryman, was authorized to receive payment for transporting Indians across the James River from Surry County to Jamestown (SAIN 17:209).

William Davis: Sometime prior to March 27, 1643, William Davis married Bridget, the widow of ancient planter and tradesman John Burrows (Burrough, Burras, Burrowes, Bourrows), who died in 1628. Bridget, who had custody of one or more of the late Rev. Richard Buck's orphans, went to court in 1642 in an attempt to assert a legal interest in the Buck estate. William Davis was then leasing 50 acres in Middle Plantation, land that belonged to Secretary Richard Kemp and abutted the palisade that spanned the James-York peninsula. Davis represented James City (probably James City County) in the assembly in March 1643 and 1647–1648. He died sometime prior to 1652, by which date Bridget had married her third husband, John Bromfield (SENIOR 1642; PB 4:81; DOR 1: 426–429; HEN I:239; STAN 63, 66; VI&A 177; LEO 21, 26).

William Davis: On May 25, 1658, William Davis, who was age 23, was identified as one of Thomas Swann's servants. On April 2, 1674, he obtained a judgment against the estate of merchant and urban Jamestown property owner Jonathan Newell (Surry County Deeds, Wills &c. 1652–1672:117; MCGC 363).

William Davis: During the summer of 1772 Captain William Davis lived in Thomas Harris's home in urban Jamestown. He died and according to an advertisement that appeared in the July 2, 1772, edition of the *Virginia Gazette*, his slave woman, household and kitchen furniture, boat, sloop, and livestock were to be sold at auction in Jamestown on July 15th. Davis's administrator was William Perkinson (Purdie-Dixon, *Virginia Gazette*, July 2, 1772). Davis may have been subletting Edward Champion Travis's home in urban Jamestown, for Travis had moved to York County by 1770.

Christopher Davison: Christopher Davison arrived in Virginia in 1621 and became established in urban Jamestown. He was a member of the Council of State and served as its clerk and as Secretary of State, holding office until 1623. In January 1622 he informed Virginia Company officials that 13 of the 20 servants he had been allocated as part of the secretary's stipend were dead. He asked for replacements, some cattle, and reimbursement for transporting his wife, Alice, to the colony. Davison probably compiled the list of those killed during the March 1622 Indian attack and the information summarized in the February 1624 census. In April 1623 he told Company officials that cape merchant Edward Blaney had brought his own brother to the colony instead of Davison's young daughter. He also said that his tenants had produced so little tobacco that he was unable to pay his debt to the Company magazine (or store of goods). Davison witnessed John Atkins' September 1623 will and testified about Captain John Martin's tendency to be boastful. He died sometime prior to February 16, 1624; his widow, Alice, continued to live in urban Jamestown (VI&A 249; STAN 21, 31; LEO xix).

Margery Dawse (Dawes): On February 16, 1624, Margery Dawse, who probably was a servant, was living in urban Jamestown in Captain William Holmes' household (VI&A 250).

Owen Dawson: Owen Dawson, a joiner from St. Martins in the Fields, arrived in Jamestown on September 5, 1623. On May 30, 1634, his land in Elizabeth City was described as being adjacent to Thomas Watts's leasehold (VI&A 251).

Edward Day: In 1674 two of Governor William Berkeley's indentured servants, Edward Day (a carpenter) and Thomas Edwards, fled in a boat which they stole from Colonel William White of urban Jamestown. When they were captured and brought before the General Court, the length of both men's contracts was extended and they were ordered to serve Colonel White, to repay him for the boat they had lost. They also were sentenced to a whipping, but by Berkeley's request Day was spared, probably because of his value as a skilled worker (MCGC 382).

John de Frizes: On February 5, 1628, John de Frizes was one of Edward Sharples's servants and lived in Jamestown (MCGC 160; VI&A 252).

Peter (Petter) de Main: Peter de Main died in Jamestown sometime after April 1623 but before February 16, 1624 (VI&A 255).

Mrs. [First Name Unknown] Deacon: Court testimony on October 3, 1672, reveals that Mrs. Sarah Bowe (Thomas Bowe's wife) called Mrs. Deacon a whore (MCGC313).

Dean: In 1769 Dean, an adult male slave, was living on Jamestown Island and was included in the late Edward Ambler I's estate (AMB-E).

Ralph Deane: On May 28, 1673, Ralph Deane, a Surry County bricklayer, was ordered to determine the value of the work that John Bird, another Surry bricklayer, had done for Richard James I of Jamestown Island. In October 1673 Philip Lightfoot had Deane arrested on account of the poor quality of the work he had done on Lightfoot's chimneys (MCGC 344, 349, 369).

Richard Death: During the early 1630s Richard Death owned some land near Pagan Point in Isle of Wight County. Sometime prior to February 1637 he patented some additional acreage in Isle of Wight and sold it to Charles Barcroft. Richard's name and those of Susan and Elizabeth Death were among the headrights that Ambrose Bennett used when acquiring some land in 1641. In 1643 and 1644 Richard Death served as a burgess for Isle of Wight County. When he prepared his will in 1647, he made bequests to his son, William, whom he identified as a London resident and merchant tailor; to his daughter, Elizabeth, the wife of John Dodman of Mulberry Island, and their children, Richard and John Dodman Jr.; and to Christopher, the son of Daniel Neale of Isle of Wight County. Death's will was recorded in the county court on March 3, 1647 (Isle of Wight Wills and Administrations A:17; LEO 21–22; PB 1:517, 746; 2:107).

Debedeavon (Native American) (see Tapatiaton)

Emanuel Dees: On June 6, 1708, Emanuel Dees was leasing the Glasshouse tract on the mainland (AMB 78).

Thomas Delamajor (Delemajor, Dillimager): In February 1624 Thomas Delamajor, a joiner and one of Sir George Yeardley's servants, was living at Flowerdew Hundred. By June 1624 he had moved to Jamestown and was still a member of the Yeardley household. It was then that he and another man reportedly were seen near the "country house" (a public building) on the night someone broke into cape merchant Abraham Peirsey's store. When a muster was made of Jamestown Island's inhabitants in early 1625, Delamajor was residing in the island's eastern end. During 1626 he made several appearances before the General Court, and in February 1628 he was ordered to pay James Parker for a deceased servant.

In March 1629 Delamajor was granted a 10-year lease for three acres at Goose Hill, in the eastern end of Jamestown Island (VI&A 252).

Lionel Delawafer: Sometime prior to March 28, 1689, Lionel Delawafer, Edward Davis, and Andrew Hinson were accused of piracy. Their goods and money were seized and they were incarcerated in Jamestown. Thanks to pressure from British merchant Micajah Perry and others, the men were released. However, a fourth of Delawafer's goods and £500 were kept, and he was forced to pay for his room and board while jailed. The accused men may have been detained in sheriff Henry Gawler's home, a unit in a brick row house on Jamestown's waterfront (CO 5/1305 ff 13–14; 1357 f 228; PRO T 11/12 f 395).

Thomas Lord Delaware (see Thomas West)

Clement Delke (Dilke): In June 1623 Clement Delke and his associates, who received a patent from the Virginia Company, planned to take 100 people to Virginia. He served as one of Flowerdew Hundred's burgesses in the assembly sessions of 1624 and 1625, and when demographic records were compiled, he and his wife were residing in the capital city. On December 13, 1624, Dr. John Pott quoted Delke as saying that he would soon be his neighbor, for he had arranged to purchase John Lightfoot's house and land in urban Jamestown. When council secretary Edward Sharples was dismissed from office in April 1625, he was ordered to serve Delke for seven years. In February 1627 Delke commenced leasing some land on the Eastern Shore that formerly had been owned by the Virginia Company. Several months later he patented 100 acres in Accomack, using the headrights of his wife, Elizabeth, and himself. The Delkes died sometime prior to June 1629, at which time administration of Elizabeth Delke's estate was granted to her sister, Catherine Kenythorpe (VI&A 254; CO 1/3 f 40; LEO 5–6).

Roger Delke (Dilke) I: Roger Delke I came to Virginia sometime prior to January 1625 when he was living at Hog Island and was one of Jamestown merchant John Chew's servants. By September 1626 Delke had moved to Jamestown Island and was lodging at Mrs. Soothey's house. When the late Henry and Elizabeth Soothey's daughter, Ann, received a headright certificate in 1643 for the people they had transported to the colony, one of those listed was Roger Delke.

In May 1627 he was fined for leaving his plantation for several days without his commander's permission. He served as a Stanley Hundred (Warwick area) burgess in the February 1633 session of the assembly but died sometime prior to June 22, 1635, and was survived by his widow, Alice, and son, Roger II. Alice Delke was in possession of land near Lawnes Creek, adjacent to that of Captain William Peirce. Sometime prior to August 28, 1637, she married Nicholas Reynolds, who repatented the property. Together they produced two sons, Francis and Robert Reynolds. After Nicholas Reynolds' death, Alice married John Gregory. In February 1664 Roger Delk II obtained a patent for1,000 acres of land on Lawnes Creek that formerly had been his father's (VI&A 255; LEO 12; AMES 2:309–310; DOR 1:815–816).

William Denson: In 1649 William Denson and another man were occupying some property on the New Town Haven (Pagan) River in Isle of Wight County. However, prior to March 1664 Denson moved to Nansemond (Lower Norfolk) County, where he acquired some land. He served as a burgess for Lower Norfolk County in 1660 and represented Nansemond County in the 1661–1662 assembly sessions. In 1664 and 1674 his acreage was mentioned in a patent for some land in Nansemond County (LEO 36, 38; Isle of Wight County Deeds, Wills, & Guardian Accounts Book A:115; PB 5:209; 6:540).

George Deverell (Deverill, Deurill): In 1624 George Deverell, who came to Virginia in 1620–1621, was living in Flowerdew Hundred, where he was a servant in Sir George Yeardley's household. By early 1625 he had moved to Yeardley's property in urban Jamestown. In February 1628 the General Court noted that Yeardley had brought Deverell to Virginia. By September 1628 his headright had been assigned to Thomas Flint of Elizabeth City (VI&A 257).

[No First Name] Devern: On April 14, 1634, Mr. Devern, master of the *William*, was accused of illegal trading (VI&A 257).

David Devries: David Devries, a Dutch mariner, came to Virginia in March 1633. He visited Samuel Mathews' plantation, Denbigh, and George Menefie's home, Littletown, which was located on Archer's Hope (College) Creek. Devries stayed in Governor John Harvey's home while visiting Jamestown in 1633. He left the colony but returned in May 1635 and cruised the James River, collecting debts. He left Virginia but returned again in 1643 and was Governor William Berkeley's houseguest in Jamestown. Devries commented that numerous Dutch and English ships were trading in the colony, and he said that the tension between Parliament and the monarchists was very much in evidence. In 1642 Devries sued the estate of Richard Stephens, a former resident of Jamestown (VI&A 257).

Thomas Dew (Dewe, Due, Dow): During 1638 Thomas Dew patented three large tracts of land on the Nansemond River in Lower Norfolk County; one of his parcels was near an old Indian town. Two years later Dew patented another 250 acres, property that was inland and contiguous to the acreage he already owned. In 1642 Thomas Dew served as a burgess for Lower Norfolk County, and in January 1643 he patented 750 acres on the south branch of the Nansemond River. He represented Nansemond County in the 1652 session of the assembly and became speaker. He was returned to the assembly in 1653, again representing Nansemond County, and he attended the sessions held in 1654–1655. In 1655 Dew was named to the Council of State and became a colonel. He patented an additional 750 acres on the Nansemond River in October 1670 (LEO 20, 29–32; STAN 37; PB 1:587, 632, 692, 942; 6:323; MCGC 559). Dew is said to have had Quaker leanings (BILL 45).

Dick: On February 15, 1768, when an inventory was made of the late Richard Ambler's slaves on Jamestown Island and his leasehold in the Governor's Land, an adult male slave named Dick was listed. In 1769 Dick was living on Jamestown Island and was included in the late Edward Ambler I's estate (York County Wills and Inventories 21: 386–391; AMB-E).

Griffin (Griffeth) Dickenson (Dickeson): In early 1656 Griffin Dickenson patented 300 acres of land on Moses Creek, a tributary of the Chickahominy River, in what is now Charles City County. On May 3, 1656, he sued John Baldwin of Jamestown Island in Surry County's monthly court. However, on October 2, 1667, Dickenson himself was censured for building a wharf on Jamestown's waterfront, contrary to law. He died sometime prior to May 1673, by which time his widow had wed Thomas Wilkinson (Surry County Deeds, Wills &c. 1652–1672:100; MCGC 344; JHB 1660–1693:48).

Jane Dickenson (Dickens, Dickinson, Digginson): Jane Dickenson and her husband, Ralph, came to Virginia in 1620 and lived at Martin's Hundred, where they were servants in Thomas Boyce's household. When the Indians attacked in 1622, Ralph was killed but Jane was taken prisoner and detained by the Pamunkey Indians for nearly a year. Dr. John Pott ransomed her for a couple pounds of glass beads, and she became his servant in Jamestown. In 1624 Jane asked Virginia's governor to set her free, claiming that her service to Dr. Pott was worse than the time she spent as a captive of the Indians (VI&A 258).

John Dier (Dyer): John Dier, a carpenter from London, arrived in Jamestown on September 12, 1623, and took the oath of supremacy (VI&A 258).

Mary Dier (Dyer): Mary Dier died in Jamestown sometime after April 1623 but before February 16, 1624 (VI&A 258).

William Dier (Dyer): William Dier, a gentleman, arrived in Jamestown in 1608 in the 1st or 2nd Supply of new settlers. Captain John Smith described Dier as a troublemaker who tried to abscond from Virginia (VI&A 259). A William Dier (perhaps the same man) died in Jamestown sometime after April 1623 but before February 16, 1624.

John Digby (Digbie): On January 24, 1677, John Digby, one of the rebel Nathaniel Bacon's most ardent supporters, was tried at a martial court held at Green Spring plantation, where he was being detained. He admitted his guilt and was sentenced to be hanged. Governor William Berkeley later said that Nathaniel Bacon had made Digby, a servant, a captain in his rebel army. When Governor Berkeley issued a proclamation on February 10, 1677, he noted that Digby already had been executed and that his estate was subject to seizure (NEVILLE 61, 274; MCGC 455, 528).

* * *

Edward Digges I: In September 1650 Edward Digges I, whose father, Sir Dudley Digges, had been a member of the Virginia Company of London, purchased Captain John West's 1,250-acre plantation in Chiskiack. The property, which Digges called the ED plantation but later was known as Bellfield, abutted west on the mouth of Kings Creek and extended in an easterly direction to a point just west of Bracken's Pond. A special strain of tobacco produced on Digges's York River plantation was noted for its mild flavor and aroma and therefore was highly saleable. During the 1650s he planted mulberry trees on his property in accord

with detailed instructions he received from experts in England, and he brought two Armenians to the colony to oversee his attempts at silk-making, which were highly successful. In fact, the Virginia assembly awarded Edward Digges I £100 in recognition of his efforts in promoting silk production. His prowess as a planter generated disposable income that enabled him to patent land in Surry, New Kent, and Gloucester counties. In 1654, while the Commonwealth government was in power, Digges was named to the Council of State. He held office for 20 years, and on March 31, 1655, the assembly chose him as governor and the successor to Richard Bennett. After Governor William Berkeley took office, Digges began serving as auditor, and in 1672 he became receiver general. On one occasion he went to England as an emissary of the Virginia government. Colonel John Page's March 1687 will reveals that Edward Digges I's wife, Elizabeth, was the testator's sister. The Digges couple produced 13 children, only 5 of whom survived. In August 1669, when 55-year-old Edward Digges I was in England preparing to set sail for Virginia, he made his will. He designated his wife, Elizabeth, as his executrix and bequeathed her £1,200. The couple's eldest son, William, was to assume control of their York River plantation, whereas the other children stood to receive legacies of money, slaves, and personal belongings. Edward Digges I died on March 15, 1676. His widow, Elizabeth, continued to occupy the property and was still living there at the time of her death 16 years later. She was survived by sons William, Dudley, and Edward II (STAN 22, 23, 36; LEO xx; PB 2:316; 3:16, 32; MEADE I:244; York County Deeds, Orders, Wills 9:53, 63, 103–107, 161–165, 249–250; MCGC 410; DOR 1:821–824; SR 350, 657, 832, 982, 6214, 7254, 7254, 7256, 7257, 7265).

Dudley Digges: Dudley Digges, one of Edward Digges I's younger sons, was around 10 years old when he lost his father. When he matured he married Susannah, the daughter of Colonel William Cole, the owner of the Boldrup plantation in Warwick County. Dudley Digges served as a factor for British merchant Jeffrey Jeffreys, who did business with the Royal African Company; in early 1677 Jeffreys sent him a large number of Africans to fulfill a contract they had made. Digges also was an agent or factor for Micajah Perry, a prominent London merchant, and served as a Warwick County burgess, attending the 1695–1696 and 1696–1697 sessions. In 1698 he was named to the Council of State and became the colony's auditor and surveyor-general. He also was a colonel in the Warwick County militia. On September 21, 1699, Dudley Digges purchased his late father's York County ED plantation from his nephew, Edward Digges, the son and heir of his eldest brother, William, who had moved to Maryland. Dudley Digges was living in Virginia when he made his will on January 13, 1711. He died five days later, leaving a widow and four children: Cole, Edward, Dudley, and Elizabeth (STAN 43; LEO 55, 57; SR 5754; York County Deeds and Bonds 1:196, 202; Deed Book 6:360; Deeds, Orders, Wills 11:210; Orders, Wills &c. 14:69–70; JHB 1695–1702:5; EJC I:391; Tyler, "Cole Family," 177; DOR 1:826–827).

William Digges: William Digges, the eldest son of Edward Digges I and his wife, the former Elizabeth Page, came into possession of his father's landholdings at age 24. He resided at the ED plantation, later known as Bellfield, the family's ancestral home in York County. In 1671 he began serving as a county justice and went on to become captain of a troop of horse soldiers. He commenced serving as a York County burgess during the latter part of the 1676 assembly session, replacing Robert Baldry, who had died in January. Digges, who staunchly supported Governor William Berkeley, fled to Maryland when Bacon's followers seemingly got the upper hand. However, he later returned to Virginia, where he remained until 1679. He married Elizabeth, the daughter of Henry Sewell of Patuxent, Maryland, and stepdaughter of Charles Calvert, the third Lord Baltimore, and became well established in Maryland. William Digges became a member of Maryland's Council, held the rank of colonel, served as the colony's deputy governor, and held several other prominent positions. He also acquired a considerable amount of real estate. When he returned to Virginia in the early 1690s, he was charged with plotting to restore James II to the monarchy. William Digges' 1694 will, which was presented for probate in 1698, distributed his property among his 10 children. He entrusted Bellfield to the management of his executors, along with the plantation's mill, slaves, and livestock. The proceeds of the plantation's agricultural and milling operations were to go toward the support of Digges' daughters until they were grown or married. Ultimately, however, the plantation was to go to his son Edward, and his slaves and livestock were to be distributed among all six of his sons. After William Digges' death, his son Edward sold Bellfield to his uncle Dudley Digges, one of Edward Digges I's younger sons (LEO 40; NEVILLE

381; DOR 1:824–825; EJC I:282–283; York County Deeds, Orders, Wills 11:210; SR 1929, 1942).

* * *

Dinah: On February 15, 1768, when an inventory was made of the late Richard Ambler's slaves on Jamestown Island and his leasehold in the Governor's Land, an adult female slave named Dinah was listed. In 1769 she and her child, Fanny, were living on the Governor's Land and were part of the late Edward Ambler I's estate (York County Wills and Inventories 21:386–391; AMB-E).

Dinah: On February 15, 1768, when an inventory was made of the late Richard Ambler's slaves on Jamestown Island and his leasehold in the Governor's Land, an adult female slave named Dinah was listed. In 1769 she was identified as Old Dinah, was living on Jamestown Island, and was attributed to the estate of Edward Ambler I (York County Wills and Inventories 21:386–391; AMB-E).

John Dinse (Dinsie): John Dinse died in Jamestown sometime after April 1623 but before February 16, 1624 (VI&A 259).

Thomas Dipnall (Dipdall, Dipnell): Thomas Dipnall served as a burgess for James City in the 1654–1655 session of the assembly. He probably represented James City County rather than Jamestown, for there is no evidence that he owned land in the capital city. A Mr. Dipnell, perhaps the same individual, was in possession of land on Skimino Creek in nearby York County (STAN 71; HEN I:386–387; NUG I:439; LEO 32).

Adam Dixon (Dixson): Adam Dixon (Dixson), a master caulker of ships and a Virginia Company servant, arrived in Virginia in 1611 with Sir Thomas Dale. In May 1622 he presented the governor and council with a list of grievances, asking that they be forwarded to the king. He went to England and returned to Virginia with his wife and daughter. In April 1623 Dixon leveled some serious allegations against Sir Samuel Argall, claiming that he had had to serve for seven years rather than the two or three to which he had agreed. Dixon went to England to press his claim and in January 1624, when testifying before Virginia Company officials, gave his age as 42. While he was away, his wife, Ann (Agnes), a resident of Jamestown Island, died. In May 1625 Adam Dixon was credited with 100 acres in Warresqueak, and in May 1626 he claimed another 200 acres, using the headrights of his wife, Ann (Agnes), and his daughter, Elizabeth, who had come to Virginia in 1622 (VI&A 259–260).

Thomas Doe: In February 1624 Thomas Doe and his wife were living in Pasbehay, the territory just west of Jamestown Island. Sometime prior to January 11, 1627, Doe, who was a planter, received permission to move from Kecoughtan to Hog Island. On October 16, 1629, when the assembly convened, he was a burgess for Archer's Hope in the corporation of James City, an indication that he or his wife had land there (VI&A 261; LEO 8).

Richard Dole: In 1608 Richard Dole, a blacksmith, arrived in Jamestown in the 2nd Supply of new settlers (VI&A 261).

Doll: On February 15, 1768, when an inventory was made of the late Richard Ambler's slaves on Jamestown Island and his leasehold in the Governor's Land, a female slave named Doll was listed. In 1769 Doll, who was included in the late Edward Ambler I's estate, was described as a girl living on the Governor's Land (York County Wills and Inventories 21:386–391; AMB-E).

George Donne: George Donne, the son of poet and dean Dr. John Donne, went to the island of St. Christopher's, where he was captured by the Spanish and taken to Madrid. He escaped, made his way to England, and came to Virginia with Governor John Harvey in 1636. While Donne was living in the colony, he wrote a tract he called "Virginia Reviewed," which he sent to the king. He also witnessed a deed of gift whereby Governor Harvey gave 500 acres of Virginia land to William Upton of Yarmouth, a mariner. Donne, one of Harvey's staunch supporters, sent a letter to the king asking for confirmation of his appointment as mustermaster general and marshal. He was named to the Council of State in 1637 and served for two years, joining those who asked for more favorable customs rates. In 1638 he informed the king that Governor Harvey had been thrust from office by headstrong members of his council. His loyalty to the deposed governor paid off, for when Harvey was restored to office, Donne (like Richard Kemp, another Harvey supporter) was given temporary custody of the substantial estate that had descended to the Rev. Richard Buck's orphan, Benomi, a mentally handicapped youth. George Donne reportedly died in Virginia sometime after 1660 (STAN 33; LEO xx; NUG I:119; SR 4, 627; CO 1/6 ff

50–51, 52ro–53vo; Stanard, "Virginia in 1637," 75–76; "Virginia in 1638," 427–428; "Virginia in 1639," 392).

Edward Douglas I: Edward Douglas I testified before the justices of Accomack County's monthly court in May 1637. When he appeared in court again on April 26, 1640, he indicated that he was age 50. Douglas served as a justice, sheriff, and burgess for Northampton County and attended the assembly sessions that were held in 1644 and 1646. In 1642 he and Edmund Scarborough II served as the late John Angood's administrators. When Douglas received a headright certificate in February 1644, he listed his own name and that of his wife, Elizabeth. Later in the year he served as a regional military commander. When Lady Elizabeth Dale's estate was being settled in 1645, Edward Douglas, who apparently was considered trustworthy and astute, served as the attorney of her administrator, William Shrimpton. Lieutenant Colonel Edward Douglas made his will on October 15, 1657. He asked his wife, Isabella, and his friends Mr. and Mrs. Edmund Boweman to see that he was interred decently if he died at the Bowemans' home. He left life-rights in his Virginia land to his wife and made generous bequests to his son, Edward II, and to his daughters, Elizabeth and Sarah, noting that Sarah had signed a marriage contract with Edward Littleton. The testator also made bequests to several other people. The late Edward Douglas I's will was proved on November 12, 1657. In October 1661 his son, Edward II, patented 3,700 acres in Northampton County. The acreage, which had belonged to the patentee's late father, stretched from the seaside toward the Chesapeake Bay and ran along the south side of Old Plantation Creek (LEO 22, 25; AMES 1:73–74, 167; 2:88–89, 161, 178, 329, 360, 426; PB 2:369; 4:128, 504; MARSHALL 10, 14, 22, 30, 34–35, 40, 47–48, 49–50).

William Douglas (Douglass, Duglas): In 1621 Captain William Douglas, a mariner, brought some passengers to Virginia on the *Margaret and John*, taking over for master John Langley, who died at sea. Afterward, Douglas was sued by John Robinson and Jamestown merchant John Chew, whose goods he detained. In May 1625 Douglas was identified as the patentee of 250 acres of land on the Appomattox River in Charles City County, acreage that was undeveloped. He made several appearances before the General Court between 1625 and 1628, usually testifying about incidents that occurred at sea. Over the years he continued to ply the

Atlantic, bringing passengers and goods to Virginia. In 1656, when William Sarsen patented some land on Jamestown Island that formerly had belonged to Lady Elizabeth Dale, William Douglas was said to have served as her attorney. He probably died sometime prior to January 1656, when Virginia merchant Peter Knight obtained a judgment against the estate of Captain William Douglas and Company (VI&A 263; Northumberland County Order Book 1652–1665:73).

William Dowman: William Dowman, a gentleman and one of the first Jamestown colonists, came to Virginia in 1608 in the 2nd Supply (VI&A 264).

George Downes: In October 1628 George Downes was identified as a merchant. By February 1632 he owned some land at the Strawberry Banks near Old Point Comfort. He was a commissioner of Elizabeth City's monthly court and served as a burgess for the lower (eastern) parish of Elizabeth City. On November 20, 1635, Downes patented some land on the lower side of the James River, near Lynnhaven, in what became Lower Norfolk and then Princess Anne County. He received his patent a month after he had transported a large group of people from London to the island of St. Christopher's aboard the *Amity* (VI&A 265; LEO 10–11; CBE 168).

John Downes: John Downes, a grocer from London, arrived in Jamestown on September 12, 1623 (VI&A 265).

John Downing: In 1668 John Downing inherited 300 acres of land and some livestock from his late father, William Downing of Great Wicocomico in Northumberland County. By 1679 Downing had become a constable for Northumberland County's Fairfield Parish, and in 1680 he became the legal guardian of John Cockrell, a minor, at the youth's request. Downing became increasingly successful, and in 1684 received a certificate that authorized him to claim land. He also began playing a more conspicuous role in public life. He served on a grand jury in 1683, and the following year he brought to court 42 yards of cloth that his household had produced, thereby documenting his eligibility to receive an award from the assembly. Downing, while churchwarden of Fairfield Parish, had a man arrested because his church taxes were in arrears. On the other hand, Downing, like many of his contemporaries, sometimes had trouble paying his own creditors and ended

up in court. In 1693 John Downing and William Jones contested the election of Richard Rodgers and Richard Flint II as Northumberland County's burgesses and were elected in their place. By April 1699 Downing was dead and his widow, Elizabeth, had begun serving as his executrix (LEO 52; Northumberland County Record Book 1666–1670:69; Order Book 1678–1698:33, 35, 37, 105, 182, 211, 224, 231, 320; 1699–1700:11, 16, 33–34, 40).

John Downman (Downeman): John Downman came to Virginia in 1611 and resided in Jamestown. He moved to Bermuda Hundred but by early 1624 had married and moved to the corporation of Elizabeth City. In 1625 he was fined and forced to make a public apology because he had slandered burgess Nicholas Martiau at Kecoughtan. In 1625 Downman and his wife, Elizabeth, were living in Elizabeth City, which he represented in the assembly. When a list of patented land was sent back to England in May 1625, John Downman was credited with 100 acres of land on the south side of the James River, acreage that was undeveloped. In March 1629 he was named a justice of Elizabeth City's court, and in October 1629 he served as that jurisdiction's burgess (VI&A 264; LEO 6, 8).

Thomas Dowse (Douse): Thomas Dowse arrived in Jamestown in 1608 in the 2nd Supply of new settlers. Captain John Smith identified him as both a laborer and taborer (drummer) and sent him to retrieve some Dutchmen who had fled to the Indians. Smith later claimed that Dowse and another man conspired with the paramount chief Powhatan. In July 1619, when the assembly convened, Thomas Dowse served as a burgess for Henrico. He was ordered to vacate some land he had seated at Arrahattock, which was made part of the College land, and settled briefly at Shirley Hundred. However, by early 1624 he had moved to Elizabeth City. Dowse and his wife, Ann, returned to England, where he abandoned her, having given her title to his real and personal property in Virginia (VI&A 266; LEO 3).

John Drason (Drayson): On April 29, 1623, John Drason, a 43-year-old sailor, testified against Edward Brewster in the lawsuit initiated by Robert Rich, the Earl of Warwick, concerning events that took place in urban Jamestown in 1618 (VI&A 267).

[First Name Unknown] Drew: Captain Drew, a miller and one of the rebel Nathaniel Bacon's supporters, was among those who seized and fortified Green Spring plantation in September 1676 (FOR I:11:45).

John Drinkard (Prichard?): John Drinkard or Prichard, a carpenter for the Company of Shipwrights, worked under the supervision of Thomas Nunn, who brought his men to Virginia in 1621. Nunn and his workers became established on Jamestown Island, where most of them died (VI&A 267).

William Drummer: On October 13, 1640, the General Court sentenced William Drummer and some other indentured servants to a whipping because they had failed to report some runaways. Drummer's time of service was to be extended by a year and he was to repay his master, who was responsible for his fine (MCGC 467).

***

William Drummond I: William Drummond I, a Scotsman and successful planter, managed to accumulate a substantial amount of wealth after he came to Virginia. He seems to have begun with a leasehold and domestic complex in the Governor's Land, just west of Jamestown. He acquired a lot in urban Jamestown sometime after May 1656, and by December 1664 had sold it to John Barber I. On March 20, 1662, Drummond's wife, Sarah, patented a half-acre lot in urban Jamestown, acreage she had inherited from Edward Prescott, a mariner with strong ties to Westmoreland County and Maryland. The Drummonds were in possession of Sarah's lot a few months later when the assembly enacted legislation subsidizing the construction of brick houses in the capital city. They may have availed themselves of the building initiative's benefits, for they purportedly owned one of the capital city's finest residences. During the 1660s, while he was governor of Carolina, Drummond patented 4,750 acres of land in Westmoreland County, purchased another 600 acres, and then laid claim to an additional 500 acres. He also acquired 1,200 acres on the east side of the Chickahominy River, near the mouth of Warrany Creek, and enhanced the size of those holdings in 1674. Drummond purchased 700 acres of James City County land from Mathew Edloe in 1668, and in 1672 he patented 960 acres in Lower Norfolk County, the same year he substantially enlarged his Governor's Land leasehold.

During the 1660s and 1670s William Drummond I clashed with several members of Virginia's ruling class, such as Theodorick Bland I and Bryan Smith. He also was involved in lawsuits with merchants in England, Scotland, and Boston, Massachusetts, and had disputes with at least two mariners. In 1672 Drummond, Mathew Page I, and Theophilus Hone agreed to construct gun carriages and a 250-foot-long brick fort in Jamestown and accepted payment in advance. However, Page died, leaving Drummond and Hone to finish the project. Ultimately, both men were brought before the General Court, whose justices ordered them to complete the job and to replace the defective brick they had used in fort construction. Drummond ran afoul of the law when he failed to respond to a summons issued by James City County sheriff Francis Kirkman, a friend of Governor William Berkeley. This encounter and conflicts with some of Berkeley's more ardent supporters may have led him to espouse the rebel Nathaniel Bacon's cause. On September 19, 1676, when Bacon's followers put Jamestown to the torch, William Drummond I set his own house ablaze. It was located on the Drummond couple's half-acre lot near the church, the only urban parcel they owned at the time of the popular uprising. Despite Drummond's role in the destruction of the colony's capital, he is credited with removing the government's records from the burning statehouse, sparing them from destruction. Even so, Drummond's active involvement in Bacon's Rebellion led to his execution for treason. According to contemporary accounts, he was hunted down and captured in the Chickahominy Swamp, tried at James Bray I's house in Middle Plantation, and hanged on January 20, 1677. Because he had been convicted of a capital crime, his estate automatically reverted to the Crown. Governor Berkeley, as the colony's highest ranking official, confiscated Drummond's personal property and had it inventoried. Later, Lady Frances Berkeley refused to relinquish Drummond's belongings and was sued by the widowed Sarah Drummond, who attempted to recover her late husband's goods (MCGC 227, 229, 312, 315, 342, 360, 365, 420, 454, 512, 527, 544; Surry County Order Book 1671–1609:13; HEN I:549; II:158, 172–176; PB 2:150; 5:634; 6:389; NUG I:177, 403, 560; II:103, 123, 140; FOR I:8:21, 23; I:9:7, 9; I:10:4; I:11:22; AND 130–131, 135; AMB 27; Soane 1683; SAIN 9:414; 10:67; 11:195; CO 1/41 f 208; 5/1355 f 186–188; 5/1371 f 218; Westmoreland County Deeds and Wills No. 1 [1653–1671]:239–240, 242, 311; Deeds, Patents &c. 1665–1677:93a–94; NEVILLE 61, 274).

Sarah Drummond (Mrs. William Drummond I): On March 20, 1662, Mrs. Sarah Drummond received a patent for a half-acre lot in urban Jamestown. Her acreage was located near the church and reportedly had been bequeathed to her by Edward Prescott, a merchant and mariner with holdings in Westmoreland County, Virginia, and in Maryland. The legitimacy of Sarah's claim was confirmed by means of a court order. Sarah and her husband, William Drummond I, were in possession of her lot in December 1662 when the assembly enacted legislation subsidizing the construction of brick houses of certain specifications. Sarah and William Drummond I very probably took advantage of the building initiative, for later they were credited with one of the capital city's finest houses. Sarah Drummond, as her late husband's administrator, vigorously attempted to recover his personal property, which Sir William Berkeley entrusted to his wife, Lady Frances, when he went to England. Mrs. Drummond, who appears to have had friends in high places, sent several letters to the Lords of Trade and Plantations asking that her property be returned, and she went to England to plead her case. She said that she had five children to support and claimed that Sir William, while governor, had acted cruelly and illegally when seizing her late husband's goods. She also filed suit against Lady Frances, whom she alleged had ordered her servants to seize and detain the Drummonds' corn, crops, claret, brandy, and cloth. In addition to the return of her late husband's belongings, Sarah Drummond demanded his back pay as a burgess. She was successful in retaining her late husband's leasehold in the Governor's Land, and it is likely that she kept her lot in Jamestown next to the churchyard, for it belonged to her personally. Sarah Drummond was survived by her sons, William II and John, and her daughter, Sarah II, who married Samuel Swann, the son of councilor and Jamestown tavern owner Colonel Thomas Swann (PB 5:634; NUG I:560; HEN II:172–176; FOR I:8:21; EEAC 19; CO 1/41 f 205–212; 1/42 ff 290–291; 5/1355 f 186; 5/1371 ff 264–269; SAIN 10:258; MCGC 519, 521, 534; Surry County Deeds and Wills 1671–1684:165; SMITH 27; Stanard, "The Randolph Manuscript," 2–3).

John Drummond: In 1704 John Drummond, one of William Drummond I's sons and heirs, paid quitrent on 700 acres of land in James City County (SMITH 27).

William Drummond II: William II, the son of Sarah and William Drummond I, inherited his late father's leasehold in the Governor's Land and perhaps his mother's lot near the church in urban Jamestown. In March 1693 Drummond was authorized to serve as

the assembly's sergeant-at-arms, a position for which he was compensated. During 1696, while he was a justice of the James City County court, he sometimes served as a messenger for the assembly. In 1701 he purchased a lot in urban Jamestown, buying it from John Harris. Drummond was still alive in 1703, at which time he was mentioned in William Broadribb's will. His lot in urban Jamestown eventually descended to his son, William Drummond III. In 1704 William Drummond II paid quitrent on 150 acres in James City County (JHB 1660–1693:413; 1695–1702:60; AMB 114; MCGH:676; SMITH 27; SAIN 17:309).

William Drummond III: William Drummond III, the son of William Drummond II, inherited his father's lot in Jamestown, which he sold to Edward Champion Travis on June 15, 1753 (AMB 114).

* * *

Robert Dudley I: Robert Dudley I of Gloucester County began serving as a justice in the monthly court of the newly formed Middlesex County and held office for many years. He also was an overseer of the public roads near his plantation. He gave his son, Robert Dudley II, a 350-acre tract in Middlesex in 1680, a year after the younger man began serving as the attorney of Robert Lancaster, a London merchant. In 1687, while he was a Middlesex County justice, Captain Robert Dudley I was among those chosen to inventory Robert Beverley I's estate. He was designated high sheriff in 1691 and by 1699 held the rank of major in the local militia. He also served as a burgess for Middlesex County and attended the assembly sessions held in 1685–1686, 1688, 1695–1696, 1696–1697, 1698, and 1699. When Edward Green, a grocer from Bristol, England, made his will on August 8, 1698, he indicated that he was staying at Captain Robert Dudley's home in Middlesex County, Virginia. He asked to be buried at the discretion of John Barnard, who was then living at John Walker's house in King and Queen County. Captain Dudley and his son, Robert II, witnessed the testator's will (LEO 48–49, 54, 56, 58–59; Middlesex County Order Book 1673–1680:114, 210, 218, 223–224; 1680–1694:128, 293, 303, 375, 466, 496, 506, 701; 1694–1705:175, 307; SR 4784).

William Dudley I: Richard Lawrence, proprietor of a popular tavern in urban Jamestown, bought suit against William Dudley I. He lost the case, which was dismissed by the General Court's justices (Governor Berkeley and his council) on October 21, 1670. On April 25, 1677, the late William Dudley I's children (James, Thomas, William II, and Elizabeth) informed London merchant James Cary that their father was dead and that his tobacco had been unlawfully seized by Berkeley's men. They said that the king's commissioners had assured them that the tobacco would be restored and delivered to Cary, who was their factor. In a separate petition to the king, the widowed Elizabeth Dudley of Middlesex County said that her late husband had been forced to take the rebel Nathaniel Bacon's oath but that he had neither supported his cause nor borne arms. Officials in England determined that Berkeley's men had wrongfully seized 15 hogsheads of tobacco from William Dudley I after the king had offered a pardon to his loyal subjects. Therefore the tobacco was to be returned (MCGC 236; NEVILLE 68, 83, 92–93, 145, 193).

Henry Duke: In October 1690 Henry Duke patented 1,000 acres in James City County, on the lower side of the Chickahominy River. Four years later he acquired more than 800 acres on Diascund Swamp and Warrany Creek. He commenced serving as a James City County burgess in 1691, replacing James Bray I, who attended the first session but resigned after refusing to take the required oaths. Duke was returned to office numerous times and attended the assembly sessions held in 1691–1692, 1693, 1696–1697, and 1699. In June 1699 he was appointed a lieutenant colonel in James City County's militia and also became county sheriff. He and Captain James Bray II made a formal complaint about a runaway slave who had become an outlaw. In 1702 Duke was named to the Council of State, on which he served until 1713. He also was appointed judge of the Vice Admiralty Court in 1704. Duke continued to acquire land and in 1704 patented 1,168 acres on the Chickahominy Swamp. Finally, in 1711 he patented 82 acres on the west side of the Chickahominy,

land that formerly belonged to surveyor John Soane (LEO xx, 50, 52–53, 56, 59; PB 8:123, 321–322; 9:611; 10:4; SR 715, 729, 1192, 1466, 3919, 14574; DES 2; EJC I:444, 446, 459).

John Dumport: John Dumport died in Jamestown sometime after April 1623 but before February 16, 1624 (VI&A 268).

Duncan: On February 15, 1768, when an inventory was made of the late Richard Ambler's slaves on Jamestown Island and his leasehold in the Governor's Land, an adult female slave named Duncan was listed. In 1769 she was living on Jamestown Island and was included in the late Edward Ambler I's estate (York County Wills and Inventories 21:386–391; AMB-E).

Thomas Dunn (Dunne): In early 1624 Thomas Dunn, who came to Virginia in 1620, was residing at Flowerdew Hundred, Sir George Yeardley's plantation. By January 1625 he had moved to Jamestown and was a servant in the Yeardley home (VI&A 269).

John Dunston: John Dunston was a burgess for James City in the October 10, 1649, session of the assembly. His ownership of land in the mainland behind Hog Island, which he acquired in 1636, suggests strongly that he represented what was then James City County. Dunston's wife was named Cicely (STAN 67; HEN I:358–359; NUG I:40, 48, 94, 109, 111; LEO 27).

John Dyus (Dyas): John Dyus reportedly provided medical treatment to the cattle belonging to the orphans of the Rev. Richard Buck of Jamestown Island. On May 8, 1626, the General Court's justices learned that Dyus had not been paid for his work. Because he was illiterate, he had asked John Southern to prepare a bill, which he took to the Buck home for acknowledgment. As no one was there, Dyus returned the bill to Southern. John Dyus died before he was compensated (VI&A 270).

E

John Eaton: On July 24, 1674, Richard Auborne, clerk of the General Court and a resident of urban Jamestown, successfully brought suit against the estate of John Eaton, an English merchant and mariner who

traded in Virginia and Maryland. In 1694 Edmund Jennings succeeded in obtaining a judgment against the Eaton estate because the decedent had agreed to supply him with a substantial quantity of shoe leather and seven pairs of shoes (York County Deeds, Orders, Wills 5:76; 10 [1694–1697]:236; SR 669, 4201, 5762, 5762a).

William Eden-Sampson (see William Sampson alias Eden)

Edith: On February 15, 1768, when an inventory was made of the late Richard Ambler's slaves on Jamestown Island and his leasehold in the Governor's Land, an enslaved girl named Edith was listed and identified as Chubby's child. In 1769 Edith, who still was described as a girl, was living on Jamestown Island and was included in the late Edward Ambler I's estate (York County Wills and Inventories 21:386–391; AMB-E).

John Edloe: In March 1676 Thomas Bowler asked the General Court to designate him John Edloe's guardian. The justices denied Bowler's request because his wife, Tabitha, was the orphan's half-sister (MCGC 387, 450).

* * *

Mathew Edloe (Edlowe) I: Mathew Edloe I came to Virginia on Lord Delaware's ship, the *Neptune*, which arrived in Jamestown in 1618. During the mid-1620s Edloe lived at the College, in the corporation of Henrico. Between April 4, 1627, and October 1628, he married Alice, the widow of Luke Boyse of Bermuda Hundred. On March 7, 1629, Mathew and Alice presented the General Court with an account of her late husband's estate. Mathew Edloe served as a burgess for the College on October 16, 1629, but died sometime prior to November 1635 (VI&A 273; LEO 8).

Mathew Edloe (Edlowe) II: On July 12, 1637, after Mathew Edloe II, the son and heir of Mathew Edloe I, attained his majority, he patented 1,200 acres in Charles City. In 1659–1660 Captain Edloe served as a burgess for James City County, a jurisdiction in which he also owned land (VI&A 273; HEN 1809–1823:I:506–507; STAN 74; NUG I:59, 88, 154; LEO 35).

* * *

Thomas Edmundson (Edmondson): In April 1666 John Gregory (Grigory) of Old Rappahannock County identified Thomas Edmundson as his son-in-law when giving him some livestock. During 1667 Edmundson patented land and quickly resold part of it. He then acquired two large tracts of land

on Piscattaway Creek in what was then Old Rappahannock County. He also patented a 513-acre tract on the south side of the Rappahannock River and seems to have settled there permanently. By 1678 Edmundson's wife, the former Anne Gregory, was dead and he had wed a woman named Mary, whose surname is unknown. During the 1680s Thomas Edmundson became increasingly involved in public life. He was among those asked to inventory and apportion estates, and he also served as a jury foreman. In 1687 he enhanced the size of his holdings by patenting 600 acres in the vicinity of some acreage he already owned. In February 1691 he testified in litigation that involved a shipment of tobacco loaded aboard the *Concord* while it was anchored in the Potomac River. Edmundson was named a justice in the monthly court of newly formed Essex County in May 1692 and served for more than a decade. In December 1693 he agreed to see that a frame courthouse was built at the Essex County seat and represented the county in its dealings with contractor Daniel Diskin. He became a burgess for Essex County and attended the assembly sessions held in 1693, 1696–1697, and 1700–1702. In 1699, while he was a court justice, Edmundson was sued for cutting timber from another landowner's property. That accusation, though substantiated, does not seem to have affected his reputation, for his appointment as justice was renewed and he continued to serve in the assembly (LEO 53, 56, 60; Old Rappahannock County Deeds and Wills 1656–1662:174–175; 1677–1682:141–142, 175–176, 244, 321, 346–348; Will Book 1682–1687:50–51, 111–112; Order Book 1683–1686: 41; Essex County Order Book 1692–1695:1, 90, 154, 159, 188; 1695–1699:5–6, 86, 158; 1699–1702:1, 3, 11, 57, 73, 122; Deeds and Wills 1692–1695:205, 302, 319, 390; PB 6:23, 149, 231; 7:237, 550; PARKS 65; SR 10736).

Edward: A laborer known as Old Edward arrived in Virginia in 1607 and was one of the first Jamestown colonists (VI&A 274).

Arthur Edwards: Arthur Edwards died in Jamestown sometime after April 1623 but before February 16, 1624 (VI&A 274).

Thomas Edwards: Thomas Edwards, one of Governor William Berkeley's indentured servants, stole Colonel William White's boat and fled. On September 28, 1674, the justices of the General Court sentenced Edwards to a public whipping and extended the length of his contract with Berkeley. He also was required to serve White, a resident of urban Jamestown, for a year and a half to compensate him for loss of his boat (MCGC 382).

* * *

William Edwards I: Sometime prior to 1648 William Edwards I, a Surry County justice of the peace and burgess who served in the assembly in 1652, 1653, and 1658, acquired 27 acres in the mainland just west of Jamestown Island. In 1652 he patented some acreage on Crouches Creek in Surry, and he may have owned one or more lots in urban Jamestown. In September 1654 a man visiting John Corker's house in Jamestown reportedly made slanderous remarks about William Edwards I's having defrauded Lieutenant Colonel Walter Chiles I. After Edwards' death, Thomas Hunt of urban Jamestown, as the decedent's executor, tried to collect funds owed to his estate. He also became the legal guardian of Edwards' minor children. William Edwards I's widow, Sarah, married William Richardson, but by June 22, 1670, she was widowed again. She eventually married Major Theophilus Hone, the owner of several lots in urban Jamestown (NUG I:353, 355; PB 2:150; STAN 69–70, 73; MCGC 216, 230, 235, 237; Surry County Deeds, Wills &c. 1652–1671:31; 1671–1684:20; LEO 30–31, 34; MCGC 223, 230).

William Edwards II: William Edwards II, his father's primary heir, enhanced his wealth by speculating in real estate and holding public offices that generated handsome fees. He began serving as clerk of the General Court in 1679 and held office until May 26, 1693. He also served as clerk of the Council of State and in 1693 became a burgess for James City County. In 1677 he purchased from Samuel Lewis a racially mixed boy, John Kikotan, a youth described as a mulatto; his name raises the possibility that he was part Indian. In 1682 Edwards was authorized to operate a ferry that ran between urban Jamestown and Crouches Creek. Several years later he patented a tiny lot on the upper side of the James River, directly across from the mouth of Crouches Creek: the perfect site for a ferry landing. Through his sister's marriage to Colonel Thomas Swann, Edwards was connected with one of Virginia's wealthiest and most powerful families. Over the years he served as the attorney of Jamestown property owners George Marable I, Thomas Rabley, and Mary Swann, and he also represented Robert Vaulx of London. During the 1680s and 1690s he patented substantial quantities of

land throughout the James River basin, from Henrico County on the west, to Nansemond on the east. Some of his newly acquired acreage was in James City County on Warrany Creek, a tributary of the Chickahominy River.

In August 1687 William Edwards II became clerk of the James City County court, a position that would have necessitated monthly trips to Jamestown and stays spanning several consecutive days. He went on to serve as a county justice, and in 1691 the assembly paid him for transcribing the legal code. He also became a trustee of the Surry County planned town called Cobham. In 1695 he purchased a house and lot in urban Jamestown from Henry Hartwell, probably because he was spending large amounts of time in the capital city attending to official duties. In 1697 Jamestown merchant and attorney William Sherwood designated Edwards as one of his executors and bequeathed him his law books and a small parcel of land that abutted Edwards' own acreage. When William Edwards II died in 1698, he was survived by his wife, Elizabeth, who hosted the Committee of Public Claims, probably utilizing the building on her late husband's lot in urban Jamestown. In 1709 she acknowledged the sale of her late husband's lot to William Broadnax I (EJC I:81, 161, 287; LJC 143; CO 5/1407 f 81; Surry County Deeds, Wills &c. 1671–1684:157, 243, 304; Order Book 1671–1691:302; Deeds and Wills 1687–1694:233; York County Deeds, Orders, Wills 9:45; NUG II:216, 285, 322, 342, 353–354, 371, 373, 389, 401; PB 8:42; PALM I:12, 38, 51; AMB 38, 55, 65, 75; MCGH 873; JHB 1695–1702:124; LEO 53).

William Edwards III: William Edwards III, like his forebears, took an active role in public life and tried to enhance his own personal wealth by patenting large quantities of frontier land. In 1699 he served as a James City County justice of the peace, succeeding his father, but he continued to reside in Surry County where he served as a burgess between 1703 and 1706. In March 1709 some of Edwards' Surry County slaves were among those who made an unsuccessful attempt to gain their freedom. By that time William Edwards III had begun having some serious financial problems. One of his creditors was William Broadnax I, to whom he mortgaged his Jamestown property. Edwards' January 9, 1722, will reveals that he bequeathed a waterfront lot in urban Jamestown to his son Benjamin, who also stood to receive some other James City County acreage. He left the remainder of his land to his son William Edwards IV, who had wed Sarah, the widow of London merchant Micajah Lowe. The testator identified Philip Ludwell II and Dr. Archibald Blair as two of his friends and Nathaniel Harrison as his father-in-law. As it turned out, William Edwards III failed to repay his debts to William Broadnax I, who gained possession of his lots in urban Jamestown (SAIN 17:309; PALM 1:129; Surry County Will Book 7:389; NUG III:37,44; STAN 95–97; AMB 63, 75, 97–98, 106–107; Tyler, "Micajah Perry," 264).

* * *

Benjamin Eggleston: On October 21, 1673, Benjamin Eggleston, whose family owned land near Governor William Berkeley's manor plantation, Green Spring, was sentenced to a whipping for impinging upon the governor's prerogative (MCGC 348). Benjamin appears to have been trespassing on Berkeley's property and may have been hunting.

Eghtop (Native American): In September 1660 the Mattaponi Indians' king and Great Men or leaders denied that they had tried to claim the Old Rappahannock County land on which Francis Brown had established a plantation. Eghtop was one of the men whose names were affixed to an affidavit attesting to their tribe's point of view (Old Rappahannock County Deed Book 1656–1664:111).

Lancelot Elay: In November 1647 Lancelot Elay, a respected member of the Jamestown community, was entrusted with the task of collecting public levies from the inhabitants of Jamestown Island, the mainland just west of Jamestown Island, and the territory bordering Powhatan Creek. In October 1649, when the parameters of urban Jamestown's market zone were set by law, the vending area's easternmost boundary line was near Lancelot Elay's house, which abutted a gut or small stream that became known as Orchard Run. Part of Elay's boundary line is shown on John Underhill's 1664 plat of a contiguous property (HEN I:342–343, 362; AMB 16, 135–136).

Elinor: On February 16, 1624, Elinor was living in urban Jamestown in merchant Edward Blaney's household, where she probably was a maid servant (VI&A 276).

Elizabeth (Mrs. John Basse [Bass, Base]) (Native American): On August 14, 1638, the king of the Nansemond Indians' daughter, Elizabeth, who was baptized and had converted to Christianity, married John Basse, the son of colonist Nathaniel Basse. John, who was born in September 1616, made note of his parents' and siblings' births and marriages in a book of sermons. His brother, Edward, also married an Indian woman (Basse Family Bible Records 1613–1699; VI&A 118).

* * *

Anthony Elliott (Elliot, Ellyott) I: Anthony Elliott I served as an Elizabeth City County burgess and attended the sessions held in 1647–1648. He then owned 300 acres near Old Point Comfort Creek in Elizabeth City. When he initiated litigation in Lancaster County's monthly court in 1654 and 1656, he was identified as a lieutenant colonel. By 1650 Elliott had begun patenting land on the Middle Peninsula, acquiring two large tracts on the North River and Mobjack Bay. He also invested in some land in Lancaster County. He was named to the Council of State in 1657, and in 1658 he represented Gloucester County in the assembly. In 1659 Elliott purchased 1,250 acres of land on the south side of the Rappahannock River in Lancaster County, near the plantation called Machapungo. A year later he bought 700 acres of adjoining property. In March 1662 he received a land certificate for having transported a large group of black and white servants into the colony. By April 1666 he had become a justice of Lancaster County's monthly court. Anthony Elliott died in Virginia sometime after July 1666 but before January 9, 1667, when administration of his estate was granted to his widow and her new husband, Christopher Wormeley II. In October 1672 the General Court authorized Anthony Elliott II and Captain Robert Beverley to patent 800 acres of land on the south side of the Rappahannock River in Lancaster County, acreage that formerly had been granted to Lieutenant Colonel Anthony Elliott, who had failed to see that it was seated (LEO 26, 34; Lancaster County Deeds &c. 1652–1657:138, 291; 1654–1661:110, 188–189, 226–227; 1661–1702:376–377; Order Book 1656–1666:172, 206, 335, 370; 1666–1680:1, 5, 21; MCGC 316; PB 1:358; 2:28, 284; 3:349; 5:428; 8:80).

David Ellis: In December 1608 David Ellis, who arrived at Jamestown in 1608 in the 2nd Supply of new colonists, accompanied Captain John Smith to Powhatan's village, Werowocomoco. Smith identified Ellis as an artisan, a soldier, and a sailor (VI&A 276).

David Ellis: David Ellis and his wife, Margaret, came to Virginia on the *Mary Marga-*

ret. In February 1624 the Ellises were living on the Governor's Land, probably in a household headed by John Carter. By early 1625 David Ellis headed his own household on the Governor's Land and probably was a tenant farmer. He purchased and patented Lieutenant Batters' acreage at Black Point in the eastern end of Jamestown Island, but promptly sold it to John Radish. By March 18, 1626, David and Margaret Ellis had a child. David was then described as John Carter's brother (brother-in-law) and an heir of Thomas Swinehow, from whom he, Margaret, and their child were to inherit rings (VI&A 277).

James Ellis: In 1682 James Ellis of Surry County relinquished his right to operate a ferry that transported passengers across the James River to Jamestown (PALM I:51).

John Ellison (Elison, Elisone, Ellyson): John Ellison had some business dealings with Nicholas Hyde, a Virginia Company investor associated with Martin's Hundred. He also had put the governor's mark on a free-ranging cow pastured on Jamestown Island, an animal that Robert Partin of Shirley Hundred claimed, and he had witnessed the agreement made by Thomas Farley and Susan Bush. John Ellison and his wife, Ellen, were living in Archer's Hope in 1624 and 1625 when their son, George, died (VI&A 277–278).

Robert Ellyson (Ellison): Robert Ellyson came to Virginia sometime prior to July 1653 and was identified as a gentleman. He represented James City County in the 1656 and 1660 sessions of the assembly and also served from 1661 to 1665. He held the rank of captain in 1657 when he patented 577 acres in New Kent County. In 1658 he became James City County's sheriff, served as sergeant-at-arms for the assembly, and became a militia captain. In 1664 he was identified as a county justice of the peace. Ellyson died in 1665 while holding office as a burgess, and in 1680 his son and heir, Garrard Robert Ellyson, repatented his New Kent County acreage. In July 1698 his daughter, Hannah, and her husband, Anthony Armistead of Elizabeth City County, sold a piece of New Kent County property that she had inherited from her late father, who was then identified as Dr. Robert Ellyson (STAN 72–73; HEN I:503; II:196–197; PB 3:26–27; 4:102; 7:22; Charles City County Order Book 1:103; LEO 33, 36, 38; NEAL 71).

John Eman (Enims): John Eman or Enims, a goldsmith from London, arrived in Jamestown on September 12, 1623, and took the oath of supremacy. He died in Jamestown sometime prior to February 16, 1624 (VI&A 278).

Ellis Emerson: Ellis Emerson and his family came to Virginia in 1623 and settled at Martin's Hundred. In February 1625, he and his wife, Ann, and son, Thomas, were still living there. Later in the year Ellis Emerson and Martin's Hundred's leader, William Harwood, offered accommodations to the people who came to Virginia to establish the East India School. Emerson served as a burgess in 1625, representing Martin's Hundred, but died sometime prior to October 31, 1626 (VI&A 279; LEO 6).

William Emerson (Emmerson): William Emerson came to Virginia in 1618 and in February 1624 was residing at Jordan's Journey, where he and his partner, John Davis, were still living a year later. Around 1629 Emerson went to England, where Captain John Smith interviewed him about conditions in the colony. On February 1, 1633, William Emerson commenced serving as a burgess for Weyanoke in the corporation of Charles City, where Jordan's Journey also was located (VI&A 279; LEO 12).

Francis Emperour: Francis Emperour of Norwick, England, a tobacco merchant, was the father of John Bland I's wife, Mary (WITH 638).

William English: William English, master of the ship *Jacob*, purchased some marketable goods on credit and transported them to Virginia. By 1625 he had immigrated to the colony and settled on the west side of the Hampton River in Elizabeth City. He appeared in court in 1625 and 1626 to testify in cases involving merchandise. In October 1626 he and William Ganey received passes authorizing them to make a trip to England. By October 16, 1629, English had been elected a burgess for Elizabeth City, and in 1632 and 1633 he represented Elizabeth City's lower or easternmost parish. During 1632 he also served as a commissioner (or justice) for the corporation of Elizabeth City's court. Like many of his peers, he invested in land on the colony's frontier, and in 1642 he patented some land on the Piankatank Bay, in what later became Gloucester (and then Mathews) County. In 1659 English served as a burgess for Isle of Wight County (VI&A 281; LEO 7–8, 11–12, 35; PB 1:825; SR 5860).

* * *

Francis Eppes (Epes) I: Francis Eppes I came to Virginia sometime prior to April 1625, when he was elected to the assembly, representing the settlers living at Shirley Hundred. During 1626 he attained the rank of ensign and was appointed a commissioner of the monthly court for the "Upper Parts," territory near the head of the James River. In July 1627 Eppes and another man were placed in command of the men ordered to attack the Weyanoke and Appomattox Indians. In 1628 Eppes served in the assembly, representing Shirley Hundred. He returned to England, but by 1632 he was back in Virginia where he served as a burgess for Shirley Hundred, Chaplin's Choice, and Jordan's Journey, then known as "Mr. Farrar's plantation." On August 26, 1635, he was granted 1,700 acres of land on the east side of the Appomattox River's mouth, within Charles City (now Prince George) County. He also had land on West and Shirley (now Eppes) Island. Captain Francis Eppes served in the assembly, representing Charles City in 1640 and 1645–1646, and in 1652 he was named to the Council of State. He consolidated his landholdings in a 1668 patent, but by September 30, 1674, was dead (VI&A 281; LEO 6, 7, 10, 18, 24; STAN 34).

Francis Eppes (Epes) II: Francis Eppes II, the son of Francis Eppes I, was born around 1627 or 1628 and resided at Bermuda Hundred. When the elder man patented 1,700 acres of land on the Appomattox River on August 26, 1635, he indicated that he had paid for son Francis II's transportation to Virginia. Sometime prior to April 20, 1658, Francis Eppes II became a justice of Charles City County's monthly court and by June 1660 had become a militia captain. A year later he was placed in command of a militia unit charged with keeping watch over the territory around Fort Henry, a military post near the falls of the Appomattox River. Eppes moved to Henrico County and around 1661 married his second wife, Elizabeth, William Worsham's widow. By February 1665 he had become a county justice. He served as a Henrico burgess and attended the assembly sessions held between 1670 and 1676. In October 1673 he received a patent for 927 acres on Swift's Creek, on the north side of the Appomattox River. He was mortally wounded or injured and died between August 20 and August 28, 1678, leaving his estate to his wife, Elizabeth, and four children (VI&A 281; PB 6:480; Charles City County Order Book 1655–1665:137, 233, 287; 1676–1679:200; Henrico County Order Book 1678–1693:56; LEO 38; DOR 1:857–858).

Francis Eppes (Epes) III: In 1678 Francis Eppes III of Bermuda Hundred, the son of Francis Eppes II and his first wife, served as administrator of his late father's and stepmother's estates. He was sworn in as a justice of Henrico County in June 1683 and was identified as a captain. Eppes was elected a burgess for Henrico County and attended the assembly sessions held in 1691–1692, 1693, 1703–1705, and 1706. Thus, he would have attended assembly meetings in Jamestown, the old capital, and in Williamsburg, the new capital. Eppes was one of the commissioners raising funds for the College of William and Mary, which was chartered in 1693. He owned 2,145 acres in Henrico County and 226 acres in Prince George. One of his friends was William Byrd II of Westover. Colonel Francis Eppes III married Anne, the daughter of Colonel Henry Isham (LEO 50, 53, 62, 64; DOR 1:858, 861–862).

* * *

Eriosinchke (Native American): In 1657 Eriosinchke, one of the Mattaponi Indians' Great Men or leaders, joined in making a peace agreement with the justices of Old Rappahannock County (Old Rappahannock County Deed Book 1656–1664:17).

Esmy Shichans (the "Laughing King") (Native American): Esmy Shichans, the Eastern Shore's chief until the 1630s, resided in what became Accomack County and most likely was the good-natured Indian leader the colonists called the "Laughing King." During 1621 he gave Sir George Yeardley all of the land between Hungars and Wissaponson creeks. In the summer of 1621 the Powhatan Indians' paramount chief, Opechancanough, sent a message to the Accomack king asking for a poisonous herb that he could use against the colonists. Esmy Shichans thwarted Opechancanough's plan by promptly disclosing it to the settlers, who took protective measures. During the early 1630s he gave some of his land to colonists he liked. One was Thomas Savage, who had lived with the Indians during his youth, learned their language, and sometimes served as an interpreter. On September 5, 1636, the justices of Accomack County's court learned that some of Esmy Shichans' men came to Daniel Cugley's house with a message "from the laughing king" and some roanoke or shell money that was intended to atone for the death of a colonist who was killed at Kent Island in 1635. Accomack's justices referred Cugley to the General Court, for he had accepted trade goods at a time all commerce with the natives was prohibited. Esmy Shichans' village was near Cheriton, but he also had sway over a town called Matoones that was located near Hungars Creek. After Esmy Shichans' death, the Accomack Indians became known as the Gingaskins. In December 1640 they received a patent for 1,500 acres (VCR 4:551; NUG I:30, 50, 77, 150, 241; MCGC 478; VCR I:579; Northampton County Deeds, Wills, Orders 2:28, 156; 3:207; Orders 9:49; AMES 1:56–58). Some respected scholars have confused Esmy Shichans, the "Laughing King," with one of his successors, Tapatiaton (Debedeavon).

Essex: In March 1710 a group of enslaved blacks, Indian servants, and indentured servants in James City, Isle of Wight, and Surry counties planned to make a break for freedom on Easter Sunday and vowed to overcome all who opposed them. One slave, a black man named Will, revealed the plot and the uprising was quelled. Among the James City County slaves jailed for complicity in the plot were males belonging to the Rev. James Blair, Philip Ludwell I, Sheriff Edward Jaquelin, George Marable II, ferryman and gunner Edward Ross, and John Broadnax, all of whom had property in urban Jamestown. Although most of the accused insurgents were jailed in Jamestown, where they were interrogated and then released into their owners' custody "to receive correction," Essex (a Ross slave) and Jamy (a Broadnax slave) were implicated in the plot and therefore were detained. Virginia's governor later reported that two slaves were executed so that "their fate will strike such a terror" that others would not attempt an uprising. The two men (one African American and one Indian) were hanged and then quartered. A quarter of the Indian, Salvador, was put on display near the "great guns" at Jamestown. There, near the ferry landing, the gruesome display would have been a grim reminder of the consequences of rebellion (Stanard, "Philip Ludwell to Edward Jenings, 1709, in regard to a Negro Plot," 23–24; EJC III:234–236, 242–243).

Ester Ederife (Evere): On February 16, 1624, Ester Ederife was residing in William Peirce's household in urban Jamestown, where she was a servant. She was still there on January 24, 1625 (VI&A 272; CBE 38, 55).

Charles Evans: On September 15, 1701, the government paid Charles Evans for the work he had done as a scribe while in Jamestown (SAIN 19:773; CO 5/1409 f 150).

He probably was employed by the Secretary of the Colony, the General Court, or the assembly.

Richard Evans (Evands): Richard Evans came to Virginia in 1618 and during the mid-1620s was living at Basses Choice, where he was a household head. When he appeared before the General Court in December 1625, he was described as Captain William Tucker's sergeant. Evans ran afoul of the law when he refused to allow his servant Arthur Avelinge to go to Jamestown, despite a summons from the General Court. He was fined and both men were summoned to Jamestown (VI&A 284).

Christopher Eveling: A dispute that Captain Christopher Eveling, a mariner, had with William Drummond I of urban Jamestown was aired before the General Court on May 24, 1673 (MCGC 339).

Robert Evelyn (Eveling, Evelin): In 1634 Robert Evelyn, who was born in England, received permission to go to Virginia. He was named to the Council of State in 1637 and served until 1640. In mid-May 1637 he witnessed a document for Captain Thomas Purfoy of Elizabeth City County. Later in the year Governor John Harvey recommended that Evelyn, a lieutenant in the militia and one of his supporters, be given a lifetime appointment as the colony's surveyor-general. Harvey's superiors agreed and Evelyn was named to the position in April 1638, replacing the late Sir Gabriel Hawley. In 1638 councilors John West, Samuel Mathews, and William Tucker, who were opponents of Governor Harvey, sent a letter to England protesting Evelyn's appointment to a judicial commission charged with deliberating the propriety of their actions. Evelyn owned land in Charles City County, where he resided, and died in Virginia sometime prior to 1655 (STAN 26, 34; LEO xx; PB 1:446; Charles City County Court Orders 1655–1658:69; SR 629, 630, 3428, 7294, 7299).

* * *

John Everett: John Everett married the widowed Mrs. Elizabeth Sikes (Sykes), who prior to April 1679 began renting and operating Colonel Thomas Swann's tavern in urban Jamestown. In January 1681 Swann's widow and son sued Everett for £26 in overdue rent, accrued while Mrs. Everett was still a widow. John Everett contended that Colonel Swann's room and board was supposed to be deducted from the rent money. In January 1681 tavern-keeper John Everett sued his near-neighbor, Mrs. Holt of Jamestown, for unlawfully detaining his steer. The Everett couple continued to serve as proprietors of Colonel Swann's tavern until around 1682. They moved to Charles City County, where in 1689 they received permission to operate a tavern at Buckland, in Westover Parish. In September 1685 John Everett was licensed by the governor to serve as an attorney, and in November 1693 he authorized William Foreman to function as his own attorney (Surry County Order Book 1671–1691:358, 488; Deeds, Wills, &c. 1672–1684:297; Deeds, Wills &c. 1687–1694:339; Charles City County Orders 1687–1695:243; EJC 10; PB 4:196).

Mrs. John Everett (see Elizabeth Sikes [Sykes])

* * *

Robert Evers (Evars, Evans, Epers): Robert Evers, guardian of the orphaned Mary Bayly, was living on her property in the eastern end of Jamestown Island in 1619. He also was present when Governor George Yeardley made a treaty with the Chickahominy Indians. On May 30, 1624, Virginia Company officials reviewed Evers' claim that Yeardley had given him 490 acres on Hog Island. Sometime after February 16, 1624, but before February 4, 1625, Robert Evers died on the lower side of the James River in Tappahanna, where he owned 100 acres (VI&A 285).

John Ewen (Ewens, Ewins): On February 19, 1627, John Ewen and Jane Hill of West and Shirley Hundred were summoned to appear before the General Court, whose justices found them guilty of lewd behavior. Ewen was sentenced to a public whipping in Jamestown and at Shirley Hundred, whereas Hill was to be publicly shamed before the congregations of the churches in Jamestown and Shirley Hundred (VI&A 286).

William Ewens (Ewins, Evans): In August 1619 William Ewens, a sea captain, transported Lieutenant William Peirce and John Rolfe to Old Point Comfort, where they bartered for the first Africans brought to Virginia. In July 1621 Ewens was identified as

captain of the *George* when the Virginia Company hired him to sail the ship *Charles* to Jamestown, and in July 1622 he brought three men to Virginia on the *James*. In May 1625 Ewens was credited with 100 acres of land on the lower side of the James River, opposite Jamestown, property that had been seated. In March 1640 he was described as a merchant, and in 1650 he identified himself as a native of Greenwich in Kent, England. Ewens' wife and daughter were both named Mary (VI&A 286).

Robert Eyre (Eyres, Eire, Eires, Eares): On July 19, 1627, Robert Eyre, a native of England, had some goods shipped from London to Virginia on the *James*. The utilitarian items he imported (cheese, salad oil, vinegar, sugar, soap, raisins, nails, gunpowder, and shot) suggest that he was then living in the colony. On February 28, 1628, Eyre, who was then in Virginia, proved the nuncupative will of Marmion Leake, who died aboard the *Samuel*, and he confirmed the court testimony of William Southey, a witness to Leake's will. In March 1629 Eyre was identified as the master of an indentured servant who lived in Edward Grindon's settlement, then part of the Treasurer's Plantation. During the late 1630s Eyre's name appeared in Lower Norfolk County's records several times, and in 1638 he was identified as a resident of the Elizabeth River, on whose south branch he patented some land in 1642. He also invested in some acreage on the south side of the Rappahannock River, on what was then Virginia's frontier. Eyre served on the assembly sessions held in 1645–1646, 1646, 1647–1648, and 1648 as a burgess for Lower Norfolk County. In February 1649 he announced that he intended to go to England and, in accord with the law, posted a notice on the courthouse door. He had returned by July 31, 1650, when he witnessed the will made by Richard Foster of the Elizabeth River. Robert Eyre died sometime prior to April 1651, at which time Elizabeth, his widow and administrator, was ordered to give one of the decedent's servants his freedom dues. By July 1651 Elizabeth Eyre had married John Custis II (LEO 25–27; Lower Norfolk County Book A:7, 11, 19, 92; B:60, 104a, 172, 184; C:4, 9, 23, 29, 40; PB 1:780; 2:159; SR 3482; VI&A 287).

F

William (Winster) Fairfax (Fierfax, Fairefax, Ffax): William Fairfax, a yeoman farmer and ancient planter who immigrated to Virginia in 1611 with his wife, Margery, built a house on a 12-acre parcel in the eastern end of Jamestown Island. When some Indians killed four people in the Fairfax household in 1617, Fairfax and his wife escaped harm because they were away from home. Fairfax patented his 12 acres in 1619 and in 1620 sold the acreage to the Rev. Richard Buck, rector of James City Parish. At that time the homestead contained two houses. During the March 1622 Indian attack, William Fairfax was killed at Ensign William Spence's house in Archer's Hope (VI&A 287–288). Wife Margery's fate is uncertain.

Fanny: On February 15, 1768, when an inventory was made of the late Richard Ambler's slaves on Jamestown Island and his leasehold in the Governor's Land, an enslaved girl named Fanny was listed and identified as Lydia's child. In 1769 Fanny was living on Jamestown Island and was included in the late Edward Ambler I's estate (York County Wills and Inventories 21:386–391; AMB-E).

Fanny: When an inventory was made in 1769 of Edward Ambler I's estate, an enslaved child named Fanny was living on the Governor's Land with her mother, Dinah (AMB-E).

John Farley (Farloe): In 1676 a man named Farley was executed at John Custis IV's Eastern Shore plantation, Arlington. Farley was described by Governor William Berkeley as one of Oliver Cromwell's soldiers who played an active role in Bacon's Rebellion. Berkeley added that John Farley and 40 men had tried to surprise him "at Accomack." On February 10, 1677, Berkeley issued a proclamation, noting that Farley's estate was not exempt from seizure (NEVILLE 61, 274; SR 660).

Thomas Farley (Fairley): Thomas Farley arrived in Jamestown on September 5, 1623. During the mid-1620s he and wife, Jane, and their daughter, Ann, were living in Archer's Hope, where he was a household head. In November 1625 Farley made arrangements to lease the late Ensign William Spence's property, which was in the same region. In

August 1626 Farley was fined for not attending church and for hunting hogs on the Sabbath. On at least one occasion, his neighbor Joseph Johnson threatened him with bodily harm because Farley's hogs had damaged Johnson's corn crop. In 1628 and 1630 Thomas Farley served as a burgess for territory that stretched from Archer's Hope to Martin's Hundred, and in 1632 he represented Archer's Hope. He was still alive in 1634. Farley was the son or brother of Roger Farley of Worcester, who died in 1622 (VI&A 289; LEO 7, 9–10; WITH 328–329).

Richard Farmar (Farmer): On March 9, 1677, Richard Farmar, an alleged supporter of the rebel Nathaniel Bacon, was put on trial at Green Spring plantation, Governor William Berkeley's home. He was found guilty and sentenced to execution (MCGC 456, 530). It is unclear whether his death sentence was carried out.

Henry Farmer (Farmor): On February 16, 1624, Henry Farmer was a servant in William Peirce's household in urban Jamestown (VI&A 289).

Richard Farmer: In February 1682 Richard Farmer was serving as Sir Henry Chicheley's clerk. His headright was used for land acquisitions on the lower side of the James River (HEN III:562; NUG II:83, 233).

Thomas Farmer: Thomas Farmer came to Virginia in 1616 and during the mid-1620s was living in Bermuda Hundred. He served as a burgess in the March 1630 session of the assembly, representing the settlers then residing on the College land in Henrico and in Bermuda Hundred (VI&A 289; LEO 9).

* * *

William Farrar (Ferrar, Ferrer) I: William Farrar I, a Virginia Company shareholder, came to Virginia in 1618 and established a plantation on the Appomattox River sometime prior to the March 1622 Indian attack. Afterward, he relocated to Jordan's Journey, a stronger and safer position, and moved into the home of Cisley Jordan, a young widow whose late husband's estate he was settling. The couple's living arrangements, termed "scandalous," resulted in a breach-of-promise suit, for she had promised to marry another. They eventually wed.

In March 1626 Farrar was named to the Council of State and later in the year was designated a commissioner of the monthly courts for the "Upper Parts," which convened at Jordan's Journey and Shirley Hundred; he served for several years. In March 1629 Farrar patented 100 acres of land on the Eastern Shore. In 1631, when he went to England to execute a real-estate transaction, he made reference to his wife, Cisley, and children Cisley II and William II, but failed to mention his son John. William Farrar I died in Virginia before June 11, 1637 (VI&A 290; STAN 31).

John Farrar (Ferrar, Ferrer): John, the youngest surviving son of William Farrar I and his wife, Cisley, probably was born around 1632 but before June 11, 1637. On October 1, 1649, John's older brother, William II, gave him a tenth of their late father's 2,000 acres in Henrico County. John Farrar outlived his brother, William II, and inherited some of his land. In February 1678 he deeded to the decedent's heirs the 200 acres he had been given in 1649. Farrar served as a burgess for Henrico County and attended the assembly sessions held in 1680–1682 and 1684 (VI&A 291; LEO 45, 47; DOR 1:929–930).

William Farrar (Ferrar, Ferrer) II: In 1631 when William Farrar I went to England to make a real-estate transaction, he mentioned his son, William II. Although his year of birth is uncertain, he probably was born in 1627. On June 27, 1637, the orphaned William Farrar II, as his late father's heir, patented 2,000 acres in Henrico County, adjoining what became known as Farrar (formerly Henricus) Island. On October 1, 1649, he gave part of that property to his brother, John. By 1655 William Farrar II had become a captain of the militia, and in 1657 he was serving as a Henrico County justice. He represented Henrico County in the assembly in 1660 and from 1661 to1676. He died in 1677 or 1678, having left some land to his younger brother, John (VI&A 291; LEO 36, 38; DOR 1:929).

* * *

Hubert Farrell: On April 7, 1674, Hubert Farrell was found guilty of slandering Tabitha, Thomas Bowler's wife, at William White's house in urban Jamestown. When the rebel Nathaniel Bacon's men attacked Jamestown on September 17, 1676, Captain Farrell, who was defending the capital city, was shot in the abdomen and died as a result of his wound. He owned some James City

County land adjoining acreage that was in the possession of William Drummond I (FOR I:11:42; PB 6:495; Stanard, "Some Colonial Records," 59; SR 6618a).

Ingram Farres: On January 24, 1629, Ingram Farres served on the jury that convened in Jamestown and tried William Reade for mortally wounding John Burrows (VI&A 291).

Moore (More) Fauntleroy (Fantelroy, Fantelary, Flantlaroy): Moore Fauntleroy, who was born in 1616, settled in Upper Norfolk (later Nansemond) County sometime prior to 1643, and in 1644 he patented 1,650 acres there. He represented Upper Norfolk in the assembly sessions that were held in 1644 and 1645, and in 1647–1648 he served as a burgess on behalf of the newly formed Nansemond County. He married Mrs. Margaret Underwood's daughter, and when Toby Smith executed a deed of gift in September 1647, he identified Fauntleroy as his brother-in-law. Smith also indicated that Fauntleroy then resided at The Forest, a Nansemond County plantation. In April 1648 Fauntleroy married Mary, the daughter of Thomas and Mary Peirsey Hill of Stanley Hundred. He began patenting land on the frontier, acquiring property along the Rappahannock River. In 1650 he laid claim to 8,850 acres in what was then Lancaster County and moved there, settling at Naylor's Hole, later the site of Tappahannock. He became a county justice and then a captain, major, and lieutenant colonel in the local militia. Fauntleroy served in 1651–1652, 1652, 1653, and 1656 as a burgess for Lancaster County, part of which was split off to form (Old) Rappahannock County. Over the years his name appeared frequently in Old Rappahannock's records, and he continued to acquire substantial quantities of land. One of his entrepreneurial efforts involved hiring a millwright from the Eastern Shore to construct a grist mill powered by oxen. In 1656 Fauntleroy clashed with John Edgecombe, who reportedly defamed him and his wife and children. As punishment, Edgecombe was made to apologize and post a bond guaranteeing his good behavior. In 1658 the king of the Rappahannock Indians confirmed an agreement that his predecessor had made with Colonel Moore Fauntleroy, authorizing him to use some land at Mangorick (Mangeright, Mangorite) and Morratico. Fauntleroy represented Old Rappahannock County in the assembly sessions held in 1659, 1660, and 1661–1662. He was dismissed from his seat at the March 1662 session because of what was considered unethical conduct. According to excerpts from assembly minutes that were entered into the records of Old Rappahannock County, Fauntleroy demanded some shell money (roanoke) from the king and Great Men of the Rappahannock Indians, a tributary tribe, and claimed that he had done so because they had refused to pay their annual tribute. After the Committee for Indian Affairs determined that Fauntleroy had lied, the assembly declared that he was ineligible to hold any civil or military office. At that time Fauntleroy had possession of 500 acres that was part of the land assigned to the Morraticund Indians. He died sometime prior to August 1663 while residing in Old Rappahannock County. An inventory of his estate was entered into Old Rappahannock County's records on July 9, 1664. Afterward, the widowed Mary Hill Fauntleroy married William Lloyd, a county justice who by 1680 had become a burgess (LEO 22–23, 26, 28–31, 33, 35–36, 39; Lancaster County Deeds &c. Book 2 [1652–1657]:3, 243–244, 267; Deeds and Wills 1654–1661:158; Orders 1656–1666:7; Old Rappahannock County Deeds and Wills 1656–1664:3, 5, 9, 22–24, 26–27, 188–191; Deeds and Wills 1665–1677:68–69; 1677–1682:279–280; Deeds, Wills, Inventories &c. 1663–1668:35; Northumberland County Deeds, Wills &c. 1661–1662:18; HEN II:35–36; PB 2:6, 8, 229–232; MCGC 280, 297, 322, 327, 338; DOR 2:806–807).

George Fawdon (Fadom, Shedam, Fawdowne): On November 1, 1624, George Fawdon informed the General Court that in 1624 he had transcribed John Phillimore's nuncupative will. He and the others who testified about the will were residents of Jamestown Island or the Neck O'Land. On February 8, 1628, Fawdon and two other men received permission to move to Warresqueak, and on June 26, 1635, he patented some land on the Nansemond River, adjacent to Richard Bennett's property. He served as James Rocke's attorney and during the 1640s witnessed a number of deeds and other legal documents for residents of Isle of Wight (formerly Warresqueak). Major George Fawdon served as an Isle of Wight burgess in 1646 and 1653, and in 1654 he gave 100 acres to the son of a fellow burgess, John George. In 1654 Fawdon signed a marriage contract with Ann Smith, Colonel Nathaniel Bacon's stepdaughter, agreeing to give her 1,500 acres on the banks of the James River in Isle of Wight County. The young couple agreed not to dispose of the land without the consent of Colonel Bacon and his wife, Ann. George Fawdon died sometime prior to July 9, 1655 (VI&A 292;

LEO 25, 31; Isle of Wight County Deeds, Wills, & Guardian Accounts Book A:88, 92).

* * *

[No First Name] Felgate (Fellgate): On January 14, 1628, Captain Felgate was fined for failing to appear before the General Court in Jamestown despite being summoned by the provost marshal (VI&A 293). It is uncertain which Captain Felgate (Robert or Tobias) disregarded the summons.

Robert Felgate (Fellgate): Robert Felgate, a mariner, arrived in Bermuda in November 1619, having survived a hurricane. According to Captain John Smith, he was Bermuda governor Nathaniel Butler's lieutenant general, and in 1620 he served on Bermuda's Council of State and held the rank of captain. Felgate returned to England but took a ship to Virginia in 1627 and settled there. In October 1629, when the Virginia assembly convened, Robert Felgate served as a burgess for the plantations on the "other side of the water," in what is now Surry County. He was returned to the assembly in March 1630 but moved downstream to Warresqueak, where he served as a commissioner of the monthly court. In 1632 Robert Felgate patented 350 acres of land at Chiskiack, acreage that fronted on the York River and abutted west on Kings Creek. He was one of the first planters to seat land on the York River frontier. His brother, Toby, a mariner, patented some adjacent land. The Felgate brothers' landholdings formed the core of what later became known as Ringfield plantation. In 1633 Captain Robert Felgate began serving as a justice, and on two or more occasions the county court convened in his home. After the death of his wife, Margaret, he married John Adkins' wife, Sibella (Isabella). In August 1637 Felgate patented 250 acres of new land in Chiskiack, most likely the additional acreage to which he was entitled once he had seated his original 350 acres. Then, in March 1639 he acquired another 400 acres, which gave him 1,000 acres in all. When Robert Felgate made his will on September 30, 1644, he left life-rights in his estate to his widow, Sibella, whom he designated his executrix. After her death Felgate's plantation in Virginia was to go to his grandson Thomas Newton, who was then living in Holland. The testator named another grandson, Thomas Burton, as reversionary heir but specified that if Newton and Burton failed to live, his property should go to the children of his brother, William Felgate. Robert Felgate died prior to November 5,

1646, by which time his widow had married George Beech. She later wed Nicholas Martiau (VI&A 293; LEO 8–9; NUG I:14–15, 71, 91, 121, 200; York County Deeds, Orders, Wills 1 [1633–1657]:267; 3 [1657–1662]:183; 2 [1691–1694]:267; DOR 2:504).

Tobias (Toby) Felgate (Fellgate): In July 1619 the Society of Berkeley Hundred's investors hired Tobias Felgate, an experienced mariner from Ratcliffe, England, to take their settlers to Virginia. He returned to the colony in 1622 as master of the *James* of London. In 1623 Felgate rebutted Bermuda Governor Nathaniel Butler's allegations about conditions in Virginia, stating that he had firsthand knowledge of the colony and had been there five times. In November 1626 he brought a shipment of goods to the colony on the *James*, commodities that London merchant Edward Bennett had sent to Richard Bennett. By February 1628 Felgate had married the former Elizabeth Fuller, who had outlived Jeremiah Clements I and merchant Ralph Hamor, both of whom had been residents of urban Jamestown. Felgate continued to ply the Atlantic but his wife, Elizabeth, died. On March 30, 1630, he wed Sarah Price, who lived in England. They produced a son, William, and a daughter, Sarah II. In 1632 Tobias Felgate patented 150 acres of land at Chiskiack. He became gravely ill and on December 24, 1634, he made a nuncupative will, designating his wife Sarah as his executrix and naming their children as his primary beneficiaries (VI&A 293–294).

* * *

Henry Fell: Henry Fell, an Oxford University student from Christchurch in Oxford, arrived in Jamestown on September 12, 1623, aboard the *Bonny Bess*. He died there sometime prior to February 16, 1624 (VI&A 294).

John Fenly (Fenley): John Fenly, one of Arthur Allen II's servants, was dispatched from Jamestown to Swann's Point on July 3, 1677 (Bruce, "Bacon's Men in Surry," 372). He may have been the John Fenley of Surry who died in 1702, leaving his widow, Ann, and son, Robert Fenley, as his heirs (Surry County Deeds, Wills, Etc. 5 [1694–1709]:268).

Francis Fenton: In November 1628 Francis Fenton and John Southern of Jamestown appeared before the General Court, where they proved the will of Thomas Gregory, purser of the *Saker* (VI&A 295).

Robert Fenton: Robert Fenton, one of the first Jamestown colonists, arrived in 1607. He was still alive in 1608 and coauthored a verse that Captain John Smith included in his *General History* (VI&A 295).

Richard Fetherstone (Featherstone): Richard Fetherstone, a gentleman, came to Virginia in January 1608 in the 1st Supply of Jamestown colonists. He became mortally ill while visiting the Rappahannock River basin and was buried at a site Captain John Smith called Featherstone's Bay (VI&A 296).

* * *

Michael Fettiplace (Phettiplace): Michael Fettiplace, a gentleman, arrived in Jamestown in January 1608 in the 1st Supply of new settlers. In 1620 Captain John Smith identified him as a Virginia Company investor and credited him and his brother, William, with coauthoring a verse that lauded Smith (VI&A 296).

William Fettiplace (Phettiplace): In January 1608 William Fettiplace, a gentleman and the brother of Michael Fettiplace, arrived in Jamestown in the 1st Supply of new colonists. Captain John Smith mentioned William Fettiplace in his account of New England. In 1622 Virginia Company officials identified him as an ancient planter when they awarded him a patent for 100 acres in exchange for his investment in the company (VI&A 296).

* * *

Peter Field (Feild): On October 21, 1678, Major Peter Field married Judith, the daughter of Henry and Judith Soane and the widow of Henry Randolph I, deceased in 1673. Field's name began appearing in Henrico County records in 1678, and in 1681 he was identified as a local resident. One of the pieces of land he owned was the "saw mill tract" on Swift Creek. In 1689 he added to his holdings in that vicinity, acquiring some acreage that had belonged to the family of wife Judith's late husband. Later, when Field resold the property, Judith relinquished her dower share. In 1681 Peter Field was among the men Charles City County's justices asked to conduct an audit, and a year later he was appointed a Henrico County justice and the county's high sheriff. Field, as guardian of his stepson, Henry Randolph II, brought suit against two men who had encroached upon the orphan's land. In October

1687 he was identified as a resident of Varina Parish when he patented 483 acres on the east side of Swift Creek in what was then Henrico (but later Chesterfield) County, adding to his acreage in that vicinity in April 1690. He also purchased a half-acre lot in Henrico County's planned town at Varina. Captain Field was elected to the assembly in 1688 and 1693, and in 1694 he commenced serving as Henrico County's coroner. On April 15, 1693, he and Captain Francis Eppes delivered several Henrico County record books to clerk of court James Cocke. When testifying in court in August 1692, he indicated that he was age 45; however, in October 1694 he stated that he was age 46 and his wife, Judith, said that she was then 48. Judith and Peter Field sold some land she had inherited from her late husband, Henry Randolph I, and witnessed the will that her brother, John Soane, made on December 16, 1695. Field also sold some of his own land on the south side of Swift Creek and had the "saw mill tract" partitioned so that his stepson would receive a share of the land. In June 1699 Field was identified as a major in the Henrico County militia, and a year later he again served as county coroner. On September 3, 1701, Major Field sent a letter to the governor about two "foreign" Indians who had been captured near Swift Creek. Afterward, the natives were sent to Williamsburg and referred to the Council of State, which decided that the assembly should determine the Indians' fate. In 1702 Field repurchased some land he had sold to his brother-in-law in 1698. He was a Henrico County justice when the court convened at Varina in June 1705, and he was still in possession of his land on Swift Creek in December 1706. On July 24, 1707, Major Peter Field died in St. Peter's Parish, which then straddled the Chickahominy River and formed part of the dividing line between Henrico and New Kent counties; he was buried on July 29th. His 1707 will, which was mentioned in subsequent land transactions and named his daughters as heirs, seems to have been lost or destroyed. In March 1708 Field's daughter Mary was identified as the wife of Thomas Jefferson of Henrico County, and Field, by then deceased, was said to have been "late of New Kent County." By 1711 Field's daughter Martha had married John Archer of Henrico County (LEO 49, 52; PB 7:610; 8:59; DOR 1:379; 2:183; Charles City County Orders 1664–1665:12; Henrico County Wills, Deeds, Etc. 1677–1692:143, 162, 168, 219, 243, 428, 501; Wills and Deeds 1688–1697:59, 73, 248, 309, 334, 387, 425, 430, 432, 518–519, 522, 581; Wills and Deeds 1697–1704:145, 201, 276, 282, 290, 439; Deeds 1706–1709:11; Wills and Deeds 1710–1714:92, 286; Wills and Deeds 1725–1737:307, 402; Court Orders 1678–1693:50, 150; EJC 1:443; 2:183; VAL IV:2303; SPVB 429).

Thomas Field: Thomas Field, an apothecary, arrived in Virginia in 1608 in the 2nd Supply of new colonists and lived in Jamestown (VI&A 297).

Henry Filmer: In March 1643 Henry Filmer was identified as a burgess for James City. He probably represented James City County rather than the capital city, because a Mr. Filmer then owned land on the east side of the Chickahominy River, within the county's boundaries. By June 1647 Henry Filmer had begun serving as a Warwick County justice. He became a burgess and from 1666 to 1676 attended the assembly on behalf of Warwick County. Filmer's wife, Elizabeth, when testifying in court in August 1650, indicated that she was age 49. In October 1676 Henry Filmer patented 360 acres in Warwick County, acreage that had formerly belonged to Anthony Barham, a resident of Mulberry Island (STAN 63; HEN I:239; LEO 21, 40; NUG I:149; PB 6:481; DUNN 24, 164).

Samuel Filmer (Filmore): Samuel Filmer of East Sutton in Kent, England, was a cousin of Frances Culpeper, who successively married Samuel Stephens, Sir William Berkeley, and Philip Ludwell I. Filmer made his will on July 17, 1667, which was proved on May 28, 1670. Probate officials noted that he had lived in Virginia but died in England (EEAC 22; SR 3544).

Henry Finch: On October 29, 1630, Henry, Sir John Finch's brother, was designated Secretary of the Colony and member of the Council of State. He retained both positions during 1632 and much of 1633, but was turned out of office around December 7th (VI&A 297; STAN 32; LEO xx).

Thomas Finch: Thomas Finch died sometime prior to April 14, 1623. He was described as the "brother" (probably a brother-in-law, stepbrother, or half-brother) of Mr. Bland and Christopher Davison, who were residents of Jamestown (VI&A 297).

Joseph Firth: On April 24, 1687, Joseph Firth's horse was pressed into service in Jamestown (York County Deeds, Orders, Wills 1687–1691:116).

Richard Firth: Richard Firth, a gentleman and investor in the Virginia Company, arrived in Virginia in 1607 and was one of the first Jamestown colonists (VI&A 298).

Samuel Firth: Samuel Firth, a merchant who by 1677 was conducting business in Surry County, was residing in urban Jamestown in July 1685 on the late Colonel Thomas Swann's property (Surry County Order Book 1671–1691:159). Firth, who does not seem to have owned land on Jamestown Island, probably used the buildings on Colonel Swann's tavern lot as a domestic complex, commercial establishment, or both. It is uncertain how long Firth was associated with the property.

Mrs. [First Name Unknown] Fisher: On September 18, 1626, the justices of the General Court were informed that on August 26th Mrs. Fisher was seen staggering drunkenly near Mrs. Henry Southey's house on Jamestown Island (VI&A 298). She may have been the widow of Thomas Fisher, who died in Jamestown between April 1623 and February 16, 1624 (VI&A 300).

Edward Fisher: During the mid-1620s Edward Fisher, his wife, Sarah, her six-year-old son, Edward Kidall, and another child were living on the mainland just west of Jamestown Island. Richard Stephens, a Jamestown merchant, hired Fisher to go on a 30-day trading voyage in his pinnace but failed to compensate him. As a result, Fisher took Stephens to court. In July 1631 Edward Fisher of Jamestown was among the planters sending a petition to England requesting relief from the customs fees then being levied on tobacco (VI&A 299).

Thomas Fisher: Thomas Fisher died in Jamestown sometime after April 1623 but before February 16, 1624 (VI&A 300).

William Fisher: By 1668 William Fisher, an English merchant, had begun sending ships to Virginia, often transporting cloth from Gloucestershire and returning with tobacco. He was living on the island of Tercera in 1675 when he filed a lawsuit claiming that a ship he had dispatched to Spain went instead to Newfoundland and then to Virginia's Eastern Shore, where it wrecked. According to Fisher his goods were recovered but Governor Berkeley seized them. Fisher moved to Virginia around 1676, established a base of operations in Jamestown, and died. Official records reveal that during 1680 the widowed Mrs. Susanne Fisher hosted one or more assembly meetings in her home, which was located on a half-acre waterfront lot in urban Jamestown. Between June 1680 and May 25, 1681, she married William Armiger, a mariner who traded extensively in the Northern Neck. After the couple wed, government officials continued to meet in their home. On January 11, 1682, Armiger went to court in an attempt to recover some funds that a Westmoreland County man, James Gaylard, owed to William Fisher's estate. Secretary of the Colony Nicholas Spencer represented the Armigers when the case was aired in the Westmoreland County court. William Armiger eventually was credited with his wife's lot in Jamestown. The couple seemingly had no heirs, for after William's death his property escheated to the Crown (SR 668, 3793b, 4194, 4564, 5588, 5762, 8857, 10031, 10722, 10919; Lancaster County Order Book 1680–1687:70; JHB 1660–1693:119; Westmoreland County Order Book 1676–1689:206, 221).

Joseph Fitch: Joseph Fitch, an apothecary, was sent to Virginia in 1621 by the Company of Mercers and accompanied Dr. John Pott, who resided in urban Jamestown. Fitch was killed at Falling Creek during the March 1622 Indian attack (VI&A 300).

Mathew Fitch (Fytch): Mathew Fitch, a mariner, was one of the first Jamestown colonists. On June 13, 1607, he was mortally wounded in Jamestown when he was shot in the chest by Indians (VI&A 300).

John Fitchett: John Fitchett immigrated to Virginia sometime prior to November 11, 1642, and secured a 21-year lease for a 32-acre parcel in the Governor's Land. In June 1654 he obtained an 8½-acre leasehold on the mainland, near the isthmus that led to Jamestown Island. Sometime prior to September 1655 he purchased the Glasshouse tract from Anthony Coleman's heirs and resold it to John Phipps and William Harris of urban Jamestown. On June 8, 1660, Fitchett patented a lot on Back Street in urban Jamestown. He renewed his claim on October 18, 1662, which suggests that his lot was still undeveloped. A few months later, when Robert Castle patented a waterfront lot in Jamestown, reference was made to Mr. Fitchett's house, which was nearby. In 1671 John Fitchett and three other men obtained a patent for 2,600 acres in what became Stafford County. Simultaneously, he and Thomas Gully received a patent for some land on Dragon Run, in what became King and Queen County. He may have had a son or kinsman who moved to Surry County, for on December 16, 1697, a John Fitchett witnessed George Foster's will. In July 1720 Jamestown lot owner William Browne (who from 1682 to 1685 was in possession of the easternmost bays of a long row house on Back Street) presented an inventory of the late John Fitchett's estate to the justices of Surry County court (PB 1:853; 3:367; 4:423; 5:272; NUG I:139, 154, 232, 313, 399; AMB 59, 78; Surry County Will Book 5:148; 7:274; MCGC 246, 270).

Robert Fitt (Fitts): Robert Fitt was in Virginia by November 1623, when he witnessed Thomas Harralde's will. During the mid-1620s he and his wife, Ann (Anne), were living in the rural part of Jamestown Island. In 1625 he was fined for public drunkenness in the same court session in which he testified against another man. On September 17, 1627, the Fitts, who had moved to Archer's Hope, were obliged to post a bond guaranteeing that they would not disturb the peace by quarreling with their neighbors. In 1628 Robert Fitt and another man commenced leasing 100 acres in Archer's Hope. Later in the year he and wife Ann sent a petition to England that stated they had been in Virginia for 14 years. If so, they would have been ancient planters (VI&A 301).

William Fitzhugh I: In 1656 William Fitzhugh, an attorney and militia commander, was designated a justice of Stafford County's monthly court. In 1679 he and Charles Brent were responsible for building a stronghold near the head of the Potomac River, where a garrison of men would serve as a defense against hostile Indians. As time went on, Fitzhugh became an immensely successful planter who between 1690 and 1696 secured titles to vast quantities of land on the fringes of the colony's frontier, particularly in Westmoreland, Stafford, and Old Rappahannock counties. One of his grants near the head of the Potomac River contained 21,996 acres. Fitzhugh leased his acreage to tenants, simultaneously securing his patents and reaping a profit. Some of the long-term rental agreements he made involved crop-sharing. Around 1674 he executed a marriage contract with Sarah, the eldest daughter of Thomas and Rose Garrard (Gerrard) of Lower Machodoc in Westmoreland County. Fitzhugh, who lived on a plantation in King George County, served as a burgess for Stafford County and attended the assembly sessions held in 1677, 1679, 1680–1682, 1684, and 1693. When Durand de Dauphine visited Virginia in 1686–1687, he spent time at Colonel Fitzhugh's home and spoke of his hospitality. In 1690, while Fitzhugh held the rank of lieutenant colonel and served as a justice of Stafford County's court, he got into a heated argument with the Rev. John Waugh, who called him a "Papist Rogue." Waugh's behavior was reported to

the General Court, which ordered him to apologize publicly. Later Waugh sold Fitzhugh two parcels of land in what became Richmond County. Early in 1700 Fitzhugh, as agent and attorney of the Northern Neck Proprietors, sued an Essex County man. When Fitzhugh was preparing to set sail for England on April 9, 1700, he prepared his will and named as heirs his wife, Sarah, and sons William II, Henry, John, Thomas, and George. By that time the testator's daughter, Rosamond, the wife of Willoughby Allerton, was dead. In Fitzhugh's absence, his representative continued the suits Fitzhugh had initiated on behalf of the proprietors. William Fitzhugh died sometime prior to December 10, 1701, when his will was proved. He reportedly had amassed approximately 54,000 acres of land in Virginia and Maryland (LEO 42–44, 46–47, 53; Stafford County Record Book 1686–1693:17a–18a, 30–31, 132–133a, 156a, 169a; 1699–1709:92–103; Old Rappahannock County Order Book 1683–1686:80; NN 1:11–14; 2:14–16, 30–31, 96–97, 141–142, 171–172, 232–233, 250–252, 282–283; Lancaster County Order Book 1680–1686:106; Essex County Order Book 1699–1702:41, 45, 122,129; Richmond County Deed Book 1 [1692–1693]:24–26, 63–69; Westmoreland County Deeds, Patents &c. 1665–1677:200–201, 205a–207; HEN 2:433; DAUPHINE 156, 158–159).

George Fitz-Jeffry (Fitzjefferys, Fitzjeffries, Fitzjeffreys): George Fitz-Jeffry, a gentleman, arrived in Jamestown on September 12, 1623. He and a Mr. Roper (probably Thomas Roper) were entitled to a patent from the Virginia Company because they were taking 100 people to the colony. Thomas Roper, who died in Jamestown sometime prior to February 16, 1624, made a will in which he asked George Fitz-Jeffry to take custody of his Virginia tobacco (VI&A 302).

William Fitz-Jeffry (Fitz-Jefferys): William Fitz-Jeffry, a gentleman, arrived in Jamestown on September 12, 1623, and died there sometime prior to February 16, 1624 (VI&A 302).

Mrs. Elizabeth Fleet: Mrs. Elizabeth Fleet had a half-acre lot in urban Jamestown. On August 1, 1655, the lot was repatented by Thomas Hunt (PB 3:367; NUG I:313, 468).

Henry Fleet (Fleete) I: Henry Fleet I, who came to Virginia around 1621, was captured by the Indians in 1623 while on a trading expedition to the Potomac River. The natives detained him for five years, during which time he learned their language and gained an understanding of their way of life. In March 1628 Fleet patented some land on the Eastern Shore near Old Plantation Creek. On a trip to England, he formed a connection with William Claiborne and his Kent Island associates, and returned to Virginia as master of one of their vessels. Fleet received a grant of 4,000 acres on the St. George's River, property he seated and then sold. He returned to Virginia and served as an official interpreter, negotiating a treaty with the Indians in 1646. Fleet went on to patent more than 13,000 acres in the Northern Neck. He also served as a Lancaster County burgess, court justice, and lieutenant colonel of militia. His name appeared frequently in local court records, alternately as a plaintiff or defendant in lawsuits. He died between April 12, 1660, and May 8, 1661, leaving a widow, Sarah, who afterward married Colonel John Walker II of Gloucester County. Lieutenant Colonel Fleet also left a son, Henry Fleet II, of Richmond County (VI&A 302; LEO 30; DOR 1:970–972; Northumberland County Record Book 1658–1662:36; Order Book 1652–1665:165, 240; Lancaster County Order Book 1652–1657:98; 1657–1666:1, 119, 143, 193; Richmond County Deed Book 1 [1692–1693]:108–112; Westmoreland County Deeds, Wills &c 1661–1662:5).

George Fletcher: George Fletcher came to Virginia sometime prior to 1652. In 1634 he was identified as a merchant in Cheshire, England, when he paid customs on goods that he had sent to the colony. On May 9, 1636, he testified in a chancery case involving London merchants Edward Bennett and Jonas Hopkins, who had shipped goods to Virginia on the *Revenge*. Fletcher said that although the ship had belonged to his late father, John Fletcher, he had claimed neither a share of the ship nor its cargo. On July 21, 1638, George Fletcher acknowledged that he had been present when Lord Baltimore received a letter from the king. In April 1652 Fletcher, who was then living in Virginia, took an oath of allegiance, swearing to uphold the Commonwealth government. Later in the year he was named a justice of the Northumberland County court and a lieutenant colonel in the local militia. He was supposed to represent Northumberland County in the assembly sessions of 1652 and 1653 but died between January 20, 1653, and November 21, 1653 (LEO 29, 31; Northumberland County Deeds and Orders 1650–1652:74, 76; Wills, Inventories &c. 1652–1658:21; Record Book 1662–1666:120; Order Book 1652–1665:1, 15, 41; SR 660, 10485, 10917, 10918).

* * *

Richard Flint (Flynt) I: Richard Flint I patented some acreage in Northumberland County in 1651, and almost immediately his name began appearing in local court records. By 1657 Flint, who was then residing on a 480-acre plantation at Cherry Point, had become clerk of Northumberland County's monthly court, a post he held for several years. As time went on, Flint added to the amount of real estate under his control, sometimes acquiring acreage and quickly reselling it. Between 1657 and 1664 he patented land on the Yeocomoco River and on Northumberland County's Mattaponi River. He also acquired some acreage between the Corotoman and Morratico rivers. In 1660 Flint was paid for apprehending David Cuffin, who had "entertained Quakers in his House contrary to the Law." Flint, who had outlived his wife, Dorothy, and had become very ill, made his will in 1664. He named as his principal heir his son Richard II, and divided the rest of his estate between sons Thomas and Peter and daughter Mary, then the wife of Thomas Smyth. Although the date of Richard Flint I's death is uncertain, he died sometime prior to October 10, 1664, and his will was proved on October 20th. An inventory of his estate indicates that he was a member of the upper middle class. In 1671 Flint's executors decided that his son Thomas would serve a six-year apprenticeship with Thomas White, a carpenter. The settlement of the late Richard Flint I's estate dragged on for many years, and in March 1694 his sons Thomas and Peter brought suit against their late father's executors, continuing litigation they had initiated in December 1681 (PB 2:317; 4:193; 5:434; NN Grants 2:69–70; Northumberland County Deeds and Orders 1650–1652:60, 82, 84; Wills, Inventories &c. 1652–1658:93, 146; Record Book 1658–1662:26, 58, 78; 1662–1666:100, 133, 172; Order Book 1652–1665:259, 395, 420, 439; 1666–1678:35, 111; 1678–1698:116; Westmoreland County Deeds, Wills, Patents &c. 1653–1659:101a; Deeds, Wills &c 1661–1662:18a).

Richard Flint (Flynt) II: In 1664 Richard Flint II, his father's namesake and principal heir, inherited Richard Flint I's plantation at Cherry Point in Northumberland County. He also received some land in Lancaster County, some livestock, and a gold signet ring. In 1668, when Flint testified before the justices of Northumberland County's monthly court, he held the rank of captain in the local militia. Like many of his contemporaries, he appeared in court from time to time to participate in lawsuits or perform civic duties. In 1677 he and another man sued John Walters and attached property, which consisted of a mare and a sloop and its rigging. Walters countersued, insisting that he had repaid his debt, and succeeded in recovering his sailing vessel. Flint was appointed the county's undersheriff in 1681, and in 1693 he and Richard Rodgers were elected to the assembly, representing Northumberland County. However, John Downing and William Jones contested the election, and when another one was held, they were chosen to replace Flint and Rodgers. In 1699 Richard Flint II bought some acreage on Totusky Creek in Richmond County (LEO 52; Northumberland County Record Book 1662–1666:133; Order Book 1666–1678:35, 89, 164, 258, 296, 322, 331, 337; 1678–1698:68, 127, 209, 333; Lancaster County Order Book 1686–1696:187; Richmond County 3 [1695–1704]:61–63).

* * *

Thomas Flint (Flynt): Thomas Flint came to Virginia in 1618 and during the mid-1620s lived at Buckroe in Elizabeth City. Later, he purchased and forfeited some land on the east side of the Hampton River, part of the defunct Virginia Company's acreage. During 1627 he took legal possession of 50 acres at Fox Hill, and in September 1628 he patented but quickly sold a large tract of land on the south side of the Warwick River in Stanley Hundred. In November 1628 Flint, whose wife, Mary, accused him of behaving lewdly with her stepdaughter, Dorothy Beheathland, was fined for contempt for treating the governor disrespectfully and was stripped of his rank as lieutenant. Even so, Flint rose in prominence and by October 1629 was serving as a burgess for the Warwick River area. In 1632 he represented the territory between Skiff's Creek and Saxon's Gaol, below Mulberry Island, and in 1633 he was the burgess for Denbigh and Stanley Hundred. He also was named a commissioner of the Warwick River monthly court. Flint represented Warwick County in the assembly sessions held in 1640, 1643, and 1647–1648. Mrs. Mary Flint outlived her husband, Thomas, and was still alive in April 1651 (VI&A 303; LEO 8–12, 18, 21, 26; DUNN 170–171).

John Flood (Flud, Fludd, Floyd): John Flood, an ancient planter, came to Virginia in 1610, and in January 1625 he and his wife, Margaret, and their son, William, were living at Jordan's Journey in what became Prince George County. He was a former servant to "Captain Whittakers," probably Isaac or Jabez Whittaker, who were Virginia Company employees. In March 1630 Flood

was Flowerdew Hundred's burgess, and in 1632 he represented the settlers living at Flowerdew, Westover, and Weyanoke. In May 1638 he patented 2,100 acres of land on the lower side of the James River. As time went on, Flood continued to acquire land on both sides of the James, and in 1640 he served as a Charles City County justice. In March 1643 and 1645 Captain Flood served as a burgess for James City County, which then included what later became Surry County. He was returned to office in 1652 and 1655–1656, representing Surry County. He was involved in Indian trade, and when a treaty was negotiated in 1646, he served as an official interpreter. Under the terms of the treaty, Colonel Flood's plantation on the lower side of the James River was one of the checkpoints through which Indians could enter the colonized area. John Flood died in 1658 (VI&A 305; LEO 9–10, 21, 24, 29, 33).

George Flower: George Flower, a gentleman who died of a "swelling," came to Virginia in 1607 and was one of the first Jamestown settlers (VI&A 307).

Thomas Follis: In January 1641 Thomas Follis served as James City's burgess (STAN 61; LEO 20). It is very likely that he represented James City County, not Jamestown, for his name is not associated with property in the capital city. Follis may have resided on the lower side of the James River, in what by 1652 had become Surry County.

John Fontaine: John Fontaine, a French Huguenot, set sail for Virginia in 1715 and stayed for four years, chronicling his visit. When he accompanied Lt. Governor Alexander Spotswood on a visit to Jamestown on April 13, 1716, they rode in a chaise and then transferred to a ferry that took them across the James River. Fontaine said that in 1716 Jamestown "chiefly consists in a church, a Court House, and three or four brick houses" and that it had formerly been the seat of government. He added that it had once been defended by "a small rampart with embrasures" that are "all gone to ruin" (FONT 10–11, 90).

Joshua Foote: In 1629 Joshua Foote, an English ironmonger, and his business partner, Richard Nicholas, agreed to supply ironware to Governor John Harvey for sale in the colony. In 1635 and 1636 Foote claimed that Harvey owed him £45 pounds and indicated that he had failed to pay for the ironware Foote had supplied (SAIN 1:225; CO 1/9 f 11).

Christopher Ford: Sometime prior to February 6, 1745, Christopher Ford came into possession of Edward Jaquelin's 122-acre leasehold in the Governor's Land. On November 6, 1756, he conveyed it to Thomas Holt (LEE MS167 b 88).

Richard Ford: On March 1660 Richard Ford began serving as a burgess for James City and probably represented James City County, not the capital city. He may have been the same individual who in October 1652 identified himself as a 38-year-old London merchant involved in trade to Virginia (STAN 73; SR 4016; LEO 36). Ford would have been eligible to serve in the assembly if he was married to a property owner in Jamestown or James City County.

Robert Ford: Robert Ford, a gentleman, came to Virginia in 1607 and was one of the first Jamestown colonists. He was clerk of the council in late December 1608 (VI&A 308).

Mr. and Mrs. Thomas Forest: Thomas Forest, a gentleman and Virginia Company investor, arrived in Jamestown in 1608 in the 2nd Supply of new colonists. He was accompanied by his wife and her maid, Anne Burras, Virginia's first female settlers (VI&A 308).

Thomas Fossett (Fawcett, Fausett): Thomas Fossett, perhaps one of Captain John Berkeley's men at the Virginia Company's ironworks, became ill with dropsy while living at Falling Creek. Afterward, he moved to Weyanoke. In 1624 he and his wife, Ann, were living on West and Shirley Hundred (Eppes) Island. In 1629 and 1630 he served as a burgess for Martin's Hundred. When John Creed of Martin's Hundred made his will in 1633, he identified Thomas Fossett as one of his masters and designated him as executor. He nominated Fossett's wife, Ann, as his administrator, noting that she was then in Virginia, thereby implying that her husband was not (VI&A 309; LEO 8–9).

Christopher Foster: On September 4, 1677, Christopher Foster of Surry County acknowledged that he was indebted to George Marable II, the owner of a waterfront lot in urban Jamestown (Surry County Order Book 1671–1691:156).

John Foster: On February 16, 1624, John Foster was an indentured servant living in Sir George Yeardley's household in urban Jamestown (VI&A 309).

Joseph Foster I: Joseph Foster I, an active member of St. Peter's Parish, served as a churchwarden, processioner, and vestryman, sometimes hosting vestry meetings in his home. He and his wife, Elizabeth I, had their daughter, Elizabeth II, baptized in 1689 and during the 1690s saw that their son, Joseph II, received the sacrament. Joseph Foster I served as New Kent County burgess and attended the assembly sessions held in 1684, 1688, 1695–1696, and 1702. He held the rank of lieutenant colonel in the New Kent County militia and was still serving as a justice in 1726. In 1701 he was among those responsible for overseeing the construction of a new parish church. In 1704 Foster paid quitrent on 800 acres in New Kent County. He was appointed New Kent County's sheriff in April 1709 and was reappointed in April 1711. In 1714 he was one of three men who served as county coroner. In 1735 a Joseph Foster patented 938 acres in what was then Hanover County but formerly had been New Kent (LEO 47, 49, 54; PB 16:286; SMITH 33; DES 4, 5, 10, 16, 26, 37, 165, 248; SPVB 7, 20, 34, 74, 81, 262, 355–356).

Richard Foster (Forster): Richard Foster began serving as an attorney in 1648 and in June 1649 became constable for the eastern shore of the Lynnhaven River, in what was then Lower Norfolk County. In November 1650 he was awarded a headright certificate for 250 acres because he had paid for his own transportation and that of his wife and daughter, who were both named Dorcas, and two servants. Foster patented 250 acres at the head of Broad Creek in November 1653 and repatented his land in March 1662. In 1655 he laid claim to 200 acres on the Severn River, a tributary of Mobjack Bay, repatenting his acreage in the early 1660s. By that time he had begun serving as a court justice in Lower Norfolk County. Surviving court records suggest that Foster was a merchant who imported cloth, hats, and shoes from mercantile firms in London. The year of Foster's death is uncertain. Burgess Richard Foster, who represented Lower Norfolk County in 1656 and 1658, may have been a kinsman of the Richard Foster of Lower Norfolk County's Elizabeth River who went to England around 1643 and in 1650 made bequests to his stepchildren, the offspring of Roger Williams and John Carraway (LEO 33, 34; Lower Norfolk County Book A:47, 104, 310, 312; B:78, 118, 122a, 155, 160, 188a; Wills, Deeds, Orders D [1656–1666]:340; PB 3:49, 336; 5:169, 262; SR 4201b, 5586, 5590, 5726).

William Foster: On March 20, 1701, William Foster of Surry County was keeper of the ferry that ran from Grays Creek to Jamestown (Surry County Order Book 1691–1713:361).

* * *

Gerrard (Gerard) Foulke (Fowke): In April 1655 Gerrard Foulke, who identified himself as a Westmoreland County merchant and lived on Potomac Creek, was appointed a justice in the county court. Over the next decade he patented literally thousands of acres in the Northern Neck, occasionally co-investing with others. On March 1658 he and Henry Corbin patented 3,000 acres. He then laid claim to 3,650 acres on Potomac Creek and 1,680 acres in Stafford County on the Rappahannock River, near the Doeg Indians' town. Finally, in October 1665 he acquired 1,050 acres in Northumberland County, on Chotanck Creek, and another 925 acres adjacent to Giles Brent's land. In 1658 Gerrard Foulke was given the task of arbitrating a dispute between Captain Giles Brent and the Doeg Indians, who were accused of killing some of Brent's cattle. Although the Indians denied any wrongdoing, they indicated that they had given Brent some roanoke (shell money) and beaver. Foulke sent a note to Brent asking him to discuss the matter, but he refused to talk and suggested ending the peace treaty with the Doegs. Foulke served as an attorney in 1656, representing London merchant Thomas Rowse. In May 1660 Gerrard Foulke and his brother, Thomas, both of whom were residents of Westmoreland County, signed a partnership agreement, merging all of their real and personal estate for seven years. At Thomas's death, which occurred prior to June 24, 1663, Gerrard inherited two-thirds of his estate and was named executor. In 1663 Colonel Gerrard Fowke served as a burgess for Westmoreland County. He was returned to the assembly in 1665, replacing Valentine Peyton, who died shortly after the 1664 session (LEO 40; Westmoreland County Deeds, Wills, Patents &c. 1653–1659:32, 36, 38, 66, 110; Deeds, Wills &c. 1661–1662:33, 51–51a; Deeds and Wills No. 1 [1653–1671]:197; Orders 1662–1664:17a; PB 4:365; 5:38, 260, 365, 505).

Thomas Foulke (Fowke): In June 1654 Thomas Foulke patented 3,350 acres on Potomac Creek in Westmoreland County. Sometime prior to 1659 he patented some land on the south side of the Potomac River, near Chappawamsick Creek. He was identified as Captain Thomas Foulke in 1659 when he served as a burgess for James City County, but he represented Westmoreland County in the 1660 and 1661–1662 sessions.

In May 1660 Gerrard and Thomas Foulke of Westmoreland County signed a partnership agreement, merging all of their real and personal estate for seven years. On May 11, 1660, Thomas Foulke, who was planning to make a trip to England, made his will. He bequeathed a third of his real and personal estate to his wife, Susanna, and left the remainder to his brother, Gerrard, who was to serve as his executor and pay his debts. While in England Thomas testified about an insurance claim involving a ship, and he was still there in February 1661 when his brother, Gerrard, mentioned their partnership when selling some Westmoreland County land to Robert Moseley. In 1661 Thomas Foulke testified about some tobacco he had shipped from Virginia. He died sometime prior to June 24, 1663, when his will was proved and his brother, Gerrard, was ordered to submit an inventory of the decedent's estate (STAN 74; HEN I:506; LEO 35–36, 40; Westmoreland County Deeds and Wills No. 1 [1653–1671]:101–102, 196–197; Deeds, Wills &c. 1661–1662:34; Orders 1662–1664:13a–14; PB 3:301; SR 3789, 10029).

* * *

Bartholomew Fowler: In spring 1699 Bartholomew Fowler, a gentleman and the colony's attorney general, stood for election as Jamestown's burgess and ran against Robert Beverley II. According to James City County's sheriff, Fowler won. However, on May 3, 1699, some of Jamestown's freeholders presented a petition in which they protested the sheriff's role in the outcome of the election. Incumbent burgesses decided that Beverley had won and ordered Fowler to withdraw his own name from consideration (SAIN 17:188; JHB 1695–1702:139, 141; STAN 25).

Francis Fowler (Fouler, Fouller): In 1624 Francis Fowler was living in urban Jamestown, where he was a servant in Captain Roger Smith's household. A year later he was residing on Smith's plantation on the lower side of the James River and was identified as a Virginia Company tenant who had been assigned to Smith. By August 1626 Fowler had obtained his freedom and had two servants of his own. In 1629 he made a couple appearances in court and agreed to build a house for his business partner, Bridges Freeman, with whom he had co-invested in some land near the mouth of the Chickahominy River. In January 1642 Francis Fowler was one of James City's burgesses, representing James City County (VI&A 310; LEO 20).

* * *

David (Davyd, Davy) Fox I: David Fox I commenced serving as a Lancaster County justice in 1652, by which time he owned a plantation bordering Morratico Creek. In 1654 the county justices convened at his home. He patented 800 acres on the north side of the Rappahannock River in June 1656, but he and his wife, Mary, quickly disposed of it. In 1664, after Mary's death, David Fox I executed a deed of gift, assigning his real and personal property to two trusted friends until his children came of age. Fox's description of his personal estate attests to his wealth and reveals that his late wife had an abundance of fine clothing. He was still serving as a Lancaster County court justice in 1666 and had just completed a term as high sheriff. By 1669 Captain David Fox I had married the widow of Richard Wright, for whom he was serving as administrator. Fox died sometime prior to January 20, 1670, when his will was proved. His widow, Anne, quickly remarried, taking St. Leger Codd as her new husband. In May 1670 Codd filed a petition on behalf of David Fox I's youngest children, William and Elizabeth, seeking custody of their portion of their late father's estate. When they matured they brought suit against Codd, claiming that he had abused his fiduciary responsibilities (Lancaster County Deeds &c. 1652–1657:1–2, 281–282, 320–321; Deeds and Wills 1656–1661:33; Deeds and Wills 1661–1702:330–333; Orders 1656–1661: 285; 1656–1666:186, 337; 1666–1680:12, 107, 133, 147; Old Rappahannock County Deeds and Wills 1656–1664:53).

David Fox II: David Fox II, the son of David Fox I, inherited his late father's household furnishings, livestock, and servants. He also stood to receive his late father's money, which was in the hands of English merchants John Jeffreys and Thomas Colclough. By 1665 David Fox II had acquired some land on the Corotoman River in Lancaster County, and by 1672 he had begun taking an active role in public life. He was identified as a militia officer when he was given the responsibility of surveying a section of highways. In September 1672 he took the oath of a county justice, a position he still held in 1691. In 1674 and 1677 he was among those frequently asked to appraise county residents' estates. By 1677 he began being identified as Captain David Fox. In December 1679 he asked the justices of Lancaster County to order a survey of some land his late father had owned: approximately half of a large tract that had formerly belonged to

Thomas Burbage, a resident of Nansemond County who invested in land along the Corotoman and Rappahannock rivers. Another Lancaster County gentleman, Colonel Edward Carter, owned the other half of the Burbage parcel. In 1680 Fox's younger brother, William, chose him as his legal guardian, and Northumberland County's justices ordered Colonel St. Leger Codd, despite his objections, to cease making use of the orphan's land. Sometime prior to October 5, 1680, David Fox II married Hannah I, the daughter of William and Hannah Ball of Lancaster County. In 1683 Fox began serving as sheriff, and in 1694 he was appointed high sheriff. Fox, who acquired some additional acreage in 1691, served as a Lancaster County burgess and attended the assembly sessions held in 1677, 1680–1682, 1684, 1685–1686, and 1693. When David Fox II made his will on June 22, 1702, he included bequests to his sons Samuel and William and named them as his executors. He left to Samuel some land on the Rappahannock River, his Manaskon Plantation, and his mill on the Corotoman River. To his son William, he left a property called the Hills Plantation, the land the testator then occupied. He also made a bequest to his daughter, Hannah II, who was married to Rodham Kenner. David Fox II left his wife, Hannah I, life-rights in his mill and some of his servants (LEO 43, 45, 47–48, 52; Lancaster County Deeds and Wills 1661–1702:283–284, 330–331; Wills 1674–1689:4, 40, 70–71, 128; 1690–1709:111–113; Order Book 1656–1666:365; 1666–1680:236–237, 427, 430, 507, 523; 1680–1686:1, 103; 1686–1696:178, 296; Northumberland County Order Book 1678–1698:75, 80–81; NN A:121, 124).

* * *

Thomas Fox: In 1608 Thomas Fox, a laborer, arrived in Virginia in the 2nd Supply of Jamestown colonists (VI&A 311).

Isaac (Isaak) Foxcroft (Foxcrofte, Foxcraft): In April 1656 Isaac Foxcroft patented 2,000 acres on the south side of the Great Wicocomoco River in Northumberland County. Two years later he was identified as a London resident when he brought suit against a Lancaster County man. By 1659 he was back in Virginia and was described as a merchant when he initiated a suit against Colonel John Washington's estate in Lancaster County's court. In early 1660 Foxcroft was still using London as his principal base of operations, but later in the year he seems to have moved to Virginia permanently and begun doing business in Northumberland County. On May 24, 1673, after he had moved to Northampton County, he sued John Newell's administrator, Elizabeth, and lodged a claim against the decedent's estate. He was residing there in 1675 when he allegedly removed part of merchant William Fisher's goods from a ship that had run aground. Isaac Foxcroft served as an attorney from time to time and appeared in Northumberland County's court, usually on account of pending litigation. He was elected a burgess and represented Northampton County in the 1677 and 1685–1686 assembly sessions. In April 1692 he claimed that, contrary to law, a ship's captain—who was defended by William Sherwood of Jamestown—had brought non-English goods into Virginia. Despite residing on the Eastern Shore, Foxcroft continued to invest in land in the Northern Neck, and in 1682 he patented 250 acres on Nuswattox Creek in Northampton County. In 1693 the justices of Accomack County's monthly court named him administrator of James Noble's estate because he was the decedent's greatest creditor (MCGC 338, 350; EJC I:228, 241–242; LEO 42, 48; Lancaster County Deeds and Wills 1654–1661:148–149, 185; Order Book 1656–1661:82, 359; 1656–1666:225; Northumberland County Order Book 1652–1665:249, 262, 295, 299, 303, 310–311; 1666–1678:176, 192, 218; SR 668, 4564; PB 4:56; 7:193; Accomack County Orders 1690–1697:121).

Frances (Native American): When Henry Williamson of Essex County prepared his will on March 30, 1699, he instructed his executors to free his Indian woman, Frances, and her mother, "being a Native Borne in this Country," if "ye Law will permit without transportation" (Essex County Deeds and Wills 1699–1702:12–13). The latter statement raises the possibility that they belonged to a tribe that was exiled from the colony.

Francis: According to Captain John Smith, during the latter part of 1608, Adam and Francis, "two stout Dutchmen" or Poles (actually, Germans) who had been living with Powhatan, came to the fort in Jamestown and requested firearms and clothing. Smith called their visit a ruse because the Indians in the group stole some additional weapons. He added that Powhatan later sent Francis, "a stout young fellow disguised like a savage," to the glasshouse, where Smith encountered and fought with the king of the Pasbehay. When Lord Delaware arrived in 1610, Francis fled to Powhatan. The savvy paramount chief realized that Francis and Adam were as likely to betray him as they had Captain Smith, so he had them executed (VI&A 311; HAI 304; 315, 337).

Thomas Francis: In 1658 Thomas Francis represented Upper Norfolk County in the assembly. He died sometime prior to October 1665, at which time his orphans (Francis, Elizabeth, Ann, and Suzanne) repatented his 900-acre plantation in what was then Nansemond County (LEO 34; PB 5:563).

Daniel Franck (Frank): In 1622 Daniel Franck, a convict, was sentenced to transportation and was sent to Virginia. In August 1623 he was identified as a laborer and resident of Jamestown Island when he killed one of Sir George Yeardley's calves and stole some personal items from provost marshal Randall Smallwood. Franck was tried, convicted, and sentenced to death for thievery. He was listed among those who had died at West and Shirley Hundred sometime after April 1623 but before February 16, 1624. In 1633 Elmer Phillips—an heir of Eleanor Phillips, who had underwritten Daniel Franck's transportation to the colony—used him as a headright (VI&A 312).

Frank (Native American): When an inventory was made of the late Mrs. Elizabeth Pinkard's estate on April 8, 1699, one of her servants was an Indian girl named Frank. Mrs. Pinkard was the widow of John Pinkard I, who in 1688 served as a Lancaster County burgess (Lancaster County Wills 1690–1709:88; LEO 49).

Ferdinand (Fardinand) Franklin: In January 1642 Ferdinand Franklin served as James City's burgess and probably represented James City County, which then encompassed what became Surry County. In April he was among those who signed the burgesses' declaration against reinstatement of the Virginia Company. Documents associated with litigation undertaken in England in 1642 and 1644 made reference to a Mr. Franklin (perhaps Ferdinand) who was involved with William Claiborne's trading activities at Kent Island. Franklin and Claiborne claimed hardships that were a result of Lord Baltimore's claiming the island for Maryland and its use by Clobbery and Company (STAN 61; LEO 20; SR 4009, 4011; BILL 44).

Fransisco (Native American): When Major George Colclough received a certificate on September 20, 1660, entitling him to patent 1,050 acres of land, one of the people he listed as a headright was "Fransisco, an Indian" (Northumberland County Order Book 1652–1665:258). Therefore, Fransisco probably was transported to Virginia from another colony.

Bridges Freeman: In 1624 Bridges Freeman was living in Elizabeth City on part of the Virginia Company's land. By 1626 he and another man were occupying a leasehold at Martin's Brandon. In 1629 Freeman, who was then serving as a burgess for Pasbehay, the territory just west of Jamestown Island, was reappointed commander of the magazine in Jamestown. By 1630 he had patented some land on the east side of the Chickahominy River's mouth, within the 3,000-acre tract that had been set aside in 1619 for the Virginia Company's use. In 1632 he was a burgess, representing the planters living along the Chickahominy River. He became that area's tobacco viewer in 1640 and later its collector of revenue. In 1647 Captain Bridges Freeman served as one of James City County's burgesses, and in 1650 he was appointed to the Council of State. He was then a lieutenant colonel in the militia (VI&A 313; STAN 35; LEO 9, 11, 26).

Ambrose Fresey: Sometime after April 1623 but before February 16, 1624, Ambrose Fresey died on Jamestown Island (VI&A 314).

Richard Frethorne (Frethram): In 1623 Richard Frethorne of Martin's Hundred, a young indentured servant, sent a letter to his parents describing the miserable living conditions in his settlement. He spoke fondly of Mr. and Mrs. John Jackson of urban Jamestown, who had built a cabin for his use whenever he came to the capital city on business. Sometime after April 1623 but before February 16, 1624, Richard Frethorne died at Martin's Hundred (VI&A 314).

Henry Fry: Sometime after April 1623 but before February 16, 1624, Henry Fry died on Jamestown Island (VI&A 314).

John Fulcher: On October 20, 1677, John Fulcher, who inherited John Baldwin's 28½-acre parcel in the western end of Jamestown Island, sold it to William Sherwood. On April 23, 1681, Fulcher confirmed the sale. Fulcher seems to have been associated with the lower side of Hampton Roads, for in 1699, 1701, and 1711 he patented large tracts of land in Norfolk and Princess Anne counties (AMB 48; PB 7:97; NUG II:222; III:27, 42, 118–119).

Francis Fulford (Fullford): Francis Fulford reportedly represented Henrico County in the assembly session held in January 1642, and in April he signed the burgesses' declaration against reinstatement of the Virginia Company (LEO 20; STAN 61; BILL 44). Unfortunately, no other documentary records have been found that mention Fulford, and Henrico County's early records have been lost or destroyed. When John Kellond of Paingsford, Devon, England, prepared his will in 1677, he made a bequest to a minor named Francis Fullford, perhaps a kinsman of the Virginia burgess (WAT 1101).

Rev. Thomas Fuller: According to court testimony taken in April and May 1622, the Rev. Thomas Fuller was living in Virginia four or five years earlier, when Sir Samuel Argall was deputy governor. Fuller stated that he was in Jamestown in 1618 when Lord Delaware's ship, the *Neptune,* arrived and that he was present when Edward Brewster was sentenced to death in a court-martial. Richard Brewster, who had brought suit against Argall, testified that Fuller arrived on the *Neptune* and spent little time in Jamestown. Fuller returned to England and in April 1622 was living in London (VI&A 315).

[No First Name] Furlow: Sometime after April 1623 but before February 16, 1624, Mr. Furlow's child died on Jamestown Island (VI&A 316).

Nicholas Fynloe: In late 1624 or early 1625, Nicholas Fynloe served on a jury impaneled to investigate the drowning death of young George Pope II, a resident of Jamestown Island (VI&A 316).

G

Elias (Ellias) Gaile (Gale): Elias Gaile, a young apprentice associated with the East India School, was sent to Virginia in 1622. The school project was abandoned on account of the recent Indian attack, and during the mid-1620s Elias was living on Jamestown Island, where he was a servant in John Burrows' household. On February 19, 1626, Elias witnessed a dispute between two men that culminated in a sword fight (VI&A 316).

Robert Gaile: In 1621 Robert Gaile filed suits against John Burrows of Jamestown Island and the estate of William Tracy of Berkeley Hundred (VI&A 316).

Robert Gaines (Native American): On December 5, 1688, George Luke was granted an attachment against the estate of the late Robert Gaines, an Indian (Old Rappahannock County Order Book 1687–1692:103).

Thomas Gaines (Native American): On October 4, 1688, George Luke successfully brought suit against Thomas Gaines, an Indian residing in Old Rappahannock County (Old Rappahannock County Order Book 1687–1692:94). He may have had a connection with a colonist named Thomas Gaines, who also was living in the county.

Stephen Galthorpe (Calthrop, Halthrop): Stephen Galthorpe died in Jamestown on August 15, 1607. President Edward Maria Winfield purportedly claimed that Galthorpe had led a mutiny (VI&A 317).

Martin Gardner: In November 1679 Stephen Procter sued Jonathan Newell, a merchant and landowner in urban Jamestown, and Martin Gardner of York County served as Procter's attorney. Gardner later represented Procter's widow, Winifred, who executed a quitclaim deed that gave William Sherwood an unencumbered title to the Newell property (AMB 20, 28, 33).

Thomas Gardner: In September 1676 Thomas Gardner, captain of the *Adam and Eve*, arrested the rebel Nathaniel Bacon and was rewarded for his service to the government. Gardner also detained Giles Bland, one of Bacon's staunchest supporters. In 1677 Captain Gardner's ship was used as a jail that housed captured rebels. Gardner served Governor William Berkeley up until the time the king's commissioners arrived in the colony (SAIN 10:192; CO 5/1307 ff 61–62).

James Garey: In March 1677 James Garey was identified as one of Governor William Berkeley's servants (SAIN 10:52). It is uncertain whether he was associated with Berkeley's property in Jamestown, with Green Spring plantation in James City County, or one of Green Spring's subsidiary farms.

Thomas Garnett: Thomas Garnett came to Virginia in 1610 and was an indentured servant. On August 3, 1619, when the assembly first convened, his master, Captain William Powell, a burgess representing Jamestown, accused him of immoral behavior and slander. He claimed that Garnett had caused him financial losses and had sought to have him deposed from office, even killed. The assembly, acting as a judicial body, sentenced Garnett to daily public whippings, and he was to stand with his ears nailed to the pillory. By early 1624 Garnett had moved to Elizabeth City, where he shared a home with his wife, Elizabeth, and their Virginia-born daughter, Susan. On July 3, 1635, he patented some land in Elizabeth City near the Little Poquoson River, acquiring his acreage by means of the headright system (VI&A 320).

William Garrett (Garret): Captain John Smith reported that William Garrett, a bricklayer, was one of the first Jamestown settlers and arrived in Virginia during the spring of 1607 (VI&A 320).

Sir Thomas Gates: Thomas Gates came to America in 1585–1586 with Sir Francis Drake and was knighted in 1597. He served in the Netherlands and in 1608 was granted a year's leave of absence to go to Virginia. He set sail from England in 1609, in a fleet that transported 500 men and women to Virginia. The vessels encountered a hurricane and his ship, the *Seaventure*, was wrecked in Bermuda. In May 1610 Gates and the other survivors continued on to Virginia in two vessels they built from Bermuda's native cedar wood. When they arrived in Jamestown, they found the surviving colonists in dire straits, and Gates realized that he did not have enough provisions to save them. Therefore, he decided to evacuate them to Newfoundland so that they could secure passage back to England. The arrival of Lord Delaware's fleet in June 1610 averted abandonment of the colony. Delaware made Gates second in command and in July 1610 sent him to England to procure additional colonists, supplies, and livestock. Gates set sail for Virginia in May 1611, accompanied by his wife and daughters. Although he and his daughters reached the colony in August 1611, his wife died at sea. In December he sent his daughters back to England. Sir Thomas Gates enforced a strict military code of justice and undertook construction of three forts at the mouth of the James River. He also erected many improvements in Jamestown, including a governor's house, the dwelling in which he lived. He returned to England in 1614, leaving Sir Thomas Dale in command. Sir Thomas Gates died in the Netherlands in September 1622. He was survived by sons Thomas and Anthony and daughters Margaret, Mary, and Elizabeth (VI&A 322; BRO 895).

Thomas Gates: Thomas Gates came to Virginia in 1609. In 1624 he identified himself as a former Virginia Company servant when he filed a petition alleging that he had been hired to make pitch and tar for three years, but that Deputy Governor Samuel Argall had detained him for eight. During the mid-1620s Thomas Gates and his wife, Elizabeth, were living at Paces Paines on the lower side of the James River, west of Grays Creek. In November 1624, when Gates sought to recover a debt from John Jackson of Jamestown, he was described as a man capable of making a house "tight." Thus, he appears to have earned some income by caulking buildings, perhaps utilizing the pitch or tar that he knew how to make. Elizabeth Gates testified in court in September 1626, in connection with allegations against Joan Wright, an accused witch. In May 1625 Thomas Gates was credited with 100 acres of land on the lower side of the James River. He appeared in court in 1626 and 1627 (VI&A 323).

John Gather (Gatter, Gaither): In early 1624 John Gather was an indentured servant in Sir Francis Wyatt's household in urban Jamestown. Within a year he had moved to Mulberry Island, where he was employed by Captain William Peirce. He went to England and returned to Virginia with his wife, Joan. In 1636 Gather patented land on the Elizabeth River and moved there, and in 1640 he served as a tobacco viewer. By February 1646 he had been widowed and remarried. He and his new wife, Mary, moved to Maryland, where he died sometime prior to November 24, 1652 (VI&A 323).

Joel Gathright: On May 31, 1793, Joel Gathright, the overseer of Champion Travis's Jamestown Island plantation, was killed by two slave women, Nelly and Daphne. They had been plowing the fields when Gathright began berating them for allowing sheep to get into a cornfield. When Nelly hotly denied it, the overseer began flailing her with a small cane. She was able to flee from his blows, despite her pregnancy, but when she stumbled and fell, he struck her repeatedly. When Nelly regained her footing, she began to fight back, at which point Daphne joined in the fray. The two women then knocked Gathright to the ground and began beating him with sticks and branches. Two young slaves heard Gathright's cries and ran for help, but by the time someone came to his aid, he was almost dead. According to the James City County coroner, the left side of Gathright's skull had been crushed with a large stone. Gathright, who was a cruel man, was the only white person residing on the Travis property at the time of his death (PALM VI:462).

Henry Gawler (Gauler): Sometime prior to July 1683, Henry Gawler married Catherine, the widow and executrix of George Marable I, who then had possession of the middle unit of a three-bay brick row house on urban Jamestown's waterfront. The Gawlers probably occupied Catherine's late husband's row house, the only property they possessed on Jamestown Island. During the early 1680s the assembly paid Henry Gawler, an ordinary-keeper, for providing room and board to some tributary Indians who were in Jamestown on official business. He also was paid for providing a meeting room to the governor and members of his council, who convened as the General Court; on another occasion he allowed the assembly to meet in his home. These rentals were necessary because Nathaniel Bacon's men had torched the statehouse in 1676. Whenever Gawler provided meeting space to government officials, he had to find accommodations for his other guests. In June 1689 William Byrd I told his agent that another shipment of claret wine was "to be put on shore at Mr. Gawler's in Jamestown." In 1685 Gawler brought suit against burgess Peter Knight I and George Bledsoe in Northumberland County, and in 1686 he sued Francis Lee in Middlesex County. It is unclear whether these men had been guests in Gawler's ordinary or were otherwise in his debt. In 1691 Henry Gawler was paid for some work he had done on the rebuilt statehouse, which was then being used as a General Courthouse. Two years later Gawler, then a James City County justice and sheriff, was paid for duties he had performed on behalf of the General Court. He probably had served as the court's sergeant-at-arms, a post traditionally assigned to the local sheriff. During the 1680s Gawler filed suit against Thomas Sowerby, Thomas Avery, and John Thompson in the Surry County court, but in 1688 he admitted owing funds for 10 pairs of shoes. Over the years he patented some land along the Blackwater River, on Moses Creek in what is now Charles City County, and in the Middle Peninsula (Surry County Order Book 1671–1691:409, 416, 469, 682; NUG II:275, 304, 329; Charles City County Order Book 1685:5; JHB 1660–1693:174, 256–257; LJC 88–89, 143, 151; Stanard, "Letters of William Byrd, First," 27; Middlesex County Order Book 1680–1694:266; Northumberland County Order Book 1678–1698:254–255).

Anthony Gay: On May 27, 1673, Anthony Gay, a London merchant, brought suit against Colonel Thomas Swann of Jamestown Island. He also sued Edward Ramsey, a James City County justice, and John Grove, a sea captain who settled in Isle of Wight County (MCGC 341).

John Geddes: In 1706 John Geddes, one of James City County's justices of the peace, asked for some of the old statehouse brick so that it could be used in constructing a new county courthouse (LJC 459).

Henry Gee: On March 17, 1677, Captain William Byrd I informed Governor William Berkeley and the members of the Council of State, who had convened as a court, that Henry Gee of Henrico County had supported the rebel Nathaniel Bacon's cause. Gee was made to appear before the king's commissioners at Swann's Point, where he stood accused of making scandalous comments and disturbing the peace. Although Gee's fate was left in the hands of the king's commissioners, he was to be turned over to the county justices in his home jurisdiction. On March 22nd the governor and council decided that Gee would be fined 1,000 pounds of pork that could be used by the king's soldiers who had come to suppress the popular uprising led by Nathaniel Bacon (MCGC 460, 532).

John Gee: Between February 14, 1624, and January 25, 1625, John Gee of Burneham in Somerset died in Jamestown. On December 22, 1626, his daughter, Jane Roode, was granted administration of his estate (VI&A 324).

Richard Genoway: On May 20, 1607, Richard Genoway, a sailor who was among

the first to arrive in Jamestown, accompanied Captain Christopher Newport on an exploratory voyage of the James River (VI&A 325).

Vallentyne Gentler: Vallentyne Gentler died in Jamestown sometime after April 1623 but before February 16, 1624 (VI&A 325).

George (Native American): In September 1661 George, an Indian leader or Great Man associated with the Nansemond tribe then living on the Rappahannock River, accompanied several men to the home of Richard White, where some settlers had been slain. George indicated he had found evidence that Indians had been present at the scene of the crime (Old Rappahannock County Deed Book 1656–1664:153–154).

George: In 1769 George, an adult male slave, was living on Jamestown Island and was included in the late Edward Ambler I's estate (AMB-E).

John George I: John George I came to Virginia prior to 1626 and was familiar with the business dealings of George Thorpe, who was killed in the 1622 Indian attack on Berkeley Hundred. In 1638 John George I patented 900 acres on Bailey's Creek in Charles City County, and two years later he acquired another 1,200 acres in that vicinity. Then, in 1642 he patented 144 acres adjacent to Captain Francis Eppes's property and Nutkins Creek in Charles City. He moved to Isle of Wight County and commenced serving as one of the county's burgesses, attending the 1647–1648 and 1652 assembly sessions. In 1650 he and fellow burgess George Hardy were ordered to inventory the estate of William Garnett, the captain of the ship *Comfort*. In October 1654 John George's son, Isaac, received a deed of gift from Major George Fawdon, a fellow burgess. John George continued to patent land and in 1667 laid claim to tracts in Isle of Wight that were located on Castle and Cypress creeks. When Colonel George made his will on August 2, 1678, he made bequests to his wife and executrix, Ann (Anne); to his son, Isaac I; to his daughters, Rebecca and Sarah; to his grandchildren, Isaac George II and John and Joyce Lewis; to kinswoman Mary Baugh; and to the children of Phillip Pardoe. He indicated that his daughter Sarah Peddington had been married to Morgan Lewis. John George's will was recorded on January 9, 1678. By June 1681 the widowed Ann George had married Nansemond County burgess John Leare. Together they conveyed the George plantation on Castle Creek, which she had inherited, to burgess Thomas Pitt. In 1695 John George II (perhaps a grandson) was identified as one of the late Colonel John Leare's heirs when merchant David Meade tried to claim some of the decedent's land in Isle of Wight and Nansemond counties, acreage that King Charles II had given to Henry Lord Maltravers (LEO 26, 29; Isle of Wight County Deeds, Wills & Guardian Accounts Book A:88; Will and Deed Book 1 [1662–1688]:170, 196, 460–461; PB 1:581, 763, 787; 6:69, 151; SR 5811, 9954, 10425).

Thomas Gibbons: On January 6, 1679, Thomas Gibbons acknowledged a debt to Thomas Rabley, a builder and the owner of a house and waterfront lot in urban Jamestown (Surry County Order Book 1671–1691: 290).

Francis Gibbs (Gibson): During the mid-1620s Francis Gibbs was living in Ralph Hamor's household in urban Jamestown (VI&A 325).

John Gibbs: In July and August 1619 Lieutenant John Gibbs served as a burgess for Captain John Ward's plantation in the corporation of Charles City. He later moved to Westover and seated his own land. On March 22, 1622, when the Indians attacked Westover, Lieutenant John Gibbs and a dozen others were slain (VI&A 325; LEO 3).

Francis Gibson (see Francis Gibbs)

Thomas Gibson: Thomas Gibson, a tradesman, arrived in Jamestown in early 1608, in the 1st Supply of new colonists. In 1608 he was one of the men sent overland to build a house for Powhatan (VI&A 326).

George Gilbert: On September 29, 1643, George Gilbert patented 50 acres in the mainland, near Walter Cooper's land and the bridge across Powhatan Creek, securing his patent on the basis of one headright. Sometime prior to August 18, 1644, Gilbert laid claim to a lot in the western end of Jamestown Island, property that abutted north upon the acreage of Rudolph Spraggon, whose one-acre lot was on the waterfront (PB 1:905, 2:11; NUG I:147, 154).

John (Jonathan, Jonathin) Giles: Jonathan Giles came to Virginia in 1619 and in 1624 was living on the Governor's Land, where he was one of Sir Francis Wyatt's servants. By early 1625 he had become part of Wyatt's household in urban Jamestown. In July 1627 Giles, whose contract had been sold to merchant Thomas Weston, sued for his freedom in Elizabeth City's court, claiming that his time of service had expired. Despite Giles' assertion, he was ordered to serve an additional six months, two of which were to cover court costs. On December 5, 1628, Giles testified about a conversation he had with Jeffrey Cornish, whose brother had been executed in Jamestown (VI&A 327).

John Giles (Gyles): In 1678 John Giles was identified as a merchant involved in transatlantic commerce. In 1680 he and his wife, Phillaritie (Phillarote, Phillarete), who were residents of Isle of Wight County, transferred 400 acres of land to Phillaritie's daughter, Jane, acreage then in the hands of a tenant. A deed the Giles couple signed in 1682 reveals that Phillaritie had been given the acreage by her late father, Thomas Woodward, and that it was part of a much larger tract. John Giles seems to have begun speculating in real estate by 1682, when he patented 1,100 acres of land in Isle of Wight County on the Blackwater or Choanoke River. He served as an attorney during the 1690s and represented Isle of Wight County in the assembly sessions of 1695–1696, 1696–1697, 1698, and 1699. During 1698 Giles acquired several tracts of land in Isle of Wight County. Some of the acreage lay between Kinsale (Kingsale) Swamp and the Blackwater River. In what seems to have been an act of kindness, in 1698 Giles gave a large tract of land he had patented to Giles Driver, its original owner, who had allowed it to escheat to the Crown. In April 1701 John and Phillaritie Giles identified themselves as residents of Isle of Wight County when they disposed of 500 acres in Carolina, on the Choanoke River (LEO 54, 56, 58–59; Isle of Wight County Will and Deed Book 1 [1662–1688]:465, 489–492; 2 [1688–1704]:270, 334; PB 7:125; 9:135, 141, 165, 180; BODIE 621, 636; SR 5762; PB 7:125; 9:135, 141, 165, 180).

Alexander Gill: Alexander Gill, Thomas Roper's servant, arrived in Jamestown in 1623. In early 1624 he was living in the home of Captain William Peirce (Perse) in urban Jamestown, but by January 1625 he had moved to Peirce's property on Mulberry Island. Sometime prior to February 5, 1627, Peirce was ordered to free Gill or compensate him for his service (VI&A 327).

John Gill: In March 1624 the General Court noted that John Gill, a merchant and Virginia Company employee who had made many trips to Virginia, was indebted to Mr.

Bennett. Gill appeared in court from time to time, trying to collect debts, and on April 3, 1626, he was released from his contract with the Virginia Company, which by then was defunct. In March 1627 Gill sued Jamestown gunsmith John Jackson, to whom he had brought an indentured servant with gunsmithing skills. In October 1627 Gill hired Joan Meatherst, a servant, and he returned to the General Court in January 1628 to bring suit against Richard Alford, a debtor (VI&A 327).

Stephen (Steven, Steeven) Gill (Gyles, Giles) I: Sometime prior to November 1636 Stephen Gill I, a surgeon, patented some land in Charles River (York) County, in the immediate vicinity of Queens Creek, using the headright of his wife, Ann, and that of her former husband, Henry Toppin. In January 1639 Gill acquired some additional acreage near Queens Creek. When he witnessed a deed on December 25, 1640, he endorsed it with his mark. By 1642 Lieutenant Gill had begun investing in land on the Middle Peninsula. One of the parcels he patented included 2,500 acres on the north side of the York River at the head of Rosewell Creek, in what became Gloucester County. When Thomas Doe gave Captain John West his power of attorney in 1644 and authorized him to administer his estate for the benefit of his daughter, Ann Doe, he indicated that he had left some papers in a chest at Stephen Gill's home in Jamestown. Gill made his will on July 15, 1646, but survived for several more years. He owned some land on the south side of the Piankatank River, became a York County burgess in 1652, and commenced serving as a justice in the county court. Like many of his peers, he went to court, often in an attempt to recover debts. During the early 1650s he was identified as a captain in the York County militia when he patented 900 acres on Fleets Bay in Northumberland County. Gill died sometime prior to August 2, 1653, when an inventory was made of his estate, which included medical paraphernalia, military equipment, and a large number of indentured servants. The testator bequeathed the York County plantation on which he then lived to his son, Stephen Gill II, and left the rest of his estate to his wife and their minor children, whom he failed to name. In 1654 Stephen Gill II laid claim to some land on the Piankatank River, acreage that had belonged to his late father (York County Record Book 1 [1633–1646]: 75, 92, 117,130, 171, 181; 2 [1633–1646]:64; PB 1:402, 722, 819, 873; 2:160, 163, 314, 319; 3:326; 5:310; 7:482; LEO 30).

Nicholas Gillman: Nicholas Gillman, a carpenter in the employ of the Company of Shipwrights, arrived in Virginia in 1622. He was supposed to work under the supervision of master boat-builder Thomas Nunn and after five years of service would be entitled to five acres of land. Nunn and his men settled on Jamestown Island, where most of them died, but in 1623 a few of the survivors were sent to Elizabeth City (VI&A 328).

Post Ginnat: Post Ginnat, a surgeon, arrived in Jamestown in 1608 in the 1st Supply of new colonists (VI&A 328).

Thomas Glasbrook: On May 25, 1671, Thomas Glasbrook's account with merchant Richard Moore was audited. In 1676 Moore imported Virginia tobacco to England and exported a large quantity of beer to the colony. He also appears to have patented some land in Lower Norfolk County (MCGC 260; SR 5592c, 5726c; PB 7:209).

Henry Glover: In February 1624 Henry Glover was living in the Jamestown Island household of John Grevett (VI&A 329).

Mathew Godfrey (Godfree): When Arthur Toppin of Lower Norfolk County's Elizabeth River Parish made his will in 1671, he made bequests to Warren, John, and Mathew Godfrey, whom he identified as his wife's brothers. Then, when Sarah Porten (Portten) made her will in 1675, she identified Warren (Warner), John, and Mathew Godfrey as her sons. They may have been the offspring of John Godfrey, who patented 300 acres on the east branch of the Elizabeth River in 1645 and 200 acres on the south branch of Daniel Tanner's Creek in 1652. In April 1685 Mathew Godfrey patented 75 acres called Cedar Island, acreage that was located in Lower Norfolk County. He witnessed a land transaction in Princess Anne County in 1692 and Richard Church's will in 1705. Three years later Godfrey's brother John indicated that he and Mathew had purchased a piece of property from William Portten. In 1699 and 1700–1702 Mathew Godfrey served in the assembly, representing Norfolk County (LEO 59–60; Lower Norfolk County Book E:106; Wills and Deeds 4:35; 7:106; 8:160; Princess Anne County Deed Book 1:31; PB 7:457).

[No First Name] Godwin: A gentleman named Godwin represented Nansemond County in the assembly sessions held in 1693 (LEO 53). Although his first name was not included in the records, he may have been Captain Thomas Godwin II, the son of Major Thomas Godwin I, who represented the county during the mid-to-late 1650s (LEO 32, 35, 41).

* * *

Thomas Godwin (Goodwyn, Godwyn) I: Thomas Godwin I, who patented 200 acres of land in Nansemond County in 1655, began serving as a justice in Lower Norfolk's court in 1653. He represented the Nansemond River area in the assembly sessions held in 1654–1655 and was returned to office in 1659, when he served as a burgess for Upper Norfolk County. When he and Richard Bennett (a Puritan) sent a letter to England in 1670, they indicated that their message was being dispatched from the Nansemond River. Godwin, who at times speculated in real estate in the Northern Neck and in the Southside, was a Nansemond County burgess in 1676 but vacated his assembly seat when he was chosen speaker. He made his will in May 1677, a document that was presented for probate in 1679 (LEO 32, 35, 41; SR 5385; BODIE 460–462; HEN I:359, 506; PB 2:244; NUG I:197, 319, 327, 392, 396; II:31, 308).

Thomas Godwin (Goodwyn, Godwyn) II: In August 1686 Thomas Godwin I's son, Thomas II, acknowledged that he had received from Colonel Joseph Bridger's estate the inheritance to which his wife, Martha, was entitled. Godwin, who was identified as a resident of Chuckatuck, purchased 400 acres on Chuckatuck Creek in December 1688. He was still alive in 1697 and held the rank of major in the militia. In May 1699 Major Thomas Godwin II and two other men were found guilty of spreading false rumors concerning the election of Nansemond County's burgesses (Isle of Wight County Wills and Deeds 1 [1688–1704]:241; 2 [1704–1715]:254; Lower Norfolk Book C:60; BODIE 460–462, 600, 640–641; EJC I:437–438, 441).

* * *

Reign Godwine: On January 13, 1627, Reign Godwine, one of the defunct Virginia Company's tenants, was assigned to provost marshal Randall Smallwood, who lived in urban Jamestown (VI&A 330).

Peter (Peeter) Gold (Gould): Peter Gold died in Jamestown sometime after April 1623 but before February 16, 1624 (VI&A 330).

Nicholas Goldsmith (Gouldsmith, Gould-finch): During the mid-1620s Nicholas Goldsmith, an indentured servant, was a member of John Burrows' Jamestown Island household. He testified at an inquest held after the death of Elizabeth Abbott, one of John Proctor's maidservants, and said that he had seen her wounds when he and his master, John Burrows, had gone to Burrows Hill, which was next door to the Proctors' plantation (VI&A 331).

Raymond Goodison: In 1608 Raymond Goodison, a laborer, arrived in Jamestown in the 1st Supply of new settlers (VI&A 331).

Benjamin Goodrich: On December 18, 1690, Benjamin Goodrich was identified as a James City County justice of the peace. Therefore, he would have attended the monthly county court sessions held in Jamestown. In 1704 he paid quitrent on 1,650 acres of land in James City County (York County Deeds, Orders, Wills 3:49; SMITH 36).

Charles Goodrich: In April 1687 Charles Goodrich patented 550 acres on the south side of the James River in what was then Charles City County but later became Prince George. During the late 1680s and throughout the 1690s he was a Charles City County justice and sometimes served as the county's high sheriff. He also appeared in court from time to time, pursuing litigation, acting as an attorney, or performing official duties. Among those for whom he served as an attorney was Edward Chilton, a prominent government official. In 1695 Captain Goodrich began representing Charles City County in the assembly, replacing Henry Batt, who left Virginia before the second session opened. Goodrich served as a Charles City burgess in the 1695–1696, 1696–1697, and 1698 assembly sessions and became a major in the county militia. Some of his disposable income came from operating a public ferry. In 1699 Goodrich ran afoul of the law when he imported a Portuguese man and an East Indian and failed to pay customs duties (LEO 54, 56, 58; Charles City County Court Orders 1687–1695:94, 316, 387, 474, 478, 534; PB 7:553; EJC I:408, 443; II:42, 235; Henrico County Will and Deed Book 1688–1697:528).

John Goodrich: Captain John Goodrich served as a justice in Isle of Wight County's monthly court in 1693 and was supposed to represent Isle of Wight in the 1695–1696 assembly sessions. He served during 1695 but died before the opening of the second session. In December 1694 he initiated a suit against Thomas and Martha Thropp, a married couple, because the husband wanted to sell a piece of property to Goodrich and the wife refused to relinquish her dower interest. A court document filed in April 1695 reveals that Captain John Goodrich's land abutted the James River. However, the patents for any land he claimed seem to have been lost or destroyed. In March 1697 Goodrich's widow, Anne, signed a marriage contract with Captain Robert Kae (Kar?) (LEO 54; Isle of Wight County Deed Book 1 [1688–1704]:150, 243; Orders 1693–1695:1, 68).

Robert Goodrich: On July 31, 1714, Robert Goodrich acquired from Philip Ludwell I a 170-acre leasehold that was adjacent to Green Spring plantation and on Checkerhouse (Gordons) Creek. On August 17, 1720, Goodrich patented 192 acres of escheat land near Ludwell's property (NUG III:223; Lee MS L 51 ff 674–675).

Thomas Goodrich: Thomas Goodrich began patenting land on the lower side of the Rappahannock River in 1657. As time went on, his holdings grew until he owned literally thousands of acres in what became Old Rappahannock County. He rose in rank in the county militia, in time serving as a major, a lieutenant colonel, and a colonel. In May 1676 he informed Governor William Berkeley that Indians had attacked some settlers living near the falls of the Rappahannock River and proffered that Virginia's tributary natives were allied with the Susquehannocks. Dissatisfied with the Berkeley government's response, Goodrich became sympathetic to the views of the rebel Nathaniel Bacon. On February 10, 1677, Governor Berkeley issued a proclamation in which he named those who were exempt from the king's pardon on account of their role in Bacon's Rebellion. Among those named was Colonel Thomas Goodrich, who was then incarcerated although he insisted that he was innocent of the charges against him (NEVILLE 61; SR 660, 12501; PB 4:148, 233, 413; 5:322, 422; 6:8, 254, 425).

Alice Goodrick (Goodrich): On November 15, 1693, Alice Goodrick submitted a claim to the assembly for building a partition in front of the secretary's office, within the statehouse. The assembly objected, for they had not authorized the work and considered it remodeling. However, on July 18, 1694, they reconsidered and agreed to pay Mrs. Goodrick for her work (LJC 206–207; EJC I:315).

James Goodwin: James Goodwin moved to York County sometime prior to December 1646, when he sued a local man. Like most of his peers, Goodwin appeared in court from time to time, initiating or responding to litigation. During the 1650s he served as a justice in the local court. Major Goodwin represented York County in the assembly session of 1658. During 1657 and 1658 he began patenting land in the Northern Neck, acreage that abutted the Potomac River in Westmoreland County (LEO 34; York County Orders Book 2 [1646–1648]:197, 207; Record Book 1 [1648–1657]:298, 324, 335; 2 [1648–1657]:383; 3 [1648–1657]:2; PB 4:264, 279, 341).

* * *

Daniel (Daniell) Gookin (Gookins, Cookins, Goegin, Coogin, Coogen, Cogan, Coogan) II: Daniel Gookin II, the son of Daniel Gookin I, arrived in Virginia sometime prior to February 1, 1631, and was living at the family's plantation, Newportes News, in 1634 when Dutch mariner Peter DeVries paid a visit. On February 25, 1635, Daniel Gookin II obtained a patent for 2,500 acres on the lower side of the James River, between the Nansemond River and Chuckatuck Creek, in what was then Upper Norfolk County and later Nansemond. He moved to the property he patented and served as a county justice and militia leader. Researcher Cynthia Leonard surmised that Gookin (Cogan) served as a burgess for Lower Norfolk County in 1642 because he was included in a list of tobacco inspectors known to have served in the assembly. In 1643 Daniel Gookin II moved to Maryland, stayed briefly, and then continued on to Massachusetts, where he became permanently established as part of the Puritan community (VI&A 333; PB 1:511; DOR 2:101–102; LEO 20).

John Gookin (Gookins, Gooken, Cookins, Goegen): John Gookin was the son of immigrant Daniel Gookin I, who became established at Newportes News but also patented land on the lower side of the James River. In October 1636 John Gookin patented 500 acres on the Nansemond River, and in 1641 he acquired 640 acres in what was then Lower Norfolk County but by 1691 had become Princess Anne County. Between March and May 1641 he married the former Sarah Offley, Adam Thorogood I's widow. Later in the year he and Captain Thomas Willoughby I built a storehouse at what became known as Willoughby's Spit. Gookin represented Lower Norfolk County in the assembly session held in 1640, and in November 1642 he informed the General Court's justices about hostile acts the Nansemond Indians committed in Upper Norfolk (later, Nansemond) County. John Gookin died prior to November 22, 1643, when his widow was granted administration of his estate. She went on to marry Francis Yeardley in 1647 (LEO 18; DOR 2:102–103, 699; 3:865; VI&A 332; PB 1:396, 785; 7:466; Lower Norfolk County Record Book A:30, 39, 87, 113).

* * *

Thomas Gordon: On September 28, 1677, Governor Herbert Jeffreys and the General Court's justices learned that Thomas Gordon, who had been found guilty of rebellion and treason on account of his involvement in Bacon's Rebellion, had failed to fulfill his court-imposed sentence. He had been ordered to kneel before the justices of Old Rappahannock County with a rope around his neck and apologize. Instead, he had appeared in court wearing small tape instead of a rope halter. Major Robert Beverley I was ordered to investigate the matter and determine whether Gordon and the county justices were in contempt of the law (MCGC 534). In November 1683 a Thomas Gordon patented 454 acres in Lower Norfolk County, land that became known as Knotts Island (PB 7:345).

John Goring: Thomas Rabley of urban Jamestown brought suit against John Goring of the Lawnes Creek Parish in the March 2, 1673, session of the Surry County Court (Surry County Order Book 1671–1691:294).

Edward Gosling (Gofling): In March 1676 George Lee of urban Jamestown brought suit against Captain Edward Gosling, a mariner, who was supposed to take Lee's tobacco to Holland. Gosling's attorney, William Sherwood of Jamestown, tried to attach enough of the mariner's estate to satisfy Lee's claim for damages. In 1683 Gosling sued two men who had tried to hire him as master of the *Concord*, a ship that was in need of repairs, and had offered to sell the vessel to him. Gosling indicated that he had expressed interest in buying the ship if he could do so with partners. He stated that he had paid for having the ship repaired, but when the work was completed, his would-be partners, William Nutt and Randolph Knipe, refused to reimburse him. As a result, Gosling was imprisoned for debt. The suit was still in progress in 1685 (MCGC 432; SR 10606).

* * *

Anthony Gosnold I: Anthony Gosnold I, a gentleman and the elder colonist of that name, came to Virginia in 1607 as one of the first Jamestown settlers. According to Captain John Smith, in late 1607 Gosnold was present when there was talk of abandoning the colony. In 1609 he went to Hog Island with Mr. Scrivener. Anthony Gosnold I apparently died in Virginia (VI&A 333).

Anthony Gosnold II: Anthony Gosnold II accompanied his father, Anthony I, to Virginia in 1607 and was one of the first colonists to become established in Jamestown. Captain John Smith said that only five of the people who accompanied the younger Anthony Gosnold to Virginia managed to survive. Smith scholar Philip Barbour surmised that Anthony Gosnold II, a cousin of Bartholomew Gosnold, returned to England and was living there in 1623 (VI&A 333).

Anthony Gosnold III: Anthony Gosnold III, the son of Anthony Gosnold II, purportedly was in Virginia in November 1615. In 1621 the Virginia Company awarded him a share of land for the money he had invested and another for his personal adventure six years earlier. Gosnold claimed that he had inherited two kinsmen's rights to Virginia land and cited his long service to the Virginia Company. He said that he had been detained as a servant long after he should have been freed and that he wanted to pass his shares of land along to his brother, Robert, and to Roger Castle. Virginia Company officials gave Anthony III and his associates a patent for a particular plantation in Virginia, but told him that before he could take possession of the land he allegedly inherited, he had to prove his claim to Governor George Yeardley's satisfaction. Anthony Gosnold III may have come to Virginia to present his case to Yeardley (VI&A 333).

Bartholomew Gosnold: Bartholomew Gosnold, Anthony Gosnold II's cousin, crossed the Atlantic in 1602. As Captain Christopher Newport's lieutenant, he explored the region that became Massachusetts and tried in vain to establish a settlement in the Elizabeth Islands. Captain John Smith described Gosnold as the prime mover in organizing the Virginia Company, and said that he had served as vice-admiral of the small fleet that brought the first colonists to Virginia in 1607. According to Smith, Gosnold, a council member, was held in high esteem by Edward Maria Wingfield, the Virginia colony's first president.

He died in Jamestown on August 22, 1607 (VI&A 333; STAN 27).

Robert Gosnold: On October 31, 1621, Robert Gosnold, the brother of Anthony Gosnold III, informed Virginia Company officials that he wanted a share of the land to which Anthony III was entitled (VI&A 334).

* * *

[No First Name] Gosnult (Gosnold?): Mr. Gosnult (Gosnold?) arrived in Jamestown on July 31, 1622, and brought along two men. He may have been Anthony Gosnold III, who was attempting to claim some Virginia land (VI&A 334).

Henry Gough (Gooch): On March 22, 1677, Lieutenant Colonel Henry Gough of York County was brought before Governor William Berkeley and the Council of State, who were holding a military tribunal. He was accused of supporting the rebel Nathaniel Bacon's cause but begged for mercy and was fined 6,000 pounds of pork that could be used by the king's soldiers. He also was supposed to post a bond guaranteeing his good behavior. During the 1660s Gough owned a large tract of land on the Chickahominy Swamp (MCGC 461, 533; PB 4:472).

John Gough (Clough, Gooch): The Rev. John Gough, rector of James City Parish, died on January 15, 1684. In 1857 Bishop William Meade commented on finding Gough's grave in the cemetery associated with the church on Jamestown Island (Tyler, "Gooch Family," 111; MEADE I:113).

Mathew Gough (Gogh, Gooch): In July 1639 Mathew Gough patented 350 acres in Henrico County on Four Mile Creek and represented Henrico County in the assembly sessions held in 1642, 1643, and 1644 (LEO 20–22; PB 1:659).

William Gough (Gooch): William Gough represented York County in the assembly sessions held in 1652 and 1654–1655. During the early to mid-1650s he invested in land in the Northern Neck, acquiring 1,050 acres on the south side of the Potomac River near Machodoc and 6,000 acres on the Corotoman River. Gough was named to the Council of State in 1655 but died on September 29th (LEO 30, 32; STAN 37; PB 2:251; 3:357).

William Gough (Gooch): William Gough patented 70 acres of land in King and Queen County in October 1694, and in 1697 he added another 1,225 acres to his holdings, which were on Arricacoe Creek. Gough represented King and Queen County in the assembly session held in 1699. In 1704 the widowed Alice Gough of King and Queen County paid quitrent on 800 acres of land and may have been William's widow (LEO 59; SMITH 37; PB 8:400; 9:96).

George Goulding: In 1607 George Goulding, a laborer, arrived in Virginia in the 1st group of colonists that settled on Jamestown Island (VI&A 334).

Thomas Goulding: Thomas Goulding's lot in urban Jamestown was adjacent to the acreage of Robert Johns, who secured a neighboring parcel in August 1638 (NUG I:96; PB 1:595).

Thomas Gouldman: Thomas Gouldman's name appeared in Old Rappahannock County's records in 1664, when he witnessed a legal document. He patented two large tracts of land there in 1666 and 1667, acreage that was on Hodskins Creek. Gouldman seems to have been living in the county in 1674, when he was serving as guardian to Ralph Warriner and his sister. When merchant George Nangle of the city of Dublin, Ireland, made his will in 1675, he left some fabric and buttons to Gouldman and named him as one of his executors. Then, in March 1679 Old Rappahannock County merchant Thomas Bowler chose Captain Thomas Gouldman as one of his executors. These designations suggest strongly that Gouldman was considered a respected and trustworthy individual. Gouldman represented Old Rappahannock County in the assembly sessions of 1680–1682. In 1714 a Thomas Gouldman, perhaps a descendant, patented some land in Essex County, territory that formerly was part of Old Rappahannock County (LEO 46; Old Rappahannock County Deeds and Wills 1656–1664:322; Deeds and Wills 1665–1677:155–156; Deeds and Wills 1677–1682:60–63, 133–137; PB 6:8, 105, 167, 526).

Edward Gourgaing (Gouynge): In the July 1619 session of the assembly, Edward Gourgaing, a burgess, represented the settlement called Argalls Gift, which was located within the 3,000 acres that had been set aside as the Governor's Land. In September 1619 the Virginia Company paid Gourgaing for some supplies he sent to Berkeley Hundred (VI&A 335; LEO 3).

Abel Gower: In November 1673 Abel Gower patented 501 acres on the lower side of the James River, abutting Sheffield's Swamp in what was then Henrico County but later became Chesterfield. He represented Henrico County in the assembly session of 1679. In 1686 Gower and Edward Stratton laid claim to 487 acres of escheat land in Henrico County. Over the years Gower witnessed wills and functioned as an attorney. One of his friends was Thomas Grendon III, who in 1685 bequeathed him a mourning ring. When Abel Gower made his will on August 25, 1688, he bequeathed life-rights in his plantation to his wife, Jane, whom he named as executrix, and designated his daughter, Tabitha Gower, as reversionary heir. If Tabitha were to die before she attained the age of 21, Obedience and Priscilla Branch were to inherit the testator's plantation. The late Abel Gower's will was proved on June 1, 1689 (LEO 44; Henrico County Will and Deed Book 1677–1692:93; Order Book 1678–1693:61; PB 6:496; 7:508; SR 3732).

Thomas Gower: Thomas Gower, a gentleman who came to Virginia in the first group of colonists, died in Jamestown on August 16, 1607 (VI&A 335).

Grace: On February 15, 1768, when an inventory was made of the late Richard Ambler's slaves on Jamestown Island and his leasehold in the Governor's Land, an adult female slave named Grace was listed with her child Jacob. In 1769 Nanny, who was identified as one of Grace's children, was living on the Governor's Land and was part of the late Edward Ambler I's estate (York County Wills and Inventories 21:386–391; AMB-E).

Amy Gramsby: On May 18, 1622, Amy Gramsby was identified as a maidservant assigned to boat builder Thomas Nunn, an employee of the Company of Shipwrights. She came to Virginia with Nunn and his wife and probably lived with them on Jamestown Island (VI&A 335).

George Graves (Grave) I: In February 1624 George Graves was living in urban Jamestown, where he was a household head. A year later he was still there and shared his home with his wife, Eleanor, a former widow, and their children from former marriages. In April 1625 George Graves claimed that his hog had been wrongfully killed. Because the accused perpetrators were prominent citizens and the man who witnessed the event was deemed unreliable, the case was dismissed. A few months later Graves was given the responsibility of seeing that Robert Wright, a resident of the eastern end of

Jamestown Island, appeared in court, and on January 8, 1627, he presented the General Court with an inventory of the late Robert Lindsey's estate. On October 9, 1627, Graves asked for some land in the Governor's Garden, which was in a more rural part of Jamestown Island, but near the governor's house. George Graves, a respected member of the community, was still alive in January 1629 (VI&A 336).

Nathaniel Graves: Nathaniel Graves, a gentleman who was living in Jamestown in December 1608, accompanied Captain John Smith on a voyage to the Pamunkey Indians' territory (VI&A 337).

Thomas Graves (Granes, Grayes) I: Thomas Graves I, a Virginia Company investor and ancient planter, came to Virginia in 1608 in the 2nd Supply of new settlers. In May 1618 he was named commander of Smyth's or Southampton Hundred, and in 1619 he served as the community's burgess. He went to Ireland and in 1622 made plans to bring 100 people to Virginia. By the mid-1620s he was living on Old Plantation Creek on the Eastern Shore, and in 1628 he was made commander of the plantation of Accomack. In March 1630, while Graves was serving as a burgess for Accomack, he was ordered to inspect the site of the fort built at Old Point Comfort. In 1632 Captain Graves, who was still a burgess for Accomack, served as a commissioner of Accomack's court and as a parish vestryman. He died between November 1635 and January 5, 1636. A 1637 patent reveals that Thomas Graves I paid for the transportation of his wife, Katherine, and sons John and Thomas II (VI&A 337; LEO 3, 9, 11; MCGC 46, 132; Northampton County Orders, Wills, Deeds 1632–1640:58, 66; DOR 1:69; 2:131–132; AMES 2:223).

[No First Name] Gray: In 1629 the justices of the General Court ordered Mrs. William Carter of Jamestown Island to apologize to Goodwife Gray in open court. Mrs. Carter reportedly had referred to Goodwife Gray as a whore when both women were in Elizabeth City. Mrs. Carter denied that Goodwife Gray was one of her cousins (VI&A 338).

* * *

Thomas Gray (Graye) I: Thomas Gray I came to Virginia sometime prior to May 1616 and probably was accompanied by his first wife, Anis (Annis, Anise), probably Anise Valentine, whom he had married in London on March 29, 1611. During the mid-1620s he lived in the eastern end of

Jamestown Island with his second wife, Margaret; his daughter Joan (Jone); and his son William, who died at a young age. Gray was widowed again but by September 11, 1626, had wed a third time, this time marrying Rebecca, a midwife, with whom he produced daughter Rebecca and sons Francis (born around 1630–1635), William (born around 1648–1649), and John (born around 1650–1651). In February 1631 Captain Thomas Gray acquired 100 acres in the corporation of Elizabeth City. In August 1635 he used the headrights of his first and third wives, Anis and Rebecca, and his sons William (the first of that name) and Thomas II when he patented 550 acres on what became known as Grays Creek in Surry County. He already owned some contiguous property that bordered William Perry's plantation. As time went on, Thomas Gray I enhanced the size of his landholdings on Grays Creek. When he testified in court in March 1654, he indicated that he was age 60. He appears to have died before November 2, 1658, having outlived his third wife. He wed a fourth time, producing some additional children who in 1662 were described as orphans. In 1672 Thomas Gray I's son John testified that he and his brother William were joint heirs of their brother Thomas Gray II. Thomas Gray I's daughter Joan (Jone) married John Hux, who outlived her, whereas his daughter Rebecca II married Daniel Hutton, who left her all of his estate (VI&A 338–339; DOR 2:198–201).

Francis Gray (Graye, Grey): Francis, the son of Thomas Gray I and his third wife, Rebecca, was born around 1630–1635. He was a merchant and planter, who in November 1653 patented 750 acres in Charles City County, land that was located on the lower side of the James River near Merchants Hope. Gray represented Charles City County in the assembly session of 1663. In 1658 he was identified as the brother of Thomas Gray II, the owner of land bordering what became known as Grays Creek. Captain Gray seems to have moved to Surry County by 1660, when his name began appearing regularly in local court records. In 1662 Francis Gray was part of a group of local men who investigated the death of a manservant whose corpse was found in the woods. On several other occasions he served on a coroner's jury. In 1662 he disposed of some of his land on Upper Chippokes Creek. Gray began speculating in real estate in the Northern Neck but continued to reside in Surry County. In 1654 he patented 1,000 acres on the south side of the Potomac River

near Rosiers Creek, renewing his claim in 1662; in November 1664 he patented 374 acres in what was then Westmoreland County. On June 16, 1675, the General Court decided that Francis Gray's disagreement with his neighbor, Colonel Thomas Swann, should be aired before the Surry County monthly court. On October 6, 1675, the General Court renewed Francis Gray's land claim. Gray died intestate sometime prior to May 1670, when his widow, Mary, was named administratrix of his estate. By July 1680 she had married Owen Mirick (LEO 37; PB 3:9, 264; 5:224, 328; MCGC 416, 421; Surry County Deed Book 1 [1652–1671]:119, 158, 165, 168, 173, 183, 197, 208, 210, 245, 267, 273, 286, 298, 314, 321, 345, 373, 389; Order Book 1671–1691:248, 305, 310, 329; PB 3:9, 264; 5:224, 328; NUG I:483; VI&A 339; DOR 2:200).

* * *

Anderton Green (Greene): Anderton Green came to Virginia with William Rowley in July 1622. In 1624 he was listed among the dead on the lower side of the James River (VI&A 340).

Dorothy Green (Greene): Dorothy Green, one of Mrs. Elizabeth Clements' servants, came to Virginia in 1617 and probably lived with the Clements family in urban Jamestown. When Mrs. Clements' son, Jeremiah, patented some land on August 26, 1633, he used the headrights of several family members and Mrs. Clements' servants (VI&A 340).

John Green (Greene): In February 1624 John Green was a servant in the Jamestown household headed by provost marshal Randall Smallwood (VI&A 340).

John Green: On December 5 and 6, 1712, John Green and his wife sold William Broadnax I a 12-acre parcel then known as the Thorny Ridge, which was located in the eastern end of Jamestown Island. No references were made to the property's prior ownership (AMB 97–98, 106–107). In 1691 a John Green, who was then living in Surry County's Lawnes Creek Parish, made a trip to England (Surry Deeds and Wills 1684–1691:145). He may have been the same man who later owned the Thorny Ridge.

Richard Green (Greene): Richard Green set sail for Virginia in 1622 and accompanied William Rowley to Jamestown. By February 1624 Green was living on the lower side of the James River, across from

Jamestown and west of Grays Creek. In January 1625 he was listed among that area's dead (VI&A 341).

Roger Green: On November 24, 1671, the vestry of James City Parish reimbursed Roger Green for transporting the Rev. Samuel Jones to Virginia. In March 1676 the General Court decided that Green's dispute with Thomas Hill II, the son of Thomas Hill I and his wife, Mary Peirsey, should be subjected to arbitration. At issue was the fact that in September 1673 Green had agreed to lease Digges Hundred to Hill but ultimately refused to vacate the property (MCGC 288, 447, 449).

Sisley (Cisley) Green (Greene): Sisley Green was living in Ralph Hamor's household in urban Jamestown on February 16, 1624 (VI&A 341).

John Greenfield: John Greenfield, one of Thomas Ludwell's servants, absconded and managed to reach England. In September 1671 he returned to Virginia as a servant to another individual. Ludwell, who was then Secretary of the Colony, recognized Greenfield and shortly after his arrival had him arrested. The General Court ordered Greenfield to complete his original term (MCGC 266, 274).

Richard Gregory: Richard Gregory came to Virginia in 1620 or 1621 and in February 1624 was living at Flowerdew Hundred, where he was one of Sir George Yeardley's servants. By January 1625 he had moved to Yeardley's home in urban Jamestown. On February 9, 1628, Sir George's widow and executrix, Lady Temperance Yeardley, testified in court that Richard Gregory was one of the servants her late husband had brought to Virginia and used as a headright when acquiring the Elizabeth City plantation known as Stanley Hundred. She said that Gregory's headright had been transferred to Thomas Flint, who purchased the plantation. Lady Temperance's statement was corroborated by Flint a few months later (VI&A 343).

Richard Gregory: In 1687 Richard Gregory began patenting land on the north side of the Mattaponi River in what was then New Kent County but later became King and Queen. Four years later he patented some escheat land in New Kent, and in 1691 he invested in some acreage on the south side of the Rappahannock River, on Piscataway Creek. When Ambrose Clare of New Kent County made his will in 1686, he asked Richard Gregory to assist his wife and executrix in settling his estate. In 1698 Richard Gregory represented King and Queen County in the assembly (LEO 58; PB 7:604, 617; 8:140, 210; SR 4777). In 1704 a Mrs. Frances Gregory, who was a widow, paid quitrent on 700 acres in King and Queen County (SMITH 38). She may have been married to Richard Gregory.

Thomas Gregson (Grigson): Thomas Gregson's name began appearing in Essex County records in 1695, when he served as an attorney. It was the first of several occasions on which he represented others. From time to time he also pursued litigation of his own and witnessed documents executed by others. When Gregson purchased some land in Essex County in December 1696, he was identified as a resident of Ware Parish in Gloucester County; however, in March 1697 he was designated an Essex County court justice. By September 1698 Gregson was living in Essex County. He continued to add to his landholdings in Essex, making four purchases in 1699, and as time went on, he spent increasing amounts of time in the county. He bought and sold acreage, which suggests that he began speculating in real estate. Captain Gregson represented Essex County in the assembly session of 1698 and continued to serve as a justice. He was still buying and patenting land in the county in 1703 and 1704. In 1704 he paid quitrent on 300 acres of land in Essex County (LEO 58; Essex County Order Book 1692–1695:242, 246, 253–254, 267, 269; 1695–1699:11, 164; 1699–1702:1; Deeds and Wills 1692–1695:389; 1695–1699:90–91, 173–174, 333; 1699–1702:4–5, 9–10, 12, 40, 42–43, 55–56, 71; 1703–1706:67; Richmond County Deed Book 3 [1697–1704]:53; PB 9:595; SMITH 38).

* * *

Edward Grendon (Grindon, Grindall) I: Edward Grendon I came to Virginia between 1611 and 1616, took an active role in public life, and was widely respected. He made a trip to England but by 1622 had returned to the colony and taken possession of some land on the south side of the James River, a plantation he called Grendon Hill. He shared his home with his wife, Elizabeth, and children Edward II and Temperance. In 1624 Edward Grendon I served as a burgess for the settlers living on the lower side of the James River, across from Jamestown. Sometime prior to August 1624 he came into possession of a ridge of land in the eastern part of Jamestown Island, and later in the year he acquired some acreage in Archer's Hope. In 1627 Grendon was second in command in an expedition against the Tappahannah Indians. He died in 1628, the year he was elected to the assembly on behalf of the people living in Shirley Hundred. He was survived by his wife, Elizabeth, and his grown son, Thomas I, who was his principal heir and lived in England at that time. In 1649, when Thomas Grendon I disposed of his late father's property on the lower side of the James, no mention was made of his Jamestown Island acreage (VI&A 343–344; LEO 5, 7).

Thomas Grendon (Grindon, Grindall) I: Thomas I, Edward Grendon's son, stayed behind in England when his parents moved to Virginia in 1622. In 1627 he sent a shipment of goods from London to Virginia, and he also invested heavily in outfitting and sending people to Virginia, especially skilled workers. By July 1631 Grendon had moved to Virginia and become a planter. In the February 1633 session of the assembly, he served as a burgess for the settlers living at Smith's Mount, Hog Island, and across from Jamestown. When he patented some land on April 12, 1638, he was identified as a London merchant. Thomas Grendon I's will, dated December 15, 1678, stated that he was a resident of Dukes Place and was a citizen and draper of London. He died prior to October 29, 1680, outliving his son, Thomas II, who had married Thomas Stegg I's widow, Elizabeth, and produced a son, Thomas Grendon III (VI&A 344; PB 1:630; LEO 12; DOR 2:225–226).

Thomas Grendon (Grindon) III: Thomas Grendon III, the son of Thomas Grendon II and his wife, Elizabeth, lived at Westover and became a Charles City County justice and lieutenant colonel. He married Sarah, the widow of Thomas Stegg II and George Harris. Sarah was so outspoken that when Governor William Berkeley issued a proclamation on February 10, 1677, naming those who had been involved in Bacon's Rebellion and were exempt from the king's pardon, he listed Sarah. Berkeley identified her as the wife and acting attorney of Thomas Grendon and indicated that she had helped the rebels "by her lyeing and scandalous" words. Thomas Grendon III died at sea on October 10, 1684, and a few months later the thrice-widowed Sarah married Edward Braine (NEVILLE 61; DOR 2:225–226).

* * *

Frances Grenville (Grevill, Grevell) (Mrs. Nathaniel West, Mrs. Abraham Peirsey, Mrs. Samuel Mathews I): Frances Grenville left England in 1620 on the *Supply*, which arrived at Berkeley Hundred in late January 1621. She married Nathaniel West I later in the year and outlived him. In February 1624 Frances and her little son, Nathaniel West II, were living in the household of her brother-in-law John West on the lower side of the James River, in the corporation of James City. By early 1625 Frances and her child had moved to the home of another brother-in-law, Francis West, then a resident of Elizabeth City. Later in the year Frances wed Abraham Peirsey of Flowerdew Hundred, a widower with two children. She outlived him and sometime after March 24, 1628, married Samuel Mathews I, who resided at the plantation known as Mathews Manor or Denbigh. Frances died prior to 1633 (VI&A 345).

John Grevett (Greevett, Gruett): John Grevett, a Virginia Company tenant and a carpenter/ sawyer, was assigned to Governor Francis Wyatt. On April 7, 1623, it was reported that prior to the March 1622 Indian attack, Grevett and Ambrose Griffin, another Virginia Company tenant and carpenter/sawyer, had been constructing a guesthouse or inn in Jamestown for the reception of newly arrived immigrants. They also had been involved in building a palisade and court of guard there. During the mid-1620s John Grevett and his wife, Ellin (Ellen), were residing in the eastern end of Jamestown Island, a rural area. On February 13, 1629, Thomas Warnett, a Jamestown merchant, made a bequest to Ellin Grevett (VI&A 345).

Ambrose Griffin (Gyffith, Griffith): Ambrose Griffin, a 30-year-old sawyer/carpenter from Gloucestershire, England, came to Virginia in 1619 and was a Virginia Company tenant. Sometime prior to the March 1622 Indian attack, Ambrose and fellow sawyer/carpenter John Grevett began constructing a guesthouse or inn in Jamestown, a building intended to provide accommodations to newcomers. Griffin also had been involved in building the palisade and court of guard in Jamestown. On December 8, 1623, Ambrose Griffin was sent to Warresqueak to assist Captain Roger Smith in building a fort there. In early 1624 he was living at Buckroe in Elizabeth City, on land that belonged to the Virginia Company, and a year later he and his wife, Joyce, were sharing Thomas Garnett's home. The Griffins seem to have moved to the lower side of the James River, for in 1629 Joyce was mentioned in a court case involving someone at the Treasurer's Plantation (VI&A 345–346).

John Griffin (Griffen): John Griffin came to Virginia in 1624, and in early 1625 he was a servant in the household of George Menefie in urban Jamestown (VI&A 346).

Ralph (Rafe) Griffin (Griphin): In February 1624 Ralph Griffin was living in the Neck O'Land, an area in which the late Rev. Richard Buck's orphans owned property. In June Griffin testified in court that when he and his mistress, Mrs. Jane Kingsmill, were at the Buck family's home, he overheard Eleanor Spradd and Robert Marshall discuss their plans to marry. Richard Kingsmill, as an overseer of Rev. Buck's will and guardian of his orphans, had temporary possession of the decedent's property in the Neck O'Land, whereas another couple occupied Buck's Jamestown Island homestead (VI&A 346).

Edward Griffith: Edward Griffith of Warwick County was among those who in May 1650 appraised the estate of a Mulberry Island resident, and in December 1656 he was designated an official surveyor. In January 1661, while he was a major in the militia and a resident of Mulberry Island, he joined James City County residents Thomas and Elizabeth Pettus of Littletown in selling a 1,000-acre tract on Potomac Creek in Northumberland County to merchant Henry Meese. Griffith represented Warwick County in the assembly sessions of 1660 and 1662–1676 and succeeded Miles Cary I, who was appointed to the Council of State in 1663. Prior to June 1661 Griffin married the widow and administratrix of Captain Henry Jackson and took custody of the decedent's orphans' goods. In 1667 Griffith witnessed a bill of sale that was recorded in Warwick County's monthly court (LEO 36, 40; Westmoreland County Deeds, Wills &c. 1661–1662: 27a–28a; MCGC 505; DUNN 30, 34, 180).

Ann Grimes: On February 16, 1624, Ann Grimes was a servant in the Yeardley household in urban Jamestown (VI&A 347).

John Grove: In January 1656 John Grove, a sea captain, was living in England, but by 1668 he had moved to Virginia and become a tithable member of Isle of Wight County's Lawnes Creek Parish. Grove was among those commissioned in 1665 to build a fort in Jamestown, as protection against a Dutch invasion. He died in 1671, at which time Edward Ramsey and colonels Nathaniel Bacon and Thomas Swann of urban Jamestown were named his executors. Among those who brought suit against Captain John Grove's estate were Richard Lynny, Francis Mason II, Thomas Pettus's guardian, and

Anthony Gay, a London merchant. Grove apparently spent a considerable amount of time in Jamestown, for his estate was charged for accommodations that had been provided to him and his slave. His estate was also indebted to Mrs. Ann Montford (Surry County Deeds, Wills &c. 1652–1672:97, 315, 383; MCGC 259, 276, 302, 310, 341).

John Grubb: On February 20, 1619, John Grubb and Joachim Andrews were in possession of land in the eastern end of Jamestown Island. When a list of patented land was sent back to England in May 1625, Grubb was credited with 100 acres in nearby Archer's Hope (VI&A 349).

Thomas Grubb: On October 31, 1622, Thomas Grubb, a joiner, agreed to serve Treasurer George Sandys for four months. In November 1624 Sandys convinced his fellow justices that Grubb should serve him another four months. By late January 1625 Grubb was living in the eastern end of Jamestown Island on a leasehold he shared with his partner, Robert Marshall; however, in April 1625 the property was partitioned so that the men could have equal shares. When Grubb made his will, which was proved on May 21, 1627, he bequeathed his part of the leasehold to Robert Wright and Andrew Rawleigh, and on October 10, 1628, the General Court transferred Grubb's property rights to them (VI&A 349).

John Gudderington: John Gudderington, a gentleman, came to Virginia in 1608 in the 2nd Supply of new settlers and would have resided in Jamestown (VI&A 349).

Thomas Guine (Gunie, Gwin?): Thomas Guine died in Jamestown sometime after April 1623 but before February 16, 1624 (VI&A 349).

Thomas Gully: On September 25, 1671, the General Court awarded Thomas Gully and John Fitchett of Jamestown some land on Dragon Swamp, in what became King and Queen County (MCGC 270).

* * *

Edward Gunstocker (Edmund Cunstocker, Indian Ned, Indian John) (Native American): On October 14, 1666, an Indian named Edward Gunstocker received a patent for 150 acres in Old Rappahannock County. He was living there on October 22, 1676, when he made his will. After professing his Christian faith, he stated that he was preparing to go on "an Expedition with the

English against my Cuntrymen [*sic*], the Indians." Gunstock bequeathed his 150-acre plantation and all of his personal property, including his household goods and livestock, to his beloved wife, Mary, and named her as his executrix. Despite the testator's concerns about participating in the 1676 military offensive, he survived and, in fact, lived for another nine or ten years. In September 1683 two men successfully brought suit against Edward Gunstocker. Then, in August 1684 he made a claim in court against the estate of Robert Gullock. However, during the winter of 1685–1686 Gunstocker (otherwise known as Indian Ned) was killed by two Indian males he had employed as servants. According to court testimony given on August 25, 1686, by Samuel Read of Westmoreland County, while Read had been in the woods searching for his livestock, he had been fired upon by two Indians "that had murdered their master Indian Ned and an Englishman in Rappahannocke." During 1686 Edward Gunstocker's will was entered into Old Rappahannock County's records. His widow, Mary, whose ethnicity is uncertain, was then serving as executrix. When two male colonists went to court in early 1688 in an attempt to retain possession of some acreage they had leased from an Indian they called Edward Gunstocker or "John," the justices upheld their right to occupy the land. By October 1688 the late Edward Gunstocker's widow and executrix, Mary, was dead, at which point his property descended to his heirs. In April 1697 an Indian man named Numpskinner, his wife, Betty alias Nonomisk (Nonomiske), and Pattiawaske sold the late Ned Gunstocker's 150 acres in Richmond County (formerly Old Rappahannock) to Nathaniel Pope alias Bridges. The deed of conveyance mentions that the acreage being transferred had been granted to Gunstocker, who was Betty's uncle, on October 14, 1666. Two patents that date to 1697 used the late Mary Gunstocker's land as a reference point (Old Rappahannock County Will Book 1682–1687:41, 100–101; Order Book 1683–1686:74, 166; 1687–1692:13, 49, 92, 71; Richmond County Deed Book 3 [1697–1704]:1–2; Westmoreland County Order Book 1676–1689:517; NN 2:264–265). Ned Gunstocker's patent seems to have been lost or destroyed.

Mary Gunstocker (Mrs. Edward [Edmund] Gunstocker [Cunstocker], wife of Indian Ned, Indian John): When Edward Gunstocker of Old Rappahannock County, a Christianized Indian, made his will on October 22, 1676, he bequeathed his 150-acre plantation and all of his personal property, including his household goods and livestock, to his beloved wife, Mary, and named her as his executrix. By 1686 he was dead, at which time his will was entered into Old Rappahannock County's court records. Gunstocker's widow, Mary, whose ethnicity is uncertain, was authorized to serve as executrix. In early 1688 she brought suit against the widowed Mrs. Crow, probably Ann Crow, a local woman. By October 1688 Mrs. Mary Gunstocker was dead and the property she and her late husband had owned, in what was then Richmond County, descended to his heirs, who were Native Americans. Two patents that date to 1697 used the late Mary Gunstocker's land as a reference point (Old Rappahannock County Will Book 1682–1687:41, 100–101; Order Book 1683–1686:74, 166; 1687–1692:13, 49, 92, 71; Richmond County Deed Book 3 [1697–1704]:1–2; Westmoreland County Order Book 1676–1689:517; NN 2:264–265).

* * *

John Gunstone: On February 4, 1674, the justices of Surry County's monthly court learned that John Gunstone had provided food to William Smith's orphaned child, who resided in urban Jamestown (Surry County Deeds, Wills &c. 1671–1684:67).

George Gwillen (Gwillum, Gwellins, Gwilliams?): George Gwillen came to Virginia sometime prior to February 1647, when he witnessed a land transaction in Nansemond County. In 1650 his headright was used by a man patenting land on the Rappahannock River. Gwillen represented Nansemond County in the assembly sessions of 1662–1665, an indication that he owned land in the county or was married to someone who did. In February 1676 he patented some escheat land, 300 acres located in Nansemond County (LEO 39; PB 2:137, 259; 6:594).

Hugh Gwyn (Gwynn, Gwin, Guinne): Sometime prior to December 1635, Hugh Gwyn patented 1,000 acres of land on the Piankatank River, in the northernmost part of what eventually became Gloucester County, but was then part of Charles River (York) County. He repatented his original acreage in 1642, when he expanded his holdings to include an additional 1,700 acres. In 1640 and 1646 Gwyn represented Charles River County in the assembly. He also was a justice in the county court and in 1648 served as a tax collector. He confirmed a deed of gift executed by his wife, Ann, in late 1640, a transaction that was registered in York County. Sometime prior to June 4, 1640, three of Gwyn's servants (a Dutchman, a Scot, and a black man) fled to Maryland. Although he asked the General Court's permission to sell them or let them be put to hire in Maryland, the justices decided that the runaways should be whipped and then returned to their master in Virginia. Hugh Gwyn was returned to the assembly in 1652, this time serving on behalf of the newly formed Gloucester County, where he owned a large quantity of land. By 1652 he was in possession of the acreage that became known as Gwynn's Island, and in 1657 he patented 165 acres close to Milford Haven Creek. Hugh Gwyn also owned 800 acres in Stafford County, acreage that his son, John, disposed of in 1689. In February 1657 Hugh Gwyn was serving as a Gloucester County justice and held the rank of colonel. By 1791 his acreage in Gloucester County had become part of Mathews County (LEO 18, 25, 29–30; PB 1:806, 865; 3:120; 4:236; York County Record Book 1633–1646:95; 1648–1657:294, 430; MCGC 466; Stafford County Record Book 1686–1693:131a–132).

John Gwyn (Gwynn, Gwin, Guinne): In April 1671 the justices of the General Court acknowledged the resolution of a suit that John Gwyn, a clergyman, had initiated in Gloucester County, litigation that was subjected to arbitration. In 1673 Gwyn, who was rector of Ware Parish in Gloucester, sued John Throgmorton, a churchwarden. A year later Gwyn was attributed to Abingdon Parish—which adjoined Ware Parish—and was identified as a clergyman and planter (MCGC 249, 331, 373, 380).

John Gwyn (Gwynn, Gwin, Guinne): John Gwyn, who was identified as a James City merchant, died in 1684. He named Henry Jenkins, his kinsman and heir, as his executor. Jenkins, a tanner and surveyor, prepared a plat of Gwyn's acreage on the mainland, a parcel that became part of the Ambler farm (WITH 276; CBE 26; AMB 167 f 91).

H

Thomas Hackett (Hacket): In June 1652 Captain Thomas Hackett patented 800 acres on the north side of the Corotoman River in Lancaster County and served as one of Lancaster's burgesses in the assembly sessions held in 1653. In August 1653 Hackett, an apparently volatile man, sent his stepson, Richard Denham (Denhawes), to the county court to deliver a challenge to David Fox, a sitting justice. Hackett proposed that he and Fox duel with eight-inch rapiers. Lancaster's justices pointed out that dueling was contrary to the laws of England and sentenced Denham to a whipping because he had delivered the message, and they also fined Hackett. Later in the year Hackett sued John Robinson's wife, Mary (Marie), and claimed that she had slandered his wife. In October 1655 Hackett executed a deed of gift whereby he gave his wife, Mary, and her children (Richard, Eleanor, William, and Suzanna Denham) his 800-acre plantation on the Corotoman River. He was still alive in August 1656 but died prior to February 11, 1657, when the widowed Mary Hackett presented an inventory of her late husband's estate (LEO 31; PB 3:206; Lancaster County Deeds &c. Book 1 [1637–1647]:125; 2 [1652– 1657]:64–65, 97, 153, 165, 226, 288; 3 [1654– 1661]:13–14, 125–126, 133).

Thomas Hackthorpe: On November 28, 1625, the General Court decided that Thomas Hackthorpe, one of ship captain Richard Page's servants, would be delivered to Abraham Peirsey in exchange for the two male servants whom Page was supposed to deliver to Peirsey but lost. Hackthorpe may have joined the Peirsey household in Jamestown or been taken to Peirsey's plantation, Flowerdew Hundred (VI&A 352).

Thomas Hadley: On October 13, 1697, Thomas Hadley purchased George Harvey's ¾-acre lot on Back Street in urban Jamestown. It included the eastern half of a two-story brick row house that was burned during Bacon's Rebellion and was partially rebuilt. Hadley may have become ill by December 1697, for he bequeathed all of his real and personal estate to his wife, Dyonysia (Dionysia), and shortly thereafter she began serving as his executrix. Mrs. Dyonysia Hadley, having inherited fee simple ownership of her late husband's property in Jamestown, sold it on June 6, 1698. It was then noted that she had transferred it to John Tullitt (Tullett) of James City Parish and County. On the cover of the deed Mrs. Hadley was listed as Dyonysia Savage Ravenscroft Hadley, and when acting as grantor, she identified herself as the "executrix and legatee of Thomas Hadley" (LEE MS 51 ff 669, 671).

Thomas Haistwell (Hastwell): In October 1686 Elizabeth Haistwell and her husband, Thomas, a London merchant and one of Micajah Perry's associates, purchased 90 acres in Nansemond County from John Hudnell and his wife, Mary. In 1699 Thomas Haistwell was identified as a friend of John Thompson of Surry County, the brother of tavern-keeper William Thompson, who prior to Bacon's Rebellion operated Colonel Thomas Swann's tavern in urban Jamestown. In 1701 Haistwell and his brother, Edward, who also was a London merchant, gave their power of attorney to John Burges of Surry (WITH 122; PB 7:528; SR 1461; Surry County Deeds, Wills &c. 5 [1694–1709]:242; Court Records 6 [1700–1711]:15).

Thomas Hakes: Thomas Hakes died on Jamestown Island sometime after April 1623 but before February 16, 1624 (VI&A 353). He may have been the individual known as Thomas Hack, who was living at Flowerdew Hundred in February 1624.

Thomas Hale (Haile, Hayle): Thomas Hale came to Virginia in 1623 and during the mid-1620s lived at West and Shirley Hundred, where he was a servant in Robert Partin's household. On June 4, 1627, the General Court's justices decided that Hale would be executed in Jamestown, for he was found guilty of raping four young girls (VI&A 353).

John Haley: John Haley of Gloucester County was among the men who in 1682 destroyed much of the year's tobacco crop in an attempt to raise prices. Although he posted a bond guaranteeing that he would appear in court, he fled and was declared an outlaw. Haley was captured and in June 1683 was incarcerated in Jamestown, in James City County's common jail. He was among those exempt from pardon for committing a treasonous offence (CO 5/1405 f 179; EJC I:40, 48–49, 488, 494).

William Halila: William Halila came to Virginia in 1617 at the expense of ancient planter Richard Kingsmill of Jamestown and was not listed in the demographic records compiled in 1624 or 1625 (VI&A 354).

[No First Name] Hall: Mr. Hall, who seems to have been associated with the Virginia

Company and went to Virginia, died sometime prior to incoming Governor George Yeardley's arrival in Jamestown on April 19, 1619 (VI&A 354).

Christopher Hall (Haule, Haul): In 1624 Christopher Hall lived on the Governor's Land, but by January 1625 he had moved to Jamestown Island. He seems to have lived on the periphery of the urbanized area, near Dr. John Pott's lot on Back Street, for he was aware that free-roaming swine and cattle had damaged the physician's tobacco crop. In August 1625 Hall argued with his Jamestown Island neighbor, Thomas Passmore, over the division of a tobacco crop and a land agreement the two men had made. By September 1627 Hall and his wife, Amy, had moved to Archer's Hope, where he and a partner, William Harman, shared a 100-acre leasehold. Amy, who had a violent temper, came to blows with Harman on at least one occasion and was punished by being towed behind a ship and being ducked in the river. By February 9, 1628, Christopher Hall was dead (VI&A 354).

George (Georg) Hall: George Hall came to Virginia in 1620. During the mid-1620s he was a servant in Governor Francis Wyatt's household in urban Jamestown (VI&A 355).

John Hall (Haule): During the mid-1620s John Hall and his wife, Susan, lived in the eastern end of Jamestown Island. On August 22, 1625, the General Court granted him a legal title to the four acres of land and dwelling he occupied, real estate he had used as collateral when securing a debt to Thomas Passmore. Hall, who outlived his wife, Susan, died before he repaid his debt. On February 6, 1626, his widowed new wife, Bridgett, was obliged to surrender his Jamestown Island property to Passmore (VI&A 355).

Susan (Susanna) Hall: Susan Hall went to Virginia in 1618 and during the mid-1620s was living in urban Jamestown, where she was a servant in Sir George Yeardley's household. On October 12, 1627, she witnessed Yeardley's will and in February 1628 verified its authenticity. Hall returned to England and on May 21, 1630, testified before the Chancery Court about Yeardley's activities while she was in Virginia (VI&A 356).

Thomas Hall: On January 11, 1677, Thomas Hall, New Kent County's clerk of court, was tried at a martial court held aboard Captain John Martin's ship, which was anchored at Tindall's Point on the upper side of the York River. He was condemned for his role in Bacon's Rebellion and was sentenced to be hanged on the river's lower shore. According to Governor William Berkeley, Hall, who died penitent, was more useful to Bacon than 40 armed men. When Berkeley issued a proclamation on February 10, 1677, in which he named those who were exempt from the king's pardon due to their role in Bacon's Rebellion, he said that Hall had already been executed (MCGC 454, 527; NEVILLE 61, 274).

William Hall: By 1654 William Hall, a cooper, had begun to acquire land in Lancaster County. In 1656 he purchased a large parcel from Richard Lawson; two years later, when he disposed of the Lawson acreage, he indicated that he was living in Rappahannock County, that is, Old Rappahannock County. In 1661 Hall patented 573 acres in Lancaster County near the head of the Rappahannock River, and then repatented his acreage two years later. Although he identified himself as a cooper in 1665 when he and his wife, Jane, sold off some of their land, he also earned income as a merchant. In 1665, when he rented two sloops from Cuthbert Potter to be used by the ship *Providence*, Hall paid Potter by giving him a substantial quantity of plank and some tobacco. Hall also consigned to Potter a substantial quantity of black cotton fabric and a large anchor intended for use by the ship *Berkeley*. When three men patented some land in 1670 in Northumberland County, at the head of the Great Wiccomoco River, it was said to be adjacent to Mr. William Hall's property. Hall represented Lancaster County in the assembly sessions held in 1677 (LEO 43; Lancaster County Record Book 2 [1637–1640]:309–310, 315, 377; Deeds &c. Book 2 [1652–1657]: 239; Deeds and Wills 1654–1661:35–36, 98; Old Rappahannock County Deeds and Wills 1656–1662:30; 1656–1664:197, 331–332, 346–347; PB 4:393, 549; NUG II:88).

William Hallet (Hallett): Official records reveal that on October 13, 1693, William Hallet was supposed to host the assembly's Committee for Public Claims. This raises the possibility that he had access to accommodations in Jamestown, property that he owned or perhaps rented. On May 4, 1724, William Hallet of Northampton County made his will, and by September 8th he was dead. He bequeathed to his wife, Lettice, life-rights in his entire estate during her widowhood. After her death or remarriage, his real and personal property was to be divided among his four children: Marshman, Sarah,

John, and Nany. Court records reveal that Lettice Hallet was the daughter of the late John Ramsbottom (JHB1660–1693:452; Northampton County Deeds, Wills &c. 1718–1725:195; MARSHALL 224, 244).

Jeremy (Jereme, Jerome, Jerime, Hierome) Ham (Hamm): In June 1655 Jeremy Ham began serving as a justice of York County's monthly court, and in July the justices convened in his home. Around that time Ham brought suit against a Charles City County man who owed him some tobacco. He represented York County in the assembly sessions held in 1658 (LEO 34; York County Deeds, Orders, Wills [1648–1657]:254, 259; Charles City County Court Orders 1655–1658:17). No patents or other land records have come to light that are attributable to Jeremy Ham, although land ownership was a prerequisite to office holding. Therefore, his wife may have been in possession of realty.

John Haman (Hamun): John Haman died in Jamestown sometime after April 1623 but before February 16, 1624. His name was listed twice among those who died in Jamestown (VI&A 357).

Stephen (Steeven) Hamlin (Hamlyn, Hamelyn, Hamblin, Hamblen, Hamblyn): Stephen Hamlin arrived in Virginia sometime prior February 1638, when he patented 250 acres of land on the east side of Queens Creek, near Middle Plantation. Then, in 1642 he patented an adjacent 400-acre tract. Thomas Philips sued Hamlin in 1640 and accused him of wrongfully keeping some of his personal belongings. In December 1645 Hamlin authorized Henry Lee to collect his debts in Charles River (later, York) County, perhaps because he was considering a move. He still had his land on Queens Creek in February 1649 when he secured a claim to 1,250 acres in Charles City County, above Weyanoke. Hamlin represented Charles City County in the assembly sessions held in 1654–1655, while the Commonwealth government was in power. He was returned to office in 1660 and served from 1661 to 1664. Hamlin also was a justice in Charles City County's monthly court in 1662. He died in 1665, and a year later his widow was awarded her dower third when his title to a 1,400-acre parcel in Charles City County was confirmed. Many years later Abraham Hamlin gave a copy of the late Stephen Hamlin's will to Charles City County's justices (LEO 32, 36–37; PB 1:618, 856; 2:266; 5:487; York County Deeds, Orders, Wills 2 [1633–1646]:119; 2 [1648–1657]:431; Court Orders 1661–1664:348; Lower Norfolk County Record Book C [1641–1654]:78; Charles City County Will and Deed Book A:77; MCGC 475).

John Hammond: John Hammond arrived in Virginia sometime prior to 1649 and became a planter in Isle of Wight County. In 1650 he was among those sued by the owners of the ship *Comfort* because he joined John George and George Hardy in taking custody of the estate of the vessel's captain, William Garnett. In 1652, while the Commonwealth government was in power, John Hammond was elected a burgess for Isle of Wight County's Lower Parish. However, he was expelled from the assembly because he was "notoriously knowne a scandalous person, and a frequent disturber of the peace of the country, by libell and other illegall practices." After he was ejected from the assembly, Isle of Wight's sheriff was ordered to hold a new election. Hammond's expulsion raises the possibility that he was a royalist who overtly opposed the Cromwell regime. In 1656 a text written by John Hammond— *Leah and Rachel, or, The Two Fruitfull Sisters Virginia and Maryland*—was published in England and was reprinted by Peter Force in 1844. In the preface he indicated that he had fled to Maryland. Hammond may have been related to the merchant John Hammond, who was living in England in 1677 and exported goods to Virginia (LEO 30; HEN I:374; SR 633, 5590, 7316, 10425; FOR III:14:1–32).

Manwarring (Manwaring, Manering, Mannaring, Mannering) Hammond (Hamond, Hamon): Manwarring Hammond, a staunch royalist, took refuge in Virginia around the time King Charles I was beheaded. In 1649 he patented 3,760 acres on the Pamunkey River, acreage that included the site of Fort Royall, a surveillance and trading post located on the upper side of the river, directly across from the bulk of his property. Hammond's acreage on the lower side of the Pamunkey extended for several miles and ran from the eastern branch of Black Creek westward to Totopotomoy Creek. In early 1650 Hammond was among a group of royalists who were lavishly entertained at Captain Christopher Wormeley I's York River plantation on Wormeley Creek in York County. As time went on, he continued to acquire land, patenting 600 acres in 1658 on Pouncey's Creek and then an additional 850 acres in 1661. Finally, in 1667 he laid claim to 4,610 acres on the eastern side of Black Creek. Most of the land he patented was on the lower side of the Pamunkey River in New Kent County. In 1660 Ham-

mond was elected a burgess for New Kent County but later in the year was named to the Council of State. He also patented some acreage in Henrico County, investing with Captain Thomas Stegg. In February 1661 Hammond was identified as a major general when he served as a Charles City County justice. On June 2, 1662, he indicated that he was at Rickahock (his plantation in New Kent) when he authorized several prominent men to serve as his attorneys in Virginia. In 1670 he sold Captain William Bassett some land on the upper side of the Pamunkey River, acreage that included the Fort Royall site. Hammond died sometime after 1670, probably in Ireland (STAN 38; LEO xx, 36; FOR III:10:49; PB 2:195; 4:342, 470, 583; 6:81; NUG I:187, 190; II:290, 306; Charles City County Court Orders 1658–1661:279; 1661–1664:314, 359, 361).

* * *

Ralph Hamor (Hamer): Ralph Hamor, a Virginia Company investor, came to Virginia in 1609 and within a year became clerk of the council. He also served as Secretary of State from 1611 to 1614. In 1614 Hamor wrote a treatise in which he described the status of the fledgling colony. He became vice-admiral and left Virginia but returned in May 1617. At the time of the March 22, 1622, Indian attack, Captain Ralph Hamor was building a home in Warresqueak. Afterward, he evacuated the surviving settlers to the safety of Jamestown Island. He patented a waterfront lot in urban Jamestown and continued to reside there with his wife, Elizabeth, who was Jeremiah Clements I's widow, and two of the children from her former marriage. Ralph Hamor became involved in a legal dispute over some Hog Island acreage that he had cleared and seated, and in January 1625 he transferred his 100 acres in Archer's Hope to Richard Kingsmill. The Hamors were actively involved in the Jamestown community's goings-on and appeared in court from time to time. Ralph Hamor died sometime prior to October 11, 1626 and was survived by his wife, Elizabeth, his sole heir. By February 8, 1628, she had married Tobias Felgate and made plans to return to England. She died prior to March 30, 1630, having bequeathed virtually all of her Virginia property to her son, Jeremiah Clements II (VI&A 358–359).

Thomas Hamor (Hamer): Sometime prior to the March 22, 1622, Indian attack, Thomas Hamor and his brother, Ralph, built homes in Warresqueak. When the Indians attacked, Thomas was at Master Harrison's house with six men and a large group of women and children. The Indians set a tobacco house ablaze and then fired on those who ventured out to quench the fire. Hamor fled back to Harrison's house, which the Indians set on fire, and finally managed to reach his own dwelling, despite an arrow that pierced his back. His wife also was seriously wounded. In the wake of the Indian attack, Thomas Hamor, his wife, and daughter were evacuated to Jamestown Island, a more secure position. By January 21, 1623, the Hamors, who were still on Jamestown Island, had become seriously ill, and he died of a burning fever shortly thereafter. According to Samuel Mole, a surgeon, Hamor's coffin was made by Nathaniel Jefferys, a Jamestown Island joiner (VI&A 359–360).

* * *

Thomas Hampton: The Rev. Thomas Hampton, rector of James City Parish from around 1639 to 1645, patented 1,100 acres of land on the Nansemond River in Upper Norfolk (later, Nansemond) County during the late 1630s, using headrights to assert his claim. It is uncertain whether Hampton was a highly successful planter or had the backing of a wealthy family. On November 4, 1639, he patented a long, narrow ridge of land in the western end of Jamestown Island, behind the church, acreage that he had to develop within six months or face forfeiture. Research suggests that Hampton's patent enveloped the ridge upon which Sir William Berkeley built a three-bay brick row house in 1645. On June 12, 1644, Hampton laid claim to an eight-acre parcel behind the church that abutted the Back Creek at a site known as "the Friggott"; his acreage was mentioned in Rudolph Spraggon's August 18, 1644, patent. Hampton's acquisitive nature seems to have extended to his life as a cleric. On October 1640 he informed the Council of State that the glebe his parish vestry had provided him contained 100 acres, not the 200 required by law. In 1646 the justices of York County censured Hampton for misappropriating the late John Powell's estate, which was supposed to be used toward the support of his orphans. Because young William Powell was left destitute, without the minimum necessities of food and clothing, the remainder of the Powell estate was seized and entrusted to a substitute guardian. The Rev. Thomas Hampton continued to acquire land. In 1654 he patented 550 acres on Diascund Creek, and in 1658 he enlarged his holdings by 400 acres. Later in the year he added another 700 acres in the same vicinity. In 1670 cartographer

Augustine Hermann labeled the Rev. Thomas Hampton's land near Diascund Creek as "Mr. Rampton's" (PB1:689; 2:11, 105; NUG I:56, 71, 154, 169, 285, 379, 387; MCGC 471; MCGH 481–482).

John Haney (Hayney, Heiny, Haine, Hemy, Henry): John Haney, a Virginia Company tenant, came to Virginia in 1621. During the mid-1620s he and his wife were living in Buckroe, in Elizabeth City. In January 1626 Haney was censured for two affronts to authority and sentenced to imprisonment in Jamestown and a public whipping. In January 1627, the defunct Virginia Company's servants and tenants were assigned to members of the Council of State, and Haney, who was still a Company tenant, was given to council member William Farrar. In December 1627 Haney acquired 150 acres at Buckroe, near Old Point Comfort Island and William Hampton's leasehold (VI&A 361).

John Haney (Haynie, Hayney): John Haney moved to Northumberland County sometime prior to 1651. He was identified as a resident of Wicocomocoe in 1654 when he patented 395 acres on the Potomac River. When he testified in court in August 1655, he said that he was age 35. In 1656 a local surgeon, William Adams, authorized Haney to serve as his attorney. Haney acquired some additional land abutting the Potomac River on May 20, 1656, and in 1662 he patented 350 acres at the head of the Wicocomocoe River. When he represented Northumberland County in the assembly sessions held in 1658, he was still living in Wicocomocoe. In 1658 he and William Presley served as the late Robert Newman's executors, and later they settled the estate of the decedent's widow, Elizabeth. In 1661 Haney became Northumberland County's official surveyor and also participated in a jury trial. As time went on, he continued to patent land on Dividing Creek, the Great Wicocomocoe River, and Chingohan Creek. A land transaction he made in 1668 reveals that he was living near the Presley plantation. Captain John Haney and his wife appeared in Northumberland County's court in July 1670, where they gave testimony. Several years later he was the defendant in a suit undertaken by a former indentured servant. In December 1677 Haney was identified as the commander of 20 soldiers who participated in an offensive against the Susquehannock Indians. He was still performing surveys in the 1670s and 1680s, when he became a county justice. In 1681 he and another man obtained permission to operate a tavern in the new county seat, and four years later

Haney was given the responsibility of seeing that the county prison was in good repair and that its boundaries were properly laid out. In 1693 and 1694 John Haney Sr.'s name appeared in county records, suggesting that he had an adult son that bore his name (LEO 34; PB 2:92–93; 3:13; 5:113; 6:165; NN 2:92–93, 169; Northumberland County Deeds and Orders 1650–1652:66; Wills, Inventories, &c. 1652–1658:103, 127; Record Book 1658–1662:14, 19, 21A–22; 1662–1666:80, 97, 111–112; 1666–1670:83–84; Order Book 1652–1665:65, 143, 185, 275, 285, 394; 1666–1678:98, 198, 218, 259, 307, 315, 329; 1678–1698:64, 68, 73, 97, 177, 183, 265, 332; 1699–1700:70). There is no known connection between John Haney of Northumberland County and Virginia Company tenant John Haney.

Richard Haney (Hanie, Hayney): In July 1664 the governor and council of the island of Mounserat called for the arrest of Richard Haney and some other armed men, who were brought in by Robert Munden, commander of the *Charles*. The accused allegedly assembled on the seashore at night and then overpowered the crew of a shallop that was loaded with sugar and anchored nearby. During the course of the attack, a seaman was wounded and several other people were imprisoned in a storehouse. After the perpetrators were rounded up, they were put aboard the *Charles* and taken to Virginia to stand trial. The bill of complaint was entered into the records of the Northumberland County court, a jurisdiction in which Captain Robert Munden did business (Northumberland County Record Book 1662–1666:131–132). This Richard Haney should not be confused with the man who became a Northumberland County burgess.

Richard Haney (Hanie, Hayney): Richard Haney was living in Northumberland County in 1681 when he was a member of a jury. A year later he served as an attorney, representing William Templar in a lawsuit. As time went on, Haney continued to appear in court, functioning as a witness or an attorney, or interacting with his own debtors and creditors. In 1687 he was the attorney of Daniel Webb, a mulatto freed by the will of his late master, Major John Mottrom. He also served as security for Alexander and Jane Wetherstone, who became responsible for a two-year-old bound servant, Rebecca Maudley. In 1691 Richard Haney patented 1,428 acres on the south side of the Rappahannock River in what was then "Old" Rappahannock County. He represented Northumberland County in the assembly sessions held in 1695–1696, 1696–1697, 1698, and

1703–1705 (LEO 54, 56, 58, 62; Northumberland County Order Book 1678–1698:100, 125, 181, 218, 262, 296, 324, 405, 407; 1699–1700:106; PB 8:199).

Hannah: On February 15, 1768, when an inventory was made of the late Richard Ambler's slaves on Jamestown Island and his leasehold in the Governor's Land, an adult female slave named Hannah was listed with her child, Charles. In 1769 Hannah and her son, Charles, were living on Jamestown Island and were attributed to the estate of Edward Ambler I (York County Wills and Inventories 21:386–391; AMB-E).

Hannah: On February 15, 1768, when an inventory was made of the late Richard Ambler's slaves on Jamestown Island and his leasehold in the Governor's Land, an adult female slave named Hannah was listed. She probably was the woman called Hannah whom Ambler bequeathed to his son, John I, and mentioned in his 1765 will. In 1769 she was identified as Old Hannah, was living on Jamestown Island, and was attributed to the estate of Edward Ambler I (York County Wills and Inventories 21:378–382, 386–391; AMB-E).

Hannah: In 1769 an enslaved woman identified as Long Hannah (probably on account of her height) was living on the Governor's Land. She and all but one of her children were attributed to the estate of the late Edward Ambler I. Long Hannah's daughter, Amy (Amey), was then living on Jamestown Island (AMB-E).

Hannah: In 1769 three adult female slaves named Hannah were living on Jamestown Island and were included in the late Edward Ambler I's estate. Each of the women had an infant (AMB-E). These three enslaved women should not be confused with the females called Old Hannah, Long Hannah, and Hannah, the mother of Charles.

Thomas Hansford (Hunsford): In 1676 Thomas Hansford of York County, whom Governor William Berkeley described as "a valiant stout man" and "resolved rebel," was executed at John Custis II's Arlington plantation on the Eastern Shore. On February 10, 1677, Governor Berkeley issued a proclamation, which noted that Hansford already had been executed and that his estate was not exempt from seizure. After Hansford's personal belongings had been confiscated, they were sold off. A significant number of the purchasers were high-ranking officials who had been Berkeley supporters. Later, Thomas Palmer, a builder, filed an appeal with the king's commissioners. He said that he had constructed a house for Hansford, who owed him 3,800 pounds of tobacco, and that Hansford's widow had only been able to pay him seven pounds. The king's commissioners decided that the seizure of Hansford's property was illegal (NEVILLE 61, 274; SR 660, 661, 749, 6618).

William Hardidge (Hardich) II: William Hardidge II, who became a Westmoreland County burgess, was the son of William Hardidge I, a highly successful merchant and planter. In October 1653 William Hardidge I, who derived part of his income from transatlantic trade, patented 1,000 acres on Poor Jack's Creek, a tributary of Nominy Bay, and added 1,450 acres to his holdings during 1664. Hardidge and his wife, Elizabeth I, the daughter of Ann Sturman, resided in Westmoreland County, where he served as a justice in the county court and as a major in the local militia. He returned to Bristol, England, but when he made his will on October 24, 1668, he described himself as "late of Nominy in the county of Westmoreland." He died sometime prior to January 8, 1669. Hardidge left the bulk of his real and personal property to his son, William Hardidge II, then a minor living in England. He bequeathed some of his household goods to his daughter, Elizabeth II, the wife of Robert Wynston, and made modest bequests to his sisters Elizabeth Boyce and Alice Foster and brother, Thomas Hardidge.

William Hardidge II, who came of age in 1673, moved to Virginia and took custody of his inheritance. By March 1680 he had married the much-widowed Frances, who had outlived Thomas Speke, Valentine Peyton, Captain John Appleton, and Colonel John Washington, all of whom had been burgesses. Hardidge, who was wealthy and prominent in his own right, became a county justice and sheriff. From time to time, the county court convened at his home in Nominy. Hardidge, who continued to serve as a county justice, represented Westmoreland County in the assembly sessions held in 1680–1682, 1685–1686, 1688, 1691–1692, and 1693. Like John and Lawrence Washington, he was a trustee of the firm that traded as Thomas Pope and Company. In March 1694 Captain William Hardidge II's will was presented to the justices of Westmoreland County's monthly court, where it was proved. Two of the four men he named as executors were chosen to serve (LEO 46, 48–49, 51–53; PB 3:62; 5:441, 454; SR 3542; Westmoreland County Deeds, Wills, Patents &c. 1653–1659:14, 20, 38, 98a–99, 116a–117; Deeds and Wills No. 1 [1653–1671]:111–112, 253–254; Deeds, Wills &c. 1661–1662:36; Deeds, Patents &c. 1665–1677:83–83a, 103a–104, 123–123a, 148; Orders 1662–1664:26, 32; 1676–1689:180, 204, 218, 240, 341, 393, 400, 405, 407, 481, 508, 589, 640; 1691–1699:103a, 129).

[No First Name] Hardwin (Hardwyn): A man named Hardwin, a laborer, came to Virginia in 1608 in the 2nd Supply of new colonists and resided in Jamestown (VI&A 363).

George Hardy (Hardey, Hardde, Hardin, Handy): George Hardy, a shipwright, represented Isle of Wight County in the assembly sessions held in 1642, 1644, 1645, 1645–1646, 1649, and 1652. In 1646 he and two other men bought a mill at the head of Lawnes Creek in Isle of Wight County. During the late 1640s Hardy and two business partners patented 1,100 acres on the Blackwater River. In 1650 he joined John George and John Hammond in taking custody of the estate of the *Comfort's* captain, William Garnett. A year later Hardy served as the administrator of William Lamb, who also was a mariner. When George Hardy made his will on March 16, 1654, he specified that after the death of his wife, who had life-rights in his estate, his personal property was to be divided between his kinsman George Hardy Jr. (perhaps a nephew) and Christian Willson. The testator's mill was to go to George Jr., who also was to get his seal ring and some land. He asked his wife to look after his kinsman Thomas Hardy, and he bequeathed to Willson his interest in some land whose ownership was being contested by Justinian Cooper's successors. Hardy apparently was a religious man, for he left a substantial sum toward the construction of a new parish church, on the condition that it would be built of brick. George Hardy's will was proved on April 14, 1655 (LEO 20, 22–24, 27, 29; Isle of Wight County Deeds, Wills, & Guardian Accounts Book A:97; Will and Deed Book 1 [1662–1688]:576–577; SR 7218, 10425; PB 2:142; BILL 45).

Anthony Harlow: On February 16, 1624, Anthony Harlow was a member of Ensign William Spence's household, which resided in the eastern end of Jamestown Island (VI&A 363).

John Harlow (Harlowe, Harloe): John Harlow, a Warwick County resident, became a churchwarden of Denbigh Parish in 1647, and his plantation was mentioned in a land transaction that occurred in 1657. Harlow represented Warwick County in the assembly sessions held in 1659, and his name appeared in local court records in 1662. On

May 26, 1671, he won a suit against Mrs. Katherine Whitby, the widow of William Whitby, who prior to March 1655 leased a bay of Governor William Berkeley's brick row house in urban Jamestown. In October 1675 Harlow again asserted a claim against Whitby's estate in an attempt to recover some funds. The suit was postponed and was still pending in March 1676 (LEO 35; DUNN 18, 34, 179, 567; MCGC 262, 278, 425, 442; HEN I:407). John Harlowe of Warwick County may have been the son of 28-year-old John Harlowe, who resided in the corporation of Elizabeth City in 1625 and eventually moved to the Eastern Shore. In 1651 that individual named his son, John, as one of his heirs (VI&A 363; PB 1:377, 790, 851; MARSHALL 31).

Thomas Harmanson: In June 1654 Thomas Harmanson patented 1,300 acres of land on the seaside, near the Matchepungo River in Northampton County. Then, in April 1667 he secured an additional 800 acres. Harmanson was among those who in 1677 protested against the somewhat meandering boundary line that separated Northampton and Accomack counties. Some of his land was thought to lie within the boundaries of the acreage assigned to the Chingoskin Indians. Harmanson represented Northampton County in the assembly sessions held in 1688 and 1691–1692. When he made his will on March 26, 1696, he described himself as "aged and weak in body." He made bequests to his wife, Elizabeth; to sons Thomas II, William, John, Henry, George, and Benjamin; to daughters Isabell (the wife of William Waters II), Elita and Elicia (the wife of Thomas Savage), and Margaret (the wife of Thomas Clay); to his grandchildren, Thomas and Elishe Harmanson; to his great grandson, Jacob Clay; and to some friends. The land, household goods, and personal effects that Harmanson bestowed on friends and kin attest to his wealth (LEO 49–50; PB 3:285; 6:30; MCGC 353, 369, 381; JHB 1659–1693:77; MARSHALL 169–170).

Ambrose Harmar (Harmer): Sometime after July 7, 1630, but before July 25, 1628, Ambrose Harmar married Richard Kingsmill's widow, Jane, and moved into a home that was located on her dower share of her late husband's Jamestown Island property. Harmar represented Jamestown in the colony's assembly in 1645 and 1646; his eligibility to serve was based on his wife's land ownership, for he never seems to have owned land there personally. Harmar was speaker of the assembly in 1646 and a member of the Council of State in 1639 and 1640. He patented marshland on the Chickahominy River and shipped a large quantity of beaver pelts to England, raising the possibility that he was involved in trapping or perhaps in Indian trade. In May 1637 Harmar asked officials in England to appoint him guardian (or custodian) of Benomi Buck, the Rev. Richard Buck's mentally handicapped son, who had just turned 21; Harmar said that he had looked after the youth for many years. Sir John Harvey disagreed with the English officials' decision, for he felt that it was his prerogative as governor to appoint custodians for the impaired. He also claimed that Jane Harmar was greedy and that she and her former husband, Richard Kingsmill, had profited handsomely from the Buck orphan's estate. In 1650 Ambrose Harmar was among those sued by the owners of the ship *Comfort* because he joined John George and George Hardy in taking custody of the estate of the vessel's deceased captain, William Garnett. Harmar died sometime prior to 1652, at which time his widow, Jane, patented some land in Northumberland County. Although she died or sold her Jamestown Island land sometime prior to June 5, 1657, "Mrs. Harmer's cart path" was identified on a Jamestown Island plat dating to the early 1660s and was mentioned in a contemporary patent (VI&A 363–364; LEO 23–25).

Charles Harmar (Harmor, Harmer, Harman): Charles Harmar, who came to the colony in 1622, oversaw Lady Elizabeth Dale's properties in Virginia and by early 1625 had settled on the Eastern Shore. In 1632 he became a burgess and a commissioner of Accomack's local court. He married Ann, the daughter and reversionary heir of Henry and Elizabeth Soothey of Jamestown Island. In June 1635, when he patented a large tract of land on the Eastern Shore, Harmar used his wife's headright. Ann, as her parents' sole surviving heir, inherited a parcel of land in the eastern half of Jamestown Island, abutting what briefly was known as Harmar Creek. Charles Harmar had business dealings with cape merchant Abraham Peirsey of Jamestown, was involved in the fur trade, and used African servants as part of his work force. He made his will in July 1639 and died prior to November 23, 1640, by which time his widow, Ann, had married Nathaniel Littleton I. Although Ann Soothey Harmar inherited a dower share of her late husband's estate, his principal heir was Dr. John Harmar of Oxford, England. On September 17, 1644, Elizabeth, the daughter of Charles and Ann

Soothey Harmar, renewed her father's patent for some acreage on the Eastern Shore, on the south side of Old Plantation Creek (VI&A 364–365; LEO 11; NUG I:28; Northampton County Deeds, Wills, &c. 7 [1655–1668]:22–24).

Gabriel Harper: On October 6, 1675, Gabriel Harper obtained a warrant for the arrest of William Drummond I of Jamestown, who had bought some andirons but never paid for them. Harper won a judgment against Drummond and also against the James City County sheriff, Francis Kirkman, because Drummond failed to appear in court (MCGC 420–421).

John Harper: John Harper, a gentleman and Virginia Company investor, came to Virginia in 1608 in the 1st Supply of new settlers and lived in Jamestown (VI&A 365).

Josyas (Josias) Harr (Hartt): On September 12, 1623, Josyas Harr, a London haberdasher, arrived in Jamestown and took the oath of supremacy (VI&A 365).

Thomas Harralde: On November 30, 1624, Hugh Hayward of the Governor's Land and Thomas Fitt of Jamestown Island testified that they witnessed Thomas Harralde's will and were present when he made it. When Richard Kingsmill of Jamestown presented the will to the justices of the General Court, he indicated that the testator lived approximately a month after preparing it (VI&A 365).

Edward Harrington (Harington): Edward Harrington came to Virginia in 1607 and was one of the first Jamestown colonists. He died on August 24, 1607, and was buried the same day (VI&A 366).

Elizabeth Harris: On March 12, 1657, the clerk of the Surry County monthly court noted that Mrs. Elizabeth Harris had made her four-year-old son, John Phipps, an apprentice to John Murray (Surry Deeds, Wills &c. 1652–1672:120). The Phipps child may have been related to the John Phipps who during the 1660s owned a large tract in urban Jamestown.

James Harris: On March 14, 1672, James Harris served as the attorney of a Bristol mercantile firm. On May 27, 1673, he appeared in the General Court as attorney of Anthony Gay, a London merchant (MCGC 328, 341).

John Harris I: John Harris I came to Virginia sometime prior to June 1623, when he held the rank of lieutenant. He and his wife, Dorothy, and their two children lived in West and Shirley Hundred. When the Harrises went to England, Dorothy gave birth to John Harris II. In May 1625, when a list of patented land was sent back to England, Sergeant John Harris I was credited with 200 acres of land in the corporation of Charles City, acreage that had been seated. In January 1629 he was identified as a resident of Shirley Hundred, and in 1628, 1629, and 1630 he served as a burgess for the Shirley Hundred Maine (mainland). In March 1629 he was a juryman (VI&A 366; LEO 7–9).

John Harris: On May 11, 1696, William Sherwood sold to John Harris, a tailor, part of a 3½-acre parcel in urban Jamestown, a lot he had purchased from John Page. Sherwood noted that the acreage he was selling had formerly been occupied by Secretary Wormeley. When George Marable II disposed of a contiguous lot on November 12, 1696, he stated that it abutted north on the house of John Harris. He may have been the John Harris who in March 1672 was an indentured servant employed by Richard Young. Harris retained his lot in urban Jamestown until November 4, 1701, when he sold it to William Drummond II (AMB 59, 62, 114; MCGC 297).

John Harris: On April 18, 1766, John Harris, a resident of urban Jamestown, placed an advertisement in the *Virginia Gazette* indicating that his horse, *Regulus*, was available there for stud service and that Harris had a good pasture and an attendant. In 1766 Harris was among those designated to appraise the late Richard Ambler's estate on Jamestown Island, and on October 24, 1776, he was ordered to take command of a brig in Jamestown. John Harris may have been related to Thomas Harris, who had a house in Jamestown in 1772 (Purdie and Dixon, April 18, 1766; July 2, 1772; York County Order Book 1765–1768:77; CLARK 6:1409).

* * *

Thomas Harris I: Thomas Harris I, an ancient planter, was associated with Bermuda Hundred and may have come to Virginia with Sir Thomas Dale, who arrived in May 1611. In February 1620 Harris inherited from Ann Gurganay (Gurganey, Gurgana) 400 acres called Longfield or Curles, in the corporation of Henrico. During the mid-1620s he and his wife, Adria, lived in Bermuda Hundred, which he represented as a burgess in 1624. Harris reputedly was a womanizer, but despite his somewhat blemished reputation, he was made a commissioner of the area's monthly court. On November 11, 1635, he received a patent for 750 acres in Henrico at Digges Hundred, land abutting that of his current wife, Joan (Joane), and the acreage he had inherited from Ann Gurganay. In January 1640 and 1647–1648, Captain Harris served as a burgess for Henrico. He died around 1649 (VI&A 367; LEO 5, 18, 26).

William Harris I: William Harris I, the son of ancient planter Thomas Harris I, was born around 1629 and inherited his father's plantation, Longfield (Curles) in Henrico. He became a county justice and served as a burgess for Henrico County in 1652, 1653, 1656, and 1658. In January 1663 he patented 450 acres on the north side of the James River and in September 1671 enhanced the size of his holdings to 1,202 acres. Harris became a major in the militias of Henrico and Charles City counties. In 1678 he and Colonel Francis Eppes II jointly commanded the horse soldiers sent out to retaliate against the hostile Indians who had attacked Henrico County settlers on August 22nd and 23rd. Harris made his will on April 20, 1678, and by October 7, 1678, was dead. He produced three sons (Thomas II, William II, and Edward), whom he named as heirs to his land, and indicated that William II and Edward were minors. He also had a daughter named Love. The decedent's second wife, Alice, upon being widowed, married George Alves of New Kent County (LEO 30–31, 33, 34; PB 5:278; 6:496; DOR 2:267; Henrico County Order Book 1694–1701:286; Deeds and Wills 1677–1692:68, 90–91, 107; SR 12501).

* * *

Thomas Harris: Thomas Harris, a man Thomas Stegg II employed as an overseer, reportedly was paid 30,000 pounds of tobacco for building a brick house in urban Jamestown, a structure he failed to finish. Official records for December 1662 reveal that Harris was supposed to provide lime. In October 1667 he was required to post a bond guaranteeing that he would complete the work he was doing for Stegg. He may have been involved in the construction of a bay that Thomas Stegg II and Thomas Ludwell added onto the end of a long brick row house, which stood on a lot the two men acquired on January 1, 1667. By September 27, 1672, Thomas Harris was dead and his widow, Alice, began settling his estate (CLARE 82 f 276; MCGC 308; JHB1660–1693:50; HEN II:156; PB 6:223).

Thomas Harris: On July 2, 1772, an advertisement published in the *Virginia Gazette* stated that there would be a sale at Thomas Harris's house in urban Jamestown on July 15th, at which time the late William Davis's personal property would be sold. Davis, a tenant, had been living in Harris's house in Jamestown (Purdie and Dixon, July 2, 1772).

William Harris: William Harris came to Virginia in 1621 at the expense of William Claiborne. On September 20, 1628, he was described as a Warwick River planter when he received a lease for 100 acres below Blunt Point. In July 1637 Harris's goods were pilfered while aboard a ship that was anchored at Jamestown (VI&A 369).

* * *

William Harris I: William Harris I, a resident of urban Jamestown, died sometime prior to October 1, 1658, when his son, William Harris II, patented a half-acre lot that was "a little above [upstream from] the dwelling house" of his late father. A building that archaeologists have dated to the mid- to late seventeenth century may have been William Harris I's residence. On September 6, 1655, Francis Morrison (Moryson) patented the 24-acre Glasshouse tract and recapitulated its chain of title; at that time he noted that he had purchased it from William Harris I. He indicated that Harris and John Phipps (a Jamestown merchant) had jointly owned the Glasshouse tract and that Phipps had assigned his interest to Harris, who later sold the property to Morrison. In 1657 the widowed Elizabeth Harris of Surry County apprenticed her four-year-old son, John Phipps, to a local man. This connection, and John Phipps' and William Harris's partnership in the Glasshouse tract, raise the possibility that William Harris I of Jamestown was related to the Harrises of Surry County (NUG I:12, 50, 313, 388, 492; II:141; PB 3:367; 4:366–367; Surry Deeds, Wills &c. Deeds, Wills &c. 1652–1672:120; 1671–1684:176; STAN 71; HCA. f 249; AMB 78).

William Harris II: On October 1, 1658, "William Harris, Son of William Harris late Deceased of James City" (that is, William Harris II, son of the late William Harris I of Jamestown) patented a half-acre lot in urban Jamestown. The wording of the Harris patent indicates that William Harris II's land was just west of his late father's dwelling. The patent stated that it had "Artificeal marked Bounds," suggesting that ditches or other man-made features (such as a fence or stakes) were used to define its perimeters. No building requirements were cited in the patent issued to William Harris II (PB 4:366–367; NUG I:388).

* * *

* * *

Benjamin Harrison I: Benjamin Harrison I patented a large tract on the lower side of the James River in 1635, and then enhanced its size in 1637 and 1643; in time, his plantation became known as Wakefield. In 1642 Harrison served as a James City burgess and tobacco viewer. He probably represented James City County, which then included what became Surry County, as there is no evidence that he owned land on Jamestown Island. Harrison was among those who in 1642 signed a declaration opposing reinstatement of the Virginia Company. He died sometime prior to 1649, when his widow, Mary, married Benjamin Sidway (LEO 20; NUG I:56, 152, 224; HEN I:230–234).

Benjamin Harrison II: Benjamin Harrison II of Wakefield in Surry County and Berkeley in Charles City was the son and heir of Benjamin Harrison I. He served as the colony's attorney general from 1697 to 1702 and was clerk of the General Court from December 12, 1698, to May 25, 1700. He also represented Surry County as a burgess in the February 1677, 1691, 1696, and 1698 sessions of the assembly. In September 1679 Harrison, as the assignee of George Marable II of Jamestown, won a suit against William Rookings, a man implicated in Bacon's Rebellion. By 1704 Harrison owned large quantities of land in Surry and Charles City counties. He served as the commander-in-chief of Surry County's militia and was responsible for seeking out frontier land that was suitable for settlement. He clashed openly with Governor Francis Nicholson. Harrison died in Surry County on January 30, 1713 (STAN 24–25, 43, 82, 87, 91–92; LEO 42, 46, 51, 57–58; HEN III:166; EJC I:401; II:10, 85, 203, 414; III:30, 131, 204, 251; Surry County Order Book 1671–1691:262; NUG I:186; II:275, 309; SMITH 41).

Benjamin Harrison III: Benjamin Harrison II's son, Benjamin III, resided at Berkeley in Charles City County. He served as a burgess in the 1705–1706 assembly session and served as treasurer of the colony from 1705–1710. Harrison, who planned to write a history of the Virginia colony, began gathering official records; however, many of those documents were destroyed when the

College of William and Mary burned in 1707. One of his official duties was to examine the boundary line between Virginia and Carolina. Benjamin Harrison III died while in office. In 1711 his widow, Elizabeth, sought the compensation he was due (LEO 64; STAN 24; LJC 517; EJC III:149, 155, 358, 537).

Nathaniel Harrison: Nathaniel Harrison, the son and heir of Benjamin Harrison II, served as a Surry County burgess in 1699. As the colony's receiver general from 1715 to 1716, he paid the gunner of the Jamestown fort (LEO 59; Stanard, "Papers from the Virginia State Auditors Office," 383).

* * *

Beverley Harrison: When an election was held on December 12, 1700, for Jamestown's seat in the assembly, Beverley Harrison and Robert Beverley II were locked in a tie vote. Beverley prevailed when the sitting burgesses made a choice between the two, and Harrison was never returned to the assembly (SAIN 18:737; LEO 60). Harrison's eligibility to hold office indicates that he or his wife had a legal interest in some land in Jamestown.

* * *

George Harrison: In March 6, 1621, the Virginia Company awarded Lieutenant George Harrison, a gentleman, 200 acres in the corporation of Charles City on the lower side of the James River. In a May 12, 1622, letter he dispatched from Jamestown, he told his brother, John, then in London, that there had been many deaths since the March 1622 Indian attack. He asked that goods be sent to him in Jamestown and indicated that only three of the four servants his brother had sent him were alive. When the ailing George Harrison prepared his will on March 17, 1624, he asked to be buried in the churchyard in Jamestown and bequeathed his land and house in Archer's Hope to his brother, John. A letter sent to England reveals that George Harrison succumbed to a wound he received in a duel with merchant Richard Stephens of Jamestown. Although he probably died as a result of infection, an inquest was held. James Harrison of Warresqueak may have been the decedent's kinsman (VI&A 369). .

John Harrison: On February 13, 1622, John Harrison of London obtained three shares of Virginia land from Sir John Wolstenholme, who had acquired them in October 1621. In September 1623 Harrison sent some goods to his brother, Lieutenant George Harrison, who already was in the colony. In August 1624, after George's death, John utilized a power-of-attorney to dispose of his late brother's servants. On January 11, 1627, John Harrison was identified as a business associate of Jamestown merchant George Menefie and Thomas Bransby of Archer's Hope (VI&A 370).

* * *

Harmon Harrison: Harmon Harrison, a gentleman and Virginia Company investor, came to the colony in 1608 in the 2nd Supply and lived in Jamestown (VI&A 370).

Harry: On February 15, 1768, when an inventory was made of the late Richard Ambler's slaves on Jamestown Island and his leasehold in the Governor's Land, an adult male slave named Harry was listed. In 1769 an enslaved man named Harry was living on the Governor's Land and was attributed to the estate of Edward Ambler I (York County Wills and Inventories 21:386–391; AMB-E).

Harry: On February 15, 1768, when an inventory was made of the late Richard Ambler's slaves at his quarter called Powhatan, a young male slave named Harry was living there. In 1769 Harry, who was described as a boy, was living on the Governor's Land and was attributed to the late Edward Ambler I's estate (York County Wills and Inventories 21:386–391; AMB-E).

[No First Name] Hart (Hartt): On February 16, 1624, Captain Hart was residing in Mr. Cann's household in urban Jamestown (VI&A 371).

Samuel Hart: On August 1, 1655, Samuel Hart and Thomas Woodhouse, who had connections with Surry County, reportedly were in possession of Mr. Chiles' land in urban Jamestown (PB 3:367; NUG I:313; CBE 252). They seem to have been Walter Chiles II's tenants.

Thomas Hart: On November 27, 1702, Thomas Hart of Surry County sought permission to operate the ferry from Swann's Point to Jamestown. He was authorized to do so as long as he provided boats of certain sizes to accommodate people and horses and saw that they were operated by a certain number of boatmen (Surry County Order Book 1619–1713:232).

William Hartley: In February 1624 William Hartley was listed as living in Edward Blaney's household in urban Jamestown. Simultaneously, he was included among the servants at Blaney's plantation on the lower side of the James River, where he was still living in 1625 (VI&A 371).

Henry Hartwell: On July 15, 1631, Henry Hartwell was among the Virginia planters who asked the king's agents to give them relief from customs duties (G&M 166). This individual may have been a kinsman of attorney Henry Hartwell of urban Jamestown, who came to Virginia sometime prior to November 1671 and lived until 1699.

* * *

Henry Hartwell: Henry Hartwell, an attorney, came to Virginia sometime prior to November 24, 1671, when James City County sheriff Francis Kirkman used him as a headright. Hartwell was one of Governor William Berkeley's favorites and probably reaped some benefits from their relationship. From December 20, 1677, through 1687, Hartwell served as clerk of the General Court. In January 1678 he functioned as the late Thomas Ludwell's executor in Virginia, and on November 22, 1678, he signed Sir William Berkeley's probate entry. In May 1679 he secured a patent for a large tract of escheat land on Warrany Creek, a tributary of the Chickahominy River, and in 1683 he patented 900 acres in Charles City. By that time he was serving as deputy escheator, an office that would have alerted him to the availability of land that had reverted to the Crown. On May 10, 1680, Hartwell took an oath as a member of the Council of State and was among those witnessing Thomas Lord Culpeper's swearing-in ceremony. On June 19, 1680, he became clerk of the council, and in September 1683 he purchased a half-acre lot in Jamestown, urban property that formerly belonged to John Custis II. In 1684 Hartwell began serving as a burgess for Jamestown, an office he held until 1686. Almost immediately he was appointed to the committee responsible for seeing that a statehouse was built for the colony. He obtained the governor's signature authorizing construction to begin, and he was among those who negotiated with William Sherwood for the use of his brick dwelling as a temporary meeting place. In November 1686 Hartwell was authorized to provide furnishings for the secretary's office and the assembly's meeting room. A respected citizen, he served as the guardian of William Broadribb.

In April 1687 Henry Hartwell secured a 1,960-acre tract in Surry County between Grays and Crouches creeks, and in April 1689 he patented two-plus acres adjacent to the turf fort on Jamestown's waterfront. His urban parcel included the Custis lot that he already owned, William May's two half-acre lots, and some vacant (unowned) land. He became a James City County justice and sheriff, and again was elected Jamestown's burgess, serving during the 1691–1692 sessions of the assembly. As a James City County justice, he asked Lieutenant Governor Francis Nicholson's permission for the county court to convene in the General Courthouse. In December 1690 Hartwell gave his power of attorney to Captain Francis Clements, who was authorized to act on his behalf in the Surry County court. In 1691 Hartwell conveyed to the government 50 acres on Grays Creek for use as a planned town, the community known as Cobham, but he retained a half-acre lot and a house there. In 1692, while he was a council member, clerk of the General Court, and a burgess for Jamestown, he filed a petition underscoring the colony's need of imported goods. In September 1692, when Virginia officials learned that the king expected council members to build houses in Jamestown, Henry Hartwell already had developed his lot in the capital city and was residing there. He was one of the councilors involved in redesigning the Secretary's Office, which was located in the refurbished statehouse. In 1694, as the assignee of Mrs. Sarah Lee of Jamestown, he brought suit against burgess William Hardidge II in Westmoreland County's monthly court. On April 23, 1695, Henry Hartwell and his wife, Jane, sold their two-plus acre Jamestown lot to William Edwards II of Surry County and went to England. While there, Hartwell was asked to respond to official queries about the council and the assembly. In October 1697 he joined the Rev. James Blair and Edward Chilton in preparing a report, "The Present State of Virginia," which addressed each of the issues raised by English officials. Hartwell was then a trustee of the College of William and Mary. In 1699 he was identified as a friend of John Thompson of Surry County. Henry Hartwell made his will on July 3, 1699, and died at Stepney in Middlesex, England, by August 2nd. In September 1699 British merchants Micajah and Richard Perry were designated his administrators. Among Hartwell's heirs were his late wife's nephews, Nicholas, Francis, and Thomas Meriwether, and William Hartwell (MCGC 287; EJC I:81, 161, 251, 269, 469; PALM I:9, 40, 42, 61; HEN II:560, 567–568; JHB 1660–1693:127, 220, 248, 283; LJC 93; SR 3719, 4788; NUG II:200, 253, 312, 331; PB 7:701; AMB 40, 55; Surry County Deeds, Wills &c. 1687–1694:181, 233; Order Book 1671–1690:509; 1692–1713:6; York County Deeds, Orders, Wills 3:49; Westmoreland County Order Book 1691–1699:149a; CO 5/1359 f 89; SAIN 15:655; WITH 122; EEAC 28; STAN 43; LEO 47–48, 50).

William Hartwell: On September 17, 1676, William Hartwell, one of Governor William Berkeley's servants, was shot in the leg while defending Jamestown from an attack by the rebel Nathaniel Bacon's men. Hartwell's contemporaries described him as staunchly loyal to Berkeley. After the rebellion subsided, he turned vigilante and reportedly jailed several James City County men and illegally seized their belongings. After Berkeley left office, some of Hartwell's victims filed formal complaints. One was John Johnson II, son of the man who during the first quarter of the seventeenth century owned a tract in the eastern end of Jamestown Island. On December 16, 1699, Hartwell sent a letter to England about some pirates who were being detained in Jamestown. He was still alive on March 27, 1702, at which time he witnessed a legal document. He died prior to August 18, 1725, leaving his daughter, Mary, as the only heir to his Surry County acreage between Grays and Crouches creeks. When she and her husband, William Macon of New Kent County, sold their land to Robert Carter of Lancaster County, the late William Hartwell was identified as Henry Hartwell's brother (AND 133; NEVILLE 67; SAIN 10:51–54; 20:156; CO 5/1371 f 171; JHB 1660–1693:219; Surry County Deeds, Wills, &c. 7 [1715–1730]:605).

* * *

John Hartwell: On October 31, 1709, George Marable II of James City County conveyed to John Hartwell of Surry County the 1,650-acre plantation known as Swann's Point and all of its improvements, property that Samuel Swann had sold to Joseph John Jackman on February 22, 1706, and that Jackman had transferred to Marable on August 11, 1709. Excluded were the 300 acres Samuel Swann had granted on February 15, 1685, to his stepmother, Mary Swann, the widow of Colonel Thomas Swann I—part of a large tract that the late Colonel Thomas Swann I had patented on February 4, 1645. John Hartwell took an active role in the local community. In November 1710, while was a burgess representing Surry County, he asked that the ferry from Swann's Point to Jamestown be moved to another location.

On October 24, 1711, he requested compensation from the Surry County court for having delivered 500 palisades to Jamestown for the construction of a line battery there. This occurred at a time when Virginia's officials were fortifying Jamestown against a possible invasion by the French. Despite Hartwell's request that the ferry landing be moved, during the years that he and his heirs owned the Swann's Point plantation, boats continued to ply a route to the western end of Jamestown Island. In June 1714 Benjamin Chapman was authorized to operate the Swann's Point ferry "until the owner of the said Point is willing to keep it." By that time, Hartwell was dead.

When John Hartwell prepared his will on February 9, 1710, he said that he was sick and weak. He survived this bout of ill health, and his will was not presented for probate until May 11, 1714. His principal heirs were his wife and daughter, both of whom were named Elizabeth. His widow, Elizabeth I, stood to receive life-rights in the eastern part of the Swann's Point tract, which contained the family home, whereas his daughter and only child, Elizabeth II, upon marrying or turning 21, was to inherit the western part of the Swann's Point tract. At the death of the elder Elizabeth, all of John Hartwell's Swann's Point property was to descend to his daughter. If she were to die while underage or unmarried, the estate was to go in equal shares to John Drummond, George Marable Jr. (III), and Henry Hartwell Marable, the children of his sister, Mary Hartwell Marable. The testator left use of a slave to his mother, Elizabeth, then the wife of Benjamin Eggleston, and he identified Thomas Rogers as his uncle. John Hartwell's inventory reveals that he was a learned man of considerable means. He owned books on law and philosophy and luxury items such as fine furniture, silver serving vessels, and looking glasses; he also had a substantial herd of livestock (Surry County Wills and Deeds 1694–1709:428–431; Deeds &c. 6 [1709–1715]:184–185, 203–204; Order Book 6 [1701–1711]:377–378; Order Book 7 [1712–1714]:27–28, 34, 60; JHB 1702–1712: 258).

Margaret Hartwell: Margaret Hartwell appeared before the General Court on October 9, 1640, to testify on behalf of her servant, Ann Belson (MCGC 465).

George Harvey: On December 7, 1696, Mrs. Sarah Lee Smith and Robert and George Nicholson of Surry County, who were George Lee's heirs, conveyed to George Harvey their respective interests in the decedent's property, part of a brick row house on Jamestown's Back Street. In December 1695 Harvey was hired to make a "platform for the great guns in Jamestown," a replacement for an old brick fort that had been torn down earlier in the year. He apparently completed his work by April 1696, when Edward Ross, "gunner of the fort at James City," requested small guns that could be used in firing salutes. Harvey kept his row house property until October 13, 1697, at which time he transferred the land and its improvements to Thomas Hadley (EJC I:322, 339, 342; LEE 51 ff 669, 671).

John Harvey: Captain John Harvey, a mariner and Virginia Company stockholder since 1620, was a hard-liner who favored martial law and a military-style government. In 1623 he informed Company officials that he planned to undertake a fishing voyage and was willing to compile information on the status of the Virginia colony. In January 1624 he obtained a patent for a large waterfront lot in urban Jamestown, one that already contained some buildings, and a month later he saw that a census was compiled. Harvey's eagerness to please the king and Privy Council paid off handsomely, for he was knighted and in August 1624 was named to the Council of State. Official records reveal that his explosive temper and autocratic attitude eventually alienated many of his fellow councilors. In March 1628 Sir John Harvey was designated Governor George Yeardley's successor. As soon as he arrived in Virginia, he purchased Sir Francis Wyatt's urban estate in Jamestown and a neighboring lot that had belonged to Sir George Yeardley. Harvey immediately began implementing the instructions he had received from the king, which included producing marketable commodities. In time, he claimed that his home, a large town stead in urban Jamestown, was serving as the colony's statehouse and that his compensation was inadequate. At the site of Governor Harvey's Jamestown mansion, National Park Service archaeologists have found fragments of plaster molding embellished with portions of Harvey's armorial crest. In 1638, when he was 54 years old, Harvey married Elizabeth, the daughter of cape merchant Abraham Peirsey and the widow of councilor Richard Stephens, with whom he often clashed. The serious differences between Governor Harvey and his council eventually became so pronounced that Harvey was ousted from office and sent back to England; however, the Privy Council reinstated him as governor, thereby upholding the king's authority. When Harvey returned to Virginia, he sought revenge on his enemies and conditions gradually deteriorated. Upon being replaced by Sir Francis Wyatt, Harvey entered a period of decline that left him physically ill, deeply in debt, and almost devoid of political power. Sir John Harvey and his wife returned to England, and his real and personal property in Jamestown and in York County were sold so that his creditors could be paid. Lady Elizabeth Harvey died in England sometime prior to September 15, 1646. Harvey died before July 16, 1650, leaving the bulk of his estate to daughters Ursula and Ann (VI&A 371–373; SR 4004; HALL 18).

Thomas Harvey (Harvy): On June 30, 1640, Thomas Harvey was ordered to pay a debt to the estate of John White of Jamestown. A few days later he secured a patent for 950 acres on the east side of the Chickahominy River in James City County. Harvey used his wife, Mary, as a headright (MCGC 471; PB 1 Pt. 2:723; 4:168).

George Harwood: Richard James I of Jamestown sued George Harwood of Warwick County on April 15, 1670. Five years later William Sherwood, who wed James' widow, Rachel, renewed the suit on her behalf. Harwood may have been the individual who in late 1642 inherited a small sum of money from London merchant Arthur Harwood, a former resident of Virginia (MCGC 205, 419; 6:218; SR 3990). None of the individuals mentioned in the testator's will suggest that he or George were related to Thomas Harwood of Mulberry Island.

* * *

Thomas Harwood: Thomas Harwood's acreage on Mulberry Island was mentioned in a patent dating to December 31, 1619. Although Harwood was living in the Neck O'Land in 1624, by early 1625 he had moved to his Mulberry Island acreage and shared a household with his wife, Grace. She may have died within a relatively short time, for he remarried, taking as his bride Anne, who became the mother of his known children, Humphrey, Grace, and Margaret Harwood. In May 1626 Harwood was awarded 100 acres of land at the mouth of Blunt Point Creek. He was elected a burgess for Mulberry Island in 1629–1630, and in 1632 and 1633 he represented the territory between Skiff's Creek and Saxon's Gaol, including the island. He enhanced the size of his Mulberry Island acreage, and as time went on, he patented large tracts on both sides of Skiff's Creek. He sided against

Governor John Harvey, who retaliated by having him arrested. Harwood resided on his Skiff's Creek plantation called Queen Hive or Hith (a word that meant "harbor") and represented Warwick County in the assembly sessions of 1640, 1642, 1645, and 1647–1648. Harwood served as speaker in 1647–1648 and was returned to office in 1649, again serving as speaker. Thomas Harwood became a tobacco viewer for Mulberry Island Parish and the Skiff's Creek area. In April 1652 he was named to the Council of State but died prior to November 26th, when his son and primary heir, Humphrey, claimed his inheritance (VI&A 375–376; LEO 9–12, 18, 20, 23, 26–27).

Humphrey Harwood: Humphrey Harwood, the son of Thomas and Anne Harwood of Warwick County, was a minor at the time of his father's death in 1652. Despite his youth, he was allowed to transfer his late father's real estate into his own name. He repatented that land on April 18, 1670, by which time he had attained his majority. In January 1677 he confiscated John Lucas's goods and livestock on behalf of Governor William Berkeley, in accord with the orders he had received. Harwood served as a justice of Warwick County's monthly court and in 1691 was sheriff. He went on to represent the county in the assembly sessions held in 1685–1686 and 1692–1693. Although William Rascow disputed the legality of Harwood's election, its validity was upheld. Harwood went on to become a major in the county militia, and he served on a special committee of burgesses charged with presenting bills to the governor and Council of State. Humphrey Harwood, who was a resident of Mulberry Island Parish, married John Needler's daughter, Ann, sometime prior to June 1687. In 1700 Major Harwood served as a judge in the special court appointed to try pirates at Elizabeth City. He died sometime prior to 1704 (LEO 48, 52; PB 3:182; 5:426; 6:218, 304; DOR 2:301–303; DUNN 3–4, 46, 149, 588–589; JHB 1660–1693:275–278, 417; York County Deeds, Orders, Wills 7 [1684–1687]:348; MCGC 213; EJC II:66; SR 660, 749). Archaeological evidence suggests that Humphrey Harwood's son, William, elected to abandon the old family home at Queen Hith during the first quarter of the eighteenth century and build a new dwelling near the head of Skiff's Creek and the road to Yorktown.

* * *

William Harwood: William Harwood came to Virginia in 1620 and was Martin's

Hundred's leader or "governor" when the Virginia Company appointed him to the Council of State. When the Indians attacked Martin's Hundred on March 22, 1622, a substantial number of colonists were killed. Although Harwood and the other survivors were evacuated to Jamestown Island, by January 1623 the Martin's Hundred plantation had been reoccupied. Living conditions were harsh, and some of the settlement's inhabitants claimed that Harwood was greedy and used the community's supplies to curry favor with influential people. In 1625, while he was a burgess for Martin's Hundred, Harwood was ordered to offer accommodations to the people sent to Virginia to establish the East India School. He was returned to the assembly in 1628. In November 1635 the Privy Council summoned him to England, where he stayed (VI&A 376; LEO 6–7).

Margaret Hatch: On June 24, 1633, Margaret Hatch was indicted for murdering her child. She was found guilty of manslaughter and sentenced to be hanged. She pled pregnancy but a jury of matrons who examined her determined that she was not an expectant mother (VI&A 377).

Thomas Hatch: Thomas Hatch came to Virginia in 1619 and was one of Sir George Yeardley's servants in urban Jamestown. In June 1624 witnesses reported that he had been seen near the fort, the "country house" (a government-owned building), and the store on the night a break-in occurred. Another witness claimed that Hatch had said that a man had been wrongfully executed for an alleged homosexual relationship. For criticizing a government decision, Hatch was arrested, whipped, pilloried, and then required to serve Yeardley an extra seven years. He also had an ear severed as part of his punishment (VI&A 377).

William Hatcher: William Hatcher, who on June 1, 1636, received a patent for 200 acres in Henrico (now Chesterfield) County and continued to acquire land, was elected to the assembly in 1644. He was returned to office in 1645–1646, 1649, 1652, and 1659, each time representing Henrico County. Apparently hotheaded, in 1654 he insulted the newly elected speaker of the assembly, Colonel Edward Hill, by calling him an atheist and blasphemer. Hatcher was censured for slandering Hill and was made to kneel and apologize. On March 15, 1677, Governor William Berkeley and his council put Hatcher on trial at Green Spring plantation, where he was accused of uttering mutinous words in support of the rebel Nathaniel Ba-

con. A jury deliberated how Hatcher should be punished and decided that he should be fined 10,000 pounds of tobacco. However, the Council of State, upon hearing the verdict, determined that he should be assessed 8,000 pounds of dressed pork that could be used by the Henrico County militia. The excuse they used was that Hatcher was an aged man (LEO 22, 24, 27, 29, 35; PB 38:353; HEN 1:387; 2:551; MCGC 458, 530).

Lazarus Haverd (Hauerd): On November 13, 1620, Lazarus Haverd, a Virginia Company employee, asked Company officials for compensation. He said that Governor George Yeardley had sent him on a fishing voyage and that he risked his life during three other voyages he had undertaken on behalf of the colony (VI&A 378).

Thomas Hawkins: Thomas Hawkins came to Virginia in 1622. During the mid-1620s he was an indentured servant who lived on the lower side of the James River, at Hugh Crowder's plantation. By February 1, 1633, Hawkins had begun serving as burgess for the settlers in the Denbigh area. He may have been the individual who patented two large tracts on the lower side of the York River, near the New Poquoson River, in 1639 and 1650 (VI&A 378; LEO 12; PB 1:666; 2:210; MCGC 53).

Gabriel (Gabriell) Hawley: In June 1636 Governor John Harvey was ordered to appoint Sir Gabriel Hawley to the post of Virginia's surveyor-general. By March 1638 Hawley was dead and Robert Evelyn (Eveling, Evelin) was named as his successor (SR 3428, 4156, 7299, 10395).

Jerome (Jerom) Hawley: In November 1633 Cecil Calvert, Lord Baltimore II, gave written instructions to his brother, Leonard, Maryland's deputy governor, and to Jerome Hawley and Thomas Cornwaleys (Cornwallis), the new colony's commissioners. He warned all three men, who were preparing to go to Maryland, to stay away from Jamestown. He also urged them not to allow the *Ark* and the *Dove* to "come within the command of the fort" at Old Point Comfort unless violent weather forced them landward. Calvert told them to anchor near Accomack so that they could find someone knowledgeable about the Potomac River who could escort them to a good place to go ashore in Maryland. Upon landing safely, Leonard Calvert was to send a messenger (a person of the Anglican faith) and gifts to Governor John Harvey in Jamestown, expressing his desire to be a good neighbor. He also was to send a letter to William Claiborne, notifying him that Kent Island lay within Maryland's boundaries. Cecil Calvert, in his instructions to Maryland's first settlers, stated that he expected to visit Governor Harvey in Virginia in 1634. In early 1636 Hawley, who was then in England, made plans to go to Virginia on the *Friendship*. He and Leonard Calvert paused in Virginia in April 1636 and then continued on to Maryland. Although Jerome Hawley went to Maryland, in 1636 King Charles I appointed him treasurer of Virginia (an office he held from 1636 to 1639), and in January 1637 he was named to the Council of State. Because Hawley was eager to bring his family to Maryland but lacked the funds to do so, he made a bargain with his brother, James, a merchant. Jerome Hawley agreed to sell James' merchandise in Maryland in exchange for his transporting Jerome's family to the colony. Jerome Hawley died intestate in Maryland in August 1638, without having sold his brother's commodities. Mrs. Hawley refused to serve as her late husband's administratrix because of the complexities of his estate and the amount of debt against it. Thomas Cornwallis, who agreed to become the late Jerome Hawley's administrator, was sued by Hawley's brother, James. Under oath, Cornwallis stated his belief that the decedent had intended to defraud his brother, James, by selling his goods on his own behalf or by sending them to Virginia where they could be sold by Gabriel Hawley and James Neale, a resident of Westmoreland County. The lawsuit was contentious and dragged on for many years (SAIN 243, 274, 285; STAN 24, 33; LEO xx; HALL 16–19; SR 630, 1438, 4004, 10394, 10395, 14604; NN 2:199–201).

William Hawley: On April 11, 1640, William Hawley was described as deputy for Henry Frederick Howard, Lord Maltravers, to whom King Charles I gave a large grant of Virginia land on the lower side of Hampton Roads, acreage that enveloped Nansemond and Norfolk counties. Governor John Harvey incurred the wrath of his council by cooperating with Hawley, even though he was obeying the king's orders (Stanard, "Council and General Court Records," 194).

William Hay (Hey): In September 1652 William Hay patented 258 acres in York County, near the New Poquoson and the stream that served as the boundary line with Denbigh (Warwick) County. As time went on, he added to his holdings and in March 1655 was in possession of 500 acres at the head of the New Poquoson River. By that time he had married John Griggs' widow,

Margery, and bestowed gifts on her children. Hay served as a York County justice during the mid-1650s and as a burgess in 1658 and 1659. In December 1663 he patented 1,695 acres in York County, near the acreage he had claimed in 1652. When the General Court convened in Jamestown on November 25, 1671, the justices noted that Captain William Hay had married John Hayward's (or Haywood's) widow. Hay's patents reveal that they were neighbors (MCGC 290; LEO 34–35; PB 4:236, 275; 5:338; York County Record Book 1 [1648–1657]:265, 293).

Robert Hayes: In 1638 Robert Hayes represented Lower Norfolk County in the assembly, and in 1640 he was named to the Lynnhaven Parish vestry. In late January 1643, when he disposed of some land on the Lynnhaven River that he had bought from Richard Popeley, he indicated that he was then living on Little Creek. Hayes patented 450 acres in Lower Norfolk County in September 1643 and added 500 acres to his holdings in November 1648, acquiring more land on Little Creek. Robert Hayes died sometime prior to March 26, 1650, when the will of his widow, Anne, was proved. She mentioned her late husband, Robert, and made bequests to her sons, Nathaniel and Adam Hayes, and to Thomas and John Workman. She also included her maidservant, Jane Nedham, in her will. By 1653 at least part of Robert Hayes' plantation at Little Creek had come into the hands of another planter (LEO 16; Lower Norfolk County Record Book A:44; B:49, 145; C:15, 48; PB 1:944; 2:174).

Thomas Haynes: Thomas Haynes became a Lancaster County justice in 1669, the same year he patented 1,300 acres of land in the fork of Corotoman Creek. In 1671 he was elected to the assembly when Raleigh Travers retired and represented Lancaster County in the assembly sessions held in 1671–1674 and 1676. He also continued to serve as a justice in the county court. In May 1678 Haynes requested compensation for a cutlass, a sword and scabbard, and another piece of military equipment that had been impressed from him when some Northern Neck men were preparing to attack the Susquehannock Indians in Maryland. In early 1679 Haynes was nominated for county sheriff. When he made his will on February 18, 1679, he mentioned the plantation on which he lived, which was located on the Corotoman River near Colonel John Carter's property. Thomas Haynes was survived by his wife, Elizabeth, whom he named as one of his executors. He made bequests to his son, James, and his daughters, Elizabeth, Margaret, and Mary. He left his property in England to his brothers, William and James Haynes; his sister, Jane; and nephews James and Thomas Haynes and Thomas Kente. Haynes died sometime prior to May 1679, when his widow presented his will to Lancaster County's court justices. An inventory of his estate, filed with the court in September 1679, reveals that the decedent was a wealthy man. By September 1680 the widowed Elizabeth Haynes married John Pinkard, also a resident of Lancaster County, who later became a burgess (LEO 38, 41; Lancaster County Wills 1674–1689:54–55, 60–64; Order Book 1666–1680:106b, 287, 291, 425, 427, 471–472; 1680–1687:6; PB 6:219).

Henry Hayrick (Heyrick, Heyrock): In March 1641 Henry Hayrick was involved in a case that appeared before the General Court, and he represented Warwick County in the assembly sessions held in 1644 and 1645. In March 1648 he witnessed a document signed by a York County planter who was securing a debt (LEO 22–23; MCGC 499; York County Court Orders 2 [1646–1648]:348).

Thomas Hayrick (Heyrick): In March 1630 Thomas Hayrick served as a burgess for the upper (or westernmost) part of the corporation of Elizabeth City, territory that in 1634 became Warwick County. He was then ordered to inspect the site of the fort built at Old Point Comfort (VI&A 379; HEN 1:149–150; LEO 9).

John Hayward (Heyward, Haywood): John Hayward married the widow of Thomas Hunt of Jamestown sometime prior to October 3, 1671, when he sued Jonathan Newell's widow, Elizabeth, on his new wife's behalf. In 1672 he brought suit against Jonathan Newell's brother and heir, David Newell, and had him arrested and jailed. In November 1671 the General Court noted that Hayward previously had wed William Hay's widow (MCGC 280, 290, 293, 307–308, 321).

Samuel Hayward: In March 1662 Samuel Hayward patented 200 acres of land that abutted the Potomac River and Chotanck Creek. As time went on, he became increasingly successful. By 1686 Hayward had been appointed a justice of Stafford County's monthly court, an indication that he was a prominent citizen, and within months he became the county's clerk of court. In December 1686 Nicholas Hayward of London brought suit against Samuel Hayward in an attempt to take custody of the late Joseph

Hayward's land and material possessions. The charges leveled by the plaintiff reveal that the decedent was a merchant and that Samuel Hayward and his wife, Martha, were then in possession of two plantations that Nicholas Hayward stood to inherit. A document Samuel Hayward filed, which was dated October 2, 1684, reveals that Samuel, Joseph, and Nicholas Hayward were brothers and that Samuel was Joseph's administrator. It also indicates that the late Joseph Hayward had borrowed money from Samuel and Martha Hayward in order to satisfy his debts to his brother Nicholas. Samuel Hayward served as a Stafford County burgess in 1685–1686 and was still a county justice in 1690. His name appeared in the records of Old Rappahannock County in 1691, when he brought suit against a local resident. In 1694 he patented 1,050 acres of land on Chotanck Creek, adjacent to the property to which he had laid claim in 1662 (LEO 48; Stafford County Record Book 1686–1693:17a–18a, 22a–23a, 26a–28, 139, 143a; Old Rappahannock County Order Book 1687–1692:226; PB 5:296; NN 2:8).

Ebenezer Hazard: Ebenezer Hazard came to Virginia and visited Jamestown in mid-June 1777, at which time he made descriptive notes about the community's appearance. He said that the former capital city was "a very small deserted Village, in a ruinous state," thanks to damage done by tenders from British men-of-war and the dozen men of the Allied army currently garrisoned there. He said that the Jamestown ferry was very dangerous whenever the wind was blowing. He visited the Ambler home, a large brick house that was "decaying fast" and was being used as a ferryhouse (SHELLEY 411–416).

George Heale (Hale) I: In 1657 George Heale I's father, Nicholas Heale, patented 500 acres on the Corotoman River in Lancaster County. As time went on, he enhanced the size of his holdings, acquiring 738 acres in 1666 and 365 acres in 1668. Nicholas Heale and his wife, Mary, died sometime after October 1669 but before March 1671, leaving their son, George I, as their primary heir. By 1679 George Heale I had begun performing surveys, work that would have enabled him to become intimately familiar with Lancaster County's landscape. In January 1683 he was paid for laying out the county's planned town, urban development initiated by the Virginia assembly, and over the years he continued to perform surveys. Heale went on to become a county justice, and he patented an additional 350 acres of land in Lancaster County in 1692. He began serving as a burgess for Lancaster County and attended the assembly sessions held in 1693, 1695–1696, and 1696–1697. When George Heale I made his will on December 30, 1697, he left his home plantation, which was near the road to Ball's Mill, to his son George II. He distributed the rest of his holdings among sons George II, John, and Nicholas, and daughters Elizabeth and Sarah Heale. The testator noted that his wife was then pregnant and that if the child survived, he/she stood to inherit some of the land that otherwise would go to George Heale II. The late George Heale I's will was presented to the justices of Lancaster County on January 12, 1698. An inventory of his estate, compiled in March 1702, reflects his affluence and included an uncommonly large quantity of cloth, raising the possibility that he was a merchant (LEO 53–54, 56; Lancaster County Wills 1690–1709:74–75, 115–118; Order Book 1666–1680:152, 219, 302–303, 473, 507; 1680–1686:41, 68, 106, 160; 1686–1696:127, 328–329; 1696–1702:32, 34; PB 4:143; 5:636; 6:260; NN 1:169–171).

Mrs. Ann Heard: On September 28, 1672, the Rev. Thomas Hampton, rector of the church in Jamestown, successfully sued Mrs. Ann Heard over the ownership of some hogs (MCGC 309).

Hearseeqe (Native American): In 1689 Hearseeqe, Herquapinck, and Paucough, the monguys or chief rulers of the Chickahominy Indians, sent a petition to the governor asking for protection from the Pamunkey Indians. They said that they had to take up residence with the Pamunkeys on the Pamunkey River because they had been attacked by the Senecas. The Chickahominy Indians' leaders asked the governor's permission to move to a place called Rickahock on the upper side of the Mattaponi River. They indicated that they had obtained the acreage from Benjamin Arnold in exchange for their own land on the lower side of the Mattaponi (PALM I:22).

James Heart: On June 12, 1762, James Heart procured a 122-acre lease for some land in the Governor's Land from Thomas Holt. On November 13, 1762, Heart conveyed his leasehold to John Ambler I, who held leases to other mainland properties and whose plantation engulfed much of Jamestown Island (AMB 167).

Thomas Hebbs (Hebb): Thomas Hebbs was living in Nathaniel Jefferys' household in urban Jamestown in February 1624. He

died sometime prior to March 31, 1628 (VI&A 381).

Robert Hedges: In February 1624 Robert Hedges, a servant, was living in William Peirce's household in urban Jamestown. However, by late January 1625 he had moved to Mulberry Island, where he was listed among Captain William Peirce's servants (VI&A 381).

John Helline (Helin): On February 16, 1624, John Helline (Helin), his wife, and their son and new baby were living in the household of merchant Delpheus Cann in urban Jamestown. Simultaneously, the Hellines were attributed to Martin's Hundred (VI&A 382).

Herquapinck (Native American): In 1689 Herquapinck, Paucough, and Hearseeqe, the monguys or chief rulers of the Chickahominy Indians, sent a petition to the governor asking for protection from the Pamunkey Indians. They said that they had to take up residence with the Pamunkeys on the Pamunkey River because they had been attacked by the Senecas. The Chickahominy Indians' leaders asked the governor's permission to move to a place called Rickahock on the upper side of the Mattaponi River. They indicated that they had obtained the acreage from Benjamin Arnold in exchange for their own land on the lower side of the Mattaponi (PALM I:22).

Mary Hewes: On April 23, 1670, it was noted that Mary Hewes, Henry Smith's indentured servant, had been sold to Walter Chiles II of Jamestown (MCGC 217).

Kilibett (Kelinet) Hichcock (Hitchcocke, Hitchcok): In February 1624 Kilibett Hichcock was listed among those in Sir George Yeardley's household in urban Jamestown. On November 21, 1625, he was identified as a gentleman. On January 13, 1627, Hichcock was described as one of Lady Temperance Yeardley's employees when he negotiated a rental agreement with John Upton, who wanted to lease some Yeardley land in the eastern end of Jamestown Island at Black Point (VI&A 385).

James Hickmore (Hickmote, Hickmoate, Hicmott, Hickmott): In 1623 James Hickmore served on a jury, an indication that he was a free man. In February 1624 he was residing in mariner John Pountis's household in urban Jamestown. In September 1624 he was fined for being drunk and disorderly, an infraction of moral law. By January 1625

Hickmore had become head of a household he shared with his wife in urban Jamestown. In March 1625 he participated in an inquest held to determine whether John Verone's death was attributable to suicide. He returned to court on February 4, 1626, to give testimony about controversial statements Peter Martin and Thomas Hatch had made at Edward Fisher's house in the Governor's Land. James Hickmore became the churchwarden of James City Parish and in August 1626 reported a man for failing to attend church (VI&A 386).

Christopher Higginson: On May 28, 1673, the General Court noted that Captain Christopher Higginson's estate was indebted to Colonel Nathaniel Bacon for his fees of office (MCGC 344).

Humphrey Higginson (Higgenson): In 1637 Humphrey Higginson, who was born in England, patented 700 acres known as Tutteys (Tutters) Neck, acreage that bordered Archer's Hope (College) Creek. He acquired the property using the headrights of his wife, Elizabeth, and 13 others he had transported to the colony. By 1648 Higginson had extended his holdings southward into the Harrop tract. He combined the Tuttey's, Kingsmill, and Farley's Necks with his Harrop plantation, unifying what eventually became the western part of Kingsmill Plantation. In 1639 Higginson and two other men were appointed to serve as tobacco viewers for the territory between Archer's Hope Creek and Wareham's Pond, to the east. In 1641 Humphrey Higginson was named to the Council of State and took the oath of supremacy. In 1654 he patented 2,000 acres on the lower side of the Potomac River in Westmoreland County. Simultaneously, he and his son, Thomas, patented 800 acres on the south side of the Piankatank River in Gloucester County. He died in England in 1665. His widow, Elizabeth, survived until at least March 1673, at which time she proved the will of their married daughter, Elizabeth Higginson Foster. In October 1670 Mrs. Elizabeth Higginson brought suit against another man's widow. On the other hand, as her late husband's executrix, she was sued by Colonel Nathaniel Bacon (STAN 35; LEO xx; SR 3551; NUG I:15, 80; II:207; PB 1:519, 834; 3:302, 304; BRU 120; MCGC 237, 344, 498).

Robert Higginson: On May 14, 1755, Robert Higginson, the ferry keeper in Jamestown, requested compensation for transporting tributary Indians across the James. On June 20, 1751, it was noted that he resided in

Jamestown. In April 1757 Higginson again ferried tributary Indians across the river (JHB 1752–1758:255, 424; Hunter, *Virginia Gazette*, June 20, 1751).

* * *

Edward Hill I: Edward Hill I, who in 1640 was a tobacco viewer for Charles City County, was speaker of the assembly in 1644–1645. In November 1647 his house at Westover was one of the sites to which tributary Indians could come when they needed to transmit an official message. By 1651 Hill had been appointed to the Council of State. In 1654 William Hatcher, a Henrico County burgess, ran afoul of the law when he described Hill as an atheist and blasphemer. In 1655 Hill, who in 1654–1655 was again speaker of the assembly, patented 4,000 acres in the upper reaches of the Rappahannock River, contingent upon its development into a fortified community and trading post. In 1656 Colonel Edward Hill, as commander of 100 colonists and a group of tributary Indians, went to the falls of the James River to fight against some warlike natives called the Riccahockians. He was later subjected to a considerable amount of criticism for his ineptitude as a military officer, for Totopotomoy, leader of the Powhatan Chiefdom, was slain while assisting the English. Because of his culpability, Hill was temporarily suspended from holding all civil and military offices. On August 5, 1658, Hill and his wife, Elizabeth, who were residents of Charles City County, conveyed their legal interest in a brick dwelling in urban Jamestown to Walter Chiles II. While it is possible that the Hills were leaseholders and that Walter Chiles II was nullifying a rental agreement his late father had made, it is perhaps more likely that Elizabeth Hill was the widow of Walter Chiles I and therefore had a dower interest in the property. In 1659 Edward Hill I again began serving as speaker of the assembly. A year later he patented nearly 2,500 acres in Charles City County, the acreage he and his descendants developed into Shirley Plantation. He died in late 1663, the same year he was paid for procuring powder and shot for the colony (AMB 6; HEN I:283, 289, 348, 387, 402, 422, 505; II:199; STAN 36, 64; NUG I:324; II:40; Lower Norfolk County Book B:204; WITH 323; MCGH 775; AMB 6; LEO 18, 20, 22–24, 26–27, 29, 32, 35).

Edward Hill II: Edward Hill II, who was born in 1637, became a Charles City County justice in 1659 and served a term as high sheriff. He married Elizabeth, the daughter of Sir Edward Williams. Hill was placed in command of a militia company in 1661 and in 1662 became a surveyor of the highways in Charles City County. He undertook construction of a small building in Charles City that was intended to serve as its courthouse, but afterward convinced his fellow justices to let him put it to use as a tavern and jail. He patented large quantities of land on the Rappahannock River and confirmed his father's patent for Shirley Plantation. He occasionally assisted in the arbitration of disputes. One involved Thomas Hill of urban Jamestown, who was in the midst of a disagreement with Roger Green, the owner of Digges Hundred. Colonel Edward Hill II was a burgess and commander of the Charles City County regiment when Bacon's Rebellion got underway. Although Bacon's men asked Hill to join them, he declined and, later, Governor Berkeley ordered him to aid in Bacon's capture. Retribution came in June 1676 when Bacon's supporters gained control of the assembly, for Hill and one of his neighbors were disbarred from holding all civil or military offices in their parishes. Hill's wife, Elizabeth, reportedly suffered many indignities at the hands of Nathaniel Bacon's men when they went to Shirley Plantation.

After the rebellion subsided, Edward Hill II served as a judge in the military tribunals held at Green Spring in January 1677. He alienated the king's commissioners by questioning the legality of a list of grievances compiled by some of Charles City County's inhabitants. He also clashed with then-Lieutenant Governor Herbert Jeffreys. Ultimately, he was removed from the council and relieved of his duties as attorney general. Among those who had problems with Hill was Mrs. Elizabeth Sykes, proprietor of Colonel Thomas Swann's tavern in urban Jamestown, for Hill failed to honor a debt. When Hill attempted to rebut the charges against him, he claimed that he had been wronged by Bacon's supporters, who used their influence to defame him and had plundered his home. In 1679 he was serving in the assembly, representing Jamestown. Sympathetic justices in nearby Henrico County rallied to Hill's support in 1680, claiming that he had been maligned. He managed to clear his name and was returned to the assembly in 1684. By March 1681 Colonel Edward Hill II had married Ann, the widow of Colonel Thomas Goodrich of Old Rappahannock County.

In 1688 Hill was named to the Council of State and served a term as attorney general. He was the first judge of the Admiralty Court of Virginia and the Carolinas, and for a time he was treasurer of the colony. He also served as collector of customs for the Upper James River District and as a vestryman of Westover Parish. In 1699, while Edward Hill II was colonel and commander of the Charles City County militia, his son, Edward III, was lieutenant colonel. During the 1680s and 1690s, Hill patented massive tracts of land in New Kent, King and Queen, Essex, Henrico, Old Rappahannock, and Charles City counties. In 1692, while Hill was a councilor, the king ordered all council members to build houses in Jamestown; it is uncertain how Hill responded. In 1695 and 1699 Hill was among those called upon to inspect the fortifications and military stores in Jamestown. He became the father-in-law of Edward Chilton, who in 1693 gave him a power of attorney. In 1696 Colonel Edward Hill II married the thrice-widowed Tabitha Scarborough Custis, whose most recent husband had been Colonel John Custis II of Arlington, in Northampton County. In October 1699 Colonel Hill was given the responsibility of pursuing the Indians on the frontiers and was authorized to choose 5,000 acres of land. Hill died on November 30, 1700, at the age of 63 (STAN 24–25, 42; LEO 41, 44, 47; NUG I:457; II:40, 268, 271, 344, 394; III:1, 11, 29, 34; HEN II:364–365; III:93; Charles City County Orders 1658–1661:34, 279–284; Wills and Deeds 1692–1694:183; MCGC 449, 521; Bruce, "Defense of Colonel Edward Hill," 239–347, 341–349; BRU 119–123;; WASH 84–91; Old Rappahannock County Deeds and Wills 1677–1682:300; EJC I:2,10, 269, 322, 423; 2:151; CO 1/42 f 111; 1/2 f 304; 5/1309 f 100; 5/1339 ff 36–37; 5/1312 f 100; SAIN 10:341; 17:279, 466; WHITE II:969; WITH 161; EEAC 31).

Edward Hill III: Edward Hill III, who was known to his contemporaries as Edward Hill Jr., took an active role in public life. He was a member of the College of William and Mary's Board of Governors and served on the vestry of Westover Parish. In 1676 he was elected to the assembly, where he represented Charles City County and probably succeeded Robert Wynne, who died in August 1675. Hill was elected speaker in 1684 and served as a burgess for Charles City in 1688. He succeeded his father as colonel of the Charles City County militia and was considered for council membership. In 1704, when a list of quitrents was sent back to England, he was credited with 2,100 acres in Charles City County, 3,000 acres in King William, and 1,000 acres in Prince George. On October 29, 1705, while Hill was a Prince George County burgess, the college's main building burned to the ground. He served as the Royal African Company's factor in 1701–1702 and had business dealings with Perry, Lane and Company of London. One of his many friends was William Byrd II of Westover, who described him as an honorable and good-natured man who lacked ambition. Edward Hill III died during the early 1720s, leaving three daughters (LEO 37, 47, 49; LJC 420; SMITH 43; BYRD passim; MEADE 110–114).

* * *

George Hill: George Hill, a gentleman, came to Virginia in 1608 as part of the 1st Supply of new settlers. Therefore, he would have resided in Jamestown (VI&A 388).

Jane Hill: Jane Hill, a young girl who came to Virginia in 1619, was living in West and Shirley Hundred in January 1625 in the household of her widowed mother, Mrs. Rebecca Rose. In February 1627 the justices of the General Court issued a warrant for the arrest of Jane Hill and John Ewen, who were to be brought to Jamestown and interrogated about their "lewd behavior" at West and Shirley Hundred. They admitted that they had begun having consensual sex and had agreed to marry, but Jane changed her mind. Both were punished for committing fornication. She was subjected to public shaming, whereas he was flogged (VI&A 388).

John Hill: John Hill came to Virginia in 1620 and in 1625 lived in Elizabeth City, where he was a 26-year-old indentured servant in the household of John Banam and Robert Sweete. Hill obtained his freedom and in April 1635 patented 350 acres on the lower side of the James River, on the Elizabeth River, in what was then Elizabeth City County but later Lower Norfolk. During April 1644 he patented 400 acres on the Elizabeth River's western branch and 200 acres on the east side of the Nansemond River. He continued to acquire acreage along the Elizabeth River's western branch and on the river's south side. Hill served as a burgess for Lower Norfolk County and attended the assembly sessions held in 1639, 1640, 1642, and 1651–1652. For reasons that are unclear, on January 20, 1648, John Hill appeared before the justices of Lower Norfolk County and provided them with detailed personal information. He indicated that he was then between 50 and 60 years of age and had lived in Virginia for more than 25 years. He said that prior to coming to the colony he had lived at the University of Oxford, where he was employed as a bookbinder. Hill added that he was in good health

and that he was the son of Stephen Hill of Oxford. In 1649 Hill witnessed the will made by John Hatton of the Elizabeth River, and in October 1655 he helped Richard Starnell with the preparation of his will. During the early 1650s, Hill's name appeared several times in the records of the county's monthly court (VI&A 389; LEO 17–18, 20, 28; Lower Norfolk Record Book A:25, 111; B:61a, 149; C:16, 28, 30, 44, 69, 179; Wills, Deeds, Orders D [1656–1666]:340; PB 1:166; 2:4–5, 122, 169).

John Hill: On April 21, 1670, the General Court's justices noted that John Hill was then in residence on the Warwick County plantation known as Boldrup, which belonged to Frances Culpeper Stephens, a former widow who had become Lady Frances Berkeley, Sir William Berkeley's wife (MCGC 211).

* * *

Nicholas Hill: In July 1658 the justices of Isle of Wight County resolved a dispute involving Major Nicholas Hill, who insisted that he had bought 900 acres on the Pagan Creek from Colonel Bernard. Earlier on, Hill laid claim to 100 acres on a tributary of the Lynnhaven River, in what was then Elizabeth City. In September 1664 he patented 750 acres in the Upper Parish of Isle of Wight County, half of the late Edward Bennett's 1,500-acre plantation, which had descended to Hill's wife, Silvestra (Sylvester), and her sister, Mary Bland. Hill went on to patent 670 acres on the Blackwater River in 1674. He served as an Isle of Wight County burgess from 1669 to 1674 and died in October 1675, a few months after his wife inherited 12,000 pounds of tobacco from her cousin, Major-General Richard Bennett. In 1680 Ralph Hill, son of the late Lieutenant Colonel Nicholas Hill, testified that the decedent had left life-rights in his plantation to his widow, Silvestra Hill, and that after her death the property was to descend to his youngest son, Richard Hill, and Richard's descendants. Ralph went on to say that his brother, Richard, had died without heirs and that he was selling his reversionary interest in the property to Major Samuel Swann of Surry County. In 1695 Silvestra Bennett Hill sold her interest in her late husband's plantation on Lawnes Creek to Lewis Burwell of York County. She survived until around 1707 (LEO 38; Isle of Wight County Deeds, Wills & Guardian Accounts Book A:77; Will and Deed Book 1 [1662–1688]:435–437; BODIE 279, 623; PB 1:506; 5:27; 6:506; SR 3568; DOR 1:228–231).

Richard Hill: Richard Hill, the son of Lieutenant Nicholas Hill and his wife, the former Silvestra (Sylvester) Bennett, lost his father in 1675. He and his siblings stood to inherit their mother's share of the property she had inherited from her father, Edward Bennett. Richard Hill, like his late father, served as an Isle of Wight County burgess and held office from 1661 to 1668. During the 1670s Richard Hill served as the attorney of two London merchants. He may have been the same man who on June 15, 1675, sued William Sherwood of Jamestown and in March 1676 filed suit against George Lee, another Jamestown resident. On September 9, 1680, Ralph Hill, another son of the late Lieutenant Colonel Nicholas Hill, testified that the decedent had left life-rights in his plantation to his widow, Silvestra Hill, and that after her death the property was to descend to his youngest son, Richard Hill, and his descendants. Ralph went on to say that his brother, Richard, had died without heirs and that he was selling his reversionary interest in the property to Major Samuel Swann of Surry County (LEO 38; BODIE 277–279, 584–585; PB 5:153; Isle of Wight County Wills and Deeds 2:133, 475; MCGC 410;.DOR 1:230–231).

* * *

Richard Hill: On July 22, 1640, Richard Hill was identified as a runaway servant in the employ of William Peirce of urban Jamestown (MCGC 467).

Robert Hill: Robert Hill served as an Isle of Wight County burgess in 1660. He and his wife, Mary, may have come to Virginia in 1642 at the expense of Francis England. In 1679 Sion Hill of Surry County, who identified himself as the late Robert Hill's son, testified about an Isle of Wight County plantation that the decedent had purchased from George Archer in 1653. A land transaction that occurred in 1694 also made reference to some acreage that Archer had sold to Hill. Robert Hill (perhaps the same man) patented some land in 1664 in Accomack County and two years later claimed 1,200 acres in Old Rappahannock County (LEO 36; Isle of Wight County Deed Book 1 [1688–1704]:97; BODIE 584–585, 614, 669; PB 5:77, 576).

Thomas Hill: On August 1, 1638, Mr. Thomas Hill secured a patent for a small lot on the north side of Back Street in urban Jamestown. He received his lot as part of the February 20, 1636, building initiative and had six months in which to commence construction. Hill, a gentleman and merchant, conducted business with many of Virginia's most prominent families. In November 1629, while he was in England, Hill witnessed the will of Francis West, Lord Delaware's brother. Hill was in Virginia during the 1630s and was among those siding with Governor John Harvey during his dispute with his councilors. In 1637 when Harvey, who was deposed as governor and then reinstated, had some of his enemies' personal property seized, Secretary Richard Kemp gave Thomas Hill some of Samuel Mathews I's goods. This prompted Mathews to seek redress in England and led to Hill's being ordered to return Mathews' belongings. It was during this period that Hill patented his lot in Jamestown. In January 1641 Hill served a term as James City's burgess and probably represented Jamestown. In April 1643 he acquired a 600-acre subunit of Richard Kemp's 4,332-acre Rich Neck tract. Hill's parcel was delineated on Kemp's plat of Rich Neck. In April 1648 Hill, a gentleman and planter, assigned his 3,000-acre Upper Chippokes tract (on the lower side of the James River) to Edward Bland. A few years later he patented some land near the head of the Potomac River. After Hill's death his wife, Mary, who was Abraham Peirsey's daughter, married Thomas Bushrod. A Northumberland County document that dates to August 1660 reveals that Thomas Hill was residing in Stanley Hundred when his daughter married Colonel Moore Fauntleroy (PB I:588; NUG I:95, 143, 159, 175, 353; WITH 52; PPR 3 Seager; SAIN 1:281; PC 2/50 f 428; CO 1/9 ff 289, 543; 1/10 ff 73–74; STAN 61; Senior 1642; MCGC 386, 447; York County Deeds, Orders, Wills 9:81, 123; Northumberland County Deeds, Wills &c. 1661–1662:18; LEO 20).

[No First Name] Hilliard (Hellyard): In 1608 a boy named Hilliard came to Virginia in the 2nd Supply of new settlers to arrive in Jamestown (VI&A 390).

Andrew Hinson: Sometime prior to March 28, 1689, Andrew Hinson, Lionel Delawafer, and Edward Davis were accused of piracy and incarcerated in Jamestown. Their goods, which were considered stolen property, were seized. Thanks to pressure from British merchant Micajah Perry and others, the men eventually were released. However, some of their goods and money were kept, and they were forced to pay for the cost of their room and board while jailed. The accused pirates may have been detained in sheriff Henry Gawler's row house on urban

Jamestown's waterfront, close to the row house unit owned by Micajah Perry (CO 5/1305 ff 13–14; 1357 f 228; PRO T 11/12 f 395).

John Hinton: On February 16, 1624, John Hinton was living in urban Jamestown in the household of Clement Dilke, a burgess (VI&A 391).

Thomas Hinton: Samuel Mathews I's father-in-law, Sir Thomas Hinton, retired to Virginia and in 1634 was appointed to the Council of State. In February 1635 Hinton's wife, Anne, was identified as the granddaughter of Anne Garrard of Upper Lambourne, Berkshire, a widow. On December 11, 1635, Governor John Harvey removed Hinton from office, simultaneously alienating Hinton and Mathews. Sir Thomas Hinton's son, a gentleman of the Privy Chamber, was considered a possible replacement for Harvey as governor (VI&A 391).

John Hitch: On July 17, 1622, Virginia Company officials noted that John Hitch of London had obtained some shares of Virginia land from Francis Carter, who had acquired them from Lord Delaware's widow. On July 31, 1622, Hitch set sail for Virginia, accompanied by Edward Pope and John Grefrihe. Hitch may have been John Hitchy, who on January 24, 1625, was living in the eastern end of Jamestown Island (VI&A 391).

John Hitchy (Hitch?): In January 1625 John Hitchy was living in the eastern end of Jamestown Island. He may have been John Hitch, who set sail for Virginia on July 31, 1622 (VI&A 391).

Francis Hobbs: In early 1647 Francis Hobbs sold his plantation on the Nansemond River to two other men. Like many of his peers, he speculated in frontier land, and in August 1650 he secured a patent for 1,000 acres on the north side of the Rappahannock River. Hobbs served as a burgess for Isle of Wight County in 1654–1655. He became Jervase Dodson's attorney in 1657, the same year that he signed a pledge promising to procure a patent for 200 acres abutting Dodson's acreage in Isle of Wight. In 1658 Captain Hobbs was among those who witnessed the codicil to Robert Bird's will. He later purchased part of Colonel Joseph Bridger's land, a parcel that Bridger had bought from Nathan Floyd. In 1674 Francis Hobbs Sr. married Nathan Floyd's widow, Mary. Hobbs made his will in March 1687 and died prior to June 9, 1688. He made bequests to his cousins Alice and John Davis and Margaret Harris and named his brother-in-law

John Harris as executor. In October Harris qualified as executor. No reference was made to Francis Hobbs' wife, raising the possibility that she was deceased (LEO 32; Isle of Wight County Deeds, Wills & Guardian Accounts Book A:14, 58–59; Wills and Deeds 1:323, 574; 2:250, 280; Administrations and Probates 1:67; PB 2:237).

John Hobson: John Hobson, who was born in England, patented some land in Isle of Wight County in March 1636. His acreage, which bordered Pagan Point (Hampstead) Creek and the Warresqueak (Pagan) River, was to be called New Town Haven. Hobson, as a shareholder of the Virginia Company, acquired the right to his land on May 2, 1621. On November 4, 1620, he was identified as one of Captain Christopher Lawne's fellow adventurers, who intended to establish what was to be called the Isle of Wight plantation. Captain Hobson was named to the Council of State in 1637, the same year that he sent a petition to England asking that the sailors aboard the *Unity* not be pressed into service. Shipping records reveal that in 1638 Hobson sent a relatively large quantity of tobacco to England in William Upton's ship. He served on the council until 1650 (VI&A 392; STAN 33; PB 1:414; LEO xx; SR 630, 3499).

William Hockaday (Hockeday): William Hockaday's name appeared in York County's records in November 1641, when he was identified as a merchant. In October 1645 he mortgaged all of his personal estate in order to cover a debt. However, he apparently was considered a reliable, trustworthy citizen, for in 1646 he served as an attorney. Over the years he made several appearances in court, usually trying to recover debts. In August 1646 he received a patent for 500 acres on the west side of Ware Creek, in what was then York County but by 1654 was New Kent. Then, in December 1648 he acquired an additional 846 acres on the basis of 17 headrights. By April 1653 Hockaday had added another 1,000 acres to his holdings, land that lay near the head of Ware Creek and extended westward to Warraney Creek. In 1652 he was among those selected to serve as county justices, and he served as a burgess for York County in 1653, while the Commonwealth government was in power. On June 3, 1663, Lieutenant Colonel William Hockaday consolidated his patents. He then possessed 5,470 acres on the south side of the York River, abutting Ware Creek, acreage on which he lived. By 1672 part of Hockaday's land belonged to his son, John (LEO 31; NUG I:167, 268, 511; PB 2:93; 5:384;

6:440; York County Deeds, Orders, Wills 1 [1633–1646]:130; 1 [1648–1657]:149; Orders, Wills, Etc. 2 [1645–1649]:56, 77, 110; Court Orders 2 [1646–1648]:155, 199, 341, 375).

John Hoddin (Holden, Hodin, Holding): In 1642 and 1643 John Hoddin represented Elizabeth City County in the assembly sessions held in 1642, 1643, and 1644. In October 1643 he began investing in land on the Middle Peninsula and patented tracts of 150 acres and 950 acres on the North River, in what was then York County but by 1651 had become Gloucester (later, Mathews) County. Hoddin continued to speculate in real estate and in 1649 secured a patent for 850 acres known as Warranucock (Goddins) Island, which is located in the Pamunkey River and was the home of the natives' paramount chief, Opechancanough. In 1653 he patented 389 acres on the lower side of the York River, to the south of the tract known as Mount Folly. Both of these parcels were in what was then York County. In January 1652 John Hoddin was still alive and witnessed a document that was recorded in Warwick County (LEO 21–22; DUNN 172).

Robert Hodge: On May 26, 1671, Robert Hodge, when acting as the attorney of Arthur Holdwort and Grace Waters, sued Theophilus Hone of urban Jamestown on account of a debt against the Richardson estate (MCGC 262).

Nicholas Hodges: When Nicholas Hodges appeared before the General Court in Jamestown on December 5, 1625, he testified that when he was in Canada, he heard Mr. Weston (a mariner) tell Nicholas Roe that, unless he would sign a release, he would put Roe's two servants ashore instead of transporting them to Virginia (VI&A 393).

Thomas Hodges (Hodgis): During the 1670s Thomas Hodges, a merchant, was active in the fur trade and exported deer, beaver, elk, otter, mink, and raccoon pelts from Virginia. He seems to have been a business associate of Richard Bennett I, for when Bennett made his will in 1675, he named Thomas Hodges as one of his overseers. On September 10, 1681, when Robert Hodge or Hodges of Lower Norfolk County made his will—which was proved a few weeks later—he named his brothers Thomas and John Hodges among his heirs and indicated that the latter was in Dartmouth. Two years later Thomas Hodges served as a witness when Adam Keeling prepared his will, and in December he was among those who went to court to prove the document's authentic-

ity. Thomas Hodges patented 787 acres on the Elizabeth River's western branch in October 1684 and served as a burgess for Norfolk County in 1693 and 1696–1697. He witnessed Thomas Hollewell's and John Powell's wills in 1687. In 1704, when quitrents were compiled, he was credited with 50 acres in Norfolk County. He may have been the same individual who paid quitrent on 250 acres in King and Queen County (LEO 53, 56; Lower Norfolk County Wills and Deeds 4:106, 155; 5:22, 66; SR 3560, 5592; PB 7:430; SMITH 45).

Anthony Hodgkins (Hodgskins, Hopskins, Hoskins, Hopkins): On April 29, 1622, Anthony Hodgkins, who was age 39 and one of Lady Delaware's servants, testified before the Chancery Court, addressing questions about Deputy Governor Samuel Argall's disposal of Lord Delaware's goods. Therefore, Hodgkins would have been in Jamestown in 1618 when Delaware's corpse arrived aboard the *Neptune*. In 1637 Hodgkins purchased a shallop on behalf of Edward Walker and Company, and three years later he received a license to keep an ordinary on the Eastern Shore. During April 1643 he made an agreement with Sir Edmond Plowden to build a partition in Plowden's store at Kecoughtan. In 1652 Hodgkins served as a burgess for Northampton County, the same year he patented 700 acres on Pungoteague Creek. A year later he patented a 400-acre tract on the north side of Kings Creek's mouth. On June 19, 1655, Hodgkins made his will, which was proved on August 16th. He left life-rights in the plantation he occupied to his wife, Joyce, and designated her as his executrix. He named his eldest daughter, Elizabeth, who was under 16, as his sole heir, with daughter Ann as reversionary heir. He made modest bequests to Ralph Dow Jr., Hugh Partridge, and servant Dorothy Young. Hodgkins asked his father (probably father-in-law), Captain William Jones, and his friend, Lieutenant William Waters, to serve as supervisors of his will and requested that they assist his wife and children (LEO 29; VI&A 393; C 24/486 Pt. 1:13; SR 9946; PB 3:124, 286; 4:503; AMES 1:136, 153; 2:30, 441, 452; Accomack County Deeds and Wills 1664–1671:15).

* * *

Rice (Ryce) Hoe (Hooe, How, Howe) I: Rice Hoe I came to Virginia in 1618 and during the mid-1620s lived at West and Shirley Hundred. He served as a burgess for Shirley Hundred Island in 1633. He went to England briefly but returned to Virginia in 1635. In

1636 he patented 1,200 acres of land near Merchant's Hope, using himself and his wife as headrights. Later, he patented land in what became Surry County. In 1640 Hoe was designated the tobacco viewer for Merchant's Hope, and he represented Charles City County in the assembly sessions of 1645, 1645–1646, and 1646. He died during the latter part of 1655 (VI&A 393–394; LEO 12, 23–25).

Rice (Ryce) Hoe (Hooe, How, Howe) III: Rice Hoe III, the grandson of early colonist Rice Hoe I, who came to Virginia in 1618, was born in 1661. His father, Rice Hoe II of Charles City County, patented 1,000 acres of land in Stafford County in 1671 and moved there shortly thereafter. A seemingly cruel man who sometimes abused his servants, he died sometime prior to October 1, 1694, having left his acreage to his son, Rice III. Colonel Rice Hoe III patented 1,100 acres in Stafford County in October 1694 and added to his holdings in 1704 and 1707. His land on the Potomac River was used as the landing for a ferry that ran to Cedar Point, Maryland. He married three times during the 1690s, wedding his first wife, the widowed Mary Massey, in October 1691. The marriage contract they signed on October 28, 1691, in anticipation of being wed that day, reveals that both parties had a child or children by a former union; the agreement was recorded on May 10, 1692. Hoe was widowed and in 1695 married Anne Howson. Upon being widowed again, he wed the former Frances Townshend, the widow of Francis Dade II and Captain John Withers. On September 8, 1699, Rice Hoe III and his bride-to-be executed a prenuptial agreement, a document that reveals that she had three living sons: Robert, Francis III, and Cadwalader Dade. On May 18, 1699 Hoe took his seat as a burgess for Stafford County and replaced the Rev. John Waugh, who was elected but declared ineligible because he was a clergyman. Hoe was returned to office in 1703 and served until 1705. He died on April 19, 1726 (LEO 59, 62–63; VI&A 393; DOR 2:338–340; 3:410; NN 2:2, 30–31; 3:58, 155; HEN 4:93; Stafford County Record Book 1686–1693:33a–34, 68a, 96, 244a–245; 1699–1709:5).

* * *

Thomas Holcroft (Howldcroft, Holdcroft, Holecroft): Thomas Holcroft arrived in Virginia in June 1610 with Lord Delaware, who designated him captain of a company. Later in the year Sir Thomas Gates ordered him to build a fort in the woods near Kecoughtan.

In October 1610 Lord Delaware commanded Captain George Yeardley and Captain Thomas Holcroft, who were in charge of the forts at Kecoughtan, to bring their men to Jamestown so that they could join him in an exploratory journey toward the mountains (VI&A 394).

Robert Holden (Holder?): On February 10, 1677, Governor William Berkeley issued a proclamation in which he named those who were exempt from the king's pardon on account of their role in Bacon's Rebellion. One was Robert Holden, who needed to be brought before a court (NEVILLE 61; SR 660). He may have been the Robert Holder who in September 1674 patented 250 acres on Skiffs Creek in James City County (PB6:521).

* * *

Richard Holder (Holden, Holdinge): On January 28, 1672, Richard Holder patented an eight-plus acre waterfront parcel that straddled Orchard Run, at the eastern limits of urban Jamestown. It included some waste (or unclaimed) land granted to him by means of an October 12, 1670, court order. Included within Holder's patent was a one-acre lot that Thomas Hunt had patented in August 1655. Holder had two children, John and Ann. In 1655 he patented 600 acres in Northumberland County, and a year later he was credited with an additional 525 acres. In 1673 he lost a case to Richard James I, a Jamestown merchant, and in 1678 he identified William Corker of Surry County as one of his debtors. Among the merchants with whom Holder dealt was Micajah Perry of London, whose agent occupied a waterfront lot just west of Holder's eight-plus acres. During 1674 Holder purchased a 37½-acre, riverfront tract from Colonel Thomas Swann. Although the men's deed has been lost or destroyed, the transaction and the year it occurred are recounted in an undated summary of Richard Ambler's mid-eighteenth-century land acquisitions. Moreover, the 37½-acre parcel, which was surveyed and drawn to scale, had by 1727 become part of a 127-plus acre parcel that belonged to William Broadnax I, described in detail in deeds executed January 1, 1744, and January 1, 1745. When Richard Holder made his will, he bequeathed his 37½ acres, the eight-plus acre parcel he patented in 1672, and a much smaller plot to his son, John, an unmarried man. On August 8, 1687, John Holder bequeathed to his married sister, Ann Holder Briscoe, the acreage he had inherited from their father and almost all of his personal estate. Holder's will, presented to the General Court on August 8, 1687, reveals that he was indebted to Ann's father-in-law, blacksmith William Briscoe, and that he bequeathed a female calf to John Hall (PB 6:442; NUG I:317, 356; II:122; MCGC 227, 247, 258, 293, 355; Surry County Will Book 2:140; AMB 22, 38, 53, 57, 63, 97–98, 106–107, 137).

Ann Holder (Holden, Holdinge) (Mrs. [No First Name] Briscoe, Mrs. James Chudley [Chudleigh]): On October 12, 1670, Ann Holder's father, Richard, patented eight-plus acres of land in urban Jamestown's easterly limits, near Orchard Run or "the orchard," which by 1681 belonged to blacksmith William Briscoe. When Richard Holder died, his Jamestown acreage descended to his son, John, who in August 1687 bequeathed it to his sister, Ann. Included were John Holder's eight-plus acres that straddled Orchard Run and 37½ acres that lay to its east. Ann also received almost all of her late brother's personal estate. Thanks to her brother's August 1687 bequest, Ann Holder Briscoe already was in possession of land on Orchard Run when her father-in-law, William Briscoe, left her the halves of two lots in urban Jamestown. On July 10, 1695, Ann, who by then had wed James Chudley, repatented the western half of one lot, supplementing it with a small amount of new land she claimed on the basis of a headright. On February 5, 1697, Ann Holder Briscoe Chudley and her husband, James, sold her reconstituted and expanded lots to William Edwards III, whose father had purchased a neighboring parcel in 1695. The Chudley couple was then residing on the residue of the eight-plus acres that Ann had inherited from her brother, John Holder (AMB 21, 22, 38, 53, 57, 63, 133; MCGC 227; PB 6:442; NUG II:122).

* * *

Rev. Robert Holderby: On May 12, 1693, the Rev. Robert Holderby was authorized to receive compensation for providing prayers to the General Assembly (LJC 143).

Arthur Holdsworth: Arthur Holdsworth, an attorney, sued William Edwards I's estate on October 2, 1671. Edwards' heirs then owned a large parcel on urban Jamestown's waterfront (MCGC 280).

Nicholas Holgrave: Nicholas Holgrave came to Virginia in 1607 and was one of the first Jamestown colonists (VI&A 394).

Thomas Holiday (Holliday): On May 21, 1679, Thomas Holiday of Jamestown, James Alsop's executor, sold the decedent's quarter-acre lot in urban Jamestown to William Briscoe, a blacksmith. At that time Holiday's wife, Hanna, released her legal interest in the Alsop land. Because Thomas Holiday was James Alsop's executor but seemingly was not an heir, Hanna may have been the decedent's widow or daughter. In December 1682 Thomas Holiday was identified as the former owner of 12 acres in the eastern end of Jamestown Island, acreage that also had belonged to William Champion. On September 20, 1686, Holiday witnessed a document, and in early May 1699 he signed a petition in which he protested the outcome of the election of Jamestown's burgess. This action indicates that he was a voter and then owned or had a legal interest in property within urban Jamestown. In 1704 he paid quitrent on 250 acres of James City County land (AMB 27, 37, 57, 133; PB 7:228; NUG II:252; SAIN 18:728; SMITH 45).

Gabriel Holland: Gabriel Holland, a yeoman who came to Virginia sometime prior to 1619, served as a burgess for the corporation of Henrico in 1623–1624. At first he lived at Shirley Hundred, where he held the rank of sergeant and was responsible for some of Berkeley Hundred's male servants. However, by February 1624 he had moved to the College. Shortly thereafter, he wed Mary, the widow of ancient planter William Pinke alias Jonas, who in August 1624 patented her late husband's 12-acre tract in the eastern end of Jamestown Island. Mary Holland died and Gabriel, who inherited her property, quickly remarried. In January 1625 he and his new wife, Rebecca, were living in rural Jamestown Island, probably on his late wife's land. Holland, a respected member of the Jamestown Island community, made several appearances in the General Court during 1627 and 1628, at which time he arbitrated disputes and collected debts attributable to merchant Humphrey Rastall's estate. He died sometime after 1632 (VI&A 394–395; LEO 5).

Richard Holland: Richard Holland came to Virginia with Edward Grindon in 1622. He may have gone to Grindon's property in the eastern end of Jamestown Island or to his plantation on the lower side of the James River, which eventually became part of the Treasurer's Plantation (VI&A 395).

Anthony Holliday (Holiday, Holloday, Halladay, Holyday, Hollyday): Anthony Holliday purchased some land in Isle of

Wight County in 1688, by which time he already resided there. He served as a burgess for Isle of Wight in 1693, 1698, and 1699 and also became a county justice of the peace. In 1694 Holliday purchased some land from two local men. When quitrent rolls were compiled in 1704, Anthony Holliday was credited with 860 acres in Isle of Wight County (LEO 52–53, 58–59; Isle of Wight County Deed Book 1 [1688–1704]:14; BODIE 600, 629; SMITH 45).

George Holmes: In 1629 George Holmes posted a bond guaranteeing another man's good behavior. On August 4, 1635, he patented some land adjoining Jockey's Neck in James City County, using his wife, Rebecca, as a headright (VI&A 396–397).

George Holmes: In September 1635 Captain George Holmes, a mariner, came to Virginia with Dutch mariner David Devries. He may have been the same individual who patented some land near Jockey's Neck in August 1635 (VI&A 397).

William Holmes: In February 1624 Captain William Holmes, a mariner, was living in urban Jamestown and headed a household he shared with a married couple and their child. During the year Holmes sold chests of medical supplies to Dr. John Pott, testified about a bargain a Jamestown merchant had made, and witnessed a will. He went to England to procure goods but died in 1627 while returning to the colony. Afterward, his widow, Elizabeth, presented the General Court with an inventory of his estate. When Captain William Holmes made his will, he named as heirs his sons William and Robert and his sisters and nephews, who were in England. He also left money to the two children of a kinsman and made a bequest that would enable his own children to come to the colony. In January 1638 Captain Samuel Mathews testified on Elizabeth Holmes' behalf. By that date she had married Joshua Mullard (VI&A 397).

John Holmwood (Holmewood): In October 1650 John Holmwood received a patent for 300 acres at the head of the Sunken Marsh on the lower side of the James River, in what was then James City County but two years later became Surry County. He became a Surry County justice and went on to marry London merchant Edward Bland's widow, Jane, who inherited 4,300 acres at the head of Upper Chippokes Creek in Surry County. On February 14, 1653, Holmwood signed an agreement with Surry County carpenter Thomas Felton, who promised to build a frame dwelling at the Bland plantation, Berkeley. Afterward, Holmwood and his wife, Jane, moved to Charles City County. On May 20, 1656, Holmwood informed Surry County's justices that although he had wed Edward Bland's widow, he was unable to account for the cargo that had been aboard the decedent's ship, with the exception of some lead, which he had sold. In 1656 John Holmwood served as a burgess for Charles City County, and by August 1659 he had become a justice in the county court. Later in the year he received permission to employ an Indian servant. In 1660 Holmwood, who was then Charles City County's sheriff, was paid for providing furniture for the county courthouse. During 1664 he was summoned to court because he had rented a defective sloop to a man whose cargo was lost when the vessel sank. Holmwood was still alive in 1666 (LEO 33; Surry County Deed Book 1:18; 2:458; Order Book 1671–1691:85; PB 2:268; SR 13838; Charles City County Orders 1655–1658:56; 1658–1661:191, 196, 253–254, 262; 1661–1664:289; 1664–1665:527, 599, 617; DOR 1:327).

James Holt: James Holt, a carpenter from London, arrived in Jamestown on September 12, 1623, and took the oath of supremacy (VI&A 397).

John Holt (Hoult): John Holt, a gentleman, came to Virginia in 1608 as part of the 2nd Supply of new settlers and would have lived in Jamestown (VI&A 397).

* * *

Randall (Randolph) Holt (Howlett) I: Randall Holt I came to Virginia in 1620–1621, probably at Dr. John Pott's expense, and in February 1624 he was a servant in the Pott household in urban Jamestown. He later moved to Pott's leasehold in the Governor's Land. Holt was freed in early January 1627. Afterward he married Mary, the daughter and sole heir of ancient planter John Bailey, who had owned land in the eastern end of Jamestown Island and on Hog Island. The couple, who resided on her property at Hog Island, produced a son and heir, Randall Holt II, shortly after their marriage. Court records reveal that before Mary's marriage, her guardians generated income on her behalf by leasing her land to tenants. In 1636 Holt patented 400 acres at the head of Lower Chippokes Creek, and in 1639 he acquired 490 acres of land on Hog Island, adding it to the 400 acres his wife had inherited there. He was still alive in July 1639 but seems to have predeceased his wife. Mary

Holt died sometime prior to August 1, 1643, at which time son Randall II repatented her acreage (VI&A 398).

Randall Holt (Howlett) II: In 1643 Randall Holt II, the son of Randall and Mary Bailey Holt, repatented his late mother's acreage in the eastern end of Jamestown Island and at Hog Island. He resided on Hog Island, and by November 5, 1654, he had sold the Jamestown Island acreage he had inherited. In May 1654 Major Randall Holt II asked Surry County's justices to compensate him for the use of his boat and servants, which had been pressed into service. Two years later he was censured for making disparaging remarks about some of the county court's justices. Around 1663 Randall Holt II married the twice-widowed Elizabeth Hansford Wilson, who had outlived John Hansford and Christopher Wilson. In 1668 Holt became a Surry County justice of the peace. When he prepared his will in April 1679, he left his personal property to his wife, Elizabeth; his land to his eldest son, John; and named sons William and Thomas as reversionary heirs. Randall Holt II's will was presented to the county court on September 2, 1679. The will made by his widow, Elizabeth, was presented for probate on May 3, 1709 (VI&A 398; DOR 2:312).

Thomas Holt: Thomas Holt, the son of Randall Holt II and grandson of Randall Holt I and his wife, ancient planter Mary Bailey, lived at Hog Island in Lawnes Creek Parish. He began serving as a Surry County justice in 1697 and went on to become sheriff, holding office in 1699, 1701, and 1707. He also was a militia captain. Holt appeared in court from time to time, witnessing documents, transacting business, and serving as an attorney. He married Frances, the daughter of Francis Mason II, sometime prior to September 1696, and upon her death wed a woman named Mary. In 1699 Thomas Holt served as a burgess for Surry County and in 1701 asked to be appointed clerk of the Committee of Propositions and Aggrievances. In 1725 he received permission to operate the ferry that ran from Hog Island to Archer's Hope. Thomas Holt's will, dated November 8, 1730, was proved on March 17, 1731 (LEO 59; DESCOG 1–3; EJC 1:446; 2:41, 135, 178; 3:146; Surry County Deeds, Wills, Etc. 4 [1694–1709]:116, 128, 353, 397, 581; DOR 2:311–313; SR 381).

* * *

Robert Holt: In 1638 Robert Holt and his partner, Richard Bell, patented 500 acres on the east side of the Chickahominy River in James City County. His acreage was near the head of Checqueroes (Gordon's) Creek and what by the early 1640s became Governor William Berkeley's plantation, Green Spring. In 1640 Holt was identified as a merchant when he repatented and enlarged Bell's share of their jointly owned patent. When Holt enhanced the size of his original acreage in 1650, amassing 1,560 acres in all, he used the headrights of his wife, Alice, and several others. As time went on, he continued to accumulate land in the vicinity of his original holdings. By July 21, 1657, Major Robert Holt was in possession of a parcel in the southeastern end of Jamestown Island, to the east of Goose Hill and south of Passmore Creek. Holt's land is mentioned in a patent for some adjoining acreage. Holt also owned a parcel in urban Jamestown, and in 1655 and 1656 he served as the capital city's burgess. His acreage was near the site on which Colonel Thomas Swann later built a tavern. Holt was returned to office after the death of Robert Ellyson and served from 1666 to 1676. Colonel Robert Holt remained loyal to Governor William Berkeley, and in 1676 he rallied 30 men and led the defense of Jamestown when the city was attacked by Nathaniel Bacon's followers. On March 16, 1677, Holt presented the James City County freeholders' grievances to the royal commissioners charged with investigating the underlying causes of Bacon's Rebellion. In 1670 Robert and Alice Holt still owned some land near Green Spring. The date of Colonel Holt's death is uncertain. However, when Thomas Abbott bequeathed Alice Holt a leasehold in the Governor's Land in 1692, he identified her as a widow and his aunt. She probably was the Mrs. Holt whom Jamestown tavern-keeper John Everett (the Swanns' tenant) accused of wrongfully detaining his steer (PB 4:100, 196; 6:42; NUG I:103, 123, 151, 202, 205, 215, 231, 347, 356, 487; II:12, 52, 206, 210; AMB 18; STAN 72; SAIN 10:44; Bruce, "Bacon's Rebellion," 171; LEE 51 f 208; Surry County Deeds, Wills &c. 1671–1684:297; LEO 33, 38).

Thomas Holt: On November 6, 1756, Thomas Holt procured from Christopher Ford a 122-acre leasehold in the Governor's Land that had been in Edward Jaquelin's possession earlier on. On November 13, 1762, Holt conveyed the Jaquelin acreage to James Heart, who immediately conveyed his leasehold to John Ambler I. By that time Ambler owned much of the urban and rural land on Jamestown Island (AMB 167).

Theophilus Hone (Howne): In November 1652 Theophilus Hone, a gentleman, served as a burgess for Elizabeth City County. Four years later he commenced representing James City, presumably Jamestown. In 1662 he was the attorney of Elizabeth Perkins, who owned a parcel on the mainland just west of Jamestown Island, and in 1664 he was identified as a James City County justice, a post he held for many years. From 1666 to 1676 Hone served as Jamestown's representative in the assembly, thereby signifying that he owned property there or was married to someone who did. In October 1667 he was among those fined for building a wharf in front of the town, an indication that he had a legal interest in a parcel of waterfront land. Over the years Hone enhanced the size of his holdings in Elizabeth City County, and he patented a large tract on the north side of the Rappahannock River. He was a respected member of the community and served as a James City Parish vestryman and a James City County sheriff. During the early 1670s Major Hone made several appearances before the General Court. In 1670 he acknowledged a debt that was attributable to Captain John Whitty's estate, and a year later he and several other men were ordered to go to Tabitha Summers Underwood's house to examine a will. He also was ordered to inventory the estate of the late Thomas Hunt, a Jamestown resident. By May 1671 Theophilus Hone had married Sarah, William Richardson's widow and executrix, who had also outlived a previous husband, William Edwards I of Surry County. In 1672 Hone gave his power of attorney to stepson William Edwards II and attorney William Sherwood, who were to conduct business on his behalf in Surry County's monthly court; both of Hone's legal representatives owned land in urban Jamestown. From June 1670 to November 1673, Major Theophilus Hone occupied a 37-foot-long brick dwelling that Walter Chiles II had built on his three-acre lot in urban Jamestown. When Chiles' widow sold the house and lot to John Page in November 1673, Hone moved next door to another dwelling, which he was occupying in 1675. By that time the house was owned by Jonathan Newell.

In 1671 Captain Christopher Wormeley, who wed the widow of James City Parish rector Justinian Aylemer, sued vestrymen Theophilus Hone and William May for the deceased clergyman's back pay. Hone and May responded by suing Walter Chiles II and Francis Kirkman, their successors on the vestry. In October 1671 Thomas Rabley (a Dutchman who eventually purchased two lots in urban Jamestown) sued Major Theophilus Hone, his former guardian. When Hone's accounts were audited, it was determined that Rabley's claim was valid. In 1672 Major Hone, William Drummond I, and Mathew Page agreed to build a 250-foot-long brick fort in urban Jamestown, near the western end of the island, and in November 1672 Hone, who agreed to see that gun carriages were built, accepted Surry County funds that were designated for fort construction. After Mathew Page died, Hone and Drummond were ordered to complete the fort and were required to replace some cracked and defective brick. Although Hone and Drummond collaborated on fort construction, there is no doubt that they were on opposing sides during Bacon's Rebellion. During 1675 and 1676, while he was high sheriff of James City County, Hone seized the rebel Nathaniel Bacon (to whom Drummond was loyal) and forcibly took him to Governor William Berkeley. Destruction of the brick dwelling that Hone was renting in September 1676, when Bacon's followers put Jamestown to the torch, resulted in the loss of Hone's goods. On February 20, 1677, Major Hone asked the assembly to allow him to lease the ruins of two brick row houses on Jamestown's Back Street, dwellings that Richard Auborne and Arnold Cassinett had occupied. The burgesses awarded Hone a 50-year lease but stipulated that he had to begin rebuilding the houses within a year and keep them in good repair; however, he failed to do so and the ruinous dwellings were assigned to others. After Bacon's Rebellion subsided, Hone was responsible for inventorying the property confiscated from certain rebels who had been executed for treason. One was William Drummond I. Hone also certified an accounting of the rebel Richard Lawrence's estate. In January 1678 Theophilus Hone, though usually not numbered among the members of the "Green Spring Faction," was named one of Thomas Ludwell's executors. Hone's daughter, Catherine, married Robert Beverley I sometime prior to April 1687. She outlived him and after 1693 married Christopher Robinson of Middlesex County (JHB 1660–1693:48, 73, 78; NUG I:322, 540; LEO 30, 33, 38; STAN 70, 72, 79; HEN II:159, 249–250; AMB 24, 26; FOR I:8:12; Bruce, "Robert Beverley," 412; "Persons Who Suffered by Bacon's Rebellion," 68; Wiseman Book of Records; MCGC 221, 236, 251, 258, 262, 277, 280, 285, 342, 344, 367; Surry County Deeds, Wills &c. 1671–1684:20; Order Book 1671–1690:13; CO 5/1371 ff 217, 247; SAIN 10:72; WITH 667; Charles City Order Book 1:33; LEO 38; EJC I:81).

Francis Hooke (Hook): Francis Hooke, who was born in England, came to Virginia sometime prior to July 1635. By that date he had secured a patent for some land in the vicinity of Ward's Creek in what was then Charles City County but later Prince George County. Two years later he patented 2,000 acres near Flowerdew Hundred and Martin's Brandon. In April 1635 Governor John Harvey recommended that Hooke be appointed captain of the fort at Old Point Comfort. Harvey's superiors agreed and in June 1636 ordered Harvey to assign Hooke to that position. By May 1637 Hooke had patented 100 acres in Elizabeth City County, on the Strawberry Banks. A few months later he acquired 50 acres known as Pascall's Neck, near the "fort field," and he received a patent for "the fort field" itself, which was situated on the Strawberry Banks. The latter parcel was to be reassigned to Hooke's successor as fort captain. Captain Francis Hooke was named to the Council of State in 1637 and died in Virginia sometime prior to May 29, 1638, when Richard Morrison succeeded him as captain of the Old Point Comfort fort. In June 1640 Captain Thomas Willoughby asked the council to replace a barrel of gunpowder that he had provided for use at Captain Francis Hooke's funeral, noting that Hooke was not only a council member but also had been "the late commander of the fort at Point Comfort" (STAN 33; LEO xx; MCGC 468; PB 1:230, 446, 473, 485; SR 629, 3427, 4156).

Jeremiah Hooke: On March 22, 1677, Jeremiah Hooke was accused of supporting the rebel Nathaniel Bacon's cause when he was brought before Governor William Berkeley and the Council of State, who were conducting a military tribunal. It was decided that Hooke would be banished from the colony for seven years rather than being tried in a courtroom. Hooke was given the option of going to New England, Barbados, Jamaica, or any of the other islands. He was ordered to leave Virginia within two months and be on good behavior until the time of his departure (MCGC 461, 533).

Edward Hooker: In 1683 Edward Hooker patented 87 acres (part of the Hot Water tract) adjacent to Philip Ludwell I's Green Spring plantation. On September 26, 1733, Hooker, or perhaps a son who bore the same name, leased 150 acres from Philip Ludwell II, who then owned the bulk of the Hot Water plantation. When a plat was prepared in 1733, reference was made to Hooker's Mill Swamp (PB 7:307; LEE 51 f 675).

Thomas Hooker: In February 1624 Thomas Hooker was a servant in the household of Governor Francis Wyatt in urban Jamestown (VI&A 399).

William Hooker: On July 21, 1657, William Hooker and Thomas Woodhouse patented 100 acres of land in the southeastern end of Jamestown Island, to the east of the Goose Hill House. The two men apparently failed to erect improvements on their property within the time allotted by law, for it escheated to the Crown and in 1667 was patented by William May (PB 4:100; NUG I:347; AMB 18).

Thomas Hope: Thomas Hope, a tailor, came to Virginia in 1608 in the 1st Supply of new settlers and lived in Jamestown (VI&A 399).

Bartholomew Hopkins (Hoskins, Hoskine, Hoskines, Hopskins): Bartholomew Hopkins, an ancient planter, was living in Elizabeth City in 1624 when he patented 100 acres of land at Buckroe, adding some acreage on the Back River in 1632. Later, he bought some land on the eastern branch of the Elizabeth River in Lower Norfolk County. He seems to have been a very successful planter, for he exported large quantities of tobacco in 1628, 1630, and 1634. Hopkins went to England in 1634 and returned with his wife, Dorcas. They went back to England in 1639 so that Bartholomew could respond to a Chancery suit. However, by August 1640 he was back in Virginia, serving as a member of the Lynnhaven Parish vestry. In 1641 a London scrivener successfully sued Hopkins in order to settle a debt, but Hopkins' wife, Dorcas, managed to have another suit delayed. In 1645 Bartholomew Hopkins patented 800 acres on the north side of the Elizabeth River's Eastern Branch, and he enhanced his holdings in that area in 1648, 1653, and 1654. He may have experienced a bout of ill health, for in August 1647 the county justices excused him from public service and taxes on account of his age and infirmities, noting that he had come to Virginia before Sir Thomas Dale's departure, that is, before May 1616. Hopkins seems to have recovered, for he represented Lower Norfolk County in the assembly sessions held in 1649, 1651–1652, 1654–1655, and 1656. In 1652 and 1653 he purchased headrights that enabled him to patent some additional land. Like many others living in Tidewater Virginia, Bartholomew Hopkins invested in acreage on the frontier, sometimes speculatively. In 1651 he patented 1,350 acres on the south side of the Rappahannock River in what was then Old Rappahannock County, and he added an identical amount of contiguous acreage by means of another patent. Hopkins identified himself as a resident of the Elizabeth River area of Lower Norfolk County in February 1654 when he disposed of part of his acreage bordering the Rappahannock River. When making his will in 1655, William Moseley of Lower Norfolk County stated that he had bought some land originally patented by Bartholomew Hopkins. In 1663, when some of Hopkins' Old Rappahannock County acreage was sold, it was described as part of a 1,350-acre patent that he had acquired in 1655 (VI&A 400; LEO 27–28, 32–33; Old Rappahannock County Deeds and Wills 1656–1664:263–265; Lower Norfolk County Record Book A:19, 27, 44, 357; B:50, 178; C:29, 31, 43, 75, 166; PB 1:45, 117; 2:157, 172, 338; 3:253, 302; SR 3487, 3490, 3784, 5624).

John Hopkins: Sometime prior to December 30, 1693, John Hopkins commenced leasing a two-acre lot from William Sherwood, part of a larger tract that Sherwood owned at the western end of Jamestown Island. Hopkins also acquired a 100-acre tract in the southeastern portion of the island. Hopkins and his son-in-law or brother-in-law, Francis Bullifant, successively were in possession of two large tracts of marshland in the eastern end of Jamestown Island and one in the island's western end that had similar characteristics. Their preference for low-lying marshy areas raises the possibility that they were trappers. In 1704 John Hopkins paid quitrent on 120 acres of James City County land (AMB 48, 49, 77, 106–107; SMITH 46).

William Hopkins: On January 6, 1694, William Hopkins was described as the son-in-law of Francis Bullifant, a Jamestown Island landowner (AMB 49). He may have been related to John Hopkins.

Horehannah (Native American): Between March 18 and June 19, 1680, when the 1677 Treaty of Middle Plantation was expanded to include additional Indian groups, Vnuntsquero, the chief man of the Maherians (Meherrins), and Horehannah, their second chief, signed on behalf of their tribe (Anonymous, 1677 treaty, Miscellaneous Virginia Records 1606–1692, Bland Manuscripts, XIV, ff 226–233).

Walter Horsefoot: On September 19, 1625, when Walter Horsefoot testified before the General Court in Jamestown, he said that the

Elizabeth had been seized at Dover for the king's service. He added that the ship's purser had sought the assistance of the lieutenant at Dover Castle and had gotten it released. On October 3, 1629, Horsefoot was ordered to post a bond guaranteeing that he would pay his debts to the purser and crew of the *Elizabeth* (VI&A 402).

Stephen Horsey (Horseye, Horsley, Horse?): In November 1642 Obedience Robins of Accomack County received headright certificates for eight people he had brought to Virginia. One was Stephen Horse, perhaps the same individual known as Stephen Horsey. Horsey witnessed Gabriell Searle's will in 1648 and in 1651 was among those who signed a pledge of loyalty to the Commonwealth government. By December 28, 1650, he had married Sarah, the widow of Michael Williams (Willyams). Joane Dresone, one of Horsey's servants, committed suicide in November 1651 by hanging herself. Horsey patented 600 acres in Northampton County in 1653. Two years later he claimed 500 acres at Onancock. He also owned land on Nussawattocks Creek and in Maryland. Stephen Horsey was elected a burgess for Northampton County in 1653. He conducted an appraisal in 1654 and later served as the overseer of Richard Vaughan's estate. In October 1658 Horsey was named in John Ellis's will. In October 1663 Colonel Edmund Scarborough sent a report to Virginia's governor and the Council of State detailing his expedition into Maryland; in the report he mentioned Stephen Horsey, whom he described as an "Ignorant, yet insolent officer, a Cooper by profession who lived long in the lower parts of Accomack." He went on to say that Horsey had been elected a burgess but later was ejected from the assembly and that he found all government repugnant. Scarborough added that Horsey also objected to the church and had not had his children baptized. He blamed Horsey for the unrest at Anamessecks, where he lived, and said that he had been arrested (LEO 31; AMES 2:222; PB 3:98; 4:21, 93; MARSHALL 22, 30, 34–35, 39, 42, 59; Scarborough 1663). Stephen Horsey seems to have moved to Maryland.

Warham (Wareham) Horsmenden (Horsemenden, Horsmanden, Horsemonden, Horsmondine): Warham Horsmenden, who was from Lenham County, Kent, arrived in Charles City County sometime prior to 1655. In April 1656, when preparing to go to England, he designated his wife as his attorney. He was named to the Council of State in 1657 and served as a Charles City County burgess in 1658 and 1659. In 1660 he and Francis Redford served as overseers of Richard Nicholas's nuncupative will, and a year later he received his commission as a military officer. When Samuel Filmer made his will in July 1667, he indicated that he was planning to marry Mary, the eldest daughter of Warham and Susan Horsmenden. Filmer bequeathed mourning rings to his future in-laws, including his future wife's uncle, Arthur Horsmenden. On May 28, 1670, when Filmer's will was presented to probate officials in England, Warham Horsmenden indicated that the decedent's wife, the former Mary Horsmenden, was then in Virginia. Warham Horsmenden died in England sometime after 1683 (LEO 34–35; STAN 37; Charles City County Order Book 1655–1658: 10, 63; 1658–1661:178, 208, 236; SR 3544, 3629). He appears to have been in possession of some land on Moses Creek, a tributary of the Chickahominy River (Charles City County Court Orders 1664–1665:593).

[No First Name] Hosier: A person named Hosier, who came to Virginia on the *Furtherance*, died in Jamestown sometime after April 1623 but before February 16, 1624 (VI&A 402).

Edward Hosier (Hosyer): Edward Hosier, a vintner from Ratcliffe, England, arrived in Jamestown in September 1623. Sometime after April 1623 but before February 16, 1624, he died on Jamestown Island (VI&A 402).

Henry Hostage (Native American): In September 1674 the justices of Middlesex County decided that Henry Hostage, an Indian who was suspected of murder, would be delivered to the James City County sheriff in Jamestown so that he could be incarcerated until he stood trial. Hostage was identified as one of Major General Robert Smith's servants (Middlesex County Order Book 1673–1680:15).

John How (Howe, Hoe, Home): John How came to Virginia in 1621. By the mid-1620s he had become a planter and headed a household on the Eastern Shore, where he was considered a gentleman. On September 20, 1628, he acquired a 30-acre leasehold in Accomack, by which time he held patents for several other tracts. Some of How's disposable income seems to have come from building ships and boats. During 1636 he made several appearances in court to testify about the estate of the late Luke Aden (Eden), which the General Court's justices authorized him to settle. Over the years How was entrusted with public duties, an indication that he was considered a responsible and respectable citizen. In 1632 he was named a commissioner of the Accomack court, and he commenced serving as a burgess, attending the assembly sessions held in 1632, 1633, and 1637. He also served on his parish vestry and was a militia commander. When How testified in court in March 1637, he said that he was age 43 or thereabouts. Shortly before his death, which occurred in November 1637, he patented 1,000 acres on Cherrystone Creek and an additional 200 acres. He was among the relatively few authorized to be interred in the chancel of his parish church. Numerous claims against his estate reveal that he was deeply in debt at the time of his death (VI&A 402; PB 1:87; NUG:I:12, 72; MCGC 46–47, 94, 101–102, 117, 138, 148; LEO 10–12, 15; AMES 1:1, 39, 43, 64, 70–71, 95–96, 101, 122, 129; 2:14).

John How: On June 13, 1640, John How, Secretary Richard Kemp's servant and cowkeeper, was censured for giving false testimony about Thomas Stroud. When free, he was to be fined for committing perjury (MCGC 477).

Dorcas Howard: In April 1629, the General Court's justices learned that Dorcas Howard, a maidservant employed by Jamestown Island resident George Ungwin, had suffered a miscarriage and admitted that Robert Gage was the baby's father. Ungwin was ordered to see that Dorcas appeared in court to answer the justices' questions (VI&A 403).

Francis Howard: Francis Howard, Lord Effingham, Virginia's governor from September 1683 to 1692, was born in 1643 and succeeded to his father's title in March 1673. He was a Roman Catholic, which set him apart from most of the Virginia colonists he governed. Governor Howard arrived in the colony in February 1684, took his oath of office, and had a council meeting at Gloucester Hall in Gloucester, the home he was renting from Colonel Thomas Pate. In April 1684, when he first met with the burgesses, he caused controversy by trying to rescind a law that allowed the assembly to serve as an appellate body, capable of overruling the General Court's decisions. Howard's intention was to reduce the assembly's power. He created a court of chancery that was distinct from the General Court and made himself Lord Chancellor. According to Robert Beverley II, Howard refused to hold court in the statehouse, where other public business was conducted, "but took the Dining-Room of a private house [the

Sherwood house] for that Use." Beverley also indicated that the court was unpopular and ceased to exist as soon as Howard left office. When Governor Howard was queried in 1690 about conditions in the colony, he indicated that in 1686 he had seen that its gun platforms and small arms were repaired and had remounted the cannon in James Fort. He filed a petition against some accused pirates and summoned a sea captain to Jamestown because he had placed his ship and crew in great peril. In February 1688 the king gave Howard a housing allowance instead of authorizing him to build an official residence. This allowed him to rent the Green Spring mansion from Philip Ludwell I. Howard left Virginia in February 1689, at which point council president Nathaniel Bacon became interim governor, serving until Lieutenant Governor Francis Nicholson took office in 1690. Francis Lord Howard died in England on March 30, 1695 (STAN 17; BEVERLEY 97; EJC I:55, 517; CO 5/1306 f 1; SAIN 12:372; 13:222; EJC I:55).

Henry Frederick Howard: During the mid-1630s King Charles I decided to bestow upon the Duke of Norfolk's son, Henry Frederick Howard, Lord Maltravers, proprietorship of a vast expanse of land in southern Virginia. Maltravers already had been received into the New England Company as a patentee and councilor, and he held a 21-year lease that authorized him to manufacture copper farthing coins for distribution to Virginia, New England, Bermuda, and other plantations. On April 11, 1636, the king sent a letter to Virginia's governor and his council stipulating that the land to be assigned to Lord Maltravers was to be located between 31 and 36 degrees latitude and was to be called Norfolk County. When Governor John Harvey issued a patent to Maltravers on January 22, 1637, the acreage he received extended southward from the lower side of the James River to a point 35 degrees north latitude, and ran for "one degree of longitude" on each side of the Nansemond River. Thus, Maltravers' patent enveloped an area that extended for approximately 55 miles on each side of the Nansemond River, and ran in a southerly direction to a point approximately 25 miles below modern-day New Bern, North Carolina. Maltravers' patent, like those issued to other would-be landowners, was conditional. He had seven years in which to seat settlers on his land, at his own expense, and he was to document the development of his property by sending a certificate to the governor for every person he transported to the colony. As soon as Maltravers' first patent was seated, he be-

came eligible for another vacant tract of comparable size. At the end of seven years, he was to commence paying quitrent to the Crown. However, he and his heirs, tenants, and servants had the right to trade with the colony's Indians and to import and export goods, paying only a modest sum each year in taxes. Residents of the Maltravers' proprietary were not required to pay taxes to the Virginia government or to perform any civil or military service other than defending the colony from foreign invasion or putting down insurrections. Moreover, Maltravers, as proprietor, had the right to make laws and ordinances pertaining to his territory and to appoint all officeholders.

It is uncertain whether Lord Maltravers ever made a serious attempt to develop the Virginia land he had been allocated. However, in 1640 his agent, William Hawley, presented the governor with a letter authorizing him to take people to Carolina. Maltravers' ephemeral association with the Nansemond River area is evidenced by several patents dating to February and March 1638, which identify the Nansemond as the Matravers (Maltravers) River. The size and scope of Lord Maltravers' patent indicate that he had a proprietary interest in what became Nansemond and Norfolk counties as well as in land in Isle of Wight County and the province of Carolina. The potential development of a vast and independent proprietorship on the south side of the James River, which would have reduced Virginia's potential tax revenues and political influence, may have encouraged Governor Harvey to ignore Maltravers' claim, for he issued several patents within that territory during the late 1630s. Lord Maltravers ultimately turned his attention to New England, and his interest in Virginia and Carolina land appears to have waned, then faded into obscurity. But in 1699 Dr. Daniel Cox, Maltravers' legal heir, asserted a claim to the land that had been assigned to the decedent. Although England's attorney general informed the Council of Trade and Plantations that the claim was legitimate, Virginia governor Francis Nicholson contended there was no evidence that Maltravers had delimited or seated his patent, and that colonists living on the south side of the James were apprehensive about any change in government. Ultimately, Dr. Cox's claim was ignored (SAIN I:153, 285; XVII:233, 572; XIX:636–638; NUG I:101–103; Stanard, "Virginia in 1638–1639," 48–49; CO 5/1359 ff 383–389).

John Howard: On February 9, 1699, John Howard, a tailor, purchased 28½ acres in the west end of Jamestown Island from the late William Sherwood's nephew, John Jarrett. Jarrett then noted that Francis Bullifant held a lease for two acres of the tract. The property was of potential commercial value, for it was traversed by the main road that crossed the isthmus linking Jamestown Island to the mainland. In May 1699 Howard appeared before the assembly, where he protested Bartholomew Fowler's election as Jamestown's burgess. By 1686 Howard had married Margaret, the daughter and administratrix of Richard Clark (Clarke), a Jamestown lot owner. In April 1671 Howard proved the will of Jamestown lot owner Thomas Hunt, and he may have been the individual who, with Robert Beverley I, was charged with trespassing in the aftermath of Bacon's Rebellion. This raises the possibility that Howard, like Beverley, was one of Sir William Berkeley's loyalists-turned-vigilante. On April 10, 1694, John Howard of James City County patented a lot in Jamestown, a parcel that extended along the rails delimiting the north side of the churchyard and abutted east upon the "great old road." On the bottom of the patent, General Court clerk William Edwards II made a notation that "The Governor wou'd not sign this patent of John Howard." In early May 1699 Howard signed a petition in which he protested the outcome of the election of Jamestown's burgess. In 1704 Howard was credited with 25 acres of land in James City County. This would have been in addition to his acreage on Jamestown Island. On May 6, 1710, Howard sold his Jamestown Island land to John Baird (JHB 1695–1702:139, 141; SMITH 46; AMB 50, 67, 82; MCGC 247, 520; WITH 60; PB 8:82, 320; NUG II:350; Stanard, "Historical and Genealogical Notes and Queries," 438).

Andrew Howell: Andrew Howell was a servant in John Burrows' Jamestown Island household during the mid-1620s (VI&A 403).

John Howell: On September 28, 1674, John Howell, one of Governor William Berkeley's indentured servants, was hauled into court as a runaway. He was whipped and time was added to his term of service. Because Howell had stolen, and then lost, the boat in which he fled, he was ordered to serve its owner, William White of Jamestown, for 1½ years to cover its cost (MCGC 382).

Robert Hubbard: On April 2, 1655, Robert Hubbard purchased a 400-acre plantation in Surry County from Thomas Woodhouse of

Jamestown. He was identified as a resident of James City, raising the possibility that he, like Woodhouse, resided in the capital city. Hubbard witnessed a document in Surry in 1652, and he returned briefly in 1657 (Surry County Deeds, Wills &c. 1652–1672:14, 61, 111). This individual may have been the Robert Hubbard who during the mid-1650s patented two large tracts of land in Westmoreland County (PB 4:99, 103).

Robert Hubbard (Hubberd): During the mid-1670s Robert Hubbard, a gentleman, sued some of his debtors in Warwick County's monthly court. However, in January 1688 he was sued by one of his own creditors. Hubbard, who was Warwick County's sheriff in 1691, represented the county in the assembly and attended the sessions held in 1691–1692 and 1696–1697. He was serving as a county justice in 1697 when his financial problems forced him to mortgage his 168-acre plantation. In 1699 Hubbard was sued by Thomas Mountford of James City County, to whom he owed a substantial sum. He seems to have been involved in the business dealings of Richard Whitaker, whose executors were sued by Dudley Digges of Warwick County (LEO 51, 57; DUNN 54, 61, 70, 75, 185, 191, 214, 272–273, 571; PB 4:99, 103; MCGC 378).

Edward Hudson: In February 1624 Edward Hudson and his wife were living in urban Jamestown in Edward Blaney's household. Simultaneously, the census-taker attributed them to the Blaney plantation on the lower side of the James River. In May 1625 Hudson held a patent for 100 acres in Henrico County, on the south side of the James River below the falls (VI&A 405).

John Hudson: John Hudson, who served as provost marshal during Sir Thomas Dale's government (1611–1616), was tried at a court-martial hearing in Jamestown and sentenced to death. However, Dale intervened and Hudson was reprieved. By June 7, 1617, Hudson had run afoul of the law again. Deputy Governor Samuel Argall banished him from Virginia, threatening him with death if he ever returned (VI&A 405).

Thomas Hudson (Huson, Husone): Thomas Hudson came to Virginia in 1621 at the expense of Governor George Yeardley and probably lived in Jamestown (VI&A 406).

Francis Huff (Huffe, Huffs, Hough): Francis Huff came to Virginia in 1624 and settled in Elizabeth City. By October 20, 1632, he had married the widow of Christopher Windmill, who owned land at Nutmeg Quarter, and in 1633 Huff served as that area's burgess. In 1635 he patented 800 acres on the Nansemond River. During the 1630s and early 1640s Huff exported tobacco from Virginia, and he did business with the Guinea Company, which was active in bringing captive Africans to Virginia and the Caribbean (VI&A 406; PB 1 Pt. 1:145, 147–148, 305; SR 3268, 3502a, 3506, 3499; LEO 12).

James Hughes: James Hughes sold his 99-year Governor's Land leasehold to Benjamin Bryan sometime after September 29, 1693. Later, it was conveyed to Governor Edmond Andros (Lee MS 51 f 672).

John Hull: On March 22, 1672, John Hull, one of William Drummond I's indentured servants, was ordered to serve some extra time (MCGC 293).

Peter Hull: Sometime prior to February 1635, Peter Hull of Blunt Point acquired a tract of land at the head of Merchants Hope Creek in Charles City and then conveyed it to another man. On November 20, 1636, he received a bequest from the Rev. Thomas Butler, rector of Elizabeth City Parish. Hull purchased 100 acres of land in Isle of Wight County from Christopher Reynolds on May 1, 1639. He seems to have moved to Isle of Wight prior to 1639–1640, when he was one of the three men charged with inspecting the tobacco grown in the territory between "the Alps," Basses Choice, and the acreage known as the Indian Field. In 1644 Hull served as a burgess for Isle of Wight County. A land transaction made in 1655 reveals that he had acquired part of John Sparkes' patent in Isle of Wight and resold it to Robert Watson. In December 1663 Hull received 400 acres of a 1,100-acre patent that he and two other men had secured in July 1651, acreage that was on the Blackwater River (VI&A 407; LEO 22; Isle of Wight County Deeds, Wills & Guardian Accounts Book A:69; PB 5:377; BODIE 172, 530).

William Humfrey: In 1621 William Humfrey was identified as one of the men going to Jamestown on the *Faulcon* (VI&A 408).

William Hunkle: On March 9, 1676, William Hunkle's will was presented to the General Court by attorney William Sherwood of Jamestown (MCGC 433).

William Hunnicutt: On May 4, 1708, William Hunnicutt and William Johnson were authorized to operate the ferry that plied a route between Swann's Point and urban Jamestown (Surry County Order Book 1691–1713:308).

Robert Hunt: The Rev. Robert Hunt, who immigrated to Virginia in the first party of settlers, was the vicar of Heathfield Parish in Sussex, England. The will he prepared on November 20, 1606, mentioned his wife, Elizabeth, and a son and daughter. Hunt became quite ill before his ship left England but survived the transatlantic crossing. When the fort accidentally caught on fire on January 1608, Hunt's books, clothing, and personal belongings were destroyed. He died within a few months, for his will was proved in England on July 14, 1608 (VI&A 408).

Thomas Hunt: On August 1, 1655, Thomas Hunt patented a one-acre lot in urban Jamestown that abutted south upon the James River. Half of the lot he claimed had formerly belonged to Mrs. Elizabeth Fleet's children, who were her heirs. The wording of Hunt's patent suggests that he was expected to construct improvements on his lot. During the 1660s and 1670s Hunt's name appeared numerous times in official records. In October 1660 he was paid for allowing the assembly to meet in his home. Hunt may have kept a tavern there, for he hosted meetings at a time when the burgesses complained about "the dishonor of our Lawes being made and judgments being given in ale-houses." He also hosted two sessions of the Quarter Court and a committee meeting, and he provided accommodations to some Indians who were in Jamestown on official business. Hunt was awarded an eight-year contract for maintaining the bridge and horse-way over his dam, which served the Powhatan Mill. In 1662 he was identified as a Jamestown resident when he made a claim against the estate of John Richards of Surry County. Four years later Hunt patented 836 acres in Surry County. His first wife was Fortune, the daughter of George Jordan of Surry County.

When the assembly decided in December 1662 to subsidize the construction of brick houses in Jamestown, Hunt agreed to erect the house that Nansemond County was required to build and to provide the brick and lime used in its fabrication. He and Jonathan Knowles, as business partners, also agreed to build two brick houses. All three structures were to be erected in the capital city as part of the 1662 building initiative. Hunt, however, reneged on his contractual obligations, and on November 9, 1666, he was censured by the assembly for accepting payment for work that he had neglected to perform. Although he was ordered to finish all three houses no later than August 1667, he failed to do so. Therefore, on October 3, 1667, the assembly ordered Hunt to post a bond guaranteeing that he would finish the three houses he had promised to build. Hunt also agreed to return the compensation he had accepted on Knowles' behalf. Despite the allegations against him, Hunt was a respected member of the Jamestown community, and William Edwards II chose him as guardian of his orphans. Thomas Hunt died sometime prior to April 5, 1671, when his will and its codicil were presented to the General Court. It was then noted that his widow, Bridget (Bridgett), had custody of his real and personal estate as well as the estate of Captain Hayes' child, who was part of her household. Two Jamestown neighbors, Walter Chiles II and William May, and two non-island residents were ordered to inventory Hunt's estate and that of Captain Hayes, Bridget's former husband. Meanwhile, John Howard of Jamestown and Abraham Sapcoate proved Hunt's will. The General Court decided that the codicil to Hunt's will was authentic; it contained instructions "about the Sale of the brick houses," perhaps the ones he had agreed to erect in Jamestown as part of the 1662 building initiative. At the time of his death, Hunt was indebted to William Sherwood. On May 24, 1671, William May, William White, Richard James I, and Major Theophilus Hone (all of Jamestown) were ordered to inventory the late Thomas Hunt's estate. The widowed Bridget Hunt married John Hayward sometime prior to October 3, 1671. The late Thomas Hunt's estate was still unsettled as late as April 1674. His leasehold in the Governor's Land was identified by surveyor John Soane on a plat he made in 1683 (NUG I:12, 313; PB 3:367; HEN II:12; JHB 1660–1693:8, 27, 44, 50; MCGC 216, 218, 247, 258, 293, 319, 327, 350, 370, 513; Surry County Deeds, Wills &c. 1655–1672:210; 1671–1684:69; Order Book 1671–1691:1; CLARE 82 f 276; Soane 1683).

Thomas Hunt: On May 26, 1630, Thomas Hunt, who indicated that he was familiar with Sir George Yeardley's handwriting, was among those who proved his October 12, 1627, will, which was made in Jamestown. Hunt may have been a Yeardley servant. In September 1636 a Thomas Hunt (perhaps the same man) patented 50 acres on Old Plantation Creek in Accomack (later, Northampton) County (VI&A 408; PB 1:376). He may have been a forebear of Thomas Hunt I, who died in Northampton County in

1656, or Thomas Hunt II, who served as an Accomack County burgess in the early 1680s.

Thomas Hunt II: In May 1655, Thomas Hunt I of Northampton County made his will, which was proved in January 1656. He divided his estate between his wife, Joane, and their son, Thomas Hunt II. Joane's death came shortly thereafter, for she made her will in January 1656 and was dead within a month. She named her son, Thomas II, as an heir but also made bequests to children attributable to previous marriages. In 1669 Thomas Hunt II patented 900 acres on Old Plantation Creek in Northampton County. He seems to have been a highly successful planter, for he exported large quantities of tobacco in 1674 and 1676. Hunt and three other men secured a patent for 2,200 acres of land called Hog Island in 1681 and added another 3,300 acres in 1687. Hunt served as a Northampton County burgess from 1680 to 1682 (LEO 46; PB 6:256; 7:113, 577; SR 3768a, 3782a; MARSHALL 41–42, 49). He may have been related to Jamestown landowner Thomas Hunt, who died around 1671.

William Hunt Sr.: On February 10, 1677, Governor William Berkeley issued a proclamation in which he named those who were exempt from the king's pardon on account of their role in Bacon's Rebellion. One of those he listed was William Hunt Sr. of Charles City County, who already was deceased. Later, Hunt's widow, Anne, filed a petition with the king's commissioners stating that her late husband had been wrongly accused of rebellion and that Governor Berkeley's men had seized his movable estate and taken it to Green Spring. She said that it had taken her late husband 25 years to build up his estate and that she and their children were dependent on it. Witnesses testified that William Hunt had died of natural causes at his own home in October 1676 and that it had not been proved that he was in rebellion against the government. Another witness stated under oath that Governor Berkeley owed Hunt 18,000 pounds of tobacco. Captain Nicholas Prynne, master of the *Richard and Elizabeth* of London, testified that the late William Hunt was the factor of Alderman Booth of London and had £265 in goods to sell on Booth's behalf. He said that Colonel Edward Hill, acting on Governor Berkeley's behalf, wrongfully seized those goods (NEVILLE 61; SR 658, 661, 662, 6618).

John Hurd: On March 10, 1676, William Sherwood of Jamestown, a merchant and attorney, swore out a warrant for the arrest of Christopher Robinson of Middlesex County, doing so as merchant John Hurd's assignee (MCGC 434).

John Hurst: On March 20, 1676, John Hurst was arrested by William Sherwood of Jamestown (MCGC 447). He may be the individual identified as John Hurd.

Robert Hutchinson: Robert Hutchinson, a mariner, came to Virginia sometime prior to February 1624, at which time he was living on the Governor's Land. During his first decade or so in the colony, he had many brushes with the law, mostly for behavioral problems like being drunk and disorderly. He also was jailed for indebtedness and fined for refusing to assist the provost marshal in carrying out his official duties. By 1639 Hutchinson apparently had achieved respectability, for he became a tobacco viewer (or inspector) for a region that encompassed Jamestown Island, Pasbehay, and the Maine. Hutchinson's upward mobility continued, and by 1640 he had become the sheriff of James City County and a local justice. A high point in his political career was election to the assembly in 1641–1642, a post he held until at least November 1647. In May 1642 he commenced leasing a parcel in the Governor's Land. Six years later he doubled the size of his leasehold and then assigned his lease to Governor William Berkeley. On February 22, 1643, Captain Robert Hutchinson obtained a patent for a lot on Jamestown Island, part of some acreage that originally belonged to Sir George Yeardley. He died sometime prior to July 1650, at which time his sister, Jane, was named his administratrix (VI&A 411; LEO 20–23, 26).

William Hutchinson: William Hutchinson came to Virginia in 1618 as an indentured servant and during the mid-1620s was living

in the corporation of Elizabeth City. By February 1632 he had settled in Warresqueak (later Isle of Wight County), where he became a commissioner of the local court and a burgess. He died there during the mid-1630s, a relatively wealthy man (VI&A 410; LEO 11).

Nathaniel Hutt: Sometime prior to August 14, 1624, ancient planter Nathaniel Hutt received a patent for 12 acres at Black Point on Jamestown Island. By January 24, 1625, he had moved or disposed of his property, for his land and tenement were in the hands of another. In May 1625, when a list of patented land was sent back to England, Hutt was credited with 200 acres near Mulberry Island (VI&A 411).

Nicholas Hyde (Hide): By May 16, 1621, Nicholas Hyde, a member of the Society of Martin's Hundred, dispatched his servant, Stephen Collins, to Virginia. On January 3, 1625, the General Court noted that Hyde had borrowed some money from John Elyson. Jamestown merchant John Southern posted a bond guaranteeing that Hyde's debt would be repaid (VI&A 412).

Thomas Hynde: Thomas Hynde left England on July 31, 1622, and came to Virginia with William Rowley. He probably was a member of the Rowley household on Jamestown Island (VI&A 412).

James Hyre: On May 23, 1671, James Hyre served as William Corker's attorney in a lawsuit against William Drummond I of urban Jamestown. In March 1672 Hyre, who was still representing Corker, renewed his suit against Drummond. The defendant was fined for failing to appear in court. In 1670 Hyre also won a suit against Richard James I, a Jamestown merchant and landowner (MCGC 215, 257, 304).

I

Iotan (see Opitchapam)

[No First Name] Isaac (Isaack): Mr. Isaac, a 26-year-old man who resided in Dr. John Pott's house in urban Jamestown, was implicated in the killing and butchering of a calf.

The case was discussed by the justices of the General Court on March 1, 1623 (VI&A 413).

John Isgrave: On February 16, 1624, John Isgrave was living in George Graves I's household in urban Jamestown (VI&A 413).

John Isles: On March 10, 1677, John Isles of Isle of Wight County, an alleged supporter of the rebel Nathaniel Bacon, was put on trial at Green Spring plantation, Governor William Berkeley's home. He was found guilty and sentenced to death (MCGC 457–458, 530; SR 660, 661, 749, 6618).

Anton Ive: On July 31, 1622 Anton Ive left England on the *James* with his master, William Rowley, a surgeon and resident of Jamestown Island (VI&A 414). All of Rowley's servants died after reaching their destination.

Abraham Iversonn (Iverson, Iveson, Ivesson): In 1653 Abraham Iversonn served as a burgess for Gloucester County. In June 1651, when Gloucester County was formed, he patented 655 acres on the south side of the North River, a tributary of Mobjack Bay. Five years later he patented 100 acres on the north side of the river, noting that he had secured his original patent on March 21, 1650. Finally, on October 1668 Abraham Iversonn acquired 985 acres on the North River and Mobjack Bay, acreage that had belonged to Anthony Elliott. In 1704 an Abraham Iversonn Sr., perhaps the same individual, was credited with 1,000 acres in Gloucester County's Ware Parish (LEO 31; HEN I:379; PB 2:327; 4:34; 5:586; SMITH 48).

J

Jack: On February 15, 1768, when an inventory was made of the late Richard Ambler's slaves on Jamestown Island and his leasehold in the Governor's Land, a male slave named Jack was listed. In 1769 he was described as a boy who lived on the Governor's Land and was attributed to the estate of the late Edward Ambler I (York County Wills and Inventories 21:386–391; AMB-E).

Christopher Jackson: In January 1718 Christopher Jackson was identified as James City County's official surveyor (EJC III:463).

Ephraim Jackson: In February 1624 Ephraim Jackson was living in gunsmith John Jackson I's household in urban Jamestown (VI&A 414).

John Jackson (Jaxon): John Jackson came to Virginia in 1619, and during the summer when the colony's assembly first convened, he served as a burgess for Martin's Hundred's settlers. Like other colonists who came to establish homes on the Society of Martin's Hundred's land, Jackson would have spent 1619 and the first part of 1620 at Argall Town, which was situated on part of the acreage set aside as the Governor's Land. During the mid-1620s Jackson and his household lived at Martin's Hundred. In a letter he wrote in May 1625, he identified himself as a bricklayer. Jackson served as a burgess for Martin's Hundred in 1628 (VI&A 415; LEO 3, 7).

John Jackson (Jaxon) I: Sometime prior to 1623 gunsmith John Jackson I patented a waterfront lot in urban Jamestown, property on which National Park Service archaeologists have found evidence of a gunmaker's workshop. Court records suggest that he was in partnership with George Clark, another gunsmith. In 1624 John Jackson I and his wife shared their home with Ephraim Jackson, an adult male. A year later the Jackson household was all-male and included John's son, 9-year-old John II, and Gercian, one of the late Rev. Richard Buck's orphans. In 1629 Jackson was named administrator of Abraham Porter's estate. His fiduciary appointment and selection as one of the Buck children's guardians suggest that he was a respected member of the community. In 1629 Jackson served as a James City Parish churchwarden and commander of the settlers in the Neck O'Land. He represented Jamestown in the assembly in 1632 and 1633, and he patented some acreage in Charles River (York) County and on the Chickahominy River in 1637 and 1638. John Jackson I of Jamestown was related to bricklayer John Jackson of Martin's Hundred (VI&A 414–415; LEO 11).

John Jackson (Jaxon): In February 1624 John Jackson was living in merchant Richard Stephens' household in urban Jamestown. He was a Virginia Company tenant who on January 12, 1627, was assigned to Sir George Yeardley, also a resident of Jamestown Island. Jackson may have been related to gunsmith John Jackson, his next-door neighbor in 1624 (VI&A 415).

Robert Jackson: On May 20, 1607, Robert Jackson, a sailor aboard one of the vessels that brought the first Jamestown colonists to Virginia, accompanied Captain Christopher Newport on an exploratory voyage of the James River (VI&A 417).

William Jackson: William Jackson came to Virginia on the *Furtherance* and died on Jamestown Island sometime after April 1623 but before February 16, 1624 (VI&A 417).

Jacob: On February 15, 1768, when an inventory was made of the late Richard Ambler's slaves on Jamestown Island and his leasehold in the Governor's Land, an enslaved boy named Jacob was listed and described as Grace's child (York County Wills and Inventories 21:386–391).

Jacob: On February 15, 1768, when an inventory was made of the late Richard Ambler's slaves on Jamestown Island and his leasehold in the Governor's Land, a male slave named Jacob was listed. In 1769 Jacob was living on Jamestown Island and was part of the late Edward Ambler I's estate. He was identified as Sylvia's son (York County Wills and Inventories 21:386–391; AMB-E).

Thomas Jacob: Thomas Jacob, a gentleman and one of the first colonists, resided in Jamestown and held the rank of sergeant. According to George Percy, he died on September 4, 1607 (VI&A 417).

Henry Jacobs: On February 7, 1628, the justices of the General Court discussed a request they had received from the Rev. Henry Jacobs' widow, Sara. She asked that administrator and merchant Richard Stephens of Jamestown be allowed to sell her late husband's goods and send the proceeds to her in England. Court testimony reveals that the Rev. Jacobs died in 1622–1623 and that afterward, Richard Stephens, the Rev. Richard Buck, and provost marshal Randall Smallwood, all of whom lived in Jamestown, assisted in settling his estate. Stephens had been named Jacobs' administrator, whereas Buck and Smallwood had inventoried his personal possessions (VI&A 417).

James Jakins: James Jakins died in Jamestown sometime after April 1623 but before February 16, 1624 (VI&A 418).

James (see "King James")

James: In 1769 James, an adult male slave, was living on Jamestown Island and was included in the late Edward Ambler I's estate. He was identified as House James, which suggests that he was one of the Amblers' house servants (AMB-E).

Martin James: On March 20, 1690, Martin James of Wapping, England, gave William Sherwood a quitclaim deed for his legal interest in the late Richard James I's 150-acre plantation in the western end of Jamestown Island (AMB 41). He probably was related to the late Richard James I.

* * *

Richard James I: Richard James I of Jamestown Island may have been the 33-year-old who came to the colony in 1635 on the *George*, which originated in London. On the other hand, several other men named Richard James came to Virginia during the second quarter of the seventeenth century, including one who in 1640 was listed as a headright of Jamestown merchant Thomas Stegg I. On June 6, 1654, Richard James I, a merchant, received a patent for 40 acres of land in urban Jamestown on the south side of the Back River, acquiring his land on the basis of one headright. On June 5, 1657, he patented 150 acres that flanked the 40-acre parcel he had claimed in 1654 and built a home. James' landholdings extended along the Back River for a considerable distance and encompassed the sites known as the Piping Point and "the Friggott," raising the possibility that he had a landing or wharf at which seagoing vessels could dock. In January 1660 he was among the prominent citizens who participated in Colonel Thomas Speke's funeral, which was held in Northumberland County. During the 1660s and 1670s Richard James I's mercantile activities extended into the Northern Neck, where he often sued debtors, especially in Lancaster County.

Sometime prior to 1660, Richard James I married a woman named Rachel, who in 1680 identified herself as Major Samuel Swann's aunt when relinquishing her legal interest in some property. This raises the possibility that she was the sister of the late Sarah Cod (Codd), Colonel Thomas Swann's second wife and Samuel Swann's mother. By 1660 Rachel and Richard James I had a son, Richard II. In 1664 Richard James I served as a Kecoughtan man's attorney in a suit against Surry County resident James Mills, litigation that involved a shipment of Africans. Then, in October

1670 he and Richard Auborne (clerk of the General Court) patented 1,000 acres of land in Northumberland County adjacent to an island attributed to the Doeg Indians. On May 28, 1673, James brought suit against Surry County bricklayer John Bird, who had constructed (or was in the process of building) a house for him. Five men were appointed to examine the work that Bird had done. James won a judgment against Bird, who may have been building a house on James' Jamestown Island property near "the Friggott," where archaeologists have found the remains of a brick dwelling.

Richard James I was a James City County justice, and during the early 1670s he and several other local men were called upon to settle estates and arbitrate disputes. His association with Jamestown property-holders Richard Auborne, Major Theophilus Hone, Colonel William White, and William May suggests that he was among the capital city's more prominent citizens. During the early 1670s Richard James I sued George Harwood (Horwood) and Job Virget as well as Robert Weeke, Raleigh Travers, and Robert Beckingham of Lancaster County. However, he was indebted to William Corker, had some of John Whitty's funds in his possession, and reputedly gave invalid bills of exchange to Barnaby Kearney, a merchant. In May 1671 James was among those appointed to inventory the estate of Thomas Hunt, a Jamestown property owner. In 1674 legal records made reference to "John a negro servant to Mr. Richard James" who had run away with five of Governor William Berkeley's men and one who belonged to Mr. George Lloyd. Richard James I was alive in September 1674 but died sometime prior to October 4, 1675, leaving his son Richard II, who was not quite 15 years old, as his principal heir. The decedent's widow, Rachel, who would have been eligible for a dower share, quickly married Jamestown merchant and attorney William Sherwood. Sherwood promptly had Giles Bland arrested on account of debts against the late Richard James I's estate, but Richard Lawrence, whose property was relatively close to James', posted a bond on Bland's behalf. Later, when Bland failed to appear in court, Sherwood obtained a judgment against Lawrence as Bland's guarantor. These proceedings, which occurred in the presence of Governor William Berkeley, probably angered Lawrence and Bland, who by that time had become staunch supporters of the rebel Nathaniel Bacon. When Bacon's men put Jamestown to the torch, Lawrence was credited with setting the James home ablaze. When Sherwood died in 1698, he left his

wife, Rachel, life-rights in almost all of his real estate and personal possessions. By 1699 she had married Edward Jaquelin, another Jamestown merchant. Stafford County records reveal that Rachel Jaquelin had a residual legal interest in the Dogue Island, property that her late husband, William Sherwood, had sold to George Mason in 1696. Reliable genealogical sources indicate that Jaquelin was born in 1668; therefore, he was eight years younger than Rachel's son, Richard James II, born in 1660. Rachel James Sherwood Jaquelin died after November 9, 1704, but before 1706, by which time Edward Jaquelin had remarried (CBE 164; PB 3:368; 4:196–197; NUG I:56, 119, 194, 314; MCGC 205, 215, 218, 225, 258, 285, 292, 343–344, 355, 382, 418–419; AMB 17; Surry County Deeds, Wills &c. 1652–1672:242; 1672–1684:273; Lancaster County Order Book 1656–1666:255, 267, 288, 298; 1666–1680:290; Northumberland County Order Book 1662–1665:325; Westmoreland County Deeds, Wills, &c. 1661–1662:19, 47–47a; Stafford County Record Book 1699–1709:250–251; WITH 534; MCGC 419; DOR 3:302; Tyler, "Historical and Genealogical Notes," 49–50).

Richard James II: Richard James II, the son of Rachel and Richard James I, was born on December 14, 1660, and lost his father during his early teens. When he came of age, he stood to inherit the decedent's 150-acre plantation on Jamestown Island. When Nathaniel Bacon's followers set Jamestown ablaze on September 19, 1676, among the structures destroyed were buildings attributed to the late Richard James I's orphaned son. William Sherwood, the boy's stepfather and guardian, sent a petition to the king, noting that the orphan's houses were worth £1,000 and that his goods and livestock had been plundered. Sherwood indicated that he and his wife and stepson had been occupying the James home and had been left homeless when rebel Richard Lawrence put the buildings to the torch. He asked for compensation so that he could rebuild in Jamestown. Richard James II died intestate without having produced an heir. Therefore, the James plantation escheated to the Crown, whereupon it was patented by his stepfather on October 23, 1690 (CO 1/41 f 32ro; AMB 17, 43; NUG I:350; PB 8:83).

* * *

Richard James: In 1663 Richard James, a Surry County, Virginia, yeoman from Curriff, in Hereford County, England, shared a home with his wife, Margery, who also was from Curriff (Surry County Deeds, Wills &c.

1652–1672:223, 228, 256). It is uncertain whether this Richard James and his contemporary, merchant Richard James I of Jamestown, were related.

Jamy: In March 1710 a group of enslaved blacks, Indian servants, and indentured servants in James City, Isle of Wight, and Surry counties planned to make a break for freedom on Easter Sunday and vowed to overcome all who opposed them. One slave, an African or African-American man named Will, revealed the plot and the uprising was quelled. Among the James City County slaves jailed for complicity in the plot were black males belonging to the Rev. James Blair, Philip Ludwell I, sheriff Edward Jaquelin, George Marable II, ferryman and gunner Edward Ross, and John Broadnax, all of whom were associated with urban Jamestown. Although most of the accused insurgents were jailed in Jamestown, where they were interrogated and then released into their owners' custody "to receive correction," Jamy (a Broadnax slave) and Essex (a Ross slave) allegedly instigated the plot and therefore were detained. Virginia's governor later reported that two slaves were executed so that "their fate will strike such a terror" that others would not attempt to rebel. The two men (an African American named Scipio and an Indian named Salvador) were hanged and then quartered. A quarter of the Indian man was put on display near the "great guns" (cannon) in Jamestown. There, near the ferry landing, the gruesome display would have been a grim reminder of the consequences of rebellion (Stanard, "Philip Ludwell to Edward Jennings, 1709, in regard to a Negro Plot," 23–24; EJC III:234–236, 242–243). During the 1950s archaeologists found part of a human skeleton, the remains of a man who had been quartered, in a well behind a long row house on Back Street.

Japazous (Native American): In January 1620 Japazous, the brother of the king of the Potomac Indians, came to Jamestown and invited the colonists to trade (VI&A 418).

Edward Jaquelin: Edward Jaquelin, a French Huguenot, was born in 1668 and was the son of John and Elizabeth Craddock Jaquelin. The family immigrated to Virginia around 1685. Around 1699 Edward Jaquelin married the wealthy and twice-widowed Rachel James Sherwood, who was many years his senior. He moved into her brick house on Back Street and on December 11, 1704, purchased London merchant Jeffrey Jeffreys' reversionary interest in the late William Sherwood's estate. Jaquelin also would have had use of wife Rachel's dower share of Richard James I's estate and perhaps William Sherwood's 260-acre leasehold in the Governor's Land. In 1699 Jaquelin and his wife, Rachel, rented their home, or the neighboring brick house they also owned, to the assembly, and they sometimes provided meeting space to the council. This would have brought Edward Jaquelin in contact with the colony's highest ranking officials, thereby enhancing his political influence. He also prepared official correspondence for the assembly. In April 1701 Jaquelin became coronet of James City County's troop of horse, and in 1702 he was clerk of the assembly's committee of propositions and grievances. After the death of his wife, Rachel, Edward Jaquelin married Martha, the daughter of Lieutenant Colonel William Cary of Elizabeth City and the widow of John Thruston of Martin's Hundred. Their marriage, which took place in 1706, seems to have enhanced Jaquelin's political influence and, in turn, his economic position. By 1710 he had become a county justice, a position he held for many years, and from time to time he served terms as sheriff and county coroner. Around the time Jaquelin took office, some of his slaves were involved in an elaborate plan to escape. In 1712 Jaquelin was elected Jamestown's delegate to the assembly and was returned to office in 1714.

Although Jaquelin did little to enhance the size of the Sherwood plantation in urban Jamestown, he purchased a half-acre lot on the waterfront, which would have enhanced his property's commercial potential and given him direct access to shipping. He also acquired a substantial amount of acreage on the mainland and in 1704 paid quitrent on 400 acres of James City County land. In 1712 he purchased the 24-acre Glasshouse tract at the entrance to Jamestown Island and began renting a 151-acre parcel in the Governor's Land, taking over Philip Ludwell II's lease. Then, in 1718 he bought a 27-acre parcel adjacent to the Glasshouse tract and the Governor's Land. This gave Jaquelin a total of 202 acres on the mainland, next to Jamestown Island. These acquisitions heralded the development of the property that later became known as "Amblers," agricultural acreage that traditionally was subsidiary to the Jaquelin (later, Ambler) plantation on Jamestown Island.

Together, Edward and Martha Cary Jaquelin produced several children. Elizabeth, the eldest, was born in 1709, married Yorktown merchant Richard Ambler in 1729, and produced sons John I, Edward, and Jaquelin. Martha Jaquelin, who remained a spinster, was born on January 31, 1711, and died on December 20, 1792. Her sister, Mary, was born in March 1714 and died on October 4, 1764, having married John Smith. Edward Jaquelin II, who was born in December 1716, died in 1734 without attaining his majority. His brother, Mathew, who was born in 1707 or 1708, died in 1727 while still a minor. Around 1733 or 1734 Martha Cary Jaquelin donated a baptismal font to the James City Parish church in Jamestown. Edward Jaquelin I died in November 1739 at the age of 71, having outlived his wife, Martha, and all of their sons. Therefore, the couple's three daughters became their only heirs. Edward Jaquelin I was buried in the churchyard in Jamestown, and his will was recorded in the James City County court. He left life-rights in a tract in the western end of Jamestown Island to his son-in-law, Yorktown merchant Richard Ambler. He bequeathed his quarter (or subsidiary farm) at Powhatan to his daughter Martha, who lived in her parents' home in Jamestown. After losing both of her parents, she moved into the Yorktown home of her sister Elizabeth and brother-in-law Richard Ambler, to whom she later sold the Powhatan quarter and gave a quitclaim deed for a tract at the western end of Jamestown Island. Edward Jaquelin I's Jamestown Island plantation and mainland farm descended through his eldest daughter, Elizabeth Ambler, to his four-year-old grandson, John Ambler I (AMB-JJ 1826; JHB 1695–1702:214, 219, 384; EJC II:132; III:243; IV:xxiii, 413; SAIN 19:162; 20:156; LEO 67; STAN 100; AMB 45, 65, 73, 77, 84, 86, 99, 101, 123; Soane 1683; MEADE I:95, 104; Smith et al. 1745; DOR 3:302; Tyler, "Historical and Genealogical Notes," 49–50; Parks, *Virginia Gazette,* November 22, 1739).

John Jarrett (Jarratt): William Sherwood was fond of his nephew, John Jarrett, and his wife, the former Joannah Lowe, niece of London merchant Micajah Perry. On April 7, 1694, he gave Jarrett some land in the western end of Jamestown Island, a parcel that extended across the isthmus connecting the island to the mainland and had great commercial value. When Sherwood made his will in August 1697, he left his clothing to John Jarrett and bequeathed his history books to Jarrett's wife, Joannah. He also left a small sum of money to the Jarrett couple's daughters, Elizabeth and Elir, and to John Jarrett's unmarried sister, Mary. Sometime prior to November 12, 1696, John and Joannah Lowe Jarrett moved into a brick row house on urban Jamestown's waterfront, a structure that was owned by her uncle's mercantile firm, Micajah Perry and Company, otherwise known as Perry, Lane and Company. On May 6, 1700, when John Jarrett disposed of the Jamestown Island parcel that the late William Sherwood had given him, Joannah waived her dower rights. John Jarrett died sometime prior to November 12, 1700, at which time the Perry firm disposed of its property in urban Jamestown. Afterward, the widowed Joannah Jarrett gained employment as housekeeper to William Byrd II of Westover, in Charles City County. Her brother, Micajah Lowe, was then a merchant in Charles City (MCGH 873; PRICE 65; WITH 43; Tyler, "Micajah Perry," 264; AMB 48, 62, 65, 67, 101).

William Jarrett: In November 1620 William Jarrett was identified as an ancient planter who had been in Virginia for 13 years. Therefore, he was one of the first Jamestown colonists. Jarrett was described as a skillful man and Virginia Company tenant. He was assigned to Captain Nuce in Elizabeth City, and his wife and children were brought to Virginia free of charge. When a list of patented land was sent back to England in May 1625, William Jarrett was credited with 200 acres at Great Weyanoke in Charles City (VI&A 418).

Arthur Jarvis: Arthur Jarvis, a James City County yeoman who had been convicted of burglary and was incarcerated in Jamestown, awaiting deportation from the colony, was thought to have set the October 20, 1698, fire that destroyed the colony's statehouse. He originally had received the death sentence, since burglary was a felony and a capital crime, but he opted for transportation. Although high-ranking officials suspected Jarvis of arson, the evidence against him was insubstantial, and he does not appear to have been prosecuted (SAIN 16:513; EJC I:397). This individual may have been a kinsman of Surry County's Arthur Jarvis, who around the same time was an associate of Thomas Swann II and had the status of gentleman.

Thomas Jarvis I: Thomas Jarvis, a merchant and mariner who settled in Elizabeth City County, was involved in international trade. In January 1674 he and fellow merchants, who owned the *Thomas and Mary,* informed officials in England that their vessel had been attacked and captured by Spanish ships while enroute from Jamaica to Virginia. Jarvis and the others sought permission to retaliate but were told to wait until the Spanish ambassador had been contacted. Jarvis went to England in 1673, intending to purchase some land. He chose the Suffolk property that Nathaniel Bacon, the soon-to-be rebel, held on behalf of his wife, the former Elizabeth Duke. Jarvis returned to Virginia, and on November 8, 1674, he and Bacon, who lived at Curles plantation in Henrico County, made a sales agreement and money changed hands. When Jarvis made another trip to England in 1676, he told Thomas Bacon, Nathaniel's father, that he was in the process of purchasing the Suffolk property. He then learned that Sir Robert Jason had a legal interest in the land. Meanwhile, Nathaniel Bacon, who got caught up in the popular uprising that bore his name, died in late 1676, before he had deeded the property to Jarvis. Jarvis returned to Virginia in August or September 1677 and by November 25, 1679, had married Elizabeth Duke Bacon, Nathaniel Bacon's widow. Between 1680 and 1682 Jarvis served as a burgess for Elizabeth City County and owned and occupied what was known as the "Tradeing Plantation," a 200-acre tract that was located on the west side of the Hampton River. He also had a 600-acre parcel on the Back River in Elizabeth City. In late 1683 the Jarvis couple went to England, where Thomas initiated a suit in an attempt to recover the funds he had paid to Bacon. He also asserted his wife's legal interest in the property. Jarvis became ill, made his will on April 6, 1684, and by April 18th was dead. He named as executors his wife, Elizabeth, brother-in-law Edward Foster, and business associate, George Richards, and specified that his real and personal property were to be sold to pay his debts. Whatever remained was to be divided equally between his wife, Elizabeth, and son, Thomas Jarvis II. Elizabeth was to retain all interest in his real estate until Thomas II attained his majority. The testator made bequests to his brother, Christopher Jarvis, and to his goddaughter, Mary Worlich, but named Edward Foster and George Richards as reversionary heirs. Four months after Thomas Jarvis I's death, his widow, Elizabeth, and the other executors began to pursue the suit that the decedent had undertaken in 1683. They prevailed and in January 1685 the defendant, Sir Robert Jason, relinquished his claim to the Bacon property. Sometime prior to July 6, 1692, Thomas Jarvis I's widow, Elizabeth, hired William Sherwood of Jamestown as her attorney. She eventually remarried, taking as her third husband Edward Mole (Hole). Later, one of the late Thomas Jarvis I's creditors brought suit against his estate and tried to make a claim against his personal property, which

Elizabeth and her third husband then possessed (WASH 18; EJC I:261; MCGC 520; LEO 45; NEAL 1–2, 21, 79, 103; SR 690, 3720, 4559, 10072, 10518, 10605, 11500, 11503).

John Jefferys (Jeffreys): John Jefferys (Jeffreys) died in Jamestown sometime after April 1623 but before February 16, 1624 (VI&A 420).

Nathaniel Jefferys (Jeffries, Jeffreys): Nathaniel Jefferys and his wife were residents of Martin's Hundred, where she was killed during the 1622 Indian attack. He was evacuated to Jamestown Island for safety's sake and continued to live there. Surgeon Samuel Mole identified Jefferys as the joiner who made Thomas Hamor's coffin. Nathaniel Jefferys seems to have remarried, for in February 1624 he and his wife were said to be residing in urban Jamestown. By early 1625 she was dead and Jefferys and Edward Cage (Cadge) were sharing a home. Court testimony taken later in the year reveals that Jefferys had been the late Robert Whitehed's servant and could be freed if he paid the decedent's heirs for his remaining time. By November 1628 Nathaniel Jefferys was dead. Because his brother and executor, John Jefferys, was not in the colony, Rowland Powell and John Cheesman (the decedent's creditors and holders of his executor's power of attorney) were authorized to act on his behalf (VI&A 420).

John Jefferson: In 1619 John Jefferson, a gentleman and ancient planter, patented 250 acres of land in Archer's Hope. He was appointed an official tobacco taster and in 1619 served as a burgess for Flowerdew Hundred, Sir George Yeardley's plantation. During 1622 Jefferson was authorized to gather information about conditions in the colony. A year later, he left for the West Indies, abandoning his Archer's Hope acreage. When John Jefferson made his will in December 1645, he identified himself as a citizen of London. He mentioned his sons John and Nathaniel and daughters Elizabeth and Dorothy, but made no reference to real or personal property in Virginia. Jefferson's will was presented for probate in 1647 (VI&A 419; LEO 3).

John Jefferson: John Jefferson, a gunsmith, came to Virginia as a Virginia Company tenant and in February 1624 was living in Elizabeth City. By January 1625, he and a partner, Walgrave Marks, who jointly headed a household, were residing on Jamestown Island just east of the urbanized area. On May 2, 1625, a warrant was issued for Jefferson's arrest because he had eloped with Captain Ralph Hamor's maidservant. In early January 1626 he was censured for deficiencies in his work as a gunsmith, which had caused Henry Booth to be injured. The General Court's justices noted that they had treated Jefferson leniently because he was "a poore man and A Tenant to the Company." In mid-January 1627, when the Council of State decided what to do with the defunct Virginia Company's tenants and servants, John Jefferson was assigned to Captain Francis West, who resided in Elizabeth City. When a plat was made in 1664 of John Knowles' acreage abutting urban Jamestown's Back Street, the name "Jno Jefferson" was written at a site just east of Orchard Run. This raises the possibility that Jefferson acquired some land close to the capital city and perhaps set up shop there (VI&A 419).

Jeffrey (Geoffrey) (Native American): In early 1653, while the Commonwealth government was in power, a Virginia colonist informed a friend in England about conditions in the colony. He said that a year or so before, Governor William Berkeley had authorized a Weyanoke Indian king to bring the Nansemond and Warresqueak tribes under the Weyanoke's subjection. However, because the Nansemond and Warresqueak refused to become subservient, the Weyanoke attacked and laid waste to their towns. Afterward, the Nansemond and Warresqueak leaders asked Governor Berkeley for permission to occupy one of their old towns, which they considered a position of greater safety. They also asked him to help them make peace with King Jeffrey, the Weyanoke leader. Governor Berkeley agreed and asked the Nansemond and Warresqueak kings to meet with King Jeffrey in Jamestown. King Jeffrey may have been Ascomowett, who was king of the Weyanoke Indians in 1649, or his successor. In September 1663 the Weyanokes sought refuge among the colonists, for King Jeffrey and six other Indians from their town had been killed by a tribe called the Pochicks. When colonists rescued the surviving Weyanoke from their palisade-enclosed fort, they found an English-style house that probably had belonged to King Jeffrey and an apple orchard. In accordance with native tradition, King Jeffrey's remains had been taken outside of the fort, laid upon a scaffold, and covered with animal skins and mats (FER 1216; Philip A. Bruce, "Colonial Letters &c.," 47–48; "Indians of Southern Virginia: Depositions in the Virginia and North Carolina Boundary Case," 4–7).

Jeffrey: On February 15, 1768, when an inventory was made of late Richard Ambler's slaves on Jamestown Island and his leasehold in the Governor's Land, an adult male slave named Jeffrey was listed. In 1769 Jeffrey was living on the Governor's Land and was included in the late Edward Ambler I's estate (York County Wills and Inventories 21:386–391; AMB-E).

* * *

Herbert Jeffreys (Jeffries, Jeffrey): Herbert Jeffreys, who was commissioned lieutenant governor of Virginia in November 1676, is believed to have been related to alderman and merchant John Jeffreys of London. He served in the English army, where he attained the rank of colonel, and early in 1677 accompanied the 1,000 royal troops the king sent to Virginia to restore order. Jeffreys was one of three special commissioners King Charles II ordered to investigate the underlying causes of Bacon's Rebellion, and he was named to succeed Governor William Berkeley, who was being recalled. Jeffreys presided over the colony until his untimely death in 1678. He was instrumental in getting the Tributary Indians to sign a major treaty on May 29, 1677, and in January 1678 he recommended that its coverage be expanded to neighboring English colonies. Jeffreys' time in office was marred by disagreements with the assembly and he was subjected to outright hostility from certain members of his council who, as part of the so-called Green Spring faction, were staunchly loyal to the late Sir William Berkeley and his policies. In fact, Philip Ludwell I, who married Berkeley's widow, once referred to Herbert Jeffreys as "a pitiful feeble Fellow with a perriwig." Jeffreys suspended some of his most outspoken critics from the public offices they held. He suffered from a recurrent illness, which by June 1678 had become debilitating, and died on December 17, 1678. He was survived by his widow, Elizabeth, and son John. In April 1679 Herbert Jeffreys' replacement, Thomas Lord Culpeper, sued his estate in an attempt to recover part of the salary the decedent had received as chief executive (STAN 16; MCGC 516, 520–521; EEAC 32; BEVERLY 86; SAIN 10:10; CO 5/1355 ff 81, 83, 243).

Sir Jeffrey Jeffreys (Jeffries, Jeffrey): London alderman and merchant Jeffrey Jeffreys, the brother and business partner of John Jeffreys, worked closely with Jamestown merchant William Sherwood. He and Micajah Perry, also of London, were the

Royal African Company's principal contractors for the sale of Africans in Virginia. By 1692 he had a plantation in Middlesex County, Virginia, where he utilized Indian and African slaves to work his land. In 1692 Jeffrey Jeffreys sent 200 guns to the colony, part of the weaponry damaged or destroyed when the statehouse burned in 1698. When William Sherwood made his will in 1697, he designated Jeffrey Jeffreys as his reversionary heir, perhaps because he was the testator's principal creditor. Jeffreys, upon learning of Sherwood's death, authorized his representative, Arthur Spicer of Richmond County, to take custody of the decedent's estate. By 1704 Jeffrey Jeffreys had been knighted. His interest in Jamestown was well known and in 1699 when Williamsburg was designated the colony's capital city, Stephen Fouace asked for his support in seeing that the former capital retained its right to assembly representation. On December 11, 1704, Sir Jeffrey Jeffreys sold the late William Sherwood's Jamestown Island holdings to Edward Jaquelin, who by 1706 had married Sherwood's widow, Rachel (MCGH 873; WITH 52; York County Deeds, Orders, Wills 9:49; SAIN 10:105, 170; EJC 1:426; AMB 65, 73; Bruce, "Bacon's Rebellion," 168; Middlesex County Order Book 1680–1694:322, 549).

John Jeffreys (Jeffries, Jeffrey): London merchant John Jeffreys, brother and business partner of alderman Jeffrey Jeffreys, had a business relationship with Richard Lee I of Gloucester County, Virginia, during the 1650s. Lancaster County records reveal that Jeffreys conducted a large volume of business in the Northern Neck, sometimes in concert with Thomas Colclough and Company, another London firm. During the mid–1670s Jeffreys used Jamestown lot owner Colonel John Page as his factor. On the eve of Bacon's Rebellion, Jeffreys had 83 pipes and hogsheads of wine stored in the cellar of Colonel Page's house in Jamestown. Governor William Berkeley reportedly confiscated 20 pipes of wine and the rest was destroyed by fire on September 19, 1676, when Nathaniel Bacon's followers set the capital city ablaze. Later, Page filed a compensatory claim on John Jeffreys' behalf, in an attempt to recover the wine's monetary value. The assembly decided to award Jeffreys half of the wine's estimated worth, for they believed that all of the stored wine would have been destroyed by fire. Jeffreys was dissatisfied with the settlement and on October 18, 1677, he appeared before the Committee for Trade and Plantations, where he attempted to obtain what he considered just compensation. He accompanied his petition with a statement from agent John Page, who said that he had sold some of Jeffreys' wine at twice the value the assembly was willing to pay and that no one had attempted to save the rest of it from the fire. The special commissioners sent to Virginia to investigate the causes of Bacon's Rebellion agreed with Page and Jeffreys and recommended that Jeffreys be fully compensated for his loss. Jeffreys continued to pursue his debtors in Virginia and in 1686 authorized Christopher Robinson to serve as his attorney. He died sometime prior to July 2, 1694, when the attorney of Jeffrey Jeffreys and a younger John Jeffreys brought suit against the late Robert Smith's executors, Ralph Wormeley II and Colonel John Armistead (CO 1/12 f 115; 1/41 f 218; 5/1355 ff 200–205; SAIN 10:167; WITH 51; Middlesex County Order Book 1673–1680:149; 1680–1694:224, 322, 697; Lancaster County Order Book 1656–1666:190).

* * *

Simon Jeffreys: Simon Jeffreys, a surveyor, made a plat for Philip Ludwell II that included part of the Governor's Land. In 1713 and 1714 Jeffreys patented three parcels of land on the west side of the Chickahominy River (AMB 84, 85; NUG III:133, 146, 149).

Peter Jemaine: Peter Jemaine left England in July 1622 and came to Virginia with William Rowley, a surgeon. It is likely that Jemaine, like Rowley, settled in Jamestown. On April 1, 1623, the Virginia Company learned that all ten of William Rowley's servants were dead (VI&A 421).

* * *

Henry Jenkins (Jinkins) I: During Bacon's Rebellion, Henry Jenkins, a James City County tanner, who leased a parcel on the Governor's Land, suffered at the hands of Nathaniel Bacon's followers and he also sustained damage from Governor William Berkeley's men. In March 1677, when Jenkins sought compensation for his losses, he informed the king's commissioners that Bacon's men had seized hides from Berkeley and brought them to him for tanning. Although he returned the tanned hides to Berkeley after the rebellion subsided, the governor's men had taken his cattle. When John Gwin, a James City merchant, made his will in July 1682, he named Henry Jenkins I as executor and sole legatee and described him as a kinsman. Jenkins, who owned property in at least three Tidewater jurisdictions, commenced serving as a burgess for York County in 1680 and attended the 1680–1682, 1695–1696, and 1696–1697 sessions. He also became an Elizabeth City County justice of the peace, holding office for many years, and he represented Elizabeth City in the 1685–1686 assembly sessions. Besides owning a tannery near Jamestown Island, Jenkins had a ketch, the *Experience*, and derived some of his income from international trade. Among the commodities he exported were tobacco and furs. He also speculated in real estate. On December 12, 1690, James City County's official surveyor, John Soane, prepared a plat of Henry Jenkins' 76-acre leasehold in the Governor's Land. Around that time, Jenkins made a trip to England. When William Sherwood made his will in August 1697, he left a horse, riding tackle, pistol, and holsters to Captain Henry Jenkins' son, Henry II. Captain Henry Jenkins I, who described himself as sick and weak, made his will in Elizabeth City on March 12, 1698. The testator made bequests to his son, Henry II, and to his brother, Daniel, and sister, Mary Jenkins Lewis, and to his nephew, Daniel, and left mourning rings to several friends. He named his son, Henry Jenkins II, and his nephew, Daniel Jenkins, as executors. Jenkins' will was proved in the General Court on September 24, 1698. On November 18, 1698, the decedent's wife, Bridgett, petitioned the court for her dower third of her late husband's estate. Two years later, Henry Jenkins II was awarded a certificate entitling him to 900 acres on behalf of some people his late father had brought to Virginia (CO 1/40 f 18; SAIN 10:52; STAN 84, 91, 110; LEO 46, 48, 55, 57, 62, 64, 68–69; NUG III:93; WITH 276–277; EEAC 26; AMB 45, 65, 77, 84–85; MCGH 874–875; NEAL 22, 48, 61, 68, 83, 92, 161, 243, 245, 283; SR 661, 749, 3731, 5762, 5763, 8520, 10520, 10587, 12627; CHAPMAN 44).

Henry Jenkins (Jinkins) II: Henry Jenkins II, the son of Henry Jenkins I, retained his late father's landholdings in Elizabeth City and patented land in Nansemond, Princess Anne, and Accomack counties. He was among the Elizabeth City vestrymen who in October 1702 accepted some acreage that had been donated to the parish for the benefit of the poor. He served as a burgess on behalf of Nansemond County in the 1703–1705 and 1705–1706 sessions but represented Elizabeth City in the 1715 and 1718 sessions. He died intestate sometime prior to August 17, 1719, at which time his widow, Mary, was designated his administratrix (LEO 62, 64, 68–69; PB 9:117, 195, 465, 480, 569; CHAPMAN 44).

* * *

Daniel Jennifer (Jenifer) I: Daniel Jennifer I seems to have secured his first patents on Virginia's Eastern Shore in 1672, around the time he married Anne (Ann) Toft, whose long-term relationship with Edmund Scarborough II is open to conjecture. He patented 5,000 acres in the vicinity of Gingoteague (Chincoteague), part of the Accomack County acreage that Edmund Scarbourough I had claimed in 1664. Jennifer and his wife, Anne, also patented 11,300 acres in Accomack County, on the seaside. During 1673 the couple began investing in land on Muddy or Guilford Creek. Part of the acreage they patented had belonged to Anne before their marriage. In 1675 Daniel Jennifer patented some additional land in Accomack County, this time acquiring 1,680 acres at Massapungo Swamp. Two years later he acquired 580 acres on the seaside next to Kekotanck Island, in the upper part of Accomack County. Then, in 1678 he laid claim to 1,680 acres on the Mesungo Swamps. During the early 1680s he patented several relatively small tracts on the seaside but he also acquired 3,500 acres on Assateague Island and 2,500 acres on the Pocomoke River. Colonel Daniel Jennifer I served as a burgess for Accomack County and attended the assembly sessions held in 1682, 1684, 1685–1686, and 1693. In June 1693 the justices of Accomack County, upon learning that he was dead, granted temporary administration of his estate to four local men who were to serve until Captain Daniel Jennifer II of St. Thomas, a mariner, attained his majority. Daniel Jennifer II was identified as master of the *Jonathan and Mary* in 1702 when a group of mariners asked the king to allow their ships to sail to foreign ports, despite an existing embargo (LEO 45, 47–48, 53; SR 3917; Accomack County Orders 1690–1697:104; JHB 1659–1693:xvi; PB 6:288, 400, 483, 533, 615, 640; 7:66, 269, 536, 537, 563; 8:129).

Edmund Jennings (Jenings): Edmund Jennings, who was born in England and lived at Ripon Hall in York County, just west of Queens Creek, was named to the Council of State in 1680. In 1681 he was designated James City County's sheriff and in 1685 was involved in securing a treaty with the Seneca Indians and other northern tribes. He served as attorney general until 1691 and was a close associate of Francis Howard, Lord Effingham. From time to time Jennings hosted council meetings in his home and he was among the several prominent men who in 1686 asked to patent some land in the Pamunkey Neck, as soon as that was legally possible. In 1687 he purchased a mill on St. Andrew's Creek, in York County, and he also bought an adjoining plantation called Poplar Neck. Over the next few years he continued to acquire acreage in that vicinity and in 1691 he served as a churchwarden of Bruton Parish. Like most of his contemporaries, Jennings appeared in court from time to time, initiating suits and defending himself. In October 1689 he secured a patent for 6,513 acres of land in Henrico County, on Tuckahoe Creek and the James River. In 1691 the assembly debated where the College of William and Mary should be built, and one of the locations considered was in Gloucester County, directly across from Edmund Jennings' plantation. When a plat was made in 1691 of Yorktown, a planned community, Colonel Jennings was credited with lot number 35, which contained a building. On September 21, 1692, while he was a council member, he was among those ordered to build a house in Jamestown. He was one of the two men authorized to view the fortifications that had been built at Yorktown and Tindall's Point, on the York River. In May 1696 Jennings and his wife, Frances, disposed of a plantation they owned in Hampton Parish, property that was in the hands of a tenant. Jennings was still on the council in 1699, when the decision was made to move the capital city from Jamestown to Williamsburg, and he served as Secretary of the Colony from 1702 to 1712. He was commander-in-chief of York County's militia, held the rank of colonel, and served as clerk of the county court. He also received income as collector of customs for the James River's Upper District and he grew and exported large shipments of tobacco. He made a trip to England in 1704, having received the king's permission to do so. He was awarded 4,000 acres of land in King William County in 1706, acreage he received in recognition of his service to the Crown. Quitrent rolls, compiled in 1704, indicate that Colonel Jennings paid taxes on 4,000 acres in King William County, 200 acres in James City County, and 1,500 acres in York County. In 1710 Jennings, who was lieutenant governor, was involved in deciding how to punish two slaves who had organized a rebellion. Afterward, he declared that they were executed so that "their fate will strike such a terror" that others would not attempt to rebel. Jennings died in Virginia on December 5, 1727 (EJC I:12, 72, 187, 269, 335, 345, 352, 354, 444, 529; II:14, 17, 151, 256, 316, 375, 391; III:81, 112, 217, 460; JHB 1660–1693:353, 466; STAN 21, 25, 43; LEO xx; PB 8:2; SR 236, 4597, 7459; York County Deeds, Or-

ders, Wills 8 [1687–1691]:27–28, 48–49, 475–478, 481, 526; 9 [1691–1694]:44–45, 70, 82, 110; 10 [1694–1607]:179, 236, 338–339, 461–462, 484–485; SMITH 49).

John Jennings: When Governor William Berkeley issued a proclamation on February 10, 1677, pardoning some of the rebel Nathaniel Bacon's followers but exempting others, John Jennings was among those he declared ineligible. Berkeley indicated that Jennings was to be tried in a court of justice. Jennings, who had been Isle of Wight County's clerk of court, filed an appeal with the special commissioners that King Charles II had ordered to investigate the underlying causes of the popular uprising. Jennings claimed that he was forced to join Bacon's army, had been incarcerated by Berkeley, and that his livestock had been seized. He asked for the right to take an oath of allegiance to the king as proof of his loyalty. On April 19, 1677, after Berkeley had left the colony, Jennings sent an appeal to Herbert Jeffreys, who had become lieutenant governor. He described himself as destitute and said that although Governor Berkeley had banished him from the colony, he was poor, aged, and sick and lacked the funds that were needed to cover the cost of his transportation. He also said that he had a wife and children who depended on him for their support. Jeffreys did not overturn Jennings' sentence, but he was allowed to postpone his departure until the following September. On September 5, 1678, John Jennings, who was preparing to leave Virginia, appointed his wife, Mary, as his attorney. However, he died before his departure (CO 1/39 ff 64–65; 1/40 f 21; Isle of Wight County Will and Deed Book 1 [1662–1688]:353–354, 361; BODIE 279; SR 660; NEVILLE 61).

Peter Jennings: Peter Jennings, who was born in England, served as a burgess in 1660 and from 1663 to 1670, representing Gloucester County, his place of residence. His land was located in the immediate vicinity of Claybank Creek. In October 1660 he patented 650 acres near the head of the Potomac River. Then, in September 1663 he and Mathew Kemp patented 1,000 acres in Lancaster County and a like amount of land in another location. In April 1662 Jennings was identified as the colony's deputy treasurer when he authorized William Horton of Westmoreland County to collect quitrents on the king's behalf. In 1663 Jennings disposed of 2,000 acres on the south side of Potomac Creek, in Westmoreland County. He was named to the Council of State in 1670 and on June 20th was sworn in. On June 26,

1670, Governor William Berkeley asked King Charles II to name Jennings as Virginia's attorney-general and pointed out that he had faithfully served the king's late father. Jennings was holding office in 1671, when he died. Sometime prior to September 23, 1674, Colonel Peter Jennings' widow, the former Catherine Lunsford, married Captain Ralph Wormeley II. A deed executed in Stafford County in November 1688 reveals that Jennings died without heirs and that his land in the county escheated to the Crown (MCGC 376; LEO xx, 36, 38; STAN 25, 39; Stafford County Record Book 1686–1693:172a–173a; Westmoreland County Deeds, Wills &c 1661–1662:9a; Deeds and Wills No. 1 [1653–1671]:204–205; PB 4:452, 484–485; 6:426; SR 646, 4389, 5624).

Jenny: On February 15, 1768, when an inventory was made of late Richard Ambler's slaves at his quarter called Powhatan, an adult female slave named Jenny was living there. In 1769 Jenny was living on Jamestown Island and was part of the late Edward Ambler I's estate (York County Wills and Inventories 21:386–391; AMB-E).

Jeremy: On February 15, 1768, when an inventory was made of late Richard Ambler's slaves on Jamestown Island and his leasehold in the Governor's Land, an adult male slave named Jeremy was listed (York County Wills and Inventories 21:386–391).

Jessee: On October 31, 1777, Edward Champion Travis placed an advertisement in the *Virginia Gazette*. He stated that "Run away from my plantation at Jamestown, sometime this last August, a likely mulatto man named Jessee, 17 or 18 years old, tall and slender. I expect he is either enlisted into the army or enlisted on board some vessel as a sailor and freeman. Whoever secures the said slave in any jail so that I get him again or delivers him to me at Queen's Creek in York County, shall have 20 dollars reward" (Purdie, *Virginia Gazette* October 31, 1777).

Joanna: In 1769 an enslaved woman named Joanna was living on the Governor's Land and shared her home with her child, Sarah. Both were attributed to the estate of Edward Ambler I (AMB-E).

Joe: On February 15, 1768, when an inventory was made of late Richard Ambler's slaves on Jamestown Island and his leasehold in the Governor's Land, an adult male slave named Joe was listed. In 1769 he was living on the Governor's Land and was included in the late Edward Ambler I's estate

(York County Wills and Inventories 21:386–391; AMB-E).

John: Mr. Pearns' servant, John, died in Jamestown sometime after April 1623 but before February 16, 1624 (VI&A 423).

John (Native American): On December 14, 1673, the justices of Lancaster County's court agreed that Captain John, an Indian, would be paid for killing a wolf. He may have been the same man who was similarly compensated in Middlesex County in 1681 (Lancaster County Order Book 1666–1680:275).

John: On September 28, 1674, the General Court heard a case involving several runaway servants, who fled in a boat that belonged to William White of urban Jamestown, and were gone for two months. Six of the absconded men were English servants and the seventh was John, "a negro servant to Richard James," a Jamestown merchant. Each of the seven was supposed to receive 39 lashes at the whipping post (MCGC 382).

John (Native American): On December 5, 1681, the justices of Middlesex County decided that Captain John, an Indian, would be paid for killing a wolf (Middlesex County Order Book 1680–1694:52).

John (Native American): On October 8, 1689, David Fox II, a Lancaster County justice, informed the court that an Indian named John, who carried a small gun and was accompanied by a black dog, had come to his house the previous week. He described John as short and around 20 years of age and indicated that he could speak good English. According to Fox, John said that when he was a child, he was captured by Seneca Indians who took him from Wiccacomicoe in Maryland. John added that he had escaped from the Seneca and that it had taken him a year and a half to reach safety. Fox expressed his concern that John might be an Indian slave who had run away from home. He also raised the possibility that John might have fled from as far away as the lower side of the James River (Lancaster County Order Book 1686–1696:111).

John: When Richard Ambler made his will on January 23, 1765, he mentioned a slave named John, who was a carpenter (York County Wills and Inventories 21:372–378).

John: When an inventory was made of the late Edward Ambler I's estate in 1769, a child named John was living with his mother, Chubby, on the decedent's leasehold in the Governor's Land (AMB-E).

John: In 1769 a man named John was living on the Governor's Land and was included in the late Edward Ambler I's estate (AMB-E). He may have been the carpenter named John that Richard Ambler mentioned in his 1765 will.

Johnny: On February 15, 1768, when an inventory was made of the late Richard Ambler's slaves on Jamestown Island and his leasehold in the Governor's Land, an adult male slave named Johnny was listed. After his name, the word "York" was listed parenthetically, suggesting that he may have been brought from Yorktown or York County. He may have been the carpenter called John that Ambler mentioned in his 1765 will (York County Wills and Inventories 21:372–378, 386–391).

Robert Johns: On August 31, 1638, Robert Johns, a merchant, secured a tiny parcel that abutted south upon the James River. Brickmaker Alexander Stomer's patent was situated to his west. Both men were obliged to develop their property within a limited period of time or face forfeiture (PB 1:595; NUG I:96).

Christopher Johnson: On July 6, 1781, Christopher Johnson, a participant in the Battle of Green Spring, which occurred near Jamestown Island, wrote a letter describing the events that occurred (Johnson 1781).

Jacob Johnson I: In May 1673 Jacob Johnson I patented 600 acres on Little Creek, in Lower Norfolk (later, Princess Anne) County. Two years later he patented 740 acres on Queens Creek in Gloucester County. Johnson served as a burgess for Princess Anne County and attended the assembly sessions held in 1693. He was one of the two men Thomas Teackle of Accomack County asked to divide his estate. When quitrent rolls were compiled in 1704, Jacob Johnson I was credited with 1,700 acres in Princess Anne County. On May 27, 1710, he made his will, which was proved on July 5th. He named his son, Jacob II, as executor and made bequests to his grandchildren: William and Jacob Johnson III and John, Mary, Jacomin, and Elizabeth Wishard. He also mentioned his married daughter, Mary, and his own wife, Ann. Jacob Johnson II outlived his father by a very short time. He made his will on April 12, 1710, and died before November 1st (LEO 52; PB 6:457, 551; Accomack County Wills &c 1692–1715:98; Princess Anne County Deed Book 2:36, 38).

* * *

John Johnson I: In January 1624, John Johnson I, an ancient planter and yeoman, patented 15 acres abutting the Back River in the eastern portion of Jamestown Island, acreage he received from Governor George Yeardley between 1619 and 1621. Johnson also was assigned 85 acres of land in Archer's Hope, behind Jamestown Island. During the mid-1620s Johnson, his wife Ann I, and their two children, Ann II and John II, were living on their farmstead in the eastern part of Jamestown Island. When a list of patented land was sent back to England in May 1625, John Johnson I was credited with 200 acres. He died sometime prior to January 25, 1638, by which time his son, John II, was grown and daughter Ann II had married Edward Travis I. Ultimately, John Johnson I's property on Jamestown Island descended to his son, John II, who on March 25, 1654, repatented it (VI&A 425).

John Johnson II: John Johnson II, the son of Ann and John Johnson I of Jamestown Island, was born around 1624. His parents died sometime prior to January 25, 1638, leaving John II and his sister, Ann II, as their heirs. On June 5, 1653, John Johnson II, who identified himself as a James City County planter, disposed of 450 acres of land in Upper Chippokes, property he seems to have inherited from his parents. Then, on March 25, 1654, he repatented his late father's 15 acres in the eastern part of Jamestown Island and his 135 acres in Archer's Hope, renewing his claim in 1662. On August 8, 1659, John Johnson II sold his parents' Jamestown Island farmstead to his brother-in-law Edward Travis I, who by that date already owned several other parcels on the north side of Passmore Creek. Johnson, a staunch supporter of the rebel Nathaniel Bacon, was among those exempted from the king's pardon in February 1677 and his estate was subject to seizure. Although Governor William Berkeley described him as "a stirrer up of the people to [Bacon's] rebellion but no fighter," and stated that he had been executed on the Eastern Shore, he had not. However, he did suffer at the hands of Berkeley's most zealous supporters and in May 1677 Johnson told the king's commissioners that he and James Barrow had been imprisoned for 17 days by William Hartwell and were only freed when they promised their captor 10,000 shingles. In 1704 John Johnson II paid quitrent on 260 acres in James City County and 350 acres in Surry (VI&A 426; NEVILLE 61, 274).

* * *

Joseph Johnson: Joseph Johnson served as a burgess for Charles City County in 1640 and 1642. In September 1642 he patented 567½ acres in Charles City County, between Bikars Bay and Merchants Hope, land that was on the lower side of the James River, in what became Prince George County. Johnson may have been the man who was living in Surry at Hog Island in February 1624. In June 1635 he patented 400 acres on the Nansemond River, having disposed of some other land he owned in Upper Norfolk County. In 1650 Joseph Johnson was a captain in the Charles City County militia and the county's high sheriff, an indication that he also would have been a justice in the local court (LEO 18, 20; Charles City Orders 1650:274; VI&A 427; PB 1:252, 418, 837). He should not be confused with the former jailbird, Joseph Johnson of Archer's Hope (VI&A 426).

Richard Johnson: By 1699 Richard Johnson, who was born in England, seems to have been involved in exporting cloth and other merchandise to Virginia. One of the London merchants with whom he was associated was John Jeffreys. In 1672 Johnson brought suit against Colonel Peter Jennings' estate in Virginia, and in 1674 he served as colonist Robert Whitehaire's administrator. Johnson patented but failed to seat some land on Monsongo Creek, acreage that later was assigned to another individual. In 1679 he claimed some land on the north side of the Mattaponi River, in what was then New Kent County. He expanded his holdings in a northerly direction and acquired some acreage on Piscattaway Creek, in what was then Old Rappahannock County. He laid claim to 3,285 acres in Pamunkey Neck in October 1695 but was obliged to surrender it the following year, presumably because the acreage he patented lay within the area assigned to the Indians or to the College of William and Mary as charter land. Johnson became a resident of King and Queen County and was named to the Council of State on January 28, 1696. He died in Virginia in 1699, having become ill while attending a council meeting. He may have been a kinsman of the Richard Johnson who patented a large tract in New Kent County in 1719 (STAN 43; MCGC 326, 365, 373; PB 6:685–686; 7:326; 9:8; 10:432; SR 239, 375, 378, 1247, 1432, 1460, 2203, 4571, 5589, 7467, 8531, 12551; EJC I:204, 251, 335, 370, 394, 398, 407, 422, 434).

Thomas Johnson: Thomas Johnson, who settled on the Eastern Shore sometime prior to 1642, became a county justice and sheriff. He also served as clerk of court and went on to become a burgess for Northampton County, attending the assembly sessions held in 1645–1646, 1646, 1652, 1653, and 1654–1655. He patented 600 acres at Naswattocks Creek in Northampton County in 1646, and a year later he secured 1,000 acres plus an additional 200 acres. Afterward he married Ann, the widow of John Major, who died in 1648. In 1651 Johnson was in the group led by Edmund Scarborough II that attacked the Indians living in the upper part of the Eastern Shore. For his participation in an offensive against peaceful natives, Johnson was obliged to make amends to the chief. In 1653 he again became embroiled in controversy, for he signed a document known as the Northampton Protest, which was written shortly after the Commonwealth government assumed power in Virginia. For his participation in the protest, he was fined and made to post a bond. Over the years Johnson was a respected citizen, who often was asked to arbitrate disputes, settle estates, and perform other functions that required good judgment. The will Colonel Thomas Johnson made on November 25, 1658, was proved on December 28th. He named his wife, Jane, as executrix and asked that his stepchildren, William, John, Alice, and Jane Major, be paid what was due them under the terms of their late father's will. The testator, who was then living on a neck of land called Matasippy, left some land to his sons Thomas and Obedience and some cattle to his son Richard. He bequeathed to stepson William Major the land called Poplar Neck (LEO 24–25, 29, 31–32; NUG I:163–164, 329; Northampton County Deeds, Wills &c. [1657–1666]:27; AMES 2:11, 180–181, 237, 264–265, 289, 366; WISE 139–140; MARSHALL 21, 59). Thomas Johnson of Accomack County may have been related to the Thomas Johnson who came to Virginia in 1628 at Adam Thorogood's expense (VI&A 427).

William Johnson: William Johnson, a laborer, was one of the first Virginia colonists and arrived in Jamestown in May 1607 (VI&A 427).

William Johnson: William Johnson, a goldsmith, came to Virginia in 1608 as part of the 2nd Supply of new settlers and would have resided in Jamestown (VI&A 427).

William Johnson: On May 4, 1708, William Johnson and William Hunnicutt, who were from Surry County, were authorized to operate a ferry between Swann's Point and Jamestown (Surry County Order Book 1691–1713:308).

William Jonas alias Pinke (see William Pinke)

Anthony Jones: Anthony Jones came to Virginia in 1620 and in 1624 was one of Sir George Yeardley's servants at Flowerdew Hundred. By January 1625 Jones had moved to urban Jamestown and was part of the Yeardley household. In June 1635 he patented 500 acres on the east side of Pagan Point Creek in Warresqueak (later, Isle of Wight) County, and in November 1636 he acquired an additional 100 acres in the same vicinity. In March 1637, when he testified in a matter involving the Admiralty Court, Jones identified himself as a 22-year-old merchant. He was described as a Virginia planter later in the year, when he was authorized to settle the estate of William Hutchinson, who died in Warresqueak. When one of Hutchinson's heirs eventually tried to claim some of Hutchinson's assets, he filed suit against Anthony Jones, Richard Bennett, and Richard Salin (Sabin), who then had custody of the decedent's estate. Jones became a burgess for Isle of Wight County and attended the assembly sessions held in 1640 and 1643. During the mid-1640s he sold a piece of land to Robert Winchell. When Anthony Jones made his will on August 16, 1649, he made bequests to his wife, Ann, brother William Jones, sister Catherine Jones, daughter-in-law Ann Smith, and godson Anthony Binford, and to Thomas and John Smith. Jones made reference to a plantation he owned that was occupied by Thomas Parker and 2,000 acres he had on the Blackwater River. A deed executed in 1655 indicates that Anthony Jones' land in Isle of Wight County adjoined that of Peter Hull and was in the eastern part of the county (VI&A 428; LEO 18, 21; Isle of Wight County Wills and Administrations A:25; Deeds, Wills & Guardian Accounts A:69; Will and Deed Book 1 [1662–1688]:338; BODIE 530; PB 1:238, 402; SR 4005, 5862, 8631).

Rev. Hugh Jones: The Rev. Hugh Jones came to Virginia in 1716 and was master of the College of William and Mary's grammar school. He became professor of natural history and mathematics in 1717, by which time he had been named rector of James City Parish. He served as chaplain of the assembly in 1718 and 1720 but returned to England in 1722. He prepared a report on conditions in Virginia, an account that was published in London in 1724. He took a very dim view of public ferries, which he considered dangerous, thanks to "sudden storms, bad boats, or unskillful or willful ferry-men . . . especially if one passes in a boat with horses." He added that his brother had died in an accident while using the Chickahominy Ferry, which crossed the river near its junction with the James. The Rev. Jones returned to the colony in 1725 and was assigned a parish in King and Queen County. Due to disagreements with the vestry, he resigned and went to Maryland, where he was residing at the time of his death in 1760 (MEADE I:160; II:393, 400–402, 405, 408–409; BRYDON 396).

Paul Jones: In 1623 Richard Norwood, who came to Virginia on the *Margaret and John*, informed his father that Paul Jones, who had accompanied him, had died because of a food shortage. It is unclear whether Jones died aboard ship or shortly after he arrived in Jamestown (VI&A 430).

Richard Jones: Richard Jones was wounded in Jamestown in September 1676, while defending the capital city from the rebel Nathaniel Bacon's followers (JHB 1660–1693:69). He may have been the Richard Jones who during the 1660s and early 1670s acquired several patents on the Elizabeth River (PB 5:32–33; 6:409, 462).

Robert Jones: On February 10, 1677, Governor William Berkeley issued a proclamation in which he named those who were exempt from the king's pardon on account of their role in Bacon's Rebellion. One of those listed was Robert Jones, who was supposed to be brought before a court of justice. On March 8, 1677, Jones was put on trial at Green Spring plantation, found guilty by a jury, and sentenced to death (NEVILLE 61; MCGC 457, 529; SR 660).

Samuel Jones: The Rev. Samuel Jones, an Anglican clergyman, was brought to Virginia by Roger Green, probably to be rector of James City Parish. On October 24, 1671, the General Court noted that James Alsop, a resident of urban Jamestown, had provided accommodations to Jones, as had Colonel John Page, also a Jamestown resident. Alsop was to be compensated and Page was to be paid to the extent parish funds would permit (MCGC 288).

William Jones: William Jones, who was from Michmanssell in Herefordshire, arrived in Jamestown on September 5, 1623. On February 16, 1624, Jones and his wife were living in the rural part of Jamestown Island, where he was a household head and a free man (VI&A 432).

William Jones alias Brooks (Brookes, Broockes) alias Morgan (see William Morgan)

William Jones (Joanes): During the 1630s William Jones' name began appearing in Accomack County court records. From time to time he initiated suits against other county residents, and he occasionally was called upon to serve as an attorney, arbitrate disputes, settle estates, and testify in court. He was a successful planter and dispatched large shipments of tobacco to England. When Jones received a patent for 100 acres of new land in March 1640, he used the headright of his wife, Elizabeth. In 1641 he was among the local men proposed to serve as the county's sheriff. He continued to patent land on Hungars Creek, where he claimed 450 acres in 1654, 300 acres in 1663, and 550 acres in 1664. In 1652 and 1659 Captain William Jones served as a burgess for Northampton County. He made his will on July 26, 1669, which was proved on August 30th. The testator identified himself as a resident of Hungars Parish and designated his wife, Anne, as executrix. He left life-rights in his land to his wife and named his grandchildren as reversionary heirs, noting that some of them lived with Anthony Hodgkins, some with Michael Ricketts, and some with Symon Carpenter of Maryland. Therefore, it appears that his daughters, Ann, Elizabeth, and Joyce, were deceased (LEO 29, 35; PB 1:725; 2:29; 5:79, 222; SR 3692; AMES 1:92, 95, 97, 102, 146, 149, 161, 165; 2:21, 37, 40, 45, 66, 88, 102–103, 196, 223, 303, 394–395; Northampton County Orders 10 [1664–1674]:71; MARSHALL 82).

William Jones (Joanes): In May 1680 William Jones began serving as a constable for the lower part of Northumberland County. He also appeared in court from time to time as a participant in lawsuits and to serve on juries. He was designated as the administrator of Mrs. Martha Jones' estate in 1681. In 1689 Captain William Jones patented some land on the south side of the Rappahannock River in Old Rappahannock County. He also may have owned land in New Kent County during the 1660s or in nearby King and Queen County during the 1690s. Jones went on to become a Northumberland County justice and was serving as the county's sheriff in June 1699, when he was replaced by Captain Rodham Kenner. William Jones and John Downing successfully contested the election of Richard Rodgers and Richard Flint as Northumberland's burgesses and in 1693 were seated in their place. Between 1704 and 1706 Jones patented a substantial amount of land in Northumberland County (LEO 52; PB 8:26; 9:207; NN 3:28, 108, 130; Middlesex County Order Book 1680–1694:246, 450; Northumberland County Order Book 1678–1698:66, 107,180, 239, 295; 1699–1700:1, 9, 16).

George Jordan: George Jordan, a burgess for James City County, attended the assembly sessions held in 1644, 1646, and 1647–1648. He lived on the lower side of the James River, in territory that in 1652 became Surry County but formerly had been part of James City. In 1659 he represented Surry in the assembly and was returned to office in 1674–1676. He was named to the Council of State in 1670 and during the early 1670s became a lieutenant colonel and Virginia's attorney general and deputy escheator. Colonel Jordan's daughter, Fortune, married Thomas Hunt of urban Jamestown, to whom Jordan sold his 400-acre Surry County plantation. On April 5, 1671, Jordan was identified as the trustee of Hunt's orphan, a youngster who may have been Jordan's grandchild. In 1673 Jordan, as Thomas Hunt's executor, sued the late John Baugh's estate; he still was serving as Hunt's executor in April 1674. In September 1674 the General Court's justices mentioned a scandalous petition against George Jordan, but the nature of those allegations was not disclosed. In May 1677 Jordan was authorized to compile a list of the men whose estates had escheated to the Crown as a result of their active role in Bacon's Rebellion. In 1677 he signed a document about the disposition of the estate of Richard Lawrence, one of Nathaniel Bacon's most ardent supporters and a resident of urban Jamestown (STAN 25, 63, 65–66; MCGC 247, 327, 370; SAIN 10:72; CO 5/1371 f 247; Surry County Court Records 1664–1671:265; LEO 22, 25–26, 35, 40).

John Jordan: On February 6, 1694, when he became seriously ill, John Jordan made his will, identifying himself as a resident of Westmoreland County's Washington Parish. He recovered his health and survived until late 1696 or early 1697. Jordan served as a burgess for Westmoreland County and attended the assembly sessions held in 1695–1696. When he prepared his will in 1694, he designated his wife, Dorcas, as his executrix. He named as heirs his grandchildren (the offspring of his stepsons, Alexander, Patrick, Thomas, and John Spence, whom he referred to as his sons) and to his daughter or stepdaughter, Eleanor Monroe. He made bequests to several godchildren and to "sons" John Sturman, Andrew Monroe, and George Weedon, and left some livestock to his pupil, Thomas Steel. In May 1702 the widowed Dorcas Spence Jordan, who described herself as "very ancient and sickly," went to court in an attempt to prevent her daughter-in-law, Jemima Spence Pope, the remarried widow of John Spence, from using Spence's portion of the late John Jordan's estate to cancel some debts. The document was endorsed by Dorcas's son, Alexander Spence (LEO 55; Westmoreland County Deeds and Wills Book 2 [1691–1699]:86a–87a; 3 [1701–1707]:94–95).

Samuel Jordan (Jordain, Jorden, Jerden): Samuel Jordan came to Virginia in 1610 and probably was aboard one of the ships in Lord Delaware's fleet. Jordan most likely resided in Charles (or Bermuda) Hundred, where he had a dwelling in 1620. In 1619 he was one of two men who represented the corporation of Charles City in Virginia's first legislative assembly. In December 1620 Jordan was credited with property in three locations. He quickly acquired another tract, which he seated and called Beggars Bush or Jordan's Journey. In July he received a share of Company stock that entitled him to 100 acres in Digges Hundred. When Indians attacked the settlements along the banks of the James River in March 1622, Samuel Jordan was living at Jordan's Journey, where he brought some of the survivors from neighboring plantations. Samuel Jordan and his wife, Cisley, produced two daughters, Mary and Margaret. He died sometime after April 1623 but before November 19, 1623 (VI&A 433; LEO 3). Extensive archaeological work has been done at Jordan's Journey.

* * *

Thomas Jordan (Jerdan) I: During the mid-1620s Thomas Jordan was living on the mainland just west of Jamestown Island, where he was one of the governor's servants. Upon completing his contract, Jordan began rising in prominence, and in 1628, 1629, and 1632 he served as a burgess for the corporation of Warresqueak, later, Isle of Wight County. He also became a commissioner of that area's monthly court. In 1635 Jordan patented 900 acres in Warresqueak, an indication that he was a successful planter. He patented some land in Nansemond County but by August 1644 was dead. Jordan and his wife, whose name is unknown, produced two children, Thomas II and Margaret. By 1660 Thomas Jordan II, who married Margaret Brasseur, had become a devout Quaker. In 1687 reference was made to his land at Chuckatuck in Nansemond County. Thomas Jordan II died in December 1699 (VI&A 435; LEO 7–8, 10–11;

PB 2:70; Isle of Wight County Deed Book 1 [1688–1704]:15, 320, 337; DOR 2:365–366). On September 6, 1681, a Thomas Jordan, perhaps Thomas II, served as the attorney of bricklayer John Bird, who was sued in the Surry County court (Surry County Order Book 1671–1691:351).

Thomas Jordan (Jerdan) III: Thomas Jordan III, who was born in March 1661, married Elizabeth, the daughter of William Burgh of Chuckatuck. He was a justice of Nansemond County's monthly court and served as sheriff. He went on to become a burgess and represented Nansemond County in the assembly sessions held in 1696–1697. In May 1699 then-sheriff Captain Thomas Jordan III (an election official) and four other men were found guilty of spreading false rumors around the time Nansemond County's new burgesses were chosen. In December 1700 Jordan purchased some land in Isle of Wight County from some residents of Nansemond's Chuckatuck Parish. In 1704, when quitrent rolls were compiled, he was credited with 700 acres in Nansemond County (LEO 56; Isle of Wight County Deed Book 1 [1688–1704]:15, 320, 337; 6:336; DOR 2:366–367; EJC I:437–438, 441).

* * *

Dorothy Jubilee (Native American): When William Sherwood prepared his will in 1697, he identified Dorothy Jubilee as his Indian servant and set her free (AMB 65; MCGH 873).

Judah: On February 15, 1768, when an inventory was made of the late Richard Ambler's slaves on Jamestown Island and his leasehold in the Governor's Land, an adult male slave named Judah was listed (York County Wills and Inventories 21:386–391).

Judith: In 1769 an enslaved girl named Judith was living on the Governor's Land and was included in the late Edward Ambler I's estate (AMB-E).

Robert Julian: In January 1625, Robert Julian was a 20-year-old servant in Thomas Passmore's household, in the eastern end of Jamestown Island (VI&A 436).

Jupiter: On February 15, 1768, when an inventory was made of the late Richard Ambler's slaves on Jamestown Island and his leasehold in the Governor's Land, an adult male slave named Jupiter was listed. In 1769 Jupiter was living on Jamestown Island and was part of the late Edward Ambler I's estate (York County Wills and Inventories 21:386–391; AMB-E).

K

Kate (Cate): On February 15, 1768, when an inventory was made of the late Richard Ambler's slaves on Jamestown Island and his leasehold in the Governor's Land, a female slave named Kate was listed. In 1769 she was described as a girl then living on the Governor's Land and was included in the late Edward Ambler I's estate (York County Wills and Inventories 21:386–391; AMB-E).

Alice Kean (Keen, Keene): In 1624 Alice Kean was a servant in the home of Mr. and Mrs. John Hall, who lived in the eastern end of Jamestown Island. By January 1625 she had joined the household of John Johnson I, also of Jamestown Island (VI&A 436).

Barnaby (Barnabe, Barnabye) Kearney (Karney, Kearne): Governor William Berkeley sued Barnaby Kearney, a merchant, for paying him with some invalid tobacco bills. When Kearney appeared before the General Court on March 21, 1672, he claimed that he had received the tobacco bills from Mr. James (probably Richard James I, a Jamestown merchant), who had received them from John Everson. Kearney was ordered to pay William White of urban Jamestown half of the freight charges associated with the transaction. In March 1676 Kearney sued Giles Bland in order to recover the funds he was owed for serving as a witness in a lawsuit. In 1684 Barnaby Kearney was one of Nansemond County's burgesses. He was still living in Nansemond in 1697 when he authorized Captain Joseph Godwin to serve as his attorney. In 1704, when quitrents were compiled, Captain Barnaby Kearney was credited with 460 acres of Nansemond County land. His acreage was mentioned in 1719 in a land transaction made by John Leare of Nansemond and in another individual's 1715 patent for land just across the boundary line between Nansemond and Isle of Wight counties. Some of Kearney's descendants moved to what became North Carolina (MCGC 292, 294, 436; LEO 47; Isle of Wight County Deed Book 2 [1704–1715]:5; Deeds, Wills, Great Book 2:247, 654; PB 10:259; SMITH 52).

John Keaton (Keeton, Keton) I: John Keaton I, a Dutch citizen, came to Virginia before April 1679, at which time he was naturalized. In 1698 he served as a burgess for Nansemond County, an indication that by that time he had acquired some real estate or was married to a landowner. In October 1702 John Keaton II patented 237 acres of land on Bennett's Creek in Nansemond County, adjacent to his father's property, and in 1704, when quitrents were compiled, a man simply identified as John Keaton paid taxes on 2,000 acres in Nansemond County. In 1720 John Keaton II patented 291 acres in Nansemond County, on Bennett's Creek, and in 1722 he added 45 acres to the land he already owned (LEO 58; HEN 2:447; PB 9:480; 11:53, 97; SMITH 52).

Rev. George Keith (Keth, Keyth, Kith, Skiffe, Cisse): The Rev. George Keith, a Scottish clergyman who spent time in Bermuda, was living in Elizabeth City in 1617 but by 1624 had moved to Martin's Hundred. His wife, Susan, was then residing in Jamestown and serving as the guardian of Ensign William Spence's orphaned daughter, Sara. On January 24, 1625, Mrs. Susan Keith and one of Mr. Keith's servants were listed among the dead in Jamestown. Her young ward, Sara Spence, had been placed in the Elizabeth City household of Mrs. Susan Bush, a young widow who may have been a kinswoman. The Rev. Keith returned to Elizabeth City, where he patented and seated 100 acres of land and became responsible for Sara Spence's estate. On March 4, 1629, the justices of the General Court noted that Keith, who had gone to England but had returned to Virginia, had been assigned to a newly formed parish that included the plantations between Marie's Mount and Water's Creek. By 1635 Keith had become the rector of Chiskiack and patented 850 acres of land on the York River, using the headrights of his second wife, Martha, and his son, John (VI&A 437–438).

William Kelloway: William Kelloway, a 20-year-old husbandman from Portsmouth, England, arrived in Jamestown on September 5, 1623 (VI&A 438).

John Kemp: On November 24, 1645, the justices of the General Court sentenced John Kemp to a whipping because he had criticized the government (MCGC 565). His punishment would have been administered in Jamestown.

* * *

Mathew Kemp I: Mathew Kemp I, the son of Edmund (Edmond) Kemp, came to Virginia sometime prior to October 1660, when he patented 500 acres at the head of the Potomac River. A year later he secured a patent for 1,100 acres on the Piankatank River, reasserting a claim to land that his late father had patented in November 1656. In September 1662 Kemp appeared in Lancaster County's monthly court as the attorney of Sir Gray Skipwith, the late Edmund Kemp's administrator. By 1663 he was residing in Lancaster and was serving as the county's high sheriff. Kemp and Captain Peter Jennings jointly patented 1,000 acres at the head of the Potomac, and they claimed another 1,000 acres on the northwest branch of the Corotoman River in Lancaster County. Mathew Kemp I eventually moved to Gloucester County and was residing there when he brought suit against Robert Beverley I. The case, which was to be heard on October 21, 1670, was postponed on account of the plaintiff's illness. As time went on, Colonel Kemp continued to acquire land. In early 1675 he claimed a 573-acre parcel in Gloucester County, and his son, Mathew II, patented an additional 229 acres. Because Colonel Kemp was one of Sir William Berkeley's supporters, the rebel Nathaniel Bacon branded him a traitor. As a result, his property sustained severe damage at the hands of Bacon's followers. After Bacon's Rebellion subsided, Kemp allegedly plundered the estates of those he assumed were Bacon supporters. In 1679 he was chosen speaker of the assembly, and he represented Gloucester County in the assembly session of June 1680. While Kemp was speaker, he and Sir Henry Chicheley sent a letter to King Charles II requesting pay for the military men sent to Virginia to quell Bacon's Rebellion. Kemp was elevated to the Council of State on July 8, 1680, and in 1682 was instrumental in preventing Gloucester's tobacco planters from destroying their crops. Mathew Kemp I died in 1683 (MCGC 236; WISE; ASPIN 172; STAN 41; LEO 44–45; Lancaster County Order Book 1656–1666:191, 234; PB 4:452, 458, 484, 528; 6:550–551; SR 235, 236, 669, 6618).

Mathew Kemp II: Mathew Kemp II, the son and heir of Mathew Kemp I, patented 229 acres in Gloucester County, on the Piankatank River, in 1675. Four years later he patented some land on the north side of the Mattaponi River, acreage formerly granted to Mrs. Elizabeth Kemp. He commenced serving as a burgess for Middlesex County in 1685, replacing Robert Beverley I, who

became clerk. By 1686 he had begun serving as a justice in Middlesex County's monthly court, and in 1687 he was designated high sheriff. In 1695, while he was a militia captain, he patented 180 acres in Middlesex County. Kemp attended the assembly sessions that were held in 1685–1686, 1693, 1695–1696, and 1696–1697, representing Middlesex. In 1694 Captain Mathew Kemp made a trip to Jamestown to deliver the tobacco that had been collected as Middlesex County's share of public levies. When he was county coroner two years later, he summoned a grand jury to investigate a female servant's death. In 1698 he officiated in an especially gruesome case that involved a young runaway slave who was brutally whipped and beaten with a branding iron. The assault was done at the orders of his master, the Rev. Samuel Gray, rector of Christ Church Parish and later a trustee of the College of William and Mary (LEO 52–54, 56; Middlesex County Order Book 1680–1694:241, 294, 354, 419, 467; 1694–1705:1, 110, 236–240, 242, 245, 320; PB 6:550; 7:10; 8:405).

* * *

Richard Kemp: Richard Kemp was named a councilor and Secretary of the Colony in August 1634. He was fiercely loyal to Governor John Harvey but clashed with the Rev. Anthony Panton, who subjected him to public ridicule by making fun of his coiffeur. After Harvey's ouster from office, Kemp continued to serve as secretary. He married Elizabeth, Christopher Wormeley I's daughter and Ralph Wormeley I's niece, and produced a daughter, Elizabeth II. During the late 1630s Kemp began to acquire massive quantities of land, and on August 1, 1638, he patented a half-acre parcel in urban Jamestown where he constructed a brick house that Governor Harvey termed "the fairest ever known in this country." Kemp also developed some land that was only a few miles from Jamestown, establishing a plantation he called Rich Neck. When Sir Francis Wyatt became governor and suspended Kemp as secretary, he slipped away to England, absconding with some of the colony's official records. When Governor William Berkeley took office in 1643, Kemp again became a councilor and Secretary of the Colony. Berkeley made a controversial move in 1646 when he gave Kemp the right to appoint each county's clerk of court. When Richard Kemp made his will on January 4, 1649, he left detailed instructions to his executors. He asked his wife, Elizabeth I, to dispose of his house in Jamestown and to leave Virginia with their daughter, Elizabeth II. Kemp died sometime prior to October 24, 1650, and his widow married Sir Thomas Lunsford, a royalist and friend of Sir William Berkeley. Lady Elizabeth Wormeley Kemp Lunsford retained Rich Neck until at least July 1654. She outlived her daughter, Elizabeth II, and on December 6, 1656, informed English probate officials that she was the late Richard Kemp's surviving executrix. By 1658 Elizabeth Wormeley Kemp Lunsford had married Major General Robert Smith (VI&A 439–440; STAN 21, 32; Lower Norfolk County Record Book B:6–6a; SR 12654).

William Kemp: William Kemp, a yeoman, came to Virginia in 1618 and settled in Elizabeth City. He quickly emerged as a community leader and in 1622 sent a list of grievances to the king on behalf of some people who had been evicted from some land that the Virginia Company had claimed for its investors. Kemp was a respected member of the community, and in March 1629 he was named a commissioner of Elizabeth City's monthly court. A year later he was elected a burgess for the upper part of Elizabeth City. He was still alive in September 1632 (VI&A 440; LEO 9).

Kemps (Native American): Kemps, an Indian who befriended the English and spent a lot of time in Jamestown, sustained abuse at the colonists' hands. Captain John Smith said that Kemps and Tassore, another Indian, were detained as fettered prisoners in 1609 and were forced to show the colonists how to plant fields. Later, both men were released; however, according to Smith, they had grown fond of the colonists and sometimes brought game animals to the fort (VI&A 441; HAI 316, 320, 322, 509, 619).

George Kendall: George Kendall, one of the first Jamestown colonists, was among the councilors who on June 22, 1607, sent a letter to officials in England containing a report on the status of the colony. He incurred the wrath of President Edward Maria Wingfield, was tried in a martial court, and executed for mutiny (VI&A 441; STAN 27).

* * *

William Kendall I: As early as 1653, William Kendall I, a mariner, began making trips to Virginia. He patented some land on the Eastern Shore during the early 1660s and over the next 25 years added to his holdings. Much of the acreage he acquired was in the vicinity of Hungars and Cheriston creeks, although he also patented land on Magothy Bay and Nussawattox Creek; at Gingoteague and Matchepungo; and on the seaside. In time, he acquired many thousands of acres in Northampton and Accomack counties, and in one transaction alone he patented 10,000 acres. Sometime after 1658 he married Susanna, the widow of Captain Francis Pott. Kendall rose in prominence over the years, and in 1670 he became a county justice. He also served as captain, lieutenant colonel, and colonel in the county militia. In October 1672 he secured 6,000 acres in the names of his son, William II, and daughter, Mary. He also served as a Northampton County burgess and attended the assembly sessions held in 1658 and between 1663 and 1676. During Bacon's Rebellion he supported the rebels' cause and was among those Governor William Berkeley declared exempt from the king's pardon. On March 3, 1677, Berkeley and the Council of State reversed their position. Kendall was, however, found guilty of uttering "scandalous & mutinous Words" that dishonored the governor and, for that transgression, was fined £50. He was returned to office and served during the assembly sessions held in 1680–1682 and 1684. In 1685 he was elected to serve as a burgess for Accomack County but vacated his seat after being chosen speaker. As it turned out, Arthur Allen II of Surry County had to finish Kendall's term as speaker, for Kendall died during 1686. William Kendall I, when preparing his will on October 29, 1685, described himself as a merchant. He added four codicils to the original document, noting on June 16, 1686, that he was "going to Rappahannock on public employ and in the hands of God as to my return." The testator named his son, William II, as his primary heir and left him the bulk of his real and personal estate. He also made significant bequests to wife, Sarah; to his daughter, Mary, the wife of Hancock Lee; and to his grandchildren, Anna, Susanna, and Kendall Lee. He also bestowed part of his personal estate upon his stepchildren, John, Mary, Esther, and Elizabeth Mathews, noting that he had custody of their late father's property. Kendall left his tannery to his son and daughter jointly, naming his kinsman, John Kendall, as reversionary heir. Colonel William Kendall I's will was proved on July 28, 1686 (LEO 34, 39, 46–48; MARSHALL 58–59, 126–128; PB 4:621–623; 5:504; 6:9–10, 29, 184–185, 259–260, 312, 316, 395, 427, 482, 510, 535, 600, 640; 7:266, 491, 495; MCGC 213, 238, 256, 295, 348–349, 402, 431, 456, 529; Northampton County Orders, Wills &c. 12 [1683–1689]:224; SR 660, 7596; NEVILLE 61).

William Kendall II: William Kendall II, the son and primary heir of William Kendall I, served as a Northampton County burgess in 1688, and also attended the first session held in 1693. In April 1692 he patented 2,750 acres in Accomack County, near Gingoteague. On January 29, 1696, Kendall made his will, which was proved on July 28th. Like his late father, the bulk of his wealth was invested in real estate. The testator named as heirs his wife, Ann; his sons William III and John; and his daughters Susanna, Mason, and Ann. All of the Kendall children were minors. He designated his wife as executrix but asked his friends Major John Custis and Daniel Neech to oversee the settlement of his estate. Like his father, William Kendall II added a codicil to his will (LEO 49, 52; MARSHALL 153–154; PB 8:235; MCGC 207, 348; Northampton County Orders, Wills &c. 13 [1689–1698]:394).

* * *

Patrick Kennede (Kennedy): On January 11, 1627, Patrick Kennede, a mariner, presented Edmund Pritchard's will to the General Court in Jamestown. He was ordered to pay Pritchard's debts to William Claiborne and George Menefie and to compensate Edward Waters of Elizabeth City for the loss of a young male servant at Cowes. On February 19, 1627, Kennede was identified as purser of the *Marmaduke*. He returned to sea, and in December 1629 he witnessed John Rayment's will, made aboard the *Friendship* of London (VI&A 442).

Samuel (Sammuel) Kennell: Samuel Kennell came to Virginia in 1621 and during the mid-1620s lived in Elizabeth City on the Virginia Company's land. By October 13, 1627, Samuel Kennell was dead and his widow had married John Barnett of Jamestown. The decedent left behind some debts, one of which was owed to Mr. Peirsey (VI&A 442).

* * *

Richard Kenner: Richard Kenner, who became established in the Northern Neck by the 1660s, may have been a kinsman of surgeon Richard Kenner who died in Lower Norfolk County during the late 1640s, leaving two orphaned sons, John and Richard. In November 1660, when Kenner sold a tract of Westmoreland County land to Richard Searles, he identified himself as a resident of Nominy, in Westmoreland. He married Elizabeth, the daughter of Matthew Rodham

(Rhoden), who in 1665 gave the Kenners a 750-acre plantation. Later in the year, the Kenner couple sold a parcel of land on the Nominy River to Peter Dunkin. As time went on, Richard Kenner acquired more land, eventually accumulating more than 2,000 acres. Some of his property was in Westmoreland County, but he also had acreage in Northumberland. In 1674 he was sued by the Rev. John Waugh, a Stafford County clergyman who had numerous business interests. Kenner served on local juries, mediated disputes, and by 1679 began serving as a Westmoreland County justice. He eventually became a burgess for Northumberland County, attending the assembly sessions held in 1688 and 1691–1692. Kenner received a land certificate in April 1683 but died sometime after July 1685, when he was serving as a county justice (LEO 49–50; Northumberland County Record Book 1662–1666:156; 1666–1670:22; Order Book 1666–1678: 2, 23, 53–56, 68, 86, 194, 303; 1678–1698:37, 53, 70, 161, 176, 273, 276; Westmoreland County Deeds, Wills &c. 1661–1662:26–26a; Deeds and Wills No. 1 [1653–1671]:282, 322; Order Book 1676–1689:278, 609; Lower Norfolk County Record Book A:303; B:67a, 164).

Rodham Kenner: Rodham Kenner, Richard Kenner's brother, served as a Northumberland County burgess in the assembly sessions held in 1695–1696, 1696–1697, and 1699. He also was a justice in the county's monthly court and in June 1699 became sheriff. By June 1702 he was married to Hannah, the daughter of David Fox II, who named her as one of his heirs. Hannah Fox Kenner was named after her mother, Hannah I, the daughter of William Ball I (LEO 50, 54, 56, 59; Lancaster County Wills 1690–1702:111–113; Northumberland County Order Book 1699–1700:1, 16).

* * *

Richard Kennon I: Richard Kennon I married Elizabeth II, the daughter of William Worsham and his wife, Elizabeth I. During her widowhood, Elizabeth I wed Colonel Francis Eppes I. When Mrs. Eppes died in 1678, she designated her son-in-law, Richard Kennon I, and her stepson, Francis Eppes II, as her executors. Kennon also served as Nathaniel Hill's executor. In 1677 Kennon witnessed a document, indicating that he was living in Bermuda Hundred. Two years later he purchased a large tract on the James River, a plantation known as Rochdale. As time went on, Kennon grew in wealth and prominence. He became a Henrico County justice in 1683 and held office for many years. When signing a document in March 1685, he indicated that he was then in England and was the factor of William Paggen, a British merchant; his relationship with the Paggen Company endured for more than a decade. Over the years Kennon continued to acquire land. One of the parcels he developed was a lot in Bermuda Hundred. When Thomas Fitzherbert made his will in 1692, he made bequests to three of Richard and Elizabeth Worsham Kennon's children: William, Elizabeth, and Sarah. Kennon served as a burgess for Henrico County in 1685–1686. In 1691 he joined Francis Eppes II, Joseph Royall, and George Archer in patenting 2,827 acres on the north side of the Appomattox River in what was then Henrico County but later became Chesterfield County. When Richard Kennon I made his will on August 6, 1694, perhaps in preparation for a trip to England he undertook a few months later, he left his wife, Elizabeth, life-rights in their plantation called The Neck and some land on Swift Creek, a parcel known as The Quarter. He bequeathed to his son, William, the rest of his real estate, which included Rochdale, a mill tract, and a lot in Bermuda Hundred, and he left a female slave to his daughter, Judith. The testator died sometime prior to August 20, 1696, at which time his will was proved in Henrico County. The widowed Elizabeth Kennon was still alive in 1719, when her son, Richard II, was preparing to marry Agnes Bolling (LEO 48; PB 8:153; Henrico County Will and Deed Book 1677–1692:25, 83, 88, 156, 243, 369, 651; 1688–1697:1, 182, 311, 376, 554, 582, 673; Order Book 1678–1693:59–60; DOR 1:858).

Thomas Kerfitt: On January 24, 1625, Thomas Kerfitt was a 24-year-old servant in Thomas Passmore's household in rural Jamestown Island (VI&A 443).

Thomas Kersie: On August 22, 1625, Thomas Kersie provided court testimony about Christopher Hall, a resident of Jamestown Island. Kersie may have lived there too (VI&A 443).

William Kerton: On January 15, 1620, it was decided that William Kerton, a vagrant from Lincolnshire who was incarcerated in Old Bailey, would be sent to Virginia. He died in Jamestown sometime after April 1623 but before February 16, 1624 (VI&A 443).

Thomas Key (Keie, Keyes, Kaye): Thomas Key came to Virginia in 1619, and during the mid-1620s he and his wife, Sarah, were living at Chaplin's Choice. By December 1628 he had married a woman named Martha, an ancient planter who had patented some land on the lower side of the James River, in Warresqueak (later, Isle of Wight County). In 1630 Key, as a burgess, represented the settlers at Denbigh, in the corporation of Elizabeth City. Court records reveal that around 1631 he fathered a child with one of his black servants, a legal offense for which he was fined. In October 1636 Key signed an agreement with Colonel Humphrey Higginson, the girl's godfather, placing her in service for nine years. He asked that she receive better treatment than a common servant or slave and be taken to England if he (Higginson) were to leave Virginia. In 1656 Elizabeth or "Black Bess," an indentured servant who was then living in Northumberland County and was part of Colonel John Mottrom's estate, asked for her freedom, stating that she was Thomas Key's daughter. Her half-brother, Jesse, also was part of the Mottrom household. Northumberland's justices noted that Elizabeth had been baptized many years earlier, could give a good account of her faith, and that Colonel Humphrey Higginson was her godfather. A copy of the agreement that Thomas Key had made with Higginson in 1636 was entered into the minutes of Northumberland County's court, and one of Higginson's former servants, Anthony Lenton (Linton), vouched for the contract's validity. Lenton added that it was commonly known that Elizabeth was Key's child and that Key and his wife had planned to go to England but had died at Kecoughtan before their departure. Mrs. Elizabeth Newman, who was age 80 and a former resident of Elizabeth City, corroborated Lenton's statements, as did Ann Clare, and said that Key had been fined for getting his black servant pregnant. On the other hand, Nicholas Jurnen claimed that Key denied fathering Elizabeth. The jury deliberating Elizabeth Key's case noted that under common law, "the Child of a woman slave begot by a free man ought to bee free," and decided that Elizabeth should be released. Shortly thereafter, she and William Greensted (Grinsted) announced their intention to marry. In July 1659 Colonel Mottrom's administrator acknowledged transferring the maidservant Elizabeth Key into William Greensted's custody and said that the couple had wed. When Elizabeth and William Greensted testified in October 1660 about some of Colonel Mottrom's livestock, she said that she was 28 and he indicated that he was 29. The Greensted couple produced at least three children: Elizabeth, William, and John (VI&A 443; LEO 9; Northumberland County Wills, Inventories &c. 1652–1658:66, 85; Record Book 1658–1662:28, 44, 62).

John Kikotan: On November 14, 1677, William Edwards II of urban Jamestown purchased a seven-year-old mulatto servant named John Kikotan from Samuel Lewis. The child's name raises the possibility that he was part Indian. He may have been the offspring of John or Jack Kecatan, one of Rice Hoe II's bond servants, who in November 1665 sued his master in order to gain his freedom (Surry County Deeds, Wills, &c. 1671–1684:157; DOR 2:338).

"King James" (Native American): On November 12, 1691, the justices of Lancaster County's monthly court authorized compensation to "King James" or James, an Indian who had killed a wolf with a gun and therefore was eligible for a bounty (Lancaster County Order Book 1686–1696:186).

* * *

Richard Kingsmill: Richard Kingsmill came to Virginia around 1610 and was a prominent member of the Jamestown community, serving as its burgess in the assemblies of 1623–1624, 1625, and 1629 and as churchwarden of the James City Parish. Although he owned a 120-acre plantation in the northwest part of Jamestown Island, by the mid-1620s Kingsmill and his wife, Jane, an ancient planter, resided on the late Rev. Richard Buck's property in the Neck O'Land, directly across the Back River from their own property. The Kingsmill household, which included daughter Elizabeth (misidentified as "Susan" when a muster was taken in February 1625) and son Nathaniel, lived on Buck's property after Richard became guardian to the deceased clergyman's children. Richard Kingsmill appeared in court regularly in various capacities and was involved in settling the estates of several prominent citizens, including cape merchant Abraham Peirsey, Vice Admiral John Pountis, Captain John Martin, and the Rev. Richard Buck. Jane Kingsmill also testified in court from time to time. By May 1625 Richard Kingsmill had come into possession of 500 acres in Archer's Hope, land that eventually became known as Kingsmill Neck. He had begun to clear and plant that acreage by 1626 and probably placed indentured servants on his property. After Kingsmill's death, which occurred after July 7, 1630, but before May 1637, his widow,

Jane, married burgess and councilor Ambrose Harmar (Harmer), who immediately sought custody of the Buck estate and the orphaned Benomi Buck, who was mentally disabled. The Harmars resided on Jamestown Island and probably occupied a home located on Jane's 40-acre dower share of her late husband's estate. Kingsmill's daughter, Elizabeth, inherited the remainder of the 120-acre plantation. In 1652 Jane Kingsmill Harmar patented 2,000 acres of land in Northumberland County. She died or sold her Jamestown Island land sometime prior to June 5, 1657 (VI&A 446–447; LEO 5–6, 8; NUG I:125, 394).

Elizabeth Kingsmill (Mrs. William Tayloe [Taylor, Tayler], Mrs. Nathaniel Bacon) (see Elizabeth Kingsmill Tayloe Bacon): Assuming that the date on her tombstone is correct, Richard Kingsmill's daughter, Elizabeth, was born in 1624. Her name was omitted from the February 1624 census, and when a muster was taken of the Neck O'Land's inhabitants in February 1625, she was misidentified as "Susan." Elizabeth outlived her brother, Nathaniel, and sometime prior to September 1638 inherited 80 acres, the bulk of her late father's Jamestown Island plantation. By that date she had married William Tayloe (Taylor, Tayler), who in 1640 purchased the Kings Creek plantation in Chiskiack, on the York River. The Tayloes, who resided on their Kings Creek property, may have placed Elizabeth's Jamestown Island property in the hands of a tenant or entrusted it to their servants. William Tayloe became a York County burgess and was named to the Council of State. When he died in 1655, he left the Kings Creek plantation to his widow, Elizabeth, who married Colonel Nathaniel Bacon, a councilor and the colony's auditor general. When the rebel Nathaniel Bacon (the colonel's cousin) built a trench in 1676 across the isthmus leading into Jamestown Island, Elizabeth was among the women he reportedly placed on the ramparts, shielding his men from those of Governor William Berkeley. On November 6, 1661, the Bacon couple sold Elizabeth's share of her late father's Jamestown Island plantation to Nicholas Meriwether (VI&A 447).

* * *

Thomas Kingston (Kingstone): In 1629 Thomas Kingston represented Martin's Hundred as a burgess in the assembly. In 1635 his acreage in James City County abutted north upon that of John Dennett, who was in possession of 200 acres and later had land in York County, on Kings Creek (VI&A 448; LEO 8; PB 1:271, 513).

Richard Kinsman: In 1649 one writer claimed that Richard Kinsman had produced good perry wine from his orchard in Virginia (FOR II:8:14).

Kiptopeke (Kiptope) (Native American): Captain John Smith's map of Virginia suggests that at the time the first colonists arrived, there were two "kings seats" or major Indian villages on the Eastern Shore. Kiptopeke, the elder brother of the Eastern Shore's principal leader, Esmy Shichans, the "Laughing King," resided at Occohannock (Aquohanock). According to Secretary John Pory, Kiptopeke was a faithful councilor and preferred to serve as his younger brother's "lieutenant" (SMITH 1610; CJS II:289, 291).

Francis Kirkman: In October 1666 Captain Francis Kirkman acquired 747 acres of land between Archer's Hope (College) and Glebe creeks, in the mainland behind Jamestown Island. He was a member of the James City Parish vestry and seems to have been friendly with Governor William Berkeley. In 1672 Kirkman patented 800 acres on the lower side of the Rappahannock River and 650 acres in Surry County, acquiring the Surry land in partnership with William White of urban Jamestown. Kirkman served as James City County's high sheriff, an indication that he also was a court justice. In October 1673 he was sued for failing to arrest Ralph Deane, who had been summoned to court. Kirkman and councilor Richard Auborne of urban Jamestown patented 250 acres of James City County land, acreage that formerly was considered part of York County. Kirkman acquired 1,000 acres of escheat land in 1674, and a year later he and Jamestown merchant William Sherwood laid claim to 1,200 acres at the head of Gray's Creek, in Surry County. By March 1676 Francis Kirkman was dead, at which time his widow, Sarah, presented his will to the General Court. She placed a lien upon the estate of merchant David Newell of urban Jamestown in an attempt to recover some unpaid sheriff's fees that the plaintiff owed her late husband's estate. When Sir William Berkeley prepared his will in 1677, he made a small bequest to Mrs. Sarah Kirkman (NUG II:44; MCGC 285, 287, 306, 318, 347, 349, 360, 394, 418, 435, 443; WITH 113).

Kissacomas (Native American): In November 1624 Edward Grindon testified that Sir Thomas Dale gave a gun to an Indian named Kissacomas, who often came to Jamestown to get powder and shot. Interpreter Robert Poole said that Kissacomas killed waterfowl and deer for Dale, who furnished him with ammunition (VI&A 448).

Kissanacomen (Native American): Kissanacomen, a Chickahominy Indian leader, lived in the village of the Ozinies. In 1611 Deputy Governor George Yeardley confronted him and his people, demanding corn (CJS II:256–257). He may have been the same man who hunted game for Sir Thomas Dale.

[No First Name] Kitchen: According to Ralph Hamor, whose narrative was written around 1614, in 1611 men named Kitchen and Cole and three others were involved in a plan to flee from the colony. They intended to go south to Ocanahowan, where they had heard some Spanish were living (VI&A 448).

Mary (Maria) Kittamaquund (Mrs. Giles Brent I) (Native American): On July 4, 1640, Father Andrew White baptized Kittamaquund, the tapac (tayac) or emperor of Maryland's Piscataway Indians, in a public ceremony in St. Mary's City that was attended by Lord Baltimore's brother, Governor Leonard Calvert. On the same day the marriage of Kittamaquund and his wife was solemnized in a Roman Catholic ceremony, and the couple took the Christian names "Charles" and "Mary." On February 15, 1641, Kittamaquund brought his young daughter to St. Mary's City and left her in the Calvert household so that she could be educated. Margaret Brent, one of the child's guardians, also was living with the Calverts. Within a year the young Piscataway girl became proficient in the English language, was baptized, and took the name "Mary" or "Maria." When Governor Calvert went to England in spring 1643, Giles Brent I commenced serving as deputy governor. Sometime prior to January 1645, he married young Mary Kittamaquund. After the couple moved to Virginia, Brent asked Calvert to deliver Mary's cattle or give him their equivalent value in tobacco. Giles Brent I patented a tract in Stafford County, across from the Piscataway Indians' town on the Maryland shore, and as time went on, he acquired numerous pieces of property along the Potomac. In mid-April 1654, when he made plans to go to England, Brent made a legal agreement with his sister, Mary. He asked her to see that his children were educated and that his wife, Mary I, was given living space in the family home. He also assigned some of his land to his sister and gave her his personal property in Virginia and Maryland, specifying that it was to be used toward the support of his wife and children. Brent and his wife, Mary, gave two calves to their daughter, Mary II, and signed their names to an April 15, 1654, document that was recorded in Westmoreland County. Mary Kittamaquund died around 1655 and Giles Brent I quickly remarried. In August 1658 he executed a deed of gift, bestowing upon his daughter, Mary II, a tract of land on the south and southwest side of the Oquio (Aquia) or Peace River. If she were to die without heirs, the land would revert back to him. When Brent made his will on August 31, 1671, he was living in Stafford County at a plantation called The Retirement. He bequeathed livestock to the living children from his first marriage: his married daughter, Mary Fitzherbert, and son, Giles Brent II. The testator, whose will was proved on February 15, 1672, left virtually all of his landholdings in Virginia, Maryland, and England to his son, Giles Brent II, but assigned reversionary rights to his late father's heirs, should there be no direct descendants. In 1684 George Talbot, who was defending the Calverts' claim from William Penn, commented that "Capt. Brent who in the right of his wife the Piscataway Emperor's daughter and only Child pretended a right to the most part of Maryland but could doe noe good . . . after a great bustle about it" (HALL 131–132, 135–136; Brown 3, "Conference Between Penn and Talbot, at New Castle in 1684," 30; Chilton, "The Brent Family," 96–102; Rowland, "Mercer Land Book," 165–168; PB 2:359; 3:134, 192, 303, 308; 4:421; 5:652; Westmoreland County Deeds, Wills, Patents &c. 1653–1659:16–17, 112).

Edward Knight: Virginia governor John Harvey (1632–1639), a proponent of industrial development, sold the Glasshouse tract to Anthony Coleman, who sometime prior to September 1655 bequeathed it to Edward Knight and William Coleman (NUG I:145, 313; PB 3:367; AMB 78).

John Knight: John Knight acquired a 27-acre tract in the Governor's Land, a parcel that had been forfeited by Alexander Stoner, a brick–maker who owned land near the isthmus that connected Jamestown Island to the mainland. Later, the Knight property came into the hands of Mrs. Jane Perkins. John Knight died in 1732 and was buried in Jamestown. Robert Sully, an artist who visited Jamestown in 1845, noted the date on Knight's tombstone (NUG I:177; PB 2:150; Sully 1845).

Joseph Knight: Sometime prior to September 1655, Joseph Knight served as William Coleman's attorney when Coleman sold his inherited interest in the Glasshouse tract to John Senior, a surveyor (NUG I:313; PB 3:367).

Nathaniel Knight: In September 1678, after the death of Nathaniel Knight of Jamestown, Joseph Knight, perhaps a kinsman, was designated to serve as his administrator. The decedent's father was Samuel Knight, who refused to officiate (EEAC 35).

Peter Knight I: In September 1643 Peter Knight, a merchant, owned land in the western end of Jamestown Island, near the isthmus that led to the mainland. He also was in possession of 225 acres in Isle of Wight County at Basses Choice and some other Isle of Wight land that he had owned since 1638. When the boundaries of Jamestown's market zone were established in October 1649, its westernmost limits were at Sandy Gut or Bay, where Knight's storehouse was situated. His mercantile interests seem to have extended throughout Tidewater Virginia, and during the 1640s, 1650s, and 1660s, Knight patented massive tracts of land in Gloucester and Northumberland counties. One of the parcels he acquired was on the south side of the Great Wicocomoco River. By 1658 he was serving as a Gloucester County justice, but he identified himself as a resident of Wicocomoco, in Northumberland. From time to time he also functioned as an attorney. In 1661 Peter Knight I admitted that he had not paid a debt that he had acknowledged in the Lower Norfolk County court on January 17, 1652. Sometime prior to 1663 he married Anne Hawley, a resident of Northumberland County. He represented Gloucester County in the assembly sessions held in 1660 and 1661–1662, but he served as a justice and burgess for Northumberland County from the mid-1660s to the late 1670s and became high sheriff. In 1670 Knight was identified as one of Philip Ludwell I's debtors. His business interests then extended into Lancaster County and other Northern Neck counties. He also participated in military affairs, in 1678 holding a captaincy. Knight was attacked and beaten by one of his indentured servants in 1674, but survived and saw that the man was punished. He served as a burgess for Northumberland County in 1684 and 1685–1686 and probably stayed in Henry Gawler's ordinary whenever he was in the capital city, for Gawler later sued him as a debtor. Although Knight was elected to attend the 1686 session of the assembly, he failed to appear. In 1699 he was serving as a county justice in Northumberland County. When he made his will on November 28, 1702, he identified himself as a resident of Wicocomoco Parish. He bequeathed land to his sons Leonard and James and gave a small amount of acreage to his daughter Elizabeth. He left her and her sister, Mary, funds they could use to buy a ring. The late Peter Knight's will was proved on July 18, 1705 (NUG I:145, 166, 184, 248, 252, 258, 340, 389, 394; II:37, 86; PB 1:889; WITH 281; MCGH 206; HEN I:362; STAN 73, 76, 83–84; MCGC 506; LEO 34, 36, 38, 47–48; Northumberland County Wills, Inventories &c. 1652–1658:54, 143; Record Book 1658–1662:54; 1662–1666:98, 168; 1706–1720:175–176; Order Book 1652–1665: 108, 147, 150, 156, 166, 276, 384, 430; 1666–1678:18, 71, 78, 93, 98, 120, 196, 203, 308, 329; 1678–1698:57, 73, 181, 183, 243, 254; 1699–1700:4; Lancaster County Order Book 1656–1666:257, 356; 1666–1680:235, 402; Lower Norfolk County Record Book C:33; Isle of Wight County Deeds, Wills, & Guardian Accounts A:65).

Richard Knight: Richard Knight died in Jamestown sometime after April 1623 but before February 16, 1624 (VI&A 449). His name was listed twice in the official records that were compiled.

Christopher Knollinge: On December 5, 1625, Christopher Knollinge testified before the General Court in Jamestown about a conversation he had with Jeffrey Cornish (VI&A 449).

Jonathan (John) Knowles: When John and Mary Phipps sold a house in urban Jamestown to Jonathan Knowles on October 5, 1661, their deed recapitulated the parcel's chain of title and noted that the property formerly had been owned by the government. Knowles was then a newly elected burgess representing Lower Norfolk County and probably considered it desirable to own a home in the capital city. On December 13, 1663, Phipps sold Knowles an adjoining 120-acre tract that enveloped the lot Phipps had bought in 1661. Knowles, a planter who continued to serve as a burgess for Lower Norfolk County, repatented his acreage on May 6, 1665. By that time he had authorized John Underhill to survey his plantation in urban Jamestown. Shown prominently on the Underhill plat, which delimited Knowles' 133-plus acres, was a dwelling labeled "Mr. Knowles." During 1662 Jonathan Knowles hosted meetings of government officials, and he provided accommodations to Indians who came to the capital city on official business. Knowles and

Thomas Hunt, the owner of a waterfront lot in Jamestown, agreed to build two houses as part of the 1662 building initiative, a government-funded program intended to improve the capital city, and both men agreed to provide large quantities of brick. On November 9, 1666, the assembly summoned Knowles and ordered him to complete the work he had agreed to do or forfeit the compensation he had received. On October 3, 1667, Knowles' business partner, Hunt, offered to post a bond guaranteeing that he would finish the three houses he was building and repay the tobacco Mr. Knowles had received for his involvement in constructing two of the houses.

Records of the Virginia Land Office reveal that around the time Jonathan Knowles acquired his land in urban Jamestown, he began investing in property in Henrico County. On December 20, 1663, he patented some land on Falling Creek in what is now Chesterfield County, adding to his holdings two years later. He moved to Henrico County sometime after 1665 but before February 16, 1667, making it his permanent home. His business interests were widespread and extended into the Middle Peninsula and the Northern Neck. In April 1667 he conveyed his Jamestown acreage to John or Jonathan Newell, a York County merchant. Knowles acknowledged that he owed Newell £500 and that he was conveying his Jamestown tract to him to settle his debt. However, Knowles' property was worth more than what he owed Newell, who agreed to pay him the difference. Mrs. Bathenia Knowles testified that she had consented to the sale "freely & voluntarily," thereby relinquishing her dower rights. Knowles seems to have been on friendly terms with Henrico County merchant Thomas Stegg II, whose will he witnessed in 1669. In October 1670 he was residing in Henrico when he successfully sued Henry Sherman, another local resident, but the judgment against Sherman was set aside by the General Court. In March 1672 Knowles returned to Jamestown to testify in court because one of his maidservants, Mary Blades, was accused of mortally wounding Philip Lettis, a fellow servant in the Knowles home; Mary was found guilty and sentenced to be hanged. In 1675 Colonel Thomas Swann of Surry, the owner of a tavern in Jamestown, sued Captain Jonathan Knowles, perhaps then a militia officer in Henrico County. In December 1685, when Mrs. Bethaniah (Bethania) Giles of Henrico County, the wife of William Giles, relinquished her dower interest in some land she and her husband had sold, she identified herself as the daughter and heiress of Captain John Knowles (AMB 10, 14, 15, 16, 19, 20, 32, 135–136; PB 7:98; NUG I:450, 537; II:123, 222; PB 5:63–65; WITH 107; JHB 1660–1693:44, 50; CLARE 82 ff 275–276; MCGC 351, 329, 411, 419; PALM I:8; SR 3546, 4023; LEO 39; Northumberland County Record Book 1662–1666:176; Order Book 1666–1678: 133; Henrico County Wills, Deeds, Etc. 1677–1692:384; Will and Deed Book 1688–1697:8; LEO 39).

Israel Knowles: On April 19, 1625, the justices of the General Court learned that Israel Knowles had named John Southern, a resident of Jamestown Island, as his executor. They designated Southern as administrator of the decedent's estate (MCGC 55).

Sands Knowles: Sands Knowles of Kingston Parish in Gloucester (later, Mathews) County was one of the rebel Nathaniel Bacon's supporters. In October 1676 he was captured by Robert Beverley I, whose men also seized his provisions, goods, servants, slaves, and shallop, and took them to Colonel John Custis II's house on the Eastern Shore, where Governor William Berkeley had taken refuge. Knowles was detained and his belongings were sold or distributed to Beverley's men. On February 10, 1677, Governor Berkeley listed Sands Knowles among those exempt from the king's pardon. However, on March 15, 1677, Berkeley and the Council of State decided that Knowles would be pardoned if he relinquished all claims to the personal belongings that had been seized and took the oath of obedience (MCGC 458–459, 531).

Kocoum (Native American): According to William Strachey, Powhatan had arranged for his young daughter, Pocahontas, to marry Kocoum, a warrior, around the time the first colonists arrived. In 1611 Pocahontas was captured and taken to Jamestown. While she was living there, she converted to Christianity and in April 1614 married John Rolfe (HAI 620).

John Kullaway (Hullaway): On February 16, 1624, John Kullaway was a servant in Dr. John Pott's household in urban Jamestown (VI&A 450).

L

Henry Lacton: In January 1625 Henry Lacton was a servant in the household of Captain Roger Smith, who occupied a waterfront lot in urban Jamestown (VI&A 450).

Daniel Lacy (Lacye, Lacey, Lucy, Lucye): In December 1624 Daniel Lacy served on the jury that investigated the death of a Jamestown Island resident. In April 1625 he was awarded four acres of land in the western end of Jamestown Island, adjacent to Richard Kingsmill's plantation. Lacy died between May 1627 and February 8, 1628 (VI&A 450).

William Lacy (Lasey): William Lacy and his wife, Susan, came to Virginia in 1624 and in January 1625 were living on Jamestown Island in a household he headed (VI&A 450).

Marquis de Lafayette: During early July 1781, the men of Marie-Joseph Paul Yves Roch Gilbert du Motier, the Marquis de La-

fayette, sustained heavy losses in what became known as the Battle of Green Spring. The letters he sent to his superiors reflected his concern for the sick and wounded and the exchanged prisoners-of-war, who were being cared for near Jamestown and in Williamsburg. On August 6, 1781, Lafayette informed General Anthony Wayne that he was having the sick and injured moved to Hanover County and that the hospital "of James Town with the prisoners is secured." In September 1781 Lafayette indicated that the French troops encamped in Jamestown lacked provisions (Bruce, "Letters of Lafayette," 59).

Robert Lamb: Robert Lamb left England in 1622 with William Rowley, who resided on Jamestown Island (VI&A 451).

Thomas Lambert (Lambart, Lambard): On June 1, 1635, Thomas Lambert patented 100 acres on the east side of the Elizabeth River in Elizabeth City (later, Lower Norfolk) County, giving his name to what is known as Lambert's Point. He was identified as a planter in September 1638 when he appeared in court to bring suit against a carpenter or joiner who had lost his boat. Lambert served as a burgess for Lower Norfolk County and attended the assembly sessions held in 1647–1648, 1649, 1652, 1656, and 1658. In 1648 Lambert patented 750 acres called Pagetts Neck in Lower Norfolk County's Lynnhaven Parish, at the head of a small creek. He held the rank of ensign in 1642, when he was identified as an Elizabeth River planter. By June 1652 he was a major in the local militia and had become a county justice, a post he held for many years. Lieutenant Colonel Thomas Lambert and his daughter, Rachel, were linked by friendship or kinship to Elizabeth Lloyd, who in 1657 left them substantial bequests and offered to cover Rachel's passage to Virginia. When Thomas Lambert of Lynnhaven Parish made his will on January 4, 1676, he left to his wife, Jane, the land he had bought from William Dyer and named her as his executrix. He also left a young heifer to Mary, the daughter of John Johnson Jr. The testator's will was proved on April 17, 1677 (VI&A; LEO 26–27, 29–30, 33–34; PB 1:171; 2:126; SR 3517; Lower Norfolk County Record Book A:8, 180, 207; B:25, 73a, 164a, 208a; C:3, 10, 31; D:1, 32; Deed Book 4:15).

John Lamoyne: In late November 1624, John Lamoyne, a merchant, testified about Simon Tuchin (Tuching), and in December 1624 he made arrangements to rent a store from John Chew, a merchant who owned a waterfront lot in urban Jamestown and a plantation at Hog Island. On January 3, 1625, Lamoyne testified about Edward and Simon Tuchin's tobacco and was censured for making some defamatory remarks about Captain Ralph Hamor (VI&A 451).

John Lampkin: In October 1618 John Lampkin testified against Captain Edward Brewster in a martial court that Deputy Governor Samuel Argall convened in Jamestown. Lampkin claimed that Brewster was guilty of mutiny because he had opposed Argall's orders. Argall, like his predecessors, favored martial law (VI&A 451).

[No First Name] Lane: In 1693 a Mr. Lane, whose first name is unknown, represented King and Queen County in the assembly. It was the first time that the new county, formed in 1691 from the northerly part of New Kent, had sent burgesses to the assembly (LEO 52). King and Queen County probably was represented by Captain John Lane,

who commenced patenting land in New Kent County in 1675 and added to his holdings there until at least 1682. Much of his land was on the north side of the Mattaponi River, within the territory that in 1691 became King and Queen County (PB 6:566; 7:25, 173, 192, 617; 8:37).

Thomas Lane: On May 23, 1673, Thomas Lane joined with Mrs. Perry in filing a suit against William Drummond I, who had possession of a lot in urban Jamestown and a farm on the Governor's Land, just west of Jamestown Island. Lane, who in 1665 patented 1,000 acres on Dennis Creek in Northumberland County, also owned 400 acres in Surry County on the Sunken Marsh and Pokatink Swamp (MCGC 337; PB 5:113; 7:184).

John Langhorne (Langhorn): John Langhorne of Warwick County was summoned to appear before the General Court in 1674 because he and another county official had seized goods belonging to the late John Grayham's estate. In 1678 he informed the county court that a man was eligible for a bounty because he had brought in a wolf's head. In September 1681 Langhorne received a patent for 1,990 acres in Denbigh Parish of Warwick County. He became a county justice and represented Warwick County in the 1680–1682 assembly sessions. In October 1681 Captain Langhorne was one of the men involved in furnishing provisions to the men in a garrison on the Potomac River, horse soldiers who were to keep watch over settlements on the frontier. In 1688 a man was fined who had verbally abused Langhorne (LEO 46; PB 7:107; EJC I:14; MCGC 384; DUNN 43). The name of John Langhorne (perhaps a descendant) appeared frequently in the records of eighteenth-century Warwick County.

Ralph Langley (Langly, Langeley): Ralph Langley was among those who inventoried Captain Stephen Gill's estate in 1653. By 1655 he had become a justice in York County's court, and in 1656 he served as a burgess for York County, an indication that he or his wife owned property in the county. Langley continued to take an active role in public life. When he obtained a headright certificate in October 1657 for 18 people he had brought to the colony, he indicated that the list included his first and second wives but he didn't identify them by name. He did, however, list others who presumably were members of his immediate family: Joseph and Ralph Langley Jr. and Agnes, Jane, and Sarah Langley. In 1657 Captain Ralph Langley was among those authorized to collect the levy. He failed to utilize the headright certificate he received in October 1657; it was sold to James Turner and Richard Littlepage, who in March 1664 patented some land on the Pamunkey River (LEO 33; York County Deeds, Orders, Wills 1 [1648–1657]:182, 251, 264, 306, 335; 3 [1648–1657]:2; PB 5:357).

Robert Langley (Langly): Sometime prior to December 19, 1625, Robert Langley, a gentleman, became ill while staying at Isabell Perry's house in urban Jamestown and died before he was able to complete his will. According to witnesses, Langley said that he wanted John Pountis and William Perry to oversee his will and that he had given Robert Tokeley (then in England) his power of attorney. Later, Tokeley, acting in that capacity, nominated Jamestown merchant Abraham Peirsey as Langley's administrator. The Rev. David Sandys delivered Robert Langley's funeral sermon. Edward Waters, Thomas Flint, Captain Whitakers, and others were indebted to the decedent's estate. Court records suggest that Langley was a merchant (VI&A 452).

Sarah Langley: In February 1624 Sarah Langley was a servant in the household of Captain Ralph Hamor in urban Jamestown (VI&A 453).

Peter (Peeter) Langman (Langden, Langdon): In 1624 Goodman Peter Langman was living at Basses Choice. However, by early 1625 he had moved to urban Jamestown where he and his wife, Mary, the 40-year-old widow of the late Peter Ascam (Ascomb, Ascombe), shared a home with her children, Abigail and Peter Ascam II, and two of the Rev. Richard Buck's orphans. In January 1626 Langman was identified as one of the Buck orphans' guardians. By August 21, 1626, he was deceased (VI&A 453).

Anthony Langston (Langstone): Anthony Langston, the son of William Langston, was an ensign in Prince Maurice's regiment during England's civil war and arrived in Virginia around 1648–1649. Like many other Englishmen who remained loyal to the monarchy, he accepted Governor William Berkeley's open invitation to take refuge in the colony, which was considered a royalist stronghold. Between 1653 and 1655 Langston began patenting land in the upper reaches of the York River, including 1,000 acres along Totopotomoy Creek, near the grants of Manwarring Hammond, Philip Honywood, and William Lewis, who also were royalist officers. In 1657 Langston and

Lewis were commissioned by the assembly to discover natural resources in the western country, one of several exploratory expeditions colonial officials authorized during the 1650s, when the Commonwealth government was in power. The Virginia assembly elected Sir William Berkeley as governor in 1660. When he went to England a year later to report on conditions in the colony, he brought along a printed text in which he promoted the colony's economic interests. Many of Berkeley's ideas were extracted from Anthony Langston's treatise on town development and manufacturing. Langston, though couching his recommendations in generalities, seems to have had a specific site in mind: 1,000 acres of land on Totopotomoy Creek, land he had acquired in 1655. In fact, that area was shown on a map that probably accompanied his treatise. By the time Governor Berkeley returned to Virginia, Anthony Langston had left for England. He was there in January 1663, when he testified in court, and by 1664 he had begun disposing of the Virginia land he had patented. Langston reportedly became a mariner and sometimes served as an official courier, transporting documents from London to Virginia and to Carolina (NUG I:312, 509; PB 3:360; 4:421; 5:376; HEN I:381; II:17; JHB 1660–1698:3–4, 106; SR 62, 4137, 6004; BILLINGS 340–341).

John Langston (Langstone): In March 1672 the justices of the General Court granted John Langston 1,600 acres of escheat land in New Kent County, acreage that formerly had belonged to Major George Lydall and Hannah Clark. He also claimed some land on the south side of the Pamunkey River, contiguous to the property royalist Manwarring Hammond had owned. On July 31, 1677, Langston asked to be pardoned on account of his role in Bacon's Rebellion; although he was given the privilege of wearing his sword, his name was not cleared. Langston was elected to the assembly in 1680 as one of New Kent County's burgesses, but he was not allowed to take his seat because of his alleged involvement in Bacon's cause. In 1682 a Privy Council committee came to his defense and recommended that he be pardoned for his offences. In early 1681 Langston patented 1,300 acres of escheat land in New Kent County, to which he added another 1,316 acres in September. In 1682 he was among those arrested for attempting to avoid paying the tax on tobacco. He died sometime prior to April 1694, when his widow, Catherine, repatented some of his acreage (LEO 45; PB 7:108, 113, 234; 8:335; MCGC 324, 516, 519; SR 1455,

6618b, 11321; NEVILLE 169–170). No familial connection between John and Anthony Langston has been found.

Peter Lansdale: In March 1660 it was announced that the Rev. Peter Lansdale and the Rev. Peter Mallory would preach at the next assembly meeting in Jamestown (HEN I:549).

Michael Lapworth: Michael Lapworth came to Virginia sometime prior to June 1621 and probably was associated with Southampton Hundred. Governor George Yeardley promised to keep Virginia Company treasurer, Sir Edwin Sandys, apprised of Lapworth's well-being. Lapworth was named to the Council of State and served during 1621 (VI&A 454; STAN 30; LEO xx).

Edward Lassells (Lassell): On June 17, 1675, the General Court heard a case involving Edward Lassells, who was being sued by Thomas Rabley, a resident of urban Jamestown. The plaintiff had purchased a sloop from Lassells, a Virginia shipwright whose property was in Kingston Parish, in what was then Gloucester, but later Mathews, County, near Milhaven (Millford Haven). On February 2, 1693, Lassells sent a letter to England in which he proposed using Virginia's cypress trees as masts in vessels he was building for the Royal Navy. Officials decided that before a decision was made, the Naval Board should consult the owners of merchant ships and others involved in the Virginia trade. Ultimately, the Lords of the Admiralty decided to have Lassells outfit two Royal Navy ships, the *Foresight* and the *Archangel,* with topmasts and crossjack yards of Virginia cypress, which they would use on their return to England. However, both vessels were to retain their own English spars as reserve. In 1707 Lassells or his son, Edward Jr., owned a lot in Gloucestertown, an urban community at Gloucester Point (MCGC 412; PB 7:222; SR 6324).

"Laughing King" (Native American) (see Esmy Shichans)

Christopher Lawne: Christopher Lawne came to Virginia in 1619. He and some fellow adventurers intended to establish a plantation in Warresqueak (later, Isle of Wight) on the east side of the mouth of what became known as Lawne's Creek. In July 1619 Captain Lawne represented his plantation in the colony's assembly, and he served as jury foreman. During the summer of 1619, he and many of his plantation's inhabitants became ill and some died. By November 1619

the survivors abandoned their property and withdrew to Charles City, where Lawne himself died, leaving two underage sons, Lovewell and Symon (VI&A 455; LEO 3).

Lawrence: On February 15, 1768, when an inventory was made of the late Richard Ambler's slaves on Jamestown Island and his leasehold in the Governor's Land, an adult male slave named Lawrence was listed. In 1769 he was living on Jamestown Island and was part of the late Edward Ambler I's estate (York County Wills and Inventories 21:386–391; AMB-E).

Richard Lawrence: Richard Lawrence arrived in Virginia sometime prior to September 10, 1662, when he appeared before Lancaster County's court justices and obtained headright certificates on behalf of several people he had brought to Virginia. He included himself, his wife, Dorothy, and his sister, Patience, plus four males who may have been servants. Only Richard Lawrence and one of the other males seem to have survived. By March 1663 Lawrence had settled in Lancaster County and begun performing surveys at the behest of its justices. From time to time his name appeared in Lancaster's court records because he was trying to collect debts or had conducted surveys. During 1663 and 1664 he patented literally thousands of acres along the Rappahannock River in Old Rappahannock County, an area that had a substantial native population. One of his patents entitled him to acreage near the Rappahannock Indian town. Another was for land in the Middle Peninsula, at the head of Dragon Swamp and bordering native-occupied territory. Besides his land in the Middle Peninsula, Lawrence owned property in Lancaster County. In March 1665 he identified himself as a resident of Old Rappahannock County when he disposed of a plantation he owned there, but in February 1667 he indicated that he was a resident of urban Jamestown. In 1668 the colony's surveyor general, Edmund Scarborough I, made him responsible for reviewing all of the plats that county surveyors sent to the Secretary's office, before they became part of a patent. Stafford County burgess Thomas Mathew, a contemporary, later said that Lawrence had acquired his property in the capital city by marrying a wealthy widow whose large and popular inn was frequented by "those of the best quality, and such others as Businesse Called to that Town."

According to Thomas Mathew, Richard Lawrence had attended Oxford University and was a charismatic man known for his intelligence and eloquence. After Lawrence wed, he became a Jamestown innkeeper, a setting that would have enabled him to interact with the public. Lawrence initiated suits in Northumberland County during the late 1660s. He also made numerous appearances before the General Court during the early to mid-1670s, often seeking to recover debts. He filed suits against several people in the Surry County court, including Thomas Clarke, a bricklayer. Lawrence continued his work as a surveyor and in July 1672 prepared a plat of Richard Lee II's plantation, Paradise, in Gloucester County. In March 1675 he was also authorized to survey Thomas Senior's land in Old Rappahannock County.

By the early 1670s Richard Lawrence had begun to clash with some of Governor William Berkeley's cronies and became increasingly frustrated with the treatment he received from members of the governor's council, who sat as General Court justices. In October 1672 Lawrence accused General Court clerk Richard Auborne of causing John Senior's death, but no action was taken. Court records fail to shed light on Lawrence's allegations, although the accuser, the accused, and the victim were Jamestown residents. In early 1673 the General Court, as an appellate body, reversed the James City County justices' decision in a suit that involved Lawrence as plaintiff and Auborne as defendant. Several months later the General Court decided to allow one of Lawrence's servants (John Bustone) to serve less time than he originally had agreed to serve. Then, in April 1674 the General Court fined Lawrence for entertaining some of Governor Berkeley's servants. As punishment, they ordered him to contribute toward the construction of a brick fort that was being built in Jamestown. When three of Lawrence's male servants stole his shallop later in the year and lost it while attempting to flee, only two were ordered to serve some extra time. In 1675 the General Court freed an indentured servant (an apprentice to a ship's carpenter) that Richard Lawrence had assigned to Arnold Cassina (Cassinett) of Jamestown in exchange for a debt. Separately and collectively, these court decisions surely heightened Lawrence's resentment of Governor William Berkeley and his council and may have provoked him to post bail for Giles Bland, who was jailed for slandering Secretary Thomas Ludwell. Then, when Bland fled to avoid standing trial, William Sherwood sued Richard Lawrence to recover the bail money.

As soon as the popular uprising known as Bacon's Rebellion got underway, Richard Lawrence, by that time a widower, emerged as a staunch supporter of the rebel Nathaniel Bacon. Most contemporary sources describe Lawrence as Bacon's friend and trusted advisor. Lawrence's contact with the patrons of his tavern, which was located close to the ferry-landing in Jamestown, would have provided him an opportunity to disseminate his views. Moreover, in 1676 he was a burgess and represented Jamestown in the assembly. He also lived next door to another Bacon supporter, William Drummond I, who had a dwelling in urban Jamestown, near the church. When Bacon brought his followers to Jamestown in June 1676, he slipped ashore and met with Lawrence. Later, Berkeley had Lawrence's tavern searched, in an attempt to capture Bacon. When Berkeley and his loyalists eventually abandoned Jamestown, Bacon's men seized the governor's goods and reportedly stashed them at Lawrence's house. In the aftermath of Bacon's Rebellion, some of Lawrence's detractors claimed that he was an atheist and had a black slave as a concubine.

When Nathaniel Bacon and his followers put Jamestown to the torch on September 19, 1676, Richard Lawrence reportedly set fire to his own house. Some writers credited him with setting the church and statehouse ablaze, and he also was said to have torched the houses that belonged to merchant William Sherwood's orphaned stepson, Richard James II. After the fire Lawrence fled with four other men, taking a pile of tobacco notes but leaving behind "a cupboard full of plate." Governor William Berkeley considered Lawrence's crimes so grievous that he declared him a traitor who was exempt from the king's pardon. Lawrence left Jamestown and vanished. Some of his contemporaries claimed that he was seen in New Kent County, but others said that he had died in the snow. Because Lawrence was considered guilty of treason, all of his real and personal property escheated to the Crown. In 1677 an inventory was made of his estate, and Major William White of Jamestown was ordered to recover whatever he could. As late as 1686 the Crown's agents were still trying to recover revenue from debtors who owed funds to Richard Lawrence's estate. Moreover, those who had purchased land from Lawrence before he ran afoul of the law had difficulty clearing their titles (MCGC 218, 222, 228, 236, 238, 297, 313, 344, 348, 372, 382, 407–408, 418, 452; Lawrence 1672; Wiseman Book of Records; SAIN 9:414; FOR I:8:15–17, 21–23, 25; I:11:22, 46; AND 49, 67; ASPIN 9:4:170; HEN II:370, 461; CO 5/1371 ff 218–219, 247; 1/39 f 65; 1/41 f 32; Beverley 96; NUG I:441,478; II:22, 265; PB 5:138, 161,

198, 201; 7:300; LEO 39, 41; Purdie and Dixon, February 23, 1769; Surry County Deeds, Wills &c. 1652–1672:301, 297, 307; Deeds, Wills &c. 1671–1684:121, 130; Order Book 1671–1691:1, 5, 8; Old Rappahannock County Deeds and Wills 1665–1677:70–71, 91–93, 104–105; Order Book 1685–1687:144; Northumberland County Record Book 1666–1670:46–47; Order Book 1666–1678:64, 106, 148, 197–198; Lancaster County Wills 1674–1689:40; Order Book 1656–1666:188, 216, 263, 316, 370; 1666–1680:40, 105, 110; 1686–1696:286, 322, 348; 1696–1702:140; Westmoreland County Deeds, Patents &c. 1665–1677:271–271a; NEVILLE 61).

Richard Lawrence: Between 1671 and 1674 Richard Lawrence served as a burgess for Lower Norfolk County. On February 6, 1681, when he made his will, Lawrence indicated that he was living on the western branch of the Elizabeth River. He made bequests to Richard and Dany Carney, his godsons; to Katherin Greene; and to John Whinsell Sr. and Jr. Richard Lawrence's will was proved on May 17, 1687 (LEO 39; Lower Norfolk County Deed Book 5:20). There is no known connection between this Richard Lawrence and the man of the same name who was a Jamestown innkeeper and an avid supporter of rebel Nathaniel Bacon.

Anthony Lawson: Sometime prior to September 1671 Anthony Lawson began occupying the late John Martin's Lower Norfolk County plantations. Martin's sister, Ann, the wife of Adam Keeling, inherited the acreage and sued Lawson in an attempt to eject him. The matter ended up in the General Court, whose justices ordered Lawson to vacate the property. Lawson began patenting land in Lower Norfolk County in 1673 and acquired nearly 500 acres on the east branch of the Elizabeth River. During the early 1680s he laid claim to 1,206 acres at the head of the Lynnhaven River, plus 300 acres of escheat land. Like many of his contemporaries on the lower side of Hampton Roads, Lawson speculated in real estate in the Northern Neck and, with a fellow investor, patented 1,250 acres near the seacoast in Northumberland County. Finally, in 1697 he patented 1,356 acres of escheat land in Charles City (later, Prince George) County. Lawson, who was Lower Norfolk County's sheriff in 1683, represented the county in the assembly sessions held in 1680–1682, 1688, and 1691–1692. When Thomas Walke of Norfolk County made his will in 1694, he named Lieutenant Colonel Anthony Lawson as one of his executors. Lawson was commander-in-chief of the Princess Anne County militia in 1699 and died sometime prior to January

7, 1703. In April 1704 Elizabeth and Thomas Lawson and Lewis Conner were identified as the decedent's surviving executors (LEO 46, 49–50; PB 6:473; 7:58, 230, 390; 8:303; 9:82; Norfolk County Wills and Deeds 5:212; MCGC 275; EJC I:443, 537; II:356).

Christopher Lawson: In February 1624 Christopher Lawson and his wife were living in Captain Roger Smith's household in urban Jamestown. By February 4, 1625, Lawson and his wife, Alice, had moved to Smith's plantation on the lower side of the James River. In January 1627 Lawson was described as a Virginia Company tenant who had been assigned to Smith, a member of the Council of State. By 1639 Lawson was a free man and was serving as the tobacco viewer for Jamestown Island and the mainland. On January 6, 1640, he still was holding that position (VI&A 456).

Thomas Lawson: Thomas Lawson, who came to Virginia with Thomas West, Lord Delaware, arrived in Jamestown on June 10, 1610. Delaware commissioned Lawson captain of a company of men, and in May 1611 Sir Thomas Dale gave Captain Thomas Lawson the responsibility of seeing that a stable was built in Jamestown (VI&A 456).

John Laydon (Layden, Leydon, Layton): John Laydon, a laborer and/or carpenter, arrived in Virginia in 1607 and was one of the first Jamestown settlers. He married Anne (Ann) Burras (Buras) in December 1608 in the colony's first wedding. Anne, who was Mrs. Thomas Forrest's maidservant, came to Virginia in 1608 in the 2nd Supply of new settlers and was one of the colony's first two women. While Sir Thomas Dale was deputy governor (1611–1616), Anne Burras Laydon and another woman were flogged because the shirts they were making were considered defective. As a result of the whipping, Anne had a miscarriage. During the mid-1620s John and Anne Laydon and their daughters Alice, Katherine, Virginia, and Margaret were living in Elizabeth City. In 1628 Laydon traded half of his 200 acres in Coxendale and Henricus Island for a 100-acre tract in Elizabeth City. He continued to acquire land in what became Warwick River (later, Warwick) County and was still alive in late March 1640 (VI&A 457–458).

[No First Name] Leach (Leech): In July 1621 Mr. Leach (Leech), the Earl of Pembroke's agent, was authorized to explore the territory on the south side of the James River, where Pembroke, a Virginia Company investor, was entitled to some land. In

December 1621 Leach was named to the Council of State (VI&A 458; STAN 30; LEO xx).

Anthony Leane: Sometime prior to May 10, 1629, Anthony Leane agreed to serve Virginia merchant Thomas Mayhew for a year and work on his boat. In exchange, Mayhew agreed to pay him £20. After Mayhew's death Leane was assigned to Mayhew's brother, Edward, with the stipulation that he was not to be put to work as a field hand. The Mayhews seem to have conducted business in Jamestown and Elizabeth City (VI&A 459).

* * *

John Leare (Lear): In October 1656 John Leare, a merchant, patented some land on the Aquia River, in Westmoreland County, a jurisdiction in which he did business. However, in November 1663 he patented some land on the Nansemond River at the head of Majors Creek, in Nansemond County, and used his wife, Mary Bastard, as a headright. Leare represented Nansemond County in the assembly sessions held between 1666 and 1676, and 1680 and 1682. In March 1676 he was among those placed in command of the local militiamen preparing a defense against the Indians. Plans were then made to build a fort at Currawaugh or New Dursley (Dursly), on the west side of the Dismal Swamp. Between 1680 and 1682 Leare added to his holdings on the Nansemond River. In 1680 he acquired 900 acres, a tract called Plumpton Park or Orapeak, which straddled the line between Nansemond and Isle of Wight counties. By June 1681 Leare had married Ann (Anne), the widow of Isle of Wight County burgess John George I. It was then that John and Anne Leare sold the late Colonel George's land to Thomas Pitt, a fellow burgess. The acreage, which was on Isle of Wight County's Castle Creek, had been leased to Lieutenant Colonel James Powell, also a burgess. In 1683 John Leare was named to the Council of State, and in 1692 he was identified as a colonel in a transaction that occurred in Isle of Wight County. He seems to have had a financial interest in the *Sarah* of Bristol, whose master was Joseph Leare, and he served as a justice in the county court. Sometime prior to 1683, when Colonel John Leare became a member of the council, he was widowed. He remarried, taking as his bride Anne, the widow of Seth Southall, the late governor of Carolina, whose administration was marred by corruption. For de-

cades Southall's creditors made repeated attempts to recover funds from his widow and her new husband. Leare became a collector of port duties for the James River's Lower District, a position that would have yielded handsome fees. It was during the early 1690s that he and his new wife, Rebecca, patented some land between the Hampton and Back rivers in Elizabeth City County. Colonel Leare made his will on November 21, 1695, by which time his son, Thomas, was deceased. Therefore, the testator left the bulk of his estate to his grandson, John, and granddaughters Elizabeth and Martha, but he also made a bequest to his stepson, John George II. Leare died in Virginia sometime prior to September 1696. In October 1743 David Meade, a Virginia merchant and the reversionary heir of Henry Lord Maltravers, asserted a legal claim to the land in Isle of Wight and Nansemond counties that previously had belonged to Colonel John Leare, acreage that Leare had bequeathed to some of his descendants (LEO 39, 45; STAN 41; Westmoreland County Deeds, Wills, Patents &c. 1653–1659:66; Isle of Wight County Will and Deed Book 1 [1662–1688]:460–461; 2 [1688–1704]:47, 79, 460; Orders 1693–1695:3; SR 236, 239, 375, 378, 679, 1460, 5811; PB 4:59; 5:313; 7:38, 196; 8:214; 11:144; HEN II:328–329).

Thomas Leare (Lear): Thomas Leare, the son of Colonel John Leare, represented Nansemond County in the assembly sessions held in 1685–1686, 1688, and 1693. He married Elizabeth, the daughter of Colonel Joseph Bridger, in 1686, and in August he acknowledged that he had received from Bridger's estate the inheritance to which his wife, Elizabeth, was entitled. Thomas Leare died sometime prior to November 21, 1695, the date on which Colonel John Leare made his will and noted that his son had predeceased him (LEO 48–49, 52; Isle of Wight County Wills and Deeds 2:254–255; SR 5811).

* * *

William Leat (Leete, Leate): The Rev. William Leat was outfitted by the Virginia Company of London and came to Virginia in 1622. He was supposed to stay with the governor until he was assigned to a church, but in February 1624 he was living in Christopher Stokes' household on Jamestown Island (VI&A 459).

Thomas Lecket: In June 1695 Thomas Lecket was renting from Francis Meriwether I the 80-acre Island House tract, which originally belonged to ancient planter

Richard Kingsmill. The property was located in the northwest portion of Jamestown Island and fronted on the Back River (AMB 56).

Christopher Lee (Lees): Christopher Lee came to Virginia in 1623. He and his wife were living at Peirsey's (Flowerdew) Hundred plantation in 1624, when his wife died. In early 1625 Lee was a servant in Abraham Peirsey's household in urban Jamestown. Lee was still working for him in November 1625 when he was ordered to deliver Peirsey's corn to a ship's purser (VI&A 459).

George Lee: George Lee probably arrived in Virginia during the mid-1650s, around the time he sent a Middlesex County man's son to Barbados as an indentured servant. By August 1660 Lee had taken up residence in Charles City County, where he stayed for nearly a decade before moving to Surry. He was heavily involved in mercantile activities and at times was identified as a London merchant. During the early 1670s John Bowler served as Lee's Virginia factor, "selling & buying of goods and Servants" on his behalf and at times functioning as Lee's attorney. During the early-to-mid 1670s Lee sued Jamestown merchants John Newell, William Sherwood, and Richard Clarke, all of whom were in possession of land in the western end of Jamestown Island. An Isle of Wight County document authorizing George Lee of Surry County to serve as an attorney reveals that he was a physician. Other court records also identify him as a doctor.

In July 1680 George Lee acquired a conditional lease for a lot and ruinous brick row house on Jamestown's Back Street, and a year later he notified the justices of Surry County that he had moved to Jamestown. The court records state that, "Whereas George Lee hath beene for these severall years last past an inhabitant in the county of Surry but now testifies as a resident of James City County, these are to inform anyone that hath any commerce, business or accounts against him that at James Towne in James City County he will and willingly answer their concerns." In January 1682 Lee was paid for providing accommodations to some Indians who came to Jamestown on official business, and in November he was compensated for hosting one of the assembly's committees. In April 1684 Lee again was paid for entertaining Indians. It is likely that when George Lee moved to Jamestown, he rebuilt a structure that was burned during Bacon's Rebellion, a row house on Back Street, for it was the only Jamestown Island property he owned. On April 7, 1685, Lee

purchased a ¾-acre parcel from William and Elizabeth Brown of Surry County, the land on which his row house stood.

When George Lee prepared his will on April 12, 1692, he left life-rights in his real estate to his wife, Sarah (Sara), to whom he also left outright ownership of his personal property. Lee's real estate then included his ¾-acre lot in Jamestown "and all houses and appurtenances thereto belonging," some acreage on the mainland, and 100 acres on the Chickahominy River. After Sarah Lee's demise, her late husband's real estate was to go to Robert and George Nicholson and their heirs. Sarah Lee, after being widowed, continued to reside in her late husband's row house on urban Jamestown's Back Street. In August 1694 councilor Henry Hartwell, as Mrs. Lee's assignee, brought suit against the executors and trustees of Westmoreland County burgess William Hardidge II and recovered £11. Four years after George Lee's death and Sarah's marriage to someone named Smith, reference was made to the suitability of "the house where Mrs. Sarah Lee alias Smith lately lived" as a meeting place for the assembly. On December 7, 1696, Sarah Lee Smith and the Nicholsons sold their respective interests in the late George Lee's house and ¾-acre lot in Jamestown to George Harvey, who kept it until October 1697. Later the property came into the hands of the Ludwells, probably Philip Ludwell II (Middlesex County Record Book 1:29–30; Surry County Deeds, Wills &c. 1652–1672:379; 1671–1684:287; Deeds, Wills &c. 1694–1709:70; Order Book 1671–1691:395; Westmoreland County Order Book 1691–1699:149a; MCGC 249, 273, 327, 382, 386, 432; AMB 37; NUG I:160; JHB 1660–1693:152, 174, 256; EJC I:410; Lee MS 51 ff 668, 669, 671; BODIE 582).

Henry Lee (Leigh, Ley): Henry Lee, a gentleman and Virginia Company investor, came to Virginia in 1608 in the 2nd Supply of Jamestown colonists. According to Captain John Smith, he died in 1609 (VI&A 459).

Hugh Lee: In May 1650 Hugh Lee was authorized to keep an ordinary in Northumberland County, and he was identified as the overseer (or guardian) of Jane Perry's orphans in November 1651. Over the years he managed to acquire a substantial amount of land. In 1651–1652 Lee represented Northumberland County in the assembly. His name appeared frequently in local records when he witnessed legal documents, sold livestock, and undertook other transactions. When testifying in court in 1653, he said that he was age 44. In August 1655 Lee was named to the vestry of what later became Chicacoan Parish, by which time he was a county justice. During the latter part of 1655 and early 1656, Northumberland County's court convened at his house. In May 1657 Lee and his wife, Hannah, signed a deed of gift in which she conveyed a calf to John Hayles. The Lees were then identified as residents of Chickacoan. Later in the year Hugh Lee brought suit against George Colclough, whom he accused of slander. In January 1658 Lee appointed his wife, Hannah, as his attorney, enabling her to initiate an appeal to the General Court. In 1660 he patented a large tract of land in the upper reaches of the Potomac River and, with his wife's consent, gave it to his cousin, Samuel Cooper, a minor. Later in the year Lee was accused of illegally removing a trunk of goods from the home of John Trussell's widow, Mary, items that belonged to Sampson Cooper, young Samuel's late father. Hugh Lee and his wife, Hannah, moved to St. Mary's County, Maryland, sometime prior to January 1662. They were living there at the time of his death, which had occurred by September 1662, when Hannah commenced serving as his administrator. The widowed Hannah Lee seems to have returned to Northumberland County. In 1675, when she testified in court about Elizabeth Rhodum's nuncupative will, she indicated that she was age 60 or thereabouts (LEO 28; Northumberland County Deeds and Orders 1650–1652:41; Wills, Inventories &c. 1652–1658:50, 108, 122, 139; Record Book 1658–1662:37, 52; 1662–1666:92; Order Book 1652–1665:27, 61, 72, 96, 149, 174, 235, 260, 318–319; 1666–1678:220, 236; NUG:I;221, 242, 319, 351).

Henry Lee: Henry Lee's name began appearing in York County records during the mid-1640s. In March 1649 he patented 247 acres on Captain West's (now Felgates) Creek in York County, and a year later he and William Clapham invested in 250 acres on the Corotoman River, in what became Lancaster County. Then, in September 1651 Lee laid claim to another 126 acres in York County, acreage near that of William Prior (Pryor), whose property bordered the York River. In 1648 Henry Lee commenced serving as a York County justice and joined Hugh Gwyn in collecting the tobacco that people in Hampton Parish (the area east of King's Creek) used to pay their taxes. In 1652 Lee, who was still a county justice, represented York County in the assembly. Like many of his contemporaries, he was sued for indebtedness, and on at least one occasion he was briefly imprisoned, but he

also brought suit against his debtors. He was among those who compiled an inventory of Captain Stephen Gill's estate. In April 1653 Lee acquired 350 acres in York County, land that lay directly behind that of Captain Francis Morgan. When John Convers made his will in 1654, he bequeathed his servant, Geromiah, to Henry Lee "of York River" and indicated that he would be "a fit master." By October 1657 Lee was dead and funds were distributed from his estate (LEO 29; PB 2:202, 238, 334; 3:20; SR 3124; York County Deeds, Orders, Wills 1 [1633–1646]:130, 134, 182; 2 [1633–1646]:100, 106; 3 [1657–1662]:4a; Orders 2 [1646–1648]:177, 218, 321, 380, 430).

* * *

Richard Lee I: Richard Lee I served as clerk of the assembly in 1640, and in 1641 he was elected speaker. The following year he was named attorney general. On May 25, 1646, William Whitby sold Richard Lee a 100-acre tract on the upper side of the York River, at the head of Tindall's Creek, noting that it was the plantation on which Lee had lived before the April 18, 1644, Indian attack. Several years later Lee's land, which was near Gloucester Point, became part of the newly formed Gloucester County. Lee served as a burgess for York County in 1647–1648. He was named to the Council of State in 1649 and served as secretary until 1652. He also was a justice in Northumberland County's monthly court and held office during the early 1660s. His name appeared in the court's minutes for October 21, 1661, when he issued a warrant for the arrest of a man charged with bigamy. Between 1651 and 1664 Lee, who had a long-term business relationship with London merchant John Jeffreys, patented an enormous quantity of land in the Northern Neck and Middle Peninsula. His holdings included a house and store in Gloucester County on the Poropotank River, buildings that in 1684 were still well-known local landmarks. In July 1672 Richard Lawrence, later known for his role in Bacon's Rebellion, prepared a plat of Lee's Poropotank property, which was called Paradise. After Colonel Lee became interested in land in the Northern Neck, he patented many thousands of acres near the head of the Potomac River and on the Machodoc. Lee died in Northumberland County sometime after February 4, 1663, but before April 20, 1664, by which time his son, John, was serving as his executor. At the time of his death, the decedent was living at Dividing Creek, in an area that later became part of Westmoreland. In 1673 Thomas Yowell's wife, Anne, was identified as one of the daughters of Colonel Richard Lee (LEO 18–19, 26; STAN 21, 25, 36; Lawrence 1672; Northumberland County Record Book 1658–1662:48, 74; 1662–1666:92; Order Book 1652–1665:243, 261, 270, 291, 343, 373; PB 2:314; 3:15, 337; 4:33, 47, 123, 139, 372, 375, 447; 5:448; Middlesex County Order Book 1680–1694:176; Westmoreland County Deeds, Patents &c 1665–1677:15a; York County Record Book 1633–1646:125).

Hancock Lee: Hancock Lee, the son of Colonel Richard Lee I, was born in 1653 at Ditchley, in Northumberland County. He married Mary, the daughter of merchant William Kendall I of Northampton County, and settled on a 700-acre tract that Kendall gave them. When Kendall made his will, he made generous bequests to Hancock and Mary Lee and to their daughters, Anna, Susanna, and Kendall Lee. Hancock Lee patented 268 acres of escheat land in Accomack County but served as a justice in Northampton County. After the death of his wife, Mary, he moved to Northumberland County, where he became a justice. He wed Sarah, the daughter of Colonel Isaac Allerton of Northumberland County. Over the next 15 years, Lee patented acreage on the Middle Peninsula and in the Northern Neck. He secured 1,750 acres in Stafford County in 1703 and claimed 1,353 acres in Richmond County in 1704. Then he added another 1,570 acres the following year. In 1707 he patented land in Stafford County, this time acquiring acreage on Occoquan Creek. Lee, who was a county justice during the late 1680s, represented Northumberland County in the assembly sessions of 1688 and 1698. In June 1699 he was appointed Naval Officer and receiver of customs duties for the Potomac River, and in 1700 he was designated Northumberland County's sheriff. When quitrent rolls were compiled in 1704, he paid taxes on 4,050 acres of land in Accomack County. In September 1706 he served on a committee that was charged with deciding which branch of the Rappahannock River formed the Northern Neck Proprietary's southern boundary line. Hancock Lee made his will on December 31, 1706, and died on May 25, 1709, at age 56. He made bequests to his wife and to his married daughter, Anna (Anne) Armstead, and to his sons, Richard, Isaac, and John. He also left funds to buy some communion silver for the Wiccomoco Parish Church. Lee's inventory attests to his immense wealth. He was buried at Ditchley (LEO 49, 59; PB 6:664; NN 3:33, 96, 101, 176, 186; EJC I:450; II:46; III:131; SMITH 55; MARSHALL 126–127; FLEET I:563–564).

John Lee: Captain John Lee, the son of Colonel Richard Lee I, served as his late father's executor in 1664. In 1672 he was named a justice of Westmoreland County's monthly court. He appeared before his fellow justices from time to time and occasionally served as an attorney. In 1673 he was appointed high sheriff and represented Westmoreland County in the assembly. Lee died sometime prior to February 25, 1674, when four men were ordered to appraise his estate. His brother, Richard Lee II, inherited the share of a mill seat the decedent had owned jointly with Isaac Allerton (LEO 40; Westmoreland County Deeds, Patents &c. 1665–1677:74a, 102–102a, 120a, 170–180c, 199a–200).

Richard Lee II: Richard Lee II, the son of Colonel Richard Lee I, served as a Westmoreland County burgess and attended the assembly sessions held in 1670–1672 and 1677. When Richard II's brother John died in 1674, Richard inherited John's interest in a Westmoreland County mill that the decedent and Isaac Allerton had owned. Richard II was made a county justice in June 1675 and held office for many years. Court testimony that he gave in August 1677 implies that he was captured and detained by followers of the rebel, Nathaniel Bacon, during the summer of 1676. Richard Lee II was named to the Council of State in 1676. In 1680, when the assembly was making plans to establish an urban community in each county, he was the person to whom Northumberland County justice and surveyor Colonel Thomas Brereton was to send a plat of the county's proposed town. Colonel Lee appeared in court from time to time, conducting personal business or acting as an attorney. On at least one occasion, legal deliberations were transacted in his home, and in 1685 he was named to a court of oyer and terminer. He was appointed Naval Officer for the Upper District of the Potomac River and was commander-in-chief of the Westmoreland County and Richmond County militias. When the colony's governing officials decided to promote cloth production, Lee and Lieutenant Colonel Isaac Allerton were made responsible for distributing flax seed to local residents. In November 1710 Lee resigned as Naval Officer of the Potomac River, citing his advanced age. Richard Lee II resided at Mount Pleasant in Westmoreland County and died on March 12, 1714 (LEO 40, 42; STAN 40; Northumberland County Order Book 1678–1698:73, 274; Westmoreland County Deeds, Patents, &c. 1665–1677:199a–200, 240, 264, 309; Order Book 1676–1689:50, 156, 167, 187, 274, 323; SR 679, I:

12501; EJC I:364, 370, 393, 398, 444–445, 506; II:22, 363, 388; III:59, 263).

William Lee: William Lee, a Virginia-born London merchant, was the son of Thomas and Hannah Ludwell Lee of Westmoreland County and was a descendant of Richard Lee. He married a cousin, Hannah Philippa Ludwell, the eldest daughter of Frances Grymes and Philip Ludwell III, and reportedly relished the opportunity to manage the property she stood to inherit from her father. After Philip Ludwell III's death in 1767, Lee, who was still in England, sought the assistance of his brother, Richard Henry Lee of Westmoreland County, in seeing that the estate was settled in a timely and equitable manner. At issue was how the inheritance of Hannah Philippa's late sister, Frances, was to be divided between Lee's wife and her sister Lucy. On July 7, 1770, Richard Henry Lee informed his brother that the Ludwell estate had been partitioned. Hannah Philippa received Green Spring, as her late father had intended, and she also inherited some real estate in Williamsburg plus "one improved and one unimproved lot in Jamestown." In January 1771 Hannah Philippa and William Lee placed her Jamestown lots and some of the other land she inherited in the hands of two trustees, merchants who were authorized to secure tenants for up to 21 years or three lifetimes. The Lee couple's "improved" lot in Jamestown most likely was the acreage that enveloped the easternmost end of a partially ruinous brick row house on Back Street. The couple had two daughters (Cornelia and Portia) and a son, William Ludwell Lee. After the close of the American Revolution, William and Hannah Philippa Ludwell Lee made plans to move to Virginia to take up residence at Hannah's ancestral home, Green Spring. However, she died on August 18, 1784, leaving William as her heir. William Lee died at Green Spring on June 27, 1795, and was buried in the churchyard in Jamestown, near the Ludwell tombs. He left to his 22-year-old son, William Ludwell Lee, "all that estate real, personal and mixed, lying in James City County, James Town, and the City of Williamsburg, which descended to his mother, my late dear wife, Hannah Philippa Lee, as co-heiress and legatee of her late father, the Honorable Philip Ludwell" (Stanard, "Virginia Gleanings in England," 288–289; "Appraisal of Estate of Philip Ludwell, Esquire," 395–416; "Some Notes on Green Spring," 293–294; Carson 7; Fredericksburg Circuit Court 1796; Lee et al. 1771; MORTON 244).

William Ludwell Lee: William Ludwell Lee, the son and primary heir of William and Hannah Philippa Ludwell Lee, was born abroad. He and his father came to Virginia right after the American Revolution and moved into the refurbished Green Spring mansion. In 1796, a year after his father's death, William Ludwell Lee told noted architect Benjamin Latrobe that he intended to replace the old Green Spring mansion and asked him to draw up plans for a new dwelling that was suitable for a young gentleman. By the time Latrobe returned to Green Spring in 1797, Lee had razed the original house and was building a new one. Although it is uncertain what he did with the Jamestown lots he inherited, he may have sold them in order to raise the money he needed to build a new house at Green Spring. William Ludwell Lee never married and died at Green Spring on January 24, 1803; he was buried near his father in the churchyard in Jamestown. When making his will, he freed his slaves and made provisions for their future support. He asked that a brick wall be built around the church cemetery in Jamestown and left his library to Bishop James Madison, a family friend. He also made a few other modest bequests, including one to the College of William and Mary. However, the bulk of his real and personal estate descended to his married sisters, Cornelia Hopkins and Portia Hodgson. Brother-in-law William Hodgson, who served as the decedent's executor, commenced settling his estate and probably disposed of his Jamestown lots, if they had not already been sold. Some of the ambiguities in William Ludwell Lee's will gave rise to disputes that were aired before Virginia's Supreme Court in 1818. The bequest he made to his former slaves gave rise to a free black community that was still in existence in 1864 (CARSON 7–8; PALM VIII:497, 507; MUMFORD VI:163–164). The Lee lots in Jamestown may have become part of the property the Amblers owned.

* * *

Major John Lee: In 1775 Major John Lee boarded a grounded British ship near Jamestown Island (Tyler, "James City County Petitions," 187).

Timothy Leeds: Timothy Leeds, a gentleman, came to Virginia in 1608 in the 1st Supply of Jamestown colonists (VI&A 460).

Francis Leigh (Lee?): Francis Leigh, who was born in England, came to Virginia sometime prior to 1670. He was named to the Council of State in 1676 and was a councilor at the time of Bacon's Rebellion. He continued to serve until August 3, 1680, and was consistently identified as Francis Leigh, Esquire. He may have been a merchant who was heavily involved in the tobacco trade with London. Leigh is thought to have died in Virginia sometime after 1680 (STAN 40; LEO xx; SR 2005, 4884, 5588a, 5592, 5726, 5728, 5732, 5762d, 5763a, 10086, 10092, 12579; MCGC 228; NEVILLE 324; EJC I:9, 11).

William Leigh: William Leigh began patenting land in New Kent County during the early 1680s and over a period of several years managed to acquire nearly 2,500 acres, most of which was on the north side of the Mattaponi River, in what later became King and Queen County. Over the years he gradually rose in prominence. In 1683 he was authorized to serve as an attorney in the General Court, an appellate body whose justices were members of the Council of State. He may have lived in Stratton Major Parish, for he witnessed a will there in 1686. In 1691 Leigh served as a burgess for New Kent County but in 1692, when the assembly sessions resumed, he began serving as a burgess for the King and Queen County and represented the newly formed county in the sessions held in 1693, 1695–1696, 1696–1697, 1698, 1699, and 1700–1702. Leigh was among those given the task of determining whether the 1698 fire that destroyed the statehouse was the work of an arsonist. In May 1699 he asked permission to patent some land in King and Queen and Essex counties, and a month later he and Benjamin Harrison II were allowed to secure 3,474 acres on Mattaponi Creek. Later in the year Leigh was designated colonel and commander-in-chief of the King and Queen County militia. He also was appointed to a committee that settled land disputes in Pamunkey Neck. Leigh gave a deposition at the King and Queen County courthouse in 1700, in a suit involving a New Kent County merchant, and in August 1700 he was among the burgesses who asked the Council of State's permission to move the assembly's records to the College of William and Mary. In 1701 and June 1702 Lee was identified as a judge of the High Court of Vice Admiralty. He seems to have had a working knowledge of seafaring and in 1701 recommended that two of the king's ships travel together as a small fleet. In 1702 he was among those called upon to determine whether the Admiralty Court's judges were to be appointed by the governor or officials in England. Colonel William Leigh died sometime prior to

July 14, 1703, when the Council of State noted that a new burgess would have to be elected for King and Queen County. He may have been the son of the merchant William Leigh who shipped tobacco to England in 1635, was Charles City County's high sheriff in 1640, and laid claim in 1642 to 1,000 acres on Poropotank Creek, in what originally was New Kent, but eventually became Gloucester and King and Queen counties (LEO 50, 52–54, 56, 58–60, 62; PB 1:802; 7:155, 390, 418, 490; 8:139; 9:214; SR 381, 4777, 10738, 10928; MCGC 491, 523; EJC I:392, 440, 444, 446; II:2, 111, 118, 126, 185, 259, 264, 268, 332).

Dionysius Leister (Lester): When the British shelled the ferry house in Jamestown in November 1775, Dionysius Leister was ferryman. In mid-November 1775 Leister's ferry boat was pressed into service to transport American troops across the James. In November 1776 he presented a claim for his services and the use of his boat (Pinkney, *Virginia Gazette*, November 2, 1775; Church #245).

Robert Leister (Lester, Leyster): In August 1622 Robert Leister, who was leaving Jamestown, said that Captain William Tucker of Elizabeth City had insulted him and that he would seek revenge if he could. This threat against Tucker was brought to light in December 1625. By January 3, 1626, Robert Leister was dead. John Heney of Elizabeth City, who claimed that Tucker's words had caused Leister's death, was punished for slandering Tucker (VI&A 461).

Thomas Leister (Lester, Leyster): In early 1624 Thomas Leister, one of Dr. John Pott's servants, was living in urban Jamestown. By January 1625 he had moved to Pott's farm on the mainland just west of Jamestown Island. Leister appeared in court during 1625 to testify about his master's misdeeds, but in 1626 he was accused of injuring Roger Stanley during a fight (VI&A 461).

William Leneve: In 1724 and on January 29, 1737, the Rev. William Leneve was identified as the rector of James City Parish. In 1738, while he was in possession of the parish glebe, he placed an advertisement in the *Virginia Gazette*, seeking an overseer or farm manager (Tyler, "Lt. Colonel Walter Chiles," 75–78; Stanard, "January 29, 1737," 352; Parks, *Virginia Gazette*, December 1, 1738).

Robert Lesley: On December 26, 1649, merchant John White, a resident of James City Parish, sold to Fleetwood Dormer 1,000 acres near the falls of the James River, including the parcels known as My Lord's Island and Prince's Island. Then, on March 18th Dormer sold his land to the Rev. Robert Lesley, the rector of James City Parish. Lesley's land eventually came into the hands of the Steggs and then the Byrds, who included it in their Title Book (WITH 149). The William Byrd Title Book is preserved at the Virginia Historical Society, in Richmond, Virginia.

Lewis: In 1769 Lewis, an adult male slave who was living on Jamestown Island, was included in the late Edward Ambler I's estate (AMB-E).

John Lewis (Lewes): John Lewis, a cooper, arrived in Virginia in January 1608 in the 1st Supply of new settlers and would have lived in Jamestown (VI&A 462).

William Lewis: William Lewis served as a James City County burgess and attended the sessions held in 1691–1692 (LEO 50). Any patents he may have secured seem to have been lost or destroyed. He may have been related to the William Lewis who patented 2,000 acres of land in New Kent County but by the early 1670s had deserted it (PB 3:345; 4:99; MCGC 264, 417).

John Lightfoot (Lightfoote, Lytefoot, Lytefoote): John Lightfoot, a yeoman, left England in 1609, was stranded in Bermuda, and did not arrive in Jamestown until 1610. On April 16, 1622, he was identified as a Jamestown resident and a free man, who in 1618 had sold corn to the late Lord Delaware's men. In early 1624 he was living in Captain William Peirce's home in urban Jamestown. In August he patented 12 acres in the eastern end of Jamestown Island, but he continued to reside in urban Jamestown, where in January 1625 he was identified as a servant in Ralph Hamor's household. Lightfoot lost his freedom because of indebtedness or an infraction of the law. By December 1624 he had come into possession of a house and some land in urban Jamestown, property that he intended to rent or sell, perhaps because he intended to move to his rural acreage. In January 1629 John Lightfoot, who was mortally ill, bequeathed his entire estate to William Spencer I, his neighbor in the eastern end of Jamestown Island (VI&A 462).

John Lightfoot (Lytefoot) I: In 1677 John Lightfoot I, who was born in England and resided on a plantation in New Kent County near the Pamunkey Indian Town (site of the current reservation), was named auditor general. In September 1696 he presented the Council of State with a letter from the king, stating that he should be added to the council. However, the incumbent council members postponed having him sworn in because of "ye said Lightfoot's General ill reputation & known misbehavior." The council deliberated the matter again in October 1696 but reached no decision. Finally, in March 1697 they acquiesced to the king's instructions and allowed Lightfoot to take office. Three years later he tried to have the council minutes amended so that the discussion of his reputation could be deleted. Lightfoot served on the Council of State until 1706. He was identified as a colonel and commander-in-chief of New Kent County's militia in 1699 and escheator of the land between the James and York rivers. In October 1703 the justices of New Kent County, on behalf of the churchwardens of St. Peter's Parish, filed a complaint against Lightfoot, claiming that he had failed to surrender one of his maidservants, who was accused of wrongdoing. In another bill of complaint, John Scott alleged that Lightfoot was detaining two shoemakers who belonged to another man's estate. Lightfoot was among the councilors who sent a protest to England in 1704, grousing about Governor Francis Nicholson's arbitrary governing style. In 1704 Lightfoot paid quitrent on 3,600 acres of land in New Kent County, 900 acres then included in Essex County, and 250 acres in James City County. When the Nanzattico Indians were punished and several of their children given to council members, Colonel John Lightfoot received a 10-year-old girl named Nanny. By November 1705 Lightfoot had begun having some medical problems that were serious enough to prevent him from attending council meetings. In October 1706 the Pamunkey Indians' queen and Great Men sent a petition to the Council of State, claiming that Lightfoot tried to lay claim to the land on which their town was located; he, in turn, denied the Indians' allegations. Lightfoot died in Virginia on May 28, 1707. When Virginia's governing officials informed the Board of Trade in 1708 that Colonel John Lightfoot was dead, they asked that William Byrd II be appointed to the receiver general's post. In September 1712 Byrd visited the New Kent County plantations of John Lightfoot I's sons, John II, Sherwood, and Goodrich, all of whom lived on the Pamunkey River (STAN 42; LEO xx; SR 238, 381, 383, 384, 385, 662, 1189, 1459, 1475, 1664, 2214, 2218, 2228, 3921, 4571, 5536, 13634; BYRD 587; SMITH 55–56; EJC I:352–353, 357, 360, 398, 433, 444–445; II:338, 414; III:5, 53, 133, 221).

Philip Lightfoot: Philip Lightfoot appears to have been living in Elizabeth City in 1667 when the Dutch attacked the tobacco fleet, for he was criticized for failing to offer resistance. In 1673 he sued Surry County bricklayer Ralph Deane for performing poor quality work on his chimneys. Lightfoot was appointed comptroller and surveyor-general of customs duties. By August 1694 he had moved to James City County where he was a justice in the local court. On October 20, 1698, Colonel Lightfoot was one of the men ordered to investigate the cause of the recent statehouse fire, believed to have been the work of an arsonist. In June 1699 he was appointed collector of customs for the James River's Upper District (SAIN 5:1507; MCGC 328, 349, 369; York County Deeds, Orders, Wills 3:31; EJC I:173, 392–393, 449, 472).

William Lightly: On October 24, 1673, William Lightly was tried by the General Court's justices, found guilty of murder, and sentenced to be hanged in Jamestown (MCGC 353).

Thomas Ligon (Liggon, Lyggon, Lygon): Thomas Ligon came to Virginia during the 1640s and by 1649 had married Mary, the daughter of Thomas Harris, a Henrico County burgess. Ligon represented Henrico County in the assembly in 1656, an indication that he or his wife owned property in the county. In 1664 he secured patents for two large tracts of land on the south side of the James River, in what was then Henrico County but eventually became Chesterfield. He acquired an additional 250 acres in 1671, and a year later he patented 1,468 acres in the same vicinity. Most of Liggon's patents were near the site Sir Thomas Dale called Mount Malada, a small settlement associated with the plantation known as Coxendale, established in 1613. However, he also had some acreage in Charles City County. By 1670 Ligon, who was Henrico County's official surveyor, held the rank of colonel in the local militia. Often, he and others were called upon to conduct surveys of land that was in dispute, and occasionally he laid claim to acreage that he patented but failed to seat. Sometimes he served as security for people being sued and occasionally he was obliged to defend himself in litigation undertaken by others. Thomas Ligon prepared his will on January 10, 1676, naming wife Mary as executrix, and died before March 16th. When the widowed Mary Harris Ligon made her will in April 1703, she named as heirs her daughter, Johan, the wife of Robert Hancock; sons Richard and Hugh; and

grandsons Thomas Farrar and Henry Ligon (LEO 33; PB 5:6, 417; 6:425; MCGC 234, 236, 251, 265, 266, 272, 288, 299, 300, 304, 321, 348, 381, 428; WINFREE 344–347; Henrico County Deeds and Wills 1688–1697:107, 231–232; Wills and Deeds 1677–1692:35; 1697–1704:366; Order Book 1678–1693:167).

Francis Limbreck (Limbrecke, Lembri): In 1611 Francis Limbreck, an English pilot, arrived at Old Point Comfort in the ship that brought Diego de Molina, a Spanish spy. After Limbreck and his companions were taken into custody, they were sent up to Jamestown, where they were detained aboard ship. In 1613 Molina informed his superiors that some people thought that Limbreck was English, but he claimed to be from Aragon, in Spain. When Sir Thomas Dale set sail for England in 1616, he took Limbreck with him. As soon as they came within sight of the English coast, Dale had him hanged (VI&A 463).

Richard Limney: On October 2, 1667, Richard Limney was fined for illegally building a wharf in front of a lot in urban Jamestown (JHB 1660–1693:48).

[No First Name] Limpanie: Robert Limpanie's son, whose first name is unknown, went to Virginia with Abraham Peirsey. On February 27, 1622, Limpanie filed a petition with the Virginia Company, asking that his son be freed. It is probable that the youth lived in Jamestown, where Peirsey had a residence and a store, although by early 1624 he may have moved to Peirsey's plantation, Flowerdew Hundred (VI&A 464).

Robert Lindsey: In February 1624 Robert Lindsey was living on the lower side of the James River, within the corporation of James City. Within the year he moved to Martin's Hundred, where he was captured by the Pamunkey Indians in April 1626 and taken to their village. He sent word that if he was not freed, he would like for his personal effects to be given to Sara Snow in Jamestown. Lindsey's fate is uncertain (VI&A 464).

George Liste: In May 1609 George Liste, John Woodall's servant, came to Virginia with a chest of surgical equipment. He would have lived in Jamestown (VI&A 465).

Richard Littlepage: Richard Littlepage began patenting land in New Kent County in 1664, co-investing with James Turner. They acquired more than 1,500 acres on the south side of the Pamunkey River, on Totopotomoy Creek, part of the land that Anthony Langston had patented earlier on. They also patented two other tracts that were in the same vicinity. On March 13, 1676, Littlepage served the attorney of Jonathan Newell's administrator; Newell, a York County merchant, had owned a large piece of property in urban Jamestown. In 1684 Richard Littlepage patented 871 acres on the north side of the Chickahominy Swamp, in a portion of New Kent County that later became Hanover County. In 1685–1686 Littlepage served as a burgess for New Kent County. He continued to acquire land and in 1701 patented 2,367 acres in Pamunkey Neck, to which he added another 4,886 acres in 1702. In 1704 he paid quitrent on 2,600 acres in King William County and 2,160 acres in New Kent. Finally, in November 1705 he laid claim to 170 acres of escheat land in King William County. On September 23, 1712, William Byrd II and several others who were visiting the Pamunkey Indians' town stopped at Captain Littlepage's plantation, which eventually became the site of a tobacco inspection warehouse (MCGC 437; LEO 50; PB 3:360; 4:421; 5:376, 379; 7:400; 9:365, 456, 684; BYRD 588; SMITH 56).

* * *

Nathaniel Littleton I: Sometime after June 1635 but before November 23, 1640, Nathaniel Littleton I, who came from a prominent English family, married Ann (Anna), the reversionary heir of Henry Soothey (Southey) of Jamestown Island. She also was the widow of Accomack County burgess Charles Harmar, who had been one of Lady Elizabeth Dale's employees on the Eastern Shore. Nathaniel Littleton I, who was exporting cloth to Virginia in 1640, became a county justice and served on the Council of State from 1642 to 1652. He also was commander of the region known as Accomack. His wife, Ann, was an astute businesswoman and sometimes served as his attorney. Colonel Nathaniel Littleton I made his will on August 1, 1654, and by September 4th was dead. His widow, Ann, survived him by only two years. Ann Soothey Harmar Littleton's will, which was proved on October 28, 1656, reveals that she and Nathaniel Littleton I had three children together, Edward, Southey, and Esther (Heaster), and that Lieutenant Colonel Edward Douglas and his wife, Isabella, were her neighbors and close friends. Another trusted friend was Captain Francis Pott (LEO xx; AMES 2:309–310; MCGC 502; Northampton County Orders, Deeds, Wills &c. 1651–1654:197; PB 4:32; AMES 2:42, 306, 309–310, 315–316; DOR 3:218–221; SR 3504; MARSHALL 48).

Southey (Southy) Littleton I: Southey Littleton I, who was born around 1646, owned two large tracts of land in Accomack County as well as some acreage in Northampton County and in Somerset, Maryland. He inherited much of his parents' property and also that of his elder brother, Edward, whom he outlived. Some of Southey Littleton's landholdings were on Nandua Creek, on Magotha Bay, and at Occocomson, Pocamoke, Machepungo, and Pungoteague. Thus, some of his acreage was in Accomack County and some was in Northampton. In 1676 and 1677 Southey Littleton served as an Accomack County burgess. He was one of three men ordered to assign a value to the goods aboard the ship *Phoenix* and on January 11, 1677, he was a member of Governor Berkeley's martial court, which tried six ringleaders of Bacon's Rebellion and then condemned them to death. On September 16, 1679, Littleton, who was then in New York on official business for the Virginia government, made his will. It was proved in New York on December 12, 1679, and in Accomack County, Virginia, on December 17, 1679. The testator left his 4,050-acre plantation on Magotha Bay in Northampton County to his son, Nathaniel II, and bequeathed his 2,270 acres at Nandua in Accomack to his youngest son, Southey II. He made more modest bequests to his daughters Gertrude, Elizabeth, Sarah, and Esther (Ester) and to his son Bowman. Southey Littleton II apparently was a widower, for he placed his children (all of whom were underage) with friends or kin (LEO 37, 42; Accomack County Wills and Deeds 1676–1690:171; Northampton County Order Book 10 [1674–1679]:234; PB 4:19, 29, 57, 150; 5:71, 181; 6:465, 492, 538, 542–543, 545, 637, 676–677; MCGC 454, 527; DOR 3:218–221).

Nathaniel Littleton II: Nathaniel Littleton II, the son of Southey Littleton I and the grandson of Nathaniel Littleton I, inherited 4,050 acres on Magotha Bay. He became a captain of the Northampton County militia and served as a Northampton County burgess in 1698 and 1699. In October 1701 he patented 150 acres on the north side of Kings Creek, acreage that his late father had owned. Nathaniel Littleton II made his will on January 25, 1703, and died sometime prior to March 1st. He made bequests to his wife, Susanna; son Southey III; and daughters Esther and Sarah. He also left portions of his property to certain friends and named his wife as executrix (LEO 58–59; VI&A 365, 655; PB 6:677; 9:400; AMES 1:42; MARSHALL 171; DOR 3:221).

* * *

Liverpool: In 1769 Liverpool, an adult male slave, was living on Jamestown Island and was included in the late Edward Ambler I's estate (AMB-E).

William Liverpool: On January 1, 1744, William Broadnax II sold William Liverpool, a slave, to Christopher Perkins. Precisely a year later, Perkins conveyed Liverpool to Richard Ambler (AMB 106–107). He may have been the same man who in 1769 was identified as Liverpool and was included in Edward Ambler I's inventory.

Daniel Llewelyn (Lluellin, Lewellyn) I: Daniel Llewelyn came to Virginia prior to September 19, 1633, when Captain William Perry used him as a headright. Sometime after May 1638 he married Ann (Anne), the widow of John Price, who died prior to 1636, and Robert Hallom, whom she also outlived. Llewelyn patented 856 acres on Turkey Island Creek in Henrico County in October 1642. By 1646 he had begun managing the Hallom family's business interests in Virginia. Like most of his contemporaries, he appeared occasionally in court as a plaintiff or defendant, and he sometimes served as a juryman. He served as a Henrico County burgess in 1643 and 1644, but when he was returned to the assembly in 1646, 1652, and 1656, he represented Charles City County and was living in Shirley Hundred. Llewelyn began serving as a Charles City County justice in 1651 and as a militia captain. He became high sheriff in April 1656, while he was living on a Charles City County plantation called Essex. In 1655 he was ordered to collect from Westover Parish's parishioners the tobacco owed as church dues; the area he covered extended from Berkeley to the upper limits of the parish. In 1657 Sheriff Daniel Llewelyn was summoned to court for allowing a prisoner to escape. When Llewelyn made his will on February 6, 1664, he indicated that he was then a resident of Chelmsford in Essex, England. He left life-rights in his Charles City County land to his wife, Ann, and named his son, Daniel II, as reversionary heir. He also made bequests to his daughters Martha and Margaret. Llewelyn's will was proved on March 11, 1664. His widow died sometime prior to May 15, 1666 (VI&A 353, 580; LEO 21–22, 25, 30, 33; PB 1:856; PB 2:352, 547; 3:379; Charles City

County Order Book 1651:273; 1655–1665:7, 13, 17, 20, 45, 56, 64, 72, 85–90, 92–95, 103, 116, 132, 601; DOR 2:231).

* * *

Cornelius Lloyd (Loyd, Lloid, Lloide): In 1637 Cornelius Lloyd, the brother of burgess and merchant Edward Lloyd, patented part of the Society of Berkeley Hundred's land. He also brought suit against John Penrise, an Elizabeth City County carpenter, summoning him to appear before New Norfolk County's justices. In November 1638 Lloyd patented 400 acres that were located approximately 10 miles up the Elizabeth River's Western Branch, on its lower side. He seems to have been a close associate of merchants Edmund Morecroft and Edward Hodge. Lloyd was elected to serve as a burgess for Lower Norfolk County and attended the assembly sessions held in 1643, 1644, 1645–1646, 1647–1648, 1651–1652, 1652, and 1653. Besides representing the county in the assembly, Lloyd served as a justice in Lower Norfolk's monthly court. By 1652 he held the rank of lieutenant colonel in the local militia. The will made by his wife, Elizabeth, in February 1657 and proved a few months later failed to mention living offspring and implies a friendship or kinship tie to the Lamberts, also of the Elizabeth River area. Elizabeth Lloyd's will suggests that her husband, Cornelius, had predeceased her (PB 1 Pt. 1:410; LEO 21–22, 24, 26, 28–31; SR 3517, 3984; Lower Norfolk County Record Book A:2a; B:119; C:10, 16, 31, 45).

Edward Lloyd (Loyd): During the mid-1620s Edward Lloyd was living in Elizabeth City, on the upper side of the James River. On March 30, 1636, he patented 400 acres on the Elizabeth River, on the lower side of the James adjacent to some acreage owned by his brother, Cornelius. Edward Lloyd served as a Lower Norfolk County court justice and as a burgess in 1645 and 1646. A land transaction that occurred in April 1651 reveals that Edward was a merchant. When John Watkins made his will in February 1648, he named Edward Lloyd as one of his executors. In 1650 Lloyd took up some land in Maryland, where he became part of the Puritan community and gradually rose in political prominence. He returned to England, where he died in 1696. He was survived by his third wife, Grace (VI&A 465; DOR 2:432–433; LEO 23, 25; Lower Norfolk County Record Book B:64a, 120a, 123a, 128; C:50; PB 1:359).

* * *

Edward Lloyd: Edward Lloyd, a black man and resident of James City County, complained about the conduct of Governor William Berkeley's men, who raided his home and frightened his pregnant wife so badly that she had a miscarriage (SAIN 10:52).

George Lloyd (Loyd, Loyde): In September 1674 George Lloyd's runaway servant was tried before the General Court. He may have been the same individual who in 1664 patented 350 acres near the head of Morgan's Creek, on the east side of the Chickahominy River in James City County. In April 1702 a George Lloyd patented 694 acres in Essex County, on the south side of the Rappahannock River, and paid quitrent on 800 acres there in 1704 (MCGC 297, 382; NUG III:58; PB 5:395; 9:442; SMITH 57).

Mathew (Matthew) Lloyd (Loyd): In February 1624 Mathew Lloyd was a servant in Edward Blaney's household in urban Jamestown (VI&A 466).

* * *

Thomas Lloyd: By 1678 Thomas Lloyd, a Virginia merchant, was exporting tobacco to England. In 1694 he appeared before the justices of Lancaster County's court, where he served as John Bertrand's attorney. Lloyd's name appeared regularly in Essex County records, usually when he took legal action on others' behalf. In 1701 he became the county's sub-sheriff. Lloyd served as a burgess for Richmond County, where he was then residing and had owned some real estate since at least the early 1690s. He also attended the assembly sessions held in 1698 and 1699. A Thomas Lloyd witnessed the will of mariner Simon Lloyd, who died in Virginia around 1656. One of the testator's brothers and heirs was William Lloyd, who like Thomas Lloyd owned land on the Middle Peninsula (LEO 58–59; Lancaster County Order Book 1686–1696:297; Essex County Order Book 1692–1695:160; 1695–1699:98; Deeds and Wills 1692–1695:262; Richmond County Deed Book 1 [1692–1693]:131–132; 2 [1693–1695]:88–89; 3 [1697–1704]:33; SR 3519, 5762d).

William Lloyd (Loyd): When mariner Simon Lloyd made his will in December 1655, he identified William Lloyd as his brother and one of his heirs. The testator's will, which was made in Virginia and witnessed by Thomas Lloyd, was proved in London in 1657. During 1666 William Lloyd married Mary Hill, the widow of Moore Fauntleroy

of Old Rappahannock County, who died prior to August 1663. In 1665 and 1666 Lloyd frequently appeared in Old Rappahannock County's court, often serving as an attorney. He began speculating in real estate and patented massive tracts of land in King and Queen and Old Rappahannock counties. In 1667 he patented 4,750 acres on the Nominy River in Westmoreland County, and by 1679 he had come into possession of land in Lancaster County. He became a major in the militia, and in 1679 he started serving as a justice in Old Rappahannock County, a post he held for many years. In 1680 he purchased a tract of land on the east side of Rappahannock Creek and in 1681, after he had become a lieutenant colonel, he and Colonel John Stone acquired some land on behalf of the county, acreage that was to be a planned town. Lloyd also sold some of his Westmoreland County land to potter Morgan Jones. After being widowed, he wed Colonel John Hull's widow, Elizabeth, by April 1684. In 1684 one of Lloyd's maidservants, a woman named Margaret, gave birth to a child she had conceived with an Indian. Lloyd, who seems to have been a compassionate man, agreed to take care of the infant, which prevented the child from becoming a ward of the parish. The county court ruled that the youngster, who was to be classified as a servant, had to serve Lloyd until age 24. Lieutenant Colonel William Lloyd, who occasionally filed lawsuits in Westmoreland County's monthly court, served as a burgess for Old Rappahannock County in 1680–1682 and 1685–1686. In 1688 he was given the responsibility of procuring four trumpets, four field drums, two staffs, colors, and other military regalia for use by the county militia. Lloyd was still acquiring real estate in 1690. In 1691 he began serving as a trustee for the town at Hobbes Hole, the community that became known as Tappahannock. Colonel William Lloyd died prior to January 4, 1693, when his son, John, began serving as his executor. In February 1693 the decedent was replaced as a town trustee. In August 1696 executor John Lloyd filed suit in Lancaster County's monthly record, in an attempt to recover some debts against his late father's estate (LEO 46, 48; Old Rappahannock County Deeds and Wills 1665–1677:25–26, 52–53, 68–69, 72–73; 1677–1682:165–167, 200, 274, 324, 337–338; Order Book 1683–1686:2, 12, 23, 133, 153; 1687–1693:49, 236–237; PB 6:50, 118; Lancaster County Order Book 1666–1680:517; 1680–1686:23, 246; 1686–1696:359; Richmond County Deed Book 1 [1692–1693]:131–132; 2 [1693–1697]:214–215; 3 [1697–1704]:18–19,

96–99; Order Book 1:76; Westmoreland County Deeds, Patents &c 1665–1677:84, 93–93a, 119–119a, 269a–270a; Order Book 1676–1689:362, 631; NN 1:16–18; SR 3519).

* * *

George Lobb: In February 1638 George Lobb, a merchant, patented 1,500 acres on the Chickahominy River in James City County, which then straddled the river and included territory now encompassed by Charles City County. His patent was near that of Jamestown merchant Thomas Warne. Lobb and Warne were among the several merchants who owned large tracts on the Chickahominy, perhaps participating in the fur trade and trading with the Indians. In 1656 Lobb served as a burgess, representing James City County (LEO 33; PB 1:608).

Loggerhead (Native American) (see Wattle Jaws)

William Love: William Love, a tailor, came to Virginia in 1607 and was one of the first Jamestown settlers. He accompanied Captain John Smith on a trip to the Pamunkey Indians' territory on December 29, 1608 (VI&A 468).

Thomas Loving (Lovinge, Loveinge, Loven): Around 1636 Thomas Loving married the widowed Frances Kaynton, whose late husband, Thomas, was the factor of Thomas Covell, a London merchant and longtime Virginia adventurer. Loving came to Virginia prior to April 1638, perhaps at George Menefie's expense, and tried to replace Kaynton as Covell's factor. However, Covell later accused Loving of taking unlawful possession of his goods. In October 1638 Loving acquired 1,500 acres in Martin's Hundred, utilizing 30 headrights. He increased his holdings in 1642 and 1653 with patents of 700 acres and 400 acres. Patentee Abraham Spencer, who owned 150 acres called Green Swamp, noted that it was adjacent to Loving's plantation, and in 1638 David Mansell acquired 250 acres that abutted west upon his land. Thomas Loving served as a James City County burgess and attended the assembly sessions held in 1644, 1646, and 1658. Over the years he was identified as a Virginia merchant when he appeared before the justices of York and Charles City counties to make claims against local citizens and contest a debt. In 1660 he witnessed a deposition that was taken in York County. In October 1640 the General Court ordered Roger Parke to serve Thomas Loving, who was then identified as the agent of Captain Corell (Covell). By 1665 Loving

had been named to the Council of State. He briefly served as surveyor-general, which gave him the responsibility of confirming the appointments of county surveyors; he was relieved of his position in March 1667. By April 18, 1670, Thomas Loving was dead and his widow and executrix, Frances, had married Edward Thruston. In April 1670 Captain Humphrey White, who had sued Thomas Loving's estate in James City County's court, appealed the justices' decision and aired his case before the General Court. He succeeded in placing a lien against Loving's property in Martin's Hundred, which was then held by Edward Thruston, and Thruston was forced to pay White a large sum. Frances Covell Loving Thruston was widowed again and by October 1675 had wed Charles Emory, who brought suit against Edward Thruston's estate. Court testimony suggests that the plaintiff's claims were associated with the late Thomas Loving's estate (LEO 22, 25, 34; STAN 26, 63, 73; Northumberland County Record Book 1662–1666:137; PB 2:362; SR 631, 3438, 3456, 3622, 4544; NUG I:30, 89, 106, 137, 224, 294; MCGC 240, 414, 426–427, 466; York County Deeds, Orders, Wills 2 [1646–1648]:375; Charles City County Orders 1658–1661:146, 164; NEILL 185, 193, 261, 287).

Michael Lowick: Michael Lowick, a gentleman, came to Virginia in 1608 in the 2nd Supply of new colonists and would have resided in Jamestown (VI&A 468).

Mrs. Bridget Lowther: On January 23, 1629, the General Court learned that Mrs. Bridget Lowther had custody of the late Nathaniel Jeffreys' servants. The justices ordered her to surrender them to Jeffreys' executor and to account for the time they had worked for her. On March 16, 1632, Mrs. Lowther, then described as a widow and resident of Pasbehay, received a 21-year lease for 250 acres on the west side of the Chickahominy River, across from the land of Bridges Freeman. Bridget Lowther's late husband's name is unknown (VI&A 469).

Thomas Lucas (Lucus, Lucar) I: In 1642 Thomas Lucas I and Thomas Gregory acquired some acreage in Middle Plantation, a parcel known as the Middle House. Their property probably was located near the midpoint of the palisade that extended across the James-York Peninsula, between the heads of Queens and Archer's Hope (College) creeks. By the early 1650s Lucas had moved to Old Rappahannock County and begun patenting large tracts of land on the south side of the Rappahannock River. In April 1655 he and Captain John Upton's widow, the former Margaret Underwood, executed a marriage contract. She and her late husband had been living in Isle of Wight County at the time of his death in 1651–1652 and had at least one child. Lucas also had been married previously and had a grown son, Thomas Lucas II, and some other children whose hereditary rights he wanted to protect. Thomas Lucas I served as a burgess for Old Rappahannock County in 1658 and 1663–1674 but died in January 1675. In October 1681 and in October 1699 references were made to his property when neighboring tracts were sold. His acreage lay within that portion of Old Rappahannock County that in 1692 became part of the newly formed Essex County (LEO 34, 39; NUG I:161; PB 2:59; 3:25, 109; 4:131; 5:444; Old Rappahannock County Deeds and Wills 1656–1664:20–21, 34, 43; 1677–1682:321–322; Essex County Deeds and Wills 1699–1702:27–29).

Lucy: On February 15, 1768, when an inventory was made of the late Richard Ambler's slaves on Jamestown Island and his leasehold in the Governor's Land, an adult female slave named Lucy was listed. In 1769 she was living on the Governor's Land and shared her home with her child, Ben (York County Wills and Inventories 21:386–391; AMB-E).

William Luddington: In 1646 William Luddington served as a burgess, representing York County. In 1647 he was paid for his service. During January 1648 a mariner doing business in the York River was authorized to collect some debts from Luddington (LEO 25; STAN 66; York County Court Orders 2 [1646–1648]:218, 370). Due to the loss of early patents and other official records, very little is known about William Luddington.

George Ludlow (Ludlowe, Ludloe): In April 1641 George Ludlow, exercising Sir John Harvey's power of attorney, conveyed the former governor's buildings and land in urban Jamestown to the Virginia government, which was trying to recover funds to repay some of Harvey's debts. In 1642 Ludlow served as a burgess for Charles River (later, York) County, but was named to the Council of State and served from 1642 to 1655. He purchased Harvey's York County plantation, on the west side of Wormeley Creek's mouth, buying it from merchant George Menefie, who held the ex-governor's mortgage. When Ludlow repatented his land in 1646, he made note of a mill that then stood on Wormeley Creek. In February 1650 royalist Henry Norwood, who had been shipwrecked on the Eastern Shore and

managed to reach the mainland, stayed briefly at George Ludlow's home on the York River; he described it as "a most pleasant situation." Like many of his peers, Ludlow speculated in real estate and invested in land in the Northern Neck and the Middle Peninsula, patenting acreage along the Potomac, Piankatank, and Rappahannock rivers, in Northumberland, Old Rappahannock, and Gloucester counties. One of the parcels he patented and then sold encompassed 500 acres at Gloucester (or Tindall's) Point. Colonel George Ludlow made his will on September 8, 1655, and died in Virginia sometime prior to August 1, 1656, when his will was proved. He left a very modest annuity to his wife, Elizabeth, and made bequests to his nephews and several other people, one of whom was Thomas Bushrod (Bushrode). The testator left his real and personal property in Virginia and his one-sixteenth interest in the ship *Mayflower* (Captain William White, commander) to his nephew Thomas Ludlow. However, on October 23, 1655, Ludlow added a codicil, bequeathing his Virginia property and interest in the *Mayflower* to another nephew, Jonathan Ludlow, the son of the testator's brother Roger. The codicil was to take effect in the event that nephew Thomas Ludlow married Mrs. Rebecca Hurst (MCGC 497; WITH 588; LEO xx, 20; STAN 35; Westmoreland County Deeds and Wills No. 1 [1653–1659]:243–244; York County Deeds, Orders, Wills 1 [1648–1657]:167; FOR III:10:49; SR 3131; NUG I:161, 164; PB 2:74, 258, 313; 3:23, 32, 38; 4:86; SR 3127, 3131).

* * *

Philip Ludwell I: Philip Ludwell I, a native of Bruton in Somerset County, England, immigrated to Virginia around 1661 and joined his brother, Secretary of the Colony Thomas Ludwell. In 1667 Philip Ludwell I was made a captain of the James City County militia and married Captain Robert Higginson's daughter, Lucy, who had outlived Major Lewis Burwell I and Colonel William Bernard. Lucy and Philip Ludwell I resided at Fairfield, the Burwell home on Carter's Creek in Gloucester County, and were living there in 1672 when son Philip Ludwell II was born. The couple also had a daughter, Jane, who married the notorious Daniel Parke II and produced Lucy II, who married William Byrd II. Between 1673 and 1675 Lewis Burwell II (Lucy's son by her first husband) probably took possession of Fairfield, for Lucy died on November 6, 1675, and young Burwell (his father's sole heir) came of age and married for the first time. Philip Ludwell I began patenting substantial quantities of land, moved to James City County, and probably joined his brother, Thomas, at Rich Neck.

During the mid-1670s Philip Ludwell I assumed an increasingly prominent role in public life. When Thomas Ludwell set sail for England in November 1674, he authorized Philip to serve as Deputy Secretary of the Colony. During the mid-1670s Philip Ludwell I made numerous appearances in the General Court, where he audited accounts, filed lawsuits, and provided testimony. In 1675 he was named to the Council of State and held office until 1677. He also was the colony's surveyor-general. The Ludwell brothers were two of Governor Berkeley's most loyal supporters throughout Bacon's Rebellion and its turbulent aftermath. Philip Ludwell I was among those who accompanied Berkeley when he fled to the Eastern Shore, and afterward he reported that his goods and those of his ward (his Burwell stepson) had been plundered. He wrote a description of Bacon's Rebellion and was among those who in March 1677 witnessed Sir William Berkeley's will. He was considered a member of the "Green Spring faction," a highly partisan group who remained staunchly loyal to Berkeley after the popular uprising was over. Philip Ludwell I's views, which he frequently voiced, placed him at odds with Lieutenant Governor Herbert Jeffreys. He also was highly critical of Jeffreys' successor, Governor Francis Howard, Lord Effingham. Ludwell's outspokenness led to his being suspended from the council but in 1688 he was elected to the assembly, serving as a burgess for James City County.

Three years after Sir William Berkeley's death, Philip Ludwell I married his widow and heir, Lady Frances Berkeley, who also had outlived her first husband, Samuel Stephens. She moved into the Ludwell home at Rich Neck but continued to identify herself as Lady Frances Berkeley. Although she became pregnant, she and Philip Ludwell I failed to produce children. Therefore, when she died in 1691 her real and personal estate descended to him and then to his son, Philip Ludwell II, the offspring of his marriage to Lucy Higginson Burwell. While Nicholas Spencer I was serving as acting governor (1683–1684), Philip Ludwell I asked the assembly for permission to lease two units of a ruinous brick row house that was located in urban Jamestown, on Back Street. The row house bays, located in the western end of the building, were government-owned, and Ludwell agreed to rebuild them but failed to do so. In 1684 and 1685, after Governor Howard's arrival, Ludwell was hired to re-

build and remodel the colony's statehouse and the secretary's office. In April 1691 he patented a 1½-acre lot adjacent to three central bays in a long, ruinous brick row house at the western end of Jamestown Island. Around the same time, he began serving as Lord Fairfax's agent for the Northern Neck Proprietary. In 1698 Ludwell was identified as the owner of a waterfront lot in urban Jamestown, adjacent to his 1½-acre lot; it was property that had belonged to his late brother, Thomas. Philip Ludwell I retired to England around 1694, entrusting his vast estate to the care of his son, Philip II, who had just come of age. He died in England sometime after 1704 (DOR 1:261, 925; 3:105–106; SHEPPERSON 453; PARKS 225; NUG II:33, 132; STAN 21, 40, 86; EJC I:40, 88, 468, 510; MCGC 355, 382, 385, 515–516, 520, 523; CO 1/2 f 304; 3/1355 ff 152–155; 5/1357 ff 260–261, 271–276, 278, 283; HEN II:560; Beverley 96; SAIN 9:414; LJC 56, 86, 97; JHB 1660–1693:245, 282; AMB 62; PB 8:315; Bruce, "The Indians of Virginia," 356; MORTON 238; CARSON 6; LEO 49; BYRD 102).

Philip Ludwell II: In 1672 Philip Ludwell II, the son of Philip Ludwell I and his first wife, Lucy Higginson Burwell Bernard, was born at Fairfield in Gloucester County. Philip II and his widowed father moved to Rich Neck around 1678 and were in residence there when Philip Ludwell I married Lady Frances Berkeley and became her heir. In 1694, around the time Philip Ludwell II came of age and his father retired to England, Philip Ludwell II moved to Green Spring plantation, making it his permanent home. As his father's heir, Philip Ludwell II inherited his landholdings and those of his stepmother, Lady Frances Berkeley. In 1694 he received a patent for the 1½-acre lot that enveloped the ruinous brick row house that his father had owned in the western end of Jamestown Island. Around 1707 he also came into possession of the eastern end of an enlarged and rebuilt row house on Back Street, a dwelling he bought from John Tullitt.

In 1697 Philip Ludwell II married Hannah, the daughter of Benjamin Harrison II, a member of the Council of State, and produced three children, one of whom was Philip Ludwell III. Like his father, Philip II took an active role in political affairs and held a number of important public offices. He was elected to the assembly in 1695 and was speaker of the 1695–1696 sessions. In 1696 he represented urban Jamestown, and in 1698 and 1699 he was a burgess for James City County. In May 1702 he was named

to the Council of State, and in 1709 he and
his friend William Byrd II of Westover were
commissioned to run the boundary line between Virginia and Carolina. The following year Lieutenant Governor Alexander
Spotswood appointed Philip Ludwell II
deputy auditor-general. Later, when the two
men's relationship became strained, Spotswood laid claim to part of Green Spring,
which he alleged had encroached upon the
Governor's Land, part of the chief executive's stipendiary support. In 1715 Philip
Ludwell II became a county lieutenant and
justice of the James City County court. He
was elected to the vestry of Bruton Parish
and was named a trustee of the College of
William and Mary, serving as rector. For
more than a decade Ludwell and his brother-
in-law, Commissary James Blair, were at
odds with Governor Francis Nicholson. This
ultimately cost Ludwell his council seat
and job as deputy auditor-general. Philip
Ludwell II died on January 11, 1727, leaving as his primary heir 11-year-old Philip
Ludwell III (MORTON 238; SHEPPERSON
1942:454; Bruce, "Title to Green Spring," 19–20,
42, 383–387; "The Indians of Southern Virginia,"
356; STAN 91; LEO 54, 56, 58–59).

Philip Ludwell III: Philip Ludwell III,
the son of Philip Ludwell II and the former
Hannah Harrison, was born at Green Spring
plantation on December 28, 1716, and was
his parents' only son and heir. Ludwell was
orphaned at age 15 and married Frances
Grymes of Morattico a few months before
he attained his majority. The young couple
made their home at Green Spring, where
their three daughters were born. Hannah
Philippa Ludwell, the couple's eldest, was
born on December 21, 1737, and married
William Lee, a London merchant and the
son of Thomas and Hannah Ludwell Lee of
Westmoreland County. Philip Ludwell III,
like his forebears, took an active role in public life and served as a burgess, councilor,
and vestryman. He became a highly valued
assistant to Governor Robert Dinwiddie,
during whose term (1751–1756) he leased
a large parcel in the Governor's Land. After
Frances Grymes Ludwell's death in 1753,
Philip III and his three daughters moved
to London, leaving the management of his
James City County properties in the hands
of overseer Cary Wilkinson. Philip Ludwell
III's health gradually declined. He made
his will on February 28, 1767, and died less
than a month later. His will stipulated that
his real and personal estate in Virginia was
to be distributed among his three daughters, only one of whom (Hannah) was an
adult. The remarkably detailed inventory

of Philip Ludwell III's personal estate lists
his belongings according to the property
with which they were associated. Although
household furnishings, agricultural equipment, livestock, and slaves were attributed
to Green Spring, none of Ludwell's personal belongings were ascribed to Jamestown, where he had one lot that contained
improvements and another that was vacant.
Because Philip Ludwell III's daughter Frances died while his estate was being settled,
her share had to be divided between her
sisters, Hannah Philippa and Lucy. Hannah
Philippa's husband, William Lee, took on
the responsibility of managing the property
she had inherited and ultimately became
her heir. The couple produced a son, William Ludwell Lee, who was heir to Hannah
Phillipa's share of her late father's estate
(Stanard, "Virginia Gleanings in England," 288–
289; "Appraisal of Estate of Philip Ludwell, Esquire," 395–416; "Some Notes on Green Spring,"
293–294; SHEPPERSON 18–19; MORTON 244;
MCGH 652).

**Frances Ludwell (see Frances Culpeper
[Culpepper] Stephens Berkeley)**

Thomas Ludwell: Thomas Ludwell immigrated to Virginia during the 1640s and in
1648 secured a patent for a large tract of land
on the Chickahominy River. He also obtained a leasehold in the Governor's Land
and some acreage in Henrico County. In
1661 he became Secretary of the Colony,
taking over from William Claiborne, and he
briefly served as interim treasurer. On April
10, 1665, Secretary Thomas Ludwell updated the Privy Council on the progress that
had been made in constructing brick houses
in Jamestown and in producing marketable
commodities. He reported that a building
had been erected for conducting government business and another structure constructed as a factory (or meetinghouse) for
merchants. In 1666 Ludwell discussed the
recently built earthen fort in Jamestown and
said that Virginia officials believed that it
was unfeasible to construct fortifications at
Old Point Comfort, at the mouth of the
James River, because of the river's width. A
year later he told his superiors why it had
been necessary to abandon the fort they had
insisted be built at Old Point Comfort, and
he described the June 5, 1667, Dutch attack
on the tobacco fleet and the devastating effects of the August 27, 1667, hurricane. On
January 1, 1667, Ludwell and Thomas Stegg
II, a Henrico County merchant, patented a
half-acre lot that enveloped a building they
had added onto the waterside end of a four-
bay brick row house in the western end of

Jamestown Island. They also purchased an adjoining row house unit from Henry Randolph, whom Ludwell had succeeded as clerk of the General Court. When Stegg II died his interest in the jointly owned row house units went to Ludwell, who in 1672 sold the Randolph dwelling to Governor William Berkeley. In April 1667 Secretary Ludwell was given the responsibility of seeing that incoming ships were cleared before they proceeded elsewhere. In 1668 he informed English officials that five forts had been built to protect the colony's shipping, one on each of the major rivers. Ludwell went on to become the colony's escheator, deputy surveyor, and council president. The lucrative fees he earned enabled him to acquire substantial quantities of land, including Rich Neck plantation in James City and large amounts of acreage in Henrico and Westmoreland counties.

During the 1670s Ludwell was embroiled in numerous personal lawsuits, mostly litigation that involved merchants trading in Virginia. In 1671 he appeared before the General Court in an attempt to recover debts from William May and Thomas Hunt, both of whom were residents of Jamestown. During the early 1670s Ludwell continued to maintain close contact with officials in England, updating them on conditions in the colony. For example, in 1673 he informed them of a Dutch attack on Virginia ships that led to the loss of several vessels. A heated argument between Thomas Ludwell and Giles Bland that occurred at Ludwell's house in 1674 culminated in the exchange of slanderous insults, the threat of a duel, and Bland's being arrested and fined. Bland, who was the son of influential British merchant John Bland, later became one of the rebel Nathaniel Bacon's staunchest supporters. Ludwell went to England in November 1674, leaving his brother, Philip I, to serve as deputy secretary. When word of Bacon's Rebellion reached England, Thomas Ludwell urged the king to send troops to quell the unrest. Ludwell's steadfast loyalty to Governor Berkeley undoubtedly fueled the desire of Bacon's men to destroy some of Ludwell's personal property and steal his livestock. After Bacon's followers set Jamestown ablaze, the General Court's and secretary's office records were stored at Ludwell's home, Rich Neck. In June 1676, when the rebel Nathaniel Bacon's men, who were positioned at the entrance to Jamestown Island, fired two great guns at the capital city, the brick row house in which Thomas Ludwell had an interest was a conspicuous target and was in relatively close range. If it withstood the bombardment, it surely sustained extensive damage on September 19, 1676, when Bacon's men put the capital city to the torch. Thomas Ludwell became ill during 1676 and died in the latter half of 1677. When he made his will on November 10, 1676, he named Thomas Thorp and Jamestown residents Theophilus Hone and Henry Hartwell as his Virginia executors and London merchant John Jeffreys as his executor in England. He bequeathed the bulk of his estate to his brother, Philip I, naming his sister, Jane, and nephew, Philip Ludwell II, as additional heirs. Thomas Ludwell's will was presented for probate in early 1678 (EEAC 37; MCGC 205, 217–218, 239, 241, 247, 290, 331, 390, 396, 399, 484, 486, 488, 490–492, 507, 510, 512, 514–516, 518–519, 521; HEN II:39, 404, 456; NUG I:145, 178, 429; II:57, 84, 92; STAN 21, 38; CO 1/19 ff 75, 213; 1/20 f 218; 1/21 f 37, 113, 116, 282–283; 1/23 f 31; 1/25 f 85; 1/30 f 120; 1/41 f 35; 5/1355 ff 60–64, 200, 202–203; SAIN 5:#975, #1250, #1410, #1506, #1508; PB 6:223; Stegg 1671; WITH 667; ASPIN 9:1:175; Wiseman Book of Records).

* * *

John Lullett: John Lullett died in Jamestown sometime after April 1623 but before February 16, 1624 (VI&A 469).

Thomas Lunn (Lun): On November 15, 1693, Thomas Lunn sought compensation from the assembly, payment for the nails and plank he had used while working on the statehouse, which also was being used as General Courthouse. The burgesses refused to pay him, claiming that they had authorized repairs to the statehouse, not remodeling, and that Lunn had changed the building into a different form. The Council of State insisted that the work was necessary and said that Lunn should be paid in currency, not tobacco. The assembly continued to voice its objections (LJC 206–208).

Sir Thomas Lunsford: Sir Thomas Lunsford, who was from Wylie in Sussex, England, reportedly was a hot-headed royalist who came to Virginia in 1649. He was named to the Council of State in 1650 and took office in 1651. In 1650 he patented more than 3,400 acres that bordered the Rappahannock River's Portobago Bay, opposite the area called Nanzattico. The land that Lunsford claimed was home to the Portobago and Nanzattico Indians. Lunsford married Secretary Richard Kemp's widow, Elizabeth, and resided at Rich Neck, where he died in 1653. Lunsford's daughter Catherine (Katherine) stayed on in Virginia; however, his other daughters, Elizabeth,

Philippa, and Mary, returned to England and were entrusted to the care of Sir John Thorogood. In 1670 the former Catherine Lunsford, who had married councilor Peter Jennings, claimed her late father's land on Portobago Bay, in what eventually became Caroline County. After Jennings' death in 1671, she went on to marry Ralph Wormeley II. Official records reveal that in 1670 the Lunsford land was part of a preserve or reservation that had been assigned to two of the colony's tributary Indian tribes, the Portobago and the Nanzattico. Catherine Lunsford Jennings Wormeley was allowed to seat her late father's patent as long as she did not disturb the Indians living there. A Northumberland County document dating to 1658 reveals that the late Thomas Lunsford also had owned land near Potomac Creek (WITH 493; Lower Norfolk Book B:142, 204; STAN 36; MCGC 227; NUG I:200; SR 2013, 6633, 12654; Northumberland County Deeds, Wills &c. 1661–1662:28a; WITH 299).

Philip Luxon: In July 1637 Philip Luxon, captain of the *Blessing*, ran afoul of the law when he and some crew members helped themselves to some "strong waters" that William Harris of Jamestown had imported. The incident occurred while the ship was anchored at Jamestown (HCA 13/53 f 249; SR 5862).

Susanna Lyall: On October 12, 1627, Susanna Lyall witnessed the will that Sir George Yeardley made in his house in urban Jamestown (VI&A 470).

George Lydall (Lidall): On June 8, 1680, George Lydall, a resident of New Kent County, was authorized to sell the government-owned weaponry that was in his possession. He was then a lieutenant colonel in the militia and was ordered to raise men to protect the frontiers. In 1684 he was given the responsibility of providing housing for a company of rangers sent to protect the frontier. The vestry records of St. Peter's Parish indicate that Colonel George Lydall died on January 19, 1705 (JHB 1660–1693:151; EJC I:7, 9, 57; VBSP 435). Lydall may have been a kinsman of New Kent County burgess John Lydall, who acquired some of his property, acreage that the decedent had deserted.

John Lydall (Lyddall, Lidall): John Lydall and William Overton patented 837 acres in St. Peter's Parish of New Kent County in 1690. Lydall already owned 2,248 acres in St. John's Parish, land that was located on the lower side of Black Creek. Part of the New Kent County tract he acquired included 1,600 acres that had been granted to Captain George Lydall, who deserted it. John Lydall, who was a New Kent County justice, sheriff, and tobacco collector, played an active role in the life of St. Peter's Parish. He served as a churchwarden and vestryman and sometimes hosted vestry meetings in his home. On occasion he also served as a processioner. As a burgess for New Kent County, he attended the assembly sessions held in 1691–1692 and 1693. When a patentee claimed land in 1698 on the south side of the Pamunkey River, he noted that it was adjacent to Lydall's plantation, Mantuen. John Lydall was on a committee that was authorized to build a new parish church, and at one point his plantation was used as the parish's glebe. John Lydall died sometime prior to July 13, 1703, and on October 1st of that year, the Council of State heard testimony about Colonel John Lightfoot's detention of two shoemakers who belonged to the decedent's estate. By September 1705 Lydall's widow and executor had married Philip Levermore. Her given name appears to have been Barbara (LEO 50, 52; PB 8:45, 121; 9:173; EJC II:338; VBSP 21, 30, 33, 35, 42–43, 74, 94–96, 112, 133, 136, 386, 671).

Lydia: On February 15, 1768, when an inventory was made of the late Richard Ambler's slaves on Jamestown Island and his leasehold in the Governor's Land, an adult female slave named Lydia was listed. In 1769 she was living on Jamestown Island and was part of the late Edward Ambler I's estate (York County Wills and Inventories 21:386–391; AMB-E).

Thomas Lyne: In August 1655 Thomas Lyne, who was mentioned in Anthony Barham's will, was identified as the guardian of Elizabeth Fleet's heirs. Sometime prior to that time, Mrs. Fleet had owned half of a waterfront lot in urban Jamestown (Barham 1641; PB 3:367; NUG I:313).

Elizabeth Lyon: In 1619 Elizabeth Lyon, a young wench, was transported to Virginia. In February 1624 she was a servant in Sir George Yeardley's household in urban Jamestown (VI&A 471).

Richard Lynny (Lynsey): On May 25, 1671, Richard Lynny sued the estate of John Grove of Surry County. On February 26, 1678, the justices of Surry County's court noted that William Corker of Jamestown was one of Lynny's debtors (MCGC 259; Surry County Will Book 2:140).

M

King of the Machodoc (Machoatick, Muchchotas) Indians (Native American): In 1650 the king of the Machodoc agreed to accept six matchcoats or cloth cloaks from six Northumberland County men in exchange for some acreage in a neck of land between the mouth of the Chacoma River (Upper Machodoc Creek) and a smaller stream (Lower Machodoc Creek), property that extended toward a location the Indians called Photomoke. In February 1656 the Machodoc Indians complained that Isaac Allerton had intruded on the land that had been set aside for their town (Northumberland County Deeds and Orders 1650–1652:50; 1652–1665:107).

Machumps (Mechumps, Muchamps, Munchumps) (Native American): In 1610–1611 Machumps, an Indian, frequently mingled with the Jamestown colonists, with Powhatan's permission. He also made one or more trips to England, and when in Virginia he sometimes dined with the colony's deputy governor, Sir Thomas Dale. According to William Strachey, Machumps told the Jamestown settlers about some fair-skinned people who were living in the countryside to the south, perhaps the "Lost Colonists." The name of Mechumps Creek in Hanover most likely is derived from that of Machumps (HAI 550, 596, 619, 655).

* * *

Machywap (Macky-wap, Machiawao) (Native American): In November 1655 the justices of Northumberland County acknowledged that Machywap, king of the Chicacoan Indians, had delivered 100 arm's lengths of roanoke (shell money) to Colonel John Mottrom, as promised. Therefore, the overseers of Mottrom's will were ordered to see that Machywap was compensated to the Indian king's satisfaction. It is uncertain what kind of bargain Machywap and Mottrom had made. In January 1656 Northumberland County's justices ordered Gervase Dodson to survey Machywap's acreage at Great Wicocomoco, to make sure that his people were provided with the amount of land to which they were entitled under the law. Machywap was then identified as king of the Chicacoan and Wicocomoco Indians. When Northumberland County's court reconvened In February 1656, it was noted

that Mackywap was then in danger from some of his own people, the Wicocomoco, because he had rendered assistance to the colonists. Six armed men were therefore ordered to protect him at the county's expense until the end of November 1656. They also were to ensure that he remained the Indians' leader or werowance. If Machywap found himself in greater danger, he was supposed to ask the local militia captain, Richard Budd, for assistance. In June 1666 Machywap's son, William, filed a petition with the justices of Northumberland County's monthly court (Northumberland County Order Book 1652–1665:69, 78, 107, 445).

William (Native American): In June 1666 William, the son of Machywap, king of the Chicacoan and Wicocomoco Indians, filed a petition with the justices of Northumberland County's monthly court (Northumberland County Order Book 1652–1665:445).

* * *

Samuel Macock (Maycock, Macocke, Morecock): Samuel Macock went to Virginia sometime prior to March 1618, when Deputy Governor Samuel Argall sought permission for him to serve as a clergyman due to the scarcity of ordained ministers. In 1619 Macock, who lived at Bermuda Hundred, became a councilor and served until 1622. He had a patent for 2,000 acres of land on the east side of Powell's Creek's mouth and established a plantation he called "Macock's Divident." Macock was killed there during the March 1622 Indian attack. During the mid-1620s, Sarah (Sara), Samuel Macock's orphaned daughter, lived in urban Jamestown in the home of Captain Roger Smith and his wife, Jane, John Rolfe's widow. In May 1626 the General Court noted that young Sarah was entitled to 200 acres of land as her late father's heir. The property she inherited probably was part of the Charles City plantation known as Macock's. Sarah Macock eventually married George Pace, the son of ancient planters Isabell and Richard Pace I of Paces Paines (VI&A 471; STAN 29; LEO xx).

Gideon Macon: Gideon Macon served as a burgess for New Kent County and attended the assembly sessions held in 1693, 1696–1697, 1698, and 1699. He may have been involved in the fur trade, for he consistently patented large expanses of swampland and marsh. In 1694 he patented a 155-acre island in the Chickahominy Swamp in New Kent County, and four years later he laid claim to three small islands in the same area, but included within the boundaries of Henrico County. In 1700 he acquired 545 acres in the fork of the Chickahominy River in New Kent County, and finally, in 1702, he patented two parcels on Pampatike Swamp in King and Queen County (LEO 53, 56, 58–59; PB 8:359; 9:172, 289, 345, 354).

* * *

Mrs. Ann (Anne) Macon (Mason) (Mrs. William Macon [Mason]): On April 16, 1684, the assembly authorized Mrs. Ann (Anne) Macon to receive payment for providing meeting space to the assembly, the council, the General Court, and certain committees, and for furnishing two upstairs rooms that served as a clerk's office (JHB 1660–1693:256). Therefore, she owned or rented a house in Jamestown, the colony's capital city. Mrs. Ann Macon may have been the widow of William Macon (Mason), whose estate was compensated for providing entertainment to an official messenger. She also may have had a familial connection with the late Thomas Rabley, who owned a fine house on Jamestown's waterfront, or with Rabley's widow, Jane, whose executor was burgess Francis Mason of Surry County.

William Macon (Mason): On April 16, 1684, the assembly authorized payment to the late William Macon's estate for the decedent's having provided entertainment to an official messenger. Macon had been a resident of Surry County in 1673 when he purchased some Nansemond County land from Thomas Ballard (JHB 1660–1693:256; Surry County Order Book 1671–1691:28; NUG II:141; PB 6:498). Macon or Mason may have been survived by a widow, Mrs. Ann (Anne) Macon, and perhaps was the brother of Francis Mason, a Surry County burgess.

* * *

Isaac (Isack) Madison (Maddeson, Maddison): Isaac Madison came to Virginia in 1611 and in 1616 was placed in command of West and Shirley Hundred. In December 1620 he sought permission to return to England, saying that he had been in Virginia for 12 years, had served Sir Thomas Dale, and had explored the colony on the Virginia Company's behalf. In July 1621 the Company rewarded Madison with free transportation for his wife and himself, two shares of land, and two apprentices. According to Captain John Smith, Isaac Madison captured the king of Potomac and his son and for a time lived with the Potomac Indians. In November 1622 Madison was given the right to serve as sole truck master or trader with the Indians. He and his wife, Mary, were living at their plantation on West and Shirley Hundred Island in 1624, when he served as the area's burgess. He also was named to the Council of State. Madison died sometime prior to January 22, 1625 (VI&A 472; LEO 5).

James Madison: Bishop James Madison, a cousin of President James Madison, was born near Staunton, Virginia, in 1749 and graduated from the College of William and Mary in 1771. He studied law and was admitted to the bar, but did not practice. Then, in 1773 he became a professor of natural philosophy and mathematics at the College of William and Mary. Two years later he set sail for England, where he undertook further study and was ordained an Anglican clergyman. He returned to William and Mary in 1777 and was elected president, a post he held until his death in 1812. Madison was a staunch patriot and organized a militia company composed of college students. He also played an important role in the reorganization of the Episcopal Church in Virginia and in 1785 was first president of the church's first Convention. In 1790 he went to England, where he was consecrated bishop by the Archbishop of Canterbury. On October 28, 1798, Bishop Madison, Dr. Philip Barraud, and two other gentlemen decided to visit John Ambler II's home on Jamestown Island. When they reached the log-and-stone causeway that linked the island to the mainland, Madison insisted on dismounting from their carriage and walking across; however, the logs were slippery and he toppled into Sandy Bay. Dr. Barraud and the others plucked him from the water. Afterward, the Bishop dined at the Ambler residence, where his companions teased him good-naturedly about his inability to walk on water (Barraud 1798; MEADE I:29; www.history.org).

Francis (Francisco) Maguel (Miguel): On July 1, 1610, Francis Maguel, an Irishman purportedly spying on behalf of Spain, prepared a written description of the Virginia colony, where he had lived for eight months. He probably left Virginia on April 19, 1608, with Captain Christopher Newport, who had brought the 1st Supply of new settlers. Maguel described the natural resources the colonists had found in Virginia. His report was enclosed in a letter that the Spanish ambassador in London sent to the king of Spain. Maguel may have used aliases such as Magill or Maguire (VI&A 473).

Edward Major (Maior): Virginia Land Office records reveal that sometime prior to August 1637 Edward Major patented some acreage in Upper Norfolk County and that he owned some land in Charles River (later, York) County. In October 1644 Major claimed 450 acres on the Nansemond River in Upper Norfolk County. When he repatented his holdings a few months later, he added another 50 acres. In September 1645 Major secured some land on the upper side of the James River, in Warwick County. In 1645–1646 Edward Major served as a burgess for Upper Norfolk County and was holding office in 1646, when the county officially became Nansemond County. He was speaker of the assembly in 1652, while the Commonwealth government was in power, and represented Nansemond County in 1653. In August 1652 a case was aired before the justices of Lower Norfolk County's monthly court that mentioned a business transaction that Major had made with Captain John Sibsey, by then deceased; the issue was resolved in February 1653 (LEO 24–25, 29, 31; Lower Norfolk County Record Book B:35a, 36, 121a; C:16, 40; PB 1:460, 659, 677; 2:17, 43, 89, 153; 5:313).

Philip Mallory: In December 1656, when the assembly decided that Virginia clergy and six of their servants would be exempt from public levies, the Rev. Philip Mallory and Mr. John Green were ordered to verify clergy exemptions. In March 1660 Mallory was paid for officiating at the last two assembly sessions, and he and the Rev. Peter Lansdale were asked to preach at the next assembly meeting (HEN I:424, 549).

Henry Lord Maltravers: Henry Lord Maltravers, the Duke of Norfolk's son, was one of King Charles I's favorites. In 1636 he authorized Maltravers to produce copper farthings that could be used in England, Ireland, Wales, and any of the American colonies except Maryland, and gave him a monopoly that was good for 21 years. The king ordered Virginia's governor, Sir John Harvey, to announce that the farthing tokens were to be considered currency. On April 18, 1637, the king gave Maltravers a large grant on the south side of the James River, acreage that encompassed what became Nansemond and Norfolk counties and parts of Isle of Wight County and Carolina. The king also ordered Governor Harvey, who had been

thrust from office and then reinstated, to assist Maltravers. Therefore, Harvey gave Maltravers the territory on the south side of the James River that became Upper and Lower Norfolk counties, today's cities of Suffolk, Norfolk, Chesapeake, and Virginia Beach. Harvey's eager acquiescence to the king's commands thoroughly alienated the Council of State, whose members strenuously objected to the loss of Virginia territory and potential tax revenues. Council members also were very critical of his blind obedience to the king. In 1700 Dr. John Cox, as Henry Lord Maltravers' heir, tried to assert a claim to Norfolk County (NEILL 134; CO 5/1359 ff 383–388; SAIN 1:153; SR 4156, 4544, 5014, 7293, 7390, 7745).

John Manby: John Manby died in Jamestown sometime after April 1623 but before February 16, 1624 (VI&A 474).

Mangopeesomon (Native American) (see Opechancanough)

David (Davy) Mansell (Mansill, Mansfield, Mainsfield, Monsell): David Mansell came to Virginia in 1619 and during the mid-1620s was living on the lower side of the James River on the Treasurer's Plantation. He was identified as one of Treasurer George Sandys' men and was a hired hand. In 1633 Mansell was a burgess for Martin's Hundred and owned land near Skiff's Creek and the parish church. He was returned to office in 1640 and represented the freeholders living in James City County—in Johnson's (i.e., Jockey's) Neck, Archer's Hope, and the Neck O'Land. In 1652 he represented James City County. As time went on, Mansell continued to acquire land in the vicinity of Martin's Hundred. By the 1650s he had moved to Old Rappahannock County and begun speculating in real estate. In 1665 Captain David Mansell disposed of half of the 460-acre plantation on which he was then living, acreage near Farnham Creek. When he prepared his will on July 24, 1672, he made bequests to his daughter, Mary, grandchild Mansell Blagrave, and a couple of friends. He died sometime prior to September 1672 (VI&A 474; STAN 68; LEO 18, 29; Old Rappahannock County Deeds and Wills 1656–1662:47, 73–74; 1665–1677:8–9, 12, 125–127; 1677–1682:215–216, 317–318).

Thomas Maples (Mayples): In September 1668 Thomas Maples and William Hitchman patented 200 acres on Warraney Creek in western James City County. A month later they patented another 536 acres. On March 22, 1677, Thomas Maples was brought before Governor William Berkeley and the Council of State, who were conducting a military tribunal. Although he was accused of supporting the rebel Nathaniel Bacon's cause, it was decided that Maples would be released if he took an oath of obedience and paid a substantial fine: 1,000 pounds of pork that could be used by the king's soldiers. In May 1679 Henry Hartwell, who had been one of Governor Berkeley's supporters, patented the 736 acres formerly claimed by Maples and Hitchman, indicating that the land had not been seated (MCGC 461, 533; PB 6:169–170, 690).

* * *

George Marable (Marble) I: When he re-patented his half-acre waterfront lot in urban Jamestown on February 25, 1663, George Marable I indicated that he had purchased it from the heirs of Mrs. Ann Talbott, who had bought her acreage from Thomas Woodhouse on September 1, 1657. In 1663 reference was made to "Marables now dwelling House," a unit or bay in a brick row house that was built in response to the 1662 building initiative. On October 31, 1673, the General Court authorized Marable to patent some vacant land that was adjacent to his house in Jamestown. During the 1670s he made numerous appearances before the General Court. In 1673 he was given the task of evaluating some work bricklayer John Bird did for Jamestown resident Richard James I, and in 1674 he and some others were told to view the brickwork done by Ralph Deane. Marable successfully sued Nicholas Wyatt, Robert Parke, Peter Dale, Alexander Spencer, William Rookings, and Christopher Foster. In 1675 he gave his power of attorney to William Edwards II of Jamestown, who on several occasions collected debts on Marable's behalf in the Surry County court. In 1676 he appealed a James City County court decision in Henry Burton's favor and lost because he failed to appear to press his case. In 1677 Marable was paid for a court appearance in Surry. He also prevailed in litigation undertaken in 1679 as Benjamin Harrison's assignee. By March 3, 1675, George Marable I had married Bennett Marjorum's widow, Agnes, and had taken possession of the decedent's estate. After Agnes's death Marable married a woman named Catherine. He died sometime prior to July 1683, leaving his widow and executrix, Catherine, who enjoyed liferights in the couple's home in Jamestown even after she remarried. He also was survived by a son, George Marable II, whom he named as reversionary heir. By 1683 the

widowed Catherine Marable had wed Henry Gawler, who used their home as an ordinary or tavern. During the mid- to late 1680s, while Henry and Catherine Marable Gawler had possession of her late husband's row house unit, the dwelling was used as a meeting place by the Council of State, the General Court, and the assembly. On at least two occasions, tributary Indians were accommodated there while they were in Jamestown on official business (MCGC 327, 344, 359, 369, 403, 447; PB 5:253–254; AMB 62; MCGH 875; Charles City County Order Book 1685:5; Surry County Deeds, Wills &c. 1671–1684:119; Order Book 1671–1691:127, 155–156, 160, 262, 409; JHB 1660–1693:256–257; LJC 88–89; Stanard, "The Randolph Manuscript," 23).

George Marable II: George Marable I's son and reversionary heir, George II, eventually came into possession of his late father's lot and brick row house on urban Jamestown's waterfront after Catherine Marable Gawler died. In 1692 he was living there when he provided room and board to three men accused of piracy. It was a politically charged case that involved London merchant Micajah Perry, who sought to have the accused men freed. Marable also was living there in late 1692 or early 1693, when he was compensated for hosting a government committee meeting "at his brick house" in Jamestown. He was married to John Hartwell I's daughter, Mary, with whom he produced two sons, George III and Henry Hartwell Marable. George Marable II became a James City County justice in 1693 and in 1697, while sheriff, attended sessions of the General Court, probably as sergeant-at-arms. The fact that he was called upon to investigate the cause of the October 1698 statehouse fire suggests that he was considered an intelligent, responsible member of the community. On November 12, 1696, Marable sold his late father's brick house and waterfront lot to William Sherwood. The east wall of the Marable dwelling abutted the brick row house then occupied by John Jarrett, William Sherwood's nephew, a dwelling that was owned by Micajah Perry and Company. The west wall of the Marable home abutted the ruins of a row house unit that belonged to Philip Ludwell I. When William Sherwood made his will in 1697, he made a bequest to George Marable II and named him an executor.

George Marable II and his brother, William, inherited their late father's 117-acre leasehold in the Governor's Land, just west of Jamestown Island, and later, George II acquired a 422-acre parcel there. Governor Francis Nicholson tried to force him to surrender his lease by having him arrested and fined. In 1707 Marable and some of the other Governor's Land tenants ran afoul of the law by refusing to pay rent while the governorship was vacant. In 1699 Marable patented 135 acres of escheat land in Jockey's Neck. He also was among those voicing objections to Bartholomew Fowler's election as Jamestown's burgess. With the exception of the 1710–1712 sessions, George Marable II served as a burgess for James City County between 1700 and 1718, and in 1707 he was part of a group serving as a court of oyer and terminer. He caused some controversy in 1708 when he closed access to "the ancient Road from the New Bridge to James City," preventing Governor's Land tenant Samuel Richardson from having access to his own leasehold. In 1706 he was among the James City County justices who asked the assembly for brick from the old statehouse for use in building a new county courthouse in Jamestown. In 1709 a group of servants and slaves planned to rise up against their masters, and some of Major George Marable II's enslaved blacks were involved. In 1712 Marable, who was then a James City County justice, was accused of malfeasance and removed from office (LJC 179, 181, 459; EJC I:363, 392–393; III:141, 160, 203, 316; SAIN 18:728; 21:285; 22:158; PALM I:45, 99, 146; AMB 62, 65; Soane 1683; NUG III:33; JHB 1695–1702:139; MCGH 873, 875; York County Deeds, Orders, Wills 3:38; Surry County Will Book 6:184; Stanard, "The Randolph Manuscript," 23; STAN 94–95, 100–102; LEO 60, 62, 64, 67–69).

William Marable: William Marable and his brother, George II, inherited their late father's 117 acre leasehold in the Governor's Land. The Marable brothers, who were George Marable I's sons, also patented a 12 acre island near the mouth of College Creek. In 1731, while William Marable was a James City County justice, he and his wife, Elizabeth, acquired 147 acres of local land that had belonged to Dr. Joseph Chermaison and his wife, Elizabeth, acreage that had escheated to the Crown. William was James City County's sheriff in 1734, an indication that he still was a justice of the peace. He went on to become a James City County burgess and attended the assembly sessions held between 1736 and 1740 (MCGH 875; Soane 1683; NUG III:170, 410; EJC IV:236, 319, 413; STAN 108, 110, 112; LEO 76).

Benjamin Marable: On August 13, 1747, Benjamin Marable, who inherited 105 acres of the late George Marable II's 422-acre leasehold in the Governor's Land, received a patent from Governor William Gooch. He immediately assigned his property to William Nugent, who on May 31, 1747, had sold his 105 acres to Richard Ambler, who was methodically enlarging his holdings on the mainland (AMB 167). Benjamin Marable's relationship to William and George Marable II is unclear. However, his entitlement to a portion of the late George II's property suggests that he may have been the decedent's brother.

* * *

Bennett Marjorum: On March 3, 1675, the General Court's justices noted that Agnes Marable, the wife of Jamestown resident and landowner George Marable I, was Bennett Marjorum's widow and heir. James Alsop of Jamestown was then in possession of Marjorum's estate (MCGC 403).

Mark: When Richard Ambler made his will in 1765, he mentioned an enslaved carpenter named Mark. On February 15, 1768, when an inventory was made of Ambler's slaves on Jamestown Island and his leasehold in the Governor's Land, an adult male slave named Mark was listed. In 1769 Mark was identified as a carpenter when he was included in the late Edward Ambler I's estate. He was then attributed to Jamestown Island (York County Wills and Inventories 21:378–382, 386–391; AMB-E).

Robert Markham: On May 20, 1607, Robert Markham, a sailor who came to Virginia in the first group of Jamestown colonists, accompanied Captain Christopher Newport when he explored the James River (VI&A 475).

Robert Markham (Marcum) alias Moutapass: In 1621 Captain John Smith identified Robert Markham alias Moutapass of the Eastern Shore as a fugitive who had lived among the northerly Indians for five years (VI&A 475).

Walgrave (Waldegrave) Marks (Markes): On December 21, 1624, Walgrave Marks served on the jury that conducted young George Pope II's inquest. In January 1625 he testified that he had witnessed an agreement between Thomas Passmore and John Hall (Haule), both of whom were residents of Jamestown. Marks and John Jefferson then jointly headed a household in urban Jamestown. On April 18, 1625, Marks witnessed an agreement made by Nathaniel Bass of Basses Choice (VI&A 475).

Thomas Marlet (Marlett, Marlott, Marloe): Thomas Marlet, a grocer from Sussex, England, came to Virginia in 1619 and in 1624 represented the College in the assembly. By January 1625 he had moved to the Maine, just west of Jamestown Island. Marlet's role in community affairs suggests that he was considered a trustworthy, responsible citizen who probably was literate (VI&A 476; LEO 5).

William Marriloe: On August 16, 1670, William Marriloe sold some Surry County land to James Alsop of Jamestown (Surry County Deeds, Wills &c. 1671–1684:73).

William Marriott: On May 3, 1658, William Marriott of Surry County testified that he went to the store (probably a storehouse) at Goose Hill, in the eastern end of Jamestown Island. In March 1660 Marriott signed a marriage contract with Susanna, the daughter of Colonel Thomas Swann I and his first wife, Margaret. In September 1665 Marriott purchased 50 acres in Surry from John Corker, a Jamestown landowner (Surry County Deeds, Wills &c. 1652–1672:119, 151, 263).

Robert Marshall: Robert Marshall came to Virginia in 1619 and in 1624 was living on the Governor's Land, just west of Jamestown Island. In June 1624 he became engaged to Eleanor Sprad, who broke the law by simultaneously agreeing to marry two men. Marshall quickly found another partner, and in January 1625 he and his wife, Ann, were living on Jamestown Island, probably on the rural parcel that he and Thomas Grubb were leasing. In April 1625 Marshall asked the General Court to partition the land he and Grubb held jointly. He seems to have struck out on his own, for during 1626 he commenced leasing a nearby 10-acre parcel, which he patented on September 20, 1628. During the mid- to late 1620s Marshall made several appearances before the General Court, where he brought suits against debtors but also was sued (VI&A 476–477).

William Marshall: When William Marshall was involved in a lawsuit in 1672, Barnaby Kearney served as his security, guaranteeing that he would appear in court when his case was tried. Marshall represented Elizabeth City County in the assembly sessions held in 1691–1692, and he also was a trustee of the town of Hampton. During the summer of 1692, while he was aboard the HMS *Assurance*, he got into a brawl with boatswain William Dolby and

Edward Legg, a member of the crew. Marshall died as a result of the fight, and Dolby and Legg were tried by the General Court, found guilty of murder, and sentenced to die. In January 1693 Dolby's wife sent a plea to England on her husband's behalf. King William intervened and ordered Virginia's governor to see that the two incarcerated men were sent to England. Captain William Marshall's wife, Hannah, served as his administratrix, an indication that he had died intestate. By March 26, 1694, she had married Richard Booker (or Brooks) of Gloucester County (LEO 50; SR 238, 375, 1187, 5010, 6324; MCGC 312, 338, 351; EJC I:266, 296; NEAL 17, 26, 36, 45, 48, 79, 94, 110, 119).

Nicholas Martiau (Marteu, Marteaw, Marteau): Nicholas Martiau, a naturalized French Protestant, came to Virginia in 1620. After the 1622 Indian attack, he lived in Jamestown for a while. By February 1624 he had moved to Kecoughtan (Elizabeth City) and commenced serving as a burgess for that area. He married Jane, the widow of Lieutenant Edward Bartley (Bartlett), and produced a daughter, Elizabeth, who was born in 1625. On July 5, 1627, Jane Bartley Martiau delivered an inventory of her late husband's estate to the General Court and attested to its accuracy. Nicholas Martiau was among the first to seat land in Chiskiack around 1629–1630, planting what became known as York Plantation. In 1640 he received a patent for 1,300 acres there: 600 acres to which he was entitled for establishing a home at Chiskiack while it was on the colony's frontier, and another 700 acres for headrights. Three of the headrights he used were for his wife, Jane; his daughter, Elizabeth; and his wife's daughter, Jane Bartley. Martiau served as a burgess for Chiskiack and the Isle of Kent (in what became Maryland) in 1632 and 1633. Around 1641 Elizabeth Martiau married George Read. Her mother, Jane Bartley Martiau, died prior to November 5, 1646, at which time Nicholas married Isabella, who had outlived Robert Felgate and George Beach. Martiau helped his new wife settle Beach's estate. Nicholas Martiau died in 1657 (VI&A 477–478; LEO 5, 10–12; DOR 2:503–505).

George Martin: George Martin, a gentleman, came to Virginia in 1607 and was one of the first Jamestown settlers (VI&A 479).

* * *

John Martin I: Captain John Martin I and his son, John Martin II, arrived in Virginia in 1607 and were among the first Jamestown settlers. Captain Martin, a Virginia Company investor, became one of the colony's first councilors and reportedly was highly opinionated. He became ill during the summer of 1607 but gradually regained his health. In 1608 Martin ventured above the falls of the James River and came back to Jamestown with samples of a mineral he mistook for gold. He went to England but returned to Virginia, and when Lord Delaware arrived in June 1610, he designated Martin the master of the battery works for steel and iron. In 1611 Martin was wounded during an offensive against the Nansemond Indians but survived. When the assembly convened in July 1619, Thomas Davis and Richard Stacy, the burgesses from his plantation, Martin's Brandon, were refused representation because Martin insisted that his property was exempt from the colony's laws. Martin proffered that Virginia would be better off as a royal colony. As time went on, he continued to spark controversy. He was a member of the Council of State in 1624–1625, while he was living in Elizabeth City. Captain John Martin made his last recorded appearance in court on January 9, 1629, when he was in his early 60s (VI&A 479; STAN 27; LEO xx, 3).

John Martin II: John Martin II, the son of Captain John Martin, arrived in Virginia in 1607 and was one of the first Jamestown settlers. Captain John Smith described him as a gentleman. According to George Percy, John Martin II died on August 18, 1607 (VI&A 480).

* * *

John Martin (Marten): John Martin, Lord Delaware's personal servant, accompanied Lord Delaware on his 1618 voyage to Virginia. Delaware died enroute and Martin continued on to Jamestown. When Sir George Yeardley arrived in April 1619 and commenced serving as governor, Martin became one of his most trusted servants. He lived in the Yeardley home in urban Jamestown and attended the governor as his personal servant. He also worked closely with Edmund Rossingham, Yeardley's factor and overseer. In 1622 Martin, who was then in England, was identified as a gentleman when he testified about the disposition of Lord Delaware's goods in Virginia. He said that he was among the men Deputy Governor Argall sent to the West Indies on the *Treasurer,* a vessel that captured an Angola ship carrying some of the very first Africans brought to Virginia. In May 1622 John Martin, who intended to return to Virginia, asked

Virginia Company officials not to consider him a "foreigner," a designation that increased the customs rates a person was obliged to pay. He reminded them that he was a Company investor and said that although he had been born in Persia, he had been baptized. In 1630 two people testified that Martin was commonly known as "the Persian," although some people thought that he was Armenian (Iranian). He had a connection with Jamestown as late as 1637 (VI&A 480).

John Martin (Marten, Martyn): In October 1651 John Martin patented 600 acres on Bennetts Creek in Lower Norfolk County. By October 1654 he had acquired an additional 1,400 acres in that area. He served as a burgess for Lower Norfolk County in 1652, and in December of that year he received compensation for his attendance at an assembly meeting. When Martin testified in court in January 1654, he said that he was age 37 or thereabouts. By 1656 he had become a justice of Lower Norfolk County's court, an office he held for several years. He was among those who in December 1655 proved the late Henry Woodhouse's will and also that of Thomas Nedham. In 1662 he repatented the 1,400 acres on Bennetts Creek that he had claimed in 1654, and a year later he patented 350 acres of escheat land. Finally, in October 1665 he patented 578 acres on the Lynnhaven River. John Martin died sometime prior to September 1671, and Anthony Lawson began occupying Martin's Lower Norfolk County plantations. The decedent's sister, Ann, the wife of Adam Keeling, inherited the acreage and sued Lawson in an attempt to eject him from the property. The matter ended up in the General Court, whose justices ordered Lawson to vacate the Martin acreage. In 1692 John Martin's son and heir, Joell, sold the decedent's "Great Plantation," which then lay within the bounds of Princess Anne County but formerly was part of Lower Norfolk County (LEO 29; Lower Norfolk County Record Book C:31, 72, 181, 204; Wills, Deeds, Orders D [1656–1666]:1, 340; Princess Anne County Deed Book 1:28; PB 2:343; 3:307; 5:336, 476, 540; MCGC 275).

Peter (Petter) Martin (Marttin): Peter Martin died in Jamestown sometime after April 1623 but before February 16, 1624, and on January 3, 1625, Richard Kingsmill presented Martin's will to the court. Martin reportedly described Richard Cornish, a condemned criminal who had been executed, as a good mariner (VI&A 481).

Ralph Martin: Ralph Martin, a husband-man from Bachain in Somershire, arrived in Jamestown on September 12, 1623 (VI&A 481).

Ruth Martin: In 1621 Ruth Martin, an indentured servant, was sent to Dr. John Pott, a resident of Jamestown, by the Company of Mercers (VI&A 481).

Mary: In 1769 an adult female slave named Mary was living on Jamestown Island and was attributed to Edward Ambler I's estate (AMB-E).

Masco (Masquran) (Native American): On May 27, 1658, Masco, one of the Rappahannock Indians' Great Men or leaders, was among the natives confirming a land transaction made by the Rappahannock's late king, Accapataugh, and Colonel Moore Fauntleroy. A few months earlier the Rappahannock had made a peace agreement with the county justices (Old Rappahannock County Deed Book 1656–1664:10–11, 26–27).

Mason (Indian Mason) (Native American): When some Richmond County land on the north side of the Rappahannock River was sold in January 1693, the acreage belonging to Indian Mason and Joseph Mason was mentioned (Richmond County Deed Book 1 [1692–1693]:192–195a).

* * *

Francis Mason I: Francis Mason I, an ancient planter, was living in Elizabeth City during the mid-1620s. By January 1625 his first wife, Mary, was dead and he had married a woman named Alice. They shared their home with his son, Francis II, who was Virginia-born. Sometime prior to November 1635, he patented some land adjacent to Thomas Willoughby, in what was then Elizabeth City (but later, Lower Norfolk) County. Lieutenant Mason became a local justice in 1637. When he testified in Lower Norfolk County's monthly court on July 19, 1641, he indicated that he was age 46. In January 1642 the county court convened in his home. Later in the year a woman was punished for calling his wife, Alice, a thief. During the next few years, Francis Mason I patented two more tracts of land in Lower Norfolk County, both of which were in the vicinity of the Lynnhaven River. He went on to serve as a tobacco viewer or inspector and became a churchwarden of the Elizabeth River Parish. By August 1647 he had begun serving as high sheriff. On November 15, 1648, it was reported that Francis Mason I

had died intestate. He was survived by his widow, Alice, and son, Lemuel, who on November 15th received letters of administration from the county court—and simultaneously orders from Governor William Berkeley—to make an inventory of the decedent's estate. The late Francis Mason I also was survived by his daughter, Elizabeth, the wife of James Thelaball of Lynnhaven Parish. On August 15, 1649, Lemuel Mason conveyed half of Hog Island to his brother-in-law, James Thelaball. However, a dispute arose and in December 1651 the Masons agreed to give Thelaball half of a 200-acre tract on the mainland abutting Hog Island, property in which they had a legal interest. Francis Mason's heirs also agreed to provide Thelaball with a large quantity of finished wood, enough glass and lead to make four windows, and six silver spoons (Lower Norfolk County Record Book A:88, 111, 142; B:52, 90, 97; C:1, 6; PB 1:312, 816, 945; 2:88; VI&A 482; DOR 2:569–570).

Lemuel (Lyonell) Mason: By February 1650 Lemuel, the late Francis Mason I's son, had married Anne (Ann), the daughter of the late Lower Norfolk County burgess Henry Seawell. In 1653 Lemuel and Anne Mason received generous bequests from Daniel Tanner to whom they had provided care during his last illness. When Lemuel Mason testified in January 1654 about Tanner's burial at his (Mason's) home, he gave his own age as 25 "or thereabouts." Major Lemuel Mason began serving as a county justice in April 1652 and held office for many years. He was elected to the assembly and attended the sessions held in 1654–1655, 1656, 1658, 1659, 1660, 1662, 1671, 1689–1682, 1684, 1685–1686, representing Lower Norfolk County. In 1656 he was paid for furnishing a case of strong drink to the assembly. Mason served on an assembly committee in June 1680 and in 1693 he attended on behalf of the newly formed Norfolk County. When Colonel Lemuel Mason made his will, which is now fragmentary, he left to his wife, Anne, life-rights in the Elizabeth River Parish plantation they then occupied and noted that it was land he had inherited from his father, Francis Mason I. The testator made bequests to his sons and to his sister, Elizabeth Thelaball, and mentioned a few others. Lemuel Mason's will was proved on September 15, 1702. On October 30, 1705, the widowed Anne Mason prepared her will, which was proved in March 1706. She made bequests to her sons, Thomas, Lemuel, and George, and to her daughters, Frances Sayer, Alice Bousch, Mary Cocke, and Dinah Thorowgood (Lower

Norfolk County Record Book B:122, 137a, 142, 152; C:1, 3, 6, 47, 65; Wills, Deeds, Orders D [1656–1666]:1.340; Wills and Deeds 6:258; 7:117; JHB 1660–1693:119; LEO 32–36, 39, 46–48, 52–53; DOR 2:570).

Thomas Mason: Thomas Mason was the son of Anne and Lemuel Mason I of Elizabeth River Parish in Norfolk County. Lemuel I, who had served as a burgess, died in 1702 and his wife, Anne, died four years later. In 1692 Thomas witnessed the will made by his uncle, James Thelaball of Norfolk County. Thomas Mason, who became a Norfolk County justice, represented the county in the 1696–1697 assembly sessions. In October 1697 he patented 53 acres called Broad Neck in Norfolk County. When quit-rent rolls were compiled in 1704, he was credited with tracts of 653 acres and 125 acres in Norfolk County, 140 acres in Princess Anne County, and 350 acres in Nansemond County. He made his will on January 9, 1711, and died before June 15th. He was survived by his wife, Elizabeth, and several children (LEO 56; SMITH 59; Norfolk County Wills and Deeds 5:208; 6:258; 7:117; PB 9:117; DOR 2:571–572).

* * *

George Mason: In November 1652 George Mason, a resident of Westmoreland County, served on a jury that had been impaneled to settle a dispute. A land transaction he executed in December 1655 reveals that he was living near the Aquia River, a tributary of the Potomac, when he sold some acreage to John Leare of Nansemond County. When Captain Mason testified in court in August 1658, he indicated that he was age 29. In 1663 he bought a 650-acre tract in Westmoreland County from Valentine Peyton. By 1667 Mason had become a major in the local militia and was a Stafford County justice. He was a member of the Association of Northumberland, Westmoreland, and Stafford Counties, a group that had been given the responsibility of building a fort as protection against the Dutch. He was also one of several prominent citizens who in 1677 were given the task of raising funds to cover the cost of suppressing Nathaniel Bacon's partisans in the Northern Neck. In 1679 Mason and two other men were authorized to see that a fort was built on the Potomac River at Niabsco and that it was equipped to accommodate a garrison of men. As a burgess for Stafford County, he attended the assembly sessions held in 1676, 1680–1682, and 1684, and he served on the committee formed in 1684 to see that a statehouse was

built. Colonel George Mason, whose name appeared occasionally in the records of Westmoreland County's monthly court, continued to represent Stafford County in the assembly sessions held in 1688, 1695–1696, 1696–1697, 1698, and 1699. He was an erudite man who sometimes served as an attorney. In 1691 he purchased a tract of land in Richmond County; when he sold it three years later, he and his wife, Mary, signed the deed (LEO 42, 46–47, 49, 51, 53–54, 57–59; HEN II:433; JHB 1660–1693:220; STAN 86; Northumberland County Record Book 1666–1670:34–36; Order Book 1652–1665:14; Stafford County Order Book 1686–1693:17a–18; Richmond County Deed Book 1 [1692–1693]:53; 2 [1693–1695]:45; Westmoreland County Deeds, Wills, Patents &c. 1653–1659:110a, 123–123a, 125a; Deeds and Wills No. 1 [1653–1671]:228–229; Deeds, Patents &c. 1665–1677:347a–350; Order Book 1676–1689:363, 381, 579).

* * *

James Mason: James Mason patented 450 acres in Isle of Wight County in 1647 and a year later began acquiring land in what by 1652 became Surry County. In 1648 he patented 250 acres at the head of Grays Creek and another 60 acres called Smith's Fort. Then, in 1653 he repatented his 250 acres, an indication that he still needed to develop the property in order to secure his claim. Finally, in 1654 he and John Bishop together patented 50 acres on Crouches Creek. Mason's name first appeared in Surry court records in November 1652, at which time he served on a coroner's jury and was identified as a planter. Over the years he appeared in court from time to time, usually when he was buying or selling livestock. However, on at least one occasion, he mortgaged his plantation. In 1654–1655 James Mason, then a resident of Mathewes Mount in Surry County, served as a burgess. In July 1655 Thomas Binns of Surry sued Mason's wife, Elizabeth, and accused her of abuse and defamation. A year later Mason began serving as a justice in the Surry County court. On December 13, 1662, the assembly's committee for "laying the levy" authorized payment to Mr. James Mason, who was compensated "for use of his house the last session of this court," which indicates that he had hosted a session of the assembly or General Court and probably owned or rented a dwelling in urban Jamestown. Mason also was paid for the "use of ye office for a year." On May 14, 1660, Mason was still serving as a justice in Surry County's monthly court. He died sometime after April or May 1665 but prior to May 1668, at which time his

21-year-old son, Francis Mason, referred to him as deceased (LEO 32; PB 2:126, 151–152; 3:14, 222; SR 3987; Surry County Deed Book I:17, 22, 24, 45–47, 65, 68, 84, 87, 102, 104, 114–120, 130, 166, 304–306, 312; Clarendon MS 82 f 276).

Francis Mason: On May 25, 1671, Francis Mason of Surry County sued the estate of John Grove, a merchant who regularly conducted business in Jamestown. In 1676, while the colony was in the throes of Bacon's Rebellion, Mason was one of Surry's burgesses. On January 24, 1677, Governor William Berkeley ordered him to assist Arthur Allen and Sheriff Samuel Swann in seizing Robert Kay's sheep, which were to be brought to Green Spring. Mason patented 300 acres on Crouches Creek in 1678 and may have been the brother of William Macon (or Mason), a resident of Surry. In 1682 Francis Mason was sheriff of Surry County, an indication that he was a justice of the peace. In November 1688 he functioned as the executor of Jane, the widow of Thomas Rabley of Jamestown, perhaps because of a familial connection. He continued to serve as a Surry County burgess and attended the 1691–1692 assembly sessions. In 1691 Mason was among those who collectively purchased the land on which the town of Cobham was built. He made his will on September 4, 1696, and died prior to March 2, 1697 (MCGC 259; STAN 81, 87; JHB 1660–1693:120; Surry County Order Book 1671–1691:682; Deeds, Wills &c. 1687–1694:233; 1694–1709:116; LEO 41, 51; PB 6:653; CO 1/39 f 24; SR 660, 6618).

* * *

Mastegonoe (Native American): Between March 18 and June 19, 1680, when the 1677 Treaty of Middle Plantation was expanded to include additional Indian groups, Mastegonoe, the king of the Sappones (Saponis) Indians, and Tachapoake, their chief man, signed on behalf of their people (Anonymous, 1677 treaty, Miscellaneous Virginia Records 1606–1692, Bland Manuscripts, XIV, ff 226–233; CO 1/40 ff 249–250).

John Matheman (Matheyman): John Matheman came to Virginia in 1619 or 1620 and in February 1624 was a young servant in Sir Francis Wyatt's household in urban Jamestown. He was still there in January 1625 and may have been the youth known as John Matheyman who was sent to Virginia by Bridewell's justices (VI&A 483).

Rowland Mathew: On May 26, 1623, Rowland Mathew of St. Clement Danes, Westminster, testified in the Earl of Warwick's suit against Edward Brewster, litigation that involved the ships *Treasurer* and *Neptune*. Mathew, a 43-year-old gentleman, vouched for the authenticity of Sir Samuel Argall's affidavit (VI&A 483).

Thomas Mathew (Mathews): Court records indicate that during the 1650s Thomas Mathew, a merchant, sometimes used Captain Thomas Cornwallis (Cornwallys) as his attorney when doing business in Northumberland County. When Mathew tried to recover a debt in March 1664 from a Northumberland County resident, a reference was made to Mathew's store at Great Wicocomoco. As time went on, Mathew claimed additional acreage in Northumberland County, and he frequently appeared in its monthly court, often trying to recover funds from debtors. In 1672 he received permission from the county's justices to erect a mill at the head of the Great Wicocomoco River or one of its branches. Among those to whom Mathew owed funds in 1674 was Jamestown innkeeper Richard Lawrence, who ultimately became one of the rebel Nathaniel Bacon's main supporters. Thomas Mathew lived at Cherry Point, in Northumberland County, where he was residing in 1674. He served as a burgess for Stafford County in 1676, but by November 1679 had become a justice of Northumberland. In an account he wrote in 1705, Mathew stated that Robert Hen, a herdsman he had hired for his plantation in Stafford, was mortally wounded by attacking Indians during the summer of 1675. He said that Hen, shortly before he died, stated that he had been attacked by tribesmen known as the Doegs. Mathew went on to explain that after Hen's death, a large party of militia pursued the Indians into Maryland, where they attacked the Susquehannock, who were friends of the English. Thomas Mathew believed that the attack on his plantation and the Susquehannock, followed by the Indians' retaliation, gave rise to the popular uprising that became known as Bacon's Rebellion. On February 10, 1677, Governor William Berkeley decided that Thomas Mathew was exempt from the king's pardon on account of his stance during Bacon's Rebellion and declared that he was to appear before a court. Captain Mathew was fortunate enough to escape with his life, and between 1679 and in 1682 he commenced serving as a justice in Old Rappahannock County's court. In 1680 he was censured for failing to send the required number of men to the garrison at the head of the Potomac River. Mathew began serving as a justice in Northumberland County, and in 1681 he became sheriff; one of his houses was used as the county prison until a suitable building was erected. In 1684, when Virginia's governing officials were encouraging the manufacture of cloth, he received a prize or bounty from the assembly because members of his household had produced 35 yards of serge, 27½ yards of woolen cloth, and 76 yards of fine linen (FOR I:8:1–26; LEO 42; Old Rappahannock County Deeds and Wills 1677–1682:251; Lancaster County Order Book 1666–1680:496; Northumberland County Order Book 1652–1665:23, 298, 361, 377–378, 412–413, 415; 1666–1678:76, 78, 164, 197–198, 208, 315, 329; 1678–1698:63–64, 77, 96, 183, 220, 333; Westmoreland County Deeds, Patents &c. 1665–1677:173a, 262a–263; AND 16–20; SR 660; NEVILLE 61).

Walter Mathew: In August 1624 Walter Mathew, a boatswain aboard the ship on which Richard Williams alias Cornish allegedly raped William Couse, testified before the General Court in Jamestown. On January 3, 1625, he continued his testimony (VI&A 483).

Jeremiah Mathewes: Jeremiah Mathewes, a servant in the employ of Jamestown innkeeper Richard Lawrence, stole a shallop and fled. On September 28, 1674, Mathewes was ordered to serve his master seven additional years (MCGC 382).

Edward Mathews: On April 19, 1667, the General Court's justices ordered Edward Mathews to ask Thomas Stegg II's forgiveness (MCGC 510). Stegg then owned a unit in a brick row house in the western end of Jamestown Island.

* * *

Samuel Mathews I: Samuel Mathews I came to Virginia prior to 1618 and at first lived in Jamestown. He moved to a settlement near the head of the James River but returned to the lower Tidewater region, and in 1624 he served as a burgess for the plantations on the lower side of the James River. He was named to the Council of State and patented land near Hog Island and at Blunt Point, near the mouth of the Warwick River. In time, he developed the Blunt Point tract into a plantation he called Denbigh or Mathews Manor. In January 1627, when foreign invasion seemed likely, Mathews Manor was considered a position of strength where people could take refuge. Sometime after March 24, 1628, Mathews married Frances Grenville, who had outlived former husbands Nathaniel West and Abraham

Peirsey. Before her death in 1633, she gave birth to sons Samuel Mathews II and Francis. During the mid-1630s, while Mathews was a councilor, he was highly instrumental in Governor John Harvey's ouster. By that time Mathews had married the daughter of Sir Thomas Hinton. As a result of his overt opposition to Harvey, Mathews was summoned to England, where he was put on trial for mutiny. He eventually was released and returned to Virginia around 1637. During the 1640s the Mathews Manor plantation, which was well developed, was home to weavers, flax makers, tanners, shoemakers, and other crafts workers. His highly successful agricultural operations enabled him to sell surplus wheat, barley, and beef to other colonies. He also hosted meetings of the Warwick County court. Lieutenant Colonel Samuel Mathews supported the Commonwealth government but continued to uphold the Virginia colony's interests. He died between November 1657 and March 1658. Mathews' son Francis went on to become a militia captain and York County justice. He married William Baldwin's daughter and died on February 16, 1675, having outlived his brother, Samuel II (SR 633; VI&A 483–485; STAN 31; LEO 5; DUNN 27; DOR 2:640; York County Deeds, Orders, Wills &c. 5 [1672–1676]:112).

Mrs. Samuel Mathews I (see Frances Grenville)

Samuel Mathews II: Samuel Mathews II, the son of Samuel Mathews I and his wife, Frances Grenville, was born around 1629. He represented Warwick River County in the 1652, 1653 and 1654–1655 sessions of the assembly and also served as a local justice. He was named to the Council of State during the Commonwealth period and held office from 1656 to 1660. In 1657 he was elected governor of Virginia and held office until his death in January 1660 (VI&A 485; STAN 36; LEO xx, 29–32; DOR 2:639–640; HEN 2:14; MCGC 209, 249, 269, 297; DUNN 18, 27, 171, 178).

John Mathews: John Mathews, the son of Samuel Mathews II and grandson of Samuel Mathews I, lived at Blunt Point, near Deep Creek in Warwick County. In October 1670 Mr. Bullock, Colonel Peter Jennings, and Major John Smith were serving as his guardians; Colonel Pritchard replaced Bullock in 1671. Although John Mathews was underage, in March 1678 he received a patent for 2,944 acres on Deep Creek. In June 1679 William Cole was identified as Mathews' guardian. John Mathews represented Warwick County in the assembly sessions held in 1680–1682 and 1684, and by March 1685 he had married Michael Tavernor's daughter, Elizabeth. He died sometime after September 15, 1686, but before May 1, 1706 (LEO 46–47; PB 6:641; DOR 2:640–641; MCGC 229, 269, 290).

* * *

William Mathews: On July 13, 1630, William Mathews, Henry Booth's servant, was found guilty of treason. Afterward, he was drawn and then hanged, probably on a gallows in Jamestown, where Booth resided (VI&A 485).

King of the Mattaponi (Mattapony) Indians (Native American): In 1657 the king and Great Men of the Mattaponi Indians made a treaty with the justices of Old Rappahannock County, agreeing not to trespass on colonists' property or kill livestock. In return, the Indians became eligible for English justice in the local court (Stanard, "Old Rappahannock County Records, Volume 1656–1664," 391). This document reveals that the Mattaponi Indians were then living within the territory that in 1692 was subdivided to form Essex and Richmond counties.

Robert Mattson: In 1621 and 1622 Robert Mattson was described as a sawyer for the Company of Shipwrights. While in Virginia he worked under the supervision of master shipwright Thomas Nunn and would have resided on Jamestown Island (VI&A 486).

Thomas Maxes: Thomas Maxes, a gentleman, came to Virginia in 1608 in the 2nd Supply of new settlers and would have resided in Jamestown (VI&A 486).

Charles Maxey: On June 4, 1627, Charles Maxey was found guilty of a sex offense and was sentenced to be whipped in Jamestown and again at Shirley Hundred, where the misconduct occurred. He also was forced to execute Thomas Hale, who had been found guilty of raping four children (VI&A 486).

William May: William May, a laborer, came to Virginia in 1608 as part of the 1st Supply of new settlers and would have lived in Jamestown (VI&A 487).

William May: In May 1661, William May patented a half-acre lot in urban Jamestown, property he was obliged to improve within six months. He apparently did so, for in December 1662 he was paid for hosting an of-

ficial meeting. National Park Service archaeologists have discovered the remains of May's house, which was fabricated of brick. In June 1670 May patented a half-acre lot that was next door to the one he acquired in 1661. Although he was not obliged to erect a building on his new lot (which in 1661 had been considered wasteland), he was ordered to plant an orchard there. On April 15, 1667, William May patented 100 acres of marshland in the eastern end of Jamestown Island, below Goose Hill. The acreage he claimed had been assigned to Thomas Woodhouse and William Hooker in 1657 but had been deserted. May probably used his rural property for pasturing livestock or other agricultural purposes. He seems to have been a respected resident of the capital city. During the late 1660s and early 1670s, the justices of the General Court frequently asked him to arbitrate disputes involving local citizens and to inventory estates. He also audited debtors' accounts and testified about a slanderous incident that occurred in Jamestown. In 1668 and 1669 he and Nicholas Meriwether served as Thomas Woodhouse's executors, collecting debts as far away as the Northern Neck. May served as first the attorney and then the administrator of Richard Woodward, a Bristol merchant, and he was a member of the James City Parish vestry. One matter he was obliged to address was Christopher Wormeley II's claim against the parish on behalf of the Rev. Justinian Aylemer's widow, Wormeley's new wife. William May made his will on March 7, 1671, and bequeathed his land in Jamestown to his attorney, Nicholas Meriwether of Jamestown, whom he also named his executor. By March 18, 1673, May was dead (MCGC 218, 221, 236, 238, 247, 251, 258–259, 277, 285, 290, 331; Surry County Deeds, Wills &c. 1652–1672:351, 386; PB 4:475; 6:42; Northumberland County Record Book 1666–1670:99; Order Book 1666–1678:49; 1666–1678:42, 49; NUG I:409; II:12; Clarendon MS 82 f 276; AMB 36, 37, 134, 135–135).

Thomas Mayhew (Mahew): Thomas Mayhew came to Virginia sometime prior to 1626 and in 1628, when he was named administrator of Daniel Lacy's estate, was identified as a merchant. Over the years Mayhew made numerous court appearances in Jamestown. He went to court in May 1629 in order to transfer servant Anthony Leane's contract to his brother, Edward Mayhew, who was planning to have Leane work aboard his boat for a year (VI&A 487).

John Meade (Mead): John Meade arrived in Virginia sometime prior to 1634 and became a planter. During the 1630s and 1640s, he and other male family members purchased tobacco and shipped it overseas, probably serving as factors for an English merchant. Sometimes, disputes over the cost of the tobacco or its quality resulted in litigation. Meade served as clerk of the assembly in 1642 and was still in office in 1644 when members of the assembly sent word to the king that the colony's shortage of coinage prevented them from establishing a functional customs house. Although no patents have come to light that indicate where assembly clerk John Meade resided when not living in Jamestown, in 1662 a landowner in Old Rappahannock County identified his property as being adjacent to Meade's (LEO 20; SR 3502b, 4003, 7377, 10740, 10489, 10949, 12875; PB 5:188).

Thomas Meares (Meeres): In 1649 Thomas Meares patented 100 acres of land on the western branch of the Elizabeth River and later added another 400 acres to his holdings. He served as a Lower Norfolk County burgess and attended the 1645, 1646, and 1647 assembly sessions but was absent from the 1648 meetings. During the 1640s he was paid for sending his boat to Jamestown to bring the county's burgesses home, and he was compensated for providing bread and meat to the boatmen. In 1646 a land dispute between Thomas Meares and Thomas Sayer was aired before Lower Norfolk County's monthly court. In 1649 Meares was among the men fined for failing to attend church, a legal obligation (LEO 23, 25–26; Lower Norfolk County Record Book A:362; B:8, 123a; PB 2:159. 173).

Joan Meatherst: In October 1627 the General Court heard testimony about Joan Meatherst, a maidservant Benjamin Sims (Syms) brought to Virginia intending to marry. As it turned out, they disliked each other intensely. Therefore, she was assigned to Jamestown merchant John Gill, whom she was to serve for two years, and Gill agreed to pay Sims, a resident of Elizabeth City, for her work (VI&A 488).

Henry Meese (Mees): Henry Meese, who was born in England, arrived in Virginia prior to 1654 and became a prosperous merchant. By 1659 his name had begun appearing in Northumberland County records. Among those with whom he traded were George Colcough, Isaac Allerton, and Peter Knight of Jamestown Island. In 1664 Meese appointed an attorney to collect a substantial sum from Colonel William

Underwood's executors, a debt that was attributable to beaver pelts. This suggests that Meese was involved in the fur trade. In January 1661 Meese purchased 1,000 acres of land on Potomac Creek in Northumberland County from Elizabeth and Thomas Pettus I of Littletown in James City County, and Major Edward Griffith of Mulberry Island in Warwick County. He patented the Pettus-Griffith acreage in October 1665, and less than a year later he patented another thousand acres in the same vicinity. In June 1666 Meese was identified as a lieutenant colonel when he patented 2,000 acres in Stafford County, on Potomac Creek. He served as a burgess for Stafford County from 1665 to 1669, at which time he returned to England, having designated a Northumberland County man as his attorney and instructed him to sue merchant Peter Knight. In 1667 Meese was a member of the Association of Northumberland, Westmoreland, and Stafford Counties, a group that was given the responsibility of building a fort as protection against the Dutch. While he was in London with mariner and merchant William Armiger, he witnessed a document before a notary public. Throughout the 1670s Meese was involved in numerous lawsuits that were the result of his involvement in mercantile activities. In 1680 he was named to the Council of State, but he died in England sometime after December 1681. On December 11, 1691, Anne Meese, who identified herself as the late Henry Meese's widow, executrix, and heir, asked Stafford County's justices to assist her in forcing the Rev. John Waugh to vacate her late husband's home plantation. She added that she wanted to sell the property, which had descended to her through right of inheritance (STAN 41; LEO 39; Old Rappahannock County Deeds and Wills 1656–1664:15–16, 287–288; Northumberland County Record Book 1662–1666:104, 130, 176; 1666–1670:34–36; Order Book 1652–1665:226, 309, 316, 331; 1666–1678:79; Stafford County Record Book 1686–1693:260a; Westmoreland County Deeds, Wills &c. 1661–1662:27a–28a; Deeds, Patents &c. 1665–1677:66a, 259a–260a; NUG I:559; PB 5:513, 630; SR 663, 3609, 3763a, 3774, 3775d, 3775f, 4201d, 4559, 5582a, 5588b, 5590, 5592c, 5594a, 5726a, 5728a, 5732, 5762d, 5764, 7072, 10059, 10102, 10494, 12553, 13788, 13855, 42029).

Meimeichcom (Native American): In 1657 Meimeichcom, one of the Mattaponi Indians' Great Men or leaders, participated in making a peace agreement with the justices of Old Rappahannock County (Old Rappahannock County Deed Book 1656–1664:17).

Thomas Melling: In June 1619 Thomas Melling, a London merchant and Virginia Company member, informed Company officials that he had sent people to Virginia. On March 13, 1622, the Company learned that Melling had obtained his property from Captain Ralph Hamor. Although the location of Melling's land is uncertain, Hamor is known to have had acreage at Warresqueak, on Jamestown Island, at Hog Island, at Blunt Point, and in Archer's Hope (VI&A 489).

William Mellinge (Mellin, Melling) I: William Mellinge I, a gentleman, served as a witness on March 13, 1633, when Captain Edmund Scarborough sold some cattle. Mellinge may have been living on the Eastern Shore at that time. Two years later he patented some land in Accomack County, and over the next few years he acquired more acreage there and in Northampton County. Mellinge, like many of his contemporaries, appeared in court from time to time to initiate litigation or defend himself from suits undertaken by others. He also witnessed wills and shipped tobacco to England. In November 1637 Thomas Hunt brought suit against Mellinge, claiming that Mellinge had rented his boat and severely damaged it. On March 25, 1651, Mellinge was among those who signed a document pledging to uphold England's Commonwealth government. He represented Northampton County in the 1653 and 1658 assembly sessions. When William Mellinge I made a nuncupative will on January 22, 1670, he nominated his wife, Anne, as executrix and left her life-rights in his plantation; he also gave her the right to use two horses and his sloop. He named his son, William II, as reversionary heir to his plantation and made bequests to his eldest daughter. He also indicated that his other children were to receive a share of his estate when they attained legal age or married, and he left remembrances to several of his friends. Mellinge died on January 30, 1670. His widow, Anne, made her will on November 20, 1676, and died on December 29th. She named as heirs her daughter Margaret and son, William II (LEO 31, 34; AMES 1:8, 25, 31, 51, 61, 91–92, 95, 114, 147; PB 1:465–466; 3:252; 4:41, 624; 5:538; 6:252; SR 3502b; MARSHALL 34, 50, 84–85, 98).

George Menefie (Menify): George Menefie, who came to Virginia in 1622, resided in urban Jamestown, on a waterfront lot he patented in 1624. As a merchant, he had close ties to several important London-based mercantile firms. In 1626 he was the corporation of James City's official merchant and factor,

and in 1629 he began serving as Jamestown's burgess. Court testimony taken during the 1620s reveals that he had an operational forge in Jamestown and that he and his wife, Elizabeth I, produced a daughter, Elizabeth II. In 1635 George Menefie patented 1,200 acres near Middle Plantation and established a plantation known as Littletown. When Dutch mariner David Devries visited Littletown in March 1633, he described its elaborate gardens. Menefie acquired land in Charles City County and developed it as his family seat, Buckland. During the early 1640s he patented a second lot in urban Jamestown and secured a patent for 3,000 acres on the north side of the York River, later the site of Rosewell plantation. Menefie served on the Council of State from 1635 to 1644. When Governor John Harvey had a heated argument with his council in April 1635, he struck Menefie on the shoulder, and accused him of treason. Although Harvey was temporarily ousted from office, he had Menefie and several other councilors arrested and sent to England to stand trial. Menefie was released after two months' detention. He probably was living at Buckland during the mid-1630s when he took a Tappahanna Indian boy into his home and reared him in the Christian faith. Sometime after August 1637, Menefie married Isabell (Izabella), the widow of Richard Pace and Captain William Perry. He outlived her, and when making his will in December 1645, he designated his third wife, Mary, as his executrix and the guardian of his daughter, Elizabeth II. Menefie's will was presented for probate in early 1646, and he was buried in the cemetery at Westover Church. When Elizabeth Menefie II matured, she married her stepbrother, Henry Perry, and resided at her late father's plantation, Buckland. Sometime prior to 1656 the Perry couple disposed of the late George Menefie's waterfront lot in urban Jamestown (VI&A 489–491; LEO 8; STAN 33).

Thomas Mentis (Meutis): In February 1624 Thomas Mentis was a servant in the household of Edward Blaney, a merchant living in urban Jamestown (VI&A 491).

John Meriday (Meredie, Meridien): John Meriday died in Jamestown sometime after April 1623 but before February 16, 1624. His name was listed twice in the accounting of the dead (VI&A 491).

* * *

Nicholas Meriwether (Merewether, Meriweather, Merryweather): In 1653 Nicholas Meriwether patented 600 acres of land in Northumberland County, on the Wicocomoco River. He also claimed 300 acres on the southeast side of the Corotoman River, in Lancaster County, and he owned some land in Westmoreland County that he sold to John Curtis and James Hare. Meriwether served as clerk when the General Court convened in Jamestown on October 10, 1655. Prior to that time he had purchased 200 acres in Westmoreland County, part of a much larger patent. By November 1661, when Meriwether—who was age 30—purchased the late Richard Kingsmill's 80-acre plantation in the eastern end of Jamestown Island from Colonel Nathaniel Bacon and his wife, Elizabeth, he already owned 200 acres on Powhatan Swamp and 297 acres on the Chickahominy River near Hog Neck. Meriwether appears to have made personal use of his Jamestown Island plantation, which lay within the capital city's limits. When a plat was made in 1664 of John Knowles' property, "Mr. Meriwether's tobacco barn" was shown in close proximity to the Knowles tract's northeasterly boundary line. On May 3, 1666, Nicholas Meriwether described himself as a resident of Jamestown Island, but in 1668 he was listed as a tithable member of Southwark Parish in Surry County. By that date, he had married Elizabeth, the daughter of Thomas Woodhouse of urban Jamestown, and was serving as his late father-in-law's executor. When the Rev. John Clayton made a schematic map of Jamestown Island in 1688, he identified the site of a brick house that was located on the west side of Kingsmill Creek's mouth. It is probable that "The Brick House" was erected by Nicholas Meriwether during the 1660s building initiative, when the construction of brick houses was subsidized by the government. Erecting the dwelling would have secured Meriwether's title to the property and provided him and his wife with a home in the capital city. In 1668 and 1669 Meriwether and William May, serving as Thomas Woodhouse's executors, collected funds from the decedent's debtors. Around 1673 Meriwether inherited May's lots in urban Jamestown, near the waterfront. He retained both parcels and the dwelling they contained for approximately four years and then sold the property to Colonel William White. It is probable that Meriwether also inherited May's 100-acre patent in the southeastern portion of Jamestown Island. Meriwether, who in 1658 was the clerk of the James City County Court, was the former clerk of Surry County, where he also owned property. He patented substantial quantities of land in the Northern Neck and some vast tracts in New Kent County and what became Hanover, Goochland, and King William counties. He appears to have died intestate around 1693–1695, leaving several children (AMB 11, 12, 25, 36, 56, 134, 135–136; PB 4:397; 7:710; NUG I:394; Clayton 1688; Surry County Deeds and Wills 1652–1672:270, 315, 351; Deeds, Wills &c. 1671–1684:117; Will Book 2:140; Northumberland County Record Book 1666–1670:99; Order Book 1652–1665:72, 404, 414; 1666–1678:42, 49; Westmoreland County Deeds, Wills, Patents &c. 1653–1659:36, 103a; Deeds, Wills &c. 1661–1662:15a–16, 33; Deeds and Wills No. 1 [1653–1671]:199–200, 229–230; NUG I: 252, 257, 316, 338, 341, 394, 556, 566; II:13; III:46, 153, 240, 247, 330–331, 362, 370–371; PB 3:63, 87; 4:90, 107, 397; HUD IV:21, 62, 78; Tyler, "Ludwell Family," 202; SMITH 60; MCGC 331; STAN 102–107).

Francis Meriwether (Merewether, Meriweather, Merryweather) I: Francis Meriwether I, one of the late Nicholas Meriwether's sons and his administrator, came into possession of the decedent's real and personal property during the mid-1690s. Despite disagreements with deputy escheator George Jordan, he managed to patent substantial quantities of land in Essex County. He became Essex's clerk of court in May 1692 and held office for many years. Meriwether continued to acquire land in Essex County, sometimes patenting land that had escheated to the Crown. On October 26, 1694, he and John Battail patented 1,091 acres in Gloucester County. Francis Meriwether I disposed of a piece of property in 1696, at which time his wife, Mary, relinquished her dower share. When Henry Hartwell made his will in July 1699, Nicholas, Francis I, and Thomas Meriwether were among his heirs, and Hartwell identified them as his late wife's nephews. Over the years Meriwether's name appeared frequently in the records of the county court, often as a plaintiff in lawsuits. In 1706 and 1712 he served as burgess for Essex County and in 1710 represented New Kent. If Nicholas Meriwether retained the 100-acre Jamestown Island patent that he inherited from William May, that acreage and a large parcel Nicholas owned on the periphery of the urbanized area (the plantation that had belonged to Richard Kingsmill) would have descended to his legal heirs. On October 21, 1695, Francis Meriwether I conveyed the Kingsmill tract to William Sherwood, to whom he owed £100, noting that he was using the property as collateral and that Thomas Lecket, a tenant, was residing there. Sherwood then owned several adjacent parcels. In January 1700 Francis Meriwether I and his wife, Mary, disposed of the Essex County plantation on which they had been living. They excluded from the sale a small plot of ground where Francis I's son, Francis II, was buried and noted that they had bought their acreage in February 1695 (AMB 56; Surry County Deeds, Wills &c. 1671–1684:117; Essex County Order Book 1692–1695:1, 90, 157–158; 1695–1699:1, 27, 87, 158; 1699–1702:2, 73, 132; Deeds and Wills 1692–1695:187–188; 1695–1699:56–57, 132–133, 346; 1699–1702:24, 68; MCGC 379; STAN 97–99; NUG II:392; III 53, 87; Tyler, "A Chain of Descent," 172; SR 4788).

* * *

John Merritt: John Merritt, who in 1621 was a passenger on the *Falcon*, went to Jamestown (VI&A 491).

William Meyer: In 1697 William Sherwood of Jamestown designated William and Elir Meyer as two of his heirs and left them some money (AMB 65).

Michaell (Michael): Michaell, a laborer, came to Virginia in 1608 in the 1st Supply of new Jamestown colonists (VI&A 492).

David Middleton: David Middleton, a Virginia Company investor, came to Virginia and was supposed to become a member of the Council of State. According to official records, he was elderly and died soon after reaching the colony (VI&A 493; STAN 29).

Thomas Middleton: On July 7, 1707, Thomas Middleton was occupying a 25-acre leasehold in the Governor's Land that eventually became part of the Ambler holdings (AMB 77).

Francis Midwinter: Francis Midwinter, a gentleman, came to Virginia in 1607 and was one of the first Jamestown colonists. According to George Percy, Midwinter died there on August 14, 1607 (VI&A 493).

Robert Migh: On April 27, 1648, Robert Migh was identified as clerk of the James City County court, whose seat was in Jamestown (Lower Norfolk Book B:85).

Edward Mihill (Myhill): Edward Mihill represented Elizabeth City County in the assembly sessions held in 1680–1682. In March 1691 he witnessed a deed for some land in Elizabeth City County, and a year or so later, he was among those chosen to sit on a Grand Jury. In 1693 he served as a court justice and participated in the division of an estate. In April 1694, while Mihill was a jus-

tice, a group of Elizabeth City County men protested against their tax assessments and the county levies. In 1697 the General Court authorized him to serve as John Lee's administrator. On December 5, 1701, Edward Mihill and Ann Johnson received a marriage license. He may have been related to the Edward Mihill who by 1650 had patented some land on the north side of the Rappahannock River in what was then a frontier area (LEO 45; PB 2:288; NEAL 7, 23, 62, 64, 86, 114, 245; EJC I:309).

Robert Miles: Sometime prior to 1648 Edward Prince assigned Robert Miles a 27-acre leasehold in the Governor's Land. Later, it came into the hands of Jane Perkins (PB 2:150; NUG I:177).

Christopher Miller: On July 22, 1640, Christopher Miller, a runaway servant in the employ of Captain William Peirce of urban Jamestown, was identified as Dutch (MCGC 467).

Henry Mills: In 1680–1682 Henry Mills served as a burgess for Nansemond County, an indication that he or his wife owned land there. In April 1685 he patented 500 acres in Nansemond's Upper Parish (LEO 45; PB 7:478).

William Mills: William Mills, an indentured servant employed by Edward Grindon of Grindon's Hill, admitted that on several occasions he had stolen from his master. On February 7, 1628, he was sentenced to be whipped "at the cart's tail" from urban Jamestown to the gallows and back (VI&A 493). The location of the gallows in Jamestown appears to have been at a site on the edge of town, overlooking Pitch and Tar Swamp.

[No First Name] Milman: Master Milman, a boy who came to Virginia in 1608 in the 2nd Supply of new settlers, lived in Jamestown (VI&A 493).

Richard Milmer: Richard Milmer, a laborer, came to Virginia in 1608 in the 1st Supply of new settlers and resided in Jamestown (VI&A 494).

Francis Milner: In 1699 Francis Milner served as a burgess for Nansemond County, and in 1700 he patented 33 acres there. Other patents he or his wife may have held that would have made him eligible to hold office seem to have been lost or destroyed. In 1706, when William Pope of Nansemond County sold some acreage on Indian Swamp, Francis Milner served as a witness. In 1704 Captain Francis Milner paid quitrent on 300 acres of land in Nansemond County (LEO 59; Isle of Wight County Deed Book 2 [1704–1715]:48; SMITH 61; PB 9:280).

Thomas Milner: In 1672 Bristol merchant John Seward designated Nansemond County merchant Thomas Milner as one of his attorneys in Virginia. By that time Milner had patented 350 acres across from Dumpling Island in Nansemond County, and he probably owned other acreage whose patents have been lost or destroyed. Then, in 1680 he and Thomas Butt invested in 3,000 acres in Lower Norfolk (later, Norfolk) County. Finally, in April 1684 he patented 12 acres of marshland in Nansemond County. Milner, who served as clerk of the assembly in 1684 and as speaker in 1693, was a Nansemond County burgess and attended the 1688, 1691–1692, 1693, 1698, and 1699 sessions. On several occasions he prepared or transcribed official documents that were sent to officials in England. He also sent a report to the Council of State, informing them that the boundary line between Virginia and Carolina had been delineated. When John Murden of Norfolk County made his will in 1694, he left to his sons some land that he had bought from Colonel Thomas Milner. In 1704 Milner paid quitrent on 1,484 acres of land in Nansemond County (LEO 47, 49–50, 52–53, 58–59; Norfolk County Wills and Deeds 5:249; Isle of Wight Will and Deed Book 1 [1662–1688]:264; PB 6:429; 7:31, 392; SR 236, 375, 376, 7303; SMITH 61).

John Milward: John Milward was sent to Virginia by the Company of Mercers. On March 10, 1622, he witnessed the will made by John Rolfe, a resident of Jamestown. When Dr. John Pott patented some land on September 1, 1632, he used Milward's headright (VI&A 494).

James Minge (Ming): In June 1670 James Minge, a surveyor then serving as London merchant Philip Manning's attorney, successfully brought suit against William Edwards I's remarried widow, Mrs. Sarah Richardson, in the General Court. Minge attempted to recover the funds that the defendant and her late husband, William Richardson, owed to Manning. Four years later Minge returned to court to testify about some tobacco that was part of John Edloe's estate but had not been inventoried. He also acknowledged that some of the tobacco was owed to William Drummond I of urban Jamestown. In 1674 Minge became clerk of

the assembly and held office until 1676. He also was clerk of the Charles City County court. In June 1675 he was ordered to survey rebel Nathaniel Bacon's land in Henrico County, his plantation at Curles. In March 1676 Minge was summoned to appear before the General Court in a case involving Thomas Bowler and his wife. Later, Minge was called upon to survey the land laid out for the Pamunkey Indians' occupancy, and he was asked to examine a plat prepared by a man who delimited a parcel for the Chickahominy Indians. In 1677 Minge and Thomas Blayton prepared the list of grievances that Charles City County's freeholders presented to the special commissioners whom King Charles II sent to the colony to investigate the underlying causes of Bacon's Rebellion. James Minge served as a burgess for Charles City County and attended the sessions held in 1680–1682 and 1684. By 1695 he had patented a massive quantity of land in New Kent County (MCGC 223, 387, 416, 436; EJC I:281, 284; LEO 37, 41, 45, 47; NUG II:170, 312, 357, 401; SR 661, 3718, 6618b).

Mingo: In 1769 Mingo, a male slave living on Jamestown Island, was included in the late Edward Ambler I's estate (AMB-E).

Richard Minter: On August 14, 1622, Virginia Company officials identified Richard Minter as Dr. Lawrence Bohunn's tenant. However, he was associated with the physician-general's office land, not with acreage that Bohunn owned personally. In 1622 Minter's wife, Ann, sent two petitions to Company officials asking that her husband be released from his contract. She insisted that he had paid for his own transportation to the colony and pointed out that he was supposed to be given 50 acres of land. Later, Ann Minter came to the colony. When Edward Minter patented some land in July 1635, he indicated that he was the son of Richard and Ann Minter and therefore was entitled to their personal adventures or headrights and that of his brother, John (VI&A 495).

"Mischief" (Native American): In March 1699 Lieutenant Governor Francis Nicholson ordered Essex County's justices to ask their county's residents whether they were fearful of the Indian "commonly called Mischief" and some other Indians who had left Maryland two years earlier and settled on an island in the Potomac River. If the residents of Essex and Stafford counties were uneasy, the militia was to be sent out (Essex County Deeds and Wills 1692–1695:323).

William Mitchell (Michell, Michael): Captain William Mitchell represented Northampton County in the assembly in March 1658 but by November 1, 1659, was dead. At that time, Northampton County's justices named his wife, Joan, as her late husband's administratrix, an indication that he had died intestate. The decedent may have been the Captain William Mitchell whose name was mentioned by Northumberland County's justices on March 10, 1653, in reference to one of his debtors (LEO 34; STAN 74; Northumberland County Records 1652–1655:12; Northampton County Order Book 8 [1657–1664]:53; MARSHALL 52).

William Mitchell: On March 9, 1676, the General Court decided that William Mitchell, one of William Drummond I's servants, was to be freed. Drummond, a Jamestown resident, had assigned Mitchell to a Mrs. Watson for three years (MCGC 423, 432).

Samuel Mole (Moll, Molt): On March 15, 1620, Samuel Mole, a surgeon, leased a house and some land from Sir George Yeardley in urban Jamestown for a term of 60 years. When Mole made plans in April 1623 to return to England, he asked incumbent Governor Francis Wyatt's permission to sell or sublet his leasehold. He said that he had spent a great deal of money repairing and modifying his house and would like to get the best profit he could. Mole's petition was granted. He left Virginia soon after April 30, 1623, and by June 11th was back in England. When testifying in court he indicated that he was age 41 and a native of Rochelle, France. He said that he had been living in Jamestown in January 1623 when Thomas Hamor died, and stated that Nathaniel Jeffereys, with whom Mole shared his home, had made Hamor's coffin. In 1643 Mole's land was in the possession of Robert Hutchinson (VI&A 497; SR 5860).

Diego de Molina (Malinos): In 1611 Diego de Molina and two other men, who were aboard a Spanish ship that entered the mouth of the James River, went ashore near Old Point Comfort and were captured. They were kept prisoner for several years because they were considered Spanish spies. In May 1613 Molina smuggled a letter to the Spanish ambassador in London, concealing it in the sole of a shoe. He described conditions in the colony and spoke disdainfully of its principal leaders. He said that he had heard that 150 settlers were living in Jamestown and described its fortifications. He added that the death rate was extremely high and

that the colonists had little food or apparel to sustain them. In an April 30, 1614, letter to the Spanish ambassador, he said that he had been sick for 17 months but was being treated kindly. Molina eventually was freed in a carefully orchestrated prisoner exchange (VI&A 497).

Richard Molineux (Mullinax, Molyneux): Richard Molineux, a gentleman, came to Virginia in 1608 in the 1st Supply of new settlers and would have resided in Jamestown (VI&A 497).

Moll: On February 15, 1768, when an inventory was made of the late Richard Ambler's slaves on Jamestown Island and his leasehold in the Governor's Land, an adult female slave named Moll was listed. She probably was Moll Cook, the dairy woman that Ambler mentioned in his 1765 will. In 1769 Moll was living on Jamestown Island and was part of the late Edward Ambler I's estate (York County Wills and Inventories 21:378–382, 386–391; AMB-E).

Moll: On February 15, 1768, when an inventory was made of the late Richard Ambler's slaves on Jamestown Island and his leasehold in the Governor's Land, an adult female slave named Moll was listed. In 1769 a female slave named Moll was living on Jamestown Island and was identified as Hannah's daughter. She was part of the late Edward Ambler I's estate (York County Wills and Inventories 21:386–391; AMB-E). She was the second Ambler slave named Moll.

* * *

William Momford (Mumford, Mountford): In May 1671 the General Court ordered William Momford, a merchant, to audit the accounts of John Stubbs, Richard Moore, and Thomas Glasbrook. In March 1675 Momford successfully sued Colonel Thomas Swann I of urban Jamestown. He claimed that he had given a pearl necklace to Swann as security, but that Swann failed to return it (MCGC 260, 403, 405).

Mrs. Ann Momford (Mrs. William Momford [Mumford, Mountford]): On September 28, 1672, Mrs. Ann Momford's attorney sued Captain John Grove's estate. Grove had a long-standing association with colonels Thomas Swann, Nathaniel Bacon, and other Jamestown property owners. His administrator was obliged to post collateral (MCGC 310).

* * *

Peter (Peeter) Montague (Montecue, Mountague, Mountegue): Peter Montague patented 100 acres on the New Town Haven (Pagan) River in Nansemond County in October 1647, and served as a Nansemond County burgess in 1652 and 1653. However, in January 1656 he patented 200 acres on the south side of the Rappahannock River, in Lancaster County, and moved there sometime prior to June 1656, when he appraised the late George Beach's estate. He patented an additional 200 acres on the south side of the Rappahannock in 1658. Throughout 1656, 1657, and 1658 Montague served as a county justice, and in 1658 he represented Lancaster County in the assembly. In February 1657 he served as the attorney of Francys Browne and his wife, Elizabeth, and conducted a real estate transaction on their behalf. When Montague made his will on March 27, 1659, he indicated that he was sick and weak; by May 25, 1659, he was dead. He left his wife, Ciceley, her dower third of his estate and left the remainder to sons Peter and William and daughters Ellen, Margaret, and Elizabeth. His daughter Anne was identified as the late wife of John Jadwyn, whereas Ellen was married to William Thompson I. Montague bequeathed his land on the Rappahannock River to his sons. In January 1664 Mrs. Ciceley Montague petitioned the justices of Lancaster County's monthly court, asking for a third of the 900 acres her late husband had owned in the county, acreage to which she was entitled as a widow (LEO 30–31, 34; Lancaster County Deeds &c. Book 2 [1652–1657]:267, 307, 331; Deeds &c. Book 2 [1654–1661]:62–63; Order Book 1656–1666:258; PB 2:130; 4:340, 350).

John Moon (Moone, O'moon, Omoonce): John Moon came to Virginia in 1623 and by January 1625 had seated some acreage on the Governor's Land, in Pasbehay. In early 1626, when he was ordered to pay his debt to Captain William Peirce of Jamestown, he was identified as "Mr.," an indication that he was considered a gentleman. By early 1629 Moon had moved to Warresqueak (later, Isle of Wight) County, which he made his permanent home, and continued to acquire land. Part of his acreage was on Warresqueak Bay. When Moon patented some additional land on October 21, 1635, he used the headright of his wife, Susan, indicating that it was for her own personal adventure. By January 1639 he had begun representing Isle of Wight County in the colony's assembly. He served as a burgess in 1640 and was reelected in 1652 and 1654–1655. After his first wife died, he married Prudence Wilson, a widow with two children. By the time of

John Moon's death in 1655, he had attained the rank of captain in the militia. It was perhaps while he served as an Isle of Wight County burgess that he first acquired a lot and house in urban Jamestown. When Moon made his will, he instructed his executors to sell his "Brew House and Land belonging to it at James Town," using the proceeds to cover his debts. He left his beloved wife, Prudence, a fourth of his personal estate, noting that the remainder was to be divided among his three daughters. He also left Prudence a third interest in his 900 acres of newly patented land. The testator made bequests to his stepson, William Wilson, and to his stepdaughter, Joan Wilson Garland, and her husband, Peter. He also made philanthropic bequests to his home parishes in England and in Isle of Wight County. Moon's land in urban Jamestown probably was sold within a relatively short time, for there is no evidence that his heirs retained the property. A land transaction made in 1694 reveals that in 1642 Captain John Moon had patented 200 acres on Pagan Creek, what became known as Red Point or Poplar Neck, and bequeathed it to his married daughter, Mary Green, from whom it descended to her son, Thomas. Prudence Moon died intestate without having remarried, and on March 9, 1663, her son, William Wilson, was appointed her administrator (VI&A 498–499; LEO 18, 29, 32; Isle of Wight County Deeds, Wills & Guardian Accounts Book A:67; Administrations and Probates 1:7; Deed Book 1 [1688–1704]:154).

John Moore: On May 28, 1673, John Moore was ordered to examine the work bricklayer John Bird had performed for Jamestown merchant Richard James I. On September 24, 1674, Moore, who was a gentleman and possibly a resident of the capital city, testified in the suit Thomas Rabley of Jamestown filed against Henry Webb (MCGC 379).

Richard Moore: On May 25, 1671, Richard Moore was identified as a merchant when he was ordered to audit the accounts of John Stubbs and Thomas Glasbrook. In 1676 Moore imported Virginia tobacco to England and exported a large quantity of beer to the colony. He appears to have patented some land in Lower Norfolk County (MCGC 260; SR 5592c, 5726c; PB 7:209).

Captain William Moore: Captain William Moore reportedly was killed in September 1676 while defending Jamestown from the rebel Nathaniel Bacon's men. His widow, Jane, survived and claimed a pension on the basis of his military service (JHB 1660–1693:69).

Richard Mopeson (Mompesson?): On March 22, 1670, it was noted that Richard Mopeson, an indentured servant, sometimes went by the name "Richard Davis" (SAIN 9:382).

Morassane (Native American): In November 1624 interpreter Robert Poole said that while Samuel Argall was deputy governor, six men were slain by natives who carried their firearms to Pamunkey, where they were used by Indians named Morassane and Nemattanew (Jack of the Feather). Governor George Yeardley sent Poole to Pamunkey to steal the guns' firing mechanisms so that the Indians would return the weapons to Jamestown to be repaired (VI&A 500).

Francis Morgan I: Francis Morgan I patented 50 acres of land in Charles River (later, York) County in September 1637 and immediately acquired an additional 100 acres. His plantation, which abutted the York River, was adjacent to the properties owned by Captain John West and William Pryor. Morgan, West, Pryor, Richard Townsend, and John Uty were among the first to settle in Chiskiack, then a frontier area. Morgan began serving as a justice as soon as a local court was established in the newly formed county. He patented an additional 100 acres of riverfront land in August 1638, this time using the acreage of his neighbor William Pryor as a reference point. The westernmost boundary of Morgan's land was a small, marshy inlet known as Morgan's Creek, which was just west of present-day Roosevelt (Brackens) Pond. In October 1640 Francis Morgan, who was then York County's high sheriff, failed to collect the levy on time. Because the delay resulted in the tobacco becoming spoiled before it was readied for shipment, he and his under sheriff were ordered to collect the proper amount. By 1642 Morgan had begun speculating in land on the Middle Peninsula, patenting 1,000 acres. In 1652 he laid claim to 510 acres on the east side of Poropotank Creek in Gloucester County, adjacent to some land he already owned. He and Ralph Green together patented 500 acres on the upper side of the Mattaponi River in what was then Gloucester County. Francis Morgan I served as a burgess for York County, the jurisdiction in which he continued to reside, and attended the assembly sessions held in 1647–1648, 1652, and 1653. By October 26, 1657, the late Captain Francis Morgan I's son and heir, Francis II, had come of age. He appeared before the justices of the General Court in June 1670, where he proved Richard Roberts' will. In 1675 the younger Francis Morgan brought suit against the sheriff of Lower Norfolk County because he had failed to compel Captain John Warner to appear. In 1676 Captain Francis Morgan II was identified as a merchant when he imported a substantial quantity of wrought iron, nails, and men's hose (LEO 26, 29, 31; PB 1:483–484, 591, 807; 3:166, 194; SR 5594a; York County Deeds, Orders, Wills 1:23, 27–30; 3:1; MCGC 222, 427, 472).

William Morgan: Ancient planter William Morgan alias Brooks (Brookes, Broockes) alias Jones arrived in Jamestown in 1610. By 1624 he and his wife, Sibile, were living in Elizabeth City where he was known as William Brooks. In a May 1638 land patent he was identified as Morgan alias Brooks. Finally, when he laid claim to some additional land in 1642, he was called William Morgan alias Brooks alias Jones (VI&A 503).

[No First Name] Morley (Morrell): In 1608 a laborer named Morley or Morrell came to Virginia in the 2nd Supply of new settlers and would have lived in Jamestown (VI&A 504).

William Morley: William Morley was a burgess for James City in the March 13, 1660, session of the assembly and in all likelihood represented James City County. He was listed among Thomas Rolfe's headrights in 1656 (STAN 73; LEO 36; PB 4:23). Any patents that Morley or his wife were assigned seem to have been lost or destroyed.

Thomas Morrice: On September 28, 1674, Thomas Morrice, one of Governor William Berkeley's servants, was tried by the General Court. Because he had stolen a boat and fled, he was sentenced to a whipping and his term of service to Berkeley was extended. Afterward, he was obliged to serve William White of urban Jamestown for a year and a half, in compensation for stealing his boat (MCGC 382).

Edward Morris (Morish): Edward Morris or Morish, a gentleman, came to Virginia in 1607 and was one of the first settlers. He was identified as a corporal when he died suddenly in Jamestown on August 14, 1607 (VI&A 504).

George Morris (Morrice): In June 1670 the General Court's justices ordered George Morris and three other men to survey some land on the Middle Peninsula in order to settle a dispute. In 1672 he and Robert Beverley I were told to conduct a survey in Gloucester County. The following year he was ordered to survey another piece of contested land. Morris began patenting land in Old Rappahannock County in 1674, and in April the General Court granted him 134 acres of escheat land in New Kent County. He got into a heated dispute with Colonel Robert Abrahall and assaulted him. As punishment, the General Court expelled George Morris from all civil and military offices until he and Abrahall could resolve their differences. He also was ordered to post a bond guaranteeing his good behavior. By March 1676 Morris had been restored to his captaincy and was appointed referee in a dispute between two local men. In 1680 he acquired a 1,190-acre tract in Old Rappahannock and added to his holdings as time went on. In 1683 he patented several large tracts in New Kent and Old Rappahannock counties, two of which collectively comprised more than 6,000 acres. In 1680–1682 George Morris served as a burgess for New Kent County. When he renewed and expanded one of his patents in New Kent County in April 1683, he was said to be occupying the 1,100-acre New Kent plantation that he had gotten in 1674 (LEO 45; PB 7:53, 236, 242, 248, 276, 380; MCGC 224, 315, 321, 332, 352, 368, 380).

Francis Morrison (Moryson, Morison): In August 1649 Francis Morrison, a royalist who had been living in Holland, set sail for Virginia with Henry Norwood, Governor William Berkeley's kinsman. The vessel they were aboard was shipwrecked near the northern part of the Eastern Shore. Berkeley befriended Morrison and made him captain of the fort at Old Point Comfort. In 1650 Morrison was named to the Council of State. In 1654, while Governor Richard Bennett held office and Virginia was under the sway of the Commonwealth government, Major Francis Morrison secured a patent for the 24-acre Glasshouse tract, which he bought from William Harris I, owner of a lot in urban Jamestown. In March 1655 Morrison also purchased a unit in Sir William Berkeley's brick row house in Jamestown, and in 1656 while he was representing James City County in the assembly he began leasing a parcel in the Governor's Land. He went on to become speaker of the assembly and held the rank of colonel for many years. In April 1661, after the Restoration, he was designated deputy governor while Governor Berkeley was in England, and he served in that capacity until Berkeley's return in autumn 1662. During that period Morrison re-

portedly donated communion silver to the church in Jamestown.

Although Morrison went to England in 1663, he continued to receive his salary as the captain of the fort at Old Point Comfort and in 1665 was named master of ordnance. As the assembly's spokesman, he communicated the colonists' concerns to Lord Arlington, who had ready access to King Charles II. Morrison indicated that the burgesses would like to see Virginia incorporated and that they were willing to purchase the Northern Neck from its proprietors. He said that the burgesses realized that the king wanted towns built and admitted that they had made a poor try, having succeeded in building only four or five houses. In 1676, while Virginia was in the throes of Bacon's Rebellion, King Charles II designated Francis Morrison, Herbert Jeffreys, and Sir John Berry as special commissioners and ordered them to investigate the popular uprising's underlying causes. Morrison arrived in the colony in late January 1677 and shortly thereafter prepared a report on conditions in Virginia. He praised Governor Berkeley and reported that Bacon's men had burned Jamestown. He was highly instrumental in drafting the Treaty of Middle Plantation, signed at Middle Plantation on May 29, 1677, and expanded in 1680. Francis Morrison died in England sometime after 1678. Cockacoeske, the Pamunkey Indians' queen, considered Morrison a good friend to her people (FOR III:10:3–4, 19, 50; NUG I:240, 305, 313, 326, 367; HEN I:426; II:159; STAN 16, 35, 51; JHB 1619–1660:20, 96). MCGC 492, 507; Tyler 1893–1894:173; CO 1/17 f 42; 1/33 f 289; 5/1355 ff 33–35, 83; 5/1371 f 19; WITH 321; Clarendon MS 110; SAIN 10:10, 13; LEO 33).

Richard Morrison (Moryson): By 1638 Richard Morrison, who was born in England, was named the captain of the fort at Old Point Comfort, also known as the "Point Comfort Castle." He was a resident of Elizabeth City and was named to the Council of State in 1641, succeeding Roger Wingate, who died in office. On April 7, 1641, Morrison asked permission to go to England. He said that he had important business to transact there and that he was sick and hoped to find better medical treatment in the Mother Country. He proposed leaving his brother, Robert, who was his deputy, in charge of the fort. Major Richard Morrison returned to Virginia and in June 1648 received a patent for 100 acres called the "Fort Field" in Elizabeth City. He made another brief trip to England but returned in 1649 with a message for Secretary Richard Kemp. It stated that the king considered the Old Point Comfort fort a very important defensive work and that he wanted it "mended" and "new works" to be added. The fort was to be staffed with 20 men and two guns were to be kept at the fort, where all incoming ships were to pay their customs duties. Richard Morrison died sometime prior to 1656 (STAN 35; LEO xx; MCGC 474–475, 479; PB 2:128; SR 133, 7811).

Ralph (Ralfe) Morton (Moorton, Murton): Ralph Morton, a gentleman, came to Virginia in 1608 in the 1st Supply of new settlers and would have lived in Jamestown. He was appointed to the Council and in 1620 was identified as a Virginia Company investor (VI&A 505; LEO xx).

***

Arthur Moseley (Mosley): Arthur Moseley, one of William Moseley I's sons, came to Virginia with his parents and brother, William II, during the 1640s, perhaps shortly before King Charles I was beheaded. In March 1650 the justices of Lower Norfolk County granted William Moseley I a land certificate that entitled him to 550 acres because he had transported himself, wife Susanna (Susan), sons William II and Arthur, and some servants to the colony. Almost immediately, the elder Moseley, who settled on the eastern branch of the Elizabeth River, began serving as a court justice in Lower Norfolk County. In 1652 he witnessed a deed whereby Lieutenant Colonel John Upton's widow, Margaret, disposed of some land on Pagan Creek. A document William Moseley I and his wife, Susanna, signed on August 1, 1650, reveals that he was a merchant who formerly had lived in Rotterdam. It also attests to the couple's immense wealth, for they traded a substantial quantity of expensive jewelry for nine head of cattle they bought from Francis Yeardley and his wife, Sarah. When William Moseley I made his will in 1655, he left some of his acreage to his sons, Arthur and William Moseley II. In March 1662 Arthur Moseley patented 200 acres on Broad Creek in Lower Norfolk County. He served as a burgess for Lower Norfolk in 1676. On February 1, 1700, he made his will, leaving to his wife, Ann, life-rights in the plantation they occupied. He also made bequests to his sons Joseph, Benjamin, William, Arthur, Edward, and George, and to his daughters Mary and Susan, who were married women. Moseley's will, which mentions four other males who may have been his grandsons, is fragmentary (Lower Norfolk County Record

Book B:141; C:10, 24, 166; Wills and Deeds 6:270; LEO 41; PB 5:176).

William Moseley (Mosley) II: William Moseley II, the son of Rotterdam merchant William Moseley I, who came to Virginia during the 1640s, settled in Old Rappahannock County sometime prior to August 1647. William II, a surveyor, began speculating in real estate, sometimes with a co-investor. Between 1663 and 1690, he acquired several large tracts of land bordering the Rappahannock River. However, he retained his holdings in Lower Norfolk County and in 1670 served as one of its burgesses. In 1672–1674 he commenced representing Old Rappahannock County in the assembly, and over the years he often performed surveys and functioned as an attorney. In 1678 his name appeared in the records of Lancaster County's court when he sued one of his debtors. In April 1684 William Moseley II was still working as a surveyor in Old Rappahannock County, but he died sometime prior to October 2nd, by which time his widow, Martha, had married Captain George Tayler (LEO 39, 54, 56; PB 4:607; 5:321; 6:15, 320, 384, 539; 7:254; 8:113; Old Rappahannock County Deeds and Wills 1656–1664:14, 18–19, 78–79; 1677–1682:228–229, 324–325; Order Book 1683–1686:11, 44, 49; Lancaster County Order Book 1666–1680:424; Northumberland County Order Book 1666–1678:89, 162; Lower Norfolk County Record Book B:141; C:10, 24, 166; Wills, Deeds, Orders D [1656–1666]:340, 343; Richmond County Deed Book 1 [1693–1693]:26; 2 [1693–1695:50–55; Isle of Wight County Deeds, Wills & Guardian Accounts Book A:41).

William Moseley (Mosley) III: Captain William Moseley III, the late William Moseley II's son, commenced serving as a justice in Essex County in May 1692, the year that Essex was formed from part of Old Rappahannock County's territory. At the end of the year he purchased some land on the lower side of the Rappahannock River, part of a tract known as Button's Range. He continued to serve as a court justice and in 1693 was one of the men authorized to purchase land on which the county's courthouse complex was to be built. Moseley, like his late father, performed numerous surveys and his name appeared frequently in the records of Richmond County, which, like Essex, was formed from Old Rappahannock County. Colonel Moseley eventually became a burgess for Essex County, attending the 1695–1696 and 1696–1697 assembly sessions. Over the years he continued to conduct surveys, often at the county's behest. On at least one occasion, he was accused of laying out a tract that encroached upon someone else's land. He was made Essex County's sheriff in July 1698 and was still serving as a justice in August 1699. However, by April 10, 1700, he was dead, at which time his will was presented to Essex County's monthly court. Moseley, who was a widower, left his late wife's three wedding rings to his daughter, Martha. He bequeathed his land to sons, John and William IV, but his personal estate was to be divided between them and their sister, Martha. The testator named his brothers Edward, Robert, and Benjamin Moseley as his executors and made bequests to his godson and two of his friends. Administration of the late William Moseley III's estate was granted to Benjamin Moseley because William Moseley IV was underage (LEO 54, 56; Essex County Order Book 1692–1695:1, 90, 109, 158, 203, 232, 261; 1695–1699:1, 3, 21, 95, 102, 155; 1699–1702:3, 29, 36, 48; Deeds and Wills 1692–1695:81, 154, 282, 376; 1695–1699:48, 157, 201–202, 206–207; 1699–1702:1, 26; Richmond County Deed Book 1 [1692–1693]:66, 96–98; 2 [1693–1695]:43–45, 107, 139–141, 152–157, 198–199).

* * *

Robert Mosely: On October 13, 1640, the General Court sentenced Robert Mosely and some other indentured servants to a whipping because they had failed to report some runaways. Moseley's time of service was extended by a year, and he was obliged to compensate his master, who had paid his fine (MCGC 467).

Theodore Moses (Moyes, Moyses, Moises, Mosses): During the mid-1620s Theodore Moses, who may have been a Virginia Company tenant, was residing at the College. By 1628 he had moved to Archer's Hope, an area for which he served as burgess in 1629 and 1630. By 1640 Moses had patented land on the west side of the Chickahominy River, abutting the tributary that became known as Moses Creek (VI&A 506; LEO 8–9).

John Mottrom (Mottram, Motram, Mottron, Mottrum, Motteram) I: John Mottrom I, who came to Virginia sometime prior to 1640, settled on the west side of Wormeley Creek, in what was then Charles River (later, York) County. In June 1640 he was among the men ordered to recover some runaway Africans who had fled from that area. By 1645 Mottrom had moved to the Northern Neck and become established at a site on the Chickacoan (or Coan) River. When the assembly convened in

1645–1646, he represented the settlers living in Chickacoan, later Northumberland County, and he was returned to the assembly in 1652. He also became a justice in the county court, which held its first meetings in his home. During the late 1640s and early 1650s, Mottrom, who was a successful planter and heavily involved in trade, patented large quantities of land in the Northern Neck, especially on the Potomac River, in time amassing many thousands of acres. He had a wharf and store or warehouse near his home, which was known as Coan Hall. Colonel John Mottrom was alive on January 20, 1653, but died prior to August 20, 1655. A detailed inventory of his estate and the accounts compiled by his executors attest to his enormous wealth and elaborate lifestyle. He was survived by his wife, Ursula, who married Colonel George Colclough of Northumberland County. John Mottrom II, his late father's principal heir, became prominent in his own right. In July 1656 the late John Mottrom I's children were identified as Anne (age 17), John II (age 14), and Frances (age 11), when they chose Colonel Thomas Speke as their legal guardian. By November 1657 Anne Mottrom had married Richard Wright of Chicacoan, who sought her share of her late father's estate and in 1661 was serving as Mottrom's administrator. In 1662 Richard and Anne Mottrom Wright sold the decedent's 900 acres on Nominy Bay to Nicholas Spencer I, who had married Anne's sister, Frances. In 1665 Nicholas and Frances Mottrom Spencer disposed of the late John Mottrom I's 1,900 acres on the Piankatank River (LEO 24, 29; Northumberland County Deeds and Orders 1650–1652:41; Wills, Inventories &c. 1652–1658:14, 21, 35, 55, 87, 94, 115–121, 123–124; Record Book 1662–1666:111–112; Order Book 1652–1665:15, 65, 96, 148, 282, 286; Westmoreland County Deeds, Wills &c. 1661–1662:20a–21a; Deeds and Wills No. 1 [1653–1659]:270–273; PB 2:185, 247; 3:64, 100; 4:49; 5:482; MCGC 468).

Thomas Moulton (Moultone, Molton, Moulston): In 1619 Thomas Moulton, a cook and gardener, set sail for Virginia. He was headed for Berkeley Hundred, where he was supposed to serve for four or five years in exchange for 25 acres of land. After the 1622 Indian attack, he became a servant in Captain William Peirce's household in urban Jamestown, where he was still living in February 1624. He was sent to Shirley Hundred to work on Berkeley Hundred's behalf, perhaps as a cow-keeper, but by February 1625 Moulton had been moved to Captain Roger Smith's plantation, where he was a servant. He testified before the General Court in October 1626 (VI&A 497).

Richard Mounford (Mumford): In June 1624 Richard Mounford testified that on the night he stood watch at the fort in Jamestown, he did not see anyone break into Mr. Peirsey's storehouse, the repository for cape merchant Abraham Peirsey's goods. In January 1625 Mounford was listed among the dead in Jamestown (VI&A 507).

Thomas Mounslie: According to George Percy's narrative, Thomas Mounslie, one of the first Jamestown colonists, died on August 17, 1607 (VI&A 507).

Peter Mountague (see Peter [Peeter] Montague (Montecue, Mountague, Mountegue)

Robert Moutapass alias Robert Markham (Marcum) (see Robert Markham [Marcum] alias Moutapass)

Thomas Mouton: Thomas Mouton, a gentleman, came to Virginia in 1607 and was one of the first settlers. According to George Percy, he died on August 17, 1607, in Jamestown (VI&A 508).

Mquanzafsi (Native American): In May 1657 Mquanzafsi, one of the Rappahannock Indians' Great Men or leaders, joined in making a peace agreement with Old Rappahannock County's justices (Old Rappahannock County Deed Book 1656–1664:10–11).

King of the Muchchotas (Native American) (see King of the Machodoc)

John Munger: On April 25, 1670, John Munger and Thomas Hunt of urban Jamestown were involved in a legal dispute that was aired before the General Court (MCGC 218).

James Murry (Murrey, Murray): In July 1654, only two years after Surry County was formed from James City, James Murry, a planter in Lawnes Creek Parish, agreed to accept Elizabeth Harris's four-year-old son, John Phipps, as his apprentice until Phipps was age 21. Murry, in turn, was to teach the boy how to read and write. Murry seems to have been considered a respectable citizen, for he occasionally served on juries. One of his associates was Randall Holt II of Jamestown Island and Hog Island. Murry seems to have died between October and November 1678. On January 7, 1679, Thomas Rabley of urban Jamestown sued the late James Murry's estate in the court of Surry County

(Surry County Court Records 1652–1663:120; 1664–1671:307, 313, 346, 351, 373, 383; 1672–1682:36, 108, 125, 228, 236, 237, 247; Order Book 1671–1691:236).

William Musgrave: On October 9, 1640, William Musgrave testified on behalf of Ann Belson, an indentured servant who was employed by Theodore Moses and wanted to be assigned to another master (MCGC 465).

George Muleston: When Jamestown merchant Thomas Warnett made his will on February 13, 1629, he named George Muleston as one of his beneficiaries (VI&A 508).

Christopher Muschamp: On March 22, 1677, Christopher Muschamp was brought before Governor William Berkeley and the Council of State, who were conducting a military tribunal. He was accused of treason and supporting the rebel Nathaniel Bacon's cause. He begged for mercy and was ordered to appear before the justices of the Warwick County court wearing a rope around his neck and pleading for forgiveness (MCGC 533).

William Mutch (Mudge, Muche): In February 1624 William Mutch was living in the urban Jamestown household of provost marshal Randall Smallwood. By December 27, 1624, Mutch had wed his wife, Margery, and become a household head in Jamestown. Mutch testified that he was one of Captain John Harvey's former servants and that Harvey had refused to give him his freedom dues and had struck him when he asked for what he was owed. In 1638 Captain Samuel Mathews I listed William Mutch among those who owed him tobacco (VI&A 509–510).

Richard Mutton: In 1607 a youth named Robert Mutton came to Virginia in the first group of settlers and would have lived in Jamestown (VI&A 510).

James Mynns: On April 6, 1671, James Mynns was said to have taken people to Mrs. Underwood's house in urban Jamestown (MCGC 251).

Mynythorne (Native American): In September 1660 the Mattaponi Indians' king and Great Men or leaders denied that they had tried to claim the Old Rappahannock County land then occupied by the plantation of Francis Brown. Mynythorne's name was affixed to the affidavit (Old Rappahannock County Deed Book 1656–1664:111).

N

Naeheoopa (Native American): On May 27, 1658, Naeheoopa, the Rappahannock Indians' king, was among the natives confirming a land transaction made by the tribe's late king, Accapataugh, and Colonel Moore Fauntleroy (Old Rappahannock County Deed Book 1656–1664:26–27).

Namenacus (Native American): In 1621 Secretary John Pory went to the Eastern Shore to search for a site at which salt could be manufactured. There he encountered Namenacus, king of the Patuxunt (Patuxent) Indians. Namenacus, who was trying to locate interpreter Thomas Savage, professed friendship and invited Pory and his group to visit his country. A few weeks later Pory's group arrived at Attoughcomoco, the village of Namenacus and his brother Wamanato (CJS II:289).

Namontack (Native American): When the English colonists visited Powhatan at Werowocomoco in 1608, Captain John Smith and Powhatan agreed to exchange Thomas Savage, a newly arrived youth, for Namontack, an Indian boy. The two young males were traded as a token of goodwill but also so that they could learn their host culture's language and serve as interpreters. Namontack was present when Powhatan and Captain Christopher Newport exchanged gifts at the paramount chief's coronation (VI&A 510; CJS II:290).

Nan: On February 15, 1768, when an inventory was made of the late Richard Ambler's slaves on Jamestown Island and his leasehold in the Governor's Land, an adult female slave named Nan was listed (York County Wills and Inventories 21:386–391).

Nancy (Nanny): On February 15, 1768, when an inventory was made of the late Richard Ambler's slaves at his quarter called Powhatan, an adult female slave named Nancy was living there. In 1769 she was still there and was part of the late Edward Ambler I's estate (York County Wills and Inventories 21:386–391; AMB-E).

Nancy (Nanny): On February 15, 1768, when an inventory was made of the late Richard Ambler's slaves at his quarter called Powhatan, a female slave named Nancy was living there. She was still there in 1769 and was described as a girl who was then part of

the late Edward Ambler I's estate (York County Wills and Inventories 21:386–391; AMB-E). She may have been related to the older woman named Nancy.

Nanny: When an inventory was made in 1769 of Edward Ambler I's estate, Nanny, Grace's child, was living in the Governor's Land. Both were enslaved (AMB-E).

King of the Nansattico Indians (Native American) (see Wattle Jaws)

King of the Nansemond Indians (Native American): On August 14, 1638, John Basse, the son of colonist Nathaniel Basse (Bass, Base), married the king of the Nansemond Indians' daughter, Elizabeth, who was baptized and had converted to Christianity. John Basse, who was born in September 1616, made notes about his parents' and siblings' births and marriages in a book of sermons. The family lived in what became Isle of Wight County (Bass Family Bible Records 1613–1699; VI&A 118).

King of the Nansemond Indians (Native American): On May 29, 1677, the king of the Nansemond Indians, whose people lived on the lower side of the James River, went to Middle Plantation (later Williamsburg) and endorsed the Treaty of Middle Plantation with a cross-like mark. He also signed the expanded version of the treaty, which was consummated between March 18 and June 19, 1680. In recognition of his loyalty to the Crown, King Charles II authorized the fabrication of a purple robe lined with scarlet shalloon, a twill-woven woolen; a crimson ermine-trimmed cap; and a coronet. The Nansemond king was described as a man "of indifferent stature and [a] very friendly Indian and much conversant amongst the English" (LC 5/108 f 8; 9/275 ff 264ro–267ro; CO 5/1371; SR 5736, 5743).

Nanticos (Native American): In November 1624 Edward Grindon said that an Indian named Nanticos was the first native he met who knew how to use firearms. He added that he did not know who had taught Nanticos how to shoot (VI&A 510).

Christopher Neale (Neal) I: In 1663 Christopher Neale I witnessed a document in Northumberland County. He married Hannah, the daughter of Matthew Rodham, and by 1665 was living in the county. In

1666 Matthew Rodham gave Hannah and Christopher Neale the 393-acre plantation on which he (Rodham) then lived, the same property that burgess Hugh Lee formerly had occupied. Although copies of any land patents that Christopher Neale secured have been lost or destroyed, in March 1695 his acreage was mentioned in John Hornsby's patent for a neighboring property on the Wicocomoco River. Like many of his contemporaries, Neale appeared in court from time to time, trying to recover funds from his debtors, and he also assisted in the settlement of estates. At least one of his indentured servants was a French youth. Neale was a constable for the Cherry Point area in 1672 and shortly thereafter obtained a license that authorized him to hire an Indian. In 1677 he brought suit against a man who had installed a dormer window in his house, an aperture that leaked and caused considerable damage. He became a county justice in 1679 and served for many years. In 1683 the county court acknowledged that Neale had produced 37 yards of woolen cloth, an achievement that made him eligible for a monetary award from the assembly. He served as a burgess for Northumberland County in 1685 but failed to appear at the 1686 session. His brother-in-law was burgess Richard Kenner, who had married Matthew Rodham's daughter Elizabeth. In 1699 a Christopher Neale, probably the son of the former burgess, was serving as a Northumberland County justice. He and his wife, Jane, were then functioning as the late Richard Rodgers' executors (LEO 48; Northumberland County Record Book 1662–1666:109; 1666–1670:22; Order Book 1652–1665:424; 1666–1678:37, 114, 133, 146, 165, 315; 1678–1698:37, 64, 164, 182–183, 225, 319, 332; 1699–1700:16; NN 2:143–144).

John Neale (Neal): In 1630 John Neale received a 50-acre leasehold at the Strawberry Banks in Elizabeth City by means of a deed of gift. He reaffirmed the title to his acreage in 1632, at which time he was identified as a merchant. Shortly thereafter, he moved to the Eastern Shore and began patenting large quantities of land in Accomack County. He laid claim to 1,500 acres on the seaside in 1636, the same year that he patented 500 acres on Smith Island. A year later he patented some land adjacent to Edmund Scarborough II's property and at the head of Kings Creek. Finally, in 1643 he patented 300 acres bordering Maggoty Bay. When Neale testified before Accomack County's justices in May 1636, he said that he was age 40 or thereabouts. A couple months later he became a vestryman. Like many of his con-

temporaries, Neale appeared in court from time to time to engage in litigation that usually involved the collection of debts. In September 1637 his wife, Elizabeth, testified against a man who had slandered a local woman. John Neale became a burgess for Accomack County and attended the assembly sessions held in 1639, 1640, and 1642 (VI&A 511; PB 1:134–135, 365, 413, 417, 465, 518; 2:365; AMES 1:52–54, 70, 86, 121–122; LEO 17–18, 20).

Neckennechehey (Native American): On May 27, 1658, Neckennechehey, one of the Rappahannock Indians' Great Men or leaders, was among the natives confirming a land transaction made by the Rappahannock's late king, Accapataugh, and Colonel Moore Fauntleroy (Old Rappahannock County Deed Book 1656–1664:26–27).

Necotowance (Native American): In October 1646 Necotowance, Opechancanough's immediate successor and the leader of several native groups that formerly had been unified under the revered paramount chief, concluded a treaty with the Virginia government. Although the colony's governing officials called him "Emperor of the Indians," his position was much weaker than that of his predecessors. As a result of the 1646 treaty, Tidewater Virginia's Indians ceded much of their territory to the English and acknowledged that their right to the remaining land was derived from the English monarch. They also agreed to pay an annual tribute to the Crown's representatives and to let Virginia's governor appoint or confirm their leaders. This was an especially important concession, for it hastened the disintegration of the Powhatan Chiefdom, which previously had been unified under a powerful paramount chief. Thanks to the 1646 treaty, the Indians ceded the eastern part of the James-York peninsula (inland to the fall line) to the Virginia government, and they relinquished their territory on the lower side of the James River, as far south as the Blackwater River and west to the old Manakin town. All natives entering the ceded territory could be lawfully slain unless they were garbed in "a coat of striped stuff," to be worn by official messengers as a badge of safe conduct. In exchange for these concessions, the Virginia government agreed to protect the tributary Indians from their enemies and to reserve for the tributaries' use all of the land north of the York River, to the west of Poropotank Creek. Colonists who had established plantations within the territory assigned to the Indians were supposed to abandon them. In accord with the terms of the 1646 treaty, Necotowance and "five more petty kings attending him" came to Jamestown in March 1648 to present 20 beaver skins, his people's first annual tribute to Virginia's governor. The fact that Necotowance had only five lesser leaders in his entourage was a reflection of the extent to which the ancient Powhatan Chiefdom had disintegrated. Many natives may not have understood the terms of the 1646 treaty or the necessity of wearing a striped coat when entering the ceded territory. A 1649 account quoted Necotowance as saying "My countrymen tell me I am a liar when I tell them the English will kill you if you goe into their bounds." The writer hastened to add that the "valiant Captain Freeman made him no liar when lately he killed three Indians without badge encroaching" (HEN I:323–329; FOR II:8:25).

Ned: In 1769, when an inventory was made of Edward Ambler I's estate in 1769, Ned, an adult male slave, was living on Jamestown Island (AMB-E).

Ned: In 1769 an enslaved boy named Ned was living on the Governor's Land. He was attributed to the late Edward Ambler I's estate (AMB-E).

Ned: In 1769 Ned and his mother, Sall (Sal), who were enslaved, were living on Jamestown Island and were part of the late Edward Ambler I's estate (York County Wills and Inventories 21:386–391; AMB-E).

John Needles: On March 12, 1627, John Needles, a sailor, testified before the General Court in Jamestown about an incident that had taken place in the West Indies involving the ship *Saker* (VI&A 512).

Nell: On February 15, 1768, when an inventory was made of the late Richard Ambler's slaves at his quarter called Powhatan, an adult female slave named Nell was living there (York County Wills and Inventories 21:386–391).

Nelly: On February 15, 1768, when an inventory was made of the late Richard Ambler's slaves at his quarter called Powhatan, an adult female slave named Nelly was living there (York County Wills and Inventories 21:386–391).

Nelly: On May 31, 1793, two of Champion Travis's slaves, Daphne and Nelly, allegedly attacked and killed their overseer, Joel Gathright. The women reportedly were plowing the fields of Travis's plantation on Jamestown Island when Gathright began berating

them for allowing sheep to get into a cornfield. When Nelly hotly denied it, the overseer began flailing her with a small cane. At first, she was able to flee from his blows, despite her pregnancy, but when she stumbled and fell, he struck her repeatedly. When Nelly regained her footing, she began to fight back, at which point Daphne joined in the fray. The two women then knocked Gathright to the ground and began beating him with sticks and branches. Two young slaves heard Gathright's cries and ran for help, but by the time someone came to his aid, he was almost dead. According to the James City County coroner, the left side of Gathright's skull had been crushed with a large stone. An inquisition (or hearing) was held in Jamestown. The enslaved women, who were tried by James City County's court justices without legal representation, were allowed to question those testifying against them. Ultimately, they were found guilty of murder and sentenced to hang. Daphne was led to the gallows on July 19th but Nelly's execution was delayed on account of her pregnancy. Although the circumstances surrounding the case are open to conjecture, the slaves' plight seems to have aroused some public sympathy. In September 1793 a group of neighborhood men asked Governor Henry Lee to commute Nelly's sentence. But simultaneously, another group of citizens filed a counter-petition, recommending that clemency be denied. William Lee of Green Spring, who favored execution, contended that "the alarming commotions in this neighborhood and the dangerous example of such a murder" might inspire other slaves to rise up against their owners. Governor Lee apparently agreed with his brother, William, for he postponed Nelly's hanging only long enough for her baby to be born. Her death sentence was carried out on October 4th, and as was customary when a slave was executed for a capital crime, her owner was compensated for her value as personal property (PALM VI:461–465, 521, 532–533, 543).

Francis Nelson: Captain Francis Nelson arrived in Jamestown in early April 1608, in the 1st Supply of new settlers. According to Captain John Smith, Nelson was a good mariner and an honest man. When Francis Nelson made his will in November 1612, he indicated that he was from St. Katherine's Precinct in London (VI&A 512).

George Nelson: In February 1624 George Nelson was a servant in the home of Governor Francis Wyatt in urban Jamestown. By January 1625 he had moved to the Governor's Land and was identified as one of the governor's servants (VI&A 512).

William Nelson alias Peter Atherton: In October 1670 William Nelson alias Peter Atherton was described as a clergyman whose right to serve as a minister had been suspended (MCGC 226).

Rowland Nelstrop: Rowland Nelstrop, a laborer who arrived in Virginia in 1608, was part of the 1st Supply of new colonists in Jamestown (VI&A 512).

Nemattanew (Nemetenew, Nenemach-anew) (Native American): Nemattanew, sometimes known as Jack of the Feather because of his feathered battle attire, was one of paramount chief Opechancanough's favorites. Some Indians were said to believe that he possessed magical powers. In 1617–1618 the firearms that belonged to six men slain by natives reportedly were carried to Pamunkey, where they were used by Nemattanew and another warrior. Sometime prior to 1621 Nemattanew killed a colonist. The deceased man's servants captured Nemattanew and put him to death. Later, some people proffered that Nemattanew's demise at the hands of the colonists was an underlying cause of the 1622 Indian attack (VI&A 512).

Edward Nevell: On December 5, 1625, Edward Nevell sued his employer, merchant and mariner Thomas Weston, in the General Court. The outcome may not have been favorable, for in January 1626, when Nevell was in Canada, he was overheard making critical remarks about the governing officials who tried his case. When he returned to Virginia, he was punished severely for having made an affront to authority. Nevell was to be pilloried in Jamestown's marketplace, lose his ears, and be made a servant for the rest of his life. In February 1626 he appeared before the General Court, where he filed a complaint against three men who allegedly stole some wine from the cabin of the ship he was aboard (VI&A 513).

Alice Newberry: Alice Newberry came to Virginia from England with William and Elizabeth Rowley (Rowsley) in 1622. The Rowley household, which included a large number of servants, resided on Jamestown Island. The Rowley couple died sometime after April 1623 but before February 16, 1624, as did one of their maidservants, perhaps Alice (VI&A 513).

John (Jonathan) Newell: On April 23, 1667, John Newell, a York County merchant, acquired a large tract of rural land that was located within Jamestown's corporate limits. The acreage formerly belonged to Jonathan (John) Knowles, one of Newell's debtors. Because Knowles' property was worth more than the sum he owed to Newell, Newell agreed to pay the balance. John Newell, like Knowles, seemingly was plagued by financial problems, for he was frequently identified as a debtor during the 1650s while he lived in Surry County. In 1653 Newell asked Surry's justices of the peace for permission to leave Virginia. He represented London merchant Joseph Beaman in the Surry County court in 1657 and a year later served as Beaman's attorney in Lower Norfolk County's monthly court. Newell was a close associate of William Marriott of Surry. In April 1667 John Newell and Ambrose Clare (Cleare) patented 2,500 acres of land in New Kent County. Later they had a major disagreement that was aired before the General Court. Although Newell acknowledged his indebtedness to Robert Whitehair in April 1670, he was arrested and incarcerated in York County's jail, but escaped. He died in 1672, and on September 24th of that year, Newell's widow, Elizabeth, was named his administratrix.

As soon as John Newell's creditors learned of his death, they flocked into court. Thomas Bushrod, Stephen Proctor, John Randall, Lieutenant Colonel Cuthbert Potter, and Isaac Foxcraft, along with John Page and George Lee of Jamestown, all filed claims against Newell's estate, as did London merchants Spencer Piggott and William Davis. On the other hand, there were quite a few people who owed money to the decedent: William Roberts, John Coale, George Distiard, and D. White. Mrs. Elizabeth Newell disputed the claim that was filed by Cuthbert Potter, and asked Robert Beverley I to assist her in dealing with him. She also contested a claim that was lodged by Mathew Page. Settlement of the Newell estate dragged on, and in 1676 Stephen Proctor's widow was still trying to recover the sum the decedent owed her late husband. In 1676 the General Court audited the accounts of John Newell's estate, which still had not been settled, and Richard Littlepage agreed to serve as the decedent's legal representative. Among the properties Newell owned at the time of his death were his 133-plus acres in urban Jamestown, 500 acres in York's Old Fields, and George Gill's mill in York County. He also had a legal interest in a mill

***

at Martin's Hundred. When John Newell died his acreage on Jamestown Island descended to his brother and heir-at-law, David Newell, a merchant who owned some land in New Kent County. Legal disputes between the decedent's widow, Elizabeth Newell, and her brother-in-law, David, continued for several years (MCGC 211, 235, 237, 247, 260, 273, 275, 307, 324–325, 328, 338, 342, 344, 350, 352, 356–357, 363, 374, 387, 437, 404, 441; CBE 41; AMB 10, 14, 15, 16, 19, 20, 28, 29, 33; Patent Book 7:98; NUG I:559; II:26, 222; Surry County Deeds, Wills &c. 1652–1672:23, 121;York County Deeds, Orders, Wills 1:397; Deeds, Orders, Wills 1665–1672:17a, 17b; Lower Norfolk County Wills, Deeds, Orders D [1656–1666]:157).

David Newell: When John (Jonathan) Newell died in 1672, his 133-plus acres in urban Jamestown descended to his brother and legal heir, David, a merchant who owned some land in New Kent County. Legal disputes between the widowed Elizabeth Newell and her brother-in-law, David, spanned a period of several years. In October 1671 John Hayward (Heyward), who had married the widow of Thomas Hunt of Jamestown, successfully brought suit against David Newell as the late Jonathan Newell's heir, and he also sued the widowed Elizabeth Newell. Although David Newell was arrested and jailed, he posted a bond and was freed. On February 7, 1677, Newell sold one acre of the "country house" lot on Jamestown's Back Street to William Sherwood. Newell already had done business with Sherwood, for in 1669 he had sold him and Thomas Rabley of Jamestown a 17-acre parcel in Middle Plantation. David Newell had a long-standing connection with the capital city, for prior to October 4, 1672, he married Letitia, the widow and administrator of John Barber I of Jamestown, who seems to have been a merchant. When John Page, Jonathan Newell, and William Monford met in Jamestown in June 1671 to review the accounts of a merchant who was being sued, they convened at David Newell's house. The dwelling likely had belonged to the late John Barber I, whose remarried widow Letitia Barber Newell probably had a dower interest (AMB 26, 29, 83; York County Deeds, Orders, Wills 1:397; MCGC 240, 262, 280–281, 293, 307–308, 314–315, 321, 342, 344, 374; WITH 82; CBE 41; NUG I:559; II:222, 261; PB 7:98).

* * *

[No First Name] Newman: In 1693 a gentleman named Newman reportedly served as a burgess for Westmoreland County. According to researcher Cynthia Leonard, his surname appeared in the official records that were sent to England. However, extant minutes of the Virginia assembly indicate that William Hardidge and Thomas Yowell were then Westmoreland's burgesses (LEO 52). The possibility exists that the nameless Mr. Newman was Alexander Newman, who later represented Richmond County.

Alexander Newman: When John Newman of Old Rappahannock County made his will in 1676, he identified Alexander Newman as his eldest son and left him 600 acres of land adjacent to the Morattico Indian town. He also named younger sons John and Samuel as heirs. Two years later Alexander Newman assigned part the decedent's estate to his brother John. Alexander Newman's name appeared numerous times in the records of Old Rappahannock County when he witnessed documents, served as an attorney, and had jury duty. He patented 580 acres in the lower part of Old Rappahannock County in April 1690 and an additional 50 acres in Richmond County in December 1694. When he gave a heifer in April 1693 to Edward and Elizabeth Jeffrey's daughter, Easter (Esther?), his goddaughter, he identified himself as a resident of the newly formed Richmond County, a descendant of the lower part of Old Rappahannock County. In 1696–1697, when the assembly convened, Captain Alexander Newman was a burgess for Richmond County. He died sometime prior to August 10, 1699, when his widow, Elizabeth, signed a marriage contract with John Trapley of Richmond County. The decedent bequeathed part of his property on Morattico Creek to Ann Glascock, the daughter of the late Gregory Glascock. He also left some additional acreage to Thomas Newman, who sold it to Captain John Trapley in 1700 (LEO 56; Old Rappahannock County Deeds and Wills 1677–1682:27–30, 137–139, 255, 315; Order Book 1683–1686:28–30; 1687–1692:131; Richmond County Deed Book 1 [1692–1693]:121; 3 [1695–1704]:63–65, 99, 120–122; PB 8:136; NN 2:98–99).

Mr. and Mrs. Christopher Newport: Captain Christopher Newport, a skillful mariner, made several voyages to the West Indies and North American coast before bringing the first colonists to Virginia, arriving at Cape Henry on April 26, 1607. He also explored the James River inland to the falls. Newport left Virginia in June 1607 but returned to the colony with the 1st Supply of new immigrants, arriving in Jamestown in January 1608. Although the fort burned shortly after the newcomers' arrival, Newport and his crew helped the colonists rebuild. Newport and Captain John Smith explored the Pamunkey River and traded with the Indians' paramount chief, Powhatan. Newport left Virginia but returned in May 1610 with Sir Thomas Gates and Sir George Somers, with whom he was shipwrecked in Bermuda. In June 1610 Lord Delaware designated Newport a vice admiral and in July named him to his council. Later, Newport and his men constructed a wharf in Jamestown while Sir Thomas Dale was having some other improvements made. He returned to England and in 1612 was employed by the East India Company. When he died in 1617, he was survived by a widow and son. In November 1619 Newport's son asked Virginia Company officials for land on behalf of his late father's investment, and in July 1621 Newport's widow was awarded land in Virginia for having paid for the transportation of six men who went to the colony in 1619 (VI&A 514; STAN 27).

Richard Newsum: On June 17, 1675, the General Court determined that Captain Richard Newsum owed money to Colonel Nathaniel Bacon of urban Jamestown (MCGC 412).

Marmaduke Newton: On April 8, 1674, Marmaduke Newton was fined for abusing Colonel Nathaniel Bacon, a member of the Council of State and Jamestown landowner (MCGC 371).

Richard Nicholas: In 1629 Richard Nicholas, an ironmonger and the partner of Joshua Foote, sold ironware to Sir John Harvey of Jamestown, who as late as March 1636 still owed him £45 for those goods (SAIN 1:225; VI&A 515).

Agnes Nicholls: On March 29, 1620, Agnes Nicholls was identified as the mother and executrix of the late Henry Davies, who went to Virginia in 1617 with Lord Delaware. She probably was in England when she drafted her petition to Virginia Company officials (VI&A 515).

John Nicholls (Nichols): John Nicholls, a gentleman, came to Virginia in 1608 in the 1st Supply of new Jamestown colonists (VI&A 516).

Francis Nicholson: Francis Nicholson was born on November 12, 1655, in Yorkshire, England, and entered the army in January 1678. In 1686 he was appointed captain of a company of foot soldiers that accompanied Sir Edmund Andros to New England, and he served as Andros's deputy in New York from 1688 to 1689. Afterward, he received a commission as lieutenant governor of Virginia, a position he held from June 1690 to September 1692. Nicholson was governor of Maryland from July 1694 to December 1698, at which time he became Virginia's governor.

In 1691, while Francis Nicholson was Virginia's lieutenant governor, James City County's justices asked permission to commence meeting in the General Courthouse because their courthouse was in disrepair. Nicholson agreed but asked the justices to relinquish their title to the acreage on which their courthouse stood. He said that if they did, he would have the building repaired and converted into a school for local children. Nicholson also sought to have the General Courthouse modified and repaired. In March 1697, while Nicholson was Maryland's governor, he spent some time in Jamestown. According to the Rev. James Blair, when Nicholson went to Middle Plantation and visited the College of William and Mary, he got into a violent quarrel with Colonel Daniel Parke II, who struck him over the head with a horsewhip. Blair said that Nicholson, who was bareheaded at the time, would have challenged Parke to a duel, had he not left his sword "in a house he dined at in Jamestown and to which he designed to return to his lodging at night." Archaeologists' discovery of "FN" bottle seals in the ruins of a brick dwelling owned by Thomas Rabley and located on urban Jamestown's waterfront suggest that Nicholson stayed there during his 1697 visit or perhaps when he returned as Virginia's governor. In October 1698, two months before Francis Nicholson took office as governor, the colony's statehouse burned. Therefore, when he arrived he had his commission read in Mrs. Rachel Sherwood's great hall in Jamestown and said that the king wanted a governor's house built. In February 1699 Nicholson sent his superiors an account of the colony's military stores, some of which had been damaged in the statehouse fire. He said that he wanted a new statehouse built soon and indicated that the colony was insufficiently fortified. Governor Francis Nicholson frequently clashed with Commissary James Blair, who ultimately used his influence to facilitate Nicholson's recall. Nicholson, who disliked Jamestown, favored moving the capital city to Middle Plantation. When some of James City County's justices opposed the move, Nicholson used his authority to repeal their rights. He also strongly opposed the old capital's having representation in the assembly, a change that would have reduced Jamestown property owners' influence, especially when it came to the issue of moving the capital. Nicholson's critics claimed that he was irrational, profane, and conniving. For example, he made threats against Lewis Burwell II whose daughter, Lucy, rejected Nicholson's romantic overtures. In 1704 Francis Nicholson, despite his disdain for Jamestown, recommended that a celebration be held there in 1707 to commemorate the first colonists' arrival. He held office in Virginia until August 1705 and in 1713 served as Nova Scotia's chief executive for several weeks. He went on to become governor of South Carolina in May 1721 and held office until 1725. On March 4, 1728, Francis Nicholson, a perennial bachelor, made his will and then died the following day (RAIMO:482–483; STAN 17, 42; EJC I:161, 167, 271, 360, 397–398, 400; PERRY I:28; SAIN 16:513, 946; 17:47, 187, 309; 22:105, 398; CO 5/1307 f 22; 5/1339 ff 36–37; 5/1359 f 325; JHB 1702–1712:43).

* * *

George Nicholson: On April 12, 1692, George Lee left George and Robert Nicholson a reversionary interest in his ¾-acre lot in urban Jamestown, which contained the rebuilt eastern bays of a brick row house on Back Street. The property was to descend to the Nicholson brothers after the death of Lee's widow, Sarah. Lee also bequeathed the rest of his real estate to the Nicholsons, who stood to receive acreage in the mainland just west of Jamestown Island and 100 acres on the Chickahominy River. Despite the late George Lee's plans, on December 7, 1696, the Nicholsons and the widowed Sarah Lee sold their respective interests in the decedent's Jamestown property and its improvements to George Harvey. At the time of the sale, George Nicholson and his wife, Hannah, were residents of Surry County (Surry County Deeds, Wills &c. 1694–1709:70; Lee 51 f 671).

Robert Nicholson: On April 12, 1692, George Lee left Robert and George Nicholson a reversionary interest in his ¾-acre lot in Jamestown, which contained the easternmost bays of a brick row house on Jamestown's Back Street. The property was to descend to the Nicholsons after the widowed Sarah Lee's demise. Lee also bequeathed to the Nicholsons the rest of his real estate. On December 7, 1696, the Nicholsons and Lee's widow sold their respective interests in the late George Lee's Jamestown property and its improvements to George Harvey. At the time of the sale, Robert Nicholson and his wife, Mary, were residents of Surry County

(Surry County Deeds, Wills &c. 1694–1709:70; Lee 51 f 671).

* * *

Betty Nonomisk (Nonomiske) (Mrs. Numpskinner) (Native American) (see Numpskinner)

Edward Normansell: Edward Normansell died in Jamestown sometime after April 1623 but before February 16, 1624 (VI&A 517).

Noroas (Native American): In June 1668 Owasewas, Appenmaw, and Chicatomen, who were Wicocomocoe Indian leaders, were summoned to court by Northumberland County's justices. They wanted an Indian named Noroas to be brought in because colonist Adam Pettegrew believed Noroas had given refuge to one of his maidservants, a runaway. Because neither Noroas nor the maidservant appeared, the court justices decided that all three Great Men should be detained (Northumberland County Order Book 1666–1678:40).

Tristram (Tristrim) Norsworthy (Naseworthy, Nosworthy, Norseworthie): In 1640 Tristram Norsworthy served as a burgess for Upper Norfolk County. He patented 150 acres in nearby Isle of Wight County in May 1643 and within two years enhanced the size of his holdings there. Lower Norfolk County's justices compensated Norsworthy for use of his boat in 1645, and a year later they designated him as one of four men who were to arbitrate a dispute. In 1654 Norsworthy became a justice of Nansemond (formerly Upper Norfolk) County. By 1650 he owned 125 acres of land on the Elizabeth River in Norfolk County, property he seems to have retained. In 1656 Lieutenant Colonel Norsworthy was identified as a resident of the Ragged Islands in Isle of Wight County (LEO 18; Tyler, "Historical and Genealogical Notes, 218–222; PB 2:28; 3:362; 5:39; 8:224; Lower Norfolk County Book A [1637–1646]:32, 70a, 72).

John Norton: By November 1, 1638, John Norton, a smith, had come into possession of a 12-acre ridge of land in the eastern end of Jamestown Island. On November 1, 1638, Norton sold his land and its improvements to Edward Sanderson, a merchant. The boundaries of the 12-acre parcel were then described in detail (PB 1:630; NUG I:105).

Thomas Norton: Thomas Norton, a gentleman who arrived in Jamestown in 1608 as part of the 2nd Supply of new colonists, was an investor in the Virginia Company (VI&A 517).

William Norton: Captain William Norton, who came to Virginia at the expense of the Virginia Company of London, took six foreign glassmakers to the colony. He was to see that the glass furnace was operational within three months and that the glassworkers were producing glass and beads. As it turned out, the project proved too costly and Norton was released from his contract. He died in late summer 1622, and in 1625 his goods were appraised. Two people to whom Norton was in debt were John Burland, a Virginia Company servant and vintner, and tailor Thomas Wilson, a servant in Dr. John Pott's Jamestown household. Captain John Smith indicated that Norton was a skillful physician and surgeon (VI&A 517).

Charles Norwood: Charles Norwood served as clerk of the assembly during its 1654–1655 and 1656 sessions but was replaced by Henry Randolph I in December 1656 (LEO 32–33). No records have been found that shed further light upon Norwood's life or career.

Henry Norwood: Henry Norwood, a royalist and one of Governor William Berkeley's kinsmen, left London in August 1649, shortly after King Charles I was beheaded. He was accompanied by Major Francis Morrison (Moryson), who had been designated captain of the fort at Old Point Comfort and eventually served as deputy governor. Norwood and his fellow passengers were shipwrecked near the northern part of the Eastern Shore. The narrative he wrote described the area's fauna and flora and its kindly natives, who literally saved their lives. He also spoke of the hospitality that was extended to him by Stephen Charlton and Argoll Yeardley, in whose homes he was a guest. Norwood crossed the Chesapeake Bay and paused at George Ludlow's home in York County. Then he went on to Captain Wormeley's house, where he encountered Sir Thomas Lunsford and three other royalists with whom he was well acquainted. He stopped in Jamestown, where he was greeted by Governor Berkeley, who invited him to his manor house, Green Spring. In May 1650 Berkeley sent Norwood to Holland to inquire about the wellbeing of the exiled monarch, Charles II, and to seek appointment as the colony's treasurer. The exiled king, who then lacked authority, gave Norwood the appointment. In 1660, after the monarchy had been restored and Norwood

took office as treasurer, King Charles II named him to the Council of State, on which he served until 1677. An Isle of Wight County document dated 1668 reveals that treasurer Henry Norwood authorized Sir William Berkeley to act on his behalf (STAN 16, 24; FOR III:10:3–4, 18, 26–30, 34–35, 38, 48–50; Isle of Wight County Will and Deed Book 1 [1662–1688]:164).

Andrew Noxe: Andrew Noxe was described on July 22, 1640, as a runaway servant and employee of William Peirce, who owned a lot on urban Jamestown's waterfront (MCGC 467).

* * *

Thomas Nuce (Newce): In 1620 Thomas Nuce was made deputy of the Virginia Company's land in Virginia, which gave him responsibility for the Company's acreage and its tenants and servants. He was given a salary and land in each of the colony's four corporations and was named to the Council of State. Nuce and his brother, William, settled in Elizabeth City. According to Captain John Smith, Thomas Nuce was a good manager, and after the March 22, 1622, Indian attack, he fortified his house at Elizabeth City, provided shelter to his neighbors, and built two houses for the reception of newly arrived immigrants. Nuce died on April 1, 1623 and was survived by a widow (VI&A 518; STAN 29; LEO xx).

William Nuce (Newce): William Nuce of Newcetown, Ireland, came to Virginia in 1620 with his brother, Thomas, and became established in Elizabeth City. In 1621 the Virginia Company made William, an associate of Daniel Gookin, the colony's new marshal. He had gotten a considerable amount of military experience in Ireland and was knowledgeable about the construction of fortifications. Governor George Yeardley had high praise for Captain Nuce and his wife. When Nuce was named to the Council of State in 1621, it was noted that he was to be knighted by the king. By January 21, 1623, William Nuce was dead, having survived the reading of his patent by only two days (VI&A 519; STAN 30; LEO xx).

* * *

William Nugent: On May 31, 1747, William Nugent sold a 105-acre leasehold in the Governor's Land to Richard Ambler, the owner of a large plantation on Jamestown Island. Nugent's leasehold formerly had belonged to the Marables. Edward Champion

Travis of Jamestown Island served as Nugent's executor in April 1750 (AMB 187).

* * *

Numpskinner (Native American): In April 1697 Numpskinner, his wife, Betty alias Nonomisk (Nonomiske), and an Indian named Pattiawaske sold the late Ned Gunstocker's 150 acres in Richmond County to Nathaniel Pope alias Bridges. The deed of conveyance reveals that the acreage had been granted to Ned Gunstocker, Betty's uncle, on October 14, 1666. The three Indians were accompanied by their interpreters, Jane Browne and Thomas Smyth (Richmond County Deed Book 3 [1697–1704]:1–2).

Betty alias Nonomisk (Nonomiske) (Mrs. Numpskinner) (Native American): In April 1697 Betty alias Nonomisk (Nonomiske) and her husband, Numpskinner, and Pattiawaske sold the late Ned Gunstocker's 150 acres in Richmond County to Nathaniel Pope alias Bridges. The deed of conveyance reveals that the acreage formerly had been granted to Ned Gunstocker, Betty's uncle, on October 14, 1666. The three Indians were accompanied by their interpreters, Jane Browne and Thomas Smyth (Richmond County Deed Book 3 [1697–1704]:1–2).

* * *

Mr. and Mrs. Thomas Nunn: In 1621 the Company of Shipwrights signed a contract with Thomas Nunn, a boat builder, who was to come to Virginia and practice his trade. If his wife performed household chores (defined as cooking, cleaning, mending, and laundry) for his workers, she would be paid. The Nunns, Thomas Nunn's workmen, and maidservant Amy Gamsby left England in 1622. Mrs. Nunn died in Elizabeth City shortly after they arrived there. Although Thomas Nunn was supposed to set up shop at Martin's Hundred, he settled on Jamestown Island, probably because it was considered a safer location after the March 1622 Indian attack. Nunn and his men were living on Jamestown Island when they built a small shallop. He was still alive in December 1623 (VI&A 520).

William Nuthead: On February 21, 1683, William Nuthead, a printer in the household of Gloucester County clerk of court and burgess John Buckner, was censured by the Council of State for printing several groups of official papers, including the November 1682 acts of the assembly, with neither authorization nor a license. Nuthead and Buckner were ordered to post a bond guaranteeing that they would never do so again. Nuthead later moved to St. Mary's City, Maryland. On February 14, 1930, the *Virginia Gazette* published an article stating that William Nuthead operated his press in Jamestown and that it was the first printing ever done in the colony. However, as noted above, primary sources place John Buckner and his servant, William Nuthead, in Gloucester County, not Jamestown, and there is no indication that printing occurred in the capital city (CO 1/51 ff 98–99; 5/1405 f 63; York County Deeds, Orders, Wills 6:483).

O

Arnold Oldesworth (Ouldsworth, Oldisworth): Arnold Oldesworth Esq. arrived at Berkeley Hundred in late January 1621. At his request, Virginia Company officials named him to the Council of State. However, he died prior to July 16, 1621 (VI&A 522; STAN 30; LEO xx).

John Oldham: On October 13, 1626, John Oldham, a merchant, testified before the General Court in Jamestown (VI&A 522).

Thomas Oldis: On November 7, 1634, Thomas Oldis attested to the accuracy of a list of goods that the late Thomas Lee had brought to Virginia, and earlier in the year he witnessed Benjamin Symms' will. In March 1639 Oldis began leasing 50 acres on the Strawberry Banks in Elizabeth City, and two years later he obtained an additional 50 acres in the county. In 1640 Oldis served as a burgess, representing Elizabeth City County. A patent issued in 1648 suggests that his house was on the east side of the Hampton River, near Old Point Comfort (VI&A 522; LEO 18; PB 1:716, 760; 2:128; NEAL 298).

Valentine Oldis: On November 19, 1627, merchant Valentine Oldis testified before the General Court in Jamestown, claiming to have loaned money to Benjamin Brown, a sick mariner who had given him a legal interest in his ship's cargo (VI&A 522).

William Olister: In 1683 William Olister was credited with a 135-acre leasehold in the Governor's Land, just west of Jamestown Island (Soane 1683).

Edward Oliver (Olliver): In February 1624 Edward Oliver, who was given a share of land by the Virginia Company, was living in the Maine or mainland, just west of Jamestown Island. In 1639 he was a tobacco inspector for Jamestown Island, the Maine, and Pasbehay (VI&A 522).

[No First Name] Omerod: On November 20, 1619, Mr. Omerod reportedly died of the flux in urban Jamestown (VI&A 523).

John Omoonce (see John Moon [Moone, O'moon, Omoonce])

George Onion (see George Ungwin [Ungwine, Unguin, Unwine, Onion, Union, Unwyn, Vinon, Vinoyn])

Opechancanough (Abochancano, Mangopeesomon) (Native American): Opechancanough, a powerful war captain, became the Powhatan Chiefdom's paramount leader, succeeding Powhatan's immediate successor, Opitchapam, around 1618–1619. Opechancanough orchestrated the March 22, 1622, attack that claimed more than a third of the colonists' lives. He resided on an island in the Pamunkey River and ruled 32 kingdoms and territory that extended from the Roanoke River to the York River. On April 18, 1644, the aged Opechancanough, who was revered as a god, led a second attack on the colonists. He was captured, incarcerated in Jamestown, and shot in the back by a guard acting without orders (VI&A 523).

Opitchapam (Itoyatin, Otiotan, Sasawpen, Iotan) (Native American): Opitchapam, Powhatan's immediate successor as paramount chief, came to power in 1618 and briefly ruled the natives living between the York and Roanoke rivers. He was succeeded by Opechancanough, a stronger, more charismatic leader (VI&A 524).

Oponamo (Native American): On May 25, 1659, the justices of Lancaster County's monthly court noted that John Milliscent owed Oponamo, an Indian, a sum equivalent to the price of a matchcoat or cloth cloak (Lancaster County Orders 1656–1666:82).

Oponomy (Oponamo?) (Native American): On April 6, 1669, Oponomy initiated a suit against Robert Jones, a Northumberland County court justice. The matter was postponed and Jones filed a countersuit, alleging that the Wicocomoco Indians had broken into his house and done some damage (Northumberland County Order Book 1666–1678:61).

John Osborne (Osborn, Osbourn): During the mid-1620s John Osborne and his wife, Mary, lived in the eastern end of Jamestown Island. By 1627 John had moved to the Governor's Land, where he was a cow-keeper. In 1643 he patented some acreage in the territory known as the Neck O'Land (VI&A 524–525).

Thomas Osborne (Osborn, Osbourn): Thomas Osborne arrived in Virginia in 1619 and probably lived on the College land, in the corporation of Henrico. During the mid-1620s he was a lieutenant at the College, and in 1625, 1628, and 1629 he served as the community's burgess. In 1627 he was put in command of the men at the College and Bermuda Hundred, and in 1630, while he was a captain, he served as a burgess for the College and Bermuda Hundred. In 1632 Osborne was named a commissioner or justice in the local court serving Henrico and Charles City, and by 1632 and 1633 he was a burgess for Bermuda Hundred, Curles, Arrahattock (the College), and Henricus (VI&A 525; LEO 6–12; STAN).

Ossakican (Wassatickon) (Native American): In 1649 Ossakican, the werowance of the Chiskiack Indians or "North Indians," received a 5,000-acre patent on behalf of his people. He was assigned "the place whereon he now liveth," near the land of Hugh Gwyn, who held a patent for some land located on the lower side of the Piankatank River, near its mouth. The Indians were supposed to be compensated for acreage that had been patented within the tract they had been assigned. This was particularly important in the territory bordering the Piankatank, where European colonists had begun establishing plantations as early as 1642. The formation of Gloucester County in 1651 is one indication of the extent to which settlement had spread north (Billings, "Some Acts Not in Hening's, April 1652, November 1652, and July 1653," 71; HEN I:323–329).

Valentine Osserby: Valentine Osserby, an indentured servant, came to Virginia in 1623. After Osserby's master died, Thomas Passmore, a carpenter, purchased the time that remained on Osserby's contract. Osserby became mortally ill in October 1623 while he was living with Passmore, whose farmstead was located in the eastern end of Jamestown Island (VI&A 526).

Thomas Ottway (Ottaway, Ottawell, Ottowell, Attowell): In 1624 Thomas Ottway, a servant, was attributed to Edward Blaney's household in urban Jamestown and to Blaney's plantation on the lower side of the James River. In early 1625 he was residing on the Blaney plantation, which belonged to William Powell's orphans. Ottway eventually obtained his freedom and on August 18, 1627, was occupying some land on the lower side of the Warwick River, within the corporation of Elizabeth City. He and Nathaniel Floyd probably were Captain Samuel Mathews' tenants (VI&A 526).

Thomas Ousley (Owsley): Thomas Ousley moved to Stafford County prior to January 1686, when he sold some of his servants, livestock, and household furnishings to another man. In August he was identified as a Stafford County merchant who had a business relationship with his brother, London merchant Newdigate Owsley. Captain Thomas Ousley grew more prosperous as time went on and took a more active role in community life. He became a county justice in 1692 but was not in court on March 9th when his wife, Anne, testified about the large group of Indians who came to her home in October 1691. In 1694 Thomas Ousley patented 1,000 acres toward the head of the Potomac River and an additional 150 acres north of Accotink Run. Then, in 1696 he claimed a 600-acre tract and 640 acres near the Anocostin Island. Ousley served as a burgess for Stafford County and attended the assembly meetings held in 1693, 1696–1697, and 1698. He was appointed county sheriff before the second session began and vacated his assembly seat. In September 1700 he gave half of a tract of land on Pohick Creek to his unmarried daughter, Sarah. He may have been in failing health, for on January 8, 1701, the justices of Stafford County's court noted that Thomas Ousley, the clerk of court, was dead. His widow, Anne, presented an inventory of his estate in December 1701 (LEO 52, 54, 58; Stafford County Record Book 1686–1693:47, 49–49a, 84, 236a–237, 253–253a; 1699–1709:44–45, 51–52, 114, 352–353; NN 2:58–60, 260–261, 267).

Owasewas (Owessewar, Owasoway?) (Native American): On April 20, 1660, Owasewas and Pewem, two of the Wicocomoco (Wecocomaka, Wicocomocoe) Indians' Great Men, made a complaint to the justices of Northumberland County's court.

They alleged that Robert Jones and George Walle (Wale, Walei) had seated illegally on the acreage that had been assigned to their tribe and that they were being deprived of the land they needed for subsistence. The justices decided to revisit the matter on May 3rd in the presence of the county militia and the accused trespassers. When the Indians returned to court on May 3, 1660, they reiterated their claim but Jones and Walle failed to appear. The justices decided that both colonists should cease developing the land they were occupying while it was determined whether they had seated acreage that had been laid out for the Wicocomoco. When George Walle appeared before the justices on May 21, 1660, he claimed that he had not intruded upon the Indians' land. Robert Jones, on the other hand, who was the late Governor Samuel Mathews II's agent, claimed that he had been assigned the property by surveyor Gervase Dodson and said that he was going to bring the matter before the General Court. On November 17, 1662, Owasewas (Owasoway) and two other Great Men of the Wicocomico Indian Town agreed that Robert Jones could use their land in exchange for twelve matchcoats or cloth cloaks. In June 1668 Owasewas, Appenmaw, and Chicatomen, who were identified as Wicocomocoe Great Men, were summoned to court by Northumberland County's justices. The Indian leaders were asked to bring in a warrior named Noroas, whom colonist Adam Pettegrew believed was harboring a runaway maidservant. Because neither Noroas nor the maidservant appeared, the court justices decided that all three Great Men should be detained (Northumberland County Order Book 1652–1665:237–238, 245, 247; 1666–1678:40; Record Book 1658–1662:86).

Hugh Owen: George Lloyd's indentured servant, Hugh Owen, fled in a boat he and some other runaways stole from William White of urban Jamestown. On September 28, 1674, the justices of the General Court decided that, as punishment, Owen would be whipped and the time he had to serve Lloyd would be extended. After that period was over, he was to be assigned to White for 18 months (MCGC 382).

Owmohowtue (Owmoh Honly) (Native American): Owmohowtue, one of the Mattaponi Indians' Great Men or leaders, participated in making a peace agreement with the justices of Old Rappahannock County in 1657 (Old Rappahannock County Deed Book 1656–1664:17).

P

Richard Pace I: Richard Pace I, a carpenter, married Isabell (Izabella) Smythe in 1608 and immigrated to Virginia sometime prior to 1616. In 1620 they patented some land and established the plantation they called Paces Paines. On the night of March 21, 1622, a Christianized native youth, probably Chanco, who lived with the Paces, revealed his people's plan to attack the colonists' settlements the next day. This enabled Richard Pace to alert the authorities in Jamestown. The Paces lived on Jamestown Island for several months after the natives' assault but eventually returned to their own plantation, making it defensible. After Richard Pace's death in early 1623, Isabell married William Perry, who shortly thereafter made a trip to England. In mid-February 1624 Isabell and an infant, probably her son, Henry Perry, were living in Jamestown. Upon being widowed again, Isabell married Jamestown merchant George Menefie. In September 1628 George Pace, the late Richard Pace's son and primary heir, received a patent for Paces Paines. He married Sarah (Sara), the daughter and heir of Samuel Macock, and in August 1650 patented 1,700 acres in Charles City County, land that became known as Macock's or Maycox. An apparently successful planter, he acquired an additional 507 acres in 1652. George and Sarah Macock Pace had a son and heir, Richard Pace II (VI&A 527–528).

George Pacy: George Pacy, a grocer from London, arrived in Jamestown on September 12, 1623 (VI&A 529).

* * *

Caleb Page: Caleb Page, Thomas and Richard Page's brother, was in Jamestown in 1625 and testified before the General Court. He became ill and died on April 2, 1627. On October 15, 1627, John Upton of Jamestown Island, the late Caleb Page's partner, said that they often purchased and resold goods they procured from Jamestown merchant George Menefie. Court testimony raises the possibility that Caleb Page was a silversmith or that he was procuring silverware that he was trading for merchandise (VI&A 529).

Richard Page: Sometime prior to May 21, 1622, Richard Page married mariner James Brett's widow, the former Elizabeth Green, and became master of Brett's ship. Richard

Page died sometime prior to November 28, 1625, when the General Court's justices ordered his brother, Caleb, to inventory his estate and pay his debts (VI&A 529).

* * *

Henry Page: On January 12, 1677, Henry Page, one of the rebel Nathaniel Bacon's most ardent supporters, was tried at a martial court held aboard Captain John Martin's ship, which was anchored in the York River. Page admitted his guilt and was sentenced to be hanged. Afterward, Governor William Berkeley identified Henry Page as a carpenter and one of his former servants and said that Bacon had made Page a colonel. On February 10, 1677, Berkeley listed Page among those deemed exempt from the king's pardon. He also indicated that Page's estate would be seized and said that Page already had been executed (MCGC 454, 527; NEVILLE 61, 274).

* * *

John Page: John Page immigrated to Virginia around 1650 and identified himself as a merchant. Within two years he had patented some land in the upper reaches of the York River, using the headrights of his wife, the former Alice Lukin (Luken), and their daughters, Mary and Elizabeth. In 1655 Page purchased a 100-acre tract in Middle Plantation, where he later built a fine brick residence, the family's ancestral home. In 1655 and 1656 he served as a burgess for York County and patented 2,700 acres in Lancaster County. As time went on, he continued to acquire land in the Northern Neck, and he laid claim to acreage on the Middle Peninsula and in Lower Norfolk County. Page frequently filed suits in the General Court, attempting to collect funds from his debtors, who included Jonathan Newell, Thomas Swann, Thomas Warren, and Thomas Hunt, some of urban Jamestown's more prominent citizens. Page was returned to the assembly and represented York County in the sessions held between 1672 and 1676. During the early to mid-1670s he appeared before the General Court, where he accused Alexander Phillis of stealing goods from his store, brought suit against Mark Warkman (Workman) of New Kent County, and obtained a warrant for Jonas Pickis's arrest. He also inventoried

Richard Stock's estate and audited the accounts of John Stubbs, Thomas Glassbrook, Thomas Swann, Thomas Hunt's administrator, and others. Page frequently served as an attorney and in 1676 was called upon to audit the estate of Jonathan Newell, a York County merchant and the owner of a large tract in urban Jamestown. On one occasion Page indicated that one of his maidservants, who had gotten pregnant in England, had returned to Virginia and become a ward of Middletown Parish. In 1671 he functioned as a vestryman for James City Parish. On October 29, 1673, Surry County bricklayer John Bird sued Colonel John Page as the executor of his brother, Mathew Page I. Three weeks later Page, who was identified as a merchant and resident of Bruton Parish, purchased the late Walter Chiles II's 3½-acre lot in urban Jamestown from his widow, Susanna, the Rev. James Wadding's new wife. Page may have had a residual interest in the property because his daughter Mary, who had been married to Chiles, had predeceased her husband. Page kept the Chiles lot for less than a decade and then sold it to William Sherwood. Although the deed of conveyance has been lost or destroyed, on October 27, 1682, when James City County surveyor John Soane delimited the property for Sherwood, he recorded detailed boundary data and noted that the 3½-acre lot was the land "bought of Coll. Page."

When the colony was in the throes of Bacon's Rebellion, Colonel John Page, a councilor, remained loyal to Governor William Berkeley. As a result, the rebel Nathaniel Bacon branded Page a traitor and allowed his men to seize and plunder Page's Middle Plantation home. Later, Page's wife, Alice, was among the women Bacon seized and used as a human shield while building his defensive trench at the entrance to Jamestown Island. Documents on file in the British Archives reveal that during the mid-1670s Colonel John Page was functioning as the factor of London merchant and alderman John Jeffreys (Jeffries), a major investor in the Royal African Company. In September 1676 Jeffreys had numerous casks and barrels of wine stored in Page's cellars in urban Jamestown. Although Governor William Berkeley confiscated part of the wine "for use in the king's service," the rest was destroyed when Bacon's followers set the capital city ablaze. Page filed a compensatory claim on Jeffreys' behalf, hoping to recover the wine's full value, but the burgesses awarded him only half of its estimated worth, for they believed that any wine the governor's men left on the premises would have been destroyed by fire. John Jeffreys

was dissatisfied with what he considered inadequate compensation and on October 18, 1677, filed an appeal with the Committee for Trade and Plantations. He accompanied his petition with a statement from his agent, John Page, who said that shortly before abandoning Jamestown, Governor Berkeley had ordered him to deliver 20 casks of Jeffreys' wine. Page indicated that he had also sold some of the wine, but that there had been no foreseeable reason to remove the rest of it. He added that as Jeffreys' agent, he had "delivered to the sd Sr Wm Berkeley 4 men negroes for 100 pounds sterling" and that he had yet to receive payment.

In mid-February 1677 the assembly authorized Colonel Page to find land at Middle Plantation that was suitable for the king's soldiers' use in planting corn. He also was supposed to oversee the construction of a powder house and guardhouse. In 1678 Page donated the York County land at Middle Plantation on which Bruton Parish Church was built. In 1679 John and Alice Page gave their son Francis 168 acres in Middle Plantation, eight slaves, and the reversionary rights to a New Kent County plantation called Mehixon. Having been returned to the assembly, Colonel Page represented York County from 1680 to 1682. He was named to the Council of State in 1681, and a year later it was decided that the colony's military stores would be taken to his house in Middle Plantation for safekeeping. On April 16, 1683, Page consolidated and repatented his 330 acres of land at Middle Plantation, which included a tract he had bought from William Sherwood and Thomas Rabley earlier on. By 1686 Page had begun serving as the colony's escheator, and in 1690 he was ordered to inventory the military stores in the fort in Jamestown. When Page died around February 1692, he was interred at Bruton Parish Church. He was survived by his wife and three of their four children: Francis, Mathew II, and Elizabeth. The widowed Alice Page inherited life-rights in her late husband's property at Middle Plantation and continued to occupy the family home, sharing it with her orphaned granddaughter, Elizabeth, Francis and Mary Digges Page's child. At Alice Lukin Page's death in 1698, the family home descended to their son Francis and his heirs. In 1704 the late Colonel John Page's estate owed quitrents on large tracts of land in James City, New Kent, King William and King and Queen counties (SMITH 67; CO 1/12 f 115; 1/41 f 218; 5/1355 ff 200–203; 5/1358 f 77; SAIN 10:167; WITH 51; FOR I:9:8; WISEMAN; ASPIN 172; MCGC 224, 247, 257, 260, 266, 288, 300, 328, 338–340, 347, 350, 358, 364, 370, 373, 410, 434, 441; STAN 41,

72; NUG I:279, 340; II:30, 261; AMB 24, 34, 37; JHB 1660–1693:71–72; EJC I:25, 117; MEADE I:146; PALM I:21; York County Deeds, Orders, Wills 3:103; 5:1, 65; 6:128; MEY 409–412; LEO 33, 40, 46; DOR 2:494–495).

Francis Page: Francis Page, the son of John and Alice Page, was born in 1657. In 1679 his parents gave him 168 acres in Middle Plantation, eight slaves, and the reversionary rights to a New Kent County plantation called Mehixon. In 1682 Page married Mary Digges of York County. Together they produced an only child, Elizabeth. By the time Francis Page married, he had become a York County justice and a member of Bruton Parish's vestry. He went on to serve as a burgess and represented York County in the assembly sessions held between 1684 and 1688. On May 12, 1684, he was named to the committee charged with rebuilding the colony's statehouse, and he was clerk of the assembly in 1688. During the 1680s he erected an ordinary, a brick malt house, and a brick barn on his 168 acres in Middle Plantation. Francis Page outlived his wife, Mary, but soon became ill. When preparing his will, he named his daughter, Elizabeth, as his sole heir, and entrusted her to the care of his widowed mother, Alice Page. He also asked his brother-in-law, Dudley Digges, to see that young Elizabeth was properly educated. The testator specified that if his daughter failed to survive, his brother, Mathew II, was to inherit his real and personal estate. By May 1692 Francis Page was dead. When his daughter, Elizabeth, grew up, she married John Page of Gloucester County, one of her late father's first cousins, and produced two children. She died on November 12, 1702, at the age of 20, probably from the complications of childbirth (MEY 410–412; JHB 1660–1693:220; York County Deeds, Orders, Wills 6:128, 9:99, 126–127; MEADE I:146; LEO 47–49).

Mathew Page II: Mathew Page II, the son of Colonel John Page and his wife, Alice, was a member of the original Board of Visitors of the College of William and Mary and served on the Council of State from 1698 to 1703. He was escheator of Gloucester, King and Queen, King William, and Middlesex counties and was colonel and commander-in-chief of the Gloucester militia. He married Mary, the daughter and heiress of John and Mary Kemp Mann of Timberneck in Gloucester County. Mary Mann Page inherited two-thirds of her late father's estate, which included the land that they developed into the plantation called Rosewell; she also bought the Timberneck tract from her

mother. Mathew and Mary Mann Page had three children: Mann I, Alice, and Martha. Mathew Page II died on January 9, 1704, and was buried at Rosewell. In 1705, when the widowed Mary Mann Page married John Page, one of her late husband's cousins, she executed a prenuptial agreement that preserved the inheritance of the children she had produced with Mathew Page II. Her primary heir was Mann Page I, who in 1725–1726 commenced construction of the Rosewell mansion. In 1734 Mathew Page II's heirs inherited his interest in Colonel John Page's property in Middle Plantation (Williamsburg) (HEN V:277–283; MEY 411–412).

Mathew Page I: Sometime prior to December 2, 1657, Mathew Page I, Colonel John Page's brother, married Elizabeth, the widow of John Crump, who was the grandson and reversionary heir of the Rev. Richard Buck of Jamestown. Afterward, Elizabeth conveyed to Mathew Page I the acreage in the Neck O'Land that she had inherited from her late husband. In March 1662 Mathew Page I repatented the 1,250-acre Crump tract in his own name. In 1672 Page began having serious medical problems, which ultimately proved fatal. His brother and executor, Colonel John Page, was ordered to fulfill the decedent's obligation to work with two other men who were building a brick fort in Jamestown. During the mid-1670s Mathew Page I's brother, John, made numerous appearances before the General Court on Mathew's behalf. In 1673 he paid Mathew's debts to Thomas Hunt's and Jonathan Newell's estates and to bricklayer John Bird of Surry County (NUG II:76, 252; PB 3:306; 6:298; 7:228–229; MCGC 298, 342, 350, 357–358, 364; DOR 1:427–428, 785; MEY 224, 410–413; BYRD 2:555).

* * *

Anthony Pagitt (Pagett): Anthony Pagitt went to Virginia in 1623 and became a servant in Abraham Peirsey's household at Flowerdew Hundred. In October 1629 he served as Flowerdew Hundred's burgess (VI&A 530; LEO 8).

Florentine Paine (Payne): Although Virginia Land Office records do not include a patent that was issued to Florentine Paine, and his name did not appear in Elizabeth City County's court records, a shipping record reveals that he had come to Virginia by 1628. In 1642 Richard Lee used him as a headright, and when William Parry patented some land in Elizabeth City in 1648, he indicated that his acreage was adjacent to Paine's property. Paine represented Elizabeth City in the assembly sessions of 1642 and 1659 (SR 3784a; LEO 20, 35; NUG I:131, 175, 219).

Ellen (Elin) Painter (Paynter): In February 1624 Ellen Painter was a maidservant in Henry Soothey's Jamestown Island household (VI&A 530).

Thomas Palmer: Thomas Palmer arrived in Virginia in 1621 with his wife, Joan, and daughter, Pricilla, and seems to have settled at Berkeley Hundred. By February 1624 he had moved to Jordan's Journey. In 1629 Palmer was named commander of the Shirley Hundred mainland and a commissioner for the monthly court serving the settlements near the head of the James River. At the end of the year, he was elected burgess for Shirley Hundred Maine. Although Palmer was supposed to represent Shirley Hundred in the March 1630 session of the assembly, he became ill while on his way to England and died there on December 29, 1629, leaving several children (VI&A 531; LEO 8–9).

Queen of Pamunkey (Native American) (see Cockacoeske)

King of Pamunkey (Native American): In 1688 the Rev. John Clayton of Jamestown indicated that the Pamunkey Indians' king had three or four horses and a saddle but did not know how to ride (FOR III:12:35). Clayton failed to mention the native leader's name.

Pantatouse (Native American): In early August 1659, Pantatouse, Yeotassa, Chakingatough, and George Caquescough, who were Machodoc Indians, were brought before the justices of Northumberland County and accused of murdering a colonist named John Cammel. A jury found all four Indians guilty and sentenced Caquescough to be hanged. However, Pantatouse and the other two men were released. All four Indians had been brought to Northumberland's justices by their own people. Nearly two years later, the Machodoc were ordered to leave their tribal land. According to Northumberland's court justices, when John Cammel was murdered, one Machodoc warrior who was implicated in the slaying was not brought in. Moreover, the justices believed that the Machodoc were conspiring with other natives "to make a Warr upon us." Therefore, Northumberland's justices decided that some local men, with the assistance of the militia,

would drive the Indians from their land (Northumberland County Order Book 1652–1665:216, 239).

Anthony Panton: The Rev. Anthony Panton, an Anglican clergyman, came to Virginia sometime prior to February 1634 at the expense of Dr. John Pott and George Menefie, residents of urban Jamestown. Panton, who became rector of York and Chiskiack parishes, openly ridiculed Secretary Richard Kemp, a staunch supporter of Governor John Harvey, and he criticized Harvey himself. The clergyman was tried, found guilty of mutiny, and fined. He also was ordered to apologize publicly in each of the colony's parishes and then banished from Virginia. Panton and his supporters protested and ultimately the case against him was dismissed (VI&A 532).

Robert Paramore (Paramour, Parramore): In February 1624 Robert Paramore was living on Hog Island, but by January 1625 he had moved to the Governor's Land. On June 25, 1627, he was fined for negligence while on sentry duty in Jamestown (VI&A 532).

Philip Pardoe: On March 5, 1675, Philip Pardoe lost a suit to William Sherwood, a Jamestown merchant and resident (MCGC 405).

* * *

Daniel Parke (Park) I: Daniel Parke I, a London gentleman who was married to Rebecca Evelyn, moved to Virginia sometime prior to 1652. In 1653 he commenced serving as a York County justice and sheriff, and he also was elected a burgess for the county. He retired from the assembly in 1667 or 1668 and in 1670 was named to the Council of State. He went on to become treasurer of the colony and eventually succeeded Thomas Ludwell as Secretary. During the 1660s Parke patented substantial quantities of land on the south side of the York River, and he acquired the Warrany Old Town, which was on the upper side of the mouth of Diascund Creek, in what was then James City County. He made occasional appearances before the General Court to testify or participate in litigation. In August 1677, when the rebel Nathaniel Bacon's men began plundering the estates of Governor William Berkeley's staunchest supporters, Colonel Daniel Parke I's goods were seized. Parke, who then was in London, prepared his will on August 11, 1677, naming his eight-year-old son, Daniel II, as heir to his Virginia land. He also designated James Bray I as his Virginia executor. Parke died on March 6, 1679, and his will was presented for probate on September 16th (WITH 164; STAN 21, 39, 78; LEO xx, 40; MCGC 349, 379, 517, 520–521; HEN II:49–51; NUG I:399, 492, 558; ASPIN 175; Bruce, "Persons Who Suffered by Bacon's Rebellion," 65; WISEMAN; EEAC 43).

Daniel Parke (Park) II: Daniel Parke II, the son of Daniel Parke I, was born in 1669 and lost his father at age 10. When he matured he distinguished himself at Blenheim, where he gained the admiration of the Duke of Marlborough. Parke served in the Parliament but was implicated in a bribery scandal. He married Jane, the daughter of Lucy and Philip Ludwell I of Fairfield in Gloucester County. Daniel Parke II and the former Jane Ludwell had a daughter Lucy, who married William Byrd II of Westover, and a daughter Frances, who wed Colonel John Custis IV of Arlington. Parke, who was handsome and was known for his volatility and love of dueling, was a notorious rake. In 1688 he was elected a burgess for James City County, replacing his father-in-law, Philip Ludwell I, who was not allowed to take his seat. Parke became a naval officer, and in 1693 he was elected to the assembly as a burgess for both Jamestown and York County. When he was told to choose between the two, he opted to represent the capital city, where his in-laws owned property. He was elected to represent New Kent County in the assembly sessions of 1695–1696 but in June 1695 he left office to become a member of the Council of State. While Parke and Maryland governor Francis Nicholson were visiting the College of William and Mary in 1696, they got into a heated argument. According to the Rev. James Blair, who witnessed the encounter, Parke struck Nicholson over the head with a horsewhip and challenged him to a duel. Only the fact that Nicholson had left his sword in Jamestown kept the two men from dueling. Daniel Parke II reportedly got along well with Governor Edmund Andros, who considered him a friend. It was during Andros's administration that Parke became the colony's escheator and collector of customs. In December 1695 he and several other men agreed to build a gun platform in Jamestown. When Daniel Parke's daughter, Frances, began making plans in March 1702 to marry John Custis IV, Parke promised to give her a dowry equal to half of what Custis could prove he was worth. He also invited his future son-in-law to live at his house in Williamsburg.

Colonel Daniel Parke II patented acreage in York County, some of which was escheat land. In 1704 he was credited with 2,750 acres in York County; 1,800 acres in James City County; 7,000 acres in New Kent County; and 4,500 acres in King William County. He also owned land in the city of Williamsburg. On April 25, 1704, Parke was named governor of the Leeward Islands. When he made his will on January 1, 1710, he left his property in Virginia and England to his daughter Frances Custis, along with any outstanding debts. Simultaneously, he bequeathed £1,000 to daughter Lucy Byrd, and he made a bequest to the illegitimate son and daughter he fathered with Mrs. Katherine Chester. Daniel Parke II was brutally slain in St. John, Antigua, on December 7, 1710, having been attacked by an angry mob. An inventory of his estate made no reference to any real or personal property he may have had in Jamestown. His will was presented for probate on May 15, 1711. Afterward, William Byrd II made an agreement with his sister-in-law Frances Custis, whereby he assumed Parke's debts along with his assets. Byrd lived to regret that decision, for the decedent's liabilities greatly outweighed his assets (STAN 43, 88; JHB 1660–1693:450; LJC 194; EJC I:339, 360; II:74; LEO 49, 52–54; PERRY I:28; NUG II:379; III:19; WITH 164, 325, 327, 335, 337, 344; BYRD xi, 102; SMITH 69; PB 4:10, 236, 399).

* * *

William Parker: In May 1636 William Parker patented 350 acres on the south side of the Nansemond River in territory then considered part of Warresqueak (Isle of Wight) County. Two years later he patented an identical amount of land in Upper Norfolk County on Powell's Creek, a tributary of the Nansemond River. In 1642 Parker served as a burgess for Upper Norfolk County, which later was renamed Nansemond County and then included a strip of land in what formerly had been Warresqueak. Parker's acreage on the western branch of the Nansemond River was used as a reference point in a 1654 patent for some nearby property (PB 1:362, 543; 3:316; LEO 20). The possibility exists that William Parker of Nansemond County was the youth who came to Virginia as one of John Bush's servants and, upon being freed, settled in Elizabeth City at Merry Point (VI&A 533).

William C. Parks: On April 24, 1745, William C. Parks witnessed Edward Jaquelin's heirs' deed to Richard Ambler for part of his property on Jamestown's waterfront (Smith et al. 1745).

* * *

William Parry (Perry): On September 22, 1638, William Parry, a resident of Kecoughtan, patented a tiny waterfront lot in urban Jamestown, a parcel that later contained a wooden warehouse situated on a brick foundation. His patent stipulated that he had to develop his lot or face forfeiture. Parry probably used his lot for commercial purposes, for the capital city was then the colony's sole port of entry. In May 1637 he acquired 350 acres of land on the Nansemond River in New Norfolk County. He also served as administrator of his late brother, John, a cooper, and inherited his wages. Sometime prior to 1643 Parry laid claim to some acreage on Pease Hill Creek (a tributary of Chickahominy River), near the "potters field dividend," a source of clay still used in pottery-making. This raises the possibility that Parry had a financial interest in a pottery kiln just west of his lot's boundary line. His property on the Chickahominy also was near some land owned by Edward Travis I of Jamestown Island. In April 1640 and October 1643, Parry was described in the records of Northampton and Surry counties as a resident of Kecoughtan (Elizabeth City). His wife was named Ann. In 1648 he patented 90 acres in Elizabeth City, and three years later he claimed 550 acres on the Potomac River. These land acquisitions, awarded on account of headrights, indicate that he was successful in generating income. He probably was the same William Parry who during the 1640s bought and then sold Dr. John Pott's 12-acre lot on Jamestown's Back Street (PB 1:598; NUG I:57, 97, 175, 221, 224, 340; PB 4:101; EEAC 44; DOR 2:132; Surry County Deeds, Wills 1652–1672:112).

John Parry: On March 24, 1637, John Parry, a cooper and single man who probably resided in Jamestown, prepared his will. He named his brother, William Parry, the owner of some Jamestown lots, as his administrator and left his wages to William. The testator bequeathed a bed and rug to Ralph Hunter, his groom, and he left clothing to John Martin and Stephen Pendle, two of the late Sir George Yeardley's servants. He gave his coopering tools and some clothing to Sam, one of Jamestown merchant George Menefie's servants. John Parry's will was presented for probate in England on July 30, 1638 (WITH 78; EEAC 44; SR 3982).

* * *

Robert Partin I: Robert Partin I came to Virginia in 1609 and may have been a Virginia Company employee. In 1620 he received a patent for acreage in the corporation of Henrico, but during the mid-1620s he was living at West and Shirley Hundred, where he also had some land. He shared a home with his wife, Margaret, and their children, Avis, Rebecca, and Robert II. Later, Margaret and Robert Partin I had another daughter, Deborah (Debora). The Partins were living at Shirley Hundred in 1627 when the General Court decided that Robert's wife and seven-year-old daughter, Avis, were to be flogged on account of a sexual offense committed by one of the household's servants. Margaret was punished because she had failed to report her young daughter's rape, and Avis received what was termed "correction" for the role she played in the incident. Robert Partin I eventually settled in Isle of Wight County, and on April 13, 1642, he and his son, Robert II, sold their Henrico County land to another individual. In 1648 Robert Partin I conveyed his Isle of Wight County plantation to John Seward, who used members of the Partin family as headrights when patenting some land (VI&A 536–537; NUG I:167–168, 171; BODIE 514–515, 674).

[No First Name] Partridge: In 1609–1610 Master Partridge, one of Captain John Smith's "old soldiers," lived in Jamestown (VI&A 537).

Thomas Passmore (Pasmore, Parsemore): On August 14, 1624, Thomas Passmore, a carpenter who came to Virginia prior to 1618, patented 12 acres in the eastern end of Jamestown Island; he also owned a 16-acre parcel that was located nearby. He probably resided on one of his patents and placed a tenant or one or more of his indentured servants on the other. In early 1624 Passmore was living in urban Jamestown in a household headed by John Southern, an experienced artisan the Society of Southampton Hundred sent to Virginia. By June 1624 Passmore had wed Jane, with whom he was residing in the rural part of Jamestown Island in January 1625. Unless she died prior to August 28, 1626, the General Court's clerk mistakenly listed her given name as Joanne when she appeared in court. Thomas Passmore was alive in January 1629 and was designated a juryman (VI&A 537–538).

* * *

John Pate: John Pate of Gloucester, who was born in Virginia, was the nephew of

Richard Pate, a highly successful planter who owned a large plantation at the head of Poropotank Creek's eastern branch. When Richard Pate died in 1657, John was named administrator of his estate. In December 1662 John Pate patented two 200-acre tracts in the immediate vicinity of the land his late uncle had owned. He also patented 1,000 acres near the head of the Potomac River. Then, in 1666 he laid claim to 300 acres in Gloucester, on the Ware River and Mobjack Bay, and three years later he acquired 1,200 acres in Old Rappahannock County on Gilson's Creek, near Robert Beverley I's holdings. In July 1669 Pate and Beverley together patented a 6,000-acre tract on the upper side of the Mattaponi River. When Secretary Thomas Ludwell sent a letter to Lord Arlington in July 1668, he entrusted it to John Pate. Pate later assured Ludwell that he had delivered the letter to one of Arlington's secretaries. At issue was concern about the price of tobacco. John Pate was named to the Council of State in 1670 and served in 1671–1672. He represented Gloucester County in the assembly from 1684 to 1692 and died in Virginia. When a list of quitrents was compiled in 1704, John Pate of Gloucester was credited with 1,000 acres in Gloucester's Petsworth Parish and 1,000 acres in King and Queen County (STAN 39; LEO xx; PB 5:201, 374, 377, 594; 6:225–226; SR 4135; SMITH 68).

Richard Pate: In November 1650 Richard Pate and another man patented 1,141 acres on the north side of the York River, at the head of Poropotank Creek's eastern branch. He sometimes did business with Richard Newport of Accomack County. Pate served as a burgess for Gloucester County in 1653. On October 30, 1657, when his will was proved, he was described as a resident of Virginia. His assets in Virginia were to be overseen by his nephew, John, the testator's brother's son (LEO 31; PB 2:271; SR 4135; AMES 2:391).

* * *

Thomas Pate: Documents in the British Archives reveal that in 1672 Thomas Pate was a Virginia merchant whose inventory included a wide variety of items. On October 26, 1676, when the rebel Nathaniel Bacon succumbed to the "bloody flux" and "a lousy disease," he was staying at the Gloucester County plantation of Colonel Thomas Pate, near the head of Poropotank Creek's eastern branch, where John Pate also owned land. In October 1678 Thomas Pate patented an ad-

ditional 200 acres in that vicinity, and in May 1679 he purchased a plantation in Old Rappahannock County. In 1678 and 1682 he initiated lawsuits in Middlesex County's monthly court. Pate served as a burgess for Gloucester County in 1684 and began renting his personal residence, Gloucester Hall, to Virginia's governor, Francis Howard, Lord Effingham. Governor Howard, who expected to bring his wife and children there, told his wife that Pate had "a very good house, and the finest ayre [*sic*] they tell me in the Country." He added that "Here is at least 2 miles round open and hilly." He also said that while he had been staying at the Pate home, he had been visited by an Indian king and his retinue. He indicated that he had asked the Indians to kill some deer and wild fowl for him because the Council of State was going to be meeting at the Pate home in the immediate future. In fact, the council met there twice more during the year. During the spring of 1684, Governor Howard wrote his wife that Colonel Pate had hoped to marry Jane Sewell Calvert, the 20-year-old widow of Maryland Chancellor Philip Calvert and the daughter of Lady Baltimore. However, the young and wealthy Mrs. Calvert returned to England with Lord and Lady Baltimore without accepting Pate's proposal, and Pate eventually married a local woman. Governor Howard gave Colonel Thomas Pate the right to issue marriage licenses in Gloucester and Middlesex counties, a duty that would have provided him with lucrative fees. When a French Huguenot traveler, Durand de Dauphine, visited Gloucester in 1686, he noted that Governor Howard had lived at Colonel Thomas Pate's home in 1684 and 1685. In May 6, 1686, Colonel Thomas Pate was designated a customs officer, replacing Philip Ludwell I, who was dismissed from office (LEO 47; Middlesex County Order Book 1673–1680:118; 1680–1694:61; Old Rappahannock County Deeds and Wills 1677–1682:238; PB 6:665; SR 1853, 4199a; AND 87, 92; NEVILLE 313, 323; EJC I:55–56, 67; DAUPHINE 30–31, 136–137, 143–144, 147; HOWARD 51, 54, 77, 82, 89, 127–128, 180–181).

Pattanochus (Native American): Between March 18 and June 19, 1680, when the 1677 Treaty of Middle Plantation was expanded to include some additional Indian groups, Pattanochus signed as King of the Nansaticoes (Nanzatticos), Nanzemunds (Nansemonds), and Portabacchoes (Portebagos). The Nansemonds listed with the Nanzatticos and Portobagos were a Rappahannock River tribe and should not be confused with the

Nansemond Indians who lived on the south side of the James River (Anonymous, 1677 treaty, Miscellaneous Virginia Records 1606–1692, Bland Manuscripts, XIV, ff 226–233).

Pattiawaske (Native American): In April 1697 Pattiawaske joined Numpskinner and his wife, Betty alias Nonomisk (Nonomiske), in selling the late Ned Gunstocker's 150 acres in Richmond County to Nathaniel Pope alias Bridges. The deed of conveyance reveals that the acreage formerly had been granted to Ned Gunstocker, Betty's uncle, on October 14, 1666. The three Indians were accompanied by their interpreters, Jane Browne and Thomas Smyth (Richmond County Deed Book 3 [1697–1704]:1–2).

Paucough (Native American): In 1689 Herquapinck, Paucough, and Hearseeqe, the monguys or chief rulers of the Chickahominy Indians, sent a petition to the governor, asking for protection from the Pamunkey Indians. They said that when they were attacked by the Senecas, they had been forced to take up residence with the Pamunkeys, on the Pamunkey River. However, in time the relationship between the Pamunkeys and Chickahominys had become contentious. Therefore, the Chickahominy Indians' leaders asked the governor's permission to move to a place called Rickahock on the north side of the Mattaponi River. They indicated that they had obtained the acreage from Benjamin Arnold in exchange for some of their own land on the south side of the Mattaponi (PALM I:22).

* * *

Francis Paul (Pall, Paule) I: Francis Paul I, a married man, came to Virginia sometime prior to 1616. He and his wife, Mathew, produced sons Thomas and Francis II and a daughter, Frances. Francis Paul I and his wife died sometime prior to January 1625, at which time six-year-old Thomas Paul and his four-year-old brother, Francis II, were living in the rural Jamestown Island household headed by George Ungwin (VI&A 539).

Thomas Paul (Pall, Paule): On May 25, 1637, Thomas Paul, the son of Francis Paul I, patented some land in James City County, using the headrights of his mother, Mathew, and sister, Frances. He failed to mention his brother, Francis II, perhaps because he was Virginia-born. Sometime prior to November 2, 1642, Thomas Paul sold 350 acres on Checkeroes (Gordon's) Creek to Captain Robert Hutchinson. When Paul patented a one-acre lot on September 20, 1643, in the western end of Jamestown Island near the Back River, he was given six months in which to develop his land (VI&A 539; PB 1 Pt. 1:430; Pt. 2:846, 890; CBE 56).

* * *

George Paul (Pall, Paule): On March 24, 1623, Virginia Company officials noted that George Paul, a member of Sir George Yeardley's household, was dead (VI&A 540). It is unclear whether he was living in Jamestown or Flowerdew Hundred.

William Paulett: On May 28, 1673, the General Court ordered William Paulett to examine the work Surry County bricklayer John Bird had done for Richard James I of Jamestown. Paulett, who probably was a brick mason, reportedly owned land near the French Ordinary in York County, as well as some acreage that had belonged to Richard Auborne, the occupant of a brick row house in urban Jamestown (MCGC 341, 344).

Robert Pawlett (Paulett, Paulette): In 1620 the Rev. Robert Pawlett, a clergyman and surgeon, set sail for Virginia and arrived at Berkeley Hundred on January 29, 1621. He was named to the Council of State on July 24, 1621. In June 1622 Virginia Company officials, who were unaware of the Indian attack that had occurred on March 22nd, decided to send Pawlett to Martin's Hundred. He died in Virginia sometime prior to 1623 (VI&A 540; STAN 30).

Thomas Pawlett (Paulett, Pawlette): Thomas Pawlett arrived in Jamestown in 1618 with some of Lord Delaware's men and in 1619 served as a burgess for Argall's Gift, a settlement situated within the Governor's Land. Pawlett returned to England but by February 1624 was back in Virginia and living at West and Shirley Hundred. From that point on, he seems to have lived in that region. In 1626 he was made a commissioner of the monthly court that served the "upper parts," which included the corporations of Henrico and Charles City, a position to which he was reappointed in 1632. In 1627 he led an expedition against the Indians, and in March 1629 he was named commander of Westover. In February 1633 Thomas Pawlett served as burgess for Westover and Flowerdew. He was returned to office in 1640 and represented Charles City County. He was named to the Council of State in 1641 and died in Virginia in January 1644 (VI&A 540; STAN 35, LEO 3, 7, 12, 18).

Dorothy Peach: On August 11, 1687, Dorothy Peach witnessed the will made by John Holder of urban Jamestown (AMB 78).

Nathaniel Peacock (Pecock): Nathaniel Peacock, a youth, came to Virginia in 1607 and was one of the first Jamestown settlers. He accompanied Captain John Smith on a voyage to the Pamunkey Indians' territory (VI&A 541).

Deuel (Dewel, Deyell) Pead (Peed): On April 28, 1684, the assembly decided that the Rev. Deuel Pead of Christ Church Parish in Middlesex County would officiate at a holy day that was to be celebrated in Jamestown. He had preached a sermon in the capital city on April 23, 1686, dedicating it to Francis Howard, Lord Effingham. During the early 1680s Pead's name appeared numerous times in the records of Middlesex's monthly court, often when defending himself from his creditors, but at least once when he had his young servants' ages determined for tax purposes. In 1686 Pead patented nearly 300 acres on the south side of the Rappahannock River. He ran afoul of the law when he told some of his servants to steal several pigs from James Curtis of Middlesex County, using their firearms if necessary. Pead was found guilty and fined for his transgression. Two years later Pead, a planter as well as a clergyman, reported Richard Willis for harboring Indians, contrary to law. In 1689 Middlesex County's sheriff summoned Pead for failing to report five tithables, a tax avoidance issue, and he was found guilty of the same type of underreporting problem in Old Rappahannock County. In 1689 Pead, who was then South Farnham Parish's rector, was arrested and brought before Old Rappahannock's justices because he had married two parishioners contrary to a specific act of assembly, which required the purchase of a marriage license, the posting of bans, the consent of witnesses or guardians, and use of the ceremony in the Book of Common Prayer. Despite these blemishes on his reputation, in 1690 the Rev. James Blair—the Church of England's Commissary in Virginia, who was trying to establish ecclesiastical courts in the colony—nominated Pead as his surrogate for the territory between the York and Rappahannock rivers (JHB 1660–1693:297; CO 5/1305; SR 7368; Middlesex County Order Book 1680–1694:173, 175, 178, 180–181, 190, 199, 203, 214, 215, 223, 243, 254, 362, 429, 480, 497, 506; Old Rappahannock County Order Book 1687–1692:119, 128, 144, 147; PB 7:650; SR 7388; HEN III:150–151).

Robert Peake: Robert Peake came to Virginia in 1623 and in February 1624 was an indentured servant at Sir George Yeardley's plantation, Flowerdew Hundred. By January 1625 he was living in urban Jamestown and was a servant in the Yeardley household (VI&A 541).

Lawrence Peal (Peale, Peele): Lawrence Peal came to Virginia in 1620 and during the mid-1620s lived in Elizabeth City. He testified that around August 1622 he was present when one of Dr. John Pott's servants, Robert Leister of Jamestown, criticized and then threatened Captain William Tucker (VI&A 541).

Gregory Pearl (Pearle): In April 1623 Gregory Pearl, a master's mate, rebutted Captain Nathaniel Butler's claims about conditions in the Virginia colony. Pearl, when testifying in Jamestown, said that he had been in the colony for 16 months (VI&A 541). Therefore, he would have been present during the March 1622 Indian attack.

[No First Name] Pearns: Mr. Pearns' servant, William, died in Jamestown sometime after April 1623 but before February 16, 1624 (VI&A 542).

Cutbert (Cuthbert) Pearson (Peirson, Peerson, Person, Seirson): Cutbert Pearson came to Virginia in 1619, and in early 1624 he was living on the east side of the Hampton River in Elizabeth City in William Barry's household. In August 1626 Pearson informed the General Court that three male residents of the Governor's Land and Jamestown Island had been drunk and disorderly. When Cutbert Pearson was assigned to the governor on January 12, 1627, he was identified as a tenant of the defunct Virginia Company (VI&A 542).

Abraham Peate: In January 1635 Abraham Peate witnessed the will made by Thomas Whaplett, a Jamestown merchant and planter. The testator bequeathed half of his property to Peate and the remainder to his sister, Rebecca Whaplett. He also asked Peate to manage her share of the plantation (VI&A 542).

John Pegden: John Pegden, a gentleman from London, arrived in Jamestown on September 12, 1623. He died sometime prior to February 16, 1624 (VI&A 543).

Pegg: In 1769, when an inventory was made of Edward Ambler I's estate, Pegg, an adult female slave, was living on Jamestown Island (AMB-E).

Richard Peirce (Pierce, Perse, Perce, Peerce): In early 1624 Richard Peirce and his wife, Elizabeth, were living in the Neck O'Land near Jamestown Island. Within a year's time, they had moved to Archer's Hope. Over the years Peirce testified before the General Court numerous times. He seems to have been a relatively successful planter and in September 1636 patented 600 acres on the east side of the Chickahominy River (VI&A 544).

Mr. and Mrs. Thomas Peirce (Pierce, Perse, Perce, Peerce): When Virginia's assembly convened in July 1619, Thomas Peirce was appointed sergeant-at-arms. Peirce, his wife, and their child were killed at Mulberry Island during the March 22, 1622, Indian attack. On October 7, 1622, Virginia Company officials noted that Peirce's brother, Edward, a London merchant tailor, was to serve as the decedent's administrator (VI&A 545).

Thomas Peirce: In January 1655 Thomas Peirce, who may have been related to Captain William Peirce of Jamestown, was living at Mulberry Island, where Captain Peirce owned land. In March 1674 a Thomas Peirce patented 155 acres of land in Mulberry Island Parish in Warwick County (Surry County Deeds, Wills &c. 1652–1672:116; DOR 2:799; NUG II:144).

William Peirce (Pierce, Pearse, Perse, Perce, Peerce): William Peirce, who had been shipwrecked in Bermuda, reached Virginia in 1610 and soon after was made captain of the guard in Jamestown. His wife, Joan I, had arrived in the colony in 1609. In 1619 Peirce witnessed Governor George Yeardley's treaty with the Chickahominy Indians, and later in the year Yeardley sent Peirce, his son-in-law John Rolfe, and another man to Old Point Comfort to meet the *Treasurer*, a vessel bearing some of the colony's first Africans. Later, Peirce's household included a black woman named Angelo, who had arrived on the *Treasurer*. In 1619 Peirce received a patent for land on Mulberry Island and some additional acreage. By 1623 he had been made lieutenant governor, captain of the governor's guard, and commander of Jamestown Island and its blockhouses. During the mid-1620s the Peirces were living in urban Jamestown on a lot that adjoined Back Street. Their house was termed "one of the fairest in Virginia."

Captain John Smith described Mrs. Joan Peirce as "an honest and industrious woman" who had a large garden in Jamestown. He quoted her as saying that she could "keep a better house in Virginia for 3 or 4 hundred pounds than in London," even though she had gone to the colony "with little or nothing." William and Joan Peirce I's daughter, Joan II, married the twice-widowed John Rolfe after his May 1617 return to the colony. They probably lived on one of the two parcels in urban Jamestown that were owned by her parents. The Rolfes' daughter, Elizabeth, was born around 1621. Upon being widowed, Joan Peirce Rolfe married Captain Roger Smith of Jamestown and moved into his home with her daughter, Elizabeth Rolfe. William Peirce was elected Jamestown's burgess in 1624 and in 1629 wrote a descriptive account of conditions in the colony. He had a store in Jamestown and was a highly successful planter who continued to acquire land, including some on the lower side of the James River. He served as a member of the Council of State from 1632 to 1643 and died before June 22, 1647. Mrs. Joan Peirce was still alive in 1641 (VI&A 545–547; LEO 5–6; DOR 2:797–800).

William Peirce (Pierce, Pearce, Pears): William Peirce patented 200 acres in Northumberland County in October 1649. He may have been living in the northwestern part of Northumberland, which in 1653 was split off to form Westmoreland County. Peirce's name first appeared in Westmoreland's court records on October 31, 1657. Over the years he went to court from time to time to witness documents or participate in lawsuits as plaintiff or defendant, or to serve as an attorney. In 1660 he was among those who inventoried the late Colonel Thomas Speke's estate, and he bought 200 acres from Richard Heabeard. In April 1661 Peirce became a justice of Westmoreland County's court, a position he held for nearly 30 years. Like many of his peers, he speculated in real estate. In December 1662 he patented 1,200 acres on the Nominy (Nomini) River in Northumberland County and seated his newly acquired property. Then, in March 1663 he sold half of it to Jamestown resident William Drummond I. At that time Peirce indicated that the acreage he was conveying to Drummond contained the plantation's housing. By June 1663 Peirce had patented 4,054 acres of land on the north side of the Rappahannock River, in what was then Old Rappahannock County. In March 1666 he acquired 1,810 acres on the east side of the Nominy River. Finally, in August 1669 he laid claim to 3,110 acres of Westmoreland County land that was adjacent to some property he already owned. One way Peirce generated income was by leasing his land to tenants. He continued to speculate in real estate and during the next few years continued to patent and then sell land. When he sold some property in 1674, his wife, Sarah, acknowledged the transaction through her attorney. In 1677 Peirce's widowed daughter, Elizabeth Vaughan, asked him to recover her debts in Maryland and Virginia and to sell her land in Westmoreland County. Major William Peirce served as a county justice throughout the 1680s and in 1681 became high sheriff. He served as a burgess for Westmoreland County from 1680 to 1682. Finally, in November 1694 he patented 50 acres between the Rappahannock and Potomac rivers, in what was then Richmond County but formerly had been Old Rappahannock. When William Peirce made his will on February 20, 1702, he identified himself as a resident of Copley Parish in Westmoreland County (LEO 46; Old Rappahannock County Deeds and Wills 1677–1682:178, 295–296, 335–338; Westmoreland County Deeds, Wills, Patents &c. 1653–1659:94a, 120a; Deeds, Wills &c. 1661–1662:4a–6a, 8a–10a, 16–16a, 22, 24, 38; Deeds and Wills 1 [1653–1671]:239–240; Wills and Deeds 3 [1701–1707]:50–51; Deeds, Patents &c. 1665–1677:22–22a, 43a, 84–84a, 122a–122, 127–127a, 178a, 209a–210, 326, 357a–358a; Order Book 1676–1689:152, 204, 253, 298, 360, 367, 471, 485, 491, 603; PB 2:187; 5:29, 356, 383, 481; 6:227; NN 2:65–66; DOR 2:799–800). No evidence has come to light linking William Peirce of Northern Neck with Captain William Peirce of Jamestown and Mulberry Island. However, the latter and his descendants invested in land on the lower side of the James River in Nansemond and Isle of Wight counties, as did many of their contemporaries who patented land in the Northern Neck during the Commonwealth period.

* * *

Abraham Peirsey (Persey, Perseye, Pearsey, Piersey): Virginia Company investor Abraham Peirsey came to Virginia in 1616 on the first magazine (store) ship and was the colony's cape merchant or official purveyor of merchandise. He served as viceadmiral during Deputy Governor Samuel Argall's government (1617–1618). As cape merchant, he participated in the colony's first assembly, which convened in July 1619. In August 1619 he accompanied Governor George Yeardley to Old Point Comfort, where they traded food for some of the colony's first Africans. Peirsey married Elizabeth Draper of London, who in November 1619 asked the Virginia Company to grant her husband some land on account of his lengthy service to the colony. In 1622 the Indians attacked the Peirsey plantation, Peirseys Toile, near Swift Creek, a tributary of the Appomattox River. Together, the Peirseys produced two children, Mary and Elizabeth II, who came to Virginia in 1623. By 1624 Abraham Peirsey had purchased the Flowerdew Hundred and Weyanoke plantations from Sir George Yeardley, changing Flowerdew's name to Peirsey's Hundred. He also was in possession of some property in urban Jamestown, the focus of his mercantile operations, and he was a member of the Council of State. Mrs. Elizabeth Peirsey died in the capital city sometime after February 16, 1624, but before January 24, 1625. In January 1625 Peirsey was living in urban Jamestown with his daughters. Later in the year he married the former Frances Grenville, the widow of Lord Delaware's brother, Nathaniel West of West and Shirley Hundred. In May 1625 Peirsey was credited with 1,150 acres on the Appomattox River; 1,000 at Flowerdew (Peirsey's) Hundred; and 2,000 acres at Weyanoke. He died in Virginia around January 16, 1628. A duplicate copy of Peirsey's will and an account of his estate were prepared by Samuel Mathews I of Denbigh, husband of the widowed Frances Grenville West Peirsey, who died sometime prior to May 10, 1633. The estate account Mathews presented to officials in England on March 15, 1634, made reference to Abraham Peirsey's house and store in Jamestown. Mathews stated that the decedent's home plantation, Peirsey's Hundred, was his most valuable property, and he noted that it contained ordnance. He also indicated that the plantation had been appraised and that nobody had been willing to pay what it was worth. In 1628, Abraham Peirsey's daughter, Elizabeth II, married Richard Stephens, a Jamestown merchant, with whom she produced two sons, Samuel and William I. After Stephens' death in 1636, Elizabeth married Governor John Harvey of Jamestown, a titled nobleman many years her senior. After Harvey was replaced as governor, he and wife Elizabeth returned to England, where she died. Abraham Peirsey's daughter, Mary, married Captain Thomas Hill of Stanley Hundred in what became Warwick County. After Hill's decease in 1657, Mary Peirsey Hill married Thomas Bushrod of York County, who outlived her (VI&A 548–550; SR 629; CO 1/8 ff 15–18).

Mrs. Abraham Peirsey (see Frances Grenville)

* * *

Abraham Pelteare (Pelterre): Abraham Pelteare, a youth, came to Virginia in 1624 and in early 1625 was living in Elizabeth City, where he was a servant. On August 28, 1626, Sir George Yeardley presented the General Court with a petition he had received from Abraham's widowed mother, Margaret. She insisted that her son had gone to Virginia to serve as an apprentice, not as an indentured servant. Pelteare was paid for his service and was entrusted to Yeardley's care. It is unclear whether he lived in the Yeardley home in Jamestown or on one of Yeardley's outlying properties (VI&A 550).

Stephen Pendle: On March 24, 1637, when cooper John Parry, William Parry's brother, made his will, he left some clothing to Stephen Pendle, identifying him as one of the late Sir George Yeardley's servants. The Parrys were residents of urban Jamestown, where Yeardley also had lived (EEAC 44).

William Penn (Pinn): In September 1683 William Briscoe patented 12 acres on Jamestown Island, acreage that formerly had belonged to the late William Penn but had escheated to the Crown. The Penn acreage seems to have been located on the east side of Orchard Run. When Briscoe made his will sometime prior to July 10, 1695, he left all of his Jamestown Island property (including the land that formerly belonged to William Penn) to his widowed daughter-in-law, the former Ann Holder (PB 7:328; NUG II:269, 372; AMB 35, 53, 133).

John Pennington (Penington): John Pennington came to Virginia in 1607 and was one of the first Jamestown colonists (VI&A 551).

Robert Pennington (Penington): Robert Pennington, a Virginia Company investor, came to Virginia in 1607 and was one of the first Jamestown colonists. He died in the capital city on August 18, 1607 (VI&A 551).

Robert Penny: On September 7, 1680, Robert Penny was identified as the bookkeeper of Thomas Rabley of Jamestown when he testified about John Goring's debt (Surry County Order Book 1671–1691:309).

Pepmngeis (Native American): In 1657 Pepmngeis, one of the Mattaponi Indians' Great Men or leaders, joined in making a peace agreement with the justices of Old Rappahannock County (Old Rappahannock County Deed Book 1656–1664:17).

Gilbert Peppett (Peppet, Pepper): Gilbert Peppett arrived in Virginia prior to May 1623. By early 1624 he was living at Sir George Yeardley's plantation, Flowerdew Hundred, where he married Alice, a woman Yeardley had brought to the colony. By December 1624 Peppett had attained the rank of lieutenant, and in 1625 he served as a burgess for Flowerdew (Peirsey's) Hundred. In May 1625 he was credited with 50 acres at Blunt Point in Elizabeth City, and two years later he added 250 acres to his holdings. By 1628 Peppett's wife, Alice, was dead, and he had wed a woman named Lucy. Gilbert Peppett died sometime prior to March 4, 1629 (VI&A 552; LEO 6).

Peracuta (Native American): In 1671 Perecuta, the Appomattock Indians' king, led European explorers Nathaniell Batts and Robert Fallom on a westerly expedition. They set out from Fort Henry, the outpost from which Abraham Wood and a party of explorers had departed in 1650 when venturing beyond the Appomattox River's head. The Appomattock Indians were then living within Charles City County, which extended across the James River, taking in what became Prince George County. They had moved to Charles City by 1665 and, according to a 1669 census of the colony's natives, had 50 warriors. In March 1675 the Appomattock Indians, who were still residing in the southerly part of Charles City County, asked that Peracuta be confirmed as their king and sought permission to hunt and gather at the heads of the rivers. Simultaneously, they asked that their old town not be burned, raising the possibility that they were becoming concerned about clashes between frontier settlers and more warlike native groups. On May 29, 1677, the day the Treaty of Middle Plantation was signed, Peracuta came to Middle Plantation prepared to endorse it, but he was turned away because some of his people were accused of murder. Between March 18 and June 19, 1680, when the original treaty was expanded to include some additional Indian groups, Peracuta, the king of the Appomattux (Appomattocks), signed on behalf of his people (JHB 1660–1693:64; SALLEY 5–20; Anonymous, 1677 treaty, Miscellaneous Virginia Records 1606–1692, Bland Manuscripts, XIV, ff 226–233; CO 1/40 ff 249–250).

George Percy: George Percy, a gentleman and one of the first Jamestown colonists, arrived in Virginia in 1607. His account of the colonists' first few weeks provides many insights into the hardships they experienced and their interaction with the Indians. Percy was president of the Virginia colony from September 1609 to May 1610, vacating office as soon as Sir Thomas Gates arrived. When Lord Delaware left the colony in March 1611, Percy became deputy governor and served in that capacity until Sir Thomas Dale's arrival in March 1611. Percy left Virginia in late April 1612 and died in England in 1632 (VI&A 553).

Perkatoan (Native American): On February 6, 1656, Perkatoan, werowance of the Machodoc Indians, joined his Great Men in making an agreement that was witnessed by some of Northumberland County's military commanders. The militia officers had been asked to investigate a complaint the Indians had made against Isaac Allerton. Under the terms of the 1656 agreement, Allerton was allowed to keep his livestock on the land but was prohibited from further development (Northumberland County Wills, Inventories &c. 1652–1658:101).

Christopher Perkins: On January 1, 1744, William Broadnax II sold all of his rural and urban property on Jamestown Island to Christopher Perkins, a Norfolk County merchant. Thanks to this transaction, Perkins controlled virtually all the frontage on the James River between Orchard Run and Passmore Creek and some urban waterfront land to the west of Orchard Run. He also owned a large parcel at the extreme western end of Jamestown Island, which included the isthmus over which passed the road to the mainland, and the lot or lots then used for the Jamestown ferry. When Broadnax conveyed his property to Perkins, he sold him a slave named William Liverpool. Perkins kept Broadnax's Jamestown Island property for precisely a year. Then, on January 1, 1745, he and his wife, Elizabeth, conveyed it to Richard Ambler, the Yorktown merchant who developed his land on Jamestown Island into a major plantation and family seat. Perkins also sold Ambler the slave named William Liverpool. On December 5, 1764, Christopher Perkins, a resident of Suffolk, prepared his will, which on December 5, 1765, was presented for probate in England (AMB 97–98, 106–107, 250; WITH 243).

* * *

Francis Perkins I: Francis Perkins I and his son, Francis II, arrived in Jamestown on January 4, 1608, in the 1st Supply of new colonists. In a March 28, 1608, letter that Francis I sent to a friend in England, he said that on January 7th a fire had consumed all but three buildings in the fort and the items that he and his son had put ashore. He asked for some clothing and expressed a desire to be appointed to the council (VI&A 554).

Francis Perkins II: Francis Perkins II, a laborer and the son of Francis Perkins I, came to Virginia in the 1st Supply of new colonists, arriving in Jamestown in January 1608 (VI&A 554).

* * *

Jane Perkins (Pirkins): Mrs. Jane Perkins patented 27 acres in the mainland on September 9, 1648. Her land, which adjoined the Glasshouse tract (then attributed to Anthony Coleman), was said to have been given to Alexander Stoner of Jamestown by Captain William Peirce, also a landowner in the capital city. The patent's text indicates that Stoner forfeited the 27-acre parcel to John Knight, who assigned it to William Edwards I, father of William Edwards II of Jamestown. He, in turn, had conveyed the acreage to Edward Prince, who assigned it to Robert Miles. Miles later transferred it to Mrs. Perkins. In 1700 Jane Perkins' acreage, which lay just outside of the Governor's Land's boundaries, escheated to the Crown and was repatented by William Woodward in October 1702. When Woodward first acquired the property, he tried to sell or lease it to William Sherwood, who had it surveyed and determined that it contained only 25 acres. Afterward, Woodward conveyed his purported 27 acres to John Tullitt of Jamestown, who in 1707 sold it to Philip Ludwell II. In 1718 Ludwell conveyed the Woodward parcel to Edward Jaquelin as 27 acres. Thanks to the marriage of Jaquelin's eldest daughter, Elizabeth, to Yorktown merchant Richard Ambler, the Perkins acreage became part of the Ambler plantation on the mainland (PB 2:177; 9:509; AMB 68, 71, 99).

Thomas Perkins: Thomas Perkins and his wife, Elizabeth, owned 27 acres in the mainland adjacent to Jamestown Island. After Thomas's death sometime prior to March 1662, Elizabeth had her attorney, Theodorick Hone of Jamestown, convey that acreage to Francis Morrison (Moryson). The Perkins property eventually became part of the Ambler plantation, as did Mrs. Jane Perkins' 27 acres, which was nearby (JHB 1660–1693:18; HEN II:159).

William Perkinson: An announcement in the July 15, 1772, issue of the *Virginia Ga-*

zette stated that William Perkinson was serving as the administrator of the late William Davis. At the time of his death, Davis was living in urban Jamestown, in Thomas Harris's house (Purdie and Dixon, July 2, 1772).

* * *

Richard Perrott (Parrott) I: Richard Perrott (Parrott) I began acquiring land along the south side of the Rappahannock River in March 1649. In 1657 and 1661 he enhanced and reaffirmed his claims, raising the possibility that he had failed to seat his property. By 1666 Perrott's property was identified as being in Lancaster County. In 1665 he patented 950 acres on the north side of the Piankatank River in Lancaster County, land adjacent to a 1,900 acre tract he had purchased from Nicholas and Frances Mottrom Spencer. By 1669 some of Perrott's landholdings were encompassed within the boundaries of the newly formed Middlesex County. In February 1673 Perrott was serving as a justice of Middlesex County's monthly court, as was his son, Richard II. In April 1680 the court convened at the elder man's house. Richard Perrott I served as a burgess for Middlesex County in 1677 and 1684, and in March 1683 he was one of three men designated to meet at the house of Ralph Wormeley II in order to inventory the estate of the late Sir Henry Chicheley. Perrott was a Middlesex County justice in April 1686 but died sometime prior to February 1687. It was then that his will was proved and his widow, Margaret, was designated his executrix. By February 1688 Margaret was dead (LEO 43, 47; Middlesex County Order Book 1673–1680:1, 219; 1680–1694:1, 103, 247, 276, 331, 388; Lancaster County Order Book 1666–1680:52; PB 4:238–239, 438; 6:196, 328; Westmoreland County Deeds and Wills No. 1 [1653–1659]:270–273).

Richard Perrott (Parrott) II: In February 1673 Richard Perrott (Parrott) II was serving as a justice of Middlesex County's monthly court, as was his father, Richard I. When Richard Perrott II was designated high sheriff in May 1675, his father served as his surety. Both men were still serving as county justices during the early 1680s (Middlesex County Order Book 1673–1680:1, 31; 1680–1694:1, 171).

* * *

* * *

Micajah Perry: In July 1690 the London mercantile firm of Micajah Perry and Company (also trading as Perry, Lane and Company) brought suit in Middlesex County's monthly court, in an attempt to recover from Robert, John, and Henry (Harry) Beverley the cost of lodging. The men probably were housed in the Perry firm's brick row house on urban Jamestown's waterfront. John Jarrett and his wife, Joannah, who was Micajah Perry's niece, were residing in the Perry-owned row house in November 1696, when George Marable II sold an adjoining unit to merchant William Sherwood. On November 12, 1710, the Perry firm disposed of its lot and dwelling. By that time John Jarrett was dead and his widow, Joannah, was living elsewhere. The firm known as Perry, Lane and Company was composed of Micajah Perry, his brother Richard, and Thomas Lane. Micajah's brother Peter, a York County merchant, and Micajah Lowe, a Charles City County merchant, also were tied into the trading network. Lowe's sister, Joannah, was the wife of John Jarrett, William Sherwood's nephew. Another member of this familial trading network probably was William Edwards IV of Surry, who was married to Micajah Lowe's widow, Sarah.

Micajah Perry's selection as attorney and/or administrator to wealthy Virginians such as Jamestown landowners Thomas and Mary Swann, Henry Hartwell, William Sherwood, and others suggests that he was trustworthy and astute. Among the records of Perry's transactions in Virginia is one for the sale of cloth to Jamestown lot owner Richard Holder. In 1688 and 1689 Micajah Perry used his influence with the Privy Council to free Edward Davis, Lionel Delawafer, and Andrew Hinson, who were accused of piracy and incarcerated in Jamestown. Perry claimed that the men's "plate, money, jewells and goods" had been illegally seized when their vessel was captured and brought in by a Maryland ship. While the alleged pirates were jailed in Jamestown, they were in the custody of the James City County sheriff, George Marable II, who eventually inherited his late father's brick row house on the Jamestown waterfront but in 1688 probably lived elsewhere. When the prisoners were released, they were forced to pay Marable for the cost of their "entertainment," an indication that the sheriff was responsible for providing them with room and board. When William Sherwood made his will in 1697, he asked Micajah Perry to administer the bequest he was making to the poor of a parish in England. British records reveal that Perry and Jeffrey Jeffreys, both of whom had a close business association with William Sherwood, were the Royal African Company's principal contractors for the sale of Africans in Virginia. In April 1704 a Virginia man urged Micajah Perry to encourage the Council of Trade to restore Jamestown's representation in the assembly, something to which Governor Francis Nicholson was adamantly opposed. When Perry died in London in October 1721, his obituary was published throughout the North American colonies. According to the *Boston Gazette,* Perry had been Virginia's greatest merchant (AMB 48, 62, 65, 101; PALM I:45; JHB 1695–1702:68; EJC I:363; MCGH 873; DAVIES 295; CO 5/1305 ff 9, 12–19; CBE 20, 28; WITH 507; P.R.O. Auditor 15/93 f 162; *Boston Gazette,* January 29–February 5, 1729; Tyler, "Micajah Perry," 264–268; SAIN 22:105; Middlesex County Order Book 1680–1694:477, 645).

Peter Perry: On February 24, 1685, Peter Perry, a merchant, was identified as Micajah Perry's brother and a resident of Virginia. He did business under the name of Peter Perry and Company and was residing on the James River when he received and sold a cargo of 190 Africans, dispatched to Virginia by merchants Micajah Perry and Thomas Lane, representatives of the Royal African Company. He went to court in early October 1689 to procure headright certificates for several people. Among them were Elizabeth Perry (perhaps his wife) and Joannah (Joanne) Lowe, his niece, who went on to marry John Jarrett, the nephew of William Sherwood. In 1688 Captain Peter Perry, a court justice, served as a burgess for Charles City County. He witnessed legal documents, sometimes served as an attorney, and like his contemporaries, went to court to collect debts. In a 1692 patent he was identified as Escheator Christopher Wormeley's deputy (Tyler, "Micajah Perry," 264–265; PB 8:240; Charles City County Will and Deed Book 1689–1690:82; 1692–1694:185; Orders 1687–1695:139, 367, 414, 545; LEO 49; SR 5754).

* * *

John Perry: In July 1627, John Perry, a London merchant, shipped cloth goods and footwear from London to Virginia. Within a year's time, he went to Virginia and by 1628 had become established at Perry's (later, Swann's) Point in the corporation of James City. When he prepared his will, he made bequests to several people in England and identified London merchant Richard Perry as his brother. John Perry died in Jamestown sometime prior to December 1628, when William Perry, a gentleman and probably a kinsman, presented his will to the

General Court and vouched for its authenticity (VI&A 555).

* * *

William Perry: William Perry came to Virginia in 1611. He patented acreage near the falls of the James River but withdrew to Jamestown Island after the 1622 Indian attack. Perhaps while he was living there, he cleared acreage at Hog Island. In 1623 he married the recently widowed Richard Pace's widow, Isabell (Izabella), of Paces Paines. When Perry went to England in 1624, he was accompanied by a Tappahanna Indian boy he was rearing in the Christian faith. Perry's wife and her infant son, perhaps Henry Perry, stayed behind and were then living in urban Jamestown. The Perrys probably resided at Paces Paines until the early 1630s when they moved to Buckland in Charles City County. Before they relocated, Perry was in command of the settlers living in the vicinity of Paces Paines and Smith's Mount and represented them in the assembly sessions held in 1629, 1630, and 1632. Lieutenant William Perry was named to the Council of State in 1632 and held office until August 1637, the time of his death. He was survived by his wife, Isabell, and their son, Henry. The twice-widowed Isabell married Jamestown merchant George Menefie, whom she predeceased (VI&A 555–556; LEO 7–10).

Henry Perry: Henry Perry was the son of Captain William Perry and his wife, the former Isabell (Izabella) Smythe, who had outlived her first husband, Richard Pace. Henry, as his late father's primary heir, inherited his 2,000-acre plantation, Buckland, in Charles City County, and repatented it in 1637. He eventually married his stepsister, Elizabeth Menefie (Menefy) II, the daughter of George Menefie (Menefy) and his first wife, Elizabeth. Henry Perry served as a Charles City County burgess in 1652 and 1654–1655 and was named to the Council of State in 1655. Elizabeth Menefie Perry inherited her late father's lot in urban Jamestown and disposed of it sometime prior to 1656. When Captain Francis Pott made his will on August 5, 1658, he made a monetary bequest to Captain Henry Perry, whom he identified as his cousin, and to Perry's wife, Elizabeth (VI&A 557; STAN 36; LEO 30, 32; MARSHALL 58–59).

* * *

William Perse (Perce): William Perse (Perce), a laborer, came to Virginia in the

1st Supply of new colonists and resided in Jamestown (VI&A 557).

Peter: On February 15, 1768, when an inventory was made of the late Richard Ambler's slaves at his quarter called Powhatan, a male slave named Peter was living there. In 1769 Peter, who was still at Powhatan, was described as a boy and was part of the late Edward Ambler I's estate (York County Wills and Inventories 21:386–391).

Arthur Pett: In 1609 Arthur Pett, a mariner and Virginia Company member, became ill on the way to Virginia in the 3rd Supply of colonists. He died aboard the *Blessing* while it was anchored in Jamestown. Pett's will, presented for probate in March 1611, mentioned his wife, Florence, and daughter, Elizabeth, who were in England (VI&A 557).

John Pettie (Pettey): In May 1622 John Pettie testified in a suit that Lord Delaware's heirs brought against Sir Samuel Argall. In 1624, when Pettie testified a second time, he identified himself as a resident of Walthamstow, in Essex (VI&A 558).

John Pettit: John Pettit, a Frenchman, was naturalized in Jamestown on October 29, 1666 (York County Deeds, Orders, Wills 1665–1672:76).

Joseph Pettit: In 1683 Joseph Pettit was in possession of a leasehold in the Governor's Land. When William Sherwood made his will in 1697, he left Pettit some of his divinity books and said that Pettit was to have free use of other volumes (Soane 1683; MCGH 873).

Theodore Pettus: Theodore Pettus, a gentleman, arrived in Jamestown on September 12, 1623, and on November 6, 1626, testified in court (VI&A 558).

Thomas Pettus I: Thomas Pettus I immigrated to Virginia sometime prior to 1641 and married Richard Durant's wealthy widow, Elizabeth. Pettus was named to the Council of State and by 1643 had begun acquiring land. He came into possession of the Utopia and Littletown tracts on the upper side of the James River in James City County, amassing 1,280 acres in all. He also acquired land in the Northern Neck. The Pettus couple resided at Littletown, which fronted on the James River and eventually became part of Kingsmill Plantation. In January 1661 Colonel Thomas Pettus I and his wife, Elizabeth, and Major Edward Griffith of Mulberry Island in Warwick County sold their jointly owned 1,000 acres of land on

Potomac Creek in Northumberland County to Henry Meese, a prominent merchant. Pettus had patented the Northumberland County acreage in March 1659. Thomas Pettus I died in Virginia around 1669. His son, Thomas II, a minor, inherited Littletown and the adjoining tract, Utopia. Accounts maintained by Thomas II's guardian reveal that Littletown was a highly productive tobacco plantation (STAN 35; LEO xx; Westmoreland County Deeds, Wills &c. 1661–1662:27a–28a; NUG I:137; II:25, 207; MCGC 253, 259, 276; Henrico Miscellaneous Court Records I [1650–1717]:73–74).

Pewem (Native American): On April 20, 1660, Pewem and Owasewas (Owessewar), two of the Wicocomocoe Indians' Great Men or leaders, made a complaint to the justices of Northumberland County's monthly court. They said that two colonists, Robert Jones and George Walle (Wale, Walei), had seated illegally upon the land that had been assigned to their tribe and that they were being deprived of the habitat they needed for subsistence. The justices decided to have the matter aired on May 3rd in the presence of the county militia. On May 3, 1660, the Indians reiterated their claim but Jones and Walle failed to appear in court. Both colonists were ordered to cease further development while local officials determined whether they had seated within the boundaries of the land laid out for the Wicocomocoe. On June 26, 1660, the land dispute resurfaced and Pewem appeared before the court. This time the justices learned that Robert Jones, who had been acting as the late Governor Samuel Mathews II's agent, claimed that the plantation he had established was outside of the Indians' boundary line. He also indicated that he was going to take the matter to the General Court. Walle, on the other hand, stated that he did not currently reside in the county and that the surveyor Gervase Dodson had given him the land. Both men were told to confine their livestock until the matter was decided (Northumberland County Order Book 1652–1665:237–238, 245, 247).

Valentine Peyton (Payton): In January 1655 Valentine Peyton patented 1,000 acres of land at the head of the Aquia River. Two years later he sold half of the tract to his brother, Henry Peyton. In 1659 Valentine Peyton and his uncle, Thomas Partington of London, served as the late Henry Peyton's executors, and the decedent's widow, Ellen (Ellinor), chose Valentine Peyton as her attorney. Peyton was among those who in 1661 made an inventory of the late Walter

Broadhurst's estate, and he later patented 650 acres on a branch of Potomac Creek. He became a justice of Westmoreland County's monthly court in 1658, and in 1663 he was designated sheriff. He went on to become a lieutenant colonel in the local militia, and he married Frances, the widow of burgess Thomas Speke I, who died sometime between December 1, 1659, and January 14, 1660. On November 27, 1662, when Peyton prepared to set sail for Jamestown, he made his will and bequeathed almost all of his real and personal estate to his wife, Frances, whom he designated his executrix. He left a mare and four cows to his underage stepson, Thomas Speke II, when he attained age 21 and named two Maryland residents as overseers of his will. Valentine Peyton represented Westmoreland County in the assembly in 1663–1664 and died shortly after the 1664 session concluded. His will was proved on June 29, 1665. His widow, Frances, married burgess Captain John Appleton, whom she also outlived. She went on to marry John Washington I, and after his death she wed William Hardidge II (LEO 40; Westmoreland County Deeds, Wills, Patents &c. 1653–1659:94a–95, 96, 116a–117; Deeds and Wills No. 1 [1653–1671]:98–99, 227–228, 259; Deeds, Wills &c. 1661–1662:16–16a, 29, 47–47a; Order Book 1662–1664:11, 15; 1676–1689:53).

John Phelps: On February 10, 1677, Governor William Berkeley issued a proclamation in which he named those who were exempt from the king's pardon on account of their role in Bacon's Rebellion. Among those named was John Phelps, whom Berkeley said needed to be brought before a court (NEVILLE 61; SR 660).

Thomas Phelps: According to Captain John Smith, Thomas Phelps, a tradesman, came to Virginia in 1608 as part of the 2nd Supply of new colonists. He would have resided in Jamestown (VI&A 558).

[No First Name] Phetiplace: When Captains Phetiplace and Ratcliffe set out from Jamestown on a trading voyage in 1609–1610, Ratcliffe was ambushed and killed at Powhatan's behest. Phetiplace may have suffered a similar fate (VI&A 558).

Thomas Phildust: Thomas Phildust, one of Sir George Yeardley's servants, came to Virginia in 1620 and in January 1625 was living in the Yeardley household in urban Jamestown (VI&A 558).

Elmer Philips (Phillips): Elmer Philips came to Virginia in 1622 and resided at West

and Shirley Hundred. By August 21, 1626, he had moved to Jamestown Island, where on September 20, 1628, he patented some land. He moved to Elizabeth City and in June 1633 patented 100 acres near Fox Hill, using his own headright and that of Daniel Franck, a servant who had been executed for thievery (VI&A 559).

Phill: On February 15, 1768, when an inventory was made of the late Richard Ambler's slaves on Jamestown Island and his leasehold in the Governor's Land, an adult male slave named Phill was listed. In 1769 Phill was living on Jamestown Island and was attributed to the household of the late Edward Ambler I (York County Wills and Inventories 21:386–391; AMB-E).

John Phillimore (Philmott, Filmore): On November 1, 1624, the General Court noted that the late John Phillimore had left his land and belongings to Elizabeth Peerce, to whom he had been engaged. He also made bequests to Mr. Constable and Thomas Sully of Jamestown. In February 1625 Phillimore was listed among those who had died on the lower side of the James River (VI&A 560).

Phillis: On February 15, 1768, when an inventory was made of the late Richard Ambler's slaves at his quarter called Powhatan, an adult female slave named Phillis was living there. She probably was the woman called Phillis whom Ambler mentioned in his 1765 will. In 1769 Phillis was living on Jamestown Island and was part of the late Edward Ambler I's estate (York County Wills and Inventories 21:378–382, 386–391; AMB-E).

Alexander Phillis: On April 18, 1670, Alexander Phillis was identified as a runaway servant who belonged to Secretary Thomas Ludwell of Jamestown. On June 22, 1670, the General Court sentenced Phillis to be burned in the hand for stealing goods from John Page's store, a retail establishment that probably was located in urban Jamestown (MCGC 207, 224).

Henry Philpot: In 1608 Henry Philpot, a gentleman and Virginia Company investor, arrived in Jamestown as part of the 2nd Supply of new colonists (VI&A 560).

Phinloe: Phinloe died in Jamestown sometime after February 16, 1624, but before January 24, 1625 (VI&A 560).

John Phipps: On February 23, 1656, John Phipps patented 120 acres of land in urban Jamestown. His acreage included a 12-acre parcel that he had purchased from Sir William Berkeley plus 108 acres he claimed on the basis of three headrights. The latter acreage probably included a one-acre lot on Pitch and Tar Swamp that Robert Brooks patented on August 28, 1644. Although Phipps' 1656 patent may have been his first land acquisition on Jamestown Island, he was a merchant and probably was already living there. In April 1652 he was ordered to repair the country house (in the New Town) and place its cellars in the hands of a tenant. John Phipps and William Harris I jointly owned the Glasshouse tract, which Harris had purchased from John Fitchett. When Francis Morrison (Moryson) patented the property on September 6, 1655, he noted that earlier on, Phipps had assigned his legal interest to Harris. The fact that Mrs. Elizabeth Harris of Surry County named her four-year-old son "John Phipps" suggests that there was a tie of friendship or kinship between the two families. On October 5, 1661, John Phipps sold his Jamestown property to Jonathan Knowles, who repatented it as 133.027 acres. Phipps' wife, Mary, relinquished her dower interest in the property her husband was selling. In March 1660 Phipps secured a patent for a half-acre lot in the western end of Jamestown Island. Because he failed to develop his property within the proscribed time, it escheated to the Crown and was repatented by another. In 1665 John Phipps patented 660 acres on the south side of the Rappahannock River, escheat land that had belonged to Henry Berry. In May 1671 Phipps sued Captain Francis Kirkman, James City County's sheriff and one of Governor William Berkeley's favorites, but the case was dismissed by the General Court. In 1674 Phipps patented 1,100 acres of land on Powhatan Swamp, seemingly the last acreage he acquired (PB 2:11; 3:367; 4:101–102, 366–367, 475; 5:63–65; 7:97; NUG I:313, 340, 388, 409, 440; II:152, 222; MCGC 58, 258; AMB 10, 61, 78, 135–136; Surry County Deeds, Wills, &c. 1652–1672:120).

Drue (Dru) Pickhouse (Piggase): Drue Pickhouse, a gentleman, arrived in Virginia in 1607 and died in Jamestown on August 19th of that year (VI&A 561).

Jonas Pickis: On May 26, 1673, Jonas Pickis of New Kent County was arrested by John Page of urban Jamestown and brought before the General Court (MCGC 340).

Spencer Piggott: In May 1673 Stephen Piggott, a London merchant, made a claim against the estate of John Newell of Jamestown by filing suit in the court of York County. Ultimately, Piggott assigned the Newell debt to Stephen Proctor, one of his own creditors. Documents in the British Archives indicate that Piggott had been trading in Virginia since the 1660s, exchanging utilitarian items for tobacco. One of his debtors was John Edwards of London, who had a plantation in the Northern Neck (MCGC 342, 356; SR 3541, 3793, 4202a, 5594a, 5726a).

Pindavako (Pindavaco) (Native American): In October 1649 Virginia officials allocated 5,000 acres of land to Ossakican, the werowance or leader of the Chiskiack (Chiskyacke), otherwise known as the "North" Indians. This decision came in response to the natives' formal acknowledgment that Virginia's land belonged to the Crown. In 1655 Pindavako, protector of the young king of the Chiskiack Indians, made a treaty in which he confirmed Edward Wyatt's right to use part of the land that had been assigned to his people as a preserve or reservation. The property was located on the lower side of the Piankatank River's mouth. By the time the land changed hands, the king of the Chiskiack already had transferred 2,000 acres of land to Colonel George Ludlow in exchange for an equal number of acres on the Piankatank (Pindavako 1655; Billings, "Some Acts Not in Hening's, April 1652, November 1652, and July 1653," 71; NUG I:239).

John Pinhorne (Pinhorn): Very little is known about John Pinhorne, who by 1657 had come into possession of some land in the southeastern end of Jamestown Island, and in 1677 was still attributed to that area. In 1652 he was listed as a headright in Nicholas George's patent for 700 acres on the Corotoman River. Pinhorne died sometime prior to October 16, 1680, when his daughter and sole heir, Ann, and her husband, William Price, sold his 300-acre Jamestown Island tract to Thomas Rabley, a Jamestown innkeeper and lot owner (NUG I:270, 347; II:12; PB 3:153; 4:150; 6:42; AMB 18; Old Rappahannock County Deeds and Wills 1677–1682:303). The land that Rabley bought would have been useful for raising agricultural crops and grazing livestock.

John Pinkard (Pinckard) I: John Pinkard I, a resident of Lancaster County's Christ Church Parish, married Sarah, the widow of Thomas Gaskins (Gaskoyne) II, who died prior to March 1, 1676. Sarah Gaskins Pinkard died within four years, and in January 1680 the Gaskins orphans' guardians sued for custody of the children and their late father's estate. Pinkard quickly remarried and by September 8, 1680, had wed Thomas Haynes' widow, Elizabeth.

In July 1680 representatives of the Haynes orphans brought suit against Pinkard in an attempt to prevent his harvesting or selling timber from their land. Over the years Pinkard, who in 1684 commenced serving as a court justice, was involved in numerous lawsuits and sometimes certified appraisals. On one occasion he filed a complaint against a local man who had verbally abused him. In 1688 Pinkard became a burgess for Lancaster County. When Robert Bristow patented some land in the county in 1697, Pinkard's property was mentioned. Pinkard made his will on March 24, 1689, and died sometime between August 1689 and December 10, 1690. He bequeathed his land and some of his personal belongings to his sons John II, Thomas, and James, and left the remainder of his estate to his daughters but failed to name them. He gave his wife, Elizabeth, use of his estate until his children were mature or she remarried. In January 1691 Elizabeth Pinkard saw that an inventory of her late husband's estate was entered into the records of the county court. The decedent's personal possessions attested to his affluence. John Pinkard II filed suit against his stepmother, Elizabeth, in an attempt to force distribution of his late father's estate, and later in the year Rebecca and Mary, the decedent's married daughters, sought their shares. When Mrs. Elizabeth Pinkard testified in court in April 1697, she indicated that she was age 50. She died prior to April 8, 1699, at which time an inventory of her estate was recorded (LEO 49; NN 2:268–269; Lancaster County Wills 1690–1709:7, 15–20, 65, 88; Wills 1674–1689:133; Order Book 1680–1687:4, 6, 68, 160, 221; 1686–1696:21, 147, 152, 159, 182; Northumberland County Record Book 1658–1666:136; Order Book 1678–1698:54, 65, 135, 174; DOR 2:55, 57 note).

William Pinke alias Jonas: William Pinke, who came to the colony before May 1616, sometimes was known as William Jonas. He acquired a 12-acre parcel near Black Point in the eastern end of Jamestown Island, where he and his wife, Mary, were living by 1623. William died prior to August 1624 and Mary, who inherited his property, secured the title in her own name. By August 14, 1624, the widowed Mary Pinke had married Gabriel Holland, a yeoman. She died shortly thereafter and by January 24, 1625, her land had descended to her new husband, Gabriel (VI&A 561).

Edward Pising: Edward Pising, a carpenter, arrived in Virginia in 1607 and was one of the first Jamestown settlers. Captain John Smith referred to Pising as a carpenter, a soldier, a gentleman, and a sergeant. He seems to have been alive in January 1609 (VI&A 562).

Edward Pitchande (Pitchard): On January 3, 1625, when he testified before the General Court, Edward Pitchande said that he had witnessed a verbal agreement between John Cooke and Peter Langman, who were residents of Jamestown. On June 7, 1625, the General Court noted that Pitchande had returned to England (VI&A 562).

Robert Pitt I: Robert Pitt I began patenting land in Isle of Wight County in 1643, when he secured 209 acres on the west side of the New Town Haven River (Pagan Creek). Five years later he patented another 300 acres in the same vicinity. In 1662 he enhanced his holdings on the river by patenting an additional 1,200 acres. Then he began investing in acreage that was far from his home in Isle of Wight. In 1662 and 1663 he or a kinsman of the same name laid claim to 4,000 acres on the Pokomoke River in Accomack County, and a year later he joined two other men in laying claim to 3,000 acres on the Blackwater River. Robert Pitt represented Isle of Wight County and served in the assembly sessions of 1649, 1652, 1653, and 1654–1655. After a brief respite, he was returned to office and served in 1659, 1660, and 1661–1662. When Colonel Pitt made his will on June 6, 1672, he made bequests to his married daughters, Mary Brassiuer and Hester Bridger, to his unwed daughter, Martha, and to his son John. He noted that his son Robert II was deceased and named as heirs grandsons Robert III and William Pitt. In a philanthropic gesture, he left his house and land for the relief of poor women, noting that it was a gift from his late wife, Martha. The testator's will was recorded on January 9, 1674 (LEO 27, 29, 31–32, 35–36, 38; Isle of Wight County Will and Deed Book 3 [1704–1715]:128; Administrations and Probates:34; PB 1:895; 2:118; 4:613–614; 5:81, 126, 254).

Thomas Pitt I: In 1667 Captain Henry Pitt's widow, Ann (Anne), who had married James Powell, conveyed to her late husband's son, Thomas Pitt I, fee simple ownership of 150 acres on Isle of Wight County's Pagan Creek. Thomas Pitt served as a burgess for Isle of Wight County from 1680 to 1682. When part of John Pitt's land on the Pagan Creek was laid out into a town site (what eventually became known as Smithfield) in 1680, Thomas Pitt was designated one of the newly established community's trustees. In June 1681 Pitt purchased the late Colonel

John George's plantation on Castle Creek from John Leare and his wife, Ann (Anne), the widow and heir of the late Colonel George. Pitt was identified as owner of the ship *Adventure* in January 1678 when he made an agreement with Virginia merchant Rowland Place, who was preparing to ship some tobacco to England. In 1684 and 1687 Pitt patented three tracts of land that had escheated to the Crown. He prepared his will on April 21, 1687, and by February 21, 1688, was dead. He made a bequest to his wife, Mary, and designated her as his executrix. He also named his children as heirs: sons Thomas II and Henry and daughters Martha, Mary, Elizabeth, Anne, and Patience. The testator's estate was appraised by burgesses Anthony Holliday and Henry Applewaite. Thomas Pitt I of Isle of Wight may have been a kinsman of Thomas Pitt or Pitts of Lower Norfolk County, who when making his will in January 1685 named as heirs his wife, Elizabeth; son, John; and daughters, Jeane and Sarah (LEO 45; Isle of Wight County Will and Deed Book 1 [1662–1688]:110–112; 391–392, 450, 460; Will and Deed Book 2:283, 296, 311; Administrations and Probates 73;.Lower Norfolk County Wills and Deeds 4:200; PB 7:396, 566, 614).

John Pittman: John Pittman, a sawyer sent to Virginia by the Company of Shipwrights in 1621, was to work under the supervision of Thomas Nunn, a master shipwright. Pittman and his fellow workers built homes on Jamestown Island (VI&A 562).

Rowland Place I: In August 1669 Rowland Place I, who was born in England, patented 1,228 acres on the north side of the James River in Henrico County. He was named to the Council of State in 1675, and in February 1676 he patented 5,579 acres in Charles City County, near Old Man's and Herring creeks. On March 21, 1676, the General Court ordered him to arbitrate a dispute between Roger Green and Thomas Hill II, the owner of a lot in urban Jamestown. At issue was Hill's lease for the plantation known as Digges Hundred and Green's refusal to vacate the property. Place briefly returned to the Mother Country but was back in Virginia by October 25, 1677, when he informed officials in England that Lieutenant Governor Herbert Jeffreys was very ill and that conditions in the colony were somewhat unsettled. In January 1678 Place was identified as a Virginia merchant when he made a bargain with Thomas Pitt I of Isle of Wight County, owner of a ship called the *Adventure*. Later in the year Place made another trip to England, carrying a letter written by Jeffreys,

who informed his superiors that Colonel Place could provide eyewitness testimony about conditions in the colony. Francis Morrison (Moryson), who was then in England, informed his superiors that Place had arrived with letters that hopefully would reach Thomas Lord Culpeper before he set sail for the colony. Rowland Place I died in England sometime after 1681. His son, Rowland II, witnessed Daniel Parke I's will on August 11, 1677 (MCGC 449; STAN 40; Isle of Wight County Will and Deed Book 1 [1662–1688]:391–392; PB 6:233; 6:590; SR 663, 690, 3720).

John Pleasants (Pleasant, Plesant) I: John Pleasants I came to Virginia sometime prior to 1670 and settled in Henrico County at Curles. He and Jane, the widow of Samuel Tucker, a clergyman, announced their wedding plans to a group of Quakers assembled in Pleasants' storehouse at Curles. Later, they visited a Quaker meeting in York County, where their marriage was formalized. This ceremony, performed beyond the pale of canon law, brought the couple to the attention of Henrico County authorities, who recognized them as religious dissenters. During the late 1670s Pleasants purchased from William Cookson a part of Curles, which had belonged to the late rebel Nathaniel Bacon and had escheated to the Crown. In 1678 John and Jane Pleasants were brought before the county's justices for failing to attend and support the Established Church, and a year later Pleasants was fined for holding Quaker meetings in his home. John Pleasants and a business partner acquired 548 acres on the upper side of the James River in Henrico County in 1679. Then, in 1690 Pleasants patented 2,625 acres near Four Mile Creek, and a year later he acquired 1,220 acres above Westham Creek. When the Act of Toleration was passed in 1689, dissenters were permitted to attend non-Anglican religious services but were obliged to render financial support to the Established Church. When John Pleasants prepared his will in September 1690, he left a small parcel at Curles to members of the Quaker faith. He presented his will in court several years before his death, apparently because he wanted to be sure that its terms would be implemented. He left to his wife, Jane, the remainder of his plantation called Curles, upon which they resided, and he left the rest of his property to his sons, John II and Joseph. He also made bequests to his daughter, Elizabeth, and several other people. Pleasants added a codicil to his will on May 3, 1697, distributing some additional land that he had purchased. In 1693 John Pleasants I was elected to the assembly on behalf of Henrico County; however, he was obliged to resign because his Quaker faith prevented him from taking the necessary oaths of office. On March 10, 1693, Pleasants and some other Quakers presented a petition to the assembly, asking for the repeal of a law levying fines for refusing to bear arms and attend militia musters. Their proposal was soundly rejected. As time went on, Pleasants continued to prosper. At the time of his death, sometime prior to June 1, 1698, when his will was proved, he owned more than 11,500 acres. The widowed Jane Pleasants made her will on January 2, 1708, and died prior to June 1, 1709 (LEO 52; JHB 1660–1693:433; SMITH 71; PB 7:12; 8:85, 173, 191, 322, 489, 627; 10:94, 157, 238–239; Henrico County Wills 3 [1688–1697]:149; 4 [1697–1704]:80, 168, 171–172; 5 [1706–1709]:166; HIN 145–147).

William Plumtree: In autumn 1669 William Plumtree and his wife, Susanna, owners of a 17-acre tract at Middle Plantation, sold their acreage to David Newell. Newell later sold the Plumtree acreage to William Sherwood and Thomas Rabley, residents of urban Jamestown. Plumtree patented 800 acres in New Kent County. He died sometime prior to April 20, 1670, at which time his widow, Susanna, was designated his administratrix. By November 1672 the widowed Susanna Plumtree had wed Charles Bryan. William Plumtree's New Kent County acreage eventually escheated to the Crown, presumably because he had produced no living heirs. The land he had owned at Middle Plantation and sold to David Newell in 1669 eventually became part of Daniel Parke II's holdings and descended to his daughter, Frances, the wife of John Custis IV of Arlington (MCGC 209, 318; PB 6:344; 7:280).

Pocahontas (Pocohunta, Matoaka, Rebecca) (Kocoum's wife, Mrs. John Rolfe) (Native American): According to William Strachey, Pocahontas, Powhatan's favorite daughter, was married to a warrior named Kocoum at a very early age. She was taken hostage by the English in 1611. Afterward, she converted to Christianity and adopted the English name Rebecca. In early April 1614 she married John Rolfe, a widower and secretary of the colony, in the church in Jamestown. In May 1616 Pocahontas and her new husband went to England, where she was introduced at court as a native princess. In March 1617, when the Rolfes and their little son, Thomas, were awaiting the ship that would take them back to Virginia, Pocahontas developed consumption (tuberculosis) and died. She was buried in the yard of St. Mary le Bow Church in Gravesend, England (VI&A 563; HAI 620).

John Polentine (Pollentin, Pollington): In July 1619 John Polentine served as burgess for the city of Henricus. By February 1624, he had moved to Warresqueak where he was sharing a home with his wife, Rachel, and Margaret Polentine. John Polentine, a planter, served in the 1624 assembly session, representing Basses Choice, and in May 1625 he was credited with 600 acres of land in Warresqueak. In 1628 his widow, Rachel, was exporting tobacco from Virginia (VI&A 564; LEO 3, 5; SR 1267, 3481, 3784a).

Richard Pomfry (Pomfrey): On March 10, 1677, Richard Pomfry, an alleged supporter of the rebel Nathaniel Bacon, was put on trial at Green Spring plantation, Governor William Berkeley's home. He was found guilty and sentenced to death (MCGC 458, 530).

Henry Poole: In 1637 Henry Poole patented 150 acres on the lower side of the James River, at Lynnhaven in Lower Norfolk County. However, by 1642 his interests seem to have shifted to the upper side of the James, for he patented 116 acres in Elizabeth City County on the east side of the Hampton River and adjoining the parish glebe. By that time he had become Elizabeth City's sheriff. Poole, who commenced serving as Elizabeth City County's clerk of court in 1648, represented the county in the 1647–1648 session of the assembly. During 1646 he disposed of his land in Lower Norfolk County, although he appeared in court there from time to time, usually to collect debts. Poole witnessed the will made in 1634 by Benjamin Syms, whose bequest established America's first free school, and Thomas Eaton's 1659 will, which established a school for the poor of Elizabeth City County (LEO 26; PB 1:444, 834; Lower Norfolk County Record Book A:191; B:33a; CHAPMAN 33, 90, 136, 155–156; NEAL 298–299).

Jonas Poole: Jonas Poole, a sailor, came to Virginia with the first group of settlers who planted a colony on Jamestown Island. In 1607 he accompanied Captain Christopher Newport on an exploratory voyage of the James River (VI&A 565).

Nathaniel Poole (see Nathaniel Powell)

* * *

Robert Poole I: Robert Poole I arrived in Jamestown in 1616 and was accompanied by his sons, Robert II and John. By September 8, 1627, Robert Poole I and his son John were dead (VI&A 565).

John Poole: John Poole arrived in Jamestown in 1616 with his father, Robert Poole I, and brother, Robert Poole II. John and Robert Poole I died prior to September 8, 1627, when Robert Poole II patented 300 acres of land on the Warwick River using his father and brother as headrights (VI&A 565).

Robert Poole II: Robert Poole II reached Virginia in 1616 and was accompanied by his brother, John, and their father, Robert Poole I. Robert Poole II became fluent in the Algonquian language and served as one of the government's official interpreters. In July 1619 he made formal accusations against Henry Spellman, another interpreter. In 1624 Robert Poole II testified that he had lived with Opechancanough during Sir Thomas Dale's government (1611–1616). Poole was residing in urban Jamestown in January 1625, where he was a household head. He went to England but returned to Virginia and seated some land on the Blunt Point (Warwick) River. He was still alive in April 1629 (VI&A 565).

* * *

William Poole: William Poole arrived in Jamestown on September 5, 1623, and took the oath of supremacy (VI&A 566).

Mr. and Mrs. George Pope I: George Pope I, his wife, and his son came to Virginia in 1622. In early 1624 he and his son, George II, were living in a Jamestown Island household headed by John Osborne. In late 1624 the youngster, who was only 4½ years old, fell into an open well and drowned. His death was ruled accidental (VI&A 566–567).

John Pope: John Pope came to Virginia in 1622 with William Rowley, who settled in Jamestown (VI&A 567). He probably was one of Rowley's servants.

Thomas Popkin: Thomas Popkin came to Virginia in 1621 at the expense of Dr. John Pott, who resided in urban Jamestown. In February 1624 Popkin was living in the Neck O'Land, but within a year's time he moved to Jamestown Island, where he died (VI&A 567).

William Popleton (Poppleton, Popkton): In July 1622 Michael Marshall (Marshott), a merchant and sea captain, brought William Popleton, an indentured servant, to Virginia. In January 1625 Popleton was living at Jordan's Journey, where he was a servant in the home of John Davis and William Emerson (Emmerson). By 1628 he had gained his freedom and was elected a burgess for Jordan's Journey. He represented the community again in 1629 and died sometime prior to July 1631 (VI&A 568; LEO 7–8).

Abraham (Abram) Porter: Abraham Porter came to Virginia in 1622 as one of the Rev. Richard Buck's servants. In early 1624 he was residing in urban Jamestown in the household of Peter Ascam (Ascomb, Ascombe), whose wife, Mary, had custody of Benomi Buck, one of the Rev. Richard Buck's orphans. Porter, who continued to reside in urban Jamestown, testified in court during the mid-1620s about duties associated with the Buck estate. In January 1625 he was a servant in the household of Peter Langman, who had wed the widowed Mary Ascam. Therefore, she probably brought Porter to the marriage as part of the Buck estate. By March 1629 Abraham Porter was dead. Reference was then made to his house, which suggests that he had obtained his freedom and was living on his own (VI&A 568).

* * *

John Porter I: John Porter I began living in Lower Norfolk County sometime prior to April 1652, when he was occupying a 400-acre tract. In January 1653 he received a land certificate that would have enabled him to patent an additional 200 acres. Although the patent Porter obtained has been lost or destroyed, the Lower Norfolk County plantation he occupied in Lynnhaven Parish in 1652 was mentioned in another landowner's claim. In August 1653 the justices of Lower Norfolk County noted that Porter had married John Cooke's widow and ordered him to pay to a debt to mariner Mathew Passett. By 1656 Porter had become a county justice and had begun serving as high sheriff. He represented Lower Norfolk County in 1662–1663 sessions of the assembly but was dismissed from his seat in 1663 because of his Quaker faith. When Porter made his will on September 18, 1672, he indicated that he resided on the eastern branch of the Elizabeth River. He made bequests to his wife, Mary, whom he named as executrix, and to his son, John Porter II, and daughter, Frances, the wife of George Fouler. In October 1673 Porter secured a patent for 3,000 acres at the head of the Elizabeth River's eastern branch, acreage that adjoined the 300 acres he had acquired on March 16, 1663. John

Porter I's will was proved on February 15, 1675. In September 1683 John Porter II patented some escheat land that formerly had belonged to the late Mary Fenwick alias Porter. This raises the possibility that John Porter I had been married to the former Mary Fenwick and that she was the mother of John Porter II (LEO 39; Lower Norfolk County Wills and Deeds Book C:36, 51, 70; Wills, Deeds, Orders D [1656–1666]:1, 32; 4:7; PB 3:24; 5:365; 6:485; SR 892).

John Porter II: John Porter II, the son of John Porter I, represented the county in the assembly in 1674, which suggests that he, unlike his father, was not a member of the Quaker faith. In September 1683 Porter laid claim to 500 acres of escheat land that formerly had belonged to the late Mary Fenwick alias Porter. This suggests that John Porter I was married to the former Mary Fenwick and that she was the mother of John Porter II (Lower Norfolk County Wills, Deeds, Orders D [1656–1666]:1, 32; 4:7; PB 7:310; LEO 39).

* * *

John Pory (Porey, Porye): John Pory was named secretary of state in 1619 and arrived in Jamestown in April of that year. In July and August 1619, when Virginia's first assembly meeting was held, he served as speaker and took minutes. He also served as a member of the council. Pory updated Virginia Company officials on conditions in the colony, and he undertook voyages to Newfoundland, Holland, and the southerly territory that became Carolina. When Pory testified in an English court in 1630, he said that he was age 56 and that he had served as secretary for three years while he was in Virginia. He died in England in 1636 (VI&A 568; LEO 3).

Peter Pory: Peter Pory, a gentleman, came to Virginia in 1608 as part of the 1st Supply of new colonists and resided in Jamestown (VI&A 569).

William Possesom (Native American): On June 26, 1661, William Possesom, an Appomattox Indian, appeared before the justices of Westmoreland County's court, whose clerk recorded the manner in which William Possesom had marked or branded his cattle and swine (Westmoreland County Deeds, Wills &c 1661–1662:42).

King of Potomac Indians (Native American): On July 14, 1655, the king of the Potomac Indians and Gerrard Foulke (Fowke)

of Westmoreland made an agreement. whereby Foulke was authorized to build a house on the land the Indians then occupied. He also was allowed to place English servants and cattle on the property and plant tobacco there. In exchange, Foulke was to give the king of the Potomac a horse, bridle, and saddle and provide him with a cow that would supply his children with milk. If the king of Potomac's Indians decided to participate in the cultivation of tobacco, the Potomacs were entitled to a share of the harvest. In 1658 the justices compensated Mr. Foulke for giving a cow to the king of the Potomac. The Potomac Indians seem to have allowed other settlers to use part of their land. On August 20, 1658, Westmoreland County's court justices attempted to settle a disagreement between the king of the Potomac and Captain Giles Brent I, which involved some land that Brent had patented. Brent claimed to have compensated the native leader for the acreage but agreed to return it to him.

In August 1661 the governor and the Council of State informed Westmoreland's justices that they had authorized colonels Edward Hill and John Carter, Henry Corbin, and Peter Ashton to arbitrate a dispute between the king of the Potomac Indians and Major General Hammond. If necessary, they were to summon the militia to preserve peace. No militiamen were to be involved who participated in trading with the Indians. As time went on, the situation became increasingly tense, and military action was taken. In October 1663 Colonel Gerrard Foulke, then a burgess, reported that the assembly had decided that the county was responsible for the expense incurred in the expedition undertaken against the king of the Potomac and his people (Westmoreland County Deeds, Wills, Patents &c. 1653–1659:110, 126; Deeds, Wills &c. 1661–1662:1, 49a; Orders 1662–1664:17).

* * *

Francis Pott: Francis Pott came to Virginia sometime prior to March 1629, when his brother, Dr. John Pott, Virginia's deputy governor, appointed him captain of the fort at Old Point Comfort, a lucrative position. Earlier in the year Francis Pott received a bequest from Thomas Warnett, a Jamestown merchant. According to Secretary Richard Kemp, Francis Pott's opposition to Governor John Harvey resulted in his being stripped of his captaincy. Loss of his position only served to fuel his hostility toward Harvey. Harvey retaliated by having Pott arrested, taken to England, and thrown into Fleet Prison. Although Pott was tried for attempting to depose the governor, he apologized and was released. Around May 1635 Francis Pott inherited Dr. John Pott's 12-acre lot on urban Jamestown's Back Street and his 500 acres in the Great Barren Neck near Middle Plantation (later, Williamsburg). He retained his Jamestown property until at least 1640 but eventually moved to the Eastern Shore, where he was living with wife, Susanna, in 1647. Pott patented 2,000 acres in Northampton County in February 1653 and another 1,000 acres in 1657. He made his will on August 5, 1658, and it was proved on October 28th of that year. He made bequests to several people, including his cousin, Captain Henry Perry, and Perry's wife, Elizabeth. He also named his widow as executrix. Susanna Pott later married Lieutenant Colonel William Kendall I, a burgess (VI&A 569; MARSHALL 58–59).

Dr. John Pott: Dr. John Pott, the colony's physician-general, came to Virginia in 1621 and was described as an experienced medical professional. He and his wife, Elizabeth, owned and occupied a 12-acre lot in urban Jamestown, acreage that was on the upper side of Back Street. Dr. Pott apparently had some serious ethical problems. While on the Council of State, he was implicated in the poisoning of a group of Indians who had assembled to sign a peace treaty. As a result of this wrongdoing, he was removed from office. He also was an accused—and convicted—cattle rustler. Mrs. Pott made several appearances in court during the 1620s, and around 1630, when her husband was accused of stealing cattle, she went to England to assert his innocence. In March 1629 Dr. John Pott's fellow councilors elected him deputy governor. However, when Sir John Harvey arrived in the colony to assume the governorship, he promptly placed Pott under house arrest for pardoning a known murderer. Besides his large lot in urban Jamestown, Pott owned a large tract of land near Middle Plantation, later known as Williamsburg (VI&A 570–571).

* * *

Cuthbert (Cutbert) Potter: In December 1655 Cuthbert Potter, a highly successful merchant, patented 1,200 acres on the south side of the Rappahannock River in Lancaster County. He acquired an additional 600 acres in that vicinity in October 1658. Then, in June 1659 he laid claim to 5,380 acres in Gloucester and Lancaster counties, land that straddled the Piankatank Swamp.

In 1661 Potter secured a patent for another 3,672 acres in Lancaster County, a 4,000-acre tract on the Piankatank. Finally, in March 1667 he acquired 270 acres on the south side of the Rappahannock in Lancaster County. In 1656 he seems to have been residing in Lancaster County near the Piankatank, but in 1663 he identified himself as a merchant of Old Rappahannock County. From time to time he served as the attorney of Sir Henry Chicheley, London merchant Thurston Withuell, and Colonel John Custis II of Northampton County. Potter was a Lancaster County merchant in 1665, when he took possession of a sloop and a flat-bottomed boat that he was keeping for another man. On May 26, 1671, he sued Letitia, the widow and administratrix of John Barber II, the owner of some waterfront lots in urban Jamestown and an outlying parcel. From 1673 through 1675 Potter pursued a claim against the estate of another merchant, the late Jonathan Newell of Jamestown, and took his widow, Elizabeth, to court. Potter, a resident of the Northern Neck, was then actively engaged in transatlantic trade and imported a wide variety of goods. In 1673 he was identified as a lieutenant colonel and in 1675 as a colonel, a rank he still held in 1690. In 1688 he was reimbursed for having arranged for 44 guns, powder, and shot to be delivered to the colony. In June 1690 Colonel Cuthbert Potter was asked to visit New England and New York to inquire into whether several recent murders on the Virginia frontier had been committed by the French and the Indians. When Potter returned a few months later, he said that some Massachusetts officials had broken open his trunk and rummaged through his letters, despite the fact that he was an official envoy of the Virginia government. Potter died sometime prior to January 4, 1692, at which time Ralph Wormeley II and Christopher Robinson were named administrators of his estate. The governor of Barbados, who was acquainted with Potter, attested to the legitimacy of his will (MCGC 262, 281, 356, 374, 387, 404; Middlesex County Order Book 1680–1694:473, 537; Lancaster County Record Book 2 [1637–1640]:116, 263, 268, 291, 309, 321, 355; PB 4:20, 276, 379; 5:48; 6:51, 147; SR 686, 3775g, 7906; EJC I:118, 121, 137).

Roger Potter: Captain Roger Potter, one of Governor William Berkeley's loyalists, served as jailer of the improvised prison at Green Spring. In 1677 Henry Gord claimed that Potter detained him there for a month, only agreeing to release him if he forfeited a cow and a calf. He said that he had a wife and five children to support and that surrendering the cattle would impose a severe hardship. Gord said that he had been forced to follow the rebel Nathaniel Bacon and that later, when he conformed to the governor's proclamation, he was forced to wear a halter while pledging his loyalty. In 1685 Potter patented 380 acres in Surry County, to which he added 268 acres in 1689. He was a respected member of the community and made occasional appearances in court. In January 1696 Potter's widow, Ann, presented his 1695 will to Surry County's justices, who authorized her to serve as his executrix. Afterward, she made several appearances in court, trying to recover funds that were owed to his estate (SAIN 10:52; CO 1/40 f 15; SR 661, 6618b; PB 7:463; 8:4; Surry County Order Book 1671–1691:481; Court Records Book 5 [1691–1700]:131, 151, 170, 173, 182).

Richard Potts: Richard Potts, a gentleman, came to Virginia in the 2nd Supply of new colonists and reached Jamestown in 1608. According to Captain John Smith, Potts was clerk of the council (VI&A 571).

William Potts: On October 26, 1677, Governor Herbert Jeffreys and the General Court's justices were informed that William Potts had not fulfilled his court-ordered sentence. He was being punished because he was found guilty of rebellion and treason on account of his involvement in Bacon's Rebellion. Potter had been ordered to appear before the justices of Old Rappahannock County with a rope halter around his neck and to apologize on bended knee. Instead, he appeared in court wearing a Manchester binding, which consisted of small tape. Potts was ordered to fulfill his sentence and to pay all court costs (MCGC 534).

King of the Potuxin Indians (Native American): In 1650 John Mottrom, a local military commander, gave the king of Potuxin six matchcoats in compensation for the two Indian women, ninety deer skins, and three beaver skins that six Northumberland County men had stolen (Northumberland County Deeds and Orders 1650–1652:42). It is likely that the king of Potuxin resided on the upper side of the Potomac River, in Maryland.

John Pountis (Pontis, Pountes, Pountis, Pontes): John Pountis, a mariner and Virginia Company investor with an interest in the northern fisheries, brought 40 passengers to Virginia in late 1619 or early 1620. He set out to procure sturgeon and intended to build cellars and special houses where they could be processed. Pountis was named to the Council of State and designated viceadmiral. He also was treasurer of Southampton Hundred. In 1621 he brought a dozen young, marriageable women to the colony to become wives for the settlers. In February 1624 Pountis was living in urban Jamestown. He set sail a few months later and died at sea (VI&A 572).

Elizabeth Powell (Pomell): On February 16, 1624, Elizabeth Powell was living in urban Jamestown in the home of Sir Francis Wyatt, where she seems to have been a servant (VI&A 573).

Henry Powell: Henry Powell, a tradesman, arrived in Jamestown in 1608 in the 2nd Supply of new settlers and lived in Jamestown. Captain John Smith later said that Powell, an "old soldier," had protected him from being ambushed. Although Smith said that Powell had served as a councilor in 1610, his name does not appear in other historical narratives (VI&A 573).

James Powell: James Powell of Isle of Wight County married Henry Pitt's widow, Ann, in 1667. The previous year, when a Dutch attack seemed imminent, Major Powell was ordered to see that the 20 men at Old Point Comfort were well armed and that the fort's ordnance was buried and guarded. In 1671 and 1675 he was one of the three men ordered by the General Court's justices to audit some disputed accounts. He was a staunch supporter of Governor William Berkeley and in September 1676 received leg wounds when the rebel Nathaniel Bacon's men attacked Jamestown. Moreover, Powell's home and livestock were plundered by Bacon's men. After Bacon's Rebellion subsided, some of Isle of Wight County's citizens presented a list of grievances to the king's special commissioners. They contended that Major James Powell had been paid too highly for subdividing their county. Powell survived the injuries he received during Bacon's Rebellion and served as an Isle of Wight County burgess in 1680 and 1682. In 1681 he was leasing a plantation on Castle Creek from John Leare and his wife, Ann (Anne), acreage that had descended to Ann from her late husband, Colonel John George. In 1691 Powell was identified as part owner of a ship that was involved in transatlantic commerce. One of his business partners was Micajah Perry of London. Powell was godfather and guardian to Richard Briggs' son, Edmund. By 1694 Colonel James Powell's widow and executrix, Ann, had married Robert Randolph (SR 6618b, 10551; LEO 45; Bruce, "Persons Who Suffered By Bacon's Rebellion," 68; Isle of Wight County Wills and Deeds 1 [1662–1688]:460–461; 2 [1688–1704]:115; 3 [1704–1715]:195; Orders 1693–1695:38; BODIE 161; MCGC 273, 420, 488).

John Powell: John Powell, a tailor, arrived in Jamestown in 1608 in the 1st Supply of new settlers. Later in the year he accompanied Captain John Smith on an exploratory voyage of the Chesapeake Bay (VI&A 573).

John Powell: John Powell came to Virginia in 1609 and lived in Jamestown. In 1622 he claimed that Deputy Governor Samuel Argall had given him some land on the east side of the Hampton River in Elizabeth City, property that Governor George Yeardley later confiscated on behalf of the Virginia Company. By February 1624 Powell and his wife, Catherene (Katherin), had moved to the west side of the Hampton River. When he patented 150 acres of land in Elizabeth City in 1624, Powell was described as a yeoman. He served as a burgess for the settlements between Waters Creek and Maries Mount in September 1632 (VI&A 573; LEO 11).

John Powell: John Powell served as a burgess for Elizabeth City County and attended the assembly sessions that were held in 1658, 1660, and from 1661 to 1676. He seems to have lived in the vicinity of the Back River. He derived some of his income from importing and selling cloth and other merchandise and seems to have speculated in real estate. In 1669 Powell testified in a lawsuit that involved the sale of tobacco. During the 1680s he patented some land on the Elizabeth River in Lower Norfolk County, in the Upper Parish of Nansemond County, and on the Eastern Shore. He died sometime prior to December 1693, at which time the justices of Elizabeth City County, who had access to his will, noted that Colonel Powell had bequeathed two cows and a horse to Moses Baker, his godson (LEO 34, 36, 38; NEAL 29, 40, 99; PB 5:521, 528; 8:10; SR 4199a, 13855).

Nathaniel Powell (Poole): Nathaniel Powell, a gentleman, came to Virginia in 1607 and was one of the first Jamestown colonists. He accompanied Captain John Smith on an exploratory voyage into the Chesapeake and embarked on a search for the Roanoke colonists. Powell was appointed sergeant major general on October 20, 1617, during Deputy Governor Samuel Argall's

administration. In April 1619, while he was living in Charles City, he served briefly as acting governor. In 1621 he was named to the Council of State. Captain Nathaniel Powell and his wife, Joyce, were killed during the 1622 Indian attack on their plantation, Powell-Brooke (VI&A 574; LEO xxi).

Philemon Powell: In January 1627 Philemon Powell, a Jamestown merchant who sued Captain John Harvey on behalf of London merchant John Sharples, was given legal possession of Harvey's acreage on the waterfront in the capital city. Powell, who was Sharples' factor, was ordered to place Harvey's property in the hands of tenants so that the rent money could satisfy his debt. By September 1627 Powell had died (VI&A 575).

Thomas Powell: In February 1629 Thomas Powell, an indentured servant, was in the employ of Edward Sharples of Jamestown (VI&A 575).

William Powell: Captain William Powell, a Virginia Company investor, came to Virginia in 1609 in the 3rd Supply of settlers and lived in Jamestown. He was George Percy's ensign, and in October 1617 he was named captain of Deputy Governor Samuel Argall's guard, commander of Jamestown and its blockhouses, and lieutenant governor. In 1619 Powell served as a burgess for James City. Early in 1620 he and a fellow colonist took possession of some acreage on Hog Island, but Powell and his wife, Margaret, continued to reside in urban Jamestown. When Powell led an expedition against the Chickahominy Indians in 1622, he lost his life. Around 1623 the widowed Margaret Powell, still a resident of urban Jamestown, married cape merchant Edward Blaney, who moved into her home. Blaney placed servants on Powell's acreage at Hog Island and at Lower Chippokes Creek in an attempt to protect the decedent's heirs' legal interest in the property. By February 1626 Margaret Powell Blaney had been widowed a second time. She married Captain Francis West, whom she predeceased. The late William Powell's orphaned son, George, inherited his late father's property on the lower side of the James River at Lower Chippokes Creek. However, because George died without heirs, the land he inherited escheated to the Crown (VI&A 576–577).

Powhatan (Wahunsunacock) (Native American): When the first colonists arrived in 1607, much of the native population of Virginia's coastal plain was under the sway of Powhatan or Wahunsunacock, a wise and aged paramount chief. The 32 districts he ruled encompassed more than 150 villages, whose inhabitants supported him in times of war and paid him tribute. Captain John Smith described Powhatan as a monarch of considerable intelligence to whom many lesser kings (or werowances) were subservient. Powhatan's daughter, Pocahontas, married John Rolfe in Jamestown in 1614, with the native monarch's consent. By 1617 Powhatan's influence over his people seems to have begun to wane, and he died the following year (VI&A 577; HAI 614–615).

Francis Poythress (Poythres, Poythers, Poytheris, Portherys): On February 9, 1633, the General Court gave Francis Poythress two letters of administration, at his request. One was for Roger Kidd's estate and the other was for Thomas Hall's. On July 13, 1637, Poythress patented some land in Charles City County, near Jordan's Point, using his own headright and those of others. He served as a burgess for Charles City County in 1644, 1645, and 1647–1648, but in 1649 he represented Northumberland County, an area in which he also owned property. In 1650 he appeared in court in Northumberland County and assigned some headrights to another individual. He was then identified as a captain. Prior to 1675 he married Woodleigh, the daughter of Robert Wynne I. By 1683 Poythress had attained the rank of major (MCGC 202; PB 1 Pt. 1:439; 2:139; NUG 2:259, 270–271, 306, 311, 333; LEO 22–23, 26–27; Northumberland County Deeds and Orders 1650–1652:42; Wills, Inventories &c.1652–1658:9; SR 3718).

John Pratt: John Pratt, a gentleman, tradesman, and Virginia Company investor, came to Virginia in 1608 in the 2nd Supply of new colonists and lived in Jamestown. In late December 1608 he was among those who accompanied Captain John Smith on a visit to the Pamunkey Indians' territory (VI&A 578).

Edward Prescott: On February 28, 1657, Edward Prescott was captain of the *Seahorse* of London, which was loaded with tobacco when it ran aground in the Potomac River during a storm and then was swamped. Aboard was business partner John Washington I, immigrant ancestor and great-grandfather of America's first president. Testimony that was taken in Westmoreland County's monthly court reveals Washington had accompanied Prescott on visits to several foreign ports. By 1659 Edward Prescott had become a resident of Westmoreland County,

and in 1661 he was among those compensated out of the late Colonel Thomas Speke I's estate. Prescott's plantation was located on the Upper Machodoc River. In December 1659 he obtained a court judgment against William Andrews, an Eastern Shore resident who reportedly owed him £420. However, in October 1660 Prescott was fined for failing to pay export duties to Captain William Kendall I, the Eastern Shore's customs officer, and he was arrested for uttering "severall scandalous mutinous and seditious words . . . against this assembly." He also was suspended "from his place in the commission," which suggests that he was a county justice. On April 4, 1661, Edward Prescott patented a half-acre of land in urban Jamestown, close to the church. On September 12, 1661, when he was getting ready to sail from New England to Madeira Island, he prepared his will, making several bequests. He left to Mary, the eldest daughter of Captain Josias Fendall of Charles County, Maryland, 1,000 acres of his land at Nangemy known as Rice Manor. He named his kinsman, Henry Alldy, and friends Nathaniel Jones and Thomas Dutton as his executors in Maryland and Westmoreland County, Virginia, who were "to possess all the rest of my estate." He may have added a codicil to his will, for on March 20, 1662, when Sarah, the wife of William Drummond I, patented Prescott's half-acre lot in Jamestown, she indicated that it had been granted to her in accord with his will and that her ownership had been confirmed by a court order. The late Edward Prescott's debts were still being settled a decade or more after his demise, and he was described as a former resident of Stafford County. Court documents indicate that on occasion he sold Virginia tobacco in Manhattan and that he sometimes transported furs to Holland. In 1680 a tract Prescott had owned in Stafford County escheated to the Crown and was reassigned by the Northern Neck's proprietors (Westmoreland County Records 1653–1657:74, 77, 128; Deeds, Wills, Patents &c. 1653–1659:74, 128–128a; Deeds, Wills, &c. 1661–1662:8a, 9a, 47–47a; Deeds, Wills, Etc. 1662–1664:8a, 22–23, 191–192; Deeds, Patents, &c.1665–1677:247a–248; Order Book 1676–1679:45; PB 5:634; Stafford County Record Book 1686–1693:49–50; NUG I:560; HEN I:549; II:15).

* * *

William Presley I: William Presley represented Northumberland County in the assembly sessions held in 1647–1648 and 1651–1652. He began serving as a county justice in early 1650, but by August he had become so ill that he prepared his will, indicating that he did not expect to live. He recovered, however, and resumed his duties as a Northumberland County justice. In March 1653 he was appointed high sheriff, and in August 1655 he was churchwarden of the parish known as the Chinckahan (Chingohan) Quarter. Presley died sometime prior to January 20, 1656, when his will was proved. He designated his sons, William II and Peter, as his principal heirs and made a bequest to his grandson, William Presley III. A court case that was aired in July 1657 reveals that when William Presley I died, he was serving as the late Robert Newman's executor. He also was administrator of the late Colonel John Mottrom's estate (LEO 26, 28; Northumberland County Deeds and Orders 1650–1652:41; Wills, Inventories &c. 1652–1658:21, 45, 95–96; Order Book 1652–1665:1, 65, 131, 137; Westmoreland County Deeds, Wills, Patents &c. 1653–1659:98).

Peter Presley: Peter Presley, the youngest son of William Presley I of Northumberland County, was a minor at the time of his father's death, which occurred prior to January 20, 1656. By September 1658 he had come of age and inherited a portion of the late Elizabeth Newman's estate. In 1660 he became a county justice and served several successive terms. He also made numerous appearances in court as a participant in litigation. In 1673 William Hartland paid him for having a tobacco house built. In August 1677 Presley and other Northumberland justices were ordered to collect the tobacco, or tax revenue, that was needed to cover the cost of suppressing Nathaniel Bacon's followers. He went on to become a burgess for Northumberland County and attended the assembly sessions that were held in 1676, 1677, and 1684. He was returned to office and served in 1691–1692. By April 1699 he was deceased (LEO 39, 43, 47, 50; Northumberland County Wills, Inventories &c. 1652–1658:95–96, 113; Record Book 1658–1662:9; Order Book 1652–1665:236, 275, 423; 1666–1678:76, 79, 190, 199, 295, 304, 316, 324; 1678–1698:64, 116, 216, 183, 198, 225; 1699–1700:8; Westmoreland County Deeds, Patents &c. 1665–1677:347a–350).

William Presley II: William Presley II, the eldest son of William Presley I, began serving as Colonel John Mottrom's administrator sometime prior to November 1657. Shortly thereafter he began serving as a county justice and held office for successive terms. As his late father's principal heir, he inherited two-thirds of his estate and served as guardian to his younger brother, Peter,

then a minor. William Presley II became as a Northumberland County burgess and attended the assembly sessions held in 1661–1668, 1676–1677, and 1680–1682. He also was among those who in August 1677 were ordered to collect the taxes needed to cover the cost of suppressing the rebel Nathaniel Bacon's supporters. In October 1669 he took an oath stating that he had transported a man's naturalization papers to Jamestown so that they could be confirmed. As time went on, Presley appeared in court, sometimes as plaintiff and sometimes as a defendant. He married and produced two sons, William III and Peter Jr. By July 1685 William Presley II was dead (LEO 39, 41, 43, 46; Northumberland County Wills, Inventories &c. 1652–1658:95–96, 143; Record Book 1658–1662:22; 1662–1666:168; 1666–1670:96; Order Book 1652–1665:153, 166, 415; 1666–1678:82, 196, 199, 212, 295, 304, 316, 324; 1678–1698:66, 78, 215, 271, 277; Westmoreland County Deeds, Patents &c. 1665–1677:347a–350).

* * *

George Pretty: George Pretty, a gentleman and Virginia Company investor, reached Jamestown in early 1608 in the 1st Supply of new colonists (VI&A 578).

[No First Name] Price: In 1607 Mr. Price and another man, who were part of the first group of Jamestown colonists, allegedly hatched a plot that Captain John Smith termed "evil" (VI&A 578).

Arthur Price (Prise) I: On June 23, 1640, Arthur Price I informed the assembly that an Indian had stolen a gun and some clothing from him and that he suspected that the thief was a native who formerly lived with the Rev. Anthony Panton. The burgesses authorized Price to detain the next Indian he encountered who admitted knowing the alleged thief. On October 17, 1640, Price, a merchant, appeared before the General Court and testified about some "scandalous" statements Francis Willis had made, defaming most of Virginia's high-ranking officials and York County's court justices. Like many of his contemporaries, Price speculated in real estate, often acquiring land on the colony's frontier. In 1642 he patented 1,000 acres on the lower side of the Piankatank River, in what became Gloucester (and later, Mathews) County, and in 1651 he laid claim to 1,700 acres on the west side of Skimino Creek in upper York County. Price represented Elizabeth City County as a burgess in 1645, but he served on behalf of York County in the 1645–1646 session. In November 1647 he was sued by Sir Edmund Plowden in a dispute over a shipment of goods. In July 1648 Price informed York County's justices that some of the settlers living to the west of Skimino Creek were allowing Indians to stay in their homes, contrary to law. Arthur Price I died sometime prior to August 1655 and was survived by his eldest son and heir, Richard, and his siblings, one of whom was Arthur II. In 1658 Captain Peter Jennings went to court in Northumberland County in an attempt to recover funds owed to the late Arthur Price I's estate. Arthur Price II's name appeared occasionally in the records generated by the General Court (LEO 23–24; Northumberland County Order Book 1652–1665:172; NUG I:131, 214, 312; II:210; PB 1:798; 3:37, 363; MCGC 321, 326, 340, 366, 476, 478; York County Deeds, Orders, Wills 2:289, 328; Court Orders 2 [1646–1648]:282).

Edward Price (Prise): Edward Price came to Virginia in 1623 and took up residence in urban Jamestown, where he was a servant in Richard Stephens' household. Price married Eleanor, Robert Brittin's (Brittaine's) widow, but died sometime prior to April 9, 1629, when the General Court ordered Eleanor to make an inventory of both men's estates (VI&A 579).

Hugh Price (Pryse): During the winter of 1609–1610, which became known as the "Starving Time," Hugh Price of Jamestown became delirious and was ranting while walking around in the settlement's marketplace. When he ventured outside of the fort, he was killed by Indians (VI&A 579).

John Price: John Price received a patent for 150 acres in the corporation of Henrico in 1620, but during the mid-1620s he and his wife and children lived in Bermuda Hundred, in the corporation of Charles City. During 1625 Price served as a burgess for Bermuda Hundred. He died in 1628, leaving his widow, Ann, and at least two children, John II and Mathew. When Mathew Price repatented his late father's land in Henrico County in May 1638, he identified the decedent as a laborer. He also indicated that Price's acreage was then in the hands of his widow, Ann, who had married Robert Hallom (VI&A 579; LEO 6; PB 1:558; DOR 2:828–829).

John Price: John Price, a gentleman and resident of Surry County, witnessed several court documents and wills in 1653. Like many of his contemporaries, he participated in litigation, sometimes as plaintiff and some-

times as a defendant. In October 1653 he signed an agreement with Edward Hurlston, a carpenter, who agreed to finish his house and construct a porch. Price may have had a violent temper, for he was accused of assaulting attorney and merchant William Sherwood, a resident of urban Jamestown. On July 4, 1679, Price, who was still a Surry County resident, testified about events that had occurred in the capital city during Bacon's Rebellion. Price reportedly was slain by William Rownan sometime prior to November 1681, and in May 2, 1682, his widow, Mary, was granted administration of his estate (Surry County Deed Book 1 [1652–1663]:28–30; Deeds, Wills &c. 1671–1684:27, 130; Order Book 1671–1691:331, 375, 369).

Walter Price (Priest): Walter Price came to Virginia in 1618 and during the mid-1620s lived at Chaplin's Choice. Court testimony reveals that Price was a member of Truelove's Company. In October 1629 Price served as a burgess for Chaplin's Choice, and in March 1630 he represented Chaplin's Choice and Jordan's Journey. He may have been related to the Walter Price who owned some land in Northumberland County in 1667 and patented 400 acres in Nansemond County in July 1684 (VI&A 580; LEO 7–9; PB 7:392; Northumberland County Order Book 1666–1678:20, 63).

John Priest: John Priest, a tailor, arrived in Jamestown in September 1623 (VI&A 582).

Ann Prince: Ann Prince left England in 1622 with William Rowley and his family and was part of their household in Jamestown (VI&A 582).

Edward Prince: When John Phipps patented a large tract in urban Jamestown on February 23, 1656, it included a 12-acre lot that had belonged to Dr. John Pott. The text of the patent indicated that Robert Bristow's widow, Joane, had assigned the Pott parcel to Edward Prince, a gentleman. In December 1639 Prince patented 500 acres of land abutting the Appomattox River, and in 1645 and 1646 he served as a burgess for Charles City County. He also owned a watermill and some houses at the head of Lawnes Creek in Isle of Wight County, and a 27-acre parcel on the mainland near the Governor's Land. When Prince made his will on April 15, 1646, he left his watermill to George Hardy and John Watkins (PB 2:177; 4:101–102; NUG I:340; MCGH 208; LEO 23–24).

John Pritchard: John Pritchard, a carpenter for the Company of Shipwrights, came to

Virginia in 1622. His supervisor, master boat-builder Thomas Nunn, was supposed to give him five acres of land when his term of indenture expired. Pritchard, like the others who came to the colony under the sponsorship of the Company of Shipwrights, built a home on Jamestown Island (VI&A 581).

Thomas Pritchard (Prichard, Pricharde, Prickett, Prickkett): Thomas Pritchard came to Virginia sometime prior to 1642 at the expense of Christopher Boyce, who used Pritchard's headright when acquiring land on the Piankatank River. Pritchard patented some land in Isle of Wight County sometime prior to 1652. Then, in 1653 he claimed some acreage on the Blackwater River. He may have been a kinsman of Walter Pritchard, who in 1654 patented 250 acres of land at Winter Harbor in Gloucester (later, Mathews) County. Thomas Pritchard represented Gloucester County in the assembly sessions of 1656, while the Commonwealth government was in power. In 1665 he patented 137 acres on the north side of Dragon Swamp in Old Rappahannock County (LEO 33; PB 1:870; 3:182, 205, 231, 268; 5:228; MCGC 94). Thomas Pritchard may have been the same individual who came to Virginia in 1620 and during the mid-1620s was one of Dr. John Pott's indentured servants (VI&A 581).

Stephen Proctor: On October 28, 1673, London merchant Stephen Proctor made a claim against the estate of John (Jonathan) Newell, a Jamestown merchant and property owner. Proctor died before the debt was satisfied but his widow and executrix, Winifred, pursued the claim in 1680 and appears to have recovered the funds that were owed. On February 6, 1682, Winifred Proctor gave a quitclaim deed to William Sherwood, who had purchased Newell's property in urban Jamestown (MCGC 357; AMB 30).

Richard Prodget: Richard Prodget, a gentleman, arrived in Virginia in early 1608 in the 1st Supply of new colonists and resided in Jamestown (VI&A 584).

Jacob Profit (Phrophett): Jacob Profit died in Jamestown sometime after April 1623 but before February 16, 1624 (VI&A 584).

Jonas Profit (Prophett): Jonas Profit, a sailor, came to Virginia in 1607 and was one of the first people to arrive at what became Jamestown. According to Captain John Smith, Profit was a soldier and fisherman (VI&A 584).

William Pryor (Prior): William Pryor began patenting land in Charles River (later, York) County in 1635. He acquired his acreage on the York River by laying claim to 300 acres by right of his adventure to Chiskiack and another 200 acres on the basis of headrights. Like his near neighbors, Richard Townsend and Francis Morgan I, William Pryor was among the first to settle in the region. In 1637 he acquired 510 acres near his original patent. Pryor was designated a county justice and served for many years. On July 28, 1636, when the county court convened for the first time, the justices met at Pryor's house, and they continued to assemble there in 1637 and 1638. Pryor served as a burgess for Charles River County and attended the 1640 assembly session. He began speculating in real estate and over the years continuously added to his holdings, sometimes acquiring land on the fringes of the colony's frontier. He patented 1,300 acres on the north side of the York River in 1642, and four years later he laid claim to 650 acres there on the basis of 13 headrights. He also acquired 600 acres on the north side of Queens Creek, in what was then very sparsely settled territory. Pryor's ability to accumulate land indicates that he was a highly successful planter, who was able to generate disposable income. William Pryor made his will on January 21, 1647, and died within four days. He designated his daughters, Mary and Margaret, as his executrixes, and left them the bulk of his estate. To his eldest daughter, Margaret, he left his interest in the ship *Honor*, some currency, and the land on which he was then living. He bequeathed the rest of his real estate to daughter Mary and stipulated that she and her sister, Margaret, were to share equally in the rest of his estate. Pryor made several monetary bequests, notably to Richard Kemp's wife, Elizabeth; to Richard Bennett; to Thomas Harwood; and to Jasper Clayton's several children. William Pryor's brother-in-law Thomas Harrison (a mariner) and Thomas Harwood were named overseers of the testator's will. They rented Pryor's York County plantation to Richard Bernard, who was obliged to keep its buildings in good repair and erect some improvements. The Pryor plantation eventually came into the hands of Thomas Ballard I. Although little information has come to light on the Pryor family, York County records suggest that one of William Pryor's daughters married a Thomas Edwards (VI&A 582; LEO 18; PB 1:223, 427, 445, 447, 802; York County Deeds, Orders, Wills 1:23, 27–30, 32, 35–39, 41–42, 47, 51, 80; 2:123, 146, 153, 202–205, 318; 3:152–153; SR 3995).

Thomas Purfoy (Purefoy, Purfray, Purfrey, Purfury, Purifoy, Purifie, Purifye, Purrifie): Thomas Purfoy came to Virginia in 1621 and by February 1624 was living on the lower side of the James River, across from Jamestown. By early 1625 he had moved to Elizabeth City. Within a year's time he became a lieutenant and was named a justice or commissioner of Elizabeth City's monthly court. He also led an expedition against the Nansemond Indians. In September 1628 Purfoy patented 100 acres in Elizabeth City near the fields called Fort Henry. By 1629 he had been named Elizabeth City's principal commander. He continued to serve as local court justice and in March 1630 was elected a burgess for the lower (eastern) part of Elizabeth City. In 1631 he obtained a 500-acre leasehold in Elizabeth City on the Back River, and a year later he was named to the Council of State. Thomas Purfoy died between September 1638 and October 1639. His wife, Lucy, outlived him and in 1640 indicated that she was age 42. Her land in Elizabeth City was mentioned in a June 1648 patent (VI&A 585; LEO xxi, 9; PB 1:103, 163, 323, 445–446, 601, 680; 2:139; DOR 2:863–864).

[No First Name] Puttock (Puttocke): In 1610 a man named Puttock, who was a lieutenant or captain, was in charge of the blockhouse in Jamestown. When he ventured out of the blockhouse, a Pasbehay Indian stabbed him to death (VI&A 586).

Pyancha (Native American): When Abraham Wood and a party of explorers ventured into the territory beyond the head of the Appomattox River in 1650, Pyancha, an Appomattock Indian warrior, served as their guide. He not only led them through the forest, he cautioned them about the dangers they might encounter (JHB 1660–1693:64; SALLEY 8–9, 13–14, 16, 18).

James Pyland (Piland): In June 1642 Francis England used James Pyland's headright when patenting some land in Isle of Wight County. In November 1652, while the Commonwealth government was in power in Virginia, Pyland was elected to the assembly as a burgess for Isle of Wight County. However, he was ejected because of his "blasphemous catechism" and his support of Thomas Woodward, a dissenter who held office in Isle of Wight but was ousted. Pyland continued to witness documents in his home county and perform official functions. He was eventually returned to the assembly in 1659, while Sir William Berkeley was governor, and was allowed to take his seat. Although only one of Pyland's patents has survived, it demonstrates that in February 1662 he laid claim to 300 acres on the James River in Isle of Wight County. In February 1663 Pyland's widow, Elizabeth, was named his executrix (LEO 30, 35; Isle of Wight County Wills and Administrations Book A:79; Will and Deed Book 1:574; Administrations and Probates 1:6; HEN I:374–375, 506; PB 1:857; 5:212; BILL 185).

Q

Ann Quaile (Mrs. Richard Quaile [Quayle]?): Ann Quaile died in Jamestown after April 1623 but before February 16, 1624. She may have been the wife of mariner Richard Quaile (Quayle) (VI&A 586).

Richard Quaile (Quayle): In February 1623 the Virginia Company authorized Captain Richard Quaile to take passengers to Virginia and then go on a fishing voyage. In March 1624, during Sir Francis Wyatt's governorship, Quaile was found guilty of making slanderous speeches against high-ranking officials. As punishment, he was to be pilloried, lose his ears, and be demoted to the status of a carpenter. Quaile promptly asked for a pardon, stating that he was sick, poor, and deeply in debt, and that his wife and servant were dead. He appears to have received clemency, for he was allowed to return to the sea. When Quaile's death was reported in November 1632, he was identified as captain of a vessel that made regular trips from the plantations to the West Indies (VI&A 586).

Queen of Pamunkey (Native American) (see Cockacoeske)

John Quigley: On June 29, 1680, John Quigley, a gentleman, asked the House of Burgesses to assign him two ruinous row houses that were located on Jamestown's Back Street, property that was publicly owned. The burgesses agreed to award him a 50-year lease if he would agree to begin repairing them within a year and complete the work within two years. Shortly thereafter, the governor and council received petitions from George Lee and Colonel Nathaniel Bacon, who were interested in leasing the same property. They seem to have been given preferential treatment, and sometime prior to July 6, 1689, Quigley withdrew his request. Very little is known about him except that on June 8, 1680, he was asked to provide medical supplies to the surgeon of the Rappahannock garrison, armed men who were stationed on the Rappahannock River frontier to protect settlers. Later, Quigley requested payment for powder and

shot he had provided to Stafford County and items he had furnished to Westmoreland County. In the latter two instances, the assembly deemed his charges excessive. In April 1680 John Quigley was identified as a Virginia merchant when his estate was sued in Middlesex County's monthly court (JHB 1660–1693:127, 136, 150; LJC 8, 10; Middlesex County Order Book 1673–1680:219–220).

Thomas Quigley: On January 21, 1624, Thomas Quigley testified that Sir Samuel Argall had forced him to relinquish compensation to which he was entitled (VI&A 587). This statement indicates that Quigley had been in Virginia during 1617–1618, while Argall was deputy governor.

R

Elizabeth Rabley: On September 24, 1674, the justices of Surry County's monthly court identified Elizabeth Rabley as an orphan and agreed that she should have a patent for certain land to which she was entitled (MCGC 379). She may have been Thomas Rabley's kinswoman, for he was still alive and had a daughter named Elizabeth.

Thomas Rabley (Radley, Rableigh, Rablais): Thomas Rabley, a Dutchman, immigrated to Virginia sometime prior to 1669. A suit he filed in 1671 against his former guardian, Major Theophilus Hone, reveals that he was a minor when he arrived in the colony, and that Hone had misappropriated some of his funds. Rabley and William Sherwood, as business partners, invested in a small tract of land at Middle Plantation (later, Williamsburg) on which they built three houses designed for garrisoning troops and storing the public supply of ammunition. The structures were still being used for military purposes in November 1682. During the 1670s Rabley, a gentleman, sued several Surry County residents in an attempt to recover funds or settle disputes. One defendant was councilor and Jamestown tavern owner Thomas Swann I. In 1674 Rabley represented his daughter, Elizabeth, in a suit against Henry Webb so that she could recover part of her deceased mother's land. He also went to court to air a disagreement about a sloop he purchased. It is unclear whether Rabley's dealings in Surry were attributable to business interests, kinship ties, or both. He may have been related to John

Rabley of York County and his children, John Jr., Elizabeth, and Thomas. In 1676 Thomas Rabley had a plantation in Middlesex County, where he maintained a personal residence, and from time to time he initiated litigation in the county court. In 1678 he was appointed constable of the county's middle precinct. In anticipation of frequent absences, he appointed an attorney to act on his behalf in Middlesex's monthly court. Rabley returned to Middlesex by June 1679, when he was reappointed constable, but in March 1680 he left again and leased his plantation to another individual.

On February 7, 1678, Rabley purchased the late John Barber I's ¾-acre waterfront parcel in urban Jamestown from his son, John Barber II. Included in the transaction was the eastern half of an adjoining lot that the late John Barber I had occupied during the mid-1660s and a contiguous half-acre lot that Barber first patented in 1656. Rabley was living in Jamestown in December 1679 when he appointed William Edwards II to act as his attorney in the Surry County court. Sometime prior to June 30, 1680, Rabley and William Sherwood began hosting official meetings in their houses in Jamestown. Both men were paid for the repairs or modifications they had made to their buildings, which were converted to public use, and they also received rent. Historical records suggest that Rabley hosted assembly meetings, whereas the Council of State met at Sherwood's. On October 16, 1680, Rabley bought a 300-acre tract in the southeastern end of Jamestown Island, below Passmore Creek, purchasing it from Ann and William Price of Old Rappahannock County. The deed of conveyance noted that Ann was the daughter and heir of the late John Pinhorne, former owner of the 300 acres.

Thomas Rabley eventually sold William Sherwood his interest in their jointly owned acreage at Middle Plantation. A Surry County court document indicates that Robert Penny served as Thomas Rabley's bookkeeper during the early 1680s. In 1682 Rabley was paid for the use of his sloop in transporting prisoners to Jamestown and for taking bedding to the men garrisoned at a fort on the colony's frontier. He was identified as a Jamestown innkeeper and resident of the capital city in 1682 when he requested compensation for providing accommodations to some Indians. He also appeared as a witness in a case involving Robert Beverley I, and he joined mariner and Jamestown resident William Armiger in a suit against George Brent of the Northern Neck. During the early 1680s Rabley made several appearances in Middlesex County's monthly court, bringing suit against local residents. In 1683 and 1684 he also initiated lawsuits in Old Rappahannock, Northumberland, Westmoreland, and Lancaster counties. His inclusion in a Middlesex County grand jury in 1685 suggests that he had returned to the county, at least temporarily.

Rabley died sometime prior to May 1685, when his widow and executrix, Jane, sued one of his debtors. On August 26, 1685, she used John Minor as her attorney when bringing suit against Robert Chamberlaine in Westmoreland County. In December 1685 the vestry of South Farnham Parish in Old Rappahannock County sued Jane Rabley in an attempt to recover some parish dues that were in arrears. As time went on, Mrs. Rabley continued to pursue her late husband's debtors and pay off his creditors. She died sometime between March 1687, when Edwin Thacker replaced her as her late husband's executor, and February 1688, when son-in-law Joseph Topping (Toppin) and Surry County resident Francis Mason began serving as her executors. They not only collected debts against her estate but also those owed to her late husband's estate. The connection between the Rabley and Mason families raises the possibility that some of the official meetings hosted by Mrs. Ann Mason of Jamestown around 1684 occurred in Thomas Rabley's brick house on urban Jamestown's waterfront. This is feasible if Mrs. Mason was one of Thomas Rabley's daughters or stepdaughters and

occupied the family home while he was in Middlesex County. When William Briscoe of Jamestown made his will, which was proved by July 10, 1695, he mentioned the fact that Joseph Topping and his wife, Elizabeth, the late Thomas Rabley's daughter, were then occupying her late father's brick house as tenants. When Briscoe's widowed daughter-in-law and heir, Ann Holder Briscoe, and her new husband, James Chudley, repatented the western portion of their Jamestown lot, a reference was made to its boundary line being near "Rablys brick house" (JHB 1660–1693:140, 174, 256–257; HEN III:562; LJC 8; MCGC 379, 412; AMB 53, 57, 63, 83, 133; Sherwood, November 8, 1698; Middlesex County Order Book 1673–1680:50, 79, 117, 138, 168, 176, 213; 1680–1694:132, 134, 173, 212, 216–217, 284, 333, 342, 344, 347, 426; York County Deeds, Orders, Wills 6:353; 9:74; NUG II:261; MCGC 280, 285, 289; Surry County Order Book 1671–1691:15, 18, 211, 236, 288, 290, 294, 302–303, 309, 395, 682; Deeds, Wills &c. 1671–1684:243; Old Rappahannock County Deeds and Wills 1677–1682:303; Order Book 1683–1686:10, 129; 1687–1692:39, 43, 72, 167; Lancaster County Order Book 1680–1687:142–143, 205, 234; Northumberland County Order Book 1678–1698:214; Westmoreland County Order Book 1676–1689:298, 305, 321, 325, 329, 443, 493, 650, 663, 678; Lower Norfolk County Record Book C:77).

William Rabnett (Ravenett): In early 1624 William Rabnett was a servant in Captain William Peirce's household in urban Jamestown, but in March 1626 he was identified as one of the late John Rolfe's servants. Rabnett's presence in the Peirce home probably was attributable to the fact that Peirce had been Rolfe's father-in-law and one of his heirs. In 1634 William Rabnett was identified as owner of a plantation on Skiff's Creek, within the Martin's Hundred Parish of James City County. He also owned some land bordering Mr. Heley's acreage in Warwick (or Denbigh) County (VI&A 586).

Rachel: On February 15, 1768, when an inventory was made of the late Richard Ambler's slaves on Jamestown Island and his leasehold in the Governor's Land, a female slave named Rachel was listed. In 1769 Rachel was included in the late Edward Ambler I's estate and was described as a girl living on the Governor's Land (York County Wills and Inventories 21:386–391).

John Radish (Reddish): John Radish, a feather-maker and indentured servant, came to Virginia in 1619. During 1624 he was residing on Jamestown Island in Robert Fitts's home. In January 1625 Radish, who had become a free man, conveyed some land in the eastern end of Jamestown Island, at Black Point, to Sir George Yeardley. Radish was then living alone in the Neck O'Land behind Jamestown Island. Later in the year he ran afoul of the law by allowing Robert Fitt (Fitts) and some of Sir George Yeardley's servants to get drunk while they were guests in his home. In May 1637 Radish purchased a 16-acre tract located in the eastern end of Jamestown Island, to the north of Goose Hill Marsh (VI&A 588).

Robert Raffe (Rasse?): Robert Raffe died in Jamestown sometime after April 1623 but before February 16, 1624 (VI&A 588).

Andrew Railey (Ralye, Rawleigh, Reily): In early 1624 Andrew Railey and Thomas Passmore were living in urban Jamestown in John Southern's household. A year later Railey was still residing on Jamestown Island, but he lived outside of the urbanized area. In 1627 he and carpenter Robert Wright inherited a leasehold in the eastern end of the island, and they also secured a lease of their own in October 1628. In January 1628 Andrew and Jonas Railey (perhaps a kinsman) were arrested as debtors of Mr. John Gill, a Jamestown merchant (VI&A 588).

James Railey (Raleley, Rylei, Rayley, Ryaly, Rylei, Reily): On the night of June 23, 1624, James Railey stood watch at the fort in Jamestown. Later, he testified that he did not see anyone break into Abraham Peirsey's store, but he saw two men "close under the Countrie howse," the term used for a building that had been erected with public funds. The loiterers claimed that they were unable to enter Sir George Yeardley's house because the door was locked (VI&A 588). They may have been near the governor's official residence, not Yeardley's personally owned dwelling, which was elsewhere on Jamestown Island.

Jonas Railey (Raleley, Rylei, Rayley, Ryaly, Rylei, Reily): In January 1625 Abraham Peirsey of urban Jamestown purchased Jonas Railey's contract from Sir George Yeardley and John Pountis. Railey, who formerly lived at West and Shirley Hundred, was eager to obtain his freedom and agreed to pay Peirsey outright or compensate him with work as a sawyer. In March 1627 Railey, then a Jamestown Island planter, was fined for failing to perform sentry duty. In January 1628 he and Andrew Railey (perhaps a kinsman) were arrested by merchant John Gill because of indebtedness (VI&A 589).

Joseph Railey (Raleley, Rylei, Rayley, Ryaly, Rylei, Reily): In late January 1625 Joseph Railey was living alone in the mainland, just west of Jamestown Island (VI&A 589). He probably was one of the governor's tenants or servants.

Edward Raleigh (Rawleigh): On May 15, 1684, Edward Raleigh was appointed the ferry keeper in Jamestown (EJC I:499).

Edward Ramsey (Ramsye): Edward Ramsey appears to have lived in James City County, although his name appeared in York County's records from time to time. In 1657 he witnessed a document that was recorded in York County, and during the 1660s he was mentioned in cases that were tried by York County's justices. On September 29, 1660, when Governor William Berkeley announced that King Charles II had been restored to the throne, he sent Captain Edward Ramsey to Pamunkey Neck to invite Colonel William Claiborne to Jamestown for a gala celebration. Ramsey served as a burgess for James City County between December 1662 and 1676, and in 1664 he was a James City County justice. By 1666 he was in possession of some land in Martin's Hundred, near Green Swamp and the boundary between James City and York counties. He and Colonel Thomas Swann I were serving as Captain John Grove's executors in 1671, when Mrs. Ann Monford, Mr. Macnen, and Colonel John Page brought suit against the decedent's estate. As time went on, Swann and Ramsey disagreed over the accuracy of the Grove estate's accounts. The General Court ordered Grove's executors to pay what the decedent owed Richard Lynny and Francis Mason. Later in the year Ramsey was among those ordered to audit the accounts generated by Theodorick Bland, the late John Holmewood's executor. In October 1675 Lieutenant Colonel Ramsey successfully sued David Morse, who reportedly slandered Ramsey's wife. He was still alive in November 1678 and had a York County man arrested for indebtedness; however, he seems to have continued to live in James City County (HEN II:196–197, 249–250; MCGC 259, 306; Charles City County Order Book:103; Tyler, "Virginia Under the Commonwealth," 196; STAN 77–78; LEO 38; NUG II:41; MCGC 259–260, 269, 276, 279, 286, 289, 290–291, 302, 306, 310, 341, 428; York County Deeds, Orders, Wills 3:12, 103; 4:107; 6:78).

Thomas Ramsey (Ramsay, Ramsy): Sometime prior to November 1637 Thomas Ramsey patented some Elizabeth City land on the lower side of the York River, near the

New Poquoson (later, Poquoson) River. As time went on, however, he shifted his interests to the upper side of the York River, where by 1642 he owned 50 acres. A bill of sale recorded in November 1656 reveals that Ramsey was then a justice in Gloucester County's monthly court. In 1657 he patented 1,000 acres in western Gloucester County, on the northeast side of the Mattaponi River. Ramsey became a burgess for Gloucester County and served in the assembly in 1656 and 1658. He probably was a forebear of the Thomas Ramsey of Petso Parish who purchased some land in Essex County in 1693 (LEO 33–34; PB 1:498, 827; 4:150; MASON 99; DUNN 587).

Thomas Ramshaw (Ramshawe, Ramshee, Ramsheer): Thomas Ramshaw, a successful planter, was living in Elizabeth City in February 1626. In 1632 he served as a burgess for the corporation of Elizabeth City, representing the Warwick River area. In 1635 he patented a tract of land in Elizabeth City County and another in Denbigh (actually, Warwick) County, using the headright of his wife, Katherine (VI&A 589; LEO 10). He may have been the same man known as Thomas Ramsey.

Anthony Randall: On November 19, 1623, Anthony Randall was mentioned in connection with a court case that involved Dr. John Pott and his wife, Elizabeth, residents of urban Jamestown. Randall seems to have lived in Jamestown, too (VI&A 589).

Mary Swann Randall (Mrs. Thomas Swann I, Mrs. Robert Randall) (see Thomas Swann I): After the death of Colonel Thomas Swann I of Surry County, his widow, Madam Mary Swann, married Robert Randall and moved to England. On July 7, 1685, she sold to her stepson, Samuel Swann, her dower interest in her late husband's house and land in urban Jamestown, then occupied by merchant Samuel Firth (Surry County Deeds, Wills &c. 1687–1694:28; WITH 507).

Edward Randolph: While Edward Randolph was in England, sometime prior to 1691, he prepared a report for the Lords of the Treasury, which described strategies that would help the American colonies produce more revenue for the kingdom. He suggested surveying (that is, inspecting) wooded areas along the seacoast, because he surmised that ships in Virginia and other colonies were avoiding ports of entry and the payment of customs duties. In early 1692 Virginia's at-torney general, Edward Chilton, reported that Randolph had been appointed their majesties' surveyor of customs in America, and shortly thereafter he arrived in Jamestown with his official papers. In April 1692 Lieutenant Governor Francis Nicholson and his council notified Virginia's county justices of Randolph's appointment. Later in the year he left Virginia and went to Maryland. During 1695 Randolph sent several pieces of official correspondence to England. He also informed Governor Nicholson that illegal trade involving ships bound for Scotland was going on in Virginia, Maryland, and Pennsylvania. He said that he had learned that the colonies' juries were not impartial and indicated that he was going to England to seek advice. Randolph followed through and submitted documents to the Board of Trade recommending that convoys escort trading ships to and from the colonies, especially Virginia and Maryland.

In 1696 Edward Randolph brought some additional issues to his superiors' attention. He said that Currituck Inlet in Carolina was a good location for New England ships to take aboard tobacco from the southern colonies and transport it back to the port of Boston for transshipping; he noted, however, that pirates and runaways posed a danger for they were sheltered at Roanoke. Randolph also addressed a more sensitive subject, for he said that the Crown had lost revenues because members of Virginia's Council of State had engrossed enormous quantities of land but failed to pay quitrents on their holdings as required by law. He suggested that a limit of 500 acres per man be imposed. Randolph also said that according to councilor Edward Chilton, in 1679 or 1680 members of the Council of State had declared themselves immune to lawsuits. As a result, British merchants were unable to collect their just debts. Randolph added that he had never been a council member but understood that some sat as judges without having taken the appropriate oath of office. When Edward Randolph made his will on June 15, 1702, he identified himself as surveyor general of customs for the American colonies and said that he was preparing to make his 17th overseas voyage. He made bequests to his daughters, Sarah, Deborah, Elizabeth Pin, and "Williams" (perhaps a married woman) and made no reference to his wife, probably because she was deceased. On December 17, 1703, the testator's will was proved. An official report filed in 1702 suggests that when Edward Randolph made his final transatlantic crossing, he clashed with others aboard the *Shelburn*, a vessel on which he had sought passage. He was then an official messenger who carried dispatches that had to be delivered to the various colonies (Essex County Orders &c. 1692–1695:158; SR 239, 1034, 1192, 1459, 1927, 1932, 1939, 1948, 2202, 4124, 5624, 7392, 7724, 7771, 7774).

* * *

Henry Randolph I: In 1662 Mrs. Sarah Drummond patented a half-acre lot in urban Jamestown, a parcel that abutted east upon the grounds of the parish church. The northwest corner of her lot abutted acreage owned by a Mr. Randolph. Research suggests that he was Henrico County merchant Henry Randolph, who came to Virginia in 1642 and within a year became clerk of the Henrico County court. From December 1656 to 1673 Randolph served as clerk of the assembly, a responsibility that would have required him to spend lengthy periods of time in Jamestown. In 1661 he also began serving as deputy escheator general. By 1670 Henry Randolph had purchased the three central units of a long brick row house in the western end of Jamestown Island, but he disposed of them within a year. The unit he sold to Thomas Ludwell and Thomas Stegg II was fully furnished. Members of Henrico's Randolph family were wealthy merchants and planters who took an active role in public life and traditionally lived at Turkey Island. During the 1650s, 1660s and 1670s Henry Randolph patented substantial quantities of land on the Appomattox River and in the Northern Neck, on both the Potomac and Rappahannock rivers. He was closely associated with merchant Thomas Stegg I of Henrico (formerly of Jamestown) and in 1668 witnessed Stegg's will. Henry Randolph died in 1673 while he was still clerk of the assembly and his widow, the former Judith Soane, was appointed his administratrix. At the time of his death, Randolph was indebted to William Drummond I and Colonel Thomas Swann I of Jamestown. In March 1676 Mrs. Judith Randolph was awarded custody of her late husband's 1,000 to 1,200 acres of land in Henrico County, acreage in which she had inherited liferights; the decedent's son, Henry II, was named as reversionary heir. Judith Soane Randolph later married Major Peter Field, a burgess and resident of Henrico County, and was still alive in 1695 (HEN I:424; II:456; Surry County Deeds, Wills &c. 1652–1672:35,98; Stegg 1668; NUG I:347, 376, 499, 560; II:57, 84, 100, 102; MCGC 225, 264, 354, 360, 372, 442, 507, 514–515; Henrico County Wills and Deeds 1688–1697:387; WITH 107; SR 3546; PB 5:634; LEO 33–37; DOR 1:379).

William Randolph I: William Randolph I came to Virginia around 1673 and succeeded his uncle, Henry Randolph I, as clerk of Henrico County's monthly court, holding that position until 1683. During that period he gained possession of Curles, the plantation that had belonged to the rebel Nathaniel Bacon, who had been found guilty of treason. He also purchased the Henrico County acreage known as Turkey Island, which became the Randolph family seat. On December 2, 1678, William Randolph I indicated that he was age 28. He married Mary Isham and was the brother-in-law of Francis Eppes III of Bermuda Hundred. Randolph commenced serving as a burgess for Henrico County and attended the assembly meetings held in 1684 and 1685–1686. When he was elected to represent Henrico and Gloucester counties in 1688, he chose to serve Henrico. He was returned to the assembly on behalf of Henrico and held office in 1691–1692, 1693, 1695–1696, and 1696–1697. In 1693 he replaced John Pleasants, a neighbor and devout Quaker who refused to take the required oaths. In 1698, while Randolph was a Henrico County burgess, he was elected speaker of the assembly. When chosen to serve as clerk in 1699, he vacated his assembly seat. In 1696 William Randolph I was named to the Council of State and became attorney general. In 1702, while he was suffering from gout, his son, William II, was authorized to serve as clerk of the assembly (STAN 25; LEO 47–50, 52–54, 56, 58–59; EJC I:57, 308, 315, 393, 397, 425, 443, 445, 459; II:33, 71, 201, 267; Henrico County Order Book 1678–1693:64–65; DOR 1:331, 858, 861; 2:230).

* * *

Richard Randolph: In 1837 Richard Randolph wrote a descriptive account of Jamestown's appearance and noted that much development had occurred during the 1660s. He said that according to extant deeds, much of the town's land lay submerged beneath the waters of the James River. In October 1856 Richard Randolph paid a second visit to Jamestown. This time, he was accompanied by Bishop William Meade (MEADE I:110; Maxwell, "Jamestown," 138–139).

Abraham (Abram) Ransack: Abraham Ransack, a refiner, arrived in Virginia in 1608 in the 1st Supply of new Jamestown settlers (VI&A 590).

* * *

Peter Ranson (Ransone, Ransom): Peter Ranson represented Elizabeth City County in the assembly sessions of 1652. During the 1650s he began speculating in real estate and in June 1653 patented 1,100 acres on the North River, Mobjack Bay, and a creek called Isle of Wight in what was then Gloucester County. He also patented 300 acres on Broad Creek in Lower Norfolk County or the Eastern Shore. In 1654 and 1656 he laid claim to 950 acres on Dividing Creek in Northumberland County. By February 1663 Peter Ranson was dead. His sons, James and George, then repatented their late father's acreage in Gloucester (later, Mathews) County. In 1672 James Ranson I brought suit against George Bledshaw, who claimed that some of the Northumberland County acreage patented by James' late father, Peter, had been deserted. In 1704 a Peter Ransom (probably burgess Peter Ranson's grandson) was credited with 1,500 acres in Essex County and 220 acres in Gloucester County's Ware Parish (LEO 29–30; PB 3:22, 108, 202, 325; 4:53; 5:326; MCGC 318; SMITH 73).

James Ranson (Ransone, Ransom) I: James Ranson I followed in the footsteps of his father, Peter Ranson, and served in the assembly. In February 1663 he and his brother, George, patented 1,100 acres on the North River, Mobjack Bay, and a creek called Isle of Wight in Gloucester (later, Mathews) County, acreage originally claimed by their late father. In 1672 the General Court decided that the Ranson brothers' land should be surveyed so that any excess acreage could be included in the patent. A few months later James Ranson sued George Bledshaw, who claimed that the Northumberland County acreage patented by James' late father, Peter, had been deserted. The matter was to be decided by the justices of the General Court. James Ranson patented some additional acreage in 1667 and served as a burgess for Gloucester County. He attended the assembly meetings held in 1691–1692, 1693, 1695–1696, 1696–1697, 1698, and 1699. Testimony he provided to the justices of Gloucester County in 1694 suggests that he was merchant Thomas Starke's factor. Ranson was identified as a colonel in 1704 when he patented 40 acres in Gloucester County's Kingston Parish, where he was churchwarden. He also paid quitrent on 1,400 acres of land in Kingston Parish in Gloucester County and his son, James II, was taxed on 310 acres in the same vicinity (LEO 50, 52–54, 56, 58–59, 62, 64; PB 5:320; 9:601; MCGC 312, 318, 324; SR 10736; SMITH 73).

* * *

King of the Rappahannock Indians (Native American): In June 1680 the justices of Old Rappahannock County's monthly court decided to summon the king of the Rappahannock Indians so that he could address a complaint against some of his people. William Harwood, a colonist, alleged that two of his Indian servants, a woman and a boy, had run away, and he suspected that they were being concealed by the Rappahannock Indians (Old Rappahannock County Order Book 1687–1692:171).

William Rascow (Rasco, Roscow): William Rascow patented some land at Blunt Point, in Warwick County sometime prior to October 1696. He represented Warwick County in the assembly sessions held in 1693 and 1695–1696. He also became a county justice and was appointed sheriff. His wife was Mary, the daughter of Colonel William Wilson of Elizabeth City County. In 1694 Governor Edmund Andros informed his superiors that William Rascow had submitted a petition concerning a debt he hoped to recover from the estate of Philip Wilcocke, master of the ship *Fortune* of Plymouth. During the spring of 1695, while Rascow was Denbigh Parish's churchwarden, he became embroiled in a dispute with the Rev. Cope Doyly, the parish minister. Rascow and the parish clerk, William Lambmot, took matters into their own hands and locked the church door, which prevented Doyly from performing the religious services that were required by law. Doyly retaliated by presenting a petition to the Council of State protesting Rascow's actions. Rascow asked for a copy of the bill of complaint and after the opposing sides were heard, the complaint against Doyly was dismissed. Rascow was ordered to allow the clergyman access to the parish church, but he was recalcitrant and failed to inform the vestry of the council's decision. As a result, in October 1696 Rascow, who in July 1696 had been named high sheriff, was stripped of his right to serve as a justice, which also meant that he lost his sheriffry. Rascow's plantation in Warwick County was mentioned in a 1696 patent for an adjacent piece of property. By 1699 William Rascow seems to have recovered his reputation. He had become a Warwick County justice once again and was returned to the assembly, where he fulfilled his term. By May 1700 he had been appointed to a judicial commission that was authorized to try a group of pirates at the Elizabeth City County courthouse, and he also was designated a trustee of Warwick Town. Rascow died on November 2, 1700, and was buried on his plantation at Blunt Point. He was survived by his wife, Mary, who served as his executrix (LEO 53, 55, 59; PB 9:45; SR 377; EJC I:322–323, 340, 356, 358; II:65–66; NEAL 22, 54, 155; DUNN 4, 63, 77, 88, 96).

Humphrey Rastall (Rastell, Roistall): Sometime prior to 1624 Humphrey Rastall, a London merchant and mariner, began transporting indentured servants to Virginia. On occasion, he hauled tobacco from Virginia to Newfoundland and made trips to Canada. During 1626 Rastall made several court appearances in suits that involved disagreements over the procurement of servants. In 1628 he became burgess for the merchants in James City. However, he died during the year (VI&A 590; LEO 7).

Elkinton Ratclife (Ratliffe): In early 1624 Elkinton Ratclife, a servant, was living in Captain Ralph Hamor's household in urban Jamestown. By February 1625 he had moved to Hamor's property on Hog Island (VI&A 590).

John Ratcliffe alias Sicklemore: John Ratcliffe, a Virginia Company investor and mariner, brought some of the first colonists to Virginia. He was appointed to the colony's council and in September 1607 was elected president. Captain John Smith later claimed that he and Ratcliffe rebuilt Jamestown after it burned in January 1608. Ratcliffe alienated his fellow council members and in July 1608 was deposed and arrested. He was restored to his council seat but left Virginia in December 1608 with Captain Christopher Newport. On June 1, 1609, when Ratcliffe was preparing to return to the colony, he made his will, naming his wife, Dorothy, as his sole heir and executrix. When Sir Thomas Gates arrived in Virginia in May 1610, he placed Ratcliffe in charge of Algernon Fort at Old Point Comfort. While on a trading voyage later in the year, he was ambushed and killed at Powhatan's behest. His widow, Dorothy, and co-executor Richard Percivall saw that his will was proved on April 25, 1611 (VI&A 590–591).

Henry Ravens: Henry Ravens, who set sail for Virginia in the fleet that brought the 3rd Supply of Jamestown settlers, was shipwrecked in Bermuda with Sir Thomas Gates and Sir George Summers. Afterward, Ravens, cape merchant Thomas Whittingham, and six sailors set out for Virginia in a longboat outfitted like a pinnace. They may have been lost at sea, for they never were heard from again. However, Powhatan later claimed that his people killed Ravens and his men (VI&A 592).

Roger Rawling (Rawlings): In 1658 Roger Rawling witnessed a legal document in Surry County, where he seems to have been living. On August 19, 1660, when he testified before Surry County's monthly court in a suit involving slanderous remarks that Bartholomew Owen had made about Captain George Jordan, he indicated that he was age 26. A year later Rawling and Fortune Mills guaranteed a debt that her husband owed. On September 4, 1677, he served as the attorney of Samuel Firth, a merchant who in July 1685 was renting the late Colonel Thomas Swann's tavern in urban Jamestown (Surry County Deed Book 1652–1663:114, 166, 168; Order Book 1671–1691:159; Deeds, Wills &c. 1687–1694:28).

Edward Rawlins: Edward Rawlins, who became an indentured servant with the understanding that he would be apprenticed to a ship's carpenter, was assigned to innkeeper Richard Lawrence of urban Jamestown. By March 6, 1675, Lawrence had turned Rawlins over to Arnold Cassinett of Jamestown, who commenced using him as a common servant. Therefore, Rawlins went to court to protest what he considered a violation of his contract. The General Court's justices agreed and ordered Cassinett to free Rawlins immediately and give him his freedom dues. During the late 1680s and early 1690s, Edward Rawlins was gunner of the fort in Jamestown (MCGC 407; EJC I:187, 255).

Mr. and Mrs. Nicholas Rayberd (Rainberte, Rayneberde, Raynbeare, Reyneberd): Nicholas Rayberd, an indentured servant employed by Captain William Eppes, came to Virginia in 1624 on the *Swann*. On November 23, 1624, when he was in Jamestown, he testified against Captain John Martin. When a muster was made of the colony's inhabitants in early 1625, Rayberd was identified as a 22-year-old servant in Eppes's household on the Eastern Shore. When Eppes obtained a patent for some land in February 1626, he used Rayberd's headright and indicated that he had paid for his transportation to Virginia. In 1633 Nicholas Rayberd appeared in the court for Accomack/Northampton, where he admitted that his taxes were in arrears. In May 1635, while he was in England, he reportedly received some tobacco from merchant Richard Bennett. Rayberd returned to Virginia and in January 1637 sued one of his own debtors. In November 1637 Farmar Jones told the justices of the Accomack/Northampton court that shortly before Rayberd died, his wife inquired what he intended to bequeath to her. He reportedly admitted that he had nothing to leave her until he had satisfied his debt to Obedience Robins I (VI&A 592).

Wassill (Wassell, Watsall) Rayner (Raynor, Royner): Wassill Rayner, a distiller, set sail for Virginia in 1619. During the mid-1620s he and his wife, Joan, were indentured servants in the urban Jamestown household of merchant Richard Stephens. The Rayner couple testified in court that John Bath, a gentleman and leather-seller who became ill while living in the Stephens home, had asked his host to serve as his administrator. On July 15, 1631, Wassill Rayner was identified as a Virginia planter when he joined others in asking for relief from the customs fees that Virginians paid on exported tobacco (VI&A 594).

Edward Read (Reade, Reed, Reid): Edward Read reportedly served as a burgess for Accomack County and attended only one session, which ran from November 10 to December 22, 1682 (LEO 45). It should be noted, however, that his name is not included in extant assembly records or other documents generated by the Virginia colony's government. Likewise, his name is not included in records generated by the Eastern Shore's court justices. In 1662 someone secured a patent near Edward Read's spring in New Kent County (PB 5:373).

* * *

George Read (Reade) I: George Read I came to Virginia with the reinstated Governor John Harvey in 1637 and shared his dwelling in urban Jamestown. After Harvey was removed from office, Read, who anticipated Secretary Richard Kemp's departure, asked his brother, Robert, to use his influence to see that he was named Secretary of the Colony. In 1640 Read succeeded Kemp and shortly thereafter married Elizabeth, the daughter of Nicholas Martiau of Elizabeth City and later Chiskiack. In 1649 Richard Kemp bequeathed a 50-acre tract in James City County, the Barren Neck, to George Read, who then lived on the property. In 1648 Read was made clerk of the Council of State, and in 1658 he became a councilor. He served as a burgess for James City County in 1649 and for York in 1656. By 1654 he had begun speculating in real estate in the Northern Neck. When Read made his will in September 1670, he left his home tract, the Martiau land in York County, to his eldest sons, George II and Robert, with reversionary rights to sons Francis and Benjamin. However, the decedent's wife, Elizabeth, had

life-rights in the property. George Read I died in 1671. In August 1691 reversionary heir Benjamin Read and his wife, Lucy, who were residents of Gloucester County, sold 50 acres of their York County land, the acreage that became Yorktown (VI&A 594; STAN 38; LEO 27, 33; Westmoreland County Deeds, Wills, Patents &c. 1653–1659:95a–96; York County Deeds, Orders, Wills 9 [1691–1694]:64–68).

Robert Read (Reade): Robert, the son of George I and Elizabeth Martiau Read, inherited half of his late father's 850-acre plantation near Yorktown. In April 1684 he patented 350 acres of land that straddled the line between York and Warwick counties. Then, in October 1688 he laid claim to 305 acres on the south side of Back Creek in York County. Read served as a burgess for York County in 1688 and in 1692 began serving as a justice in the county court. He married Mary, the daughter of John Lilly. When quitrent rolls were compiled in 1704, Robert Read was credited with 750 acres. The will he made on December 30, 1712, was proved on March 16, 1713. His widow's will, proved on November 20, 1722, named their children (LEO 49; PB 7:353, 680; York County Deeds, Orders, Wills 1:241–243; Orders, Wills &c. 14:241–242; 16:165; SMITH 74; DOR 2:508).

* * *

Humfrey Read (Reade, Reede): Humfrey Read—who was shipwrecked in Bermuda with Sir Thomas Gates and part of the 3rd Supply of settlers—told Gates that Stephen Hopkins had tried to pervert the Scriptures and use them for his own purposes, in disobedience of the law (VI&A 595).

James Read (Reade): James Read, a blacksmith, was one of the first Jamestown settlers. Sometime after September 17, 1607, then-president of the colony John Ratcliffe alias Sicklemore struck him. He retaliated by returning the blow. For this affront to authority, Read was sentenced to hanging. He was reprieved and in 1608 accompanied Captain John Smith on a voyage to explore the Chesapeake Bay. Later in the year Smith sent him overland to Werowocomoco, on the York River, to build a house for Powhatan. Smith then referred to him as a soldier (VI&A 595).

John Reding (Redding, Reading): John Reding died in Jamestown sometime after April 1623 but before February 16, 1624 (VI&A 596).

Stephen Reeks: Stephen Reeks ran afoul of the law in 1640 by insulting the king's religion (HEN I:552). This raises the possibility that Reeks had Puritan leanings.

Randall (Randal, Randol) Revell (Revel, Reavell): On January 13, 1634, when Randall Revell testified before Accomack's justices to verify the authenticity of William Batts' nuncupative will, he said that he was age 20. When Revell and another man appeared in court the following year, they reported that they had heard Henry Charleton call clergyman Mr. Cotton a "black cotted raskoll" and threaten to kick him over the palisades. When Randall Revell testified again in September 1636, he gave his age as 28. He returned to court to testify in a lawsuit in February 1645 and used a signature mark to endorse his deposition. Later in the year he and three other men certified the accuracy of the late Philip Chapman's inventory. Revell occasionally served as an attorney, and he frequently performed appraisals. In July 1645 he went to court in an attempt to collect a debt. He was among those who in March 1651 signed a document pledging loyalty to the Commonwealth government. On January 16, 1656, Revell was among those witnessing the will made by Wackawamp, then the native emperor of the Eastern Shore. He served as a burgess for Northampton County in 1658. Although Randall Revell's patents seem to have been lost or destroyed, in 1652 and 1654 his son, Edward Revell, repatented his 1,500 acres on the south side of the Pungoteague River, and during the 1670s and 1680s claimed some acreage of his own (LEO 34; AMES I:9, 28, 58–59; 2:405, 418, 434, 445–448; PB 3:12, 170; 6:392; 7:524; MARSHALL 23–25, 30, 34, 57).

Charles [Christopher?] Reynolds: According to minutes generated by the clerk of the assembly, Charles Reynolds served as a burgess for Isle of Wight County when the legislature convened on November 25, 1652 (LEO 30; STAN 69; HEN I:373). However, because his name does not appear in extant land patents, Isle of Wight County court documents, or in other official sources, the possibility exists that his first name was misspelled. If so, the burgess may have been Christopher Reynolds, a prominent Isle of Wight citizen who arrived in Virginia in 1622 and died in 1654 (VI&A 597; BODIE 521).

John Reynolds (Rennolds): John Reynolds, a husbandman, arrived in Jamestown in 1619 and was one of the Virginia Company's servants or tenants. He died in the capital city sometime after April 1623 but before February 16, 1624 (VI&A 598).

Nathaniel Reynolds (Reignolds, Reighnolds): In 1623 Nathaniel Reynolds served on a jury and as a James City Parish churchwarden, indications that he was a respected member of the community. In February 1624 he was identified as a gentleman living in urban Jamestown in the home of mariner and vice admiral John Pountis. Reynolds was summoned to court in March 1625 because his sow had damaged corn belonging to another resident of Jamestown Island. In 1626 the General Court noted that Nathaniel Reynolds had appraised the estate of the Rev. Richard Buck, who died in late 1623 or early 1624 (VI&A 598).

Nicholas Reynolds: On April 24, 1623, Nicholas Reynolds, who had come to Virginia on the *Margaret and John*, sent a petition to the governor (VI&A 598).

Richard Richards: Richard Richards came to Virginia in 1620, and within a year he and a partner, Richard Dolphenby, had purchased a 100-acre tract at Paces Paines and sold it to Isabell Pace Perry. In June 1624 Richards testified that he did not intend to marry Mara Buck, one of the late Rev. Richard Buck's orphans and a resident of Jamestown Island. In January 1625 Richards and his partner were living at Burrows Hill, just west of Paces Paines. By 1632 he had been elected a burgess for the territory that extended from Captain William Perry's plantation (at Swann's Point) to Hog Island. In 1640 he served on behalf of the settlers living on the upper side of the James River, between Farley's Neck and Wareham's Ponds. Richards was still serving as a James City County burgess in 1642. In 1648 Richard Richards patented a 350-acre tract he called Littletown (Little Town) on the upper side of the James River, to the east of Kingsmill Neck, in close proximity to Farley's Neck and Wareham's Ponds. By 1660 the Richards patent had been absorbed into Thomas Pettus I's plantation, Littletown (VI&A 599; LEO 10–11, 18, 20; NUG I:80–81, 166, 178).

John Richardson (Richason, Richinson, Recheson): John Richardson was a Virginia merchant who in 1677 was involved in importing cloth. On July 4, 1683, he witnessed a codicil to the will made by Adam Keeling of Lower Norfolk County, and in 1688 he patented a large tract of land near Machepongo Bay in what was then Lower Norfolk County. Later, he patented some land in

Lynnhaven Parish. In November 1689 Richardson and his wife, Ann, sold some of their land in what became Princess Anne County, but in 1695 he laid claim to 128 acres of oceanfront land in the same vicinity. Richardson served as a Princess Anne County burgess and attended the 1691–1692 sessions of the assembly and the sessions that were held from March 2 to April 3 and October 10 to November 18, 1693. In January 1695 he was among those who inventoried the late Francis Land's estate, and he appeared in court from time to time, usually witnessing legal documents. Richardson made his will on August 20, 1714, and died sometime prior to October 4th. He made bequests to his sons, Thomas and John; to his daughter, Ann, the wife of Francis Morse; and to his grandsons Richardson and John Jackson Morse. The testator failed to mention his wife, which suggests that she was deceased (LEO 50, 52–53; Lower Norfolk County Wills and Deeds Book 4:155; Princess Anne County Deed Book 1:11, 75, 263; 2:102; 3:8; SR 5586, 5590; PB 7:677, 694; 8:424).

William Richardson: Mrs. Sarah Richardson, the widow of William Edwards I of Surry County, married William Richardson. He died sometime prior to June 22, 1670, and by May 1671 Sarah had married Major Theophilus Hone, a resident of urban Jamestown (MCGC 223, 262). The Hone couple would have been residing in the capital city at the time of Bacon's Rebellion.

Richard Ricks (Rix, Reeks, Reekes, Reakes): Sometime prior to August 5, 1658, Richard Ricks purchased from Major Richard Webster a structure known as "the country house" (a building that had been erected with public funds) and the lot on which it stood. When Ricks died, the house and lot descended to his son, John, a minor. The property was entrusted to the care of the late Richard Ricks' widow, Elizabeth, who served as the boy's legal guardian. On August 5, 1658, when Edward Hill and his wife disposed of their interest in Richard Kemp's brick house, the Kemp dwelling was described as being next door to Mrs. Ricks' house. Plats made by surveyors John Underhill in 1664 and John Soane in 1681 suggest strongly that the "country house" and the brick house William Sherwood built on its ruins were in the immediate vicinity of buildings that have been excavated by archaeologists. Sometime after August 5, 1658, but before October 17, 1660, Richard Ricks' widow, Elizabeth, who had married Edmund Shipdam, got the General Court's permission to sell her late husband's prop-

erty, which she held in trust for his son, John Ricks. The Shipdams indicated that the house was in disrepair and that the estate the orphan stood to inherit would be devalued if the property were kept. The court justices agreed, and shortly thereafter Elizabeth and Edmund Shipdam sold "the country house" and lot to John Phipps, who already owned some neighboring property. In February 1679 Mrs. Elizabeth Shipdam, who was deceased, was identified as the mother of Elizabeth Moseby and John Ricks (AMB 6, 7, 10, 134, 135–136; Charles City County Orders 1677–1679:353).

William Ricks: On September 20, 1686, William Ricks witnessed a legal document for William Sherwood (AMB 37).

Sara Riddall (Ruddell): In February 1624 Sara Riddall was living in the household of Mr. and Mrs. Hickmore in urban Jamestown and may have been a servant (VI&A 600).

Peter Ridley (Ridely): In September 1639 Peter Ridley patented 200 acres of land in Martin's Hundred, near the boundary line between James City and Charles River (later, York) counties. He served as a burgess for James City County in 1645 and attended the assembly sessions held in 1645–1646 and 1647–1648 (STAN 64; HEN I:289; LEO 23–24, 26; PB 1:672). Although no further information has come to light on Ridley, a Peter Rigby (Rigbye, Riggby), perhaps the same man, patented 100 acres in Charles River (later, York) County in December 1639 and acreage in the Middle Peninsula and Northern Neck during the 1640s and 1650s. Rigby, whose wife was named Dorothy, was literate. His name appeared from time to time in York County's records during the 1640s and early 1650s (PB 1:731, 811; 3:269, 384; York County Deeds, Orders, Wills 1:82; Court Orders 2 [1646–1648]:273, 355; 1 [1648–1652]:169).

Joseph Ring I: Joseph Ring I, a merchant who owned some land in Warwick County on the east side of Skiffs Creek, began serving as a York County burgess in 1684. He was paid "for mending Armes" for the colony and in 1691 stored part of the county's supply of powder. He played an active role in community life and seems to have been an intelligent and respected citizen. In 1691 he was called upon to inventory the estate of the widow of Edward Digges of Bellfield, and in 1692 he witnessed the will of Colonel Nathaniel Bacon of the Kings Creek plantation. In 1686 he made repairs to the French Ordinary, the tavern in which York

County's court justices convened for official meetings, and he served on the Committee of Public Claims when the last statehouse was built in Jamestown. Ring, who was returned to the assembly and represented York County in the sessions that were held in 1691–1692, and 1693, was present in 1691 when a petition was sent to King William and Queen Mary asking them to establish a college in Virginia. He also was present when a town-founding act was passed in 1691, which led to the establishment of Yorktown, and afterward he became a town trustee. Sometime prior to 1688 Joseph Ring I married Sarah, the daughter of Edmund and Mary Kemp Berkeley. His connection with the Berkeley family would have enhanced his political capital. His widowed mother-in-law, Mary Kemp Berkeley, went on to marry John Mann of nearby Gloucester County. Although Joseph Ring I was recommended for appointment to the Council of State in 1699, he was passed over by his superiors in the Mother Country. When he prepared his will on December 3, 1698, he conveyed to his wife, Sarah, life-rights in the dwelling and plantation they then occupied. Ring died on February 26, 1703, at age 57, leaving a widow and young children. A detailed inventory made of his estate on August 24, 1704, attests to his wealth. The widowed Sarah Berkeley Ring married Joseph Walker, a Yorktown merchant (LEO 47, 51, 53; NUG II:255; PB 7:243; York County Deeds, Orders, Wills [1702–1706]:105–107, 277–280; MCGC 197, 202; JHB 1659–1693:188, 191–198, 245, 254, 347, 353, 357, 493; EJC I:185).

William Riscom: In July 1707 William Riscom was occupying a 75-acre leasehold on the Governor's Land, near Powhatan Mill (AMB 77).

Robert: When writing about life in the colony in 1616, Captain John Smith made reference to Robert, a Polish man, who would have been one of the first Jamestown settlers (VI&A 601).

Robert (Native American): On February 19, 1678, the justices of Northumberland County ordered those who had possession of guns that belonged to the Wicococomoco Indian Town's inhabitants to return them to Robert, the town's Great Man or leader (Northumberland County Order Book 1678–1698:23).

Robert: On February 15, 1768, when an inventory was made of the late Richard Ambler's slaves at his quarter called Powhatan, an adult male slave named Robert was living

there (York County Wills and Inventories 21:386–391).

James Roberts: James Roberts, a servant, was living in Ensign William Spence's household on Jamestown Island on February 16, 1624 (VI&A 602).

William Roberts: On March 14, 1672, William Roberts acknowledged a debt to the estate of John (Jonathan) Newell, a Jamestown merchant and landowner, doing so in the presence of Elizabeth Newell, the decedent's administratrix (MCGC 328). Roberts may have been the same individual who during the early 1650s and 1660s invested in some land in Gloucester and Northumberland counties (PB 3:160; 4:180, 497, 533).

John Robins (Robbins, Robyns, Robinson) II: In April 1639 John Robins II, who came to Virginia with his father, John Robins I, in 1623, secured a patent for 300 acres on the west side of the Chickahominy River, above Pease Hill. Simultaneously he patented 200 acres on the Back River in Elizabeth City County, adjacent to some land he already owned. In 1642 and 1645 he began acquiring property on the Middle Peninsula in what became Gloucester County, securing 2,000 acres that abutted Mobjack Bay and the Ware River, an area that became known as Robins Neck. In 1649 he patented 400 acres on the north side of the Rappahannock River. Robins served as a burgess for Elizabeth City County in 1646 and 1649 and was a county justice in 1652. When he prepared his will on November 22, 1655, he devised his land to his son, Thomas I, and named grandsons Benjamin, Thomas II, and William Robins as reversionary heirs, noting that another grandson (John) was deceased (VI&A 603–604; LEO 25, 27; PB 1:119, 638, 833; 2:43, 206; NEAL 75, 130). Burgess John Robins may have been related to the John Robins who came to Virginia in 1625 at Captain William Eppes's expense and settled on the Eastern Shore in what became Northampton County (PB 1 Pt. 1:49).

* * *

Obedience Robins I: In January 1628 Obedience Robins I, a surgeon and resident of the Eastern Shore, testified in court. In March 1630 he began serving as a burgess for Accomack County and by 1632 had become a commissioner of the local court and a vestryman. Two years later he became the county's deputy lieutenant. Sometime after September 10, 1630, probably around 1634, he married Grace, Edward Waters' widow. When Robins testified before Accomack County's justices in September 1636, he gave his age as 35 or thereabouts. In 1642 he and John Wilkins hired millwright Anthony Lynney to build a windmill and install the ironwork it required. Robins' stubborn refusal to issue warrants for the collection of his parish's church taxes raises the possibility that he had Puritan leanings. He served as an Accomack County burgess in 1640 and 1642 and represented Northampton County in 1652. He began serving on the Council of State in 1655 during the Commonwealth era and held office until 1660. He made a nuncupative will, which was presented to the county court on December 30, 1662. Major William Waters, who transcribed Robins' final words, said that the testator had wanted his estate to be divided among his wife and children. Robins wanted his wife, Grace, to have life-rights in the estate and said that his younger son, Obedience Robins II, was to have the 900 acres on which John Daniel then resided. The testator asked Major Waters (his stepson) and Captain William Andrews (his son-in-law) to assist the widowed Grace Robins in settling the estate (VI&A 602; LEO xxi, 9, 18, 20, 22, 29–30; STAN 37; MCGC 159, 504; NUG I:84, 152, 224–225, 401, 407; AMES 1:1, 4–6, 18, 39, 44, 57, 59, 66; 2:39–41, 54, 86, 88, 141, 154–155; 453; PB 1:539; 2:364; MARSHALL 70; DOR 2:702–703).

John Robins: John Robins, the son of Obedience Robins and his wife, the former Grace O'Neill Waters, was born in Northampton County during the mid-1630s and was the Robins couple's eldest son. Captain John Robins, like his father, gradually rose in prominence and, at the time of Bacon's Rebellion, was a staunch supporter of Governor William Berkeley. In February 1677 Robins was appointed Northampton County's high sheriff, and less than a decade later, he was given the responsibility of maintaining a register of patents on the king's behalf. He served as a burgess for Northampton County in 1691–1692. When a list of quitrents was compiled in 1704, Major John Robins was credited with 1,180 acres in Northampton County and 2,700 acres in Accomack. Robins, who had married Esther Littleton, was survived by eight children (Obedience II, John, Edward, Thomas, Littleton, Esther, Grace, and Elizabeth) and seven grandchildren, whom he named in his December 5, 1707, will, which was proved on May 28, 1709. The testator's wife, Esther, seems to have predeceased him (LEO 50; DOR 2:703–704; Northampton County

Deeds, Wills &c. 1655–1657:22–24; 1658–1666: 179; Order Book 10 [1674–1679]:161–162; Will Book 19:27; PB 3:251; 4:541; 6:435, 541; 8:168, 242–243; SR 3457; MARSHALL 184).

* * *

Christopher Robinson: Christopher Robinson, who was born in England, immigrated to Virginia and eventually settled at Hewick in Middlesex County. His name began appearing in Middlesex records in 1673, at which time he was identified as a lieutenant colonel of the militia. In June 1675 the colony's deputy secretary, Philip Ludwell I, recommended Robinson as clerk of the Middlesex County court. Robinson represented Middlesex County in the assembly sessions that were held in 1680–1682, 1685–1686, and 1691–1692. In 1686 he served as the attorney of British merchant John Jeffreys, who was pursuing a debtor in Middlesex County. Later in the year he was appointed Middlesex's coroner. In April 1692 Robinson patented 959 acres on the south side of the Rappahannock River in Middlesex County. Later, he and another man patented 3,288 acres in Essex County. Records on file in the British Archives reveal that much of Christopher Robinson's income was derived from the slave trade. During the 1680s and early 1690s, he served as a representative or factor of John and Jeffrey Jeffreys, prominent British merchants who were associated with the Royal African Company and exported large numbers of Africans to Virginia. He served as an executor of Richard Perrott I of Middlesex, and in 1690 he and his wife, Catherine, the widow of Robert Beverley I, served as the decedent's co-executors. In 1691, while Robinson was a Middlesex County justice, he served as a trustee of the town laid out on the land of Ralph Wormeley II, the community that became known as Urbanna. Robinson was named to the Council of State and became Secretary of the Colony, holding office in 1692–1693. In September 1692, when the colony's statehouse was being rebuilt, Robinson was involved in redesigning the Secretary's office. Like other members of the council, he was supposed to build a house in Jamestown. Robinson then owned part of the land associated with Powhatan Plantation in James City County. He died in Virginia in early 1693, and on March 6, 1693, his will was proved in Middlesex County's monthly court. As late as 1697 his executors were still attempting to settle his estate (EJC I:251; STAN 21, 42; LEO 45, 48–50; Middlesex County Order Book 1673–1680:3, 32; 1680–

1694:244, 257, 338, 373, 477, 515, 565, 613; Lancaster County Order Book 1696–1702:24; PB 8:221; 9:651; SR 5580, 5754, 5873, 5874). The Colonial Williamsburg Foundation owns a collection of rare documents known as the Robinson Papers, records that contain genealogical information.

James Robinson: James Robinson came to Virginia in 1621 as an indentured servant. Court testimony taken in 1629 indicates that William Spencer of Jamestown Island was entitled to use Robinson as a headright. When Spencer patented some land in Warresqueak three years later, he used Robinson's headright and indicated that he had paid Mr. Weston, a merchant, for his passage (VI&A 603).

John Robinson: John Robinson, a gentleman and investor in the Virginia Company of London, arrived in Virginia in 1607 in the first group of Jamestown settlers. He joined Captain John Smith in exploring the Chickahominy River and, according to Smith, was slain by the Indians while sleeping beside a canoe (VI&A 603).

Tully Robinson: In November 1685 Tully Robinson patented a tract of land on the south branch of the Elizabeth River in Lower Norfolk County, as well as 350 acres in Lynnhaven Parish, acreage that extended toward the North River. He served as an Accomack County burgess in 1699 and would have been in office when the colony's capital city moved from Jamestown to Williamsburg. When Richard Robinson of Northampton County made his will in 1695, he designated his kinsman Tully Robinson as a trustee. In 1712 another kinsman, Benjamin Robinson, bequeathed Tully his spectacles. By February 1703 Tully Robinson was a captain in the militia and had married Sarah, the daughter of John West, a prominent Eastern Shore landowner and Edmund Scarborough II's son-in-law. In 1706 Robinson and his brother-in-law, Jonathan West, patented 500 acres in Accomack County. When John West made his will in 1719, he asked his son-in-law Tully Robinson and two other men to assist his wife. Robert Howsen also remembered Robinson in his will. On November 1, 1723, Colonel Tully Robinson made his will, which was proved on August 5, 1724. He designated his wife as his executrix but failed to reveal her name. He made bequests to his son, William Robinson, and to his daughters, two of whom (Mary and Ann) were unmarried. Robinson's married daughters included West Smith, Scarburgh Wise, Sarah Smith,

Susanna McClenahan (McClanahan), and Elizabeth Smith. Grandson William Robinson Smith, the son of Elizabeth and John Smith, also was named as an heir (LEO 59; Accomack County Wills &c. 1692–1715:317; Wills, Deeds &c. 1715–1729:558; PB 7:483–484; 9:716; MARSHALL 151, 206, 225, 230).

William Robinson II: William Robinson II, a well-to-do planter, served as a burgess for Lower Norfolk County and attended the assembly sessions held in 1684 and 1685–1686. He was the son of William Robinson I, who brought him to Virginia sometime prior to 1653 and went on to become a Lower Norfolk County constable. In 1652 William Robinson I patented 500 acres along the Eastern Branch of the Elizabeth River, and two years later he joined Cornelius Johnson in patenting 400 acres on the lower side of the Potomac River. During the early 1680s William Robinson II, who inherited his late father's property, began patenting land along the Elizabeth River. After Lower Norfolk's boundary lines were adjusted and the county's name was changed, Captain William Robinson II began representing newly formed Norfolk County in the assembly meetings held in 1691–1692 and 1695–1696. He died before the opening of the second session of the 1695–1696 assembly (LEO 47–48, 50, 54; Lower Norfolk County Wills and Deeds Book C:7, 48; 5:12, 46; PB 3:111, 180, 284; 4:498; 5:54, 221, 366; 6:92, 402; 7:139, 286, 348, 410).

Christopher Rodes: Christopher Rodes, a laborer, arrived in Jamestown in January 1608 as part of the 1st Supply of new settlers (VI&A 604).

Roger Rodes (Redes, Roeds): Roger Rodes, an indentured servant employed by a Mr. Fitzjeffrey, arrived in Jamestown in 1623. In early 1624 he was living in Thomas Allnutt's household in the Neck O'Land behind Jamestown Island, but by January 1625 he had moved to urban Jamestown, where he was a servant in the Allnutt home. On March 7, 1626, the General Court added an additional year of service onto Rodes' contract with Allnutt because he had wagered a year of his time and lost (VI&A 605).

William Rodes (Roods): Diarist George Percy indicated that William Rodes, one of the first Virginia planters, died in Jamestown on August 27, 1607 (VI&A 605).

Richard Rodgers (Rogers): By 1683 Richard Rodgers, the brother of Northumberland County justice William Rodgers, began taking a role in public life. In 1685, after William was no longer a member of Northumberland's monthly court, Richard began serving as a justice. Shortly after his appointment, he and some of his fellow justices dissented from a majority decision, a somewhat controversial move. Like many of his peers, Richard Rogers took part in litigation, alternately as a plaintiff and as a defendant. In 1692 he was elected to the assembly, representing Northumberland County. However, John Downing and William Jones successfully contested Rodgers' and Richard Flint II's election and were chosen in their place. By June 1699 Richard Rodgers was dead, at which time Christopher Neale and his wife, Jane, were serving as the decedent's surviving executors (LEO 52; Northumberland County Order Book 1678–1698:187, 204, 266, 314–315; 1699–1700:29, 40, 101).

John Rodis: According to the minutes of the General Court for March 2, 1629, John Rodis became indebted to Abraham Porter of Jamestown Island. However, Porter forgave Rodis's debt when on his deathbed (VI&A 605).

Edward Roecroft alias Stallings (see Edward Stallings alias Roecroft)

Willimot Rogerman: On October 25, 1670, the General Court was informed that Willimot Rogerman, one of Jamestown lot owner Thomas Ludwell's maidservants, was pregnant (MCGC 238).

Edward Rogers (Rogeres): Edward Rogers, a carpenter, arrived in Jamestown in 1623. When a muster was made of the colony's inhabitants in early 1625, he was living on the Eastern Shore in the household of William Eppes, where he was a servant (VI&A 605).

John Rogers (Rodgers): John Rogers, a planter, was identified as a James City burgess in February 1645. He probably represented the territory that in 1652 became Surry County, for he does not seem to have owned land in urban Jamestown or on the upper side of the James River. Rogers, who in 1659 inherited some hogs and wearing apparel from Arthur Jordan of Surry County, participated in a coroner's jury that was impaneled there in 1662. He patented 200 acres in Surry County in May 1666. He or perhaps a descendant may have begun speculating in real estate, for during the 1650s a John Rogers patented a large tract of York County land on Skimino Creek and began claiming

land in Northumberland County (STAN 64; HEN I:289; LEO 23; PB 3:104, 227, 277; 4:61, 204, 542, 569, 641; 5:641; SR 3499b; Surry County Record Book 1:141, 197, 314, 374; Order Book 2:).

* * *

John Rolfe: John Rolfe and his pregnant wife left England in 1609 in the 3rd Supply of settlers. They were shipwrecked in Bermuda, where Mrs. Rolfe gave birth to a daughter they named Bermuda. When the infant was christened in February 1610, Captain Christopher Newport and William Strachey served as witnesses; the child and her mother died a short time later. John Rolfe reached Virginia in May 1610. During the next few years he conducted agricultural experiments that led to the development of a palatable and marketable strain of tobacco, the colonists' money crop. Rolfe, a member of the Council of State, served as the colony's secretary of state from 1614 to 1619 and wrote an account of life in Virginia. Around April 1, 1614, he married the Indian princess Pocahontas, who had been taken hostage by the colonists in 1611, then converted to Christianity and adopted the English name Rebecca. In May 1616 the Rolfes and their infant son, Thomas, set sail for England, where Pocahontas was introduced at court and treated as a native princess, and encountered her old friend Captain John Smith. Pocahontas died of consumption (tuberculosis) in March 1617, while she and her husband and child were in Gravesend awaiting the ship that would take them back to Virginia. Rolfe entrusted his son, Thomas, to the care of his brother, Henry, and returned to Virginia. Within a year or two the twice-widowed John Rolfe married Joan (Joane), Captain William Peirce's daughter. The Rolfes resided in urban Jamestown, probably on one of the two parcels that Joan's parents owned. The couple and their daughter, Elizabeth, who was born around 1621, were sharing a home when John and his father-in-law, William Peirce, went to Old Point Comfort and encountered Virginia's first Africans. When Rolfe made his will in March 1622, he was living in urban Jamestown, although he owned land on the lower side of the James River on Mulberry Island, and at Bermuda Hundred. He died sometime prior to October 1622, having left his wife, Joan, an interest in his land on Mulberry Island. Sometime prior to 1623, Joan married Captain Roger Smith of Jamestown and moved into his home. She was living there with daughter Elizabeth Rolfe during the mid-1620s (VI&A 606–608).

Rebecca Rolfe (Mrs. John Rolfe). See Pocahontas (Pocohunta, Matoaka, Rebecca) (Native American)

Thomas Rolfe: Thomas Rolfe, who was born in 1615, was the son of John Rolfe and his wife, Pocahontas (Rebecca), and accompanied them on their May 1616 trip to England. After Pocahontas's death, John Rolfe returned to Virginia, leaving little Thomas in England to be reared by his uncle, Henry Rolfe. When John Rolfe prepared his will in March 1622, he left son Thomas 400 acres of land on the lower side of the James River, acreage that included the site of a fort that Captain John Smith had built in 1608. In 1618 Virginia Company officials heard a rumor that the Indians had given their country to Thomas Rolfe and were reserving it for him until he came of age. When he returned to Virginia, he married a woman with whom he produced a daughter named Jane. In 1635 Thomas Rolfe was listed among the headrights of his step-grandfather, Captain William Peirce, and sometime prior to March 1640 he took possession of his father's land on the lower side of the James River. On October 6, 1646, Rolfe agreed to build a fortified stronghold or blockhouse at Moysenac, on the upper side of Diascund Creek's mouth within what is now New Kent County. He promised to see that it was manned and maintained for three years, and in exchange he received 400 acres. Rolfe's fort, Fort James, was built where it could maintain surveillance over the Indians (VI&A 608).

* * *

William Rookings (Rookeings) I: On October 18, 1670, William Rookings I made a claim against the estate of John Newell, a Jamestown resident, seeking compensation for his funeral charges. Rookings became a follower of the rebel Nathaniel Bacon and commander of his loyalists in Surry County. During July 1676 he and his men seized Major Arthur Allen II's brick home in Surry, occupying the property for several months. On January 24, 1677, after the popular uprising was quelled, Rookings was tried in a court martial hearing at Green Spring and sentenced to death. However, he died on February 27, 1677, while imprisoned there. Rookings left behind two orphaned children, William II and Elizabeth. On September 2, 1679, Captain Nicholas Wyatt, the late William Rookings I's executor, was sued by Benjamin Harrison, an assignee of George Marable I of Jamestown (Surry County Deeds, Wills &c. 2 [1671–1684]:135; Order Book 1671–1691:262; MCGC 235, 455, 528; NEVILLE 70; DOR 3:38).

Thomas Roper: Thomas Roper, a gentleman, came to Jamestown in September 1623. A few months earlier he and George Fitz-Jeffry, who were planning to bring 100 people to Virginia, received a patent for some land in the colony. Roper became ill within months of his arrival and died on Jamestown Island sometime prior to February 16, 1624. When preparing his will, Roper bequeathed two of his male servants their freedom, noting that one was then in the employ of William Peirce of Jamestown. He bequeathed a pair of linen breeches to William Smith of Jamestown, and he left some money to the Rev. Haute Wyatt, whom he identified as the minister there. Roper's will was presented for probate in England on February 5, 1627 (VI&A 609).

William Roper: In June 1635 William Roper received a certificate that entitled him to two headrights. Two years later he received a patent, using the headrights of his wife and a manservant. His 150-acre plantation, in what was then Accomack County, was located on a relatively small neck of land then known as Aquasca or Aqusca, on Old Plantation Creek. Roper, who was a merchant, carried on a profitable trade in Chesapeake waters, often with Maryland colonists. He became a commissioner of Accomack County's monthly court in September 1636, and in 1637 he appraised Henry Charleton's estate and assisted in selling the late Mary Bibby's personal effects. Roper served as a burgess for Accomack County in 1637 and during the early 1640s continued to perform appraisals, witness wills, and carry out other public and private duties. In 1642 he began serving as a justice for Northampton County, the lower portion of what formerly had been Accomack. He was returned to the assembly in 1644 and attended on behalf of Northampton County. In 1645 he was among those who viewed the land occupied by Philip Taylor's plantation and the acreage that belonged to the Indians who lived on the opposite side of Mattawomes Creek. Captain William Roper died sometime prior to December 3, 1650, and was survived by his widow, the former Katheryn Graves, and a daughter (NUG I:46, 295, 418; AMES 1:xxxiv; 36, 58, 64, 71, 81, 89; 2:xiii, 56, 178; PB 1:375; 3:289; 4:538; 7:196; SR 4201e; MARSHALL 3, 8, 11–12, 14, 16, 19, 26; LEO 15, 22).

[No First Name] Rose: According to Captain John Smith, a male laborer whose surname was Rose arrived in Virginia in 1608 in the 2nd Supply. He would have lived in Jamestown (VI&A 610).

Edward Ross: On October 29, 1696, Lieutenant Edward Ross patented a lot in the western end of Jamestown Island. His patent enveloped a half-acre lot that John Phipps had claimed on May 4, 1661, and then deserted. Ross reportedly was living on the property at the time he received his patent and sometime prior to 1702 began operating a ferry from Jamestown to Swann's Point, in Surry County. During the early-to mid-1680s Ross summoned the burgesses to assembly meetings and the justices to the General Court by beating a drum at the appointed hour. He was still official drummer in 1693. Ross occasionally served as a government messenger and in 1696 carried some of the king's letters from Virginia to Maryland, Pennsylvania, New York, and Jersey. In 1696 he was asked to serve as the General Court's sergeant-at-arms, at a time when the James City County sheriff (who usually held that post) was engaged in a pay dispute.

By June 1695 Ross had been designated gunner of Jamestown's fortifications, which then consisted of a platform with "great guns," and he also was responsible for the colony's supply of ammunition. The fort was located in a swale to the south of Edward Ross's home lot, near the southwest corner of Edward Chilton's property. The military stores for which Ross was responsible were kept in a magazine or powder house, which according to the Rev. James Blair, stood "all alone without any Garrison to defend it" and was "a ready prey for any foreign or domestic enemy." Mid-nineteenth-century paintings by Robert Sully and his descriptive notes suggest that the small brick building stood upon a bluff overlooking the river, about 120 feet west of the fort, whereas an early-twentieth-century plat of the APVA (Preservation Virginia) property, which shows the powder magazine's ruins, indicates that it was near the southwest corner of a long brick row house. Ross served as the Jamestown fort's gunner until around 1708, and he performed related duties, such as having powder barrels rehooped and accounting for the military stores kept in Jamestown. When the French posed a threat to the colony around 1708, the military stores in Jamestown were moved to Williamsburg, which was then considered a safer location. Throughout the years Edward Ross was gunner of the Jamestown fort, he was proprietor of the ferry to Swann's Point. In 1703 he requested an increase in the fare

he was allowed to charge. On May 24, 1726, Edward Ross's widow, Sarah, who seems to have had life-rights in her late husband's property at the western end of Jamestown Island and in his ferrying concession, requested a rate increase for conveying people and horses across the James. When Sarah Ross died, her late husband's "lots or parcels . . . where the Ferry is now kept" descended to his reversionary heir, William Broadnax II (NUG III:8–9; PB 9:49; SAIN 14:132; 15:454; 17:51; 18:263; 21:310; HEN III:319; JHB 1660–1693:191; 1712–1726:411; Surry County Order Book 1691–1713:232; James City County Plat Book 2:6; LJC 143; CO 5/1308:150; 5/1309 ff 223–224; PERRY I:14; EJC I:331, 344–345, 349, 356, 410, 423; II:208, 276; III:13–14, 102, 202; AMB 53, 61, 97–98, 106–107; Stanard, "The House of Burgesses," 236; "Council Papers," 401).

Edmund Rossingham (Roffingham): Edmund Rossingham, Sir George Yeardley's nephew, arrived in Virginia in April 1619. He served as a burgess for Yeardley's plantation, Flowerdew Hundred, in the July–August 1619 assembly meeting. Eight years later he testified in court that in 1619 Governor Yeardley had dispatched him on a trading voyage within the Chesapeake Bay, and that in January 1620 Yeardley had given him a power of attorney when sending him to Newfoundland to trade. He also said that Yeardley had sent him to Holland in 1621 and 1623 with authorization to serve as his factor. While Rossingham was in England, he testified against Captain John Martin, one of Yeardley's detractors. After Sir George Yeardley's death in early November 1627, Rossingham sought to recover funds from his estate, compensation for services he had performed on the decedent's behalf. When administrator Ralph Yeardley refused to pay him, Rossingham sent a petition to the Privy Council, which ordered a payment of £200. Because Yeardley still refused to comply, Rossingham initiated a chancery suit (VI&A 611; LEO 3).

Lionell (Lyonell) Roulston (Rowlston, Rowlstone): Lionell Roulston came to Virginia in 1623, and in early 1625 he was living in Elizabeth City, where he was an indentured servant. By 1627 he had obtained his freedom. In 1629 Roulston was named a justice of Elizabeth City's monthly court, and he was elected a burgess for the corporation of Elizabeth City. He represented the York River plantations in the September 1632 and February 1633 sessions of the colony's assembly, an indication that he then owned property in what by 1634 had become Charles River or York County (VI&A 611; LEO 8, 11–12).

Claude Rouniere: Claude Rouniere married Joseph Chermaison's widow, Elizabeth, sometime prior to January 1713. On January 12, 1713, Rouniere indicated that he was functioning as Chermaison's executor when he disposed of the Glasshouse tract on the mainland adjacent to the Governor's Land and Jamestown Island (EJC II:339; AMB 78; NUG II:140).

Robert Rouse: On October 13, 1640, the General Court sentenced Robert Rouse and some other indentured servants to a whipping because they had failed to report some runaways. Rouse's time of service was to be extended by a year and he was to repay his master, who was responsible for his fine (MCGC 467).

[No First Name] Rouslie (Rowley?): In January 1638 Captain Samuel Mathews testified that in 1624 he had received some tobacco from Captain William Holmes of Jamestown. He admitted that when he accepted the tobacco, he still owed Holmes for the house he had purchased from him, a structure that formerly belonged to Holmes' brother (probably his brother-in-law or stepbrother), Rouslie (EAE 89; MCGC 143). Mathews may have been referring to William Rowley, a Jamestown resident who died prior to February 16, 1624.

William Rowland: In 1677 William Rowland and another Surry County resident sent a petition to the king's special commissioners, stating that they had been forced to support the rebel Nathaniel Bacon. They said that they had been imprisoned by Governor William Berkeley's men and had to promise to pay many thousand pounds of tobacco in order to obtain their freedom. During the 1670s and 1680s Rowland made numerous appearances in court, often to deal with his creditors. On March 20, 1701, Rowland was authorized to keep the ferry that ran from Crouches Creek to Jamestown (Surry County Order Book 1671–1691:86, 256, 279, 286, 291, 327–328, 385; 1691–1713:361; SR 661, 6618b).

William Rowley (Rowsley): In July 1622 William Rowley, a surgeon, and his wife, Elizabeth, set sail for Virginia with their ten servants. On April 3, 1623, Rowley informed Virginia Company officials that his wife was eager to return to England because there was much famine and death in urban Jamestown, where they lived. He added that his servants

were dead, that the colonists' livestock were depleted, and that they needed help from England. He indicated that he had purchased a cow for an exorbitant price and that the woods were very dangerous because of the Indians. William and Elizabeth Rowley died at their home in urban Jamestown sometime prior to February 16, 1624, and their maidservant also perished. On December 12, 1625, several people testified that Mrs. Rowley made a nuncupative will while she lay ill and that she had freed Anthony West, a servant (VI&A 614).

Thomas Rowse: In 1683 Thomas Rowse was in possession of a 20-acre leasehold in the Governor's Land (Soane 1683).

Sibil (Sybil, Sybill) Royall: In November 1623 Sybil Royall, a widow, testified in court about some items stored in a trunk at Dr. John Pott's house in urban Jamestown. When she died sometime prior to October 4, 1624, having made a nuncupative will, she left almost all of her belongings to the widowed Mary Ascam (Ascomb), a resident of Jamestown. On January 24, 1625, Mrs. Sibil Royall was listed among those who had died in Jamestown since February 16, 1624. Although the identity of Mrs. Royall's late husband is uncertain, he may have been Roger Royall, who perished at Bermuda Hundred in the March 1622 Indian attack (VI&A 615).

Roger Ruce (Reuse, Ruse): In February 1624 Roger Ruce was a servant in Captain William Peirce's household in urban Jamestown. By January 1625 he had moved to Captain Peirce's property on Mulberry Island (VI&A 615).

John Russell: John Russell, a gentleman and Virginia Company investor who came to Virginia in 1608 in the 2nd Supply of Jamestown settlers, learned how to fell trees and make clapboard. In January 1609 he and Captain John Smith went to Werowocomoco on the York River. The weather was very cold and Russell, who was obese, over-exerted himself onshore and became ill (VI&A 616).

Walter Russell: Walter Russell, a doctor of physic, reportedly arrived in Jamestown in 1608 in the 1st or 2nd Supply of new settlers. He explored the Chesapeake Bay with Captain John Smith and was co-author of an account of their travels. When Smith was wounded by a stingray, Dr. Russell gave him first aid and offered medical assistance (VI&A 617).

William Russell: William Russell, a gentleman who came to Virginia in 1608 in the 2nd Supply of colonists, was captured by Powhatan but escaped and returned to Jamestown (VI&A 617).

Ruth: When Dr. John Pott of urban Jamestown patented some land on September 1, 1632, he used the headright of a maidservant named Ruth (VI&A 617).

John Rutherford: On February 10, 1677, Governor William Berkeley issued a procla-

mation in which he named those who were exempt from the king's pardon on account of their role in Bacon's Rebellion. One of those named was John Rutherford, who was then incarcerated at Green Spring. He probably was the same individual who in 1655 had patented 500 acres on Ohoreek Swamp, a tributary of Upper Chippokes Creek. His acreage was on the lower side of the James River in what was then Charles City County and later Prince George (NEVILLE 61; SR 660; PB 4:40).

S

Robert Sabin (Sabyn, Savin): Robert Sabin came to Virginia in 1622 and during the mid-1620s was residing in Elizabeth City. He served as a burgess for Warresqueak (later, Isle of Wight) in 1629, 1630, and 1633 and in July 1631 was one of the Virginia planters who asked the king for relief from customs duties. When Sabin testified before the Admiralty Court in 1637, he identified himself as a 45-year-old tallow chandler from Maides Mill in Herts (VI&A 618; SR 4005; LEO 8–9, 12).

Rowland Sadler: Rowland Sadler, a planter, had become established in Virginia by 1638. On March 2, 1643, he served as a burgess for James City County, which until 1652 spanned both sides of the James River, encompassing what became Surry County. In November 1657 he witnessed a document that was signed in Surry County, which raises the possibility that he was associated with that area (STAN 63; HEN I:239; LEO 21; SR 3499b; Surry County Deed Book 1 [1652–1663]:108).

Sall (Sal): On February 15, 1768, an adult female named Sall was included in an inventory of the late Richard Ambler's slaves who lived on Jamestown Island or in his leasehold in the Governor's Land. In 1769 Sall and her child, Ned, were living on Jamestown Island and were part of the late Edward Ambler I's estate (York County Wills and Inventories 21:386–391; AMB-E).

John Salmon: In April 1622 John Salmon testified that he was one of the late Lord Delaware's servants and accompanied his lordship to Virginia in 1618. Salmon lived in Jamestown until 1619 when Deputy Gover-

nor Samuel Argall sent him to sea on the *Treasurer*. Salmon said that he disembarked in Bermuda and returned to England, although the *Treasurer* continued on to the West Indies (VI&A 620).

Joseph Salmon (Sammon): Sometime prior to 1636 Joseph Salmon acquired land on the south side of the Nansemond River in what became Isle of Wight County. In 1639–1640 he was a tobacco viewer for the territory between Redd Point and Pagan Point Creek. In 1642 Salmon served as a burgess for Isle of Wight County (LEO 20; NUG I:47, 55, 69; BODIE 172).

Elizabeth Salter: During the mid-1620s Elizabeth Salter, a child, was living in Captain Roger Smith's household in urban Jamestown. She may have been entrusted to the care of Smith's wife, Joan (Joane), who was John Rolfe's widow (VI&A 620).

John Saltman: John Saltman left England in July 1622 and came to Virginia with Edward Grindon (VI&A 620).

Salvadore (Native American): In March 1710 a group of indentured servants and enslaved blacks and Indians in James City, Isle of Wight, and Surry counties planned to make a break for freedom on Easter Sunday and vowed to overcome all opposition. One slave, a black man named Will, revealed the plot and the uprising was quelled. Among the slaves jailed for complicity in the plot were black men belonging to the Rev. James Blair, Philip Ludwell I, Sheriff Edward Jaquelin, George Marable II, John Broadnax, and ferryman and gunner Edward Ross, all of whom were associated with property in urban Jamestown. Although most of the accused insurgents were jailed in Jamestown, where they were interrogated and then released into their owners' custody "to receive correction," Jamy (a Broadnax slave) and Essex (a Ross slave) were implicated in the plot and therefore were detained. Virginia's governor later reported that two other slaves were executed so that "their fate will strike such a terror" that others would not attempt an uprising. The two men (one African American and one Indian) were hanged and then quartered. Salvadore, an Indian, was to be executed at Surry Courthouse on the first Tuesday in May. Surry County's justices were to decide where two of Salvadore's quarters were to be displayed, but they were to deliver his head and the remaining two quarters to the sheriff of James City County. The deceased Indian's head was displayed in a public place in the city of Williamsburg and one of his quarters was placed near the "great guns" in Jamestown, near the ferry landing. Salvadore's remaining quarter was to be delivered to the sheriff of New Kent County, who was to display it in a public place. These gruesome displays would have been a grim reminder of the consequences of rebellion (Stanard, "Philip Ludwell to Edward Jenings, 1709, in regard to a Negro Plot," 23–24; EJC III:234–236, 242–243). Salvadore's name raises the possibility that he had been brought to Virginia from the Caribbean or South America. During the 1950s National Park Service archaeologists found a quarter of a human skeleton in an abandoned well behind a brick row house on Jamestown's Back Street.

Sam: On February 15, 1768, when an inventory was made of the late Richard Ambler's slaves on Jamestown Island and on his leasehold in the Governor's Land, an adult male slave named Sam was listed. In 1769 a man named Sam was living on the Governor's Land and was attributed to the late Edward Ambler I's estate (York County Wills and Inventories 21:386–391; AMB-E).

William Sambage: William Sambage, a gentleman, arrived in Jamestown in 1608 as part of the 2nd Supply of new colonists (VI&A 620).

William Sampson alias Eden: Captain William Sampson alias Eden, a mariner and probable Virginia Company employee, made several trips to Virginia and in 1622 was authorized to trade with the Indians. In 1627 he brought some Indians from the Caribbean Islands to Jamestown. They escaped into the forest, and because they were considered dangerous, the General Court decided that they should be captured and hanged (VI&A 620).

Samuel: According to Captain John Smith, in 1608 Samuel, a "Dutchman" or Pole (actually, a German), who was one of the first colonists, gave some firearms to the Indians. Like two of his countrymen, Adam and Francis, Samuel was implicated in a plot to provide weapons and tools to the Indians. Smith said that in 1609 Samuel was living with Powhatan at Werowocomoco. Powhatan later had him killed (VI&A 621, HAI 304, 325, 485).

Edward Sanders (Saunders): On April 30, 1623, Edward Sanders testified that he had been in the colony for three years (VI&A 621).

John Sanders: On March 1, 1677, John Sanders, an alleged supporter of the rebel Nathaniel Bacon, was put on trial at Green Spring plantation, Governor William Berkeley's home. He entered a plea for mercy and was pardoned, although he was fined 2,000 pounds of tobacco. Sanders appears to have been from Isle of Wight County, where he owned land (MCGC 456, 528; PB 7:72).

Richard Sanders (Saunders): On August 28, 1644, Richard Sanders received a patent for a one-acre waterfront lot in the western end of Jamestown Island, near the site of the old block house. No building requirements were cited in his patent, which was near the isthmus that led to the mainland. His acreage also extended eastward into the marshland abutting the Back River. A man named Richard Sanders, perhaps the patentee, came to Virginia sometime prior to February 1624 and took up residence on the Governor's Land, where he was one of the governor's indentured servants (VI&A 622; PB 2:11; NUG I:154).

Roger Sanders (Saunders): On January 20, 1626, Roger Sanders, one of George Medcalf's servants, was living in Elizabeth City. By March 1628 he was free. By then he married Frances, the widow of ancient planter John Blore (Blower), and was identified as an Accomack County mariner when he obtained a 50-acre leasehold on Old Plantation Creek. By February 1632 Sanders had become a commissioner of Accomack's monthly court. He began serving as a burgess for Accomack in February 1633 but died sometime prior to October 20, 1634 (VI&A 622; MCGC 91, 95, 189; LEO 12; AMES 1:1–2, 27, 98, 118).

Edward Sanderson: Edward Sanderson, a merchant, purchased a parcel in the eastern end of Jamestown Island from John Norton, who also was a merchant. In February 1638 Sanderson patented 200 acres near Piney Point, on the east side of the Chickahominy River's mouth, and quickly enlarged his holdings to 2,000 acres. Part of the land he acquired had formerly belonged to Edward Morecroft (a merchant) and it was near the acreage of Major Robert Holt of Jamestown, who also was a merchant. These men's persistent interest in the Chickahominy River basin, an area that until the late 1640s had a substantial native population, raises the possibility that they were involved in Indian trade. Court testimony heard in 1638 by England's High Court of Admiralty involved a dispute between an English merchant and two Virginians: Jamestown merchant George Menefie and Edward Sanderson, who allegedly loaded 20 tons of tobacco aboard the ship *Dove* while it was in the colony. In 1650 Sanderson added to his holdings on the Chickahominy River in James City County, and by September 1665 he had amassed 3,000 acres in that area. Sanderson's 1665 patent cites his new acreage's proximity to Checkerous Creek and Governor Berkeley's trees, revealing that his 3,000 acres abutted Gordon's Creek and lay inland behind Green Spring plantation. In August 1663, when Sanderson filed a suit in Northumberland County's monthly court in an attempt to recover a debt, Thomas Brereton I, a former clerk of the General Court and a resident of Lancaster County, served as Sanderson's attorney. Brereton was still pursuing the case in early 1664, by which time the plaintiff was dead (PB 1:630; NUG I:101, 105, 112, 123, 205, 524, 527; Northumberland County Order Book 1652–1665: 358, 372; SR 8901).

Christopher Sandford: On January 3, 1625, Christopher Sandford was identified as one of the men who worked as a Jamestown Island cow-keeper after the March 1622 Indian attack (VI&A 622).

* * *

John Sandford (Sandiford, Sanford): In 1672 John Sandford witnessed the will made by James Johnson, a Lower Norfolk County planter who resided on the western branch of the Elizabeth River. He proved Thomas Axwell's will in 1678, Adam Keeling's in 1683, and Richard Chambers' in 1687. As time went on, Sandford acquired substantial quantities of land in Lower Norfolk County. He patented 1,680 acres on

Currituck Bay in September 1680, and in April 1688 he patented 1,517 acres near Currituck. He may have been related to the individual who in 1687 and 1703 patented two parcels of land in Middlesex County. Sandford became a burgess for Lower Norfolk County and attended the assembly sessions that were held in 1691–1692. He died intestate sometime prior to April 29, 1693, at which time administration of his estate was granted to his widow, Sarah. An inventory of the decedent's estate was presented to the justices of Princess Anne County on May 22, 1693 (LEO 50; Lower Norfolk County Record Book E:143; 4:41, 155; 5:26; PB 7:57, 582, 659; 9:533; Princess Anne County Deeds 1:11, 38, 55; PB 7:57, 582, 659).

Samuel Sandford (Sanford): Samuel Sandford, a London merchant, began doing business in Virginia by the 1670s and often collaborated with the London firm Perry and Lane, which owned a lot on urban Jamestown's waterfront. Sandford served as an Accomack County burgess in 1693, an indication that he owned property in the county or was married to someone who did, and he also was appointed high sheriff. In 1702 he patented 2,870 acres of land on the Eastern Shore, and two years later patented another 2,950 acres. During the early eighteenth century he became involved in a lawsuit with the Perry and Lane firm, a dispute over his share of certain customs fees. He was identified as the owner of a ship called the *Richard and Sarah*, which carried freight for Perry and Lane. On March 27, 1711, Sandford, who was then living in London, made his will, which was proved on January 1, 1712. He made no reference to a wife or children and distributed his estate among his siblings and their offspring, almost all of whom lived in England. He indicated that his brother John Sandford, and John's daughter, Susannah, sometimes lived in Princess Anne County, Virginia; he also mentioned his brother Giles Sandford and his daughter, Katherine, and said that his kinsman Thomas Parry resided in Maryland. The testator gave much of his Accomack County land to his parish for use in the education of poor children (LEO 52; Accomack County Wills &c. 1692–1715:556; PB 9:506, 642; SR 4348, 5736, 8525, 10123, 10610; 10752, 11551, 11553).

* * *

Thomas Sands: Thomas Sands, a gentleman, came to Virginia in 1607 and was one of the first Jamestown colonists (VI&A 622).

* * *

David Sandys (Sands, Sanders): The Rev. David Sandys, whose brother, George, was Virginia's treasurer, arrived in the colony in 1622. In 1624, while he was residing on Hog Island, he was accused of trying to take advantage of Mara Buck, a young orphan and heiress who lived in Jamestown. Thomas Allnutt of Jamestown, who made the allegations, was found guilty of slander and fined, perhaps on account of George Sandys' influence. The Rev. Sandys continued to live at Samuel Mathews' plantation on Hog Island, but he died in early August 1625, shortly after becoming minister to the Martin's Hundred settlers. His parishioners were ordered to pay the remainder of his salary, even though he died before fulfilling a year of service (VI&A 622–623).

George Sandys (Sands, Sanders): George Sandys, treasurer of the Virginia colony from 1621 to 1625, resided in the urban Jamestown home of Captain William Peirce. He corresponded with Virginia Company officials on a regular basis, tried to raise silk worms, and oversaw the industrial enterprises of Company-sponsored workers. Sandys reported the famine and diseases that followed the March 1622 Indian attack and informed the Company about the colony's glassworks and the shipwrights' business. Sandys, a merchant, patented three adjacent parcels on the lower side of the James River, combining them into the Treasurer's Plantation. He also acquired acreage in Archer's Hope and in Upper Chippokes. When the Virginia government sent Sandys to England in 1639 to oppose the Virginia Company's re-establishment, he duplicitously urged the authorities to revive it. He died there in 1644 (VI&A 623; STAN 24, 30).

* * *

Robin Santy: In 1694 Robin Santy, who was black and one of Philip Ludwell I's indentured servants, petitioned the General Court in order to obtain his freedom. His suit was dismissed because he failed to appear on the day his case was to be heard. Ludwell, a General Court judge, made no apparent attempt to recuse himself from the decision-making process (EJC I:310).

Abraham Sapcoate: On April 5, 1671, Abraham Sapcoate proved the will of the late Thomas Hunt of urban Jamestown (MCGC 247).

Sarah: On February 15, 1768, an adult female slave named Sarah was included in an inventory of the late Richard Ambler's slaves on Jamestown Island and his leasehold in the Governor's Land. She may have been the woman called Old Sarah whose name appeared in a 1769 inventory of Edward Ambler I's estate (York County Wills and Inventories 21:386–391; AMB-E).

Sarah: On February 15, 1768, when an inventory was made of the late Richard Ambler's slaves on Jamestown Island and his leasehold in the Governor's Land, an enslaved girl named Sarah was listed and described as Young Hannah's child (York County Wills and Inventories 21:386–391).

Sarah: On February 15, 1768, when an inventory was made of the late Richard Ambler's slaves on Jamestown Island and his leasehold in the Governor's Land, an enslaved girl named Sarah was listed and identified as Hannah's child (York County Wills and Inventories 21:386–391). She was listed separately from the youngster known as Young Hannah's child.

Sarah: In 1769 an enslaved child named Sarah was living on the Governor's Land and was included in the late Edward Ambler I's estate. She was then living with her mother, Joanna (AMB-E).

Sarah: When an inventory was made of Edward Ambler I's estate in 1769, an adult female slave known as Little Sarah was living on Jamestown Island (AMB-E).

William Sarson (Sarsnett): William Sarson arrived in Virginia sometime prior to May 1638, at which time his headright was used by Indian interpreter and trader John Fludd (Flood) of Westover in Charles City County. On October 2, 1656, Sarson patented 107 acres in the eastern end of Jamestown Island: 100 acres he acquired on the basis of two headrights plus 7 acres he purchased from Captain William Douglas (Dowglass), Lady Elizabeth Dale's administrator. Sarson's patent was located on the south side of Passmore Creek, to the south of the Goose Hill house. On March 18, 1662, Sarson renewed his patent, thereby gaining time to erect improvements on his property. He was still credited with his acreage in April 1667. Prior to 1680 his acreage came into the hands of John Pinhorne (NUG I:86, 319, 347, 469; PB 1:548; 3:391; 4:150; 5:145; MEY 290; AMB 18; Old Rappahannock County Deeds and Wills 1677–1682:303).

Richard Savage: Richard Savage, a laborer, arrived in Virginia in 1608 as part of the 1st Supply of new settlers. Captain John

Smith said that Savage saw certain Dutchmen (fellow colonists) give weapons to the Indians and tried to reach Jamestown to inform the authorities (VI&A 624).

* * *

Thomas Savage (Savadge, Salvadge): Thomas Savage, a young laborer and one of Captain John Martin's servants, arrived in Jamestown in 1608. Captain Christopher Newport gave him to Powhatan in exchange for Namontack, a young Indian he took back to England. Savage became fluent in the natives' language and often served as an official interpreter. By 1625 he and his wife, Hannah (Ann), were living on the Eastern Shore, on land given to him by the region's native leader, Esmy Shichans, often known as the Laughing King. The Savage household included son John I, born around 1624. Ensign Thomas Savage died sometime after March 1632, when he commenced leasing 100 acres on Old Plantation Creek, but before September 1633. By 1638 Hannah Savage had married Daniel Cugley, with whom she had a daughter, Margery (VI&A 624).

John Savage (Savadge, Salvadge) I: In 1637 John Savage I renewed his late father's patent for the land given him by the Eastern Shore's Laughing King. He violated church law in 1643 when he had sexual relations with a maidservant. Savage served as a burgess for Northampton County and attended the assembly sessions that were held between 1665 and 1676. In 1673 he repatented an aggregate of 9,000 acres in Northampton County, land that bordered Cheriston Creek and spanned across the Eastern Shore from east to west. The patent's text states that it had been renewed by the widowed Hannah Savage in 1635 and by her son, John, in 1637 and 1664. In 1674 a dispute between some of Savage's tenants and the Accomack Indians was brought to the attention of the General Court. Savage, who was identified as a merchant in 1677, imported cloth, buttons, hats, wrought iron, upholstery ware, and other saleable goods. When he testified in court in November 1677, Savage indicated that he was age 53. He married Ann Elkington and then, after being widowed, wed Mary, the daughter of Grace O'Neill Waters and Obedience Robins I. The will Captain John Savage made on August 26, 1678, was proved on December 11th. He divided his enormous landholdings among his seven living children (sons John II, Thomas, and Elkington and daughters Mary, Susanna, Grace, and an infant girl yet unnamed) and also left them some of his personal belongings. The testator made bequests to his grandchildren, the offspring of his daughters, Susannah and Grace, and left his wife, Mary, only £20 or 200 pounds of tobacco. Mary Robins Savage later married William Cordrey, who eventually abandoned her. She was said to have been of unsound mind (VI&A 625; PB 1:275, 449; 6:495; Northampton County Order book 10 [1674–1679]:315–320; 11 [1678–1683]:285; 13 [1689–1698]:22; DOR 3:118–120; LEO 39; MCGC 369, 373, 381, 402, 442; SR 5726a; MARSHALL 103–104).

* * *

Francis Sawyer [Sayer, Sayres]: Francis Sawyer came to Virginia sometime prior to August 1650 at Thomas Sawyer's expense. Sometime prior to 1667 Francis came into possession of some land on the Southern Branch of the Elizabeth River in Lower Norfolk County. County records suggest that he was a respectable citizen who was held in high esteem by his contemporaries. When William Odeon made his will in 1662, he asked Sawyer to serve as overseer of his estate. Sawyer performed the same duty for Richard Pinner, who died in 1667, and witnessed several wills in 1666. When Richard Russell made a new will in 1667, he indicated that it nullified the old one that he had left with Francis Sawyer. Sawyer witnessed John Hebert's will in 1669 and that of Thomas Axwell around 1678. He also witnessed and proved several wills during the 1680s and on at least one occasion served as an executor. In 1684, while Sawyer was a major, he laid claim to two tracts in Lower Norfolk County: 610 acres between the south and east branches of the Elizabeth River and 1,000 acres at the head of Pizzle Creek. Finally, in 1692 he patented 147 acres on the west side of the Elizabeth River's Southern Branch, in what was then Norfolk County. Francis Sawyer served as a Norfolk County burgess from 1691 to 1693 and was still alive on July 1, 1700. He was identified as Major Francis Sawyer when he executed a deed of gift to his daughter, Mary Thorogood (LEO 50, 52–53; PB 6:112; 7:409, 415; 8:224; Lower Norfolk County Wills and Deeds B:153; D:368; E:19, 22, 29, 185; Norfolk County Wills and Deeds 4:42, 128, 155; 5:6, 12, 164, 168, 170; 6:170).

Thomas Sawyer (Sawier): In February 1624 Thomas Sawyer was living at the Bennett plantation in Warresqueak, but by January 1625 he had moved to Jamestown, where he was a servant in Peter Langman's household. In January 1628 two Jamestown merchants, Edward Sharples and Mr. Gill, arrested Sawyer for indebtedness. The following month he and two other men received permission to move to Warresqueak (later known as Isle of Wight) (VI&A 626). There may have been a connection between this Thomas Sawyer and the man of the same name who received a land certificate from Lower Norfolk County's justices in August 1650 (Lower Norfolk County Wills and Deeds B:153).

William Sawyer (Sawier): In 1624 William Sawyer, a servant, was simultaneously attributed to Edward Blaney's household in urban Jamestown and to Blaney's land on the lower side of the James River. The duplicate listing probably occurred because Blaney shifted his servants from one property to the other. In February 1625 Sawyer was associated with the Blaney plantation on the lower side of the river (VI&A 626).

* * *

Edmund (Edmond) Scarborough (Scarburgh) I: Edmund Scarborough I came to Virginia prior to March 1630, when he commenced serving as a burgess for Accomack. His eligibility to hold office indicates that he or his wife owned land in the county. Scarborough sat in the assembly until at least 1633, and he also served as a justice in the local court. He died intestate after April 1634, but before January 9, 1635. On February 19, 1635, Mrs. Hannah Scarborough identified herself as Edmund's widow when she appeared before Accomack's monthly court to sell some cattle. On November 28, 1635, son and heir Edmund Scarborough II repatented some his late father's land (VI&A 626; LEO 9–10, 12; PB 1 Pt. 1:322–323; AMES 1:1, 12–13, 30).

Edmund (Edmond) Scarborough (Scarburgh) II: Captain Edmund Scarborough II, the son of Edmund Scarborough I, began serving in the local court held at Accomack in January 1633. He repatented some of his late father's land on November 28, 1635, and began acquiring acreage in his own right. He represented Northampton County as a burgess in the sessions that were held from 1643 through 1648 and served as speaker of the assembly meetings that were held in 1645–1646. He was returned to the assembly in 1652 and 1656, while the Commonwealth government was in power. In 1654 he and John Walton invested in 3,900 acres of land called Peckincke in Westmoreland County, acreage they held on behalf of John Bagnall of London, a merchant-tailor.

Scarborough was reelected to the assembly and attended the sessions held in 1660 and in 1661–1662. As time went on, he seems to have begun considering himself above the law. In October 1663 he took it upon himself to lead a large party of horse soldiers into Maryland. In his account of that expedition, he railed against Quakers and other religious dissenters. Scarborough was returned to the assembly and represented Accomack County from 1666 to 1670. He became the colony's official surveyor (surveyor general) and held office from 1665 to 1670. He surveyed the boundary line between Virginia and Maryland but made some unauthorized changes for which he was later held accountable. Scarborough was a merchant whose business ethics were as questionable as his morality. Although he was a married man, he maintained a long-term relationship with Mrs. Ann Toft, a much younger single woman, who produced three children. He also saw that she acquired literally thousands of acres of land. Some of Scarborough's contemporaries considered him a cruel and highly controversial figure. In 1670 Governor Berkeley issued a warrant for his arrest, alleging that he had mistreated the neighboring Indians. Specifically, Scarborough was accused of abusing the Indians "by Murthering [*sic*], Whipping & burning them, [and] By taking their children from them who are their parents." When he was tried before the General Court, he was found guilty and barred from holding civil and military offices until reinstated by the governor. In 1672, when the Accomack County's court justices were informed of Edmund Scarborough II's death, they named his son-in-law, Devoreau Browne, as his sole administrator. However, the General Court designated the decedent's son, Charles Scarborough, and sons-in-law Devoreau Browne and John West as joint administrators. Colonel Edmund Scarborough II was survived by his wife, Mary, who declined the right to serve as his administratrix (LEO 21, 23–24, 26, 29, 33, 36–37, 39; STAN 26; PB 1 Pt. 1:322–323; Westmoreland County Deeds, Wills, Patents &c. 1653–1659; Accomack County Orders 1671–1673:188; Deeds and Wills 1664–1671:166; MCGC 212, 230, 238, 256, 517; NUG I:67, 102, 107; PB 1:322–323, 615; 5:522; 6:392; SR 237, 455, 644, 646, 653, 687, 1409, 1456, 4348, 4557, 7982, 10066, 11301; AMES 1:1, 7, 68; Scarborough 1663; MARSHALL 48).

Charles Scarborough: Charles Scarborough, the son of Colonel Edmund Scarborough II, was among those who served as administrators of his late father's estate. On February 10, 1677, then Governor William

Berkeley listed Charles Scarborough among those he declared exempt from the king's pardon on account of their role in Bacon's Rebellion. However, on March 3, 1677, Berkeley and the Council of State granted him a pardon and fined him £40. Scarborough represented Accomack County in the assembly and served in the sessions held 1680–1682, 1684, 1688, and 1691–1692. He was named to the Council of State in 1691, although Governor Francis Howard would have preferred another candidate. In a letter Howard sent to the king, he described Scarborough as "inconsiderable in his estate," an indication that he preferred councilors to be men of substantial wealth. In 1698, when Scarborough was appointed the customs officer for Accomack, he was given a salary of £40 a year. He made his will on August 6, 1701, and died in Virginia prior to October 6, 1702. The testator divided his landholdings among his wife, Mary, and numerous children: Bennett, Charles, Henry, Ann (the wife of George Parker), Mary, Sarah, and Tabitha (LEO 45, 47, 49–50; STAN 42; Accomack County Wills &c 1692–1715:292; PB 6:392; SR 239, 375, 378, 2202, 2203, 3627, 4571, 4597, 5624, 7982; NEVILLE 61; MCGC 456, 529).

* * *

William Scarborough (Starbrough): On March 16, 1677, William Scarborough, one of the rebel Nathaniel Bacon's supporters, was put on trial at Green Spring plantation, Governor William Berkeley's home. He was found guilty and sentenced to death. Later, Berkeley declared that he was exempt from the king's pardon and that his estate was subject to seizure. However, Scarborough was reprieved, and in 1682 and 1684 he patented some land on the Piankatank River in Middlesex County (NEVILLE 147; SR 660, 661, 749, 6618; MCGC 460, 532; PB 7:43, 363, 692; Surry County Deed Book 1 [1664–1671]: 236, 240, 248, 316; Deeds &c. 1671–1691:74).

Martin Scarlett (Scarlet): Martin Scarlett moved to Stafford County prior to September 1686, when he witnessed a will. Documents his wife signed in 1688 and 1691 reveal that her first name was Ann (Anne), but they fail to disclose her maiden name. Over the years Martin Scarlett's name appeared frequently in the records of Stafford's monthly court. In March 1692 he patented 320 acres on Morumscoe Creek (a tributary of Occoquan Bay), bordering some land he already owned. He served as a Stafford County burgess, attending the sessions held in 1680–1682, 1685–1686, 1691–1692, and

1693. He succeeded Thomas Ousley, who was appointed county sheriff. Scarlett was supposed to attend the 1695–1696 session but died before the assembly convened (LEO 46, 48, 51–52, 54; Stafford County Record Book 1686–1693:2a–3, 83, 105, 187a–189, 216a–217; NN 1:150).

Scipio: In 1769, when an inventory was made of the late Edward Ambler I's estate, an enslaved boy named Scipio was living on the Governor's Land (AMB-E).

Scipio: In March 1710 a group of indentured servants and enslaved blacks and Indians in James City, Isle of Wight, and Surry counties planned to make a break for freedom on Easter Sunday and vowed to overcome all opposition. One slave, a black man named Will, revealed the plot and the uprising was quelled. Among the slaves jailed for complicity in the plot were black men belonging to the Rev. James Blair, Philip Ludwell I, Sheriff Edward Jaquelin, George Marable II, ferryman and gunner Edward Ross, and John Broadnax, all of whom were associated with property in urban Jamestown. Although most of the accused insurgents were jailed in Jamestown, where they were interrogated and then released into their owners' custody "to receive correction," there were two exceptions: Jamy (a Broadnax slave) and Essex (a Ross slave) were implicated in the plot and therefore were detained. Virginia's governor later reported that two other slaves were executed so that "their fate will strike such a terror" that others would not attempt an uprising. The two men (an African American named Scipio and an Indian named Salvadore) were hanged and then quartered. Scipio was executed at Gloucester Courthouse and then dismembered. His head and one of his quarters were to be put on public display in Gloucester and his remaining quarters were to be sent to Middlesex, King and Queen, and Lancaster counties, where they could be displayed prominently (Stanard, "Philip Ludwell to Edward Jenings, 1709, in regard to a Negro Plot," 23–24; EJC III:234–236, 242–243, 246).

Robert Scotchmore (Scotsmore, Scottesmore): Robert Scotchmore came to Virginia in 1623 and in February 1624 was living on the mainland or Governor's Land, just west of Jamestown Island. Within a year he and his household moved to Martin's Hundred. In 1630, 1632, and 1633 he served as a burgess and represented the Martin's Hundred community in the assembly (VI&A 627; LEO 9, 11–12).

[No First Name] Scott (Scot): In 1608 a laborer identified only as Master Scott arrived in the 2nd Supply of Jamestown colonists (VI&A 627).

Anthony Scott (Scot): When Thomas West, Lord Delaware, arrived in Jamestown on June 10, 1610, his ensign, Anthony Scott, read his commission aloud (VI&A 627).

Henry Scott (Scot): On February 16, 1624, Henry Scott was a servant in Captain William Holmes' household in urban Jamestown. He died on the mainland, just west of Jamestown Island, sometime prior to January 30, 1625 (VI&A 627).

John Scott I: John Scott I, a merchant and planter, may have been in Virginia in 1666 when Governor William Berkeley designated him vice admiral of the tobacco fleet. In 1671 he was a resident of Westmoreland County and a highly successful planter who sent a large shipment of tobacco to England. He purchased some land in Westmoreland County near Pope's Creek in 1695 and patented another 400 acres there in January 1696. He also seems to have owned an interest in some acreage in Charles City and Henrico counties. In 1698 Scott, whose home was on Mattox (Appomattox) Creek, a tributary of the Potomac River, served as a burgess for Westmoreland County. His May 28, 1700, will was presented for probate on November 21, 1701. Scott left his plantation at the head of Pope's Creek to his wife, Sara (Sarah), if she would accept it as her dower share of his real estate. He also left her the bulk of his household goods and furnishings. The testator left his home tract to his son, John II, who was then a young child, and also bequeathed a plantation in Maryland to his daughter, Jane. He made bequests to his sisters, Jane and Rebecca, and to his brother, Gustavus Scott, who was his business partner in the ship *Potomac Galley*. John Scott I designated his widow, Sara, as his executrix and trustee, and specified that his son, John II, was to be sent to school in England as soon as he was eight or nine years old and entrusted to the care of his uncle Gustavus. Scott noted that his wife, Sara, stood to receive £100 from the estate of her late husband, George Cross. He also made a monetary bequest to his young stepson, George Cross Jr., noting that if he failed to reach his majority or marry, those funds should revert to his mother and the Scott children, Jane and John II. John Scott I made bequests to his kinsman William Graham; to his godson, John Hore; and to his friends

Andrew Monroe and David Wilson. On November 26, 1701, the widowed Sara Cross Scott, who already had remarried, was named her late husband's executrix. She was then the wife of Jacob Martyn or Martin, a mariner. In March 1702 Mrs. Sara Martyn presented a partial inventory of the late John Scott I's estate; she supplemented that information in August (LEO 58; Westmoreland County Deeds and Wills Book 2 [1691–1699]:45–46; 3 [1701–1707]:27–29, 51–54, 87, 258–260; SR 641, 3593c, 5874; PB 7:466; 8:35, 46; NN 2:218–219).

Nicholas Scott (Scot): Nicholas Scott, a drummer, came to Virginia in 1607 and was one of the first Jamestown colonists (VI&A 627).

John Scrimgeour (Native American): On June 26, 1695, 30-year-old John Scrimgeour, who identified himself as "an Indian native of this country" and a servant who had been employed by the Rev. John Scrimgeour of Westmoreland County, went to court to seek his own freedom. He insisted that he was being unlawfully detained by the deceased clergyman's heir, Mrs. Frances Spencer, and declared that under the law he was not a slave. To prove the point, he cited Act 12 of the October 3, 1670, session of Virginia's assembly. However, Mrs. Spencer refused to relinquish custody of the Rev. Scrimgeour's estate, which she and her new husband, the Rev. John Bolton, contended included the Indian servant. To further complicate matters, William Scrimgeour, the deceased clergyman's brother, contested the validity of the decedent's nuncupative will, which was made while the Rev. John Scrimgeour was living in Mrs. Spencer's home. Despite the testimony of the servant John Scrimgeour and his wife, Mary, Westmoreland's justices eventually awarded the Rev. John Scrimgeour's estate to his brother, William, and named him administrator. He, like Mrs. Frances Spencer, stubbornly refused to release his late brother's Indian servant. In May 1696 John Scrimgeour returned to court, where he initiated a suit against William Scrimgeour and again tried to obtain his freedom. In July he won a suit he had filed against a local resident for whom he had done some work, an indication that he continued to function as a free man. John Scrimgeour's perceptiveness and knowledge of the law was quite remarkable for an individual who probably had very few educational opportunities (Westmoreland County Order Book 1691–1699:182, 185a, 201a, 207, 211, 221).

Mathew Scrivener (Scrivenor): Mathew Scrivener, a gentleman and Virginia Company investor, arrived in Jamestown in January 1608 in the 1st Supply of new colonists. He was named to the Council of State, eventually serving as secretary. He accompanied Captains John Smith and Christopher Newport on several voyages of discovery and became acting president of the colony, serving from July 1608 to September 1609. He set off for Hog Island in early 1609/1610 but was caught in a winter storm and drowned when his boat sank. Scrivener, a wise and intelligent man, was helpful in rebuilding the Jamestown fort after it burned in January 1608 (VI&A 628; STAN 27).

George Seaton: George Seaton patented some land in Westmoreland County in 1657 but eventually settled in Gloucester County, where he became a court justice. On March 15, 1677, Seaton, who was living in Kingston Parish in Gloucester (later, Mathews) County, was put on trial at Green Spring plantation, the home of Governor William Berkeley. Court testimony reveals that in November 1676, when Seaton was captured by Robert Beverley I, his personal property was seized and carried off. Seaton begged for clemency and the General Court's justices agreed that he could receive the king's pardon if he relinquished all claims to the property that had been confiscated by Beverley and his men, with the exception of four hogsheads of tobacco (MCGC 459, 531; PB 4:191; 7:553).

Henry (Henery, Henrie) Seawell (Sewell) I: In September 1632 Henry Seawell I served as a burgess for the upper (or westernmost) parish of Elizabeth City. In 1639 and 1640 he represented Lower Norfolk County, was a justice in the county court, and served as a churchwarden. During 1641 the governor and his council decided to have a parish church built at Mr. Seawell's Point, a location now known as Sewell's Point. The county justices convened in the Seawell home from time to time. In 1642, while Henry Seawell I was a sitting justice, Elizabeth Mills, who had claimed that Sewell's wife, Alice, was a thief, was found guilty of defamation. Mills was obliged to apologize to the Seawells and was sentenced to ten lashes. Henry and Alice Seawell died sometime prior to February 14, 1645. Later in the year their underage son and heir, Henry II, was identified as an orphan. By February 27, 1650, the Seawell couple's daughter, Anne (Ann), had married Lemuel Mason (VI&A

629; HEN I:179; LEO 11, 17–18; Lower Norfolk County Book A:16, 25, 50, 64, 75, 79, 86, 235, 283; B:137a, 138, 161a, 163a, 167).

Cutbert (Cuthbert) Seirson (see Cutbert [Cuthbert] Pearson, Peirson [Peirson, Peerson, Person])

J. Selloan: On May 15, 1622, a man known as J. Selloan was identified as an employee of the Company of Shipwrights. He worked with Thomas Nunn and his men, who lived on Jamestown Island (VI&A 629).

John Senior (Seneor): Sometime prior to 1624 John Senior patented 12 acres in the eastern end of Jamestown Island, an area where many ancient planters had homesteads. He later settled on the lower side of the James River, in what became Surry County. Senior surveyed Secretary Richard Kemp's property at Middle Plantation in 1643 and shortly thereafter surveyed the Governor's Land and Green Spring Plantation, Governor William Berkeley's estate. Between 1644 and 1652 Senior patented three tracts of Surry County land, and he acquired some acreage along the north side of the Piankatank River in what became Middlesex County. For a time, he also owned the Glasshouse tract on the mainland adjacent to Jamestown Island. On November 5, 1654, Edward Travis I bought 150 acres on Jamestown Island from John Senior, a tract that included Senior's original 12 acres. During the early 1670s Richard Lawrence, a Jamestown innkeeper, accused Richard Auborne, clerk of the General Court, of causing John Senior's death. Although Auborne was arrested, he was released after he posted a bond. When the case against Auborne was presented by the attorney general in October 1672, it was determined that there were no grounds for an indictment (VI&A 629).

William Senior: In October 1669 William Senior, a carpenter who lived on the Eastern Shore, patented 300 acres in Northampton County. He was killed in Jamestown in September 1676 while defending the capital city from an attack by the rebel Nathaniel Bacon's men. Afterward, his widow, Eleanor (Ellinor, Ellenor), sought a pension from the government. On May 15, 1677, the justices of Northampton County appointed Eleanor Senior as administratrix of her late husband's estate, which was appraised by several local men. Afterward, she married John Hundson, and the decedent's daughter, Dorothy, wed Jacob Bishop (NUG II:65; PB 6:259; JHB 1660–1693:69; MARSHALL 99).

Seosteyn (Native American): In 1677 Seosteyn, chief counselor to Cockacoeske, the Queen of the Pamunkey Indians, and a member of her entourage, was among the natives recognized for their loyalty to the Crown during Bacon's Rebellion. King Charles II authorized the fabrication of a purple robe for Seosteyn; it was lined with scarlet shalloon, a twill-woven woolen. Seosteyn was described as "a man of a goodly presence and long of stature, in great esteeme with the Queen [of Pamunkey] and her people and a constant lover and friend to the English" (LC 5/108 f 8; 9/275 ff 264ro–267ro; CO 5/1371; SR 5736, 5743).

Richard Serjeant (Serieant): Richard Serjeant came to Virginia in 1623. In January 1625 he was living in urban Jamestown, where he was a servant in cape merchant Abraham Peirsey's household (VI&A 630).

Serrahohque (Native American): On May 29, 1677, Serrahohque, king of the Nottoway Indians, went to Middle Plantation (later Williamsburg) and signed the Treaty of Middle Plantation, using three diagonal lines as his mark. He also endorsed the expanded version of the treaty, which was consummated between March 18 and June 19, 1680. In recognition of Serrahohque's loyalty to the Crown, King Charles II authorized the fabrication of a purple robe lined with scarlet shalloon, a twill-woven woolen; a crimson ermine-trimmed cap; and a coronet. The Nottoway king was described as "a very old man and one that govern[s] his people with prudence and good discipline, so that they are very obedient unto him and inoffensive to the English. He is a big boned man streight [*sic*] and tall of stature" (LC 5/108 f 8; 9/275 ff 264ro–267ro; CO 5/1371; SR 5736, 5743).

John Seward (Seaward) I: John Seward I came to Virginia in 1622 and during the mid-1629s lived in Elizabeth City, where he was an indentured servant. In 1635 he patented some land in Warresqueak (or Isle of Wight) County and enhanced the size of his holdings in 1636 and 1638. Seward represented Isle of Wight County in the 1645–1646 assembly sessions. In March 1648 he purchased Robert Partin's Isle of Wight County plantation, making it his home tract. A month later he patented 1,200 acres on the Blackwater River, which was considered a branch of the Roanoke River, and he acquired an additional 400 acres on the south side of the Roanoke. Both tracts then lay within Isle of Wight County. When Seward made his will on September 16, 1651, he identified himself as a Bristol merchant who had land in Isle of Wight, Virginia. In April 1665 John Seward II patented his late father's 1,600 acres in Isle of Wight. In 1672 he was identified as a Bristol merchant and John Seward I's son when he sold Levy Neck to another merchant. On March 22, 1672, a warrant was issued for the arrest of John Seward II of Isle of Wight County, who was being sued by Theophilus Hone of Jamestown. Seward, who was away from of the colony at the time, had designated Thomas Milner of Nansemond County and Edmond Wickens of Isle of Wight to serve as his attorneys in Virginia (VI&A 630; LEO 24; MCGC 293; BODIE 514, 565–567, 655, 662, 664, 665, 668, 674, 680; Isle of Wight Will and Deed Book 1 [1662–1688]:264; Deeds, Wills & Guardian Accounts Book A:14; PB 2:116–117; 5:3).

Thomas Sexton: Thomas Sexton, a youth from London who formerly lived at Christ Church's Hospital, arrived in Jamestown in September 12, 1623. He died in Jamestown sometime prior to February 16, 1624 (VI&A 630).

Shacrow (Chacrow) (Native American): In November 1624 Edward Grindon said that during Sir Thomas Dale's government (1611–1616), an Indian named Shacrow, who lived with Lieutenant Skarse (John Sharpe), the commander of Jamestown, often used firearms. According to interpreter Robert Poole, Shacrow also stayed with captains William Pierce and William Powell (VI&A 630).

George Sharks (Shurke): George Sharks reportedly died on Jamestown Island after April 1623 but before February 16, 1624. Despite being listed as deceased, he was identified as a member of Ensign William Spence's household (VI&A 630).

John Sharpe (Skarfe, Scarpe): John Sharpe, a Virginia Company investor, arrived in Jamestown sometime prior to 1614 when Captain Francis West, Lord Delaware's brother, designated him a lieutenant and placed him in command of the capital city. When Sir Thomas Dale left Virginia in May 1616, he placed Lieutenant Sharpe in charge of Jamestown. He was later identified as one of those who had taught Indians how to shoot firearms (VI&A 630).

Judith Sharpe: Judith Sharpe died in Jamestown after April 1623 but before February 16, 1624 (VI&A 631).

Samuel Sharpe (Sharp): Samuel Sharpe set sail for Virginia in 1609 and was shipwrecked in Bermuda with Sir Thomas Gates and the colony's other leaders. In July 1619 Sharpe represented Bermuda (or Charles) City in the assembly. In 1624 he was a burgess for Flowerdew Hundred, where he and his wife were living. When a list of patented land was sent back to England in May 1625, Sharpe was credited with 100 acres on the Appomattox River. In 1629 he served as a burgess for Bermuda Hundred (VI&A 631; LEO 3, 5, 8).

Sharper: On February 15, 1768, when an inventory was made of the late Richard Ambler's slaves at his quarter called Powhatan, an adult male slave named Sharper was living there. In 1769 Sharper, a carpenter then living on Jamestown Island, was considered part of the late Edward Ambler I's estate (York County Wills and Inventories 21:386–391; AMB-E).

* * *

Edward Sharples (Sharpless): Edward Sharples arrived in Virginia sometime prior to September 1623 and in February 1624 was named clerk of the Council of State. He was then living in a Jamestown household headed by Alice Davison, the widow of former clerk Christopher Davison. Sharples angered his superiors by surreptitiously sending some official documents to the king and Privy Council. As punishment, he was sentenced to losing his ears and was ordered to serve Jamestown resident Clement Delke for seven years. However, Sharples regained his freedom within two years time and began conducting business as a merchant. Sharples' political, legal, and business transactions suggest that he lived in urban Jamestown while he was in Virginia (VI&A 632; LEO 5).

John Sharples (Sharpless): In January 1627 London merchant John Sharples, the brother of Council of State clerk Edward Sharples, brought suit against Captain John Harvey of urban Jamestown, one of his debtors. Philemon Powell served as his attorney (VI&A 633).

* * *

Annis Shaw: Annis Shaw came to Virginia in 1623 and in January 1625 was a maidservant in Abraham Peirsey's Jamestown household (VI&A 633).

Philip Shelly (Shelley): On July 6, 1680, the justices of Surry County's monthly court noted that Philip Shelly had married Ann Mason (Macon), a widow. She should not be confused with the Ann Macon who was still widowed in 1684 and possibly had been married to William Macon, or was Lemuel Mason's widow, Anne. In November 1682 Surry's justices noted that Shelly had completed his work on the county courthouse and should be paid. In 1687 he was identified as a member of the county militia, and in 1690 he was named Ann Mugget's executor. As time went on, he continued to make appearances in court, sometimes as a juryman and sometimes as a participant in suits. In 1695 and 1696 Shelly was involved in the construction of the Lawnes Creek Parish Church. He died sometime prior to July 1704, having been survived by his current wife, Sarah (Surry County Order Book 1671–1691:302, 390, 601, 622, 753; Court Records 1691–1700:16, 18, 84, 131, 135, 138, 146, 152, 163, 166, 172, 176, 185, 188, 249, 258, 266; Court Records 1700–1711:50).

Walter Shelly (Shelley): In July 1619 Walter Shelly served as a burgess for Southampton or Smyth's Hundred, in the corporation of Charles City. He died in Jamestown on August 1, 1619, while the assembly was in session (VI&A 634; LEO 3).

Baldwin (Balldwin, Bauldwin) Shepherd (Sheppard, Shepard): Baldwin Shepherd, a successful planter, patented 1,000 acres in Northumberland County in 1665. Then, in 1672 he laid claim to 360 acres in Elizabeth City County, at the head of Harris Creek. Shepherd served as an Elizabeth City County burgess and attended the 1680–1682 assembly sessions. He played an active role in the Elizabeth City community, where he witnessed wills and legal transactions and occasionally served as an attorney. In 1689 he was a county justice, and by 1695 he had become high sheriff. Shepherd made his will on February 27, 1697 and died sometime prior to September 20, 1697. He was survived by his wife, Elizabeth; son, John; and daughter, Elizabeth Cofield (LEO 45; PB 5:83; 7:229; NEAL 7, 12, 16, 19, 22, 44, 47, 53, 55, 61, 68–70, 86, 153, 158, 161, 168, 177, 187, 219).

John Shepherd: On October 1, 1644, John Shepherd was a burgess for James City (STAN 63; LEO 22). He probably represented James City County rather than the capital city, for there is no indication that he or his spouse (if he was married) owned land there.

In 1644 James City County spanned both sides of the James River, encompassing the territory that by 1652 became Surry County.

John Shepherd (Sheppard, Shepard): John Shepherd patented 175 acres in York County in June 1645. He served as an Elizabeth City County burgess and attended the assembly sessions that were held from 1652 to 1655. In 1652 he patented 1,000 acres of land in Northumberland County and reasserted his claim ten years later (LEO 29, 31–32; PB 2:23; 3:91; 4:417). John Shepherd of Elizabeth City County may have been related to Elizabeth City County burgess Baldwin Shepherd, whose land straddled the boundary line between York and Elizabeth City counties and whose son was named John.

[No First Name] Sheppard: In February 1624 the son of a man identified only as "Old Sheppard" was living at the Glasshouse (VI&A 634).

Robert Sheppard (Shepheard, Shepard, Sheapard): Robert Sheppard, who came to Virginia on the *George* in 1621 and appears to have been free, lived on the lower side of the James River during the mid-1620s. In February 1625 he resided on the Treasurer's Plantation. In 1635 he patented some land at the head of Lower Chippokes Creek, using headrights that belonged to his wife, Priscilla I, and himself. He was a lieutenant in 1638 when he significantly enhanced his holdings in that area. In 1646 and 1647–1648 Shepherd served as a burgess for James City County, which then spanned both sides of the James River and included the territory that in 1652 became Surry County. In January 1653 he sold some land on the west side of Lawnes Creek, in what was then James City County, identifying the acreage as his former home. Major Sheppard died sometime prior to November 1654, when his widow, the former Elizabeth Spencer, signed a marriage contract with Thomas Warren of Smith's Fort plantation in Surry. Warren agreed to provide for Sheppard's underage children, Anne, John, Robert, and William, and preserve their inheritance. He also agreed to give the decedent's daughters, Priscilla II and Susanna, their portion of their late father's estate. The widowed Elizabeth Sheppard had the right to dispose of certain personal items, notably a gold seal ring bearing the initials *DS*, a pair of silver tongs marked *RS*, and a silver inkhorn marked *JS*. Elizabeth Spencer Sheppard Warren died between 1655 and 1658 (VI&A 635; LEO 25–26; PB 1:548; Surry County

Deed Book 1 [1652–1663]:19, 50, 54, 56–58, 60–61, 204; DOR 3:227).

Robert Sheppard (Shepheard, Shepard, Sheapard): In February 1624 Robert Sheppard, who came to Virginia on the *Hopewell*, was living in Edward Blaney's household in urban Jamestown. A year later he was residing at the Blaney/Powell plantation on the lower side of the James River, where he was one of Blaney's servants (VI&A 635).

James Sherlock: From May 26, 1693, to December 12, 1698, James Sherlock was clerk of the Governor's Council and the General Court. During the late 1670s he was a merchant who imported tobacco into England. In 1675 Henry Aubery used his headright when patenting some land in the Northern Neck (EJC I:287, 401; SR 575a, 5592e, 5762f; PB 6:565).

Michael Sherman: In November 1693 Michael Sherman served as a burgess and justice for James City County. As county sheriff, he was paid for keeping prisoners. Sherman served another term as burgess in 1696–1697 (STAN 63; LEO 52, 56; LJC 207). He may have been related to the Elizabeth Sherman who in 1704 paid quitrent on 500 acres of James City County land (SMITH 80).

Peaceable (Peceable) Sherwood: In February 1624 Peaceable Sherwood was residing in the urban Jamestown household headed by Captain William Holmes and Mr. Calker. In December 1624 he testified before the General Court in a case that involved some missing legal documents. On February 5, 1625, he was listed among those who had died on the lower side of the James River, within the corporation of James City (VI&A 636).

William Sherwood: William Sherwood, an attorney who immigrated to Virginia sometime prior to 1669, was born around 1641 and was from White Chapel, near London. Before he left England, he marred his reputation by misappropriating some funds from Sir Joseph Williamson. In a June 17, 1671, letter to Williamson, Sherwood said he was ashamed of the "fowl [*sic*] act" he had committed, which was a felony, and thanked Williamson profusely for sparing him "three years time," presumably referring to a jail sentence. Sherwood also promised to turn evil into good. Over the years he continued to express his gratitude to Williamson and kept him apprised of events in the colony. As Williamson was Lord Arlington's secretary and a major investor in the Royal African

Company, he was in a good position to serve as Sherwood's mentor. The tone of the men's correspondence suggests that they were friends. Sometime prior to 1669 William Sherwood and Thomas Rabley (a naturalized Dutchman who owned a brick house on Jamestown's waterfront) purchased two small parcels in Middle Plantation, which they eventually developed and rented to the government. Sherwood may have then been a resident of Surry County, for he frequently witnessed court documents there and during the early 1670s served as the county's subsheriff. He also functioned as John George I's attorney and audited documents associated with a dispute between Thomas Rabley and Theophilus Hone of Jamestown. In 1673 Sherwood told Sir Joseph Williamson about the recent Dutch invasion, during which part of Virginia's tobacco fleet sustained damage. He also arbitrated disputes between James Minge and Ralph Poole, and between Thomas Hunt's executors and George Jordan and James Wadding. As an attorney, he conveyed John Salway's Surry County plantation to Colonel Thomas Swann I, the owner of a tavern in Jamestown. In 1673 William Sherwood claimed that John Price of Surry County, who had a reputation for volatility, had assaulted him. He also said that he had seen Roger Delk threaten another man. He obtained a judgment against Philip Pardoe but was sued by Richard Hill. He represented Robert Jones of Surry as an attorney in a suit against Robert Beverley I and in October 1675 issued a warrant for Giles Bland's arrest after his confrontation with Secretary Thomas Ludwell of Jamestown. It was around that time that Sherwood, a merchant, and James City County sheriff Francis Kirkman patented 1,200 acres near the head of Gray's Creek in Surry.

By October 4, 1675, William Sherwood had married Jamestown merchant Richard James I's widow, Rachel. He took charge of the real and personal estate his 15-year-old stepson, Richard James II, stood to inherit upon attaining his majority. He also attempted to collect debts that were accruable to the late Richard James I's estate. One of James' debtors whom Sherwood had arrested was Giles Bland, the son of London merchant John Bland II and his wife, Sarah. William and Rachel James Sherwood and young Richard James II resided in Jamestown in a brick dwelling Rachel's late husband had built close to the Back River. Although very little is known about Rachel's family background, a Surry County record dating to October 1680, in which Rachel relinquished her legal interest in some property, reveals that she was the aunt of Major Samuel Swann. This raises the possibility that she was the sister of Major Swann's mother, the former Sarah Cod (Codd), who was Colonel Thomas Swann's second wife and who died in 1654.

William Sherwood's business affairs were severely disrupted by Bacon's Rebellion, and ultimately he alienated the rebel Nathaniel Bacon and Bacon's nemesis, Governor William Berkeley. Sherwood, who was unsympathetic to Bacon because he had acted outside of the law, forced Jamestown innkeeper and Bacon supporter Richard Lawrence to post a bond guaranteeing Giles Bland's appearance in court; when Bland failed to appear, Sherwood kept the funds. After the popular uprising subsided, Governor Berkeley became angry with Sherwood because he served as the attorney of some people accused of being Bacon supporters. Sherwood, on the other hand, claimed that he was abused by Berkeley, who called him a jailbird and rogue, and at one point barred him from practicing law in Virginia or serving as a burgess. Sherwood told Sir Joseph Williamson that Berkeley was vindictive and had ordered the execution of some people who were Sherwood's debtors. He said that the aging governor had punished him for submitting James City County freeholders' list of grievances to the king's commissioners, and he claimed that the so-called Green Spring faction was at the root of many of the colony's problems.

On September 19, 1676, the day William Sherwood set sail for England to report on conditions to the colony, Nathaniel Bacon's men set Jamestown ablaze. Sherwood later said that during the conflagration the houses he possessed as Richard James II's guardian, which were worth £1,000, were among the buildings burned. Sherwood sought to attach part of the estate of Richard Lawrence, the rebel who allegedly set fire to the James/Sherwood home, and he told the king's commissioners that those funds would enable him "to rebuild in James City." In a separate petition Sherwood said that several men executed for their role in the rebellion were his debtors, and he asked to be reimbursed from the condemned men's estates. Some of the debts Sherwood attempted to collect were due to him in the right of the orphan, Richard James II. Sherwood purchased a one-acre lot from David Newell on February 6, 1677, a parcel that contained the ruins of "the country house." Newell's deed to Sherwood was acknowledged in court on April 23, 1678, by James Alsop of Jamestown and Richard James II,

William Sherwood's 17-year-old stepson. On April 23, 1681, Sherwood received a patent for the Newell lot, by which time he had "built a faire howse & Appurtenances" on the property. Then, sometime prior to August 1681, he purchased 66 acres that bordered his one-acre lot's northern and eastern boundary lines. The compensatory funds Sherwood received as a sufferer in Bacon's Rebellion probably enabled him to construct the brick dwelling and a kitchen he erected on part of the "country house" lot on Jamestown's Back Street, buildings that are depicted and identified on John Soane's August 1681 plat.

In October 1677 William Sherwood purchased John Fulcher's 28½ acres in the western end of Jamestown Island and had his patent confirmed in April 1681. Between 1677 and 1682 he also acquired some land that was contiguous to the urban property he already owned, and he purchased 3½ acres from John Page. On October 23, 1690, Sherwood patented the 150-acre tract that his wife's late husband, Richard James I, had acquired on June 5, 1657. That land had descended to the decedent's son, Richard James II, who had died unmarried and without heirs, with the result that his acreage had escheated to the Crown. On April 20, 1694, William Sherwood patented a 308-acre aggregate that encompassed much of the western end of Jamestown Island, within Jamestown's corporate limits. Besides the James orphan's land, the parcel also included an additional 40 acres that comprised the widowed Rachel James' dower share of her late husband's estate. The Rev. John Clayton, a dedicated naturalist, informed a friend in England that he had advised Sherwood to drain his 150 acres of marsh land (which ran diagonally across his plantation) and convert it into pasture. In addition to his acreage on Jamestown Island, William Sherwood had a 260-acre leasehold on the mainland, in the Governor's Land.

After Governor William Berkeley was recalled to England, Sherwood gradually became more active in politics. In 1678 he served as a James City County justice and as Virginia's attorney general. However, in 1679 he was accused of malpractice and was declared ineligible to serve as a burgess because he had previously been convicted of a felony. Sherwood weathered the criticism and began to practice law as a private citizen. He did business in Westmoreland County and sometimes hired John Minor, a local attorney, to represent him when pursuing debtors. By April 1682 Sherwood had been elected a burgess for James City County. It was in that capacity that he was authorized to draft a contract with Philip Ludwell I for rebuilding the statehouse, which had been torched by Bacon's rebels. In August 1684 Sherwood was told to draft a document that the assembly was planning to send to officials in England. When he was in London during 1690, he gave court testimony in which he described himself as a 49-year-old gentleman and Jamestown resident. After his return to Virginia he resumed work as a practicing attorney. He also continued to serve as a burgess for Jamestown and was among those who protested Daniel Parke II's election as a burgess. In 1692 he authorized Isaac Merill of London to act as his attorney in England, and in 1693 he patented 3,000 acres of land in what was then New Kent County, acreage that straddled Totopotomoy Creek. In 1695 Sherwood sponsored a bill outlawing free-ranging swine in urban Jamestown. He was the Royal African Company's official representative in Virginia and part of his income was derived from the slave trade. His mentor, Sir Joseph Williamson, was one of that firm's original stockholders, and his friend Jeffrey Jeffreys and his niece's uncle, Micajah Perry, were the Royal African Company's principal contractors for the importation of Africans into Virginia. Sherwood had a financial interest in a ship called the *Nansemond*.

Throughout the 1680s and 1690s William Sherwood (and later, his widow, Rachel) derived income from renting portions of one of their houses to the government for official meetings. The Council of State convened there in June 1680, perhaps for the first time, and afterward it became a regular occurrence. Sherwood also continued to host committee meetings. His services as an attorney extended into the Middle Peninsula and Northern Neck, and he continued to work with London merchant Micajah Perry and his business associates. In March 1697 Sherwood sent word to James Blaise in Middlesex County, urging him to see that a deceased Essex resident's debts to the Perry and Lane mercantile firm were paid promptly, ahead of his other obligations. Sherwood closed his letter by saying that he hoped to visit Blaise in Middlesex before the summer's end. Ill health intervened, however, and on August 18, 1697, while Sherwood was visiting Captain Henry Jenkins' house in the Governor's Land, he made his will, stating that he was sick and weak. He left his divinity books to his wife, Rachel, along with a life-interest in all of his real and personal estate. He named British merchant and Royal African Company contractor Jeffrey Jeffreys as his reversionary heir and made a bequest to the poor of James City Parish and of White Chapel Parish in England. He stipulated that wife Rachel, William Edwards II, and George Marable II, all of whom lived in Jamestown, were to decide which local paupers were to be helped. He asked to be buried at the east end of the church in Jamestown, outside of the walls. Sherwood bequeathed his Indian servant, Dorothy Jubilee, her freedom and left a sum of money to Mary Anthrobus, another servant. He also made bequests to Micajah Perry of London, his niece Joanna Jarrett, Dionysius Wright, William Edwards II, Joseph Pettit, Governor Edmund Andros, Hugh Davis, Captain Arthur Spicer, and Captain Henry Jenkins and his son. He named William Edwards II, George Marable II, and Dionysius Wright as overseers of his will and asked them to inventory his estate. William Sherwood died sometime prior to September 10, 1697, and his will was presented for probate in February 1698. In accordance with his wishes, he was buried in the churchyard in Jamestown. According to Robert Sully's 1865 narrative, Sherwood's epitaph described him as a great sinner awaiting a joyful resurrection. After Sherwood's death the widowed Rachel James Sherwood continued to reside in Jamestown and rent meeting-space to government officials. On May 10, 1699, she presented a claim "for the use of her house where his Excellency and council sit and also for the other roomes [*sic*] since the statehouse was fired, made use of for the secretarys office and assembly records." Around 1699 Mrs. Sherwood married Edward Jaquelin, a merchant who was nine years younger than her deceased son, Richard James II. Jaquelin moved into her brick home in Jamestown and on December 11, 1704, purchased Jeffrey Jeffreys' legal interest in the late William Sherwood's approximately 400-acre estate. He also commenced making compensatory claims on wife Rachel's behalf, submitting a final one on December 16, 1700, by which time Williamsburg had become the capital city.

Edward Jaquelin did little to enhance the size of the Sherwood plantation on Jamestown Island, other than buying a half-acre lot on the waterfront; however, he acquired a substantial amount of acreage on the mainland. In 1712 he purchased the 24-acre Glasshouse tract at the entrance to Jamestown Island, and in 1718 he bought an adjacent 27-acre parcel. In 1712 he also began leasing a 151-acre parcel in the Governor's Land, which he sublet from Philip Ludwell II. This gave Jaquelin a total of 202 acres adjacent to Jamestown Island. These acquisitions seemingly heralded the development of the mainland farm known as "Amblers," which traditionally served as a subsidiary to the Jaquelin/Ambler plantation on Jamestown Island. After Rachel James Sherwood Jaquelin's death, Edward Jaquelin married Martha Cary of Elizabeth City County, with whom he produced several heirs (NUG II:222, 261, 380, 394; PB 7:97–98; 8:83, 384–386; AMB 17, 23, 26, 29, 33, 34, 41, 43, 45, 65, 73, 77, 84, 86, 99, 134, 135–136; AMB-JJ 1826:26; WITH 534; FOR III:12:23; SAIN 7:564, 801, 1124; 9:965; 10:43, 61, 114, 269; CO 1/26 f 194; 1/27 f 83; 1/30 f 121; 1/37 f 39; 1/40 f 51; 1/41 ff 31–32ro; 1/42 ff 60, 304; 1/55 ff 1–2; Surry County Deeds, Wills &c. 1652–1671:354, 378, 383, 385; 1671–1684:27, 41, 44; 1672–1684:273; Order Book 1671–1691:158; MCGC 285, 289, 341, 405, 410, 415, 418–419, 432–434, 447, 452, 519–521; LJC 19, 92–93, 247; MCGH 873; JHB 1660–1693:121, 127, 131, 225, 245, 248, 257, 282, 325, 450, 452; 1695–1702:8, 20, 22, 48, 62, 104, 124, 142, 154, 198, 214, 219; York County Deeds, Orders, Wills 3:48; 6:412; 9:48–49, 134; Lancaster County Order Book 1687–1696:35–36; Essex County Order Book 1695–1699:48, 66; Deeds and Wills 1 [1695–1699]:100; Westmoreland County Order Book 1676–1689:392, 414, 437, 444, 460, 481, 491; EJC I:227; II:52; HCA 70/57 f 120; STAN 86; LEO 45, 47, 49, 54, 56; Soane 1683; DAVIES 62, 295; Bruce, "Bacon's Rebellion,"170–174; ASPIN 172).

Edmund (Edmond) Shipdam (Shipham?): Sometime after August 5, 1658, but before October 17, 1660, Edmund Shipdam married Elizabeth, the widow of Richard Ricks (Rix, Reeks, Reekes, Reakes). It was then that the Shipdam couple received the General Court's permission to sell an urban lot and building known as "the country house" that Ricks' orphaned son, John, stood to inherit. The Shipdams indicated that the building was in disrepair and that the value of the orphan's property was dwindling. Shortly thereafter, Elizabeth and Edmund Shipdam sold the lot and its improvements to merchant John Phipps, the owner of some contiguous acreage. Edmund Shipdam died sometime prior to April 1673, having named his wife, Elizabeth, as executrix. Richard James I, a Jamestown merchant and creditor, brought suit against his estate. In February 1679 Mrs. Elizabeth Shipdam, who was then deceased, was identified as the mother of Elizabeth Moseby and John Ricks (AMS 7, 10; Charles City County Orders 1650–1696:513; 1677–1679:353).

John Short: John Short, a gentleman, arrived in Virginia in 1607 and was one of the first Jamestown colonists. In 1608 Edward Maria Wingfield referred to him as "old Short," a bricklayer, who had remained loyal to him when others did not (VI&A 637).

Jeffrey Shortridge: Jeffrey Shortridge, a tradesman, came to Virginia in 1608 as part of the 2nd Supply of new settlers to Jamestown. In late 1608 Captain John Smith referred to him as a soldier (VI&A 637).

Margaret Shrawley: Margaret Shrawley died in Jamestown sometime after April 1623 but before February 16, 1624 (VI&A 637).

Shurenough (Native American): Between March 18 and June 19, 1680, when the 1677 Treaty of Middle Plantation was expanded to include additional Indian groups, Shurenough, the king of the Manakin Indians, signed on behalf of his people (Anonymous, 1677 treaty, Miscellaneous Virginia Records 1606–1692, Bland Manuscripts, XIV, ff 226–233).

George Shurke (see George Sharks)

John Sibley (Sipsey, Sipse, Sypsey, Sibsey, Sibseyy, Shipsie): In February 1624 John Sibley, a yeoman, was living in Elizabeth City when he patented some land, utilizing the headright system. The acreage he acquired was on the south side of the James River, in what was then the corporation of Elizabeth City but later Elizabeth City County. During the late 1630s and throughout the 1640s, he continued to patent land in that area. Two of his large tracts abutted the Elizabeth River's Western Branch, and he also owned Craney Island. Sibley was co-owner of the *America*, a ship that during the 1630s was involved in the tobacco trade with England. In 1632 and 1633 he was a burgess for the upper parish of Elizabeth City. When Lower Norfolk County was formed from the southern part of Elizabeth City County, Captain John Sibley was designated a justice of the new county's monthly court, which held its first session on May 15, 1637. He continued to serve as a Lower Norfolk County justice, and in 1646 he became high sheriff. The county court sometimes convened in his home. By 1637 Sibley had been made a member of the Council of State; however, in 1638 and 1640 he represented Lower Norfolk County in the assembly. Captain Sibley was still serving as a justice in Lower Norfolk County's monthly court in April 1652, but made his will on July 15, 1652. He died before August 16, 1652, when his widow, Elizabeth, presented his will to the local court. Several local men were given

the responsibility of appraising Sibley's estate. His will reveals that he still owned land at Craney Point, which was then in the possession of a tenant or servant. Besides his widow, the testator was survived by his daughter, Mary, who was married to Richard Conquest. Sibley referred to Thomas Lambert as his "beloved brother-in-law." By April 1653 the widowed Elizabeth Sibley and her son-in-law, Richard Conquest, were involved in a dispute over custody of an indentured servant. An inventory of the late John Sibley's estate, presented to the court in August 1653, attests to his wealth and socioeconomic standing (VI&A 638; LEO 11–12, 16, 18, 20; Lower Norfolk County Record Book A:1, 4, 13, 100, 127, 153, 331; C:9, 16–17, 42, 53; STAN 33; SR 4007; PB 1:453; 2:158–159).

John Sicklemore alias Ratcliffe (see John Ratcliffe alias Sicklemore)

Michael Sicklemore: Michael Sicklemore, a gentleman, came to Virginia in 1608 in the 1st or 2nd Supply of Jamestown settlers. Captain John Smith described him as an honest, valiant, and conscientious soldier and sent him into the territory on the south side of the James River to search for evidence of the Roanoke colonists. In 1609, while he and some other colonists were on an island in the Nansemond River, he was killed by attacking Indians (VI&A 638).

Thomas Sides: Thomas Sides, who was living in the Neck O'Land in early 1624, died on Jamestown Island sometime prior to January 24, 1625 (VI&A 638).

John Sidney (Sydney): In 1642 John Sidney, a gentleman and highly successful planter, was the sheriff of Lower Norfolk County. A year later he was among a group of men appointed to conduct a survey of the Lynnhaven area. In September 1644 he patented 200 acres on the upper side of the Elizabeth River, and in August 1647 he acquired 300 acres on the lower side of the same river. During the 1640s and 1650s, while he resided on a plantation bordering the Elizabeth River, he raised livestock for sale to others. In 1646 Sidney was a commander of the county militia, and by 1654 he held the rank of lieutenant colonel. He also was appointed a tobacco inspector. In April 1651 he became a county justice, a post he held for many years. He was "of the quorum," that is he was one of a limited number who had to be present whenever cases were tried. Sidney served as a burgess for Lower Norfolk County and attended the sessions held in 1640, 1644, 1647–1648, and 1651–1652. He was returned to office in 1656 and served from 1658 to 1660. He sold some of his land at the head of the Elizabeth River's Eastern Branch in 1652. Colonel John Sidney made a nuncupative will that was recorded on October 17, 1663. He made bequests to his goddaughter, Kate Joy, and his cousins, whose surname also was Joy. When George Fouler's widow, Frances, made her will in January 1678, she identified Colonel John Sidney as her father and indicated that he had given her a parcel of land that she was leaving to her daughter, Pembroke Fouler. She also mentioned her other two children, George and Sidney Fouler (LEO 18, 22, 26, 18, 33; Lower Norfolk County Wills and Deeds Book A [1637–1646]:110–111, 129, 134, 145, 149, 156, 159, 164, 166, 202, 230, 238, 243; B 1646–1652]: 10, 10a, 18, 20, 50, 55a, 63, 67, 70, 134, 158–158a, 162, 163a, 167a, 170–172, 175a, 176, 179, 187, 188a, 190a, 200a, 208a; C:10, 17, 80; D [1656–1666]:1, 32, 385; 4:58; NUG I:156, 169, 328, 415; PB 2:15, 102).

Elizabeth Sikes (Sykes) (Mrs. John Everett): Mrs. Elizabeth Sikes, a widow, leased and operated Colonel Thomas Swann I's tavern in urban Jamestown in the years immediately following Bacon's Rebellion. Swann's tavern, which was damaged in the September 1676 fire that largely destroyed Jamestown, had been restored to usable condition by September 1679. Mrs. Sikes married John Everett in 1680, and in January 1681 Swann's widow and son sued Everett for £26 "for the rent of a House leased by the above said Elizabeth Sikes whilst she was a widow." Everett, on the other hand, contended that "the sd Tho Swann dec'd did accept what he [Swann] expended at the said house as part of the rent for the said House." Mrs. Elizabeth Sikes Everett seems to have had trouble collecting funds from another patron, Colonel Edward Hill II of Charles City, for in July 1680 she filed a complaint against him in the General Court. The Everetts still had possession of the tavern in 1681 (Surry County Deeds, Wills &c. 1672–1684:297; Order Book 1671–1691:358; EJC I:10).

Silvy: In 1769 an enslaved woman named Silvy, and her child, Sukey, were living on the Governor's Land and were included in the late Edward Ambler I's estate (AMB-E).

William Simkler: In September 1676 William Simkler lost his life defending Jamestown from Nathaniel Bacon's men. Afterward, his widow, Margaret, claimed a government pension on his behalf (JHB 1660–1693:69).

Richard Simmons: Richard Simmons, one of the first Jamestown colonists, died on September 18, 1607 (VI&A 639).

William Simon: William Simon, a laborer, came to Virginia in 1608 in the 1st Supply of Jamestown settlers (VI&A 639).

[No First Name] Simons: In 1614 a colonist named Simons reportedly was in the hands of the Indians. Sir Thomas Dale wanted to recover him but learned that Simons had fled to Nandtaughtacund, an Indian village on the Rappahannock River (VI&A 639).

Frank Sisco (Native American): In September 1662, when an inventory was made of the late Colonel John Mottrom's estate in Northumberland County, an Indian servant named Frank Sisco was listed along with the decedent's other indentured servants, who also were identified by race (Northumberland County Record Book 1658–1662:82).

Thomas Sisson: Thomas Sisson, a haberdasher from London, arrived in Jamestown on September 5, 1623 (VI&A 640).

Thomas Skinner (Skynner): On May 20, 1607, Thomas Skinner, a sailor, came to Virginia with the first Jamestown colonists (VI&A 641).

Robert Small: Robert Small, a carpenter, came to Virginia in 1607 and was one of the first Jamestown colonists. (VI&A 642).

Robert Smalley: Robert Smalley probably arrived in Jamestown in 1609 in the 3rd Supply of new colonists. Sir Thomas Dale (1611–1616) placed him in command at Henrico. When Smalley made his December 19, 1617, will, he left his real and personal property to his wife, Elizabeth, who was then living with him at Bermuda Hundred. When Mrs. Smalley asked the Virginia Company for a widow's pension on July 12, 1620, she claimed that Sir Samuel Argall had seized her late husband's property. She also said that the decedent had served in Virginia for 11 years. Elizabeth Smalley presented Robert Smalley's will for probate in November 1621 and was appointed substitute executrix of his estate. She also was authorized to inquire into the disposition of his property. In January 1623 the Virginia Company decided that Mrs. Smalley's complaints against Argall should be settled in Virginia. By January 11, 1627, she had married Randall Crew, who pursued her case against Argall (VI&A 642).

Randall Smallwood (Smalwood, Smale-wood): Randall Smallwood came to Virginia prior to August 1623 and resided in urban Jamestown. He became provost marshal of the corporation of James City and during the 1620s and early 1630s made numerous appearances in court to testify in an official capacity. On January 30, 1626, he stated that he had taken a muster of the colony's inhabitants in the presence of Governor George Yeardley. Smallwood acquired some land in Warwick County sometime prior to June 1639, and he was still alive in March 1640 (VI&A 643).

William Smethes: William Smethes, a gentleman, came to Virginia in 1607 and was one of the first Jamestown colonists (VI&A 644).

[No First Name] Smith: Mrs. Smith died in Jamestown sometime after April 1623 but before February 16, 1624 (VI&A 644).

Ann Smith (Mrs. [No First Name] Smith; Mrs. Nathaniel Bacon): By 1654 Mrs. Ann Smith, a wealthy widow, had married Colonel Nathaniel Bacon, the owner of property in urban Jamestown and the Kings Creek plantation on the York River. She was the mother of Ann Smith, who in 1654 married Isle of Wight County burgess George Fawdon. In a marriage contract Fawdon made with his bride-to-be, he mentioned his future wife's brother, William Smith (MCGH 159; Isle of Wight County Book A:93; BODIE 528–529).

* * *

Arthur Smith I: In September 1637 Arthur Smith I patented 1,450 acres, a neck of land that lay on a tributary of the Pagan River; he renewed his patent in 1643, an indication that he had not developed his property. In March 1643 he patented 350 acres on Cypress Swamp, in what was then Isle of Wight County, and in 1645 he served as a burgess for Isle of Wight. When Smith made his will on October 1, 1645, he indicated that he was a resident of Warresqueak, the Indians' name for what became Isle of Wight County. He made bequests to his sons, Arthur II, George, Richard, and Thomas, and to his daughter, Jane, and noted that his wife had predeceased him. He also left remembrances to his godsons, Arthur Taylor and Arthur Virgin. The testator named as overseers of his will Peter Hull, merchant Peter Knight, and shipwright George Hardy, all of whom were burgesses (LEO 23; Isle of Wight County Will and Deed Book 1 [1662–1688]:51–52, 154; 2 [1688–1704]:330; PB 1:529; 6:683).

Arthur Smith II: In 1661 Arthur Smith II, who was born in Isle of Wight around 1638 and went on to become a county justice, executed a deed that allowed his brother George Smith to sell a piece of land. In 1666 Arthur Smith II and his wife, Sarah, who lived on the Pagan River, sold some land on the Blackwater River to George Hardy. They indicated that Sarah was the daughter and heir of the late Richard Jackson and the granddaughter of the late Alice Bennett. Arthur Smith II served successive terms in the assembly, representing Isle of Wight County in 1680–1682, 1685–1686, 1688, and 1691–1692. In 1683 he patented 1,100 acres on the south side of Currewaugh Swamp in Isle of Wight County. Then, in October 1689 he laid claim to 310 acres in Isle of Wight, land that lay adjacent to that of William Oldis. In 1692, when Smith was a colonel in the local militia, he served as a trustee of the town called Newport, later Smithfield. In 1693 he appraised the estate of Joseph Worry, a former burgess. When Arthur Smith II made his will on December 2, 1696, he indicated that he was a resident of Isle of Wight's Lower Parish and named his wife, Mary, as his executrix. He made bequests to his sons, Thomas, George, and Arthur III; to his daughters, Jane Benn, Sarah Monro, and Mary Pitt; and to his grandson, Arthur Benn. The testator's will was proved on June 10, 1697 (LEO 45, 48–50; Isle of Wight Will and Deed Book 1 [1662–1688]:52–53, 69–70; 2 [1688–1704]:54; 2 [1704–1715]:336, 377; PB 7:333; 8:22).

* * *

Austen (Osten) Smith: Austen Smith, a carpenter, arrived in Jamestown on September 12, 1623, and in February 1624 was living in Richard Stephens' home in the capital city (VI&A 644).

Bryan Smith: Bryan Smith, who patented some acreage in Henrico County, owned the Mount Folly and Taskinask plantations, which abutted the lower side of the York River in what is now James City County. In May 1673 he filed suit against William Drummond I of Jamestown, accusing him of slander. Smith was then representing Perry and Lane, a British mercantile firm that had a business presence on urban Jamestown's waterfront. Several months earlier Smith and Drummond had been involved in another legal dispute. During Bacon's Rebellion, Bryan Smith was staunchly loyal to Governor William Berkeley and turned vigilante after the popular uprising was quelled. He may have feared retribution because of his extreme partisanship, for he seems to have erected a fortified stronghold, a stone house, on an elevated promontory overlooking Ware Creek, near the back line of his Mount Folly property. Smith eventually became deeply indebted to Daniel Parke II, who took legal possession of his property. As a result, Smith's landholdings eventually came into the hands of William Byrd II of Westover, who married Parke's daughter, Lucy (MCGC 312, 337; Byrd Title Book:233; NEVILLE 1976:67, 69; PB 1:552, 783; 6:560; 7:127; SR 661, 6618b).

Christopher Smith: The Rev. Christopher Smith, the rector of James City Parish, married William Broadribb's widow, Lydia, sometime after May 1703 but before 1709. In 1706 Smith offered instruction to Indian children at the College of William and Mary. When a list of quitrents was compiled in 1704, Smith was paying taxes on 450 acres of land in James City County. A man of the same name was paying quitrent on 200 acres in King and Queen County and 800 acres in King William (MCGH 76; SMITH 82).

Edward Smith: When the ship *Falcon* set sail for Jamestown in 1621, Edward Smith was a member of the crew (VI&A 644).

Henry Smith (Native American): On January 3, 1698, the justices of Middlesex County's monthly court ordered John Byrd to take an inventory of the personal estate of an Indian man named Henry Smith. On February 7, 1698, the decedent's inventory reportedly was submitted and recorded (Middlesex County Order Book 1694–1705:207, 212).

John Smith: Captain John Smith, one of Virginia's best-known early settlers, traveled extensively and came to Virginia in 1607 in the first group of colonists. He was implicated in a mutiny and kept in irons for several months. He was admitted to the council in June 1607 and in September began serving as cape merchant. He undertook several exploratory voyages and was captured and detained by the Indians. In September 1608 Smith became president of the Virginia colony. During his time in office he rebuilt and strengthened Jamestown, forced the colonists to work toward their own support, and interacted extensively with the natives. Smith eventually was arrested and sent to England, where he stayed until March 1614. Afterward, he went to New

England. Captain John Smith died in England on June 21, 1631. His published works, though largely drawn from the writings of others, provide many insights into the early years of colonization and offer his perspective on Native American life (VI&A 644; STAN 27).

John Smith (Smyth): John Smith came to Virginia in 1611. By February 1624 he, his wife, and child had moved to Burrows Hill on the lower side of the James River. In October 1629 Smith served as a burgess for the settlement generally known as Paces Paines, and in 1632 and 1633 he represented the settlers living in the same vicinity, which included the plantations called Burrows Hill (or Smith's Mount) and Perry's (Swann's) Point (VI&A 645; LEO 7–8, 11).

John Smith (Smithe, Smyth): In 1639 John Smith and Christopher Bea patented 100 acres at the head of the Old Poquoson River in Elizabeth City County. He may have been the same individual who patented land on the lower side of the James River, across from Newport News Point. In 1648 Smith served as merchant William Dade's attorney and on occasion appraised decedents' estates. When he testified before Warwick County's justices in 1650, he indicated that he was 30 years old. In September 1654 John Smith of Stanley Hundred in Warwick County joined Nicholas Smith in patenting 3,000 acres in Westmoreland County. The following month he was designated Warwick County's sheriff. Smith served as a Warwick County burgess in 1658 and was chosen speaker of the assembly (LEO 34; PB 1:126, 679; 2:121; 3:374; CHAPMAN 135; DUNN 164, 166, 174,180; MCGC 504).

John Smith: In January 1681 Madam Mary Swann and her stepson Samuel, co-heirs of the late Colonel Thomas Swann I, who had owned a Jamestown tavern, sued tavernkeeper John Everett and his wife, Elizabeth, in attempt to recover some back rent. Everett contended that Swann's room-and-board at the tavern was supposed to be deducted from that sum. Although the plaintiffs won a preliminary judgment against Everett, he was given the right to substantiate his claim. Therefore, he summoned carpenter John Smith (who then lived near the Blackwater River) to Surry County's monthly court to testify about Colonel Swann's agreement to swap room-and-board for rent. On February 25, 1682, Smith was interrogated by Everett in the presence of Surry County's court justices. He testified that he had made an agreement with the late Colonel Swann to perform carpentry at the house in Jamestown, the tavern that Everett rented from Swann. Smith went on to say that he had gone to Jamestown to examine Swann's building so that he could determine how much repair-work was required. He admitted hearing that Swann was renting accommodations in the capital city but said that he was uncertain who provided them (Surry County Deeds, Wills, &c. 1672–1684:297, 304; Order Book 1671–1691:358).

John Smith II: Gloucester County burgess John Smith II was the son of John Smith I, who in 1652 patented 150 acres on Horn Harbor and Mobjack Bay in Gloucester (later, Mathews) County. Three years later the elder man acquired 400 acres on Milford Haven, close to the land he had patented in 1652. Finally, in 1657 he laid claim to 500 acres that bordered the York River and Poro-potank Creek, property on which he built his home. When a group of indentured servants planned an insurrection in 1663, Birkenhead (Berkenhead), a manservant who belonged to John Smith I, revealed the plot, averting what could have been a major tragedy. Smith may have patented some land on the south side of the Rappahannock River in Old Rap-pahannock County during the early 1660s. John Smith II, who inherited his father's property and became a prosperous mer-chant, represented Gloucester County in the assembly meetings that were held in 1685–1686, 1688, and 1691–1692. In 1693 he owned some land on the lower side of the York River, near Yorktown, acreage that was proposed as a possible site for the College of William and Mary. During the latter part of the seventeenth century and the early eigh-teenth century, while he was surveyor-gen-eral, he invested in acreage in the Northern Neck and the Middle Peninsula, acquiring land in Gloucester, Middlesex, Essex, King and Queen, and Richmond counties, some-times in partnership with Harry Beverley. When a list of quitrents was compiled in 1704, Smith was credited with literally thousands of acres of land. John Smith II of Gloucester County married Elizabeth Cox, the great-great-granddaughter of William Strachey. He authorized London merchants Micajah and Richard Perry and Thomas Lane to collect the annual rent on the prop-erty his wife had inherited from the Stracheys. Smith became a member of the Council of State and served until 1720. He was appointed commander-in-chief of the Gloucester County militia in October 1706 and died sometime after February 22, 1720, but before 1730 (LEO xxi, 48–50; BEVERLEY 68–69; PB3:117; 4:82,184, 604; 6:204; 7:385,

612; 9:459, 536; 10:6, 13; NN 3:122, 241; SMITH 82; SR 3775i, 3782, 4242, 11593; EJC I:366, 411; II:348–350, 388, 450; III:132, 521; DOR 3:255).

John Smith: On August 17, 1720, John Smith patented 192 acres of escheat land in James City County, near the Ludwell estate. On November 17, 1737, he married Edward Jaquelin's daughter, Mary, who was born on March 1, 1714. On April 24, 1745, John and Mary Jaquelin Smith relinquished their life-rights in a two-acre parcel in the western end of Jamestown Island, conveying their legal interest to brother-in-law Richard Ambler. The Smiths were then residents of Shooter's Hill in Middlesex County. Mary Ambler Smith died on October 4, 1764. The wid-owed John Smith represented Goochland County in the assembly sessions held be-tween 1752–1758 and 1759–1761, and he served on behalf of Middlesex County from 1761 to 1768. He made his will on January 7, 1771, and died on November 19, 1771, at Harewood in Jefferson County (Smith et al. 1745; MCGH 661; NUG III:223; AMB 116; DOR 3:321).

John Hill Smith: John Hill Smith, a Wil-liamsburg attorney, married Mary, John Am-bler II's daughter. Afterward, Ambler gave Mary his farm in the mainland just west of Jamestown Island. On January 28, 1832, Smith presented a petition to the state legis-lature in which he protested Goodrich Durfey and William Edloe's proposal to build a toll bridge linking Jamestown Island to the mainland and to move the ferry land-ing from Smith's mainland farm to James-town Island. Smith, in his counter-petition, said that he had built a house on his property to accommodate steamboat passengers. Durfey and Edloe's proposal prevailed and a bridge was built to replace the badly eroded isthmus that once connected Jamestown Is-land to the mainland (James City County Leg-islative Petitions 1832:137).

Lawrence Smith: In 1657 Lawrence Smith, a surveyor, patented some acreage at the head of the Ware River in Glouces-ter County. During the 1660s and 1670s he began speculating in real estate in Glouces-ter and Old Rappahannock counties, often claiming tracts encompassing literally thou-sands of acres. He also patented vast amounts of acreage in New Kent County, sometimes investing with Robert Beverley I. Finally, in 1691 he laid claim to 1,200 acres at the head of the Severn River in Gloucester. Some-times Smith's real estate investments paid off handsomely, for in 1680 he was gener-ously compensated when part of his land was selected as the site of Gloucestertown, a planned urban community and official port. Major Lawrence Smith was among those who suffered during Bacon's Rebellion. When seeking compensatory damages, he said that his estate had been plundered and that Nathaniel Bacon's men had imprisoned him. The vast quantity of acreage that Smith and another colonist (William Byrd I) were acquiring attracted the attention of English authorities, who ordered Virginia's acting governor to cease awarding them land. In 1686 and 1688 Smith appeared before Middlesex County's justices. By the latter date he held the rank of colonel. He served as a burgess in 1691–1692, representing Gloucester County (LEO 50; Middlesex County Order Book 1680–1694:272, 351; PB 4:253; 5:587; 6:41, 144, 240, 356, 444, 516, 547; 8:212; SR 235, 4563, 6618b; HEN II:405; EJC I:18, 193, 260, 310; BILLINGS 271–272).

Nicholas Smith: Documents on file in the British Archives reveal that in 1640 Nicholas Smith was shipping cloth and clothing from London to Virginia. In 1652 he lost 31 hogsheads of tobacco that were aboard the *Golden Lion*, which was anchored in the James River when it was seized by a London ship. Admiralty records reveal that, contrary to law, Smith's tobacco was being shipped to a merchant in Amsterdam, in the Netherlands. In 1655 Smith, who was then a merchant and planter, patented 200 acres on the James River in Isle of Wight County. He represented Isle of Wight in the assembly meetings that were held in 1656 and from 1660 to 1662 (LEO 33, 36, 38; PB 4:39; SR 3506, 4016).

Osmond Smith: Osmond Smith, an indentured servant, came to Virginia in 1620, and in early 1625 he was a young indentured servant in the urban Jamestown household of Dr. John Pott (VI&A 646).

Robert Smith (Smyth): By 1658 Robert Smith, who was born in England and became Virginia's major general, had married Christopher Wormeley I's twice-widowed daughter, Elizabeth, who had outlived Secretary Richard Kemp and Sir Thomas Lunsford. Marriage to a wealthy and well-connected woman seems to have helped Smith's financial position. He began patenting land in 1661, acquiring 1,299 acres on the upper side of the Piankatank River in Lancaster (by 1669, Middlesex) County, and a year later he and Nicholas Smith, as co-investors, patented more acreage in the Northern Neck. Robert Smith became a councilor in

1663 and served throughout Sir William Berkeley's second term in office. He eventually moved to Middlesex County, and served successive terms as a county justice. During the late 1660s he patented 1,900 acres of land on the lower side of the Rappahannock River, south of Portobago Bay, and he laid claim to a large tract of escheat land in Lancaster County. He patented some acreage on the Lynnhaven River and eventually acquired some land on the Nominy River in Westmoreland County. Smith was highly respected, and over the years he was involved in some of the major decisions made by Virginia's governing officials. In 1666 he was among those endorsing Maryland and Virginia officials' agreement not to plant tobacco for a year, an attempt to improve the price of the colonies' tobacco. In 1667 he was authorized to seize powder that could be used in the colony's defense. He also was among the officials who informed the king that they had built fortifications (a turf fort) in Jamestown instead of at Old Point Comfort, the site that British merchants favored. In 1668 Smith's handling of the estates of Mary Cliff and Henry and Samuel Vassal was challenged by their heirs, who confronted him in the General Court. In 1673 Smith, who often was called upon to arbitrate disputes, was authorized by the Virginia government to buy shares of land in the Northern Neck Proprietary. In November 1676 Smith and Secretary Thomas Ludwell asked the king for 200 men to help put down the rebel Nathaniel Bacon's insurgents and said that loyalists and perhaps the Indians would assist. Smith added that using local militiamen to quell the insurrection was preferable to bringing in large numbers of troops from overseas. He also urged the king to pardon those who had been minor participants in the popular uprising. Smith paid a personal toll for his loyalty to Governor Berkeley, for Bacon's men plundered his estate. He and other high-ranking officials who owned property in the Northern Neck Proprietary asked the king for reassurance that their land rights would be preserved. In February 1683 Secretary Nicholas Spencer informed his superiors that Major General Robert Smith was dangerously ill. However, Smith seems to have overcome whatever health problems he was experiencing, for he lived several more years. In late 1683 and early 1684, he sent a petition to officials in England, pointing out that he had not received his annual salary of £300 a year since 1679, although he had continued to serve as Virginia's major general. He also pointed out that when he had suppressed the plant cutters, who in 1678–1679 had tried to decimate the tobacco crop, they had taken revenge by damaging his plantations. Smith was named to Virginia's court of oyer and terminer in late 1685 and reportedly died around 1687 (STAN 39; CO 1/20 Part I f 119; 1/38 f 35; MCGC 230, 486, 488, 490–491, 518; ASPIN 175; SAIN 9:1098; Middlesex County Order Book 1673–1680:11; 1680–1694:1; PB 4:382; 5:202; 6:115–116, 215; 7:427; NN 2:269–270; SR 641, 655, 657, 659, 672, 679, 2654, 3828, 4386, 4559, 4560, 7819, 10476, 12501; MCGC 208, 214, 224, 230, 256, 295, 302, 347, 442, 489, 518).

Roger Smith: Captain Roger Smith, who served in the Netherlands with Thomas West, Lord Delaware, came to Virginia sometime prior to 1616. As soon as he reached Virginia, he began serving on the Council of State. He went to England but returned to the colony in 1621. His military expertise was highly valued, and after the 1622 Indian attack he was given the means and authority to build a fort on the lower side of the James River in Warresqueak. Sometime prior to 1623 Smith married William Peirce's daughter, Joan, who had outlived her former husband, John Rolfe. During 1624 and 1625 Smith played an active role in the Virginia government. He had a home on the waterfront in urban Jamestown but also owned a plantation on the lower side of the James River and some land in Archer's Hope. He was still alive in June 1629 and serving on the Council of State (VI&A 648–649; STAN 30; LEO xxi).

Sarah Lee Smith (Mrs. George Lee; Mrs. [First Name Unknown] Smith): On April 12, 1692, George Lee bequeathed to his wife, Sarah, life-rights in all of his real estate. That realty included a ¾-acre parcel on Back Street in urban Jamestown, which contained the reconstructed bay of a brick row house that was burned during Bacon's Rebellion; some acreage in the mainland just west of Jamestown Island; and 100 acres on the Chickahominy River. Testator George Lee named Robert and George Nicholson as reversionary heirs to all of his real estate but he left his widow, Sarah, outright ownership of his personal property. Mrs. Sarah Lee apparently continued to reside in the Jamestown row house that she and her late husband had occupied. Four years after George Lee's death and Sarah's remarriage to someone named Smith, "the house where Mrs. Sarah Lee alias Smith lately lived" was considered as a possible meeting place for the assembly. On December 7, 1696, Sarah Lee Smith and her late husband's reversionary heirs, Robert and George Nicholson, sold

their respective interests in the late George Lee's house and lot in Jamestown to George Harvey, who kept the property until October 1697 (Lee MS 51 ff 669, 671; Surry County Deeds, Wills &c. 1694–1709:70; EJC I:410).

Thomas Smith (Smyth): Thomas Smith came to Virginia and during the mid-1620s was living in urban Jamestown, where he was a servant in Captain William Peirce's household (VI&A 650).

Thomas Smith: In November 1677 Thomas and William Smith were mentioned in the will of William White of Surry. In 1691 Thomas Smith, who owned several pieces of land in Surry, was a justice of the county's monthly court. He probably was related to fellow legatee William Smith, who had a house "at Towne," that is, in urban Jamestown (Surry County Deeds, Wills &c. 1671–1684:67, 203; Order Book 1671–1691:428, 562, 814).

Toby (Tobias, Tobyas) Smith (Smyth): In 1640 Toby Smith identified himself as a 25-year-old Virginia planter when he testified in an English court. Later in the year he had some cloth goods shipped to the colony. Smith then owned a 650-acre plantation in Warwick County, at the head of the Back River, and in 1643 he served as a Warwick County burgess. However, in 1644 he represented Lower Norfolk County and in 1649 served as a burgess for Nansemond County, an indication that he or his spouse owned land in those jurisdictions. When Smith executed a gift in September 1647, bestowing some cattle upon his children, Toby and Phebe II, he identified Moore Fauntleroy of The Forest in Nansemond County as his brother-in-law. By the early 1650s Toby Smith began speculating in real estate. He patented 350 acres on the west side of Mattahunk Neck, in what was then James City County but later became Charles City. In 1652 he began claiming land on both sides of the Rappahannock River in what was then Lancaster County. Finally, in 1657 he acquired 1,350 acres on the south side of the Rappahannock River in Old Rappahannock County. Smith moved to Old Rappahannock County, where his brother-in-law Moore Fauntleroy lived, and rose to the rank of lieutenant colonel in the militia. When Smith made his will in 1657, he mentioned sons Henry and William and his 1,600-acre plantation called Rockingham, which was located on the north side of the Rappahannock River. Toby Smith died sometime prior to April 15, 1658. In 1659 his widow, Phebe I, asked for her dower share of her late husband's Rockingham tract (LEO 21–22, 27; Old Rappahannock County Deeds and Wills 1656–1664:22–23, 66, 77; SR 3504, 4007; PB 1:749, 943; 2:13, 329; 3:24, 174, 328; 4:155).

William Smith: William Smith, a blacksmith and Virginia Company servant, set sail for Virginia in April 1619. By 1623 he had been assigned to Governor Francis Wyatt's guard. Therefore, he would have resided in urban Jamestown or on the Governor's Land. In February 1627 William Smith of Jamestown was identified as an heir of Thomas Roper, a gentleman (VI&A 651).

William Smith: On February 4, 1674, William Smith was said to possess a house and a child "at Towne," an indication that he had a dwelling in Jamestown, then the colony's only urban community. In November 1677 William and Thomas Smith were mentioned in the will of William White of Surry and may have been related. William Smith was still alive in 1696 (Surry County Deeds, Wills &c. 1671–1684:67, 203; Order Book 1671–1691:784; 1691–1700:150).

William Smith Jr.: On February 10, 1774, William Smith Jr. was described as proprietor of the ferry that ran from Jamestown to Cobham, where he had an ordinary (Purdie and Dixon, February 17, 1774).

J. F. D. Smyth: In 1773 J. F. D. Smyth, who visited Jamestown, described the former capital city as a "paltry place" that was too small to be considered a village. He said that he obtained horses from Mr. Travis (probably Champion Travis or his brother Edward IV) and went to Williamsburg. Smyth noted that Jamestown, despite its insignificant size, still had the right to representation in the assembly. He incorrectly surmised that Champion Travis was "the proprietor of the whole town" and that he probably was its only voter (Maxwell, "A Tour in the United States of America &c. by J. F. D. Smyth," 12–13).

Eleanor (Elinor, Ellenor) Snow (Snowe) (Mrs. [John?] Snow [Snowe]; Mrs. George Graves [Grave]) (see George Graves [Grave]): In February 1624 Eleanor, then the wife of George Graves (Grave), was living in urban Jamestown with her daughters, Rebecca and Sara Snow. She was still there a year later. Eleanor probably was the widow of John Snow, who perished at Weyanoke during the March 1622 Indian attack. When Robert Lindsey was captured and detained by the Pamunkey Indians in 1626, he sent word to Jamestown that his locked chest and personal possessions were to be given to

Sara Snow if he was not freed (VI&A 652–653).

* * *

Henry Soane (Soanes, Sonne?) I: Henry Soane I started speculating in real estate during the early 1650s. He began patenting land on the upper side of the Chickahominy River in 1651 and then began adding to his holdings in that area. Some of his acreage was in the vicinity of Diascund Creek, which eventually became the dividing line between James City and New Kent counties. He also began laying claim to land on the northeast side of the Mattaponi River, in what was then New Kent County, and on the south side of the Rappahannock River. Soane was a burgess for James City County from 1652 through 1654 and from 1658 to 1661. He and his wife, Judith, produced at least three children: John, Judith II, and William. Henry Soane I served as speaker of the assembly's March 1661 session but died before that body reconvened. He probably was the same Henry Soane or Sonne who in November 1655 witnessed Captain Roger Webster's sale of a Surry County mill to John Corker. Burgess Henry Soane I's daughter, Judith, married Henry Randolph I and at Randolph's death wed Major Peter Field of Henrico County (STAN 68–71, 73; HEN I:386–387; LEO 29–32, 34, 36–38; Surry County Deed Book I {1652–1661]:74–75; PB 2:351; 3:26–27, 199, 213; 4:80, 87; DOR 1:379).

John Soane (Soanes): John Soane, the son of burgess Henry Soane I, was a highly skilled surveyor and prepared plats of several James City County properties during the 1670s, 1680s, and 1690s. In October 1679 he surveyed the Iron Mine Meadows tract at Green Spring for Lady Frances Berkeley, and in 1681 he undertook surveys and prepared plats of two parcels that William Sherwood owned in the western end of Jamestown Island. In October 1682 Soane described the metes and bounds of another property Sherwood owned in urban Jamestown, and in 1684 he made a plat of Christopher Wormeley II's land, part of the plantation known as Powhatan. In 1683 Thomas Lord Culpeper hired John Soane to survey the Governor's Land, and in 1690 Henry Jenkins commissioned him to make a plat of his leasehold there. In 1695 Soane prepared an affidavit in which he described the boundaries of some property James and Ann Holder Chudley owned in urban Jamestown. These examples of Soane's work reveal that he was a meticulous draftsman whose work had a high degree of accuracy. The compass roses that appear on his plats reflect his experience as a mariner. In June 1699 Soane was designated James City County's official surveyor.

During the 1680s John Soane patented several pieces of land on the west side of the Chickahominy River, in what is now Charles City County. In 1683 he acquired a 457-acre tract, and a year later he patented 710 acres in the same vicinity. Finally, in 1687 and 1690 he patented two small parcels near Pease Hill Creek. Some of Soane's income was derived from the slave trade. As captain of the ship *Jeffrey*, he went to Old or New Callabar in August 1693 to exchange the Royal African Company's cargo for 340 Africans that he brought to Virginia. He also was sent to Africa by London merchant and slave trader Jeffrey Jeffreys, one of the Royal African Company's principal contractors in Virginia. On December 16, 1695, John Soane of James City County prepared his will, which was recorded in the Henrico County monthly court on August 1, 1699. He left his mother, Judith Soane, a modest sum of money, and he gave to his brother, William, his plantation called Poplar Spring, located on the east side of the Chickahominy River, and asked him to serve as his executor. The testator bequeathed his surveying and mathematical instruments to his "cousin" (actually, nephew) Henry Soane II. In June 1701, when some questions arose about the boundaries of the Governor's Land, the late John Soane's executors were ordered to search his papers to see whether they included a plat of the 3,000-acre publicly owned parcel. By that time the Governor's Land plat already had been sent to England and had become part of Lord Culpeper's papers (AMB 134, 135–136; Soane 1679, 1681, 1683, 1684, 1690, 1695; SAIN 17:293; 19:292; PRO T.70/61 f 106ro; NUG II:273, 280, 313, 344; Henrico County Wills and Deeds 1697–1704:145; EJC II:149–150; SR 5754).

William Soane (Soanes): In 1680 William Soane patented land on the upper side of the Chickahominy River, near the mouth of Diascund Creek in James City County. He appears to have resided in Henrico County, where he served as an agent of the county court. In 1695 he laid claim to some land in Varina Parish, acreage adjoining the property owned by the Rev. James Blair and two other men, a site that in 1680 was selected for urban development. Soane's acreage was located to the east of Farrar Island, in the immediate vicinity of historic Varina Farm. In April 1690 Henrico County official issued Soane a license that authorized him to keep an ordinary at Varina, sell liquor, and operate a ferry. He also received permission from the county justices to use the loft in the courthouse as extra lodging for his tavern guests. William Soane, who was age 41 in 1691, represented Henrico County in the assembly meetings that were held from 1695 to 1697. In 1695 when James City County surveyor John Soane made his will, he identified William Soane as his brother and left him some land on the Chickahominy. In 1702 William Soane patented 51 acres near the Varina acreage he already owned, and in 1704 he paid quitrent on 3,841 acres of Henrico County land. When he made his will on April 18, 1714, he made bequests to his wife, Mary; sons John, Henry, and Samuel; and daughters Martha Soane and Judith Thweatt. His holdings then included land in Henrico and Charles City counties. Captain William Soane's will was proved on January 3, 1715, and an inventory of his estate was made later in the year (LEO 54, 56; PB 7:22; 8:404; 9:432; MCGC 103; Henrico County Wills and Deeds 1688–1697:262, 305, 491, 559, 609; 1697–1704:145, 442; 1714–1718:9, 48; Orders and Wills 1678–1693:331, 340). William Soane of Henrico County may have been related to the man of the same name who came to Virginia in 1621 or 1622 on the *George*, at the expense of John Southern (VI&A 653; SMITH 83).

Henry Soane (Soanes): In 1695 James City County surveyor John Soane left his surveying and mathematical instruments to his nephew, Henry, the son of Henrico County burgess William Soane. In 1704 Henry Soane paid quitrent on 750 acres of James City County land. In October 1714 he was given weights and scales for one of the tobacco inspection warehouses in James City County, and on November 16, 1714, he commenced serving as one of the county's burgesses. Henry Soane made his will on May 21, 1722 (EJC III:381; PB 10:393; STAN 100; LEO 67; Henrico County Wills and Deeds 1697–1704:145; SMITH 83).

* * *

Sir George Somers: Sir George Somers set sail for Virginia in early June 1609 and was shipwrecked in Bermuda with Sir Thomas Gates. When they arrived in Virginia in May 1610, Gates designated him one of his councilors. Shortly after Lord Delaware's arrival in Jamestown in June, he sent Somers to Bermuda to bring back food for the colonists. He became ill there and died in November 1610 (VI&A 653; STAN 28).

Thomas Somersall: Thomas Somersall died on Jamestown Island sometime after April 1623 but before February 16, 1624 (VI&A 654).

Henry Soney (Soane, Sonne?): In 1629 James City Parish churchwarden John Jackson reported Henry Soney and three others to the General Court because their church dues were in arrears. In September 1632 Soney's bond was revoked at his request. In 1655 a man named Henry Sonne or Soane (perhaps the same individual) witnessed a deed in which Captain Richard Webster of Jamestown sold a mill on Gray's Creek in Surry County to John Corker, who was associated with Jamestown and Surry (VI&A 654; Surry County Deed Book I (1652–1661):74–75).

Henry Soothey (Southey, Sothey) I: In 1622 the Virginia Company gave Henry Soothey I a patent for 900 acres and noted that he and his associates planned to bring 100 people to Virginia. He and his wife, Elizabeth, arrived in the colony later in the year with their six children and ten servants. Between April 1623 and February 16, 1624, while the Sootheys were residing in urban Jamestown, Mr. Soothey and all but one of the couple's children (Mary, Thomas, Henry II, and two others whose first names are unknown) became ill and died. Elizabeth Soothey and daughter Ann were still living in Jamestown in January 1625. In May 1626 the justices of the General Court, apparently unaware that Henry Soothey II was dead, authorized him to take up 900 acres, the quantity of land to which his late father was entitled for transporting 18 people to Virginia. On September 10, 1627, after learning that Henry Soothey I and his son were dead, the General Court's justices awarded Mrs. Elizabeth Soothey a parcel of land near the late Rev. Richard Buck's house, in the east-central portion of Jamestown Island. On September 18, 1626, the court's justices heard testimony about an event witnessed by a man who had been residing at Mrs. Soothey's house in August 1626. Sometime prior to November 1635 Elizabeth and Henry Soothey I's daughter, Ann, married Charles Harmar (Harmor, Harmer, Harman) of Accomack, overseer of Lady Elizabeth Dale's property. Upon being widowed again, Ann wed Nathaniel Littleton I, also of Accomack and one of the Eastern Shore's most prominent citizens. In 1643 Ann Soothey Harmar Littleton received a headright certificate for the people her parents had transported to the colony (VI&A 654–656; AMES 2:309–310).

Robert Sorrell: In 1651 Robert Sorrell began patenting land on Warraney Creek in what was then James City County and added to his holdings within two years' time. On April 25, 1670, his dispute with Jonathan Newell's assignee, burgess and councilor Thomas Ballard, was aired before the General Court. In September 1676 Sorrell, who was in Jamestown, wounded some of the rebel Nathaniel Bacon's men who were trying to seize provisions set aside for use in marches against the Indians. He was killed while defending the capital city from a frontal attack by Bacon's men. Afterward, his widow, Rebecca, sought a widow's pension (PB 2:310; 3:26; SR 6618b; MCGC 218; JHB1660–1693:69).

Thomas Southcot (Southcoat, Southcote, Southcott, Southcoote): Captain Thomas Southcot served as a burgess from 1665 to 1671 and represented Charles City County. He died in 1671 and probably was succeeded by Nicholas Wyatt (LEO 37; HEN II:249). Thomas Southcot may have had a connection with Captain Otho Southcot, a Charles City County justice, who was living in the county in 1661, and in September 1672 was ordered to examine some records in a suit involving some Charles City residents (MCGC 309; Charles City County Orders 1658–1661:252; 1661–1664:402).

John Southern (Sotherne): John Southern, an experienced artisan, came to Virginia in 1620 and brought along the men and equipment needed to erect an ironworks at Southampton Hundred, which he represented in the assembly. During the mid-1620s he resided in urban Jamestown, but he may have begun developing some property in the eastern end of Jamestown Island, acreage he patented in 1626. As a burgess he represented Jamestown during 1630 and 1632 assembly meetings (VI&A 656; LEO 5, 9–10).

William Southey (Southeree): When William Southey, a surgeon on the ship *Samuel*, was in Jamestown on February 27, 1628, he informed the justices of the General Court that he had witnessed the wills Samuel Gilpin and Marmion Leake made while they were aboard (VI&A 657).

Thomas Sowerby: On July 3, 1683, Henry Gawler of urban Jamestown sued Thomas Sowerby in Surry County's monthly court. The suit was dismissed (Surry County Order Book 1671–1691:409).

Mr. and Mrs. Edward Spalding: On February 16, 1624, Edward Spalding, his wife, a son, and a daughter were living in urban Jamestown in Mr. Cann's household (VI&A 657).

Spark: In 1769 when an inventory was made of the late Edward Ambler I's estate, an adult male slave named Spark was living on Jamestown Island (AMB-E).

Robert Sparkes: Robert Sparkes came to Virginia prior to 1611 and would have lived in Jamestown. In January 1613 Captain Samuel Argall left Sparkes and four other males as hostages when trading with the Indians for corn along the Potomac River (VI&A 658).

Charles Sparrow (Sparrowe): Around 1649 Charles Sparrow patented 750 acres of land on the lower side of the James River, in what was then Charles City County but later became Prince George. His acreage was on the west side of Upper Chippokes Creek and abutted Martin's Brandon. Sparrow represented Charles City County in the assembly in 1645–1646, 1649, 1652, and 1660. He became a county justice in 1656 and held office for the rest of his life. He was nominated as sheriff in 1657 but was passed over. Throughout the years he arbitrated disputes, served on coroner's juries, and performed other public duties. When London merchant John Sadler made his will in 1658, leaving some cattle and goods to the minister of Martin's Brandon Parish, he entrusted his bequest to the custody of Charles Sparrow. In 1659 Sparrow went to court, where he transferred to Captain Richard Tye's eldest daughter, Elizabeth, his share of 2,500 acres near Merchant's Hope, acreage that he and Tye had patented jointly. If Elizabeth died, the property was to descend to her younger siblings. Charles Sparrow died on September 11, 1660, and five days later his widow, Jane, married William Rawlinson (Rollinson). On October 3, 1660, Charles City County's justices decided that an inventory of the decedent's estate should be compiled immediately, and an acting administrator was ordered to pay the surgeon who had attended Sparrow in his final illness. On February 11, 1661, William Rawlinson was named trustee of the decedent's estate until the arrival of Charles Sparrow's son and heir, Selby Sparrow, and Rawlinson was authorized to pay for the medical care provided to Jane Sparrow before her husband's death. In August 1661 William Byrd I, who was then living at Martin's Brandon, was authorized to sell the late Charles Sparrow's property. In December 1661 Selby Sparrow, who was a minor, asked Charles City County's justices for an account of the property he stood to inherit. The justices also were obliged to appoint a guardian for him. By August 1663 Selby Sparrow was dead and his stepfather, William Rawlinson, asked that the late Charles Sparrow's real and personal estate be divided among Charles' surviving orphans and that he (Rawlinson) be given custody of his wife's dower share (LEO 24, 27, 30, 36; PB 2:168, 248; Charles City County Order Book 1655–1658:46, 83; 1658–1661:154, 203, 235, 245, 247, 254, 258, 266, 270; 1661–1664:303, 319, 402, 414; WAT 621).

John Spearman: John Spearman, a laborer, arrived in Jamestown in early 1608 as part of the 1st Supply of new settlers (VI&A 659).

Henry Speed (Speede): On May 30, 1625, Henry Speed, a sailor on the *Temperance*, testified before the General Court about the disposition of the late Henry Wilkinson's personal effects. On March 12, 1627, he offered testimony about an incident in the West Indies that involved the ship *Saker* (VI&A 659).

Thomas Speke (Speake, Speak, Spake) I: By 1650 Thomas Speke I had begun serving as a justice in Northumberland County's monthly court, a position he held for many years. His eligibility to serve indicates that he or his wife owned property in the county. In 1651–1652 Speke represented the county in the assembly. During 1651 he patented two large tracts of land in Northumberland County, one of which was on the Nominy River, and in 1653 he patented another 1,000 acres on the Potomac. In November 1653 Speke's first wife, Ann, when testifying in court about an event that had occurred four or five years earlier, said that she was approximately age 42. By April 1655 Thomas Speke had become a militia colonel, and he was appointed a justice of Westmoreland County's monthly court. He was one of the overseers of the late Colonel John Mottrom I's will and kept some of his livestock at Mottrom's plantation. In July 1656 Mottrom's underage children chose Colonel Speke as their legal guardian. Like most of his peers, Speke appeared in court from time to time to participate in litigation that usually involved debt. When he made his will on December 1, 1659, he indicated that he was in failing health. He bequeathed life-rights in his home plantation to his second wife, Frances, who also stood to receive some servants and livestock. However, half of the orchard on the property and a moiety of its profits were to go to the testator's son and primary heir, Thomas II, to whom he also left 700 acres of his plantation called Curriwoman. Thomas Speke I bequeathed 200 acres and some livestock to his brother, John, who was then in England, and urged him to move to Virginia. He also left remembrances to his father-in-law, Thomas Gerrard, and his wife, Susanna; brother-in-law Robert Slye; and godson Thomas Gerrard. Speke died sometime prior to January 14, 1660, when his will was proved. Later in the month his widow, Frances, presented an inventory of his estate to the county court. An account of his estate reveals that a gunner was injured at his funeral, probably when a salute was fired, and that attendees included an array of prominent individuals, including one member of the Council of State. By November 1662 Thomas Speke's widow, Frances, had married Valentine Peyton, who died sometime prior to June 1665. She went on to marry John Washington I (LEO 28; Northumberland County Deeds and Orders 1650–1652:41; Wills, Inventories &c. 1652–1658:21, 36, 87, 114; Record Book 1658–1662:62; Order Book 1652–1665:1, 94, 96, 145, 170, 219; Westmoreland County Deeds, Wills, Patents &c. 1653–1659:36, 94, 116a; Deeds, Wills, &c. 1661–1662:4a–6a, 47–47a; Deeds and Wills No. 1 [1653–1671]:103–105, 259; PB 2:337; 3:68).

Henry Spellman (Spillman, Spilman, Spelman): Henry Spellman, a youth, arrived in Jamestown in 1609 in the 3rd Supply of new colonists. Captain John Smith sold him to an Indian tribe called the Little Powhatan, but he escaped and fled to the Patomeck Indians, who detained him. Some of Spellman's contemporaries considered him the colony's most skillful linguist. Spellman left Virginia but returned by 1616 and again began serving as an interpreter. During the late spring or early summer 1619, Captain Henry Spellman angered high-ranking officials by making some inflammatory statements to the Indian leader Opechancanough. As a result, he was censured and his rank was reduced to Company servant. He also was ordered to serve the governor for seven years as a public interpreter. In March 1623 Spellman was killed by the Anacostan Indians (VI&A 659).

Thomas Spellman (Spillman, Spilman, Spelman): Thomas Spellman came to Virginia in 1623 and in February 1624 was a servant in the household of Richard Stephens, a Jamestown merchant. He was still there a year later (VI&A 660).

Alexander Spence: Alexander Spence, the stepson of Westmoreland burgess John Jordan, was a Westmoreland County justice

during the 1690s. In October 1694 he patented 47 acres in Richmond County, and in July 1695 he acquired 328 acres in Westmoreland. He went on to represent Westmoreland County in the assembly meetings that were held in 1695–1696, 1696–1697, 1698, and 1699. He also served as the county's official surveyor. When he prepared his will on May 2, 1704, he described himself as a resident of Yeowocomico and "sick and weak." He made bequests to his son, Patrick, and to his daughters, Dorcas, Mary, and Elizabeth, but specified that his wife was to have nothing but her own wearing apparel and her dower share of the profits of his plantation. Alexander Spence's will was proved on May 2, 1704, and an inventory of his estate was presented in August (LEO 53, 55, 57–59; Westmoreland County Deeds and Wills Book 2 [1691–1699]:9a,10a–12a; 3 [1701–1707]:11–13, 250–252, 301–305, 390–391; NN 2:47–48, 175–176; SMITH 112).

Mr. and Mrs. William Spence (Spense): William Spence arrived in Jamestown in 1608 in the 1st Supply of new settlers. His contemporaries described him variously as a laborer, farmer, and gentleman who was honest and valiant. During Sir Thomas Dale's government (1611–1616), Ensign Spence was the first farmer to seat his own land, which was located in the eastern end of Jamestown Island. In July 1619 he represented Jamestown in Virginia's first legislative assembly. Although Spence and a partner secured a patent for 300 acres in Archer's Hope, Spence continued to reside on Jamestown Island. In February 1624 Spence, his wife, and their Virginia-born daughter, Sara (Sarah), were said to be residing on Jamestown Island, but at the same time the Spence couple was listed among those who had died since February 1623. The orphaned Sara Spence was entrusted to the care of a guardian, Mrs. Susan Bush, a young widow and resident of Elizabeth City. In 1624 John Johnson I was ordered to make repairs to the late Ensign Spence's property, presumably rendering it tenantable, and Sara's guardians were told to have her Archer's Hope property surveyed. By April 3, 1627, Sara Spence was dead (VI&A 661).

Alexander Spencer (Sponsor, Spenser): In January 1672 Alexander Spencer, who appears to have come to Virginia around 1668, appeared before the justices of Surry County's monthly court, where he acknowledged a debt to Colonel Thomas Swann I. On October 12, 1675, Spencer initiated a suit against Jamestown innkeeper Richard Lawrence, but it was dismissed. Spencer had property in Surry County, where he was a tithe. In 1677 he was identified as a debtor to George Marable II and Colonel Thomas Swann I, both of whom owned property in urban Jamestown. Spencer was still alive in 1680, but afterward his name disappeared from the records, suggesting that he left the colony or moved to a county whose records have been destroyed (MCGC 427; Surry County Order Book 1671–1691:19, 105, 155, 181, 218, 235, 321; NUG II:32).

Kathren Spencer (Spenser): On February 16, 1624, Kathren Spencer (Spenser) was a servant in Governor Francis Wyatt's urban Jamestown household (VI&A 662).

Nicholas Spencer I: Nicholas Spencer I and his brother, Robert, came to Virginia in 1657 aboard the *Sea Horse* with John and Lawrence Washington, forebears of America's first president. Nicholas Spencer I became the Washingtons' neighbor, and in 1677 he and John Washington I jointly patented 5,000 acres of land in Stafford County. A power of attorney dated September 1659 referred to Spencer as a London merchant, which suggests that although he was living in Virginia, he maintained close ties to the English mercantile community. In August 1658 Spencer and another Westmoreland County man acquired 1,000 acres of land at Turkey Point, in what is now Calvert County, Maryland. On August 18, 1662, Anne Mottrom Wright, the eldest daughter of Colonel John Mottrom I, conveyed to Nicholas Spencer of Chickacone (Chicacoan) 900 acres of land bordering Nominy Bay, part of the acreage that Mottrom, a wealthy and powerful planter, had patented in August 1650. Spencer may have already married Anne's younger sister, Frances. When Richard Wright made his will on August 16, 1663, he referred to Nicholas Spencer I and John Mottrom II as his brothers, that is, brothers-in-law, leaving no doubt that Nicholas and Frances were then husband and wife. Together, Nicholas and Frances Mottrom Spencer produced several sons, all of whom were born between 1665 and 1685–1687.

Surviving patents reveal that Nicholas Spencer I, a successful planter, began speculating in land in the Northern Neck. He also enhanced his financial wellbeing by trading in imported goods and holding public offices. On October 27, 1664, he was among those sworn in as justices of Westmoreland County's monthly court. He was a burgess during the Commonwealth period (1652–1662), and in 1666 he was returned to the assembly, holding office until 1676. Thus,

between 1671 and 1676 Nicholas Spencer simultaneously held three important public positions, for he was a county justice, burgess, and a member of the Council of State. In June 1666, when the Grand Assembly decided to suspend the planting of tobacco for a year, Governor William Berkeley authorized Colonel Spencer and other emissaries to make cessation agreements with the governors of Maryland and Carolina. When the Dutch threatened to attack in November 1667, Spencer attended a meeting of the Association of Northumberland, Westmoreland, and Stafford Counties, which decided to erect a fort at Yeomocomico. He relinquished his seat in the county court in 1678, shortly before he became Secretary of the Colony. After Governor William Berkeley died, Spencer asked his brother to use his influence at court to see that he was reappointed Collector of Customs for the Lower Potomac River, a very lucrative position.

When the rebel Nathaniel Bacon railed against Governor Berkeley and his loyalists during Bacon's Rebellion, he described Spencer as one of his "wicked and pernicious councilors and assistants." In January 1677 King Charles II's Special Commissioners described Spencer as someone whose personal estate "was much impaired . . . by the late rebels." A petition filed on August 25, 1677, by Major Isaac Allerton, whose property had sustained damage during Bacon's Rebellion, reveals that Nicholas and Frances Spencer's home in Nominy was occupied by some of Bacon's followers. Allerton's testimony made reference to "the rebels' garrison at Spencers" and Bacon's men's presence at the residence of Colonel John Washington I. In May 1677, when the colonial government and the tributary Indians made a formal peace agreement at Middle Plantation, Colonel Nicholas Spencer was on the Council of State, and he held office when the treaty was expanded in 1680. He served as Secretary of the Colony from 1679 to September 1689, and during the summer of 1680 he sent word to England that the Indians were at peace, probably because of the garrisons at the rivers' heads. As council president, he became acting head of the Virginia government in 1683, when Thomas Lord Culpeper went to England, and he served until February 1684.

On April 25, 1688, Nicholas Spencer of Nominy in Westmoreland County, Virginia, made his last will and testament; he asked to be buried "without pomp or shew [*sic*] or the indecencies of funerals in this Country accustomed." He seems to have exercised his right to have his will proved in the General

Court, a privilege extended to those whose assets were known to exceed their debts. Although Spencer's original will has been lost or destroyed, along with most of the General Court's other records, a copy was filed in England, where he also had significant financial assets. The widowed Frances Mottrom Spencer received life-rights in the Westmoreland County tract called "Kingcopsco," which included the family home, and relinquished her dower rights in a third of the decedent's realty. The rest of Nicholas Spencer's personal property in Virginia was to be divided equally among his wife, Frances, and sons Nicholas II, John, and Francis. On October 22, 1689, Virginia's Council of State sent word to the Lords of Trade and Plantations that Secretary Nicholas Spencer died on September 23, 1689. Correspondence Spencer sent to English officials in April 1689 reveals that he was then residing in James City County on a plantation he was renting from Lady Frances Berkeley and her husband, Philip Ludwell I. The Spencer household appears to have returned to Westmoreland County by January 1690. In late November 1691 Madam Frances Spencer presented Westmoreland County's court justices with the Rev. John Scrimgeour's nuncupative will, which named her as heir. He had been living in Mrs. Spencer's home in Nominy and serving as her farm manager or overseer. He also kept all of his clothing, personal effects, household furnishings, livestock, and servants there. Although Mrs. Spencer was authorized to settle his estate, that arrangement soon proved controversial, for the deceased clergyman's brother arrived from England and successfully contested the validity of the will. Sometime prior to November 30, 1693, the widowed Frances Mottrom Spencer married the Rev. John Bolton, the rector of Westmoreland County's Cople Parish. Court testimony taken in July 1694 suggests that within months of the time they wed, the Bolton couple began having marital problems. Other court records suggest that Bolton, who was Irish, was very aggressive toward women (NUG I:395, 547; II:6, 48, 60, 82, 86, 178; Westmoreland County Deeds and Wills 1 [1653–1671]:265, 314, 317–318; Deeds, Wills, etc. 1661–1662:18, 20–21; 1662–1664:9–10, 27, 33–34, 36, 38–39, 41; [1665–1677]:27–29, 33–35, 39–40, 45, 49, 54–55, 57, 63–64, 66–67, 83, 89–90, 93–95, 102, 105, 111, 118–119, 127, 134–135, 140, 142–143, 146, 159, 184–185, 264–266, 271, 318–319, 325a–326, 364; Order Book 1676–1679:69, 75–76, 103, 129; 1679–1682:220, 231, 250; 1691–1692:1, 11, 18, 42; 1692–1694:88, 106, 144; HEN II:225–226, 255–258, 275; STAN 17, 21, 40; SR 69, 641, 740, 4790, 6618, 7366; SAIN 9:437–438; 10:92–93, 108, 498; 11:241, 613; 13: 32–33, 162; NEVILLE 378–379; PPR Register Books 14–15 Noel; EJC I:53; 1924:522; LEO 40).

Robert Spencer (Spenser, Spensor): In 1672 Captain Robert Spencer patented 300 acres in Surry County, approximately a mile up Crouches Creek. On March 6, 1675, the General Court deferred hearing his suit against Captain William Corker, the son of John Corker, a property owner in urban Jamestown. Spencer, who was married to Elizabeth, the daughter of Captain John White I of Jamestown, was attempting to recover a bed and furniture that his wife stood to inherit. When the case again appeared on the court docket on June 17th, it was dismissed. After the death of Spencer's wife, Elizabeth, he remarried. By May 1679 he himself was deceased and his widow and executrix, Jane, had married Thomas Jordan. The decedent was survived by his daughter, Elizabeth, who chose her stepfather as her guardian (MCGC 407, 413; Surry County Will Book 2:140, 203; Order Book 1671–1691:247, 265, 288, 301, 335–336, 349; PB 6:404). Robert Spencer of Surry County does not appear to have been related to Secretary Nicholas Spencer, who had a brother named Robert.

William Spencer (Spenser) I: In 1624 William Spencer I, a yeoman and ancient planter, secured a patent for a narrow ridge of land in the eastern end of Jamestown Island, a parcel that bordered the James River. By January 1625 he was residing there with his wife, Alice I, and daughter, Alice II, but his son, William II, was dead. In 1629 Spencer inherited the property of his neighbor John Lightfoot. Later that year, when he patented 290 acres, he used the headright of his wife, Dorothy, indicating that she had come to the colony in 1619. Spencer probably married Dorothy before he wed Alice I, with whom he was living in 1625. Spencer and his wife went on to produce at least two more daughters, Elizabeth and Anne. In 1633 William Spencer served as a burgess for Mulberry Island. During the early 1630s he patented 1,350 acres of land on Lawnes Creek, the lower side of the James River, and in 1640 he served as official tobacco viewer for territory that extended from Lawnes Creek to Hog Island. Spencer retained his Jamestown Island property until around 1637–1638 and conducted business on Captain William Peirce's behalf as late as January 1655. By 1654 Spencer's daughter, Anne, had married William Cockerham. His daughter, Elizabeth, wed three times in succession, taking as her husband Robert Sheppard, Thomas Warren, and John Hunnicutt. She died between 1655 and 1658 (VI&A 662–663; DOR 3:227–228; LEO 12).

Arthur Spicer: Captain Arthur Spicer moved to Old Rappahannock County sometime prior to November 1680 and from time to time appeared in the local court, often as an attorney. He frequently did business in Lancaster and Westmoreland counties, where he initiated lawsuits and often served as an attorney. One of the people he represented was Robert Beverley II. Spicer represented Old Rappahannock County in the assembly meetings held in 1685–1686 and 1688, and in 1693 he served on behalf of the newly formed Richmond County. When George Talbot of Maryland was brought to Jamestown in 1686 and tried for murder, Arthur Spicer and Colonel Thomas Ballard served as his attorneys. In March 1692 Spicer patented 1,174 acres on the north side of the Rappahannock River, in a portion of Old Rappahannock County that became Richmond County. The following year he patented 2,750 acres in Essex County on the south side of the Rappahannock, toward the head of Peumansend Creek. By September 1693 Captain Spicer had married Elizabeth, the daughter and only heir of Thomas Jones, who joined him in selling a piece of Richmond County property. In April 1695 Spicer bought 343 acres of Richmond County land, a plantation commonly known as the New Courthouse. He identified himself as a resident of Richmond County in April 1696 when filing a suit in Essex County's monthly court. In 1697 merchant and attorney William Sherwood of urban Jamestown, who had served with Spicer in the assembly, bequeathed him some money to buy a mourning ring. As London merchant Jeffrey Jeffreys' representative, Captain Spicer eventually took custody of Sherwood's estate. He was still pursuing litigation in Essex County in 1698 and 1699, when he served as the attorney of a Bristol merchant. Spicer died sometime prior to April 12, 1700 (AMB 65; MCGH 873; LEO 48–49, 52–54; Old Rappahannock County Deeds and Wills 1677–1682:290; Order Book 1683–1686:141, 149, 155; 1687–1692:148, 226; Lancaster County Order Book 1680–1687:3, 82; PB 8:271; Essex County Deeds and Wills 1 [1696–1699]:36–37; Order Book 1695–1699:9, 166, 333; 1699–1702:37; Richmond County Deed Book 1 [1692–1693]:79, 186–189; 2 [1693–1695]:17, 162–166; Westmoreland County Order Book 1676–1689: 278, 283–288, 301, 316, 327, 365, 462, 485, 511, 632; NN 1:158; SR 237, 680).

John Spier (Spiers, Spiors): In March 1676 the General Court authorized John Spier to patent approximately 600 acres of land in Nansemond County, acreage that George Abbott had claimed and then deserted. When Richard Briggs of Surry County made his will in 1679, he instructed his executors to see that his son, Edmund, was placed with Dr. John Spier of Nansemond County. Spier served as a burgess from 1680 to 1682, representing Nansemond County. In February 1696 he invested in some land in Essex County, and in 1704 he paid quitrent on 160 acres that were located there (LEO 45; Essex County Deeds and Wills 1695–1699:24; Isle of Wight County Wills and Deeds 2:195; MCGC 444; SMITH 84).

Alexander Spotswood: Lieutenant Governor Alexander Spotswood, who took office on June 23, 1710, was concerned about the insufficiency of Jamestown's fortifications. During August and September 1711, he made six trips to the former capital to inspect the line battery. On June 30, 1713, he proposed trading some grazing land near Jamestown (acreage reserved for the governor's use) for 40 acres near Williamsburg. In July 1718 Spotswood tried to remove Rev. James Blair and Philip Ludwell II—two men he intensely disliked—from his council. He also alleged that the southerly boundary of Ludwell's Green Spring plantation had encroached upon the Governor's Land and brought suit in an attempt to restore it to its original size of 3,000 acres. Ludwell's attorney succeeded in demonstrating that the boundary line between the two properties had remained fixed and that whatever land had been lost was attributable to erosion (STAN 18; CO 5/1316 ff 440–441; WMQ 3[2]:41. Spotswood built forts and personal residences on the Virginia frontier at Fort Christanna in today's Brunswick County and at Germanna in Orange County. In 1716 he led a party of horsemen who set out from Germanna and ventured as far west as the Shenandoah River. Spotswood and his fellow travelers called themselves the Knights of the Golden Horseshoe.

Eleanor (Elinor) Sprad (Spradd, Sprade, Sprage): In 1624 Eleanor Sprad, a maidservant in merchant Edward Blaney's household in urban Jamestown, ran afoul of the law when she became engaged to two men. For this infraction of moral law, she was ordered to apologize to the congregation of the church in Jamestown (VI&A 663).

Rudolph (Rudalph, Radolph, Radulph) Spraggon (Spragon, Spragling): In June 1635 Rudolph Spraggon set sail for Virginia with Captain William Barker, a mariner who owned and occupied a waterfront lot in urban Jamestown. Like the other men and women aboard the ship, Spraggon probably was an indentured servant. On August 18, 1644, he patented a one-acre lot in the western end of Jamestown Island, a parcel he seems to have occupied. He was still alive in April 1649 and was identified as a resident "of James City" and a debtor (VI&A 663).

Robert Spring: Robert Spring, a London merchant, set out for Virginia during the early 1670s with his servants and some goods. They reached Barbados, where Spring made a bargain with mariner Robert Browning, who agreed to take them to Virginia on the *Hercules* in exchange for some sugar and tobacco. Later, Spring and Browning got into a dispute over the terms of their bargain. On February 10, 1677, when Governor William Berkeley named those who were exempt from the king's pardon on account of their role in Bacon's Rebellion, he listed Robert Spring, who was supposed to be brought before a court. Later in the year Secretary Coventry asked Lieutenant Governor Herbert Jeffreys to collect some funds from Spring, who owed him a large sum. Coventry said that Spring had formerly lived in London but had settled in Virginia. Robert Spring, or perhaps a relative, patented 300 acres at the head of the Elizabeth River's western branch in 1653 and repatented that acreage in 1665 (NEVILLE 61; SR 660, 832, 10434; PB 3:17; 5:548).

William Spring: William Spring, an indentured servant employed by Thomas Rabley of urban Jamestown, allegedly was taken out of Virginia by Colonel Thomas Swann I, also a Jamestown property owner. On July 2, 1678, Rabley brought suit against Swann in the Surry County monthly court (Surry County Order Book 1671–1691:211).

[No First Name] Stacie (Stacy): According to Captain John Smith, in 1610 Master Stacie, one of the first Jamestown colonists, sought revenge against the Pasbehay Indians (VI&A 664).

Robert Stacie (Stacy, Stacey): In 1619 Robert Stacy was one of the two burgesses who represented Martin's Brandon. Both men were denied seats because the legality of Captain John Martin's patent was questioned. Stacie may have been related to Thomas Stacie, a Virginia Company investor (VI&A 664; LEO 3).

Peter Stafferton (Stasserton): In September 1623 Peter Stafferton, a gentleman, witnessed the will of John Atkins of Warresqueak. By February 1624 Stafferton and his wife, Mary, were living on the mainland or Governor's Land, just west of Jamestown Island. Later in the year he appeared in court twice to address legal matters. In 1627 he shipped goods from London to Virginia and was involved in a lawsuit that involved goods exchanged for tobacco. In 1635 and 1638 Stafferton patented land in Elizabeth City, and in 1640 he represented that jurisdiction in the assembly (VI&A 664; LEO 18).

Daniel Stallings: Daniel Stallings, a jeweler, arrived in Jamestown in 1608 in the 1st Supply of new colonists (VI&A 665).

Edward Stallings alias Roecroft: Edward Stallings alias Roecroft visited New England with Captain John Smith in 1615 and co-authored an account of their adventures. Stallings was hired to undertake a fishing voyage and returned to New England in December 1619. Afterward, he cruised down the coast, heading for Jamestown, where he intended to spend the winter. Shortly after his arrival he engaged in a heated dispute with Captain William Eppes, which resulted in a duel. Stallings, who received a blow to the head from Eppes's sheathed sword, collapsed and died (VI&A 665).

Roger Stanley: Roger Stanley, who came to Virginia in 1620, was a servant of Dr. John Pott, a resident of urban Jamestown. Stanley was living on the Maine in 1625. In 1626, when he and Thomas Lister (Leyster) got into a heated dispute, they fought with swords and then with their bare hands. Afterward, Stanley died of a wound to his arm (VI&A 666).

Elizabeth Starkey: Elizabeth Starkey, a young maid who came to Virginia in 1621, was living in urban Jamestown in 1624 and was a member of merchant Edward Blaney's household (VI&A 666).

Jane Steckie: Sometime prior to September 1625, Jane Steckie became one of cape merchant Abraham Peirsey's servants. She probably resided in the Peirsey home in urban Jamestown or at Flowerdew Hundred, where Peirsey also had a residence (VI&A 667).

* * *

Thomas Stegg I: Thomas Stegg I, a Jamestown merchant and avid supporter of Governor John Harvey, ran afoul of the authorities in 1640 when he helped Secretary Richard

Kemp slip out of Virginia with some public documents. In 1643 Stegg became a burgess for Charles City County, where he had a plantation on Old Man's Creek. He became a member of the Council of State in 1642 and in 1643 became a burgess and speaker of the assembly. When John Watson patented a one-acre lot "neare the Brewere poynt" on August 28, 1644, his land abutted that of Thomas Stegg I. A document dated June 18, 1650, and entered into the records of Lower Norfolk County's monthly court, reveals that Captain Stegg imported indentured servants into the colony and sold them; his son, Thomas Stegg II, served as security. Thomas Stegg I made his will on October 6, 1651, when he was preparing to set sail for Virginia. He was in the Parliamentary fleet sent to force the colony to submit to the Commonwealth government. Stegg died before July 14, 1652, and his will was proved by his widow, sole executrix, and heir, Elizabeth. The testator designated his son, Thomas Stegg II, as his reversionary heir and made bequests to his daughter, Grace Byrd, and her children. The widowed Elizabeth Stegg married Thomas Grendon II, with whom she produced a son, Thomas Grendon III (MCGC 482, 492, 495; HEN I:239, 375; STAN 35, 63; LEO 21; Lower Norfolk County Book A:191; C:43; WAT 101–102; FOR II:9:19; EEAC 55; PB 2:10; NUG I:154).

Thomas Stegg II: Thomas Stegg II was the son of Thomas Stegg I, a Jamestown merchant, burgess, and member of the Council of State. As reversionary heir, he inherited his late father's property in Virginia, which included some Charles City County acreage. Thomas Stegg II began patenting land in Henrico County, which he made his home, and he married Sarah, George Harris's widow. Stegg was named to the Council of State in 1662 and from 1664 to 1667 served as auditor general. While he was a councilor, he and Secretary Thomas Ludwell collaborated on the construction of a brick row house on the waterfront in the western end of Jamestown Island. He and Ludwell also purchased a neighboring row house unit from Henry Randolph I. In October 1665, while auditor general, Stegg summoned the colony's sheriffs and other tax officials to Jamestown to present their accounts. When he made his will on March 31, 1669, he left his Jamestown property to Thomas Ludwell and noted that he was including his interest in the land, furniture, and neighboring row house that he and Ludwell had purchased from Henry Randolph I. Stegg bestowed the rest of his property upon his nephew, William Byrd I, who was the son of John and

Grace Stegg Byrd; included was a fine stone house near the falls of the James River. After Stegg's death in Virginia in 1670, his widow, Sarah, married Thomas Grendon III of Charles City County. During Bacon's Rebellion Sarah's outspokenness and endorsement of the rebel Nathaniel Bacon's views made Governor William Berkeley despise her. In February 1677 Berkeley declared her exempt from the king's pardon (HEN I:239; STAN 35, 63; Lower Norfolk County Book A:191; FOR 9:19; MCGC 225, 507, 482, 484, 486, 488, 490–492, 495, 509–510; NEVILLE 61; STAN 22, 39; NUG I:154, 230, 425, 478, 537; II:69; PB 6:223; WITH 107; CO 1/20 Part I f 199; EEAC 55; WAT 102–103; Old Rappahannock County Deeds and Wills 1665–1677:37–38; DOR 2:226).

* * *

John Stegg: On March 15, 1643, the sheriff of Elizabeth City County was ordered to seize the estate of Sir Edmund Plowden so that John Stegg could pay Plowden's debt to William Parry, a Jamestown merchant. On June 6, 1644, Parry was ordered to give security for the powder, sack (wine), and steel he obtained from Plowden's store (MCGC 561).

Stephen: According to Captain John Smith, on May 20, 1607, Stephen, a sailor, accompanied Captain Christopher Newport on an exploratory voyage up the James River. Therefore, Stephen would have lived in Jamestown (VI&A 667).

Stephen: A man named Stephen came to Virginia on the *Furtherance* and died in Jamestown sometime after April 1623 but before February 16, 1624 (VI&A 667).

George Stephens (Stevens, Steephens, Steevens): George Stephens, who owned some land on Lawnes Creek in what is now Surry County, served as a burgess for James City County and attended the assembly sessions held in 1645, in 1645–1646, and in March 1652. When the legislature reconvened in November 1652, Stephens was representing Surry County, which had been formed from the southerly part of James City. In 1653 he purchased 950 acres in Upper Chippokes at Cabin Point from John Johnson of James City County. He retained that acreage until 1659. Stephens became a court justice in 1664 and died sometime prior to May 7, 1667. He was survived by his sister, Elizabeth Pitt, and by his son, James, who in 1667 was gravely ill (STAN 64, 68; LEO 23–24, 29–30; HEN I:289; Surry

Deed Book 1 [1652–1663]:16, 28, 83–84, 108, 141; 2 [1664–1671]:280–281, 319, 411, 458).

* * *

Richard Stephens: Richard Stephens, a merchant and Virginia Company investor, came to Virginia in 1623. Shortly after his arrival he secured and developed a waterfront lot in urban Jamestown. He resided there and in 1624 became a burgess, representing the community's merchants. Around 1628 Stephens married cape-merchant Abraham Peirsey's daughter, Elizabeth II. As Peirsey's surviving heir, she inherited Flowerdew Hundred. Together Richard and Elizabeth Peirsey Stephens produced two sons, Samuel and William I. William, the younger son, was born around 1630. When he died around 1656, he was identified as a cooper and was survived by his wife, Margaret, and their son, William Stephens II. In 1630, while Sir John Harvey was governor, Richard Stephens was named to the Council of State and served until 1636. By that time he had patented some land in Elizabeth City. He clashed openly with Harvey, whom he sought to have ousted from office, and in 1635 the two came to blows. Stephens died around 1636, leaving his wife, Elizabeth, life-rights in his 500-acre Warwick River plantation called Boldrup, which he had acquired from William Claiborne. Elizabeth Peirsey Stephens was living there in 1638 when she married Governor John Harvey, who was many years her senior and one of her late husband's enemies. The Harveys lived in Jamestown, probably in the residence that sometimes served as the colony's statehouse. When Harvey left office in 1639 and returned to England, Elizabeth accompanied him and died there sometime prior to September 1646 (VI&A 667–668; DOR 3:249; STAN 32; LEO 5; NUG I:72).

Samuel Stephens: Samuel, the son of Richard and Elizabeth Peirsey Stephens, was born around 1629 and as his father's primary heir stood to inherit his home lot in urban Jamestown and plantations in Elizabeth City, Upper Norfolk (Nansemond) County, and Warwick County. When Stephens married Frances Culpeper in 1653, he agreed to give her his Warwick County plantation, Boldrup, if he died before producing an heir. In 1662 Stephens was designated commander of Albemarle (in Carolina), and in 1667 he commenced serving a three-year term as the proprietary's governor. While Stephens held office in Carolina, a turf fort was built on the western part of his Jamestown lot. Samuel Stephens died sometime

prior to March 1670, and in accord with the marriage contract he had signed in 1653, Boldrup descended to his widow, Frances, who successively married Sir William Berkeley and Philip Ludwell I (VI&A 668; DOR 3:248).

Frances Culpeper Stephens (Mrs. Samuel Stephens, Mrs. William Berkeley, Mrs. Philip Ludwell I) (see Frances Culpeper Stephens Berkeley)

* * *

John Stevenson: John Stevenson, a gentleman, came to Virginia in 1607 and was one of the first Jamestown colonists (VI&A 669).

Augustine (Augustin) Steward: In May 1622 Augustine Steward, who set out for Virginia with Lord Delaware in 1618 but returned to England, testified in court. He said that when he and Edward Brewster were in Jamestown, Brewster had behaved harshly toward Delaware's men. He also described the *Neptune's* encounter with the *Treasurer* while both ships were at sea (VI&A 669).

John Stirring: On January 26, 1650, John Stirring wrote a letter to John Ferrar in which he described many of the Virginia colony's natural resources and its economic potential. He also described the extent to which the colony was developed and said that there had been two or three brew-houses in Jamestown, but that they had failed because their proprietors were unable to collect whatever their patrons owed (FER 1152).

John Stith: John Stith came to Virginia sometime prior to 1656. He settled in Charles City County where he became a lieutenant, captain, and then major of the local militia. In 1663 Stith and Samuel Eale, a business partner, began patenting land on the upper side of the James River in Charles City County. Their 500-acre tract was near Herring Creek and Captain Henry Perry's plantation, Buckland. A year later Stith, who was a merchant and county justice, laid claim to another 550 acres on the upper side of the James, and he expanded his holdings in 1675 and 1683. Because Stith was a staunch supporter of Governor William Berkeley, his conduct was questioned during 1677 and 1678 by three Charles City County men. They claimed that Stith and Edward Hill had tried to get local citizens to recant the grievances they had presented to the king's commissioners who were investigating the underlying causes of Bacon's Rebellion. In 1692 Stith acquired a 471-acre tract of Charles City land that formerly belonged to James Waradine, and he patented 595 acres on the east side of the Chickahominy River in James City County. Captain Stith represented Charles City County in the assembly meetings that were held in 1685–1686 and 1693. He made his will on November 13, 1690, and added a codicil on October 3, 1693. On April 3, 1694, probate was granted to his widow, Jane, and sons John and Drury (LEO 48, 52; PB 5:268, 278; 6:555; 7:2448:237, 240; SR 661, 663; NEVILLE 75, 87; Charles City County Orders 1687–1695:491).

Lieutenant Stokes: On May 12, 1619, Lieutenant Stokes requested land in compensation for his lengthy service on behalf of the colony (VI&A 671). His first name is unknown.

Christopher Stokes (Stoaks, Stocks, Stoiks, Stoakes): Christopher Stokes, his wife, Mary, and their three-year-old son, William, came to Virginia in 1622 at the expense of merchant Edward Bennett. They were expected to settle at Southampton Hundred, but because they arrived after the March 1622 Indian attack, they settled on Jamestown Island, where their presence is well documented. In 1624 five-year-old William Stokes witnessed the drowning death of George Pope II, a Jamestown Island youngster. By 1629–1630 Christopher Stokes had moved to what eventually became Warwick County, and he began representing the Denbigh area as a burgess. In 1635 he patented some land in Elizabeth City. Stokes died sometime prior to July 25, 1646, at which time his widow, Abettris, and his brother, William, relinquished their joint executorships and Abettris became her late husband's administratrix. Four men were appointed to appraise the decedent's estate, and his widow, Abettris, agreed to pay his funeral expenses and compensate Dr. Henry Waldron for providing Stokes with medical treatment (VI&A 671; LEO 8–9; York County Record Book 2 [1646–1648]:152).

John Stokes (Stoaks, Stocks, Stoiks, Stoakes): In February 1624 John Stokes and his wife, Ann, were living in the eastern end of Jamestown Island with their infant. The Stokes couple was still there a year later, but their baby seems to have died (VI&A 671–672).

Robert Stokes (Stookes, Stoakes): On March 9, 1677, Robert Stokes, an alleged supporter of the rebel Nathaniel Bacon, was put on trial at Green Spring plantation, Governor William Berkeley's home. He was found guilty and sentenced to death. An inventory of Stokes' estate was compiled later in the year (MCGC 456, 530; HEN II:551; SR 749).

John Stokeley alias Taylor (see John Taylor alias Stokeley)

James Stone: On February 13, 1629, James Stone was designated overseer of Jamestown merchant Thomas Warnett's will (VI&A 673).

John Stone: Prior to 1623 John Stone, a mariner, came to Virginia and settled at Martin's Hundred; he was still living there in February 1624. In September 1626 the General Court determined that Martin's Hundred's leader William Harwood had evicted Captain Stone from the dwelling he had built there at his own expense. Stone, who was employed in the king's service, was provided with 30 servants who were not to be taken from him by mariners or others. In 1626 he was authorized to trade with friendly Indians on the Eastern Shore, and he was allowed to make voyages to the West Indies. During the late 1620s, he was bringing large quantities of imported goods into Virginia. Stone was among those who in March 1633 dined at Governor John Harvey's home in urban Jamestown. Shortly thereafter, when Stone was transporting grain and cattle to Boston, he was killed by Indians on the Connecticut River. His trading partner was Stephen Charlton, an Eastern Shore resident. Captain John Stone's estate was still being settled in 1648, for he was deeply in debt at the time of his death and had sold to his creditors his legal interests in three ships (VI&A 672; SR 3482, 4529, 10416; MCGC 104, 114, 134, 169–171).

John Stone: John Stone, a merchant, began doing business in Virginia during the 1650s. He became quite successful and seems to have undertaken commercial activities in Warwick County, where he witnessed a will in 1652. Over a period of many years, he imported European goods and sold them in Virginia. Sometime after February 3, 1669, but before September 1671, he married Colonel John Walker II's widow, Sarah, who also had outlived Lieutenant Colonel Henry Fleet. John Daingerfield, who was married to one of Walker's daughters, sued Stone in an attempt to recover her share of her late father's estate. Mrs. Daingerfield's sisters, Anne Payne (Paine) and Frances Walker, also joined in the suit. Although the case was aired in Old Rappahannock County, ultimately it was forwarded to the General

Court, whose justices sided with John Stone. He eventually became an Old Rappahannock County justice, and sometime prior to 1679 he became a colonel in the local militia. As a burgess, he represented the county in the assembly meetings that were held in 1680–1682 and 1691–1692. When he filed a suit in Westmoreland County in 1678, he appointed Anthony Bridges to serve as his attorney. He was among those authorized to be involved in Indian affairs in the Middle Peninsula and Northern Neck. In 1691 Colonel Stone served as a trustee for the town at Hobbes Hole, a community that became known as Tappahannock (LEO 46, 50; Old Rappahannock County Deeds and Wills 1677–1682:204; Order Book 1683–1686:110, 153; 1687–1692:236–237; Westmoreland County Order Book 1676–1689:131; MCGC 277; SR 3775, 4106, 4199, 12623; EJC I:52, 57, 168, 194).

Maximillian Stone I: Maximillian Stone I came to Virginia in 1620–1621 at the expense of Sir George Yeardley and was one of his indentured servants. In 1625 Stone, his wife, Elizabeth, and son, Maximillian II, were living at Hog Island. He was obliged to serve Yeardley until February 1627. In 1628 Maximillian Stone I represented Hog Island in the assembly (VI&A 673; LEO 7).

Moses (Moyses) Stone (Stones, Ston): Moses Stone arrived in Jamestown in September 1623. In early 1624 he was residing in urban Jamestown in merchant George Menefie's household, where he was a servant. By early 1625 he had moved to Elizabeth City and was living in a household headed by John Downman (VI&A 674).

Robert Stone: In 1622 Robert Stone testified that he was in Virginia in August 1618 when there was a dispute between Edward Brewster and Richard Beamond of the *Neptune*. He said that he was in Jamestown when Brewster was tried in a martial court (VI&A 674).

Alexander Stoner (Stomer, Stommer, Stonar, Stonnar): Alexander Stoner, a brickmaker, came to Virginia sometime prior to June 22, 1635, and married Jane, the widow and heir of John Cooke, a Virginia Company servant. Using Jane's inheritance and some headrights of his own, he patented 350 acres that abutted the James City Parish glebe in Archer's Hope. In 1638 he used his land as collateral when securing a debt to Jamestown merchant John Chew. In August 1637 Stoner received a patent for a one-acre lot on the isthmus then connecting Jamestown Island to the mainland. He also had 27 acres

contiguous to the Governor's Land and Glasshouse Point, plus some acreage on the Chickahominy River. In 1646 Bartholomew Hoskins of Lower Norfolk County, who had served as Alexander Stoner's guarantor, was ordered to pay a debt Stoner owed to the late Stephen Pennell's administrator, William Barker (VI&A 674–675; Lower Norfolk County Book A:68a).

John Stoner: John Stoner, who was named to the Council of State in 1634, died on his way to Virginia (STAN 33; LEO xx).

Joshua Story (Storey): Joshua Story, a merchant, came to Virginia sometime prior to 1675 and began selling imported cloth from a ship that traded in the York River. He became highly successful and by 1680 had begun investing in large tracts of land on the north side of the Mattaponi River, in what by 1691 had become King and Queen County. As time went on, Story continued to increase his holdings, sometimes collaborating with others when patenting land. In 1683 he and another man laid claim to a 5,000-acre tract on the north side of the Mattaponi River, and in 1688 he patented 400 acres in the vicinity of Dragon Swamp. Then, in 1689 he patented an additional 2,500 acres. During the early 1690s he continued to acquire land in the upper reaches of the Mattaponi River, near the property of Robert Beverley II, at one time clerk of the assembly and clerk of the General Court. Story patented tracts of 4,270 and 7,440 acres in 1691 and then acquired an additional 9,150 acres in 1693. The largest amount of acreage he patented at one time was a 11,620-acre tract that he patented in 1691. He probably placed indentured servants on his newly patented property, although the requirements for "seating" or substantiating a land claim were very lenient. Joshua Story represented King and Queen County in the assembly meetings that were held in 1691–1692, 1693, 1695–1696, and 1696–1697 (LEO 50, 53–54, 56; SR 3774; PB 7:34–35, 65, 243, 646, 702; 8:131, 138, 150, 266, 268).

Robert Story (Storye): According to court testimony given in England in 1622, Robert Story, a gentleman, lived in Deputy Governor Samuel Argall's house in urban Jamestown. He indicated that he went to Virginia with Argall and left with him in spring 1619. Story was a witness in the suit Lady Cecily Delaware (Lady Cecily West) undertook against Sir Samuel Argall (VI&A 675).

Samuel Stoughton (Stoughter): On March 10, 1645, Samuel Stoughton patented 800 acres in Upper Norfolk (later, Nansemond) County, part of a larger tract that had belonged to the late Michael Wilcox and had descended to his widow, Elinor. Stoughton, who married Elinor Wilcox, had the property surveyed and probably made his home upon the tract, the only land in which he had a legal interest. Stoughton patented his wife's legacy less than a month after some newly enacted legislation required patentees to reoccupy their outlying property or consider it abandoned. Property owners whose landholdings were in "places of danger" were authorized to return to their homes as long as there were at least ten able men in the group equipped with arms and ammunition and the local military commander approved. These factors combine to suggest that Samuel Stoughton built the fortified compound or bawn that archaeologists have unearthed within the confines of his patent. Stoughton served as an Upper Norfolk County burgess and attended the sessions that commenced in October 1646, November 1647, and November 1654. Therefore, he held office when the assembly drafted the 1646 Indian treaty, which required the natives to withdraw south of the Blackwater River. Stoughton may have moved to Lower Norfolk County, where he witnessed a document in June 1650 (LEO 25–26, 32; NUG I:125, 162; PB2:66; HEN I:285–286, 291–292; Lower Norfolk County Record Book B:160).

William Strachey: William Strachey came to Virginia with Sir Thomas Gates and Sir George Somers and was aboard the *Seaventure*, which ran aground in Bermuda. Strachey and his shipmates arrived in Jamestown in May 1610. Strachey was already a member of the Council of State when Lord Delaware arrived and made him secretary of the colony. He held that post until he left Virginia in 1611. A letter Strachey wrote in mid-July 1610 describes the Jamestown fort's size and appearance at that time. Strachey died in England around 1634 (VI&A 675).

William Strange (Strainge, Straunge): In 1619 William Strange, a boy who was being detained at Bridewell Prison, was sent to Virginia. In February 1624 he was living at Flowerdew Hundred, but within a year's time he had moved to urban Jamestown, where he was a servant in Sir George Yeardley's household (VI&A 676).

John Stratton: In June 1641 John Stratton's widow, Joanna, was designated his administratrix (EEAC 56).

Joseph Stratton: In March 1630 Joseph Stratton began serving as a burgess for Nutmeg Quarter, in what was then part of the corporation of Elizabeth City but later became Warwick County. In September 1632 Stratton became the burgess for the territory between Waters Creek and Marie's Mount. Warwick County records indicate that he was still alive in 1656 (VI&A 676; LEO 9, 11).

Edward Streater (Stretter, Streeter): Captain Edward Streater, who was serving as a burgess for Nansemond County in 1656, brought suit against the late Captain William Brocas's estate. He also sued two men in Northumberland County's monthly court. By March 1657 Streater had patented 3,000 acres on the Potomac River in Westmoreland County. A few months later, when he sold 14 head of cattle to a Lancaster County man, he identified himself as a Nansemond County merchant but noted that the livestock was on his own plantation on the Rappahannock River. Captain Edward Streater married Elizabeth, the widow of Colonel Thomas Burbage of Nansemond County. When Thomas Oldis II's guardian brought suit against Streater in the General Court in July 1658, he indicated that Streater was retaining Oldis's inheritance. This suggests that Streater's wife, Elizabeth, had been widowed at least twice by the time he married her. By May 9, 1660, Edward Streater was dead. During 1663 and 1664 his widow, Elizabeth, tried to recover funds from her late husband's debtors and defend his estate from the claims of David Burke, one of the decedent's former servants. By April 1670 Elizabeth had wed John Barber II of urban Jamestown. He brought suit against Thomas Bowler in an attempt to recover debts to the Streater estate. Barber pursued the litigation after Elizabeth's death and eventually won the case (LEO 33; Lancaster County Deeds &c. Book 2 [1652–1657]:255, 305; [1654–1661]:130–131; Order Book 1656–1666:73, 112, 232, 259, 263; PB 4:210; Northumberland County Wills, Inventories &c. 1652–1658:121; Record Book 1658–1662:4; MCGC 206–207).

John Strechley (Stretchley): In May 1674 John Strechley was sworn in as Lancaster County's clerk of court and held office for many years. In March 1682 he informed the county's justices that he was planning to make a trip to England and asked them to find a deputy clerk while he was absent. He returned within a year and resumed his clerkship. Strechley represented Lancaster County in the assembly sessions held in 1693 and 1695–1696, and in December

1696 he was still serving as Lancaster's clerk of court. In 1695 he and his wife, Alice, were living on a Lancaster County plantation that belonged to his stepson, Raleigh Chinn. Strechley purchased 700 acres in Richmond County, on Totosky Creek, in December 1697. When he made his will on December 6, 1698, he left his Richmond County plantation to his wife, Alice, and named her as his executrix. He also made bequests to his stepchildren, Kathrine, Anne, and Raleigh Chinn, the offspring of the late John Chinn, and to his own sister, Sarah Bambridg. Strechley's will was proved on December 14, 1698. The widowed Alice Strechley became ill and made her will on August 29, 1701. She made bequests to her daughters, Catherine Heale and Anne Fox, and her son, Raleigh Chinn; to her sisters, Dorothy Durham and Tomazin Marshall; and to her cousin, Mary Dodson. Mrs. Alice Strechley's will was proved on October 8, 1701 (LEO 52, 54; Lancaster County Deeds and Wills 1661–1702:429–430, 445–446, 448–450; Wills 1674–1689:16, 131; 1690–1709: 1, 6, 87, 106; Order Book 1666–1680:282, 293, 429; 1680–1686:75, 82, 90, 142; 1686–1696:163, 319; 1696–1702:62; Old Rappahannock County Deeds and Wills 1677–1682:51–53; Richmond County Deed Book 3 [1697–1704]:22–25, 33).

John Stringer: John Stringer was practicing medicine in Accomack County by the 1630s and sometimes had problems collecting what he was owed. A reference to his ownership of a silver crucifix suggests that he or a family member may have been of the Catholic faith. By 1661 Stringer had acquired 2,900 acres on the seaside, in Northampton County. Then, in 1667 he patented 150 acres in Accomack County at Occocomson, a tract near the head of Occocohannock Creek, and enlarged it by 1,050 acres in 1673. In August 1672 Stringer and two other men invested in 2,100 acres called Foster's Neck, and later in the year he laid claim to a 400-acre tract on Savages Creek. By 1659 Stringer was elected to the assembly, representing Northampton County, and he served in the sessions that were held from then until 1662. In October 1663 he was among those accompanying Colonel Edmund Scarborough II on an expedition into Maryland. In April 1670, while Sir Henry Chicheley was deputy governor, Stringer was ordered to tell Colonel Edmund Scarborough II, the colony's surveyor general, not to alter the Eastern Shore boundary line between Virginia and Maryland. Stringer also was told to take custody of the *Hope* of Amsterdam, a Dutch ship that had entered Virginia waters contrary to the navigation acts. He was rewarded for his service by being made sheriff of the Eastern Shore, whose counties were then unified. In 1673 Stringer and Colonel John Custis were authorized to investigate a boundary line dispute. A year later both men were added to a commission charged with investigating whether Captain Savage's plantation had intruded upon the Eastern Shore Indians' land. During the mid-1670s Colonel Stringer, who continued to practice medicine, served as an attorney, and he also reported on a ship that had wrecked after entering Cherrystone Creek. Probably because of his loyalty to the Crown during Bacon's Rebellion, Stringer was made the Eastern Shore's customs officer, a position that generated an abundance of disposable income. He served until June 29, 1687, when he was replaced by John Custis III. On February 10, 1689, Colonel John Stringer made his will, which was proved on December 21, 1689. He asked to be buried beside his late wife but failed to provide her given name, and he made bequests to his son, Hillary Stringer, and to his married daughters, Frances Mosley and Ann Thorogood. He also made bequests to his three grandsons, Hillary, John, and Thomas Stringer, and granddaughters Ann and Mary Stringer. One of the tracts that the decedent left to his grandson Hillary Stringer was part of a plantation he had purchased from the late William Taylor (LEO 35–36, 39; MCGC 212, 216, 241, 373, 381, 444–446, 507; AMES 1:102, 121, 144–146; 2:385, 395; PB 4:536; 6:30, 64, 414, 424; SR 668, 1854, 3173, 6618, 7813; Scarborough 1663; MARSHALL 141–142).

Samuel Stringer: Samuel Stringer, a 27-year-old merchant tailor from Cheshire, England, came to Virginia in 1619 and landed in Jamestown (VI&A 676).

Thomas Strowd: On June 13, 1640, the General Court determined that Thomas Strowd had been wrongly convicted and fined for committing slander. In 1642 John Ewens used Strowd's headright when patenting some land on the Appomattox River (MCGC 477; NUG:I:139).

John Stubbs (Stubb?): On May 25, 1671, the General Court decided to audit John Stubbs' account with merchant Richard Moore. He may have been the John Stubb whose headright was used by John Chandler when patenting some land in Northumberland County. From 1675 through at least 1677, Stubbs was a merchant who imported into Virginia large quantities of canvas and other cloth, and exported tobacco and furs. One of his trading partners was Thomas

Stubbs, who sometimes did business in Jamaica and Maryland (MCGC 260; NUG:I:341; SR 3775i, 3793f, 5588b, 5593a).

Thomas Studley (Stoodie): Thomas Studley, a gentleman, came to Virginia in 1607 and was one of the first Jamestown colonists. He served briefly as cape merchant and died on August 28, 1607 (VI&A 676).

William Stufton: On October 2, 1667, the General Court fined William Stufton for "building a wharf before town," contrary to law. Because Stufton's property is not mentioned in extant land ownership records, the location of his property in urban Jamestown is uncertain. He may have been married to someone who owned or had life-rights to a waterfront lot in the capital city (JHB 1660–1693:48).

John Sturdivant (Sturdevant): On February 10, 1677, Governor William Berkeley issued a proclamation in which he named those who were exempt from the king's pardon on account of their role in Bacon's Rebellion. One of those named was John Sturdivant, who was supposed to be brought before a court of justice. He was the same individual who in 1653 patented 600 acres on the north side of Swift Creek in Henrico County. Sometime after February 1659 but before September 1660, John Sturdivant married Sarah, the widow of Samuel Woodward and the daughter of Robert Hallom. By 1663 Sturdivant owned some land on the lower side of the Appomattox River in what was then Charles City County, enhancing his holdings in 1673. In February 1680 John Sturdivant and his wife, Sarah, who then lived in Charles City County, executed a deed of gift, bestowing on her son, Samuel Woodward, some acreage at Turkey Island. The deed noted that Sarah's mother, who was Robert Hallom's widow, had patented the acreage and left it to her three children. John Sturdivant seems to have been involved in Indian trade and probably was employed by William Byrd I. In 1684 he and several others were killed while on a trading mission that led them through the Occaneechee Indians' territory. Sturdivant's widow, Sarah, seems to have died in late 1690 or early 1691 (NEVILLE 51, 61; SR 660; PB 3:172; 5:350; 6:480; Charles City County Order Book 1655–1665:112, 240, 275; 1687–1695:322; Henrico County Wills, Deeds &c. 1677–1692:123, 282–290, 447; DOR 2:232–233).

Sukey: In 1769 a child named Sukey was living with her mother, Silvy, on the Governor's Land and was included in the late Edward Ambler I's estate (AMB-E).

Suky (Sukey): On February 15, 1768, when an inventory was made of the late Richard Ambler's slaves on Jamestown Island and his leasehold in the Governor's Land, an adult female slave named Suky was listed. In 1769 she was living on the Governor's Land and was included in the late Edward Ambler I's estate (York County Wills and Inventories 21:386–391; AMB-E).

Thomas Sully (Sulley): Thomas Sully came to Virginia in 1611. When a census was made of the colony's inhabitants in March 1620, he was on a trading voyage to Accomack and Acohanock. In February 1624 Sully and his wife were living in the Neck O'Land behind Jamestown Island. When he patented six acres on the extreme western end of Jamestown Island in August 1624, he was identified as a yeoman. He already owned a parcel at Black Point in the eastern end of Jamestown Island, which he sold to Sir George Yeardley in January 1625. By early 1625 Sully and his wife, Maudlyn, had moved to the corporation of Elizabeth City, where he eventually patented some land near the head of the Hampton River (VI&A 677).

Thomas Sully: No information has come to light about the Thomas Sully who during the early 1670s rented from Walter Chiles II's remarried widow, Susanna Wadding, and her husband James, the brick house that Secretary Richard Kemp had built in Jamestown (AMB 24). Sully may have been a kinsman of the ancient planter Thomas Sully, who in 1625 was age 36.

Arthur Swaine (Swayne): In November 1621 the Virginia Company issued a patent to Arthur Swaine and his associates, who were planning to take 100 people to Virginia. In July 1622 he was identified as master of the *Flying Hart*. Swaine's plans seem to have fallen apart, for in October 1624 Company officials were still discussing his taking people to the colony. Governor Francis Wyatt sent word to England that the *Flying Hart* of Flushing (in the Netherlands), sent out by Arthur Swaine and William Constable on the Virginia Company's authority, had arrived in Jamestown in December 1625. By that time the Company's charter had been revoked. Wyatt said that half of the ship's passengers, which included servants, were poorly provisioned and were famished when they came ashore (VI&A 678).

Alexander Swann (Swan): Alexander Swann, who witnessed several court documents in 1692, patented 226 acres on Richmond County's Farnham Creek in 1695. By that time he already had owned, but sold, a large tract near the falls of the Rappahannock River. He joined Elizabeth and Margaret Swann in witnessing John Cone's will in December 1697, and in August 1698 he proved John Gibson's will in Lancaster County's monthly court, shortly after becoming a justice. Swann began serving as a Lancaster burgess in 1699. In October 1700 he and his wife, Elizabeth, who were then identified as residents of Christ Church Parish, sold some of their land on Corotoman Creek. Mrs. Elizabeth Swann was summoned to court by Robert Carter, who questioned her about the nuncupative will made by Carter's niece, Elizabeth, the wife of John Lloyd. In 1701 Swann was identified as a captain in the militia. In 1704 he patented 1,200 acres on the main run of the Rappahannock River in Richmond County and an additional 150 acres on the Corotoman River in Lancaster County and paid quitrent on both pieces of property (LEO 59; Lancaster County Deeds and Wills 1661–1700: 403–404, 419–421, 436, 439–440; Wills 1690–1709:82, 107; Order Book 1696–1702:42, 93, 121, 128, 132; Richmond County Deed Book 1 [1692–1693]:54, 80, 86–90, 146–151; 2 [1693–1695]:56–58, 146–150; NN 2:123–125; 3:31, 43; SMITH 112).

Ann Swann: On March 20, 1630, Ann Swann testified in the suit involving Edward Rossingham and Ralph Yeardley, Sir George Yeardley's administrator and brother. She said that she had been living in Virginia 12 years earlier when Rossingham and Captain John Martin had arrived from England. She probably was a member of the Yeardley household in Jamestown (VI&A 678).

Mathew Swann: Mathew Swann, a tithable member of the Lawnes Creek Parish in Surry, was part of the "giddy-headed multitude" who gathered in 1673 to protest the taxes imposed by the Berkeley government. He was a resident of the plantation known as Lower Chippokes and was accused of being a ringleader of "mutinous persons" during Bacon's Rebellion (Surry County Deeds, Wills &c. 1652–1672:315, 1672–1684:27, 40; MCGC 367).

* * *

Thomas Swann (Swan) I: Thomas, the son of William and Judith Swann, was born in May 1616. In November 1635 he repatented 1,200 acres on the lower side of the James River, land that had belonged to his father and included the plantation that became

known as Swann's Point. In 1639 he married his first wife, Margaret Debton, who died in 1646. By 1640 Swann had been appointed the official tobacco viewer for the territory between Smith's Fort and Grindon Hill, and served as a burgess in 1645–1646, 1649, and 1658. In January 1649 he married Sarah Cod (Codd), who gave birth to a son, Samuel Swann, in 1653 and died in 1654. When Surry County was formed in 1652, Swann became high sheriff, an indication that he already was a county justice. In March 1655, shortly before Swann married his third wife, Sarah Chandler, he was held responsible for the death of his servant, Elizabeth Buck, although her demise was ruled involuntary. In 1656 and 1658 he patented two large tracts of land in Surry County, and in 1668 he claimed 500 acres in James City County. Colonel Thomas Swann I continued to make his home at Swann's Point in Surry and had a tavern at Wareneck. He made numerous appearances before the Surry County court and from time to time undertook action in the General Court. He occasionally was sued, and in March 1660 he was fined for failing to collect some of the tobacco owed as taxes. On November 9, 1662, Swann signed a marriage contract with Ann Brown, the widow of Colonel Henry Brown of Four Mile Tree plantation. He posted a bond, agreeing to see that the decedent's son, Berkeley, would receive his inheritance. Only four months after Ann's death in August 1668, Colonel Swann wed for a fifth time, taking as his wife Mary, George Mansfield's sister. Together, Mary and Thomas Swann produced four children, three of whom reached adulthood.

Colonel Swann occasionally was called on to audit accounts and arbitrate disputes. He lost a suit against William Momford, from whom he had accepted an expensive necklace as collateral, and he was sued by Thomas Rabley of Jamestown. Swann was named to the Council of State in 1659 and served through the late 1660s. When the assembly decided in 1661 that tan houses were to be built in each county, the vestries of Southwark and Lawnes Creek parishes agreed that Surry's should be built on Colonel Swann's land. In 1671 Swann purchased part of a Jamestown row house from his son-in-law, Henry Randolph I, and a year later he was named to a government commission given the task of building a brick fort in Jamestown. He acquired two pieces of land in Jamestown, one urban and one rural, and erected a tavern on his urban lot. Swann's tavern in urban Jamestown opened for business sometime prior to Bacon's Rebellion. At first, his hired servants ran the establishment, but he eventually made a rental agreement with Surry County tavern-keeper William Thompson I, who turned its day-to-day management over to his under-age son, William II. On November 17, 1677, Colonel Swann sued William Thompson I for failing to cover the debts incurred by his son "in ye sd Col Swanns Ordinary at James City." The younger man also refused to deliver the account books in which those debts were recorded, "including some authorized by Swann's hired servants before Thompson Jr. kept ye sd Ordinary." The business dealings between Swann and Thompson not only involved Swann's tavern in Jamestown but also his tavern at Wareneck in Surry County. Again, Swann was the owner and Thompson was the licensed tavern-keeper. Colonel Swann reportedly was sympathetic to the rebel Nathaniel Bacon's views, and his son, Samuel, was married to Sarah II, the daughter of Bacon supporter William Drummond I. However, Swann's popular house of entertainment in Jamestown was torched on September 19, 1676, when Bacon and his followers set the capital city ablaze. Some of Swann's detractors dubbed him "ye great toad." In January 1677 the king's special commissioners, sent to investigate the causes of Bacon's Rebellion, stayed in the Swann home at Swann's Point. When Governor William Berkeley issued a proclamation on February 10, 1677, naming those who were exempt from the king's pardon on account of their role in Bacon's Rebellion, one of those he listed was Thomas Swann. After Berkeley left office, Swann regained his council seat and rebuilt his tavern in Jamestown. He also served as a Surry County burgess in 1679.

Swann died on September 16, 1680, at age 64 and was buried at Swann's Point. On November 2, 1680, the widowed Mary Swann, who informed the justices of the Surry County court that she was unable to find her husband's will, was given temporary custody of his estate. As administratrix of her late husband's estate, she brought suit against bricklayer John Bird on July 5, 1681, and sought punitive damages that were twice the size of Bird's February 1, 1674, bonds. Her action followed in the wake of a September 7, 1680, countersuit Bird filed against Colonel Swann's estate. Bird insisted that he had satisfied part of his debt with tobacco and paid off the remainder with work he had done as a builder. Four men were to meet at Mrs. Swann's to examine Bird's accounts. By November 1, 1681, she had obtained a judgment against him. Bird, on the other hand, swore that "he was

to have 8,000 lb. of tobacco and cask for two months work of a bricklayer for building a brick house in Jamestown for the said Thomas Swann Esq. dec'd." He admitted, however, that he still owed funds to Colonel Swann's estate. Because Swann lived until September 1680, it is unclear whether the brick house Bird agreed to build for him in Jamestown was erected before Bacon's Rebellion or afterward, perhaps as a replacement for a structure that had burned.

In January 1681 Mrs. Mary Swann and her stepson, Samuel, as the late Colonel Thomas Swann's co-heirs, brought suit against tavern-keeper John Everett in attempt to recover some back rent. Everett, on the other hand, contended that the decedent's room-and-board at the tavern were to be deducted from that sum. On January 3, 1682, the plaintiffs were awarded a judgment against Everett, but he was given the right to prove that Swann had agreed to deduct his room-and-board from the rent money. Everett called witnesses, and it was determined that a binding agreement had been made. On February 25, 1682, Mrs. Swann relinquished her dower interest in all of her late husband's property to her stepson, Samuel, except for her "right and title of dower of, in and to the housing and land that my sd. husband was seized of in James City, lately in the possession of John Everett, excepting also my right and title of dower of the house and land at Wareneck where tavern was kept." Thus, the widowed Mary Swann decided to retain her interest in her late husband's taverns, which were income-producing properties. She appointed William Edwards II as her attorney and described him as her brother. Finally, on July 7, 1685, Robert Randall and his wife, Mary, who identified herself as the widow of the Honorable Thomas Swann, relinquished to her stepson, Samuel Swann, her dower interest "in a certain house and all the land thereunto belonging situate and being in James City and now is in the possession of Mr. Samuel Firth, merchant." She received £20 in exchange for surrendering her property rights (VI&A 679; STAN 38; LEO xxi, 24, 27, 34, 44; NEVILLE 61; Surry County Deed Book 1 [1652–1672]:195; Deeds, Wills &c. 1671–1684:297, 304; 1687–1694:28; Order Book 1671–1691: 210, 314, 343, 352, 358; WITH 525, 534–535). Archaeological evidence suggests that the Swann tavern in Jamestown was in use until around 1700.

Samuel Swann (Swan): Samuel, the son of Colonel Thomas Swann I and his second wife, Sarah Cod (Codd), was born on May 11, 1653, and married William Drummond

I's daughter, Sarah II, in 1673. He became high sheriff of Surry County in 1675 and two years later commenced serving as a burgess. He was returned to office repeatedly and served in the assembly sessions that were held in 1680–1682, 1684, 1685–1686, 1688, and 1693. The faith that the widowed Sarah Drummond placed in her son-in-law, Major Samuel Swann, is evidenced by her giving him a power of attorney. He also was the nephew of Rachel, the wife of William Sherwood, whose Jamestown home he agreed to rent on behalf of the Council of State. Swann patented 248 acres of land in Surry County in 1668, acreage that had belonged to his half-brother, Thomas Swann II. Later, he patented 960 acres in Lower Norfolk County. During the early 1680s Samuel Swann and his widowed stepmother, Mary, shared ownership of his late father's property in urban Jamestown and some land in Surry at Wareneck, each of which parcels contained a tavern. As joint heirs, they went to court to collect sums that were owed to the decedent's estate, which included debts attributable to bricklayer John Bird and Jamestown tavern-keeper John Everett. On July 7, 1685, Robert Randall and his wife, Mary, who identified herself as the widow of the Honorable Thomas Swann, relinquished to her stepson, Samuel Swann, her dower interest "in a certain house and all the land thereunto belonging situate and being in James City and now is in the possession of Mr. Samuel Firth, merchant." When and how Samuel Swann disposed of his late father's property in Jamestown is open to conjecture. Governor Francis Nicholson intensely disliked him and he eventually moved to Carolina. After the death of his wife, Sarah, he married a Carolinian, Elizabeth Lillington. Since Swann got rid of the ancestral plantation at Swann's Point prior to 1710, selling it to Joseph John Jackman, he may have disposed of his Jamestown property around the same time. Swann died on September 14, 1707, at his plantation, Perquimans (Surry County Deeds, Wills &c. 1671–1684:115, 165, 272, 297, 304; 1687–1694: 28; Order Book 1671–1691:28, 358; STAN 82, 84, 88, 89; LJC 93; NUG II:55, 303; SAIN 22:158; WITH 42, 534–536; LEO 43, 46–49, 52).

Thomas Swann II: Thomas Swann II, the son of Mary Mansfield and Colonel Thomas Swann I, was born in October 1669 and was a fraternal twin. In 1679 he served his first term as burgess for Surry in 1695 and held office through 1698. In September 1682 he relinquished to his half-brother, Samuel, his legal interest in his late father's tavern in Wareneck. In June 1685 he issued a warrant

for the arrest of Captain John Knowles of Jamestown. He married Eliza Thompson, the daughter of tavern keeper William Thompson I of Surry, who had rented and operated the late Colonel Thomas Swann I's taverns in Wareneck and urban Jamestown. From 1703 through 1705 Thomas Swann II was a Nansemond County burgess (WITH 535; STAN 83, 90, 92, 95; Surry County Deeds, Wills &c. 1687–1694:273; NUG I:465; HEN III:166; MCGC 411; LEO 53–54, 57–58, 62).

* * *

John Swarbeck (Swarbrooke, Swartbrick): In April 1623 John Swarbeck, a Virginia Company servant, was a cow keeper for Governor Francis Wyatt and Captain William Powell, who were residents of Jamestown Island. In early January 1625 he told the General Court that he had served as Powell's cow keeper immediately after the 1622 Indian attack but relinquished his position after Powell's widow married Jamestown merchant Edward Blaney. In January 1625 John Swarbeck was living in Pasbehay, on the Governor's Land (VI&A 679).

Robert Sweet (Sweete, Sweat): Robert Sweet came to Virginia in 1618, and in 1622 he identified himself as an ancient planter and adventurer in New England. In 1624 and 1625 he was living in Elizabeth City, which he made his permanent home. He served as one of that area's burgesses in 1628. In 1640 he ran afoul of the law when he reportedly got a black woman servant pregnant (VI&A 680; LEO 7).

William Swett: On February 4, 1674, William Swett was described as having a house and a child "at Towne," Jamestown, then the colony's only urban community. Swett attested to the accuracy of that information (Surry County Deeds, Wills &c. 1671–1684:67, 203).

James Swift: James Swift, who was with Sir Thomas Gates and Sir George Somers aboard the *Seaventure* when it ran aground in Bermuda in 1609, continued on to Jamestown. He was one of the hostages whom Captain Samuel Argall left with the Indians in January 1613 when trading for corn in the Potomac River basin. Ensign James Swift, who was with Argall when Pocahontas was captured, was still alive in 1620 (VI&A 680).

George Syberry (Syberrye): George Syberry, a tallow-chandler from London, arrived in Jamestown in September 1623 (VI&A 681).

Henry Syberry (Syberrye): Henry Syberry, a chandler from London, arrived in Jamestown in September 1623 (VI&A 681).

Syla: On February 15, 1768, when an inventory was made of the late Richard Ambler's slaves on Jamestown Island and his leasehold in the Governor's Land, an adult female slave named Sylva was listed with her child, Tom (York County Wills and Inventories 21:386–391).

T

Richard Taborer: On February 16, 1624, Richard Taborer was living at the Glasshouse, just west of Jamestown Island (VI&A 682).

Thomas Taborer (Taberor, Taberer, Tabenor, Taberrer, Taboror, Tabirir): In April 1652 Thomas Taborer patented 250 acres in Isle of Wight County, on a branch of the Blackwater River. When James Roche of Warresqueak prepared his will, he referred to a May 4, 1652, letter from Taborer stating that he had shipped some of Roche's tobacco to England. Sometime after 1656 Taborer, then a resident of Isle of Wight County, married John Wood's widow, Margaret, a member of the Quaker faith. In 1658 he served as a burgess for Isle of Wight County. He also functioned as the attorney of Nicholas George of Lancaster County, who in 1656 sold some Isle of Wight County land that was on the Blackwater River. When Joshua Taborer made his will in November 1656, he identified Thomas as his brother and one of his heirs. He also indicated that their father was William Taborer of the county of Derby. By February 1657 Thomas Taborer had joined his brothers, Nicholas and George, and another man in disposing of a 900-acre tract they had patented jointly. Then, in 1663 the four men repatented the same 900 acres. By 1675 Taborer had purchased some of John Bland's property in Isle of Wight County. Then, in April 1681 he patented 400 acres near the mouth of the Pagan River. He represented Isle of Wight County in the assembly sessions held in 1680–1682, and he also was a county justice. When the legislature enacted town-founding legislation in 1680, and each of Virginia's counties was supposed to set aside a 50-acre tract for urban development, part of John Pitt's land (what was known as Pates Field) on the Pagan River was laid out as a town site. That acreage, sometimes called Newtown, eventually became known as Smithfield. Major Thomas Taborer and Thomas Pitt, who were then Isle of Wight

burgesses, were designated the new community's trustees. When Richard Bennett made his will in 1674, he made a bequest to Taborer's wife, perhaps on account of her faith. In 1689 Bartholomew Greene, a mariner from Charlestown in New England, authorized Major Taborer to serve as his attorney. Taborer seems to have become a Quaker. When he made his will on January 24, 1692, he left his land at Basses Choice to his grandson, Joseph Copeland, and divided his other holdings among his daughters and grandchildren. The testator died sometime prior to February 9, 1695, when his will was proved. In 1694 John Newman was granted administration of the decedent's estate during the minority of his ward, Joseph Copeland. Taborer's estate was distributed to John Williams' wife, Elizabeth; Robert Jordan's wife, Christian; and William Webb's wife, Mary. Ruth Newman, who received a third of Taborer's estate and was identified as the decedent's executrix, may have been his remarried widow (LEO 34, 45; BODIE 214, 346–347, 521, 523, 526, 535, 583, 629–630; Isle of Wight County Deeds, Wills & Guardian Accounts A:65; Will and Deed Book 1 [1662–1688]:450; 2[1688–1704]:18; 2 [1704–1715]: 350; Orders 1693–1695:75; PB 3:206; 5:347; 7:71; SR 3560, 4107).

Tachapoake (Native American): Between March 18 and June 19, 1680, when the 1677 Treaty of Middle Plantation was expanded to include additional Indian groups, Tachapoake, chief man of the Sappones (Saponis) Indians, and Mastegonoe, their king, signed on behalf of their people (Anonymous, 1677 treaty, Miscellaneous Virginia Records 1606–1692, Bland Manuscripts, XIV, ff 226–233).

Tahocks (Native American): Toward the latter part of 1655 Northumberland County's military commanders were asked to investigate a complaint the Machodoc Indians had made against Isaac Allerton. On February 6, 1656, Tahocks and the Machodoc Indians' other Great Men joined their werow-ance, Perkatoan, in making an agreement that was witnessed by some of Northumberland County's military men. Under its terms, Allerton was allowed to keep his livestock on the Indians' land but was prohibited from further development (Northumberland County Wills, Inventories &c. 1652–1658:101).

John Talbent (Tallent): On September 28, 1674, the General Court decided that John Talbent, one of Governor William Berkeley's runaway servants, was to be whipped because he had fled in a boat he had stolen from Colonel William White, a resident of urban Jamestown. Talbent's contract with Berkeley was extended, and he was made to serve Colonel White for a year and a half to pay for the boat he had lost. In 1683 Talbent was in possession of a 50-acre leasehold in the Governor's Land (MCGC 382; Soane 1683).

Ann Talbott (Mrs. [No First Name] Talbott): On March 1, 1655, Mrs. Ann Talbott patented a one-acre waterfront lot in urban Jamestown, property that may have already been developed. On September 1, 1657, when Thomas Woodhouse subdivided his one-acre waterfront lot, which was located a short distance to the east of the acreage Mrs. Talbott already owned, he sold the western half of his property to Mrs. Talbott. She died sometime prior to February 25, 1663, and her heirs sold her part of the Woodhouse lot and its improvements to George Marable I (PB 3:331; 5:253–254; NUG I:305).

John Taliaferro (Tollifer): When John Taliaferro and Cadwallader Jones explored the periphery of the Virginia Piedmont in 1682, they "saw an Indian yt made a periauger at the mountain and brought her down to the garrison with skins and venison, where the said Jones commanded." They were referring to one of the garrisons built on the frontier in 1679, at the heads of the colony's four major rivers. John Taliaferro was considered an intelligent and trustworthy citizen, and over the years he performed public duties on behalf of the county court and local citizens. In 1688 he appeared before Old Rappahannock County's justices and posted a bond guaranteeing that Robert Taliaferro's widow, Sarah, would perform her duties as her late husband's administratrix. In June 1692 he took the required oath of office and became a justice of the newly formed Essex County's monthly court, serving several consecutive terms. Like many of his peers, he appeared in court to file petitions, testify, and present inventories of the estates he had

appraised. In August 1692 he was identified as a resident of St. Mary's Parish when he purchased some Essex County land from John Smith of Gloucester County. He sold some of his acreage on the north side of the Rappahannock River to a Richmond County man in 1698. In 1699, while Captain Taliaferro was Essex County's high sheriff, he also served as one of the county's burgesses (LEO 59; CO 5/1315; Old Rappahannock County Order Book 1687–1692:74, 80; Essex County Order Book 1692–1695:7, 52, 188; 1695–1699:1, 152, 154, 162; 1699–1702:5, 33, 89, 99, 132; Deeds and Wills 1692–1695:38–41, 146–150, 340; 1695–1699:120, 334, 343–344; 1699–1702:1, 35, 45; Richmond County Deed Book 3 [1697–1704]:36–38).

Josias Tanner: On January 24, 1625, Josias Tanner, who was age 24, was residing in the eastern part of Jamestown Island (VI&A 682).

Tapatiaton (Debedeavon) (Native American): In 1648 an Eastern Shore Indian leader called Tapatiaton was werowance or leader of the natives around Nandua, and by 1649 he had begun identifying himself as their "great king." He was described as the leader of the Nassawaddox in 1651, and in 1660 he claimed to be werowance of the Onancock. Then, in 1662 he began calling himself "Great Emperour of the Eastern Shore." Therefore, Tapatiaton appears to have displaced Wackawamp's heirs or perhaps was an heir who changed his name after assuming a very important leadership position. During the 1650s and 1660s Tapatiaton sold off portions of his people's land. As a result, their acreage was greatly reduced (Northampton County Deeds, Wills, and Orders 3:135, 166, 223; Deeds, Wills &c. 4:90, 125, 174, 225; 7/8:10, 13–14, 51; Deeds and Wills 1657–1666:6, 44, 73–74, 78; Orders 8:88; Accomack County Deeds and Wills 1663–1666:22, 39–40, 45, 53, 57, 64, 74; MCGC 369). Some respected scholars have confused Esmy Shichans, the "Laughing King," with one of his successors, Tapatiaton, who also was known as Debedeavon.

Taptico (Native American): On April 27, 1693, the governor and his council reviewed a petition that Taptico and some other Wicocomico Indians had submitted concerning colonists' intrusion upon their lands. Council members reviewed a June 7, 1678, order of the General Court, and a May 22, 1683, statement by the council, and decided that Captain John Smith and certain others who had disturbed the Indians would be ordered to cease and desist (EJC I:284). The Captain John Smith who appears to have been intruding upon the Indians' land most likely was Gloucester County burgess John Smith II, who then owned land in the Middle Peninsula and Northern Neck.

Tasreifern (Native American): In 1657 Tasreifern, the king of the Mattaponi Indians, joined the tribe's Great Men or leaders in making a peace agreement with the justices of Old Rappahannock County (Old Rappahannock County Deed Book 1656–1664:17).

Tassore (Native American): Tassore, an Indian who befriended the English and spent a lot of time in Jamestown, suffered abuse at the colonists' hands. Captain John Smith said that in 1609 Tassore and an Indian named Kemps were shackled and detained as prisoners and were forced to show the colonists how to plant agricultural crops. Although both native men were eventually released, Smith said that they had grown fond of the colonists and often brought game animals to the fort (HAI 316, 320, 322).

Tatenenoug (Native American): On November 17, 1662, Tatenenoug and two other Great Men of the Wicocomico Indian Town acknowledged that Robert Jones could use part of their land in exchange for 12 matchcoats or cloaks (Northumberland County Record Book 1658–1662:86).

John Taverner (Tavernor): John Taverner, a gentleman and Virginia Company investor, came to Virginia in 1608 in the 1st Supply of Jamestown colonists. In May 1609 he was identified as the former cape merchant of the fort and store. Taverner's friends asked the Virginia Company to allow him to return to England (VI&A 683).

Henry Tavin: Henry Tavin, a laborer, came to Virginia in 1607 and was one of the first Jamestown colonists (VI&A 683).

Tawcren (Towerozen, Towerezen) (Native American): On September 12, 1660, the justices of Lancaster County's monthly court assigned a tract of land on Rappahannock Creek to Tawcren, king of the Rappahannock Indians. They indicated that they were responding to an order they had received from the colony's assembly. Lancaster's justices agreed to build an English-style house for Tawcren, as he and his chief men had requested. The Rappahannock Indian leaders agreed to air their disputes before the county court and to report any of their people found trespassing or stealing livestock from the settlers (Lancaster County Orders 1656–1666:126).

Henry Tawney (Tawny, Towney): Henry Tawney, a barber surgeon, set sail for Virginia in 1618. After he lived in Virginia for a year or so, he returned to England. During the early 1620s he testified in a series of lawsuits that involved the disposition of the late Lord Delaware's goods. According to one witness, Captain Edward Brewster gave Tawney the key to the storehouse in which the decedent's belongings were kept. He added that Deputy Governor Samuel Argall took the key away from Tawney, yet continued to hold him accountable for Delaware's goods. When Tawney protested, Argall assigned the duty to another man. After Tawney returned to England, he testified in a suit that Argall supporter Robert Rich, the Earl of Warwick, brought against Edward Brewster (VI&A 683).

* * *

William Tayloe (Taylor, Tayler): Captain William Tayloe, a merchant, wed Elizabeth, the daughter and heir of ancient planter Richard Kingsmill of Jamestown. In April 1640 Tayloe purchased the 1,200-acre Kings Creek plantation, which abutted the York River and extended in an easterly direction from Queens Creek to Utimaria Point, which was located on the west side of Kings Creek's mouth. In 1643 and 1647–1648 Tayloe served as a York County burgess. In November 1647, after the 1646 Treaty had been signed and the native population was prohibited from entering the James-York Peninsula except at certain checkpoints, Tayloe's plantation was designated an official point of entry. In 1651 Tayloe was named to the Council of State. He died sometime after 1655 and left the bulk of his Kings Creek plantation to his widow, Elizabeth, who later married Colonel Nathaniel Bacon (VI&A 686; STAN 36; LEO 21, 26; York County Deeds, Orders, Wills 1:71, 153; 9:113).

Elizabeth Kingsmill (Mrs. William Tayloe [Taylor, Tayler]) (see Elizabeth Kingsmill Tayloe Bacon)

William Tayloe: William Tayloe began doing business in Virginia sometime prior to 1689, when the Royal African Company rejected a bill of exchange he had received from Gawen Corbin, a resident of the Middle Peninsula. Tayloe eventually settled in Richmond County, where he patented 184 acres of land in August 1695, and he represented the county in the assembly sessions that were held in 1695–1696. He witnessed a deed for land on Taylor's Creek in Richmond County in November 1694 and served as a court witness in 1697 and 1698. In September 1704 Tayloe, who was then a colonel in the Richmond County militia, informed the Council of State that a frontier family had been attacked by hostile natives and that several Nanzattico Indians had confessed to the crime. Other Nanzattico had been taken into custody but were kept separate from those who had confessed to the murders. At first, plans were made to bring the Indians to Williamsburg to stand trial. Ultimately, however, the accused were remanded to the justices of Richmond County, who on October 5th convened in a Court of Oyer and Terminer, which had the right to make life and death decisions. Although some of the accused warriors were executed, at least two others were considered potentially worthy of clemency and were brought to Williamsburg to stand trial. Colonists who had unlawfully helped themselves to the Nanzatticos' belongings while the Indians were incarcerated were ordered to give those items to Colonel William Tayloe. Mentioned were skins, wampum, peake (shell money), and other chattels "lately taken from the Indian town." Tayloe continued to represent Richmond County in the assembly and served in 1700–1702 and 1705–1706 sessions. He was reelected to the 1710–1712 session of the assembly but died before the opening of the first meeting. William Tayloe of Richmond County was the nephew of merchant William Tayloe of Kings Creek plantation in York County (LEO 54, 60, 64–65; NN 2:183–184; SR 5879; Richmond County Deed Book 2 [1692–1693]:106–107; 3 [1697–1704]:22–25, 33; DOR 2:419; EJC II:384–388, 396–398).

***

Fortune Taylor: Fortune Taylor, a young marriageable maid, came to Virginia in 1621 and in early 1624 was a servant in the urban Jamestown household of Dr. John Pott (VI&A 684).

Francis Taylor: On January 6, 1679, Francis Taylor, a gentleman, lost a lawsuit against Thomas Rabley of urban Jamestown. Taylor, who was a resident of Surry County, made numerous court appearances over the years, often as a debtor. He appears to have been capable of rendering medical treatment, perhaps because he was a doctor or an apothecary (Surry County Order Book 1671–1691:1, 23, 83, 190, 194, 221, 235, 288, 339).

George Taylor (Tayler) II: George Taylor II served as a burgess for Old Rappahannock County and attended the assembly sessions held in 1684. He was the son of George Taylor I, a successful planter, who in 1650 patented two large tracts of land on the north side of the Rappahannock River, in what became Lancaster County. The elder man added to his holdings in 1653 and 1656. George Taylor I and his son, George Taylor II, resided in Old Rappahannock County, where both men witnessed a land transaction in February 1666. George Taylor II went on to become a militia captain and held that position for many years. He often served as an attorney and from time to time witnessed documents. As a trustee he participated in a land transaction that occurred in June 1693 in what was then Richmond County, but formerly had been Old Rappahannock. Later in the year Taylor and a partner purchased some land from burgess Arthur Spicer and his wife, Elizabeth. In November 1694 Taylor identified himself as a resident of Richmond County's Sittenborne Parish when he transferred property on Taylor's Creek to George Tomlin. His land was mentioned again in 1696, when John Weir's daughter sold her land. George Taylor II was still alive in October 1700 (LEO 47; PB 2:239, 259; 3:36, 393; 4:11; SR 3512; Richmond County Deed Book 1 [1692–1693]:186–189; 2 [1692–1693]:106–107; 3 [1697–1704]:9–11, 22–25, 33, 119; Old Rappahannock County Deed Book 3:203–207).

Henry Taylor: On January 25, 1800, Henry Taylor signed a one-year contract with John Ambler II, agreeing to be the overseer (or farm manager) of his Jamestown Island plantation and the Ambler property on the mainland. Taylor agreed to make the slaves "rise early and to do each day as good a days work as the weather and their circumstances permit" and to obey orders. Taylor himself was to take good care of his employer's livestock. He was paid in crop shares, which meant that if he performed his duties satisfactorily, he was entitled to keep a twelfth of the grain, cotton, and tobacco that was produced on the plantation, and a twelfth of the cider (Ambler, January 25, 1800).

John Taylor: John Taylor, a yeoman, came to Virginia in 1610 and lived in Jamestown. He patented some land in Elizabeth City in September 1624, while he was a resident of Newportes News. In early 1625 he and his wife, Rebecca, who came to the colony in 1623, were living in the Elizabeth City household headed by William Gayne and

Robert Newman. In November 1633 Taylor relinquished the patent he had received in 1624 and asked for 150 acres. He noted that he was entitled to a 100-acre dividend as an ancient planter and said that he was using the headright of his wife, the former Rebecca Ravening, whose transportation costs he had paid. He was ordered to provide proof that he had paid for his wife's passage (VI&A 684).

John Taylor (Taylour, Tayler): John Taylor, son of the late Richard Taylor of Flowerdew Hundred plantation in Charles City County (now Prince George), was orphaned sometime prior to 1680. After being widowed, his mother, Sarah, married Captain Robert Lucy, who moved to Flowerdew and hosted a session of Charles City's court in their home on February 3, 1680. Later in the year the Virginia assembly enacted legislation promoting urban development and acreage was to be set aside in each of Virginia's counties as the site of a planned town. At that time a 50-acre tract was laid out on the east side of the point of land at Flowerdew, across the James River from the plantation known as Swineyards. By June 1688 John Taylor, who had come of age, was made a justice of the Charles City County court and quickly began performing civic duties. He seems to have maintained close ties with Colonel Edward Hill II of Shirley, his former guardian. In August 1688 Hill came into court and said that Robert Lucy was dead and that the Taylor orphans wanted to relinquish all claims they had against property held by their mother, the widowed Sarah Taylor Lucy. Hill noted that in October 1684, he had been John Taylor's guardian and administrator of the estate that the late Richard Taylor's youngest daughters, Sarah and Katherine, stood to receive. He also made reference to two older Taylor daughters: Elizabeth, the wife of Captain John Hamblin, and Frances, the wife of Richard Bradford.

As time went on, John Taylor became increasingly involved in maximizing the productivity of the properties he had inherited from his late father. He purchased some land on Powells Creek and began making plans to erect a mill. Then, in April 1688 he submitted a petition to Charles City County's justices in which he claimed that in 1680 his late stepfather, Robert Lucy, had wrongfully sold some of his most valuable agricultural land at Flowerdew, acreage that had been designated a town site. He said that the 50-acre parcel, which was close to his home and was part of his inheritance, was worth much more than Lucy had been paid. Taylor also noted that Charles City's justices had moved the county seat from the town site to Westover, and asked to be given the old courthouse, which was in ruinous condition, so that he could use it for drying tobacco. Although Taylor was authorized to use the old courthouse, he was not compensated for the 50 acres his late stepfather had sold to the government as a town site. In August 1690 Taylor again requested payment for the 50-acre town site. Two months later Captain James Bisse, who had married the twice-widowed Sarah Taylor Lucy, agreed to give him the funds he was owed from his late stepfather's estate for the sale of the 50 acres. Charles City's justices decided to have a deed drafted so that John Taylor and his wife, Henrietta Marie (Mary), could acknowledge the sale. These legal maneuvers came only months before the assembly enacted some new town-founding legislation, again designating Flowerdew Towne an official port. This time, the burgesses noted that the little urban community included several dwellings and warehouses. Afterward, Charles City's justices ordered James Minge, the county surveyor, to lay off the 50-acre town site, Charles Towne, at Flowerdew, and in December 1692 Captain John Taylor purchased three half-acre lots in the town site—numbers 67, 68, and 69.

Taylor served as a witness in January 1693 when Edward Chilton of Jamestown and Charles City County executed an agreement naming Charles City burgess Edward Hill II as his attorney. Taylor, who by 1694 was Charles City County's high sheriff, represented the county in the assembly sessions that were held in 1693, 1696–1697, 1698, and 1699. In October 1698 he was one of the men given the task of investigating the fire that destroyed the colony's statehouse. In February 1699 he filed a petition with the Council of State claiming that he had been authorized to serve as clerk of the Charles City County court but that the incumbent, James Minge, had refused to relinquish the office. Interestingly, a decade earlier Minge had refused to release the county's court record books, which he insisted on keeping in his home. Taylor agreed to serve as the monarchy's advocate in the colony's admiralty court later in the year, and finally in May 1699 he took office as Charles City County's clerk. On June 1, 1700, Captain John Taylor sent a message to the governor asking to be excused from a meeting of the admiralty court. A year later he again requested permission to be absent, citing his continual sickness. Then, on June 20, 1702, Taylor asked to be relieved of his position as clerk of Charles City County's court, noting that "for several years he hath been very much afflicted with the Gripes of the Belly and Pain in his Limbs." He said that he had been advised to go to England "to the Bath" so that his health might be restored. Taylor closed by requesting that his deputy clerk be authorized to serve in his absence. In 1704 he paid quitrent on 1,700 acres in what became Prince George County and was among the men authorized to certify the affidavits of people making complaints against the governor. When the assembly initiated new town-founding legislation in October 1705, the burgesses decided that the small urban community at Flowerdew was to be called Powhatan (LEO 52–53, 56, 58–59; EJC I:392, 407–408, 414, 439, 449; II:64, 89, 138, 256–257, 438; Charles City County Will and Deed Book A [1692–1694]:183; Orders 1687–1695:107–108, 125, 149, 171, 200, 239, 302, 314, 352, 358, 365–367, 380, 439, 554, 556, 592; SMITH 87; HEN II:472; III:58, 415–416).

Philip (Phillip, Phillipe) Taylor (Tayler): Philip Taylor settled on the Eastern Shore prior to April 1634, when a bargain he had made with Captain Edmund Scarborough was discussed by Accomack County's court justices. Later in the year he went to court to protest the behavior of a local man, who had had sex with his maidservant. Taylor patented 500 acres in Accomack County in 1637 and 1,000 acres on the seaside in 1643. When he testified in May 1635 about a large quantity of beaver pelts that Captain William Claiborne had brought from Kent Isle, he gave his age as 24. Two years later Taylor again was summoned to court because he had shipped some rotten tobacco to John Neale's store at Kecoughtan. In February 1638 Taylor was away from Virginia when a man tried to collect on a debt. Later that year the county justices learned that he and Mr. Neale had made a bargain involving the purchase of 21–22 hogsheads of salt. When Philip Taylor testified at Kecoughtan in 1640, he discussed the sacrifices that William Claiborne had made when establishing a trading post at Kent Island. He also identified himself as one of the original free men at Kent Island. In 1641 Accomack's justices ordered Taylor not to disturb the Indians living on Mattawomes (Mattawoman) Creek, directly across from his plantation. In 1642 Taylor was designated a churchwarden and took the oath of office; he also became a justice and sheriff of Northampton County, newly named in 1643. While sheriff, he was obliged to detain prisoners in his home because there was no jail. He served as a burgess for Northampton County in 1643 and died intestate sometime prior to February 25, 1645. His widow, Jane, who served as his administratrix, later married William Eltonhead of Maryland. Philip Taylor's heirs included two children, Zarah and Thomas. Court testimony taken in September 1645 reveals that in July 1645 one of Taylor's African servants was Anthony (Antonio) or Anthony Johnson, who came to Virginia in 1621 as one of the Bennett family's servants and eventually moved to the Eastern Shore, where he became a free man and landowner (LEO 21; AMES 1:12, 14, 20, 35, 85, 102–103, 121, 161; 2:56, 178, 202, 457; PB 1:496, 935; SR 11330; MARSHALL 8, 10, 14, 17–18, 37, 45; DOR 1:48; VI&A 87).

Richard Taylor (Tailor, Tiler, Tyler): Richard Taylor arrived in Virginia in September 1608 and in December 1623 was living at Bermuda Hundred. He and his wife, Dorothy, were still living there when a list of patented land was sent back to England in May 1625 and Taylor was credited with 100 acres in Charles City, acreage that was planted. Over the next several years Taylor made several court appearances. In 1625 and 1628 he served as a burgess for the College, an indication that he or his wife had acreage that was located in the corporation of Henrico. He was still alive in January 1629. Taylor's land, which was near 4 Mile Creek in Henrico County, was used as a reference point in John Cookeney's 1638 patent (VI&A 685; PB 1:555; LEO 6–7).

Steven Taylor (Tailor): When Steven Taylor testified in court On October 11, 1627, he identified himself as one of Mrs. John Pott's servants. He said that he had been hired by Allen Keniston but became lame while in his employ. Taylor was returned to Mrs. Pott's urban Jamestown household so that he could be cured (VI&A 686).

Thomas Taylor: Thomas Taylor patented 250 acres in Warwick County in March 1642. He added another 350 acres in October 1643, this time claiming land that abutted the Warwick River. He was a successful planter and shipped tobacco to England during the mid-to-late 1630s, often using Thomas Jeffreys as his factor. In 1646 Taylor served as a burgess for Warwick County. Like many of his contemporaries, he initiated litigation in order to collect debts. In 1647, while he was a county justice, he lost a suit to John Phillips; afterward, he appealed the county court's decision to the General Court. Taylor was still a sitting justice in Warwick County's court in 1651 (LEO 25; PB 1:903, 923; SR 3490a, 11328; DUNN 18, 21–22, 24–25, 165–167, 176, 179).

William Taylor (Taler): William Taylor, a laborer, came to Virginia in 1608, in the 2nd Supply of Jamestown colonists (VI&A 686).

Terhoffamoh (Native American): On February 6, 1656, Terhoffamoh and the Machodoc Indians' other Great Men joined their werowance, Perkatoan, in making an agreement that was witnessed by some of Northumberland County's military commanders. The military officers had been asked to investigate a complaint the Indians had made against Isaac Allerton. Under the terms of the 1656 agreement, Allerton was allowed to keep his livestock on the Indians' land but was prohibited from further development (Northumberland County Wills, Inventories &c. 1652–1658:101).

Edward Thomas: In April 1683 Edward Thomas, a successful merchant, began patenting land in Old Rappahannock County, acreage that was on the south side of the Rappahannock River. As time went on, he added to his holdings in that area. In 1691 he acquired 450 acres on Dragon Swamp, and in 1697 he patented 2,750 acres at the heads of Peumansend and Portobago creeks in what was then Essex County, a descendant of Old Rappahannock. Captain Thomas began serving as an Essex County justice in May 1692, an office he held for seven years, and he became a burgess for Essex in 1693. In early 1693 he purchased a 250-acre Essex County plantation that belonged to Vincent and Anne Vause. The Vause couple's deed noted that the acreage was descended from a 2,000-acre tract that Richard Bennett had patented in 1642. In December 1693 Edward Thomas was one of the Essex County justices involved in finding a proper location for the jurisdiction's new courthouse, and in 1696 he became high sheriff. A year later he provided some furnishings for the new courthouse—a table and chair for the clerk of court. In 1698 he was identified as a merchant and was compensated as county coroner. He was paid by the county for transporting an official messenger to Jamestown. Edward Thomas died sometime after June 1699 but before August 10, 1699. His will, which was dated May 23, 1699, and proved on November 10, 1699, suggests that he was unmarried at the time of his death and had neither living children nor grandchildren. In December an inventory was made of his estate. Thomas, as testator, bequeathed some land and slaves to Thomas Meriwether's wife, Elizabeth, and he gave his housekeeper, Mary Peterson, the use of five slaves and his plantation called Cox's Quarter. He left money and slaves to several young people, including his godsons, and he gave the plantation on which he was then living to South Farnham Parish for a glebe. Thomas Meriwether was named Captain Edward Thomas's administrator while Katherine and Frances Williamson, the designated executors, were minors (LEO 52; PB 7:285, 653; 8:198; 9:80, 668; Essex County Order Book 1692–1695:1, 90, 114, 158, 188; 1695–1699:3, 18, 41, 47, 138; 1699–1702:1–2, 6, 18, 29, 76, 103; Deeds and Wills 1692–1695:42–43, 115–118, 229–230, 240, 318; 1695–1699:133, 165–166, 267–270; 1699–1702:1, 21).

John Thomas: In May 1622 John Thomas, a sawyer sent to Virginia by the Company of Shipwrights, set sail for Virginia with Thomas Nunn. Like Nunn, he probably lived and died on Jamestown Island (VI&A 688).

William Thomas: William Thomas served as a burgess for Surry County in 1652, the year the county was formed. It is uncertain when he came to Virginia. On January 16, 1652, he purchased from Benjamin Siddway a tract on Upper Chippokes Creek that contained 350 acres, acreage that formerly had belonged to Jeremiah Clements II and had passed into the hands of Benjamin Harrison's orphan, Peter. Thomas appeared in Surry County's court on July 19, 1652, when he witnessed a document, and in July 1653 William Lea, Gregory Rawlings' executor, authorized Thomas to serve as his attorney. By January 1653, however, Captain William Thomas seems to have violated the trust of London merchants Henry and John Richards, for whom he served as factor in Surry County. They successfully sued him and attached some of the tobacco that he was planning to ship overseas. They also secured an attachment against his personal estate, which, like Thomas, was "like[ly] to be Conveighed [sic] out of this Collonye." Surry County records reveal that William Thomas left other creditors in his wake. On November 5, 1656, London merchant John Richards sold to Arthur Allen of Lawnes Creek the late William Thomas's 350-acre plantation, which Thomas had bought at a public outcry. Thomas's property, which was on the east side of Upper Chippokes Creek, eventually was developed as Claremont Manor (LEO 30; Surry County Deeds, Wills &c. [1652–1663] Book I:4, 23, 27, 83–84, 86, 89, 97, 112, 136, 158).

William Thomas: William Thomas had begun having business dealings in Northumberland County by 1652, the same year he patented 700 acres on the northeast side of

Mobjack Bay. He moved to his newly patented property and within a year claimed 100 acres on the north side of the Rappahannock River in Lancaster County. Thomas represented Northumberland County as a burgess in 1656 and also began serving as a justice in the county's monthly court. He maintained his legal interest in his land on Mobjack Bay and repatented it in 1662. However, he continued to live in Northumberland County, where he played an active role in public life and continued to acquire land. Although Thomas was considered a gentleman of superior social status, he appears to have been very volatile and prone to violent outbursts. In 1661 the justices of Northumberland County fined him for defaming Lieutenant Daniel Neale and physically attacking him with "such blowes as impaired his health." For this transgression Mr. Thomas was fined 200 pounds of tobacco. In 1669 Richard Lawrence, a Jamestown innkeeper, brought suit against William Thomas in an attempt to recover funds. Thomas continued to acquire headrights, and in 1669 he received a land certificate from the justices of Northumberland County's monthly court. By August 1678 William Thomas was dead, at which time his widow, Mary, was designated his administratrix, an indication that he died intestate. Simultaneously, Mrs. Thomas was named guardian of her son, Edward Sanders. Two months later, when settling her late husband's estate, she asked the court to give her certain household items, notably her bed and bedding, some shoes, and a warming pan. In November 1683 Mary Thomas was still settling her late husband's estate. She died sometime prior to March 1684 and was survived by her son, Edward Sanders; her daughters by William Thomas, Mary and Elizabeth, who were married to Edward White and Benjamin Cotman, respectively; and her stepdaughter, Rebecca, then married to Josias Pitts (LEO 33; Northumberland County Deeds and Orders 1650–1652:67; Wills, Inventories &c. 1652–1658:10, 74, 86, 94; Record Book 1658–1662:21, 82; 1662–1666:98, 112; Order Book 1652–1665:89, 148, 150–151, 262, 273, 278–279, 410; 1666–1678:64, 74, 80, 198; 1678–1698:6, 135, 201–202, 209, 223, 242; PB 3:20, 146; 4:416). It should be noted that there were two men named William Thomas who lived in Northumberland County at the same time. One was a gentleman and burgess, who always was identified as "Mr." and the other was a planter and fiddler from Yeocomoco, who occasionally ran afoul of the law.

[First Name Unknown] Thomson (Thompson): On March 3, 1674, the justices of Surry County noted that Mr. Thomson or Thompson of Surry's boat had been trimmed by James Alsop of urban Jamestown (Surry County Deeds, Wills &c. 1671–1684:46). He may have been the merchant John Thompson, a Surry resident who traded in London.

George Thompson (Thomson): George Thompson, the brother of prominent merchant and mariner Maurice Thompson, came to Virginia prior to March 1621. He returned to the colony in 1623 and in 1624 was living in Elizabeth City, where he was a young indentured servant. By May 1626 he had become a free man, and in October 1627 he held the rank of ensign. In March 1629 Lieutenant George Thompson was named a commissioner of Elizabeth City's monthly court, and he was made commander of the territory between Lieutenant Lupo's Creek and Chamberlaine's Creek. In October 1629 Thompson served as one of Elizabeth City's burgesses (VI&A 689; LEO 8).

John Thompson (Thomson): Merchant John Thompson of Surry County, the Rev. William Thompson's son, was elected to the assembly in 1693 and served in the sessions held in 1693, 1695–1696, and 1696–1697. In 1699 he successfully sued tavern-keeper and jailer Henry Gawler of urban Jamestown in the Surry County monthly court. Thompson's will, prepared on January 27, 1699, while he was in London, was presented for probate on March 16, 1699. It reveals that William and Samuel Thompson were his brothers and that his sister Katherine was married to Robert Paine, whereas his sister Elizabeth was the wife of William Catlet. Among the late John Thompson's close friends were Henry Hartwell of Jamestown, Arthur Allen II of Surry, William Haistwell, and Francis Clements. Clements also was closely associated with Henry Hartwell (Surry County Order Book 1671–1691:458, 469, 472; WITH 122; LEO 53–54, 57; SR 4786).

Roger Thompson (Thomson): In 1620 Roger Thompson, a vagrant, was brought to Bridewell, where officials decided that he would be sent to Virginia. In February 1624 he was living at Flowerdew Hundred, but by January 1625 he had moved to urban Jamestown, where he and his wife, Ann, were servants in Sir George Yeardley's household. On February 26, 1627, he testified about some cattle he had delivered to John Pountis of Jamestown and accounted for the number of Sir George Yeardley's animals that had been slaughtered. When Jamestown merchant Thomas Warnett made his will on February 13, 1629, he named Ann Thompson as one of his beneficiaries (VI&A 690).

* * *

William Thompson I: Colonel Thomas Swann I's tavern in urban Jamestown opened for business sometime prior to Bacon's Rebellion. At first, his hired servants ran the establishment, but he eventually made a rental agreement with Surry County tavern-keeper William Thompson I. Thompson held the tavern's license but turned the tavern's day-to-day management over to his underage son, William II. On November 17, 1677, Swann sued William Thompson I for failing to cover the debts incurred by his son "in ye sd Col Swanns Ordinary at James City." The plaintiff also contended that William Thompson II refused to deliver the account books in which those debts were recorded, "including some authorized by Swann's hired servants before Thompson Jr. kept ye sd Ordinary." The matter was aired before Surry County's monthly court, whose justices referred it to a jury. After a lengthy debate the jurors agreed that William Thompson I should provide Swann with an accurate account of his business dealings in the ordinary in Jamestown. Thompson also was ordered to deliver the account books or else pay a fine. On the back of the Surry County document summarizing the jury's verdict, someone noted that the suit between Swann and Thompson had been "presented on the other side," a probable reference to the General Court, which convened regularly in Jamestown and sometimes served as an appellate body. The notation also stated that "Coll. Thos. Swann sued William Thompson Sr. to recover bond guaranteeing that his son would perform a condition made between him and ye sd. Coll Swann concerning ye sd Coll Swann's ordinary in Jamestown, most of which branches in ye sd condition have been broken." Again, the matter was referred to a jury, which concluded that Bacon's Rebellion had prevented Thompson and his son from providing Swann with the accounts. They decided, however, that William Thompson I was to give Swann a full account by February 24, 1678, or forfeit his bond.

Swann and Thompson had business dealings together involving not only Swann's tavern in Jamestown but also the tavern he owned in Surry County at Wareneck. On January 2, 1678, when Thompson sued Swann over matters concerning the Wareneck tavern, Surry County's justices decided that the dispute should be settled via formal arbitration. On July 22, 1678, a jury convened at Wareneck to examine the differences between Swann and Thompson, who agreed to abide by their decision. The matter was still unresolved on November 5, 1678. Despite the on-going disagreements between Colonel Thomas Swann and William Thompson I, Swann's son Thomas II and Thompson's daughter, Eliza, eventually wed. One Jamestown lot owner with whom William Thompson I worked closely was Edward Chilton, with whom he patented a 1,160-acre parcel in Surry County (Surry County Order Book 1671–1691:179–180, 210; WITH 535; NUG II:304).

William Thompson II: William Thompson II, the underage son of Surry County tavern-keeper William Thompson I, managed Colonel Thomas Swann I's tavern in urban Jamestown, which opened for business sometime prior to Bacon's Rebellion. On November 17, 1677, Swann sued William II's father for failing to cover his share of certain debts incurred "in ye sd Col Swanns Ordinary at James City." William Thompson II also refused to deliver the account books that documented those debts, some of which predated the Thompsons' rental of the ordinary. The suit, which was aired before the Surry County monthly court, was referred to a jury, which agreed that William Thompson I should give Swann an accurate account of his business dealings at the tavern. That accounting was postponed until February 24, 1678, because of disruption attributable to Bacon's Rebellion. William Thompson II's sister, Eliza, eventually married Colonel Swann's son Thomas II (WITH 535; Surry County Order Book 1671–1691:179–180).

* * *

Thomas Thornbury (Thornebury, Thornburrow, Thornborough): Thomas Thornbury, a free man, came to Virginia in 1616 and in 1620 went on one of several trading voyages. In 1625 he was living in Elizabeth City in the household of Edward Waters. When Thornbury brought Waters' boat up to Jamestown in January 1626 so that he could take Waters back to Elizabeth City, he ran afoul of the law by becoming inebriated, setting sail in a small boat, and losing a man overboard. When John Gundry sold some land in Elizabeth City on December 30, 1626, he noted that Thornbury was then leasing part of the property. By 1634 he had patented some land of his own in Elizabeth City on the Back River. He was elected a burgess for Elizabeth City in 1653 (VI&A

691; LEO 31). He may have been the late husband of Eliza Thornborough, a widow who died in Elizabeth City prior to August 18, 1659 (NEAL 299).

* * *

Adam Thorogood (Thorowgood, Thorugood) I: Adam Thorogood I came to Virginia in 1621 and by February 1624 was living in Elizabeth City, where he was an indentured servant in Edward Waters' household. By December 1626 he had gained his freedom and purchased some land in Elizabeth City. Despite some legal problems, he rose in the ranks of society and in 1627 was named a commissioner of Elizabeth City's court. He returned to England and in July 1627 married Sarah Offley. Thorogood was elected to the assembly and served on behalf of Elizabeth City in 1629, 1630, and 1632. In 1634 the Privy Council ordered Virginia's governor to grant Thorogood a large patent on the lower side of Hampton Roads at Lynnhaven, in what became Lower Norfolk (later, Princess Anne) County. He was awarded 5,350 acres of land in 1635 and built a home on his property. On May 15, 1637, when Lower Norfolk County's justices began convening as a monthly court, Thorogood was serving as a justice and as a member of the Lynnhaven Parish vestry. In 1637 he was named to the Council of State, and as time went on, he added to his holdings in the vicinity of Lynnhaven Bay. Adam Thorogood I made his will on February 17, 1640, and died shortly thereafter. The General Court ordered his widow, Sarah, who by May 2, 1641, had married John Gookin, to make an inventory of her late husband's estate. After Gookin's death, Sarah wed Captain Francis Yeardley (VI&A 691; LEO 8–9, 11; PB 1:179; Lower Norfolk County Record Book A:1, 9, 39, 59; B:52a, 53a; C:13, 18; DOR 3:326–328).

Adam Thorogood (Thoroughgood, Thorowgood) II: Between 1664 and 1670 Adam Thorogood II, the son of Adam Thorogood I, served as a burgess for Lower Norfolk County. He also was a lieutenant colonel in the militia and served as a county justice and sheriff. Although he made his will on October 31, 1679, he lived for several more years. He bequeathed to his wife, Frances, life-rights in the plantation on which they lived, and designated his son Argoll Thorogood as reversionary heir. The rest of his land was to be divided among his five sons: Argoll, John, Adam III, Francis, and Robert. He left a young black servant to his daughter, Rose. The remainder of the testator's

personal property was to be divided in equal shares among his wife and six children when they came of age. Thorogood asked his friends Lemuel (Lyonell) Mason, Anthony Lawson, Malachi Thruston I, and William Porten to serve as guardians for his children and overseers of his will. He instructed his executrix, Frances, to see that he was buried with his parents in the church at Lynnhaven. John Thorogood and Malachi Thruston proved Adam Thorogood II's will on February 1, 1686 (LEO 39; Lower Norfolk County Wills and Deeds 4:217; DOR 3:330).

John Thorogood (Thoroughgood, Thorowgood): John Thorogood, the son of Adam Thorogood II, represented Princess Anne County in the assembly sessions that were held in 1695–1696, 1696–1697, 1698, and 1699. Around 1679 he married Ann, the daughter of Colonel John Stringer of Northampton County. After being widowed, he wed Margaret Lawson. Thorogood served as a justice and sheriff of Princess Anne County, and successively held the ranks of captain, major, and colonel in the local militia. On December 9, 1701, Colonel Thorogood made his will, which was proved on January 7, 1702. He designated his wife, Margaret, as his executrix and made bequests to sons Anthony and John and daughters Ann and Elizabeth (LEO 54, 56, 58–59; Princess Anne County Deed Book 1:312; DOR 3:335).

* * *

Thomas Thorogood (Thorowgood): On January 24, 1625, 17-year-old Thomas Thorogood was a servant in the household of John Burrows of Jamestown Island (VI&A 692). When Adam Thorogood I patented a large tract of land in 1635 on the lower side of the James River, he used Thomas Thorogood's headright; he may have been the same individual who had been John Burrows' servant (PB 1:179).

Thomas Thorp: On January 17, 1678, Thomas Ludwell, the owner of two units in a brick row house at the western end of Jamestown Island, designated Thomas Thorp as one of his executors in Virginia (SR 3719).

George Thorpe: In 1618 George Thorpe, a member of the Virginia Company and an investor in Bermuda, joined several others in forming a partnership known as the Society of Berkeley Hundred. Its purpose was to establish a private plantation in Virginia, the settlement called Berkeley Hundred. Thorpe, who set sail for Virginia in September 1619, was named to the Council of State and was supposed to serve as deputy for the College land. He briefly returned to England but in September 1620 went back to Virginia with William Tracy, with whom he jointly governed Berkeley Hundred. On March 22, 1622, when the Indians attacked the settlements sparsely scattered along the James River, George Thorpe and ten others were killed at Berkeley Hundred (VI&A 693; STAN 30; LEO xxi).

Otho (Otto) Thorpe (Thorp): Otho Thorpe came to Virginia sometime prior to 1672 when he participated in a suit that was aired before the General Court. At issue was ownership of an 850-acre tract of land that had been claimed by John Clarke. The matter was still pending four years later. In May 1673 Thorpe sued Thomas Warren, commander of the ship *Daniell,* in an attempt to recover the value of some goods that were damaged on the way from London. Thorpe was residing at Middle Plantation when Bacon's Rebellion got underway, and an assembly meeting was held at his home on October 2, 1677, after the popular uprising was quelled. He asked to be compensated for the losses he had sustained at the hands of Nathaniel Bacon's men and described his losses. He indicated that six of his servants were carried off and that his estate had been plundered of goods worth £1,200. The king's commissioners were hesitant to approve Thorpe's claim because he had signed the written oath the rebels had endorsed. He, on the other hand, claimed that he was drunk when he signed the oath and said that he had consistently supported Virginia's governing officials. He admitted, however, that he had questioned the wisdom of Governor Berkeley's decision to raise troops in Gloucester County while it was under the control of Bacon's men. Thorpe said that his tobacco had been seized by Berkeley's men and loaded aboard an outgoing ship and that he was owed an additional £400. Colonel John Page sued Major Otho Thorpe, claiming that Thorpe had refused to pay a just debt. Thorpe served as a burgess for York County and attended the sessions held in 1680–1682. He moved to London, and when he made his will on June 28, 1686, he identified himself as a merchant. He died sometime prior to December 1697 and was survived by his wife, Frances, who married John Annesley of Westminster, Middlesex County, England. Thorpe left money to his niece, Hannah, the wife of John Pell of London, and as the testator's surviving heir, she eventually inherited an interest in his landholdings in York and James City counties.

On January 25, 1700, Hannah conveyed her 450 acres of land called Middle Plantation in "York River County" to James Whaley, a Virginia merchant. However, Otho Thorpe's widow, Frances, and her new husband, John Annesley, brought suit against Whaley, for they believed he was occupying the decedent's property illegally (LEO 46; SR 662, 749, 4561, 6618c; MCGC 312, 321, 339, 402, 424, 451; York County Deeds, Orders, Wills 4 [1665–1672]:272–273; 6 [1677–1684]:333, 342; 7:285; 10 [1694–1697]:182–183; 11 [1698–1702]: 116, 121, 132, 272, 466–467; Deeds, Administrations, Bonds 1 [1694–1701]:259–260, 313–321).

Kenelm (Kenelme) Throgmorton: Kenelm Throgmorton, a gentleman, came to Virginia in 1607 and was one of the first Jamestown colonists. He died at the end of summer 1607 (VI&A 695).

Clement Thrush: Clement Thrush came to Virginia in 1623 at the expense of his master, John Moone, who owned a lot and brewhouse in urban Jamestown and some acreage in the corporation of Warresqueak, later known as Warresqueak (then Isle of Wight) County (VI&A 695).

Thomas Thurston: On November 27, 1657, Thomas Thurston and Josias Cole, who were Quaker ministers, were incarcerated in Jamestown because they were religious dissenters. They described Jamestown's jail as "a dirty dungeon." It probably was a windowless basement in one of the capital city's brick buildings. The men were denied access to pen, ink, or paper and the opportunity to speak with others. Eventually it was decided that they would be sent to Maryland (MCGC 506; Tyler, *Cradle,* 61).

Malachi (Malachy, Mallachi, Mallachy) Thruston I: Malachi Thruston I represented Lower Norfolk County in the assembly in 1676, by which time he had begun patenting land in the county. He was returned to office and served as a burgess in the sessions held in 1680–1682. Thruston continued to patent land, amassing a number of modest-sized tracts in Lower Norfolk County, part of which acreage was in Lynnhaven Parish. Several of the parcels he acquired were escheat land, small tracts that had reverted to the Crown. In 1685 he patented more than 900 acres at the head of the Elizabeth River's Eastern Branch, and in January 1687 he witnessed the will made by Henry Woodhouse of Lower Norfolk County. During 1691–1692 Thruston represented one of Lower Norfolk County's descendants, Princess Anne County, in the assembly. However, by 1695 he had begun serving as Norfolk County's clerk of court, and in 1698 he was a burgess for Norfolk County. Although the names and boundary lines of the jurisdictions Thruston represented experienced significant changes, he also relocated, for he moved his household from rural Princess Anne County to the town of Norfolk. When Malachi Thruston made his will on March 14, 1699, he identified himself as a resident of Norfolk. He left lots to his sons, John, James, and Malachi II, although his wife, Martha I, the daughter of James Porter, was to retain life-rights in the property. He also stipulated that his land called Brushy Neck, which he had inherited from Richard Jones, would be retained for the use of his wife and sons. He specified that his son Malachi II was to have "my Plantation I lately lived on at Linhaven [Lynnhaven] in Princess Anne County" and he left to his daughter Sarah a plantation called Currituck that also was in Princess Anne. Daughters Jeane and Martha II also received bequests. The testator gave his personal property to his wife, Martha I, and their sons and daughters. He also named his wife and sister-in-law Jeane (Jane) Porter as co-executrixes. Malachi Thruston I's will was proved on November 15, 1699 (LEO 39, 46, 50, 58; SR 3740, 3742; Norfolk County Wills and Deeds 4:156; 5:164, 247; 7:170; PB 6:408; 7:313, 363, 383, 458; 8:39; 9:90).

William Tiballs (Tibbalds?): On March 17, 1677, Captain William Byrd I informed Governor William Berkeley and the members of the Council of State, who had convened as a court, that William Tiballs had supported the rebel Nathaniel Bacon's cause. Tiballs was made to appear before the king's commissioners at Swann's Point, where he was accused of disturbing the peace and making scandalous comments. Although the king's commissioners had the right to determine Tiball's fate, they decided that he was to be turned over to the county justices in his home jurisdiction. On March 22nd the governor and council decided that Tiballs would be fined 1,000 pounds of pork that could be used by the king's soldiers (MCGC 460, 532). He may have been the William Tibbalds whose headright was used by four men who patented more than 10,000 acres in New Kent County in 1674 (PB 6:518).

Robert Tindall (Tyndall): Robert Tindall, a gunner, came to Virginia in 1607 in the first group of colonists that planted a settlement at Jamestown. He prepared a map of Virginia in 1608, showing Jamestown Island

and some of the sites at which the natives were living. He made a second voyage to Virginia between May and November 1609 and a third trip between April 1610 and June 1611, as captain of Lord Delaware's ship, the *Delaware*. On June 17, 1610, Delaware sent Tindall into the Chesapeake Bay on a fishing expedition and on July 7, 1610, Delaware dispatched him to capes Henry and Charles (VI&A 696; SR 48, 112).

Thomas Tindall (Tyndall): Thomas Tindall died in Jamestown sometime after April 1623 but before February 16, 1624. In May 1625 he was credited with 100 acres, which suggests that he was an ancient planter. His land was located in Coxendale, in the corporation of Henrico (VI&A 696).

Thomas Todd: On April 22, 1670, the General Court noted that William Whitby II, a teenage orphan, had nominated Thomas Todd as his guardian. On October 21st of that year, Todd represented the orphan in a dispute with John Harlow (Harloe). William Whitby II was the son of William Whitby I, a burgess and speaker of the assembly, who died sometime prior to April 1670 and was survived by his widow, Katherine (MCGC 215, 236, 503; HEN I:407; JHB 1619–1660:97).

Anas Todkill: Anas Todkill, a carpenter who came to Virginia in 1607, was one of the first Jamestown colonists and, with another man, chronicled the settlers' first year. He accompanied Captain John Smith on a voyage of discovery in the Chesapeake Bay, and was captured by the Indians when he went ashore while exploring the countryside along the Rappahannock River. He was rescued and in 1608 accompanied Nathaniel Powell and some Indian guides on an expedition, the objective of which was finding the so-called "lost colonists." On December 29, 1608, Todkill went with Smith to Werowocomoco, Powhatan's principal seat, and he accompanied Captain John Martin on his two trips to the Pasbehay Indians' village. Later, Tindall identified himself as one of Martin's servants (VI&A 696).

Robert Tokeley: On January 3, 1626, the General Court's justices learned that the late Robert Langley, a Jamestown merchant, had given his power of attorney to Robert Tokeley, who was then in England. Tokeley nominated cape merchant Abraham Peirsey of Jamestown as the decedent's administrator in Virginia and authorized him to collect Langley's debts. The justices of the General Court decided to require Tokeley to produce a copy of the letters of administration that gave him authority over Langley's estate (VI&A 697).

Henry Tolton: On July 25, 1637, Henry Tolton of Bristol was identified as a servant employed by Walter Chiles I, who owned lots and houses in urban Jamestown and some land in the eastern end of the island (HCA f 273).

Tom (Native American): In July 1689 John Waters appeared before the justices of Old Rappahannock County's court and swore that a Rappahannock Indian named Tom had asked Daniel Disking to look after his son in the event of his death (Old Rappahannock County Order Book 1687–1692:118).

Tom: On February 15, 1768, when an inventory was made of the late Richard Ambler's slaves on Jamestown Island and his leasehold in the Governor's Land, an adult male named Tom was listed. In 1769 he was living on the Governor's Land and was part of the late Edward Ambler I's estate (York County Wills and Inventories 21:386–391; AMB-E).

Tom: On February 15, 1768, when an inventory was made of the late Richard Ambler's slaves on Jamestown Island and his leasehold in the Governor's Land, an enslaved boy named Tom was listed and described as Sylva's child. In 1769 Tom, who was still described as a boy, was living on the Governor's Land and was part of the late Edward Ambler I's estate (York County Wills and Inventories 21:386–391; AMB-E).

John Tomlinson (Tompkinson): On October 13, 1640, John Tomlinson was sentenced to a whipping because he failed to report some runaway servants (MCGC 467).

Tommy: In 1769 an adult male slave known as Gardener Tommy was living on Jamestown Island and was attributed to Edward Ambler I's estate (AMB-E).

James Tooke (Took, Tuke): James Tooke came to Virginia in 1621, at the expense of William Dum, a ship's carpenter. In early 1624 Tooke was living in the eastern end of Jamestown Island, where he was a servant in William Spence's household. Within the year he moved to the Governor's Land and became a household head. In January 1627 he was given permission to move to Mulberry Island. Tooke, a planter, served as a burgess for Isle of Wight (Warresqueak) County in 1640, and in 1646 he became a county justice. Sometime prior to 1642 he acquired 500 acres on the east side of

Lawnes Creek, which he resold four years later. Surviving records reveal that he secured some land at the head of the Blackwater River prior to September 1653. In 1659 James Tooke made his will, which was proved in early 1662. He was survived by his sons, Thomas and William, and daughter, Dorothy. In March Thomas Tooke repatented his late father's land on the Blackwater River (VI&A 697; LEO 18; STAN 61; PB 1:793, 820; 3:231; 5:228; BODDIE 260–262, 515, 704; Isle of Wight County Record Book A:12).

Joseph Topping (Toppin): On September 24, 1674, the justices of Surry County's monthly court identified Joseph Topping's wife, the former Elizabeth Rabley, as her late mother's heir. They also agreed that she was entitled to certain land for which she should have a patent. By November 6, 1688, Topping was functioning as the executor of his wife's deceased parents, Thomas and Jane Rabley of Jamestown. Among the people he sued on the Rableys' behalf were Christopher Robinson and his wife, who were Major Robert Beverley I's co-executors. Topping also had former Jamestown tavern-keeper John Everett serve as his attorney in Charles City County. Topping, who frequently filed suits in the monthly courts of Charles City, Old Rappahannock, and Westmoreland counties, died sometime prior to November 11, 1689. When Jamestown blacksmith William Briscoe bequeathed his property to his daughter-in-law, Ann, around 1695, he indicated that his acreage in urban Jamestown was next door to the brick house formerly occupied by Joseph and Elizabeth Topping, who had been living in Elizabeth's late father's dwelling (AMB 53, 133; MCGC 379; Surry County Order Book 1671–1691:682; Middlesex County Order Book 1680–1694:333, 356, 426; Charles City County Order Book 1687–1695:447, 453; Old Rappahannock County Order Book 1687–1692:43, 72; Westmoreland County Order Book 1676–1689: 650, 663, 678).

Totopotomoy (Tatapatamoi) (Native American): By 1649 Totopotomoy, a Pamunkey warrior, had become king of the Pamunkey Indians. He replaced Necotowance, who was identified as "Emperor of the Indians" in 1646 when he signed a treaty with the Virginia government. This change in titles suggests that the Indians of Virginia's coastal plain were no longer unified under a paramount chief or principal leader. Totopotomoy, a staunch ally of the English, was killed in 1656 in a conflict that became known as the Battle of Bloody Run. Contemporary sources suggest that bungling actions on the part of Colonel Edward Hill I led to the death of Totopotomoy and many of his warriors, who were fighting alongside the English in opposition to some hostile, outlying tribes. After Totopotomoy's death, his widow, Cockacoeske, became the leader or queen of the Pamunkeys, a role she held for the rest of her life. She was described by one contemporary as a descendant of Opechancanough, Powhatan's brother. If Totopotomoy was also a descendant, he and his wife may have been cousins.

In October 1649, a month after the native territory north of the York River was officially opened to settlement, the Virginia assembly enacted legislation allocating a 5,000-acre tract to each of the three Indian leaders whose territory was enveloped by colonized land. This decision came in response to the natives' acknowledgment that Virginia's land belonged to the Crown and to their request to receive a patent for specific tracts. The act of assembly specified that one of the 5,000-acre tracts was to be laid out and surveyed for Totopotomoy adjacent to the place where he was living, and that he would be issued a patent. However, a patent apparently was not forthcoming, for in July 1653 Totopotomoy again petitioned the assembly for a legal title to his people's land. This time, the assembly agreed to give him a choice between the land he was then occupying and a tract called Ramomak (Romancoke). The acreage he chose is part of today's Pamunkey Indian Reservation (HEN I:293–295, 325, 354–355, 402–403; FOR I:8:13–15, 25; Billings, "Some Acts Not in Hening's, April 1652, November 1652, and July 1653," 229; MCGC 499). In 1654 the northwesterly part of York County was split off to form New Kent County, an indication of how rapidly the Pamunkeys' territory was being colonized. Today, a creek in Hanover County bears Totopotomoy's name.

William Towne: On May 28, 1673, the General Court's justices discussed a lawsuit that William Towne initiated against Thomas Wilkinson of urban Jamestown, who had married Griffin Dickenson's (Dickeson's) widow (MCGC 344).

Richard Townsend (Townshend, Townscend): Richard Townsend came to Virginia in 1620 and signed a contract with Dr. John Pott, who agreed to teach him the apothecary's art in exchange for his labor. During the mid-1620s, when he was living in urban Jamestown in Pott's household, Townsend sued Pott, claiming that he had failed to fulfill his part of their bargain. The General Court agreed and ordered Pott to train Townsend or pay for his services. In October 1629 Townsend served as a burgess for the territory between Archer's Hope and Martin's Hundred, and by 1637 he had been named to the Council of State. In 1639 he patented 650 acres that extended along the York River from Yorktown (formerly Martiau's and Smith's) Creek to Ballard (formerly Townsend) Creek. Captain Richard Townsend received his land as one of the first adventurers to seat land in Chiskiack, then a frontier area. Like his near neighbors, William Pryor and Francis Morgan I, he served as a justice of the peace as soon as a court was established in the newly formed Charles River (York) County, which he represented in the assembly in 1642. Townsend died in Virginia in 1645. His son and heir, Francis Townsend, repatented his acreage on the York River, which descended to Robert Townsend I, whose widow, Mary, and son Robert II sold it to Augustine and Mildred Read Warner (VI&A 698; LEO xxi, 8, 20; NUG I:120, 271; York County Deeds, Orders, Wills 1:23, 27–30; 7:257; 10:69, 470, 50112:314–315).

Thomas Townsend (Townson): When galley-pot maker Christian Whithelme I made his will in England in March 1629, he identified Thomas Townsend as his son-in-law and one of his principal heirs. Whithelme was an investor in one of Governor John Harvey's entrepreneurial schemes. Townsend, a potter, went to Virginia in 1635, but he eventually returned to England and carried on the family tradition of manufacturing delftware (VI&A 698).

Lawrence Towtales: Lawrence Towtales, a tailor, came to Virginia in 1608 as part of the 1st Supply of new settlers and lived in Jamestown (VI&A 698).

William Tracy: In 1620 William Tracy, a Virginia Company investor, made an agreement with the Society of Berkeley Hundred, asking for some land, cattle, and horses if a smithery or bloomery were to be built. Within a month, Sir William Throgmorton, a member of the Society, assigned Tracy some land in Berkeley Hundred and upon reaching Virginia, Tracy was to be made a member of the Council of State. Tracy set sail for Virginia with his wife, Mary, and children, Joyce and Thomas, in September 1620 and arrived at Berkeley Hundred on January 29, 1621. He died sometime prior to April 8, 1621, leaving behind a substantial amount of debt (VI&A 698; STAN 29; LEO xxi).

* * *

Raleigh (Rawleigh, Raughley, Rawley) Travers (Traverse) I: Raleigh Travers I, the brother of William Travers I and one of his heirs, came to Virginia sometime prior to 1651–1652, when he commenced serving as a burgess for Lancaster County. He was returned to office in 1661 and represented the county until 1670. In 1666 Travers was authorized to purchase a drum for the assembly's use in summoning its members to meetings. He was a successful planter and over the years patented substantial quantities of land in the Middle Peninsula and Northern Neck. During the 1660s he served as a justice in Lancaster County's monthly court. In 1663 he purchased from Gerrard Foulke 3,350 acres called Aquicreek (Accokeek) in Westmoreland (later, Stafford) County, a tract that already had several tenants. Travers died sometime after May 11, 1670, but before early December 1670. At that time a court-appointed administrator awarded the decedent's estate to his widow, Elizabeth, who later married Colonel John Taverner. A notation in Lancaster County court minutes for March 12, 1673, indicates that Raleigh Travers I's estate was indebted to John Sympson "for his trouble in goeing aboute Mr. Traverse his funeral att Portan," which lasted for 21 days. By March 1674 Travers' widow, Elizabeth, had married Robert Beckinham (Beckingham). Later in the year, Travers' estate was sued by Richard James I, a Jamestown merchant whose business dealings extended to the Northern Neck (Stanard, "Travis Family," 246; NUG I: 241, 300, 333, 374, 430, 469; II:50, 359; DOR 3:653; Old Rappahannock County Wills 1682–1687:115–116; Lancaster County Order Book 1656–1666:175; 1666–1680:9, 50, 143, 174, 258, 277, 290; Westmoreland County Deeds and Wills No. 1 [1653–1671]:217–219; LEO 28, 28).

William Travers (Traverse, Travars) I: William Travers I patented some land on the Rappahannock River sometime prior to 1665. He became a highly successful planter and in 1677 served as speaker of the assembly. He also was a skillful attorney and in 1674 represented Henry Corbin in a matter that was aired before Lancaster County's monthly court. On May 13, 1676, he sent a letter to England informing the authorities that Governor Berkeley had gone to the falls of the James River, where he expected to encounter hostile Indians, especially the Susquehannocks. In 1678 Colonel Travers patented a large tract of land in what was then Old Rappahannock County. He died intestate prior to September 11, 1678, and was survived by his widow, Rebecca, and sons Samuel, William II, and Raleigh Travers II.

By October 1678 the widowed Rebecca Travers, as her late husband's administratrix, had begun settling his estate. On November 14, 1679, Rebecca and Virginia merchant John Rice, who were planning to wed, executed a marriage contract, a document that reveals she was a wealthy widow. In November 5, 1680, Rice served as her representative in litigation involving the settlement of her late husband's estate. Litigation was still underway in 1684, when Rice defended the Travers estate against the claims of William Smith of Dublin. In 1685 Rice conveyed to his stepson, Samuel Travers, his share of the late William Travers I's estate, which was encumbered by some quitrents that were in arrears. When Raleigh Travers II made his will in 1687, he made a bequest to his mother, Rebecca Rice, and named as reversionary heirs his brother Samuel and son Raleigh III (LEO 43; NUG I:463; II:31, 55; Westmoreland County Order Book 1676–1689:183, 198, 202, 206; Old Rappahannock County Deeds and Wills 1677–1682:240–241, 289–294; Wills 1682–1687: 73–77, 115–116; Order Book 1683–1686:34, 125–126; 1687–1692:62; Middlesex County Order Book 1673–1680:95, 107; Lancaster County Order Book 1666–1680:288, 290, 435; Northumberland County Order Book 1678–1698:11; SR 657).

Samuel Travers (Traverse): In 1685, John Rice, who had married William Travers I's widow, Rebecca, transferred to Samuel Travers, one of the decedent's sons, the real and personal estate he stood to inherit from his late father. Samuel's inherited realty was encumbered by some overdue quitrents, taxes that were owed on the property. Old Rappahannock County's justices were asked to determine whether John Rice, as custodian of the property, should have paid the quitrents or whether they were Samuel Travers' responsibility. By 1686 Travers had become a justice of Old Rappahannock County's monthly court and two years later, a captain of militia. By 1689 he had become the county's sheriff. When his term as sheriff was due to be extended two years later, he refused to take the Crown's oath of allegiance and supremacy. In March 1692 when Captain Samuel Travers, then deputy escheator, repatented some of the land he had inherited, he identified himself as William Travers I's son and one of his heirs. Later in the year Samuel deeded some of his late father's land in Stafford County to his brother, Raleigh II, who promptly sold it. When Samuel Travers and his wife, Frances, disposed of some land on Totosky Creek in Richmond County in January 1694, Travers said that the land transaction was unencumbered by any claims that his father's other heirs might make. During 1696–1697 Samuel Travers represented Richmond County in the assembly (NN 1:128, 198; Old Rappahannock County Wills 1682–1687:115–116; Order Book 1683–1686:115, 125–126, 158; 1687–1692:64, 117, 151, 165, 211; Stafford County Record Book 1686–1693:274a–275; Richmond County Deed Book 2 [1693–1695]:4–6; LEO 56).

* * *

* * *

Edward Travis (Travers) I: Sometime prior to January 25, 1638, Edward Travis I married Ann II, the daughter of John Johnson I, who lived in the eastern end of Jamestown Island. In 1644 Travis commenced serving as a James City County burgess. By that time he was in possession of 1,080 acres of land on the west side of the Chickahominy River, abutting Pease Hill Creek in what was then James City County but is now Charles City. On March 10, 1652, Travis patented 196 acres in the eastern end of Jamestown Island, acreage that was "near black Poynt" and was bound north and east upon the Back River. Included were 24 acres formerly granted to John Southern, 16 acres that had belonged to Thomas Passmore, 12 acres patented by John Senior I, and 144 acres Travis had received on the basis of headrights. Then, on March 10, 1653, Travis patented 326 acres that included the 196 acres he had acquired the previous year plus 130 acres of marsh and arable land "lying southerly from his now dwelling house." Thus, it was on Edward Travis I's original 196 acres that he built his home, not on the acreage of his late father-in-law, John Johnson I, as traditionally has been assumed. On November 5, 1654, Travis patented 150 acres that he had acquired from John Senior I, a parcel that included some additional acreage in the eastern end of Jamestown Island and some marshland north of Passmore Creek. A month later, on December 4, 1654, he patented a 12-acre parcel that he had purchased from John Crump (Crumfort), the late Rev. Richard Buck's grandson and reversionary heir. Finally, on August 8, 1659, Travis purchased his wife's parents' home tract from his brother-in-law John Johnson II. Ann Johnson Travis and her husband, Edward I, produced a son, Edward II. At Edward Travis I's death, which occurred prior to February 10, 1664, his Jamestown Island landholdings descended to his son, Edward Travis II (VI&A 425–426; PB 1:531; 3:8, 158; 7:228–229; NUG I:83, 224, 231, 270–271; II:252; STAN 63; DOR 2:358; LEO 22).

Edward Travis II: Edward Travis II was the son of John Johnson I's daughter, Ann II, and her husband, Edward Travis I. Some genealogists have surmised that Edward Travis II was married to Elizabeth Champion because John Champion was interred in the Travis graveyard on Jamestown Island. Edward Travis II inherited his father's 396-acre plantation on Jamestown Island, which he repatented on February 10, 1664. He also purchased 70 acres from Walter Chiles II's widow, Susanna, which he patented on August 7, 1672. Then, on November 15, 1677, he acquired 12 acres from William Champion. All of these parcels became part of the Travis plantation, an aggregate of 550 acres, which Edward Travis II patented on December 22, 1682. He went on to acquire some land along the east side of Kingsmill Creek, which gave him just over 802 acres, a large plantation that encompassed the southeast end of Jamestown Island and included all of the territory east of Kingsmill Creek and north of Passmore Creek. In 1678 Travis gave his wife, Elizabeth, his power of attorney in the Surry County monthly court. After her death he married a woman named Rebecca, who was born around 1677. Edward Travis II was a respected member of the Jamestown community, and in May 1699 he was James City Parish's churchwarden. He died on November 2, 1700, and was buried in the family cemetery on Jamestown Island. He was survived by his widow, Rebecca, and his young son, Edward Travis III. Rebecca Travis inherited life-rights in her late husband's plantation on Jamestown Island, but the decedent's son was his reversionary heir. Upon being widowed, Rebecca married Jamestown's burgess, William Broadnax I, who owned three parcels on the east side of Orchard Run and some acreage within urban Jamestown's corporate limits. Together, the former Rebecca Travis and William Broadnax I had three children: Edward, Elizabeth, and William Broadnax II. Documentary sources suggest that the Broadnax couple and their respective children continued to occupy the Travis family home on Jamestown Island. Rebecca died on December 19, 1723, at age 46 and was buried in the Travis family cemetery near the family home. William Broadnax I, his three children, and his stepson most likely were sharing the Travis family home on Jamestown Island at the time of Broadnax's death in February 1727 (DOR 2:358–360; PB 5:342; 7:228–229; NUG I:503; II:252; York County Deeds, Orders, Wills 1698–1702:455–456; Surry County Deeds, Wills &c. 1671–1684:170; LJC 263).

Edward Travis III: Edward Travis III, the young son of Edward Travis II, lost his father in November 1700. Although Edward III, as his late father's reversionary heir, stood to inherit the ancestral plantation in the eastern end of Jamestown Island, the decedent's widow, Rebecca, had life-rights in the property and was living there at the time of her death in 1723. Edward Travis III would have shared the family home with the remarried Rebecca Travis, his stepfather William Broadnax I, and the Broadnax couple's three young children. When Edward Travis III matured, he married Elizabeth Marable. Together, they produced a son, Edward Champion Travis, who was born around 1720, and a daughter, Rebecca Elizabeth, who was born in 1727. When Edward Travis III assumed control of his late father's plantation, he did not enhance its size, but he purchased some acreage within urban Jamestown's corporate limits, parcels that bordered the road leading across the isthmus then connecting Jamestown Island to the mainland. On January 13, 1717, he bought a 28½-acre tract at the western end of the island, near the isthmus, and he also acquired John Baird's lot by James City Parish's churchyard. On July 17, 1719, he conveyed both plots to his stepfather, William Broadnax I, and he also purchased some of his step-uncle John Broadnax's personal property. When Edward Travis III died, he left his wife, Elizabeth, life-rights in their Jamestown Island plantation, naming son Edward Champion Travis as reversionary heir (DOR 2:358–361; Stanard, "Travis Family," 142; Tyler, "The Broadnax Family," 56; AMB 92, 106–107; York County Deeds, Orders, Wills 15:510).

Edward Champion Travis: Edward Champion Travis, the son and heir of Elizabeth and Edward Travis III, was born in 1720 and died in August 1779 at age 59. When Edward Champion Travis came of age around 1741–1742, he married Susannah Hutchings of Norfolk, the daughter of John and Amy Hutchings. Together, Susannah and Edward Champion Travis produced sons Champion, Edward IV, and John I, and a daughter, Susannah II. When Travis wrote a letter to a kinsman in 1747, he made reference to his "mother," perhaps a reference to a woman his stepfather, William Broadnax I, had married after Rebecca Travis's death. Besides the ancestral plantation in the eastern end of Jamestown Island, Edward Champion Travis came into possession of a waterfront lot in urban Jamestown. In September 1755 he patented a neighboring half-acre parcel, acreage that had escheated to

the Crown. On the Travis lots, archaeologists have discovered the remains of a one-story brick dwelling that had an English basement. Travis would have found it advantageous to own property within Jamestown's corporate limits, for it would have made him eligible to hold office as the community's burgess. Also, the former capital was an official port of entry that had access to deepwater shipping.

By 1750 Travis had become involved in the slave trade, and his sloop, the *Jamestown*, commenced transporting Africans from Barbados to Virginia. The firm known as Edward C. Travis and Company was involved in the slave trade until at least 1758. While Travis was residing on Jamestown Island, he played an active role in public life. In 1752 he began serving as burgess for Jamestown and retained his seat through 1765. He also became a James City County justice in 1752 and served as county coroner in 1759. In 1745 he witnessed a deed whereby Edward Jaquelin's heirs transferred their land to Richard Ambler, and in 1750 (while serving as William Nugent's executor) he assigned a 105-acre leasehold in the Governor's Land to Richard Ambler. In June 1753 he bought a half-acre lot in urban Jamestown from William Drummond III and sold it to Richard Ambler the following October. His purchase was shrewd, for Ambler already owned the neighboring properties that formerly belonged to Christopher Perkins and Edward Jaquelin's heirs. Therefore, the Travis lot was directly in front of the site upon which Ambler was building a brick mansion for his son John Ambler I. Edward Champion Travis's wife, Susannah, died on October 28, 1761, at age 33.

In 1766 Edward Champion Travis was among those appointed to appraise the late Richard Ambler's personal property in James City County. In 1768 and 1769 the county tax assessor credited Travis with around 40 slaves of tithable age and 1,652 acres of James City County land. His acreage included his 802¾-acre plantation in the eastern end of Jamestown Island and a tract known as Piney Grove, which was situated between Deep Creek (now known as Lake Pasbehay) and the mouth of the Chickahominy River. When a hurricane struck eastern Virginia in mid-September 1769, destroying numerous buildings and ruining crops, the *Virginia Gazette* reported that "A schooner of Major Travis's, lying before his house" on Jamestown Island "was drove from her anchors and went ashore on the other side." On June 14, 1770, shortly before Edward

Champion Travis moved to York County and took up residence on his recently purchased riverfront plantation, Timson's Neck, he offered a seagoing vessel for sale "at Jamestown," where it was available for examination. When Travis vacated his Jamestown Island property, which included the ancestral plantation and his home in urban Jamestown, he left it to the occupancy of his sons, Edward Travis IV and Champion, but did not give them outright ownership. In 1772 Major Travis was deemed ineligible to hold office in James City County because he was living in York County. In late October 1777, when he sought to recover a slave who had fled from his Jamestown Island plantation, he placed an advertisement in the *Virginia Gazette* and indicated that he was living at Timson's Neck.

By late summer 1775 the breach between Great Britain and her American colonies had become irreparable, and King George III declared that the colonies were in "open and avowed rebellion." This announcement came a few days after two British tenders fired upon some American sentinels stationed in Jamestown, "driving two or three small balls through the ferry-house." Because Jamestown Island protruded toward the James River's channel and therefore was strategically important, the Travis plantation and the family's urban home were in the midst of a war zone. When a boatload of British soldiers tried to land on Jamestown Island in mid-November 1775, about half a mile below the American battery, they were driven off. However, a British man-of-war reportedly fired upon the Travis family's home and sent a shot through the kitchen chimney. The building that was shelled probably was the family's urban dwelling, which was located just east of the American battery and on the bank of the James, where it would have been a conspicuous target. When Edward Champion Travis of Timson's Neck made his will on December 15, 1778, he left virtually all of his James City County land to his son Champion and gave the Timson's Neck plantation to son John. He bequeathed his land in Brunswick and Surry counties to son Edward Travis IV, a naval officer. In 1779 Edward Champion Travis reportedly assaulted the Rev. William Bland and gave him a severe beating. Travis died of dropsy at age 59 on August 21, 1779, and his will was presented for probate on September 20th. An inventory of his estate, filed in York County, omitted all references to any personal possessions, slaves, or livestock he may have had in James City County, probably because he had already passed them along to son Champion (Stanard,

"Travis Family," 134, 141–145; DOR 2:360–361; Purdie, June 14, 1770; November 17, 1775; October 31, 1777; Purdie and Dixon, September 14, 1769; Dixon, August 21, 1779; BLAND n.d.; Thompson [1780]; Smith et al. 1745; AMB 114, 115; PB 31:635; York County Order Book 3 [1765–1768]:77; Wills and Inventories 22 [1771–1783]:458–459; Williamsburg-James City County Tax Lists 1768–1769; MIN 145, 159; STAN 128–170; EJC 5:391; 6:512; LEO 84, 87, 89, 92).

Champion Travis: Champion Travis, the eldest son of Susannah Hutchings and Edward Champion Travis, probably was born on Jamestown Island, for his birth occurred before his parents moved to Timson's Neck in York County. In November 1772 he married Elizabeth (Betsey), the daughter of Captain Samuel Boush of Norfolk and his wife, the former Alice Mason. Together, Champion and Elizabeth produced several children, the eldest of whom was their son and principal heir, Samuel. In 1769 Champion Travis was credited with 10 tithable slaves in James City County but no land, probably because the slaves were residing on one of the properties owned by his father. On December 15, 1778, Edward Champion Travis made his will, leaving virtually all of his James City County land to his son Champion. Included in the bequest were the decedent's Williamsburg residence, his Jamestown Island plantation, his dwelling in urban Jamestown, and his plantation called Piney Grove, a subsidiary farm that was located a few miles west of Jamestown Island and extended to the east side of the Chickahominy River's mouth.

Champion Travis, like his forebears, took an active role in public life. He served as a James City County justice and sheriff and represented Jamestown in the House of Burgesses from 1768 to 1771. He also participated in the Conventions of 1774 and 1775. During the Revolutionary War he was a colonel in the state regiment, and in 1776 he was appointed a naval commissioner. At the onset of the American Revolution, Champion Travis probably was living in his father's plantation house in the eastern part of Jamestown Island, for his brother Edward Travis IV was then occupying their father's residence in urban Jamestown. The Travis brothers also may have spent time at their father's house in Williamsburg. In 1776, however, Champion Travis informed the Virginia Convention that "his dwelling-house and offices thereunto belonging in the town of Jamestown for many months past have been and are now occupied and appropriated by a detachment from the Virginia army as guardhouses." When real estate tax rolls were compiled for James City County in 1782, Champion Travis was in possession of 2,038 acres of rural land. His holdings then included the ancestral plantation on Jamestown Island and Piney Grove, along with his house and lot in urban Jamestown and a dwelling in the city of Williamsburg. Travis went on to serve in the House of Delegates in 1781–1782 and from 1800 to 1806, representing James City County.

When Champion Travis's brother John Travis I died around 1795, his personal effects at Timson's Neck were offered for sale at a public auction. Champion then purchased two slaves (a man named Nero and a boy named Bob), a phaeton, a bed, a gun, a bullet mold, and several other items. He may have taken the slaves and some of his other acquisitions to his Jamestown Island plantation or to Piney Grove. When personal property tax records were compiled in 1782, Champion Travis of James City County was credited with 24 slaves who were age 16 or older, 32 cattle, and a two-wheeled vehicle. By 1783 Travis owned fewer slaves but a larger herd of livestock, and in 1784 he had a four-wheeled carriage. It is very likely that he divided his time between Jamestown Island and his home in Williamsburg. Personal property tax rolls for 1787 reveal that Champion Travis employed an underage white male overseer named William Steiff, who assisted with Travis's farming operations. Travis paid taxes on two groups of slaves and two herds of livestock, which probably were divided between his Jamestown Island and Piney Grove plantations.

On May 31, 1793, Nelly and Daphne, two of Champion Travis's slaves who were plowing his fields on Jamestown Island, attacked and killed their overseer, Joel Gathright. The circumstances surrounding this emotionally charged case, which resulted in the enslaved women's being executed, are open to conjecture. From 1794 through 1796 a substantial number of slaves continued to live on Travis's James City County property, along with two or three free white males. By 1797 the number of slaves in Travis's possession began to dwindle, perhaps a reflection of hard economic times. He disposed of his Piney Grove tract in 1800–1801 and seems to have invested very little in his plantation on Jamestown Island, which lacked a resident overseer.

When artist Louis Girardin published a work entitled *Amoenitates Graphicae* in 1805, he included a sophisticated watercolor painting that depicted part of urban Jamestown. Overlooking the riverbank was a story-and-a-half dwelling in the vicinity of the urban lots that had been owned successively by Edward Champion Travis and Champion Travis. In a position analogous to the Ambler house, whose towering ruins still stand, was a large, two-story dwelling with a mansard roof. Champion Travis died in August 1810, and the following year the names of his underage sons, Samuel and Robert Travis, commenced appearing in James City County's personal property tax rolls. However, the decedent's Jamestown Island plantation was attributed to his estate through 1817. Finally, in 1818 the late Champion Travis's Jamestown Island property was transferred to his eldest son, Samuel Travis. The decedent's daughter, Susan, married famed agricultural reformer Edmund Ruffin, whereas Champion and Elizabeth's daughter, Catherine, married Jessee Cole of Williamsburg. Champion and Elizabeth's sons, Robert, William L. and John, survived to adulthood (James City County Land Tax Lists 1782–1821; Personal Property Tax Lists 1782–1818; Stanard, "Travis Family," 141–145; TRAVIS 68; Dixon, August 21, 1779; York County Wills and Inventories 22 [1771–1783]:458–459; 23 [1783–1811]:465–471; SCHRE 6:9–10; PALM VI:461–465, 521, 532–533, 543; LEO 97, 100, 103, 106, 110, 112, 142, 220, 224, 228, 232, 236, 240; Girardin 1805; DOR 2:359–360, 605; Rind, December 3, 1772).

Edward Travis IV: Edward Travis IV, who in 1772 was described as a resident "of Jamestown," was the son of Edward Champion Travis and his wife, Susannah, and the brother of Champion Travis. Edward IV seems to have moved into his father's house in urban Jamestown around 1770, probably when the elder man moved to Timson's Neck in York County. Sometime prior to April 2, 1772, he wed Miss Elizabeth (Betsy) Taite. The couple's marriage was brief, for she died prior to January 28, 1773. During the American Revolution Edward Travis IV, who was a 1st lieutenant in the 2nd Virginia Regiment when the war began, became a naval officer. He was based in Jamestown, where he outfitted American naval vessels. The Travis house in urban Jamestown, depicted by artist Louis Girardin in 1805, was located upon the bank of the James River. It was shelled by a British vessel in 1775, the same year that Edward Travis IV took command of a British ship that had run aground. In 1776 he was placed in command of the *Manley* galley, and later in the year he was made commander of the brig *Raleigh*. In April 1777, when Travis was ordered to harass enemy naval vessels, he was captured by the frigate *Thames*.

Upon being paroled, he was promoted to captain.

In February 1779 Edward Travis IV married Clarissa, the daughter of Benjamin Waller of Williamsburg. Perhaps hoping to provide her with what he considered a suitable home, he signed a lease on November 27, 1779, agreeing to rent Mrs. Mary Ambler's Jamestown mansion and plantation for four years, commencing January 13, 1780. By that time Edward's elder brother, Champion, had inherited virtually all of their late father's property in James City County, including the decedent's house in Williamsburg. On April 1, 1780, while Edward Travis IV was residing "at Jamestown," probably in the Ambler house, he placed an advertisement in the *Virginia Gazette* offering for sale his dwelling and some lots in Williamsburg. He still was in Jamestown on March 6, 1784, when he announced that he had "four very likely slaves" to sell. One was "a young fellow well acquainted with the business of a house carpenter and cooper; also his wife, a very likely wench of middle age, accustomed to cook and domestic work, with two healthy children, a boy and a girl." Edward Travis IV died on March 28, 1784, while on his way to the Virginia springs to recover his health. On July 1, 1804, when his son, Joseph H. Travis, sought to obtain his military warrant for 5,333⅓ acres of land, he certified "that he is the only heir at law of Edward Travis, dec'd, his father, who was a Captain in Virginia State Navy and who died intestate." In 1784 the late Edward Travis IV's estate was credited with five young slaves and six cattle (Purdie and Dixon, April 2, 1772; January 28, 1773; Dixon, May 9, 1777; February 26, 1779; April 1, 1780; Purdie, November 17, 1775; *Virginia Gazette and Weekly Advertiser*, March 6, 1784; James City County Legislative Petitions 1775; Personal Property Tax Lists 1784–1786; AMB 129; CLAGHORN:14, 314; HEITMAN 547; CLARK 6:1409; BURGESS 1148–1149; DOR 2:360–361).

John Travis I: John Travis I, the son of Edward Champion Travis and his wife, Susannah, was born around 1760. He married Judith Langhorn and in 1779 inherited his late father's York County plantation, Timson's Neck, which was located on the west side of Queens Creek's mouth. Together, John Travis I and his wife, Judith, produced four children: John II, Mary, Champion II, and Judith II. Travis died sometime prior to 1787, after which time his personal property in James City County was attributed to his widow, Judith, and his York County property was associated with his estate. In October 1795,

when the decedent's estate was appraised and some of his personal belongings were sold at auction, his oldest brother, Champion Travis, purchased several items and two of his slaves. Between 1806 and 1817 Judith Langhorn Travis, who then owned 257 acres in the western part of James City County, was credited with six or seven slaves age 12 or over, one or more horses, a wheeled vehicle, and some cattle. In 1815 she was taxed on several luxury items, including a mahogany tea table, three large pieces of artwork, and a chest of drawers. Her household also had use of a carriage (TRAVIS 71; James City County Personal Property Tax Lists 1806–1824; Land Tax Lists 1811–1814; York County Deeds, Orders, Wills 1783–1811:II:465).

Samuel Travis: Samuel, Champion and Elizabeth Boush Travis's eldest son, was born sometime after 1772. By 1818 he was in possession of his late father's Jamestown Island plantation, having purchased his siblings' interest in the property. The tax assessor noted that the acreage in Samuel's possession had been deeded to him "by Blunt Cole and others and is the same land formerly charged to Champion Travis." Tax rolls for 1820 indicate that there were no buildings on Samuel Travis's Jamestown Island property that were deemed worthy of taxation. Thus, the dwelling the Travises had occupied for successive generations seemingly was uninhabitable. Traditionally, any buildings occupied by Travis slaves (and perhaps any barns or tobacco houses that were present) would have been excluded from the tax officials' assessment. Over the years the number of slaves and quantity of livestock in Samuel Travis's possession gradually increased, but he never added taxable improvements to his Jamestown Island property.

Samuel Travis, a resident of Williamsburg, was married to Elizabeth Bright of Hampton, the daughter of Captain Francis Bright of the Virginia Navy. Travis served in the War of 1812 and was a member of the House of Delegates, representing Williamsburg. He made his will on July 21, 1821, and it was presented for probate two days later. Although he mentioned some land in Kentucky that he had inherited from his father, he failed to mention his property on Jamestown Island. Samuel's brother Robert and brother-in-law Jessee Cole served as his executors. He was survived by his wife, Elizabeth, and their five daughters (Susan, Elizabeth II, Virginia, Catherine, and Julia). The late Samuel Travis's Jamestown Island plantation remained intact and from 1822 through 1830 was attributed to his estate. In

1831 the Travis property was purchased by David Bullock, who already owned the Amblers' holdings on Jamestown Island. When a celebration was held in 1822 to commemorate the arrival of Virginia's first colonists, some of the celebrants, in their unbridled enthusiasm, "burnt down one of the two large brick houses on the island." A newspaper reporter stated that, "Just as I am writing this, the old brick building belonging to Colonel Travis' estate has taken fire and the roof is already in a blaze. It was an uninhabitable ruin, to be sure, but I am sorry, as it is one of the few remaining monuments of antiquity here, to see it disappearing from the scene." In 1854 the artist Robert Sully sketched the towering ruins of the Travis family's ancestral home in the eastern end of Jamestown Island (TRAVIS 68–69; Williamsburg Hustings Court I:48; James City County Personal Property Tax Lists 1811–1821; Land Tax Lists 1810–1831; *Richmond Times-Dispatch* 1822; AMB-JJ 1828; Tyler, "Glimpses of Old College Life," 222; LEO 291, 296, 301, 306).

* * *

Richard Tree: Richard Tree, a carpenter who claimed to be an ancient planter, came to Virginia in 1618, perhaps on a return trip. In 1624 he patented an 8-acre ridge of land in the eastern end of Jamestown Island and acquired 42 acres about a mile below Blunt Point. In January 1625 he was residing in rural Jamestown Island with his son, John. Tree was a respected member of the Jamestown Island community and served on juries, participated in an inquest, and was churchwarden of James City Parish in 1626. By October 1628 he had moved to the lower side of the James River, where he was hired to build a frame church for the parishioners of Hog Island. In 1629 and 1632 he served as that area's burgess. Tree retained his Jamestown Island property until at least February 1638, and it continued to be used as a reference point in the island's landscape. By August 1638 he had acquired a half-acre lot in urban Jamestown, acreage that he was obliged to develop or forfeit (VI&A 700; LEO 8, 11).

John Trehearne (Trachern, Trahorne): John Trehearne came to Virginia in 1622 with the settlers whom Rowland Truelove and his fellow investors, known as the Truelove's Company, sent to the colony. During the mid-1620s he was living at Chaplin's Choice in the corporation of Charles City. Trehearne survived until at least March 24, 1630, at which time he was serving as a burgess for the territory around Weyanoke (VI&A 700; LEO 9).

Edward Trew: On November 15, 1620, William Potterton informed Virginia Company officials that his apprentice, Edward Trew, had gone to Virginia with Thomas West, Lord Delaware, and was still in the colony as a Company servant. Potterton was told to discuss the matter with Lady Delaware (VI&A 701).

George Trotter: On July 1, 1683, George Trotter sued Surry County bricklayer John Bird and won (Surry County Order Book 1671–1691:420, 429). Bird was involved in constructing at least two brick buildings in urban Jamestown.

John Trussell: During the mid-1620s John Trussell was living at West and Shirley Hundred and was an indentured servant in Thomas Pawlett's household. In late 1634 he purchased some of the late Thomas Lee's goods, which were sold by Bartholomew Hopkins. He patented some land in Elizabeth City County in 1635 but retained it for only three years. While in Elizabeth City he served as undersheriff. By 1644 he had moved to Northumberland County, of which he had become commander. In 1649 he acquired some land on the Chicacoan River in Northumberland County, near the wealthy and influential John Mottrom, and shortly thereafter he purchased some additional acreage. By 1650 Trussell had begun serving as a county justice and retained that position for nearly a decade. In 1651 he patented some land on the Chicacoan River and two years later transferred it to Richard and Mary Rice, utilizing a deed of gift. When Trussell testified in court in May 1653, he said that he was age 50 or thereabouts. As time went on, he continued to add to his landholdings. He served as a Northumberland County burgess in 1649, 1651–1652, and 1654–1655 and regularly submitted requests for compensation and reimbursement. By 1655 he had become a lieutenant colonel in the local militia, and in 1658 he held the rank of colonel. He also was a vestryman for the Anglican congregation in the Chicacoan area. In January 1656 Trussell was identified as Northumberland County's high sheriff and coroner. During the latter part of 1659, he prepared his will and made bequests to sons John and William, daughter Elizabeth (Betty), and pregnant wife Mary, who probably was expecting their daughter Anne. John Trussell died prior to February 20, 1660, when his widow, Mary, was granted a commission of administration. His will was proved in July. An inventory of the decedent's estate reveals that his home was well furnished and equipped with luxury items; however, he left behind a significant amount of debt. By February 1662 the widowed Mary Trussell had remarried (VI&A 702; LEO 27–28, 32; NUG I:32, 88, 185, 205, 362, 382; Northumberland County Deeds and Orders 1650–1652:41; Wills, Inventories &c. 1652–1658:53, 60, 62, 67, 94; Record Book 1658–1662:9, 40, 43–44, 64, 78, 86; 1662–1666:104; Order Book 1652–1665:21, 28, 65, 71, 143, 154, 234, 241–242; DOR 3:428–429).

* * *

Daniel Tucker (Tooker): According to Captain John Smith, Daniel Tucker, a gentleman and Virginia Company investor, came to Virginia in 1608 in the 2nd Supply of new colonists and lived in Jamestown. When Lord Delaware arrived in Virginia in June 1610, he made Tucker provost marshal, truck-master, vice-admiral, and clerk of the store. Tucker also served on the Council of State. He acquired some land in Bermuda and in 1616 became Bermuda's governor, holding office until 1619. In April 1619 Tucker informed the Virginia Company that he had spent five years in Virginia and was one of Lord Delaware's associates. In November 1620, when he asked the Company for compensation for services performed during Delaware's administration, he received some shares of land. In March 1622 Tucker was authorized to receive a patent because he was transporting 100 people to the colony. He identified himself in May 1622 as a resident of Milton, in Kent, when he gave false testimony about Captain Edward Brewster's court martial in Virginia. Captain Daniel Tucker returned to Bermuda and died there in February 1625 (VI&A 702).

William Tucker (Tooker, Tuker) I: William Tucker I, a Virginia Company investor, came to Virginia in 1610, and in 1619 he served as a burgess for the corporation of Kecoughtan (Elizabeth City). After the March 1622 Indian attack, he was placed in command of Elizabeth City's inhabitants. Tucker's wife, Mary I, came to Virginia in 1623 with her brothers, George, Paul, and William Thompson. William Tucker, like his brother, Daniel, had a distinguished military and political career and in 1623 was named to the Council of State. He represented Elizabeth City in the assembly sessions held in 1624–1625. He undertook trading voyages in the Chesapeake Bay and

in the Pamunkey and Potomac rivers, and in May 1623 he led an expedition against the Indians on the lower side of the James River. Tucker was actively involved in the infamous scheme of serving poisonous wine to natives signing a peace treaty. As a military leader he led expeditions against the Nansemond and Warresqueak Indians. Captain William Tucker and his wife, Mary, continued to reside in Kecoughtan. From 1625 through 1629 he was Kecoughtan's commander, and during the 1630s he continued to acquire property in Elizabeth City, including some on the lower side of the James. Mary Thompson Tucker predeceased her husband, but the date of her death is uncertain. In August 1639 Captain Tucker was among those arrested and sent to England by Governor John Harvey. Afterward, he claimed that he had been detained in England for three years because of false allegations. He seems to have remarried there. When he prepared his will on October 12, 1642, he named his wife, Frances, as an heir and divided the remainder of his estate among his three children: sons William II and Thomas and daughter Mary II. The testator left all of his Virginia land to his son William II. No mention was made of Mary and William Tucker I's daughter Elizabeth, who was born in August 1624 and may have been deceased when her father made his will (VI&A 703–704; LEO 3, 5–6; WITH 367).

* * *

Mary Tucker (Mrs. Edward Basse [Bass, Base]) (Native American): In 1644 Mary Tucker, an Indian who had converted to the Christian faith, married Edward, Nathaniel and Mary Jordan Basse's son. Edward was born on May 8, 1622, in what became Isle of Wight County (Bass Family Bible Records 1613–1699; CJS 2:296; VI&A 118).

St. George Tucker: St. George Tucker, renowned for his knowledge of the law, was born in 1752 at Port Royal, Bermuda. He came to Virginia in 1771 and enrolled at the College of William and Mary, where he studied law under George Wythe. After service in the American Revolution, he succeeded Wythe as professor of law. Tucker sat as a judge on the Virginia General Court from 1785 to 1802 and served on the Virginia Supreme Court of Appeals from 1803 to 1811. In 1813 he was appointed a judge of the United States District Court, a position he retained until his death in 1827. In August 1781 St. George Tucker reported that the French were landing in Jamestown (Tucker 1781; www.history.org).

Elizabeth Tudman: On March 23, 1662, the assembly denied Mrs. Elizabeth Tudman's claim to 27 acres on the mainland near Jamestown Island, a tract formerly owned by Thomas Perkins. The burgesses agreed that her patent, which was fragmentary, lacked the proper endorsements. On April 9, 1666, when a jury deliberated the matter, it was decided that the 27 acres should be declared escheat land because Perkins had produced no heirs. Afterward, Mrs. Elizabeth Tudman renounced her claim and Francis Morrison's (Moryson's) title to the 27-acre tract was confirmed (AMB 51 f 671). It is likely that Mrs. Tudman was Thomas Perkins' widow and that her rights to his property expired upon remarriage.

John Tullitt (Tullett, Tullit, Tulitt): On June 6, 1698, John Tullitt purchased from Mrs. Dyonysia Hadley the eastern units of a long brick row house on urban Jamestown's Back Street, the former home of Mrs. Sarah Lee, and began occupying the property. On February 25, 1699, the Council of State decided that "the house where Mrs. Sarah Lee alias Smith lately lived now in the possession of Mr. John Tullitt" was the most convenient place for the assembly to meet. Therefore, Tullitt was ordered to "repair and fit up the said house" in accord with the governor's directions. On May 11, 1699, Tullitt requested compensation for readying his home for assembly meetings. He was dissatisfied with the sum the assembly offered and on May 22nd asked for an increase. Although relatively little is known about John Tullitt as a private individual, he seems to have been a builder, for governing officials frequently hired him to undertake construction projects. In June 1695 he was paid to raze the old brick fort built in Jamestown in the 1670s and replace it with a new gun platform. He also was compensated for mending the gun carriages and mounting the weapons on the new platform. In 1700 Tullitt was authorized to supply brick for the new capitol building that was being erected in Williamsburg. Then, in October 1709 he offered to construct the College of William and Mary's main building for £2,000, as long as he was allowed to harvest wood from the college's property and skilled workmen were brought from England. Tullitt received permission to proceed with construction of the college, and in November 1711 he was paid £500. Two months later he received £400 for building the college hall. He may have found it difficult to maintain accurate business records, for he and Auditor William Byrd II of Westover reviewed them several times. The two men apparently became friends, for they continued to keep in touch after they ceased being involved in government-sponsored projects.

In October 1702 John Tullitt purchased 27 acres near Jamestown Island, adjacent to the Governor's Land, and retained the property for many years. In 1703, while Tullitt was renting William Broadribb's mill near Jamestown, he patented 391 acres on the south side of King's Creek's head. He paid quitrent on 625 acres in James City County (property he either owned or rented) in 1704, and in November 1705 he patented 17,653 acres in Henrico County near Falling Creek, and moved there. He gradually began divesting himself of his property in James City County. In July 1707 he conveyed to Philip Ludwell II the remaining 16 years of his 21-year lease for the Goose Hill plantation in the eastern end of Jamestown Island; three leaseholds in the Governor's Land; and his lease for William Broadribb's mill. It probably was around 1707 that Tullitt disposed of his Jamestown row house, conveying it to Philip Ludwell II. He also sold Ludwell his 27 acres on the mainland, near the entrance to Jamestown Island. John Tullitt died sometime prior to December 1719, when his widow, Hannah, was ordered to present an inventory of his estate, which she did on September 5, 1727. On May 20, 1736, when she made her will, she mentioned several cousins and a brother who were members of the Brummall (Bromer) family; her will was recorded in June 1737 (MCGH 676; NUG III:80, 109; AMB 77, 99; SMITH 90; LEE 51 f 671; EJC I:331, 410; JHB 1695–1702:160,175; SAIN 17:209; Byrd 2:99, 116, 286, 351, 384, 434, 476, 522, 551–552; Henrico County Wills and Deeds 1714–1737:51, 631; Minute Book 1719–1724:5, 7).

Edward Tunstall (Tonstall): By the mid-1630s Edward Tunstall began patenting acreage that abutted south upon the falls of the Appomattox River. His land was in what was then Henrico County but is now Chesterfield. In 1640 he served as a burgess for Henrico County. In October 1686 an Edward Tunstall (probably a descendant) patented some land on the upper side of the Mattaponi River, in what was then New Kent County but later, King and Queen (NUG I:111; PB 1:397, 455, 659, 815, 884; 7:519; LEO 18).

Charles Turner: In 1671 Charles Turner, who had posted a bond guaranteeing that John Waters would appear before the General Court, was obliged to forfeit the funds he had pledged because the defendant failed to show up. In 1680–1682 Turner served as a burgess for New Kent County, where he had patented 2,400 acres of land on the south side of Totopotomoy Creek. On May 22, 1686, the vestry of St. Peter's Parish authorized Turner to officiate as clerk of the vestry and reader, a paid position he held for many years. Charles Turner married Mary Cox on August 12, 1691, and on October 30, 1692, their daughter, Susannah, was baptized. Turner died sometime after January 19, 1697, but before December 18, 1697 (LEO 45; PB 7:80; MCGC 265, 284; SPVB 5–6, 53–54, 396, 416).

James Turner: When Governor William Berkeley issued a proclamation on February 10, 1677, naming those who were exempt from the king's pardon, one of the people he listed was James Turner, whose estate was subject to seizure. Like others who were declared traitors, Turner's estate was confiscated and inventoried. During the 1660s and early 1670s, James Turner patented some land on the south side of the Pamunkey River in New Kent County (NEVILLE 61; PB 5:367, 379; 6:290; SR 660, 3560).

John Turner: On January 24, 1677, John Turner, one of the rebel Nathaniel Bacon's most ardent supporters, was tried at a martial court held at Green Spring plantation, where he was being detained. Turner admitted his guilt and was sentenced to be hanged.

On February 10, 1677, Governor William Berkeley issued a proclamation in which he named those who were exempt from the king's pardon on account of their role in Bacon's Rebellion. One of those named was John Turner, who had escaped from prison before he could be punished. Afterward, his estate was confiscated and inventoried (MCGC 455, 528; NEVILLE 61; SR 660, 3560). Turner may have been a servant of Richard Bennett of the Nansemond River. When Bennett made his will in 1674, he made bequests to some of his servants but purposefully excluded John Turner (SR 749).

Roger Turner (Turnor): Roger Turner died on Jamestown Island sometime after April 1623 but before February 16, 1624 (VI&A 705).

John Twine (Twyne): In 1618 Deputy Governor Samuel Argall placed John Twine in charge of the late Lord Delaware's store of goods after the decedent's servant, Henry Tawney, refused to be held accountable for them. Although Twine accepted responsibility for Delaware's goods, Argall kept the only key to the storeroom and purportedly sold some of his beer, wine, and vinegar. In July and August 1619 John Twine served as clerk of Virginia's first assembly (VI&A 706; LEO 3).

U

John Underhill I: John Underhill I, a surveyor, married Mary Felgate sometime prior to 1662. She had outlived her second husband, William Felgate Jr., the owner of Ringfield, a 350-acre plantation in York County. Underhill, who became a York County justice, repatented the acreage that Mary had inherited. The property fronted on the York River and had been acquired in 1637 by William Felgate Jr.'s uncle and benefactor, Robert Felgate. When governing officials enacted building initiatives in December 1662 that were intended to turn Jamestown into a thriving urban community, they authorized payment to Captain John Underhill for surveying the acreage that was to be developed. If Underhill did indeed produce a plat of urban Jamestown, it awaits discovery. In 1664 he surveyed Jonathan Knowles' farmstead, which lay within Jamestown's corporate limits, and prepared a plat of the property. It eventually became part of the Ambler plantation. Captain John Underhill of York County prepared his will on November 20, 1672, and by January 13, 1673, was dead. He left his widow, Mary, life-rights to the York River plantation on which they lived, but at her decease the property was to revert to his son John Underhill II. In the event of John II's demise, the plantation was to descend to the testator's other son, Nathaniel, to whom he left some property in New Kent County. The testator also made bequests to his daughters Jane and Mary (AMB 135–136; York County Deeds, Orders, Wills 3:183; 5:37; JHB 1659–1693:8; MCGC 246, 301, 314; Clarendon 82 f 275). John Underhill was interred at Ringfield, where fragments of his tombstone were visible in 1893. The tombstone reportedly had a coat of arms and an inscription stating that Underhill had immigrated to Virginia from the city of Worcester, England

William Underwood I: During the 1630s William Underwood, a merchant, began importing shoes and other utilitarian items to Virginia and sending large shipments of tobacco to England. Overseas records reveal that he was engaged in transatlantic trade until the mid-1650s. He had business dealings with Henry Mountfort of Rotterdam and William and John Drake, who were London merchants. He was also a business associate of James Williamson. Underwood's disposable income enabled him to acquire large quantities of land. In 1650 he patented 1,400 acres on the north side of the Rappahannock River, and by August 12, 1650, he was living there. In 1652 Underwood represented Lancaster County in the assembly and commenced serving as a county justice. When the justices of Lancaster County convened at Captain William Underwood I's house in January 1657, they authorized him to serve as the late James Williamson's administrator, noting that Underwood's sister was the decedent's widow. In 1658 Underwood patented a 2,784-acre tract in Old Rappahannock County near Nanzattico, and another large parcel in Westmoreland. As time went on, he continued to add to his holdings, and in 1662 he patented 2,561 acres in Old Rappahannock County. By 1675 Major William Underwood I was dead. He was survived by his widow, Elizabeth, and son, William Underwood II. When William II sold part of his late father's land near Peumansend Creek in 1692, the property's history was recounted in the deed of conveyance. It stated that William Underwood I had acquired the acreage from his brother-in-law, Ammaree Butler, when he married Butler's sister, Elizabeth. After Underwood's death a dower third descended to his widow, Elizabeth, who remarried, taking as her husband Archdale Combes (Coumbes). When Elizabeth Butler Underwood Combes made her will, she bequeathed her property to William Underwood II and John and William Combes (LEO 30; Lancaster County Deeds &c. Book 2 [1652–1657]:83, 288, 308; 2 [1653–1702]:14; Richmond County Deed Book 1 [1692–1693]:7; PB 2:213; 4:119, 344, 598; 6:688; SR 633, 3499c, 3852c, 10913, 10942, 13850).

George Ungwin (Ungwine, Unguin, Unwine, Onion, Union, Unwyn, Vinon, Vinoyn): George Ungwin, who was residing on Hog Island in 1624, testified about seeing Abraham Peirsey's storehouse being robbed while he was standing watch at the Jamestown fort. By January 1625 Ungwin and his wife, Elizabeth I, were living in the eastern end of Jamestown Island. Ungwin was arrested for indebtedness in 1628. His wife died and he remarried sometime prior to May 1637, when he patented 250 acres on the Chickahominy River, using his new wife, Katherine I, and daughters Elizabeth II and Katherine II as headrights. He sold that property in 1646 but may have retained some nearby acreage, for as late as 1653 Ungwin's Chickahominy River plantation, near Checroes (now Gordon's) Creek, was considered a local landmark (VI&A 707–708; PB 1 Pt. 1:430).

Michael Upchurch: In 1650 Michael Upchurch, a Virginia colonist, sent a letter to John Ferrar, who was in England. When describing conditions in the colony, he said that a good cow was worth 500 to 600 weight of tobacco in the summer or 300 weight in the winter. He added that most people killed their own cattle and swine and did their own butchering, and said that there was an abundance of swine and poultry. Upchurch indicated that coopers and tailors were the most successful at making a living and that carpenters, joiners, and smiths (if equipped with the tools of their trade) fared well. He estimated that at least 30 to 40 ships visited Virginia each year, bringing necessities to the colonists. In a March 1651 letter, Upchurch told John Ferrar's daughter, Virginia, that he had sent her an Indian basket and some fauna he had collected in the colony. Then, in May 1652 he sent a letter to Nicholas Ferrar, noting that he had sent John Ferrar some tobacco and tobacco seeds and six Indian pipes. Michael Upchurch and his wife, Frances, appear to have been residents of the Northern Neck (FER 1031, 1182, 1203; PB 3:272, 313).

John Upton (Uptone) I: John Upton I came to Virginia as a servant to cape merchant Abraham Peirsey, and in February 1624 and January 1625 he was living in Peirsey's household at Flowerdew Hundred. He gained his freedom in April 1625 by paying Peirsey for the eight months remaining on his contract. In April 1626 Upton approached one of Sir George Yeardley's servants about renting a dwelling and some land at Black Point, at the eastern tip of Jamestown Island. He probably was living on the property later in the year when he made arrangements to purchase some corn from Richard Tree, a Jamestown Island resident. By February 1629 Upton had wed one of Jamestown merchant Thomas Warnet's

(Warnett's) heirs. She may have owned some land in Warresqueak (Isle of Wight), for in 1630 Upton commenced representing that area in the assembly, three years prior to his owning land there. John Upton I was returned to office repeatedly and attended the assembly meetings that were held in 1633, 1640, 1642, and from 1645 through 1648. He continued to add to his landholdings and during the 1640s transferred modest-sized parcels to people who seem to have been his tenants. Among those to whom he transferred land were Christopher Benn and his wife, Anne, whose son, James, later became a burgess. Upton, who became a captain in the local militia and a local justice of the peace, made his will on January 16, 1651. In November and his wife, Margaret, transferred 400 acres to his stepson William Underwood. Upton died before April 9, 1652, at which time his widow, Margaret, disposed of part of his land. The late John Upton I bequeathed his landholdings to his wife, Margaret, and son, John II, and named his stepchildren, William, Elizabeth, Sarah, and Margaret Underwood, as reversionary heirs. Margaret Underwood Upton was still alive in March 1655 (VI&A 708–709; LEO 9, 12, 18, 20, 24, 26; Isle of Wight County Deeds, Wills and Guardian Accounts Book A:20, 32, 38, 40–41, 62; BODIE 513–514, 516). It is uncertain whether there was a familial connection between Margaret Underwood Upton and merchant William Underwood I, a resident of the Northern Neck.

Ann Usher: Ann Usher, an eight-year-old child who had been born in Virginia, was living in West and Shirley Hundred on January 1625 and was a member of John and Susan Collins' household. In June 1627 Ann, who was still living in West and Shirley Hundred, was sentenced to a whipping in the fort in Jamestown because she and another young girl had been raped by a young male servant (VI&A 709).

Benjamin Usher: Benjamin Usher died on Jamestown Island sometime after April 1623 but before February 16, 1624. Simultaneously, he was listed among the dead at one of the plantations on the lower side of the James River, within the corporation of James City (VI&A 709).

Uttamatomakkin (Tomocomo) (Native American): Uttamatomakkin, who was a counselor to Opechancanough, accompanied Sir Thomas Dale when he left Virginia in May 1616. Dale's entourage also included Pocahontas and her husband, John Rolfe, and several other natives. While in England, Uttamatomakkin was supposed to learn about the country and how many inhabitants it had. During 1616–1617 he was interviewed by the Rev. Samuel Purchas, who communicated by means of a translator provided by Dale. Purchas recorded portions of his conversation with Uttamatomakkin and tried to recount the Indian's statements about religion. He indicated that Uttamatomakkin was married to Matachanna, one of Powhatan's daughters (HAI 880–884).

John Uty (Utie, Utey) I: In February 1623 John Uty I was living on Hog Island with some other settlers who had been associated with the Society of Southampton Hundred's settlement in Charles City. He and his wife, Ann, and their young son, John II, were still there a year later, when he represented the community in the assembly. In November 1624 Uty patented some land he called "Utopia" at the neck of Hog Island. He made several court appearances during 1625 and 1626, often testifying about matters that involved Southampton Hundred. In 1628 he was granted 250 acres of escheat land in Archer's Hope, and in March 1629 he was placed in command of the plantations between that area and Martin's Hundred. He served as that territory's burgess in 1628 and 1629, and in 1630 he became a burgess for Hog Island. Uty agreed to plant a settlement in Chiskiack in exchange for a 1,250-acre patent, and in 1632 he was named to the Council of State. Like most of his fellow councilors, he had irreconcilable differences with Governor John Harvey and was among those who helped thrust Harvey from office and send him back to England. When Harvey regained his power, he had Uty arrested and sent to England to stand trial. John Uty I died in 1639 at his York River home, Kings Creek plantation or "Utimaria" (VI&A 709–710; LEO 5, 7–9).

V

Michael Vanlandingham (Vanlandigame, Vanlandigham): On September 20, 1668, Michael Vanlandingham, an alien and long-time resident of Virginia, was naturalized and granted denization by the assembly. In 1666 he was in possession of some acreage on the Mattaponi River, in what was presumed to be Northumberland County (Northumberland County Record Book 1666–1670:1, 51). He may have been related to Benjamin and Richard Vanlandingham, who patented acreage in nearby Old Rappahannock County in 1679 (PB 6:674–675).

Henry Vaughan: On May 3, 1699, Henry Vaughan joined Jamestown landowners George Marable II, John Howard, Thomas Holiday (Holliday), and other freeholders in protesting the James City County sheriff's actions in the election of Jamestown's burgess, a contest in which Robert Beverley II and Bartholomew Fowler received an equal number of votes. Vaughan's protest suggests that he or his wife owned land in the capital city. Incumbent assembly members chose Beverley, and the freeholders' petition was forwarded to officials in England on December 9, 1700. In February 1717, Vaughan and his wife, Katherine, who were then residents of Wallingford Parish, which straddled the Chickahominy River, sold some James City County land to William Broadnax I of urban Jamestown (JHB 1695–1702:139; SAIN 18:728; AMB 83).

Nicholas Ven: Nicholas Ven, a laborer, came to Jamestown in 1608 in the 1st Supply of new colonists (VI&A 711).

Vincencio (Vicentio) (see Vincencio [Vicentio] Castine [Castillian])

Job Virgett: On November 22, 1671, Job Virgett, who was indebted to Jamestown merchant Richard James I, was arrested (MCGC 285).

Vnuntsquero (Native American): Between March 18 and June 19, 1680, when the 1677 Treaty of Middle Plantation was expanded to include some additional Indian tribes, Vnuntsquero, the chief man of the Maherians (Meherrins), and Horehannah, their second chief, signed on behalf of their people (Anonymous, 1677 treaty, Miscellaneous Virginia Records 1606–1692, Bland Manuscripts, XIV, ff 226–233).

William Volday (Volda, Voldo, William Henrick Faldoe, "Faldoe the Heletian"): William Volday, a Swiss citizen, came to Virginia in 1607 and was one of the first Jamestown colonists. Although Captain John Smith accused Volday of furnishing some fugitives with what they needed to destroy the colony, Volday claimed that the runaways he had been sent to retrieve were angry and uncooperative. Smith later said that Volday left the colony with Lord Delaware in 1610 and that he died very miserably (VI&A 713; HAI 323, 337, 521, 687).

W

Wackawamp (Wachiowamp) (Native American): Wackawamp, replaced the late Esmy Shichans, the Eastern Shore's principal leader or chief, around 1641 and in 1642 he was identified as "the great Kinge of ye Eastern Shore." On July 4, 1643, the justices of Accomack County ordered three men to pay Wackawamp a certain quantity of roanoke (shell money) in exchange for the land in their possession. When Colonel Henry Norwood and his shipmates were marooned on the upper part of Virginia's Eastern Shore during the winter of 1649, they were be-

friended by "the great Kinge," who gave them food, lodging, and warm garments. They also met his brother, Kickotank. In the early 1650s Wackawamp began selling off the lands that had belonged to the Occohannock chiefdom. By 1656 the Eastern Shore had become so densely populated that he was obliged to ask the county court for protected land on which his people could live. Wackawamp died in 1657, at which time his will was recorded in the county court. He bequeathed his kingdom to his daughter but failed to identify her by name, and indicated that at her decease, his dominions would descend to his brother's sons, Akomepen and Quiemacketo (Northampton County Deeds, Wills, and Orders 2:156; 3:226; Deeds, Wills &c 4:35; 7/8:51; 9 [1657–1666]:51; AMES 2:289; FOR III:10:39–49).

Rev. James Wadding: Sometime prior to August 7, 1672, the Rev. James Wadding, rector of James City Parish, married Walter Chiles II's widow, Susanna. Together, the Wadding couple sold Chiles' 70 acres at Black Point to Edward Travis II. Then, on November 20, 1673, they disposed of the decedent's 3½-acre lot and its improvements in urban Jamestown, conveying the property to Colonel John Page, a York County merchant. Wadding went on to become the rector of Gloucester County's Ware Parish. In September 1676, when he was at Gloucester County's seat, some of the rebel Nathaniel Bacon's followers tried to force him to subscribe to an oath of fidelity, which declared that Governor William Berkeley was a traitor. Because Wadding refused to sign and urged others not to do so, he was imprisoned for his audacity. Bacon denounced him and informed him that he could say what he pleased in church but not in camp, unless he could fight better than he could preach. However, when Bacon became deathly ill, he asked for Wadding's ministerial assistance (AMB 24; MCGC 370; NUG:I:252; PB 7:228–229; WASH 84, 238; AND 73–75; Middlesex County Order Book 1673–1680:40).

Armiger Wade: Armiger Wade was living in York County in 1648 when he was granted administration of the late Robert Halsey's estate. In 1656 Wade served as a burgess, representing York County, and he also was a county justice. In August 1657 he witnessed a document that involved a land transaction in New Poquoson Parish. Wade's will was proved on April 24, 1677. He named his son, Armiger Wade II, as his executor and gave him some land in the New Poquoson. He also made bequests to the children of his daughters Mary Hay and Dorothy Lilly. In October 1691 the testator's son and executor, Armiger Wade II, patented 165 acres near the head of Robin's Creek, in the New Poquoson Parish of York County (LEO 33; PB 3:54; York County Order Book 2 [1646–1648]:327; 3 [1648–1657]:2, 347).

Wahunsunacock (Native American) (see Powhatan)

Richard Waldo (Waldoe): Richard Waldo, a gentleman, came to Virginia in 1608 in the 2nd Supply of new settlers. Shortly after he arrived in Jamestown, he became a member of the governor's council. Sir Thomas Gates designated Waldo master of the works in May 1609 (VI&A 715).

[No First Name] Walker: Master Walker, a tradesman, came to Virginia in 1608, in the 2nd Supply of new settlers and lived in Jamestown (VI&A 716).

George Walker: George Walker, a Virginia Company investor and a gentleman, came to Virginia in 1607 and was one of the first Jamestown settlers. He died on August 24, 1607 (VI&A 716).

James Wallace: On October 1, 1674, James Wallace, the owner of land in Charles City County, was involved in a lawsuit with Thomas Hill II of urban Jamestown. At issue were discrepancies in certain accounts that both men had kept (MCGC 387; PB 6:248, 553).

John Walker: John Walker died on Jamestown Island sometime after April 1623 but before February 16, 1624 (VI&A 716).

John Walker: John Walker, who was born in England, represented Warwick County in the assembly from 1644 to 1646, and 1649 (LEO 22, 24–25, 27; HEN I:283, 299, 359). Records documenting his public and private life in Warwick County seem to have been lost or destroyed. He may have moved to the Middle Peninsula.

* * *

John Walker I: John Walker I began investing in land in the Middle Peninsula in 1651 and patented two large tracts on the Ware River in Gloucester County. He continued to acquire land in the region, securing acreage on the Milford Haven Inlet, on the Corotoman River, and in Old Rappahannock County. By 1654, he had settled in Gloucester County. He became a Gloucester County justice and in 1656, while he was a member of the county court, he was involved in a case that concerned ownership of some cattle in the Denbigh (Warwick County) area (PB 2:356–357; 3:346; 4:268; 6:151; DUNN 587). This raises the possibility that he was the individual who had served as a Warwick County burgess during the 1640s.

John Walker II: Lieutenant Colonel John Walker II was named to the Council of State in late 1656 while the Commonwealth government was in power, and he held his council seat during 1657–1661. According to one respected researcher, when Walker was named to the Council of State, he vacated his seat in the assembly, where he had been representing Charles City County. Walker married Sarah, the widow of councilor and Lieutenant Colonel Henry Fleet, who died prior to May 8, 1661. Walker patented 2,000 acres of land on the north side of the Rappahannock River, in Old Rappahannock County, in 1663. Colonel John Walker settled in Richmond County (a descendant of Old Rappahannock County) and was residing there at the time of his death. He made his will on February 22, 1666, and between July 6, 1668, and February 3, 1669, added a codicil to it. In 1669 when Sarah Fleet Walker prepared her will, she made bequests to her stepdaughters: Elizabeth, Esther, Frances, Jane, and Sarah Walker and Anne Payne (Paine). Sometime after Colonel John Walker's death, which occurred sometime after February 3, 1669, but before September 1671, the twice widowed Sarah Fleet Walker, married Colonel John Stone (STAN 37; LEO 22, 24–25, 27, 33; HEN I:283, 299, 323, 359, 422, 432, 499, 505, 512, 526; Old Rappahannock County Deeds and Wills 1656–1664:274, 309–310, 322; Deeds and Wills 1677–1682:142–144; Northumberland County Wills, Inventories &c.1652–1658:54; Westmoreland County Deeds, Wills &c 1661–1662:5; York County Deeds, Orders, Wills 3 [1657–1662]:140; 4 [1665–1672]:311; Charles City County Orders 1658–1661:232; PB 4:234; 5:216; 6:65, 147; 7:624; SR 4784; MCGC 245, 277; DOR 1:972; Richmond County Will Book 2:108). Colonel John Walker should not be confused with John Walker of Westmoreland County, a man of much more modest means.

* * *

Peter Walker: The records of Accomack County's monthly court for November 26, 1638, contain a transcription of a promissory note in which Peter Walker was identified as a London merchant. Walker, when doing business in the colony, had made a bargain with another London merchant, William Holmes, who used as collateral some livestock, a boat, and a plantation he owned on Maggoty Bay. In February 1640 when Walker returned to the Accomack County court to claim Holmes' assets, he indicated that he was 22 years old. Later in the year, Walker, who moved to Virginia, was obliged to go to court to account for the death of one of his servants. Although it was determined that the youth died of scurvy, some witnesses testified that he had been beaten by his master, Peter Walker. An angry

exchange between Captain William Stone and Peter Walker in 1644, while Stone was visiting Walker's dwelling, reveals that Walker was quick-tempered, prone to violence, and proud of his upbringing. In 1645 Walker patented 150 acres on Old Plantation Creek, land that had formerly belonged to John Blore, and four years later he witnessed Walter Walton's will, which was made in Accomack County. Peter Walker married Alice or Alicia Travellor, who had outlived William Burdett, her former husband. Walker represented Northampton County in the assembly, serving as a burgess from 1654 to 1656. He died prior to January 1656 and was survived by his widow and administratrix, Alice, who went on to marry John Custis I (LEO 32–33; Accomack County Wills &c 1692–1715:129, 351; PB 2:44; SR 3499c, 4099; AMES 1:130, 159, 167; 2:22–26, 383–384; MARSHALL 43).

Richard Walker: Richard Walker died on Jamestown Island sometime after April 1623 but before February 16, 1624 (VI&A 716).

Thomas Walker I: In February 1665 Thomas Walker I of Gloucester County patented 2,350 acres on the Mattaponi River, escheat land located in what became New Kent County and then King and Queen. He was designated the late Thomas Perry's administrator in 1670 and was ordered to take custody of his estate. Later in the year Major Walker became involved in a dispute over some land on the Piankatank River. Over the years his name appeared frequently in cases handled by the General Court. In April 1687 Lieutenant Colonel Walker enhanced the size of his acreage, known as Fort Mattapony and later, as Ryefield, which was located in King and Queen County. Between 1662 and 1676 he represented Gloucester County in the assembly. In 1704 he paid quitrent on 600 acres in King and Queen County and was a captain in the militia. He died sometime prior to October 12, 1709. His son, Thomas II., married Susannah, the niece of Mary Peachy of St. Stephen's Parish (LEO 38; PB 5:616; 7:559; SR 4335; DOR 1:774–775; MCGC 209, 213, 240, 258, 336, 396, 404, 439).

William Walker: On March 22, 1677, William Walker was brought before Governor William Berkeley and the Council of State, who were conducting a military tribunal, and accused of treating a county justice contemptuously. It was decided that he would be released if he posted a bond, guaranteeing his good behavior (MCGC 461). He may have been the William Walker who patented land in Northumberland County in 1655 and renewed his patent in 1662 (PB 4:427).

Charles Waller: Charles Waller, an indentured servant, came to Virginia in 1620 and in 1624–1625 was living in the urban Jamestown household of Captain Roger Smith. Waller and some others ran afoul of the law in 1629 when they refused to help the provost marshal place an unruly person in the stocks (VI&A 716).

John Waller: John Waller, a gentleman and Virginia Company investor, came to Virginia in 1607 and was one of the first Jamestown colonists. He reportedly seized the King of the Pasbehay Indians and stabbed him with his sword (VI&A 717).

John Waller: In 1618 John Waller set sail for Virginia with Lord Delaware. He witnessed Edward Brewster's attack on George Perrin and was present when Brewster struck the Earl of Northumberland's younger brother, George Percy. Waller also was in the colony when Deputy Governor Samuel Argall had Brewster tried at a court martial hearing (VI&A 717).

George Wallings (Wallins): George Wallings represented Nansemond County in the assembly between 1662 and 1665 and died after the 1665 session (LEO 39; STAN 77). No documentary records have come to light that are associated with Wallings' public or private life or the land that he or his wife would have owned.

Wamanto (Native American): Wamanto and his brother, Namenacus, king of the Patuxunt (Patuxent) Indians, lived on the Eastern Shore in a village called Attoughcomoco. In 1621 when Secretary John Pory and a group of men visited the region, looking for a convenient place to manufacture salt, they met Namenacus who invited them to visit his country. A few weeks later when Pory arrived at Attoughcomoco, he met Wamanto, whom he described as hospitable and accommodating. Wamanto introduced Pory to his wife and children and took him hunting. He also showed him the natives' numerous corn fields (CJS II:289–290).

William Wanerton: William Wanerton died on Jamestown Island sometime after February 16, 1624, but before January 24, 1625 (VI&A 718).

Evan Ward: Evan Ward, an indentured servant employed by Jamestown innkeeper Richard Lawrence, stole a shallop and fled. Because he was a runaway and lost the vessel he took, he was sentenced to serve seven additional years (MCGC 382).

John Ward (Warde): In 1619 John Ward and his associates transported some people to Virginia and received a patent from the Virginia Company. Later in the year, Ward represented his plantation in the assembly despite Speaker John Pory's insistence that he had seated his land illegally. Ward sent his ship into the Potomac River to trade with the King of the Patawomack Indians and later claimed that he had been cheated. He left Virginia in 1620 but returned after the 1622 Indian attack and settled on part of the Virginia Company's land in Elizabeth City. By February 1627 Captain John Ward was back in England (VI&A 718; LEO 3).

Lawrence Ward: On February 7, 1653, while the Commonwealth government was in power, Lawrence Ward, who lived in Isle of Wight County, sent a letter to England in which he described conditions in the colony. He said that around January 26th he encountered a gentleman who had been sent by the governor and Colonel William Claiborne to explore the country that lay to the south. Ward said that he reached the Roanoke River and when he was on his way home, he encountered the king of the Nansemond Indians and the king of the Chowan Indians, who were on their way to Jamestown to meet with the governor to make peace. Ward said that Colonel Bernard (probably councilor William Bernard) had informed him about Governor William Berkeley's failed attempt to make the Nansemond and Warresqueak Indians subservient to the Weyanoke and how the tribal leaders went to Jamestown to negotiate peace. During the mid-to-late 1640s Lawrence Ward patented two tracts of land in Isle of Wight County (FER 1216; PB2:76, 87).

William Ward (Warde): William Ward, a tailor and Virginia Company investor, came to Virginia in 1608 in the 2nd Supply of Jamestown settlers. Captain John Smith described Ward as a soldier (VI&A 719).

William Ward (Warde): In February 1624 William Ward, a servant, was living in urban Jamestown in Edward Blaney's household. Simultaneously, he was attributed to the Blaney plantation on the lower side of the James River. He was still at the Blaney plantation in February 1625 and may have been the boy named William Ward who was sent to Virginia by officials at Bridewell (VI&A 719).

John Wareham: John Wareham, a merchant, came to Virginia sometime prior to January 1629 and in 1632 he served as a burgess for Mounts Bay, an area in the eastern part of Archer's Hope. In 1633 he represented the settlements from Harrop to Martin's Hundred, territory that stretched from the east side of Archer's Hope (now College) Creek to Skiffs Creek. Sometime prior to 1638 Wareham acquired land at Mounts Bay, within what eventually became Kingsmill Plantation. In 1652 he patented land in Northumberland County, acreage that by 1666 had descended to his daughter, Elizabeth, who was named after her mother (VI&A 720; PB 1:2:629; 3:126; 5:533; LEO 11–12).

Mark (Marke) Warkman (Warkeman, Workman, Warkeham) I: Sometime prior to 1669 Mark Warkman I patented some land in Gloucester County's Ware Parish. In June 1675 he was described as deceased and the former owner of some land adjacent to a patent secured by Robert Beverley I. On June 16, 1675, the lawsuit Jamestown merchant and planter John Page filed against Warkman was postponed. The decedent's son and namesake, Mark II, went on to patent Pampertike in Pamunkey Neck in New Kent County, and during the early 1680s served as the colony's deputy escheator (MCGC 410; NUG I:72, 163, 196, 203, 224–225, 228, 253, 290, 357).

* * *

Augustine (Austin) Warner I: Augustine Warner came to Virginia in the *Hopewell* in 1628 at the expense of Adam Thorogood. In October 1635, Warner patented 250 acres in the New Poquoson in Elizabeth City. He served as a burgess in 1652, representing York County. In 1654 he patented some land in Gloucester County, acreage on which the ancestral home, Warner Hall, eventually was built. Warner was a member of the assembly in 1659, representing Gloucester, and he was named to the Council of State in 1660. In November 1672 when the assembly decided to have a bridge built across Dragon Run, Lieutenant Colonel John Carter II and Robert Beckingham of Lancaster County were ordered to meet at Warner's home. Warner died in Virginia on December 24, 1674 (VI&A; DOR 3:18; LEO 29, 35; STAN 38; Lancaster County Order Book 1666–1680:242; NEVILLE 45).

Augustine Warner II: Augustine Warner II, the Virginia-born son of Augustine Warner I, served as a burgess from 1672 to 1676, representing Gloucester County. He was speaker of the 1676 and 1677 assembly sessions and resided at Warner Hall in Gloucester County's Abingdon Parish. In a petition he sent to the king, John Thornbush, a London merchant, claimed that in late September 1676, during Bacon's Rebellion, William Byrd I of Henrico County entered Colonel Warner's Gloucester County home and carried off goods worth more than £845. Warner later tried to claim £1,000, a sum that included damages. In 1677 Warner was named to the Council of State. He died in Virginia on June 19, 1681. His daughter, Mildred, married John Washington I's son, Lawrence. Together, Lawrence and Mildred Warner Washington produced three surviving children: John, Augustine, and Mildred II (STAN 41; LEO 37–38, 42; NEVILLE 88–89, 92, 125, 167; Westmoreland County Deeds and Wills 1691–1699:133–135).

* * *

Thomas Warnet (Warnett): On February 13, 1629, when Thomas Warnet, a merchant and mariner, made his will, he was a resident of urban Jamestown. His widow and executrix, Thomasine, who also was one of his heirs, presented his will for probate on November 8, 1630. The testator made bequests to several Jamestown Island residents and to people who lived in Elizabeth City and Martin's Hundred (VI&A 720).

Thomas Warr: On March 22, 1677, when Governor William Berkeley and the Council of State conducted a military tribunal and considered the extent of Thomas Warr's involvement in Bacon's Rebellion, they found Warr guilty. Warr and two other men asked to be transported out of colony rather than being tried in a courtroom. The justices agreed that they should be banished for seven years and gave them the option of going to New England, or to Barbados, Jamaica, or any of the other islands. Warr was ordered to leave Virginia within two months and to be on good behavior until the time of his departure (MCGC 461, 533; HEN II:555).

Anthony Warren: On February 8, 1628, Anthony Warren was identified as the co-administrator of the late Daniel Lacey's estate. Lacey was a gentleman and resident of Jamestown Island (VI&A 720).

John Warren: John Warren served as a burgess for Lower Norfolk County and sat in the assembly sessions that were held between 1658 and 1661. He died in office in 1661 (LEO 34–36, 39). The decedent may have been related to the John Warren who was living in the Lawnes Creek Parish of Surry County in 1669 and purchased some land there in 1671 (PB 6:386; Surry County Deed Book I:313, 337).

Thomas Warren (Warrin, Warne): Edward Prescott's April 4, 1661, patent for a ½ acre lot in the western end of Jamestown Island, a parcel that descended to Mrs. Sarah Drummond, made reference to "Mr. Warren's lot." The Warren acreage probably belonged to Thomas Warren who in 1644 served as one of the several burgesses attributed to James City. Although he may have represented the capital city, it is more likely that he served on behalf of James City County, which included then the territory that later became Surry County. In 1654 Thomas Warren of Smith's Fort plantation in Surry County married ancient planter William Spencer's daughter and heir, Elizabeth, the widow of Major Robert Sheppard of Lower Chippokes. Sheppard, who served as a James City County burgess from 1644–1646, had an ongoing business relationship with London merchant John White I, then owner of a 1-acre lot near the church, in the western end of Jamestown Island. On September 23, 1654, when the widowed Elizabeth Spencer Sheppard signed a marriage contract with Thomas Warren, she agreed that he could "have and enjoy all the estate of Major Robert Sheppard, deceased, now in the possession of the said Elizabeth, his relict" with the exception of certain items of personal property and the decedent's children's inheritance. This raises the possibility that Elizabeth's new husband, Thomas Warren, acquired the right to use a Jamestown lot that had belonged to the estate of her late husband, Robert Sheppard: property that by 1661 had become known as "Mr. Warren's lot" and was next door to the 1-acre lot John White I owned in 1644.

In 1659 Thomas Warren was elected a burgess for Surry County and in 1660 he served on the commission charged with seeing that a statehouse was built. He was returned to the assembly and served from 1662 to 1669. He died prior to April 21, 1670, at which time his will was proved by John Corker and William Thomson I (Thompson), both of whom had ties to Jamestown and Surry County. Surviving records fail to indicate what happened to "Mr. Warren's lot" in Jamestown. However, Thomas Warren's will reveals that he bestowed upon his Shepperd stepchildren some of the property in which he had a legal interest. Therefore, the lot may have descended to Elizabeth Spencer Shepperd Warren's grandson,

Thomas Hart II, who in 1702 was authorized to keep a ferry from Swann's Point to Jamestown (DOR 3:227–229; STAN 63–64; MCGC 213, 339; PB 5:634; NUG I:560; Surry County Deeds, Wills &c. 1652–1672:60; Order Book 1691–1713:232; LEO 22, 24, 35, 40).

Thomas Warwell: On May 28, 1673, Thomas Warwell was ordered to examine the work that bricklayer John Bird had done for Richard James I of urban Jamestown. He also was to determine its value. By March 16, 1674, Warwell was dead and his widow, Elizabeth, was given administration of his estate. Attorney William Sherwood, who had married the late Richard James I's widow, Rachel, brought suit against Thomas Warwell's estate in September 1675. Colonel Thomas Swann I also sued the decedent (MCGC 344; Surry County Order Book 1671–1691: 91, 99, 119).

John Washbourne (Washburne, Washburn, Wasborne): In April 1679 John Washbourne, who became Accomack County's clerk of court in 1675, patented 600 acres at Pokamock, in Accomack County. A month later he acquired 644 acres on the south side of the Pungoteague River, in Northampton County. In 1687 while he was still Accomack's clerk of court, he certified the nuncupative will made by Simon Keeth, master of the ship *Truelove* of London. Between 1693 and 1697 Washbourne represented Accomack County in the assembly. He continued to acquire land and in 1696 patented 644 acres on the Pungoteague River. Washbourne was appointed the customs officer for Cape Charles in 1698, a post he held until 1706, and was given a salary of £25 a year. On March 28, 1721, Captain Washbourne made his will, which was proved on June 6, 1721. He left to his widow, Susanna, life-rights in the plantation on which the family home was located. After her death, the property was to descend to grandson Washbourne Johnson. Washbourne made bequests to his other grandchildren, Richard, Temperance, and Bridgett Johnson, all of whom were the children of his married daughter, Dorothy Johnson. The testator may have been a descendant of 29-year-old John Washbourne, an indentured servant who was living on the Eastern Shore in 1624 and was still residing there in 1634 (LEO 53–54, 56; Accomack County 1632–1637:28; Wills, Deeds &c 1715–1729:347; SR 2153, 3621, 3743; PB 6:676, 686; 9:34; MARSHALL 171; VI&A 721).

[No First Name] Washer: In July 1619 when Virginia's first assembly convened,

Ensign Washer, whose first name is unknown, served as burgess for Captain Christopher Lawne's plantation. In November 1619, he and Lawne were planning to secure the neck of land they were occupying on Warresqueak Bay (VI&A 721; LEO 3).

* * *

John Washington I: John Washington I, great-grandfather of the first president of the United States, arrived in Virginia in 1657. Before he left England he formed a business partnership with mariner and Jamestown lot owner Edward Prescott. They sailed together through the Baltic Sea, paused in Germany, continued on to Denmark, and then set out for Virginia on a ketch called the *Seahorse* of London. Prescott and Washington disposed of their cargo and then took aboard some tobacco they planned to sell in Europe. However, in February 1657 the ship ran aground in the Potomac River and a winter storm led to its sinking and the loss of its cargo. Although the *Seahorse* was repaired and put afloat, Washington decided to stay on in Virginia and asked Prescott to return the funds he had invested in the voyage. Prescott refused, claiming that Washington owed him money. Court testimony reveals that the two men exchanged heated words while in the Westmoreland County home of Nathaniel Pope. Although Pope offered to settle Washington's account with Prescott, Washington went to the local court and placed a lien on Prescott's vessel. The disagreement was still viable in September 1659. By that date Washington had married Pope's daughter, Ann, and fathered the couple's eldest son, Lawrence. In May 1659 Pope gave the Washingtons 700 acres of land on the east side of Appomattox (Mattox) Creek. John and Ann Pope Washington had at least three children together: Lawrence, John II, and Ann.

Over time, John Washington I, a highly successful planter and entrepreneur, amassed a substantial quantity of acreage and placed tenants or servants on his property. Much (but not all) of that land eventually came into the hands of his descendants. Among his landholdings was the tract on Little Hunting Creek that became known as Mount Vernon. Washington and his brother-in-law, Thomas Pope, patented ten islands in the mouth of Cedar (or Popes) Creek and laid claim to 1,200 acres on the branches of Appomattox (Mattox) Creek. Through this means, Washington came into exclusive possession of a tract known as the "Indian Town." In 1661 he was elected a vestryman,

and a year later he became a county justice and a major in the militia. He went on to become a lieutenant colonel in the county militia and, eventually, a colonel. When Westmoreland County was subdivided into three parishes in May 1664, one was designated Washington Parish. He became a burgess in 1665, the same year he secured a patent for 320 acres that fronted on the Potomac River and lay between Mattox and Bridges creeks. The plantation he established there became the site of the family's ancestral home and burial ground. In 1666 he acquired some land that straddled the boundary line between the northerly part of Old Rappahannock and Westmoreland counties, a parcel that abutted south upon the Rappahannock River and was part of the acreage set aside for the Nanzattico Indians.

After Ann Pope Washington's death in 1668, John Washington I married a wealthy widow, Anne, who had outlived Walter Broadhurst I and Henry Brett. She brought to the marriage the Broadhurst plantation, which contained the county seat, an ordinary, a shop, and some other buildings. When John Washington leased the Broadhurst property in January 1670 to Lewis Markham for three years, he indicated that the plantation's dwelling was furnished. He stipulated that Markham could have half of the ordinary's profits, but Washington himself retained the courthouse and prison, a shop, and a loft. In 1670 Washington patented 450 acres in Northumberland County, near the head of the Nominy River. He continued to take an active role in public life and served as a county justice and burgess. He also was a trustee of the Westmoreland County trading firm, Thomas Pope and Company, which had dealings in Barbados and England.

Anne Broadhurst Brett Washington died around 1675, and shortly thereafter John Washington I married her sister, Frances Gerrard, who had outlived three former husbands, one of whom was Thomas Speke I, a prominent public official. Before the couple wed in May 1676, they signed a marriage contract, whereby John agreed to give Frances 500 acres and a one-third interest in her mill, should she outlive him. When he testified in court in January 1676, Washington gave his age as 45. During the popular uprising known as Bacon's Rebellion, Washington, who was still serving as a burgess, remained loyal to Governor William Berkeley and suffered the consequences. Stephen Mannering, one of Nathaniel Bacon's followers, tried to prevent Washington's overseers from removing food and tobacco from his plantations at "ye Round Hills" (on the Upper Machodoc) and "at ye river side" (Bridges Creek). Another Bacon loyalist, Daniel White, attempted to seize Washington's corn, tobacco, livestock, and watercraft. In August 1677 Colonel Isaac Allerton informed a Westmoreland County jury that some of Bacon's men had gained control of Colonel John Washington's home. After Bacon's supporters were captured and brought to trial, Washington was compensated for his losses. Later, Edward Blagg Jr. successfully sued Washington for the loss of his sloop. He claimed that during Bacon's Rebellion, Washington had used the vessel to convey his goods and estate to Maryland but had failed to return it and had allowed it to rot at another man's landing.

John Washington I made his will on September 21, 1675, but lived two more years. During that interval, he lost his wife Frances and remarried. On May 10, 1676, Washington executed a marriage contract in anticipation of marrying the late John Appleton's widow, Frances. Under that agreement, Washington deeded a tract of land to two trustees, who were serving on Frances's behalf. Colonel John Washington I died between August 25, 1677, when the monthly court convened in his home, and its next monthly session, which was held on September 26th. He was interred in the nearby graveyard beside his first wife, Ann, and the two children of theirs who had failed to survive. He made bequests to children John, Lawrence, and Ann, who were minors; to his wife; and to his own siblings, Lawrence and Martha. In 1677 Washington's widow, Frances, received eight black servants who were part of his personal estate. The decedent's estate was divided in 1683 at the request of his heirs, but in November 1684 Lawrence Washington was still serving as his late father's executor (JHB 1660–1693:41; Meade II:166–169; Westmoreland County Deeds, Wills, Patents &c. 1653–1659:77, 89–90, 95–97, 127, 168, 226, 252, 294, 351–352; Deeds and Wills 1661–1662:4–4a, 16, 134; 1691–1699:124–125a; Deeds, Patents &c. 1665–1677:49a–51, 73, 102, 121a–122, 184, 231–232, 247a, 274, 278, 325a–326, 365a–367; Order Book 1662–1664:32; 1676–1689:100, 256, 269, 380, 405; Stafford County Record Book 1686–1693:195a; PB 3:70; 5:161, 168, 170–171, 250, 286; 6:187, 615; Old Rappahannock County Order Book 1683–1686:56; MCGC 225, 278, 347, 444, 446, 517; NEVILLE 50, 54; LEO 40–42).

Lawrence Washington: Lawrence, the eldest son of Ann Pope and John Washington I and the nephew of immigrant Lawrence Washington, was 18 years old in 1677 when he lost his father. Even before he attained his majority and became his late father's executor, he began playing an active role in public life. During the summer of 1679 he saw military service, for he was among those sent to a fort or garrison that was built near the mouth of Occoquan Creek. In June 1680, when he was only 21, he began serving as one of Westmoreland County's justices and held that office for the remainder of his life; he also served as high sheriff and frequently functioned as an attorney. The need to enforce the law occasionally required him to summon his own kin to court. In January 1683 Lawrence Washington asked the justices of Westmoreland County to appoint special commissioners to divide his late father's estate. Sometime after February 1684 he was designated a militia captain, a rank he retained for 15 years. He appeared in Old Rappahannock County's monthly court when serving as Colonel John Washington I's executor. He also was called upon to defend some of his late father's actions that had resulted in lawsuits. He succeeded his father as a trustee of the trading firm Thomas Pope and Company.

In 1684, when he was only 25, Lawrence Washington became a Westmoreland County burgess. He served in the assembly in 1686 and again in the sessions of 1691–1692. During the 1680s and 1690s his need to attend assembly meetings occasionally interfered with his ability to serve as a local court justice. In May 1686 he asked to defer taking his oath as a county justice because he was planning "to Ship himself for England." He returned within a year and in 1687 was among the local justices who took the obligatory oath of office. In 1691 Washington was Westmoreland County's coroner, and in 1697, while he was a justice, he was ordered have a ducking stool constructed at his mill dam in Washington Parish. In July 1692 he was ordered to procure from England a printed copy of the latest laws enacted by Parliament. He apparently failed to do so, despite having accepted payment in advance. Occasionally he was sued. George Harwick, from whom Lawrence Washington regularly obtained "meat, drink & lodging" and pasturage during court sessions, sued to recover what he was owed and contended that the defendant had little regard for the premises he was renting.

When Lawrence Washington was in his late 20s, he married Mildred, the daughter of burgess and councilor Augustine Warner II of Gloucester County. The couple produced three surviving children: John (born around

1690), Augustine (born in ca. 1694), and Mildred II. Lawrence Washington appears to have made very few land acquisitions. He was short-lived and died in 1698 at the age of 38. The fact that his will was made on March 11, 1698, approximately two weeks before his March 30th death, suggests that he was suddenly taken ill. At the time of his demise, he and his household resided on the east side of Upper Machodoc Creek's mouth near the Round Hills, probably on part of the acreage his late father, John Washington I, purchased from John Hillier. The opening paragraphs of Lawrence Washington's will suggest that he was deeply religious and committed to the Anglican faith. He bequeathed a pulpit cloth and cushion to the upper and lower churches of Washington Parish. He divided his real estate among his three children (John, Augustine, and Mildred II). He also gave wife Mildred liferights in the property that contained the family home but named their eldest son, John, as reversionary heir. In 1700 Mildred Warner Washington married George Gale of Whitehaven in Cumberland, England, who had business interests in Virginia and Maryland. The newly married Gales moved to Westmoreland, England, taking the Washington children with them. Mildred Warner Washington Gale died there in 1701, leaving the youngsters in the custody of their stepfather, George Gale (Westmoreland County Order Book 1676–1689:102, 155, 165–166, 183, 216, 255–256, 302, 314, 360, 367, 380, 404–405, 412, 468, 476–477, 502, 578, 594; 1690–1698:6, 23, 31, 38, 44, 62–63, 66, 68, 95, 105, 129, 156–157, 182, 185, 221, 242–243, 251, 269, 502, 578; Deeds and Wills 1691–1699:133–135; Deeds, Wills, and Patents 3:369; Deeds, Patents &c. 1665–1677:365a–367; LEO 47–48, 51, 84; Stafford County Record Book 1686–1693:195a–196; Old Rappahannock County Order Book 1683–1686:56, 92).

George Washington: George Washington, the great-grandson of John Washington I, married the former Martha Dandridge, the young widow of Daniel Parke Custis. On October 10, 1778, Washington, the first president of the United States, dispatched a letter to his stepson, John Parke Custis, who had just come of age. He acknowledged John's desire to sell the lots John owned in urban Jamestown, which the younger man considered useless, but advised against it. He said that he considered the monetary system unstable and urged John to trade the lots for some real estate rather than currency. Washington held a legal interest in the property because they were part of the dower lands of his wife, Martha (CUSTIS 1778; WASHING-TON 13:56–58; BYRD xi, 82, 249). The fate of the Custis lots, which had descended from John Custis II, is uncertain. However, they probably became part of the Ambler family's landholdings in urban Jamestown.

* * *

Thomas Waterman: On April 20, 1624, Ralph Hamor of Jamestown asked William Harwood of Martin's Hundred to return his manservant Thomas Waterman, who reportedly was at Harwood's plantation (VI&A 721).

Andrew Waters: The General Court's minutes for April 25, 1626, note that surgeon Thomas Bunn provided medical treatment to Andrew Waters, one of Richard Stephens' servants in urban Jamestown (VI&A 721).

* * *

Edward Waters (Watters, Walters): Edward Waters was shipwrecked in Bermuda and arrived in Virginia in 1610. When the Bermuda Company was formed, he was one of six men named to the council of governors. During the 1622 Indian assault, Waters and his family, who lived in Elizabeth City, were captured by the Indians, taken across the James River to Nansemond, and kept prisoner. They managed to escape and made their way back across the river and reached Kecoughtan. In 1624 Waters, his wife (the former Grace O'Neill), and their son, William I, were living near Waters Creek, but by 1625 they had moved to Blunt Point. In August 1626 Waters was named a justice of Elizabeth City's monthly court, and in 1628 he served as one of the area's burgesses. In March 1629 he was made a lieutenant and placed in command of the Elizabeth City plantations located between the east side of the Hampton River and Fox Hill. In 1630, while the Waters family was in England, Grace testified that she had been living in Sir George Yeardley's household in 1621. When Edward Waters made his will on August 20, 1630, he named as heirs his wife, Grace, and their children, William I and Margaret. The testator died shortly thereafter. Upon being widowed, Grace O'Neill Waters married Obedience Robins I and moved to the Eastern Shore (VI&A 722–723; LEO 7).

William Waters I: In 1652 William Waters I, the Virginia-born son of ancient planters Edward Waters and his wife, the former Grace O'Neill, survived the 1622 Indian attack and in 1624–1625 was living with his parents in Elizabeth City. In September 1630 he was identified as the minor son and primary heir of Edward Waters of Elizabeth City. After the widowed Grace Waters married Obedience Robins I, William Waters I and his sister, Margaret, moved to the Eastern Shore. He patented 700 acres in Northampton County near the head of Old Plantation Creek and in 1650 married Dr. George Clarke's widow, Margaret. On March 25, 1652, Waters and his stepfather, Obedience Robins I, were among the local men who pledged their support to England's newly formed Commonwealth government. It is likely that Robins, who was on the Council of State, served as his stepson's mentor and assisted him in becoming well established socially, politically, and economically. Waters served his first term in the assembly in 1654–1655, while his stepfather was a councilor. He continued to take an active role in public life and served as a county justice and high sheriff in 1664. He also served as one of Northampton County's burgesses in 1660–1662. When Waters testified in court on December 30, 1662, he indicated that he was age 39. It was around that time that Virginia's Eastern Shore was divided into two counties, and some of Northampton County's residents contended that Colonel Edmund Scarborough II had outwitted Colonel William Waters "to our great detriment and loss." In February 1661 Waters purchased from Hugh Yeo a tract of land in Old Plantation Neck, acreage that formerly had belonged to Randall Revell, and in 1662 he patented a large tract in Maryland. In 1664 he was asked to undertake construction of a courthouse in the "Town Field," and by June 1665 he had wed Dorothy Marriott. On May 26, 1671, Lieutenant Colonel William Waters I patented 700 acres on Kings Creek and established what became his descendants' ancestral home. His landholdings eventually included land that was further north, on Gingoteague and Onancock creeks. Waters was returned to the assembly in 1680. His will, made on October 8, 1685, was proved on July 29, 1689. The wording of that document, which states that it was made the "10th Month 8th Day 1685," suggests that he had become a Quaker. The testator said that his estate included holdings in Virginia, Maryland, and Europe. He made bequests to his sons, William II, Edward, Richard, John, Obedience, and Thomas, but made no reference to a wife or daughters. When Waters added a codicil to his will in December 1688, he noted that he had chosen to re-sign it in the presence of new witnesses because all of the original witnesses were dead. Wil-

liam Waters I and his descendants were heavily involved in trade (LEO 32, 36, 39, 46; PB 3:102; 6:404; Northampton County Orders, Deeds, and Wills 1645–1651:208, 224; Deeds, and Wills &c. 1657–1666:76, 111; Orders and Wills 12 [1683–1689]:451–454; Accomack County Deed Book 1664–1671:13A; PB 3:102; 4:536; 5:421; 6:404; 9:33; AMES 2:141–142; NUG I:163–164, 260, 418; VI&A 723; DOR 3:473–475; MARSHALL 138; SR 39641).

William Waters II: William Waters II, the son of William Waters I and his second wife, the former Dorothy Marriott, was in his mid-20s when his father died. He inherited his father's Kings Creek plantation and made it his home. Like his late father, he took an active role in public life and during the 1690s served as a Northampton County justice, sheriff, and coroner. Waters' fellow justices hired him to construct a new county prison. William Waters II married Thomas Harmanson's daughter, Isabell, sometime prior to 1696. After her death he wed Benjamin Baynton's widow, Mary, who had three children. When Waters testified in court in July 1694, he said that he was age 30. He served as a burgess for Northampton County in 1693 and attended the sessions held from 1695 to 1697, 1700–1702, 1712–1714, and 1718–1720. In 1695 he patented 200 acres on Messango Creek in Accomack County. In 1704, when a list of quitrents was sent back to England, Waters paid taxes on 700 acres of land, his Kings Creek plantation in Northampton County. Over the years Waters continued to add to his landholdings. He also served as a naval officer of the Eastern Shore, and as a major and lieutenant colonel in the county militia. One of Waters' friends was William Byrd II of Westover, who said that he enjoyed visiting Waters' plantation and described him as "a very honest man." When Colonel William Waters II made his will on July 3, 1720, he left to his son, William III, the family home, a sloop, a two-masted boat, a gold ring, and an escritoire. He also made bequests to his daughter, Margaret Presson, and her children, Thomas and Isabell. Waters' foreign assets and his keen interest in commerce and trade suggest that the scope of his investments was considerable. The testator's will was proved in Northampton County on April 19, 1721 (LEO 53–54, 56, 60, 64, 67, 69, 71; DOR 3:475–476; Northampton County Order Book 13 [1689–1698]:283, 300; Orders and Wills 14 [1698–1710]:112–119; Deeds, Wills &c. 13 [1718–1725]:122; SR 11578; PB 9:33; MARSHALL 238).

* * *

Robert Waters: In May 1671, Robert Waters' widow and administratrix, Grace, brought suit against the late William Richardson's executrix, who had married Major Theophilus Hone of urban Jamestown. The case was deferred and on October 2, 1671, the attorney for the late Robert Waters' estate won a judgment against William Edwards II of Jamestown (MCGC 262, 280).

Henry Watkins: Henry Watkins came to Virginia sometime prior to the 1622 Indian attack and was the overseer of Lady Elizabeth Dale's property on the Eastern Shore. In 1624 he was one of two men representing the Eastern Shore in the assembly (VI&A 724; LEO 5).

James Watkins: James Watkins, a laborer, came to Virginia in 1608 in the 2nd Supply of Jamestown colonists. According to Captain John Smith, he was an "old soldier" and had killed an Indian during an ambush (VI&A 724).

* * *

John Watkins I: In March 1638 John Watkins patented 150 acres near Lower Chippokes Creek, land that was located beside the Sunken Marsh, better known as College Run. Ten years later he laid claim to 850 acres above the head of Gray's Creek. His land acquisitions, which were made by means of the headright system, suggest that he was a successful planter. On November 24, 1674, John Watkins I of Surry County was identified as Henry Watkins' late father (NUG I:103, 176; Surry County Order Book 1671–1691:76).

Henry Watkins: On November 24, 1674, Henry Watkins of Surry, who was the late John Watkins' son and had recently come of age, brought suit against Francis Mason and Richard Lawrence, a Jamestown innkeeper and surveyor. By March 4, 1679, Henry Watkins was dead. His brother, John II, was then given administration of his estate (Surry County Order Book 1671–1691:76, 240–241).

* * *

Rice (Rys) Watkins: During the mid-1620s Rice Watkins, a servant employed by Edward Blaney of Jamestown, was living on Hog Island. In August 1626 Watkins, who was then Martin Turner's administrator and principal heir, was ordered to inventory his goods. Two years later he was appointed administrator of the late Hugh Crowder's estate (VI&A 725).

Mr. [Abraham?] Watson (Wattson): When Mrs. Ann Talbott patented her one-acre waterfront lot in urban Jamestown on March 1, 1655, a Mr. Watson was in possession of a contiguous parcel to her west, a lot that John Corker had claimed in 1640. Although Mr. Watson's identity is uncertain, his identification as "Mr." indicates that he was a gentleman. At least three adult males with the Watson surname were associated with Jamestown during the mid-seventeenth century, but only one seems to have been classified as a gentleman: Mr. Abraham Watson, who served as a James City burgess from 1652 through 1655. This raises the possibility that during the early 1650s, when John Corker moved to Surry and began serving as one of its burgesses, he sold his Jamestown lot to Abraham Watson, who commenced representing James City. It is unclear whether he represented James City County or Jamestown, the capital city (STAN 69–71; HEN I:386–387; NUG I:305; PB 3:331; LEO 30–32). Office-holders or their spouses were required to own land in the area they represented.

Abraham Watson (Wattson): Abraham Watson came to Virginia sometime prior to December 1650 when Thomas Tilsey of James City County used him as a headright. Watson served as a James City burgess from 1652 through 1655 and may have represented Jamestown, the capital city. On February 10, 1657, he patented 150 acres of land in James City County, a tract then known as the Bachelor's Bank. His property was on the mainland, just east of Jamestown Island, and abutted the James City Parish glebe and David Mansell's land in the Neck O'Land (LEO 30–32; STAN 69–71; PB 4:248; NUG I:204, 343, 364).

Isaac Watson (Wattson): When John Watson patented a one-acre lot on August 28, 1644, "neare the Brewere poynt" in the western end of Jamestown Island, his land abutted northeast upon that of Isaac Watson. As Isaac Watson's patent has been lost or destroyed, its precise location is uncertain. Very little is known about Isaac Watson other than the fact that in 1655 he acquired Richard Codsford's acreage in Westmoreland County and that he and a partner patented some land on Aquia Creek in 1662 (PB 2:10; NUG I:154, 312, 512). In 1671 a mariner named Isaac Watson was identified as master of the ship *Richard and Anne* of Faversham when he transported tobacco to England (SR 3593d).

John Watson (Wattson): On August 23, 1644, John Watson received a patent for one acre of ground in the eastern end of Jamestown Island "neare the Brewers Point." Watson's parcel, which abutted west on the James River, was nearly square and was well suited for commercial or industrial development. By 1656 Watson's patent had become part of a much larger tract that belonged to John Baldwin. John Watson received his land as part of the 1642 building initiative, which was intended to fuel development in the capital city. If he failed to construct improvements on his property, it could be assigned to another (NUG I:145; PB I:889). During the second and third quarters of the seventeenth century, there were at least two men named John Watson who had a connection with Jamestown Island. In 1625 an indentured servant named John Watson (age 24) was living in Elizabeth City in the home of the Rev. Jonas Stockton. By 1635 he was free and had patented 150 acres in Elizabeth City in "the New Poquoson," using himself, wife Elizabeth, and a man servant as headrights. Watson's property then abutted the acreage of Christopher Stokes, a former resident of Jamestown Island. On the other hand, John Watson, who was living on the College land during the mid-1620s, purchased some cloth from Jamestown merchant Edward Blaney. A third man named John Watson was living in Isle of Wight County in November 1651 when he made his will, mentioning his brothers Robert and James and sister-in-law Ann (NUG I:26; PB I:225; HEN I:362; HOT 256; MCGC 97; MCGH 156, 225; VI&A 725).

William Watson: William Watson died in August 1659 while he was aboard a ship that was anchored in Jamestown. He was survived by his wife, Sarah (EEAC 61).

Wattle Jaws (Loggerhead, King of the Nanzattico) (Native American): When John Knotts of Westmoreland County testified on February 20, 1654, before the county's justices, he said that approximately two years earlier he had seen Daniel Lisson give a gun to an Indian who went by the name of Wattle Jaws or Loggerhead and was a king of the Nanzattico. When Knotts asked the Indian why he did not bring the gun home, he said that he had bought it (Westmoreland County Deeds, Wills, Patents &c. 1653–1659:15). It is unclear whether Wattle Jaws, when referring to "home," meant his people's village or Lisson's house.

John Watton: John Watton died on Jamestown Island sometime after April 1623 but before February 16, 1624 (VI&A 725).

Mathew (Matthew) Watts: Mathew Watts served as an Elizabeth City County burgess during the sessions that commenced in April 1695 and ended in May 1696. He succeeded William Wilson, who left Virginia before the opening of the 1696 session. Watts was not returned to the assembly, but he served as a county justice and was surveyor of roads for the area near Elizabeth City's Back River. In 1704 he paid quitrent on 454 acres of Elizabeth City County land. Mathew Watts made a will that was recorded in Elizabeth City County on August 15, 1716. Legatees included his son, Samuel, and daughter, Ann II. Although he named his wife, Ann I, and Charles Tucker as co-executors, local court justices designated Hannah Armistead as the decedent's executrix. Watts' estate was appraised by three men, who saw that it was recorded on June 15, 1717 (LEO 54; Elizabeth City County Deeds, Wills, and Orders 1715–1721:41; 1723–1730:21; NEAL 73, 95, 137, 211, 238, 280; SMITH 94).

John Waugh (Wough): The Rev. John Waugh, an Anglican clergyman, arrived in Stafford County in the late 1660s. He quickly ran afoul of the law because he married a Maryland couple who had failed to procure a license or post bans. Waugh was suspended from his duties but apologized, promising never to do it again, and posted a bond guaranteeing his good behavior. In 1674 he brought suit against Richard Kenner of Northumberland County. Four years later he sued Dominick Rice for defamation, alleging that when Rice appeared before Westmoreland County's justices, he had accused Waugh of hog-stealing. Waugh and his wife, Elizabeth, made their home in Stafford County's Stafford Parish during the 1670s and 1680s and were living there in 1686 when they disposed of 300 acres on Choppawomsick Creek. Waugh's name appeared in Stafford County's records from time to time because he witnessed documents. He also was frequently involved in lawsuits. In 1689, when tensions between France and England were high, Waugh and two other men added to the unrest by spreading rumors that Maryland's Roman Catholics were plotting with the Indians and were planning to invade Stafford County and overrun Virginia. Waugh and his companions were arrested and imprisoned because of their inflammatory remarks and rumor mongering. In 1690 Waugh made some ill-advised comments about an incoming governor and in the heat of the moment called Colonel William Fitzhugh I "a Papist Rogue." Waugh's behavior came to the attention of the General Court, and he was made to apologize publicly. In December 1691 Anne, the late Henry Meese's widow, executrix, and heir, asked Stafford County's justices for assistance in evicting the Rev. John Waugh from her late husband's plantation. She said that she wanted to sell the property and that Waugh refused to leave. In 1692 Waugh sold some of his land to William Fitzhugh I, acreage that was located near the head of the Rappahannock River. Although the freeholders of Stafford County elected Waugh to the assembly and he was supposed to attend the 1699 session, he was declared ineligible because he was a clergyman. On May 9, 1700, Waugh gave a large tract of land on the Potomac River to his sons, Joseph and John. He retired that year, after his license was revoked (LEO 59; EJC 104–106, 519, 522; Stafford County Record Book 1686–1693:34–34a, 119–119a, 157, 169a, 219a–220, 260a; 1699–1709:32; Richmond County Deed Book 1 [1692–1693]:24–26, 66–70; Northumberland County Order Book 1666–1678:194, 338; 1678–1698:9, 16–17; Westmoreland County Deeds, Patents &c. 1665–1677:217–217a, 234a–236).

Wawoscon (Wawoseons) (Native American): On July 2, 1658, the justices of Lancaster County's monthly court ordered John Meredith to pay Wawoscon and his brother four yards of trading cloth. In 1665 Meredith patented land on the Corotoman River (Lancaster County Orders 1656–1666:53; PB 5:490).

Robert Weatherall (Wetherall): In 1645–1646 and 1652, Robert Weatherall served as a burgess for James City, probably representing James City County rather than Jamestown, for he does not appear to have owned property in the capital city. In 1652 he sold Sir William Berkeley 1,000 acres of land that he had patented in 1648, acreage that abutted Green Spring. Weatherall sometimes served as Thomas Ludwell's attorney (STAN 64, 68–69; NUG I:160, 173, 203, 415; HEN I:298; II:319–321; MCGC 503; LEO 24, 29–30).

Samuel Weaver: Samuel Weaver arrived in Jamestown on September 12, 1623, aboard the *Bonny Bess* (VI&A 726).

[No First Name] Webb: On February 16, 1624, Goodman Webb, whose first name is unknown, headed a household in the eastern half of Jamestown Island (VI&A 726).

George Webb: George Webb was captain of a ship that brought the 3rd Supply of new colonists to Jamestown. In June 1610 Lord Delaware designated him sergeant-major of the fort. In January 1613 Captain Samuel Argall captured some Indian boys and exchanged them for Captain George Webb and some other men the natives were detaining. In 1614 Webb was named commander of forts Henry and Charles in Kecoughtan and held that post for at least two years. When Virginia officials reviewed in 1624 the events that preceded the 1622 Indian attack, they criticized Captain George Webb for allowing one of his servants to teach Indians how to use firearms (VI&A 726).

Giles (Gyles) Webb: Giles Webb arrived in Virginia sometime prior to 1649, when he became embroiled in a lawsuit involving the loss of a large quantity of tobacco that he was sending overseas. In August 1652 he was identified as a Virginia planter when he lost another shipment that was sent to London in a New England ship. When a man in Surrey County, England, gave Webb a promissory note on August 8, 1656, he referred to his "well beloved friend Mr. Giles Webb of Chuckatuck." Webb served as a burgess from 1658 to 1660, representing Upper Norfolk County. During 1661–1662 he attended assembly meetings on behalf of Nansemond County, Upper Norfolk's successor (LEO 34–36, 39; Lower Norfolk County Record Book B [1646–1652]:111; SR 4012, 4016). A Giles Webb patented 681 acres of land on the north side of the Rappahannock River in Lancaster County in February 1667. He may have been former burgess Giles Webb, for a significant number of other residents of the lower side of the James River invested in land in the Northern Neck (PB 6:111; Lancaster County Record Book 2 [1637–1640]:202).

Henry Webb: On September 24, 1674, the General Court noted that Thomas Rabley of urban Jamestown had brought suit against Henry Webb on behalf of his wife, Elizabeth Rabley (MCGC 379). Webb may have been a former resident of eastern York County (PB 8:137).

Stephen Webb: In February 1624 Stephen Webb was living on the Governor's Land in George Fryer's household. A year later he had been moved to the lower side of the James River, where he was a servant on Captain Roger Smith's plantation. Court testimony dating to 1627 reveals that Webb was a Virginia Company tenant who had been assigned to Captain Roger Smith of Jamestown after the Company was defunct. On June 30, 1635, Webb and his wife, Clare, leased from George Powell 300 acres at the mouth of Lower Chippokes Creek, in what was then James City County but eventually became Surry County, and agreed to erect improvements on the property. He served as one of James City's burgesses in 1643 and 1644, representing the territory on the lower side of the James River. Stephen Webb died sometime prior to January 3, 1656, when his son, Robert, appeared before Surry County's justices and testified that he was born on November 16, 1636, and that his brother, William, was born on February 15, 1645. Robert Webb indicated that he had found the information about their birth dates written his late father's handwriting in an old Bible. On July 24, 1659, the late Stephen Webb's younger brother, William, a merchant of Tuksbury in Gloucester County, England, sent a document to Surry County's justices in which he provided information that could be used to prove that he was his brother's legitimate heir. An affidavit from the minister and churchwardens of Bushly Parish in Gloucester stated that Stephen Webb (the Virginia colonist) had been baptized there on September 1, 1598, and that his brother, William, had been baptized there on May 10, 1601. Both were the sons of Ann and Stephen Webb of Bushly Parish. When trying to claim his late brother's estate, William Webb indicated that he was the uncle of Robert Webb, who also was deceased, and therefore he had a right to both men's Virginia property (VI&A 727; LEO 21–22; Surry County Deed Book 1652–1663:73, 137–138, 174–175).

Thomas Webb: In 1607 Thomas Webb came to Virginia and was one of the first Jamestown colonists. Captain John Smith described him appreciatively as a carpenter and a gentleman and as one of his "old soldiers" (VI&A 727).

Wingfield (Winfield) Webb (Webbe): In November 1650 Wingfield Webb and Richard Pate patented 1,141 acres on the north side of the York River, at the head of the eastern branch of the Poropotank River. A Winifred Webb reportedly made three trips to Virginia and was listed among the headrights that secured the Webb-Pate patent; it may be a corruption of the name "Wingfield." In 1654–1655, while the Commonwealth government was in power, Wingfield Webb served as a burgess representing Gloucester County (LEO 32; PB 2:271).

John Webber (Webbar): When the Association of Northumberland, Westmoreland, and Stafford Counties met in November 1667 to select a site on which to build a fort, John Webber, an engineer, was given the responsibility of laying out the fort and overseeing its construction. The fort was to be built at what was then known as Levy Neck Point, where the Yeocomico River meets the Potomac River. Men were to be pressed into service and wood was to be procured, as were cannon and other weaponry. The fort was being built in response to a mandate from the assembly, at a time when a Dutch attack was anticipated. When John Webber made his will on February 12, 1671, he bequeathed to his son, Peter, 100 acres of land near Little Choptanke and instructed his executors to send home to England the proceeds of whatever goods he had. Webber died sometime prior to March 28, 1671, at which time his will was proved (Northumberland County Record Book 1666–1670:34–36, 41; Deeds and Wills 1670–1672:166; HEN II:255–256).

Wassell (Wessell) Weblin (Webling): Wassell Weblin, the son of a London brewer, arrived in Jamestown in 1622. He signed a contract with Edward Bennett of Warresqueak, agreeing to serve as an apprentice for three years. On November 13, 1626, the General Court, upon reviewing Weblin's contract, ordered Bennett to uphold his end of the bargain. On January 14, 1628, Wassell Weblin was arrested by Jamestown merchant Edward Sharples for unpaid debt (VI&A 728).

Richard Webster: Major Richard Webster, who by 1653 had become a resident of Jamestown, purchased a house from the government sometime between 1652 and 1658. The structure, commonly known as "the country house," had been erected with public funds. Webster seems to have had a connection to Roger Williams of Lower Norfolk County, for he gave Williams' orphan a cow. Webster had a mill and plantation on Swann's Creek in Surry County but represented Jamestown in the March 1658 session of the assembly. By August 1658 he had assigned the "country house" and the lot on which it stood to Richard Ricks (Rix). Sometime after August 5, 1658, but before October 17, 1660, Ricks's widow received official permission to sell it (AMB 6, 7, 10, 32; Surry County Deeds, Wills &c. 1652–1672:76; Lancaster County Deed and Will Book 1652–1657:87; HEN I:439; Lower Norfolk County Record Book C:23; PB 7:98; NUG II:222; LEO 34).

Roger Webster: Roger Webster came to Virginia sometime prior to February 1624. He lived at Hog Island and may have been employed by the Virginia Company or the Society of Southampton Hundred, in which many Company investors were involved. Although Webster was still living on Hog Island in 1628, by 1632 he had moved to Archer's Hope and was serving as the burgess for that area's settlers and the people living in the vicinity of the James City Glebe. In November 1655 Captain Roger Webster sold a Surry County mill to John Corker (Surry County Deed Book I [1652–1661]: 74–75; VI&A 728; LEO 11).

Abraham Weeks (Weekes): In April 1662 Abraham Weeks patented 450 acres in Lancaster County, on the north side of the Rappahannock River. He moved there and later in the year appeared in county court. He began to take an increasingly active role in public life, and in March 1666 he was nominated as a justice for the county court. He was approved, and in May 1666 he took the oath of office. Weeks was still living in Lancaster County in 1669. When a London merchant named Weeks as an heir in October 1676, he identified Weeks as a Middlesex County resident whose home was on the Rappahannock River. The change in jurisdiction probably was the result of Middlesex County's being formed from part of Lancaster's territory. Abraham Weeks represented Middlesex County in the assembly sessions of 1677, 1680–1682, and 1684, and during the early 1680s he served as a justice of the Middlesex County court. He continued to acquire land, and in 1680 he and another man patented 1,091 acres adjacent to Henry Corbin's property. In 1680 Weeks was one of the trustees authorized to purchase a 50-acre town site from Ralph Wormeley II. When Middlesex County's justices convened in May 1690, they authorized fellow justice Abraham Weeks to compile a list of the tithables in the county's upper precinct. In March 1692 Weeks' widow, Millicent, and Mathew Lydford presented his will to the county court and were identified as his executors. In December of that year, Mrs. Millicent Weeks returned to court and confirmed the terms of her late husband's will, which included bequests to several people. When Henry Williamson of Essex County made his will in 1699, he bequeathed to one of his daughters half of a Middlesex County plantation that he had bought from Abraham and Millicent Weeks in 1688 (LEO 43, 45, 47; Middlesex County Order Book 1673–1680:63; 1680–1694:13, 241, 470, 474, 546, 599; Lancaster County Order Book 1656–1666:179; 1666–1680:1, 100; Essex County Deeds and Wills 1699–1701:12–13; PB 4:380; 7:52).

Robert Weeks (Weekes): In May 1673 John Davis's son, Thomas, sued Robert Weeks. Later in the year Weeks sued Richard James I of urban Jamestown in an attempt to recover funds from the estate of Richard Holder, also of Jamestown. Because the General Court concluded that Weeks had no case against Holder, Weeks forwarded his case to the assembly, which occasionally served as an appellate body. In 1662 Robert Weeks patented 50 acres at Middle Plantation. Part of his acreage was in James City County and part was in York (MCGC 341, 355; PB 5:174).

John Weir (Weire, Weyre, Weye): John Weir represented Old Rappahannock County in the assembly sessions of 1659–1660 and from 1661 to 1670. Although he was reelected to the assembly, he died before the 1671 session commenced. Weir held the rank of captain in 1663 and 1664 when he patented several large tracts of land on the north side of the Rappahannock River, in what was then Old Rappahannock County but later became Richmond County. One of the parcels he acquired adjoined the land on which he was then living. In 1665 Weir purchased a mill on Gilson's Creek, a tributary of the Rappahannock River, and in 1667 he patented some land on Occupacia Creek, in what became Essex County. By that time he was a major in the local militia. In 1696 the late Major John Weir's widowed daughter and heir, Elizabeth Gardner, then a resident of St. Mary's County, Maryland, conveyed some of her late father's acreage to Jeffrey Jeffreys, a London merchant (LEO 35–36, 39; Old Rappahannock County Deeds and Wills 1665–1677:111–112; Richmond County Deed Book 2 [1693–1695]:162–166; 3 [1697–1704]:9–13; PB 4:106; 5:128, 232, 234; 6:77).

Richard Welbeck: Richard Welbeck moved to Surry County sometime prior to January 1665, when he purchased a horse. In 1667 he appeared in court, where he witnessed a document in an official capacity, and over the next few years he went to court occasionally in pursuit of debtors. However, in January 1675 Colonel Thomas Swann of Surry County and urban Jamestown filed suit against Welbeck, whom he claimed had failed to pay the quitrent that was owed on the property he was renting from Swann. On March 5, 1675, Swann's case against Welbeck, who was a gentleman, was dismissed because Welbeck proved that he had given the quitrent to Colonel Thomas Stegg II, a deceased councilor. Welbeck appears to have been a merchant, for he sold shoes, beer, and other items. On one occasion he ran afoul of the law for selling beer without a license. He died intestate sometime prior to January 1, 1678, and Major William Brown was authorized to serve as his administrator (MCGC 406; Surry County Deed Book 1 [1652–1671]:245, 297–298, 330, 351, 361, 378, 389, 464; Order Book 1671–1691:1, 18, 65, 81, 88, 91, 102, 107, 176, 187, 258).

Thomas Welbourne (Wellbourn, Welburn, Welburne): When London merchant Thomas Cox sued mariner George Pattison in 1676, he identified Thomas Welbourne as his factor and asked him to testify about the cargo's condition. Other court documents described Welbourne as a merchant. In April 1678 Welbourne patented 83 acres called Fox Island, near Watts Island in the Chesapeake Bay, and he and a man named Peter Walker laid claim to Gengoteague (Chincoteague) Island. Over the years Welbourne gradually rose in prominence. Sometime prior to 1686 he married Arcadia (Arcadis), the daughter of Mrs. Ann Toft, whose long-term relationship with Edmund Scarborough II was highly controversial. Welbourne's brother-in-law was Captain John Osborne of Somerset County, Maryland, who was married to the former Attlanta Toft. Captain Thomas Welbourne became a county justice, and in 1699 he represented Accomack County in the assembly. He died intestate and on February 3, 1703, his widow, Arcadia, was granted administration of his estate. Sometime prior to August 1703 she joined Francis Mackennie, John West, and Daniel Jennifer II in patenting 3,804 acres in Accomack County (LEO 59; Accomack County Wills and Deeds 1676–1680:479; Orders 1697–1703:136; Wills &c 1692–1715:6, 129, 300; PB 6:637; 9:545; SR 7420, 7421, 7422).

Poynes Weldon (Welden): Poynes Weldon served as a James City County burgess in 1695–1696 and may have been related to merchant Samuel Weldon, a James City County justice and sheriff who came to Virginia in 1675. Samuel Weldon's wife, the former Sarah Efford, inherited several hundred acres of land approximately four miles west of Middle Plantation (later, Williamsburg) and left it to her son, Benjamin (LEO 54; Stanard, "Virginia Gleanings in England," 195–196).

Richard Wells: Richard Wells represented Lower Norfolk County in the assembly sessions held between 1645 and 1648. He may have moved to the Northern Neck, where a Richard Wells patented 500 acres of land in Northumberland County in 1653 and 100 acres in Westmoreland County in 1658. In

1655 Wells' wife, who was living in Westmoreland, ran afoul of the law by altering the identification mark on a hog (LEO 24, 26; PB 3:3; 4:318; Westmoreland County Deeds, Wills, Patents &c. 1653–1659:42, 93).

Thomas Wells II: On October 26, 1699, Thomas Wells II patented a fraction of Philip Ludwell I's half-acre waterfront lot in urban Jamestown. His lot line, which was adjacent to Captain George Marable II's brick row house, passed through the wall of Marable's kitchen. Wells was a Henrico County planter with holdings on the James and Appomattox rivers. He was the son of Thomas Wells I of Bristol Parish in Henrico, who by 1665 was living in Henrico County and owned some land on the upper side of the Appomattox River, in what eventually became Chesterfield County. When Thomas Wells I made his will on January 21, 1695, he made bequests to his son, Thomas II, and daughter, Mary, giving them his Indian servants and other personal property (PB 9:232; NUG II:114, 181; III:32; Henrico County Wills, Deeds, Etc. 1677–1692:119, 394; 1688–1697:174, 226, 570; Deeds and Wills 1688–1697:664, 710; Miscellaneous Records Book 1:29).

* * *

Anthony West: Sixteen-year-old Anthony West came to Virginia in 1622 as a servant of surgeon William Rowley and his wife, Elizabeth, who died within a year or so of their arrival. West was residing in urban Jamestown in Captain William Holmes' household in February 1624, but within the year moved to Treasurer's Plantation on the lower side of the James River. Jamestown resident John Southern informed the General Court that shortly before Mrs. Rowsley died, she said that she intended to give West his freedom and had asked Captain Sampson to take him back to England. The General Court freed West, a surgeon, and allowed him to leave the colony. In 1634, while he was in England, he married Anne (Ann), the 26-year-old widow of Anthony Huffe. When he returned to Virginia, he and his wife took up residence in Northampton County, where he died between October 12, 1651, and May 25, 1652, naming as heirs his wife, Anne, son John, and daughter Katherine. The testator's widow, Anne, married Captain Stephen Charlton, a burgess (VI&A 730; PB 2:185; MARSHALL 31; DOR 3:509–511).

John West: John West, the son of surgeon Anthony West and his wife, Anne, was born in 1638; when testifying in court in November 1663, he indicated that he was age 25. Though underage at the time of his father's death, he came into possession of 1,600 acres on the Great Naswattock River. John West, who was a carpenter and shipbuilder, served as an Accomack county justice and sheriff and as a captain, major, and lieutenant colonel in the militia. Around 1660 he married Matilda, the young daughter of land baron Edmund Scarborough II and his wife, Mary. West commenced patenting large quantities of land, and over the next two decades he accumulated literally thousands of acres. During the 1660s he patented acreage on Deep and Pungoteague creeks. He expanded his holdings in those areas during the 1670s but also acquired land at Onancock, at Gingoteague (Chincoteague), and on the seaside. Although he patented land independently, he sometimes co-invested with members of the Scarborough family. He also repatented acreage that originally had been his wife's. John West represented Accomack County in the assembly sessions that were held in 1676. He also was a customs official for Accomack and in that capacity participated in a chancery suit that involved London merchant Thomas Cox and his factor, Thomas Welbourne. On February 6, 1703, John West made his will, which was proved on August 4, 1703. He made bequests to his wife, Matilda, and to his numerous children: two sons named John, plus Anthony, Alexander, Benomy, and Jonathan, and daughters Ann, Catherine, Frances, Mary, Matilda, Sarah, and Scarburgh. The testator also made bequests to his numerous grandchildren. Matilda Scarborough West, a prominent member of the Society of Friends, died intestate sometime after August 2, 1720 (LEO 37; DOR 3:509–511; Accomack County Wills &c. 1692–1715:317; Order Book 1719–1724:22; PB 4:23, 52, 499; 5:75; 6:390, 392, 398, 423, 533, 610, 639; 7:14; 8:64).

* * *

* * *

Henry West: Henry West of Isle of Wight County, who was considered one of the rebel Nathaniel Bacon's most ardent supporters, was captured and detained at Governor Berkeley's Green Spring plantation in James City County. On January 24, 1677, when West was tried at a martial court held at Green Spring, he was found guilty of treason and rebellion. However, his crimes were not considered as heinous as those of the others being tried. Therefore, he was sentenced to banishment rather than death by hanging. West had the option of going to

England, Jamaica, Barbados, or any of the other islands for seven years. He was obliged to forfeit his estate, preserving only the funds he needed to secure passage out of Virginia. In November 1677 Henry West, who was then staying with a relative in London, sent a petition to the king. He asked to be allowed to return to Virginia where his wife and children were living and said that Bacon's men had forced him to join their army. He also asked the king to pardon his brother, William West. Henry's petition was referred to the Privy Council, which forwarded it to Virginia's governor, Thomas Lord Culpeper, who granted him a pardon (MCGC 455, 528; NEVILLE 81, 87, 186–187, 192, 194).

William West: On January 24, 1677, William West, one of the rebel Nathaniel Bacon's most ardent supporters, was tried at a martial court held at Green Spring plantation, where he was being detained. He admitted his guilt and was sentenced to be hanged, but managed to escape from prison. Later, Isle of Wight County officials sent a petition to the king asking that West's life be spared and that his estate be given to his wife and children. The request seems to have come too late, for an account of William West's estate was compiled in May 1677. In November 1677 Henry West, a convicted rebel who had been transported out of Virginia, entered a plea on behalf of his brother, William West (MCGC 455, 528; NEVILLE 66, 81, 147).

* * *

John West: John West, a husbandman, arrived in Jamestown in 1623. In early 1624 he and Thomas West (perhaps a kinsman), who had accompanied him to Virginia, were residing on Jamestown Island in John Grevett's household. In January 1625 West and Thomas Crompe jointly headed a household on Jamestown Island (VI&A 735).

Richard West: On October 13, 1640, the General Court sentenced Richard West, a free man, to a whipping because he failed to disclose a plot that involved some servants who planned to run away. West was ordered to serve the colony for two years (MCGC 467).

* * *

Thomas West: Sir Thomas West, Lord Delaware, succeeded to his father's peerage in 1602 and became a member of the Privy Council. He was on the Virginia Company's

Council and in February 1609 married Cecily Sherley. As the first Lord Governor and Captain General of Virginia, West set sail for Virginia in 1610. When he arrived in Jamestown, he found the settlement's fort and buildings in disrepair and resolved to place the colony on a much firmer footing. However, after a few months sickness forced him to withdraw to the West Indies and then to England. When Sir Thomas Dale brought Pocahontas (then Mrs. John Rolfe) to England in 1616, Lord and Lady Delaware reportedly befriended her and introduced her at court. In 1618 West set out for Virginia but died at sea. His remains were brought to Jamestown, where they were interred. After her husband's death, Lady Cecily West tried to recover his goods and the debts accruable to his estate. She died in 1662 (VI&A 734).

Francis West I: In 1608 Francis West I, Lord Delaware's brother and a Virginia Company investor, arrived in Jamestown in the 2nd Supply of new settlers. When Captain John Smith was removed as chief executive in September 1609, council president Francis West became acting governor and served for only two weeks. In 1612 he was designated commander of Jamestown, and in 1617 he received a lifetime appointment as "maker of Ordnance." By April 1623 he had married Margaret, the widow of Captain William Powell and Edward Blaney and a resident of urban Jamestown. Together they produced a son, Francis West II. In 1624 Francis West I was residing at West and Shirley Hundred Island, but by 1625 he had moved to Elizabeth City and was living on the Virginia Company's land. When a list of patented land was sent back to England in May 1625, Captain West was credited with 500 acres at Westover and some land on Lower Chippokes Creek. He continued to serve on the council and during the mid-1620s was a member of the Quarter Court. West became acting governor on November 14, 1627, and held office for two years. His wife, Margaret, died and in late March 1628 he married Sir George Yeardley's widow, Lady Temperance. She died intestate the following December, before she had finished settling her late husband's estate. West, in an attempt to recover Temperance's dower share of Sir George Yeardley's estate, sued Ralph Yeardley. West remarried, taking as his bride Sir Henry Davye's daughter, Jane. When Francis West I made his will on November 17, 1629, before setting sail for England, he authorized his wife, Jane, to sell his Virginia land. He died in the colony in 1633–1634, possibly in a drowning accident, and his will was presented for probate

on April 28, 1634, Francis West II stood to inherit half of his late father's property at age 21 (VI&A 731–732; SR 3968).

Nathaniel West: Nathaniel West was the brother of Thomas West, the third Lord Delaware, who became Virginia's governor. On October 20, 1617, the Virginia Company designated Nathaniel West the captain of the Lord General's Company. He came to Virginia around 1618 and three years later married Frances Grenville. After his death, which occurred sometime prior to February 16, 1624, his widow, Frances, and their little son, Nathaniel II, took up temporary residence with her brothers-in-law, captains John and Francis West. In late 1625 the widowed Frances Grenville West married cape merchant Abraham Peirsey of Flowerdew Hundred and Jamestown (VI&A 733).

Mrs. Nathaniel West (see Frances Grenville)

John West I: John West I, the son of Thomas West, Lord Delaware, came to Virginia in 1618 and established Westover, which was attacked by the Indians in 1622. By 1624 he had moved to a plantation on the lower side of the James River, across from Jamestown and to the east of Gray's Creek. He continued to live there and represented that area in the assembly from 1628 to 1630. Colonel John West I was among the first to patent land in Chiskiack, receiving a patent for 600 acres on October 8, 1630. His acreage, which extended along the York River, ran from the mouth of Kings Creek (on the west) east to a point just west of Bracken's Pond, where it interfaced with a tract assigned to Captain Francis Morgan. At first, Felgates Creek was known as West's. West became a member of the Council of State in 1631 and held office until 1659. In 1633 he commenced serving as a justice of York County. When Governor John Harvey was thrust from office in 1635, West (as senior member of the council) was elected as his replacement until a new royal appointee took office. In 1650 he sold his York River plantation to Edward Digges I and moved to a 1,550-acre tract that he had patented at the junction of the Pamunkey and Mattaponi rivers. John West I died in Virginia in 1659 (VI&A 732; LEO 7–9; HEN I:257; NUG I:20, 24, 29–30, 80, 136; MCGC 11, 479, 481; York County Deeds, Orders, Wills 1:23, 27–30, 32, 35–39, 41–42, 47, 51, 80; 2:146, 153; JHB 1659–1693:4).

John West II: John West II, the son of John West I, was born around 1632, probably at Chiskiack, and lived on his father's plantation at West Point, where the Pamunkey and Mattaponi rivers converge to form the York. He went on to serve as a captain, major, and lieutenant colonel of the militia. Sometime prior to November 4, 1664, Colonel John West II married Unity, the daughter of Major Joseph Croshaw and the granddaughter of ancient planter Raleigh Croshaw. The West couple, as Croshaw's legatees, eventually inherited his land. Together, they produced three sons (John III, Thomas, and Nathaniel) and a daughter, Anne. Lieutenant Colonel West, a member of the Council of State, remained loyal to Governor William Berkeley during Bacon's Rebellion and was among those who tried Bacon supporters in a military tribunal. He was known to have fathered a son with the widowed Cockacoeske, queen of the Pamunkey Indians. The youth was called "Captain John West" and was a signatory to the 1677 Treaty of Middle Plantation. By 1685 John West II and his wife, Unity, "lived asunder," presumably because of his liaison with the Indian queen. Colonel West, a New Kent County justice, represented New Kent in the assembly, serving in 1680–1682, 1684–1686, and 1688. When he and a fellow New Kent burgess, Joseph Foster, violated some of the assembly's procedural rules in 1684, they refused to apologize to their fellow burgesses. As a result, they were arrested and detained until they did. West made his will on November 15, 1689. He was returned to office and attended the first session of the 1691–1692 assembly. On October 30, 1693, Unity Croshaw West relinquished her dower interest in the York County tract called Poplar Neck, the Croshaw home place (VI&A 733; LEO 37, 45, 47–50; FOR 1:8:14–15; JHB 1659–1693:210, 212, 214–215; DOR 1:773; 3:490; NEVILLE 61; MCGC 456, 529; York County Deeds, Orders, Wills I:290; Deeds, Wills, Orders &c. 4:251; HEN 6:428).

John West ("Captain John West") (Native American): Early in 1676 Virginia's governing officials met with Cockacoeske, queen of the Pamunkey Indians, in Jamestown and sought her aid in defending the colony against hostile Indian tribes. She brought along her interpreter, Cornelius Dabney, and her son, a youth described as the offspring of an English colonel. Later, the young man, who was identified as "Captain John West," joined Cockacoeske in signing the Treaty of Middle Plantation, which was consummated at the site of what became Williamsburg. The mark he made, signifying his approval, was "I W." When King Charles II commissioned gifts for Cockacoeske and "the Prince, her son and successor," her son was described as a "good, brave young man pretty full of stature and slender body, a great war captain among the Indians and one that has been very active in the service of the English." Young West received a scarlet suit lined with sky-blue morella tabby and decorated with silver and gold lace and silver and gold buttons. His outfit included scarlet stockings embellished with black silk embroidery; a belt embroidered with silver and gold; a white beaver hat trimmed with a silver and gold band; a fine sword and scabbard; and a pair of pistols inlaid with silver and gold. He was presumed to be the son of John West II, who owned land in Pamunkey Neck near the village of Cockacoeske, who was widowed in 1656. According to one of John West II's descendants, his wife, Unity, deserted him because of his liaison with the queen of the Pamunkey Indians. By 1678 "Captain John West" had married a Pamunkey Indian girl who was born in the Chickahominy Indians' village. When Cockacoeske and her son compiled a list of complaints against the Chickahominy Indians, whom the 1677 treaty had rendered subservient to the Pamunkey Indians, they alleged that young West's wife had fled to the Chickahominies and refused to return (FOR 1:8:14–15; AND 125–127; LC 5/108 f 8; 9/275 ff 264ro–267ro; SR 5736, 5743; CO 1/42 177; 5/1371; DOR 1:773; 3:490).

* * *

Thomas West: Thomas West, a cooper from London, arrived in Jamestown in September 1623 and took the oath of allegiance. In February 1624 he and John West (perhaps a kinsman) were residing in the Jamestown Island household of sawyer and carpenter John Grevett. West died sometime prior to January 24, 1625 (VI&A 736).

William West (Weste): Around 1610 William West, a gentleman, prepared a nuncupative will shortly before he set sail for Virginia. He accompanied George Percy on a trip to the Pasbehay Indians' village at the mouth of the Chickahominy River. Later, West was killed by the Indians when he and Captain Edward Brewster went to the falls of the James River (VI&A 736).

Thomas Weston: Thomas Weston, a merchant, was an adventurer in New England before he undertook trading activities in Virginia. He was involved in transporting and selling indentured servants and made regular trips to Canada, exchanging tobacco for cargoes of fish. Weston's trading activities in

Virginia took place in Newportes News, Elizabeth City, and Jamestown. In 1628 he served as a burgess, representing Kecoughtan and the merchants. He eventually moved to Maryland but ultimately returned to England (VI&A 736; LEO 7).

John Westropp (Westhope, Westhrope): In 1644 John Westropp served as a burgess, representing Charles City County. His only surviving patent, which dates to November 1653, was for 600 acres near Burchen Swamp, on the south side of the James River in what was then Charles City County, but later Prince George. When Westropp made his will on September 24, 1655, he identified himself as a London merchant. He left a large sum of money to Martin's Hundred Parish so that the vestry could repair the existing church or build a new one on the same ground. He bequeathed to the parish his own "Great Bible" and a copy of Bishop Andrewe's sermons, texts that were in his house in Virginia, and left the parish some tobacco that could be used to purchase a communion cup. The testator gave four cows to John Sadler, one of the merchants who had invested in the Virginia plantations known as Merchant's Hope and Martin's Brandon, and identified him as his father, perhaps his stepfather. He bequeathed a cow to Thomas, the son of Walter Cooper (Couper), who then lived in the mainland near Jamestown. Westropp left his servants, Joshua Clarke and Thomas Smith, part of their time, and bequeathed his goods in England to his sisters, Anner (the wife of Edmond Beckford), Frances (the wife of Edward Henshaw), Bridget (the wife of Richard Bickerton), and Dorothy (the wife of Mark Gibson). He gave to his sister, Judith (the wife of William Thomas), and his other sisters the shipment of goods he had aboard a ship that was bound for Virginia. Court testimony taken in Charles City County on March 3, 1656, reveals that Major John Westropp died in Virginia and that he probably was ill prior to his death. Three men who visited Westropp's home asked him whether he had made a will. Westropp indicated that he had done so but wanted to make a new one. He nominated Captain Richard Tye, Charles Sparrow, and Francis Grey as overseers, and later, Sparrow and Captain Thomas Stegg II officiated as administrators. If Westropp did indeed make a new will, it seems to have been lost or destroyed, for on June 12, 1656, his original will, which named another group of overseers, was proved in London (LEO 22; PB 3:54; SR 3130; Charles City County Order Book 1655–1658:41, 80).

Ferdinando Weyman (Weynman, Wayneman): Sir Ferdinando Weyman, an investor in the Virginia Company, went to Virginia with incoming Governor Thomas West, Lord Delaware, and arrived in Jamestown in June 1610. Delaware immediately appointed him master of the ordnance and named him to his council. Weyman died before the end of the year (VI&A 738).

Thomas Whaley: On February 10, 1677, Governor William Berkeley issued a proclamation in which he named those who were exempt from the king's pardon on account of their role in Bacon's Rebellion. Among those named was Thomas Whaley, a major in the rebel Nathaniel Bacon's army, who was supposed to be brought before a court. His property also was confiscated. Surviving records indicate that he had been in Virginia since the late 1630s. Thomas Whaley's son, James, a merchant, married Mary, the daughter of Mathew Page I and the niece of Colonel John Page, sometime prior to November 1695 (NEVILLE 61; York County Deeds, Administrations, Bonds 2 [1701–1713]:235–236; Deeds, Orders, Wills [1691–1694]:103; SR 660, 749, 10010).

Wharoy (Native American): On May 27, 1658, Wharoy, one of the Rappahannock Indians' Great Men or leaders, was among the natives confirming a land transaction made by the Rappahannock's late king, Accapataugh, and Colonel Moore Fauntleroy (Old Rappahannock County Deed Book 1656–1664: 26–27).

Nevett (Nevet, Neuett, Nevit) Wheeler: Nevett Wheeler arrived in Charles City County sometime prior to the late 1650s, when he testified that he had received the tobacco another man paid to some merchants as rent. He appeared in court in March 1664 to make a claim against one of his servants, who had run away. He went to court from time to time, pursuing debtors and responding to his own creditors' claims, and he also served on juries. In 1673 Wheeler and two other men ran afoul of the law when they initiated a brawl with two others outside of the Charles City courthouse. On March 15, 1677, Nevett Wheeler, an alleged supporter of the rebel Nathaniel Bacon, was put on trial at Green Spring plantation, Governor William Berkeley's home. He availed himself of the king's pardon and took an oath of loyalty (Charles City County Order Book 1661–1664:316; 1664–1665:490; 1672–1674:503, 525, 528–530, 537, 543; MCGC 458, 531; SR 6618c).

Jabez Whitaker (Whittaker, Whitakers): In November 1619 Jabez Whitaker, the Rev.

Alexander Whitaker's brother, was put in charge of some Virginia Company tenants and servants who were being sent to the land set aside for the Company's use. Because the men arrived in the midwinter and were unaccustomed to frontier living conditions, half were assigned to established planters and the other half were assigned to the Company Land in James City, where Whitaker had built a guesthouse to shelter newcomers. By February 1624 he and his wife, Mary, had moved to Elizabeth City, a community he commenced representing in the assembly. In 1626 Jabez Whitaker was appointed to the Council of State (VI&A 739–740; LEO 5).

Richard Whitaker (Whittaker): In 1666 Richard Whitaker, a resident of Warwick County, purchased 135 acres of land in James City County, acreage at Grices Run's head that formerly belonged to Thomas Loving. Three years later Whitaker sold his property to David Crafford, who by that time had bought 86 acres from Loving. In 1671 the churchwardens of Martin's Hundred Parish took Richard Whitaker to court on a charge of bastardry. The General Court ordered him to maintain the child and to reimburse Martin's Hundred Parish's churchwardens for what they had spent on the youngster's upkeep. During 1671 and 1672 Whitaker engaged in a land dispute with some of his neighbors in Warwick County. At issue was a 650-acre parcel near Skiff's Creek that he and John Saunders both claimed. Ultimately the General Court ordered Whitaker to have John Underhill survey 150 acres near Mr. Harwood's old field in Warwick County. He also was to have Underhill survey a 100-acre parcel adjoining that of Anthony Haynes. Afterward, Whitaker was to notify his neighbors if surplus land was found in either of those plots. A suit undertaken in 1671 and 1672 by a Dr. Burgany and his wife, Jane, suggests that Richard Whitaker's wife and Jane Burgany were the sisters of Captain Robert Pyland. William Bogue (Boague), an attorney, persuaded the General Court's judges to require Whitaker to present an account of the Pyland estate, listing the distributions he had made on the decedent's behalf. In October 1674 Whitaker went to court, where he acknowledged a £15 debt to Lieutenant Colonel William Farrar II of Henrico County. Whitaker's name frequently appeared in the records of nearby York County, where he collected debts, settled estates, bought and sold land, and served as an attorney, executor, and court-appointed administrator. In December 1675 he appeared before the justices of York

County's monthly court and verified Josias Stacy's power of attorney. In 1679 Whitaker, who was identified as a resident of Warwick County, was granted a commission of administration for York's clerk of court, Thomas Finney, who had made a nuncupative will and named him as primary beneficiary. Richard Whitaker served as a burgess, representing Warwick County in the assembly sessions held in 1680–1682, 1685–1686, 1688, 1691–1693, and 1695–1696. By 1691 he had become a county justice, and in 1696 he left the assembly when he was designated Warwick County's high sheriff. He also served as a military officer. In 1678 he recorded the taxes that had been collected in Warwick County during the year, and in 1691 he made an account of the muskets that had been issued to local military men. In 1687 Whitaker went to court to settle a disagreement with Benjamin Brock, a neighbor with whom he clashed over ownership of some land and cattle. In 1690 he admitted that he was indebted to John Meade, a merchant. By 1698 Richard Whitaker was deceased and his widow, Elizabeth, was serving as his executrix (LEO 46, 48–49, 51, 55, 57; PB10:341; NUG III:195; MCGC 246, 248, 261, 265, 273–274, 307–308; STAN 85, 86, 91; DUNN 2000:1, 43, 49–50, 56, 75, 185, 187, 193; York County Deeds, Orders, Wills 5:138, 199; 7:245, 250–251, 256, 262, 293, 295; 8:207; 14:72, 79).

Walter Whitaker (Whittaker): In March 1674 Walter Whitaker, who was a doctor, began serving as a justice of the Middlesex County court. He also was a captain in the county militia, and in 1671 he was Middlesex's high sheriff. From 1669 to 1676 he represented Middlesex County in the assembly. In 1676 and 1677, while Bacon's Rebellion was in progress, he remained loyal to Governor William Berkeley. As a result, he was captured by Nathaniel Bacon's men and imprisoned for two days. Later he and William Ball claimed that Major Robert Beverley I had freed a Middlesex County shoemaker named Bentley, who was a Bacon supporter. During the summer of 1677 he provided shipboard medical care to the acting governor, Herbert Jeffreys, who was suffering from ague (malaria). In May 1678 Whitaker used his plantation, Abraham's Neck, and all of his servants, livestock, and household furnishings as collateral when covering debts to the acting governor's brother, London merchant John Jeffreys. In October 1684 Whitaker, who was age 45, testified in court about a man who died at Colonel Richard Lee's house on the Poropotank River. He said that as a physician, he had attended the decedent and been present when he made a nuncupative will. Whitaker, who in 1686 served another term as Middlesex County's high sheriff, sued Edward Chilton of Jamestown. Dr. Whittaker died between December 1691 and September 1692, at which time his widow, Sibella (Sybella, Sebellah), presented his nuncupative will, which was proved by the oaths of witnesses. Afterward, three local officials convened at the decedent's house to make an inventory of his estate. Mrs. Whitaker was granted administration of her late husband's estate (LEO 38; Middlesex County Order Book 1673–1680:4, 26, 110, 128–131; 1680–1694:16, 40, 76, 177, 241, 252, 533, 562, 575; SR 661, 6402, 6618c).

William Whitaker (Whittaker): William Whitaker began representing James City County in the assembly in 1649 and held office until 1660. During the mid-to-late 1650s he was a captain and then a lieutenant colonel in the local militia. In June 1656 he laid claim to 90 acres in eastern James City County, acreage that abutted Thomas Loving's boundary lines and lay behind Robert Leonard's house. Whitaker was named to the Council of State in 1659. In 1673 the General Court authorized William Whitaker to patent any unclaimed "waste land" he could find between the parcels owned by Robert Harres and William Buckes, whose acreage straddled the boundary line between James City and York counties. He died in Virginia sometime after that time (STAN 67–70, 72, 74; HEN I:358–359, 506–507; LEO 27, 29–33, 35; NUG I:317, 471; MCGC 329).

* * *

William Whitby (Whittby, Whittbey) I: William Whitby I arrived in Virginia sometime prior to 1642, when he took office as a burgess, representing Warwick County. He was returned to the assembly in 1644 and served from 1652 to 1655. During the 1640s he also was a Warwick County justice. Whitby owned some land near the mouth of Waters Creek. During the 1640s he invested in some property at the head of Tindall's Creek, acreage near Gloucester Point that he and George Ludlow had bought from Argoll Yeardley. In May 1646 Whitby confirmed the sale of his Gloucester property to Richard Lee I. In July 1653, while Whitby was representing Warwick County in the assembly, he replaced Walter Chiles I as speaker. As time went on, he patented literally thousands of acres of land in Warwick County, on the Middle Peninsula and in the Northern

Neck. In 1653 he witnessed a document acknowledging that Sir William Berkeley and his wife, Lady Frances, had received 26 oxen from Colonel Francis Yeardley of Lower Norfolk County. Whitby also tried to recover some funds that the late Captain John Sipsey of Lower Norfolk County had owed him. A March 30, 1655, land transaction reveals that William Whitby I had rented a row house in urban Jamestown, part of a three-bay structure that Sir William Berkeley had built in the capital city around 1645. Although it is uncertain when Whitby began leasing the property and when he ceased, it probably was during the early 1650s, when the Commonwealth government was in power and he was serving in the assembly. Whitby died sometime prior to April 1670, leaving a widow, Katherine, and a teenage son, William II. On May 26, 1671, Katherine Whitby was sued by Theophilus Hone of Jamestown (NUG I:80, 224, 229, 258; HEN I:353, 375, 378, 386–387, 407; MCGC 215, 262, 278, 415, 425, 503; JHB 1619–1660:92, 97; STAN 70; DUNN 17–19, 22, 24–26, 163, 170–171, 445; Lower Norfolk County Record Book C:64, 66; LEO 20, 22, 29–32; York County Record Book 2 [1633–1646]:125).

William Whitby (Whittby, Whittbey) II: William Whitby II, the orphaned son of William Whitby I, burgess, speaker of the assembly, and one-time tenant of Sir William Berkeley, chose Thomas Todd as his guardian. In 1675 the General Court's justices decided the late William Whitby I's land could not be sold to pay his debts until his son came of age. They noted, however, that the youth's majority was close at hand and that although he formerly had been one of Robert Beverley's servants (probably Robert Beverley I), he was free, having fulfilled his term of indenture. By March 1676 William Whitby II had come of age. He was ordered to examine his late father's accounts so that a dispute with John Harlow could be settled. The General Court's justices also informed him that William Whitby I had some of William Haddock's money in his possession at the time of his death. When William Whitby II made his will in 1676, he identified himself as a Middlesex County planter who lived on the Piankatank River. He made bequests to several people, giving them tracts of land in Warwick, Stafford, and Old Rappahannock counties. One of Whitby's legatees was Major Robert Beverley, whom he designated as one of his executors. William Whitby II's will was proved in July 1677 (MCGC 215, 262, 278, 415, 425, 442; SR 3998; Middlesex County Order Book 1673–1680:74).

* * *

George White: On October 20, 1617, George White was tried in Jamestown and was pardoned for having fled to the Indians, taking weaponry (VI&A 741).

Jeremy (Jereme) White (Whitt): During the mid-1620s Jeremy White, a servant in Edward Blaney's household, was living on the lower side of the James River. On August 28, 1626, Thomas Passmore's widow, Joanne or Jane, informed the General Court that she preferred to employ Jeremy White, a servant then living in her Jamestown Island household, to the maidservant Mrs. Margaret West had taken from her. White, who was part of the late Thomas Passmore's estate, was supposed to serve Mrs. Passmore until December 1, 1627 (VI&A 741).

John White: On August 28, 1644, John White, a London merchant who spent much of his time in Virginia, received a patent for a one-acre lot in urban Jamestown, next to the churchyard. His patent noted that if he or his assignees failed to improve the property, it would revert to the Crown. White represented "James City" (James City County or Jamestown) in the January 12, 1641, session of the colony's assembly, an indication that he or his wife was a property owner. In June 1640 Richard Popeley (who had land in Middle Plantation) and Thomas Harvey (whose property lay just west of the Governor's Land) were ordered to pay their debts to John White. He seems to have had business dealings with the prominent merchant and councilor George Menefie of Jamestown, who in his December 31, 1645, will left "to Jo: White, Merchant, £10, provided he continue one year longer in Virginia and collect my debts as formerly." The business relationship between Menefie and White suggests that they may have been tied into the same trading network. On September 14, 1646, White, who was then in London and serving as factor for Robert Sheppard of Chippokes in Surry County, informed Sheppard that 17 Dutch ships and 8 larger vessels were then enroute to Virginia with goods to trade. In 1654 Sheppard's widow, the former Elizabeth Spencer, signed a marriage contract with Thomas Warren, authorizing White "to have and enjoy all the estate of Major Robert Sheppard, deceased, now in the possession of the said Elizabeth, his relict" with certain minor exceptions. This may explain when and how John White and Thomas Warren came to be next-door neighbors in Jamestown and probable co-owners of a building that straddles their property line. On October 17, 1654, White, who was then in England, sought official permission to send some merchandise to Virginia on a Dutch ship, the *Peace* of Amsterdam. Again, he was described as a merchant. In December 1649 John White "of James [City] Parish in Virginia, merchant," disposed of some land at the falls of the James River, acreage later owned by Thomas Stegg I and William Byrd I and his descendants. All three of the men who witnessed White's deed were recently arrived royalists who had been befriended by Sir William Berkeley; therefore, John White most likely was loyal to the Crown and to Governor Berkeley.

Official records reveal that John White was killed in Jamestown during Bacon's Rebellion, probably in mid-September 1676 when Nathaniel Bacon's men attacked the capital city. It was then that the rebel army fortified a position on the isthmus leading to Jamestown Island, facing the palisades that Governor Berkeley's men had erected 100 to 150 paces away. On September 14th Berkeley's loyalists made an assault on Bacon's men but were obliged to retreat, and several of Berkeley's men were killed in the foray. On February 20, 1677, Mrs. Mary White asked the assembly for compensation because her husband, John, had lost his life in Jamestown while in service to the king. White, when defending Jamestown, would have been under the command of his near-neighbor, Colonel Robert Holt. Although very little reliable genealogical information has come to light about merchant John White of Jamestown, he may have been a sibling of London haberdasher William White, who in 1676 left £10 to his brother, John, then in Virginia. He also may have been a kinsman of the late Captain John White of Surry County, who died prior to March 1675 (PB 2:10–11; NUG I:154; AND 71; WITH 149, 180, 194; CO 1/12 f 74; SR 633; MCGC 407, 413, 471; Surry County Deeds, Wills &c. 1 [1652–1672]:60; 2 [1672–1691]:140, 203; DOR 3:227; HLOP 1625–1641:113; STAN 61; JHB 1660–1693:69; FOR I:11:24–25; LEO 20).

John White: John White was the son and heir of Captain John White of Surry County. In March 1675 Captain White's son, John, and John's brother-in-law, Robert Spencer, tried to recover their share of the late Captain White's estate. Captain John White's widow, Mary, married William Corker of Jamestown. When John White of Surry County prepared his will on April 1, 1679, he made bequests to his sister Mary White and stepsister Lucy Corker, but did not mention his sister Elizabeth White, who had married Captain Robert Spencer. White's will was presented for probate on May 6, 1679 (Surry County Deeds, Wills &c. 2 [1672–

1691]:140, 203).

John White: On August 8, 1687, John White witnessed the will of John Holder, owner of a lot in urban Jamestown. According to records of the Council of State, on May 12, 1693, White was paid for ringing the bell that summoned council members to meetings. Two months later he asked to be appointed door-keeper for the assembly. His availability to perform these duties, which would have required his presence in Jamestown on a regular basis, raises the possibility that he was residing there (LJC 143; JHB 1660–1693:442; AMB 38).

William White: William White, a laborer, came to Virginia in 1607 in the first group of Jamestown colonists (VI&A 742).

William White: When George Ludlow of York County made his will on September 8, 1655, he bequeathed his sixteenth-part interest in the ship *Mayflower* to Thomas Bushrod and noted that Captain William White was then the ship's commander (SR 3131). White, a trader to Virginia, may have been the same individual who by the 1670s had settled in urban Jamestown.

William White: William White, a highly successful merchant and planter who moved to Jamestown during the 1670s, patented literally thousands of acres of land in counties throughout eastern Virginia during the 1660s, 1670s, and early 1680s. His landholdings included acreage on the lower side of the James River, in Surry, Lower Norfolk, and Isle of Wight counties. By 1668 he had wed the widow of William Barbribb of Surry County. White took an active role in public life. In 1671 he was ordered to inventory the estate of Jamestown resident and landowner Thomas Hunt, and in 1672 he received funds for the construction of a brick fort in the capital city. In November 1673 Hubert Farrell and Mrs. Tabitha Bowler, who reportedly were visiting William White's house in Jamestown, began squabbling and exchanging insults. Later, Mrs. Bowler's husband sued Farrell for slandering her. During 1674 some runaway servants absconded from Jamestown in a boat they stole from William White.

On February 6, 1677, Major William White bought the late William May's home and two half-acre lots abutting Back Street in urban Jamestown. When surveyor John Soane made a plat of William Sherwood's property in 1681, he depicted White's house, which he indicated was at a location analogous to a site where archaeologists have found the remains of a dwelling. Because White commenced residing in Jamestown sometime prior to 1673, he may have begun renting the late William May's dwelling shortly after May's death, which occurred between 1671 and 1673. In 1677 William White was ordered to recover and inventory the estate of an absconded rebel, Jamestown innkeeper and surveyor Richard Lawrence. From 1680 to 1682 White, who had attained the rank of colonel, served as a burgess representing James City, probably Jamestown. As church warden of James City Parish, he requested funds from the assembly so that the church, which had been torched by Bacon's rebels, could be rebuilt. In August 1682 the will of Colonel William White of Jamestown was presented for probate. Because White's widow, Jane, had left the colony, London merchant and Jamestown lot owner Micajah Perry was named administrator of the decedent's Virginia estate. On September 20, 1686, escheator John Page held an inquisition in order to determine whether the late Colonel White's Jamestown lots should revert to the Crown. The jurymen who deliberated the matter decided that since White had no heirs living in Virginia and had neither sold nor bequeathed his lots to anyone, the property should be considered abandoned. For that reason both parcels were declared escheat land (AMB 25, 36, 134; NUG I:510, II:24, 64, 225, 233; Surry County Deeds, Wills &c. 1 [1652–1672]:351; 2 [1671–1691]:180; Order Book 1671–1690:13; MCGC 252, 271, 318, 335, 368, 382; CO 5/1371 f 247; JHB 1660–1693:120, 128, 151; LEO 45; EEAC 63).

William White I: When William White I, a haberdasher of St. Brides in London, England, prepared his will in November 1676, he made bequests to his brother, John White, and his own son, William White II, who were then in Virginia (WITH 194).

William White: When William White of Surry County made his will on September 1, 1677, he left a heifer and some clothing to Thomas and William Smith. He bequeathed the remainder of his personal estate to his wife, whom he failed to identify (Surry County Deeds, Wills &c. 2 [1671–1691]:153).

Robert Whitehed (Whitehead?): On April 4, 1625, it was reported that Robert Whitehed was deceased and that Nathaniel Jeffreys of Jamestown had been one of his servants (VI&A 742).

* * *

Christian Whithelme (Whitehelm, Withelm) I: Christian Whithelme I, a Dutch vinegar-maker who moved to England and became a galley-pot maker (delftware potter) and distiller of aquavitae, unsuccessfully sought the right to be the sole producer of smalt, the cobalt blue pigment used in decorating tin-glazed pottery and in starch. He decided to cut his losses by investing in the production of potash, one of the principal compounds used in smalt-making. Whithelme's March 1629 will reveals that he had joined Virginia's governor, Sir John Harvey of Jamestown, in investing in the production of soap ashes, potashes, and other commodities. Whithelme specified that his estate was to be divided equally between his son, Christian II, who was then in Virginia, and his son-in-law, Thomas Townsend. He died within a month of making his will (VI&A 743).

Christian Whithelme (Whitehelm, Withelm) II: Christian Whithelme II was the son of galley-pot maker Christian Whithelme I, a Dutch artisan living in England. When the elder man made his will in March 1629, he indicated that his son, who was living in Virginia, was to get half of his estate unless he returned from overseas "lewd, bad and not obedient" (VI&A 743).

* * *

Henry Whiting (Whiteing): Henry Whiting, who was born in England, settled in Gloucester County. In May 1672 he purchased two plantations in Middlesex County from the Rev. James Wadding, then rector of Gloucester's Ware Parish. In February 1674 Whiting and his wife, Aphia, sold both parcels to John Armistead of Kingston Parish. In 1672, when the original transaction occurred, Whiting was identified as a surgeon. He was among those who heard witnesses testify against Colonel Philip Ludwell I in 1678. Whiting served in the assembly from 1680 to 1684 and was married to the daughter of Peter Beverley, Gloucester County's clerk of court. Between 1682 and 1686 Whiting and John Buckner secured three large patents in Gloucester County. In 1682 the two men acquired 2,673 acres in the vicinity of Cow Creek and the North River, and in 1686 they patented two more tracts in the same vicinity, consisting of 280 acres and 2,400 acres. During the early 1680s Major Henry Whiting was censured for supporting the planters who destroyed much of Virginia's tobacco crop in an attempt to elevate prices. In 1683 officials in England responded by banning him from

holding all public offices. However, by 1690 the political climate had changed and Whiting was named to the Council of State, on which he served from 1691 to 1694. He also was Virginia's treasurer from 1692 to 1693. In 1694 Essex County's justices noted that Colonel Whiting was Mathew Nelson's executor. When quitrent rolls were compiled in 1704, Henry Whiting (perhaps the colonel's son) was credited with paying taxes on 800 acres in Gloucester County's Ware Parish, whereas Madam Whiting paid the taxes that were owed on 950 acres. Colonel Whiting also was credited with a Gloucestertown lot in 1707 (STAN 24, 42; LEO xxi, 45, 47; Essex County Order Book 1692–1695:190, 210; Deeds and Wills 1692–1695:319, 340; SR 181, 6618c; EJC I:39, 41, 193, 251, 266, 472–474, 493, 530; Middlesex County Order Book 1673–1680:40; SMITH 97).

Robert Whitmore: Robert Whitmore, a youth detained in Bridewell Prison, went to Virginia in 1620. In February 1624 he was a servant in the urban Jamestown household of merchant Edward Blaney, but by the following year he had relocated to Blaney's plantation on the lower side of the James River (VI&A 743).

John Whitson (Whitsen): John Whitson became a resident of Surry County sometime prior to June 1668, when he was listed as a tithe living in the territory between the Smith's Fort plantation and College Run. A year later he and Arthur Long had some business dealings with merchant George Foxwell, which culminated in an appearance before Surry's justices. When tax lists were compiled, Whitson was listed with his father-in-law, Robert Spencer, the husband of Captain John White's daughter Elizabeth. In July 1671 Spencer executed a deed of gift, which bestowed some livestock on his granddaughter, Martha Whitson, specifying that the child's father, John Whitson, was obliged to give her a like amount. Robert Spencer indicated that Whitson had been married to his daughter Anne, who was then deceased. A little over a year later, Spencer went to court to seek custody of his granddaughter, Martha, claiming that her father's behavior had put her at risk. On September 14, 1672, Whitson received a patent for 200 acres near the head of Grays Creek. In 1673 he paid taxes on a free white male who resided at the Ware Neck mill, which Whitson was renting from Colonel Thomas Swann I. In 1674 Swann sued Whitson for breach of contract, claiming that he had failed to finish a house he had agreed to build. Swann also sued him in an attempt to recover some funds. In late 1675 Whitson was ordered to appear before the General Court to answer a complaint made by one of his servants. On March 16, 1677, Whitson, a supporter of the rebel Nathaniel Bacon, was put on trial at Green Spring plantation, Governor William Berkeley's home. He was found guilty and sentenced to death. Afterward, his real and personal estate was inventoried and then confiscated. By 1690 Whitson's 200 acres near the head of Grays Creek had been granted to William Wray, whose wife, Mary, was identified as the late John Whitson's only daughter. The patent to Wray noted that Whitson had been executed as a participant in Bacon's Rebellion and that his land had escheated to the Crown (MCGC 459, 531–532; SR 749; Surry County Deed Book 1 [1652–1671]:315, 326, 345, 373, 390; Deeds, Wills &c. 5 [1694–1709]:235, 413; Order Book 1671–1691:11, 33, 73, 103, 106, 137, 266; PB 8:87–88).

William Whittington II: In October 1661 William Whittington II repatented the 800 acres in Accomack County that his late father, Captain William Whittington I, had claimed in March 1653 and bequeathed to him in May 1659, along with the rest of his landholdings. In October 1669 William Whittington II patented 3,600 acres abutting the seaside of the Eastern Shore peninsula, acreage that also included some of his late father's property. During the 1670s and 1680s he continued to acquire large tracts of land on the Eastern Shore, including Gengoteague (Chincoteague) Island, which he patented in its entirety. William Whittington II served as a burgess representing Northampton County from 1680 to 1682. In 1687 he sent a petition to the Council of Maryland, alleging that some people were planning to take up land on Assoawagen (possibly Assawoman) Island utilizing Virginia patents. He pointed out that the island was in Maryland, although a boundary line with Virginia had not been established. William Whittington II's sisters or half-sisters were named Urselie and Elizabeth (LEO 46; PB 3:286; 4:506; 6:256, 421, 439; 7:526, 633; SR 1942; MARSHALL 60, 63).

John Whitty: Richard James I of Jamestown was indebted to Captain John Whitty, a London mariner who was involved in business dealings with several residents of the capital city and Surry County. One of Whitty's close friends was the Rev. Philip Mallory, who had lived in Virginia but by 1661 had returned to London. Mallory made his will in 1661, naming Captain John Whitty as an executor. When Whitty died in the late 1660s, he owed money to Thomas Ludwell

and William Drummond I, both of whom lived in urban Jamestown. In May 1671 the General Court noted that Whitty's widow, Susan, was planning to marry Jamestown lot owner William Corker. She was the daughter of Arthur Blackmore of St. Gregory in London. In 1672 Major Theophilus Hone of Jamestown placed a lien against the late Captain John Whitty's estate (MCGC 215, 218, 257, 270, 318; Surry County Deed Book 1 [1652–1671]:23, 26, 30; SR 3521).

James Wickham: On February 24, 1623, James Wickham, a servant in Dr. John Pott's household in urban Jamestown, was involved in killing and dressing a stolen calf (VI&A 744).

William Wickham: In March 1618 Deputy Governor Samuel Argall said that he would like Mr. William Wickham to be ordained, although his eyesight was poor and he needed someone to read to him. Wickham was a councilor in 1619 when Sir George Yeardley commenced serving as governor (VI&A 744; LEO xxi).

King of the Wicocomoco (Wecocomaka) and the Chicacoan Indians (Native American) (see King of the Chicacoan and the Wicocomoco Indians)

Richard Wiffin (Wyffing, Wyffin): Richard Wiffin, a gentleman and Virginia Company investor, arrived in Jamestown in early 1608 in the 1st Supply of new settlers. Captain John Smith authorized Richard Wiffin and Sergeant Jeffrey Abbott to capture and kill the Dutchmen who had fled to the Indians. Wiffin was coauthor of a verse that accompanied Smith's *Proceedings* (VI&A 744).

Peter Wilcocke: On July 22, 1640, Peter Wilcocke was identified as a runaway servant in the employ of William Peirce of urban Jamestown (MCGC 467).

Edward Wigg: Edward Wigg came to Virginia in 1621 and settled at Basses Choice. He seems to have been associated with several Jamestown residents, notably merchant Edward Sharples, Abraham Porter, John Jackson, Robert Hutchinson, and George Ungwin. In 1629 Wigg married one of Stephen Barker's maidservants and by the 1630s he had become a planter (VI&A 744–745).

John Wilcox (Wilcocks, Wilcocke, Wilcockes): John Wilcox, who was from Plymouth, England, came to Virginia in 1620 and shortly after his arrival established a plantation on the Virginia Company's land on the

Eastern Shore. On September 10, 1622, when he was preparing to go on a march against the Indians, he prepared his will. He made bequests to his wife and executrix, Temperance, to his sisters Katherin and Susana Wilcox, and to his stepdaughter, Grace Burges. Captain Wilcox survived the offensive against the Indians. He continued to live on the Eastern Shore and in 1624 represented that area as a burgess. In March 1627 he asked for 500 acres on the upper side of Old Plantation Creek. By January 21, 1628, he was dead, reportedly having perished while crossing the Chesapeake Bay (VI&A 745; SR 3117; LEO 5).

John Wilcox: In 1656 John Wilcox served as a burgess, representing Nansemond County (LEO 33). No patents have come to light that disclose where Wilcox was living. He may have been the same individual who moved to Northampton County and began serving as a burgess in 1658.

John Wilcox (Willcox, Willcocks, Wilcocks): In 1658, while the Commonwealth government was in power, John Wilcox represented Northampton County in the assembly. He married Captain Argoll Yeardley's widow, the former Anne Custis, sometime after October 1655 and purchased a 400-acre plantation in 1660. On May 7, 1661, Wilcox, a resident of Hungars Parish, made his will and named as heirs his wife, Anne, and her children, Henry and Edward Yeardley. He left his wife life-rights in his entire estate, which was to descend to the child she was then expecting. In the event of the child's death, his stepsons Henry and Edward Yeardley were to inherit his property. The testator made provisions for Henry and Edward Yeardley's brother, Argoll II, and noted that John Custis II was his stepsons' uncle. Wilcox added a codicil to his will on May 23, 1662, shortly before he died, again naming as an heir the child with whom his wife was pregnant. He also bequeathed 200 acres to any offspring that his own brother, Henry, might have. John Wilcox died sometime prior to May 28, 1662, at which time his will was proved. Parish records reveal that John and Anne Wilcox's son, William, was born on July 21, 1662. The widowed Anne Custis Wilcox appears to have married John Luke. She died sometime prior to October 20, 1686 (LEO 34; DOR 3:866; MARSHALL 45, 68–69; Northampton County Deeds, Wills &c. 7 [1657–1666]:117; PB 7:533; STAN 74; HEN I:429).

Daniel Wild (Wilde, Wyld): Daniel Wild patented a large tract of land in York County

in June 1654, securing 750 acres with co-investor Philip Chesley. Two years later he witnessed a document whereby Robert Wild (probably a kinsman) sold some land to Chesley. Daniel Wild was fined in 1661 for failing to appear in court. In 1662 he patented 1,484 acres on the Old Mill Swamp, near the head of Queens Creek. The following year he and James City County sheriff Francis Kirkman patented 2,000 acres on the south side of the Potomac River, near Yeocomoco Creek. From 1669 to 1671 Wild served as a burgess and represented York County in the assembly. Among those with whom he had complex business dealings were merchant and physician George Lee (of Jamestown, Surry County, and London) and Lee's factor, John Bowler. Court testimony aired in England in 1669 reveals that Lee entrusted the oversight of his plantation to Bowler, who died while on a trip to England. Bowler's mother and administrator designated Daniel Wild as her attorney and made him responsible for Lee's property. However, Lee was dissatisfied with the arrangement and initiated a lawsuit. Court testimony reveals that Wild had three plantations of his own, some cattle and household goods, and a share in 12 black servants. Like many of his contemporaries, he was occasionally involved in litigation, usually over debt. In 1672 he became embroiled in a land dispute with Robert Bullock of Warwick County. When Captain Wild's business partner Philip Chesley prepared his will in 1674, he named Wild and his sister, Margaret, as heirs. On October 25, 1676, Daniel Wild made his will, indicating that he was a resident of Bruton Parish in York County, Virginia, but was then in Stepney Parish, Middlesex, England. He left his Queens Creek plantations to his married daughter, Margaret, the wife of John Martin, a mariner from Ratclyff in Middlesex. He also named the Martin couple as his executors and gave them all of his real and personal property in Virginia. He stipulated that if neither his daughter nor her husband lived to inherit his estate, it was to be divided among Nicholas Harrison of London and his children. The testator indicated that his servant and apprentice, Valentine Harvey, was then occupying his property in Virginia, and he named several other people as heirs. One was his widowed sister, Margaret Wild Chichley of London. Daniel Wild died sometime prior to October 25, 1676, when his married daughter, Margaret, presented his will to probate officials in England. After Wild's death, George Lee brought suit against his estate in an attempt to recover the value of the property Bowler had left in the decedent's hands.

By that time, both John and Margaret Wild Martin were dead (LEO 40; PB 3:274; 5:239; 6:123; York County Deeds, Orders, Wills 1 [1648–1657]:281; 3 [1657–1662]:1; SR 3354, 3561, 3751, 10429, 11482, 12555; MCGC 312, 321, 326–327, 343, 352, 368).

Robert Wilde: In June 1610 Lord Delaware appointed Robert Wilde as master of the store in Jamestown, a job that gave him the responsibility of distributing provisions and supplies. He left Virginia but returned to the colony in July 1622 (VI&A 747). There is no known connection between this individual and the Robert Wild who resided in York County during the early 1640s and served as the parish clerk.

Bishop Wiles: Bishop Wiles, a laborer, came to Virginia in the 1st Supply of new settlers and arrived in Jamestown in 1608 (VI&A 747).

Thomas Wilford (Wilsford, Willsford): In 1651–1652 Thomas Wilford served as a burgess, representing Northumberland County. By that time he had purchased some land on Perry's Creek, at Cherry Point Neck. In 1655 he was among those responsible for collecting taxes in the county. When acquiring another piece of property in 1655, he indicated that he was age 39. He owned land in Westmoreland County and appeared before the county's justices in February 1654. In June 1656, shortly after Wilford married Margaret, the widow of John Browne of Maryland, he executed a deed of trust, assigning his plantation at Appomattox in Westmoreland County to his trustee, Job Chandler, a Marylander, along with part of his personal property. In August 1658 Wilford executed two deeds of gift, conveying two calves to his son, Andrew, and one to his stepdaughter, Sarah Browne. John Washington I was then young Sarah's guardian and conservator of her late father's estate. In January 1662 Thomas Wilford, who identified himself as a "reader to the parish" or vestry clerk, presented the justices of Westmoreland County with a list of the christenings and burials that had taken place in Appomattox Parish during 1661. From time to time he served as an attorney, and in 1663 he was made clerk of Westmoreland County's court. When proving the late Thomas Foulke's will on June 24, 1663, Wilford, who identified himself as a notary public, said that he was age 45 and had prepared the testator's will. Wilford served as the late Richard Heaberd's trustee and made two land transactions on behalf of the decedent's widow. When Thomas Wilford made his

own will on September 1, 1666, he left the property he had bought from John Watts to his son Andrew. He bequeathed to sons Andrew and James equal shares of the plantation at Appomattox on which the family then lived; he also stipulated that if Andrew died without heirs, his share would descend to son Thomas. Wilford's will was proved on September 11, 1667. In March 1672 Colonel St. Leger Codd sought custody of Thomas Wilford's orphan and the estate he stood to inherit. The child, whose name and age are unknown, was thought to be mentally disabled. When the General Court convened later in the year, they decided to return the orphan to his former guardian, Mr. John Watts, who also was to be entrusted with his inheritance (LEO 28; MCGC 294, 307; Northumberland County Wills, Inventories &c.1652–1658:21, 50, 80, 95–95, 128; Deeds and Wills 1670–1672:164; Order Book 1652–1665:3, 64; Westmoreland County Deeds, Wills, Patents &c. 1653–1659:15, 56–57, 112a–113; Deeds, Wills &c. 1661–1662:2a, 39, 53a, 54a; Deeds and Wills No. 1 [1653–1671]:196–197, 232–233, 315–316; Orders 1662–1664:16, 23a).

Thomas Wilford (Wilsford, Wilsfoode): During Bacon's Rebellion, which got underway in 1676 and ended in 1677, Captain Thomas Wilford sided with Nathaniel Bacon and was one of his staunchest supporters. According to a contemporary account, Wilford was the second son of a knight and royalist. He was captured by Governor Berkeley's men who ambushed some of the rebels holed up in Captain Thomas Cheesman's house on the York River. During the fight that ensued, Wilford lost one of his eyes. He was described as a small but very courageous man who had spent a number of years serving as an interpreter to the Indians. He also was said to have driven the queen of the Pamunkey Indians and her people from the land they had been given by the assembly. In February 1677 Thomas Wilford was tried in a court martial hearing that was held at Green Spring Plantation, found guilty, and hanged. His estate was subject to seizure, and he was declared exempt from the king's pardon (AND 80–81; HEN II:370; NEVILLE 61, 274; SR 658, 660, 749, 6618c).

John Wilkins (Wilkines): John Wilkins came to Virginia in 1618 and settled on the Eastern Shore with his wife, Bridgett. He became a commissioner of the Accomack court in 1633 and two years later became a vestryman. Although he invested in land on the Nansemond River, he quickly sold it and patented two large tracts in Accomack near Kings Creek. Sometime after 1634 but before September 1637, he remarried, taking as his bride a woman named Anne. Over the years Wilkins made numerous appearances in the Accomack County court, sometimes as a plaintiff and sometimes as a defendant. He seems to have had an explosive temper and on at least one occasion was fined for swearing. He served as a burgess for the Eastern Shore in 1641–1642. In 1642 he and a neighboring property owner, Obedience Robins I, made an agreement with Anthony Lynney, a millwright, to build a windmill on their acreage. Over the years Wilkins made trips to England, Amsterdam, and Hamburg. His will, made on December 23, 1649, and proved in January 1651, named his wife, Anne, and his children as heirs. The decedent was around age 57 at the time of his death. His surviving heirs were his married daughter, Mary Baldwin, a child of his first marriage, and daughters Lydia, Anne II, and Frances, the offspring of his second wife. He and his second wife, Anne, also had sons John, Argoll, and Nathaniel (VI&A 747; LEO 20; AMES 1:5–7, 9–10, 13, 19–20, 41–42, 53–54, 59, 67, 77, 83, 96, 98–100, 118, 122–123, 139, 143, 154–155, 163, 165–166, 170, 178, 182, 202, 210, 275–276, 301, 325–326, 407; 2:5, 19, 77, 118, 154–155, 202, 275–276, 325–326, 412–413, 453; Northampton County Orders, Deeds, Wills II:128–129; DOR 1:71; 3:573–575; MARSHALL 26–27).

James Wilkinson (Wilkenson): When the rebel Nathaniel Bacon seized control of Jamestown in 1676, he captured James Wilkinson and the Rev. John Clough, the rector of James City Parish. Bacon condemned both men to death, exercising martial law. He decided to release the clergyman but had Wilkinson executed (SR 6618).

Thomas Wilkinson (Wilkenson): In 1650 Thomas Wilkinson, who was relatively wealthy and successful, acquired 500 acres on the Potomac River, and three years later he claimed 320 acres on the Rappahannock. Finally, in 1658 he patented 6,000 acres on Potomac Creek on the basis of 120 headrights. He may have been the same individual who sometime prior to August 1, 1655, purchased the late Mrs. Elizabeth Fleet's half-acre lot in urban Jamestown from her children's guardian, Thomas Lyne, and later sold the property to Thomas Hunt. Thomas Wilkinson made his will on April 25, 1668, and died several months later. He bequeathed his 6,000 acres on Potomac Creek to his wife, Anne, and daughter, Elizabeth. As it turned out, Elizabeth died and Wilkinson's widow, Anne, married John Goodall of James City County, whom she also outlived

(NUG I:201, 240, 313, 335, 378; PB 3:367; Stafford County Record Book 1686–1693:268–268a).

Thomas Wilkinson: By 1673 Thomas Wilkinson had married the widow of Griffin (Griffeth) Dickenson (Dickeson), the owner of a waterfront lot in urban Jamestown. In October 1667 Dickenson was censured and then fined for building a wharf "before the town" contrary to law (MCGC 344; JHB1660–1693:48; PB 3:367; NUG I:313).

William Wilkinson: William Wilkinson, a surgeon, came to Virginia in 1607 in the first group of Jamestown colonists (VI&A 748).

William Wilkinson: According to John Soane's 1683 plat, William Wilkinson had two leaseholds in the Governor's Land. One comprised 31 acres and the other 25 acres (Soane 1683).

Will: On July 2, 1673, Will, a runaway African slave who belonged to Robert Bryan of Gloucester County, was sentenced to be whipped in Jamestown. Bryan patented some acreage in Gloucester in 1662 and in 1671 laid claim to a large tract in Old Rappahannock County (MCGC 347; PB 5:296; 6:518).

Hugh Willastone (Willeston, Wooleston): Hugh Willastone, a gentleman and Virginia Company investor, arrived in the colony in 1608 in the 2nd Supply of new settlers and lived in Jamestown. He died in Virginia sometime prior to February 2, 1624, having neither wife nor children (VI&A 748).

William: Mr. Pearns' servant, William, died in Jamestown sometime after April 1623 but before February 16, 1624 (VI&A 749).

William (Native American) (see Machywap)

[No First Name] Williams: In 1608 Master Williams, a laborer, came to Virginia in the 2nd Supply of new Jamestown settlers (VI&A 749).

Christopher Williams: On July 22, 1640, Christopher Williams, a servant in William Peirce's household in urban Jamestown, was described as a surgeon and a Dutchman. He came to Virginia sometime prior to 1638 at John George's expense. By 1642 Williams and John Edwards had a leasehold in James City County, in the western part of Governor's Land (MCGC 467; PB 1:2:581, 772).

Edward Williams: Edward Williams came to Virginia in 1624 and in January 1625 was a servant in merchant George Menefie's household in urban Jamestown (VI&A 749).

Hugh Williams (Winge): Hugh Williams came to Virginia in 1620 and in February 1624 was an indentured servant in William Peirce's household in urban Jamestown. By January 1625 he had moved to Mulberry Island, where he was a servant in the Peirce household. By November 1635 he had acquired and then sold some land on the lower side of the James River in what became Isle of Wight County (VI&A 750; PB 1:1:316).

John Williams: On July 22, 1640, John Williams was described as a runaway servant who belonged to William Peirce of urban Jamestown (MCGC 467).

Richard Williams alias Cornish (see Richard Cornish)

James Williamson: In 1652 James Williamson, a merchant, commenced serving as a burgess for Lancaster County. He had business dealings with firms in Rotterdam and sometimes served as an agent for other Virginia merchants. In 1654 he obtained permission to leave Virginia, but it is unclear whether he ever departed. In 1656 Williamson sold part of a vast tract he owned on the north side of the Rappahannock River and at the same time acquired some additional land. He died intestate sometime prior to December 8, 1656 (LEO 29–30; Lancaster County Deed and Will Book 1652–1657: 1, 84–86, 26, 279–282, 308, 333–334; 1654–1661:17, 36–38, 83, 95, 112).

Robert Williamson I: Between 1662 and 1676 Dr. Robert Williamson I, a physician, represented Isle of Wight County in the assembly. He purchased 350 acres from William Richardson and his wife in 1666, the same year he patented 3,350 acres on the Blackwater River. In 1669 Williamson married Joan (Jone), the daughter of Arthur Allen I of Surry County. When Williamson made his will on February 16, 1669, he identified himself as a medical doctor and said that he wanted to be buried near his late father-in-law, Arthur Allen I. The testator made bequests to his wife, Joan, and to his sons, Robert II, George, Arthur, and Francis, and asked Major Nicholas Hill and Captain John Grove to serve as executors and trustees. Jamestown merchant and attorney William Sherwood witnessed Williamson's will, which was proved on May 2, 1670. Sometime prior to November 2, 1672, the widowed Joan Allen Williamson married Robert Burnett. A month later the late Dr. Williamson's estate was appraised and divided among his widow and four orphans. The decedent's son Robert II inherited the family's plantation on Pagan Creek. However, because he died before he had produced an heir, the Williamson land escheated to the Crown (LEO 38; Isle of Wight Wills and Deeds 1 [1662–1688]:13, 94–95, 504–505; 2:85, 116; PB5:626; 7:472, 544).

Ann Willis: Ann Willis came to the colony in 1620 and in January 1625 was a maidservant living in Sir George Yeardley's household in urban Jamestown (VI&A 752).

* * *

Francis Willis: Francis Willis, who was born in England, settled in Charles River (York) County and in 1640 was serving as the clerk of court. He ran afoul of the law by making disparaging comments about the governor, the Council of State, and the assembly, and he also criticized the county's justices. Willis was fined, relieved of his office, and made to stand at the courthouse door beneath a paper describing his offenses. By 1649 he had patented some land near the head of the Severn River in what by 1651 had become Gloucester County, and in 1652 he represented that county in the assembly. On behalf of Gloucester County, he attended the assemblies that convened in 1659, 1660, and 1661–1662, but he served as a York County burgess in 1656. In 1666 Willis laid claim to some acreage on the Ware River. He was appointed to the Council of State in 1658, while the Commonwealth government was in power, and served until 1671. Like other council members, he was a justice of the General Court and sometimes audited accounts or served as a referee in disputes. Colonel Willis, who considered himself a resident of Ware River Parish in Gloucester County, Virginia, eventually returned to East Greenwich, Kent County, England. He was living there on July 6, 1689, when he made his will, which was proved on April 25, 1691. He left his widow, Jane, a large sum of money and the personal property in their home and what they had brought from Virginia, and gave other realty and personal goods to his siblings, nieces and nephews, and cousins (STAN 38; LEO xxi, 29–30, 33, 35–36, 38; PB 2:199; 5:654; MCGC 207, 253, 427, 435, 476; SR 3749).

Henry Willis: On March 2, 1679, Thomas Rabley of Jamestown sued Henry Willis, a merchant trading in Virginia. Willis, on the other hand, brought suit against George Lee, a physician and resident of Jamestown. Henry Willis died sometime prior to July 6, 1689, when his brother, former council member Francis Willis, made his will (Surry County Order Book 1671–1691:303; SR 3749, 5728).

* * *

Edward Willmoth: On January 21, 1629, Edward Willmoth, a youth, testified that when John Lightfoot was on his deathbed, he told Nicholas Spencer that he wanted William Spencer to have his tobacco and cattle. Willmoth may have lived in the eastern end of Jamestown Island, where Lightfoot resided (VI&A 752).

Thomas Willoughby (Willoby, Willowby, Willowbye) I: Thomas Willoughby I came to Virginia in 1610 and settled in Elizabeth City, on the east side of the Hampton River. He was ousted from his acreage in 1619 by Governor George Yeardley, who claimed the land on behalf of the Virginia Company. Willoughby then moved to the west side of the Hampton River. He served as a burgess for Elizabeth City, holding office in 1628, 1630, and 1632. In 1629, while he was a lieutenant, he was named commander of the area from Newportes News to Captain William Tucker's plantation. He also became a commissioner of Elizabeth City's monthly court. By 1635 Willoughby had built a house on his property on the south side of the James River and commenced making Lower Norfolk County his permanent home. He became a county justice and served several successive terms. He was named to the Council of State in 1639, and in 1641 he and John Gookin built an officially sanctioned tobacco warehouse on a point of land that belonged to Willoughby. In a deposition taken on November 26, 1650, Thomas Willoughby said that he was age 52. He died in England sometime prior to April 15, 1657, at which time administration of his estate was granted to his nephew, Thomas Middleton. On August 16, 1658, the decedent's son, Thomas Willoughby II, was granted a commission of administration and went on to become a Lower Norfolk County justice. Willoughby Spit, in the City of Norfolk, gets its name from Thomas Willoughby I (VI&A 752; LEO 7, 9–11; DOR 3:649–651; PB 1:311, 410–411, 696; SR 4213; Lower Norfolk County Record Book A:86–87, 104; B;174, 210; D [1656–1666]:340, 342).

Benjamin Wilson: On December 12, 1766, Benjamin Wilson conveyed the late Walter Chiles II's 200-acre leasehold in the Gover-

nor's Land to Cary Wilkinson. Jean-Nicholas Desandrouins identified Wilkinson's farm on a map he made in 1781 (AMB 24; LEE 51 f 673).

George Wilson: From November 1661 until at least May 1662, George Wilson, a Quaker, was incarcerated in Jamestown, where he was "chained to an Indian wch is in prison for murder." Wilson said that they "had our Legs on one bolt made fast to a post with an ox chaine," and he referred to the jail as "that dirty dungeon Jamestown" (Chandler et al., "George Wilson," 266–267).

James Wilson: On January 12, 1677, James Wilson, who was accused of treason and rebellion, was hauled before a military tribunal that was held aboard Captain John Martin's ship while it was anchored in the York River at Tindall's (Gloucester) Point. Wilson was found guilty due to his involvement in Bacon's Rebellion and was sentenced to be hanged. On February 10, 1677, when Governor William Berkeley named the men exempt from the king's pardon and whose property would be seized, James Wilson was listed. Berkeley indicated that Wilson already had been executed (SR 660; NEVILLE 61; MCGC 527).

James Wilson (Willson): In October 1688 James Wilson patented 1,083 acres on Cypress Swamp, a tributary of the Northwest River and Currituck Sound. The land he patented was located in Lower Norfolk County, later Norfolk County. In 1698 Wilson represented Norfolk County in the assembly. In 1702 he patented 212 acres in Norfolk County adjoining some land he already owned. When quitrents were compiled in 1704, he was credited with 2,800 acres in Norfolk County and was identified as a colonel. In 1708 he witnessed the will made by the Rev. Roger Kellsall of Elizabeth River Parish in Norfolk County (LEO 58; PB 7:694; 9:477; Norfolk County Wills and Deeds 8:51; SMITH 98).

Robert Wilson: On April 16, 1684, Robert Wilson received one year's pay as a drummer (JHB 1660–1693:255). This raises the possibility that he lived in or near Jamestown.

Susan Wilson: On October 11, 1627, Susan Wilson testified in court about Allen Kineston's hiring Mrs. John Pott's servant, Steven Taylor. Wilson said that when Taylor became lame, Kineston returned him to Mrs. Pott, a resident of urban Jamestown, so that he could receive medical treatment. Susan

Wilson may have been the wife of Thomas Wilson, a Pott servant (VI&A 754).

Thomas Wilson: Thomas Wilson, a tailor, came to Virginia in 1620 and by January 1625 had become a servant living in Dr. John Pott's home in urban Jamestown. Wilson plied his trade in other nearby settlements and eventually became one of Pott's tenants, perhaps on the Governor's Land. Because Wilson became drunk and beat his wife, he was hauled into court and then punished (VI&A 754).

William Wilson: In May 1609 Virginia Company officials authorized William Wilson, who was then in Jamestown, to return to England so that he could tell them what the colonists needed in the way of medical supplies and equipment (VI&A 755).

William Wilson (Willson): During the late seventeenth century William Wilson, a merchant, owned land on the south side of the Back River, near Thomas Eaton's free school in Elizabeth City County. He also had property on the waterfront and on the lower side of the James River in Norfolk County. Like many of his contemporaries, Wilson made numerous appearances before the justices of Elizabeth City County, usually in pursuit of debtors. He also served as an attorney and administrator and occasionally became the guardian of minor children. In 1689 Wilson witnessed the will made by John Grave, a Quaker. William Wilson of Elizabeth City County held the rank of captain in 1692 and by 1698 had become a major. He also was a justice in the county court and by 1699 had become a lieutenant colonel and commander-in-chief of the Elizabeth City County militia. At the same time, Wilson was also a naval officer and the receiver of customs duties. He represented Elizabeth City in the assembly sessions held in 1684, 1685–1686, 1688, 1691–1692, 1693, and 1695–1696. In 1690 he and several other Elizabeth City men were ordered to depose some accused pirates, and he also was among those told to auction off a publicly owned naval vessel. In 1692 William Wilson and attorney William Sherwood presented the governor with a petition from Thomas Jarvis I's widow, Elizabeth, who also was the widow of the rebel Nathaniel Bacon. On June 1, 1695, Wilson was a witness when Francis Meriwether I of Jamestown deeded his Jamestown property to William Sherwood. However, he left Virginia before the opening of the assembly's final session and was replaced by Mathew Watts.

On September 16, 1698, William Wilson and Jane Davis obtained a marriage license in Elizabeth City County. A year later he asked the Council of State for permission to rent Old Point Comfort Island. He was returned to the assembly and served in the sessions held from 1700 to 1702. In 1705 he was a member of the Elizabeth City Parish vestry. He resigned as the Lower District's naval officer in 1710, citing his age and bodily infirmities (AMB 56; LEO 47–50, 53–54; PB 8:246, 406, 417, 428; CHAPMAN 161; NEAL 1, 3, 17, 20, 25, 33, 47, 55, 82–83, 85–86; SR 3755; EJC I:113, 121, 186, 232, 237, 309, 381, 444, 449, 464; II:3–4, 50, 63, 66, 113, 126, 439; III:59, 101, 215, 253).

Willis Wilson (Willson) II: Willis Wilson II came to Virginia at the expense of James Wilson, who used his (and probably his father's) headrights in 1693 and 1694 when patenting land in Elizabeth City County. In August 1695 Willis Wilson witnessed a document that was recorded in the county court, and a year later he asked Elizabeth City's justices to have some of his tobacco, which had been damaged in shipment from Gloucester to Hampton, inspected. He was identified as a captain when he was designated the late John Poulson's administrator, and in 1697 he was described as James Wilson's kinsman. From 1693 to 1699 Willis Wilson, who was identified as "Willis Wilson Jr.," served as a burgess and represented Elizabeth City County in the assembly. He also was heavily involved in maritime activities that occasionally resulted in his appearing before the Admiralty Court. In 1698 Captain Willis Wilson and some fellow investors asked the Council of State to sell them a ship that a British man-of-war had captured in the West Indies and brought to Virginia. Later, he asked to be compensated for salvaging materials from two other naval vessels that had been recovered. When Wilson, who had business dealings with London merchant Micajah Perry, was sued in 1699 on account of a debt that involved the lading of the brigantine *Speedwell*, he was identified as a burgess. Wilson became a justice of King and Queen County in 1699. In December 1701 the Royal African Company identified him as their factor and the intended recipient of a shipment from Angola. He made his will in 1706 and died a short time later, having made a substantial bequest to Lucy Halbert, a minor. The late Willis Wilson II's son, Willis III, went on to serve as a burgess for Norfolk County in 1718 and 1720–1722 (PB 8:256, 354; LEO 52, 56, 58–59, 69–70; SR 5722, 10626, 10629; NEAL

56–58, 65; CHAPMAN 70; EJC I:380–382, 411, 414–415, 424, 431; II:43, 52, 54–55, 84, 155, 251).

John Winchester: On October 13, 1640, the General Court sentenced John Winchester and some other indentured servants to a whipping because they had failed to report some runaways. Winchester's time of service was extended by a year and he was told to repay his master, who was responsible for his fine. He may have been in the employ of William Hatcher, who transported him to Virginia and used his headright when patenting land in 1636 and 1637 (MCGC 467; NUG I:40, 59).

Edward Windham (Windom): On May 15, 1637, when Lower Norfolk County's justices began convening as a monthly court, Edward Windham was serving as a justice, a post he held for several years. In August 1640 he was named to the Lynnhaven Parish vestry. In 1642 and 1643 he represented the county in the assembly and was compensated for his service. When Windham testified before the county court in November 1642 in a dispute involving land ownership, he stated that he was age 26 "or thereabouts." The following summer he identified himself as a resident of Lynnhaven in Lower (or New) Norfolk County when he sold 250 acres on the western branch of Samuel Bennett's Creek, near Adam Thorogood's land. In 1646 Windham became Lower Norfolk's high sheriff, an indication that he was continuing to serve as a justice. He was reimbursed by the county court for providing iron bolts and chains that were used to secure prisoners. He also furnished a sloop and a crew of men who transported the county's burgesses to an assembly meeting in Jamestown in 1647. In 1651 Windham was identified as "secretary" (probably scribe) when the Rev. Robert Powyes of Lynnhaven made his will. Captain Windham, who was still serving as a county justice in November 1652, witnessed some legal documents (LEO 20–21; Lower Norfolk County Record Book A:1, 44, 153, 157, 331; B:7a, 55a, 70a, 186a, 208; C:2–3, 13, 24–25).

Barbara (Barbary) Wingbrough: When the justices of the General Court convened on December 1, 1657, Barbara Wingbrough, who had been charged with witchcraft, was arraigned but acquitted (MCGC 506).

Edward Maria Wingfield: Edward Maria Wingfield, a Virginia Company investor, came to Virginia in 1607 in the first group of Jamestown colonists. He was a member of the colony's first council and on May 14, 1607, was chosen president. While he was in office, colonists began to die in droves because of food shortages and disease. On September 10, 1607, he was removed from office and incarcerated until he could be sent back to England with Captain Christopher Newport. He arrived there in May 1608 (VI&A 756).

Roger Wingate: Roger Wingate, who was born in England, was named to the Council of State in 1639 and in August was designated the colony's treasurer. In October 1640 Virginia's sheriffs were ordered to collect the year's quitrents and give them to Wingate. He was alive on March 10, 1640, when the council convened but died shortly thereafter. He was replaced as councilor by Richard Morrison. In April 1642 William Claiborne was appointed Wingate's successor as treasurer after word of Wingate's death reached England. On July 21, 1648, Roger Wingate's widow, Dorothy (Dorithy), gave to her "only and welbeloved sonn Lewis Burwell" the quitrents due to her late husband, which had been granted to her by King Charles I. Lewis Burwell I was the son of Edward and Dorothy Bedell Burwell. After being widowed, Dorothy had married Roger Wingate (STAN 24, 34; LEO xxi; SR 3430, 3431, 5014; MCGC 472, 479, 495, 500; York County Record Book 2 [1648–1657]:394).

John Winsloe (Winslow?): On September 27, 1671, the General Court confirmed the patent that John Winsloe and Richard Auborne of urban Jamestown had received in February 1667, entitling them to 2,000 acres in the upper (or western) part of New Kent County. In April 1677 Winsloe laid claim to 600 acres on the south side of the Mattaponi River in New Kent County, and two years later he patented 600 acres on the south side of the Piankatank River, also in New Kent (MCGC 276; PB 6:109, 213, 245).

John Wisdom (Wisedom, Wisdome): On March 22, 1677, John Wisdom was brought before Governor William Berkeley and the Council of State, who were conducting a military tribunal. He was accused and found guilty of supporting the rebel Nathaniel Bacon's cause. Wisdom and two other men asked to be transported out of the colony rather than being tried in a courtroom. The justices agreed that they should be banished for seven years and gave them the option of going to New England, Barbados, Jamaica, or any of the other islands. Wisdom was ordered to leave Virginia within two months and to be on good behavior until the time of his departure. He may have been a newly arrived servant, since Mr. Henry Aubery used his headright when patenting some land in Old Rappahannock County (MCGC 461, 533; HEN II:555; PB 6:565).

Simon (Symon) Withe (With): Simon Withe, a bricklayer from London, arrived in Jamestown on September 5, 1623. He died in Elizabeth City sometime prior to February 16, 1624 (VI&A 757).

Edward Withers: In 1622 Edward Withers testified in the Earl of Warwick's suit against Edward Brewster, indicating that he came to Virginia in 1618 on Lord Delaware's ship as one of Delaware's attendants. He described portions of Brewster's court martial hearing, conducted by Deputy-Governor Samuel Argall in Jamestown (VI&A 758).

John Withers (Wythers, Wyther): In October 1654 John Withers patented 1,000 acres on Potomac Creek in a part of Westmoreland County that in 1664 became Stafford County. Over the next few years he continued to add to his holdings in that area. Finally, in July 1668 he added another 320 acres. He seems to have been a merchant and planter, who generated disposable income by exporting tobacco and selling imported goods. By December 1686 Withers had become a lieutenant in Stafford County's militia and a justice in the county's monthly court. In August 1688 he used his 330-acre plantation on Accokeek Run as collateral when covering a debt. When executing an agreement with his creditor, he promised to defend the property from his wife's dower rights or those of his mother, who was then married to Thomas O'Donell. Withers continued to serve as a county justice and in 1691 was paid for holding a court session in his home. He also witnessed documents from time to time. He served as a burgess and represented Stafford County in the assembly sessions held in 1691–1692 and 1696–1697. Like many of his contemporaries, his business dealings extended across county boundary lines. Captain John Withers died sometime prior to September 8, 1699, when his widow, Frances, executed a prenuptial agreement before marrying Rice Hoe III. That document reveals that she had three sons: Robert, Francis, and Cadwalder Dade (LEO 51, 57; Stafford County Record Book 1686–1693:16–18, 119–119a, 145a, 216a–217; 1699–1709:5; Richmond County Deed Book 1 [1692–1704]:34; Old Rappahannock County Order Book 1683–1686:92; Westmoreland County Deeds, Wills, Patents &c.

1653–1659:38, 85, 92; PB 3:364, 373; 4:342; 6:179). There may have been a connection between John Withers of Westmoreland and Stafford counties and a John Withers who came to Virginia in 1638 and a few months later was identified as a surgeon's mate (SR 10723, 10876).

Thomas Wittingham: In May 1609 Thomas Wittingham was appointed cape merchant of the Jamestown fort and store, replacing John Tavernor (VI&A 758).

[No First Name] Witts: Goodman Witts, whose first name is unknown, died on Jamestown Island sometime after April 1623 but before February 16, 1624 (VI&A 758).

Wonuffacomen (Native American): On February 6, 1656, Wonuffacomen and the Machodoc Indians' other Great Men, joined their werowance, Perkatoan, in making an agreement that was witnessed by some of Northumberland County's military commanders. The militia leaders, who had been asked to investigate a complaint the Indians had made against Isaac Allerton, concluded that Allerton was allowed to keep his livestock on the land but was prohibited from undertaking further development (Northumberland County Wills, Inventories &c. 1652–1658:101).

[No First Name] Wood: Captain Wood, one of Captain John Smith's "old soldiers," came to Virginia in the fleet that brought Sir Thomas Gates. He was named to the Council of State in May 1609 and was captain of a ship that brought part of the 3rd Supply of new colonists to Jamestown (VI&A 759).

Abraham (Abram) Wood: Abraham Wood, who came to Virginia at age 10, went on to become a very successful planter and during the 1630s patented substantial quantities on both sides of the Appomattox River. In the wake of the 1644 Indian attack, Captain Wood agreed to build Fort Henry at the falls of the Appomattox River. By 1652 he had attained the rank of major and was placed in command of the Charles City and Henrico militias. He became a Henrico County justice and served as one of its burgesses from 1644–1646. He represented Charles City from 1652–1656 and in 1657 was named to the Council of State. In 1680 he helped negotiate an important peace agreement with the Indians, an expansion of the 1677 Treaty of Middle Plantation. Major-General Abraham Wood died sometime prior to 1682, having witnessed the maturation of the colony, two major Indian attacks, Bacon's Rebellion, and other pivotal events. He was survived by a son, Abraham II; a married daughter, Mary Chamberlayne; and his wife, whose name is unknown (VI&A 759; LEO 22–25, 30, 32–33; DOR 3:674–677).

Percival (Percivall, Percivell) Wood: In 1624 Percival and Ann Wood were residing on the lower side of the James, to the west of Gray's Creek, but a year later they were living on Mulberry Island. It was then that the Woods sold a house and 12 acres of land at Black Point, on the eastern end of Jamestown Island, to Sir George Yeardley. In 1628 Percival Wood served as Mulberry Island's burgess, but in February 21, 1632, he represented Archer's Hope. Then, on September 4, 1632, he attended the assembly on behalf of the settlers living in Martin's Hundred (VI&A 760; LEO 7, 10–11).

William Wood: When John Barber I first patented a lot in urban Jamestown on May 14, 1656, William Wood was in possession of a neighboring parcel (PB 5:228; NUG I:468).

John Woodall: In May 1609 John Woodall, a Virginia Company investor, sent some livestock and indentured servants to the colony. One servant was Christopher Best, a surgeon, who in 1623 was living in urban Jamestown in the household of John Pountis. Woodall's cattle may have been kept on Jamestown Island or on the Governor's Land, for they were entrusted to the care of the governor's former cow-keeper, John Osborne. As time went on, Woodall, as an absentee owner, continued to have problems with the people to whom he had entrusted his real and personal property in Virginia, and in 1634 he asked the colony's governor to intervene on his behalf. He also asked for a monopoly on apiculture—what he termed "the commodity of bees" (VI&A 761).

Henry Woodhouse II: Henry Woodhouse II was born around 1607. He was the eldest son of Captain Henry Woodhouse I, the Bermuda governor (1623–1627) who aspired to become governor of Virginia and was acquainted with Sir George Yeardley. Henry Woodhouse II moved to Virginia sometime prior to May 22, 1637, when he secured his first patent. He used the headrights of his wife, Mary, daughter, Elizabeth, and seven other people. Woodhouse, a gentleman, was named to the Lynnhaven Parish vestry in Lower Norfolk County in August 1640. When he testified before the justices of

Lower Norfolk County's monthly court in November 1642, he said that he was age 35 "or thereabouts." When the assembly convened in 1647, Woodhouse served as a burgess for Lower Norfolk County. The following year he was named a tax collector for the territory on the east side of the Lynnhaven River, an area in which he had patented some acreage. As time went on, he continued to claim land in that vicinity. His property on the eastern shore of the Lynnhaven River was near the western branch of the Elizabeth River and eventually lay within the bounds of Princess Anne County. Woodhouse was returned to the assembly in 1652 and continued to represent Lower Norfolk County; he also served as a justice in the county's monthly court. When Henry Woodhouse II made his will on July 16, 1655, he left his wife, Mary (Maria), a third of his moveable estate and life-rights in the plantation they occupied, which ultimately was to go to their son Henry III. He bequeathed the rest of his Virginia acreage to his sons Horatio and John. The testator left his reversionary interest in two shares of land in Bermuda to his son William and specified that the remaining two-thirds of his personal estate was to be distributed among his sons (at age 20) and daughters (at age 16). He also bequeathed 5 shillings to daughter Elizabeth Collins and a like amount to a female named Judith. Henry Woodhouse II's will was proved on November 15, 1655. His son Henry III survived until 1686 (LEO 26, 29; Lower Norfolk County Record Book A:44, 164; B:93; C:22, 31–32; PB 1:1:424; 2:167, 3:254; 6:581; 8:180; SR 629, 3742, 4529; James, "Henry Woodhouse," 229).

Thomas Woodhouse: In 1640 Thomas Woodhouse patented and developed some land near Gray's Creek in what was then James City County but later Surry County. By 1655 he had moved to urban Jamestown. While living in Surry he had at least one young male Indian servant. Woodhouse seems to have prospered, for in July 1657 he and a partner, William Hooker, patented 100 acres of land in the southeastern end of Jamestown Island, and during 1658 and 1659 he laid claim to 6,000 acres of land on the Potomac River and 100 acres in Isle of Wight County. Woodhouse's land in Isle of Wight abutted that of two other members of the Jamestown community: John Moon (Omoonce) and the late John Upton I. On March 24, 1655, Sir William Berkeley sold Thomas Woodhouse part of a brick row house he had built in the western end of Jamestown Island, describing it as the "late statehouse." Woodhouse was paid for renting his house to the Council of State and the Quarter Court twice in 1656, and on October 11, 1660, he was compensated for hosting council meetings. The assembly also convened at Woodhouse's from time to time. He probably kept a tavern, for it was during this period that the burgesses decided to build a statehouse because of "the dishonor of our Lawes being made and judgments being given in ale-houses." On October 17, 1655 Woodhouse patented a one-acre waterfront lot in urban Jamestown. He failed to develop his property, which he subdivided and sold in 1657. Woodhouse seems to have had more success acquiring property than in retaining it. The 100 acres he owned in the eastern end of Jamestown Island escheated to the Crown sometime prior to 1667, and he lost ownership of his row house unit. Documents filed in Northumberland County's monthly court reveal that Woodhouse was alive in March 1662 but dead by May 1665 and that William May and son-in-law Nicholas Meriwether (both of Jamestown) were then serving as his executors. In 1668 and 1669 two prominent Northumberland County citizens, with the authorization of May and Meriwether, were allowed to collect funds from Woodhouse's debtors there and in nearby Westmoreland County. In 1694 Woodhouse was mentioned as the former owner of some acreage in urban Jamestown, near Colonel Thomas Swann's property (JHB 1619–1660:96, 101; 1660–1693:8, 27; AMB 18; 64; MCGC 514; Surry County Deeds and Wills 1652–1672:6, 23, 39, 63; PB 3:380; 4:100; 5:253; Northumberland County Record Book 1666–1670:99; Order Book 1652–1665:414; 1666–1678:42, 49; NUG I:317, 347, 375, 391; HEN I:424).

Thomas Woodhurst (Woodhouse?): When William and Elizabeth Brown I of Surry County sold their ¾-acre lot and its improvements in urban Jamestown to George Lee on April 7, 1685, their property was described as "formerly the estate of Thomas Woodhurst." The northern and western boundaries of the Browns' property, which bordered Back Street and had contained two bays of a long brick row house, ran "as far as the two houses extend of the said George Lee, the one being by him built and inhabited, the other ruinous being westerly." This indicates that Lee had improved the Browns' land prior to purchasing it. It is uncertain whether Woodhurst owned the property before or after Bacon's Rebellion. However, if he owned it beforehand, he would have been

Richard Auborne's landlord (LEE MS 51 f 668; JHB 1660–1693:73, 152). Because the Browns' deed to George Lee is the only known documentary reference to Thomas Woodhurst, the possibility exists that he was Thomas Woodhouse, whose name is associated with at least four other properties on Jamestown Island and who, like the Browns, had ties to Surry County.

John Woodlief (Woodliffe, Woodlase) II: John Woodlief II, the son of ancient planter John Woodlief I, was born around 1615. In August 1637 he identified himself as the late John Woodlief's son and heir when patenting the decedent's 550-acre plantation in what was then Charles City County but later became Prince George County. A year later Woodlief acquired an additional 200 acres on the basis of headrights. When he repatented his landholdings in 1642, he noted that 20 of his 750 acres were at Bermuda Hundred. John Woodlief II served as a burgess in 1652, representing Charles City County. In 1661 he was placed in command of a company of militia that served under Colonel Abraham Wood (VI&A 762; LEO 30; DOR 3:706).

Christopher Woodward: Christopher Woodward came to Virginia in 1620 and in 1625 was living at West and Shirley Hundred, where he owned some land. In October 1629 Woodward served as a burgess for Westover, which like West and Shirley Hundred was in the corporation of Charles City. In 1635 he patented 300 acres on the Appomattox River, enhancing the size of his acreage in 1637. This time he listed his late wife, Margaret, and current wife, Dorothy, as headrights. A few months later Woodward claimed a total of 600 acres. He may have been alive in 1642 when his land was used as a reference point in a neighboring patent, but he died sometime prior to October 1650, when his son and heir, Samuel Woodward, disposed of his property (VI&A 763; PB 1:301–302, 414, 469, 862; SR 3114; LEO 8; DOR 3:844).

George Woodward: Court records dating to September 27, 1672, indicate that when George Woodward died, he was indebted to Thomas Harris, whose widow, Alice, was in the process of collecting from her late husband's debtors. Harris seems to have been a bricklayer, for during the 1660s Thomas Stegg II paid him a substantial sum for building a house. In 1653 Woodward patented some land on Diascund Swamp in James City County (MCGC 308; HEN II:156; PB 6:620).

Mary Woodward: In February 1624 Mary Woodward was a servant in Governor Francis Wyatt's household in urban Jamestown (VI&A 764).

Richard Woodward (Woodard): On November 25, 1671, the General Court noted that Richard Woodward, a Bristol merchant and owner of the ship *Virginia Merchant*, was deceased and that his estate was in the custody of William May of urban Jamestown. In March 1673 May was still representing Woodward's interests (MCGC 290, 293, 331).

William Woodward: On October 10, 1670, William Woodward acquired some Henrico County land from Thomas Stegg II, part-owner of a brick row house unit in the western end of Jamestown Island. In October 1702 Woodward patented 25–27 acres of escheat land (formerly Jane Perkins' property) on the mainland just west of Jamestown Island, and quickly resold it to John Tullitt. The Perkins' parcel eventually became part of the Ambler plantation on the mainland (MCGC 222; PB 9:509; NUG III:67).

Thomas Wooten (Wotton): Thomas Wooten, a surgeon and gentleman, came to Virginia in 1607 in the first group of Jamestown colonists. According to Captain John Smith, Wooten was a skillful surgeon and saved many lives. Edward Maria Wingfield disliked Wooten because he wanted to live aboard the pinnace instead of residing on Jamestown Island (VI&A 764).

William Wooten (Wootton): On October 13, 1640, the General Court identified two indentured servants, John Bradye and William Wooten, as the instigators of a conspiracy that involved running away and enticing others to do so. Both men were sentenced to be whipped from the gallows to the courthouse door. Wooten, who seems to have been considered more culpable, was to be branded on the forehead and made to serve the colony for seven years, all the while working in irons. This was to be done after he had completed his service to Mr. Sanderson, probably Edward Sanderson, a merchant, who purchased a Jamestown Island parcel from John Norton, a smith (MCGC 467; PB 1:630; NUG I:105).

Daniel Workman (Warkeman, Warkman): When surveyor John Soane made a plat of the Governor's Land in 1683, he indicated that Daniel Workman was then in possession of a leasehold. However, he failed to indicate how much land Workman was renting. By April 1684 Workman had patented 228 acres on the Chickahominy River in what was then Charles City County's Weyanoke Parish (Soane 1683; PB 7:384). He may have been related to merchant Mark Workman.

George Worleigh (Worledge, Worley, Worldridge, Worleich, Worldige, Worlidge): In 1642 George Worleigh served as a burgess for Charles River (York) County and may have been the "Mr. Worlidge" who owned land in eastern York County. In April 1642 he signed a written protest against reinstatement of the Virginia Company. In October 1643 George Worleigh's acreage was mentioned in a patent for land near Mobjack Bay in what by 1651 had become Gloucester County. He died prior to June 7, 1644, when Richard Duning obtained an attachment against his estate for failing to deliver a manservant. This raises the possibility that Worleigh imported and sold indentured servants. William Pryor also secured an attachment against Worleigh's estate (LEO 20; York County Deeds, Orders, Wills 2 [1646–1648]:151, 174; PB 1:343, 949; 3:91; BILL 45).

William Worleigh (Worldige, Worlidge, Woolrich, Worlich, Woeleich, Wooldridge, Worleich): William Worleigh came to Virginia in 1622 as a young indentured servant and in 1624 and 1625 was living in Elizabeth City. On June 17, 1635, he received a patent for 400 acres of land in Elizabeth City County. He did business on the Eastern Shore, and in 1642 John Neale served as his attorney in Accomac County's monthly court. Worleigh represented Elizabeth City in the assembly in 1644, 1649, and in 1654–1655 and also attended the sessions held in 1658 and 1660–1662 (VI&A 765; LEO 22, 27, 32, 34, 36, 38; AMES 2:207).

Richard Worley (Worlie): Richard Worley, a gentleman, arrived in Jamestown in 1608 in the 2nd Supply of new settlers (VI&A 764).

* * *

Christopher Wormeley I: Christopher Wormeley I, the governor of Tortuga from 1632 to 1635, served as Virginia's Secretary of State from 1635 to 1649. In 1638 he was appointed captain of the fort at Old Point Comfort. By that time he had patented 1,420 acres fronting on the York River, on the east side of what already was known as Wormeley Creek, and established a plantation. In 1650 several prominent royalists who had just come from England, notably,

Sir Thomas Lunsford, Sir Henry Chicheley, Sir Philip Honywood, and Colonel Manwarring Hammond, visited Wormeley's home and were treated very hospitably. Another exiled royalist, Henry Norwood, who had been shipwrecked on the Eastern Shore and arrived at Wormeley's house in February 1650, said the house was the scene of "feasting and carousing." Wormeley died in 1656, leaving a son, Christopher Wormeley II, and a daughter, Elizabeth, who successively married Secretary of the Colony Richard Kemp of Jamestown, Sir Thomas Lunsford, and Major General Robert Smith (VI&A 765; FOR III:10:49).

Christopher Wormeley II: Christopher Wormeley II married the widow of Anthony Elliott I, who died sometime after July 1666 but before January 9, 1667. After her demise, which occurred before May 12, 1669, he wed the former Frances Armistead, the widow of the Rev. Justinian Aylemer, rector of James City Parish. Because the vestry failed to give Aylemer's widow her back pay, on September 29, 1671, Wormeley brought suit against vestrymen Theophilus Hone and William May, both of whom lived in urban Jamestown. Wormeley was then a justice in Lancaster County's monthly court. In 1676 the rebel Nathaniel Bacon called Christopher Wormeley II (a councilor and supporter of Governor William Berkeley) a traitor, and Bacon's men reportedly plundered Wormeley's estate. Wormeley also was imprisoned for a time at the Mehixon fort in King William County. Wormeley's loyalty to the Virginia government paid off, and in 1683 he was named to the Council of State. During the early 1680s he was a justice of Middlesex County's monthly court and 1681 was designated high sheriff. By 1684 Colonel Wormeley owned 660 acres called Powhatan, which lay on the south and east side of the Drinking Swamp, a branch of Powhatan Creek. His acreage, which was surveyed by John Soane, was part of a nearly 2,300-acre tract formerly owned by Richard Eggleston. In 1687 Ralph Wormeley II and Christopher Wormeley II were ordered to bring the assembly records from Middlesex County to Jamestown. Sometime prior to October 1690, Christopher Wormeley II married Elizabeth, the widow of Colonel John Carter II of Lancaster County. He temporarily served as one of the decedent's executors but relinquished his role when Carter's daughter, Elizabeth, came of age. Afterward, Wormeley took legal action on his new wife's behalf, in an attempt to force Robert Carter to give her a dower third of Colonel John Carter II's estate. However,

Robert Carter, in lawyerly fashion, utilized a delaying tactic. In 1692 the Privy Council ordered the members of Virginia's Council of State to construct houses in urban Jamestown; however, there is no evidence that Wormeley did so. On March 5, 1694, Mrs. Million Downman presented the will of Madam Elizabeth Wormeley, wife of Christopher Wormeley II, to the justices of the Middlesex County court, at which time it was validated. Later in the day Colonel Wormeley, the decedent's widower who also was an executor, indicated that he was going to contest the will in the General Court. Colonel Christopher Wormeley II died in 1701. The will he made on June 20, 1690, perhaps around the time he married Elizabeth Carter, specified that his plantation called Powhatan was to descend to his son William. The testator left half-shares of his plantation in Middlesex to his son Thomas and daughter, Judith. A will he made at a later date stated that he wanted to be buried in his garden in Middlesex, between his first and second wives (MCGC 277, 285; WISEMAN; SR 7366; ASPIN 172; NUG II:345; CO 5/1407 f 81; EJC I:269; STAN 42; Soane 1684; Wormeley, June 20, 1690; Middlesex County Order Book 1680–1694:1, 20, 22, 482, 679; Old Rappahannock County Order Book 1683–1686:9; Lancaster County Order Book 1666–1680:21, 35, 109; 1686–1696:149, 185, 199–200, 241).

William Wormeley: William Wormeley, the son of Christopher Wormeley II, stood to inherit 660 acres of the James City County plantation known as Powhatan. On October 25, 1695, he patented 712 acres on the east side of Powhatan Creek. Because Wormeley died without legal heirs, his land at Powhatan descended to his sister, Judith, the wife of Corbin Griffin. In 1698 William Wormeley and his siblings, Thomas Wormeley and Judith Wormeley Griffin, asked the justices of Middlesex County to determine which of the wills made by their father, the late Christopher Wormeley II, should be considered valid. In 1699 William Wormeley was a Middlesex justice (Wormeley, June 20, 1690; Griffin, February 2, 1701; NUG III:4; Middlesex County Order Book 1694–1705:230, 296).

Ralph Wormeley I: In 1649 Ralph Wormeley I patented more than 3,000 acres of land along the lower side of the Rappahannock River, on the east side of Nimcock (Rosegill) Creek. His property, which contained the old and new Nimcock Indian towns, was in what around 1669 became Middlesex County. Within a year he built a dwelling on his plantation and acquired some additional acreage that lay directly across the creek. He patented 3,500 acres on Mobjack Bay and part of a 1,645-acre tract in York County that he obtained from Christopher Wormeley I. Ralph Wormeley I also claimed a large tract in Pamunkey Neck that impinged upon native territory. On July 2, 1645, he signed a marriage contract with Agatha, the widow of Luke Stubbinge of Northampton County. Besides servants, livestock, and household goods, Wormeley agreed to give his bride-to-be his 500-acre plantation in York County, the property on which he resided and had purchased from Jeffrey Power. Ralph Wormeley I served as a York County burgess in 1649 and was named to the Council of State in 1650, but died a year later. He was survived by his widow, Agatha Eltonhead Stubbinge Wormeley, who married Sir Henry Chicheley, and an infant son, Ralph Wormeley II (NUG I:181–182, 206; III:7; STAN 35; Lower Norfolk Book B:140, 142; AMES 2:433–434; LEO 27).

Ralph Wormeley II: Ralph Wormeley II, the son of Ralph I and Agatha Eltonhead Stubbinge Wormeley, was born in 1650 and lost his father a year later. He stood to inherit his late father's plantation, Rosegill, upon attaining his majority. In 1674 Wormeley married Colonel Peter Jennings' widow, the former Catherine Lunsford, and became a burgess for Middlesex County, serving from 1669 to 1674. He also patented 2,870 acres of land in Middlesex. In 1675 he was named a member of the Council of State. In March 1677 Wormeley impelled Sir Henry Chicheley to sign a document in which he agreed to account for the income he had received from the estate of the late Ralph Wormeley I over a 20-year period. Chicheley also was obliged to account for the disbursements he had made on his stepson's behalf. Attached to the agreement was a detailed list of valuable personal property (servants, livestock, and household furnishings) that young Wormeley expected to receive as part of his late father's estate. In 1680 he laid claim to 2,200 acres on the upper side of the Rappahannock River, a tract called Nanzattico, part of the territory laid off as the Nanzattico Indians' preserve. Through his marriage to Catherine Lunsford, he acquired control of a large tract directly across the river, bordering Portobago Bay.

During Bacon's Rebellion, Ralph Wormeley II, like his stepfather, sided with Governor William Berkeley. As a result, his estate was plundered and he was imprisoned for a time. After the rebellion subsided, he continued to serve as a councilor and as a justice of the Middlesex County court. In 1686 he entertained Durand de Dauphine, a French Huguenot, who stayed at Rosegill and also visited the Wormeley plantations at Nanzattico and on Portobago Bay, then the home of some natives. In 1687 Ralph Wormeley II and Christopher Wormeley II were asked to bring the assembly's records, which had been in Robert Beverley I's possession, from Middlesex County to Jamestown. When an act was passed promoting urban development in 1680, plans were made to establish a town in Middlesex County, on the west side of Rosegill Creek. Wormeley, who owned the proposed town site, known as Urbanna, agreed to sell it and accepted payment. Within a year the acreage was laid out into streets and lots. However, in November 1681, when workmen were hired to build a county courthouse in the new town, construction was delayed because Wormeley refused to transfer the property's title to the county justices. In 1691, when a second town act was passed, the justices again attempted to procure a deed to the town site. This time Wormeley agreed to release the land if the justices acknowledged that he had certain entitlements. They refused to acquiesce to his demands, which they likened to creating a fiefdom, and resolved to take possession of the land via condemnation. Although some of Urbanna's town lots were sold, Wormeley interfered when some lot owners tried to begin construction, and he also obstructed the building of a courthouse and jail. In an unrelated matter, he sued a mariner, whom he accused of seizing and abandoning his sloop.

During the late 1680s and the 1690s, Ralph Wormeley II continued to acquire land in the Middle Peninsula. In 1695 he patented (but was obliged to surrender) 13,500 acres of land in King and Queen County. The following year he obtained 3,400 acres in Middlesex. In 1693, as Secretary of the Colony, he informed overseas officials that the Virginia colonists were too impoverished to send assistance to the settlers in New York. He also complained about Commissary James Blair's continuous lobbying on behalf of Virginia's Anglican clergy. In October 1693 Wormeley, who was then council president, served briefly as acting governor. In 1694 and 1695 he supplemented his income with the fees he was paid for having carriages and a horser made for the cannon in Jamestown. It was during this period that he resided part time in a home located in urban Jamestown. By 1697 Wormeley had begun having some serious medical problems and in 1699 was too sick to commute to council meetings. On at least one occasion, the council convened at his home, Rosegill. Despite ill health, Ralph Wormeley II continued to acquire massive tracts of land in the Middle Peninsula and managed to enhance his landholdings significantly. He prepared his will on February 22, 1700, and died on December 5th. Afterward, he was criticized for relegating many of his official duties as secretary to his junior clerk (NUG I:169; II:208, 313, 330, 357, 373; III:3, 6–7, 11, 19, 23, 28, 31, 33; EJC I:315, 331, 426; II:131; STAN 21, 41, 80; CO 5/1307 ff 54, 59–68, 191–209; 5/1312 ff 90, 100; 5/1339 ff 36–37; 5/1358 f 294; 5/1359 ff 11–12; 5/1407 f 81; AMB 50, 59; LEO 38; RUT 216–221; MCGC 260, 376; HEN II:568; WISEMAN; Middlesex County Order Book 1673–1680:104–107, 224; 1680–1694:13, 510, 516, 559, 573; 1694–1705:154; Lancaster County Order Book 1686–1696:224, 230; DURAND 141–144).

* * *

Joseph Worry (Woory): In 1679 Joseph Worry purchased 360 acres of land on Cypress Swamp in Isle of Wight County from Richard Jordan Sr. Worry represented Isle of Wight County in the assembly in 1684. When appearing before Isle of Wight County's monthly court in April 1690, he identified himself as a resident of Chuckatuck. He was residing there in 1691 when he inherited £200 from his brother, Robert, then a resident of London. Joseph Worry eventually married James Webb's widow, Elizabeth. He made his will on February 15, 1693, and by October was dead. The twice-widowed Elizabeth quickly remarried and served as Worry's administratrix after she had wed Lieutenant Colonel Samuel Bridger (LEO 47; Isle of Wight County Will and Deed Book 1 [1662–1688]: 35, 336, 414; Wills and Deeds 2 [1688–1704]:336; Orders 1693–1695:3, 18; BODIE 605). If Joseph Worry claimed any land in his own right, the patent or patents he secured have been lost or destroyed.

Benjamin Worsley: Benjamin Worsley, who was named to the Council of State, appears to have been fiercely ambitious. In 1644 he asked King Charles I to appoint him Virginia's governor and claimed that people wanted him to forcibly oust Governor William Berkeley. After the Roundheads began to gain the upper hand, Worsley became a vocal proponent of their cause. He claimed that Governor Berkeley preferred to trade with the Netherlands than with England because Dutch goods and shipping costs were cheaper. He also alleged that the only clergy Berkeley would tolerate were Anglican. Worsley, like Berkeley, promoted the pro-

duction of marketable commodities in Virginia and was knowledgeable about manufacturing wine and linen. Around 1650 he urged the Commonwealth government to assert its authority over Virginia, which he felt could be subdued peacefully (HAR 26/33/7A; 28/2/2A; 43/19A; 61/5/1A; 61/8/1A).

[No First Name] Wright: Mr. Wright died in Jamestown sometime after April 1623 but before February 16, 1624 (VI&A 766).

[No First Name] Wright: In 1656 a Mr. Wright, whose first name is unknown, served in the assembly. Surviving historical records fail to identify the area he represented (LEO 33; STAN 72–73). He may have been from New Kent, Westmoreland, or Surry County, jurisdictions whose delegates' names are not included in surviving documentation.

Dionisius Wright (Write): In 1697 William Sherwood, a James City County justice of the peace and Jamestown resident, bequeathed some law books to Dionisius Wright, the county's clerk of court and clerk of the Council of State in 1701–1702 (AMB 65; MCGH 873; SR 381, 729, 2272).

John Wright: On September 4, 1667, John Wright was identified as the Surry County attorney of William Sherwood of urban Jamestown. In 1697 Sherwood chose Wright as his executor (Surry County Order Book 1671–1691:158; AMB 65).

John Wright: In November 1678 John Wright patented 1,040 acres of land in Nansemond County near Dumpling Island Creek, a tributary of the Nansemond River. Then, in April 1694 he patented two more large tracts on Bennett's Creek in Nansemond County. Finally, in 1696 he laid claim to another 1,450 acres on Bennett's Creek and some additional land near Dumpling Island. Collectively, these land acquisitions made him one of the county's largest landowners. During 1695–1696 Wright represented Nansemond County in the assembly. When Francis Hatton, a Lower Norfolk County planter, made his will in 1687, he made a bequest to his cousin John Wright, perhaps the individual who later became a burgess. In 1711 John Wright bought some acreage in the lower (or easternmost) part of Isle of Wight County, near the Nansemond County line, and seems to have moved there with his wife, Martha. Burgess John Wright may have been related to the John Wright who in 1638 and 1643 patented land on the Nansemond River, in what was then Upper Norfolk County but later Nansemond County (LEO 54; Lower Norfolk County Wills and Deeds Book 5:67; Isle of Wight County Deed Book 2 [1704–1715]:193, 214; Deeds, Wills 2 [1715–1726]:45; PB 1:683, 878; 6:669; 8:325, 339; 9:15, 45).

Robert Wright: Robert Wright, a sawyer, arrived in Jamestown in 1609 and a year later married a woman named Joane (Joan, Jane), who was a midwife. Court testimony reveals that while the colony was under martial law, Joane was flogged for hemming a shirt improperly. In February 1624 the Wrights and their daughter were living in the corporation of Elizabeth City. By early 1625 they had a second child and were living on the lower side of the Hampton River, on the Virginia Company's land. Robert Wright often paid his creditors with labor. By September 1626 the Wrights had moved to what eventually became Surry County, where Joane, who was left-handed and perhaps clairvoyant, was accused of practicing witchcraft. Due to persistent rumors about Joane's supernatural powers, the Wrights were brought before the Quarter Court. Finally, in January 1627 Robert Wright requested permission to move to Jamestown Island, where he could have land on which to build a home. In August 1627 he received a patent for a 12-acre waterfront parcel in the eastern end of Jamestown Island. Wright and his partner, Andrew Rawleigh, also received a lease for another parcel in that vicinity. Robert Wright, who repeatedly was jailed as a debtor, died sometime after March 2, 1629 (VI&A 766–767).

* * *

Anthony Wyatt (Wyat, Wiatt) I: Anthony Wyatt I came to Virginia sometime prior to 1628, when he exported tobacco from Virginia in the *Truelove*, a vessel owned by some Virginia Company investors whose settlers lived at Chaplin's Choice. In 1635 he was identified as a merchant doing business in London, and during 1638 and 1639 he obtained a license to sell tobacco in London, Northamptonshire, and Leistershire. Wyatt was a resident of Jordan's (later, Flowerdew Hundred) Parish, on the lower side of the James River. He served as a Charles City County burgess and sat in the assembly meetings that were held in 1645–1646, 1653, and 1656. In October 1650 he purchased 450 acres on the south side of the Appomattox River from Christopher Woodward's heir. He appeared before the justices of Charles City County in June 1655. In 1665 Wyatt patented 282 acres in Charles City County near Deep Bottom, and in 1669 he claimed 398 acres that formerly had belonged to George Potter. Wyatt also acquired the plantation called Chaplin's (formerly Chaplin's Choice) on the lower side of the James River, just east of Jordan's Point. When Anthony Wyatt's eldest son, Nicholas, repatented the property in 1686, he said that his late father had owned it for many years and that his original patent (one that had been issued to Chaplin) was destroyed when his house burned (LEO 22, 24, 31; PB 5:510; 6:247; 7:531; SR 3784b, 10915, 10938, 10945; Charles City County Order Book 1655–1665:1, 5, 196).

Nicholas Wyatt (Wyat, Wiatt): Nicholas Wyatt, the son of burgess Anthony Wyatt I, represented Charles City County in the assembly from 1672 to 1676 and probably succeeded Thomas Southcot, who died in 1671. On March 12, 1673, Wyatt's attorney, who appeared in Charles City County's monthly court, acknowledged his client's debt to George Marable II, the owner of a house and waterfront lot in urban Jamestown. In January 1679 Wyatt sued Surry County bricklayer Thomas Clarke, and later in the year he served as the executor of William Rookings, one of the late Nathaniel Bacon's supporters. In 1677 Wyatt and three other Charles City County men presented testimony to the special commissioners whom King Charles II sent to Virginia to investigate the underlying causes of Bacon's Rebellion. A patent Wyatt received in April 1686 reveals that he lived near Martin's Brandon in Charles City (later Prince George) County. A few months later he patented the plantation called Chaplin's (Chaplin's Choice) on the lower side of the James River, near Jordan's Point. He indicated that he was the son and heir of the late Anthony Wyatt, who died in possession of the property and lost his patent in a house fire. Nicholas Wyatt initiated a suit in June 1690 on behalf of his brother, Anthony Wyatt II. He accused John Good of dispossessing Anthony II and his wife of property she had inherited from her grandmother, Elizabeth Tatem. In 1693 Captain Nicholas Wyatt and John Tirrey served as overseers of the will made by Henry Gerrard of Martin's Brandon. Wyatt was still alive in 1695 and in 1704 was credited with 700 acres of land in Prince George County (LEO 37; PB 7:510, 531; SR 661, 3951; MCGC 327; Surry County Order Book 1671–1691:235, 262; Charles City County Order Book 1687–1695:145, 288, 574; SMITH 101).

* * *

***

Francis Wyatt: Francis Wyatt was knighted in 1618 and married Margaret, Sir Samuel Sandys' daughter and the niece of Virginia Company Treasurer Sir Edwin Sandys. Sir Francis became Virginia's governor in 1621 and arrived in Virginia shortly before the March 1622 Indian attack. Lady Margaret came over in 1622. Governor Wyatt responded to the crisis forcefully and effectively. During his first term he resided in urban Jamestown, ultimately in a townstead of his own. In February 1624 he was sharing his home with his wife, his brother, and ten servants. Lady Margaret Wyatt returned to England sometime prior to January 24, 1625. Governor Wyatt had 500 acres below Blunt Point and some land in Elizabeth City. His intelligence and evenhandedness facilitated Virginia's transition to a Crown colony. He went to England in 1626 but returned to Virginia in November 1639 as Governor John Harvey's successor. In October 1641 Wyatt received a patent for a lot in urban Jamestown and a 50-acre leasehold on the Governor's Land. On December 16, 1641, he transferred his leasehold to his eldest son, Henry. The Wyatt property on the Governor's Land abutted the parcels leased by Robert Hutchinson and John White, who owned acreage on Jamestown Island. After incoming governor Sir William Berkeley arrived in February 1642, Sir Francis Wyatt became a councilor. He returned to England in early 1644 and died there later in the year (VI&A 768–769).

Hautt (Hawt, Hant) Wyatt: The Rev. Haute Wyatt, the brother of incoming governor Sir Francis Wyatt, came to Virginia in 1621 and was minister to those who occupied the Governor's Land. In February 1624, while the Rev. Wyatt was living in his brother's home in urban Jamestown, he became rector of James City Parish, succeeding the late Rev. Richard Buck. Hautt Wyatt returned to England with his brother in 1626 (VI&A 769).

***

William Wyatt (Wiatt) I: William Wyatt I commenced patenting large tracts of land on the Mattaponi River during the mid-1650s, acreage that eventually was included in King and Queen and King William counties but at that time lay in Gloucester and New Kent. As time went on, Wyatt continued to add to his holdings in those areas. In 1670 he began transferring some of his acreage to his son, William II. On March 8, 1676, Major

William Wyatt I lost a lawsuit to Theophilus Hone, the owner of several lots in urban Jamestown. In June 1677 Wyatt prepared a petition on behalf of William and Elizabeth Rookings and submitted it to the special commissioners whom King Charles II sent to Virginia to inquire into the causes of Bacon's Rebellion (MCGC 432; PB 3:4, 233, 354; 5:286, 439, 453; 6:276, 322; 7:32; SR 661).

Hugh Wynne (Winne): In 1608 Hugh Wynne, a tradesman, arrived in Jamestown in the 2nd Supply of new colonists (VI&A 770).

Peter Wynne (Winne): Peter Wynne, a gentleman and shareholder in the Virginia Company, came to Virginia in 1608 in the 2nd Supply of new settlers. Shortly after he arrived in Jamestown, he became a member of the Council of State. On November 26, 1608, Wynne, who was living in the capital city, wrote a letter to Sir John Egerton describing the colony's attributes. Captain Peter Wynne died in Virginia in 1609. In May 1609 Sir Thomas Gates, who was unaware of Wynne's death, designated him sergeant-major of the fort and lieutenant governor (VI&A 770).

Robert Wynne I: In 1658 Robert Wynne I began serving as a burgess for Charles City County. He was returned to office repeatedly and served in the assembly from 1661 to 1674. He became speaker in March 1662 and held that post through October 1674. The locations of Wynne's landholdings are uncertain because any patents he received seem to have been lost or destroyed. When Robert Wynne made his will on July 1, 1675, he stated that he was a resident of Jordan's Parish in Charles City County, an indication that he lived on the south side of the James River. He said that he wanted to be buried at Jordans Church near the grave of his son Robert II. The testator left cattle to his sons Thomas and Joshua and a servant to his married daughter, Woodleigh Poythress, and bequeathed to all three of them his real estate in England. Son Joshua Wynne was to receive the testator's Virginia plantation called Georges. Robert Wynne I's wife, Mary, whom he named as administratrix, stood to inherit whatever remained of his real and personal estate in Virginia and elsewhere. He bestowed gifts upon a number of friends and chose merchant Thomas Grendon and son-in-law Francis Poythress to oversee his will. Robert Wynne's will was proved in Charles City County court on August 3, 1675 (LEO 34, 36–37; SR 3718, 12501).

Thomas Wythe (Wyth): Thomas Wythe came to Virginia sometime prior to 1674, at which point he dispatched a large quantity of tobacco to England. In 1678 he and Thomas Arnold were identified as merchants when they sent a shipment of goods from England to Virginia. In 1684 Wythe, who was then in London, sent imported goods to the colony in the ships *Recovery* and *Endeavor*. During 1680–1682 he served as a burgess on behalf of Elizabeth City County, and he also was a justice in the county court. On December 14, 1693, Wythe made his will, which was proved on March 19, 1694. On September 18, 1694, his widow, Ann I, was designated executrix and captains Anthony and William Armistead agreed to serve as her security. Wythe divided his plantation between his wife and son, Thomas II, and made bequests to his grandson, Thomas III, and granddaughter, Ann II. He also left some personal possessions to certain servants and friends. The testator's reference to his merchandise implies that he was still employed as a merchant at the time he made his will. On September 7, 1695, Mrs. Ann Wythe Sr. and Mr. Thomas Harwood were granted a marriage license (LEO 45; NEAL 32, 38–39, 104; SR 2005a, 3768d; 5763b; CHAPMAN 106–107, 161).

Y

George Yarington: George Yarington, a gentleman, arrived in Jamestown in 1608 in the 2nd Supply of colonists (VI&A 770).

William Yates: When William Yates made his will on September 5, 1764, he mentioned his daughter, Elizabeth, who was married to the Rev. William Bland, rector of James City Parish. Yates was a resident of Williamsburg and president of the College of William and Mary (MEADE 113; Purdie and Dixon, *Virginia Gazette,* December 17, 1772).

* * *

Sir George Yeardley (Yardley): George Yeardley, who set out for Virginia in 1609 and was shipwrecked in Bermuda with Sir Thomas Gates, arrived in the colony in 1610 and was made captain of Gates's guard. He married Temperance Flowerdew three years later. When Sir Thomas Dale left Virginia in May 1616, he named Yeardley as acting governor, a position he held for a year. The Yeardleys returned to England, but in October 1618 Yeardley was designated Virginia's governor and a month later was knighted. Governor Yeardley and his wife arrived in Jamestown in April 1619. Yeardley presided over the colony during a pivotal period in its history, when the New World's first representative assembly convened and the headright system was established. In mid-summer 1619 Yeardley learned that his titles to two large tracts of land, Weyanoke and Flowerdew Hundred, had been confirmed, and in August 1619 he procured some Africans from a Dutch mariner who entered Hampton Roads. Yeardley's first term as governor expired in November 1621, and as soon as his successor took office, he channeled his energies into developing his own properties. However, he served as a member of the Council of State, and in 1624 he was named acting governor. Despite his substantial investment in his outlying properties, Sir George Yeardley, Lady Temperance, and their sons, Francis and Argoll, and daughter, Elizabeth, lived in urban Jamestown. Their home occupied a 7¼-acre parcel in the northwestern part of Jamestown Island. Yeardley sold his Flowerdew Hundred and Weyanoke plantations to cape merchant Abraham Peirsey in 1624 but retained some land on Hog Island, and in 1625 he purchased three parcels in the eastern end of Jamestown Island. Then, in 1627 he patented 1,000 acres near Blunt Point and acquired 3,700 acres of land on the Eastern Shore. Lady Temperance, a woman of considerable intelligence, took an active role in her household's business affairs, especially after her husband became seriously ill. When Sir George Yeardley, who was "weak and sick in body," made his will on October 12, 1627, he bequeathed to his wife life-rights in their dwelling in urban Jamestown, along with their home's contents, but specified that the rest of his real and personal property was to be sold and the proceeds divided into thirds. On October 29th he added a codicil to his will, instructing his wife to sell their Jamestown Island property so that the proceeds could be added to his estate. He died within two weeks and on November 13, 1627, was interred at Jamestown. In November 1627 Lady Temperance renounced her dower interest in Flowerdew Hundred and Weyanoke, which her late husband had sold to Abraham Peirsey in 1624. She married interim Governor Francis West I in late March 1628 and died intestate in December 1628 (VI&A 771–775).

Argoll (Argall) Yeardley (Yardley): Argoll Yeardley, the eldest son of Sir George and Lady Temperance Flowerdew Yeardley, was born in Virginia around 1620 and during the 1620s resided in the family home in Jamestown. He lost his father in November 1627 and his mother a year later. Argoll, as the eldest son, stood to inherit a third of his late father's estate, the bulk of which was in the hands of his uncle, Ralph Yeardley. From 1639 to 1655 Argoll Yeardley served on the Council of State, and in 1642 he became a commissioner of the Accomack County court. While visiting the Netherlands in 1649, he met and married Anne Custis, his second wife, and brought her to Virginia. The Yeardley couple lived on the Eastern Shore in Northampton County, as did his politically powerful brother-in-law, Colonel John Custis II of Arlington. In 1649–1650 Henry Norwood, a kinsman of Governor William Berkeley who had been shipwrecked on the Eastern Shore, spent some time in the Yeardley home while awaiting transportation across the Chesapeake Bay. The Yeardleys lived in Old Town Neck, where Argoll patented 2,000 acres. He died sometime prior to October 29, 1655 (VI&A 775; LEO 31; FOR III:10:49).

Francis Yeardley (Yardley): Francis, the youngest son of Sir George and Lady Temperance Flowerdew Yeardley, was born in Virginia around 1624 and resided in urban Jamestown with his parents, brother Argoll, and sister Elizabeth. The Yeardley children lost their father in 1627 and their mother a year later. In January 1643 Francis Yeardley received a patent for 3,000 acres of land on the Eastern Shore, but he married the twice-widowed Sarah Offley Thorogood Gookin in 1647 and began residing at Lynnhaven, in what was then Lower Norfolk County. In 1650 he sold some cattle to William Moseley I and his wife in exchange for some fine jewelry. Yeardley continued to patent land in the Lynnhaven area and served as a Lower Norfolk County justice from 1651 until at least 1653. He also was a member of the Maryland Council and became a burgess for Lower Norfolk County in 1653. Yeardley may have been volatile, for in 1652 surgeon Edward Hall asked the justices of Lower Norfolk County court for protection from Colonel Yeardley, whom he feared "will doe him some bodily harme, or burne his houses." Later in the year Yeardley and Lieutenant Colonel Lloyd posted a bond to cover some debts against the late Colonel John Sibsey's estate. Yeardley was given command of the militia company drawn from the territory on the western side of the Lynnhaven River. In 1654 he visited Roanoke Island and the site the "Lost Colonists" had occupied. Later, he and his wife, Sarah, entertained some of that area's Indians in their home in Lynnhaven. Francis Yeardley died in 1656 (VI&A 775; LEO 31; Lower Norfolk County Record Book B:55; C:10, 13, 16, 20, 62, 64).

* * *

James Yemanson: In February 1624 James Yemanson, an indentured servant, was living in Captain Ralph Hamor's household in urban Jamestown (VI&A 776).

Hugh Yeo: Hugh Yeo was living on the Eastern Shore in 1652 when he dispatched a shipment of tobacco to a Bristol merchant, putting it aboard the *Mary* of Accomack, with William Chappell as master. In 1655 Yeo patented 644 acres on the Pungoteague River in Northampton County and significantly added to his holdings in that vicinity in 1661 and 1664. Finally, in 1674 he laid claim to 2,050 acres on Matchapungo Creek and the Matchapungo River. Yeo represented Accomack County in the assembly from 1663 to 1670. He died intestate sometime prior to March 17, 1678, at which time William Yeo asked Accomack County's court justices to grant him administration of the decedent's estate. They denied his petition and gave Edward Revell custody of the estate (LEO 37; Accomack County Wills and Deeds 1676–1680:62; SR 6578; PB 4:2, 541; 5:398; 6:540).

Leonard Yeo I: In August 1637 Leonard Yeo patented 850 acres on Old Poquoson Creek in Elizabeth City County. He added to his holdings in 1644 by patenting 350 acres at the head of the Hampton River. During 1645 and 1646 Yeo served as a burgess for Elizabeth City County. He was returned to the assembly and represented Elizabeth City from 1662 to 1670. He seems to have had some business dealings with William Burdett of the Eastern Shore, to whom he loaned plow chains. Colonel Yeo's property on the Back River descended to his son, Leonard II, whose July 1690 will was presented to the General Court on April 28th and recorded in Elizabeth City County's monthly court on November 18, 1690. Leonard Yeo II, who said that he lived on the Back River and was sick and weak, named his wife, Mary, as his sole beneficiary and designated her as his executrix (LEO 23–24, 38; AMES 2:308; PB 1:444; 2:201; NEAL 5, 15, 40–41).

Yeotassa (Native American): In early August 1659 Yeotassa, Pantatouse, Chakingatough, and George Caquescough, four Machodoc Indians who stood accused of murdering colonist John Cammel, were brought to the justices of Northumberland County by their own people. Although a jury found all four Indians guilty and sentenced George Caquescough to be hanged, Yeotassa and the other two men were released. Nearly two years later Northumberland County's justices ordered the Machodoc to leave their tribal land. They indicated that when Cammel was killed, one Machodoc warrior, who purportedly was involved in the slaying, was not brought in. Moreover, the justices believed that the Machodoc were conspiring with other natives "to make a Warr upon us." Because of those suspicions, the justices decided that some local men, with the assistance of the militia, should drive the Indians from their land (Northumberland County Order Book 1652–1665:216, 239).

York: On February 15, 1768, when an inventory was made of the late Richard Ambler's slaves on Jamestown Island and his leasehold in the Governor's Land, a male slave named York was listed. In 1769 a boy named York was living on the Governor's Land and was attributed to the late Edward Ambler I's estate (York County Wills and Inventories 21:386–391; AMB-E).

[No First Name] Young (Younge, Yonge): In February 1624 a servant whose surname was Young was part of Sir George Yeardley's household in urban Jamestown (VI&A 776).

Richard Young: Richard Young came to Virginia in 1616, and in early 1624 he and his wife, Joan I, and their young daughter, Joan II, were living in Thomas Gray's household in urban Jamestown. By early 1625 the Youngs had moved to Elizabeth City and were sharing their home with a 12-year-old girl named Susan, whose connection with the family is uncertain (VI&A 776–777).

Robert Young: On July 31, 1622, Robert Young set sail for Virginia with William Rowley, a resident of urban Jamestown (VI&A 777).

Thomas Young (Yonge, Younge): In September 1632 or 1633, Thomas Young, a Londoner, was authorized to undertake a voyage of discovery in Virginia. In April 1634 he informed England's governing officials that he and his nephew, Robert Evelyn (Evelin), wanted to trade in America, especially in Virginia. Sometime prior to July 13, 1634, Young arrived in Jamestown. He sent a letter home, indicating that there was a great deal of tension between Lord Baltimore's supporters and opponents (VI&A 777).

Thomas Young: On January 12, 1677, Thomas Young, one of the rebel Nathaniel Bacon's most ardent supporters, was tried at a martial court held aboard Captain John Martin's ship while at anchor in the York River. Young admitted his guilt and was sentenced to be hanged. Governor William Berkeley later declared that Young had been commissioned by one of Bacon's followers, a General Monke. On February 10, 1677, Governor William Berkeley issued a proclamation in which he named those who were exempt from the king's pardon on account of their role in Bacon's Rebellion. One of those was Young, who already had been executed. He was said to have furnished provisions to Bacon's men (MCGC 454, 527; NEVILLE 61, 274; SR 658, 660, 749).

William Young: William Young, a Virginia Company investor, arrived in Jamestown in 1608 in the 1st Supply of new colonists (VI&A 777).

Thomas Yowell (Youell, Youll, Youlle) II: Thomas Yowell II was the son of Thomas Yowell I of Northumberland County, who died in 1655 at age 40. He was survived by his sons, Thomas II and Richard, and his widow, Ann, the daughter of Ann Sturman (Stereman). In 1671 Captain Thomas Yowell II of Westmoreland County presented the late William Hardidge I's will to the county court and asked the decedent's widow, Elizabeth, whether she would accept his bequest instead of her dower third. Yowell was named guardian of the decedent's children, and in May 1673 he gave William Hardidge II custody of his inheritance. Thomas Yowell II was married to Anne (Ann, Anna), one of the late Colonel Richard Lee I's daughters. In June 1673 the Yowell couple, who resided in Nominy, relinquished their legal interest in the Lee estate, transferring it into the hands of Colonel Lee's primary heir, his son, John. When Captain Thomas Yowell II testified before Westmoreland County's justices a year later, he said that he was 30 years old. He became a county justice shortly thereafter and served for many years. In 1677, while he was high sheriff, he sold a piece of property on the Lower Machodoc River to Westmoreland County potter Morgan Jones. Richard Mitchell sued Yowell in 1681, claiming that Yowell was unlawfully detaining his sloop. Yowell, on the other hand, claimed that he had purchased the vessel from a third party. Although a jury decided in favor of the plaintiff, Yowell stated that he planned to appeal the decision to the General Court. In September 1684 Thomas Yowell II was authorized to keep the public ferry at Nominy, which was free for Westmoreland residents. During the assemblies held in 1685–1686, 1688, and 1693, he rep-

resented Westmoreland County in the assembly. On December 7, 1694, when Yowell, a resident of Cople Parish, made his will, he indicated that he was seriously ill. He bequeathed to his wife, Anne, life-rights in the 950-acre plantation on which they lived, as well all of his personal estate. He also made bequests to his surviving daughters, Ann Watts and Winefred Spence, and to his grandsons, Yowell Watts, Thomas Spence, and Yowell English. The testator named his wife, Anne, as executrix. The decedent's will was proved in May 1695 and an inventory of his estate, compiled in March 1696, reflects his wealth (LEO 48–49, 52; Northumberland County Order Book 1652–1665:68, 75, 85; Westmoreland County Deeds, Wills, Patents &c. 1653–1659:14, 20, 23, 38, 42, 65; Deeds, Patents &c. 1665–1677:83–83a, 147–149, 151a, 210a, 284–285a; Deeds and Wills 1691–1699:22a–23, 59a–60; Order Book 1676–1689:66, 152, 155, 187, 201, 235, 247, 257, 359, 373, 491, 526).

Z

Zeb: In 1769 Zeb, an adult male slave, was living on Jamestown Island and was included in the late Edward Ambler I's estate (AMB-E).

John Zouch II: During the 1620s John Zouch II and his sister, Isabella, came to Virginia with their father, John Zouch I, a titled nobleman, and tried to establish a plantation and ironworks at Rochdale, in the corporation of Henrico. When Sir John Zouch made his will in 1636, he left his Virginia land and much of his personal property to his son and namesake, who was a co-investor. By October 1642 John Zouch II had come into possession of some land on the upper side of the Appomattox River, and in 1644 he

served as a burgess for Henrico County. He died without living heirs and the property he inherited from his father escheated to the Crown (VI&A 777; LEO 22; PB 7:127).

Pedro De Zuniga: Don Pedro de Zuniga, Spain's unpopular ambassador to England, prided himself on passing along intelligence information. On June 16, 1608, Zuniga sent word to Spain that the Virginia colonists had fortified their settlement and were prepared to become pirates. On September 10, 1608, he sent another letter, plus a crude map of Tidewater Virginia, which shows the Jamestown fort. That drawing has become known as the Zuniga map. In May 1610 Don Alonso de Velasco replaced Zuniga as ambassador (VI&A 711, 778).

INDEX

A

Abbay, Thomas, 29
Abbes, Edward, 58
Abbott [Abbot]
  Elizabeth, 174
  George, 382
  Jeffrey, 29, 445
  Samuel, 29
  Thomas, 212
Abell (slave), 29
Aberdeen (slave), 29
Abochancano (Native
  American), see
  Opechancanough
Abrell [Abraell, Abrahall]
  Richard, 29
  Robert, 29, 290
Accapataugh (Native
  American), 29, 104, 277,
  294, 295, 341, 439
Acrig, George, 30
Adams [Addams]
  Ann, 30
  Peter, 30
  Robert, 30
  Robert (Mrs.), 30
  Thomas, 30
  William, 188
  _____, 30
Aden [Eden], Luke, 216
Adkins
  John, 157
  Sibella [Isabella] (_____),
  157, 158, 275
Adling, Henry, 30
Akomepen (Native American),
  421
Alder [Aldon], Richard, 30
Aldridge, Francis, 81
Alford, Richard, 30, 173
Alice (slave), 30, 133
Alicock [Allicock], Jeremy
  [Herome], 30
Allainby [Allamby], see
  Allomby
Alldy, Henry, 331
Allen [Allin]
  Arthur, 71, 279, 400
  Arthur I, 30, 449
  Arthur II, 30, 31, 50, 158,
  240, 350, 401
  Catherine [Katherine]
  (Baker), 31, 50
  Joan [Jone], 449
  William, 31
Allerton
  Elizabeth, 32
  Elizabeth (Willoughby)
  (Overzee) (Colclough),
  31, 32, 121
  Hannah (Keene) (Bushrod),
  32

Isaac, 31, 32, 43, 83, 121,
  256, 270, 282, 317, 380,
  394, 395, 400, 427, 453
Isaac II, 32
Rosamond (Fitzhugh), 32,
  161
Sarah, 256
Sarah (Taverner) (Travers),
  32
Willoughby, 32, 161
Allicock, see Alicock
Allin, see Allen
Allnutt (Alnut, Alnutt)
  Joan [Joane] (_____), 32,
  49
  Thomas, 32, 49, 55, 91,
  348, 356
Allomby [Allainby, Allamby]
  Eleanor [Ellynor], 33
  Elizabeth (_____), 32, 33
  Thomas, 32, 33
Alsop [Allsop, Alsope]
  James, 33, 70, 210, 235,
  274, 275, 365, 401
  Judith (_____), 33
Alves
  Alice (_____) (Harris), 193
  George, 193
Ambler
  Catherine (Bush) (Norton),
  36, 37
  Catherine Cary, 36, 37
  Edward, 225
  Edward I, 30, 33, 34, 35,
  37, 62, 67, 70, 75, 86,
  109, 113, 115, 136, 139,
  140, 142, 143, 147, 148,
  155, 171, 178, 189, 195,
  222, 223, 228, 232, 233,
  237, 238, 250, 259, 262,
  269, 274, 277, 286, 287,
  294, 296, 313, 320, 321,
  337, 353, 354, 356, 359,
  363, 369, 378, 390, 406,
  464, 465
  Edward II, 27, 36, 37, 89
  Elizabeth, 33, 36, 37
  Elizabeth (Birkard), 33
  Elizabeth (Jaquelin), 26, 33,
  34, 35, 225, 226, 317
  Frances (Armistead), 35, 36
  Jaquelin, 33, 35, 226
  John, 33, 131
  John I, 26, 33, 34, 35, 137,
  189, 202, 212, 225, 226,
  410
  John II, 27, 34, 35, 36, 37,
  56, 89, 108, 112, 271,
  372, 397
  John Jaquelin, 34, 36, 37
  Lucy (Marshall), 36
  Mary, 372
  Mary (Cary), 34, 35

Mary (_____), 413
Mary Cary, 36, 37
Philip St. George, 36, 37
Rebecca (Burwell), 35
Richard, 26, 29, 30, 33, 34,
  35, 37, 61, 62, 67, 70,
  75, 86, 109, 113, 115,
  131, 137, 140, 142, 143,
  147, 148, 155, 178, 189,
  192, 195, 209, 222, 223,
  225, 226, 228, 232, 233,
  237, 238, 250, 262, 265,
  269, 274, 287, 294, 296,
  301, 309, 317, 320, 321,
  337, 346, 353, 354, 356,
  363, 372, 390, 394, 406,
  410, 464
  Richard Cary, 36, 37
  Sarah (Taylor) (Holcombe),
  37
  Sarah Jaquelin, 36, 37
  Thomas Marshall, 36, 37
  William Marshall, 36, 37
Ambler Family, 27, 37, 89,
  126, 184, 285, 414, 428,
  456
Amry, Charles, 37
Amy [Amey] (slave), 37, 189
Anderson
  Comfort, 37
  Mary (_____), 37
  Naomi, 37
  William, 37
Andrews [Andrewes], see also
  Andros
  Dorothea (Robins)
  (Evelyn), 38
  Elizabeth (Travellor), 38
  Joachim [Jocomb, Joakim,
  Jockey, Jenkin], 37, 182
  Joachim (Mrs.), 37
  Robin (Native American),
  38
  William, 38, 331, 347
  William I, 38
  William II, 38
  _____ (Bishop), 439
Andros [Andrus], see also
  Andrews
  Edmond [Edmund], 38,
  72, 113, 219, 299, 309,
  341, 367
Angelo (slave), 9, 38, 314
Angood, John, 143
Anne, Queen of England, 25
Annesley
  Frances (_____) (Thorpe),
  404
  John, 404
Anscomb, _____, 89
Anthrobus, Mary, 38, 367
Apleby, see Appleby

Appenmaw (Native American), 38, 111, 300, 304
Appleby [Apleby], William, 38
Appleton
  Frances (Gerrard) (Speke) (Peyton), 39, 190, 321, 378, 379, 426, 427
  John, 38, 39, 190, 321, 427
Applewaite [Applewayte, Applewhaite]
  Anne, 39
  Henry, 39, 324
  Henry (Mrs.), 39
  John, 39
  Thomas, 39
  William, 39
Archer
  Gabriel, 3, 4, 39
  George, 206, 242
  John, 159
  Martha (Field), 159
Argall [Argal, Argoll, Argyle], Samuel, 7, 39, 49, 59, 70, 84, 123, 128, 142, 168, 170, 208, 218, 248, 270, 276, 279, 289, 315, 320, 330, 336, 353, 369, 378, 387, 393, 396, 417, 423, 432, 445, 453
Arlington (Lord), 290, 311, 364
Armiger [Armager]
  Suzanne (_____) (Fisher), 40, 160
  William, 40, 44, 160, 282, 337
Armistead [Armestead, Armstead, Armsted]
  Anna [Anne] (Lee), 256
  Anthony, 40, 151, 462
  Anthony I, 41
  Anthony II, 40, 41
  Frances, 35, 36, 45, 213, 281, 457
  Hannah, 431
  Hannah (Ellyson), 40, 41, 151
  Hind, 41
  John, 41, 229, 444
  Judith, 40
  Moss, 41
  Rebecca (_____), 41
  Robert, 40, 41
  Symon, 39
  William, 80, 462
  William I, 40, 41
  William II, 41
  William III, 41
  _____, 41
Arndell, *see Arrundell*
Arnold
  Anthony, 29, 41
  Benedict, 126, 312
  Benjamin, 202
  Thomas, 462
Awrrey, *see Awbrey*

Arrundell [Arndell, Arondell, Arundel, Arundell, Arundelle]
  Elizabeth, 41, 42
  John, 42
  Peter, 42
  Richard, 42
Arthur, Richard, 42
Asbie, John, 42
Ascam [Ascomb, Ascombe]
  Abigail [Abigall], 42, 249
  Mary (_____), 42, 91, 115, 249, 326, 352
  Peter, 115, 249, 326
  Peter I, 42
  Peter II, 42, 249
Ascomowett (Native American), *see Jeffrey [Geoffrey]*
Ashley, Ann, 42
Ashton [Aston]
  Hannah (_____), 43
  John, 43
  Mary, 119
  Peter, 39, 42, 43, 83, 327
  Walter I, 43, 119
  Walter II, 43
  Warbowe (_____), 43
Aston, *see Austin*
Atherton, Peter, *see Nelson, William*
Atkins
  John, 43, 138, 383
  Richard, 43, 137
  William, 43
  _____, 43
Attahune (Native American), 43
Attowell, *see Ottway*
Atwell, Nicholas, 44
Auborne [Awborne]
  Mary (_____), 44
  Richard, 44, 46, 116, 147, 213, 224, 244, 251, 312, 361, 452, 455
Aubrey, *see Awbrey*
Austin (Austen, Austine, Aston)
  Robert, 44
  Samuel, 97
Avelinge, Arthur, 153
Avery, Thomas, 171
Awborne, *see Auborne*
Awbrey [Aubrey, Awbry, Awrrey]
  Henry, 44, 45, 364, 453, 456
  Mary, 45
  Mary (_____), 45
  Richard, 45
Axwell, Thomas, 355, 357
Aylemer [Aylmer]
  Frances (Armistead), 35, 36, 45, 213, 281, 457
  Justinian, 45, 213, 281, 457

B

Backer, *see Baker*
Bacon
  Ann (_____) (Smith), 45, 61, 157, 235, 370
  Elizabeth (Duke), 47, 48, 227, 451
  Elizabeth (Kingsmill) (Tayloe), 45, 46, 47, 243, 284, 396
  Mary, 48
  Nathaniel (Col.), 45, 46, 47, 48, 96, 103, 131, 157, 182, 203, 217, 243, 284, 287, 299, 336, 345, 370, 396
  Nathaniel (the rebel), 19, 20, 21, 31, 32, 33, 40, 41, 44, 45, 46, 47, 48, 50, 53, 54, 65, 67, 73, 74, 78, 81, 83, 85, 87, 90, 97, 102, 104, 110, 112, 117, 118, 124, 128, 134, 141, 142, 144, 145, 147, 155, 156, 169, 170, 171, 175, 176, 177, 184, 186, 196, 199, 204, 212, 213, 214, 222, 224, 227, 229, 231, 233, 235, 236, 239, 243, 247, 249, 251, 252, 256, 268, 273, 278, 279, 286, 288, 290, 293, 299, 305, 306, 308, 311, 324, 325, 329, 332, 340, 350, 352, 354, 359, 361, 365, 366, 369, 373, 377, 380, 384, 386, 392, 404, 405, 417, 421, 426, 427, 436, 439, 440, 442, 445, 447, 448, 452, 457, 460, 464
  Nicholas, 286
  Thomas, 47, 227
  _____, 46
Baglen, Thomas, 48
Bagley, *see Bagness*
Bagnall [Bagnell]
  Anne [Ann] (Braswell), 48, 80
  James, 48, 80
  John, 358
  Rebecca (Izard), 48
Bagness [Bagley], Anthony, 48
Bagwell
  Alice (_____) (Stratton), 48
  Henry, 48
  James, 48
  Joan [Joane] (_____) (Alnutt), 32, 49
  John, 44, 48
  Thomas, 32, 48
Bailey [Bailie, Baile, Baily, Baylie, Baly, Baley, Bayley, Bayly]
  Arthur, 49, 129

Avarilla (Bristow), 87
Edmund, 49
Henry, 49
John, 49, 211
Joyce, 49
Lacy, 49
Lewis, 123
Mary, 49, 154, 211, 212
Mary (_____), 50
Richard I, 49
Temperance, 90, 118, 119
Thomas, 49, 50
Ursilla, 49
Ursilla (_____), 49
Whittington, 49
William, 49, 50
Baird
John, 50, 116, 218, 410
Margaret (_____), 50
Baker [Backer]
Catherine [Katherine],
31, 50
Elizabeth (_____), 50
Henry I, 50
Henry II, 50
James, 50
John, 50
Lawrence, 31, 50
Mary (_____), 50
Moses, 330
Thomas, 50
Baldridge
James, 51
Thomas, 50, 51
Baldry [Baldrey, Baldrye],
Robert, 51, 142
Baldwin [Baldwine, Baldwyn,
Bauldwin]
John, 51, 140, 168, 431
Mary (Wilkins), 448
William, 280
_____, 280
Baley, *see Bailey*
Ball [Baul, Baule]
David, 52
George, 52
Hannah, 52, 166, 241
Hannah (_____), 51, 52,
166
Henry, 51
James, 52
Joseph, 51, 52
Margaret, 52
Margaret (_____), 52
Richard, 52
Samuel, 52
Stretchley, 52
William, 134, 166, 440
William I, 51, 52, 241
William II, 51, 52
William III, 52
Ballard
Anna (_____), 53
Mathew, 53
Thomas, 271, 377, 382

Thomas I, 52, 53, 334
Thomas II, 53
Ballard Family, 53
Baltimore, *see also Calvert*
(Lady), 311
(Lord), 311
Baly, *see Bailey*
Bamford [Bramford,
Brampford], John, 53
Banam, John, 205
Banbridg, Sarah (Strechley),
389
Banckton [Bankton], John, 53
Bandage, Phillip, 53
Banister
Henry, 58
John, 76
Banks [Bancks, Bankus,
Bincks, Binks, Byncks]
Ann (_____), 53
Christopher, 53, 54
Francis, 53
William, 53
Bankton, *see Banckton*
Baptista, John, 54
Baram, *see Barham*
Barber [Barbar, Barbour,
Barker]
Christopher, 55
Elizabeth (_____)
(Burbage) (Streater),
54, 388
Henry, 55
John I, 33, 54, 145, 298,
336, 454
John II, 54, 78, 125, 328,
336, 388
Letitia (_____), 33, 54, 125,
298, 328
Mary, 55
Philip, 176
Prudence (_____), 54
Stephen, 55, 445
Thomas, 54
William, 55, 125, 126, 382,
387
William I, 54
William II, 55
William III, 55
Barbribb
Jane (_____), 443
William, 443
Barcroft, Charles, 139
Barefoot, William, 55
Bargrave, John, 55
Barham [Baram, Barram]
Anthony, 55, 97, 159, 269
Elizabeth, 55
Elizabeth (Benne), 55
Barker, *see Barber*
Barnard, *see Bernard*
Barnes
Alice (_____), 75
Edward, 51, 75
Lancelot [Launcelott], 56

Richard, 56
Robert, 56
Barnett [Barnet, Barnitt]
John, 56, 241
Mary (_____) (Kennell),
56, 241
Thomas, 56
Barney
Edward E., 28
Louise (_____), 28
Barnitt, *see Barnett*
Barram, *see Barham*
Barraud, Philip, 56, 271
Barrett [Barret]
Thomas, 56
William, 56
Barrington, Robert, 56
Barrow, James, 233
Barry, William, 313
Bartley [Bartlett]
Edward, 57, 275
Jane, 275
Jane (_____), 57, 275
Richard, 56
Barwick
Elizabeth (_____), 57
John, 93
Thomas, 57, 135
Base, *see Basse*
Baskerville
John, 55
Mary (Barber), 55
Basse [Bass, Base]
Edward, 57, 150, 415
Elizabeth, 150, 294 (Native
American)
John, 57, 150, 294
Mary (Jordan), 57, 415
Mary (Tucker) (Native
American), 415
Nathaniel, 57, 80, 150, 274,
294, 415
Bassett
Bridget [Bridgett] (Cary),
57
Joanna (Burwell), 57
William, 187
William I, 57
William II, 57
William III, 57
Bastard, Mary, 253
Bateman
Hastings, 57, 58
John, 57, 58
Bates, Thomas, 58
Bath, *see Booth*
Batt [Batte, Battes, Batts, Bats]
Ellen [Ellin] (_____), 58
Henry, 58, 174
Mary (Lound), 58
Michael, 58
Nathaniel, 316
Thomas, 59
William, 58, 344

Battail [Battaile],
Catherine [Katherine]
(Taliaferro), 58, 59
John, 58, 59, 284
Batters, _____ (Lt.), 59, 151
Batts, *see Batt*
Baugh
John, 59, 236
Mary, 171
Baughan [Boughan]
James I, 59
James II, 59
John, 59
Baul [Baule], *see Ball*
Bauldwin, *see Baldwin*
Bawdreye, Mary, 59
Baylie [Bayley, Bayly], *see*
Bailey
Baylor
John, 59, 60
Lucy (Todd) (O'Brien), 60
_____, 60
Baynes, Richard, 60
Baynton
Benjamin, 429
Mary (_____), 429
_____, 429
Bea, Christopher, 371
Beach [Beech]
George, 157, 288, 275
Sibella [Isabella] (_____)
(Adkins) (Felgate), 157,
158, 275
Beadle
Gabriel, 60
John, 60
Beale
Alice (_____), 60
George, 60
Thomas, 60, 81
Beaman, Joseph, 297
Beamond, Richard, 387
Beard
Joan [Joane] (_____), 60
Margaret (_____), 58, 60
William, 58, 60
Bearly, *see Beazley*
Beasley [Beaslie, Beasly], *see*
Beazley
Beaston [Beastone, Beriston,
Berristone, Boriston], Theo-
philus, 61
Beaumont, _____, 39
Beazley [Beasley, Beaslie,
Beasly, Bearly], Jacob
[Job], 61
Beckett, *see Leckett*
Beckford
Anner (Westropp), 439
Edward, 439
Beckinham [Beckingham]
Elizabeth (_____)
(Travers), 61, 408
Robert, 61, 125, 224, 408,
424

Bedell, Dorothy [Dorithy], 96,
452
Beech, *see Beach*
Beheathland [Bethlehem]
Dorothy, 61, 128, 163
Mary, 61, 66, 134
Mary (_____), 61, 163
Robert, 61, 66, 134
Behoute, Ann, 61
Belfield, Richard, 61
Bell [Bel]
Henry, 61
John, 61
Richard, 61, 212
Belson, Ann, 61, 197, 293
Ben (slave), 61, 62, 265
Benn [Ben, Benne]
Anne, 62
Anne (_____), 62, 419
Arthur, 62, 370
Christopher, 62, 419
George, 62
James, 419
James I, 62
James II, 62
Jane (Smith), 370
Jeane, 62
Mary, 62
Sarah, 62
Bennett
Alice (_____), 370
Ambrose, 139
Anna [Anne], 63, 74
Edward, 53, 62, 158, 162,
205, 206, 386, 433
Elizabeth, 55
Katherine (_____), 128
Mary, 62, 205
Mary Ann (_____), 101
Philip, 63
Richard, 55, 63, 74, 101,
141, 157, 158, 174, 205,
235, 290, 334, 342, 394,
400, 417
Richard I, 62, 63, 208
Richard III, 63
Robert, 62, 63, 99
Samuel, 452
Silvestra [Sylvester], 62,
205, 206
Thomas, 63
William, 63
_____, 173
Bennett Family, 63, 111, 399
Bentley [Bentlie, Bently]
William, 63, 64
_____, 440
Beriston, *see Beaston*
Berkeley
Edmund, 346
Frances (Culpeper)
(Stephens), 46, 65, 66,
121, 130, 145, 146, 159,
205, 228, 266, 267, 375,
381, 385, 441

John, 64, 164
Mary (Kemp), 346
Maurice, 64
Sarah, 346
William, 13, 14, 16, 18, 19,
20, 30, 31, 33, 39, 41,
44, 45, 46, 47, 50, 53,
54, 59, 60, 63, 64, 65,
66, 67, 68, 69, 70, 73,
74, 75, 81, 83, 85, 87,
97, 100, 102, 105, 110,
111, 112, 115, 117, 121,
124, 125, 128, 130, 132,
138, 140, 141, 142, 145,
146, 147, 148, 150, 155,
159, 160, 169, 171, 175,
177, 181, 186, 188, 189,
191, 195, 196, 198, 199,
204, 205, 209, 212, 213,
214, 218, 220, 221, 222,
224, 228, 229, 231, 232,
233, 235, 238, 239, 240,
243, 244, 247, 249, 251,
261, 263, 266, 268, 273,
277, 279, 289, 290, 293,
301, 305, 306, 308, 321,
322, 325, 328, 329, 335,
338, 347, 352, 353, 354,
355, 358, 359, 360, 361,
365, 366, 371, 373, 380,
383, 384, 385, 386, 390,
392, 395, 404, 405, 408,
417, 421, 422, 423, 424,
426, 432, 436, 438, 439,
440, 441, 442, 445, 447,
450, 452, 454, 457, 458,
459, 461, 463, 464
William (Mrs.), 64
Berkeley Family, 64, 66
Bernard [Barnard]
Beheathland, 66, 134
John, 55, 56, 146
Lucy (Higginson)
(Burwell), 66, 96, 265,
266, 309
Mary (Beheathland), 61,
66, 134
Richard, 334
Thomas, 61, 66, 134
William, 56, 96, 265, 423
_____ (Col.), 205, 423
Bernardo
Peirce (_____), 66
_____, 66
Berristone, *see Beaston*
Berry
Henry, 322
John, 66, 67, 290
Bertrand, John, 263
Bess (slave), 52
Best, Christopher, 67, 454
Bethlehem, *see Beheathland*
Betsey (slave), 67
Betty (Native American) alias
Nonomisk, *see Nonomisk*

Betty (slave), 67
Beverley [Beverly]
  Catherine, 68, 69
  Catherine (Hone), 68, 69,
    213, 347, 406
  Elizabeth (_____), 68
  Henry "Harry," 68, 69, 318,
    372
  John, 318
  Margaret (_____), 67
  Mary, 68
  Peter, 68, 69, 444
  Robert, 48, 69, 150, 318,
    441
  Robert I, 41, 53, 60, 67, 68,
    78, 92, 94, 114, 116,
    118, 132, 146, 176, 213,
    218, 239, 247, 290, 297,
    311, 337, 347, 361, 365,
    372, 406, 424, 440, 441,
    458
  Robert II, 68, 69, 98, 165,
    194, 216, 217, 382, 387,
    420
  Ursula (Byrd), 69, 98
  William, 69, 70, 186
  _____, 444
Biard, Peter, 70
Bibbie [Bibby]
  Mary, 350
  Thomas, 70
Bickerton
  Bridget (Westropp), 439
  Richard, 439
Biggs
  Rebecca, 70
  Richard I, 70
  Richard II, 70
  Sarah (_____), 70
  Timothy, 105
  _____ (_____)
    (Catchmaid), 105
Billington, Luke, 132
Billy (slave), 70
Binford, Anthony, 235
Bincks [Binks], see Banks
Binns [Binns], Thomas, 70,
  278
Bird, see Byrd
Birkard, Elizabeth, 33
Bishop [Bishopp, Bushopp]
  Dorothy (Senior), 361
  Henry, 70
  Jacob, 361
  John, 70, 278
  John I, 70
  John II, 70
Biss [Bisse]
  James, 71, 398
  Sarah (_____) (Taylor)
    (Lucy), 398
"Black Bess," (slave), 242
Black [Blacke, Blackey,
  Blackley, Blacky]
  Margaret (Gybson), 71
  William, 71

Blackmore
  Arthur, 126, 445
  James, 67
  Susan, 125, 126, 445
Blackwood, Susan, 71
Blacky, see Black
Blades, Mary, 71, 246
Blagg, Edward, Jr., 427
Blagrave, Mansell, 272
Blainy, see Blaney
Blair
  Archibald, 71, 72, 96, 103,
    150
  James, 23, 38, 41, 71, 72,
    98, 103, 113, 153, 196,
    225, 267, 299, 309, 313,
    351, 353, 359, 376, 382,
    458
  John, 71, 72, 133
  Mary (Wilson) (Roscoe)
    (Cary), 71, 103, 341,
    342
  Sarah (Harrison), 72
Blaise, James, 366
Blake
  Bartholomew, 72
  John, 72, 73
  _____, 72
Blanckevile, Charles, 73
Bland
  Adam, 73
  Anna (_____), 73, 120
  Anna [Anne] (Bennett),
    63, 74
  Edward, 73, 206, 211
  Elizabeth (Yates), 74, 462
  Giles, 73, 74, 132, 169,
    224, 238, 251, 268, 365
  Jane, 73
  Jane (Bland), 73, 211
  John, 64, 120, 268, 394
  John I, 73, 74, 116, 151
  John II, 73, 74, 365
  Mary (Bennett), 62, 205
  Mary (Emperour), 151
  Peregrine [Perregrin,
    Perigreene, Perygreene],
    74
  Richard, 74
  Sarah (_____), 73, 74, 116,
    120, 365
  Theodorick, 63, 73, 120,
    338
  Theodorick I, 74, 145
  Theodorick II, 74
  Thomas, 62
  William, 74, 411, 462
  _____, 159
Blaney [Blainy, Blanie, Blany,
  Blanye, Blayny]
  Edward, 74, 75, 106, 129,
    138, 150, 195, 218, 263,
    283, 304, 330, 358, 364,
    382, 383, 423, 430, 431,
    437, 442, 444

Margaret (_____) (Powell),
  74, 75, 106, 330, 393,
  437, 442
Blayton, Thomas, 75, 286
Bledshaw, George, 341
Bledsoe, George, 170
Blesse [Bliss], John, 75
Blewitt [Blewett, Bluett, Bluet]
  Benjamin, 75
  Elizabeth, 75
  _____ (Capt.), 75
Bliss, see Blesse
Blois, Charles, 48
Blore [Blower]
  Frances [Francis] (_____),
    93, 354
  John, 93, 354, 422
Bluett [Bluet], see Blewitt
Blunt, Humphrey [Henry], 75
Bly
  John, 107
  Mary (Wood), 107, 454
Boague, see Bogue
Bob (slave), 75, 412
Bock, Humphrey, 75
Bogue [Boague], William, 440
Bohun [Bohune, Bohunn,
  Bohunne]
  Alice (_____) (Barnes), 75
  Lawrence, 75, 111, 286
Boice [Boise], see Boyse
Bolling
  Agnes, 242
  Anne [Ann] (Stith), 75
  Jane (Rolfe), 75
  John, 75
  Robert, 75, 76
  Stith, 76
Bolt [Boult], Amias [Annis], 76
Bolton [Boulton]
  Frances (Mottrom)
    (Spencer), 292, 318,
    360, 380, 381
  Francis, 76
  John, 360, 381
  Joseph, 76
Bond
  Dorothy (_____), 76
  John I, 76
  John II, 76
Boodington, John, 82
Booker, see also Brooks
  Hannah (_____) (Marshall),
    275
  Richard, 275
Booth [Bath, Boothe, Bouth,
  Buth]
  Alderman, 220
  Elizabeth (_____), 77
  Frances (_____), 77
  Henry [Henery], 76, 228,
    281
  John, 58, 76, 77, 343
  Mary, 77
  Reynold, 77

Robert I, 77
Robert II, 77
_____ (Sgt.), 76
Boriston, *see Beaston*
Bouch, *see Boush*
Boucher
    Daniel, 77
    Elizabeth, 77
    Elizabeth (_____), 77
    Robert, 77
Boughan, *see Baughan*
Boult, *see Bolt*
Boulton, *see Bolton*
Bourcher, George, 77
Bourne [Borne]
    James, 77
    John, 78
    Robert, 77, 78
Bourrows, *see Burrows*
Boush [Bouch]
    Alice (Mason), 277, 411
    Elizabeth "Betsey"
        ["Betsy"], 411, 413
    Samuel, 128, 411
Bouth, *see Booth*
Bowe
    Jeoffrey, 78
    Sarah (_____), 78, 138
    Thomas, 138
Boweman, *see Bowman*
Bowland, Robert, 78
Bowler
    Anne, 79
    Elizabeth, 79
    James, 79
    John, 78, 254, 446
    John (Mrs.), 446
    Sarah (_____), 78
    Tabitha (_____), 78, 79,
        148, 156, 286, 443
    Thomas, 54, 78, 148, 156,
        177, 286, 388
    _____, 443
Bowman [Boweman]
    Grace, 51
    Edmund, 143
    Edmund (Mrs.), 143
    Sarah, 79
Boyse [Boice, Boise, Boyce,
    Boys]
    Alice (_____), 79, 148
    Cheney [Chyna, Chene,
        Cheyney], 79
    Christopher, 334
    Elizabeth (Hardidge), 190
    Hannah, 79
    Humphrey [Humpry], 79
    John [Johnny], 79
    John (Mrs.), 79
    Luke, 43, 79, 148
    Thomas, 141
    _____, 79
Bradford [Braford, Brodsil,
    Brodsul]
    Frances (Taylor), 398

Henry, 79
John, 79
Richard, 398
William, 89
Bradley, Thomas, 79
Bradwell, John, 80
Bradye, John, 80, 456
Braford, *see Bradford*
Braine
    Edward, 181
    Sarah (_____) (Harris)
        (Stegg) (Grendon), 181,
        384
Bramford [Brampford], *see
    Bamford*
Branch
    Christopher, 80
    John, 80
    Mary (_____), 80
    Obedience, 178
    Patience, 178
    Thomas, 80
    _____, 80
Bransby, Thomas, 195
Brashear [Brasseur, Brassier,
    Brassieur]
    John, 80
    Margaret, 237
    Mary, 119
    Mary (Pitt), 80, 323, 324
    Robert, 80
Brass [Brase] (slave), 80
Brasseur {Brassier, Brassieur],
    see Brashear
Braswell [Bracewell]
    Anne [Ann], 48, 80
    Jane, 80
    Rebecca, 80
    Richard, 81
    Robert, 48, 80, 81
Bray
    Angelica (_____), 81
    Ann, 81
    Ann (_____), 81
    David I, 81
    Edward, 81
    James, 54
    James I, 60, 81, 145, 147,
        309
    James II, 81, 127, 147
    John, 81
    Mourning (Glenn) (Pettus),
        81
    Plomer [Plumer, Plummer],
        82
    Robert, 81, 82
    Samuel, 82
    Sarah (_____), 82
    Thomas I, 81
Breman [Breeman, Bremo,
    Bremor, Bremore]
    Margaret (_____), 82
    Thomas, 82
Brent
    Charles, 161

Frances (_____) (Harrison),
    82
George, 337
George II, 83
Giles [Gyles], 165
Giles [Gyles] I, 82, 83, 99,
    244, 245, 327
Giles [Gyles] II, 82, 83, 245
Margaret, 82, 99, 244
Mary, 82, 244, 245
Mary [Maria]
    (Kittamaquund) (Native
    American), 82, 244, 245
Richard, 82
Brereton [Brerreton,
    Brewerton]
    Elizabeth, 83
    Jane (Claiborne), 83
    Marie [Mary] (_____), 84
    Thomas, 43, 256
    Thomas I, 83, 355
    Thomas II, 83, 84
Brett
    Anne (Gerrard)
        (Broadhurst), 87, 207,
        426
    Elizabeth (Green), 305
    Henry, 87, 426
    James, 305
Bretton [Brittaine, Brittin,
    Britton]
    Eleanor (_____), 333
    Robert, 333
    Temperance (_____), 70
    William, 70
Brewer [Bower, Brower]
    Ann, 84
    John I, 84
    John II, 84
    John III, 84
    Margaret, 84
    Marie [Mary] (_____), 84
    Roger, 84
    Thomas, 84
Brewster
    Edward, 84, 144, 168, 248,
        279, 385, 387, 396, 415,
        423, 438, 453
    Henry, 85
    Richard, 84, 85, 168
    Richard (Mrs.), 84, 85
    William, 85
Bricke [Britt], Edward, 85
Bricken [Britain, Brechen]
    James, 128
    _____ (Crafford), 128
Bridger
    Elizabeth, 85, 253
    Elizabeth (_____) (Webb)
        (Worry), 459
    Hester, 85
    Hester (Pitt), 85, 323
    Joseph, 73, 76, 131, 174,
        207, 253
    Joseph I, 85

Joseph II, 85
Martha, 85, 174
Mary, 85
Mary (_____), 85
Samuel, 85, 459
William, 85
Bridges
  Anthony, 387
  Nathaniel, *see Pope,*
    Nathaniel
Bridget [Bridgett] (slave), 86
Briggs
  Edmund, 329, 382
  Richard, 329, 382
Bright
  Elizabeth, 413
  Francis, 413
Brinton [Brynton], Edward, 86
Briscoe [Brisco]
  Ann (Holder), 86, 87, 114,
    209, 210, 316, 337, 375
  Ann (_____), 406
  William, 33, 86, 87, 114,
    210, 316, 337, 406
  _____, 86
Brishitt [Briskitt], Peter
  [Peeter], 86
Brislow, Richard, 86
Bristow
  Avarilla, 87
  Avarilla [Averilla] (Curtis),
    87
  Joane (_____), 86, 333
  Peter, 87
  Robert, 49, 60, 86, 323, 333
  Robert I, 86
  Robert II, 87
  Susanna (_____), 87
Brittaine [Brittin, Britton], *see*
  Bretton
Broadhurst [Brodhurst]
  Anne (Gerrard), 87, 207,
    426
  Elizabeth, 87
  Gerrard, 87
  Walter, 320, 321
  Walter I, 87, 96, 426
  Walter II, 87
Broadnax [Brodnax]
  Ann (_____), 88
  Edward, 87, 409
  Elizabeth, 87, 409
  John, 88, 153, 225, 353,
    359, 410
  Rebecca (_____) (Travis),
    87, 409, 410
  William I, 33, 87, 88, 149,
    150, 179, 209, 409, 410,
    420
  William II, 33, 87, 88, 93,
    262, 317, 351, 409
Broadnax Family, 25, 354, 359
Broadribb
  Lydia (_____), 88, 371
  William, 88, 110, 146, 195,
    371, 416

_____, 88
Brocas [Brocus]
  Elinor [Elnor] (_____), 88,
    89, 101
  Mary (_____), 88
  William, 88, 89, 101, 388
Brock, Benjamin, 440
Brockenbrough, William, 89
Brocus, *see Brocas*
Brodnax, *see Broadnax*
Brodsil [Brodsul], *see Bradford*
Bromer, *see Brummall*
Bromfield
  Bridget (Buck) (Burrows)
    (Davis), 89, 95, 130,
    138
  John, 89, 95, 130, 138
Brooks [Broockes, Brookes],
  see also Booker
  Richard, 89, 275
  Robert, 322
  William [alias Jones, alias
    Morgan], *see Morgan,*
    William
Broomer, Thomas, 89
Brown [Browne]
  Ann (_____), 90, 391
  Benjamin, 303
  Berkeley, 90, 391
  Devereau [Deborae,
    Deverax, Devereaux,
    Devereux, Deveroux],
    89, 90, 358
  Elizabeth (_____), 90, 254,
    288, 455
  Francis [Francys], 120, 150,
    288, 293
  Henry, 90, 391
  Henry II, 90
  Jane, 302, 312
  John, 90, 118, 447
  John (Mrs.), 90
  Margaret (_____), 447
  Original, 86
  Sarah, 447
  Tabitha (Scarborough)
    (Smart), 89, 90, 132,
    204, 359
  Temperance (Bailey), 90,
    118, 119
  Thomas, 90
  William, 160, 254, 435
  William I, 74, 90, 113, 455
  _____, 89
Browning [Browninge]
  John, 90
  Robert, 91, 383
  William, 91
Brummall [Bromer] Family,
  416
Bryan
  Benjamin, 219
  Charles, 325
  Robert, 448
  Susanna (_____)
    (Plumtree), 325

Brynton, *see Brinton*
Buck [Buckes]
  Benomi [Benomy], 91,130,
    143, 191, 243, 326
  Bridget, 89, 91, 95, 130,
    138
  Elizabeth, 89, 91, 130, 307,
    391
  Gercian, 91, 130, 222
  Mara, 91, 95, 344, 356
  Maria (Thorowgood), 91
  Peleg, 91, 130
  Richard, 9, 89, 91, 95, 102,
    130, 138, 143, 147, 155,
    182, 191, 222, 223, 243,
    249, 307, 326, 344, 377,
    409, 461
  William, 441
  _____, 349
Buck Family, 147
Buckingham
  Edward, 92
  _____, 91, 92
Buckler, Andrew, 92
Buckmaster [Buckmuster],
  John, 92
Buckner
  Ann (_____), 92
  John, 302, 444
  John I, 92
  John II, 92
  Sarah (_____), 92
  Thomas, 92
  William, 92
Buckridge, Ralph, 93
Budd, Richard, 270
Budworth, James, 93
Bullen, Silvester [Sylvester],
  93
Bullifant
  Francis, 88, 93, 215, 218
  Joyce (Hopkins), 93
Bullock [Bullocke]
  David, 27, 28, 414
  Hugh, 93
  Mary (_____), 93
  Robert, 93, 446
  Thomas, 95
  William, 93
  _____, 280
Bunn, Thomas, 428
Burbage
  Elizabeth (_____), 54,
    388
  Thomas, 166, 388
Burchitt, *see Burdett*
Burd [Burde], *see Byrd*
Burdett [Burchitt, Burditt]
  Alice [Alicia] (Travellor),
    93, 94, 422
  Frances [Francis] (Blore)
    (Sanders), 93, 354
  Thomas, 94
  William, 93, 94, 463
Burfoot, William, 94

Burgany
  Jane (Pyland), 440
  _____ (Dr.), 440
Burgess [Burges, Burgis]
  Grace, 446
  John, 185
  Temperance (_____), 446
  Thomas, 94
Burgh
  Elizabeth, 237
  William, 237
Burgis, *see Burgess*
Burke, David, 388
Burland, John, 94, 301
Burnett
  Joan [Jone] (Allen)
    (Williamson), 449
  Robert, 449
Burnham
  John, 68, 94
  Rowland, 94
Burras, *see Burrows*
Burrin, Anthony, 94
Burrows [Bourrows, Burrough,
  Burroughs, Burras,
  Burrowes]
  Anne [Ann], 164, 252
  Anthony, 94
  Barbary [Barbara], 95
  Benjamin, 95
  Benomi [Benomy], 95
  Bridget (Buck), 89, 91, 95,
    130, 138
  Christopher, 95
  Elizabeth, 95
  John, 42, 79, 89, 91, 94, 95,
    123, 138, 156, 169, 174,
    218, 403
  Mary, 95
  Mary (_____), 95
  Robert, 95
  William, 95
Burt [Burte, Burtt]
  Jane, 95
  Robert, 95
Burton
  George, 95
  Henry, 95, 273
  Thomas, 157
Burtt, *see Burt*
Burwell
  Abigail (Smith), 46, 57, 96
  Dorothy [Dorithy] (Bedell),
    96, 452
  Edward, 96, 452
  Elizabeth (Carter), 96
  James, 46, 96
  Joanna, 57
  Lewis, 205
  Lewis I, 71, 96, 265, 452
  Lewis II, 46, 57, 94, 96,
    265, 266, 300
  Lewis III, 96
  Lucy, 300
  Lucy (Higginson), 66, 96,
    265, 266, 309

Nathaniel, 46, 96
Rebecca, 35
_____, 96
Burwell Family, 27, 46, 71
Bush
  Catherine, 36, 37
  John, 309
  Susan, 151
  Susan (_____), 238, 379
Bushopp, *see Bishop*
Bushrod [Bushrode]
  Elizabeth (Farlow), 97
  Hannah (Keene), 32
  John, 32
  Mary (Peirsey) (Hill), 97,
    156, 180, 206, 315
  Richard, 97
  Thomas, 97, 206, 265, 297,
    315, 443
Bustone, John, 97, 251
Butler [Buttler]
  Ammaree, 418
  Elizabeth, 418
  Marie [Mary] (_____)
    (Brereton), 84
  Nathaniel, 9, 97, 157, 158,
    313
  Sara, 97
  Thomas, 56, 84, 219
  William, 97
Butt, Thomas, 286
Buttler, *see Butler*
Byncks, *see Banks*
Byrd [Bird, Burd]
  Ann (_____), 70
  Grace (Stegg), 384
  John, 33, 50, 70, 139, 224,
    237, 273, 288, 306, 307,
    312, 371, 384, 392, 393,
    414, 425
  Lucy (Parke), 98, 133, 265,
    309, 371
  Maria (Taylor), 98
  Mary (Horsemenden), 97
  Robert, 93, 207
  Ursula, 69, 98
  William I, 69, 97, 98, 170,
    171, 373, 378, 384, 390,
    405, 424, 442
  William II, 69, 72, 76, 96,
    98, 116, 133, 152, 205,
    226, 259, 261, 265, 267,
    309, 371, 416, 429
  _____, 384
Byrd Family, 71, 259

C

Cage [Cadge], Edward, 98, 227
Calcker [Calcar, Calker]
  _____ (Mrs.), 99
  _____, 99, 364
Caldwell, William, 98
Calker, *see Calcker*
Calthrop [Colethorpe], *see also
  Galthorpe*

Ann (_____), 99
Christopher, 99
Calver, James, 106
Calvert
  Anne (Mynne), 99
  Cecil, 2nd Lord Baltimore,
    82, 99, 199, 200, 311,
    464
  Charles, 3rd Lord Baltimore,
    142, 162, 167
  George I, 1st Lord
    Baltimore, 99
  George II, 99
  Jane (Sewell), 311
  Joane (_____), 99
  Leonard, 82, 99, 199, 200,
    244
  Philip, 311
Calvert Family, 245
Cammel, John, 100, 107, 308,
  464
Cann
  Delpheus, 99, 202
  _____, 195, 378
Cannion, Ralph, 99
Cant
  David I, 100
  David II, 100
  John, 100
Cantrell [Cantrill], William,
  100
Capp [Cappe], *see Capps*
Capper, John, 100
Capps [Capp, Cappe, Caps],
  William, 100
"Captain John" (Native
  American Indian), 232
Caquescough, George (Native
  American), 100, 107, 308,
  464
Carey, *see Cary*
Carleton, Stephen, 100
Carman, Henry, 101, 107
Carney
  Dany, 252
  Richard, 252
Carpenter, Symon, 236
Carraway
  John, 164
  _____, 164
Carter
  Alice (Croxon), 102
  Ann (Mathis), 102
  Avis (Turtley), 102
  Charles, 101, 102
  Edward, 101, 135, 166
  Elinor [Elnor] (_____)
    (Brocas), 88, 89, 101
  Elizabeth, 96, 101, 102,
    135, 391, 457
  Elizabeth (Hull), 101
  Elizabeth (Travers), 102,
    457
  Elizabeth (_____), 101
  Elizabeth "Betty" (Landon)
    (Willis), 102

Francis, 207
John, 51, 89, 135, 151, 200, 327
John I, 63, 101, 102
John II, 101, 102, 424, 457
Joseph, 135
Katherine, 135
Katherine (Dale), 135
Margaret, 150, 151
Peter, 135
Robert, 76, 101, 102, 196, 391, 457
Robert "King," 96, 102
Thomas, 135
William, 102
William (Mrs.), 178
_____, 102
Cartwright, John, 102
Carver
Richard, 82, 102
William, 102, 132
Carwithey, Richard, 103
Cary [Carey]
Anne [Ann] (Taylor), 57, 103, 104
Bridget [Bridgett], 57, 103
Harwood, 104
Henry, 103
James, 147
John, 104
Martha, 33, 104, 225, 226, 367
Martha (_____), 104
Mary, 34, 35
Mary (Milner), 103
Mary (Wilson) (Roscoe), 71, 103, 341, 342
Miles, 57, 104
Miles I, 45, 103, 104, 182
Miles II, 24, 71, 103
Thomas, 103
William, 103, 104, 225
Wilson, 34
Caskameno [Caskamin, "Esquire John"] (Native American), 104
Cassen
George, 104
Thomas, 104
William, 104
Cassinett [Cassina, Cossina], Arnold [Arnall], 46, 104, 213, 251, 342
Castine [Castillian]
Vencentia (_____), 104
Vincencio [Vicentio, Vincentio], 104, 420
Castle
Robert, 105, 160
Roger, 176
Caswell, William, 105
Cate (slave), *see Kate (slave)*
Catchmaid [Cathmaie, Catchmade]
Edward, 155

George, 105
George (Mrs.), 105
Cater, Edward, 166
Catesbie, Dorcas, 105
Catherine, Queen of the Weyanoke (Native American), 105
Catlett [Catlet]
Elizabeth, 105
Elizabeth (Thompson), 401
Elizabeth (_____), 105
John I, 105
John II, 105
Sarah, 105
William, 401
_____, 105
Caufield, *see Cawfield*
Caught [Cawt], Bryan, 106
Cauntrie [Chantry, Channtree], Robert, 106
Causey [Cawsey]
John, 106
Nathaniel, 106
Thomas, 106
Thomasine (_____), 106
Cawfield [Caufield]
Dorcas (_____), 106
Elizabeth, 106
Robert, 106
William, 106
Cawsey, *see Causey*
Cawt, *see Caught*
Ceely [Seely, Seelie], Thomas, 106
Ceny, Henry, 106
Chacrow (Native American), *see Shacrow*
Chakingatough (Native American), 100, 107, 308, 464
Challis [Challice], Edward, 107
Chamberlain [Chamberlin, Chamberlaine, Chamberlayne]
Edmund, 107
Elizabeth (Stratton), 107
Mary (Wood) (Bly), 107, 454
Robert, 337
Thomas, 107
Chambers
Alice, 107
Richard, 355
Chambly [Chambley], Robert, 107
Champion
Elizabeth, 87, 108, 409
John, 87, 107, 108, 409
William, 108, 210, 409
Chancellor, Robert, 108
Chanco [Chauco] (Native American), 108, 122, 305
Chandler [Chaundler, Chandeler]
Job, 447
John, 108, 389

Samuel, 108
Sarah, 391
Chantry [Chantree], *see Cauntrie*
Chaplin [Chaplain, Chaplaine, Chapline, Chaplyn], Isaac [Isaak], 108
Chapman
Benjamin, 108, 197
Francis, 108, 109
Philip, 344
William, 109, 115
Chappell, William, 463
Charles (slave), 109, 189
Charles I, King of England, xii, 16, 64, 85, 99, 111, 136, 187, 200, 217, 272, 291, 301, 459
Charles II, King of England, 16, 23, 66, 71, 105, 118, 130, 136, 172, 228, 231, 232, 239, 286, 290, 294, 301, 338, 362, 380, 438, 460, 461
Charlton [Charleton, Charleston]
Anne [Ann] (_____) (Huffe) (West), 109, 435
Bridgett, 109
Bridgett (_____) (Severne), 109
Elizabeth, 109
Henry [Henrie], 109, 344, 350
Stephen, 109, 127, 301, 386, 435
Chauco (Native American), *see Chanco (Native American)*
Cheesman [Cheaseman, Cheasman, Chisman]
Edmund [Edmond, Edward] I, 109, 110
Edmund II [Edmond, Edward], 109, 110
Elizabeth (Read), 110
John, 109, 110, 227
Lydia (_____), 110
Margaret (_____), 109, 110
Mary (_____) (Lilly), 109
Thomas, 109, 110, 447
_____, 102
Chermaison [Chermeson]
Elizabeth, 110
Elizabeth (_____), 110, 274, 352
John, 110
Joseph, 88, 274, 352
Chermant, Thomas, 111
Chermeson, *see Chermaison*
Chesley, Philip, 446
Chester
Anthony, 111
Katherine (_____), 309
Chew
John, 53, 57, 63, 99, 111, 139, 143, 248, 387

Rachel [Rachael] (_____)
  (Constable), 111
Samuel, 111
Sarah (_____), 111
Cheyney, Henry, 111
Chicacoans and Wicocomocos
  [Wecocomaka,
  Wicocomocoe] (King of
  the), *see Machywap*
Chicatomen (Native
  American), 38, 111, 300,
  304
Chicheley [Chichley]
  Agatha (Eltonhead)
    (Stubbinge)
    (Wormeley), 88, 89,
    111, 458
  Henry, 88, 111, 112, 131,
    155, 239, 318, 328, 389,
    457, 458
  Margaret (Wild), 446, 447
  Thomas, 111
Chick, William, 36, 112
Child, John, 90
Chiles [Childs, Giles], *see also*
  Gill
  Elizabeth (_____), 112, 203
  Henry, 113
  John, 113
  Mary (Page), 112, 306
  Mary (_____), 113
  Susanna (_____), 113, 213,
    306, 390, 409, 421
  Walter I, 112, 125, 149,
    203, 406, 441
  Walter II, 112, 113, 195,
    202, 203, 213, 220, 306,
    390, 409, 421, 450
  William, 112
  _____, 195
Chilton
  Edward, 23, 72, 113, 122,
    174, 196, 204, 339, 351,
    398, 402, 441
  Hannah (Hill), 113
Chinn
  Alice (_____), 389
  Anne, 389
  Catherine [Kathrine], 389
  John, 389
  Raleigh, 389
Chisman, *see Cheesman*
Chiste Cuttewans (Native
  American), 113
Chowans (King of the), 423
Chubby (slave), 75, 113, 114,
  148, 232
Chudley [Chudleigh]
  Ann (Holder) (Briscoe), 86,
    87, 114, 209, 210, 316,
    337, 375
  James, 86, 87, 114, 210,
    337, 375
Church
  Abigail, 114

Ann, 114
Elizabeth (_____), 114
Joseph, 114
Mary, 114
Patience, 114
Richard, 114, 173
Sarah, 114
_____, 114
Churchill, William, 114
Cisse, *see Keith*
Claiborne [Claiborn,
  Clayborne, Cleyborn]
  Jane, 83
  William, 11, 83, 99, 114,
    115, 162, 167, 193, 200,
    241, 267, 338, 385, 399,
    423, 452
Clapham, William, 255
Clara [Clary] (slave), 115
Clare [Cleare]
  Ambrose, 115, 180, 297
  Ann, 242
Clark [Clarke]
  Bridgett, 115
  George, 115, 222, 429
  Hannah, 249
  John, 115, 404
  John (Mrs.), 115
  Joshua, 439
  Margaret, 116, 218
  Margaret (_____), 429
  Richard, 109, 115, 116,
    218, 254
  Thomas, 116, 251, 460
  _____, 115
Claus, John, 116
Clay
  Jacob, 191
  Margaret (Harmanson), 191
  Thomas, 191
Clayborne, *see Claiborne*
Clayton
  Jasper, 334
  John, 23, 116, 284, 308,
    366
  John II, 116
  Thomas, 117
  _____, 334
Cleare, *see Clare*
Clements [Clemons]
  Ann (Meriwether), 117
  Edye (_____), 117
  Elizabeth, 117
  Elizabeth (Fuller), 117, 158,
    179, 187
  Ezeckiell, 117
  Francis, 116, 117, 196, 401
  Francis I, 117
  Francis II, 117
  Jeremiah, 179
  Jeremiah [Jeffrey, Jereme,
    Jeremie, Jeremy,
    Joreme] I, 117, 158, 187
  Jeremiah [Jeffrey, Jereme,
    Jeremie, Jeremy,

Joreme] II, 117, 187,
    400
  Lydia (_____), 117
  Nicholas, 117
  _____, 187
Clever, John, 104
Cleyborn, *see Claiborne*
Cliff, Mary, 373
Close, Phettiplace [Petiplace,
  Pettiplace, Phetiplace], 117
Clough, *see Gough*
Coale, *see Cole*
Cobb, Joseph, 116
Cockacoeske, Queen of
  the Pamunkeys (Native
  American), 21, 22, 118,
  129, 134, 290, 362, 407,
  438, 447
Cocke [Cock], *see also Cox*
  Agnes, 119
  Elizabeth, 119
  Elizabeth (Pleasants), 119
  Frances (_____) (Herbert),
    119
  James, 119, 128, 159
  Mary (Aston), 119
  Mary (Brasseur), 119
  Mary (Mason), 277
  Nicholas, 118
  Richard, 90, 119
  Richard I, 118, 119
  Stephen, 119
  Temperance, 119
  Temperance (Bailey)
    (Brown), 90, 118, 119
  Thomas, 119
  Thomas I, 119
  Thomas II, 119
  William, 119
Cockerham [Cockeram]
  Ann (Spencer), 381
  Thomas, 120
  William, 50, 381
  William I, 119, 120
  William II, 120
Cockrell, John, 144
Cod [Codd]
  Anna (_____) (Bland), 120
  Anne (_____) (Wright)
    (Fox), 120, 166
  Sarah, 223, 365, 391, 392
  St. Leger, 120, 124, 166,
    447
  William, 120
Codsford, Richard, 430
Cofield, Elizabeth (Shepherd),
  363
Cogan [Coogan, Coogin,
  Coogen, Cooking], *see*
  Gookin
Coght (Native American), 120
Colclough [Collclough]
  Elizabeth (Willoughby)
    (Overzee), 31, 32, 121
  George, 31, 120, 121, 167,
    255, 282, 292

Thomas, 166, 229
Ursula (_____) (Thompson)
    (Mottrom), 121, 292
Cole [Coale]
    Ann (Digges), 121
    Blunt, 413
    Catherine (Travis), 412
    Francis, 121
    Jessee, 412, 413
    John, 297
    Josiah, 121
    Josias, 404
    Martha (_____), 121
    Richard, 39, 43, 51
    Susannah, 141
    William, 65, 141, 280
    William I, 121
    William II, 121
    _____, 244
Coleman
    Anthony, 121, 122, 160,
        245, 317
    William, 122, 245
Colethorpe, *see Calthrop*
Colfer, _____, 122
Collclough, *see Colclough*
Collier, Samuel, 122
Collins
    Elizabeth (Woodhouse),
        454
    John, 419
    Stephen, 221
    Susan (_____), 419
    _____ (Mrs.), 122
    _____, 122
Colston [Coulson, Costnol]
    Ann (Hull), 122
    William, 122
Comahum (Native American),
    108, 122
Combes [Coumbes]
    Archdale, 418
    Austen, 122
    Elizabeth (Butler)
        (Underwood), 418
    John, 418
    William, 418
Cone, John, 391
Connaway
    Edwin, 88
    Eltonhead, 88
    Martha (_____), 88
Conner, Lewis, 252
Conquest
    Mary (Sibley), 368
    Richard, 368
Constable [Cunstable]
    Edward, 123
    Philip, 123
    Rachel [Rachael] (_____),
        111
    Robert, 123
    Sibell (_____), 123
    William, 123, 390
    _____, 321

Convers, John, 255
Cooke [Cook]
    Arthur, 123
    Christopher, 123
    Edward, 123
    Jane (_____), 123, 387
    John, 123, 323, 326, 387
    Mary (_____), 326
    Moll (slave), 287
    Mordecai [Mordecay], 123
    Richard, 123
    Roger, 123
    Thomas, 123
    William, 124
Cookeney, John, 399
Cookeson [Cookson]
    Richard, 124
    William, 124, 324
Cooking, *see Gookin*
Cooksey
    William, 124
    William (Mrs.), 124
    _____, 124
Cookson, *see Cookeson*
Cooper [Couper, Cowper]
    George, 124
    Justinian, 190
    Sampson, 255
    Samuel, 255
    Thomas, 124, 439
    Walter, 172, 439
    _____, 124
Copeland
    Joseph, 124, 394
    Joseph I, 124
    Joseph II, 124
    Mary (_____), 124
    _____, 124
Copsco (Native American), 125
Corbin [Corben, Corbyn,
    Corbitt]
    Alice (_____), 125
    Gawen, 396
    Henry, 42, 54, 125, 165,
        327, 408, 434
    Richard, 114
    _____ (Church), 114
Corbitt, *see Corbin*
Cordrey
    Mary (Robins) (Savage),
        357
    William, 357
Corell, *see Covell*
Corker
    Dorothy (_____), 125
    John, 112, 125, 149, 275,
        375, 377, 381, 425, 430,
        434
    Lucy, 126, 442
    Mary (_____) (White), 442
    Susan (Blackmore)
        (Whitty), 125, 126, 445
    Susanna, 126
    William, 54, 112, 125, 126,
        209, 221, 224, 269, 381,
        442, 445

Cornish
    Jeffrey, 172, 246
    Richard, 276
    Richard, alias Williams,
        Richard, 126, 127, 280
    _____, 172
Cornwallis [Cornwaleys,
    Cornwallys]
    Charles, Lord Cornwallis,
        27, 126
    Thomas, 199, 200, 279
Corstenstam [Corsten Stam,
    Corstin Stam, Corssin
    Stamm, Curson Stame, Van
    Corensten, Costence]
    Arent [Around], 126, 127
    Arent (Mrs.), 126
    Derrick [Derricke, Dirck],
        126, 127
Cossina, *see Cassinett*
Costence, *see Corstenstam*
Costnol, *see Colston*
Cotman
    Benjamin, 401
    Elizabeth (Thomas), 401
Cotton, _____, 344
Coumbes, *see Combes*
Councill, Hodges, Jr., 77
Countwayne [Countrivane,
    Countway], John, 127
Couper, *see Cooper*
Courtney, William, 127
Couse, *see Cowse*
Covell [Corell]
    Frances, 264
    Thomas, 264
Coventry, _____ (Sec.), 383
Cowles [Cowels], Thomas,
    81, 127
Cowling, Christopher, 127
Cowper, *see Cooper*
Cowse [Couse], William, 126,
    127, 280
Cox [Coxe], *see also Cocke*
    Daniel, 217
    Elizabeth, 372
    John, xii, 272
    Mary, 417
    Richard, 127
    Thomas, 435, 436
Craddock, Elizabeth (_____),
    225
Crafford [Crawford]
    Abigail, 128
    David, 127, 128, 440
    Elizabeth, 128
    Margaret (_____), 128
    Sarah, 128
    William, 128
    William I, 128
    William II, 128
    William III, 128
Crakeplace, *see Crapplace*
Crampe, *see Crump*
Crapplace [Crakeplace],
    William, 128

Crawshawe, *see Croshaw*
Creed, John, 164
Creete
  Alice (_____) (Corbin), 125
  Henry, 125
Crew [Crews, Crewes]
  Dorothy (Beheathland), 128
  Elizabeth (_____)
    (Smalley), 128, 369
  James, 128
  Mary (_____)
    (Beheathland) (Flint),
    61, 163
  Randall, 61, 128, 369
Crispe [Cripps], Zachary
  [Zacharia], 129
Croft, _____, 100
Crompe, *see Crump*
Crompe, Thomas, 436
Cromwell
  Oliver, 16, 129, 155, 187
  Richard, 129
Crosby [Crosbie]
  Daniel, 129
  Thomas, 129
  _____, 129
Croshair, *see Croshaw*
Croshaw [Crawshawe,
  Croshair, Crowshawe]
  Joseph, 129, 438
  Raleigh [Raughley,
    Rawleigh], 123, 129,
    438
  Unity, 129, 438
  _____ (Capt.), 123
Cross [Crosse]
  George, 360
  George, Jr., 360
  Sarah [Sara] (_____), 360
  Thomas, 129
Crouch [Crouth]
  Richard, 129
  Thomas, 129
Crow, Ann (_____), 183
Crowder [Cruder], Hugh, 130,
  199, 430
Crowdick, John, 42
Crowshawe, *see Croshaw*
Croxon, Alice, 102
Crumfort, *see Crump*
Crump [Crampe, Crompe,
  Crumfort, Crumpe]
  Elizabeth, 130
  Elizabeth (Buck), 89, 91,
    130, 307, 391
  John, 91, 130, 307, 409
  Thomas, 91, 130
Crust, Thomas, 130
Cuffin, David, 162
Cugley
  Hannah [Ann] (_____)
    (Savage), 357
  Daniel, 152, 357
  Margery, 357
Culpeper [Culpepper]

Alexander, 130
Catherine, xi
Frances, 46, 65, 66, 121,
  130, 145, 146, 159, 205,
  228, 266, 267, 375, 381,
  385, 441
John, 133
Thomas, 65, 130
Thomas, Lord Culpeper, 46,
  130, 131, 195, 228, 324,
  375, 380, 436
Cunstable, *see Constable*
Cunstocker, *see Gunstocker*
Cupid (slave), 131
Currer, John, 131
Curtis [Curtys]
  Anne (_____), 131
  Avarilla [Averilla], 87
  James, 313
  John, 131, 284
  Thomas, 87
Custis [Custise]
  Alice [Alicia] (Travellor)
    (Burdett) (Walker), 93,
    94, 422
  Anne, 131, 446, 463
  Bridget, 133
  Bridget (_____), 133
  Daniel Parke, 133, 428
  Elizabeth, 133
  Elizabeth (Custis), 133
  Elizabeth (_____) (Eyre),
    131, 154
  Frances, 133
  Frances (Parke), 133, 309,
    325
  Hancock, 133
  Henry, 131, 133
  Joan (_____), 131
  Joanna Mary, 133
  John, 241, 389
  John I, 131, 132, 422
  John II, 20, 65, 90, 94, 102,
    131, 132, 133, 154, 189,
    195, 204, 247, 328, 428,
    446, 463
  John III, 132, 133, 389
  John IV, 132, 133, 155,
    309, 325
  John Parke, 133, 428
  John Parke (Mrs.), 133
  Joseph, 132
  Martha (Dandridge), 133,
    428
  Sarah (_____), 132
  Sorrowful Margaret, 133
  Tabitha (Scarborough)
    (Smart) (Brown), 89,
    90, 132, 204, 359
  Thomas, 133
  William, 132
  William II, 133
  _____, 133
Custis Family, 27
Cutler, Robert, 134

D

Dabney [Dabamy, Dabony,
  Debony], Cornelius, 22,
  118, 134, 438
Dade
  Beheathland (Bernard),
    66, 134
  Cadwalder, 209, 453
  Frances (Townshend), 209,
    453
  Francis, 453
  Francis I, 134, *see also
    Smith, John, alias
    Francis Dade*
  Francis II, 134, 209
  Francis III, 209
  Robert, 209, 453
  William, 371
  _____ (Pinkard), 135
Daingerfield
  John, 386
  _____ (Walker), 386
Dale
  Edward, 134, 135
  Elizabeth, 135
  Elizabeth (Throgmorten),
    108, 122, 135, 143, 144,
    191, 261, 356, 377, 430
  Katherine, 135
  Peter, 273
  Thomas, 6, 7, 39, 49, 70,
    84, 135, 136, 142, 170,
    192, 214, 218, 244, 252,
    260, 270, 271, 299, 317,
    326, 362, 369, 379, 419,
    437, 462
d'Ancteville, Louis Floxel, 37
Dandridge, Martha, 133, 428
Danes, John, 93, 135
Daniel [Danyell]
  John, 347
  Richard, 135
Daphne (slave), 135, 170, 296,
  412
Dauphine, Durand de, 161,
  311, 458
Davenant, William, 136
Davenport, Joseph, 136
David (slave), 136
Davis [Davies, Davye, Davys]
  Agnes (_____), 299
  Alice, 207
  Bridget (Buck) (Burrows),
    89, 91, 95, 130, 138
  Edward, 136, 139, 206, 318
  Elizabeth, 77
  Henry, 299, 437
  Hugh, 136, 367
  James, 136, 137
  Jane, 137, 437, 451
  Joan [Jone], 137
  John, 77, 137, 138, 151,
    207, 326, 434
  Rachell (_____), 136

Richard, 137, *see also*
    Mopeson, Richard
Robert, 136, 137
Thomas, 136, 137, 138,
    276, 434
Walter, 137
William, 27, 89, 95, 138,
    193, 297, 318
Davison
    Alice (_____), 137, 138,
        363
    Christopher, 43, 137, 138,
        159, 363
Davye, *see Davis*
Dawe, George, 123
Dawse [Daws], Margery, 138
Dawson, Owen, 138
Day, Edward, 138
De Frizes, John, 138, *see also*
    Devries
De Main, Peter [Petter], 138
Deacon, _____ (Mrs.), 78,
    138
Dean (slave), 139
Deane, Ralph, 139, 244, 260,
    273
Death
    Elizabeth, 139
    Richard, 139
    Susan, 139
    William, 139
Debedeavon (Native
    American), *see Tapatiaton
    (Native American)*
Debony, *see Dabney*
Debton, Margaret, 391
Dees, Emanuel, 88, 139
Delamajor [Delemajor,
    Dillimager], Thomas, 139
Delawafer, Lionel, 136, 139,
    206, 318
Delaware (Lady), *see West,
    Cecily (Sherley)*
Delaware (Lord), *see West,
    Thomas*
Delke [Dilke]
    Alice (_____), 140
    Clement, 139, 207, 363
    Elizabeth (_____), 139
    Roger, 365
    Roger I, 139, 140
    Roger II, 140
Denham [Denhawes]
    Richard, 184
    Suzanna (Hackett), 184
Dennett, John, 243
Denny, Robert, 98
Denson, William, 140
Desandrouins, Jean-Nicholas,
    450
Deverell [Deverill, Deurill],
    George, 140
Devern, _____, 140
Devries [DeVries]
    David, 140, 211, 283

Peter, 175
Dew [Dewe, Due], *see also*
    Dow
    Thomas, 140
Dickenson [Dickens, Dickeson,
    Dickinson, Digginson]
    Griffin [Griffeth], 140, 407,
        448
    Griffin [Griffeth] (Mrs.),
        140, 448
    Jane (_____), 140, 141
    Ralph, 140, 141
Dick (slave), 140
Dier [Dyer]
    John, 141
    Mary, 141
    William, 141, 248
Digby [Digbie], John, 141
Digges
    Ann, 121
    Cole, 142
    Dudley, 141, 142, 218,
        307
    Edward, 142, 345
    Edward I, 111, 121, 141,
        142, 437
    Edward II, 141
    Edward (Mrs.), 345
    Elizabeth, 142
    Elizabeth (Page), 141, 142
    Elizabeth (Sewell), 142
    Martha (Lear), 121
    Mary, 306, 307
    Susannah (Cole), 141
    William, 141, 142
    _____, 141
Digges Family, 53
Digginson, *see Dickenson*
Dilke, *see Delke*
Dinah (slave), 142, 155
Dinse [Dinsie], John, 142
Dinwiddie, Robert, 267
Dipnall [Dipdall, Dipnell]
    Thomas, 142
    _____, 142
Diskin, Daniel, 148, 406
Distiard, George, 297
Dixon [Dixson]
    Adam, 142
    Ann [Agnes], 142, 143
    Elizabeth, 143
Dodman
    Elizabeth (Death), 139
    John, 139
    John, Jr., 139
    Richard, 139
Dodson
    Gervase [Jervase], 207,
        270, 304, 320
    Mary, 389
Doe
    Ann (_____) (Toppin)
        (Gill), 173
    Thomas, 143, 173
    Thomas (Mrs.), 143

Dolby
    John, 127
    William, 275
    William (Mrs.), 275
Dole, Richard, 143
Doll (slave), 143
Dolphenby, Richard, 108, 344
Donne [Dunn, Dunne]
    George, 91, 143
    John, 143
    Thomas, 147
Dormer, Fleetwood, 258, 259
Douglas [Douglass, Dowglass,
    Duglas]
    Edward, 261
    Edward I, 143
    Edward II, 143
    Elizabeth, 143
    Elizabeth (_____), 143
    Isabella (_____), 143, 261
    Sarah, 143
    William, 126, 143, 144, 356
Douse, *see Dowse*
Dow, *see also Dew*
    Ralph, Jr., 208
Dowglass, *see Douglas*
Dowman, William, 144
Downeman, *see Downman*
Downes
    George, 144
    John, 144
Downing
    Elizabeth (_____), 144
    John, 144, 163, 236, 349
    William, 144
Downman [Downeman]
    Elizabeth (_____), 144
    John, 144, 387
    Million (_____), 457
Dowse [Douse]
    Ann (_____), 144
    Thomas, 144
Doyly, Cope, 341
Drake
    Francis, 169
    John, 418
    William, 418
Draper, Elizabeth, 315
Drason [Drayson], John, 144
Dresone, Joane, 215
Drew, _____, 144
Drinkard, John, 145, *see also
    Prichard, John*
Driver, Giles, 172
Drummer, William, 145
Drummond
    John, 146, 197
    Sarah, 146, 392
    Sarah (_____), 66, 67, 145,
        146, 331, 340, 393, 425
    William I, 20, 45, 66, 67,
        74, 81, 91, 97, 125, 131,
        145, 146, 153, 156, 192,
        213, 219, 221, 248, 251,
        286, 287, 314, 331, 340,
        370, 392, 445

William II, 88, 146, 192
William III, 146, 410
_____ (Mrs.), 88
Drysdale, Hugh, 102
Dudley
    Elizabeth, 147
    Elizabeth (_____), 147
    James, 147
    Robert I, 146
    Robert II, 146
    Thomas, 147
    William I, 146, 147
    William II, 147
Due, *see Dew*
Duglas, *see Douglas*
Duke
    Edward, 47
    Elizabeth, 47, 48, 227, 451
    Ellen (Panton), 47
    Henry, 147
    John, 47
Dum, William, 406
Dumport, John, 147
Duncan (slave), 147
Duning, Richard, 456
Dunkin, Peter, 241
Dunmore (Lord), 78
Dunn [Dunne], *see Donne*
Dunston
    Cicely (_____), 147
    John, 147
Durant
    Elizabeth (_____), 320
    George, 105
    Richard, 320
Durfey, Goodrich, 372
Durham, Dorothy (_____), 389
Dutton, Thomas, 331
Dyas, *see Dyus*
Dyer, *see Dier*
Dyus [Dyas], John, 147

E

Eale, Samuel, 385
Eares, *see Eyre*
Eaton
    John, 147
    Thomas, 325, 451
Eden, *see Aden*
Eden [Eden-Sampson],
    William, *see Sampson,
    William*
Ederife [Evere], Ester, 153
Edgecombe, John, 156
Edith (slave), 148
Edloe [Edlow, Edlowe]
    Alice (_____) (Boyse), 79,
        148
    John, 78, 148, 286
    Mathew, 145
    Mathew I, 79, 148
    Mathew II, 148
    William, 372
Edmundson [Edmondson]
    Anne (Gregory), 148

Mary (_____), 148
Thomas, 148
William, 63
Edwards
    Arthur, 148
    Benjamin, 149
    Elizabeth (_____), 149
    John, 322, 448
    Sarah (Harrison) (Lowe),
        150, 318
    Sarah (_____), 149, 213,
        286, 345, 430, 449
    Thomas, 99, 138, 148, 334
    William I, 105, 112, 125,
        149, 210, 213, 286, 317,
        345
    William II, 31, 112, 124,
        125, 149, 196, 213, 218,
        220, 243, 273, 317, 336,
        367, 392, 430
    William III, 112, 114, 149,
        150, 210
    William IV, 150, 318
    _____ (Pryor), 334
    _____, 149
Effingham (Lord), *see Howard,
    Francis*
Efford, Sarah, 435
Egerton, John, 461
Eggleston
    Benjamin, 88, 150, 197
    Elizabeth (_____)
        (Hartwell), 197
    Richard, 457
Eghtop (Native American), 150
Eire [Eires], *see Eyre*
Elay, Lancelot, 150
Elison [Elisone], *see Ellison*
Elizabeth (Native American),
    see Basse, Elizabeth
Elizabeth I, Queen of England,
    85
Elizabeth (slave), 242
Elkington, Ann, 357
Elliott [Elliot, Ellyott]
    Anthony, 222
    Anthony I, 150, 457
    Anthony I (Mrs.), 150, 457
    Anthony II, 150
Ellis
    David, 59, 129, 150, 151
    James, 151
    John, 215
    Margaret (Carter), 150, 151
Ellison [Elison, Elisone,
    Ellyson, Elyson]
    Ellen (_____), 151
    Garrard Robert, 151
    George, 151
    Hannah, 40, 41, 151
    John, 151, 221
    Robert, 40, 151, 212
Ellyott, *see Elliott*
Eltonhead
    Agatha, 88, 89, 111, 458
    Edward, 101

Jane (_____) (Taylor), 399
William, 399
Elyson [Ellyson], *see Ellison*
Eman [Enims], John, 151
Emerson [Emmerson]
    Ann (_____), 151
    Ellis, 151
    Thomas, 151
    William, 151, 326
Emory
    Charles, 264
    Frances (Covell) (Kaynton)
        (Loving) (Thruston),
        264
"Emperor of the Indians,"
    *see Necotowance (Native
    American)*
Emperour
    Francis, 151
    Mary, 151
England
    Francis, 76, 206, 335
    John, 61
English
    William, 151
    Yowell, 465
Epers, *see Evers*
Eppes [Epes]
    Anne (Isham), 152
    Elizabeth (Worsham)
        (Kennon), 152, 241, 242
    Francis, 159, 171, 241
    Francis I, 152, 242
    Francis II, 152, 193, 241,
        242
    Francis III, 152, 340
    William, 50, 56, 93, 342,
        346, 349, 383
    _____, 152
Eriosinchke (Native American),
    152
Esmy Shichans, the "Laughing
    King" (Native American),
    152, 153, 244, 357, 395,
    420
"Esquire John" (Native
    American), *see Caskameno
    (Native American)*
Essex (slave), 153, 225, 354,
    359
Evans [Evands], *see also
    Evers; Ewens*
    Charles, 153
    Richard, 153
    Thomas, 109
Evars, *see Evers*
Evelyn [Eveling, Evelin]
    Christopher, 153
    Dorothea (Robins), 38
    George, 70
    Rebecca, 308
    Robert, 153, 199, 464
Evere, *see Ederife*
Everett
    Elizabeth (_____) (Sikes),
        153, 154, 204, 369, 371

John, 153, 154, 212, 369, 371, 372, 392, 393, 406
Evers [Evars, Epers], *see also Evans*
Richard, 49
Robert, 154
Everson, John, 238
Ewens [Ewen, Ewins], *see also Evans*
John, 154, 205, 389
Mary, 154
Mary (_____), 154
William, 9, 154
Eyre [Eares, Eire, Eires, Eyres]
Elizabeth (_____), 131, 154
Robert, 131, 154

F

Fadom, *see Fawdon*
Fairfax [Fairefax, Fierfax, Ffax]
Margery (_____), 155
Catherine (Culpeper), xi
Thomas, Lord Fairfax, xi, 102, 130, 266
William [Winster], 91, 155
Fairley, *see Farley; see also Farlow*
Faldoe, William Henrick [Faldoe the Heletian], *see Volday, William*
Fallom, Robert, 316
Fanny (slave), 142, 155
Fantelroy, Fantelary, *see Fauntleroy*
Farley [Fairley], *see also Farlow*
Ann, 155
Jane (_____), 155
Roger, 155
Thomas, 151, 155
Farlow [Farloe], *see also Farley*
Elizabeth, 97
John, 155
Farmer [Farmar, Farmor]
Henry, 155
Richard, 155
Thomas, 155
Farrar [Ferrar, Ferrer]
Cisley, 156
Cisley (_____) (Jordan), 155, 156
John, 156, 385, 418
Nicholas, 418
Thomas, 260
Virginia, 64, 418
William, 101, 188
William I, 61, 155, 156
William II, 156, 440
_____, 152
Farrell, Hubert, 78, 156, 443
Farres, Ingram, 156
Fausett, *see Fossett*
Fauntleroy [Fantelroy,

Fantelary, Flantlaroy]
Mary, 104
Mary (Hill), 156, 206, 263
Moore [More], 29, 60, 104, 156, 157, 206, 263, 277, 294, 295, 374, 439
_____ (Smith), 156
_____, 60
Fawcett, *see Fossett*
Fawdon [Fadom, Shedam, Fawdowne]
Ann (_____) (Smith), 45, 61, 157, 235, 370
George, 45, 61, 157, 171, 370
Feild, *see Field*
Felgate [Fellgate]
Elizabeth (Fuller) (Clements) (Hamor), 117, 158, 187
Isabella, *see Sibella*
Margaret (_____), 157
Mary (_____), 417
Robert, 157, 275, 417
Sarah, 158
Sarah (Price), 158
Sibella [Isabella] (_____) (Adkins), 157, 158, 275
Tobias "Toby," 117, 157, 158, 187
William, 53, 157, 158
William, Jr., 417
_____ (Capt.), 157
Fell, Henry, 158
Felton, Thomas, 211
Fendall
Josias, 331
Mary, 331
Fenly [Fenley]
Ann (_____), 158
John, 158
Robert, 158
Fenton
Francis, 158
Robert, 158
Fenwick, Mary, 327
Ferrar, *see Farrar*
Ferrar Family, 123
Fetherstone [Featherstone], Richard, 158
Fettiplace [Petiplace, Pettiplace, Phetiplace Phettiplace]
Michael, 158
William, 158
_____ (Capt.), 321
Ffax, *see Fairfax*
Field [Feild]
Judith (Soane) (Randolph), 158, 159, 340, 375
Martha, 159
Mary, 159
Peter, 158, 159, 340, 375, 376
Thomas, 159
Fierfax, *see Fairfax*

Filmer [Filmore], *see also Phillimore*
Elizabeth (_____), 159
Henry, 159
Mary (Horsmenden), 216
Samuel, 65, 159, 216
_____, 159
Finch
Henry, 159
John, 159
Thomas, 159
Finney, Thomas, 440
Firth
Joseph, 159
Richard, 159
Samuel, 160, 339, 342, 392, 393
Fisher
Edward, 160, 203
Sarah (_____) (Kidall), 160
Suzanne (_____), 40, 160
Thomas, 160
Thomas (Mrs.), 160
William, 40, 160, 167
_____, 160
Fitch [Fytch]
Joseph, 160
Mathew, 160
Fitchett, John, 113, 160, 161, 182, 322
Fitt [Fitts]
Ann [Anne] (_____), 161
Robert, 161, 337, 338
Thomas, 192
Fitz-Jeffry [Fitz-Jefferys, Fitzjeffrey, Fitzjefferys, Fitzjeffreys, Fitzjeffries]
George, 161, 350
William, 161
_____, 348
Fitzherbert
Mary (Brent), 82, 244, 245
Thomas, 242
Fitzhugh
George, 161
Henry, 161
John, 161
Rosamond, 32, 161
Sarah (Garrard), 161
Thomas, 161
William, 32
William I, 161, 431, 432
William II, 161
Fitzjeffrey [Fitzjefferys, Fitzjeffries, Fitzjeffreys], *see Fitz-Jeffry*
Flantlaroy, *see Fauntleroy*
Fleet [Fleete]
Elizabeth (_____), 161, 219, 269, 448
Henry, 386, 422
Henry I, 161, 162
Henry II, 162
Sarah (_____), 162, 386, 422
_____, 219

Fletcher
  George, 162
  John, 162
Flint [Flynt]
  Dorothy (_____), 162
  Mary, 162
  Mary (_____)
    (Beheathland), 61, 163
  Peter, 162
  Richard, 236
  Richard I, 162
  Richard II, 144, 162, 163,
    349
  Thomas, 61, 66, 79, 140,
    162, 163, 180, 249
Flinton, Farrar (Pharaoh), 63,
  116
Flood [Flud, Fludd], *see also*
  Floyd
  John, 163, 356
  Margaret (_____), 163
  Thomas, 117
  William, 163
Flower, George, 163
Flowerdew, Temperance, 55,
  75, 80, 180, 202, 208, 437,
  462, 463
Floyd, *see also Flood*
  Mary (_____), 207
  Nathan, 207
  Nathaniel, 304
Flud [Fludd], *see Flood*
Flynt, *see Flint*
Follis, Thomas, 163
Fontaine, John, 25, 163
Foote, Joshua, 163, 299
Force, Peter, 187
Ford
  Christopher, 164, 212
  Richard, 164
  Robert, 164
Foreman, William, 154
Forest [Forrest]
  Thomas, 164
  Thomas (Mrs.), 164, 252
Forster, *see Foster*
Fossett [Fawcett, Fausett]
  Ann (_____), 164
  Thomas, 164
Foster [Forster]
  Alice (Hardidge), 190
  Christopher, 164, 273
  Dorcas, 164
  Dorcas (_____), 164
  Edward, 227
  Elizabeth, 164
  Elizabeth (Higginson), 203
  Elizabeth (_____), 164
  George, 160
  John, 164
  Joseph, 164, 438
  Joseph I, 164
  Joseph II, 164
  Richard, 154, 164
  William, 164

Fouace, Stephen, 110, 229
Fouler [Fouller], *see Fowler*
Foulke [Fowke]
  Gerrard [Gerard], 165, 327,
    408
  Susanna (_____), 165
  Thomas, 165, 447
Fowke, *see Foulke*
Fowler [Fouler, Fouller]
  Bartholomew, 69, 165, 218,
    274, 420
  Frances (Porter), 326
  Frances (Sidney), 369
  Francis, 165
  George, 326, 369
  Pembroke, 369
  Sidney, 369
Fox
  Anne (Chinn), 389
  Anne (_____) (Wright), 166
  Anne (_____), 120
  David, 52, 184
  David [Davyd, Davy] I,
    120, 166
  David II, 166, 232, 241
  Elizabeth, 120, 166
  George, 63
  Hannah, 166, 241
  Hannah (Ball), 52, 166, 241
  Mary (_____), 166
  Samuel, 166
  Thomas, 166
  William, 120, 166
Foxcroft [Foxcraft, Foxcrofte],
  Isaac [Isaak], 166, 167, 297
Foxwell, George, 444
Frances (Native American),
  167
Francis
  Ann, 167
  Elizabeth, 167
  Francis, 167
  Suzanne, 167
  Thomas, 167
Franck [Frank], Daniel, 167,
  321
Frank (Native American), 167
Franklin
  Ferdinand [Fardinand], 167
  _____, 167
Fransisco (Native American),
  167, 168
Freeman
  Bridges, 165, 168, 264
  _____ (Capt.), 296
Fresey, Ambrose, 168
Frethorne [Frethram], Richard,
  168
Fry, Henry, 168
Fryer, George, 432
Fulcher, John, 51, 168, 366
Fulford [Fullford], Francis, 168
Fuller
  Elizabeth, 117, 158, 178,
    187
  Thomas, 168

Furlow, _____, 168
Fynloe, Nicholas, 168
Fytch, *see Fitch*

G

Gage, Robert, 216
Gaile, *see Gale*
Gaines
  Robert (Native American),
    169
  Thomas, 169
  Thomas (Native American),
    169
Gaither, *see Gather*
Gale [Gaile]
  Elias [Ellias], 169
  George, 428
  Mildred (Warner)
    (Washington), 428
  Robert, 169
Galt, James, 36
Galthorpe [Halthrop], *see also*
  Calthrop
  Stephen, 169
Gamsby, Amy, 302
Ganey, William, 151
"Gardener Tommy" (slave),
  406
Gardner
  Elizabeth (Weir), 434
  Martin, 169
  Thomas, 74, 169
Garey, James, 169
Garland
  Joan (Wilson), 288
  Peter, 288
Garnett
  Elizabeth (_____), 169
  Susan, 169
  Thomas, 10, 169, 181
  William, 76, 171, 187, 190,
    191
Garrard, *see Gerrard*
Garrett [Garret], William, 169
Gaskins [Gaskoyne]
  Sarah (_____), 322
  Thomas II, 322
  _____, 322
Gates
  Anthony, 170
  Elizabeth, 170
  Elizabeth (_____), 170
  Margaret, 170
  Mary, 170
  Thomas, 6, 7, 39, 75, 135,
    136, 169, 170, 209, 299,
    317, 342, 343, 363, 376,
    388, 393, 421, 453, 461,
    462
Gather [Gatter, Gaither]
  Joan (_____), 170
  John, 170
  Mary (_____), 170
Gathright, Joel, 135, 170, 296,
  412

Gatter, *see Gather*
Gawler [Gauler]
   Catherine (_____)
     (Marable), 170, 273
   Henry, 23, 62, 97, 98, 122,
     136, 139, 170, 171, 206,
     245, 273, 377, 401
Gay, Anthony, 171, 182, 192
Gaylard, James, 160
Gayne, William, 397
Geddes, John, 171
Gee
   Henry, 171
   Jane, 171
   John, 171
Genoway, Richard, 171
Gentler, Vallentyne, 171
Geogin, *see Gookin*
George
   Ann [Anne] (_____), 171,
     172, 253, 324, 329
   Isaac I, 171
   Isaac II, 171
   John, 157, 187, 190, 191,
     324, 329, 448
   John I, 171, 253, 365
   John II, 172, 253
   Nicholas, 322, 394
   Rebecca, 171
   Sarah, 171
George (Native American), 171
George (slave), 171
George III, King of England,
   411
Geromiah (slave), 255
Gerrard [Garrard, Gerard]
   Anne, 87, 207, 426
   Frances, 39, 190, 321, 378,
     379, 426, 427
   Henry, 460
   Rose (_____), 161
   Sarah, 161
   Susanna (_____), 379
   Thomas, 161, 379
Gibbons, Thomas, 172
Gibbs [Gibson, Gybson]
   Dorothy (Westropp), 439
   Francis, 172
   John, 172, 391
   Margaret, 71
   Mark, 439
   Thomas, 71, 172
Gilbert, George, 172
Gill [Gyles, Giles], *see also*
   Chiles
   Alexander, 172
   Ann (_____) (Toppin), 173
   Bethaniah [Bethania]
     (Knowles), 246
   Francis, 128
   George, 297
   Jane, 172
   John [Jonathan, Jonathin],
     106, 172, 173, 282, 338

Phillaritie [Pillarote,
   Phillarete] (Woodward),
   172
Stephen, 248, 255
Stephen I, 173
Stephen II, 173
William, 246
_____, 358
Gillman, Nicholas, 173
Gilpin, Samuel, 377
Gilson
   Andrew, 134
   Beheathland (Bernard)
     (Dade), 66, 134
Ginnat, Post, 173
Girardin
   Louis, 36, 412
   Louis Hue, 27
Glasbrook [Glassbrook],
   Thomas, 173, 287, 288, 306
Glascock
   Ann, 298
   Gregory, 298
Glenn, Mourning, 81
Glover, Henry, 173
Godfrey [Godfree]
   John, 173
   Mathew, 173
   Sarah (_____), 173
   Warren [Warner], 173
Godwin [Godwine, Godwyn,
   Goodwyn]
   Joseph, 238
   Martha (Bridger), 85, 174
   Reign, 174
   Thomas I, 174
   Thomas II, 174
   _____, 173
Gogh, *see Gough*
Gold [Gould], Peter [Peeter],
   174
Goldsmith [Gouldfinch,
   Gouldsmith], Nicholas, 174
Gooch, *see also Gough*
   William, 72, 274
Good, John, 460
Goodall
   Anne (_____) (Wilkinson),
     448
   John, 448
Goodison, Raymond, 174
Goodrich [Goodrick]
   Alice (_____), 175
   Anne (_____), 175, 204
   Benjamin, 174
   Charles, 174
   John, 174, 175
   Robert, 175
   Thomas, 175, 204
Goodwin, James, 175
Gookin [Cogan, Coogan,
   Coogen, Coogin, Cooking,
   Gookins, Geogin]
   Daniel, 301
   Daniel I, 175

Daniel II, 175
   John, 175, 176, 403, 450
   Sarah (Offley) (Thorogood),
     175, 176, 291, 403, 463
Gord
   Henry, 328, 329
   Henry (Mrs.), 328
   _____, 329
Gordon, Thomas, 176
Goring
   Charles, 33
   Eleanor [Ellynor]
     (Allomby), 33
   John, 176, 316
Gosling [Gofling], Edward,
   176
Gosnold [Gosnult]
   Anthony I, 176
   Anthony II, 176
   Anthony III, 176, 177
   Bartholomew, 3, 176
   Robert, 176, 177
   _____, 177
Goss, Susanna, 59
Gough [Clough, Gogh], *see*
   also Gooch
   Alice (_____), 177
   Henry, 177
   John, 117, 177, 448
   Mathew, 177
   William, 177
Gouldfinch, *see Goldsmith*
Goulding
   George, 177
   Thomas, 177
Gouldman, Thomas, 79, 177
Gourgaing [Gouynge], Edward,
   177
Gower
   Abel, 177, 178
   Jane (_____), 178
   Tabitha, 178
   Thomas, 178
Grace (slave), 178, 223, 294
Graham, William, 360
Gramsby, Amy, 178
Graves [Granes, Grave,
   Grayes]
   Eleanor [Elinor, Ellenor]
     (_____) (Snow), 178,
     375
   George, 375
   George I, 178, 221
   John, 178, 451
   Katherine (_____), 178
   Katheryn, 350
   Nathaniel, 178
   Thomas I, 178
   Thomas II, 178
Gray [Graye, Grey]
   Anis [Annis, Anise]
     (Valentine), 178, 179
   Francis, 179
   Henry, 123
   Joan [Jone], 179

John, 179
Margaret (_____), 179
Mary (_____), 179
Rebecca, 179
Rebecca (_____), 179
Samuel, 114, 239
Samuel (Mrs.), 114
Thomas, 179, 464
Thomas I, 178, 179
Thomas II, 179
William, 105, 179
_____, 102, 178
Grayes, *see Graves*
Grayham, John, 248
"Great Kinge of ye Eastern
    Shore," *see Wackawamp
    (Native American)*
Green [Greene]
    Anderton, 179
    Bartholomew, 394
    Dorothy, 179
    Edward, 146
    Elizabeth, 305
    John, 179, 272
    Katherin, 252
    Mary (Moon), 288
    Nathaniel, 27
    Ralph, 289
    Richard, 179
    Robert, 235
    Roger, 180, 204, 324
    Sisley [Cisley], 180
    Thomas, 288
Greenfield, John, 180
Greensted [Grinsted]
    Elizabeth, 242
    Elizabeth (Key), 242
    John, 243
    William, 242
Greevett, *see Grevett*
Grefrihe, John, 207
Gregory [Grigory]
    Alice (_____) (Delke)
        (Reynolds), 140
    Anne, 148
    Frances (_____), 180
    John, 140, 148
    Richard, 180
    Richard (Mrs.), 180
    Thomas, 158, 264
Gregson [Grigson], Thomas,
    59, 180
Grendon [Grindall, Grindon]
    Edward, 49, 91, 154, 210,
        244, 285, 294, 353,
        362
    Edward I, 111, 180
    Edward II, 180
    Elizabeth (_____) (Stegg),
        181, 384
    Elizabeth (_____), 180, 181
    Sarah (_____) (Harris)
        (Stegg), 181, 384
    Temperance, 180
    Thomas, 181, 461

Thomas I, 181
Thomas II, 181, 384
Thomas III, 178, 181, 384
Grenville [Grevell, Grevill],
    Frances, 181, 280, 315,
    437
Grevett [Greevett, Gruett]
    Ellin [Ellen] (_____), 181
    John, 173, 181, 436, 438
Grevell [Grevill], *see Grenville*
Grey, Francis, 439
Griffin [Griffen, Griffeth,
    Griffith, Griphin, Gyffith]
    Ambrose, 181
    Corbin, 457
    Edward, 134, 182, 282, 320
    John, 182
    Joyce (_____), 181
    Judith (Wormeley), 457
    Ralph [Rafe], 182
    _____ (_____) (Jackson),
        182
Griggs
    John, 200
    Margery (_____), 200
Grimes [Grymes]
    Ann, 182
    Frances, 257, 267
    John, 100
Grindall, *see Grendon*
Grindon, *see Grendon*
Grinstead, *see Greensted*
Griphin, *see Griffin*
Grove, John, 171, 182, 269,
    279, 287, 338, 449
Grubb
    John, 182
    Thomas, 182, 275
Gruett, *see Grevett*
Grymes, *see Grimes*
Gudderington, John, 182
Guine [Guinne], *see Gwyn*
Gullock, Robert, 183
Gully, Thomas, 160, 182
Gundry, John, 402
Gunstocker [Cunstocker]
    Edward ["Indian John,"
        "Indian Ned"] (Native
        American), 182, 183
    Mary (_____), 183
    Ned, 302, 312
Gunstone, John, 183
Gurganay [Gurganey,
    Gurgana], Ann, 192, 193
Gwillen [Gwilliam, Gwilliams,
    Gwellins, Gwillum],
    George, 81, 183
Gwyn [Guine, Guinne, Gwin,
    Gwynn]
    Ann (_____), 183
    Hugh, 183, 184, 255, 303
    John, 184, 229
    Thomas, 182
Gybson, *see Gibbs*
Gyffith, *see Griffin*

H

Hack [Hakes], Thomas, 185
Hackett [Hacket]
    Eleanor, 184
    Mary (_____), 184
    Richard, 184
    Suzanna, 184
    Thomas, 184
    William, 184
Hackthorpe, Thomas, 184
Haddock, William, 441
Hadley
    Dyonysia [Dionysia]
        (Savage) (Ravenscroft),
        184, 185, 416
    Thomas, 184, 185, 197
Haile, *see Hale*
Haine, *see Haney*
Haistwell [Hastwell]
    Edward, 185
    Elizabeth (_____), 185
    Thomas, 185
    William, 401
Hakes, *see Hack*
Halbert, Lucy, 451
Hale [Haile, Hales, Hayle,
    Hayles], *see also Heale*
    John, 255
    Thomas, 185, 281
Haley, John, 185
Halila, William, 185
Hall [Haule, Haul]
    Amy (_____), 185
    Bridgett (_____), 185
    Christopher, 185, 242
    George [Georg], 185
    Jane (_____), 186
    John, 89, 124, 185, 210,
        238, 274
    John (Mrs.), 238
    Susan [Susanna], 185
    Susan (_____), 185
    Thomas, 185, 186, 331
    William, 186
    _____, 185
Hallet [Hallett]
    John, 186
    Lettice (Ramsbottom), 186
    Marshman, 186
    Nany, 186
    Sarah, 186
    William, 186
Hallom
    Ann [Anne] (_____)
        (Price), 262, 333, 390
    Robert, 262, 333, 390
    Sarah, 390
Halsey, Robert, 421
Halthrop, *see Galthorpe*
Ham [Hamm], Jeremy
    [Hierome, Jereme, Jerime,
    Jerome], 186
Haman [Hamun], John, 186
Hamar, *see Hamor*

Hamblin [Hamblen, Hamelyn], *see Hamlin*
Hamer, *see Hamor*
Hamlin [Hamlyn, Hamelyn, Hamblin, Hamblen, Hamblyn]
  Abraham, 186
  Elizabeth (Taylor), 398
  John, 398
  Stephen [Steeven], 186
Hamm, *see Ham*
Hammond [Hamond, Hamon]
  John, 187, 190
  Manwarring [Manwaring, Manering, Mannaring, Mannering], 42, 187, 249, 457
  _____ (Maj. Gen.), 125, 327
Hamor [Hamar, Hamer]
  Elizabeth (Fuller) (Clements), 117, 158, 187
  Ralph, 7, 30, 62, 102, 106, 117, 127, 137, 158, 172, 180, 187, 228, 244, 248, 249, 259, 283, 342, 428, 463
  Thomas, 187, 188, 227, 287
  Thomas (Mrs.), 188
  _____, 188
Hampton, Thomas, 188, 202
Hamun, *see Haman*
Hanby Family, 135
Hancock
  Johan (Ligon), 260
  Robert, 260
Handy, *see Hardy*
Haney [Haine, Hanie, Hayney, Heiny, Hemy, Henry]
  John, 188, 189
  John (Mrs.), 188
  John, Sr., 189
  Richard, 189
Hannah (slave), 37, 109, 189, 287, 356
Hansford [Hunsford]
  Elizabeth (_____), 212
  John, 212
  Thomas, 189, 190
Hardde [Hardey], *see Hardy*
Hardidge [Hardich], 190
  Alice, 190
  Elizabeth, 190
  Elizabeth (Sturman), 190
  Elizabeth (_____), 464
  Frances (Gerrard) (Speke) (Peyton) (Appleton) (Washington), 39, 190, 321, 378, 379, 426, 427
  Thomas, 190
  William, 39, 298
  William I, 190, 464
  William II, 190, 196, 254, 321, 464
Hardin, *see Hardy*

Hardwin [Hardwyn], _____, 190
Hardy [Hardde, Hardey, Hardin, Handy]
  George, 171, 187, 190, 191, 333, 370
  George (Mrs.), 190
  George, Jr., 190
  John, 77
  Thomas, 190
Hare, John, 284
Harington, *see Harrington*
Harlow [Harloe, Harlowe]
  Anthony, 190
  John, 190, 191, 405, 441
Harman, *see Harmar*
Harmanson
  Benjamin, 191
  Elishe, 191
  Elita [Elicia], 191
  Elizabeth (_____), 191
  George, 191
  Henry, 191
  Isabell, 191, 429
  John, 191
  Margaret, 191
  Thomas, 191, 429
  Thomas II, 191
  William, 191
Harmar [Harman, Harmer, Harmor]
  Ambrose, 91, 191, 243
  Ann [Anna] (Soothey), 139, 191, 192, 261, 377
  Charles, 122, 191, 261, 377
  Elizabeth, 191
  Jane (_____) (Kingsmill), 91, 182, 191, 243
  John, 191
  William, 185
Harper
  Gabriel, 192
  John, 192
  Thomas, 59
Harr, *see Hart*
Harralde, Thomas, 161, 192
Harres, Robert, 441
Harrington [Harington],
  Edward, 192
Harris
  Adria (_____), 192
  Alice (_____), 193, 455
  Dorothy (_____), 192
  Edward, 193
  Elizabeth (_____) (Phipps), 192, 193, 293, 322
  George, 181, 384
  James, 192
  Joan [Joane] (_____), 193
  John, 146, 192, 207
  John I, 192
  John II, 192
  Love, 193
  Margaret (_____), 207
  Mary, 260
  Sarah (_____), 181, 384

  Thomas, 62, 76, 138, 192, 193, 260, 318, 455
  Thomas I, 192, 193
  Thomas II, 193
  William, 160, 193, 269
  William I, 193, 290, 322
  William II, 193, 194
  _____, 192
Harris Family, 27, 193
Harrison
  Benjamin, 69, 72, 137, 273, 350, 400
  Benjamin I, 194
  Benjamin II, 31, 194, 258, 266
  Benjamin III, 194
  Beverley, 194
  Beverley (Mrs.), 194
  Elizabeth (_____), 194
  Frances (_____), 82
  George, 194, 195
  Hannah, 72, 266, 267
  Harmon, 195
  James, 194
  John, 194, 195
  Mary, 194
  Nathaniel, 150, 194
  Nicholas, 446
  Peter, 400
  Sarah, 72, 150
  Thomas, 88, 334
  _____, 187, 188, 446
Harrison Family, 71, 72
Harry (slave), 195
Hart [Harr, Hartt]
  Josyas [Josias], 192
  Samuel, 195
  Thomas, 195
  Thomas II, 425
  _____, 195
Hartland, William, 332
Hartley, William, 195
Hartt, *see Hart*
Hartwell
  Elizabeth, 197
  Elizabeth (_____), 197
  Henry, 23, 72, 86, 88, 113, 116, 132, 149, 195, 196, 254, 268, 273, 284, 318, 401
  Jane (_____), 196
  John, 196, 197
  John I, 273
  Margaret, 197
  Mary, 76, 196, 197, 273
  William, 196, 233
Harvey [Harvy]
  Ann, 198
  Elizabeth (Peirsey) (Stephens), 197, 198, 315, 385
  George, 184, 197, 254, 300, 374
  John, xii, 11, 13, 55, 56, 64, 79, 91, 99, 111, 121, 127, 140, 143, 153, 163,

191, 197, 198, 199, 200,
   206, 207, 214, 217, 239,
   245, 265, 272, 280, 283,
   293, 299, 308, 315, 327,
   328, 330, 343, 363, 383,
   385, 386, 407, 415, 419,
   437, 444, 461
Mary (_____), 198
Thomas, 198, 442
Ursula, 198
Valentine, 446
Harwick, George, 427
Harwood [Horwood]
   Ann (Needler), 198
   Ann (_____) (Wythe), 462
   Anne (_____), 198
   Arthur, 198
   George, 198, 224
   Grace, 198
   Grace (_____), 198
   Humphrey, 198
   Lydia (_____) (Cheesman),
      110
   Margaret, 198
   Thomas, 110, 198, 334, 462
   William, 151, 198, 199,
      341, 386, 428
   _____, 137, 440
Hatch
   Margaret, 199
   Thomas, 199, 203
Hatcher, William, 199, 203,
   452
Hatton
   Francis, 459
   John, 205
Haverd [Hauerd], Lazarus, 199
Hawkins, Thomas, 199
Hawley
   Anne, 245
   Gabriel [Gabriell], 153,
      199, 200
   James, 200
   Jerome [Jerom], 199, 200
   Jerome [Jerom] (Mrs.), 200
   William, 200, 217
Hay [Hayes, Hey]
   Adam, 200
   Anne (_____), 200
   Bridget [Bridgett] (_____)
      (Hunt), 201, 220, 298
   Joseph, 123
   Margery (_____) (Griggs),
      200
   Mary (Wade), 421
   Nathaniel, 200
   Robert, 200
   William, 200, 201, 220
   _____, 220
Hayes, *see Hay*
Hayle [Hayles], *see Hale*
Haynes
   Anthony, 440
   Elizabeth, 201
   Elizabeth (_____), 167,
      200, 201, 322, 323

James, 201
Jane, 201
Margaret, 201
Mary, 201
Thomas, 200, 201, 322
William, 201
_____, 323
Hayney, *see Haney*
Hayrick [Heyrick, Heyrock]
   Henry, 201
   Thomas, 201
Hayward [Haywood, Heyward]
   Bridget [Bridgett] (_____)
      (Hunt) (Hay), 200, 201,
      220, 298
   Hugh, 192
   John, 200, 201, 220, 298
   Joseph, 201
   Martha (_____), 201
   Nicholas, 201
   Samuel, 201
Hazard, Ebenezer, 34, 201
Heabeard [Heaberd, Hebert]
   John, 357
   Richard, 447
Heale, *see also Hale*
   Catherine [Katherine]
      (Chinn), 389
   Elizabeth, 202
   George (Mrs.), 202
   George I, 201, 202
   George II, 202
   John, 202
   Mary (_____), 201
   Nicholas, 201, 202
   Sarah, 202
   _____, 202
Heard, Ann (_____), 202
Hearseeqe (Native American),
   202, 312
Heart, James, 202, 212
Heaster, Esther [Ester]
   (Littleton), 261, 347
Hebbs [Hebb], Thomas, 202
Hebert, *see Heabeard*
Hedges, Robert, 202
Heiny, *see Haney*
Heley, _____, 337
Helline [Helin]
   John, 202
   John (Mrs.), 202
   _____, 202
Hellyard, *see Hilliard*
Hemy, *see Haney*
Hen, Robert, 279
Heney, John, 258
Henry, *see Haney*
Henshaw
   Edward, 439
   Frances (Westropp), 439
Herbert
   Frances (_____), 119
   John, 119
Hermann, Augustine, 188
Herquapinck (Native
   American), 202, 312

Hethersoll, Thomas, 124
Hewes, Mary, 202
Hey, *see Hay*
Heyrick [Heyrock], *see
   Hayrick*
Heyward, *see Hayward*
Hichcock [Hitchcocke,
   Hitchcok], Kilibett
   [Kelinet], 202
Hickmore [Hickmote,
   Hickmoate, Hicmott,
   Hickmott]
   James, 202, 203, 345
   James (Mrs.), 203, 345
Hide, *see Hyde*
Higginson [Higgenson]
   Christopher, 203
   Elizabeth, 203
   Elizabeth (_____), 203
   Humphrey, 203, 242
   Lucy, 66, 96, 265, 266,
      309
   Robert, 96, 203, 265
   Thomas, 203
Hill
   Anne (_____) (Goodrich),
      204
   Edward, 72, 132, 199, 220,
      327, 345, 385
   Edward (Mrs.), 345
   Edward I, 112, 203, 407
   Edward II, 112, 203, 204,
      369, 398
   Edward, III [Jr.], 113, 204,
      205
   Elizabeth (_____) (Chiles),
      112, 203
   Elizabeth (Williams), 203,
      204
   George, 205
   Hannah, 113
   Jane, 154, 205
   John, 205
   Mary, 156, 206, 263
   Mary (Peirsey), 97, 156,
      180, 206, 315
   Nathaniel, 241
   Nicholas, 62, 205, 206,
      449
   Ralph, 205, 206
   Rebecca (_____), 205
   Richard, 86, 107, 114, 205,
      206, 365
   Robert, 206
   Silvestra [Sylvester]
      (Bennett), 62, 205, 206
   Sion, 206
   Stephen, 205
   Sylvester, 63
   Tabitha (Scarborough)
      (Smart) (Brown)
      (Custis), 89, 90, 132,
      204, 359
   Thomas, 73, 97, 156, 204,
      206, 315
   Thomas I, 180

Thomas II, 97, 180, 324, 421
_____, 205
Hilliard [Hellyard], _____, 206
Hillier, John, 428
Hinson, Andrew, 136, 139, 206, 318
Hinton
Anne (_____), 207
John, 207
Thomas, 207, 280
_____, 207, 280
Hitch [Hitchy], John, 207
Hitchcocke [Hitchcok], *see Hichcock*
Hitchman, William, 272, 273
Hitchy, *see Hitch*
Hobbs
Francis, 207
Francis, Sr., 207
Mary (_____) (Floyd), 207
Hobson
Henry, 103
John, 207
Hockaday [Hockeday]
John, 207
William, 207
Hoddin [Hodin], *see Holder*
Hodges [Hodge, Hodgis]
Edward, 262
John, 208
Nicholas, 208
Robert, 208
Thomas, 128, 208
Hodgkins [Hodgskins, Hopskins, Hoskins, Hopkins]
Ann, 208
Anthony, 208, 236
Elizabeth, 208
Joyce (_____), 208
Hodgson
Portia (Lee), 257
William, 257
Hoe [Hooe, Home, How, Howe]
Anne (Howson), 209
Frances (Townshend) (Dade) (Withers), 209, 453
John, 216
Mary (_____) (Massey), 209
Rice [Ryce] I, 208, 209
Rice [Ryce] II, 209, 243
Rice [Ryce] III, 209, 453
Holcombe, Sarah (Taylor), 37
Holcroft [Howldcroft, Holdcroft, Holecroft], Thomas, 209
Holden, Robert, 209
Holder [Hoddin, Hodin, Holden, Holdinge]
Ann, 86, 87, 114, 209, 210, 316, 337, 375

John, 114, 208, 209, 210, 313, 443
Richard, 114, 126, 209, 210, 318, 434
Robert, 209
Holderby, Robert, 210
Holdinge, *see Holder*
Holdsworth [Holdwort], Arthur, 208, 210
Hole, *see Mole*
Holecroft, *see Holcroft*
Holgrave, Nicholas, 210
Holiday, *see Holliday*
Holland
Elizabeth (_____), 211
Gabriel, 61, 210, 323
Mary, 80
Mary (_____) (Pinke), 210, 323
Rebecca (_____), 210
Richard, 210
Hollewell, Thomas, 208
Holliday [Holiday, Holladay, Holloday, Hollyday, Holyday]
Ann (Brewer), 84
Anthony, 210, 211, 324
Hanna (_____), 210
Thomas, 33, 86, 210, 420
Holmes
Elizabeth (_____), 211
George, 211
Rebecca (_____), 211
Robert, 211
William, 55, 99, 138, 211, 352, 360, 364, 422, 435
_____, 352
Holmwood [Holmewood]
Jane (Bland) (Bland), 73, 211
John, 73, 211, 338
Holt [Howlett, Hoult]
Alice (_____), 212
Elizabeth (_____) (Hansford) (Wilson), 212
Frances (Mason), 212
James, 211
John, 211, 212
Mary (Bailey), 49, 211, 212
Mary (_____), 212
Randall I, 49, 211, 212
Randall II, 49, 211, 212, 293
Robert, 54, 212, 355, 442
Thomas, 164, 202, 212
William, 212
_____ (Mrs.), 154, 212
Holyday, *see Holiday*
Home, *see Hoe*
Hone [Howne]
Catherine, 68, 69, 213, 347, 406
Sarah (_____) (Edwards) (Richardson), 149, 213, 286, 345, 430, 449

Theodorick, 317
Theophilus, 67, 68, 113, 145, 149, 208, 213, 220, 224, 268, 336, 345, 362, 365, 430, 441, 445, 457, 461
Honywood, Philip, 249, 457
Hooe, *see Hoe*
Hooke [Hook]
Francis, 214
Jeremiah, 214
Hooker
Edward, 214
Thomas, 214
William, 214, 281, 454
Hope
George, 37
Joanna Custis, 133
Joanna Mary (Custis), 133
Temperance (_____), 37
Thomas, 214
William, 37
Hopkins [Hopskins, Hoskine, Hoskines, Hoskins]
Bartholomew, 214, 215, 387, 414
Cornelia (Lee), 257
Dorcas (_____), 214
John, 93, 215
Jonas, 162
Joyce, 93
Stephen, 343
William, 215
Hore, John, 360
Horehannah (Native American), 215, 420
Hornsby, John, 295
Horse [Horseye], *see Horsey*
Horsefoot, Walter, 215
Horsey [Horse, Horseye, Horsley]
Sarah (_____) (Williams), 215
Stephen, 215
Horsmenden [Horsemenden, Horsemonden, Horsmanden, Horsmondine]
Arthur, 216
Mary, 97, 216
Susan (_____), 215, 216
Warham [Wareham], 97, 215, 216
Horton, William, 231
Hosier [Hoyser]
Edward, 216
_____, 216
Hoskins [Hoskine, Hoskines], *see Hopkins*
Hostage, Henry (Native American), 216
Hough, *see Huff*
Hoult, *see Holt*
"House James" (slave), 223

How [Howe], *see Hoe*
Howard
  Dorcas, 216
  Francis, Lord Effingham,
    37, 68, 132, 216, 217,
    230, 266, 311, 313, 359
  Henry Frederick, Lord
    Maltravers, xii, 172,
    200, 217, 253, 272
  John, 50, 116, 217, 218,
    420
  Margaret (Clark), 116, 218
Howell
  Andrew, 218
  Edward, 33
  John, 218
Howldcroft, *see Holcroft*
Howlett, *see Holt*
Howne, *see Hone*
Howsen [Howson]
  Anne, 209
  Robert, 348
Hoyser, *see Hosier*
Hubbard [Hubberd], Robert,
  218
Huddleston, John, 130
Hudnell
  John, 185
  Mary (_____), 185
Hudson [Huson, Husone]
  Edward, 218
  Edward (Mrs.), 218
  John, 218
  Thomas, 218
Huff [Huffe, Huffs, Hough]
  Anne [Ann] (_____), 109,
    435
  Anthony, 435
  Francis, 218, 219
  Stephen, 109
  _____ (_____) (Windmill),
    219
Hughes, James, 219
Hull
  Ann, 122
  Elizabeth, 101
  Elizabeth (_____), 263
  John, 219, 263
  Peter, 219, 235, 370
Hullaway, *see Kullaway*
Humfrey, William, 219
Hundson
  Eleanor [Ellinor, Ellenor]
    (_____) (Senior), 361
  John, 361
Hunkle, William, 219
Hunnicutt
  Elizabeth (Spencer)
    (Sheppard) (Warren),
    119, 120, 364, 381, 382,
    425, 442
  John, 382
  William, 219, 234
Hunsford, *see Hansford*

Hunt
  Anne (_____), 220
  Bridget [Bridgett] (_____),
    200, 201, 220, 298
  Elizabeth (_____), 219
  Fortune (Jordan), 219, 236
  Joane (_____), 220
  Mary (_____), 77
  Robert, 91, 219
  Thomas, 30, 88, 113, 127,
    149, 161, 201, 209, 213,
    218, 219, 220, 224, 236,
    246, 268, 283, 293, 298,
    305, 306, 307, 356, 365,
    443, 448
  Thomas I, 220
  Thomas II, 220
  Thomas, Sr., 220
  William, 77
  William, Sr., 77, 220
  _____, 219
Hunter, Ralph, 310
Hurd, John, 220, 221
Hurlston, Edward, 333
Hurst
  John, 221
  Rebecca (_____), 265
Huson [Husone], *see Hudson*
Hutchings
  Amy (_____), 410
  John, 410
  Susannah, 410, 411, 412,
    413
Hutchinson
  Jane, 221
  Robert, 221, 287, 312, 445,
    461
  William, 221, 235
Hutt, Nathaniel, 221
Hutton
  Daniel, 179
  Rebecca (Gray), 179
Hux
  Joane [Jone] (Gray), 179
  John, 179
Hyde [Hide], Nicholas, 151,
  221
Hynde, Thomas, 221
Hyre, James, 221

I

"Indian John" (Native
  American), *see Gunstocker,
  Edward*
"Indian Mason" (Native
  American), *see Mason
  (Native American)*
"Indian Ned" (Native
  American), *see Gunstocker,
  Edward*
Innis
  Elizabeth (_____)
    (Allomby), 32, 33
  Walter, 33

Iotan (Native American),
  *see Opitchapam (Native
  American)*
Isaac [Isaack], _____, 221
Isgrave, John, 221
Isham
  Anne, 152
  Henry, 152
  Mary, 340
Isles, John, 222
Ison, Edward, 72
Itoyatin (Native American),
  *see Opitchapam (Native
  American)*
Ive, Anton, 222
Iversonn [Iverson, Iveson,
  Ivesson]
  Abraham, 222
  Abraham, Sr., 222
Izard
  Rebecca, 48
  Richard, 48, 81

J

Jack (slave), *see John (slave)*
Jackman, Joseph John, 196,
  393
"Jack of the Feather" (Native
  American), *see Nemattanew
  (Native American)*
Jackson [Jaxon]
  Christopher, 222
  Ephraim, 222
  Henry, 182
  Henry (Mrs.), 182
  John, 12, 89, 91, 115, 168,
    170, 173, 222, 223, 377,
    445
  John (Mrs.), 222
  John I, 222
  John I (Mrs.), 168
  John II, 222
  Richard, 370
  Robert, 223
  Sarah, 370
  William, 223
Jacob (slave), 178, 223
Jacobs [Jacob]
  Henry, 223
  Sarah (_____), 223
  Thomas, 223
Jadwyn
  Anne (Montague), 288
  John, 288
Jakins, James, 223
James
  Margery (_____), 224
  Martin, 223
  Rachel (_____), 38, 69,
    198, 223, 224, 225, 229,
    299, 365, 366, 367, 393,
    425
  Richard, 223, 224, 225, 232
  Richard I, 44, 61, 70, 73,
    139, 198, 209, 220, 221,

223, 224, 225, 238, 273,
  288, 312, 365, 366, 367,
  408, 420, 425, 434
Richard II, 223, 224, 251,
  365, 366, 367
_____, 238
James (Native American), 243
James (slave), 223
James I, King of England, 85
Jamy (slave), 88, 153, 225,
  354, 359
Japazous (Native American),
  225
Jaquelin
  Edward, 25, 26, 33, 34, 35,
    104, 110, 133, 137, 153,
    164, 212, 224, 225, 229,
    309, 317, 353, 359, 367,
    372, 410
  Edward I, 226
  Edward II, 226
  Elizabeth, 26, 33, 34, 35,
    225, 226, 317
  Elizabeth (Craddock), 225
  John, 225
  Martha, 33, 226
  Martha (Cary) (Thruston),
    33, 104, 225, 226, 367
  Mary, 33, 226, 372
  Mathew, 226
  Rachel (_____) (James)
    (Sherwood), 38, 69,
    198, 223, 224, 225, 229,
    299, 365, 366, 367, 393,
    425
Jaquelin Family, 33
Jarrett [Jarratt]
  Elir, 226
  Elizabeth, 226
  Joanna, 367
  Joannah (Lowe), 226, 318,
    319
  John, 218, 226, 273, 318
  Mary, 226
  William, 226
  William (Mrs.), 226
  _____, 226
Jarvis
  Arthur, 226
  Christopher, 227
  Elizabeth (Duke) (Bacon),
    47, 48, 227, 451
  Thomas I, 47, 48, 226, 227,
    451
  Thomas II, 227
Jason, Robert, 47, 48, 227
Jaxon, *see Jackson*
Jefferson
  Dorothy, 227
  Elizabeth, 227
  John, 102, 227, 228, 274
  Mary (Field), 159
  Nathaniel, 227
  Thomas, 159
Jefferys [Jeffrey, Jeffereys,
  Jeffries, Jeffreys]

Easter [Esther], 298
Edward, 298
Elizabeth (_____), 228, 298
Herbert, 48, 53, 68, 130,
  176, 204, 228, 231, 266,
  290, 324, 329, 383, 440
Jeffrey, 114, 141, 225, 228,
  229, 318, 347, 366, 367,
  376, 382, 434
John, 94, 114, 120, 124,
  125, 166, 227, 228, 229,
  234, 255, 268, 306, 347,
  440
Nathaniel, 93, 98, 188, 202,
  227, 264, 287, 443
Nathaniel (Mrs.), 227
Simon, 229
Thomas, 399
Jeffrey (slave), 228
Jeffrey [Geoffrey], King of
  the Weyanokes, (Native
  American), 228
Jenifer, *see Jennifer*
Jenkins [Jinkins]
  Bridgett (_____), 230
  Daniel, 230
  Henry, 184, 366, 367, 375
  Henry I, 229, 230
  Henry II, 230
  Mary, 230
  Mary (_____), 230
  _____, 367
Jennifer [Jenifer]
  Anne [Ann] (Toft), 230
  Daniel, 133
  Daniel I, 230
  Daniel II, 230, 435
Jennings [Jenings]
  Catherine [Katherine]
    (Lunsford), 232, 268,
    269, 458
  Edmund, 147, 230, 231
  Frances (_____), 231
  John, 231
  Mary (_____), 231
  Peter, 92, 231, 232, 234,
    239, 269, 280, 333, 458
Jenny (slave), 232
Jeremy (slave), 232
Jermaine, Peter, 229
Jessee [Jesse] (slave), 232, 242
Jinkins, *see Jenkins*
Joan (slave), 82, 83
Joanna [Johanna] (slave), 232,
  356
Joe (slave), 232
John (Native American), 232
John (slave), 113, 114, 133,
  222, 223, 224, 232
Johnny (slave), 233
Johnny "York" (slave), 233
Johns, Robert, 177, 233
Johnson
  Ambrose, 89
  Ann, 233, 285, 409

Ann (_____) (Major), 234
Ann (_____), 233
Anthony [Antonio], 399
Bridgett, 425
Christopher, 233
Cornelius, 348
Dorothy (Washbourne), 425
Jacob I, 233
Jacob II, 233
Jacob III, 233
Jacomin, 233
James, 355
Jane (_____), 234
John, 233, 384
John I, 233, 238, 379, 409
John II, 196, 233, 409
John, Jr., 248
Joseph, 155, 234
Mary, 233, 248
Obedience, 234
Richard, 234, 425
Temperance, 425
Thomas, 234
Washbourne, 425
William, 219, 233, 234
Johnson Family, 80
Jolley, James, 125
Jonas, William, alias Pinke, *see
  Pinke, William*
Jones [Joanes]
  Ann, 236
  Ann (_____) (Smith), 235
  Ann [Anne] (_____), 235,
    236
  Anthony, 235
  Cadwallader, 395
  Catherine, 235
  Elizabeth, 236, 382, 397
  Elizabeth (_____), 236
  Farmar, 342
  Hugh, 26, 235
  Joyce, 236
  Martha (_____), 236
  Morgan, 263, 465
  Nathaniel, 331
  Paul, 235
  Richard, 235, 405
  Robert, 113, 235, 303, 304,
    320, 365, 396
  Samuel, 33, 180, 235
  Thomas, 382
  William, 144, 163, 208,
    235, 236, 349
  William (Mrs.), 235
  William, alias Brooks
    [Brookes, Broockes],
    alias Morgan, *see
    Morgan, William*
  _____ (Capt.), 80
Jordan [Jerden, Jordain,
  Jorden]
  Arthur, 349
  Christian (_____), 394
  Cisley (_____), 155, 156,
    237

Dorcas (_____) (Spence), 236, 237
Elizabeth (Burgh), 237
Fortune, 219, 236
George, 219, 236, 284, 342, 365
Jane (_____) (Spencer), 381
John, 236, 237, 379
Margaret, 237
Margaret (Brasseur), 237
Mary, 57, 237, 415
Richard, Sr., 459
Robert, 394
Samuel, 237
Thomas, 381
Thomas I, 237
Thomas I (Mrs.), 237
Thomas II, 237
Thomas III, 237
_____, 236
Joy
Kate, 369
_____, 369
Jubilee, Dorothy (Native American), 237, 367
Judah (slave), 237
Judith (slave), 237
Julian, Robert, 237
Jupiter (slave), 237
Jurnen, Nicholas, 242

K

Kae [Kar]
Anne (_____) (Goodrich), 175
Robert, 175
Karney, *see Kearney*
Kate [Cate] (slave), 238
Kay [Kaye], *see Key*
Kaynton
Frances (Covell), 264
Thomas, 264
Kean [Keen, Keene]
Alice, 238
Hannah, 32
Kearney [Karney, Kearne], Barnaby [Barnabe, Barnabye], 224, 238, 275
Keaton [Keeton, Keton]
John, 238
John I, 238
John II, 238
Kecatan, John [Jack], 243
Keeling
Adam, 208, 252, 276, 344, 355
Ann (Martin), 252, 276
Elizabeth, 81
Thorowgood, 81
Keene, *see Kean*
Keeth, *see Keith*
Keeton, *see Keaton*
Keie, *see Key*

Keith [Cisse, Keth, Keeth, Keyth, Kith, Skiffe]
George, 238
John, 238
Martha (_____), 238
Simon, 425
Susan (_____), 238
Kellond, John, 168
Kelloway, William, 238
Kellsall, Roger, 450
Kemp
Edmund [Edmond], 239
Elizabeth, 239, 240
Elizabeth (Wormeley), 239, 240, 268, 334, 373, 457
Elizabeth (_____), 239
John, 238
Mary, 307, 346
Mathew, 231
Mathew I, 239
Mathew II, 239
Richard, 13, 64, 82, 91, 99, 101, 112, 123, 138, 143, 206, 216, 239, 240, 268, 290, 308, 327, 334, 343, 345, 361, 373, 383, 384, 390, 457
William, 240
Kemps (Native American), 240, 396
Kendall
Ann, 241
Ann (_____), 241
George, 240
John, 240, 241
Mary, 240, 256
Mason, 241
Sarah (_____), 240
Sorrowful Margaret (Custis), 133
Susanna, 241
Susanna (_____) (Pott), 240, 328
William, 133
William I, 240, 241, 256, 328, 331
William II, 240, 241
William III, 241
Keniston, Allen, 399
Kennede [Kennedy], Patrick, 241
Kennell
Mary (_____), 56, 241
Samuel [Sammuel], 56, 241
Kenner
Elizabeth (Rodham), 241, 295
Hannah (Fox), 166, 241
John, 241
Richard, 241, 295, 431
Rodham, 166, 236, 241
Kennon
Agnes (Bolling), 242
Elizabeth, 242
Elizabeth (Worsham), 152, 241, 242

Judith, 242
Richard I, 241, 242
Richard II, 242
Sarah, 242
William, 242
Kente, Thomas, 201
Kenythorpe, Catherine (_____), 139
Kerfitt, Thomas, 242
Kersie, Thomas, 242
Kerton, William, 242
Keth, *see Keith*
Keton, *see Keaton*
Key [Kay, Kaye, Keie, Keyes]
Elizabeth, 242
Martha (_____), 242
Robert, 31, 279
Sarah (_____), 242
Thomas, 242
Kickotank (Native American), 420
Kidall
Edward, 160
Sarah (_____), 160
Kidd, Roger, 331
Kikotan, John (slave), 149, 243
Killbee, William, 114
Kineston, Allen, 450
"King James" (Native American), 243
"King Jeffrey," (Native American), *see Jeffrey [Geoffrey]*
King, John, 64
Kingsmill
Elizabeth, 45, 46, 47, 243, 284, 396
Jane (_____), 91, 182, 191, 243
Nathaniel, 46, 243
Richard, 11, 45, 46, 47, 91, 95, 182, 185, 187, 191, 192, 243, 247, 254, 276, 284, 396
Susan, *see Kingsmill, Elizabeth*
Kingston [Kingstone], Thomas, 243
Kinsman, Richard, 244
Kiptopeke [Kiptope] (Native American), 244
Kirkman
Francis, 44, 59, 145, 192, 195, 213, 244, 322, 365, 446
Sarah (_____), 244
Kissacomas (Native American), 244
Kissanacomen (Native American), 244
Kitchen, _____, 244
Kith, *see Keith*
Kittamaquund
Charles, (Native American), 82, 244, 245

Mary [Maria] (Native
 American), 82, 244, 245
Knight
 Anne (Hawley), 245
 Edward, 122, 245
 Elizabeth, 246
 James, 246
 John, 109, 245, 317
 Joseph, 122, 245
 Leonard, 246
 Mary, 62, 246
 Nathaniel, 245
 Peter, 83, 144, 282, 370
 Peter I, 170, 245, 246
 Richard, 246
 Samuel, 245
Knipe, Randolph, 176
Knollinge, Christopher, 246
Knotts, John, 431
Knowles
 Bathenia (_____), 246
 Bethaniah [Bethania], 246
 Israel, 247
 Jonathan [John], 54, 71,
  219, 220, 228, 246, 247,
  284, 297, 322, 393, 417
 Sands, 132, 247
 _____, 246
Kocoum (Native American),
 247, 325
Kullaway [Hullaway], John,
 247

L

Lacton, Henry, 247
Lacy [Lacey, Lacye, Lasey,
 Lucy, Lucye]
 Daniel, 247, 281, 424
 Robert, 398
 Sarah (_____) (Taylor), 398
 Susan (_____), 247
 William, 247
Lafayette, Marquis de, *see
 Motier, Marie-Joseph Paul
 Yves Roch Gilbert*
Lamb
 Robert, 247
 William, 190
Lambert [Lambard, Lambart]
 Jane (_____), 248
 Rachel, 248
 Thomas, 81, 247, 248, 368
Lambert Family, 262
Lamberton, George, 127
Lambmot, William, 341
Lamoyne, John, 248
Lampkin, John, 248
Lancaster, Robert, 146
Land, Francis, 345
Landon, Elizabeth "Betty," 102
Lane
 John, 248
 Thomas, 248, 318, 319, 372
 _____, 248

Langden [Langdon], *see
 Langman*
Langeley, *see Langley*
Langhorne [Langhorn]
 Judith, 413
 John, 248
Langley [Langly, Langeley]
 Agnes, 248
 Jane, 248
 John, 143
 Joseph, 248
 Ralph, 248, 249
 Ralph, Jr., 248
 Robert, 249, 405, 406
 Sarah, 248, 249
 Stephen (Mrs.), 248
Langman [Langden, Langdon]
 Mary (_____) (Ascam), 42,
  91, 115, 249, 326, 352
 Peter [Peeter], 42, 123, 249,
  323, 326, 357
Langston [Langstone]
 Anthony, 249, 250, 261
 Catherine (_____), 249
 John, 249, 250
 William, 249
Lansdale, Peter, 250, 272
Lapworth, Michael, 250
Lasey, *see Lacy*
Lassells [Lassell]
 Edward, 250
 Edward, Jr., 250
Latrobe, Benjamin, 257
"Laughing King" (Native
 American), *see Esmy
 Shichans*
Lawne
 Christopher, 57, 207, 250,
  426
 Lovewell, 250
 Symon, 250
Lawrence
 Dorothy (_____), 250
 Patience, 250
 Richard, 20, 33, 39, 44, 46,
  74, 97, 104, 116, 146,
  213, 224, 236, 250, 251,
  252, 255, 279, 280, 342,
  361, 365, 379, 401, 423,
  430, 443
Lawrence (slave), 250
Lawrie, Thomas, 97
Lawson
 Alice (_____), 252
 Anthony, 82, 252, 276, 403
 Christopher, 252
 Elizabeth, 252
 Margaret, 403
 Richard, 186
 Thomas, 252
Laydon [Layden, Layton,
 Leydon]
 Alice, 252
 Anne [Ann] (Burras), 252
 John, 252

Katherine, 252
 Margaret, 252
 Virginia, 252
Lea, William, 400
Leach [Leech], _____, 252,
 253
Leake, Marmion, 154, 377
Leane, Anthony, 253, 281
Leare [Lear]
 Ann [Anne] (_____)
  (George), 171, 172, 253,
  324, 329
 Anne (_____) (Southall),
  253
 Elizabeth, 253
 Elizabeth (Bridger), 253
 John, 78, 121, 171, 172,
  238, 253, 278, 324, 329
 Joseph, 253
 Martha, 121, 253
 Mary (Bastard), 253
 Rebecca (_____), 253
 Thomas, 253
Leat [Leate, Leete], William,
 253
Le Briton, John, 43
Leckett [Lecket], *see also
 Beckett*
 Thomas, 61, 253
 William, 284
Lee [Leigh, Lees, Ley]
 Anna [Ann, Anne], 240,
  255, 256, 464, 465
 Christopher, 254
 Christopher (Mrs.), 254
 Cornelia, 257
 Francis, 170, 257, 258
 George, 29, 46, 78, 81, 90,
  116, 176, 197, 206, 254,
  297, 300, 336, 374, 446,
  449, 455
 Godfrey, 117
 Hancock, 240, 256
 Hannah (Ludwell), 257,
  267
 Hannah (_____), 255
 Hannah Philippa (Ludwell),
  257, 267
 Henry, 136, 186, 254, 255,
  296
 Hugh, 121, 254, 255, 295
 Isaac, 256
 John, 31, 255, 256, 257,
  285, 465
 Kendall, 240, 256
 Mary (Kendall), 240, 256
 Portia, 257
 Richard, 32, 83, 94, 256,
  257, 307, 440
 Richard I, 229, 255, 256,
  441, 464, 465
 Richard II, 251, 256
 Richard Henry, 257
 Sarah, 197
 Sarah (Allerton), 256

Sarah [Sara] (_____), 196,
  254, 300, 374, 416
Susanna, 240, 256
Thomas, 257, 258, 267,
  302, 414
William, 136, 257, 258,
  267, 296
William Ludwell, 257, 267
Leech, *see Leach*
Leeds, Timothy, 257
Leete, *see Leat*
Legg, Edward, 275
Leigh, *see Lee*
Leister [Lester, Leyster, Lister]
  Dionysius, 258
  Robert, 258, 313
  Thomas, 258, 383
Lembri, *see Limbreck*
Leneve, William, 258
Lenton [Linton], Anthony, 242
Leonard
  Cynthia, 175, 298
  Robert, 441
Lesley, Robert, 258, 259
Lester, *see Leister*
Lettice, Philip, 71
Lettis, Philip, 246
Levermore
  Barbara (_____) (Lydall),
    269
  Philip, 269
Lewellyn, *see Llewelyn*
Lewis [Lewes]
  John, 92, 171, 259
  Joyce, 171
  Mary (Jenkins), 230
  Morgan, 171
  Samuel, 149, 243
  Sarah (George)
    (Peddington), 171
  William, 249, 259
Lewis (slave), 259
Ley, *see Lee*
Leydon, *see Laydon*
Leyster, *see Leister*
Lightfoot [Lightfoote, Lytefoot,
  Lytefoote]
  Goodrich, 259
  John, 44, 53, 78, 139, 259,
    269, 381, 450
  John I, 259
  John II, 259
  Philip, 139, 260
  Sherwood, 259
Lightly, William, 260
Ligon [Liggon, Lyggon,
  Lygon]
  Henry, 260
  Hugh, 260
  Johan, 260
  Mary (Harris), 260
  Richard, 260
  Thomas, 260
Lillington, Elizabeth, 393
Lilly
  Dorothy (Wade), 421

John, 109, 343
Mary (_____), 109
Mary, 343
Limbreck [Limbrecke,
  Lembri], Francis, 260
Limney, Richard, 260
Limpanie
  Robert, 260
  _____, 260
Lindsey, Robert, 178, 260, 375
Lisson, Daniel, 431
Liste, George, 260
Lister, *see Leister*
Littlepage, Richard, 249, 260,
  297
"Little Sarah" (slave), 356
Littleton
  Ann [Anna] (Soothey)
    (Harmar), 139, 191,
    192, 261, 377
  Bowman, 261
  Edward, 143, 261
  Elizabeth, 261
  Esther [Ester], 261, 347
  Gertrude, 261
  Nathaniel, 126, 127
  Nathaniel I, 191, 261, 377
  Nathaniel II, 261
  Richard, 261
  Sarah, 261
  Sarah (Douglas), 143
  Southey, 261
  Southey [Southy] I, 261
  Southey II, 261
  Southey III, 261
  Susanna (_____), 261
Liverpool (slave), 262
Liverpool, William (slave), 88,
  262, 317
Llewelyn [Lluellin, Lewellyn]
  Ann [Anne] (_____) (Price)
    (Hallom), 262, 333, 390
  Daniel I, 262
  Daniel II, 262
  Margaret, 262
  Martha, 262
Lloyd [Loyd, Lloide, Loyde]
  Cornelius, 262
  Edward, 63, 262, 263
  Elizabeth, 248
  Elizabeth (Carter), 391
  Elizabeth (_____) (Hull),
    263
  Elizabeth (_____), 262
  George, 224, 263, 304
  Grace (_____), 262
  Humphrey, 66
  John, 263, 391
  Mary (Hill) (Fauntleroy),
    156, 157, 263
  Mathew [Matthew], 263
  Simon, 263
  Thomas, 263
  William, 157, 263
  _____ (Lt. Col.), 463

Lluellin, *see Llewelyn*
Lobb, George, 84, 264
Loggerhead (Native American),
  see Wattle Jaws
Long, Arthur, 444
"Long Hannah" (slave), 189
Lound
  Henry, 58
  Mary, 58
Love, William, 264
Loving [Loveinge, Loven,
  Lovinge]
  Frances (Covell) (Kaynton),
    264
  Thomas, 127, 264, 440, 441
Lowe
  Joannah [Joanne], 226, 318,
    319
  Micajah, 150, 226, 318, 319
  Sarah (Harrison), 150, 318
Lowick, Michael, 264
Lowther
  Bridget (_____), 264
  _____, 264
Loyd [Loyde], *see Lloyd*
Lucas [Lucar, Lucus]
  John, 198
  Margaret (Underwood)
    (Upton), 264, 265, 291,
    418, 419
  Samuel, 126
  Thomas I, 264, 265
  Thomas II, 265
Lucy (slave), 62, 265
Lucy [Lucye], *see Lacy*
Luddington, William, 265
Ludlow [Ludloe, Ludlowe]
  Elizabeth (_____), 265
  George, 97, 265, 301, 322,
    441, 443
  Jonathan, 265
  Rebecca (Hurst), 265
  Roger, 265
  Thomas, 265
Ludwell
  Frances, 257, 267
  Frances (Culpeper)
    (Stephens) (Berkeley),
    46, 65, 66, 121, 130,
    145, 146, 159, 205, 228,
    266, 267, 375, 381, 385,
    441
  Frances (Grymes), 257, 267
  Hannah, 257, 267
  Hannah (Harrison), 72,
    266, 267
  Hannah Philippa, 257, 267
  Jane, 98, 265, 268, 309
  Lucy, 257, 267
  Lucy (Higginson) (Burwell)
    (Bernard), 66, 96, 265,
    266, 309
  Philip I, 45, 46, 57, 66, 73,
    96, 130, 153, 159, 175,
    214, 217, 225, 228, 245,

265, 266, 268, 273, 309,
311, 347, 353, 356, 359,
366, 381, 385, 435, 444
Philip II, 72, 88, 96, 98,
150, 214, 225, 229, 254,
265, 266, 267, 268, 317,
367, 382, 416
Philip III, 257, 266, 267
Thomas, 14, 65, 66, 73, 74,
122, 180, 193, 195, 213,
251, 265, 266, 267, 268,
308, 311, 321, 340, 349,
365, 373, 384, 432, 445
Ludwell Family, 27, 53, 71,
98, 254
Luke
Anne (Custis) (Yeardley)
(Wilcox), 131, 446, 463
George, 169
John, 446
Lukin [Luken], Alice, 305,
306, 307
Lullett, John, 268
Lunn [Lun], Thomas, 268
Lunsford
Catherine [Katherine], 232,
268, 269, 458
Elizabeth, 268
Elizabeth (Wormeley)
(Kemp), 239, 240, 268,
334, 373, 457
Mary, 269
Philippa, 269
Thomas, 240, 268, 269,
301, 373, 457
Luxon, Philip, 269
Lyall, Susanna, 269
Lydall [Lyddall, Lidall]
Barbara (_____), 269
George, 249, 269
John, 269
Lydford, Mathew, 434
Lydia (slave), 155, 269
Lyggon [Lygon], *see Ligon*
Lyne, Thomas, 269, 448
Lynny [Lynney, Lynsey]
Anthony, 347, 448
Richard, 182, 269, 338
Lyon, Elizabeth, 269
Lytefoot [Lytefoote], *see
Lightfoot*

M

Machiawao (Native American),
see Machywap
Machodocs [Machoatick,
Muchchotas] (King of the)
(Native American), 270
Machumps [Mechumps,
Muchamps, Munchumps]
(Native American), 270
Machywap [Macky-wap,
Machiawao] (Native
American], 111, 270, 448
Mackennie, Francis, 435

Macnen, _____, 338
Macock [Macocke, Maycock,
Morecock]
Samuel, 79, 270, 305
Sarah [Sara], 270, 305
Macon, *see also Mason*
Ann [Anne] (_____), 271,
363
Gideon, 270
Mary (Hartwell), 76, 196
William, 76, 196, 271, 279,
363
Madison [Maddeson,
Maddison]
Isaac [Isack], 271
James, 37, 257, 271
Mary (_____), 271
Maguel [Migeul, Magill,
Maguire], Francis
[Francisco], 271, 272
Major [Maior]
Alice, 234
Ann (_____), 234
Edward, 97, 272
Jane, 234
John, 234
William, 234
Makemie
Francis, 37
Naomi (Anderson), 37
Malinos, *see Molina*
Mallory
Peter, 250
Philip, 272, 445
Maltravers (Lord), *see Howard,
Henry Frederick*
Manby, John, 272
Mangopeesomon (Native
American), *see
Opechancanough*
Mann
John, 307, 346
Mary, 307
Mary (Kemp) (Berkeley),
307, 346
Mannering, Stephen, 426
Manning, Philip, 286
Mansell [Mansill, Monsell],
see also Mansfield
David "Davy," 264, 272,
430
Mary, 272, 339
Mansfield [Mainsfield], *see
also Mansell*
George, 391
Mary, 196, 318, 339, 371,
391, 392, 393
Maples [Mayples], Thomas,
272, 273
Marable [Marble]
Agnes (_____) (Marjorum),
273, 274
Benjamin, 274
Catherine (_____), 170, 273
Elizabeth, 410

Elizabeth (_____), 274
George I, 37, 95, 124, 149,
170, 273, 274, 350, 395
George II, 88, 153, 164,
192, 194, 196, 225, 273,
274, 318, 353, 359, 367,
380, 420, 435, 460
George III [Jr.], 197, 273
Henry Hartwell, 197, 273
Mary (Hartwell), 197, 273
William, 273, 274
Marable Family, 301
Marjorum [Marjoram]
Agnes (_____), 273, 274
Bennett, 33, 273, 274
Markham [Marcum]
Lewis, 87, 426
Robert, 274
Robert, alias Moutapass,
Robert, 274
Mark (slave), 274
Marks [Markes], Walgrave
[Waldegrave], 227, 274
Marlborough (Duke of), 309
Marlet [Marlett, Marlott,
Marloe], Thomas, 275
Marriloe, William, 275
Marriot [Marriott]
Dorothy, 429
Susanna (Swann), 275
William, 97, 275, 297
_____ (_____) (Butler), 97
Marshall [Marshott]
Ann (_____), 275
Eleanor (Spradd), 182
Hannah (_____), 275
Lucy, 36
Michael, 326
Robert, 182, 275
Tomazin (_____), 389
William, 275
Marteau [Marteaw], *see
Martiau*
Marten, *see Martin*
Martiau [Marteu, Marteau,
Marteaw]
Elizabeth, 275, 343
Jane (_____) (Bartley), 57,
275
Nicholas, 110, 144, 158,
275, 343
Sibella [Isabella] (_____)
(Adkins) (Felgate), 157,
158, 275
Martin [Marten, Martyn]
Ann, 252, 276
George, 275
Jacob, 360
Joell, 276
John, 40, 137, 138, 185,
243, 252, 276, 305, 310,
342, 351, 357, 383, 391,
405, 446, 447, 450, 464
John I, 275, 276
John II, 275, 276

Margaret (Wild), 446, 447
Peter [Petter], 203, 276
Ralph, 277
Ruth, 277
Sarah [Sara] (_____) (Cross
     (Scott), 360
Thomas, 89
Mary (slave), 277
Mary, Queen of England, 346
Masco [Masquran] (Native
     American), 277
Mason, *see also Macon*
Alice, 277, 411
Alice (_____), 277
Anne [Ann] (Seawell), 277,
     278, 361
Anne [Ann] (_____), 337,
     363
Dinah, 277
Elizabeth, 277
Elizabeth (_____), 278
Frances, 212, 277
Francis, 271, 279, 337, 338,
     430
Francis I, 277
Francis II, 182, 212, 277
George, 224, 277, 278
James, 278
Joseph, 277
Lemuel [Lyonell], 277, 361,
     363, 403
Lemuel [Lyonell] I, 278
Mary, 277
Mary (_____), 277, 278
Thomas, 277, 278
William, 279
Mason ["Indian Mason"]
     (Native American), 277
Massey, Mary (_____), 209
Mastegonoe (Native
     American), 279, 394
Matachanna (Native
     American), 419
Matheman [Matheyman], John,
     279
Mathews [Mathew, Mathewes]
Edward, 280
Elizabeth, 240
Elizabeth (Tavernor), 281
Esther, 240
Frances (Grenville) (West)
     (Peirsey), 181, 280,
     315, 437
Francis, 280
Jeremiah, 280
John, 240, 280, 281
Mary, 240
Rowland, 279
Samuel, 30, 56, 65, 66, 74,
     140, 153, 211, 304, 352,
     356
Samuel I, 181, 206, 207,
     280, 293, 315
Samuel II, 121, 129, 280,
     304, 320
Thomas, 83, 250, 279

Walter, 280
William, 281
_____ (Baldwin), 280
_____ (Hinton), 280
Matheyman, *see Matheman*
Mathis, Ann, 102
Mattaponi [Mattapony] (King
     of the) (Native American),
     281
Mattson, Robert, 281
Maudley, Rebecca, 189
Maurice (Prince), 249
Maxes, Thomas, 281
Maxey, Charles, 281
May, William, 43, 196, 213,
     214, 220, 224, 268, 281,
     284, 443, 455, 456, 457
Maycock, *see Macock*
Mayhew [Mahew]
Edward, 253, 281
Thomas, 253, 281
McClenahan [McClanahan],
     Susanna (Robinson), 348
Meade [Mead]
David, 172, 253
John, 281, 282, 440
William, 59, 177, 340
Meares [Meeres], Thomas, 282
Meatherst, Joan, 173, 282
Mechumps (Native American),
     see Machumps
Medcalf, George, 354
Meeres, *see Meares*
Meese [Mees]
Ann [Anne] (_____), 282,
     432
Henry, 182, 282, 320, 432
Meimeichcom (Native
     American), 282
Mellinge [Mellin, Melling]
Anne (_____), 283
Margaret, 283
Thomas, 283
William I, 283
William II, 283
Menefie [Menefy, Menify]
Elizabeth, 283, 319, 328
Elizabeth (_____), 283, 319
George, 11, 62, 77, 102,
     115, 123, 140, 182, 195,
     241, 264, 265, 283, 305,
     308, 310, 319, 355, 387,
     442, 449
Isabell [Izabella] (Smythe)
     (Pace) (Perry), 109, 270,
     283, 305, 319, 344
Mary (_____), 283
Mentis [Meutis], Thomas, 283
Meredith, John, 432
Meriday [Meredie, Meridien],
     John, 283
Merill, Isaac, 366
Meriwether [Merewether,
     Meriweather,
     Merryweather]

Ann, 117
Elizabeth (Crafford), 128
Elizabeth (Woodhouse),
     284
Elizabeth (_____), 400
Francis, 59, 61, 196
Francis I, 253, 284, 285,
     451
Francis II, 285
Mary (_____), 284, 285
Nicholas, 43, 45, 46, 47, 59,
     117, 126, 196, 243, 281,
     283, 284, 455
Thomas, 196, 284, 400
_____, 284
Meriwether Family, 128
Merritt, John, 285
Merryweather, *see Meriwether*
Meutis, *see Mentis*
Meyer
Elir, 285
William, 285
Michael [Michel], *see Mitchell*
Middleton
David, 285
Thomas, 285, 450
Midwinter, Francis, 285
Migh, Robert, 285
Mihill [Myhill]
Ann (Johnson), 285
Edward, 285
Miles, Robert, 285, 317
Miller, Christopher, 285
Milliscent, John, 303
Mills
Elizabeth, 361
Fortune (_____), 342
Henry, 285
James, 223
William, 285
Milman, _____, 285
Milmer, Richard, 285
Milner
Francis, 285, 286
Francis (Mrs.), 285
Mary, 103
Thomas, 103, 286, 362
Milward, John, 286
Minge [Ming], James, 78, 286,
     365, 398
Mingo (slave), 286
Minor, John, 337, 366
Minter
Ann (_____), 286
Edward, 286
John, 286
Richard, 286
Mirick
Mary (_____) (Gray), 179
Owen, 179
"Mischief" (Native American),
     286
Mitchell [Michael, Michell]
Joan (_____), 287
Richard, 465
William, 287

Mode, Gyles, 77
Moises, *see Moses*
Mole [Hole, Moll, Molt]
Edward, 48, 227
Elizabeth (Duke) (Bacon)
(Jarvis), 47, 48, 227,
451
Samuel, 188, 227, 287
Molina [Malinos], Diego de,
260, 287
Molineux [Molyneux,
Mullinax], Richard, 287
Moll (slave), 287
Molt, *see Mole*
Molton, *see Moulton*
Molyneux, *see Molineux*
Momford [Monford, Montford,
Mountford, Mumford]
Ann (_____), 182, 287, 338
Henry, 418
Richard, 293
Thomas, 218
William, 287, 298, 391
Mompesson, *see Mopeson*
Monguy (Native American), 41
Monke, _____ (Gen.), 464
Monroe [Monro]
Andrew, 236, 360
Eleanor, 236
Sarah (Smith), 370
Montague [Montecue,
Mountague, Mountegue]
Anne, 288
Ciceley (_____), 288
Elizabeth, 288
Ellen, 288
Margaret, 288
Peter [Peeter], 288
William, 288
Montford, *see Momford*
Moon [Moone, O'moon,
Omoonce]
Abraham, 29, 131
John, 13, 288, 404, 454
Mary, 288
Prudence (_____) (Wilson),
288
Susan (_____), 288
Moore
Jane (_____), 288
John, 288
Richard, 173, 287, 288, 389
William, 288
Moorton, *see Morton*
Mopeson [Mompesson],
Richard, 137, 289
Morassane (Native American),
289
Morecock, *see Macock*
Morecroft
Edmund, 262
Edward, 355
Morell, *see Morley*
Morgan
Francis, 53, 255, 437
Francis I, 289, 334, 407

Francis II, 289
Sibile (_____), 289
William, alias Brooks
[Brookes, Broockes],
William, 32, 289
Morish, *see Morris*
Morison, *see Morrison*
Morley [Morell]
William, 289
William (Mrs.), 289
_____, 289
Morris [Morrice, Morish]
Edward, 289
George, 29, 289, 290
Thomas, 289
Morrison [Morison, Moryson]
Francis, 22, 67, 134, 193,
290, 301, 317, 322, 324,
416
Richard, 214, 290, 291, 452
Robert, 290
Morse
Ann (Richardson), 345
David, 338
Francis, 345
John Jackson, 345
Richardson, 345
Morton [Moorton, Murton],
Ralph [Ralfe], 291
Moryson, *see Morrison*
Moseby, Elizabeth (Ricks),
345, 367
Moseley [Mosley]
Ann (_____), 291
Arthur, 291
Benjamin, 291, 292
Edward, 291, 292
Frances (Stringer), 389
George, 291
John, 292
Joseph, 291
Martha, 292
Martha (_____), 291
Mary, 291
Robert, 165, 292
Susanna [Susan] (_____),
291, 463
William, 215, 291
William I, 291, 463
William II, 291
William III, 291, 292
William III (Mrs.), 292
William IV, 292
Moses [Moises, Mosses,
Moyes, Moyses], Theodore,
61, 292, 293
Mosley, *see Moseley*
Mosses, *see Moses*
Motier, Marie-Joseph Paul
Yves Roch Gilbert, Marquis
de Lafayette, 27, 126, 247
Mottrom [Motram, Motron,
Motteram, Mottram,
Mottrum]
Anne, 292, 380

Frances, 292, 318, 360,
380, 381
John, 121, 189, 242, 270,
329, 332, 369, 414
John I, 292, 378, 380
John II, 292, 380
Ursula (_____)
(Thompson), 121, 292
Moulton [Molton, Moulston,
Moultone], Thomas, 292
Mounslie, Thomas, 293
Mountague [Mountegue], *see
Montague*
Mountford, *see Momford*
Moutapass, Robert, *see
Markham, Robert*
Mouton, Thomas, 293
Moyes [Moyses], *see Moses*
Mquanzafsi (Native American),
293
Muchchotas (King of the)
(Native American), *see
Machodocs (King of the)*
Muche, *see Mutch*
Muchumps (Native American),
see Machumps
Mudge, *see Mutch*
Mugget, Ann, 363
Muleston, George, 293
Mullard
Elizabeth (_____)
(Holland), 211
Joshua, 211
Mullinax, *see Molineux*
Mumford, *see Momford*
Munchumps (Native
American), *see Machumps*
Munden, Robert, 189
Munger
Elizabeth, 77
John, 77, 293
Murden, John, 286
Murray [Murrey, Murry]
James, 293
John, 192
Murrow, Mary (Church), 114
Murry, *see Murray*
Murton, *see Morton*
Muschamp, Christopher, 293
Musgrave, William, 293
Mutch [Mudge, Muche]
Margery (_____), 293
William, 293
Mutton, Richard, 293
Myhill, *see Mihill*
Mynne, Anne, 99
Mynns, James, 293
Mynythorne (Native
American), 293

N

Naeheoopa (Native American),
29, 294
Namenacus (Native American),
294, 423

Namontack (Native American), 294, 357
Nan (slave), 294
Nancy (slave), 294
Nangle, George, 177
Nanny (Native American), 259
Nanny (slave), 178, 294
Nansemond (King of the), 294, 423
Nanticos (Native American), 294
Nanzattico (King of the) (Native American), *see* *Wattle Jaws*
Naseworthy, *see Norsworthy*
Neale [Neal]
 Christopher, 139, 295, 349
 Christopher I, 294, 295
 Daniel, 139, 401
 Elizabeth (_____), 295
 Hannah (Rodham), 294, 295
 James, 200
 Jane (_____), 295, 349
 John, 295, 399, 456
Neckennechehey (Native American), 295
Necotowance (Native American), 14, 295, 296, 406
Ned (slave), 296, 353
Nedham
 Jane, 200
 Thomas, 276
Neech, Daniel, 241
Needler
 Ann, 198
 John, 198
Needles, John, 296
Nell (slave), 296
Nelly (slave), 135, 136, 170, 296, 412
Nelson
 Francis, 296
 George, 296
 Mathew, 444
 William, 297
 William, alias Atherton, Peter, 43
Nelstrop, Rowland, 297
Nemattanew [Nemetenew, Nenemachanew, "Jack of the Feather"] (Native American), 289, 297
Nero (slave), 412
Nevell, Edward, 297
Nevett, William, 78
Newberry, Alice, 297
Newce, *see Nuce*
Newell
 Christopher, 384
 David, 54, 201, 244, 298, 325, 365
 Elizabeth (_____), 60, 167, 201, 297, 298, 328, 346

John [Jonathan, Jonathin], 53, 54, 97, 115, 138, 167, 169, 201, 213, 246, 254, 261, 297, 298, 305, 306, 307, 322, 328, 334, 346, 350, 377
 Letitia (_____) (Barber), 33, 54, 125, 298, 328
Newman
 Alexander, 298
 Elizabeth (_____), 188, 242, 298, 332
 John, 298, 394
 Robert, 188, 332, 398
 Ruth (_____), 394
 Samuel, 298
 Thomas, 298
 _____, 298
Newport
 Christopher, 3, 4, 39, 171, 176, 223, 271, 274, 294, 298, 299, 325, 342, 349, 357, 361, 384, 452
 Christopher (Mrs.), 298, 299
 Richard, 311
 _____, 299
Newsum, Richard, 299
Newton
 Marmaduke, 299
 Thomas, 157
Nicholas, Richard, 163, 216, 299
Nicholls [Nichols]
 Agnes (_____) (Davies), 299
 John, 299
 Sarah (Church), 114
Nicholson
 Francis, 25, 46, 69, 72, 81, 194, 196, 217, 259, 267, 273, 286, 299, 300, 309, 319, 339, 393
 George, 197, 254, 300, 374
 Hannah (_____), 300
 Mary (_____), 300
 Robert, 66, 197, 254, 300, 374
Noble, James, 167
Nonomisk [Nonomiske], alias Betty (Native American), 183, 300, 302, 312
Norfolk (Duke of), xii, 217, 272
Normansell, Edward, 300
Noroas (Native American), 38, 111, 300, 304
Norsworthy [Naseworthy, Norseworthie, Nosworthy], Tristram [Tristrim], 300
Northumberland (Earl of), *see* *Percy, Henry*
Norton
 Catherine (Bush), 36, 37
 John, 104, 300, 355, 456

Thomas, 300
 William, 66, 94, 301
Norwood
 Charles, 301
 Henry, 109, 265, 290, 301, 420, 457, 463
 Richard, 235
Nosworthy, *see Norsworthy*
Nott, Edward, 25
Noxe, Andrew, 301
Nuce [Newce]
 Thomas, 301
 Thomas (Mrs.), 301
 William, 55, 301
 William (Mrs.), 301
 _____ (Capt.), 226
Nugent, William, 274, 301, 302, 410
Numpskinner (Native American), 183, 302, 312
 Betty, alias Nonomisk (Native American), 183, 300, 302, 312
Nunn
 Thomas, 115, 145, 173, 178, 281, 302, 324, 334, 361, 400
 Thomas (Mrs.), 302
Nuthead, William, 92, 302
Nutt, William, 176

O

O'Brien, Lucy (Todd), 60
Odeon, William, 114, 357
O'Donell
 Thomas, 453
 _____ (_____) (Withers), 453
Offley, Sarah, 175, 176, 291, 403, 463
"Old Ben" (slave), 61
"Old Dinah" (slave), 142
"Old Edward," 148
"Old Hannah" (slave), 189
"Old Sarah," 356
"Old Sheppard," 364
"Old Short," *see Short, John*
Oldesworth [Oldisworth, Ouldsworth], Arnold, 302
Oldham, John, 302
Oldis
 Thomas, 302
 Thomas II, 388
 Valentine, 302
 William, 370
Oldisworth, *see Oldesworth*
Olister, William, 303
Oliver [Olliver], Edward, 303
Omerod, _____, 303
O'moon [Omoonce], *see Moon*
O'Neill, Grace, 347, 357, 428, 429, 430
Onion, *see Ungwin*
Opechancanough

[Abochancano, Mangopeesomon] (Native American), 12, 14, 64, 108, 118, 152, 208, 272, 295, 297, 303, 326, 407, 419
Opitchapam [Iotan, Itoyatin, Otiotan, Sasawpen] (Native American], 12, 303
Oponomo [Oponamo] (Native American), 303
Osborne [Osborn, Osbourn, Osbourne]
  Attlanta (Toft), 435
  John, 123, 303, 326, 435, 454
  Mary (_____), 303
  Thomas, 303
Ossakican [Wassatickon] (Native American), 303, 322
Osserby, Valentine, 303
Otiotan (Native American), *see Opitchapam*
Ottway [Attowell, Ottaway, Ottawell, Ottowell], Thomas, 304
Ouldsworth, *see Oldesworth*
Ousley [Owsley]
  Anne (_____), 304
  Newdigate, 304
  Sarah, 304
  Thomas, 304, 359
Overton, William, 269
Overzee
  Elizabeth (Willoughby), 31, 32, 121
  Simon, 31, 121
Owasewas [Owasosway, Owessewar] (Native American), 38, 111, 300, 304, 320
Owen
  Bartholomew, 342
  Hugh, 304
Owmohowtue [Owmoh Honly] (Native American), 304
Owsley, *see Ousley*

P

Pace
  George, 270, 305
  Isabell [Izabella] (Smythe), 109, 270, 283, 305, 319, 344
  Richard, 108, 283, 319
  Richard I, 270, 305
  Richard II, 305
  Sarah [Sara] (Macock), 270, 305
Pacy, George, 305
Page
  Alice, 307
  Alice (Lukin/Luken), 305, 306, 307
  Caleb, 305

Elizabeth, 141, 142, 305, 306, 307
Elizabeth (Buck) (Crump), 89, 91, 130, 307, 391
Elizabeth (Green) (Brett), 305
Elizabeth (Page), 307
Francis, 306, 307
Henry, 305
John, 70, 81, 86, 89, 112, 141, 192, 213, 229, 235, 297, 298, 305, 306, 307, 321, 322, 338, 366, 404, 421, 424, 439, 443
Mann I, 307
Martha, 307
Mary, 112, 305, 306, 439
Mary (Digges), 306, 307
Mary (Mann), 307
Mathew, 91, 213, 297
Mathew I, 130, 145, 306, 307, 439
Mathew II, 306, 307
Richard, 184, 305
Thomas, 305
Pagen, William, 242
Pagitt [Pagett], Anthony, 307
Paine [Payne]
  Anne (Walker), 386, 422
  Florentine, 307, 308
  John, 29
  Katherine (Thompson), 401
  Robert, 401
  Thomas, 78
Painter [Paynter], Ellen [Elin], 308
Pall, *see Paul*
Palmer
  Joan (_____), 308
  Pricilla, 308
  Thomas, 189, 308
  _____, 308
Pamunkey (King of the) (Native American), 308
Pamunkey (Queen of the) (Native American), *see Cockacoeske*
Pantatouse (Native American), 100, 107, 308, 464
Panton
  Anthony, 239, 308, 332
  Ellen, 47
Paramore [Paramour, Parramore], Robert, 308
Pardoe
  Philip [Phillip], 171, 308, 365
  _____, 171
Parke [Park]
  Daniel I, 77, 101, 116, 308, 309, 324
  Daniel II, 24, 98, 133, 265, 299, 309, 325, 366, 371
  Frances, 133, 309, 325
  Jane (Ludwell), 98, 265, 268, 309

Lucy, 98, 133, 265, 309, 371
Rebecca (Evelyn), 308
Robert, 273
Roger, 264
William, 77
Parker
  Anderson, 37
  Ann (Scarborough), 359
  George, 359
  James, 139
  John, 122
  Mathew, 37
  Thomas, 37, 235
  Thomas I, 122
  Thomas II, 122
  William, 37, 309
Parks, William C., 309
Parramore, *see Paramore*
Parrott, *see Perrott*
Parry, *see also Perry*
  Ann (_____), 310
  John, 310, 316
  Thomas, 355
  William, 307, 310, 316, 384
Parsemore, *see Passmore*
Partin
  Avis, 310
  Deborah [Debora], 310
  Margaret (_____), 310
  Rebecca, 310
  Robert, 151, 185, 362
  Robert I, 310
  Robert II, 310
Partin Family, 310
Partington, Thomas, 320
Partridge
  Hugh, 208
  _____, 310
Pasbehay (King of the) (Native American), 423
Pasmore, *see Passmore*
Passett, Mathew, 326
Passmore [Parsemore, Pasmore]
  Jane [Joanne] (_____), 310, 442
  Thomas, 89, 92, 185, 237, 242, 274, 303, 310, 338, 409, 442
Patawomack (King of the) (Native American), 423
Pate
  John, 41, 310, 311
  Richard, 311, 433
  Thomas, 41, 216, 311
  Thomas (Mrs.), 311
Pattanochus (Native American), 311
Pattiawaske (Native American), 183, 302, 312
Pattison
  Alexander, 55
  George, 435
Paucough (Native American), 202, 312

Paul [Pall, Paule]
Frances, 312
Francis I, 312
Francis II, 312
George, 312
Mathew (_____), 312
Thomas, 312
Pawlett [Paulett, Paulette, Pawlette]
Robert, 312
Thomas, 312, 414
William, 312
Payne, *see Paine*
Peach, Dorothy, 313
Peachy, Mary, 422
Peacock [Pecock], Nathaniel, 313
Pead [Peed], Deuel [Dewel, Deyell], 313
Peake, Robert, 313
Peal [Peale, Peele]
Lawrence, 313
Malachi, 97
Pearl [Pearle], Gregory, 313
Pearns, _____, 232, 313, 448
Pears [Pearse], *see Peirce*
Pearsey, *see Peirsey*
Pearson [Peerson, Peirson, Person, Seirson], Cutbert [Cuthbert], 313
Peate, Abraham, 313
Pecock, *see Peacock*
Peddington, Sarah (George), 171
Peed, *see Pead*
Peele, *see Peal*
Peerce, *see Pearson*
Peerson, *see Pearson*
Pegden, John, 313
Pegg (slave), 313
Peirce [Pears, Pearse, Peerce, Perce, Perse, Pierce]
Edward, 314
Elizabeth, 315, 321
Elizabeth (_____), 314
Joan [Joane], 314, 349, 353, 374, 437
Joan (_____), 11, 55, 314
Richard, 314
Sarah (_____), 315
Thomas, 314
Thomas (Mrs.), 314
William, 9, 11, 30, 37, 38, 44, 55, 79, 85, 102, 124, 140, 153, 154, 155, 170, 172, 202, 206, 259, 285, 288, 292, 301, 314, 315, 317, 319, 337, 349, 350, 352, 356, 362, 374, 381, 445, 448, 449
_____, 314
Peirsey [Persey, Perseye, Pearsey, Piersey]
Abraham, 8, 31, 53, 56, 59, 97, 101, 107, 139, 181,

184, 191, 197, 198, 206, 243, 249, 254, 260, 280, 307, 315, 338, 362, 363, 383, 385, 405, 418, 437, 462, 463
Elizabeth, 197, 198, 315, 385
Elizabeth (Draper), 315
Frances (Grenville) (West), 181, 280, 315, 437
Mary, 97, 156, 180, 206, 315
William, 293
_____, 241, 293
Peirson, *see Pearson*
Pell
Hannah (Thorpe), 404
John, 404
Pelteare [Pelterre]
Abraham, 316
Margaret (_____), 316
Pembroke (Earl of), 252
Pendle, Stephen, 310, 316
Penington, *see Pennington*
Penn [Pin, Pinn]
Elizabeth (Randolph), 339
William, 82, 86, 245, 316
Pennell, Stephen, 387
Pennington [Penington]
John, 316
Robert, 316
Penny, Robert, 316, 337
Penrise, John, 262
Pepmngeis (Native American), 316
Peppett [Peppet, Pepper]
Alice (_____), 316
Gilbert, 316
Lucy (_____), 316
Peracuta (Native American), 316
Perce, *see Peirce*
Percivall, Richard, 342
Percy
George, 4, 42, 122, 136, 223, 276, 285, 293, 316, 317, 330, 348, 423, 438
Henry, 9th Earl of Northumberland, 423
Perkatoan (Native American), 317, 395, 400, 453
Perkins [Pirkins]
Christopher, 33, 88, 262, 317, 410
Elizabeth, 213
Elizabeth (_____), 317, 416
Francis I, 317
Francis II, 317
Jane, 285, 456
Jane (_____), 245, 317
Thomas, 317, 416
Perkins Family, 33
Perkinson, William, 138, 317, 318

Perrin
George, 423
Sebastin, 32
Perrott [Parrott]
Margaret (_____), 318
Richard I, 318, 347
Richard II, 318
Perry, *see also Parry*
Elizabeth, 137, 319
Elizabeth (Menefie), 283, 319, 328
Henry, 283, 305, 319, 328, 385
Isabell, 249
Isabell [Izabella] (Smythe) (Pace), 109, 270, 283, 305, 319, 344
Jane (_____), 254
John, 319
Micajah, 68, 69, 116, 136, 139, 141, 185, 196, 206, 207, 209, 226, 228, 273, 318, 319, 329, 366, 367, 372, 443, 451
Peter, 318, 319
Richard, 196, 318, 319, 372
Thomas, 422
William, 179, 249, 262, 283, 305, 319, 344
_____ (Mrs.), 248
Perse, *see Peirce*
Persey [Perseye], *see Peirsey*
Person, *see Pearson*
Peter (slave), 320
Peterson, Mary, 400
Petiplace, *see Fettiplace*
Pett
Arthur, 320
Elizabeth, 320
Florence (_____), 320
Pettegrew [Pettigrew]
Adam, 38, 111, 300, 304
Elizabeth, 120
Pettie [Pettey], John, 320
Pettiplace, *see Fettiplace*
Pettit
John, 320
Joseph, 320, 367
Pettus
Elizabeth, 46
Elizabeth (_____) (Durant), 182, 183, 320
Mourning (Glenn), 81
Theodore, 320
Thomas, 182
Thomas I, 282, 320, 344
Thomas II, 81, 320
Pewem (Native American), 304, 320
Peyton [Payton]
Ellen [Ellinor] (_____), 320
Frances (Gerrard) (Speke), 39, 190, 321, 378, 379, 426, 427
Henry, 320

Valentine, 39, 165, 190, 278, 320, 379
Phelps
John, 321
Thomas, 321
Phettiplace [Phetiplace], *see* Fettiplace
Phildust, Thomas, 321
Philips, *see Phillips*
Phill (slave), 321
Phillimore [Philmott], John, 123, 157, 321, *see also Filmer [Filmore]*
Phillips [Philips]
Eleanor, 167
Elmer, 167, 321
John, 399
Thomas, 186
_____, 126
Phillis (slave), 321
Phillis, Alexander, 305, 321
Philpot, Henry, 321
Phinloe, 321
Phipps
Elizabeth (_____), 192, 193, 293, 322
John, 89, 160, 192, 193, 246, 293, 321, 322, 333, 345, 351, 367
Mary (_____), 246, 322
Pickhouse [Piggase], Drue [Dru], 322
Pickis
Jonas, 305, 322
Joseph, 41
Joseph (Mrs.), 41
Pierce, *see Peirce*
Piersey, *see Peirsey*
Piggase, *see Pickhouse*
Piggott, Spencer, 297, 322
Piland, *see Pyland*
Pin [Pinn], *see Penn*
Pindavako [Pindavaco] (Native American), 17, 322
Pinhorne [Pinhorn]
Ann [Anne], 322, 337
John, 322, 337, 356
Pinkard [Pinckard]
Elizabeth (_____) (Haynes), 167, 200, 201, 322, 323
James, 323
John, 201
John I, 167, 322, 323
John II, 135, 323
Mary, 323
Rebecca, 323
Sarah (_____) (Gaskins), 322
Thomas, 323
_____, 135, 323
Pinke
Mary (_____), 210, 323
William, alias Jonas, William, 210, 323

Pinner, Richard, 357
Pirkins, *see Perkins*
Pising, Edward, 323
Pitchande [Pitchard], Edward, 323
Pitt [Pitts]
Ann [Anne] (_____), 323, 329, 330
Anne, 324
Elizabeth, 324
Elizabeth (Stephens), 384
Elizabeth (_____), 324
Henry, 323, 324, 329
Hester, 85, 323
Jeane, 324
John, 31, 85, 323, 324, 394
Josiah, 401
Martha, 323, 324
Martha (_____), 323
Mary, 80, 323, 324
Mary (Smith), 370
Mary (_____), 85, 324
Patience, 324
Rebecca (Sanders), 401
Robert, 80, 85
Robert I, 323
Robert II, 323
Robert III, 323
Sarah, 324
Thomas, 85, 172, 253, 324, 394
Thomas I, 323, 324
Thomas II, 324
William, 85, 323
Pittman, John, 324
Place
Rowland, 324
Rowland I, 324
Rowland II, 324
_____ (Mrs.), 123
Pleasants [Pleasant]
Elizabeth, 119, 324
Jane (_____) (Tucker), 324, 325
John, 119, 340
John I, 324, 325
John II, 324
Joseph, 324
Plowden, Edmond [Edmund], 208, 333, 384
Plumtree
Frances, 325
Susanna (_____), 325
William, 325
Pocahontas [Pocohunta, Matoaka, Rebecca Rolfe] (Native American), 5, 55, 75, 247, 325, 331, 349, 350, 393, 419, 437
Polentine [Pollentin, Pollington]
John, 325
Margaret, 325
Rachel (_____), 325
Pomell, *see Powell*

Pomfry [Pomfrey], Richard, 325
Poole
Henry, 325
John, 326
Jonas, 325
Nathaniel, *see Powell, Nathaniel*
Ralph, 365
Richard, 81
Robert, 244, 289, 362
Robert I, 326
Robert II, 326
William, 326
Pope
Ann, 426, 427
Edward, 207
George, 107
George I, 326
George I (Mrs.), 326
George II, 168, 274, 326, 386
Jemima (_____) (Spence), 237
John, 326
Nathaniel, 426
Nathaniel, alias Bridges, Nathaniel, 183, 302, 312
Thomas, 190, 426, 427
William, 285
Popeley, Richard, 200, 442
Popkin, Thomas, 326
Popleton [Popkton, Poppleton], William, 326
Porey, *see Pory*
Porten [Portten]
Sarah (_____) (Godfrey), 173
William, 173, 403
Porter
Abraham [Abram], 55, 222, 326, 349, 445
Frances, 326
James, 405
Jeane [Jane], 405
John I, 326, 327
John II, 326, 327
Martha, 405
Mary Fenwick, 327
Mary (_____) (Cooke), 326
Porteus, Edward, 92
Portheris, *see Poythress*
Portten, *see Porten*
Pory [Porey, Porye]
John, 7, 9, 244, 294, 327, 423
Peter, 327
Possesom, William (Native American), 327
Potomac (King of the) (Native American), 271, 327
Pott [Potts]
Elizabeth (_____), 328, 339
Francis, 85, 86, 240, 261, 319, 327, 328

John, 11, 60, 63, 71, 85, 86,
  89, 102, 129, 139, 141,
  160, 185, 211, 221, 247,
  258, 277, 286, 301, 308,
  310, 313, 326, 327, 328,
  333, 339, 352, 353, 373,
  383, 397, 407, 445, 451
John (Mrs.), 399, 450
Richard, 329
Susanna (_____), 240, 328
William, 329
Pott Family, 451
Potter
  Ann (_____), 329
  Cuthbert [Cutbert], 54, 101,
    111, 132, 186, 297, 328
  George, 460
  Roger, 328, 329
Potterton, William, 414
Potuxin (King of the) (Native
  American), 329
Poulson, John, 451
Pountis [Pontis, Pountes,
  Pountis, Pontes], John, 67,
  98, 116, 202, 243, 249, 329,
  338, 344, 401, 454
Povey, Thomas, 120
Powell [Pomell]
  Ann [Anne] (_____) (Pitt),
    324, 329, 330
  Catherene [Katherin]
    (_____), 330
  Elizabeth, 329
  George, 330, 433
  Henry, 329
  James, 253, 323, 329
  John, 188, 208, 330
  Joyce (_____), 330
  Margaret (_____), 74, 75,
    106, 330, 393, 437, 442
  Nathaniel, 330, 405
  Philemon, 330, 363
  Rowland, 227
  Thomas, 330
  William, 9, 10, 58, 74, 75,
    80, 106, 169, 188, 304,
    330, 362, 393, 437
Power, Jeffrey, 458
Powhatan (Wahunsunacock)
  (Native American), 5, 12,
  30, 86, 118, 122, 144, 150,
  167, 172, 247, 270, 294,
  299, 303, 321, 325, 330,
  331, 342, 353, 354, 357,
  405, 407, 419
Powyes, Robert, 452
Poythress [Poytheris, Poythers,
  Poythres, Portherys]
  Francis, 331, 461
  Woodleigh (Wynne), 331,
    461
Pratt, John, 331
Preene, John, 123
Prescott, Edward, 38, 145, 146,
  331, 425, 426

Presley
  Peter, 332
  Peter, Jr., 332
  William, 188
  William I, 331, 332
  William II, 332
  William III, 332
Presson
  Isabell, 429
  Margaret (Waters), 428, 429
  Thomas, 429
Pretty, George, 332
Price [Priest, Prise, Pryse]
  Ann [Anne] (Pinhorne),
    322, 337
  Ann [Anne] (_____), 262,
    333, 390
  Arthur I, 332, 333
  Arthur II, 333
  Edward, 333
  Eleanor (_____) (Brittin),
    333
  Hugh, 333
  John, 262, 333, 365
  John II, 333
  Mary (_____), 333
  Mathew, 333
  Richard, 134, 333
  Sarah, 158
  Walter, 333
  William, 322, 337
  _____, 332
Prichard [Pricharde, Prickett,
  Prickkett]
  Edmund, 241
  Edward, 98
  John, 333, 334, *see also
    Drinkard, John*
  Thomas, 334
  Walter, 334
  _____ (Col.), 280
Priest, *see Price*
Prince
  Ann, 333
  Edward, 285, 317, 333
Prior, *see Pryor*
Prise, *see Price*
Procter [Proctor]
  Alice (_____), 129
  John, 129, 174
  Stephen, 169, 297, 322, 334
  Stephen (Mrs.), 297
  Winifred (_____), 169, 334
Prodget, Richard, 334
Profit [Prophett]
  Jacob, 334
  Jonas, 334
Prynne, Nicholas, 220
Pryor [Prior]
  Margaret, 334
  Mary, 334
  William, 53, 255, 289, 334,
    407, 456
Pryse, *see Price*
Purchas, Samuel, 419

Purfoy [Purefoy, Purfray,
  Purfrey Purfury, Purifie,
  Purifoy, Purifye, Purrifie]
  Lucy (_____), 335
  Thomas, 99, 153, 335
Puttock [Puttocke], _____, 335
Pyancha (Native American),
  335
Pyland [Piland]
  Elizabeth, 440
  Elizabeth (_____), 335
  James, 335
  Jane, 440
  Robert, 440

Q

Quaile [Quayle]
  Ann (_____), 335
  Richard, 335
Quiemacketo (Native
  American), 421
Quigley
  John, 335, 336
  Thomas, 336

R

Rabley [Radley, Rableigh,
  Rablais]
  Elizabeth, 86, 336, 337, 406
  Elizabeth (_____), 432
  Jane (_____), 271, 279,
    337, 406
  John, 336
  John, Jr., 336
  Thomas, 54, 67, 125, 149,
    172, 176, 213, 250, 271,
    279, 288, 293, 298, 299,
    306, 316, 322, 325, 336,
    337, 365, 383, 391, 397,
    406, 432, 449
Rabnett [Ravenett], William,
  337
Rachel (slave), 337
Radish [Reddish], John, 80,
  151, 337, 338
Radley, *see Rabley*
Raffe [Rasse], Robert, 338
Railey [Raleley, Ralye, Rayley,
  Reily, Ryaly, Rylei], *see also
  Rawleigh*
  Andrew, 338
  James, 338
  Jonas, 338
  Joseph, 338
Rainberte, *see Rayberd*
Raleley [Ralye], *see Railey*
Rampton, *see Hampton*
Ramsay, *see Ramsey*
Ramsbottom
  John, 186
  Lettice, 186
Ramsey [Ramsay, Ramsy,
  Ramsye]
  Edward, 171, 182, 338

Edward (Mrs.), 338
Thomas, 338, 339, *see also Ramshaw, Thomas*
Ramshaw [Ramshawe, Ramshee, Ramsheer]
Katherine (_____), 339
Thomas, 339
Ramsy [Ramsye], *see Ramsey*
Randall
Anthony, 339
John, 297
Mary (Mansfield) (Swann), 339, 196, 318, 371, 391, 392, 393
Robert, 339, 392, 393
Randolph
Ann [Anne] (_____) (Pitt) (Powell), 324, 329, 330
Deborah, 339
Edward, 339
Elizabeth, 339
Henry, 45, 49, 103, 268
Henry I, 158, 159, 301, 340, 375, 384, 391
Henry II, 158, 340
Judith (Soane), 158, 159, 340, 375, 376
Mary (Isham), 340
Richard, 340
Robert, 330
Sarah, 339
William, 119
William I, 340
William II, 340
_____, 340
Ransack, Abraham [Abram], 340
Ranson [Ransone, Ransom]
George, 341
James, 341
James I, 341
James II, 341
Peter, 341
Rappahanock (King of the) (Native American), *see Accapataugh*
Rascow [Rasco, Roscoe, Roscow]
Mary (Wilson), 71, 103, 341, 342
William, 71, 103, 198, 341
Rasse, *see Raffe*
Rastall [Rastell, Roistall], Humphrey, 210, 342
Ratcliffe [Ratcliff, Ratcliffe]
Dorothy (_____), 342
Elkinton, 342
John, alias Sicklemore, John, 342
Michael, 94
_____ (Capt.), 321
Ravenett, *see Rabnett*
Ravening, Rebecca, 397, 398
Ravens
Henry, 342

Ravenscroft
Dyonysia [Dionysia] (Savage), 184, 185, 416
Rawleigh [Raleigh], *see also Railey*
Andrew, 182, 460
Edward, 338
Rawlings [Rawling, Rawlins]
Edward, 104, 342
Gregory, 400
John, 80
Roger, 342
Rawlinson [Rollinson]
Jane (_____) (Sparrow), 378
William, 378
Rayberd [Rainberte, Raynbeare, Rayneberde, Reyneberd]
Nicholas, 342
Nicholas (Mrs.), 342
Rayley, *see Railey*
Rayment, John, 241
Raynbeare [Rayneberde], *see Rayberd*
Rayner [Raynor, Royner]
Joan (_____), 343
Wassill [Wassell, Watsall], 12, 343
Read [Reade, Reed, Reede, Reid]
Benjamin, 343
Edward, 343
Elizabeth, 110
Elizabeth (Martiau), 275, 343
Francis, 54, 343
George, 275
George I, 343
George II, 343
Humfrey, 343
James, 343
Lucy (_____), 343
Mary (Lilly), 343
Mildred, 407
Robert, 343
Samuel, 183
William, 156
_____, 343
Reading [Redding], *see Reding*
Reakes, *see Ricks*
Reavell, *see Revell*
Recheson, *see Richardson*
Reddish, *see Radish*
Redes, *see Rodes*
Redford, Francis, 216
Reding [Redding, Reading], John, 343
Reed [Reede], *see Read*
Reeks [Reekes], *see Ricks*
Reid, *see Read*
Reighnolds [Reignolds], *see Reynolds*
Reily, *see Railey*
Rennolds, *see Reynolds*

Revell [Reavell, Revel]
Edward, 344, 463
Randall [Randal, Randol], 344, 429
Reyneberd, *see Rayberd*
Reynolds [Reighnolds, Reignolds, Rennolds]
Alice (_____) (Delke), 140
Charles, 344
Christopher, 219, 344
Francis, 140
John, 344
Nathaniel, 344
Nicholas, 140, 344
Robert, 140
Rhoden [Rhodum], *see Rodham*
Rice
Dominick, 431
John, 408
Mary (_____), 414
Rebecca (_____) (Travers), 408
Richard, 414
Rich
Nathaniel, 55
Robert, Earl of Warwick, 123, 144, 279, 396, 453
Richards
Fortune (Jordan), 219
George, 227
Henry, 400
John, 219, 400
Richard, 108, 344
Richardson [Richason, Recheson, Richinson]
Ann, 345
Ann (_____), 345
John, 344, 345
Samuel, 274
Sarah (_____) (Edwards), 149, 213, 286, 345, 430, 449
Thomas, 345
William, 149, 213, 286, 345, 430, 449
Richardson Family, 208
Richason, *see Richardson*
Richinson, *see Richardson*
Richman [Richmand]
Elizabeth (Watkins), 52
George, 52
Ricketts, Michael, 236
Ricks [Reakes, Reeks, Reekes, Rix]
Elizabeth, 345, 367
Elizabeth (_____), 345, 367, 433
John, 345, 367
Richard, 345, 367, 433
Stephen, 344
William, 345
Riddall [Ruddell], Sara, 345
Ridley [Ridely], Peter, 345
Rigby [Rigbye, Riggby]

Dorothy (_____), 345
Peter, 345
Ring
Joseph I, 345, 346
Sarah (Berkeley), 346
_____, 346
Riscom, William, 346
Rix, *see Ricks*
Robbins, *see Robins*
Robert (Native American), 346
Robert (slave), 346
Roberts
James, 346
Richard, 289
William, 297, 346
Robins [Robbins, Robinson, Robyns]
Ann, 348
Benjamin, 346, 348
Catherine (Hone) (Beverley), 68, 69, 213, 247, 406
Christopher, 41, 68, 69, 114, 120, 213, 221, 229, 328, 347, 406
Dorothea, 38
Edward, 347
Elizabeth, 347, 348
Esther, 347
Esther (Littleton), 347
Grace, 347
Grace (O'Neill) (Waters), 347, 357, 428, 429, 430
James, 348
John, 143, 184, 346, 347, 348
John I, 346
John II, 346
Littleton, 347
Mary, 348, 357
Mary [Marie] (_____), 184
Obedience, 215
Obedience I, 343, 346, 347, 357, 428, 429, 448
Obedience II, 347
Richard, 131, 348
Sarah, 348
Sarah (West), 348
Scarburgh, 348
Susanna, 348
Thomas, 347
Thomas I, 346
Thomas II, 346
Tully, 348
West, 348
William, 86, 346, 348
William I, 348
William II, 348
_____ (_____) (Hill), 86
Robinson, *see Robins*
Rochambeau (Comte de), 37
Roche, James, 394
Rocke, James, 157
Rodes [Redes, Roeds, Roods]
Christopher, 348

Roger, 348
William, 348
Rodgers [Rogers, Rogeres]
Edward, 349
Elizabeth (Dale), 135
John, 349
Richard, 144, 163, 236, 295, 348, 349
Thomas, 197
William, 135, 348, 349
Rodham [Rhoden, Rhodum]
Elizabeth, 241, 255, 295
Hannah, 294, 295
Matthew [Mathew], 241, 294, 295
Rodis, John, 349
Roe, Nicholas, 208
Roecroft, Edward, alias Stallings, *see Stallings, Edward*
Roeds, *see Rodes*
Rogerman, Willimot, 349
Rogers [Rogeres], *see Rodgers*
Roistall, *see Rastall*
Rolfe
Bermuda, 349
Elizabeth, 314, 349
Henry, 349, 350
Jane, 75, 350
Jane (_____), 270
Joan [Joane] (Peirce), 314, 349, 353, 374, 437
John, 7, 8, 9, 38, 75, 85, 102, 137, 154, 247, 270, 286, 314, 325, 331, 337, 349, 350, 353, 374, 419
Rebecca, *see Pocahontas*
Thomas, 55, 75, 126, 289, 325, 349, 350
_____, 349
Rollinson, *see Rawlinson*
Roode, Jane (Gee), 171
Roods, *see Rodes*
Rookings [Rookeings)
Elizabeth, 350, 461
William, 194, 273, 460, 461
William I, 350
William II, 350
Roper
Katheryn (Graves), 350
Thomas, 161, 172, 350, 375
William, 350
_____, 161, 350
Roscoe [Roscow], *see Rascow*
Rose
Rebecca (Biggs), 70
Rebecca (_____) (Hill), 205
_____, 350
Ross
Edward, 88, 153, 197, 225, 351, 353, 359
Sarah (_____), 351
Ross Family, 354, 359
Rossingham [Roffingham]
Edmund, 276, 351
Edward, 391

Roulston [Rowlston, Rowlstone], Lionell [Lyonell], 351
Rouniere
Claude, 110, 352
Elizabeth (_____) (Chermaison), 110, 274, 352
Rouse [Rowse]
Robert, 352
Thomas, 165, 352
Rouslie, *see Rowley*
Rowland, William, 352
Rowley [Rouslie, Rowsley]
Elizabeth (_____), 297, 352, 435
William, 70, 105, 179, 221, 222, 229, 247, 297, 326, 333, 352, 435, 464
_____, 352
Rowley Family, 105, 333
Rowlsey, *see Rowley*
Rowlston [Rowlstone], *see Roulston*
Rownan, William, 333
Rowse, *see Rouse*
Royall
Joseph, 242
Roger, 352
Sibil [Sybil, Sybill] (_____), 352
Royner, *see Rayner*
Ruce [Ruese, Ruse], Roger, 352
Ruddell, *see Riddall*
Ruese, *see Ruce*
Ruffin
Edmund, 412
Susan (Travis), 412
Ruse, *see Ruce*
Russell
John, 352
Richard, 357
Walter, 352
William, 353
Rutherford, John, 353
Ryaly [Rylei], *see Railey*

S

Sabin [Sabyn, Salin, Savin]
Richard, 235
Robert, 353
Sadler
John, 378, 439
Rowland, 353
Saier, *see Sayer*
Salin, *see Sabin*
Sall [Sal, Sel] (slave), 296, 353
Salmon [Sammon]
John, 353
Joseph, 353
Salter, Elizabeth, 353
Saltman, John, 353
Salvadore [Salvador] (Native American), 153, 225, 353, 354, 359

Salway, John, 365
Sam (slave), 310, 354
Sambage, William, 354
Sammon, *see Salmon*
Sampson
    William, alias Eden,
        William, 354
    _____ (Capt.), 435
Sanders [Saunders], *see also*
    Sandys
    Edward, 354, 401
    Frances [Francis] (Blore),
        93, 354
    John, 354, 440
    Mary (_____), 401
    Rebecca, 401
    Richard, 354
    Roger, 93, 354
Sanderson
    Edward, 107, 300, 355, 456
    _____, 456
Sandford [Sandiford, Sanford]
    Christopher, 355
    Giles, 355
    John, 355
    Katherine, 355
    Samuel, 355
    Sarah (_____), 355
Sandys [Sands], *see also*
    Sanders
    David, 249, 356
    Edwin, 250, 461
    George, 51, 91, 104, 182,
        272, 356
    Margaret, 461
    Samuel, 461
    Susannah, 355
    Thomas, 355
Sanford, *see Sandford*
Santy, Robin, 356
Sapcoate, Abraham, 220, 356
Sarah (slave), 29, 67, 232,
    356
Sarson [Sarsen, Sarsnett],
    William, 88, 93, 144, 356
Sasawpen (Native American),
    see Opitchapam
Saunders, *see Sanders*
Savage [Savadge, Salvadge]
    Ann (Elkington), 357
    Dyonysia [Dionysia], 184,
        185, 416
    Elita [Elicia] (Harmanson),
        191
    Elkington, 357
    Grace, 357
    Hannah [Ann] (_____), 357
    John I, 357
    John II, 357
    Mary, 357
    Mary (Robins), 357
    Richard, 356
    Susanna, 357
    Thomas, 152, 191, 294, 357
    _____ (Capt.), 389

Savin, *see Salin*
Sawyer [Sawier], *see also*
    Sayer
    Francis, 357
    Mary, 357
    Thomas, 357, 358
    William, 115, 358
Sayer [Saier, Sayers], *see also*
    Sawyer
    Frances (Mason), 277
    Thomas, 282
Scarborough [Scarburgh,
    Starbrough]
    Ann, 359
    Bennett, 359
    Charles, 89, 358, 359
    Edmund, 215, 283, 399
    Edmund [Edmond] I, 250,
        358
    Edmund II, 89, 133, 143,
        230, 234, 295, 348, 358,
        389, 429, 435, 436
    Edmund III, 89
    Hannah (_____), 358
    Henry, 359
    Mary, 359
    Mary (_____), 358, 359,
        436
    Matilda, 436
    Sarah, 359
    Tabitha, 89, 90, 132, 204,
        359
    William, 359
Scarborough Family, 436
Scarlett [Scarlet]
    Ann [Anne] (_____), 359
    Martin, 359
Scarpe, *see Sharpe*
Scipio (slave), 225, 359
Scotchmore [Scotsmore,
    Scottesmore], Robert, 359
Scott [Scot]
    Anthony, 360
    Comfort (Anderson), 37
    Gustavus, 360
    Henry, 360
    Jane, 360
    John, 259
    John I, 360
    John II, 360
    Nicholas, 360
    Rebecca, 360
    Sarah [Sara] (_____)
        (Cross), 360
    _____, 128, 360
Scottesmore, *see Scotchmore*
Scrimgeour
    John, 361, 381
    John (Native American),
        360
    Mary (_____), 360
    William, 360
Scrivener [Scrivenor]
    Mathew, 361
    _____, 176

Searle [Searles]
    Gabriell, 215
    Richard, 241
Seaton, George, 361
Seaward, *see Seward*
Seawell [Sewell]
    Alice (_____), 361
    Anne [Ann], 277, 278, 361
    Elizabeth, 142
    Henry, 142, 277
    Henry [Henery, Henrie]
        I, 361
    Henry II, 361
    Jane, 311
Seirson, *see Pearson*
Selloan, J., 361
Senior [Seneor]
    Dorothy, 361
    Eleanor [Ellinor, Ellenor]
        (_____), 361
    John, 44, 122, 245, 251,
        361
    John I, 409
    Thomas, 251
    William, 361
Seosteyn (Native American),
    118, 362
Serjeant [Serieant], Richard,
    362
Serrahohque (Native
    American), 362
Severne
    Bridgett (_____), 109
    John I, 109
    John II, 109
Seward [Seaward]
    John, 286, 310
    John I, 362
    John II, 362
Sewell, *see Seawell*
Sexton, Thomas, 362
Shacrow [Chacrow] (Native
    American), 362
Sharks [Shurke], George, 362
Sharpe [Scarpe, Sharp, Skarfe,
    Skarse]
    John, 362
    Judith, 362
    Samuel, 101, 363
    Samuel (Mrs.), 363
Sharper (slave), 363
Sharples [Sharpless]
    Edward, 43, 63, 93, 100,
        116, 138, 139, 330, 358,
        363, 433, 445
    John, 330, 363
Shaw, Annis, 363
Sheapard, *see Shepherd*
Shedam, *see Fawdon*
Sheffield, Thomas, 80
Shelly [Shelley]
    Ann (_____) (Macon), 363
    Philip, 363
    Sarah (_____), 363
    Walter, 363

Shepherd [Sheapard, Shepard, Shepheard, Sheppard]
Anne, 364
Baldwin [Balldwin, Bauldwin], 363, 364
Elizabeth, 363
Elizabeth (Spencer), 119, 120, 364, 381, 382, 425, 442
Elizabeth (_____), 363
John, 363, 364
Priscilla, 364
Priscilla (_____), 364
Robert, 106, 119, 120, 364, 381, 382, 425, 442
Susanna, 364
William, 119, 364
_____, 364
Sheppey, Martha, 107
Sherley, Cecily, 207, 208, 387, 414, 437
Sherlock, James, 364
Sherman
Elizabeth, 364
Henry, 246
Michael, 364
Sherwood
Peaceable [Peceable], 364
Rachel (_____) (James), 38, 69, 198, 224, 225, 229, 299, 365, 366, 367, 393, 425
William, 23, 38, 44, 48, 53, 86, 93, 114, 116, 120, 131, 136, 149, 167, 168, 169, 176, 192, 195, 198, 206, 213, 215, 218, 219, 220, 221, 223, 224, 225, 226, 227, 228, 229, 230, 237, 244, 251, 254, 273, 284, 285, 298, 306, 308, 317, 318, 320, 325, 333, 334, 336, 337, 345, 364, 365, 366, 367, 375, 382, 393, 425, 443, 449, 451, 459
_____ (Mrs.), 38
Sherwood Family, 217
Shipdam [Shipham]
Edmund [Edmond], 345, 367
Elizabeth (_____) (Ricks), 345, 367, 433
Shipsie, see Sibley
Short, John, 367
Shortridge, Jeffrey, 368
Shrawley, Margaret, 368
Shrimpton, William, 143
Shurenough (Native American), 368
Shurke, see Sharks
Sibley [Shipsie, Sibsey, Sibseyy, Sipse, Sipsey, Sypsey]
Elizabeth (_____), 368

John, 95, 272, 368, 411, 463
Mary, 368
Sicklemore
John, alias Ratcliffe, see Ratcliffe, John
Michael, 368
Siddway, see Sidway
Sides, Thomas, 368
Sidney [Sydney]
Frances, 369
John, 368, 369
Sidway [Siddway]
Benjamin, 194, 400
Mary (Harrison), 194
Sierson, see Pearson
Sikes [Sykes], Elizabeth (_____), 153, 154, 204, 369, 371
Silvy (slave), 369, 390
Simkler
Margaret (_____), 369
William, 369
Simmons, Richard, 369
Simon [Simons]
William, 369
_____, 369
Sims [Syms, Symms], Benjamin, 282, 302, 325
Sipsey [Sipse], see Sibley
Sisco, Frank (Native American), 369
Sisson, Thomas, 369
Skarfe [Skarse], see Sharpe
Skiffe, see Keith
Skinner [Skyner, Skynner]
Margaret (Brewer), 84
Thomas, 369
Skipwith, Gray, 239
Skyner, see Skinner
Slye, Robert, 379
Smalewood [Smalwood], see Smallwood
Small, Robert, 369
Smalley
Elizabeth (_____), 128, 369
Robert, 128, 369
Smallwood [Smalwood, Smalewood]
Mathew, 59
Randall, 167, 174, 179, 223, 293, 370
Smart
John, 132
Tabitha (Scarborough), 89, 90, 132, 204, 359
Smethes, William, 370
Smith [Smithe, Smyth, Smythe]
Abigail, 46, 57, 96
Ann, 45, 157, 370
Ann (_____), 45, 61, 157, 235, 370
Arthur, 76, 85
Arthur I, 370

Arthur II, 370
Arthur III, 370
Austen [Osten], 370
Bryan, 145, 370, 371
Christopher, 88, 371
Edward, 371
Elizabeth (Cox), 372
Elizabeth (Robinson), 348
Elizabeth (Wormeley) (Kemp) (Lunsford), 239, 240, 268, 334, 373, 457
Gabriel, 51
George, 370
Henry, 202, 374
Henry (Native American), 371
Isabell [Izabella], 109, 270, 283, 305, 319, 344
J. F. D., 375
Jane, 370
Joan [Joane] (Peirce) (Rolfe), 270, 314, 349, 353, 374, 437
John, 3, 4, 5, 10, 29, 30, 33, 34, 42, 48, 60, 76, 77, 86, 92, 104, 122, 123, 124, 129, 141, 144, 150, 151, 157, 158, 167, 169, 176, 178, 220, 226, 235, 240, 244, 254, 264, 271, 274, 276, 280, 294, 296, 299, 301, 310, 313, 314, 321, 323, 329, 330, 331, 332, 334, 342, 343, 346, 348, 349, 350, 352, 354, 356, 357, 361, 368, 371, 372, 379, 383, 384, 395, 396, 405, 415, 420, 423, 430, 433, 437, 445, 453, 456
John, alias Dade, Francis I, 134
John (Mrs.), 371
John I, 372
John II, 372, 396
John Hill, 36, 37, 372
Lawrence, 372, 373
Lydia (_____) (Broadribb), 88, 371
Mary, 370
Mary (Ambler), 372
Mary (Flint), 162
Mary (Jaquelin), 33, 226, 372
Mary (_____), 370
Mary Cary (Ambler), 36, 37
Nicholas, 371, 373
Osmond, 373
Phebe, 374
Phebe (_____), 374
Richard, 370
Robert, 216, 229, 240, 373, 374, 457

Roger, 11, 30, 53, 76, 165, 181, 247, 252, 270, 292, 314, 349, 353, 374, 423, 432
Sarah, 370
Sarah (Jackson), 370
Sarah (Robinson), 348
Sarah [Sara] (_____) (Lee), 196, 254, 300, 374, 416
Thomas, 162, 235, 302, 312, 370, 374, 375, 439, 443
Toby [Tobias, Tobyas], 156, 374
West (Robinson), 348
William, 183, 350, 370, 374, 375, 408, 443
William, Jr., 375
William Robinson, 348
_____ (Mrs.), 370
_____, 183, 254, 371, 374, 375
Snow [Snowe]
Eleanor [Elinor, Ellenor] (_____) (Graves), 178, 375
John, 375
Rebecca, 375
Sara, 260, 375
Soane [Soanes, Soney, Sonne]
Henry, 158, 375, 376, 377
Henry I, 375
Henry II, 376
John, 86, 147, 159, 220, 230, 306, 345, 366, 375, 376, 443, 448, 456, 457
Judith, 158, 159, 340, 375, 376
Judith (_____), 158, 375, 376
Martha, 376
Mary (_____), 376
Samuel, 376
William, 375, 376
Soikes, *see Stokes*
Somers [Summers]
George, 6, 299, 342, 376, 388, 393
Tabitha, 213
Somersall, Thomas, 377
Somes, Mary [Marie], 95
Soney [Sonne], *see Soane*
Soothey [Southey, Sothey, Southeree]
Ann [Anna], 139, 191, 192, 261, 377
Elizabeth (_____), 139, 191, 377
Henry, 139, 191, 261, 308
Henry I, 377
Henry II, 377
Henry (Mrs.), 160
Mary, 377
Thomas, 377
William, 154, 377

Sorrell
Rebecca (_____), 377
Robert, 377
Sotherne, *see Southern*
Southall
Anne (_____), 253
Seth, 253
Southcot [Southcoat, Southcote, Southcott, Southcoote]
Otho, 377
Thomas, 377, 460
Southern [Sotherne], John, 93, 130, 147, 158, 221, 247, 310, 338, 376, 377, 409, 435
Sowerby, Thomas, 171, 377
Spake, *see Speke*
Spalding
Edward, 377
Edward (Mrs.), 377
_____, 378
Spark (slave), 378
Sparkes
John, 219
Robert, 378
Sparrow [Sparrowe]
Charles, 378, 439
Jane (_____), 378
Selby, 378
_____, 378
Speake [Speak], *see Speke*
Spearman, John, 378
Speed [Speede], Henry, 378
Speke [Spake, Speake, Speak]
Ann (_____), 378
Frances (_____) (Gerrard), 39, 190, 321, 378, 379, 426, 427
John, 379
Thomas, 121, 190, 223, 292, 314
Thomas I, 321, 331, 378, 379, 426
Thomas II, 321, 378
Spellman [Spelman, Spilman, Spillman]
Henry, 326, 379
Thomas, 379
Spence [Spense]
Alexander, 236, 237, 379
Alexander (Mrs.), 379
Dorcas, 379
Dorcas (_____), 236, 237
Elizabeth, 379
Jemima (_____), 237
John, 236, 237
Mary, 379
Patrick, 236, 379
Sara [Sarah], 238, 379
Thomas, 236, 465
William, 9, 63, 77, 155, 190, 238, 346, 362, 379, 406
William (Mrs.), 379
Winifred (Yowell), 465

Spencer [Spenser, Spensor]
Abraham, 264
Alexander, 273, 379, 380
Alice, 381
Alice (_____), 381
Anne, 381, 444
Dorothy (_____), 381
Elizabeth, 119, 364, 381, 382, 425, 442
Elizabeth (White), 381, 442, 444
Frances (Mottrom), 292, 318, 360, 380, 381
Francis, 381
Jane (_____), 381
John, 125, 381
Kathren, 380
Nicholas, 32, 40, 79, 120, 160, 318, 373, 450
Nicholas I, 266, 292, 380, 381
Nicholas II, 381
Robert, 126, 380, 381, 442, 444
William, 38, 44, 75, 87, 348, 425, 450
William I, 259, 381
William II, 381
_____, 75, 87
Spense, *see Spence*
Spenser [Spensor], *see Spencer*
Spicer
Arthur, 229, 367, 382, 397
Elizabeth (Jones), 382, 397
Spier [Spiers, Spiors], John, 382
Spillman [Spilman], *see Spellman*
Spiors, *see Spier*
Spotswood, Alexander, 26, 72, 163, 267, 382
Spradd [Sprad, Sprade, Sprage], Eleanor, 182, 275, 382
Spraggon [Spragling, Spragon], Rudolph [Radolph, Radulph, Rudalph], 172, 188, 382, 383
Spring
Robert, 54, 383
William, 383
Stacie [Stacy, Stacey]
Josias, 440
Richard, 276
Robert, 383
Thomas, 383
_____, 383
Stafferton [Stasserton]
Mary (_____), 383
Peter, 43, 383
Stallings
Daniel, 383
Edward, alias Roecroft, Edward, 383
Stanley, Roger, 258, 383

Starbrough, *see Scarborough*
Starke, Thomas, 341
Starkey, Elizabeth, 383
Starnell, Richard, 205
Stasserton, *see Stafferton*
Steckie, Jane, 383
Steel, Thomas, 236
Steephens [Steevens], *see Stephens*
Stegg
    Elizabeth (_____), 188, 384
    Grace, 384
    John, 384
    Sarah (_____) (Harris), 181, 384
    Thomas, 187
    Thomas I, 181, 223, 340, 383, 384, 442
    Thomas II, 65, 97, 180, 193, 246, 267, 268, 280, 340, 384, 434, 439, 455, 456
Stegg Family, 259
Steiff, William, 412
Stephens [Steephens, Steevens, Stevens]
    Elizabeth, 384
    Elizabeth (Peirsey), 197, 198, 315, 385
    Frances (Culpeper), 46, 65, 66, 121, 130, 145, 146, 159, 205, 228, 266, 267, 375, 381, 385, 441
    George, 80, 384
    James, 384
    Margaret (_____), 385
    Richard, 58, 106, 108, 140, 160, 194, 197, 222, 223, 315, 333, 343, 370, 379, 385, 428
    Samuel, 65, 121, 130, 159, 266, 315, 385
    William I, 315, 385
    William II, 385
Stereman, *see Sturman*
Stevenson, John, 385
Steward, Augustine [Augustin], 385
Stirring, John, 385
Stith
    Anne [Ann], 75
    Drury, 386
    Jane (_____), 386
    John, 385, 386
    John, Sr., 75
Stoaks [Stoakes], *see Stokes*
Stock [Stocks], *see Stokes*
Stockton, Jonas, 431
Stoiks, *see Stokes*
Stokeley, John, alias Taylor, *see Taylor, John*
Stokes [Stoaks, Stocks, Stoiks, Soikes, Stoakes], *see also Stock*
    Abettris (_____), 386
    Ann (_____), 386

Christopher, 253, 386, 431
Jane (Braswell), 80
John, 30, 386
Mary (_____), 386
Richard, 81, 306
Robert, 386
William, 386
_____, 30, 386
_____ (Lt.), 386
Stomer [Stommer], *see Stoner*
Stonar, *see Stoner*
Stone [Stones, Ston]
    Elizabeth (_____), 387
    Francis, 122
    James, 386
    John, 109, 263, 386, 387, 422
    Maximillian I, 387
    Maximillian II, 387
    Moses [Moyses], 387
    Robert, 387
    Sarah (_____) (Fleet) (Walker), 162, 386, 422
    Theophilus, 61
    William, 422
Stoner [Stomer, Stommer, Stonar, Stonnar]
    Alexander, 61, 123, 233, 245, 317, 387
    Jane (_____) (Cooke), 123, 387
    John, 387
Stoodie, *see Studley*
Story [Storey]
    Joshua, 387
    Robert, 387
Stoughton [Stoughter]
    Elinor (_____) (Wilcox), 388
    Samuel, 387, 388
Strachey, William, 247, 270, 325, 349, 372, 388
Strachey Family, 372
Strange [Strainge, Straunge], William, 388
Stratton
    Alice (_____), 48
    Benjamin, 48
    Edward, 178
    Edward, Jr., 107
    Elizabeth, 107
    Joanna (_____), 388
    John, 388
    Joseph, 388
    Martha (Sheppey), 107
Straunge, *see Strange*
Streater [Stretter, Streeter]
    Edward, 54, 388
    Elizabeth (_____) (Burbage), 54, 388
Strechley [Stretchley]
    Alice (_____) (Chinn), 389
    John, 120, 134, 388, 389
    Sarah, 389
Streeter [Stretter], *see Streater*
Stretchley, *see Strechley*

Stringer
    Ann, 389, 403
    Frances, 389
    Hillary, 389
    John, 109, 389, 403
    Mary, 389
    Samuel, 389
    Thomas, 389
    _____, 109
Strobia, John Henry, 27
Stroud [Strowd], Thomas, 216, 389
Stubbinge
    Agatha (Eltonhead), 88, 89, 111, 458
    Luke, 458
Stubbs [Stubb]
    John, 287, 288, 306, 389
    Thomas, 389, 390
Studley [Stoodie], Thomas, 390
Stufton, William, 390
Sturdivant [Sturdevant]
    John, 390
    Sarah (Hallom) (Woodward), 390
Sturman [Stereman]
    Ann (_____), 190, 464
    Elizabeth, 190
    John, 236
Suky [Sukey] (slave), 369, 390
Sully [Sulley]
    Maudlyn (_____), 390
    Robert, 245, 351, 367, 414
    Thomas, 113, 321, 390
Summers, *see Somers*
Swaine [Swayne], Arthur, 123, 390
Swann [Swan]
    Alexander, 390, 391
    Ann, 391
    Ann (_____) (Brown), 90, 391
    Elizabeth, 391
    Elizabeth (Lillington), 393
    Elizabeth (_____), 391
    Eliza (Thompson), 393, 402
    Judith (_____), 391
    Margaret, 391
    Margaret (Debton), 391
    Margaret (_____), 275
    Mary, 149
    Mary (Mansfield), 196, 318, 339, 371, 391, 392, 393
    Mathew, 391
    Samuel, 50, 146, 196, 205, 206, 223, 279, 339, 365, 371, 391, 392, 393
    Sarah (Chandler), 391
    Sarah (Cod/Codd), 223, 365, 391, 392
    Sarah (Drummond), 146, 393
    Susanna, 275
    Thomas, 45, 70, 90, 91, 125, 138, 146, 149, 153,

154, 160, 171, 179, 182,
185, 204, 209, 212, 223,
246, 287, 305, 306, 318,
342, 365, 434, 455
Thomas I, 23, 196, 275,
287, 336, 338, 339, 340,
365, 369, 371, 372, 379,
380, 383, 391, 392, 393,
402, 425, 444
Thomas II, 226, 393, 402
William, 391
_____ (Edwards), 149, 153,
369
Swarbeck [Swarbrooke,
Swartbrick], John, 393
Swayne, *see Swain*
Sweet [Sweat, Sweete], Robert,
205, 393
Swett, William, 393
Swift [Swyft]
James, 393
Thomas, 105
Swinehowe [Swinhow],
Thomas, 53, 58, 129, 151
Swyft, *see Swift*
Syberry [Syberrye]
George, 393
Henry, 394
Sydney, *see Sidney*
Sykes, *see Sikes*
Sylva [Syla] (slave), 394, 406
Sylvia (slave), 223
Sympson, John, 408
Syms [Symms], *see Sims*
Sypsey, *see Sibley*

T

Taborer [Taberor, Taberer,
Tabenor, Taberrer, Tabirir,
Taboror]
George, 394
Joshua, 394
Margaret (_____) (Wood),
394
Nicholas, 394
Richard, 394
Thomas, 77, 124, 394
William, 394
Tachapoake (Native American),
394
Tahocks (Native American),
394
Taite, Elizabeth "Betsy," 412
Talbent [Tallent], John, 395
Talbott [Talbot]
Ann (_____), 49, 124, 273,
395, 430
George, 82, 245, 382
_____, 395
Taler, *see Tayloe*
Taliaferro [Tollifer]
Catherine [Katherine],
58, 59
Charles, 59
John, 395

Robert I, 59, 395
Robert II, 59
Sarah (_____), 395
Tallent, *see Talbent*
Tanner
Daniel, 173, 277
Josias, 395
Tapatiaton [Debedeavon]
(Native American), 153,
395
Taptico (Native American), 395
Tasreifern (Native American),
396
Tassore (Native American),
240, 396
Tatapatamoi (Native
American), *see
Totopotomoy*
Tatem, Elizabeth (_____), 460
Tatenenoug (Native American),
396
Taverner [Tavernor]
Elizabeth, 281
Elizabeth (_____)
(Travers), 408
John, 396, 408, 453
Michael, 281
Sarah, 32
Tavin, Henry, 396
Tawcren [Towerozen,
Towerezen] (Native
American), 396
Tawney [Tawny, Towney],
Henry, 396, 417
Tayloe [Taler, Tayler, Taylor,
Taylour, Tiler, Tyler]
Anne [Ann], 57, 103, 104
Arthur, 370
Comfort, 37
Comfort (Anderson), 37
Dorothy (_____), 399
Elias, 37
Elizabeth, 37, 398
Elizabeth (Kingsmill), 45,
46, 47, 243, 284, 396
Fortune, 397
Frances, 398
Francis, 397
George, 291
George I, 397
George II, 397
Henrietta Marie [Mary]
(_____), 398
Henry, 36, 77, 78, 397
James, 50, 60
Jane (_____), 399
John, 397, 398, 399
Joseph, 125
Katherine, 398
Maria, 98
Martha (_____) (Moseley),
291
Naomi, 37
Philip [Phillip, Phillipe],
350, 399

Rebecca (Ravening), 397,
398
Richard, 398, 399
Sarah, 37, 398
Sarah (_____), 398
Stephen [Steven], 399, 450
Thomas, 103, 399
William, 45, 46, 243, 389,
396, 397, 400
Zarah, 399
Tayloe Family, 46
Teackle, Thomas, 233
Templar, William, 189
Terhoffamoh (Native
American), 400
Tew
Grace (Bowman), 51
John, 51
Thacker
Edward, 337
Edwin, 114
Thelaball
Elizabeth (Mason), 277
James, 277, 278
Thomas
Edward, 400
Elizabeth, 401
John, 400
Judith (Westropp), 439
Mary, 401
Mary (_____) (Sanders),
401
William, 42, 400, 401, 439
Thomas, Lord Delaware, *see
West, Thomas*
Thompson [Thomson]
Ann (_____), 401, 402
Eliza, 393, 402
Elizabeth, 401
Ellen (Montague), 288
George, 401, 415
John, 31, 117, 171, 185,
196, 401
Katherine, 401
Mary, 415
Maurice, 401
Paul, 415
Richard, 121
Roger, 401
Samuel, 401
Ursula (_____), 121, 292
William, 185, 401, 415
William I [Sr.], 125, 288,
392, 393, 402, 425
William II [Jr.], 392, 402
_____, 401
Thornbury [Thornborough,
Thornburrow, Thornebury]
Eliza (_____), 403
Thomas, 402, 403
Thornbush, John, 424
Thorogood [Thorowgood,
Thorugood]
Adam, 234, 424, 452
Adam I, 175, 403

Adam II, 403
Adam III, 403
Ann, 403
Ann (Stringer), 389, 403
Anthony, 403
Argoll, 403
Dinah (Mason), 277
Elizabeth, 403
Frances (_____), 403
Francis, 403
John, 269, 403
Margaret (Lawson), 403
Maria, 91
Mary (Sawyer), 357
Robert, 403
Rose, 403
Sarah (Offley), 175, 176,
  291, 403, 463
Thomas, 403
Thorpe [Thorp]
Frances (_____), 404
George, 171, 403, 404
Hannah, 404
Otho [Otto], 404
Thomas, 268, 403
Throgmorten [Throgmorton]
Elizabeth, 108, 122, 135,
  143, 144, 191, 261, 356,
  377, 430
Henry, 31
John, 184
Kenelm [Kenelme], 404
William, 407
Throgmorten Family, 135
Thropp
Martha (_____), 175
Thomas, 175
Thrush, Clement, 404
Thruston [Thurston]
Edward, 264
Frances (Covell) (Kaynton)
  (Loving), 264
James, 205
Jeane, 405
John, 104, 225, 405
Malachi [Malachy,
  Mallachi, Mallachy] I,
  403, 404, 405
Malachi II, 405
Martha, 405
Martha (Cary), 33, 104,
  225, 226, 367
Martha (Porter), 405
Sarah, 405
Thomas, 121, 404
Thweatt
James, 58
Judith (Soane), 376
Tiballs [Tibbalds], William,
  405
Tiler, *see Tayloe*
Tilsey, Thomas, 430
Tindall [Tyndall]
Robert, 405
Thomas, 405

Tirrey, John, 460
Todd
Lucy, 60
Thomas, 405, 441
Todkill, Anas, 405
Toft
Ann [Anne], 230
Ann (_____), 358, 435
Arcadia [Arcadis], 435
Attlanta, 435
Tokeley, Robert, 249, 405
Tollifer, *see Taliaferro*
Tolton, Henry, 406
Tom (Native American), 406
Tom (slave), 394, 406
Tomkings, Thomas, 82
Tomlin, George, 397
Tomlinson [Tompkinson],
John, 406
Tommy (slave), 406
Tomocomo (Native American),
  see Uttamatomakkin
Tompkinson, *see Tomlinson*
Tonstall, *see Tunstall*
Tooke [Took, Tuke]
Dorothy, 406
James, 406
Thomas, 406
William, 406
Tooker, *see Tucker*
Topping [Toppin]
Ann (_____), 173
Arthur, 173
Elizabeth (Rabley), 86, 336,
  337, 406
Henry, 173
Joseph, 86, 337, 406
Totopotomoy [Tatapatamoi]
  (Native American), 21, 118,
  203, 406, 407
Towerezen [Towerozen], *see
  Tawcren*
Towne, William, 407
Towney, *see Tawney*
Townsend [Townscend,
  Townshend, Townson]
Frances, 209, 453
Francis, 407
Mary (_____), 407
Richard, 289, 334, 407
Robert I, 407
Robert II, 407
Thomas, 407, 444
Towtales, Lawrence, 407
Trachern, *see Trehearne*
Tracy
Joyce, 407
Mary (_____), 407
William, 169, 404, 407
Trahorne, *see Trehearne*
Trapley
Elizabeth (_____)
  (Newman), 298
John, 298
Travellor

Alice [Alicia], 93, 94, 422
Alisha (_____), 38
Elizabeth, 38
George, 38
Travers [Travars, Traverse], *see
  also Travis*
Elizabeth, 102, 457
Elizabeth (_____), 61, 408
Frances (_____), 408
Raleigh [Rawleigh,
  Raughley, Rawley],
  125, 200, 224, 408
Raleigh I, 61
Raleigh II, 408
Raleigh III, 408
Rebecca (_____), 408
Samuel, 408, 409
Sarah (Taverner), 32
William, 125
William I, 408
William II, 408
Travis, *see also Travers*
Ann (Johnson), 233, 409
Catherine, 412, 413
Champion, 135, 170, 296,
  375, 410, 411, 412, 413
Champion II, 413
Clarissa (Waller), 413
Edward, 80
Edward I, 129, 130, 233,
  310, 361, 409
Edward II, 87, 108, 409,
  410, 421
Edward III, 50, 87, 88, 409,
  410
Edward IV, 27, 35, 375,
  410, 411, 412, 413
Edward Champion, 26, 33,
  74, 78, 138, 146, 232,
  301, 302, 410, 411, 412,
  413
Elizabeth, 413
Elizabeth (Bright), 413
Elizabeth (Champion), 87,
  108, 409
Elizabeth (Marable), 410
Elizabeth "Betsy" (Boush),
  411, 413
Elizabeth "Betsy" (Taite),
  412
John, 411, 412
John I, 410, 412, 413
John II, 413
Joseph H., 413
Judith, 413
Judith (Langhorn), 413
Julia, 413
Mary, 413
Rebecca (_____), 87, 409,
  410
Rebecca Elizabeth, 410
Robert, 412, 413
Samuel, 411, 412, 413, 414
Susan, 412, 413
Susannah, 410

Susannah (Hutchings), 410, 411, 412, 413
Virginia, 413
William L., 412
_____, 375
Travis Family, 25, 26, 27, 28, 40, 108, 411, 413
Tree
John, 414
Richard, 93, 124, 414, 418
Trehearne [Trachern, Trahorne], John, 414
Trevathan, Ann (Church), 114
Trew, Edward, 414
Trotter, George, 414
Truelove, Rowland, 90, 414
Trussell
Anne, 414
Elizabeth "Betty," 414
John, 255, 414, 415
Mary (_____), 255, 414, 415
William, 414
Tuchin [Tuching]
Edward, 248
Simon, 248
Tucker [Tooker, Tuker]
Charles, 431
Daniel, 415
Elizabeth, 415
Frances (_____), 415
Jane (_____), 324, 325
Mary, 415
Mary (Native American), 415
Mary (Thompson), 415
Samuel, 324
St. George, 415
Thomas, 415
William, 56, 153, 258, 313, 450
William I, 415
William II, 415
Tudman, Elizabeth (_____) (Perkins), 416
Tuke, *see* Tooke
Tuker, *see* Tucker
Tullitt [Tulitt, Tullett, Tullit]
Hannah (_____), 416
John, 88, 184, 185, 266, 317, 416, 456
Tunstall [Tonstall], Edward, 416
Turner [Turnor]
Charles, 416, 417
James, 249, 260, 417
John, 417
Martin, 102, 430
Mary (Cox), 417
Roger, 417
Susannah, 417
Turtley, Avis, 102
Twine [Twyne], John, 417
Tye
Elizabeth, 378
Richard, 378, 439

Tyler, *see Tayloe*
Tyndall, *see Tindall*

U

Underhill
Jane, 417
John, 150, 246, 345, 417, 440
John I, 417, 418
John II, 417
Mary, 417
Mary (_____) (Felgate), 417
Nathaniel, 417
Underwood
Elizabeth, 419
Elizabeth (Butler), 418
Margaret, 264, 265, 291, 418, 419
Margaret (_____), 156, 419
Sarah, 419
Tabitha (Summers), 213
William, 282, 419
William I, 418
William II, 418
_____ (Mrs.), 293
Ungwin [Onion, Unguin, Ungwine, Union, Unwine, Unwyn, Vinon, Vinoyn]
Elizabeth, 418
Elizabeth (_____), 418
George, 216, 312, 418, 445
Katherine, 418
Katherine (_____), 418
Upchurch
Frances (_____), 418
Michael, 418
Upton [Uptone]
John, 48, 62, 85, 202, 264, 291, 305
John I, 418, 419, 454
John II, 419
Margaret (Underwood), 264, 265, 291, 418, 419
William, 143, 207
Usher
Ann, 419
Benjamin, 419
Utie [Utey], *see* Uty
Uttamatomakkin [Tomocomo] (Native American, 419
Uty [Utie, Utey]
Ann (_____), 419
John, 46, 53, 91, 106, 289
John I, 419
John II, 419
_____, 46

V

Valentine
Anise, 178
James, 84
Valux, Robert, 149
Van Corensten, *see Corstentam*

Van der Donck, Adriaen, 127
Vanlandingham [Vanlandigame, Vanlandigham]
Benjamin, 420
Michael, 420
Richard, 420
Vassal
Henry, 373
Samuel, 373
Vaughan
Elizabeth (Peirce), 315
Henry, 420
Katherine (_____), 420
Richard, 215
Vause
Ann (_____), 400
Vincent, 400
Velasco, Alonso de, 465
Ven, Nicholas, 420
Verone, John, 99, 203
Vicars, John, 62
Vincencio [Vicentio], *see Castine, Vincencio*
Vinon [Vinoyn], *see Ungwin*
Virget [Virgett], Job, 224, 420
Virgin, Arthur, 370
Vnuntsquero (Native American), 215, 420
Volday [Volda, Voldo], William, 420

W

Wackawamp [Wachiowamp] (Native American), 344, 395, 420
Wadding
James, 113, 306, 365, 390, 421, 444
Susanna (_____) (Chiles), 113, 213, 306, 390, 409, 421
Wade
Armiger [Armager], 421
Armiger II, 421
Dorothy, 421
Mary, 421
Wahunsunacock, *see Powhatan*
Wake, Richard, 116
Walden, Humphrey, 55
Waldo [Waldoe], Richard, 421
Waldron, Henry, 386
Wale [Walei], *see Walle*
Walke, Thomas, 114, 252
Walker
Alice [Alicia] (Travellor) (Burdett), 93, 94, 422
Anne, 386, 422
Arcadia [Arcadis] (Toft), 435
Edward, 208
Elizabeth, 422
Esther, 422
Frances, 386, 422
George, 421

Jane, 422
John, 60, 146, 421, 422
John I, 421
John II, 162, 386, 421, 422
Joseph, 346
Peter, 422, 435
Peter I, 94
Richard, 422
Sarah, 422
Sarah (Berkeley) (Ring),
    346
Sarah (_____) (Fleet), 162,
    386, 422
Susannah (_____), 422
Thomas I, 422
Thomas II, 422
William, 422, 423
_____, 386, 421
Wallace, James, 41, 421
Walle [Wale, Walei], George,
    304, 320
Waller
    Benjamin, 413
    Charles, 423
    Clarissa, 413
    John, 423
Wallings [Wallins]
    George, 423
    George (Mrs.), 423
Walters, *see Waters*
Walton
    John, 109, 358
    Walter, 422
Wamanto (Native American),
    294, 423
Wanerton, William, 423
Waradine, James, 386
Ward [Warde]
    Evan, 423
    John, 55, 172, 423
    Lawrence, 423
    William, 423
Wardley
    Jane (_____), 60
    Thomas, 60
Wareham
    Elizabeth, 424
    Elizabeth (_____), 424
    John, 424
Warkman [Warkeman], *see*
    Workman
Warne, *see Warren*
Warner
    Augustine, 407
    Augustine [Austin] I, 424
    Augustine II, 424, 427
    John, 289
    Mildred, 424, 427, 428
    Mildred (Read), 407
Warnett [Warnet]
    Thomas, 58, 94, 181, 293,
        327, 386, 401, 418, 424
    Thomasine (_____), 424
    _____, 419
Warr, Thomas, 424

Warren [Warrin, Warne]
    Anthony, 424
    Elizabeth (Spencer)
        (Sheppard), 120, 364,
        382, 425, 442
    John, 424, 425
    Thomas, 120, 125, 264,
        305, 364, 382, 404, 425,
        442
Warriner
    Ralph, 177
    _____, 177
Warwell
    Elizabeth (_____), 425
    Thomas, 425
Warwick (Earl of), *see Rich,*
    Robert
Washbourne [Wasborne,
    Washburn, Washburne]
    Dorothy, 425
    John, 425
    Susanna (_____), 425
Washer, _____ (Ens.), 425, 426
Washington
    Ann, 426, 427
    Ann (Pope), 426, 427
    Anne (Gerrard)
        (Broadhurst) (Brett), 87,
        207, 426
    Augustine, 424, 428
    Frances (Gerrard) (Speke)
        (Peyton) (Appleton),
        39, 190, 321, 378, 379,
        426, 427
    George, 133, 428
    John, 32, 39, 40, 166, 190,
        380, 424, 427, 428
    John I, 87, 321, 331, 379,
        380, 424, 426, 427, 428,
        447
    John II, 87, 426
    Lawrence, 190, 380, 424,
        426, 427, 428
    Lawrence I, 427
    Martha, 427
    Martha (Dandridge)
        (Custis), 133, 428
    Mildred, 424, 428
    Mildred (Warner), 424,
        427, 428
Wassatickon (Native
    American), *see Ossakican*
Waterman, Thomas, 428
Waters [Walters, Watters]
    Andrew, 428
    Dorothy (Marriott), 429
    Edward, 241, 249, 347,
        402, 403, 428, 429
    Grace, 208
    Grace (O'Neill), 347, 357,
        428, 429, 430
    Isabell (Harmanson), 191,
        429
    John, 162, 163, 406, 416,
        429

Margaret, 428, 429
Margaret (_____) (Clarke),
    429
Mary (_____) (Baynton),
    429
Obedience, 429
Richard, 429
Robert, 430
Thomas, 429
William, 208, 347
William I, 428, 429
William II, 191, 429
William III, 429
_____ (Maj.), 347
Waters Family, 428
Watkins
    Elizabeth, 52
    Henry, 430
    James, 430
    John, 63, 262, 333
    John I, 430
    John II, 430
    Nicholas, 52
    Rice [Rys], 430
Watson [Wattson]
    Abraham, 430
    Ann (_____), 431
    Elizabeth (_____), 431
    Isaac, 430
    James, 431
    John, 384, 430, 431
    Robert, 219, 431
    Sarah (_____), 431
    William, 431
    _____, 430
    _____ (Mrs.), 287
Wattle Jaws [Loggerhead, King
    of the Nanzattico] (Native
    American), 431
Watton, John, 431
Watts
    Ann, 431
    Ann (Yowell), 465
    John, 447
    Mathew [Matthew], 431,
        451
    Samuel, 431
    Thomas, 80, 138
    Yowell, 465
Wattson, *see Watson*
Waugh [Wough]
    Elizabeth (_____), 431
    John, 161, 209, 241, 282,
        431, 432
    Joseph, 432
Wawoscon [Wawoseons]
    (Native American), 432
Wayne, Anthony, 126, 247
Wayneman, *see Weyman*
Weatherall [Wetherall], Robert,
    432
Weaver, Samuel, 432
Webb [Webbe]
    Ann (_____), 433
    Clare (_____), 432

Daniel, 189
Elizabeth (_____), 459
George, 432
Giles [Gyles], 432
Henry, 288, 336, 432
James, 459
Mary (_____), 394
Robert, 433
Stephen, 432, 433
Thomas, 89, 433
William, 394, 433
Wingfield [Winfield], 433
Winifred, 433
_____, 432
Webber [Webbar]
John, 433
Peter, 433
Weblin [Webling], Wassell
[Wessell], 433
Webster
Richard, 125, 345, 377, 433
Roger, 375, 433, 434
William, 116
Weedon, George, 236
Weeks [Weeke, Weekes]
Abraham, 434
Millicent (_____), 434
Robert, 138, 224, 434
Thomas, 116
_____, 434
Weir [Weire, Weye, Weyre]
Elizabeth, 434
John, 397, 434
_____, 397
Welbeck, Richard, 434, 435
Welbourne [Wellbourn,
Welburn, Welburne]
Arcadia [Arcadis] (Toft),
435
Thomas, 435, 436
Welch, _____, 39
Weldon [Welden]
Benjamin, 435
Poynes, 435
Samuel, 435
Sarah (Efford), 435
Wells
Mary, 435
Richard, 435
Richard (Mrs.), 435
Thomas I, 435
Thomas II, 435
West [Weste]
Alexander, 436
Ann [Anne], 435, 436, 438
Anne [Ann] (_____)
(Huffe), 109, 435
Anthony, 109, 352, 435,
436
Benomy, 436
Catherine, 436
Cecily (Sherley), Lady
Delaware, 207, 208,
387, 414, 437
Frances, 436

Frances (Grenville), 181,
280, 315, 437
Francis, 75, 130, 181, 206,
228, 330, 362, 437
Francis I, 437, 463
Francis II, 437
Henry, 436
Henry (Mrs.), 436
Jane (Davye), 437
John, 127, 134, 141, 153,
173, 181, 289, 348, 358,
435, 436, 437, 438
John [Captain John] (Native
American), 22, 89, 118,
438
John I, 437
John II, 129, 437, 438
John III, 438
Jonathan, 348, 436
Katherine, 435
Margaret (_____) (Powell)
(Blaney), 74, 75, 106,
330, 393, 437, 442
Mary, 436
Matilda, 436
Matilda (Scarborough), 436
Nathaniel, 280, 315, 437, 438
Nathaniel I, 181
Nathaniel II, 181, 437
Rebecca (Braswell), 80
Richard, 436
Sarah, 348, 436
Scarburgh, 436
Temperance (Flowerdew)
(Yeardley), 55, 75, 80,
180, 202, 208, 437, 462,
463
Thomas, 438
Thomas, 3rd Lord Delaware,
6, 30, 39, 61, 75, 84, 89,
148, 167, 168, 169, 206,
208, 209, 237, 252, 259,
276, 299, 312, 317, 320,
353, 360, 362, 374, 376,
385, 388, 396, 405, 414,
415, 417, 420, 423, 432,
436, 437, 439, 447, 453
Unity (Croshaw), 129, 438
William, 48, 436, 438
William (Mrs.), 436
_____, 436
Weston
Thomas, 172, 297, 438, 439
_____, 208, 348
Westropp [Westhope,
Wethrope]
Anner, 439
Bridget, 439
Dorothy, 439
Frances, 439
John, 439
Judith, 439
Wetherall, *see Weatherall*
Wetherstone
Anthony, 189
Jane (_____), 189

Weye, *see Weir*
Weylie, _____, 89
Weyman [Wayneman,
Weynman], Fernando,
439
Weyre, *see Weir*
Whaley
James, 404, 439
Mary (Page), 439
Mary (_____), 133
Thomas, 46, 439
Whaplett
Rebecca, 313
Thomas, 313
Wharoy (Native American),
439
Wheeler, Nevett [Neuett,
Nevet, Nevit], 439
Whinnsell
John, Sr., 252
John, Jr., 252
Whitaker [Whitakers,
Whittaker, Whittakers]
Alexander, 440
Elizabeth (Pyland), 440
Isaac, 99, 163
Jabez, 163, 439, 440
Mary (_____), 440
Richard, 127, 218, 440
Sibella [Sybella, Sebellah]
(_____), 441
Walter, 94, 440, 441
William, 441
_____ (Capt.), 163, 249
Whitby [Whittbey, Whittby]
Katherine (_____), 191,
405, 441
William, 191, 255
William I, 405, 441
William II, 405, 441
White [Whitt]
Andrew, 244
D., 297
Daniel, 427
Edward, 401
Elizabeth, 381, 442, 444
George, 442
Humphrey, 264
Jane (_____) (Barbribb),
443
Jeremy [Jereme], 42
John, 126, 198, 258, 442,
443, 444, 461
John I, 381, 425
Mary (_____), 442
Mary, 442
Mary (Thomas), 401
Richard, 171
Thomas, 162
William, 44, 78, 86, 104,
138, 148, 156, 218, 220,
224, 232, 238, 244, 251,
265, 284, 289, 304, 374,
375, 395, 442, 443
William (Mrs.), 443

William I, 443
William II, 443
Whitehaire, Robert, 78, 234,
 297
Whitehed, Robert, 227, 443
Whiteing, *see Whiting*
Whithelme [Whitehelm,
 Withelm]
 Christian I, 407, 444
 Christian II, 444
Whiting [Whiteing]
 Aphia (_____), 444
 Henry, 444
 _____ (Beverley), 444
Whitmore, Robert, 444
Whitson [Whitsen]
 Anne (Spencer), 444
 John, 444, 445
 Martha, 444
 Mary, 445
Whitt, *see White*
Whittaker [Whittakers], *see
 Whitaker*
Whittingham, Thomas, 342
Whittington
 Elizabeth, 445
 Urselie, 445
 William I, 445
 William II, 445
Whitty
 John, 125, 126, 213, 224,
  445
 Susan (Blackmore), 125,
  126, 445
Wiatt, *see Wyatt*
Wickens, Edmond, 362
Wickham
 James, 445
 William, 445
Wicocomoco [Wecocomaka]
 (King of the) (Native
 American), *see Chicacoans
 and Wicocomocos (King
 of the)*
Wiffin [Wyffing, Wyffin],
 Richard, 445
Wigg
 Edward, 55, 445
 Edward (Mrs.), 445
Wilcox [Wilcocks, Wilcocke,
 Wilcockes, Willcocks,
 Willcox]
 Anne (Custis) (Yeardley),
  131, 446, 463
 Elinor (_____), 388
 Henry, 446
 John, 445, 446
 Katherin, 446
 Michael, 388
 Peter, 445
 Philip, 341
 Susana, 446
 Temperance (_____)
  (Burges), 446
 William, 446
 _____ (Capt.), 42

Wild [Wilde, Wyld]
 Daniel, 78, 446
 Margaret, 446, 447
 Robert, 446, 447
Wiles, Bishop, 447
Wilford [Wilsford, Wilsfoode,
 Willsford]
 Andrew, 447
 James, 447
 Margaret (_____)
  (Browne), 447
 Thomas, 110, 447
Wilkenson, *see Wilkinson*
Wilkins [Wilkines]
 Anne, 448
 Anne (_____), 448
 Argoll, 448
 Bridgett (_____), 447
 Frances, 448
 John, 347, 447, 448
 Lydia, 448
 Mary, 448
 Nathaniel, 448
Wilkinson [Wilkenson]
 Anne (_____), 448
 Cary, 267, 450
 Elizabeth, 448
 Henry, 378
 James, 448
 Thomas, 140, 407, 448
 William, 448
 William Jr., 36
 _____ (_____)
  (Dickenson),140, 407,
  448
Will (slave), 153, 225, 353,
 359, 448
Willastone [Willeston,
 Wooleston], Hugh, 448
William, King of England,
 275, 346
William (Native American),
 see Machywap
William (servant), 448
Williams [Willyams, Winge]
 Christopher, 448
 Edward, 203, 448
 Elizabeth, 203, 204
 Elizabeth (_____), 394
 Hugh, 449
 John, 394, 449
 Michael, 215
 Richard alias Cornish, *see
  Cornish, Richard*
 Roger, 164, 433
 Sarah (_____), 215
 _____, 164, 339, 448
Williamson
 Arthur, 449
 Frances, 400
 Francis, 449
 George, 449
 Henry, 167, 434
 James, 418, 449
 Joan [Jone] (Allen), 449

Joseph, 364, 365, 366
Katherine, 400
Robert I, 449
Robert II, 449
 _____ (Underwood), 418
 _____, 434
Willis
 Ann, 449
 Elizabeth "Betty" (Landon),
  102
 Francis, 332, 449, 450
 Henry, 449, 450
 Jane (_____), 449
 Richard, 38, 102, 313
Willmoth, Edward, 450
Willoughby [Willoby,
 Willowby, Willobye]
 Elizabeth, 31, 32, 121
 Thomas, 31, 108, 121, 214,
  277
 Thomas I, 175, 450
 Thomas II, 450
Willsford [Wilsford,
 Wilsfoode], *see Wilford*
Willson, *see Wilson*
Willyams, *see Williams*
Wilson [Willson]
 Benjamin, 450
 Charles, 190
 Christian, 190
 Christopher, 212
 David, 360
 Elizabeth (_____)
  (Hansford), 212
 George, 450
 Goodwin, 27
 James, 450, 451
 Jane (Davis), 451
 Joan, 288
 Mary, 71, 103, 341, 342
 Prudence (_____), 288
 Robert, 450
 Samuel, 431
 Susan, 450, 451
 Thomas, 27, 37, 66, 100,
  301, 451
 Thomas (Mrs.), 451
 William, 71, 103, 288, 341,
  431, 451
 Willis II, 451
 Willis III, 451
 Willis, Jr., 451
Winchell, Robert, 235
Winchester, John, 452
Windham [Windom], Edward,
 452
Windmill
 Christopher, 219
 Christopher (Mrs.), 219
Windom, *see Windham*
Wingate
 Dorothy [Dorithy] (Bedell)
  (Burwell), 96, 452
 Roger, 290, 452
Wingbrough, Barbara
 [Barbary], 452

Winge, *see Williams*
Wingfield, Edward Maria, 4, 30, 100, 169, 176, 240, 368, 452, 456
Winne, *see Wynne*
Winsloe [Winslow], John, 44, 452
Wisdom [Wisedom, Wisdome], John, 452, 453
Wise, Scarburgh (Robinson), 348
Wisedom, *see Wisdom*
Wishard
  Elizabeth, 233
  Mary, 233
  Jacomen, 233
  John, 233
With [With], *see Wythe*
Withers [Wythers, Wyther]
  Edward, 453
  Frances (Townshend) (Dade), 209, 453
  John, 209, 453
  _____ (Mrs.), 453
Withuell, Thurston, 328
Wittingham, Thomas, 453
Witts, _____, 453
Woeleich, *see Worleigh*
Wolstenholme, John, 194, 195
Wonuffacomen (Native American), 453
Wood
  Abraham [Abram], 316, 335, 453, 454, 455
  Abraham [Abram] (Mrs.), 454
  Abraham II, 454
  Ann (_____), 454
  John, 394
  Margaret (_____), 394
  Mary, 107, 454
  Percival [Percivall, Percivell], 454
  William, 454
  _____ (Capt.), 453
Woodall, John, 67, 260, 454
Woodard, *see Woodward*
Woodhouse, *see also Woodhurst*
  Abraham, 107
  Elizabeth, 284, 454
  Henry, 276, 404
  Henry I, 454
  Henry II, 454
  Henry III, 454
  Horatio, 454
  John, 454
  Mary [Maria] (_____), 454
  Thomas, 43, 49, 105, 125, 195, 214, 218, 273, 281, 284, 395, 454, 455
  William, 454
Woodhurst, Thomas, 90, 455, *see also Woodhouse*

Woodlief [Woodliffe, Woodlase]
  John I, 455
  John II, 455
Woodward [Woodard]
  Christopher, 455, 460
  Dorothy (_____), 455
  George, 455
  Henry, 91
  Margaret (_____), 455
  Mary, 456
  Phillaritie [Phillarete, Pillarote], 172
  Richard, 281, 456
  Samuel, 390, 455
  Sarah (Hallom), 390
  Thomas, 172, 335
  William, 317, 456
Wooldridge [Woolrich], *see Worleigh*
Wooleston, *see Willastone*
Woory, *see Worry*
Wooten [Wootton, Wotton]
  Thomas, 456
  William, 80, 456
Workman [Warkman, Warkeman]
  Daniel, 456
  John, 200
  Mark, 305
  Mark I, 424
  Mark II, 424
  Thomas, 200
Worleigh [Woeleich, Wooldridge, Woolrich, Worledge, Worley, Worldige, Worldridge, Worleich, Worlich, Worlidge, Worlie]
  George, 456
  Mary, 227
  Richard, 456
  William, 456
  _____, 456
Wormeley
  Agatha (Eltonhead) (Stubbinge), 88, 89, 111, 458
  Catherine [Katherine] (Lunsford) (Jennings), 232, 268, 269, 458
  Christopher, 150, 213, 239, 319
  Christopher I, 187, 373, 456, 457, 458
  Christopher II, 45, 102, 281, 375, 457, 458
  Elizabeth, 239, 240, 268, 334, 373, 457
  Elizabeth (Travers) (Carter), 102, 457
  Frances (Armistead) (Aylemer), 45, 213, 281, 457
  Judith, 457

Ralph, 68, 88, 101
Ralph I, 111, 112, 239, 457, 458
Ralph II, 68, 94, 111, 112, 229, 232, 269, 318, 328, 347, 434, 457, 458, 459
Thomas, 457
William, 457
  _____ (Capt.), 301
  _____ (Secretary), 192
  _____ (_____) (Elliott), 150, 457
Worry [Woory]
  Elizabeth (_____) (Webb), 459
  Joseph, 370, 459
  Robert, 459
Worsham
  Elizabeth, 241, 242
  Elizabeth (_____), 152, 241, 242
  William, 152, 241
Worsley, Benjamin, 459
Wotton, *see Wooten*
Wough, *see Waugh*
Wray
  Mary (Whitson), 445
  William, 445
Wright [Write]
  Ann [Anne] (Mottrom), 292, 380
  Anne (_____), 120, 166
  Dionysius, 367, 459
  Joan, 41, 42, 77, 170
  Joane [Joan, Jane] (_____), 42, 460
  John, 459
  Martha (_____), 459
  Richard, 166, 292, 380
  Robert, 123, 178, 182, 338, 460
  _____, 459
Wright Family, 460
Wroughton, William, 51
Wyatt [Wiatt, Wyat]
  Anthony, 460
  Anthony I, 460
  Anthony II, 460
  Edward, 322
  Francis, 11, 56, 64, 75, 80, 95, 112, 122, 123, 128, 137, 170, 172, 181, 185, 197, 198, 214, 239, 279, 287, 296, 329, 335, 375, 380, 390, 393, 456, 461
  Haute [Hant, Hante, Hautt, Hawt], 350, 461
  Henry, 461
  Margaret (Sandys), 461
  Nicholas, 116, 273, 350, 377, 460
  Nicholas (Mrs.), 460
  William, 41
  William I, 461
  William II, 461

Wyffin [Wyffing], *see Wiffin*
Wyld, *see Wild*
Wynne [Winne]
  Hugh, 461
  Joshua, 461
  Mary (_____), 461
  Peter, 461
  Robert, 204
  Robert I, 331, 461
  Robert II, 461
  Thomas, 461
  Woodleigh, 331, 461
Wynston
  Elizabeth (Hardidge), 190
  Robert, 190
Wythe [With, Withe, Wyth]
  Ann, 462
  Ann (_____), 462
  George, 415
  Simon [Symon], 453
  Thomas, 462
  Thomas II, 462
  Thomas III, 462
Wythers [Wyther], *see Withers*

Y

Yarborough, Richard, 22
Yardley, *see Yeardley*
Yarington, George, 462
Yates
  Elizabeth, 74, 462
  William, 74, 462
Yeardley [Yardley]
  Anne (Custis), 131, 446, 463
  Argoll [Argall], 131, 301, 441, 446, 462, 463
  Argoll II, 446
  Edward, 446
  Elizabeth, 462, 463
  Francis, 176, 291, 403, 441, 462, 463
  George, 6, 8, 9, 11, 41, 42, 49, 56, 61, 62, 63, 75, 79, 84, 92, 100, 102,

115, 122, 123, 128, 139, 140, 147, 152, 154, 164, 167, 176, 180, 185, 197, 199, 202, 209, 218, 220, 221, 222, 227, 233, 235, 244, 250, 269, 276, 287, 289, 301, 310, 312, 313, 314, 315, 316, 321, 330, 338, 351, 370, 387, 388, 390, 391, 401, 418, 428, 437, 445, 449, 450, 454, 462, 463, 464
  Henry, 446
  Ralph, 351, 391, 437, 463
  Sarah (Offley) (Thorogood) (Gookin), 175, 176, 291, 403, 463
  Temperance (Flowerdew), 55, 75, 80, 180, 202, 208, 437, 462, 463
Yeardley Family, 182
Yemanson, James, 463
Yeo
  Hugh, 429, 463
  Leonard I, 463
  Leonard II, 463, 464
  Mary (_____), 464
  William, 463
Yeotassa (Native American), 100, 107, 308, 464
Yonge, *see Young*
York (slave), 464
Youell, *see Yowell*
Young [Younge, Yonge]
  Dorothy, 208
  Joan, 464
  Joan (_____), 464
  Richard, 192, 464
  Robert, 464
  Thomas, 464
  William, 464
  _____, 464
"Young Ben" (slave), 62
"Young Hannah" (slave), 356
Yowell [Youell, Youll, Youlle]

Ann, 465
Anne [Ann, Anna] (Lee), 255, 464, 465
Ann (_____) (Sturman), 190, 464
Richard, 464
Thomas, 255, 298
Thomas I, 464
Thomas II, 464, 465
Winifred, 465

Z

Zeb (slave), 465
Zouch
  Isabella, 465
  John I, 465
  John II, 465
Zuniga
  Pedro de, 465

No Last Name

Adam, 30, 167, 354
Alice, 297
Anthony [Antonio], 38, 399
Birkenhead [Berkenhead], 372
Dorothy, 61
Edward, 148
Elinor, 150
Francis, 30, 167, 354
Jane, 172
Jeffrey [Geoffrey], 42
John, 232, 233
Judith, 454
Margaret, 263
Mary, 61
Michaell [Michael], 285
Robert, 346
Ruth, 353
Samuel, 354
Stephen, 384
Susan, 464
William, 313, 448

Printed in the USA
CPSIA information can be obtained
at www.ICGtesting.com
JSHW061636210224
57720JS00016B/151